McCarthy's
DESK ENCYCLOPEDIA
of
INTELLECTUAL
PROPERTY

Second Edition

McCarthy's
DESK ENCYCLOPEDIA
of
INTELLECTUAL
PROPERTY

Second Edition

J. Thomas McCarthy

The Bureau of National Affairs, Inc., Washington, D.C.

Library of Congress Cataloging-in-Publication Data

McCarthy, J. Thomas, 1937-
   McCarthy's desk encyclopedia of intellectual property — 2. ed
      p.   cm.
   Includes bibliographical references.
   ISBN 0–87179–899–9
   1. Intellectual property—United States—Encyclopedias.
   2. Intellectual property—Encyclopedias.   I. Title.
   KF2976.4.M38   1995
   346.7304'8'03—dc20
   [347.3064803]   95-37468
                          CIP

Published by BNA Books
1231 25th St., NW, Washington, D.C. 20037

Printed in the United States of America
International Standard Book Number: 0-87179-899-9

Preface to the Second Edition

In the four years since the First Edition, significant changes in intellectual property law have occurred. The most notable event was the GATT TRIPS agreement and its incorporation into U.S. law through the Uruguay Round Agreements Act of 1994. Several new entries explain the far-reaching impact of the GATT TRIPS accord and its implementation in the United States. The agreement reflects the increased globalization of the field, which is also indicated in new entries in this edition for terms such as "NAFTA," "Trademark Law Treaty," "European Trademark," "World Trade Organization," and "harmonization."

Globalization is an increased concern in the field because intellectual property has increased its role as a key part of American exports. This has made Americans more concerned with relatively lower levels of intellectual property protection and enforcement in nations to which the United States sells intellectual-property-intensive products. These include high-tech goods like computer programs and such entertainment products as motion pictures on cassette and music on compact discs.

In this edition, I have not only updated existing entries with recent legislative and case-law developments, but I have also added 70 new entries.

Grateful acknowledgement is given to my student researchers, who were of great assistance to me in the preparation of this edition: Cynthia R. Baroumand, Susan Kay Faris, Heather Friedman, Elizabeth E. Launer, Lisa A. Palter, and Nazanin Parvizi. Special thanks go to my chief student researcher on this project, Benjamin P. Oelsner.

J. THOMAS McCARTHY

San Francisco
October 1995

Preface to the First Edition

My basic goal in writing this reference book was to help make intellectual property law understandable and easily accessible, to demystify it. Law that is incomprehensible and inaccessible to all but a few seasoned experts is not the "rule of law" of a democratic and free society.

Intellectual property basically consists of certain creations of the intellect. Technological, marketing, literary, and artistic information are given the legal aspects of property and are more commonly recognized under specific labels such as patent, trademark, and copyright. A strong and readily understood system of intellectual property laws is not a luxury in today's shrinking world of accelerating growth in technology development and worldwide marketing and communications. Such a system of laws is necessary to ensure survival of the domestic economy in an increasingly rigorous world market. If interested persons cannot readily retrieve and comprehend the law, then intellectual property law becomes part of the problem, not part of the solution.

In this book, I have tried to pack as much useful information in as small a space as possible. This proved to be more difficult that I anticipated, given the constraint of the need to make the explanations clear and understandable and, at the same time, legally and technically accurate. I felt that the traditional dictionary or encyclopedia entry system would be most familiar to users and would be the structure that provides the most information with the least amount of search time.

This book is intended to be regularly *used*. This is a desk book, to be kept close at hand, not filed away in the library. Lawyers are often expected to quickly opine on the phone, in meetings, or in response to the ubiquitous fax message. Often, one needs to have the memory refreshed on the relevant basic legal rules. In those situations or when one does not have time to delve into a multivolume treatise, this book is available.

I wrote this book to be useful to a wide potential audience. Likely users of this book range from the novice attorney to the seasoned expert. It should provide a practical reference book to both the in-house counsel and law firm litigator who only now and then deal in intellectual property matters. This book may also be valuable to the business client who wants to be informed, and could prove to be an ideal business gift from the intellectual property attorney to the sophisticated business client. Attorney-client communication is always easier if both sides of the conversation use the same terms of art to mean the same thing.

This book can also be used as an introductory text on intellectual property by the student and beginner by starting with the basic entries such as "patent," "trademark," "copyright," and "trade secret" and then delving into greater depth by following the cross-references to entries defining and explaining more complex concepts.

In recent years, intellectual property law has become more diverse and complex. Unlike the usual practice of 25 years ago, not everyone in the field is expected to be facile in all aspects of patent, trademark, and copyright law. Today, for example, many attorneys deal mainly in trademark law, and less frequently handle patent and copyright matters. This book can enable everyone to brush up on basic rules quickly and to catch up on recent changes in the law.

In 1989 significant statutory changes occurred in trademark and copyright law and are incorporated into the entries in this book. Effective in March 1989, the Berne Convention Implementation Act made important changes in U.S. copyright law so that the United States could become a member of the Berne Union. Effective in November 1989, the Trademark Law Revision Act made significant changes in U.S. trademark law, especially the adoption for the first time in the United States of an "intent-to-use" system for applying to register a mark. Since 1982, the Court of Appeals for the Federal Circuit (CAFC) has had exclusive appellate power over patent infringement appeals and has made several decisive changes in the direction of U.S. patent law and policy. I have tried in the patent law entries to emphasize the newer case law interpretations made by the CAFC.

The structure of this book generally follows that of the familiar dictionary or encyclopedia format. Each word entry is immediately followed by an indication in brackets as to the field or fields of intellectual property into which the concept falls. Each word is then defined and explained, followed by references to those sections of the leading treatises in which the matter can be explored further. Most entries also contain references to and quotations from the important cases, legislation, rules, and any other useful sources, such as the Manual of Patent Examining Procedure. Entries for particularly difficult concepts also contain factual examples drawn from the litigated cases. In the definitions and explanations, a word appearing in small capitals indicates that the word is defined elsewhere in this encyclopedia. While the general structure of entries is uniform throughout the encyclopedia, the length and complexity of the entries vary with the difficulty and intricacy of the concepts explained. My working rule was to include as many diverse research materials and quotations within the space available as I thought would advance understanding of a concept.

A reference work like this is never complete. As technology, marketing, art, and communications change and grow into the twenty-first century, associated concepts in intellectual property will develop and evolve. I call upon the readers and users of this book to become part of the on-going process of change and improvement that will be reflected in future editions of this encyclopedia. Please alert me to ways to improve the usefulness of this book and to additional entries you think would be appropriate and helpful.

Grateful acknowledgement is given to my student researchers Camden L. Collins, Laura A. Newman, and Thomas M. Onda. The Westlaw legal research system was used in the preparation of this book.

J. THOMAS MCCARTHY

San Francisco
March 1991

Contents

Contents

List of Entries

Note: Entries are alphabetized letter-by-letter; e.g., publication *precedes* public use.

---

*Indicates that the entry is a cross-reference
†Indicates that the entry is new to the second edition

---

*Indicates that the entry is a cross-refernece
†Indicates that the entry is new to the second edition

*Indicates that the entry is a cross-reference
†Indicates that the entry is new to the second edition

---

*Indicates that the entry is a cross-refernece
†Indicates that the entry is new to the second edition

---

*Indicates that the entry is a cross-reference
†Indicates that the entry is new to the second edition

*Indicates that the entry is a cross-refernece
†Indicates that the entry is new to the second edition

M

Madrid Arrangement
Madrid Protocol
Madrid Union *
maintenance fees
Manual of Patent Examining Procedure *
manufacturing clause
march in †
mark
marking estoppel
marking of patent
Markush claim
mask work
means for claim *
means-plus-function claim
mechanical licensing agent
mechanical rights
mechanic skilled in the art *
mediation *†
merchandising
merchant's mark
merger
   copyright
   trademark
method claim *
Mexico City Convention
microcode
microorganism depository *
minitrial *†
misappropriation
misdescriptive mark *
mismarking
misuse
   patent
   trademark
   copyright
MITI
monopoly
   patent
   trademark
moral rights

motion picture
moveover
MPEP
multimedia †
multiple dependent claim
multiple performances doctrine *
Muncie Gear doctrine *
musical work
mutilation

N

NAFTA †
naked license *
nanotechnology †
National Film Preservation Act
neighboring rights
new matter
new use for old product *†
Nice Agreement
nonobviousness *
nonprofit organization
nonstaple *
nose of wax
notice
   patent *
   trademark
   copyright
novelty
nunc pro tunc

O

object code
objective evidence
obviousness
obvious to try
office action
Official Gazette
off-shore assembly
OG *
old combination *

---

*Indicates that the entry is a cross-reference
†Indicates that the entry is new to the second edition

---

*Indicates that the entry is a cross-refernece
†Indicates that the entry is new to the second edition

---

*Indicates that the entry is a cross-reference
†Indicates that the entry is new to the second edition

---

*Indicates that the entry is a cross-refernece
†Indicates that the entry is new to the second edition

---

*Indicates that the entry is a cross-reference
†Indicates that the entry is new to the second edition

Table of Cases

Cases are referenced to page number. Alphabetization is letter-by-letter.

B

E

H

I

L

M

N

O

U

Y

Z

A

AAU [trademark]

See AMENDMENT TO ALLEGE USE.

abandonment [patent–trademark]

1. Abandonment of Invention. Acts by an inventor to withhold an invention from public knowledge by either (1) deliberately hiding the invention or (2) failing to apply for a patent within a reasonable time after invention. Such conduct can extinguish a first inventor's priority of invention such that a patent is granted to a later rival inventor. Abandonment is often regarded as synonymous with its statutory siblings: SUPPRESSION and CONCEALMENT. Patent Code §102(g) states that one who is the first to complete the invention by CONCEPTION and REDUCTION TO PRACTICE will lose the right of priority and the patent if that inventor thereafter abandons, suppresses, or conceals the invention.

The most common situation by which the first inventor loses out to a second inventor by abandonment is where after reduction to practice by the first inventor, no patent application is filed for an unreasonable period, and during that interval of inactivity the second inventor enters the scene.

• *Statutory Reference:* 35 U.S.C. §102(c) & (g): "A person shall be entitled to a patent unless— … (c) he has abandoned the invention, or … (g) before the applicant's invention thereof the invention was made in this country by another who had not abandoned, suppressed, or concealed it."

• *Treatise Reference*: 3 D. Chisum, *Patents* §10.08 (1994 rev.).

• *Case Reference*: "Actual abandonment under 35 U.S.C. 102(c) requires that the inventor *intend* to abandon the invention, and intent can be implied from the inventor's conduct with respect to the invention …. Such intent to abandon an invention will not be imputed, and every reasonable doubt should be resolved in favor of the inventor.… Delay in filing alone is not a sufficient basis from which to infer the requisite intent to abandon under 35 U.S.C. 102(c)." *Ex parte Dunne*, 20 USPQ2d 1479, 1480 (Bd. Pat. App. & Int'f. 1991) (reversing rejection on ground of abandonment where inventor conceived invention in June 1982 but did not file application until September 1987).

• *Example*: In an interference proceeding, Murphy completed his jet plane vent invention by a REDUCTION TO PRACTICE in September 1974 but rival inventor Correge was first to file a patent application in April 1975. Correge alleged that the delay from Murphy's reduction to practice until Murphy's December 1975 filing date constituted an unreasonable delay sufficient to create an inference of intent to abandon. The court held that the period of delay should only be counted as the seven months from the completion of Murphy's invention in September 1974 until the first public disclosure in April 1975 made at a meeting of airline industry representatives. During that seven-month period, Murphy's employer evaluated the invention, a patent search was made and evaluated, and a patent application was authorized. This was held not to be an abandonment, and Murphy was given priority and the patent. "The only question left to resolve is whether the seven month period between Murphy's reduction to practice and his public disclosure was an excessive delay sufficient to raise the presumption of an intent to abandon.… On this record, we hold that there was sufficient disclosure-directed activity during the seven months between reduction to practice and first public disclosure to rebut any inference, if inference there were, of abandonment." *Correge, Dominique & Ciprian v. Murphy*, 705 F.2d 1326, 1330–31, 217 USPQ 753, 756 (Fed. Cir. 1983).

• *Note*: There is some authority indicating that "suppression or concealment" indicate a concept different from "abandonment." "Under the statute an applicant's suppression or concealment not amounting to abandonment prevents him from establishing priority over a subsequent inventor, but does not destroy his right to a patent.... While [the inventor] may not use his 1962 reduction to practice to prove priority, because of the suppression or concealment found by the Board, it is nevertheless his de facto date of invention." *Steierman v. Connelly*, 197 USPQ 288 (Comm. Pat. & T.M. 1976).

2. Abandonment of Patent Application. An application for patent can become abandoned either by a formal abandonment by the applicant or by failure of the applicant to take appropriate action (failure to prosecute) within a specified time at some stage in the prosecution of the case. For example, under 37 C.F.R. §1.135 a patent application can become abandoned by a failure to respond within the time provided to an action by the Patent and Trademark Office (OFFICE ACTION). An abandoned application is removed from the Patent and Trademark Office docket of pending cases. In certain circumstances REVIVAL of an application abandoned for failure to prosecute is permitted.

See *Manual of Patent Examining Procedure* §711 (1994).

3. Abandonment of Trademark. The loss of all rights to exclude others from use of a trademark, resulting from either: (1) ceasing use with intent not to resume use; (2) LICENSING of a mark without quality control, causing the term or symbol to lose significance as a mark; (3) assigning a mark without also transferring associated goodwill (ASSIGNMENT in gross); or (4) the mark falling into majority usage as a GENERIC NAME of a type of goods or services.

Abandonment Through Nonuse. Since rights in a trademark are acquired through use, these rights may be lost through nonuse. The two elements of such abandonment are: (1) ceasing use with (2) the intent not to resume use. Under federal law, the kind of "use" needed is use made in the "ordinary course of trade," not just token, nominal use made in a gesture to prevent loss of rights. A challenger's proof of nonuse for three consecutive years raises a statutory presumption of abandonment, which shifts the burden of rebuttal to the registrant. *Cerveceria Centroamericana S.A. v. Cerveceria India Inc.*, 892 F.2d 1021, 13 USPQ2d 1307 (Fed. Cir. 1989). The URUGUAY ROUND AGREEMENTS ACT of 1994 increased the statutory term of nonuse that triggers the presumption from two to three years, effective January 1, 1996. Once a mark has been abandoned by nonuse, a subsequent use does not retroactively cure the abandonment. *AmBrit Inc. v. Kraft Inc.*, 805 F.2d 974, 1 USPQ2d 1161 (11th Cir. 1986).

Balance of Factors. Generally, courts will balance the following two factors: (1) the user's state of mind concerning resumption of use; and (2) the public's state of mind concerning the degree to which the term or symbol still has the power to identify and distinguish. However, a trademark can be instantaneously abandoned by stopping use accompanied by a public announcement that there will be no further use. See, e.g., *Hiland Potato Chip Co. v. Culbro Snack Foods*, 221 USPQ 142 (S.D. Iowa 1982), *aff'd*, 720 F.2d 981, 222 USPQ 790 (8th Cir. 1983). Since abandonment results in a forfeiture of rights, most courts require the challenger to prove abandonment by clear and convincing evidence. A change of format or appearance of a mark over time generally will not result in an abandonment or a break in the chain of priority of title if the change preserves continuity of image and carries forward the basic commercial impression of the mark.

Abandonment From Loss of Trademark Rights. In addition to nonuse, abandonment can result from any acts of commission or omission that cause a mark to lose its significance as a mark or to become the generic name for a type of goods or services. Such acts include:

(1) "naked licensing"—the licensing of a mark without quality control (see LICENSING);

(2) "assignment in gross"—the assignment of a mark divorced from the goodwill associated with the mark (see ASSIGNMENT); and

(3) majority customer usage of the word or symbol mark as a generic name for a type of goods or services (see GENERIC NAME). Concerning generic name use, a 1984 revision to the Lanham Act forbids the use of "purchaser motivation" as a test for abandonment. This was to preclude any future use of a Ninth Circuit test, which inferred that a term is a generic name unless a majority of customers are motivated to buy the product because they know the corporate trade name of the producer and like that company's products. *Anti-Monopoly, Inc. v. General Mills, Inc.*, 684 F.2d 1326, 216 USPQ 588 (9th Cir. 1982).

Significance of Abandonment. Alleged abandonment of a mark is significant in the following contexts: (1) an alleged infringer can challenge the validity of the mark on the ground that it has been abandoned; (2) abandonment may result in a break in the chain of priority where another party claims an intervening use; and (3) an abandoned mark cannot be federally registered and once a mark is registered and later abandoned, the registration can be canceled at any time. Only very rarely is a mark ever "abandoned" because of a failure to prosecute infringers. The usual result is some loss of strength, not total abandonment. *Sweetheart Plastics, Inc. v. Detroit Forming, Inc.*, 743 F.2d 1039, 223 USPQ 1291 (4th Cir. 1984); 2 J.T. McCarthy, *Trademarks and Unfair Competition* §17.05 (3d ed. 1995 rev.).

• *Treatise Reference*: 2 J.T. McCarthy, *Trademarks & Unfair Competition* §§17.01– .10 (3d ed. 1995 rev.).

• *Statutory Reference*: Lanham Act §45, 15 U.S.C. §1127:

Abandonment. A mark shall be deemed to be "abandoned" when either of the following occurs:

(1) When its use has been discontinued with intent not to resume such use. Intent not to resume may be inferred from circumstances.

Nonuse for three consecutive years shall be prima facie evidence of abandonment. "Use" of a mark means the bona fide use of that mark made in the ordinary course of trade, and not made merely to reserve a right in a mark.

(2) When any course of conduct of the owner, including acts of omission as well as commission, causes the mark to become the generic name for the goods or services on or in connection with which it is used or otherwise to lose its significance as a mark. Purchaser motivation shall not be a test for determining abandonment under this paragraph.

• *Case Reference*: "[G]oodwill does not ordinarily disappear or completely lose its value overnight. Erosion from non-use is a gradual process. As long as the mark has significant remaining value and the owner intends to use it in connection with substantially the same business or service, the public is not deceived." *Defiance Button Mach. Co. v. C&C Metal Prods. Corp.*, 759 F.2d 1053, 1060, 225 USPQ 797, 801 (2d Cir. 1985).

4. Abandonment of Application to Register Trademark. An application to register a mark can become abandoned either by a formal abandonment by the applicant or by failure of the applicant to take appropriate action (failure to prosecute) within a specified time at some stage in the prosecution of the case. Under 37 C.F.R. §2.65, an application to register can become abandoned by a failure to respond within the six-month period provided for response to an action by the Patent and Trademark Office (OFFICE ACTION). Also, an INTENT TO USE application can become abandoned by failure to file timely a Statement of Use. 37 C.F.R. §2.65(c). In certain circumstances one is permitted to seek REVIVAL of an application abandoned for failure to prosecute.

abstract of the disclosure [patent] A part of a patent consisting of a concise technical summary of the disclosure of the invention. The abstract enables a searcher to obtain quickly information about the essential contents of the invention disclosed in the patent. The abstract is usually confined to about 100 words.

Because of its conciseness, the abstract is easily translated into different languages and, therefore, plays an important role in the international exchange of technical information contained in patent documents.

The "abstract" is to be distinguished from the "summary of the invention," which is also a part of the patent but is a longer, albeit still brief, summary of the nature, substance, and object of the invention. 37 C.F.R. §1.73.

The abstract of the disclosure has been interpreted as being a part of the specification for the purpose of complying with the enablement requirement. Thus, disclosures in the abstract can assist in enabling one skilled in the art to make and use the invention. *In re Armbruster*, 512 F.2d 676, 185 USPQ 152 (C.C.P.A. 1975).

See DISCLOSURE, SPECIFICATION.

• *Rule Reference*: "A brief abstract of the technical disclosure in the specification must be set forth on a separate sheet, preferably following the claims under the heading 'Abstract of the Disclosure.' The purpose of the abstract is to enable the Patent and Trademark Office and the public generally to determine quickly from a cursory inspection the nature and gist of the technical disclosure. The abstract shall not be used for interpreting the scope of the claims." 37 C.F.R. §1.72(b).

• *Manual Reference*: "When applicable, the abstract should include the following: (1) if a machine or apparatus, its organization and operation; (2) if an article, its method of making; (3) if a chemical compound, its identity and use; (4) if a mixture, its ingredients; (5) if a process, the steps…. The abstract should be in narrative form and generally limited to a single paragraph within the range of 50 to 250 words…. The form and legal phraseology often used in patent claims, such as 'means' and 'said,' should be avoided. The abstract should sufficiently describe the disclosure to assist readers in deciding whether there is a need for consulting the full patent text for details." *Manual of Patent Examining Procedure* §608.01(b) (1994).

• *Commentary Reference*: "[The abstract] starts by an indication of the technical field to which the invention pertains and has to be drafted in a way which allows clear understanding of the technical problem, the gist of the solution of that problem through the invention and the principal use or uses of the invention." WIPO, *Background Reading Material on Intellectual Property* 91 (1988).

• *Example 1*: The abstract for the first patent on a TRANSGENIC animal granted by the U.S. Patent and Trademark Office: "A transgenic non-human eukaryotic animal whose germ cells and somatic cells contain an activated oncogene sequence introduced into the animal, or an ancestor of the animal, at an embryonic stage." U.S. Patent No. 4,736,866, granted April 12, 1988.

• *Example 2*: "A heart valve which has an annular valve body defining an orifice and a plurality of struts forming a pair of cages on opposite sides of the orifice. A spherical closure member is captively held within the cages and is moved by blood flow between open and closed positions in check valve fashion. A slight leak or backflow is provided in the closed position by making the orifice slightly larger than the closure member. Blood flow is maximized in the open position of the value by providing an inwardly convex contour on the orifice-defining surfaces of the body. An annular rib is formed in a channel around the periphery of the valve body to anchor a suture ring used to secure the valve within a heart." *Manual of Patent Examining Procedure* §608.01(b), Example 1 of "Sample Abstracts" (1994).

access [copyright] The reasonable opportunity to copy by seeing or hearing the copyrighted work that is allegedly infringed. Proof of COPYING usually consists of evidence that (1) the defendant has access to the copyrighted work and (2) the defendant's work is SUBSTANTIALLY SIMILAR to the copyrighted work. *Sid & Marty Krofft Television Prods., Inc. v. McDonald's Corp.*, 562 F.2d 1157, 1163, 196 USPQ 97, 101 (9th Cir. 1977); *Reyher v. Children's Television Workshop*, 533 F.2d 87, 90, 190 USPQ 387, 390 (2d Cir. 1976).

Proof of Access. Access must be proven: it cannot be arrived at through mere speculation or conjecture. A "bare possibility" of access is not sufficient. For example, the mere fact that the defendant and a copy of the work were at one time in the same city is not sufficient proof of a reasonable opportunity to view. Mere evidence that an unsolicited script was received by one office on the lot of a large motion picture studio is not sufficient proof of access.

See CORPORATE RECEIPT DOCTRINE.

Performance as Providing Access. The fact that a popular song was widely broadcast on the radio for some time was held to be sufficient proof of its access to Beatle George Harrison, who was found to have unconsciously infringed *He's So Fine* when he composed *My Sweet Lord. Bright Tunes Music Corp. v. Harrisongs Music Ltd.*, 420 F. Supp. 177, 180 (S.D.N.Y. 1976), *aff'd sub nom. Abko Music Inc. v. Harrisongs Music Ltd.*, 722 F.2d 968, 221 USPQ 490 (2d Cir. 1983). On the other hand, it was held that two or three performances of a song by the composer in Chicago and a tape sent to some music publishers was proof of only a "bare possibility" of access to the song where the famous songwriter-performers The Bee Gees wrote the allegedly infringing work *How Deep Is Your Love.* No infringement was found on the ground that the plaintiff was unable to prove more than mere "speculation" or a "bare possibility" of the defendants' access to the copyrighted work. *Selle v. Gibb*, 741 F.2d 896, 901, 223 USPQ 195, 199 (7th Cir. 1984).

Striking Similarity and Access. In some cases, there will be such a striking similarity of detail between the copyrighted work and the accused work that copying seems to be the only reasonable inference to draw. In those cases, the strength of evidence to prove access becomes much less important. In effect, striking similarity creates a presumption requiring the defendant to come forward with evidence of independent creation. However, if the striking similarity is only on the level of trite, stock elements, then "striking similarity is just one piece of circumstantial evidence tending to show access" and "must be considered together with other types of circumstantial evidence relating to access." *Selle v. Gibb*, 741 F.2d 896, 901, 223 USPQ 195, 198 (7th Cir. 1984). Thus, absent persuasive evidence of access, copying can be inferred only if the similarity in detail between the works is so striking as to preclude the possibility that the defendant arrived at the accused work by coincidental independent creation. Sometimes this is the case where there are many common errors in the two works, whether those errors were intentionally planted by the plaintiff or not. See 3 *Nimmer on Copyright* §13.03[C] (1994 rev.).

Reasons for Similarity of Works. In a copyright infringement suit, similarity between the works will usually be due to one of three possibilities: (1) the defendant had access to the plaintiff's work and copied from it, either consciously or unconsciously; (2) the defendant did not copy from the plaintiff's work and independent creation has resulted in a work which is coincidentally similar; or (3) both the plaintiff and the defendant based their works on a common prior source.

See COPYING, INFRINGEMENT OF COPYRIGHT.

• *Treatise References*: 3 *Nimmer on Copyright* §13.02 (1994 rev.); 2 P. Goldstein, *Copyright* §7.2.1.1 (1989); M. Leaffer, *Understanding Copyright* §9.3 (1989); 1 W. Patry, *Copyright Law and Practice* 694 (1994).

• *Case Reference*: "Proof of copying is crucial to any claim of copyright infringement because no matter how similar the two works may be (even to the point of identity), if the defendant did not copy the [copyrighted] work, there is no infringement.... However, because direct evidence of copying is rarely available, the plaintiff can rely upon circumstantial evidence to prove this essential element, and the most important component of this sort of circumstantial evidence is proof of access.... The plaintiff may be able to introduce direct evidence of access when, for example, the work was sent directly to the defendant (whether a musician or a publishing company) or a close associate of the defendant. On the other hand, the plaintiff may be able to establish a reasonable possibility of access when, for example, the complaining work has been widely disseminated to the public." *Selle v. Gibb*, 741 F.2d 896, 901, 223 USPQ 195, 198 (7th Cir. 1984).

accused device [patent] A product or device that is alleged by the owner of a patent to infringe a claim of the patent. The term "device" in this context is also often used generically to include an accused process.

- *Usage Example*: The test of literal infringement is whether each element of the claim is found in the accused device.

- *Case Reference*: "[To ascertain if there is patent infringement] it must be determined whether the claim 'reads on' the accused product or process, that is, whether the claimed invention is being made, used or sold by the alleged infringer." *Standard Oil Co. v. American Cyanamid Co.*, 774 F.2d 448, 452, 227 USPQ 293, 295 (Fed. Cir. 1985).

accused work [copyright] A work, such as a book, motion picture, song, or computer program, which is alleged by the owner of a copyright to infringe the copyright.

- *Usage Examples*:

"[W]here such substantial similarity is found, slight differences between a protected work and an accused work will not preclude a finding of infringement.... Identity or near identity between the accused work and the protected work is definitely not required for a determination of infringement." *Durham Indus., Inc. v. Tomy Corp.*, 630 F.2d 905, 913, 208 USPQ 10, 18 (2d Cir. 1980).

"Because direct evidence of copying often is unavailable, copying may be inferred where the defendant had access to the copyrighted work and the accused work is substantially similar to the copyrighted work." *Atari, Inc. v. North Am. Philips Consumer Elecs. Corp.*, 672 F.2d 607, 614, 214 USPQ 33, 38 (7th Cir. 1982).

ad interim copyright [copyright]
See MANUFACTURING CLAUSE.

ADR [general legal]
See ALTERNATIVE DISPUTE RESOLUTION.

aesthetic functionality [trademark]
See FUNCTIONALITY (subhead 2: *Functionality and Trademark–Trade Dress*).

affixation [trademark] The physical application or attachment of a trademark to the goods, to their container, or to displays associated with the goods.

Common-Law Affixation. At early common law, priority of use was not attained unless and until the goods with the trademark physically affixed were sold in the open market. A mark not physically affixed (i.e., used only in advertising) was not protected as a TECHNICAL TRADEMARK but was protected under the separate law of unfair competition. *American Steel Foundries v. Robertson*, 269 U.S. 372, 380 (1926). With the gradual dissolution of the line between "trademark" law and "unfair competition" law, the common-law requirement of affixation is of little significance today.

Federal Trademark Registration Affixation. To be registrable, a trademark must be "affixed" to the goods according to the federal definition of affixation, which permits any of the following alternatives as to where the mark is placed: (1) on the goods or their containers; (2) on "displays associated" with the goods or containers; or (3) if the nature of the goods makes the foregoing methods "impracticable," then on "documents associated with the goods or their sale." The last alternative was added in 1989 as part of the Trademark Law Revision Act to cover situations such as the shipping of bulk goods (e.g., grain) or goods shipped in tank cars (e.g., petroleum or milk). It has been held that use of a mark on point-of-purchase displays and counter or window displays is a use on "displays associated" with the goods. The Court of Customs and Patent Appeals rejected the notion that there had to be some physical contact or close physical association between the display and the goods. *Appl. of Marriott Corp.*, 459 F.2d 525, 173 USPQ 799 (C.C.P.A. 1972).

Federal Service Mark Registration Affixation. For service marks, there is no physical "thing" to which the mark can be affixed. Therefore, the Lanham Act does not specify any type of physical association that must exist between the service and the mark. Sufficient service mark usage includes use of the mark in advertising and promotional materials, use on the letterhead of a letter describing or promoting the service, and use on a business card. While at one time the Court of Customs and Patent Appeals said that to prove that a certain term was being used to identify services, there must be a "direct association" in the advertising between the term and the service, the Court of Appeals for the Federal Circuit later made it clear that the term "direct association" is merely a metaphorical guide and "does not create an additional or more stringent requirement for registration" of a service mark beyond that defined in the statute itself. *In re Advertising & Marketing Dev. Inc.*, 821 F.2d 614, 620, 2 USPQ2d 2010, 2014 (Fed. Cir. 1987).

• *Treatise Reference*: 1 J.T. McCarthy, *Trademarks and Unfair Competition* §§16.08–.11 (3d ed. 1995 rev.).

• *Statutory Reference*: Lanham Act §45, 15 U.S.C. §1127:

Use in Commerce. The term "use in commerce" means the bona fide use of a mark in the ordinary course of trade and not made merely to reserve a right in a mark. For purposes of this Act, a mark shall be deemed to be in use in commerce—

(1) on goods when—

(A) it is placed in any manner on the goods or their containers or the displays associated therewith or on the tags or labels affixed thereto, or if the nature of the goods makes such placement impracticable, then on documents associated with the goods or their sale, and

(B) the goods are sold or transported in commerce, and

(2) on services when it is used or displayed in the sale or advertising of services and the services are rendered in commerce, or the services are rendered in more than one State or in the United States and a foreign country and the person rendering the services is engaged in commerce in connection with the services.

aggregation [patent] (1) A COMBINATION of parts or elements into an invention that is unpatentable because obvious. (2) A combination of parts into an invention in which the parts do not cooperate or interact with each other.

Definition One. "In course of time the profession came to employ the term 'combination' to imply … [the presence of a patentable invention] and the term 'aggregation' to signify its absence, thus making antonyms in legal art of words which in ordinary speech are more nearly synonyms." *Great Atl. & Pac. Tea Co. v. Supermarket Equip. Corp.*, 340 U.S. 147, 151, 87 USPQ 303, 305 (1950). Since the 1952 Patent Code, "aggregation" is occasionally, but only rarely, used as a synonym for an "obvious" combination of prior art elements. See, e.g., *Lindemann Masch. GmbH v. American Hoist & Derrick Co.*, 730 F.2d 1452, 1462, 221 USPQ 481, 488 (Fed. Cir. 1984).

See OBVIOUSNESS.

Definition Two. In this type of invention, the component parts are merely "aggregated" together and do not interact in a way that produces a new result. Perhaps the most famous example of an unpatentable "aggregation" is the invention of attaching an eraser at the end of a pencil. The Supreme Court said that this was no more a patentable combination than putting a screwdriver at the end of a hammer handle. The Court held that since the pencil and the eraser did not combine to produce any new joint result, the bringing together was an unpatentable aggregation: "No effect is produced, no result follows, from the joint use of the two.… The combination, to be patentable, must produce a different force or effect, or result in the combined forces or processes, from that given by their separate parts. There must be a new result produced by their union: if not so, it is only an aggregation of separate elements.… It may be more convenient to turn over the different ends of the same stick than to lay down one stick and take up another. This, however, is not invention within the patent law.…" *Reckendorfer v. Faber*, 92 U.S. 347, 356–57 (1876).

• *Manual Reference*: "Rejections on the ground of aggregation should be based upon a lack of cooperation between the elements of the claim.... Example of aggregation: A washing machine associated with a dial telephone.... A claim is not necessarily aggregative because the various elements do not function simultaneously. A typewriter, for example, is a good combination." *Manual of Patent Examining Procedure* §706.03(i) (1994).

aid or abet infringement [patent]   One who "actively induces" infringement of a patent, as defined in Patent Code §271(b), is often said to "aid or abet" the infringement. "To 'actively induce' patent infringement means in essence to aid and abet such infringement by another." *Marston v. Gant*, 351 F. Supp. 1122, 1125 (E.D. Va. 1972).

See INDUCE INFRINGEMENT.

• *Case References*:
"Paragraph (b) [of Patent Code §271] recites in broad terms that one who aids and abets an infringement is likewise an infringer.... [This] may include liability of corporate officials who actively aid and abet their corporation's infringements." *Power Lift, Inc. v. Lang Tools, Inc.*, 774 F.2d 478, 481, 227 USPQ 435, 437 (Fed. Cir. 1985) (Rich, J., quoting from S. Rep. No. 1979, 82d Cong., 2d Sess. 9 (1952)).

"[I]t is well settled that corporate officers who actively aid and abet their corporation's infringement may be personally liable for inducing infringement under §271(b) regardless of whether the corporation is the alter ego of the corporate officer." *Orthokentics Inc. v. Safety Travel Chairs, Inc.*, 806 F.2d 1565, 1578, 1 USPQ2d 1081, 1090 (Fed. Cir. 1986).

Aiken exemption [copyright] An exemption in Copyright Act §110(5) from copyright liability for small retail establishments that play an ordinary radio or television receiver for the benefit of patrons or workers. However, to fall within the exemption, the retail establishment must not be any larger in size than that in the *Aiken* case, the receiving apparatus must be of a kind commonly used in private homes, there can be no direct charge to see or hear the broadcast, and there can be no equipment that transmits the broadcast to other places.

Aiken's Chicken Shop. The statutory exemption is sometimes known as the "Aiken" (or "store receiver") exemption because it is designed to codify the result of a case decided by the U.S. Supreme Court in 1975. In that case, the owner of Aiken's Chicken Shop, a small restaurant in Pittsburgh with a floor area of 1,055 square feet, 620 square feet open to the public, used an ordinary FM radio receiver with four ceiling-mounted speakers to play music for the enjoyment of patrons. The Supreme Court held that this was not an infringing performance of copyrighted music that was broadcast over the station. *Twentieth Century Music Corp. v. Aiken*, 422 U.S. 151, 186 USPQ 65 (1975).

Scope of the Exemption. Congress in enacting the Copyright Act §110(5) exemption stated that the factual situation in the *Aiken* case is intended to "represent the outer limit of the exemption and ... the line should be drawn at that point." H.R. Rep. No. 94-1476, 94th Cong., 2d Sess. 87 (1976). Neither larger retail establishments nor places that use receiving apparatus of a kind not commonly used in private homes fall within the *Aiken* exemption. For example, the reception of television programs in a bar via a satellite dish is not within the exemption because satellite dishes are not "commonly found in private homes." *National Football League v. McBee & Bruno's, Inc.*, 792 F.2d 726, 731, 230 USPQ 30, 34 (8th Cir. 1986). And a chain of over 400 retail stores, each store averaging 3,500 square feet, was held to be too large to come within the §110(5) exemption. *Sailor Music v. The Gap Stores, Inc.*, 668 F.2d 84 (2d Cir. 1981). But one court has held that the §110(5) exception is not limited to the square footage in the *Aiken* case, stating that the focus of the exemption is the equipment being used in the store. A store could exceed the *Aiken* size and still be exempt if it uses "homestyle" equipment. *Edison Brothers Stores Inc. v. Broadcast Music Inc.*, 954 F.2d 1419, 1425, 21 USPQ 2d 1440, 1445 (8th Cir. 1992). It has been held that the financial size and strength of the alleged infringer is not relevant to the §110(5) exemption. "No case has relied solely on the financial size or ability of the defendant as a reason for denying the application of §110(5)." *Broadcast Music Inc. v. Claire's Boutiques*, 949

F.2d 1482, 1492, 21 USPQ 2d 1181, 1189 (2d Cir. 1991).

Exemption Is Measured on a Store-by-Store Basis. For the purposes of the exception, all the receivers owned by a chain of stores are not counted together but on a per-store basis. If each store has a single receiver, the owner does not exceed the "single receiving apparatus" requirement of §110(5). *Broadcast Music Inc. v. Claire's Boutiques Inc.*, 949 F.2d 1482, 1490–91, 21 USPQ2d 1181, 1188 (2d Cir. 1991). "It is not appropriate to focus on the number of stores involved, but rather on whether each store duplicates the requirements of the homestyle exception." *Edison Bros. Stores, Inc. v. Broadcast Music, Inc.*, 954 F.2d 1419, 1422, 21 USPQ2d 1440, 1442 (8th Cir. 1992).

See PERFORMANCE, TRANSMISSION.

• *Treatise References:* 2 *Nimmer on Copyright* §8.18[C][2] (1994 rev.); 1 P. Goldstein, *Copyright* §5.8.1.5 (1989); M. Leaffer, *Understanding Copyright* §8.18[B] (1989); W. Patry, *Copyright Law and Practice* 917–24 (1994) ("The emphasis on size obscures the practical thrust of the section, which is to exempt a simple, single, ordinary radio or television used to keep store clerks or patrons amused."); 1 N. Boorstyn, *Copyright* §6.26[5] (2d ed. 1994).

• *Statutory Reference:* 17 U.S.C. §110: "Notwithstanding the provisions of section 106, the following are not infringements of copyright: ... (5) communication of a transmission embodying a performance or display of a work by the public reception of the transmission on a single receiving apparatus of a kind commonly used in private homes, unless—(A) a direct charge is made to see or hear the transmission; or (B) the transmission thus received is further transmitted to the public...."

AIPLA [general intellectual property] American Intellectual Property Law Association, a national society of more than 5,000 lawyers engaged in the practice of intellectual property law. AIPLA was formerly known as the American Patent Law Association (APLA). AIPLA publishes the scholarly journal *AIPLA Quarterly Journal.* AIPLA headquarters is located at 2001 Jefferson Davis Highway, Arlington, Virginia 22202.

AIPPI [international] Association Internationale pour la Protection de la Propriété Industrielle. AIPPI is an international association to promote the study and protection of INDUSTRIAL PROPERTY.

algorithm [computer–patent]   (1) In the broadest, nonlegal sense, a fixed step-by-step procedure for accomplishing a given result. (2) In patent law, "algorithm" as used in (1) in a nonlegal sense is a much broader category than a "mathematical algorithm." The former is in a patentable category, and the latter is not. In patent law, a "mathematical algorithm" or so-called "Benson algorithm" is not patentable. First so defined in *Gottschalk v. Benson*, 409 U.S. 63, 175 USPQ 673 (1972), the Supreme Court later stated that in the *Benson* case, "[w]e defined 'algorithm' as a 'procedure for solving a given type of mathematical problem,' and we concluded that such an algorithm, or mathematical formula, is like a law of nature, which cannot be the subject of a patent." *Diamond v. Diehr*, 450 U.S. 175, 186, 209 USPQ 1, 8 (1981).

• *Case References:*

The Supreme Court stated the general rule for patent protection for a process implemented by a computer program: "[A patent] claim drawn to subject matter otherwise statutory does not become nonstatutory simply because it uses a mathematical formula, computer program or digital computer.... [W]hen a claim containing a mathematical formula implements or applies that formula in a structure or process which, considered as a whole, is performing a function which the patent laws were designed to protect (e.g., transforming or reducing an article to a different state or thing), then the claim satisfies the requirements of [Patent Code] §101." *Diamond v. Diehr*, 450 U.S. 175, 192, 209 USPQ 1, 10 (1981).

"We note these discussions of the meaning of 'algorithm' to take the mystery out of the term and we point out once again that every step-by-step process, be it electronic or chemical or mechanical, involves an algorithm in the broad sense of the term.… [I]t is no ground for holding a claim is directed to nonstatutory subject matter to say it includes or is directed to an algorithm. This is why the proscription against patenting has been limited to *mathematical* algorithms and abstract *mathematical* formulae which, like the laws of nature, are not patentable subject matter." *In re Iwahashi*, 888 F.2d 1370, 1374, 12 USPQ2d 1908, 1911 (Fed. Cir. 1989) (apparatus MEANS PLUS FUNCTION CLAIM directed to a voice recognition device held to be patentable subject matter even though a mathematical formula was recited as part of the claim).

The Federal Circuit held unpatentable as an algorithm a claim reciting the process of performing clinical laboratory tests on a person in order to obtain data for defined parameters (e.g., sodium content), and analyzing the data to determine if there is an abnormality and possible causes. While expressed in words, not mathematical notation, it was still classified as an algorithm. "[M]athematical algorithms join the list of non-patentable subject matter not within the scope of section 101, including methods of doing business, naturally occurring phenomenon, and laws of nature.… On the other hand, 'the mere presence of a mathematical exercise, as a step or steps in a process involving nonmathematical steps, should not slam the door of the Patent and Trademark Office upon an applicant.' … Thus, if there are physical steps included in the claim in addition to the algorithm, the claim might be eligible for patent protection.… The sole physical process step in Grams' claim 1 is step [a], i.e., performing clinical tests on individuals to obtain data.… [A]pplicants are, in essence, claiming the mathematical algorithm, which they cannot do under *Gottschalk v. Benson*. The presence of a physical step in the claim to derive data for the algorithm will not render the claim statutory." *In re Grams*, 888 F.2d 835, 836–37, 12 USPQ2d 1824, 1826–28 (Fed. Cir. 1989).

"[A]t the core of the [Supreme] Court's analysis in each of these cases lies an attempt by the court to explain a rather straightforward concept, namely, that certain types of mathematical subject matters, standing alone, represent nothing more than *abstract ideas* until reduced to some type of practical application, and this that subject matter is not, in and of itself, entitled to patent protection. … [T]he proper enquiry in dealing with the so-called mathematical subject matter exception to §101 alleged herein is to see whether the claimed subject matter *as a whole* is a disembodied mathematical concept, whether categorized as a mathematical formula, mathematical equation, mathematical algorithm, or the like, which in essence represents nothing more than a 'law of nature,' 'natural phenomenon,' or 'abstract idea.' If so, *Diehr* precludes the patenting of that subject matter." *In re Alappat*, 33 F.3d 1526, 1542, 31 USPQ2d 1545, 1556–57 (Fed. Cir. 1994) (Rich, J. for majority of court en banc).

• *Example*: Schrader filed a patent application claiming a method for selecting the most profitable combination of bids at an auction, such as an auction of various parcels of real estate. After the items for sale have been offered to the bidders, bids are received and entered into a record. Then, the winning bids are determined by assembling a combination which yields the greatest total price from all the entered bids. The Federal Circuit said that a mathematical algorithm was implicit in the claim because it claimed the solving of a mathematical problem: determining the optimal combination of bids. In order for an algorithm to be the statutory subject matter of a patent, there must be some kind of transformation or reduction of subject matter. Schrader's claim did not recite sufficient physical activity to meet this burden. Data gathering is insufficient as it is implicit in any application of a mathematical algorithm. The grouping or regrouping of bids did not constitute a physical change, effect or result. As there was no data manipulation or transformation effected in the process claim, it was rejected for lack of statutory subject matter under 35 U.S.C. §101. *In re Schrader*, 22 F.3d 290, 30 USPQ2d 1455 (Fed. Cir. 1994).

all claims rule [patent] Under the law followed by some courts prior to the 1984 amendments to the Patent Code concerning joint inventors, a patent was invalid for failure to name the proper inventors unless each joint inventor named made an inventive contribution to *every* claim in a patent containing more than one claim. This was known as the "all claims" rule. The 1984 amendment to Patent Code §116 "clearly repudiates the [all claims] rule." *Smithkline Diagnostics Inc. v. Helena Labs. Corp.*, 859 F.2d 878, 889, 8 USPQ2d 1468, 1477 (Fed. Cir. 1988).

See JOINT INVENTORS.

all elements rule [patent] An aspect of the doctrine of EQUIVALENTS, under which each ELEMENT of a claim or its substantial equivalent must be found in the ACCUSED DEVICE to constitute infringement. When applying the all elements rule, the word "element" is "used in the sense of a *limitation* of a claim." *Corning Glass Works v. Sumitomo Elec. USA Inc.*, 868 F.2d 1251, 1259, 9 USPQ2d 1962, 1968 (Fed. Cir. 1989).

The all elements rule rejects the approach of applying the doctrine of equivalents by comparing the accused device as a whole with the claimed invention as a whole.

See EQUIVALENTS, DOCTRINE OF.

- *Case References*:

"In the All Elements rule, 'element' is used in the sense of a *limitation* of a claim.... An equivalent must be found for every limitation of the claim somewhere in an accused device, but not necessarily in a corresponding component, although that is generally the case." *Corning Glass Works v. Sumitomo Elec. USA Inc.*, 868 F.2d 1251, 1259, 9 USPQ2d 1962, 1968 (Fed. Cir. 1989). The Court of Appeals for the Federal Circuit affirmed a finding that in a claim to an optical wave guide type of telecommunications optical fiber, the substitution in the accused device of a negative dopant chemical in the cladding was the equivalent of the claimed element of a positive dopant chemical in the core of the fiber.

" '[I]nfringement can only be found if the different elements and operations are the legal equivalents of those disclosed in the patent-in-suit.' It is clear from this that the district court correctly relied on an element-by-element comparison to conclude that there was no infringe-

ment under the doctrine of equivalents...." *Pennwalt Corp. v. Durand-Wayland Inc.*, 833 F.2d 931, 935, 4 USPQ2d 1737, 1740 (Fed. Cir. 1987) (en banc).

"It is ... well settled that each element of a claim is material and essential, and that in order for a court to find infringement, the plaintiff must show the presence of every element or its substantial equivalent in the accused device. ... To be a 'substantial equivalent,' the element substituted in the accused device for the element set forth in the claim must not be such as would substantially change the way in which the function of the claimed invention is performed." *Perkin-Elmer Corp. v. Westinghouse Elec. Corp.*, 822 F.2d 1528, 1533, 3 USPQ2d 1321, 1325 (Fed. Cir. 1987).

- *Example*. A patent claim for a frame to hold a piece of fabric to serve as a wall covering recited as a limitation in the claim that the frame included two elements: (1) linear pieces and (2) preformed right-angled corner pieces. The court held that there was no infringement where the accused frame, while using the linear pieces of element (1) above, did not use the preformed corner pieces of element (2) above. Rather, to form a corner, the accused device used two linear pieces cut at a 45 degree angle which were to be placed together to form a right angle. The court said that if the accused frame formed only of linear pieces was to be viewed as an infringement of the claimed two elements of linear and right angle pieces, it would violate the all elements rule, which requires that every element in the claim be found in the accused device, either literally or equivalently. Since the limitation of element (2) above was not found in the accused device there was no infringement. "Both types of pieces are required by the claim." *Unique Concepts Inc. v. Brown*, 939 F.2d 1558, 1561–62, 19 USPQ2d 1500, 1503–04 (Fed. Cir. 1991) (Rich, J., dissenting, would find that element (2) was not limited to unitary or preformed corner pieces and was infringed by using two linear pieces to form a right angle).

all rights reserved [copyright–international] A provision of the BUENOS AIRES CONVENTION on Literary and Artistic Copyright of 1910 is the source of the often-seen legend "All Rights

Reserved" or its equivalents "Copyright Reserved" and "Todos los derechos reservados." The Buenos Aires Convention is a treaty entered into among 16 Central and South American nations and the United States. The author from any member country who has secured copyright in the author's own country will enjoy in each of the other Convention countries the copyright rights accorded to its own citizens if the specified notice is used.

In Buenos Aires nations that have become members of the UNIVERSAL COPYRIGHT CONVENTION (UCC), the UCC notice supersedes the "All Rights Reserved" notice. Only in those three Buenos Aires nations that are not parties to the UCC would the "All Rights Reserved" notice still seem to be necessary. Those are Bolivia, Honduras, and Uruguay. See 1 *Nimmer on Copyright* §5.05[B][2][c] (1994 rev.); W. Patry, *Copyright Law and Practice* 1252 (1994).

See UNIVERSAL COPYRIGHT CONVENTION, BERNE CONVENTION.

alternative dispute resolution (ADR)

[general legal] A means other than litigation for resolving conflicts between parties; it is generally less expensive, faster, and more confidential than traditional litigation. ADR takes several forms, including:

Mediation. A settlement process in which a neutral party facilitates communication between the parties, listens to their arguments, and assists them in reaching a mutually satisfactory result.

Arbitration. A decision-making process in which a neutral factfinder listens to arguments and makes a decision on relevant issues. The decision may be binding or nonbinding depending on the parties' previous agreement.

Minitrial or Summary Jury Trial. A settlement device requiring a formal case presentation generally presented by the counsel for each side. Arguments are heard by a panel of jurors presided over by a magistrate or a judge. The jury makes a nonbinding decision and is often then made available for interviews by the parties. Such an approach allows each side to see the strengths and weaknesses of its case and its opponent's case thus tending to lead them to settle.

Early Neutral Evaluation. An alternative dispute resolution procedure in which the parties and their counsel present the factual and legal grounds of their case to one another and to an impartial attorney with expertise in the subject matter at issue. The conference is confidential and nonbinding and allows the parties to receive a neutral evaluation identifying the primary issues, the areas of agreement, and the possibilities for settlement.

• *Book References*: Jay Folberg, *Mediation: A Comprehensive Guide to Resolving Conflicts Without Litigation* (1984); Stephen B. Goldberg et al., *Dispute Resolution* (1985 & Supp. 1987); Linda R. Singer, *Settling Disputes, Conflict Resolution in Business, Families, and the Legal System* (1990); T. Creel (ed.), *Guide to Patent Arbitration* (1987).

ambush marketing [trademark] A type of advertising by a company that is not an official sponsor of an event, the advertisor using the event to attract customers to pay attention to the ad. The ad may also only remind customers of the event or may create the misleading impression that the company is an official sponsor or is affiliated with the event.

For example, an athletic shoe manufacturer who is not an official sponsor of a World Cup soccer finals round may use a television advertisement featuring soccer players from various nations. This reminds viewers of the World Cup, presumably to the detriment of a competitor who paid to be an official sponsor of the World Cup and expected to have certain exclusive advertising rights.

• *Commentary Reference*: Ambush marketers are "companies that compete with official sponsors and hope to profit by giving the impression that they are officially part of the [Olympic] Games." R. Frank, *Olympic Flame Singes Some Atlanta Businesses,* Wall St. J., Mar. 22, 1995, at B1.

amendment [patent-trademark-copyright] A modification of either: (1) a patent application; (2) an application for registration of a mark; or (3) a registration of a claim to copyright.

1. Amendment of Patent Application. The applicant for a patent can amend the specification, drawings, or claims of an application. 37 C.F.R. §1.115. The most common amendment is one that narrows the scope of the patent CLAIMS in order to avoid the PRIOR ART references cited by the examiner in the Patent and Trademark Office.

While the specification of the patent application may be amended, no amendment can introduce NEW MATTER into the disclosure of the invention. 35 U.S.C. §133; 37 C.F.R. §118(a).

A granted patent cannot be amended except by a CERTIFICATE OF CORRECTION or through REISSUE.

See NEW MATTER; CORRECTION, CERTIFICATE OF; REISSUE.

• *Rule Reference*: "The claims may be amended by canceling particular claims, by presenting new claims, or by rewriting particular claims.… The requirements of §1.111 must be complied with by pointing out the specific distinctions believed to render the claims patentable over the references in presenting arguments in support of new claims and amendments." 37 C.F.R. §1.119.

2. Amendment of Application and Registration of Mark. The applicant for registration can amend any part of the application to correct minor errors or to avoid objections made by the examiner. However, no amendment of the dates of use or addition to the specification of goods or services is permitted without supplementary proof through declarations. 37 C.F.R. §2.71. An application for registration on the principal register can be amended to be an application for the supplemental register, or vice versa. 37 C.F.R. §2.75.

Mistakes in an issued registration of a mark can be corrected by the issuance of a CERTIFICATE OF CORRECTION.

In certain circumstances an issued registration of a mark can be amended to reflect changes. Upon application, the registration may be amended or disclaimed in part. 37 C.F.R. §2.173. However, an amendment cannot make changes that would materially alter the character of the mark itself such that would require a republication of the mark. Lanham Act §7(e), 15 U.S.C. §1057(e). This is to prevent competitors being presented with an amended registered mark which they have never had an opportunity to oppose. See *In re Holland Am. Wafer Co.*, 737 F.2d 1015, 222 USPQ 273 (Fed. Cir. 1984) (amended version of trademark held to be an unpermitted "material alteration" of old version). In the case of a change of ownership of a registration, the assignee may request that a new certificate of registration be issued in the name of the assignee. Lanham Act §7(d), 15 U.S.C. §1057(d); 37 C.F.R. §2.171.

See CORRECTION, CERTIFICATE OF.

• *Statutory Reference*: Lanham Act §7(e), 15 U.S.C. §1057(e): "Upon application of the registrant and payment of the prescribed fee, the Commission for good cause may permit any registration to be amended or to be disclaimed in part: *Provided*, That the amendment or disclaimer does not materially alter the character of the mark.…"

3. Amendment of Copyright Registration. A SUPPLEMENTARY REGISTRATION may be made either to correct or to amplify the information in a basic registration. 7 U.S.C. §408(d); 37 C.F.R. §201.5(b). A "correction" is appropriate if the information was incorrect at the time of the original registration. An "amplification" should reflect new facts or clarify information previously given.

Supplementary copyright registration is not appropriate to indicate changes in ownership or licensing of rights in the work, to correct errors in copyright notices on copies of the work, or to reflect changes in the content of the work. 37 C.F.R. §201.5(b)(2)(iii).

A supplementary registration augments but does not supersede the original, basic registration. 17 U.S.C. §408(d). The basic registration is not expunged or canceled.

• *Rule Reference*: "After a basic registration has been completed, any author or other copyright claimant of the work, or the owner of any exclusive right in the work, or the duly authorized agent of any such author, other claimant, or owner, who wishes to correct or amplify the information given in the basic registration for the work may file an application for supplementary registration." 37 C.F.R. §201.5(b)(1).

Amendment to Allege Use [trademark]

A change in an INTENT TO USE (ITU) application for trademark registration, by which an applicant who has used the mark during prosecution can change the ITU application into a use-based application.

Use Must Precede Registration. A U.S. trademark registration will not be granted unless and until an applicant files a verified statement, together with specimens, that it has used the mark in United States interstate or foreign commerce. The only exception is that qualified foreign companies are permitted to obtain a U.S. registration merely upon stating an intent to use without ever actually using or proving use in the United States. Proof of use is accomplished by filing either an Amendment to Allege Use (AAU), or a Statement of Use (SOU). The difference between these two methods of proving use of the mark is their timing. It is fundamental to United States trademark registration practice that use must precede registration. Without use, there is no "trademark" to be recorded on the federal register of marks. The "use" necessary is use in the "ordinary course of trade," not just token use.

Proof of Use. There are two methods for an ITU applicant to offer proof of use of the mark: (1) via an Amendment to Allege Use (AAU) during the pre approval-for-publication period; and (2) via a Statement of Use (SOU) during the post notice-of-allowance period.

The time gap between approval for publication and issuance of the notice of allowance is known as the BLACKOUT PERIOD because during this period neither the SOU nor an AAU can be filed.

Advantage of Amendment to Allege Use. The advantage to using an AAU to prove use of the mark rather than waiting for publication and allowance and then filing a Statement of Use is that the AAU procedure permits the applicant who uses soon after applying to obtain registration faster.

- *Treatise Reference*: 2 J.T. McCarthy, *Trademarks and Unfair Competition* §19.07[4] (3d ed. 1995 rev.).

- *Statutory Reference*: Lanham Act §1(c), 15 U.S.C. §1051(c): "At any time during examination of an application filed under subsection (b), an applicant who has made use of the mark in commerce may claim the benefits of such use for purposes of this Act, by amending his or her application to bring it into conformity with the requirements of subsection (a)."

- *Rule Reference*: 37 C.F.R. §2.76(a): "An application under section 1(b) of the Act may be amended to allege use of the mark in commerce under section 1(c) of the Act at any time between the filing of the application and the date the examiner approves the mark for publication or the date of expiration of the six-month response period after issuance of a final action. Thereafter, an allegation of use may be submitted only as a statement of use under §2.88 after the issuance of a notice of allowance under section 13(b)(2) of the Act. If an amendment to allege use is filed outside the time period specified in this paragraph, it will be returned to the applicant."

analogous art [patent] Information from a technological field which is not within the field of the invention in question but is still so reasonably pertinent to the technological problem that persons working in the field would turn to this information to seek a solution to the problem. Art which is found to be "analogous" will be considered in determining obviousness of the invention under §103. On the other hand, information from a technology that is so far removed from the field to which an invention pertains that the information is not considered to be PRIOR ART is dubbed a reference from a "nonanalogous art." "Art" is used here in the sense of "technology."

The Test of Obviousness. Under Patent Code §103, an invention is "obvious" and unpatentable if the difference between the invention and the prior art are such that "the subject matter as a whole would have been obvious at the time the invention was made" to a person having ordinary "skill in the art" to which the invention "pertains."

Skill Only in the Art to Which the Invention "Pertains." Patent Code §103 states that the hypothetical person is expected to be skilled only in the art "to which such subject matter pertains," not to be skilled in every branch of technology, science and human knowledge. "[A]n inventor could not possibly be aware of every teaching in every art." *In re Wood*, 599 F.2d 1032, 1036, 202 USPQ 171, 174 (C.C.P.A. 1979). Art B is analogous to art A if the hypothetical person seeking a solution to a problem in technology A would be likely to seek the solution by referring to information in technology B.

Test of Analogous Art. Whether a reference is "analogous" art is a fact question, with two questions asked: (1) is the art from the same field of endeavor, regardless of the problem addressed? and (2) if the art is not within the same field of endeavor, is it still reasonably pertinent to the particular problem involved? *In re Clay*, 966 F.2d 656, 658–59, 23 USPQ2d 1058, 1060 (Fed. Cir. 1992). "A reference is reasonably pertinent, if even though it may be in a different field from that of the inventor's endeavor, it is one which, because of the matter with which it deals, logically would have commended itself to an inventor's attention in considering his problem. Thus, the purposes of both the invention and the prior art are important in determining whether the reference is reasonably pertinent to the problem the invention attempts to solve." *In re Clay*, 966 F.2d at 659, 23 USPQ2d at 1060–61.

See ART, OBVIOUSNESS, SKILL IN THE ART, PRIOR ART.

• *Statutory Reference*: 35 U.S.C. §103: "A patent may not be obtained though the invention is not identically disclosed or described as set forth in section 102 of this title, if the differences between the subject matter sought to be patented and the prior art are such that the subject matter as a whole would have been obvious at the time the invention was made to a person having ordinary skill in the art to which such subject matter pertains."

• *Case References*:
"In resolving the question of obviousness under 35 U.S.C. §103, we presume full knowledge by the inventor of all the prior art in the field of his endeavor. However, with regard to prior art outside the field of his endeavor, we only presume knowledge from those arts reasonably pertinent to the particular problem with which the inventor was involved…. The rationale behind this rule precluding rejections based on combinations of teachings of references from nonanalogous arts is the realization that an inventor could not possibly be aware of every teaching in every art." *In re Wood*, 599 F.2d 1032, 1036, 202 USPQ 171, 174 (C.C.P.A. 1979).

The court held that a pump is analogous prior art to a compressor as both have essentially the same function and structure. "In [the inventor's view] the examiner and the board defined the problem too broadly by including both compressors and pumps in the prior art. [The inventor] cites *Stratoflex, Inc. v. Aeroquip Corp.*, in which this court … [was faced with the question] whether rubber hose should be considered as prior art relevant to the claimed PTFE [Teflon] tubing. In finding that rubber hose was prior art, the court focused on only the second step of the two-step test for nonanalogous art which test had been stated in *Wood*. …[See case reference above.] Here, the references satisfy the first inquiry because they are 'within the field of the inventor's endeavor' of horizontally reciprocating, double-acting piston devices for moving fluids …. [T]he cited pumps and compressors have essentially the same function and structure: they move fluids by means of a double-acting piston, a cylinder, and valves." *In re Deminski*, 796 F.2d 436, 441–42, 230 USPQ 313, 315 (Fed. Cir. 1986).

• *Treatise Reference*: "Analogous art is simply that which is not too remote to be treated as prior art, and so labeling it merely connotes that it is relevant to a consideration of obviousness under §103." R. Harmon, *Patents and the Federal Circuit* §4.4 (3d ed. 1994).

• *Example 1: Art Held Not to Be Analogous:* The Court of Customs and Patent Appeals held that an ancient Japanese sword-making method was not analogous prior art to an invention for reducing turbulence in the flow of propellant to a rocket engine. The invention essentially consisted of putting a thin layer of thermal insulating plastic on the inner walls of pipes carrying super-cold (cryogenic) rocket propellant from the fuel tank to the rocket engine. This solved a problem of flow turbulence by quickly cooling the temperature of the warmer metal pipe walls down to the cold temperature of the liquid cryogenic fuel. The reference cited as prior art consisted of the ancient Japanese method of quickly cooling steel swords and cutlery in the water-quenching process by coating the steel with a thin layer of powdered clay. This coating increased the quick cooling of the hot metal blade as it was thrust into the cold quenching water. The court found that the reference was not from an analogous art, and was not to be considered, holding the invention to be nonobvious and patentable. "[The inventors] are of course not charged with the teachings in all arts. Where is the dividing line? ... [The] invention is manifestly far removed from the art of manufacturing Japanese cutlery.... [I]t does not seem to us that one seeking to eliminate pump cavitation problems *and* the problem of vapor in cryogenic liquid propellant flow systems would turn to the cutlery art." *Appl. of Van Wanderham*, 378 F.2d 981, 986, 988, 154 USPQ 20, 25 (C.C.P.A. 1967).

• *Example 2: Art Held Not to Be Analogous:* Oetiker invented an improvement in a metal clamp with a hook structure, the clamp used to secure commercial hose used on an assembly line. A cited reference was Lauro's patent, which disclosed a plastic hook and eye fastener used on garments. The Court of Appeals for the Federal Circuit held that the Lauro garment fastener was not analogous art and rejected the contention that all hooking problems are analogous. "It has not seen shown that a person of ordinary skill, seeking to avoid a problem of fastening a hose clamp, would reasonably be expected or motivated to look to fasteners for garments. The combination of elements from non-analogous sources, in a manner that reconstructs the applicant's invention only with the benefit of hindsight, is insufficient to present a prima facie case of obviousness." *In re Oetiker*,

977 F.2d 1443, 1447, 24 USPQ2d 1443, 1446 (Fed. Cir. 1992).

• *Example 3: Art Held to Be Analogous*: Paulsen and others invented a form of laptop computer housing. Several claims were rejected as obvious in light of prior art of hinges and latches as used in a desktop telephone directory, a piano lid, a kitchen cabinet, a washing machine cabinet, a wooden furniture cabinet and a housing for storing audio cassettes. The Federal Circuit affirmed the rejection of claims, holding that while such prior art references were not within the same field of endeavor as portable computer housings, they were analogous art because they related to the same technical problems as faced by these inventors. "The problems encountered by the inventors ... were problems that were not unique to portable computers. They concerned how to connect and secure the computer's display housing to the computer while meeting certain size constraints and functional requirements. The prior art cited by the examiner discloses various means of connecting a cover (or lid) to a device so that the cover is free to swing radially along the connection axis, as well as means of securing the cover in an open or closed position. ... [O]ne of ordinary skill in the art 'would have consulted the mechanical arts for housings, hinges, latches, springs, etc.' Thus, the cited references are 'reasonably pertinent' and we therefore conclude that the Board's finding that the references are analogous was not clearly erroneous." *In re Paulsen*, 30 F.3d 1475, 1481–82, 31 USPQ2d 1671, 1676 (Fed. Cir. 1994).

• *Example 4: Art Held to Be Analogous:* The Court of Appeals for the Federal Circuit affirmed a holding of invalidity of a patent on a form of photosensitive night light, finding that a person of ordinary skill in the art would be aware of prior art in the related field of shades for overhead lighting fixtures. "In evaluating obviousness, the hypothetical person of ordinary skill in the pertinent art is presumed to have the 'ability to select and utilize knowledge from other arts reasonably pertinent to [the] particular problem' to which the claimed invention is directed.... Assuming arguendo that these four references [relating to shades for overhead lighting fixtures] are not strictly within the field of [electric night lights], they are easily within a field analogous thereto, and their teachings are properly combinable with the earlier references...." *Cable Elec. Prods., Inc. v. Genmark, Inc.*, 770 F.2d 1015, 1025, 226 USPQ 881, 886 (Fed. Cir. 1985).

annuity [patent]
See MAINTENANCE FEES.

anonymous work [copyright] A work in which no person is identified as author. Copyright in an anonymous work created after January 1, 1978, lasts for a term of 75 years from first publication of the work or a term of 100 years from creation of the work, whichever expires first. But if, before the end of that term, the identity of the author is revealed in a registration of copyright or in the public records of the Copyright Office, then the term of copyright is the life of the author plus 50 years.

See DURATION OF COPYRIGHT.

• *Statutory Reference*: 17 U.S.C. §101: "An 'anonymous work' is a work on the copies or phonorecords of which no natural person is identified as author." Regarding duration, see 17 U.S.C. §302(c).

anticipation [patent] A bar to the validity of a patent that exists when the disclosure of a single piece of PRIOR ART reveals every element of the claimed invention. When that bar exists, there is "anticipation." The legal source of the bar is Patent Code §102, which sets down a list of conditions that will prevent the granting of a valid patent. If one of those conditions is satisfied, there is "anticipation." Another way of phrasing it is to state that if there is "anticipation," then the invention lacks NOVELTY and cannot be validly patented.

Identity of Invention. For a piece of PRIOR ART to constitute anticipation, it must not merely approximate or be almost the same as the patent claim in question. There must be an IDENTITY OF INVENTION between the prior art and the claim in question.

Nonanticipation Is Not Synonymous With Patentability. Merely because an invention is not anticipated by one piece of the PRIOR ART, i.e., is not identical to it, does not mean that the invention is patentable. Rather, it must then meet the condition of OBVIOUSNESS; the invention must not be obvious in view of all the prior art combined. Referring to another court's erroneous use of the term "anticipation," the Court of Customs and Patent Appeals remarked: "[T]he Fifth Circuit used the term 'anticipation' broadly to mean that the subject matter of the claims was not patentable over Stow, rather than as a term of art in patent law to mean that the basis of invalidity was 35 U.S.C. §102.... [C]ourts occasionally fail to understand the jargon of patent law." *In re Clark*, 522 F.2d 623, 635 n.9, 187 USPQ 209, 219 n.9 (C.C.P.A. 1975) (Miller, J., concurring).

Anticipation of "Means Plus Function" Claims: "Anticipation is determined by comparison of the reference with the claims. The claims here define the invention in terms of several specific 'means-plus-function' elements. The limitations which must be met by anticipatory reference are those set forth in each statement of function.... Such a limitation cannot be met by an element in a reference that performs a different function, even though it may be part of a device embodying the same general overall concept." *RCA Corp. v. Applied Digital Data Sys., Inc.*, 730 F.2d 1440, 1445 n.5, 221 USPQ 385, 389 n.5 (Fed. Cir. 1984).

• *Usage Note*: Prior to the 1952 Patent Code, the term "anticipation" was often used as a synonym for "unpatentable," regardless of the statutory basis for nonpatentability of the invention. But with passage of §§102–03 of the 1952 Patent Code, the word "anticipation" took on a narrower and more definite meaning, as defined above.

See NOVELTY; THAT WHICH INFRINGES IF LATER, ANTICIPATES IF EARLIER.

• *Treatise Reference*: "At some risk of oversimplification, the rule may be stated as follows: lack of originality, or lack of priority, or a statutory bar, can be established only where the prior invention is identical to, or 'anticipates' the invention sought to be patented. If there are differences between the prior work and the invention for which a patent is sought, §103 automatically comes into play, and the inquiry then becomes whether those differences are such that the invention would have been obvious. All this sounds logical enough. But it does not take much exposure to patents and patent law until one realizes that instances of complete identity are comparatively rare." R. Harmon, *Patents and the Federal Circuit* §3.2 (3d ed. 1994).

- *Case References*:

"Anticipation under 35 U.S.C. §102 requires the presence in a single prior art disclosure of each and every element of a claimed invention.... [P]rior to the Patent Act of 1952, the term 'anticipation' was used in a broader sense than it is today. The pre-1952 cases often used the term 'anticipation' to mean that the subject matter of the claims was found exactly in the prior art (lacked novelty) or, though different, was not 'inventive' over the prior art.... In the 1952 Act, Congress replaced the latter concept with 35 U.S.C. §103, the requirement of nonobviousness.... 'Anticipation' thereafter became a restricted term of art in patent law meaning that the claimed invention lacked novelty, or was unpatentable under 35 U.S.C. §102." *Lewmar Marine, Inc. v. Barient, Inc.*, 827 F.2d 744, 747–48, 3 USPQ2d 1766, 1768 (Fed. Cir. 1987).

"Anticipation is established only when a single prior art reference discloses, expressly or under principles of inherency, each and every element of a claimed invention." *RCA Corp. v. Applied Digital Data Sys., Inc.*, 730 F.2d 1440, 1444, 221 USPQ 385, 388 (Fed. Cir. 1984). *Accord In re Paulsen*, 30 F.3d 1475, 1478, 31 USPQ2d 1671, 1673 (Fed. Cir. 1994).

"Anticipation requires the presence in a single prior art disclosure of all elements of a claimed invention arranged as in the claim.... A prior art disclosure that 'almost' meets that standard does not 'anticipate.' Though it is never necessary to so hold, a disclosure that anticipates under §102 also renders the claim invalid under §103, for 'anticipation is the epitome of obviousness.'... The reverse is not true, for the need to determine obviousness presumes anticipation is lacking." *Connell v. Sears, Roebuck & Co.*, 722 F.2d 1542, 1548, 220 USPQ 193, 198 (Fed. Cir. 1983).

"The law of anticipation does not require that the reference 'teach' what the subject patent teaches. Assuming that a reference is properly 'prior art,' it is only necessary that the claims under attack, as construed by the court, 'read on' something disclosed in the reference, i.e., all limitations of the claim are found in the reference, or 'fully met' by it." *Kalman v. Kimberly-Clark Corp.*, 713 F.2d 760, 772, 218 USPQ 781, 789 (Fed. Cir. 1984).

antidissection rule [trademark]
See COMPOSITE MARK.

antlike persistency [patent]   A famous phrase used by Judge Learned Hand in 1924 to refer to the allegedly unrelenting perseverance of patent attorneys in obtaining patent claims favorable to their clients when dealing with the examiners of the U.S. Patent and Trademark Office. Judge Hand made the remark in the context of dealing with the doctrine of CLAIM DIFFERENTIATION.

- *Case Reference*: "I turn now to the claims. The case is the common one of needless elaboration of distinctions which are verbal and details which are trivial. It is absurd to apply in all such cases the rule that claims must at any cost be treated as patentably differentiated. Courts have descanted upon the abuse again and again, but the antlike persistency of solicitors has overcome, and I suppose will continue to overcome, the patience of examiners, and there is apparently always but one outcome." *Lyon v. Boh*, 1 F.2d 48, 49–50 (S.D.N.Y. 1924).

apostille [international] A standard form used to authenticate documents from foreign countries. The apostille may be placed on the document itself as with a stamp or on a separate piece of paper attached to the document. The apostille must be in the form of a square at least 9 centimeters long. The title, "Apostille (Convention de La Haye du 5 octobre 1961)" must be on the document and in the French language. The word apostille is French, meaning an addition, a marginal note or observation.

Purpose of an Apostille. The apostille is provided for by the Convention Abolishing the

Requirement of Legalization for Foreign Public Documents (signed at the Hague in 1961 and acceded to by the United States in 1981). Almost fifty nations are members of the Convention. An apostille replaces the final certification by consular or diplomatic officials of public documents prepared in Convention member countries. The official designated by the foreign government to issue the apostille, when signing it, certifies that the signature of the notary public, or attesting officer, is genuine.

Patent and Trademark Documents. In Patent and Trademark Office practice, an apostille must accompany all documents, which are to be filed or recorded, from Convention member countries that must be sworn to or acknowledged by a notary public. These include patent documents such as the inventor's oath on a patent application and the assignor's signature on a patent assignment document. The apostille must be issued by a competent official of the country where the documents to be filed were prepared.

- *Example 1*: An inventor is a French citizen, residing in France and signs the inventor's oath for a United States patent application. The inventor's signature is attested to by a French notary. The French notary's authority must then be legalized by an official of the United States embassy or consulate in France. But if an apostille is used, it replaces the need for legalization by a U.S. consular officer in France. The apostille can be signed by an employee of the appropriate government office in France, such as an authorized clerk of the law courts in the vicinity of the notary.

- *Example 2*: An inventor is a U.S. citizen residing in California and signs the inventor's oath for a French patent application. The inventor's signature is attested to by a California notary. The California notary's authority must then be legalized by an official of the French consulate in California. But if an apostille is used, it replaces the need for an attestation by a French consular officer. The apostille can be signed by an employee of the appropriate government office in California, such as an authorized employee of the California Secretary of State's office.

- *Statutory References*:

15 U.S.C. §1061: "Acknowledgments and verifications required under this chapter may be made before any person within the United States authorized by law to administer oaths, or, when made in a foreign country, before any diplomatic or consular officer of the United States or before any official authorized to administer oaths in the foreign country concerned whose authority is proved by a certificate of a diplomatic or consular officer of the United States, or apostille of an official designated by a foreign country which, by treaty or convention, accords like effect to apostilles of designated officials in the United States, and shall be valid if they comply with the laws of the state or country where made."

35 U.S.C. §115: "The applicant shall make oath that he believes himself to be the original and first inventor of the process, machine, manufacture, or composition of matter, or improvement thereof, for which he solicits a patent; and shall state of what country he is a citizen. Such oath may be made before any person within the United States authorized by law to administer oaths, or when made in a foreign country, before any diplomatic or consular officer of the United States authorized to administer oaths, or before any officer having an official seal and authorized to administer oaths in the foreign country in which the applicant may be, whose authority is proved by a certificate of a diplomatic or consular officer of the United States, or apostille of an official designated by a foreign country which, by treaty or convention, accords like effect to apostilles of designated officials in the United States, and such oath shall be valid if it complies with the laws of the state or country where made. When the application is made as provided in this title by a person other than the inventor, the oath may be so varied in form that it can be made by him."

- *Manual Reference*: "On Oct. 15, 1981, the Hague 'Convention Abolishing the Requirement of Legalization for Foreign Public Documents' entered into force between the United States and thirty-eight foreign countries that are parties to the Convention. The Convention applies to any document submitted to the United

States Patent and Trademark Office for filing or recording, which is sworn to or acknowledged by a notary public in any one of the member countries. The Convention abolishes the certification of the authority of the notary public in a member country by a diplomatic or consular officer of the United States and substitutes certification by a special certificate, or apostille, executed by an officer of the member country. Accordingly, the Office will accept for filing or recording a document sworn to or acknowledged before a notary public in a member country if the document bears, or has appended to it, an apostille certifying the notary's authority." *Manual of Patent Examining Procedure* §602.04(a) (1994).

apparatus claim [patent] A claim of a patent that covers a product, machine, or structure. This is in contrast to a PROCESS CLAIM, which covers a method or process.

A product whose structure is difficult to describe can sometimes be claimed by defining the process that produces the product. This is a PRODUCT-BY-PROCESS claim.

• *Case Reference*: "Claim 1 of [the patent] is an apparatus claim, and apparatus claims cover what a device *is*, not what a device *does*. An invention need not *operate* differently than the prior art to be patentable, but need only *be* different." *Hewlett-Packard Co. v. Bausch & Lomb Inc.,* 909 F.2d 1464, 1468, 15 USPQ2d 1525, 1528 (Fed. Cir 1990) (Rich. J.).

appellation of origin [trademark–unfair competition] A term that refers to both a product's geographic origin and to its distinctive product characteristics caused by particular geographic conditions or methods of production. Some distinguish an appellation of origin from an INDICATION OF SOURCE, which refers solely to the geographic origin of production. ROQUEFORT cheese is an example of an appellation of origin because it designates both geographic origin and product characteristics. "Paris" perfume is an indication of source, which refers only to geographic origin. The term GEOGRAPHIC DENOMINATION encompasses both categories.

Ladas suggests that the semantic difficulty between "appellation of origin" and "indication of source" is caused by the lack of direct English translation of the French terms "indications de provenance" (indications of source) and "appellations d'origine" (appellations of origin). "Source" in English does not have the same definite meaning of geographical origin that the word "provenance" has in French. 3 S. Ladas, *Patents, Trademarks and Related Rights: National and International Protection* §842 (1975). The second paragraph of Article 1 of the PARIS CONVENTION includes in the definition of INDUSTRIAL PROPERTY the categories of "indications of source or appellations of origin."

• *Commentary Reference*: "Indications of source and appellations of origin both serve to identify the source or origin of the products or services for which they are used. Appellations of origin, however, have an additional function. Whereas an indication of source shows only from where a product comes, an appellation of origin indicates, in addition, the characteristic qualities of a product which are determined by the geographical area from which it comes and to which the appellation refers." WIPO, *Background Reading Material on Intellectual Property* 14 (1988).

application program [computer–copyright] A COMPUTER PROGRAM that performs a certain job for the user, such as a word processing program or a data base program. There is no doubt that the expression of an application program is protectable by copyright law.

See OPERATING SYSTEM PROGRAM.

• *Case Reference*: "Computer programs can be categorized by function as either application programs or operating system programs. Application programs usually perform a specific task for the computer user, such as word processing, checkbook balancing, or playing a game." *Apple Computer, Inc. v. Franklin Computer Corp.,* 714 F.2d 1240, 1243, 219 USPQ 113, 116 (3d Cir. 1983).

apportionment of profits [patent–trademark–copyright]

See PROFITS.

APS [patent] Automated Patent Search system. The Patent and Trademark Office collection of PRIOR ART on a data base can be searched by computer methods, as contrasted with the older "paper system."

arbitrary mark [trademark]   A word or picture that is in common linguistic use but which, when used in connection with certain goods or services, neither suggests nor describes any quality or characteristic of those particular goods or services. Arbitrary marks are inherently distinctive and need no proof of SECONDARY MEANING to be regarded as valid for registration or legal protection. Arbitrary marks are inherently relatively strong marks, in that their intrinsic distinctiveness likely will have a substantial impact on the buyer's mind. Commonly recognized examples would be APPLE personal computers, ARM & HAMMER baking soda, NOVA television series, and SHELL gasoline.

• *Treatise Reference*: 1 J.T. McCarthy, *Trademarks and Unfair Competition* §11.04 (3d ed. 1995 rev.).

arbitration [general legal]
See ALTERNATIVE DISPUTE RESOLUTION.

art [patent] Technology. The term "art" as synonymous with "technology" is standard usage in patent law by itself and as used in the terminology PRIOR ART and STATE OF THE ART. This use of "art" as synonymous with the more modern word "technology" harkens back to an earlier use of "art" as denoting the technical skill or adeptness associated with the "artisan" rather than the "artistic" inspiration associated with the "fine arts." This older meaning of "art" is still preserved in some popular uses, e.g., "state of the art," "artisan," "the art of baking," and "the art of sailing."

Constitutional Usage. In eighteenth century usage as reflected in the Patent and Copyright Clause of the U.S. Constitution, the term "useful arts" referred to technology, which was the domain of "discoveries" made by "inventors," while the term "science" referred to knowledge,

which was the domain of "writings" made by "authors."

See CONSTITUTION.

Skill in the Art. The term SKILL IN THE ART denotes an ordinary level of proficiency in the particular technology in which an invention is made. Under Patent Code §103, an invention is "obvious" and unpatentable if the differences between the invention and the PRIOR ART are such that "the subject matter as a whole would have been obvious at the time the invention was made" to a person having ordinary skill in the art to which the invention relates.

See also ANALOGOUS ART.

• *U.S. Constitution*: Article 1, section 8, clause 8: "The Congress shall have power ... To promote the progress of science and useful arts, by securing for limited times to authors and inventors the exclusive rights to their respective writings and discoveries."

• *Case References*:

"We have previously pointed out that the present day equivalent of the term 'useful arts' employed by the Founding Fathers [in the U.S. Constitution] is 'technological arts.' " *In re Bergy*, 596 F.2d 952, 959, 201 USPQ 352, 359 (C.C.P.A. 1979), *dismissed as moot*, 444 U.S. 924 (1980). *Accord In re Waldbaum*, 457 F.2d 997, 1003, 173 USPQ 430, 434 (Fed. Cir. 1972) ("The phrase 'technological arts,' as we have used it, is synonymous with the phrase 'useful arts' as it appears in Article I, Section 8 of the Constitution.").

"This ... furthers the basic purpose of the patent system. The exclusive right, constitutionally derived, was for the national purpose of advancing the useful arts—the process today called technological innovation." *Paulik v. Rizkalla*, 760 F.2d 1270, 1276, 226 USPQ 224, 228 (Fed. Cir. 1985).

• *Usage Examples*:

"A §103 determination involves fact and law. There may be these facts: what a prior art patent as a whole discloses; what it in fact disclosed to workers in the art; what differences exist between the entire prior art, or a whole prior art structure, and the whole claimed invention...." *Panduit Corp. v. Dennison Mfg. Co.*,

810 F.2d 1561, 1566, 1 USPQ2d 1593, 1595 (Fed. Cir. 1987).

"[T]he units designated 'ROM' and 'RAM' are, respectively, a read only memory and a random access memory, terms well understood by those skilled in the art." *In re Iwahashi*, 888 F.2d 1370, 1372, 12 USPQ2d 1908, 1909 (Fed. Cir. 1989).

ASCAP [copyright] The American Society of Composers, Authors and Publishers. One of the main PERFORMING RIGHTS SOCIETIES that licenses certain performing rights in copyrighted musical works. The over 40,000 songwriter and publisher members of ASCAP grant to ASCAP the nonexclusive right to license nondramatic public performances of the copyrighted musical works of its members. ASCAP issues licenses, including BLANKET LICENSES, of the nondramatic performing rights in those copyrighted musical works to users who perform copyrighted music. ASCAP then distributes the resulting royalties to its members according to a schedule reflecting the amount of use of their music. ASCAP has over 3,000,000 musical compositions in its repertory and its licenses enable a licensee to perform any of those compositions. While radio and television broadcasters are the largest licensees of ASCAP, other licensees include operators of entertainment establishments where live or recorded music is played and larger commercial stores which play radio and television broadcasts of music. Rights *not* licensed by ASCAP and therefore licensed only by the individual copyright owners include: dramatic performing rights (GRAND RIGHTS) such as for operas and musical plays; printed sheet music; MECHANICAL RECORDING RIGHTS in phonograph records, tapes, and discs; and SYNCHRONIZATION RIGHTS for music sound tracks for motion pictures.

See also BMI, SESAC, GRAND RIGHTS, BLANKET LICENSE.

• *Case References*: *Broadcast Music, Inc. v. Columbia Broadcasting Sys., Inc.*, 441 U.S. 1, 5, 201 USPQ 497, 499 (1979); *Robert Stigwood Group v. Sperber*, 457 F.2d 50, 173 USPQ 258 (2d Cir. 1972).

• *Treatise References*: 2 *Nimmer on Copyright* §8.19 (1994 rev.); M. Leaffer, *Understanding Copyright* §8.22 (1989); S. Shemel & M.W. Krasilovsky, *This Business of Music* ch. 18 (1985).

ASMP [copyright] The American Society of Magazine Photographers is a 5,500 member organization founded in 1944. It was established to further the trade practices for photographers in communications fields including providing business advice and promoting ethical conduct. A recent concern is the use of members' works in multimedia formats. There is a move towards setting up a clearinghouse which will sell members' rights to multimedia producers, collect royalties and monitor for possible infringements.

assignment [patent–trademark–copyright] A sale of rights in intellectual property.

1. Assignment of Patent. An assignment of a patent is a transfer of sufficient rights such that the transferee has title to the patent. Under the classic rule of *Waterman v. Mackenzie*, 138 U.S. 252 (1891), a patent LICENSE is any transfer of rights that does not amount to an assignment of the patent. An assignment is a transfer of either: (1) all rights of exclusivity in the patent; (2) an undivided fractional portion (e.g., a 50 percent interest); or (3) all rights within a specified portion of the United States. Transfer of anything less than that is dubbed a "license." *Waterman v. Mackenzie*, 138 U.S. 252, 255 (1891) (see case reference below). "To determine whether a provision in an agreement constitutes an assignment or a license, one must ascertain the intention of the parties and examine the substance of what was granted." *Vaupel Textilmaschinen v. Meccanica Euro Italia*, 944 F.2d 870, 874, 20 USPQ2d 1045, 1048 (Fed. Cir. 1991).

The Right to Sue Infringers. The right to sue infringers is normally the privilege of the party that has title to the patent, and a licensee usually cannot sue for infringement in its own name. *United States v. General Elec. Co.*, 272 U.S. 476, 489 (1926). However, an exclusive licensee can sue for infringement in the name of the patentee by joining the patentee as an involuntary party. *Independent Wireless Tel. Co. v. Radio Corp. of Am.*, 269 U.S. 459, 469 (1926). The assignee has standing to sue an infringer only if he holds legal title to the patent during the time of the infringement. *Crown Die & Tool Co. v. Nye Tool & Mach. Works*, 261 U.S. 24, 40–41 (1923).

See LICENSE OF PATENT.

"Patentee" Includes an Assignee. Patent Code §261 specifically authorizes the assignment and grant of exclusive licenses of patents. The title PATENTEE is given to the inventor to whom the patent was granted and to all persons to whom the patent is subsequently assigned. 35 U.S.C. §100(d).

Assignment Prior to Invention and Prior to Patent. An assignment of rights in an invention can be made after the time of invention but prior to the issuance of a patent. Legal title to the patent will pass to the assignee upon the grant of the patent. Assignment of rights in an invention can also be made prior to the existence of the invention. This is an assignment of an expectant interest and the assignee would hold only equitable title to the patent. "Once the invention is made and the application for patent is filed, however, legal title to the rights accruing thereunder would be in the assignee (subject to the rights of a subsequent purchaser under §261), and the assignor-inventor would have nothing remaining to assign." *FilmTec Corp. v. Allied-Signal Inc.*, 939 F.2d 1568, 1572, 19 USPQ2d 1508, 1511 (Fed. Cir. 1991) (if an inventor granted its employer rights in inventions made during employment, then inventor had nothing to assign to a subsequent assignee and such an assignment would be a nullity).

Purchase of Patent Rights Subsequent to an Assignment. A subsequent bona fide assignee will become the owner of the patent if a prior assignee fails to file a RECORDATION OF TRANSFER of patent ownership with the Patent and Trademark Office (PTO) within three months of the assignment or prior to a later assignment. See RECORDATION OF TRANSFERS.

Assignor Estoppel. The doctrine of ASSIGNOR ESTOPPEL is an equitable rule prevent-

ing the assignor of a patent from challenging the validity of the patent in a suit for infringement brought by the assignee against the assignor.

See LICENSE OF PATENT, ASSIGNOR ESTOPPEL.

• *Statutory Reference*: 35 U.S.C. §261: "Subject to the provisions of this title, patents shall have the attributes of personal property. Applications for patent, patents, or any interest therein, shall be assignable in law by an instrument in writing. The applicant, patentee, or his assigns or legal representatives may in like manner grant and convey an exclusive right under his application for patent, or patents, to the whole or any specified part of the United States. ..."

• *Case References*:

"The patentee or his assigns may, by instrument in writing, assign, grant and convey, either, 1st, the whole patent, comprising the exclusive right to make, use and vend the invention through the United States; or, 2nd, an undivided part or share of that exclusive right; or, 3rd, the exclusive right under the patent within and throughout a specified part of the United States. A transfer of either of these three kinds of interests is an assignment, properly speaking, and vests in the assignee a title in so much of the patent itself, with a right to sue infringers; in the second case, jointly with the assignor; in the first and third cases, in the name of the assignee alone. Any assignment or transfer, short of one of these, is a mere license, giving the licensee no title in the patent, and no right to sue at law in his own name for infringement. In equity, as at law, when the transfer amounts to a license only, the title remains in the owner of the patent; and suit must be brought in his name, and never in the name of the licensee alone, unless that is necessary to prevent an absolute failure of justice, as where the patentee is the infringer, and cannot sue himself. Any rights of the licensee must be enforced through or in the name of the owner of the patent, and perhaps, if necessary to protect the rights of all parties, joining the licensee with him as a plaintiff." *Waterman v. Mackenzie*, 138 U.S. 252, 255 (1891).

"The owner of a patent may assign it to another and convey, (1) the exclusive right to make, use and vend the invention throughout the United States, or, (2) an undivided part or share of that exclusive right, or (3) the exclusive right under the patent within and through a specific part of the United States. But any assignment or transfer short of one of these is a license, giving the licensee no title in the patent and no right to sue at law in his own name for infringement." *United States v. General Elec. Co.*, 272 U.S. 476, 489 (1926).

"And 35 U.S.C. §261 makes clear that an application for patent as well as the patent itself may be assigned. Further, it is settled law that between the time of an invention and the issuance of a patent, rights in an invention may be assigned and legal title to the ensuing patent will pass to the assignee upon grant of the patent. If an assignment of rights in an invention is made prior to the existence of the invention, this may be viewed as an assignment of the expectant interest. An assignment of an expectant interest can be a valid assignment." *FilmTec Corp. v. Allied-Signal Inc.*, 939 F.2d 1568, 1572, 19 USPQ2d 1508, 1511 (Fed. Cir. 1991).

• *Treatise References*: R. Nordhaus, *Patent License Agreements* §11 (1994 rev.); 6 D. Chisum, *Patents* §21.03[2] (1994 rev.); 1 H. Einhorn, *Patent Licensing Transactions* §1.01 (1994 rev.); 3 P. Rosenberg, *Patent Law Fundamentals* §§16.01[1][a], 17.09[1][b] (1994 rev.); H. Mayers & B. Brunsvold, *Drafting Patent License Agreements* (3rd ed. 1991); R. Ellis, *Patent Assignments* §74 (3d ed. 1955).

2. Assignment of Trademark. A trademark or service mark can be validly assigned only in connection with the goodwill that is symbolized by that mark. An assignment of a mark without an accompanying transfer of associated goodwill is known as an "assignment in gross," which is invalid to transfer any rights in the mark. If the purported assignor then ceases to use the mark, as is usually the case, the purported assignor abandons its rights. The purported assignee cannot rely upon the priority-of-use date of the purported assignor and must start with a new first-use date. On the other hand, after a valid assignment of the mark and its goodwill, the assignee succeeds to all the rights and priority of the assignor. *Premier Den-*

tal Prods. Co. v. Darby Dental Supply Co., 794 F.2d 850, 230 USPQ 233 (3d Cir. 1986) ("[F]ollowing a proper assignment, the assignee steps into the shoes of the assignor.").

The "Anti-Assignment-in-Gross Rule." The "anti-assignment-in-gross rule" is a prophylactic prohibition designed to avoid the customer deception that could result from an abrupt and radical change in the nature and quality of the goods and services after assignment of the mark. By requiring that the ability to carry on producing or selling the same quality of goods or services be transferred along with the mark, the rule does not guarantee continuity, but only facilitates it. Under a strict view, some courts require that the assignor transfer to the assignee sufficient tangible assets to enable the assignee to continue in real continuity with the past expectations of customers. Under a more liberal view, the focus is placed not on a formalistic transfer of tangible assets, but on whether in fact the assignee can and does carry on in continuity so as to reasonably meet the expectations customers attach to the trademark or service mark symbol. The liberal view is especially appropriate for the assignment of service marks. *Visa, USA Inc. v. Birmingham Trust Nat'l Bank*, 696 F.2d 1371, 216 USPQ 649 (Fed. Cir. 1982).

Intent-to-Use Applications. When providing for intent-to-use applications in the Lanham Act in 1989, Congress required in Lanham Act §10 that an intent-to-use application cannot be assigned before the applicant files a verified statement of use, unless that part of the "business" connected with the mark is also transferred. The "business" must be "ongoing and existing." The purpose of this new limitation on assignments is to prohibit "trafficking" in marks: the buying and selling of inchoate marks, which as yet have no real existence because they are not yet in use, have no customer recognition and goodwill, and presently have no indicia of legally protectable trademarks.

See ABANDONMENT, LICENSING, CONSENT AGREEMENT.

• *Statutory Reference*: Lanham Act §10, 15 U.S.C. §1060: "A registered mark or a mark for which application to register has been filed shall be assignable with the goodwill of the business in which the mark is used, or with that part of the goodwill of the business connected with the use of and symbolized by the mark. However, no application to register a mark under section 1(b) shall be assignable prior to the filing of the verified statement of use under section 1(d) except to a successor to the business of the applicant, or portion thereof, to which the mark pertains, if that business is ongoing and existing. In any assignment authorized by this section, it shall not be necessary to include the goodwill of the business connected with the use of and symbolized by any other mark used in the business or by the name or style under which the business is conducted. Assignments shall be by instruments in writing duly executed. Acknowledgement shall be prima facie evidence of the execution of an assignment...."

• *Treatise Reference*: 2 J. T. McCarthy, *Trademarks and Unfair Competition* §18.01–.12 (3d ed. 1995 rev.).

• *Case References*:

"A trademark is a mere symbol of the goodwill of the business with which it is associated.... As [defendants] correctly observe, the transfer of a trademark or trade name without the attendant goodwill of the business which it represents is, in general, an invalid, 'in gross' transfer of rights.... We agree with the [defendants] that the [plaintiffs'] contentions run afoul of the well-established principle that a mark is not property that may be assigned 'in gross.' ... Of course the question whether a mark has been severed from its goodwill may not always be an easy one." *Berni v. International Gourmet Restaurants, Inc.*, 838 F.2d 642, 646, 5 USPQ2d 1723, 1726 (2d Cir. 1988) (owners of business did not retain any rights in mark after sale of business and lacked ownership and standing to sue for infringement of mark).

"[W]e find that it is not necessary to the continuing validity of the mark that tangible assets of the assignor pass to the assignee.... The plaintiff contends that controlling weight should be given to whether there was a transfer of tangible assets.... The cases cited by both sides of this controversy are consistent with the underlying purpose of why a transfer of goodwill is required in order for an assignment of a

mark to be effective. The cases all seek to protect customers from deception and confusion. In the case of a service mark, such confusion would result if an assignee offered a service different from that offered by the assignor of the mark. Such is not the case here." *Money Store v. Harriscorp Fin. Inc.*, 689 F.2d 666, 676, 216 USPQ 11, 20–21 (7th Cir. 1982).

"A trademark cannot be sold 'in gross,' that is, separately from the essential assets used to make the product or service that the trademark identifies.... The discontinuity would be too great. The consumer would have no assurance that he was getting the same thing (more or less) in buying the product or service from its new maker." *Green River Bottling Co. v. Green River Corp.*, 997 F2d 359, 361, 27 USPQ2d 1304, 1306 (7th Cir. 1993).

3. Assignment of Copyright. The rule governing assignment of copyright under the 1909 Copyright Act was one of "indivisibility" of copyright: a copyright was an indivisible property right which was not capable of being split up into smaller units and sold or exclusively licensed. The rule of indivisibility was done away with in the 1978 Copyright Act by §201(d)(2), which permits the assignment or exclusive license of any part or subpart of the bundle of rights comprising a copyright. H.R. Rep. No. 94-1476, 94th Cong., 2d Sess. 123 (1976). This and other provisions of the 1978 Act have largely done away with any practical distinction between an assignment and an exclusive license of the same rights of copyright. Both are categorized as a "transfer" of copyright ownership. An exclusive licensee of a right of copyright is regarded as the copyright owner of the particular right that is licensed.

• *Example*: An author of a series of illustrated children's books can grant an exclusive license to Alpha Studios to produce a feature length DERIVATIVE WORK motion picture using the copyrightable elements of the books, an exclusive license to Beta to create a daily newspaper cartoon based upon the illustrations in the books, an exclusive license to Gamma to use the characters from the books in puppet shows performed in California for a one-year period, and an exclusive license to Zeta to make plush dolls smaller than 12 inches tall of characters from the books. Each license is a "transfer" of rights of copyright, and each transferee has "all of the protection and remedies accorded to the copyright owner" by law. 17 U.S.C. §201(d)(2). For example, each transferee (exclusive licensee) has standing to sue third parties for copyright infringement for an invasion of its scope of exclusive rights within the original copyrighted work.

One Copyright Per Work. There is never more than a single copyright in a work regardless of the owner's exclusive license of various rights to different persons. "Section 201(d)(2) provides for divisibility of rights, not divisibility of copyright." 3 *Nimmer on Copyright* §10.02[C][2] (1994 rev.). There is only one registration per copyrightable work. However, if a licensee creates a copyrightable DERIVATIVE WORK, that derivative copyright can be separately owned and registered by the licensee.

Formalities. To be valid, a copyright transfer must be in writing and signed by the person conveying rights. 17 U.S.C. §204(a). This applies to assignments and exclusive licenses, but not to nonexclusive licenses.

Copyright Distinct From Copyrighted Object. Since 1978, Copyright Act §202 has made it clear that ownership of copyright is distinct from ownership of physical objects in which copyrightable works are embodied, recorded, or stored. The sale of ownership of a material object does not implicitly convey any rights of copyright. For example, when an artist sells an original work of art, it is presumed that there is no sale of copyright in that work of art unless the artist clearly assigns copyright in a writing signed by the artist.

- *Treatise References*: 3 *Nimmer on Copyright* §10.01 *et seq.* (1994 rev.); 1 N. Boorstyn, *Copyright* §§3.08–.09 (2d ed. 1994); M. Leaffer, *Understanding Copyright* §5.8 (1989); 1 P. Goldstein, *Copyright* §4.4 (1989); W. Patry, *Copyright Law and Practice* 385 (1994).

- *Statutory References*:

17 U.S.C. §101: "A 'transfer of copyright ownership' is an assignment, mortgage, exclusive license, or any other conveyance, alienation or hypothecation of a copyright, whether or not it is limited in time or place of effect, but not including a nonexclusive license."

17 U.S.C. §201(d):

Transfer of Ownership—

(1) The ownership of copyright may be transferred in whole or in part by any means of conveyance or by operation of law, and may be bequeathed by will or pass as personal property by the applicable laws of intestate succession.

(2) Any of the exclusive rights comprised in copyright, including any subdivision of any of the rights specified by section 106, may be transferred as provided by clause (1) and owned separately. The owner of any particular exclusive right is entitled, to the extent of that right, to all of the protection and remedies accorded to the copyright owner by this title.

17 U.S.C. §204(a): "A transfer of copyright ownership, other than by operation of law, is not valid unless an instrument of conveyance, or a note or memorandum of the transfer, is in writing and signed by the owner of the rights conveyed or such owner's duly authorized agent."

assignor estoppel [patent–trademark]

1. Patent Assignor Estoppel. An equitable rule preventing the assignor of a patent from challenging the validity of the assigned patent in a subsequent suit for infringement brought by the assignee against the assignor.

History of the Rule. The U.S. Supreme Court upheld the rule itself but carved out an exception allowing the assignor to present evidence of prior art for the purpose of construing and narrowing the scope of the claims of the assigned patent, which may bring the accused device outside the scope of those claims. But this does not permit the assignor to argue that those claims are invalid. *Westinghouse Elec. & Mfg. Co. v. Formica Insulation Co.*, 266 U.S. 342 (1924). The Supreme Court created a further exception to the rule by allowing the assignor to show that the invention was a copy of an expired patent and hence invalid. *Scott Paper Co. v. Marcalus Mfg. Co.*, 326 U.S. 249 (1945).

After the 1969 Supreme Court decision in *Lear, Inc. v. Adkins*, 395 U.S. 653 (1969), striking down the rule of LICENSEE ESTOPPEL, the lower courts split on whether assignor estoppel should similarly be held preempted by patent policy. In 1988 the Court of Appeals for the Federal Circuit resolved the conflict by distinguishing *Lear v. Adkins* and upholding the rule of assignor estoppel. *Diamond Scientific Co. v. Ambico, Inc.*, 848 F.2d 1220, 6 USPQ2d 2028 (Fed. Cir. 1988).

- *Case References*: "Assignor estoppel is an equitable doctrine that prevents one who has assigned the rights to a patent (or patent application) from later contending that what was assigned is a nullity.... [A]n assignor should not be permitted to sell something and later to assert that what was sold is worthless, all to the detriment of the assignee.... [T]he equities of the contractual relationships between the parties should deprive one party (as well as others in privity with it) of the right to bring that challenge [against the validity of the patent]." *Diamond Scientific Co. v. Ambico, Inc.*, 848 F.2d 1220, 1224–25, 6 USPQ2d 2028, 2030–31 (Fed. Cir. 1988).

The rule of assignor estoppel is a doctrine " 'that is mainly concerned with the balance of equities between the parties.' ... Those in privity with the assignor partake in that balance; hence, extension of the estoppel to those in privity [inventor's new employers] is justified." *Shamrock Technologies Inc. v. Medical Sterilization Inc.*, 903 F.2d 789, 793, 14 USPQ2d 1728, 1732 (Fed.Cir. 1990).

- *Example*: While employed by the Alpha Chemical Co., Dr. X invents a new and valuable form of animal vaccine. Pursuant to the X-Alpha employment agreement, Dr. X assigns the patent application to Alpha. Later, Dr. X leaves employment to start her own company, the Omega Vaccine Co., which begins making a vaccine. Alpha sues Omega and Dr. X for infringement of the patent. The doctrine of assignor estoppel precludes Dr. X and the Omega company (in privity with Dr. X) from challenging the validity of the assigned patent.

2. Trademark Registration Assignor Estoppel. An equitable rule that prevents the assignor of a registered trademark from challenging the validity of the assigned trademark in a subsequent suit for infringement brought by an assignee against the assignor. The rule is largely undeveloped in the case law, and its scope remains uncertain in the trademark context.

- *Case Reference*: The three members of a singing group jointly applied for a federal registration of the name of their group as a service mark and then assigned their rights to their manager. One of the members left and formed a competing group under the same name. The manager sued for infringement of the registered mark. The defendant, as an original joint applicant for the registration, was held estopped from challenging the validity of the mark on the ground of failure to make exclusive and continuous use as of the date claimed in the registration. *Marshak v. Green*, 505 F. Supp. 1054, 212 USPQ 493 (S.D.N.Y. 1981).

ATRIP [international] The International Association for Advancement of Teaching and Research in Intellectual Property. The international association was formed under the aegis of World Intellectual Property Organization (WIPO) and is composed of professors, teachers, and researchers from around the world who are active in the field of intellectual property.

attorney-client privilege [general legal] To encourage full and frank communications between attorneys and their clients, attorney-client communications are privileged from disclosure in discovery and at trial. This privilege also extends to communications between corporate employees and in-house counsel. *Upjohn Co. v. United States*, 449 U.S. 383, 389 (1981). Unlike the ATTORNEY WORK PRODUCT immunity, the attorney-client privilege is that of the client, not the attorney. However, the attorney may sometimes be under a duty to assert the privilege on the client's behalf.

Patent Validity Opinions. In-house and outside patent counsel's opinions on patent validity are as eligible for the attorney-client privilege as any other communication from attorney to client. "[C]ounsel's opinions on patent validity are not denied the client's privilege merely because validity must be evaluated against publicly available information." *American Standard Inc. v. Pfizer, Inc.*, 828 F.2d 734, 3 USPQ2d 1817, 1825 (Fed. Cir. 1987) (opinion letter that relied on nonconfidential data in public records and did not reveal a confidential communication from the client is not privileged).

Communications Related to Patent Prosecution. Earlier district court decisions held that the attorney-client privilege should not usually protect communications from inventors to their lawyers since these communications consist largely of technical information which would be made public in the patent. See *Jack Winter, Inc. v. Koraton Co.*, 172 USPQ 201 (N.D. Cal. 1971); *Hercules Inc. v. Exxon Corp.*, 434 F. Supp. 136, 196 USPQ 401 (D. Del. 1977). More recently, the trend in the district courts is to permit assertion of the attorney-client privilege even though much of the communication between the inventor and his attorney is technical information which will be made public when the patent issues. See *Advanced Cardiovascular Sys. Inc. v. C.R Bard Inc.*, 144 F.R.D. 372, 25 USPQ2d 1354, 1359 (N.D. Cal. 1992) ("[T]he communications from inventor to patent lawyer, even those that are entirely technical, remain presumptively protected by the attorney-client privilege."); *Burroughs Wellcome Co. v. Barr Labs. Inc.*, 143 F.R.D. 611, 25 USPQ2d 1274, 1276 (E.D.N.C. 1992) ("[T]he privilege protects from discovery drafts of replies and responses prepared in response to questions or decisions of a patent examiner.").

Governing Law. In federal question cases, the federal courts apply a federal common law of privilege, guided, but not bound, by state law. Fed. R. Evid. 501.

- *Case References:*

"The [patent] attorney is not a mere conduit for either the client's communications containing the technical information or the technical information itself. He does not file his client's communications with the Patent Office. He does not file transcripts of his conversations with the client regarding technical matters and then await the issuance of the patent. ... The fact that much of the technical information in one form or another finds its way into the patent

application, to be made public when the patent issues, should not preclude the assertion of the privilege over the communication in which the information was disclosed to the attorney." *Burroughs Wellcome Co. v. Barr Labs. Inc.*, 143 F.R.D. 611, 25 USPQ2d 1274, 1276 (E.D.N.C. 1992), quoting *Knogo Corp. v. United States*, 213 USPQ 936, 940–41 (Ct. Cl. 1980).

"[T]he communications from inventor to patent lawyer, even those that are entirely technical, remain presumptively protected by the attorney-client privilege. We would consider ordering these communications disclosed only on a very compelling showing, [for example], that despite the presumption of confidentiality, the inventor in fact expected specific communications he or she made to the patent counsel to be disclosed, without editing, to the PTO." *Advanced Cardiovascular Sys. Inc. v. C.R. Bard Inc.*, 144 F.R.D. 372, 25 USPQ2d 1354, 1359 (N.D. Cal. 1992).

attorney fees award   [patent–trademark copyright] An order by the court that the losing party must reimburse the winning party's reasonable attorney fees expended in winning the case. Ordinarily, U.S. courts have rejected the "English rule," which requires the loser to pay the winner's attorney fees in most civil cases. Rather, the "American rule" is that the prevailing party is ordinarily not entitled to any attorney fees unless there is a specific statute that authorizes it. One reason for this rule is that one should not be penalized for merely defending or prosecuting a civil lawsuit. *Machinery Corp. of Am. v. Gullfiber AB*, 774 F.2d 467, 471, 227 USPQ 368, 371 (Fed. Cir. 1985).

Federal statutes permit the award of attorney fees in patent, trademark, and copyright infringement cases. The starting point for measuring the amount of a reasonable attorney fee award is the number of attorney hours expended on the litigation multiplied by a reasonable hourly rate. *Hensley v. Eckerhart*, 461 U.S. 424, 433–34 (1983).

1. Award of Attorney Fees in Patent Cases. Federal law permits the court to award reasonable attorney fees to the prevailing party in "exceptional cases." While the usual award of attorney fees is to a prevailing patentee against a willful and egregious patent infringer, an award can also be made to a prevailing defendant against a patentee who has litigated in bad faith or has committed fraud or other inequitable conduct during prosecution of the patent. *Machinery Corp. of Am. v. Gullfiber AB*, 774 F.2d 467, 472, 227 USPQ 368, 372 (Fed. Cir. 1985).

The Requirement of "Willfulness." Willfulness is required for an award of increased damages in patent cases. While a finding of willfulness does not automatically lead to an award of attorney fees, willfulness may be sufficient for declaring this to be an "exceptional case" sufficient for the award of attorney fees to the prevailing patent owner. *Avia Group Inc. v. L.A. Gear Cal., Inc.*, 853 F.2d 1557, 1566, 7 USPQ2d 1548, 1556 (Fed. Cir. 1988).

There is no difference in the standard applied to patentees and infringers in evaluating the kind of conduct needed to constitute an "exceptional" case. "The balance is not tipped in favor of either side when each is required to prove the other guilty of bad faith litigation by clear and convincing evidence in light of the totality of the circumstances." *Eltech Sys. Corp. v. PPG Indus. Inc.*, 903 F.2d 805, 811, 14 USPQ2d 1965, 1970 (Fed. Cir. 1990).

See WILLFULNESS.

• *Statutory Reference*: 35 U.S.C. §285: "The court in exceptional cases may award reasonable attorney fees to the prevailing party."

• *Treatise Reference*: R. Harmon, *Patents and the Federal Circuit* §14.4 (3d ed. 1994) ("Not all successful defendants are entitled to attorney fees. The requirement in §285 of establishing an exceptional case remains a formidable and adequate barrier to unwarranted awards.").

• *Case References*:

"This standard [of 35 U.S.C. §285] may be broken down into four parts: (1) the case must be exceptional; (2) the district court may exercise its discretion; (3) the fees must be reasonable; and (4) the fees may be awarded only to the prevailing party." *Machinery Corp. of Am. v. Gullfiber AB*, 774 F.2d 467, 470, 227 USPQ 368, 371 (Fed. Cir. 1985).

"[A]wards of increased damages and attorney fees [should] not be allowed to thwart efforts to challenge the validity of patents believed in good faith to be invalid. A party who has obtained advice of competent counsel, or otherwise acquired a basis for a bona fide belief that a patent is invalid, can be said to serve the patent system in challenging that patent in a law suit conducted fairly, honestly, and in good faith. Such a party should not have increased damages or attorney fees imposed solely because a court subsequently holds that belief unfounded, particularly when the issues may be fairly described as 'close.'" *Kloster Speedsteel AB v. Crucible Inc.*, 793 F.2d 1565, 1581, 230 USPQ 81, 91–92 (Fed. Cir. 1986).

"Provisions for increased damages under 35 U.S.C. §284 and attorney fees under 35 U.S.C. §285 are available as deterrents to blatant, blind, willful infringement of valid patents. The only deterrent to the equally improper bringing of clearly unwarranted suits on obviously invalid or unenforceable patents is Section 285. No award under Section 285 can fully compensate a defendant subjected to bad faith litigation, e.g., for loss of executives' time and missed business opportunities.... In determining the compensatory quantum of an award under Section 285 in such an egregious case, therefore, courts should not be, and have not been, limited to ordinary reimbursement of only those amounts paid by the injured party for purely legal services of lawyers, or precluded from ordinary reimbursement of legitimate expenses defendant was unfairly forced to pay." *Mathis v. Spears*, 857 F.2d 749, 754, 8 USPQ2d 1029, 1033 (Fed. Cir. 1988).

The finding that a patentee knew, or should have known, that the infringement suit it filed was baseless is sufficient to support a conclusion that the case is "extraordinary" for purposes of awarding attorney fees to the prevailing alleged infringer. "The 'should know' rubric obviously applies when a party attempts to escape the consequences of his conduct with the bare statement, 'I didn't know.' A party confronted with the difficulty of proving what is in an adversary's mind must be at liberty to prove facts establishing that that adversary should have known, i.e. to prove facts that render the 'I didn't know' excuse unacceptable." *Eltech Sys. Corp. v. PPG Indus. Inc.*, 903 F.2d 805, 810, 14 USPQ2d 1965, 1969 (Fed. Cir. 1990).

2. Award of Attorney Fees in Trademark Cases. The federal trademark act authorizes an award of attorney fees to the prevailing party in exceptional cases. This provision was added in 1975 after the U.S. Supreme Court held that the previous version of the statute did not permit an award of attorney fees. *Fleischmann Distilling Corp. v. Maier Brewing Corp.*, 386 U.S. 714, 153 USPQ 432 (1967).

"Exceptional" Cases. The 1975 statutory authorization was intended to allow the recovery of fees "in infringement cases where the acts of infringement can be characterized as 'malicious,' 'fraudulent,' 'deliberate,' or 'willful.'" S. Rep. No. 93-1400, 93d Cong., 2d Sess. 2, reprinted in 1974 U.S. Code Cong. & Admin. News 7132, 7133. Most courts have found that an "exceptional" case justifying an award of fees to a prevailing plaintiff is where there are acts of intentional and deliberate infringement. See, e.g., *Centaur Communications, Ltd. v. A/S/M Communications, Inc.*, 830 F.2d 1217, 1229, 4 USPQ2d 1541, 1551 (2d Cir. 1987) ("Of course, deliberate and willful infringement can render a case 'exceptional' and thus support an award of attorneys' fees.").

Types of Cases. Attorney fees have been awarded to a prevailing defendant where the plaintiff's conduct is not as egregious as "bad faith," but does fall within the category of bringing a lawsuit totally lacking in merit or merely as a means of competitive harassment. See, e.g., *Mennen Co. v. Gillette Co.*, 565 F. Supp. 648, 220 USPQ 354 (S.D.N.Y. 1983), *aff'd*, 742 F.2d 1437 (2d Cir. 1984) (suit filed as "competitive ploy"); *Noxell Corp. v. Firehouse No.1 Bar-B-Que Restaurant*, 771 F.2d 521, 221 USPQ 115 (D.C. Cir. 1985) (fees awarded to defendant who prevailed on a change of venue motion where it is "exceptional" that plaintiff filed suit in a district that was so clearly improper).

Lanham Act §43(a) Cases. The 1988 Trademark Law Revision Act codifies the nearly unanimous judicial view that all those statutory remedies, including attorney fee awards, which are available for infringement of registered marks are equally available to the plaintiff who uses Lanham Act §43(a) as the vehicle to assert claims of infringement of unregistered marks, trade names, or trade dress as well as claims of false advertising and trade libel.

Counterfeiting. In cases of trademark counterfeiting, the award of the trademark owner's reasonable attorney fee is mandatory unless there are extenuating circumstances. Lanham Act §35(b), 15 U.S.C. §1117(b).

• *Statutory Reference*: Lanham Act §35(a), 15 U.S.C. §1117(a): "The court in exceptional cases may award reasonable attorney fees to the prevailing party."

• *Treatise Reference*: 3 J.T. McCarthy, *Trademarks and Unfair Competition* §30.30 (3d ed. 1995 rev.).

3. Award of Attorney Fees in Copyright Cases. The Copyright Act authorizes an award of attorney fees to the prevailing party. Unlike parallel provisions in the patent and trademark laws, there is no statutory requirement that the case be "exceptional" before attorney fees may be awarded. The federal courts differ on what criteria justify an award of attorney fees in copyright cases.

"Dual" Standard Gives Way to "Evenhanded" Standard. Prior to 1994, some courts used a "dual" standard which treated prevailing plaintiffs and defendants differently. Such courts held that while a prevailing plaintiff should be routinely (but not invariably) awarded attorney fees, a prevailing defendant should be awarded attorney fees only if the lawsuit was baseless, frivolous, or in bad faith. See, e.g., *McCulloch v. Albert E. Price, Inc.*, 823 F.2d 316, 323, 3 USPQ2d 1503, 1508 (9th Cir. 1987). Other courts made no distinction between prevailing plaintiffs and defendants and generally rejected the need for bad faith as a condition to the award of attorney fees. See, e.g., *Original Appalachian Artworks, Inc. v. Toy Loft, Inc.*, 684 F.2d 821, 832, 215 USPQ 745, 755 (11th Cir. 1982) (prevailing plaintiff); *Original Appalachian Artworks, Inc. v. McCall*

Pattern Co., 825 F.2d 355, 356, 3 USPQ2d 1815, 1816 (11th Cir. 1987) (prevailing defendant). In the 1994 *Fogerty v. Fantasy* decision, the U.S. Supreme Court rejected the "dual" standard and held that prevailing plaintiffs and defendants are to be treated alike in that either side, if it prevails, is to be awarded attorney fees "only as a matter of the court's discretion." *Fogerty v. Fantasy, Inc.*, 114 S.Ct. 1023, 1033, 29 USPQ2d 1881, 1888 (1994). (See quotation below.)

Registration Prior to Infringement. Under Copyright Act §412, a court has no discretion whatever to award statutory damages or attorney fees unless the work was registered prior to the time that the defendant commenced the infringing act. The object of this provision is to encourage the early registration of claims to copyright. As to infringing acts that begin very soon after first publication of a work, the copyright owner is given a grace period of three months within which to register without losing these remedies. Even if registration does not occur within the three-month period after first publication, these remedies are available so long as registration precedes the commencement of infringement.

• *Statutory References*:

17 U.S.C. §505: "In any civil action under this title, the court in its discretion may allow the recovery of full costs by or against any party other than the United States or an officer thereof. Except as otherwise provided by this title, the court may also award a reasonable attorney's fee to the prevailing party as part of the costs."

17 U.S.C. §412: "In any action under this title, ... no award of statutory damages or of attorney's fees, as provided by sections 504 and 505, shall be made for—(1) any infringement of copyright in an unpublished work commenced before the effective date of its registration; or (2) any infringement of copyright commenced after first publication of the work and before the effective date of its registration, unless such registration is made within three months after the first publication of the work."

• *Treatise Reference*: 2 P. Goldstein, *Copyright* §12.3.2.2 (1989); 3 *Nimmer on Copyright* §14.10 (1994 rev.); 1 N. Boorstyn, *Copyright* §13.06 (2d ed. 1994); W. Patry, *Copyright Law and Practice* 1175 (1994).

• *Case Reference*: "Some courts following the evenhanded standard have suggested several nonexclusive factors to guide courts' discretion. For example, the Third Circuit has listed several nonexclusive factors that courts should consider in making awards of attorney's fees to any prevailing party. These factors include 'frivolousness, motivation, objective unreasonableness (both in the factual and in the legal components of the case) and the need in particular circumstances to advance considerations of compensation and deterrence.' *Lieb v. Topstone Industries, Inc.*, 788 F.2d 151, 156 (3rd. Cir. 1986). We agree that such factors may be used to guide courts' discretion, so long as such factors are faithful to the purposes of the Copyright Act and are applied to prevailing plaintiffs and defendants in an evenhanded manner." *Fogerty v. Fantasy, Inc.*, 114 S. Ct. 1023, 1033 n.19, 29 USPQ2d 1881, 1888 n.19 (1994).

attorney work product   [general legal] Documents prepared by an attorney or an agent of an attorney in anticipation of litigation or preparation for trial.

Qualified Immunity From Discovery. The law creates a qualified immunity from discovery as to certain documents created by an attorney or the attorney's agent in preparation for litigation. The reasons are to prevent the opposing attorney from taking a free ride on the diligent attorney's efforts and also to create a modest zone of privacy for an attorney's notes of his or her thoughts and strategy for the case. However, some documents can be disclosed upon a showing of need. For example, if an attorney's agent obtained a verbatim statement from a nonparty witness who has since left the country and is unavailable, the opposing attorney may obtain in discovery a copy of that statement because there is no other way to obtain this information without undue hardship.

Absolute Immunity From Discovery. Under federal law, documents that reflect an attorney's mental impressions, conclusions, opinions, or legal theories are almost always immune from discovery by the opposition. If such things were discoverable, the "effect on the legal profession would be demoralizing" and "the interests of the clients and the cause of justice would be poorly served." *Hickman v. Taylor*, 329 U.S. 495, 511 (1947). This principle is codified in Federal Rule of Civil Procedure 26(b)(3). Some courts hold that this immunity is absolute and no showing of need can ever justify production of the attorney's mental impressions or legal theories. For example, it has been held that there can be no discovery of documents revealing a patent attorney's advice when a defendant counterclaims that the patent infringement claim was brought in bad faith, that is, knowing there was no merit to the allegations of patent infringement. *Duplan Corp. v. Moulinage de Chavanoz*, 509 F.2d 730, 734 (4th Cir. 1974). But cf. *Handgards, Inc. v. Johnson & Johnson*, 192 USPQ 316 (N.D. Cal. 1976) (discovery of attorney's advice permitted where the patent owner claimed good faith on the basis of legal advice given to it).

• *Treatise Reference*: C. Wright, *Law of Federal Courts* §82 (4th ed. 1983).

• *Rule Reference*: Fed. R. Civ. Proc. 26(b)(3): "[A] party may obtain discovery of documents and tangible things otherwise discoverable ... prepared in anticipation of litigation or for trial by or for another party or by or for that party's representative (including the other party's attorney, consultant, surety, indemnitor, insurer or agent) only upon a showing that the party seeking discovery has substantial need of the materials in the preparation of the party's case and that the party is unable without undue hardship to obtain the substantial equivalent of the materials by other means. In ordering discovery of such materials when the required showing has been made, the court shall protect against disclosure of the mental impression, conclusions, opinions or legal theories of an attorney or other representative of a party concerning the litigation."

audience test [copyright]

See SUBSTANTIAL SIMILARITY, ORDINARY OBSERVER TEST.

Audio Home Recording Act [copyright]

See DIGITAL AUDIO RECORDING TECHNOLOGY.

audiovisual work [copyright] A general category of copyrightable works that consist of images which are related, presented in a series, and intended to be shown by the use of a machine. Any sound accompanying the work is included within this category of work.

A common example of an audiovisual work is a slide show, such as is commonly displayed in a sales presentation, a lecture, or an introduction to a museum. While intuition would lead to the conclusion that a silent movie or a slide show without sound are not audiovisual works, in fact they are audiovisual works because they fit within the statutory definition. MOTION PICTURES are a statutorily defined subcategory of audiovisual work. Video games have often been held to be audiovisual works. See, e.g., *M. Kramer Mfg. Co. v. Andrews*, 783 F.2d 421, 435, 228 USPQ 705, 714 (4th Cir. 1986).

• *Statutory Reference*: 17 U.S.C. §101: " 'Audiovisual works' are works that consist of a series of related images which are intrinsically intended to be shown by the use of machines or devices such as projectors, viewers, or electronic equipment, together with accompanying sounds, if any, regardless of the nature of the material objects, such as films or tapes, in which the works are embodied."

• *Case References*:

A news program and a thematically related textual display (teletext) transmitted on the same television signal but broadcast on different television channels were held to constitute a single audiovisual work. "Congress probably wanted the courts to interpret the definitional provisions of the new act flexibly, so that it would cover new technologies as they appeared, rather than to interpret those provisions narrowly and so force Congress periodically to update the act." *WGN Continental Broadcasting Co. v. United Video, Inc.*, 693 F.2d 622, 627, 216 USPQ 97, 102 (7th Cir. 1982).

"It is not immediately obvious that video games fall within this definition. The phrase 'series of related images' might be construed to refer only to a set of images displayed in a fixed sequence. Construed that way, video games do not qualify as audiovisual works. Each time a video game is played, a different sequence of images appears on the screen.... But the phrase might also be construed more broadly to refer to any set of images displayed as some kind of unit. This is how we [construe] it...." *Midway Mfg. Co. v. Artic Int'l, Inc.*, 704 F.2d 1009, 1011, 218 USPQ 791, 792 (7th Cir. 1983).

author [copyright] Either the real person who creates a copyrightable work or the real person or corporate employer of a person who creates a copyrightable work within the scope of employment.

Statute Does Not Define "Author." The Copyright Act consistently uses the phrase "original works of authorship" as the basic subject matter of copyright protection. See, e.g., 17 U.S.C. §102(a). The Copyright Act also consistently uses the term "author" as indicating the creator of a work. See, e.g., 17 U.S.C. §201(a) ("Copyright in a work protected under this title vests initially in the author...."). However, the Act never explicitly defines "author" in the definitions section, 17 U.S.C. §101, or elsewhere.

Sweeping Significance. "Author" in copyright law is used in its broadest possible meaning and includes not only writers of novels, plays, and treatises, but also those who create computer programs, arrange data in telephone books, choreograph dances, take photographs, sculpt stone, paint murals, write songs, record sounds, and translate books from one language to another. All these creators are "authors" in the copyright sense. "Author" is also a word of constitutional dimension, for the Patent and Copyright Clause of the Constitution gives Congress the power to promote the progress of "science" by securing for limited times to "authors" the exclusive right to their "writings." See CONSTITUTION.

Supreme Court Definitions. In holding that a photographer is an "author" of a photograph, the Supreme Court approved of this definition of "author": "He to whom anything owes its origin; originator, maker; one who completes a work of science of literature." *Burrow-Giles Lithographic Co. v. Sarony,* 111 U.S. 53, 58 (1884). Similarly, in the 1973 *Goldstein* case, the Supreme Court said that the constitutional word "author" should not be construed in a "narrow literal sense," but more broadly: "While an 'author' may be viewed as an individual who writes an original composition, the term, in its constitutional sense, has been construed to mean an 'originator,' 'he to whom anything owes its origin.' " *Goldstein v. California,* 412 U.S. 546, 561, 178 USPQ 129, 135 (1973). In further refining the definition, the Supreme Court observed: "As a general rule, the author is the party who actually creates the work, that is, the person who translates an idea into a fixed, tangible expression entitled to copyright protection." *Community for Creative Non-Violence v. Reid,* 490 U.S. 730, 737, 10 USPQ2d 1985, 1989 (1989). The Supreme Court has held that one who merely collects and arranges uncopyrightable data cannot own copyright in that data because he is not an "author" of them; "facts do not owe their origin to an act of authorship." *Feist Publications v. Rural Tel. Serv.,* 499 U.S. 340, 347, 18 USPQ2d 1275, 1278 (1991).

Computer-Generated Works. If a computer program significantly contributes to the creation of a work, such as machine-generated art or music, can a computer be an author? The answer is no, for "machines do not need these monopoly incentives; they just need electricity." M. Leaffer, *Understanding Copyright* §3.7 (1989). Either the programmer or the user of such a computer would be designated the "author."

Works Made for Hire. The only situation in which someone other than the actual creator of the work is the "author" is with WORKS MADE FOR HIRE. In the case of a work made for hire, the employer is considered to be the "author" when an employee creates a work on the job. The real person, partnership, or corporation for whom the work was prepared is considered to be both the "author" and the owner of copyright from the moment of creation of the work. 17 U.S.C. §201(a). A work made for hire is a work prepared "by an employee within the scope of his or her employment" or a commissioned work that falls within a specified category of works and the parties agree in writing to treat it as a work made for hire. 17 U.S.C. §101.

See WORK MADE FOR HIRE, JOINT AUTHORS.

B

back door to Berne [copyright] A method used by United States authors and publishers to achieve the benefits of the BERNE CONVENTION prior to 1989 when the United States became a member of the Berne Convention.

Description of the Back Door. The Berne Convention extends its benefits not only to authors in member nations but also to authors in nonmember nations (such as the United States prior to 1989) if such authors publish their works for the first time in a nation that is a member of Berne or "simultaneously" in a non-Berne and a Berne nation. Under later revisions of the Berne Convention, "simultaneously" includes two publications made within 30 days of each other. Thus, a U.S. author or publisher could obtain the benefits of the Berne Convention through the "back door" by making first publication "simultaneously" in the United States and in a Berne nation such as Canada or the United Kingdom. The U.S. author or publisher then obtained Berne benefits equal to those of a national of the country where the publication occurred.

Drawbacks of the Back Door and the Advent of the Front Door. This back door method proved not to be as advantageous as it sounds. There was a legal question as to whether a nation adhered to the Berne Convention text that permitted a 30-day window for a "simultaneous" publication, rather than the almost impossible task of first publication on the exact same day in different nations. There were also the obvious practical problems of the expense of arranging first publication abroad and the legal issue of how many copies need be distributed abroad to meet the Berne Convention's definition of "publication." The need to face these difficulties came to an end with U.S. membership in the Berne Convention on March

1, 1989. Thereafter, U.S. nationals could enter Berne through the front door.

See BERNE CONVENTION, BCIA.

- *Treatise References*: 3 *Nimmer on Copyright* §17.04[D][2] (1994 rev.); 2 P. Goldstein, *Copyright* §16.7 (1989).

based on [copyright] (1) In the copyright infringement context, a later work is "based on" a previous work so long as the later work is so SUBSTANTIALLY SIMILAR to the previous work that the later work would be an infringement. (2) In the context of an author's contractual agreement to receive payment or credit for a production "based on" the author's work, the term has sometimes been given a broader meaning, including later works bearing any perceptible similarity to the author's work.

In the copyright context, "based on" is used in the Copyright Act as part of the definition of a DERIVATIVE WORK. 17 U.S.C. §101. That is, a derivative work is one "based on" a preexisting work. One view is that a work is not considered to be "derivative" of another work unless, absent a license, it is so "substantially similar" to the underlying work that it would be a copyright infringement of it.

Contractual Credit to Author. Some decisions have implied that in the context of an author's contractual right to credit for a motion picture "based on" the author's work, a later product will be viewed as "based on" if there is any perceptible similarity between the works. 2 *Nimmer on Copyright* §8.21[E] (1993 rev.). Nimmer, while recognizing that the parties may contract to the contrary, recommends that "based on" should be confined to the copyright infringement standard of similarity because "credit to an author short of this standard would tend to deceive the public." *Id.*

Misleading and Truthful Credit. In *King v. Innovation Books*, 976 F.2d 824, 24 USPQ2d 1435 (2d Cir. 1992), the court held that using "based upon" credit was appropriate. While it was false to advertise a film as "Steven King's The Lawnmower Man" where author Stephen King had no involvement in and gave no approval to either the screenplay or the movie, separate advertising stating that the movie was based upon a short story by Stephen King was not false or misleading because a scene that was the "core" of King's story was used in the movie.

- *Case Reference*: "Where a movie draws in material respects from a literary work, both quantitatively and qualitatively, a 'based upon' credit should not be viewed as misleading absent persuasive countervailing facts and circumstances." *King v. Innovation Books,* 976 F.2d 824, 830, 24 USPQ 2d 1435, 1439 (2d Cir. 1992).

See DERIVATIVE WORK.

Bayh-Dole Act [patent] The 1980 Bayh-Dole Act amended the patent code to encourage commercialization and public availability of inventions resulting from federally supported research. The law allows universities, small businesses, and nonprofit organizations to patent the results of their research and license them to the private sector subject to government MARCH-IN RIGHTS. Prior to Bayh-Dole, rights to those inventions were either assigned to the Federal funding agency or dedicated to the public through publication of research results. The Act has resulted in an increased number of patents issued to universities.

- *Statutory Reference*: 35 U.S.C. §202(a): "Each nonprofit organization or small business firm may ... elect to retain title to any subject invention."

See MARCH-IN RIGHTS.

BCIA [copyright] The Berne Convention Implementation Act of 1988. This Act created important revisions to U.S. copyright law so that the United States could become a member of the Berne Union, an international copyright treaty organization created by the BERNE CONVENTION. The revisions in U.S. law made by the BCIA became effective March 1, 1989. Berne Convention Implementation Act of 1988, Pub. L. No. 100-568, 102 Stat. 2853, enacted October 31, 1988.

A Nonself-Executing Treaty. The principle followed by Congress in enacting the BCIA was known as a "minimalist" philosophy: domestic U.S. copyright law would be amended only to the minimal extent absolutely necessary to just come within the standards required for the United States to become a member of the Berne Union. Congress went out of its way to prevent any claims that the Berne Convention is self-executing under U.S. law. Thus, Congress clearly intended that a private party litigating in federal court could only state a claim or defense based directly on U.S. copyright statutes, not on the Berne Convention provisions themselves. (See statutory reference below.)

The "Elimination" of Formalities of Copyright. While the BCIA made several changes in U.S. law, the two major changes were the elimination of copyright notice as a condition subsequent to the existence of copyright and the elimination of registration as a condition precedent to the filing of a copyright infringement lawsuit for foreign works. The 17 U.S.C. §411 requirement of registration as a condition for filing such a lawsuit was retained only as to domestic works, i.e., works first published in the United States. However, both the use of copyright notice and prompt registration of copyright are still strongly recommended even after the BCIA, for such actions will significantly maximize the remedies available against infringers.

See BERNE CONVENTION, NOTICE OF COPYRIGHT, REGISTRATION OF COPYRIGHT, UNIVERSAL COPYRIGHT CONVENTION.

- *Treatise References*: 1 Nimmer on Copyright §1.12[A] (1994 rev.); M. Leaffer, *Understanding Copyright* §12.4 (1989); 2 P. Goldstein, *Copyright* §16.7 (1989); W. Patry, *Copyright Law and Practice* 1287 (1994).

• *Statutory Reference*: Berne Convention Implementation Act of 1988, Pub. L. No. 100-568, 102 Stat. 2853, enacted October 31, 1988, effective March 1, 1989:

Section 2. Declarations. The Congress makes the following declarations:

(1) The Convention for the Protection of Literary and Artistic Works, signed at Berne, Switzerland on September 9, 1886, and all acts, protocols, and revisions thereto (hereinafter in this Act referred to as the "Berne Convention") are not self-executing under the Constitution and laws of the United States.

(2) The obligations of the United States under the Berne Convention may be performed only pursuant to appropriate domestic law.

(3) The amendments made by this Act, together with the law as it exists on the date of the enactment of this Act, satisfy the obligations of the United States in adhering to the Berne Convention and no further rights or interest shall be recognized or created for that purpose.

Benson algorithm [computer–patent]

See ALGORITHM.

Berne Convention [copyright–international]

The major multilateral copyright treaty. The Berne Convention, whose members form the Berne Union, is adhered to by over 75 nations, including the United States. The World Intellectual Property Organization (WIPO) serves as the administering agency for the activities of the Berne Union.

U.S. Entrance Into the Berne Union. For many years, the United States was the only large western nation not a member of the Berne Union. The United States did not join until March 1, 1989. The legislation implementing U.S. entrance is known as the Berne Convention Implementation Act. See BCIA.

The principle followed by Congress in enacting the BCIA was known as a "minimalist" philosophy: domestic U.S. copyright law would be amended only to the minimal extent absolutely necessary to come within the standards required for the United States to become a member of the Berne Union. Congress went out of its way to prevent any claims that the Berne Convention is self-executing under U.S. law. Thus, Congress clearly intended that a private party litigating in federal court could only state a claim or defense based directly on U.S. copyright statutes, not on the Berne Convention provisions themselves. (See statutory reference below.)

Prior to U.S. entrance into Berne, U.S. authors and publishers could obtain the benefits of Berne through a procedure known as the BACK DOOR TO BERNE.

Main Points of Treaty. There are five major principles of the Berne Convention:

(1) National treatment. A work originating in one of the nations that is a member of the Berne Union must be given at least the same level of protection in each member nation as that nation gives to works of its own citizens.

(2) No formalities. Copyright must be granted automatically and cannot be conditioned on formalities such as registration or the giving of notice of copyright. However, a nation may condition certain judicial remedies on observance of formalities, as the United States does with respect to conditioning statutory damages and attorney fees upon prompt registration.

(3) Minimum duration of copyright. The minimum term is life of the author plus 50 years.

(4) Moral rights. Certain defined MORAL RIGHTS are required to be protected under national law.

(5) Independence. Copyright protection is independent of the existence of protection in the country of origin.

Dates of Revisions. The Berne Convention is the oldest multilateral copyright treaty, having been created in 1886. The original text has been revised several times to cope with all the revolutionary changes in the technology of information recordation, storage, and transmission. Revisions took place in Berlin (1908), Rome (1928), Brussels (1948), Stockholm (1967), and Paris (1971).

See BCIA (Berne Convention Implementation Act), BACK DOOR TO BERNE, UNIVERSAL COPYRIGHT CONVENTION (UCC).

• *Treatise References*: 2 *Nimmer on Copyright* §17.01[B][1] (1994 rev.) (text of Berne Convention at Appendix 27); 2 P. Goldstein, *Copyright* §16.7 (1989) (text of Berne Convention at Appendix B-6); M. Leaffer, *International Treaties on Intellectual Property* §339 (1990); M. Leaffer, *Understanding Copyright* §12.4 (1989); WIPO, *Background Reading Material on Intellectual Property* 66–70, 230–36 (1988); W. Patry, *Copyright Law and Practice* 1267 (1994) (text of Berne Convention at 2013); 1 N. Boorstyn, *Copyright* §17.01 (2d ed. 1994).

best mode [patent] A condition of the grant of a valid patent, under which the inventor is required to describe the best method known to the inventor of carrying out the claimed invention. The inventor must not conceal from the public the best physical way to make use of the invention.

Disclosure of the Best Mode Is Part of What the Patentee Owes to the Public. Disclosure of the best mode is a crucial condition of a valid patent, because what the inventor must give to the public in return for the grant of a limited period of exclusive rights (the patent) is a complete and candid description of the invention so as to enable others to understand it and to be able to develop the technology further. Also, once the patent expires, the public is entitled to use the invention and is entitled to a full and complete description of it in order to do so. The public, in exchange for the exclusive rights given the inventor under the patent laws, is entitled to receive from the inventor a full disclosure of the inventor's preferred way to make and use the invention. "The purpose of the best mode requirement 'is to restrain inventors from applying for patents while at the same time concealing from the public preferred embodiments of their inventions.' " *DeGeorge v. Bernier*, 768 F.2d 1318, 1324, 226 USPQ 758, 763 (Fed. Cir. 1985).

Requirements of Proper Disclosure of Best Mode. Best mode analysis consists of two questions: (1) Did the inventor know of a better mode of carrying out the claimed invention than that disclosed in the specification; and (2) did the inventor conceal that better mode. *Engel Indus. Inc. v. The Lockformer Co.*, 946 F.2d 1528, 20 USPQ2d 1300 (Fed. Cir. 1991). The first question goes to the issue of whether, at the time of filing the patent application, the inventor knew of a method of practicing the invention that he considered better than any other. This is a purely subjective issue and concerns whether the inventor had to disclose any facts beyond those required by the ENABLEMENT requirement. If the inventor did know of a preferred method or mode, one must compare the method that the inventor knew of and preferred with that disclosed in the patent specification. The issue is whether the inventor disclosed the best mode adequately to enable one skilled in the relevant art to practice the best mode. *Chemcast Corp. v. Arco Indus. Corp.*, 913 F.2d 923, 927–28, 16 USPQ2d 1033, 1036 (Fed. Cir. 1990).

Continuation Application. It has been held that there is no requirement that best mode be updated in a continuation application. The date for evaluating a best mode disclosure in a continuing application is the date of the earlier application with respect to common subject matter. *Transco Prods. Inc. v. Performance Contracting, Inc.*, 38 F.3d 551, 32 USPQ2d 1077 (Fed. Cir. 1994).

Requirements of Patent Code §112. Patent Code §112 sets forth three distinct requirements:

(1) The DESCRIPTION requirement. The invention that is claimed must be the invention that is described.

(2) The ENABLEMENT requirement. The description must be in such full, clear, and concise terms as to enable any person skilled in the art to make and use the invention.

(3) The "best mode" requirement. The description must be of the best embodiment of the invention known to the inventor at the time of the patent application.

The best mode requirement is imposed in addition to the enablement obligation. While disclosure of *any* mode of carrying out the claimed invention satisfies the enablement requirement, disclosure of the *best* mode is needed to satisfy the best mode obligation. "A specification can be enabling and yet fail to disclose an applicant's contemplated best mode." *Chemcast Corp. v. Arco Indus. Corp.*, 913 F.2d 923, 928, 16 USPQ2d 1033, 1037 (Fed. Cir. 1990). Each claim must be considered individually for compliance with the best mode requirement.

- *Statutory Reference*: 35 U.S.C. §112: "The specification shall contain a written description of the invention, and of the manner and process of making and using it, in such full, clear, concise, and exact terms as to enable any person skilled in the art to which it pertains, or with which it is most nearly connected, to make and use the same, and shall set forth the best mode contemplated by the inventor of carrying out his invention."

- *Case References*:
"Not complying with the best mode requirement amounts to concealing the preferred mode contemplated by the applicant at the time of filing.... '[T]here is no objective standard by which to judge the adequacy of a best mode disclosure.' ... Instead, 'only evidence of concealment (accidental or intentional) is to be considered. That evidence ... must tend to show that the quality of an applicant's best mode disclosure is so poor as to effectively result in concealment.' " *DeGeorge v. Bernier*, 768 F.2d 1318, 1324, 226 USPQ 758, 763 (Fed. Cir. 1985).

"Because not complying with the best mode requirement amounts to concealing the preferred mode contemplated by the applicant at the time of filing, in order to find that the best mode requirement is not satisfied, it must be shown that the applicant knew of and concealed a better mode than he disclosed." *Hybritech Inc. v. Monoclonal Antibodies, Inc.*, 802 F.2d 1367, 1384–85, 231 USPQ 81, 94 (Fed. Cir. 1986).

"Enablement looks to placing the subject matter of the claims generally in the possession of the public. If, however, the applicant develops specific instrumentalities or techniques which are recognized at the time of filing as the best way of carrying out the invention, then the best mode requirement imposes an obligation to

disclose that information to the public as well." *Spectra-Physics Inc. v. Coherent, Inc.*, 827 F.2d 1524, 1532, 3 USPQ2d 1737, 1742 (Fed. Cir. 1987).

- *Treatise References:*
"The best mode requirement is a subjective test in that the statute requires a disclosure only of that which the inventor, not someone else, contemplates as the best mode of carrying out the invention. Not surprisingly then, best mode is a question of fact...." R. Harmon, *Patents and the Federal Circuit* §5.3 (3d ed. 1994). See 2 D. Chisum, *Patents* §7.05 (1994 rev.).

- *Example 1: Best Mode Requirement Satisfied*. In the specification of a patent for a portable apparatus for cleaning computer disk packs, the applicant disclosed the following data regarding the cleaning solution needed to use the invention: "The cleaning solution employed should be of a type adequate to clean grease and oil from the disc surfaces, such as a 91 percent alcohol solution or a non-residue detergent solution such as Randomex Cleaner No. 50281." Randomex Cleaner was the patent owner's proprietary brand. The president of the patent owner testified that he intentionally failed in the patent to give the chemical formula for his brand as "a good advertising gimmick" that might induce users of his machine to also buy his brand of cleaning solution. While the cleaning solution was needed to use the invention, it was not claimed as part of the invention itself. The district court found the patent invalid for failure to disclose the best mode for a cleaning solution.

The Court of Appeals for the Federal Circuit reversed, finding that the disclosure was adequate. The court of appeals found that reference to the preferred cleaner as "a non-residue detergent solution" was an adequate disclosure of the best mode: there was no need to go further to disclose details of the chemical formula. By way of analogy, the court of appeals said that if one invents a new form of internal combustion engine, the best mode requirement would demand that the inventor divulge the general type of commercially available fuel on which the engine would run best. There would be no requirement to disclose the chemical formula of that gasoline. *Randomex Inc. v. Scopus Corp.*, 849 F.2d 585, 7 USPQ2d 1050 (Fed. Cir. 1988).

• *Example 2: Best Mode Requirement Not Satisfied.* Wilson invented and patented an improved form of valve stem seal for an automobile engine to prevent oil leakage into the cylinders of the engine. The patent claim included an elastomeric (rubber) ring extending around the seal. In a report made some months before the patent application was filed, inventor Wilson said that tests revealed that treating the seal surface with fluoride was necessary for satisfactory performance. Patented seals sold by the patent owner were fluoride-treated. The patent specification mentioned that useful "in some instances" was the coating of the elastomeric seal with various lubricating materials such as graphite. The patent specification did not disclose the need for fluoride treatment of the seal. The Court of Appeals for the Federal Circuit held that although fluoride treatment was well known to persons skilled in this art, the patent was invalid for failure to meet the best mode requirement. The uncontroverted evidence proved that at the time of filing the application for patent, "Mr. Wilson believed that the best way of carrying out his invention included fluoride treating the surface of the valve seals." Since this was not disclosed, the patent was invalid for failure to comply with the best mode requirement of Patent Code §112. *Dana Corp. v. IPC Ltd. Partnership*, 860 F.2d 415, 419, 8 USPQ2d 1692, 1695–96 (Fed. Cir. 1988).

• *Example 3: Best Mode Requirement Not Satisfied.* In the late 1960s Irwin and Levine invented a new method of computerized data processing, with the final step being storage of data on a magnetic tape cassette. The inventors built a major business on the invention of the patent. In reviewing the appeal of an infringement suit, the Federal Circuit held that seven claims of the patent were not proven to be invalid and were infringed, but that eight of the claims were invalid for failure to comply with the best mode requirement. One of the objectives of the claimed invention disclosed in the specification was to store data on "magnetic tape cassettes of the general type presently [the application was filed in 1969] finding extensive

and widespread usage in audio entertainment equipment, but never heretofore used in data handling apparatus." The Federal Circuit affirmed the trial court finding that the patentee knew prior to filing the application that standard audio tape was not in fact the best mode for carrying out the invention. The patentee used tape and cassettes of its own design and specification that were substantially different from standard audio tape in yield strength and magnetic characteristics. *Northern Telecom Inc. v. Datapoint Corp.*, 908 F.2d 931, 15 USPQ2d 1321 (Fed. Cir. 1990) (Judge Newman dissenting on this point).

biogenetics [patent]

See BIOTECHNOLOGY, GENETIC ENGINEERING.

biotechnology [patent] The science of changing the genetic structure (genotype) of living organisms in the manufacture of drugs or other products or in producing new forms of living organisms. A synonym is GENETIC ENGINEERING. Products and processes involving biotechnology are patentable. See, e.g., *Hybritech Inc. v. Monoclonal Antibodies, Inc.*, 802 F.2d 1367, 231 USPQ 81 (Fed. Cir. 1986). A patent may be obtained on a living organism that has been genetically altered. In 1994 the Patent and Trademark Offfice proposed new guidelines for the examination of biotechnology patent applications. See 49 Pat. Trademark & Copyright J. (BNA) 223 (Jan. 5, 1995).

See GENETIC ENGINEERING, TRANSGENIC.

BIRPI [copyright–international] Bureaux Internationaux Réunis pour la Protection de la Propriété Intellectuelle was an organization to promote the protection of copyright. BIRPI once published the copyright periodical *Droit d'Auteur* and was the predecessor organization to *WIPO*, the World Intellectual Property Organization.

blackout period [trademark] In an INTENT TO USE APPLICATION to register a trademark, the time between PTO approval for PUBLICATION FOR OPPOSITION and issuance of the notice of allowance during which neither the "Statement of Use" nor an Amendment to Allege Use can be filed. 37 C.F.R. §§2.76(a), 2.77, 2.88. The only amendment permitted during the blackout period is an amendment to delete goods or services.

The blackout period does not begin until the day after the mark is approved for publication. An intent to use applicant who wishes to file an amendment to allege use can beat the onset of the blackout period if a call to the Trademark Status Line reveals that the application has not entered the blackout period and the amendment to allege use is filed that same day in accordance with 37 C.F.R. §1.10. *In re Sovran Fin. Corp.*, 25 USPQ2d 1537, 1538 (Comm. Pat. 1992).

See INTENT TO USE APPLICATION.

• *Rule Reference*: 37 C.F.R. §2.76(a): "An application under section 1(b) of the Act may be amended to allege use of the mark in commerce under section 1(c) of the Act at any time between the filing of the application and the date the examiner approves the mark for publication or the date of expiration of the six-month response period after issuance of a final action. Thereafter, an allegation of use may be submitted only as a statement of use under §2.88 after the issuance of a notice of allowance under section 13(b)(2) of the Act. If an amendment to allege use is filed outside the time period specified in this paragraph, it will be returned to the applicant."

blanket license [copyright] A license from a PERFORMING RIGHTS SOCIETY to a performer of music, such as a radio station, charging a flat amount or a percentage of revenues, to perform any of the songs in the repertory of the society subject to the conditions of the license.

Performing Rights Societies. A PERFORMING RIGHTS SOCIETY, such as *ASCAP*, generally grants licenses to perform MUSICAL WORKS in its repertory only on a collective, pooled basis, with the grant of a license to perform all the compositions in the repertory. License fees are ordinarily a percentage of total revenues or a flat dollar amount according to the type of use made of the music. Radio and television networks and individual stations hold blanket licenses from both ASCAP and BMI.

Early Challenges to Blanket Licenses. A major conflict between the music and broadcasting industries was ended by the entry of consent decrees in 1941. These decrees, amended in 1951, laid down the rules by which ASCAP and BMI could license users and broadcasters of music consistent with the antitrust laws. In one of the continuing disputes that followed, the Court of Appeals for the Ninth Circuit held that the blanket licenses did not restrain trade because the consent decree preserved the right of individual ASCAP members to directly deal with licensees as to nondramatic performing rights, so that ASCAP was not the exclusive source of licenses. *K-91 Inc. v. Gershwin Publishing Co.*, 372 F.2d 1 (9th Cir. 1967). The Department of Justice agreed.

The CBS Challenge. In another antitrust attack on the blanket license program, CBS offered to negotiate with the PERFORMING RIGHTS SOCIETIES for licenses based on individual musical compositions actually used by CBS, was refused, and sued the performing rights societies for violation of the Sherman Antitrust Act. The district court dismissed the complaint, finding that there existed a free market in which CBS could negotiate directly with the copyright owner for a "per composition" license and that, similar to a patent PACKAGE LICENSE, a copyright blanket license was legal so long as it was noncoercive and administratively convenient. The Court of Appeals for the Second Circuit upheld the district court on all grounds except one: it held that the blanket license constituted illegal per se price fixing. The U.S. Supreme Court reversed this holding that the blanket license plan was illegal per se price fixing and remanded for a determination under the rule of reason. *Broadcast Music, Inc. v. CBS, Inc.*, 441 U.S. 1, 201 USPQ 497 (1979). On remand, the court of appeals found the blanket licensing system to be reasonable under the antitrust RULE OF REASON. *CBS Inc. v. ASCAP*, 620 F.2d 930, 205 USPQ 880 (2d Cir. 1980). Additional antitrust challenges to the blanket license system have continued but been unsuccessful. See, e.g., *Buffalo Broadcasting Co. v. ASCAP*, 744 F.2d 917, 223 USPQ 478 (2d Cir. 1984).

Fee Determination and the Consent Decree. As amended in 1950, the consent decree provides that in the event of a dispute concerning the amount of a fee for the blanket license, the District Court for the Southern District of New York is authorized to determine a reasonable fee. A challenge to a blanket license fee determination under the ASCAP consent decree was decided in *American Soc'y of Composers, Authors and Publishers v. Showtime/The Movie Channel, Inc.*, 912 F.2d 563, 567, 16 USPQ2d 1026, 1029 (2d Cir. 1990). The court set a "reasonable" fee and recognized that lack of competition in the market for copyrighted music enhanced ASCAP's bargaining power in negotiating rates.

See PERFORMING RIGHTS SOCIETIES.

• *Treatise References*: 2 *Nimmer on Copyright* §8.19 (1994 rev.); 1 P. Goldstein, *Copyright* §5.9 (1989); M. Leaffer, *Understanding Copyright* §8.22[B]–[D] (1989).

blind bidding [copyright–entertainment law] In the distribution of motion pictures for exhibition in theaters, blind bidding is the practice of distributors requiring exhibitors to submit bids for the right to exhibit films without the bidding exhibitor first having an opportunity to view the films. See Note, *Blind Bidding and the Motion Picture Industry*, 92 Harv. L. Rev. 1128 (1979).

Blind bidding has been prohibited by statute in several states. Such statutes have been challenged unsuccessfully as unconstitutional on several grounds, including preemption by the federal copyright laws. See *Allied Artists Pictures Corp. v. Rhodes*, 496 F. Supp. 408, 207 USPQ 630 (S.D. Ohio 1980), *aff'd*, 679 F.2d 656, 215 USPQ 1097 (6th Cir. 1982) (rejecting constitutional challenge to Ohio anti-blind-bidding statute); *Associated Film Distrib. Corp. v. Thornburgh*, 683 F.2d 808 (3d Cir. 1982), 800 F.2d 369, 231 USPQ 143 (3d Cir. 1986) (Pennsylvania anti-blind-bidding statute not preempted by the federal Copyright Act). A claim that blind-bidding practices constituted a violation of federal antitrust laws was dismissed in *Harkins Amusement Enters., Inc. v. General Cinema Corp.*, 850 F.2d 477, 489 (9th Cir. 1988).

block booking [copyright–antitrust] Conditioning the license of desirable copyrighted motion picture films on also taking a license of undesirable films. Such conduct has been held to constitute a TIE-IN illegal under the antitrust laws. *United States v. Loew's Inc.*, 371 U.S. 38 (1962) (block booking of films for license for showing on television held illegal).

See TIE-IN OF COPYRIGHTS, PACKAGE LICENSING.

• *Treatise Reference*: W. Holmes, *Intellectual Property and Antitrust Law* §36.05 (1994 rev.).

blocking patents [patent] Separately owned patents that so overlap or interlock in coverage that the collective technology of the patents cannot practicably be used without a license under each patent. Patents can overlap such that there is DOMINATION by one over another.

Blocking patents can be unblocked by cross-licensing or depositing the patents in a PATENT POOL.

BMI [copyright] Broadcast Music, Inc. One of the main PERFORMING RIGHTS SOCIETIES, which licenses certain performing rights in copyrighted musical works. Similar in operation to *ASCAP*, BMI is organized along different lines: it is a nonprofit corporation owned by members of the broadcasting industry and is affiliated with or represents thousands of authors, composers, and music publishing companies. BMI grants licenses, such as BLANKET LICENSES, for the right to nondramatic public performances of the copyrighted MUSICAL WORKS of the members. BMI has about 2,000,000 musical compositions in its repertory. Its BLANKET LICENSES enable a licensee to perform any of those musical works. The license covers only the right to perform the music in a nondramatic manner: the GRAND RIGHTS or dramatic performing rights are not licensed by BMI.

See PERFORMING RIGHTS SOCIETIES, *ASCAP, SESAC*, GRAND RIGHTS, BLANKET LICENSE, PERFORMANCE.

• *Treatise References*: 2 *Nimmer on Copyright* §8.19 (1994 rev.); M. Leaffer, *Under-*

standing Copyright §8.22 (1989); S. Shemel & M.W. Krasilovsky, *This Business of Music* ch. 18 (1985).

Board of Patent Appeals and Interferences [patent] An administrative board that is part of the Patent and Trademark Office (PTO), which hears (1) appeals from PTO decisions by EXAMINERS rejecting the patentability of claims to new inventions; (2) questions of patentability and priority in INTERFERENCE proceedings between rival claimants for a patent on the same invention (see 37 C.F.R. §1.191); and (3) NASA entitlement proceedings.

See INTERFERENCE, PATENT, ENTITLEMENT PROCEEDINGS.

• *Statutory Reference*: 35 U.S.C. §7(b): "The Board of Patent Appeals and Interferences shall, on written appeal of an applicant, review adverse decisions of examiners upon applications for patents and shall determine priority and patentability of invention in interferences declared under section 135(a) of this title. Each appeal and interference shall be heard by at least three members of the Board of Patent Appeals and Interferences, who shall be designated by the Commissioner...."

bootleg merchandise [trademark–unfair competition] Unauthorized merchandise bearing the names, trademarks, logos, and/or likenesses of performers or musical groups.

For example, bootleg merchandise is created when the name of a musical group is affixed to posters, caps, t-shirts, etc., without the permission of the members of the group and sold as if properly licensed. If the use of the images or names of the performers or groups without authorization is likely to cause confusion, mistake, or deception as to the source of the product, it will constitute a violation of LANHAM ACT §43(a). See *Nice Man Merchandising, Inc. v. Logocraft, Ltd.*, 23 USPQ2d 1290, 1292 (E.D. Pa. 1992).

Licensed products are distributed by companies that have been specifically licensed to produced such merchandise. Such merchandise by performers and groups is sometimes referred to as "popular music novelty merchandise" or "PMNM." The manufacture and sale of bootleg merchandise can also be a violation of performers' RIGHT OF PUBLICITY as an unauthorized commercial exploitation of their names or likenesses.

bootleg recording [copyright–unfair competition] An unauthorized recording of a live performance.

For example, a bootleg copy of a performance is made if a member of an audience at a live performance conceals a recording device, records the performance, and sells the resulting discs, records, or tapes. This would not constitute infringement of a SOUND RECORDING copyright because there is no recapture of the actual sounds on a record; rather it is the capture of live sounds. If the performance is of music previously written down or recorded, the unauthorized recorder has made an unauthorized reproduction of that FIXED work and is liable for traditional copyright infringement under federal law. But if the performance is of extemporaneous speech or improvised music, there is no reproduction of a fixed work unless there is transmission and simultaneous recording by the performing artists. Even if there is no performance of a fixed work, there is still federal liability for infringement under the URUGUAY ROUND AGREEMENTS ACT OF 1994.

Uruguay Round Agreements Act. Until the December 8, 1994, enactment of the URUGUAY ROUND AGREEMENTS ACT, there was no specific federal law relating to the unauthorized recording of a live performance. Under that Act, 17 U.S.C. §1101 was added imposing liability on a person who makes an unauthorized recording of a live musical performance. Such a person is liable for all the civil remedies available against a copyright infringer. Also, the addition of 18 U.S.C. §2319A makes bootlegging "knowingly and for purposes of commercial advantage or private gain" a federal crime.

State Law. The provision added by the URUGUAY ROUND AGREEMENTS ACT, 17 U.S.C. §1101(d), provides that the federal remedies are in addition to, not in lieu of, federal law. Thus, parallel state protection against bootlegging continues after the 1994 federal law. Such protection would be available under state MISAP-

PROPRIATION law. Some states have statutes specifically aimed at bootlegging, e.g., California Penal Code §653s.

Bootleg Versus Pirate Recording. A bootleg recording differs from a pirate recording in that a pirate recording is one illegally reproduced from a genuine, authorized recording, not from a live performance. However, "bootleg recording" is occasionally misused as an apparent synonym for "pirate recording." See *United States v. Powell*, 701 F.2d 70, 217 USPQ 609 (8th Cir. 1983).

Word Origin. The word "bootleg" is borrowed from the American slang word for alcoholic liquor illegally produced without the payment of the proper taxes. The word has been adopted for direct use without translation in other nations as denoting the unlawful reproduction of live performances. See WIPO, *Glossary of Terms of the Law of Copyright and Neighboring Rights* 190 (1980).

• *Case Reference*: *United States v. 1934 Stereo Eight-Track Tape Sound Recordings*, 213 USPQ 437 n.2 (D. Mass. 1980).

brand name [trademark] (1) In business and marketing, variously used to indicate an advertising image, corporate identifier, or trademark. (2) In law, "brand" or "brand name" is not a term of art, but only a colloquial way to refer to a trademark. See *Philip Morris Inc. v. Imperial Tobacco Co.*, 251 F. Supp. 362, 377, 148 USPQ 255, 265 (E.D. Va. 1965), *aff'd*, 401 F.2d 179, 158 USPQ 561, 159 USPQ 257 (4th Cir. 1968).

brevet [patent] French term for patent.

Brussels Satellite Convention [international–copyright] The Convention Relating to Distribution of Programme-Carrying Signals Transmitted by Satellite is a multilateral treaty that obligates member nations to take adequate measures to prevent the unauthorized distribution or retransmission on their territory of signals carried by satellite. Developed in Brussels in 1974 and ratified by the United States in 1984, the convention has nine member states.

The convention focuses on the unauthorized distribution of signals rather than on their unauthorized reception. The convention exempts signals intended for direct reception from satellite by the general public. Since the convention leaves each nation free to choose its own method of implementation, the United States took the position that existing copyright and communications law sufficiently fulfilled the obligations of the convention, and therefore no new legislation was passed upon ratification of the treaty. See text of treaty at 3 P. Goldstein, *Copyright* App. B-10 (1989).

• *Treatise References*: "[T]he signal is the object of protection, not the content of the material sent by the signal. Accordingly, the Convention is designed to protect the emitter or carrier, not the copyright owner of the program material." M. Leaffer, *Understanding Copyright Law* 357 (1989). See 2 P. Goldstein, *Copyright* §16.9 (1989); W. Patry, *Copyright Law and Practice* 1263 (1994).

Budapest Treaty [patent] A treaty that enables those applying for a patent on an invention involving biological materials to satisfy the EN-ABLEMENT requirement of the patent offices of several nations by depositing a sample of the microorganism or cell culture with a single international cell depository. The full name of the treaty is The Budapest Treaty on the International Recognition of the Deposit of Microorganisms for the Purposes of Patent Procedure. It entered into force in 1980, and about 22 nations are party to the treaty.

International Depository. The main feature of the Budapest Treaty is that a nation must recognize the deposit of a microorganism with any "international depository authority," regardless of its location in the world. Thus, one deposit with one international depository will suffice for a patent application filed in the patent offices of all nations that are parties to the treaty.

Cell Depository. A CELL DEPOSITORY is a scientific institution that receives and maintains biological microorganisms and cultured cells and provides samples to interested persons on request. When an invention involves a microorganism that is not readily available to the public, a written description of the invention in the patent SPECIFICATION is not a sufficient disclosure to satisfy the ENABLEMENT requirement. In such cases, it is necessary for the inventor to deposit with a specialized institution a sample of the cells or microorganism. This will enable others to reproduce the invention.

The treaty sets up procedures for a cell depository to qualify as an "international depository authority" under the treaty. The regulations under the treaty contain detailed provisions on who is entitled, and when, to receive samples of the deposited microorganism.

See BIOTECHNOLOGY, GENETIC ENGINEERING.

• *Treatise Reference*: "When protection is sought in several countries for an invention involving a microorganism or the use of a microorganism, the complex and costly procedures of the deposit of the microorganism might have to be repeated in each of those countries. It was in order to eliminate or reduce such multiplication, in order to enable one deposit to serve the purpose of all the deposits which would otherwise be necessary, that the Treaty was concluded.... The Treaty is primarily advantageous to the depositor who is an applicant for patents in several countries; the deposit of a microorganism under the procedures provided for in the Treaty will save him money and strengthen his security." WIPO, *Background Reading Material on Intellectual Property* 379–80 (1988). See text of treaty at 7 D. Chisum, *Patents* App. 22 (1994 rev.).

Buenos Aires Convention [patent–copyright–international] There are two international treaties of this name:

(1) *Buenos Aires Convention on Inventions, Patents, and Designs and Industrial Models* of 1910, entered into among 19 Central and South American nations and the United States. See text of convention at 3 S. Ladas, *Patents, Trade-*

marks and Related Rights: National and International Protection App. 9, at p. 1964 (1975).

(2) *Buenos Aires Convention on Literary and Artistic Copyright* of 1910, entered into among 16 Central and South American nations and the United States. A provision of this convention is the source of the often-seen legend: "All Rights Reserved" or its equivalents "Copyright Reserved" and "Todos los derechos reservados." The author of any contracting county who has secured copyright in its own country will enjoy in each of the other convention countries the copyright rights accorded to its own citizens if the specified notice is used. See W. Patry, *Copyright Law and Practice* 1252 (1994) (text of convention in appendix); 1 *Nimmer on Copyright* §5.05[B][2][c]; text of convention at App. 28 (1994 rev.); text of convention at 3 P. Goldstein, *Copyright* App. B-14 (1989).

See ALL RIGHTS RESERVED.

bundling [antitrust] Conditioning the lease or purchase of item A on the lease or purchase of separate item B. Such conduct can be held to constitute a TIE-IN illegal under antitrust law.

By analogy to the motion picture block booking tie-in cases, it has been held to be an illegal copyright tie-in for a computer manufacturer to "bundle" or tie-in the purchase of computer hardware to the purchase of copyrighted software programs (i.e., where the programs can contractually only be used on hardware made by the seller of the software). *Digidyne Corp. v. Data Gen. Corp.*, 734 F.2d 1336 (9th Cir. 1984).

See TIE-IN, BLOCK BOOKING.

• *Treatise Reference:* W. Holmes, *Intellectual Property and Antitrust Law* §36.05 (1994 rev.).

bursting bubble [general legal]
See PRESUMPTIONS.

C

CAFC [patent–trademark]

See COURT OF APPEALS FOR THE FEDERAL CIRCUIT.

cancellation proceeding [trademark] An administrative INTER PARTES proceeding before the TRADEMARK TRIAL AND APPEAL BOARD (TTAB) in which a person with a reasonable belief that he or she will be damaged petitions for the cancellation of the federal registration of a mark. Cancellations are governed by Lanham Act §§14, 18, and 19.

Standing. Standing to petition to cancel is conferred on anyone other than a mere inter-meddler. Anyone with "a personal interest in the outcome beyond that of the general public" has standing. *Lipton Indus., Inc. v. Ralston Purina Co.*, 670 F.2d 1024, 1028, 213 USPQ 185, 188 (C.C.P.A. 1982).

Grounds. A petition to cancel a mark that has been on the principal register less than five years may be based on any ground that would have barred registration in the first instance. *Lipton Indus., Inc. v. Ralston Purina Co.*, 670 F.2d 1024, 1029–30, 213 USPQ 185, 190 (C.C.P.A. 1982). Most often these grounds will be those bars to registration listed in Lanham Act §2. Once a registration is over five years old, Lanham Act §14 narrows the grounds for a petition to cancel to those specifically listed in §14. Those grounds are: (1) the mark has become a generic name; (2) the mark has been abandoned; (3) the registration was obtained fraudulently; (4) the mark is barred by the provisions of §§2(a), 2(b), 2(c), or 4; (5) the mark is used to misrepresent the source of the goods or services; or (6) a CERTIFICATION MARK is used in violation of the special requirements for such marks. The equitable defenses of LACHES, estoppel, and acquiescence are made available by Lanham Act §19, 15 U.S.C. §1069.

Cancellation in Federal Litigation. In cases in which a federally registered mark is already in issue, federal courts have the power to order the cancellation of federal registrations under Lanham Act §37, 15 U.S.C. §1119. See 3 J.T. McCarthy, *Trademarks and Unfair Competition* §30.32 (3d ed. 1995 rev.).

Cancellation of Part of a Registration. While at one time it was held that the TTAB could not cancel a registration in part, that rule was nullified by a 1989 amendment to Lanham Act §18, which permits the Patent and Trademark Office to order cancellation "in whole or in part," to "modify" a registration by "limiting the goods or services specified," and to "otherwise restrict or rectify" the register.

Evidence. The testimonial evidence in a cancellation proceeding consists of the written transcript of a testimonial deposition resembling a discovery deposition; it does not consist of live testimony before the Trademark Board. The "trial" before the board consists of what in a court trial would be closing arguments by counsel supplementing their trial briefs.

• *Treatise Reference*: 2 J.T. McCarthy, *Trademarks and Unfair Competition* §§20.12–.21 (3d ed. 1995 rev.).

captive chip [computer] A SEMI-CONDUCTOR CHIP used by its manufacturer only in its own products and not sold on the open market. See R. Stern, *Semiconductor Chip Protection* (1986).

CARP [copyright]

See COPYRIGHT ARBITRATION ROYALTY PANEL.

carry back [patent–trademark]

1. Patent Carry Back. To carry back is to claim a date of actual REDUCTION TO PRACTICE of the invention earlier than the date of the patent application. The date when an application that adequately discloses the invention is filed with the Patent and Trademark Office is presumed to be the date of invention. The inventor always bears the burden of proving an earlier date of invention.

When challenged with a PRIOR ART reference relied upon to show OBVIOUSNESS, the applicant or patentee may carry back his date of invention to show a date of invention earlier than the date of the reference. This form of carry back is known as SWEARING BACK.

• *Treatise References*: D. Chisum, *Patents* §§3.08[1], 10.03[1][c] (1994 rev.); 2 P. Rosenberg, *Patent Law Fundamentals* §10.02[2] (1994 rev.).

See SWEARING BACK.

2. Trademark Registration Carry Back. To carry back is to claim a date of first use of a mark earlier than the date of first use stated in an application for registration. In an INTER PARTES opposition or petition to cancel proceeding in the Patent and Trademark Office, an applicant or registrant who wishes to carry back the date of first use to a date prior to the date of first use claimed in the application for registration has the burden of doing so by clear and convincing evidence.

• *Case Reference*: "Where an applicant seeks to prove a date earlier than the date alleged in its application, a heavier burden has been imposed on the applicant than the common law burden of preponderance of the evidence.... The reason for such an increased evidentiary burden, supported by common sense, is that a change of position from one 'considered to have been made against interest at the time of filing of the application' ... requires enhanced substantiation." *Hydro-Dynamics Inc. v. George Putnam & Co.*, 811 F.2d 1470, 1473, 1 USPQ2d 1772, 1774 (Fed. Cir. 1987) (applicant failed to carry evidentiary burden).

CCC [copyright]
See COPYRIGHT CLEARANCE CENTER.

CCPA [patent–trademark]
See COURT OF CUSTOMS AND PATENT APPEALS.

cell depository [patent] A scientific institution that receives and maintains biological microorganisms and cultured cells and provides samples to interested persons on request. When an invention involves a microorganism or cell line that is not readily available to the public or cannot be reproduced without undue experimentation, a written description of the invention in the patent SPECIFICATION is not a sufficient disclosure to satisfy the ENABLEMENT requirement. In such cases, it is necessary for the inventor to deposit with a specialized institution a sample of the cells or microorganism to enable others to make and use the invention.

The United States is a signatory of the Budapest Treaty on the International Recognition of the Deposit of Microorganisms for the Purposes of Patent Procedure (BUDAPEST TREATY). The main feature of the treaty is that a nation must recognize the deposit of a microorganism with any "international depository authority," regardless of its location in the world. Thus, one deposit with one international depository will suffice for a patent application filed in the patent offices of all nations that are parties to the treaty. See Hall & Chwang, *Deposit Requirements for Biological Materials*, 14 Hous. J. Int'l L. 565 (1992).

See ENABLEMENT, BUDAPEST TREATY

• *Case References*:
"When an invention relates to a new biological material, the material may not be reproducible even when detailed procedures and a complete taxonomic description are included in the specification. Thus the then Patent Office established the requirement that physical samples of such material be made available to the public as a condition of the patent grant." *In re Lundak*, 773 F.2d 1216, 1220, 227 USPQ 90, 93 (Fed. Cir. 1985).

"Where an invention depends on the use of living materials such as microorganisms or cultured cells, it may be impossible to enable the public to make the invention (i.e., to obtain these living materials) solely by means of the written disclosure. One means that has been developed for complying with the enablement requirement is to deposit the living materials in cell depositories which will distribute samples to the public who wish to practice the invention after the patent issues.... A deposit has been held necessary for enablement where the starting materials (i.e., the living cells used to practice the invention, or cells from which the required cells can be produced) are not readily available to the public. Even when starting materials are available, a deposit has been necessary where it would require undue experimentation to make the cells of the invention from the starting material.... [A] deposit is not always necessary to satisfy the enablement requirement. No deposit is necessary if the biological organisms can be obtained from readily available sources or derived from readily available starting materials through routine screening that does not require undue experimentation." *In re Wands*, 858 F.2d 731, 735, 8 USPQ2d 1400, 1402–03 (Fed. Cir. 1988).

"[A] deposit has been considered adequate to satisfy the *enablement* requirement of 35 U.S.C. §112, when a written description alone would not place the invention in the hands of the public and physical possession of a unique biological material is required.... [W]hen ... the organism is created by insertion of genetic material into a cell obtained from generally available sources, then all that is required is a description of the best mode and an adequate description of the means of carrying out the invention, not the deposit of the cells. If the cells can be prepared without undue experimentation from known materials, based on the description in the patent specification, a deposit is not required." *Amgen, Inc. v. Chugai Phamaceutical Co.*, 927 F.2d 1200, 1210–11, 18 USPQ2d 1016, 1024–25 (Fed. Cir. 1991).

• *Treatise References*: 2 D. Chisum, *Patents* §7.03[5][b] (1994 rev.); 1 I. Cooper, *Biotechnology and the Law* §5.05[1][a] (1994 rev.).

• *Rule Reference*: "Biological material need not be deposited, inter alia, if it is known and readily available to the public or can be made or isolated without undue experimentation." 37 C.F.R. §1.801 (1993).

cell library [computer] A "cell" is a unit or module within a SEMICONDUCTOR CHIP that performs a certain electronic function, such as an oscillator, amplifier, or register. Cells are of varying sizes and may contain from one to many thousands of transistors. A "cell library" is a collection of cells available for licensing by customers who combine the cells in their semiconductor chips to achieve the desired functions. The physical design of a semiconductor chip is protectible under the Semiconductor Chip Protection Act (see SCPA).

• *Reference*: R. Stern, *Semiconductor Chip Protection* §12.5 (1986) (discussing licensing of cell libraries).

certificate of correction [patent]
See CORRECTION.

certification mark [trademark] A mark used to attest that goods or services sold under the mark either meet the standards set, come from the region named, or were made or performed by union labor.

Types of Certification Marks. There are three basic types of certification marks.

(1) The "Good Housekeeping Seal"-type of certification of goods or services. A well-known example is the UNDERWRITERS LABORATORIES (UL) standards and testing certification mark. The owner of the mark does not sell the certified goods but sets standards, tests goods, and certifies that the goods meet the standards.

(2) The "Roquefort Cheese"-type of certification of regional origin. For example, the mark ROQUEFORT certifies that cheese bearing the mark has been made from sheep's milk and cured in the natural caves in Roquefort, France.

(3) The "Union Label"-type certification that goods were made or services performed by union labor.

Special Requirements for Registration of a Certification Mark. It is a ground for cancellation of a certification mark registration, and a bar to registration in the first instance, if the registrant either: (1) does not control or is not able to exercise control over the use of the mark; (2) permits the use of the certification mark for other than certification purposes; (3) refuses to certify or to continue to certify the goods or services of any person who maintains the standards or conditions the mark certifies; or (4) engages in the production or marketing of any goods or services to which the certification mark is applied. Lanham Act §14(5), 15 U.S.C. §1064(5). The requirement of (4) above is known as the "anti-use-by-owner" rule. It prohibits a certifier from engaging in the sale of goods or services that it certifies, for to do so would compromise the objectivity of the certifier. The requirement of (3) above imposes a kind of limited "compulsory license" in that it requires the certifier to permit use of the certification mark by anyone who meets the standards. There is no governmental control over the standards the certifier uses. That is up to the certifier.

- *Treatise Reference*: 2 J.T. McCarthy, *Trademarks and Unfair Competition* §19.32 (3d ed. 1995 rev.).

- *Statutory References*:

Lanham Act §4, 15 U.S.C. §1054: "Subject to the provisions relating to the registration of trademarks, so far as they are applicable, collective and certification marks, including indications of regional origin, shall be registerable under this Act, in the same manner and with the same effect as are trademarks, by persons, and nations, States, municipalities, and the like, exercising legitimate control over the use of the marks sought to be registered, even though not possessing an industrial or commercial establishment, and when registered they shall be entitled to the protection provided herein in the case of trademarks, except in the case of certification marks when used so as to represent falsely that the owner or a user thereof makes or sells the goods or performs the services on or in connection with which such mark is used...."

Lanham Act §45, 15 U.S.C. §1127:

The term "certification mark" means any word, name, symbol, or device, or any combination thereof—

(1) used by a person other than its owner, or

(2) which its owner has a bona fide intention to permit a person other than the owner to use in commerce and files an application to register on the principal register established by this Act,

to certify regional or other origin, material, mode of manufacture, quality, accuracy, or other characteristics of such person's goods or services or that the work or labor on the goods or services was performed by members of a union or other organization.

challenge [patent] Some unequivocal act evidencing a patent licensee's position that the licensed patent is invalid. The refusal to continue to pay royalties for the explicitly expressed reason that the patent is believed to be invalid constitutes a sufficient "challenge." *P.P.G. Indus., Inc. v. Westwood Chem. Co.*, 530 F.2d 700, 706, 189 USPQ 399, 404 (6th Cir. 1976). Some have argued that a challenge must occur in court by the filing of a pleading alleging patent invalidity. McCarthy, *"Unmuzzling" the Patent Licensee: Chaos in the Wake of Lear v. Adkins*, 45 Geo. Wash. L. Rev. 429, 472 (1977).

The Rule of Lear v. Adkins. According to the case law decided in the wake of *Lear, Inc. v. Adkins*, 395 U.S. 653, 162 USPQ 1 (1969), it is the timing of the licensee's "challenge" to the validity of the patent that is crucial to the payment of royalties. One of the policies of the *Lear* decision is the encouragement of an early adjudication of patent invalidity. *Lear v. Adkins* held that a licensee cannot be forced to pay royalties pending its challenge to validity in court. 395 U.S. at 673. Even if the patent is ultimately held invalid as a result of the challenge, there can be no refund of prechallenge royalties, because such a refund would discourage an early challenge to the patent. There is uncertainty as to whether postchallenge royalties paid by the successful paying and challenging licensee are refundable or not. See *Cordis Corp. v. Medtronic,*

Inc., 780 F.2d 991, 228 USPQ 189 (Fed. Cir. 1985) (issue not decided).

See LICENSE ESTOPPEL.

Chinese copy

[patent–trademark–copyright] An identical copy of a work or product protected by patent, trademark, trade dress, or copyright.

Some courts consider the term inappropriate as implying an ethic slur. "The court must note that plaintiff's repeated reference of [defendant's] packaging as a Chinese copy is dated, ethnocentric, and wholly unnecessary. While the phrase may have been (or, sadly, continues to be a common reference among practitioners, its use remains entirely inappropriate." Patel J. in *Carol Cable Co. v. Grand Auto Inc.*, 4 USPQ2d 1056, 1059 n.2 (N.D. Cal. 1987)

Synonyms: KNOCK OFF, COUNTERFEIT,

- *Usage Examples*:

Patent Law:

"As to [the patentee's] suggestions that the district court should have found literal infringement because the accused sensor employs the 'principle teachings of the '819 patent' and is with one exception virtually 'a Chinese copy of Figure 13 of the '819 patent,' we think the district court prudently rejected any such theories." *Environmental Instruments, Inc. v. Sutron Corp.*, 877 F.2d 1561, 1564, 11 USPQ2d 1132, 1134 (Fed. Cir. 1989).

"[I]t would appear that the only purpose served by the contour seam in the [accused] Russell foot covers is to avoid being a Chinese copy of the foot covers described in Claims 4 and 5 of the Sarbo Reissue Patent.... [T]he addition of a useless or unimportant item cannot avoid infringement.... [E]very essential element of the foot cover described in the claims of the Reissue Patent is embodied in the Russell products and clearly infringes those claims." *Wayne-Rossard Corp. v. Russell Hosiery Mills, Inc.*, 483 F.2d 770, 772–73, 179 USPQ 193, 195 (4th Cir. 1973).

Copyright Law:

"[The case of *Pellegrini v. Allegrini*, 2 F.2d 610 (E.D. Pa. 1924)] holds, however, that it is not necessary to infringement that the accused work should be a 'Chinese Copy' of the copyrighted work." *Rosenthal v. Stein*, 205 F.2d 633, 636, 98 USPQ 180, 183 (9th Cir. 1953).

Trademark/Trade Dress Law:

"Confusion or invited substitution is indicated by the showing that [defendants] advertising circular ... encloses two samples of heart-shaped tablets which are Chinese copies of [plaintiff's] Dexedrine tablet...." *Ross-Whitney Corp. v. Smith Kline & French Labs.*, 207 F.2d 190, 197, 99 USPQ 1, 6 (9th Cir. 1953).

"Relying on Sears and Compco, defendant herein asserts that 'a defendant may legally copy a plaintiff's article of manufacture and/or wrapper and package, which are not covered by a valid patent or copyright, slavishly down to the minutest detail and to the extent of making a "Chinese copy" thereof.... ' " *Spangler Candy Co. v. Crystal Pure Candy Co.*, 353 F.2d 641, 645, 147 USPQ 434, 437 (7th Cir. 1965).

Chinese wall

[general legal] A method by which a law firm attempts to prevent firm disqualification in a situation where a member of the firm possesses information that may create a conflict of interest. An effective Chinese wall prevents the flow of information from an attorney with knowledge of a former client's confidences and secrets to other attorneys in the law firm. The Chinese wall is an attempt to rebut the presumption of shared confidences: the presumption that every attorney in a law firm shares in every other attorney's knowledge.

- *Example*: If the Alpha & Alpha law firm represents the plaintiff in a patent infringement suit against Zeta Industries Co., and Alpha & Alpha hires as an associate Joan Jones, an in-house counsel for Zeta Industries, then there is an obvious conflict of interest resulting from confidential information Joan Jones may know that bears on the litigation. Confidences and secrets obtained by a single attorney in an adverse representation can disqualify every member of his or her law firm because the law presumes that every attorney in a law firm shares in every other attorney's knowledge.

The creation of a Chinese wall is designed to rebut this presumption and prevent intrafirm communication about a specific matter. The object of the wall is to create an impermeable barrier to exchange of client confidences. The wall is created by procedures such as prohibiting the target attorney from having any connection with the case and banning relevant discussions with, and circulation of relevant documents to, the target attorney.

Whether the wall is sufficient to rebut the presumption of intrafirm sharing of confidences is a factual determination guided by factors such as the degree of sensitivity of the information; the size of the law firm and the number of disqualified target attorneys; how seriously constructed and administered the wall is; and whether the entire law firm was adequately notified of the requirement to screen the target attorney or attorneys.

- *Case References*:

During patent litigation, two attorneys left the plaintiff's law firm and joined the defendant's law firm. The offer of defense counsel three months later to construct a Chinese wall around the two new attorneys was rejected as too late, and the law firm was disqualified from further representation of the defendant. *EZ Painter Corp. v. Padco, Inc.*, 746 F.2d 1459, 223 USPQ 1065 (Fed. Cir. 1984).

"Circuits which allow rebuttal of the presumption [of shared confidences] require evidence of an effective screening of the tainted attorney from the rest of the firm in order for the presumption to be successfully rebutted. This is generally known as the Chinese Wall defense." The evidence in this case was held inadequate to construct a Chinese wall and disqualification was ordered. *Atasi Corp. v. Seagate Technology*, 847 F.2d 826, 831, 6 USPQ2d 1955, 1958 (Fed. Cir. 1988).

Plaintiff in a patent infringement suit moved to disqualify the defendant's law firm because two of the law firm's lawyers had previously worked on plaintiff's legal affairs while they were with other law firms and they obtained confidences substantially related to the subject of the infringement suit. The court denied the motion to disqualify because the defendant's law firm had erected a Chinese wall around the two attorneys. "The day that the Willian firm

was notified of the current action, each attorney that posed a potential conflict was immediately notified that a Chinese wall was being erected around them." *North Am. Philips Corp. v. American Vending Sales Inc.*, 29 USPQ2d 1817, 1822 (N.D. Ill. 1993).

- *Law Review Reference*: Comment, *The Chinese Wall Defense to Law Firm Disqualification*, 128 U. Pa. L. Rev. 677 (1980).

See CONE OF SILENCE.

chip [computer–copyright] A semiconductor chip is a multilayer semiconductor device that performs various electronic functions in a circuit. A chip may contain as many as millions of transistors. A semiconductor chip product is defined in the Semiconductor Chip Protection Act (see SCPA), 17 U.S.C. §901(a)(1), as a product "having two or more layers of metallic, insulating or semiconductor material deposited or otherwise placed on, or etched away or otherwise removed from, a piece of semiconductor material in accordance with a predetermined pattern; and intended to perform electronic circuitry functions."

chip pirate [computer–copyright] One who copies exactly or almost exactly a competitor's semiconductor chip product without permission. While the term is used pejoratively, certain forms of chip copying are not piracy and are permitted under the Semiconductor Chip Protection Act (see SCPA), 17 U.S.C. §906. See R. Stern, *Semiconductor Chip Protection* §5.5 *et seq.* (1986).

See PIRACY.

CIP [patent] A CONTINUATION-IN-PART application.

claim [patent] The part of a patent that defines the technology which is the exclusive property of the patentee for the duration of the patent. A patent claim sets the bounds of the technical area within which the patent owner has the legal right to exclude others from making, using, and selling. Each claim must precisely define the limits of the invention it covers. The claims of a patent are analogous to the metes and bounds of a real estate deed spelling out the exact dimensions of ownership in a piece of property. "It is elementary that the property right bestowed by a patent is measured in the first instance by the claims." *A.B. Dick Co. v. Burroughs Corp.*, 713 F.2d 700, 702, 218 USPQ 965, 967 (Fed. Cir. 1983).

Each Claim Stands on Its Own as a Property Right. For purposes of infringement, each claim of a patent defines a separate invention. *Jones v. Hardy*, 727 F.2d 1524, 1528, 220 USPQ 1021, 1024 (Fed. Cir. 1984). That is, each claim of a patent defines a separate right to exclude. One claim of a patent may be infringed without another being infringed.

Subparts of a Claim Are Not Separate Claims. A claim is an entity that must be considered as a whole. A part of a claim is not "claimed" subject matter. For example, a claim to a process comprising of step A followed by step B followed by step C defines, as a matter of law, only the A-B-C process. No single step is being "claimed." All that is claimed is the process consisting of the combination of all three steps. Such a claim creates no patent right or monopoly in step A. There is no right to prevent others from using step A apart from the combination of steps A-B-C. Step A is not patented. *General Foods Corp. v. Studiengesellschaft Kohle mbH*, 972 F.2d 1272, 1274, 23 USPQ2d 1839, 1840 (Fed. Cir. 1992).

Infringement Is Determined by the Wording of the Claims. It is only the claims that define the exclusive rights of a patent. "The disclosure of a patent is in the public domain save as the claims forbid. The claims alone delimit the right to exclude; only they may be infringed." *Environmental Instruments Inc. v. Sutron Corp.*, 877 F.2d 1561, 1564, 11 USPQ2d 1132, 1134 (Fed. Cir. 1989). It is not proper to attempt to find the GIST or HEART OF THE INVENTION and then compare that to the ACCUSED DEVICE to determine patent INFRINGEMENT. The first step in determining patent infringement is to interpret the claim in question to ascertain its precise scope and meaning before comparing it to the accused device. In the second step, the court determines whether the claims "READ ON" the accused device; that is, are all ELEMENTS of the claim found in the product or process of the

person charged with being an infringer. Patent infringement can be found through LITERAL INFRINGEMENT or infringement by the doctrine of EQUIVALENTS.

Claim Construction Is for the Judge, Not the Jury. In 1995, the Federal Circuit held that construing the meaning of language in a patent claim is solely a question of law to be determined by a judge, not a question of fact for a jury. "[C]ompetitors should be able to rest assured, if infringement litigation occurs, that a judge, trained in the law, will similarly analyze the text of the patent and its associated public record and apply the established rules of construction, and in that way arrive at the true and consistent scope of the patent owner's rights to be given legal effect." *Markman v. Westview Instruments, Inc.*, 52 F.3d 967, 979, 34 USPQ2d 1321, 1329 (Fed. Cir. 1995).

Scope of Claims. Claims are generally written in a series of narrowing scope. An INDEPENDENT CLAIM stands on its own, whereas a DEPENDENT CLAIM adds further limitations to the claim on which it depends. A MULTIPLE DEPENDENT CLAIM depends on more than one prior claim in the alternative.

Interpretation of Claims. The terms of a claim are given their ordinary meaning to one of skill in the art unless it appears from the patent and file history that the terms were used differently by the inventor. *Envirotech v. Al George, Inc.*, 730 F.2d 753, 759, 221 USPQ 473, 477 (Fed. Cir. 1984). In drafting the claims, the inventor may be his own "lexicographer" when there is a need to coin new expressions with which to precisely delineate a new technological development. Where the inventor chooses to be his own lexicographer and to give terms uncommon meanings, he must set out his uncommon definition in some manner within the patent disclosure. The patent specification must support the new definition of terms. The general maxim of claim interpretation is that the claims must be read in the light of the SPECIFICATION.

Claims Distinct From the Specification. A strict reading of Patent Code §112 could lead to the conclusion that the claims of a patent are a part of the specification. ("The specification shall conclude with one or more claims....")

But, in practice, the specification and the claims are always referred to by the courts and practitioners as separate and distinct parts of a patent. E.g., "the claim must be read in light of the specification." See *General Foods Corp. v. Studiengesellschaft Kohle mbH*, 972 F.2d 1272, 1274, 23 USPQ2d 1839, 1840 (Fed. Cir. 1992) (Rich, J.) (Specification is distinct from the claims.).

Elements Within a Claim. Each claim recites a number of limitations or ELEMENTS, which define the technical boundaries of the invention. Under the ALL ELEMENTS RULE, each element of a claim or its equivalent must be found in the accused device to constitute infringement. An element in a claim is a definition of a technological feature that is a discrete limitation on the scope of the claim.

Varieties of Claims. Various terms of art refer to several recognized types of claims. See JEPSON CLAIM, MARKUSH CLAIM, PRODUCT BY PROCESS CLAIM, MEANS PLUS FUNCTION CLAIM, SINGLE MEANS CLAIM. Indefinite claims are invalid (see INDEFINITENESS OF CLAIM), and the doctrine of CLAIM DIFFERENTIATION relates to interpretation of words in a claim.

- *Statutory References*:

35 U.S.C. §112, second paragraph:

"The specification shall conclude with one or more claims particularly pointing out and distinctly claiming the subject matter which the applicant regards as his invention."

35 U.S.C. §282:

"Each claim of a patent (whether in independent, dependent or multiple dependent form) shall be presumed valid independently of the validity of other claims...."

- *Manual Reference*: "The meaning of every term used in any of the claims should be apparent from the descriptive portion of the specification with clear disclosure as to its import.... A term used in the claims may be given a special meaning in the description. No term may be given a meaning repugnant to the usual meaning of the term." *Manual of Patent Examining Procedure* §608.01(o) (1994).

- *Case References*:

"Another way of stating the legal truism [that a part of a claim is not 'claimed' subject matter] is that patent claims, being definitions which must be read *as a whole*, do not 'claim' or cover or protect all that their words may *disclose*. Even though the claim to the A-B-C combination of steps contains a detailed description of step A, that does not give the patentee any patent right in step A and it is legally incorrect to say that step A is 'patented.' " *General Foods Corp. v. Studiengesellschaft Kohle mbH*, 972 F.2d 1272, 1274–75, 23 USPQ2d 1839, 1840 (Fed. Cir. 1992).

"Infringement, literal or by equivalence, is determined by comparing an accused product not with a preferred embodiment described in the specification, or with a commercialized embodiment of the patentee, but with the properly and previously construed claims in suit." *SRI Int'l v. Matsushita Elec. Corp. of Am.*, 775 F.2d 1107, 1121, 227 USPQ 577, 586 (Fed. Cir. 1985).

"The terms of a claim will be given their ordinary meaning unless it appears that the inventor used them differently.... The ordinary meaning of claim language, however, is not dispositive and resort must still be had to the specification and prosecution history to determine if the inventor used the disputed terms differently than their ordinary accustomed meaning.... Patent law allows an inventor to be his own lexicographer. '[T]he specification aids in ascertaining the scope and meaning of the language employed in the claims inasmuch as words must be used in the same way in both the claims and the specification.' " *ZMI Corp. v. Cardiac Resuscitator Corp.*, 844 F.2d 1576, 6 USPQ2d 1557, 1560 (Fed. Cir. 1988).

"All [a patentee] need do is convey his thoughts, in his own language, but somehow make his invention clear and do so in such a way that his counsel cannot give a different meaning to his words, before the Patent Office than he does before the courts. He should not be allowed to stretch his words so that they are inclusive when infringement is being considered and restricted and narrowed when validity is challenged by disclosures of the prior art." *Chicago Steel Foundry Co. v. Burnside Steel*

Foundry Co., 132 F.2d 812, 814–15, 56 USPQ 283, 286 (7th Cir. 1943).

"[A]n inventor is permitted to define the terms of his claims.... Nevertheless, the place to do so is in the specification, of the inventor's application, and the time to do so is prior to that application acquiring its own independent life as a technical disclosure through its issuance as a United States patent. The litigation-induced pronouncements of [the inventor], coming nearly at the end of the term of his patent, have no effect on what the words of that document in fact do convey and have conveyed during its term to the public." *Lear Seigler, Inc. v. Aeroquip Corp.*, 733 F.2d 881, 889, 221 USPQ 1025, 1031 (Fed. Cir. 1984).

"It is entirely proper to use the specification to interpret what the patentee meant by a word or phrase in the claim.... But this is not to be confused with adding an extraneous limitation appearing in the specification, which is improper. By 'extraneous,' we mean a limitation read into a claim from the specification wholly apart from any need to interpret what the patentee meant by particular words or phrases in the claim." *E.I. Du Pont & Co. v. Phillips Petroleum Co.*, 849 F.2d 1430, 1433, 7 USPQ2d 1129, 1131 (Fed. Cir. 1988).

"This does not mean there is never a need for extrinsic evidence in a patent infringement suit. A judge is not usually a person conversant in the particular technical art involved and is not the hypothetical person skilled in the art to whom a patent is addressed. Extrinsic evidence, therefore, may be necessary to inform the court about the language in which the patent is written. But this evidence is not for the purpose of clarifying ambiguity in claim terminology. It is not ambiguity in the document that creates the need for extrinsic evidence but rather the unfamiliarity of the court with the terminology of the art to which the patent is addressed." *Markman v. Westview Instruments, Inc.*, 52 F.3d 967, 986, 34 USPQ2d 1321, 1335 (Fed. Cir. 1995).

• *Treatise References*:

"[C]laims are not technical descriptions of the disclosed inventions but are legal documents like the descriptions of lands by metes and bounds in a deed which define the area conveyed but do not describe the land.... It is the claim, not the specification, that distinguishes what infringes from what does not." R. Harmon, *Patents and the Federal Circuit* §5.4 (3d ed. 1994).

"Unlike many European countries, in the United States, a modern patent claim is characterized by a so-called peripheral definition, i.e., a delineation of the outer limits or boundaries of the invention defined by the claim. This peripheral definition is often analogized to defining real property by a metes and bounds deed." R. Choat, W. Francis, & R. Collins, *Patent Law* 414 (3d ed. 1987).

"Claims in patents are typically drafted in the form of a preamble, transition and one or more elements. Each element constitutes a limitation or narrowing of the scope of the claim." 4 D. Chisum, *Patents* §18.04[4] (1994 rev.).

claim differentiation, doctrine of

[patent] This doctrine creates a presumption: when different words or phrases are used in separate CLAIMS of a patent, the words are presumed to mean significantly different things and the claims are presumed to have a different scope. The limitations in a narrow claim cannot be used to narrow the meaning of a broader claim. However, this doctrine does not allow a claim to be interpreted so as to be broader in scope than what is contained in the claims in view of the specification.

Often, DEPENDENT CLAIMS are written so as to progressively narrow the scope of the independent claim on which they depend. For example, if the independent claim recites as an element a "fastener," and if two dependent claims narrow that to a "nut and bolt" and a "rivet," respectively, then the doctrine of claim differentiation dictates that the term "fastener" in the main claim must be broader in scope than just a "nut and bolt" and a "rivet." Thus, "fastener" could well include "plastic adhesive," "welding," or "removable clamp." "Where some claims are broad and others narrow, the narrow claim limitations cannot be read into the broad whether to avoid invalidity or to escape infringement." *United States v. Telectronics Inc.*, 857 F.2d 778, 783, 8 USPQ2d 1217, 1221 (Fed. Cir. 1988).

See CLAIMS, DEPENDENT CLAIM, ANTLIKE PERSISTENCY.

• *Case Reference*: "There is presumed to be a difference in means and scope when different words or phrases are used in separate claims. To the extent that the absence of such differentiation in meaning and scope would make a claim superfluous, the doctrine of claim differentiation states the presumption that the difference between claims is significant." *Tandon Corp. v. U.S. International Trade Comm'n*, 831 F.2d 1017, 1023, 4 USPQ2d 1283, 1288 (Fed. Cir. 1987).

• *Example*: In a patent covering a drive shaft assembly for a chain link conveyor belt, one element of claim 1 is defined as "a drive shaft with a substantially uniform, non-circular cross section." Claim 3 is limited to a square drive shaft and claim 6 is limited to a regular polygonal drive shaft. In determining infringement of claim 1, it would be improper to interpret the claim so as to limit it to a square or regular polygonal drive shaft. "The doctrine of claim differentiation precludes a reading of those limitations into claim 1 in determining literal infringement." The Court of Appeals for the Federal Circuit held that the district court committed legal error in interpreting claim 1 as though it were limited to a square or other regular polygonal shaft. Thus, it was error to refuse to find that an accused device with a round drive shaft with notches cut for keys was an "equivalent" of the drive shaft of claim 1 and hence an infringement. *Laitram Corp. v. Cambridge Wire Cloth Co.*, 863 F.2d 855, 866, 9 USPQ2d 1289, 1299 (Fed. Cir. 1988).

clean room [computer–copyright] A secure place in which a computer program is written free from access to the SOURCE CODE or OBJECT CODE of a previously copyrighted computer program, which is referred to herein as the "target program." A computer programmer working in a clean room is provided with only the functional specifications of the target program. The computer program produced in the clean room is then compared to the target program and used as the basis for defensive or offensive legal arguments in computer program copyright litigation in the instances listed below.

The term "clean room" is borrowed from its use in high technology to denote a manufacturing or assembly area that is scrupulously kept free from dust and dirt which would interfere with the operation of delicate electronic components or satellites.

Defensive Use to Argue No Access. A computer program is not an infringement of a prior copyrighted program (the "target" program) unless the later program was actually copied. It was not copied, no matter how similar it is, if the author of the later program had no ACCESS to the previously copyrighted target program. In attempting to avoid any charges of copyright infringement, a software developer will have a new computer program written in a clean room in which the program writers are sealed off from any access to all but the functional specifications of the target program. No matter how similar the resulting clean room program is to the target program, there will be no copyright infringement if the clean room was in fact secure.

In practice, a "specifications team" of programmers will analyze the target software, distill the ideas and functions, and prepare a list of engineering specifications. These specifications will be given to a "coding team" of programmers who have no access to the copyrighted expression of the target program. From these specifications the "coding team" will write the "clean room program," which may be immune from a charge of copyright infringement by the owner of copyright in the target program. See Reback & Siegel, *Toward a Comprehensive Test for Software Infringement*, 1 Computer Law., No. 11, pp. 1, 6 (Dec. 1984).

• *Case Reference*: "A 'clean room' is a procedure used in the computer industry in order to prevent direct copying of a competitor's code during the development of a competing product. Programmers in clean rooms are provided only with the functional specifications for the desired program. As Dr. Tredennick explained, the use of a clean room would not have avoided the need for disassembly [of plaintiff's program] because disassembly was necessary in order to discover the functional specifications for a Genesis-compatible game." *Sega Enters. Ltd. v. Accolade*, 977 F.2d 1510, 1526, 24 USPQ2d 1561, 1572 (9th Cir. 1992).

Defensive Use to Provide Evidence That Similarity Is Dictated by Functional Aspects. The defendant in copyright litigation provides an expert witness program writer with the functional specifications of the plaintiff's computer program. The expert witness writes a program in a clean room environment. The clean room program proves to be as similar in expression to the plaintiff's program as is the defendant's accused program. This similarity of the clean room program is evidence that functional engineering constraints and the nature of the idea of the program require the similarity that is found between the plaintiff's program and the accused program. This is evidence supporting the argument that the defendant did not copy or that the defendant only copied functional ideas from the plaintiff or that there is only one way, or a few ways, to express the idea of the plaintiff's program (MERGER of idea and expression) and thus no protection at all or only virtually identical copying will be infringement.

• *Case Reference*: "The Clean Room microcode constitutes compelling evidence that the similarities between the [plaintiff's] microcode and the [defendant's] microcode resulted from constraints.... [T]he shorter, simpler microroutines can be expressed only in a few limited ways.... The Clean Room and [plaintiff's] version are identical, which is evidence of its constrained nature.... [Defendant] properly used the underlying ideas, without virtually identically copying [the plaintiff's program's] limited expression." *NEC Corp. v. Intel Corp.*, 10 USPQ2d 1177, 1188 (N.D. Cal. 1989).

Offensive Use to Provide Evidence That Functional Idea Can Be Expressed in Several Ways. The plaintiff in copyright litigation provides an expert witness program writer with the functional specifications of the plaintiff's computer program. The expert witness writes a program in a clean room environment with no access to the plaintiff's computer program. The clean room program is able to perform the same engineering functions as does the plaintiff's program, but does so by way of a different "expression." The plaintiff relies on this evidence to argue the opposite of the elements mentioned in the second instance discussed above. For example, the clean room program is relied upon to prove that there is no merger of idea and expression.

• *Case Reference*: The clean-room-produced software proved that "alternative system level designs could have been used to avoid this similarity" between the plaintiff and the defendant and that "the idea did not have only one necessary form of expression, but many." *Pearl Sys. Inc. v. Competition Elecs., Inc.*, 8 USPQ2d 1520, 1522 (S.D. Fla. 1988).

Remedial Use to Achieve Compatibility. In resolution of the IBM-Fujitsu dispute, the arbitrators permitted Fujitsu to have access to IBM source code in a clean room in which functional specifications would be developed and given to Fujitsu software developers to write Fujitsu software compatible with IBM, but not a copyright infringement of IBM software. See Parker, *"Secured Facility" Solves Compatibility Conflicts*, Infoworld, p. 41 (Sept. 28, 1987).

clearance   [copyright–entertainment law]
In the distribution of motion pictures for exhibition in theaters, a contract term giving a film exhibitor a degree of exclusivity in the exhibition of a film within a particular market. A clearance prevents a distributor from licensing other theaters, either specifically named or within a named geographic area, to exhibit a movie while it is being exhibited by the theater with the clearance.

As vertical nonprice restraints, clearances are evaluated for possible antitrust law illegality under the RULE OF REASON. Clearances that are unduly extended as to area or duration might be unreasonable restraints of trade under Sherman Act §1. See *Harkins Amusement Enters., Inc. v. General Cinema Corp.*, 850 F.2d 477, 486 (9th Cir. 1988).

clear and convincing [general legal]
A level of proof in between the usual civil law "preponderance of the evidence" standard and the higher criminal law "beyond a reason-

able doubt" standard. While many different word formulations have been used by the courts, the most popular is that "clear and convincing" evidence is evidence that produces in the mind of the judge or jury a firm conviction that the fact has been established.

One important part of intellectual property law where a "clear and convincing" standard of proof is required is in challenging the validity of a patent. A patent is presumed valid and the burden is always on the challenger to prove facts that lead to invalidity by "clear and convincing" evidence.

See PRESUMPTION OF PATENT VALIDITY.

• *Case References*:

The Supreme Court has defined clear and convincing evidence as proofs which "place in the ultimate factfinder an abiding conviction that the truth of [the] factual contentions are 'highly probable.' " *Colorado v. New Mexico*, 467 U.S. 310, 316 (1984). This definition is quoted with approval in *Price v. Symsek*, 988 F.2d 1187, 1191, 26 USPQ2d 1031, 1034 (Fed. Cir. 1993).

"The 'clear and convincing' standard of proof of facts is an intermediate standard which lies somewhere between 'beyond a reasonable doubt' and a 'preponderance of the evidence.' … Although not susceptible to precise definition, 'clear and convincing' evidence has been described as evidence which produces in the mind of the trier of fact 'an abiding conviction that the truth of [the] factual contentions are "highly probable." ' … But even under the 'clear and convincing' standard, proof need not be airtight. 'The law requires persuasion, not perfection.' " *Buildex Inc. v. Kason Indus. Inc.*, 849 F.2d 1461, 1464, 7 USPQ2d 1325, 1327–28 (Fed. Cir. 1988).

"[T]here is a presumption of validity, a presumption not to be overthrown except by clear and cogent evidence.… A patent regularly issued … is presumed to be valid until the presumption has been overcome by convincing evidence of error.… [O]ne otherwise an infringer who assails the validity of a patent fair upon its face bears a heavy burden of persuasion, and fails unless his evidence has more than a dubious preponderance." *Radio Corp. of Am.*

v. Radio Eng'g Labs., 293 U.S. 1, 2, 7–8, 21 USPQ 353, 355–56 (1934).

co-branding [trademark] The use of two or more trademarks on a single product. Where two companies agree to create and market a product with both of their trademarks they are said to have co-branded the product. Co-branding can be accomplished through licensing or via a separate company set up to make and market the new product.

See LICENSE OF TRADEMARK.

Code on Technology Transfer [patent–international] In 1974 the GROUP OF 77 submitted to The United Nations Conference on Trade and Development (UNCTAD) a proposed code of conduct covering international transfers of technology. The proposed code lists 20 license restrictions to be discouraged. Several years of discussion and draft revisions followed. When finally adopted, the code is likely to be in the nature of guidelines, not legally binding rules.

coined mark [trademark]

See FANCIFUL MARK.

collective mark [trademark] A mark used to indicate either that (1) goods or services were made or performed by the members of an organization; or (2) a person or company is a member of a union, association, or any other organization.

1. Collective Trademarks and Service Marks. These are marks used only by members of an organization to identify and distinguish the goods and services as coming from a member of the collective organization. Examples include an agricultural cooperative or sellers of farm produce, a professional medical or legal organization, or an organization like the Professional Golfer Association. While some courts had imported from the law of CERTIFICATION MARKS the "anti-use-by-owner" rule, the 1989 Trademark Law Revision Act expressly changed Lanham Act §4 to make it clear that there is no bar to the collective organization itself selling the same kind of goods and services under the mark as are sold by its individual members under the collective mark.

2. Collective Membership Marks. These are marks used by individuals to indicate that they are members of a union, association, or any other organization. These are the only kind of symbols federally registrable under the Lanham Act that are not necessarily used by a seller of goods or services. Rather, a collective membership type of mark need only be used by an individual to signify membership. This type of use can include use of an organization name or symbol on membership cards, wall plaques, personal rings and jewelry, and wearing apparel. However, use of a term merely to indicate that a person is a recipient of an award, title, or degree from an organization does not suffice to evidence use as a collective membership mark. *In re National Ass'n of Purchasing Mgt.*, 228 USPQ 768 (T.T.A.B. 1986). There is no reason why the name or emblem of an organization cannot, given proper usage and advertising, serve simultaneously as a collective membership mark and as a trademark for merchandise bearing the name or emblem.

• *Treatise Reference*: 2 J.T. McCarthy, *Trademarks and Unfair Competition* §19.34 (3d ed. 1995 rev.).

• *Statutory References*:

Lanham Act §45, 15 U.S.C. §1127. *Collective Mark.*

The term "collective mark" means a trademark or service mark—

(1) used by the members of a cooperative, an association, or other collective group or organization, or

(2) which such cooperative, association, or other collective group or organization has a bona fide intention to use in commerce and applies to register on the principal register established by this Act,

and includes marks indicating membership in a union, an association, or other organization.

Lanham Act §4, 15 U.S.C. §1054: "Subject to the provisions relating to the registration of

trademarks, so far as they are applicable, collective and certification marks, including indications of regional origin, shall be registerable under this Act, in the same manner and with the same effect as are trademarks, by persons, and nations, States, municipalities, and the like, exercising legitimate control over the use of the marks sought to be registered, even though not possessing an industrial or commercial establishment, and when registered they shall be entitled to the protection provided herein in the case of trademarks, except in the case of certification marks when used so as to represent falsely that the owner or a user thereof makes or sells the goods or performs the services on or in connection with which such mark is used...."

collective work [copyright]

See COMPILATION.

colorable imitation [trademark] A spurious mark that so resembles the genuine mark as to be likely to cause confusion.

"Colorable imitation" is a somewhat dated, but still used, synonym for "infringing mark" or "confusingly similar mark." It is sometimes used in legal briefs and judicial opinions as a colorful alternative to repetitive use of "confusingly similar."

"Colorable imitation," although appearing in the introduction to the federal definition of trademark infringement in Lanham Act §32(1), has no independent legal significance.

• *Statutory Reference*:

Lanham Act §45, 15 U.S.C. §1127: *Colorable Imitation.* "The term 'colorable imitation' includes any mark which so resembles a registered mark as to be likely to cause confusion or mistake or to deceive."

Lanham Act §32(1), 15 U.S.C. §1114(1):

Any person who shall, without the consent of the registrant—

(a) use in commerce any reproduction, counterfeit, copy, or colorable imitation of a registered mark in connection with the sale, offering for sale, distribution, or advertising of any goods or services on or in connection with which such use is likely to cause confusion, or to cause mistake, or to deceive; ...

shall be liable in a civil action by the registrant for the remedies hereinafter provided....

• *Case Reference*: "Difficulty frequently arises in determining the question of infringement; but it is clear that exact similarity is not required, as that requirement would always enable the wrong-doer to evade responsibility for his wrongful acts. Colorable imitation, which requires careful inspection to distinguish the spurious trade-mark from the genuine, is sufficient to maintain the issue; but a court of equity will not interfere, when ordinary attention by the purchaser of the article would enable him to at once discriminate the one from the other. Where the similarity is sufficient to convey a false impression to the public mind and is of a character to mislead and deceive the ordinary purchaser in the exercise of ordinary care and caution in such matters, it is sufficient to give the injured party a right to redress." *McLean v. Flemming*, 96 U.S. 245, 255 (1878).

combination [patent] Almost every patentable invention consists of a combination or bringing together of elements or parts that cooperate to produce a new result, structure, or process. At one time, the courts espoused a theory that combination inventions should be scrutinized with great care before a patent was granted or upheld. Today, the theory of a higher patentability hurdle for "combination" inventions has been rejected, the courts recognizing that almost every invention consists of a "combination" of known parts.

The bringing together of parts in such a manner that the parts do not cooperate or interact is called an unpatentable AGGREGATION.

Previous View of "Combination Patents." In a 1950 decision, the U.S. Supreme Court remarked: "In course of time the profession came to employ the term 'combination' to imply ... [the presence of a patentable invention] and the term 'aggregation' to signify its absence.... Courts should scrutinize combination patent claims with a care proportioned to the difficulty and improbability of finding invention in an assembly of old elements." *Great Atl. & Pac. Tea Co. v. Supermarket Equip. Corp.*, 340 U.S. 147, 151–52, 87 USPQ 303, 305 (1950).

Rejection of the Previous View. The statement quoted above that combination patent claims should be given special scrutiny cannot be construed as "a rule of law applicable broadly to patent cases because virtually every claimed invention is a combination of old elements.... There is neither a statutory distinction between 'combination patents' and some other, never defined type of patent, nor a reason to treat the conditions for patentability differently with respect to 'combination patents.' It but obfuscates the law to posit a non-statutory, judge-created classification labeled 'combination patents.' " *Medtronic Inc. v. Cardiac Pacemakers, Inc.*, 721 F.2d 1563, 1566, 220 USPQ 97, 99–100 (Fed. Cir. 1983).

• *Case References*: "The reference to a 'combination patent' is equally without support in the statute.... Virtually *all* patents are 'combination patents.' ... It is difficult to visualize, at least in the mechanical-structural arts, a 'non-combination' invention, i.e., an invention consisting of a *single* element. Such inventions, if they exist, are rare indeed." *Stratoflex, Inc. v. Aeroquip Corp.*, 713 F.2d 1530, 1540, 218 USPQ 871, 880 (Fed. Cir. 1983).

"Virtually all inventions are necessarily combinations of old elements. The notion, therefore, that combination claims can be declared invalid merely upon finding similar elements in separate prior patents would necessarily destroy virtually all patents and cannot be the law under the statute, §103." *Panduit Corp. v. Dennison Mfg. Co.*, 810 F.2d 1561, 1575, 1 USPQ2d 1593, 1603 (Fed. Cir. 1987).

combining prior art [patent] While various references of the PRIOR ART may be combined to argue that the present invention is unpatentable as obvious in view of that prior art, it is not proper to combine references unless there is something in the prior art suggesting the desirability of such a combination.

The "critical enquiry" in combining various prior art references is whether there is something in the prior art as a whole that suggests the desirability, and thus the obviousness, of making the combination of those references. *In re Newell*, 891 F.2d 899, 901, 13 USPQ2d 1248, 1250 (Fed. Cir. 1989). When the party challenging validity relies upon a combination of prior art references to establish invalidity, that party bears the burden of showing some teaching or suggestion in these references which supported their use in combination. *Ashland Oil Inc. v. Delta Resins & Refractories, Inc.*, 776 F.2d 281, 293, 227 USPQ 657, 664 (Fed. Cir. 1985).

See PRIOR ART, OBVIOUSNESS.

• *Case References*:

"Obviousness cannot be established by combining the teachings of the prior art to produce the claimed invention, absent some teaching or suggestion supporting the combination. Under section 103, teachings of references can be combined *only* if there is some suggestion or incentive to do so." *ACS Hosp. Sys. Inc. v. Montefiore Hosp.*, 732 F.2d 1572, 1577, 221 USPQ 929, 933 (Fed. Cir. 1984).

" 'When prior art references require selective combination by the court to render obvious a subsequent invention, there must be some reason for the combination other than the hindsight gleaned from the invention itself.' ... Something in the prior art as a whole must suggest the desirability, and thus the obviousness, of making the combination." *Uniroyal, Inc. v. Rudkin-Wiley Corp.*, 837 F.2d 1044, 1051, 5 USPQ2d 1434, 1438 (Fed. Cir. 1988).

"It is insufficient that the prior art disclosed the components of the patented device, either separately or used in other combinations; there must be some teaching, suggestion, or incentive to make the combination made by the inventor." *Northern Telecom Inc. v. Datapoint Corp.*, 908 F.2d 931, 934, 15 USPQ2d 1321, 1323 (Fed. Cir. 1990).

• *Treatise Reference*: "It is improper to use the inventor's patent as an instruction book on how to reconstruct the prior art.... To properly combine references, there must have been some teaching, suggestion, or inference in the references, or knowledge generally available to one of ordinary skill in the art, that would have led one to combine the relevant teachings." R. Har-

mon, *Patents and the Federal Circuit* §4.7 (3d ed. 1994).

• *Example*: Fine's invention related to a system for detecting and measuring minute quantities of nitrogen compounds as small as one part in one billion. This would have use in detecting drugs and explosives concealed in luggage and closed containers. The Patent and Trademark Office (PTO) rejected Fine's patent application on the ground that it would be "obvious" under §103 to substitute the nitric oxide detector disclosed in the PRIOR ART Warnick patent for the sulphur dioxide detector in the Eads' prior art sulfur detector to arrive at the Fine nitrogen detector invention. The Court of Appeals for the Federal Circuit reversed and ordered the PTO to grant to Fine the contested patent claims. The court held that it was improper to combine the prior art references in this case because there was nothing in the prior art to suggest combining the references in this way. "There is no suggestion in [the prior art] Eads [patent], which focuses on the unique difficulties inherent in the measurement of sulfur, to use that arrangement to detect nitrogen compounds. In fact Eads says that the presence of nitrogen is undesirable.... So instead of suggesting that the system be used to detect nitrogen compounds, Eads deliberately seeks to avoid them; it warns against rather than teaches Fine's invention. See *W.L. Gore & Assoc. v. Garlock, Inc.*, 721 F.2d 1540, 1550, 220 USPQ 303, 311 (Fed. Cir. 1983) (error to find obviousness where references 'diverge from and teach away from the invention at hand.'). In the face of this, one skilled in the art would not be expected to combine a nitrogen-related detector with the Eads system. Accordingly, there is no suggestion to combine [the] Eads and Warnick [prior art references]." *In re Fine*, 837 F.2d 1071, 1074, 5 USPQ2d 1596, 1599 (Fed. Cir. 1988).

commercial success [patent] A showing of the commercial success of a product which is attributable to the excellence of the patented invention that the product embodies is relevant evidence of the NONOBVIOUSNESS of the invention. Commercial success is one of the types of objective evidence of marketplace recognition of the invention, which are known as SECONDARY CONSIDERATIONS.

Evidence of Commercial Success and Its Rebuttal. The burden is on the patentee to prove commercial success and that there is a nexus between that commercial success and the invention claimed in the patent. It is then the challenger's burden to rebut with evidence that the commercial success was due to other factors such as advantages of the product unrelated to the invention, superior marketing practices, superior manufacturing quality, advertising and promotion, and lower prices.

Delay Between Invention and Commercial Success. The mere fact that there was a gap in time between the invention and the commercial success of products using it is not a reason to discount the relevance of commercial success. "Absent some intervening event to which success must be attributed, the delay in achieving the great commercial success of the claimed invention in this case does not detract from the probative value of the evidence of that success." *Windsurfing Int'l Inc. v. AMF, Inc.,* 782 F.2d 995, 1000, 228 USPQ 562, 565 (Fed. Cir. 1986).

• *Case Reference*: "When a patentee asserts that commercial success supports its contention of nonobviousness, there must of course be a sufficient relationship between the commercial success and the patented invention. The term 'nexus' is often used in this context to designate a legally and factually sufficient connection between the proven success and the patented invention, such that the objective evidence should be considered in the determination of nonobviousness. The burden of proof as to this connection or nexus resides with the patentee.... A prima facie case of nexus is generally made out when the patentee shows both that there is commercial success, and that the thing (product or method) that is commercially successful is the invention disclosed and claimed in the patent.... When the patentee has presented a prima facie case of nexus, the burden of coming forward with evidence in rebuttal shifts to the challenger.... It is thus the task of the challenger to adduce evidence to show that the commercial success was due to extraneous factors other than the patented invention, such

as advertising, superior workmanship, etc.... A patentee is not required to prove as part of its prima facie case that the commercial success of the patented invention is *not* due to factors other than the patented invention." *Demaco Corp. v. F. von Langsdorff Licensing Ltd.,* 851 F.2d 1387, 1392–94, 7 USPQ2d 1222, 1226–27 (Fed. Cir. 1988).

• *Treatise Reference*: "There is no doubt that a strong showing of commercial success, attributable to the merits of the claimed invention, is powerful and persuasive evidence of nonobviousness. And there is no doubt that the commercial success of the infringer's product is as relevant as that of the patentee. As the Court [of Appeals for the Federal Circuit] has observed, an attack on commercial success evidence comes with poor grace from an infringer who achieved its own great commercial success and became one of the industry leaders by making and selling its own copy of the patented invention." R. Harmon, *Patents and the Federal Circuit* §4.6(b) (3d ed. 1994).

• *Example 1*: The patent being litigated claimed a huge machine for cutting large pieces of scrap metal into small pieces for recycling. The evidence showed that 30 machines using the claimed invention sold at about $667,000 each. In reversing a finding of invalidity, the Court of Appeals for the Federal Circuit stated: "The commercial success here shown is evidence that the claimed invention was not obvious to those who paid 2/3 of a million dollars for each machine to escape the previously perceived need for pretreatment of massive scrap." *Lindemann Maschinenfabrik GmbH v. American Hoist & Derrick Co.,* 730 F.2d 1452, 1461, 221 USPQ 481, 488 (Fed. Cir. 1984).

• *Example 2*: The patent in issue claimed a method that produced a high-strength synthetic polyamide fiber marketed by patent owner Du Pont under the trademark "Kevlar." "The commercial success of Du Pont's Kevlar patent has been enormous and its range of uses substantial. Du Pont is still developing commercial applications for Kevlar, having spent significant amounts of money in developing both new uses and new markets for the product. Commercial success is, of course, a strong factor favoring non-obviousness...." *Akzo N.V. v. International Trade Comm'n*, 808 F.2d 1471, 1481, 1 USPQ2d 1241, 1246 (Fed. Cir. 1986) (challenge to validity of patent rejected).

common descriptive name [trademark] A
GENERIC NAME. Prior to the 1989 amendments, the Lanham Act used the term "common descriptive name." Several courts, including the U.S. Supreme Court, read "common descriptive name" as meaning a "generic name," distinct from a "descriptive" term. *Park 'N Fly Inc. v. Dollar Park & Fly*, 469 U.S. 189, 194, 224 USPQ 327, 329 (1985). In the 1989 amendments, the archaic and confusing term "common descriptive name" was replaced with the more modern term "generic name," thus codifying the interpretation of the courts.

See GENERIC NAME.

Community Trademark
[international-trademark]

See EUROPEAN COMMUNITY TRADEMARK.

compilation [copyright] A copyrightable
work consisting of an assembly of preexisting material, the assembly resulting from at least some minimal originality and creativity in selecting, organizing, and arranging the preexisting material without making any internal changes in that material.

Compilation Compared to a Derivative Work. A compilation differs from a DERIVATIVE WORK in that in a compilation, preexisting material is brought together without change, while in a derivative work, the preexisting material is changed in some way.

Types of Compilations. In the nomenclature of the Copyright Act, there are two categories of compilations: collective and noncollective works. A COLLECTIVE WORK is a compilation in which copyrightable materials have been gathered together without change, such as an anthology of short stories or a collage of photographs. A noncollective work is one in which noncopyrightable materials have been gathered together without change, such as unprotectible facts in an almanac; unprotectible names, addresses, and phone numbers in a telephone book; or unprotectible stock market prices in a computerized data base.

Compilation Copyright Gives No Exclusive Right to Underlying Materials. The owner of copyright in a compilation acquires no exclusive rights at all in the underlying materials that are brought together. The only protection is against another person arranging the material in the same manner as in the protected compilation. If the same materials are arranged in a substantially different fashion, there is no infringement. If the compilation consists of material in copyright, the copyrights in individual works and in the compilation are separate from and independent of each other. 17 U.S.C. §103(b).

Sweat of the Brow Theory Rejected. Under the "sweat of the brow" theory, the hard work and "industrious collection" of public domain facts and data is rewarded with a copyright on the facts and data themselves. The Supreme Court in 1991 rejected this theory, saying that it "flouted basic copyright principles" because it created exclusive rights in information that the "author" did not create, but only collected. *Feist Publications v. Rural Tel. Serv.*, 499 U.S. 340, 18 USPQ2d 1275 (1991).

Selection and Arrangement of Data. The required ORIGINALITY and CREATIVITY in a compilation consists in the selection or arrangement of the preexisting material. Originality in *selection* may exist in works in which the compiler has spent effort in selecting which data to include in its list or collection, e.g., a social register, a list of reasonably priced motels, a directory of intellectual property attorneys. Typical and common selection does not rise to the level of creativity required. For example, the act of taking data provided by telephone service subscribers, such as name, town, and telephone number, to list in a white-pages directory lacks the requisite selection, originality, and creativity to transform it into copyrightable expression. *Feist Publications v. Rural Tel. Serv.*, 499 U.S. 340, 363, 18 USPQ2d 1275, 1284 (1991) (Such a selection "lacks the modicum of creativity necessary to transform mere selection into copyrightable expression.").

Originality in *arrangement* may exist in works in which the compiler has spent effort in the particular arrangement of data in its collection, e.g., collecting data in chronological order in an almanac, arranging historical dates and events in a study guide for history students, collecting and arranging corporate data in an industrial directory. Commonplace or inevitable arrangement, such as listing names alphabetically in a white-pages telephone directory, does not meet the minimal creativity required for copyrightability. *Feist Publications v. Rural Tel. Serv.,* 499 U.S. 340, 363, 18 USPQ2d 1275, 1285 (1991) ("[T]here is nothing remotely creative about arranging names alphabetically in a white pages directory. It is an age-old practice, firmly rooted in tradition and so commonplace that it has come to be expected as a matter of course.").

In most cases, compilations involve elements of both selection and arrangement originality. See, e.g., *Eckes v. Card Prices Update,* 736 F.2d 859, 863, 222 USPQ 762, 765 (2d Cir. 1984) (sufficient selection and arrangement originality existed in collectors' guide listing 18,000 baseball cards and their market prices, together with a list of the 5,000 most valuable cards); *West Publishing Co. v. Mead Data Central Inc.,* 799 F.2d 1219, 1226, 230 USPQ 801, 805 (8th Cir. 1986) (West "used sufficient talent and industry in compiling and arranging cases to entitle it to copyright protection" in West case reporters); *Bellsouth Advertising & Publishing Corp. v. Donnelley Information Publishing Inc.,* 999 F.2d 1436, 28 USPQ2d 1001 (11th Cir. 1993) (court en banc found insufficient originality and creativity and denied compilation copyright protection for a yellow-pages classified business directory which used an alphabetized list of business types and used standard divisions such as arranging churches by denomination or attorneys by area of specialty).

Making a Compilation of Works Without a License. A compilation that is a collective work and brings together preexisting works which are individually protected by copyright would be a copyright infringement in the absence of a license. Thus, one who wishes to exploit that type of compilation needs a copyright license from the owner of copyright in the underlying work or works. If there is no such license, then the use of the underlying work in the compilation is illegal under copyright law. The Copyright Act states that copyright does not extend to any part of the compilation work in which such preexisting material is unlawfully used. 17 U.S.C. §103(a). However, because the compiler's copyrighted work is only the particular selection and arrangement of material, there is no "part of the work" in which the preexisting copyrighted material is unlawfully used and enforcement of the compilation copyright should not be precluded. See 1 P. Goldstein, *Copyright* §2.16 (1989).

Selection and Arrangement Applied to Audiovisual Works. Audiovisual works, such as video games and computer USER INTERFACES, are analogous to factual compilations in that both involve a choice and ordering of elements that, in themselves, may not qualify for copyright protection. The "author's" selection and arrangement of those elements may yield a work that is sufficiently original and creative to be protected by copyright law. For example, the D.C. Circuit held that while the individual graphic elements of each screen display of Atari's BREAKOUT video game were not copyrightable, the selection and arrangement of elements were original and creative, not conventional, obvious, or inevitable. *Atari Games Corp. v. Oman,* 979 F.2d 242, 246–47, 24 USPQ2d 1933, 1937–38 (D.C. Cir. 1992).

See DERIVATIVE WORK, DATA BASE.

- *Treatise References*: 1 *Nimmer on Copyright* §3.02 (1994 rev.); 1 P. Goldstein, *Copyright* §2.16.1 (1989); 1 N. Boorstyn, *Copyright* §2.16 (2d ed. 1994); M. Leaffer, *Understanding Copyright* §2.11 (1989); W. Patry, *Copyright Law and Practice* 189 (1994).

- *Statutory References*:

17 U.S.C. §101: "A 'compilation' is a work formed by the collection and assembling of preexisting materials or of data that are selected, coordinated, or arranged in such a way that the resulting work as a whole constitutes an original work of authorship. The term 'compilation' includes collective works."

17 U.S.C. §101: "A 'collective work' is a work, such as a periodical issue, anthology, or encyclopedia, in which a number of contribu-

tions, constituting separate and independent works in themselves, are assembled into a collective whole."

17 U.S.C. §103: "(a) The subject matter of copyright as specified by section 102 includes compilations and derivative works, but protection for a work employing preexisting material in which copyright subsists does not extend to any part of the work in which such material has been used unlawfully. (b) The copyright in a compilation or derivative work extends only to the material contributed by the author of such work, and does not imply any exclusive right in the preexisting material. The copyright in such work is independent of, and does not affect or enlarge the scope, duration, ownership, or subsistence of, any copyright protection in the preexisting material."

• *Legislative History*: "Between them the terms 'compilations' and 'derivative works' … comprehend every copyrightable work that employs preexisting material or data of any kind.… A 'compilation' results from a process of selecting, bringing together, organizing, and arranging previously existing material of all kinds, regardless of whether the individual items in the material have been or ever could have been subject to copyright.… [Section 103(a)] prevents an infringer from benefiting, through copyright protection, from committing an unlawful act, but preserves copyright protection for those parts of the work that do not employ the preexisting work. Thus, an unauthorized translation of a novel could not be copyrighted at all, but the owner of copyright in an unauthorized anthology of poetry could sue someone who infringed the whole anthology, even though the infringer proves that publication of one of the poems was unauthorized." H. Rep. No. 94-1476, 94th Cong., 2d Sess. 57–58 (1976).

• *Case Reference*: "[C]hoices as to selection and arrangement, so long as they are made independently by the compiler and entail a minimal degree of creativity, are sufficiently original that Congress may protect such compilations through the copyright laws. … Thus, even a directory that contains absolutely no protectible written expression, only facts, meets the constitutional minimum for copyright protection if it features an original selection or arrangement … [T]he copyright in a factual compilation is thin. Notwithstanding a valid copyright, a subsequent compiler remains free to use the facts contained in another's publication to aid in preparing a competing work, so long as the competing work does not feature the same selection and arrangement." *Feist Publications v. Rural Tel. Serv.*, 499 U.S. 340, 348, 18 USPQ2d 1275, 1279 (1991).

• *International Reference*: GATT Agreement, Article 10(2). "Compilations of data or other material, whether in machine readable or other form, which by reason of the selection or arrangement of their contents constitute intellectual creations shall be protected as such. Such protection, which shall not extend to the data or material itself, shall be without prejudice to any copyright subsisting in the data or material itself."

composite mark [trademark] A mark composed of more than one distinct element, such as two words, words and a design, letters and a picture, or a design formed of several distinct elements.

The "Antidissection" Rule. A composite mark is tested for validity, distinctiveness, and infringement by looking at it as a whole, rather than breaking it up into its component parts. This is known as the "antidissection rule." "The commercial impression of a trademark is derived from it as a whole, not from its elements separated and considered in detail. For this reason it should be considered in its entirety.…" *Estate of P.D. Beckwith, Inc. v. Commissioner of Patents*, 252 U.S. 538, 545–46 (1920). However, it is not a violation of the antidissection rule to separately view the component parts of a composite as a preliminary step on the way to an ultimate determination of probable customer reaction to the composite as a whole.

Judging the Validity of Composite Marks. Composite terms with a generic component can be either strong trademarks (e.g., COCA-COLA) or merely a generic composite of generic parts (e.g., turbodiesel). It is possible to combine two or more admittedly descriptive elements into a composite mark that is not a descriptive mark as a whole. For example, the composite MOUSE SEED for a rodent exterminator was held to be nondescriptive, as was ROACH MOTEL for an insect trap, the court noting that "its very incongruity is what catches one's attention." *American Home Prods. Corp. v. Johnson Chem. Co.*, 589 F.2d 103, 106, 200 USPQ 417, 420 (2d Cir. 1978). A composite mark that contains a surname, when considered in its entirety, may be classified for registration purposes as primarily not being merely a surname. *In re Hutchinson Technology, Inc.*, 852 F.2d 552, 7 USPQ2d 1490 (Fed. Cir. 1988) (HUTCHINSON TECHNOLOGY held to be a composite that is not primarily merely a surname).

Judging the Infringement of Composite Marks. The antidissection rule dictates that a composite mark should not be split up into its components, each of which is compared with components of the accused mark to determine the issue of likelihood of confusion. It is the impression the mark creates as a whole on the ordinary purchaser in the marketplace that will or will not be likely to create confusion, not the impression gleaned from a painstaking comparison of each separate element of the composite as expressed in carefully weighed words in legal briefs. The rationale of the antidissection rule is based upon a commonsense observation of customer behavior: the average buyer does not retain all the individual details of a composite mark, but rather retains only the overall, general impression created by the composite. It is, however, appropriate in determining the confusion issue to give greater weight to the "dominant" part of a composite mark, for it is that which may make the greatest impression on the ordinary customer. Similarly, it is appropriate to downplay the similarity of generic or highly descriptive portions of conflicting marks.

Presumption of Validity. The statutory presumptions of validity extend only to a registered composite mark as a whole, not to any one component part of the composite. *In re National Data Corp.*, 753 F.2d 1056, 224 USPQ 749 (Fed. Cir. 1985).

See PRESUMPTION OF TRADEMARK VALIDITY.

Disclaimer of Unregistrable Parts of a Composite Mark. The Patent and Trademark Office (PTO) will sometimes require that an applicant disclaim unregistrable matter that forms part of a registrable composite mark. A disclaimer makes it clear on the public record that the registration is presumptive evidence of the validity only of the composite mark as a whole, not of any individual unregistrable element of the composite.

See DISCLAIMER.

• *Treatise Reference*: J.T. McCarthy, *Trademarks and Unfair Competition* §§11.10 (descriptive composites), 12.12[3] (generic composites), 13.11[4] (composite surname marks), 14.06 (composite geographic marks), 23.15 (comparing conflicting marks to determine the likelihood of confusion) (3d ed. 1995 rev.).

• *Case References*:

"Plaintiff's second argument, that a composite trademark should not be broken into its component parts in determining whether it is generic, is also disposed of easily. This circuit has noted: 'Dissecting marks often leads to error. Words which could not individually become a trademark may become one when taken together.' … Certain terms may connote more than the sum of their parts and we must take care to decide the genericness of these terms by looking to the whole…. Other composite terms are nothing more than the sum of their parts, such as 'multistate bar examination' and 'light beer.' 'Liquid controls' falls in the latter category. In any case, we do not believe that the principle that the validity of a mark is to be determined by looking at the mark as a whole precludes a court from examining the meanings of the component words in determining the meaning of the mark as a whole." *Liquid Controls Corp. v. Liquid Control Corp.*, 802 F.2d 934, 938, 231 USPQ 579, 582–83 (7th Cir. 1986) ("liquid controls" held to be a generic composite term).

"The basic principle in determining confusion between marks is that marks must be compared in their entireties…. It follows from that principle that likelihood of confusion cannot be predicated on dissection of a mark, that is, on only part of a mark. On the other hand, in articulating reasons for reaching a conclusion on the issue of confusion, there is nothing improper in stating that, for rational reasons, more or less weight has been given to a particular feature of a mark, provided the ultimate conclusion rests on consideration of the marks in their entireties. Indeed, this type of analysis appears to be unavoidable." *In re National Data Corp.*, 753 F.2d 1056, 224 USPQ 749, 750–51 (Fed. Cir. 1985).

comprehensive nonliteral similarity
[copyright] See SUBSTANTIAL SIMILARITY.

comprising
[patent] An open-ended term used in patent claims that commonly follows the claim PREAMBLE and introduces the ELEMENTS making up the claim.

An Open Introductory Term. The open-ended connotation of "comprises" in patent law has long been recognized. It has become a term of art. "Comprising" is a synonym for "including" or "containing." Thus, the presence in the ACCUSED DEVICE of additional elements not found in the patent claim does not avoid LITERAL INFRINGEMENT of the claim. The mere addition of components, parts, or process steps to an infringing product or process does not avoid infringement. "The presence of additional elements is irrelevant if all the claimed elements are present in the accused structure." *Mannesmann Demag Corp. v. Engineered Metal Prods. Co.*, 793 F.2d 1279, 1282, 230 USPQ 45, 47 (Fed. Cir. 1986) (claim elements introduced by term "characterized by"). Thus, if the invention is claimed in the patent as "comprising" elements A + B + C, the claim is infringed by a device having elements A + B + C + X.

"Comprising" Compared to "Consisting." "Consisting of" is a closed introductory term, while "comprising" has the opposite significance of an open introductory term. A "consisting of" claim is narrower and is infringed only if the accused device has all of, but no more than, the elements recited in the patent claim.

See CONSISTING OF, CONSISTING ESSENTIALLY OF.

• *Treatise Reference*: 2 D. Chisum, *Patents* §8.06[1][b] (1994 rev.).

• *Case References*:
"The [claim] is a comprising-type [claim], which, by definition, does not exclude the presence of other steps, elements or materials." *Reese v. Hurst*, 661 F.2d 1222, 1229, 211 USPQ 936, 943 (C.C.P.A. 1981).

"The transitional phrase, which joins the preamble of a claim with the body of a claim, is a term of art and as such affects the legal scope of a claim.... [A] transitional term such as 'comprising' or, as in the present case 'which comprises,' does not exclude additional unrecited elements, or steps (in the case of a method claim)...." *Moleculon Research Corp. v. CBS, Inc.*, 793 F.2d 1261, 1271, 229 USPQ 805, 812 (Fed. Cir. 1986).

compulsory licensing
[patent–trademark–copyright] A permission to use intellectual property, compelled by the government in order to accomplish some political or social objective. Compulsory licensing forces an intellectual property owner to allow others to use that property at a fee set by the government. The owner is not allowed to refuse to license or to negotiate voluntary license fees in a free market, but is compelled to license at a rate thought to be "reasonable" by the government.

1. Compulsory Licensing of a Patent. Government-mandated licensing is required in only rare instances in the United States. The use of compulsory licensing as a remedy for some types of antitrust violations is the most well-known instance. In infringement cases, the refusal of a court to enjoin a proven patent infringer because of some other social or economic policy amounts to ad hoc compulsory licensing. Such instances are very rare.

Foreign Compulsory Licensing. In some foreign nations, a compulsory license is available from the owner of a dominant patent to the owner of a dependent, improvement patent that cannot be practiced without permission from the owner of the dominant patent. 1 S. Ladas, *Patents, Trademarks and Related Rights: National and International Protection* §246 (1975). See DOMINATION. The 1995 GATT TRIPS agreement in Article 31(l) places three conditions on compulsory licensing in such cases of domination.

Working a Patent. Many nations require a compulsory license in the event the patentee does not use the patented technology domestically. Article 31 of the 1995 GATT TRIPS agreement places certain conditions on a nation's ability to order compulsory licensing for failure to work. Unlike most nations, the United States does not have a patent working requirement and hence no statutory compulsory licensing enforcement system. The failure to use a patented invention has been held not to be "inequitable" conduct sufficient to be a bar to obtaining an injunction against an infringer. *Continental Paper Bag Co. v. Eastern Paper Bag Co.*, 210 U.S. 405, 429 (1908). In 1988, 35 U.S.C. §271(d)(4) was added to provide that it is not a MISUSE of patent sufficient to deny relief against infringement if the patent owner has "refused to license or use any rights to the patent." Thus, the statute prohibits using nonuse or a failure to work as a ground of defense in any patent infringement case.

Limited Compulsory Licensing in the United States. Congress has required patent owners to license their patent rights in only rare instances. Examples include certain patents relating to nuclear energy and air pollution control devices. The United States provides for compulsory licenses only under three statutes: the Atomic Energy Act, the Clean Air Act, and the Energy Policy Act. As a result of the 1995 GATT TRIPS agreement, regulations under those acts were amended to comply with the conditions specified in Article 31 of the GATT TRIPS agreement. Various other nations provide for the grant of a compulsory license in cases of national defense, the needs of the national economy, or public health. Compulsory licensing has been ordered by a court in the United States for public health reasons in only a few extraordinary cases. For example, one court found infringement and awarded damages but refused to enjoin an infringing sewage treatment plant when such an injunction would result in dumping raw sewage into Lake Michigan near the city of Milwaukee. *City of Milwaukee v. Activated Sludge Inc.*, 69 F.2d 577 (7th Cir. 1934).

Antitrust Remedy. The most common instance of government-mandated patent licensing is as a remedy for certain types of antitrust violations. Where patents have been used in violation of the antitrust laws, they may, like any other form of property, be subject to provisions of an antitrust decree designed to cure the effects of the unlawful conduct and to restore effective competition in the particular industry. These provisions may take the form of compulsory licensing on a reasonable-royalty basis, compulsory licensing on a royalty-free basis, an injunction against enforcement of patent rights, or dedication of the patents to the public. Compulsory licensing can be viewed as a form of partial divestiture of assets: "[C]ompulsory licensing, on a reasonable royalty basis, is in effect a partial dissolution on a nonconfiscatory basis." *United States v. United Shoe Mach. Corp.*, 110 F. Supp. 295, 351 (D. Mass. 1953), *aff'd per curiam*, 347 U.S. 521 (1954). In 1972 the Supreme Court concluded that compulsory patent licensing at court-set rates is a "recognized" antitrust remedy which is appropriate to "pry open to competition" the market that has been closed by the defendant's illegal actions. *United States v. Glaxo Group Ltd.*, 410 U.S. 52, 64 (1972).

See WORKING.

- *Treatise References*: ABA, *Antitrust Law Developments* 521 (2d ed. 1984); C. Hills, *Antitrust Advisor* §6.56 (3d ed. 1985); 1 S. Ladas, *Patents, Trademarks and Related Rights: National and International Protection* §245 *et seq.* (1975).

- *Case Reference*: "A patent owner is not in the position of a quasi-trustee for the public or under any obligation to see that the public acquires the free right to use the invention. He has no obligation either to use it or to grant its use to others. If he discloses the invention in his application so that it will come into the public domain at the end of the 17-year period of exclusive right he has fulfilled the only obligation imposed by the statute. 35 U.S.C. §33. This has been settled doctrine since at least 1896. Congress has repeatedly been asked, and has refused, to change the statutory policy by imposing a forfeiture or by a provision for compulsory licensing if the patent is not used within a specified time." *Hartford-Empire Co. v. United States*, 323 U.S. 386, 432 (1945).

2. Compulsory Licensing of a Trademark. There is no general statutory or case law rule permitting the compulsory licensing of trademarks in the United States.

Antitrust Remedy. In antitrust cases, the remedy of compulsory licensing of a trademark has been proposed. While in no reported private antitrust litigation has a plaintiff received the sanction of compulsory trademark licensing, the remedy of forfeiture of a trademark as an antitrust remedy has been requested and rejected. See 3 J.T. McCarthy, *Trademarks and Unfair Competition* §31.26[6] (3d ed. 1995 rev.). In government antitrust suits, the remedy of an injunction against the use of a trademark has been utilized in only rare instances. *Ford Motor Co. v. United States*, 405 U.S. 562 (1972) (Ford ordered to refrain from use of FORD trademark on spark plugs for five years). In the controversial 1978 "ReaLemon" case, the Federal Trade Commission's compulsory licensing remedy was reversed by the full FTC. *In re Borden Inc.*, 92 FTC 669, Trade Reg. Rep. 21490 (1978), *aff'd sub nom. Borden Inc. v. Federal Trade Comm'n*, 674 F.2d 498 (6th Cir. 1982), *vacated*, 461 U.S. 940 (1983), *on remand*, 711 F.2d 758 (6th Cir. 1984).

Certification Mark. The statutory provisions for a CERTIFICATION MARK embody what might be referred to as a very limited form of compulsory licensing. One who has registered a term as a certification mark must license or permit use of the mark by anyone who maintains the standards or conditions the mark certifies. Lanham Act §14(5)(D), 15 U.S.C. §1064(5)(D). See 2 J.T. McCarthy, *Trademarks and Unfair Competition* §19.32 (3d ed. 1995 rev.).

3. Compulsory Licensing of a Copyright. As a result of the many years of protracted hearings and revised bills preceding enactment of the copyright revision act effective in 1978, Congress compromised on several points between advocates of full copyright protection and advocates of free use. Originally, a new agency, called the Copyright Royalty Tribunal, was set up to set and process royalty rates for compul-

sory licenses. In December 1993, the Copyright Royalty Tribunal was abolished and replaced by a series of ad hoc COPYRIGHT ARBITRATION ROYALTY TRIBUNALS appointed by the Librarian of Congress.

As modified in recent years, this compromise takes the form of a compulsory license for five types of uses of copyrighted works: (1) cable television; (2) the use of musical works on jukeboxes if voluntary licenses cannot be achieved; (3) use of musical works on jukeboxes (now repealed); (4) the use of certain works on public broadcasting; and (5) the use of copyrighted works in satellite retransmissions to the public for private viewing.

(1) *Cable Television.* Congress adopted a compromise between copyright owners and cable operators under which cable operators need not obtain consent from or negotiate fees with copyright owners, but copyright owners must receive government-set royalties from the cable operators for certain retransmissions of their copyrighted works on cable television. Copyright Act §111(c) creates a compulsory licensing system for cable operators who retransmit broadcast signals. The cable operator cannot change the content of the transmission: if it does, it is acting outside of the compulsory license. Royalty fees are set by and paid to the Copyright Office for distribution to the appropriate copyright owners. Royalty distributions have led to challenges in the courts, which have generally upheld distribution decisions. See 1 N. Boorstyn, *Copyright* §§6.30–.33 (2d ed. 1994); M. Leaffer, *Understanding Copyright* §8.19[D] (1989); 2 *Nimmer on Copyright* §8.18[E] (1994 rev.); 2 P. Goldstein, *Copyright* §5.8.2.2 (1989).

(2) *Making Phonorecords of Musical Works.* In Copyright Act §115, Congress continued a compulsory license system (MECHANICAL LICENSE) established in 1909 for the making of PHONORECORDS that record nondramatic musical works. The term "phonorecord" includes vinyl discs, tapes, compact discs, or any other object in which sound is recorded. It does not include the soundtrack of a motion picture, video tape, or video disc. The first recording of a song is the subject of a voluntary license and free market bargaining between copyright

owner and record company. But under Copyright Act §115, the distribution to the public of that first recording triggers a compulsory license to all others to also record that song. To obtain the compulsory license, a subsequent recording company must follow the statutory reporting procedures and pay the government-set royalty fee to the copyright owner. Prior to 1994, the Copyright Royalty Tribunal set the royalty, which as of 1994 was 6.6 cents per work or 1.25 cents per minute of playing time, whichever is more. To obtain the compulsory license, the recorder must assemble musicians and/or vocalists to perform anew and cannot merely electronically reproduce the original recording unless it has an express license to do so. In practice, record companies usually do not directly utilize the statutory scheme, but rather obtain licenses through an agent such as the HARRY FOX AGENCY, which represents most of the owners of musical works. See 2 P. Goldstein, *Copyright* §5.2.1.1 (1989); 1 N. Boorstyn, *Copyright* §6.10 (2d ed. 1994).

(3) *Use of Musical Works on Jukeboxes.* Copyright Act §116, as originally enacted, created a compulsory license for the use of musical works played on jukeboxes, i.e., coin-operated phonorecord players. Royalties were set by and paid to the COPYRIGHT ROYALTY TRIBUNAL for distribution. The 1988 Berne Revision amendments replaced this with a voluntarily negotiated system of licenses. The Copyright Royalty Tribunal Reform Act of 1993 changed the system again, eliminating the compulsory license, authorizing the parties to negotiate terms and rates of royalties, and ending oversight by the COPYRIGHT ROYALTY TRIBUNAL. Only if a negotiated license cannot be achieved would it be necessary for a copyright royalty arbitration panel to establish a royalty rate. See 2 P. Goldstein, *Copyright* §5.8.4 (1994 Supp.); 1 N. Boorstyn, *Copyright* §6.37 (2d ed. 1994); W. Patry, *Copyright Law and Practice* 977–87 (1994).

(4) *Use of Works on Public Broadcasting Stations.* Copyright Act §118 created a compulsory licensing system for the broadcast of nondramatic musical works and pictorial works on public noncommercial broadcasting stations. In the absence of voluntary licenses between public broadcasting representatives and copyright owners, the Copyright Office sets royalties, which are to be paid directly to copyright owners.

(5) *Satellite Retransmission.* Those who rent satellite facilities for the retransmission of broadcasting containing copyrighted material are engaging in a "performance" of the material for which a license is needed. Because satellite carriers do not qualify for the cable system compulsory license, Congress created in §119 of the Copyright Act, effective in 1989, a special compulsory license for certain satellite retransmissions for private home viewing of broadcasts of copyrighted material. A satellite carrier must pay to the Copyright Office a statutory royalty per subscriber. The Copyright Office then distributes the proceeds to copyright owners. The satellite compulsory licensing system had a sunset provision of December 31, 1994, which was extended by Congress to December 31, 1999, in the Satellite Home Viewer Act of 1994, which also made substantive changes in the statutory scheme (Pub. L. No. 103-369). See 1 N. Boorstyn, *Copyright* §6.36 (2d ed. 1994); M. Leaffer, *Understanding Copyright* §8.20 (1989); 2 P. Goldstein, *Copyright* §5.8.3 (1989); W. Patry, *Copyright Law and Practice* 989 (1994).

computer program [computer–copyright–patent–trade secret] Computer program was defined in a 1980 amendment to the Copyright Act, 17 U.S.C. §101, as "a set of statements or instructions to be used directly or indirectly in a computer to bring about a certain result." This definition was enacted by Congress to implement a recommendation of CONTU.

See CONTU.

1. Copyright on Computer Programs. Copyright protection is available for the "expression," but not the "idea," of a computer program. The CLEAN ROOM technique is sometimes used to prove one side or the other of disputes as to the idea and expression of programs. Copyright protects both applications programs and OPERATING SYSTEM PROGRAMS in both OBJECT CODE and SOURCE CODE versions, whether stored in a disk or in a ROM, or loaded into RAM.

See ROM, RAM.

Scope of Protection. There is controversy as to the extent to which copyright protection extends beyond the literal listings of a program to the overall STRUCTURE, SEQUENCE, AND ORGANIZATION of the program. There is even more controversy as to whether copyright protects the LOOK AND FEEL of a computer program. See Samuelson, Davis, Kapor & Reichman, *A Manifesto Concerning the Legal Protection of Computer Programs*, 94 Colum. L. Rev. 2308 (1994).

International Protection. Adopted in 1991, the European Union Software Directive requires member nations to treat computer programs as literary works within the meaning of the Berne Convention. A 1993 European Union Directive provided that computer programs are to be protected for the new term granted literary works: life of the author plus 70 years. The NAFTA and GATT agreements required protection of computer programs as "literary works" under the Berne Convention. See W. Patry, *Copyright Law and Practice* 233 (1994); 42 BNA PTCJ 93, 109 (May 23, 1991).

- *Case References:*

"[A] computer program, whether in object code or source code, is a 'literary work' and is protected from unauthorized copying, whether from its object or source code version." *Apple Computer, Inc. v. Franklin Computer Corp.,* 714 F.2d 1240, 1249, 219 USPQ 113, 121 (3d Cir. 1983).

"A computer program is made up of several different components, including the source and object code, the structure, sequence and/or organization of the program, the user interface, and the function, or purpose of the program.... Whether the nonliteral components of a [computer] program, including the structure, sequence and organization and user interface, are protected depends on whether, on the particular facts of each case, the component in question qualifies as an expression of an idea or an idea itself." *Johnson Controls Inc. v. Phoenix Control Sys. Inc.,* 886 F.2d 1173, 1175, 12 USPQ2d 1566, 1568 (9th Cir. 1989).

"[W]e think that district courts would be well-advised to undertake a three-step procedure.... In ascertaining a substantial similarity under this approach, a court would first break down the allegedly infringed [computer] program into its constituent structural parts. Then, by examining each of these parts for such things as incorporated ideas, expression that is necessarily incidental to those ideas, and elements that are taken from the public domain, a court would then be able to sift out all non-protectable material. Left with a kernel, or possible kernels, of creative expression after following this process of elimination, the court's last step would be to compare this material with the structure of an allegedly infringing program. The result of this comparison will determine whether the protectable elements of the programs at issue are substantially similar so as to warrant a finding of infringement." *Computer Assocs. Int'l Inc. v. Altai Inc.,* 982 F.2d 693, 706, 23 USPQ2d 1241, 1252–53 (2d Cir. 1992).

- *Treatise References:* 3 *Nimmer on Copyright* §13.03[A][1][d] (1994 rev.); 2 P. Goldstein, *Copyright* §8.5.1.2 (1989); 1 N. Boorstyn, *Copyright* §11.06 (2d ed. 1994); W. Patry, *Copyright Law and Practice* 213 (1994).

See IDEA-EXPRESSION DICHOTOMY; CLEAN ROOM; LOOK AND FEEL; OBJECT CODE; OPERATING SYSTEM PROGRAM; SOURCE CODE; STRUCTURE, SEQUENCE, AND ORGANIZATION.

2. Patent on Computer Programs. Patent protection is available for a process that uses a computer program to carry it out. Patent protection is not available for an ALGORITHM or mathematical formula used to define the steps in a computer program.

Freeman-Walter-Abele Test. A test sometimes used to determine whether claims to a computer program are directed at statutory subject matter under Patent Code §101 is called the "Freeman-Walter-Abele" test, named after three CCPA cases that created the test. The test proceeds in two steps: First, it is determined whether a mathematical algorithm is recited directly or indirectly in the claim. If so, the second step is to determine whether the claimed invention as a whole is no more than the algorithm itself, in which case it is not in a patentable category. That is, the second step determines whether the claim is directed to a mathematical algorithm that is not applied to or limited by physical elements or process steps. If the claim comes within this definition, then the claim does not define patentable subject matter under Patent Code §101.

• *Case References*:

"[A]n algorithm, or mathematical formula, is like a law of nature, which cannot be the subject of a patent.... [A patent] claim drawn to subject matter otherwise statutory does not become nonstatutory simply because it uses a mathematical formula, computer program or digital computer.... [W]hen a claim containing a mathematical formula implements or applies that formula in a structure or process which, considered as a whole, is performing a function which the patent laws were designed to protect (e.g., transforming or reducing an article to a different state or thing), then the claim satisfies the requirements of [Patent Code] §101." *Diamond v. Diehr*, 450 U.S. 175, 186–92, 209 USPQ 1, 8–10 (1981).

The Court of Appeals for the Federal Circuit held that a claim to a computer-implemented voice-recognition apparatus is in a patentable category even if it recites a mathematical algorithm, so long as it defines apparatus. "[E]very step-by-step process, be it electronic or chemical or mechanical, involves an algorithm in the broad sense of the term.... This is why the proscription against patenting has been limited to *mathematical* algorithms and abstract *mathematical* formulae which, like the laws of nature, are not patentable subject matter.... The fact that the apparatus operates according to an algorithm does not make it nonstatutory." *In re Iwahashi*, 888 F.2d 1370, 1374–75, 12 USPQ2d 1908, 1911 (Fed. Cir. 1989).

"[The inventor] admits that claim 15 would read on a general purpose computer programmed to carry out the claimed invention, but argues that this alone does not justify holding claim 15 unpatentable as directed to nonstatutory subject matter. We agree. We have held that such programming creates a new machine, because a general purpose computer in effect becomes a special purpose computer once it is programmed to perform particular functions pursuant to instructions from program software.... Under the Board's reasoning, a programmed general purpose computer could never be viewed as patentable subject matter under §101. This reasoning is without basis in the law.... [A] computer operating pursuant to software *may* represent patentable subject matter, provided, of course, that the claimed subject matter meets all of the other requirements of [the Patent Code]." *In re Alappat*, 33 F.3d 1526, 1545, 31 USPQ2d 1545, 1558 (Fed. Cir. 1994) (en banc, majority opinion of Rich, J.).

See ALGORITHM.

3. Trade Secret Protection for Computer Programs. If a computer program has been kept confidential and if that confidentiality has been breached through improper means such as by a disloyal employee, a double-dealing prospective licensee, or industrial espionage, then there is a valid claim for infringement of TRADE SECRETS in a computer program. Because of the requirement of confidentiality, mass-marketed computer programs (subsequent to the period of secret in-house development) are generally not protectible by trade secret law. Rather, trade secret protection is generally available only for the custom-made or limited-edition programs sold to only a few customers under a promise of secrecy. See *Trandes Corp. v. Guy F. Atkinson Co.*, 996 F.2d 655, 27 USPQ2d 1014 (4th Cir. 1993) (Source and object code of computer program used to perform survey calculations for construction of subway tunnels is protectable trade secret under Maryland law.). Trade secret law is state, not federal, law.

• *Case Reference*: The plaintiff developed the "POBAS III" accounting computer program designed for school districts and county governments. Employees of the plaintiff left and formed their own company, came out with a substantially identical program, and solicited several of the plaintiff's clients. Damages and an injunction were affirmed on appeal. "[Plaintiff's] POBAS III system is a trade secret. The system derived independent economic value from being generally unknown and available solely from [plaintiff].... [Plaintiff] can assert POBAS III was a trade secret only if they made reasonable efforts to maintain the secrecy of POBAS III.... [Plaintiff] took reasonable efforts to maintain the secrecy of POBAS III. The efforts constituted more than mere intent: (a) all of the source code listing and magnetic tapes incorporating the POBAS system bore proprietary notices; (b) the [plaintiff's] user manuals were copyrighted and stated that all system information was proprietary; and (c) every client contract stated that POBAS was the exclusive proprietary property of [plaintiff]. Although absolute security was not achieved, [plaintiff] took reasonable efforts to protect the secret of POBAS III from third parties." *Aries Information Sys., Inc. v. Pacific Management Sys. Corp.*, 366 N.W.2d 366, 368, 226 USPQ 440, 442 (Minn. App. 1985).

concealment [patent] Acts by an inventor to withhold an invention from public knowledge by either (1) deliberately hiding the invention or (2) failing to apply for a patent within a reasonable time after invention. Such conduct can extinguish a first inventor's priority of invention such that a patent is granted to a later rival inventor. Concealment is generally regarded as synonymous with its statutory siblings ABANDONMENT and SUPPRESSION. Patent Code §102(g) states that one who is the first to complete the invention by CONCEPTION and REDUCTION TO PRACTICE will lose the right of priority and the patent if that inventor thereafter abandons, suppresses, or conceals the invention.

Failure to Timely File a Patent Application. The most common situation in which the first inventor loses out to a second inventor because of concealment is where after reduction to practice by the first inventor, no patent application is filed for an unreasonable period and during that interval of inactivity the second inventor enters the scene.

The Mason v. Hepburn Decision. The classic case, the holding of which is codified in Patent Code §102(g), is *Mason v. Hepburn*, 13 App. D.C. 86 (D.C. Cir. 1898). Mason completed his invention of a gun clip in 1887 by building a working model. For seven years thereafter, Mason did nothing about the invention. After 1887, Hepburn independently made the same inven-

tion, promptly filed for a patent application, and was granted a patent in September 1894. Learning of Hepburn's patent, Mason was spurred to file his patent application in December 1894. In an INTERFERENCE proceeding, Mason in effect claimed: "I invented that first." The court held that while Mason may have negligently rather than willfully concealed or suppressed his invention, the "indifference, supineness, or wilful act" of a first inventor is the basis for "the equity" that favors the second inventor when that person made and disclosed to the public the invention during the period of prolonged inactivity of the first inventor.

• *Statutory Reference*: 35 U.S.C. §102(g): "A person shall be entitled to a patent unless— (g) before the applicant's invention thereof the invention was made in this country by another who had not abandoned, suppressed, or concealed it...."

• *Treatise Reference*: 3 D. Chisum, *Patents* §10.08 (1994 rev.).

• *Case References*:

"The result of applying the suppression and concealment doctrine is that the inventor who did not conceal (but was the de facto last inventor) is treated legally as the first to invent, while the de facto first inventor who suppressed or concealed is treated legally as a later inventor." *In re Suska*, 589 F.2d 527, 529, 200 USPQ 497, 499 (C.C.P.A. 1979).

"The courts have consistently held that an invention, though completed, is deemed abandoned, suppressed or concealed if, within a reasonable time after completion, no steps are taken to make the invention publicly known. Thus, failure to file a patent application; to describe the invention in a publicly disseminated document; or to use the invention publicly, have been held to constitute abandonment, suppression or concealment." *International Glass Co. v. United States*, 408 F.2d 395, 403, 159 USPQ 434, 441 (Ct. Cl. 1968), quoted with approval in *Lutzker v. Plet*, 843 F.2d 1364, 1366, 6 USPQ2d 1370, 1371 (Fed. Cir. 1988).

"The cases show either intentional concealment or an unduly long delay after the first inventor's reduction to practice. Some cases excused the delay, and some did not.... The decisions applying section 102(g) balanced the law and policy favoring the first person to make an invention, against equitable considerations when more than one person had made the same invention; in each case where the court deprived the de facto first inventor of the right to the patent, the second inventor had entered the field during a period of either inactivity or deliberate concealment by the first inventor. Often the first inventor had been spurred to file a patent application by news of the second inventor's activities. Although 'spurring' is not necessary to a finding of suppression or concealment... the courts' frequent references to spurring indicate their concern with this equitable factor.... We affirm the long-standing rule that too long a delay may bar the first inventor from reliance on an early reduction to practice in a priority contest. But we hold that the first inventor will not be barred from relying on later, resumed activity antedating an opponent's entry into the field, merely because the work done before the delay occurred was sufficient to amount to a reduction to practice." *Paulik v. Rizkalla*, 760 F.2d 1270, 1274–76, 226 USPQ 224, 226–28 (Fed. Cir. 1985).

- *Example*: In February 1976 Lutzker conceived of and in March 1976 reduced to practice an invention consisting of a device for making canapes. Thereafter, Plet invented the same device and filed a patent application for it in March 1980. A commercially acceptable version of Lutzker's device was first disclosed to the public at a trade show in July 1980, and he filed a patent application the following November. Even though he was the first inventor, Lutzker had to overcome the presumption of abandonment, suppression, or concealment that arose from the 51-month period from his reduction to practice to first public disclosure. Lutzker's explanation that he was working to improve his invention for commercial introduction was rejected and the patent was awarded to Plet. "Since Lutzker's activities were directed to commercialization of his invention and since none of his activities were reflected in his patent application, such activities will not excuse the delay or rebut the presumption of suppression or concealment.... Moreover, in this case the Board also found that 'Lutzker's actions ... constitute more than an inference of suppression or concealment' because of his deliberate policy not to disclose his invention to the public until he is ready to go into commercial production. Such a policy is evidence of an intent to suppress or conceal the invention under 35 U.S.C. §102(g)." *Lutzker v. Plet*, 843 F.2d 1364, 1368, 6 USPQ2d 1370, 1372 (Fed. Cir. 1988).

See ABANDONMENT, INTERFERENCE.

concept [patent–copyright] Neither patents nor copyrights create exclusive rights in a mere idea, theory, or concept.

No Protection to a Mere Concept or Idea. Patents only protect certain explicit and tangible inventions and copyrights only protect certain concrete expressions. Patents do not protect "ideas," only specific structures and methods. "Reducing a claimed invention to an 'idea,' and then determining patentability of that 'idea' is error." *Jones v. Hardy*, 727 F.2d 1524, 1528, 220 USPQ 1021, 1026 (Fed. Cir. 1984). The copyright statute is explicit: "In no case does copyright protection for an original work of authorship extend to any idea, procedure, process...." 17 U.S.C. §102(b).

See HEART OF THE INVENTION, GIST OF THE INVENTION.

- *Case References*: "It is hornbook law that abstractions, i.e., concepts, are not patentable subject matter." *RCA Corp. v. Applied Digital Data Sys., Inc.*, 730 F.2d 1440, 1445 n.5, 221 USPQ 385, 389 n.5 (Fed. Cir. 1984).

"[I]t is elementary that however new and useful, or even revolutionary and beneficial to humanity, an idea may be, it is not of itself patentable.... Thus a system for the transaction of business, such, for example, as the cafeteria system for transacting the restaurant business, or similarly the open-air drive-in system for conducting the motion picture theatre business, however novel, useful, or commercially successful is not patentable apart from the means for making the system practically useful or carrying it out." *Lowe's Drive-In Theatres, Inc. v. Park-In Theatres, Inc.*, 174 F.2d 547, 551–52, 81 USPQ 149, 153 (1st Cir. 1949) (patent on drive-in movie system held invalid).

conception [patent] The formulation in the inventor's mind of a definite perception of the complete invention. While conception is a purely mental act, it cannot be proven in court merely by the inventor's testimony: there must be some additional evidence in corroboration of the inventor's testimony. Conception marks the beginning of the inventive process and reduction to practice marks the end of the inventive process.

The Concept Must be Specific, Not Vague. To sufficiently mark the beginning of the inventive process and give priority, the conception must be of a specific method of solving a problem or of carrying out a result, not just of the result itself. The concept must be sufficiently complete so that one of ordinary skill in the art could understand the concept and bring it to reality through a reduction to practice. See 3 D. Chisum, *Patents* §10.04 (1994 rev.). Neither a mere recognition of a problem to be solved nor a vague, general approach to solving it are sufficient for "conception" to occur. See 2 P. Rosenberg, *Patent Law Fundamentals* §10.01[1] (1994 rev.). Conception only occurs when the inventor has all the needed data and details for carrying out the invention. See 1 S. Ladas, *Patents, Trademarks and Related Rights: National and International Protection* §188 (1975). Thus, if one merely recognizes the problem of transmission of electrical power through high power lines and conceives of the general idea of broadcasting electrical power by means of radio waves, that vague idea without any specific notion of the means of accomplishing it is not a "conception" in patent law.

Simultaneous Conception and Reduction to Practice. For some complex chemical compounds, conception will not occur until the invention has been reduced to practice. "We hold that when an inventor is unable to envision the detailed constitution of a gene so as to distinguish it from other materials, as well as a method for obtaining it, conception has not been achieved until reduction to practice has occurred, i.e., until after the gene has been isolated." *Amgen Inc. v. Chugai Pharmaceutical Co.,* 927 F.2d 1200, 1206, 18 USPQ2d 1016, 1021 (Fed. Cir. 1991).

See INVENTIVE PROCESS, CORROBORATION, REDUCTION TO PRACTICE, PRIORITY OF INVENTION.

• *Statutory Reference*: 35 U.S.C. §102(g): "In determining priority of invention there shall be considered not only the respective dates of conception and reduction to practice of the invention, but also the reasonable diligence of one who was first to conceive and last to reduce to practice, from a time prior to conception by the other."

• *Treatise References*: 3 D. Chisum, *Patents* §10.04 (1994 rev.); 2 P. Rosenberg, *Patent Law Fundamentals* §10.01[1] (1994 rev.); 1 S. Ladas, *Patents, Trademarks and Related Rights: National and International Protection* §188 (1975).

• *Case References*:

The seminal and most famous definition of conception and one that has been adopted by modern courts is the following: "The conception of the invention consists in the complete performance of the mental part of the inventive act. All that remains to be accomplished, in order to perfect the act or instrument, belongs to the department of construction, not invention. It is therefore the formation, in the mind of the inventor, of a definite and permanent idea of the complete and operative invention, as it is thereafter to be applied in practice, that constitutes an available conception, within the meaning of the patent law." *Mergenthaler v. Scudder,* 11 App. D.C. 264, 276, 1897 C.D. 724, 731 (1897), adopted with approval in *Gunter v. Stream* 573 F.2d 77, 80, 197 USPQ 482, 484 (C.C.P.A. 1978); *Coleman v. Dines,* 754 F.2d 353, 359, 224 USPQ 857, 862 (Fed. Cir. 1985).

"It is settled that in establishing conception a party must show possession of every feature recited in the [interference] count, and that every limitation of the count must have been known to the inventor at the time of the alleged conception.... Conception must be proved by corroborating evidence which shows that the inventor disclosed to others his 'completed thought expressed in such clear terms as to enable those skilled in the art' to make the invention." *Coleman v. Dines*, 754 F.2d 353, 359, 224 USPQ 857, 862 (Fed. Cir. 1985).

"Conception is the touchstone of inventorship, the completion of the mental part of invention.... [T]he test for conception is whether the inventor had an idea that was definite and permanent enough that one skilled in the art could understand the invention.... An idea is definite and permanent when the inventor has a specific, settled idea, a particular solution to the problem at hand, not just a general goal or research plan he hopes to pursue. ... But, an inventor need not know that his invention will work for conception to be complete. ... He need only show that he had the idea; the discovery that an invention actually works is part of its reduction to practice.... A conception is not complete if the subsequent course of experimentation, especially experimental failures, reveals uncertainty that so undermines the specificity of the inventor's idea that it is not yet a definite and permanent reflection of the complete invention as it will be used in practice." *Burroughs Wellcome Co. v. Barr Labs. Inc.*, 40 F.2d 1223, 1227–28, 32 USPQ2d 1915, 1919–20 (Fed. Cir. 1994).

concurrent use proceeding [trademark]
An administrative INTER PARTES proceeding before the TRADEMARK TRIAL AND APPEAL BOARD (TTAB) initiated by an applicant for registration who files an application that is limited to a defined territory within the United States. The applicant must state, to the best of its knowledge, the extent of the concurrent use by others of the mark for similar goods or services in other parts of the nation. Under §2(d) of the Lanham Act, more than one person can obtain registration of the same or a similar mark for the same or similar goods or services, but only if the parties are so geographically separated that there will not be a likelihood of confusion between the concurrent uses. A determination of these issues is made by the TTAB in a concurrent use proceeding.
The Burden to Negate a Likelihood of Confusion. A junior user applicant for concurrent registration has the burden to show that there will be no likelihood of confusion in the territories of actual use, not merely in the territory claimed by the junior user. *Gray v. Daffy Dan's*

Bargaintown, 823 F.2d 522, 3 USPQ2d 1306 (Fed. Cir. 1987). An agreement by the parties that delineates their respective territories of use and that consents to a concurrent registration is entitled to "substantial weight." *Amalgamated Bank of New York v. Amalgamated Trust & Savs. Bank*, 842 F.2d 1270, 6 USPQ2d 1305 (Fed. Cir. 1988).

Administrative Versus Court-Ordered Concurrent Registration. Lanham Act §2(d) provides two alternative routes to concurrent registration: an INTER PARTES concurrent use proceeding before the TTAB or issuance of a concurrent registration by the Commissioner of Patents and Trademarks upon the direction of a court. After a court determination of the respective territorial rights of the contesting parties, the Patent and Trademark Office is bound and must issue a concurrent registration with limitations that correspond to the judgment of the court.

Only Covers Territorially Separated Concurrent Use. A TTAB concurrent use proceeding is usually for territorial disputes and is not ordinarily used to resolve a dispute by two parties using a similar mark in the same territory but for different goods or services. *Tamarkin Co. v. Seaway Food Town Inc.,* 34 USPQ2d 1587 (TTAB 1995).

Evidence. The testimonial evidence in a concurrent use proceeding consists of the written transcript of a testimonial deposition resembling a discovery deposition rather than live testimony before the Trademark Board. The "trial" before the board consists of what in a court trial would be closing arguments by counsel supplementing their trial briefs.

• *Treatise Reference*: 2 J.T. McCarthy, *Trademarks and Unfair Competition* §20.22–.23 (3d ed. 1995 rev.).

cone of silence [general legal] A method by which an attorney attempts to prevent law firm disqualification in a situation where the attorney switches law firms and possesses information that may create a conflict of interest. Unlike the CHINESE WALL, which requires the cooperation of all members of the new law firm in screening the attorney from sensitive information, the cone of silence is a self-imposed silence on sensitive information and provides less assurance against shared confidences. Like the Chinese wall, the cone of silence is an attempt to rebut the presumption of shared confidences, i.e., that every attorney in a law firm shares in every other attorney's knowledge.

• *Case Reference*:

"Atasi contends the so-called 'cone of silence' is sufficient to rebut the presumption [of shared confidences]. Under this method screening is sufficient to rebut the presumption where the attorney switching firms, but not the other members of the firm, agrees not to share confidences of prior clients with his new associates.... Since the Ninth Circuit has yet to approve the Chinese Wall, which provides more assurance against shared confidences than the cone of silence, we do not now approve the latter method of rebuttal." *Atasi Corp. v. Seagate Technology*, 847 F.2d 826, 831–32, 6 USPQ2d 1955, 1958 (Fed. Cir. 1988).

See CHINESE WALL.

confusingly similar [trademark] Shorthand for saying that concurrent use of conflicting marks will create a likelihood of confusion and hence infringement. "[Not] 'confusingly similar' ... is a shorthand expression indicating that we do not think concurrent use of the marks is likely to *cause* confusion." Judge Rich in *Motorola, Inc. v. Griffiths Elecs., Inc.*, 317 F.2d 397, 400, 137 USPQ 551, 554 (C.C.P.A. 1963).

Sometimes, when appropriately modified in context, "confusingly similar" is used only to refer to similarity of the marks themselves, not to the ultimate conclusion of likelihood of confusion of customers as to source or sponsorship. For example: "[W]e are satisfied that, if the marks themselves are confusingly similar, customers of the fast-food restaurant would be likely to believe that opposer [who is the owner of a supermarket chain] owned, sponsored or supplied that business." *Giant Food, Inc. v. Nation's Foodservice, Inc.*, 710 F.2d 1565, 1570, 218 USPQ 390, 394 (Fed. Cir. 1983). Of course, the test of infringement is likelihood of confusion, not just whether the marks themselves are "confusingly similar." *Myurgia, S.A. v. Comptoir De La Parfumerie S.A.*, 441 F.2d 673, 675, 169 USPQ 587, 588 (C.C.P.A. 1971).

See INFRINGEMENT OF A TRADEMARK.

• *Treatise Reference*: 2 J.T. McCarthy, *Trademarks and Unfair Competition* §23.01[3][b] (3d ed. 1995 rev.).

consent agreement [patent–trademark] An agreement between two or more parties regarding the legality of the use of the intellectual property in dispute.

1. *Consent Agreement for Patent.* If in a patent dispute the parties settle the case and the agreement becomes embodied in a judicial consent decree stating that the patent in dispute is valid, in a later dispute principles of the finality of judgments can bar that same party from claiming that the patent is invalid. The Federal Circuit has held that if a consent decree would foreclose subsequent challenges to the validity of a patent under general rules of res judicata, then the LEAR RULE favoring challenges to validity does not overrule that foreclosure effect. *Foster v. Hallco Mfg. Co.*, 947 F.2d 469, 20 USPQ 2d 1241 (Fed. Cir. 1991).

• *Case Reference*: "A binding consent judgment encourages patent owners to agree to settlement and to remove its force would have an adverse effect on settlement negotiations. Thus, unlike *Lear*, where there was a conflict between federal patent policy and state law of contracts, here we have strong competing policies that do not implicate questions of the primacy of federal over state law.... [W]e cannot conclude that the public policy expressed in *Lear* is so overriding that challenges to validity must be allowed when under normal principles of *res judicata* applicable to a consent judgment, such challenges would be precluded." *Foster v. Hallco Mfg. Co.*, 947 F.2d 469, 477, 20 USPQ2d 1241, 1247 (Fed. Cir. 1991).

2. *Consent Agreement for Trademark.* A contract in which trademark owner A consents to party B's usage of a mark within certain defined conditions of use measured by format, line of goods, services, and/or territory. By consenting, A either explicitly or implicitly admits

that B's defined usage is not likely to cause confusion with A's usage. Often, a consent agreement is used as the legal vehicle to settle a trademark dispute.

A Consent Is Neither an Assignment Nor a License. A consent agreement is neither an ASSIGNMENT nor a LICENSE. No transfer of title of any mark takes place, and there is no grant of a right to use the mark. In a consent, A is not granting B a license because in a license the licensee is engaging in acts that would infringe the licensor's mark but for the permission granted in the license. *In re Mastic Inc.*, 829 F.2d 1114, 4 USPQ2d 1292 (Fed. Cir. 1987). But in a consent, A is stating that B's use, if confined to the defined format, market, or territory, is not likely to cause confusion with A's mark. As between the contracting parties, a consent agreement will be voided as against public policy for permitting conduct that will confuse only if such confusion is clear and unavoidable. *T & T Mfg. Co. v. A.T. Cross Co.*, 449 F. Supp. 813, 197 USPQ 763 (D.R.I.), *aff'd*, 587 F.2d 533, 201 USPQ 561 (1st Cir. 1978) (overzealous judicial scrutiny of consent agreements would violate policy favoring settlement of trademark disputes).

Impact on Third Parties. A consent admits at least implicitly that the permitted use is not likely to cause confusion. In a future infringement suit against a nonparty to the consent agreement, the defendant may point to the consent as an admission by the plaintiff that the defined use is noninfringing and may argue that its own use is not much different. The leading case is one in which company A using SUNKIST on citrus fruits and company B using SUNKIST on canned fruit and vegetables entered into a consent agreement consenting to each other's usage. A and B later sued a bakery using SUNKIST on bread. The court stated that where A and B agree that there will be no confusion by use of the same mark on closely related food products, they cannot claim that there will be confusion from use of the mark on bread. *California Fruit Growers Exch. v. Sunkist Baking Co.*, 166 F.2d 971, 975, 76 USPQ 85, 89 (7th Cir. 1947).

"Letters of Consent" and the Likelihood of Confusion Issue. An applicant who was refused registration of a mark because of an alleged conflict with a prior registration may obtain a "letter of consent" from the owner of the cited registered mark to convince the Patent and Trademark Office examiner to reverse the refusal. The Court of Customs and Patent Appeals and the Court of Appeals for the Federal Circuit have generally been supportive of giving very strong evidentiary weight to such letters of consent, pointing out that when merchants say that their uses will not cause confusion, it is a bold step for a court to hold that the uses will cause confusion. *In re E.I. du Pont de Nemours & Co.*, 476 F.2d 1357, 1363, 177 USPQ 563, 568 (C.C.P.A. 1973). The Federal Circuit has pointed out that the businesspeople who enter into consent agreements "are in a much better position to know the real life situation than bureaucrats or judges and therefore such agreements may, depending on the circumstances, carry great weight." *Bongrain Int'l (Am.) Corp. v. Delice de France, Inc.*, 811 F.2d 1479, 1484, 1 USPQ2d 1775, 1778 (Fed. Cir. 1987). On the other hand, if a consent agreement is "naked," in that it does not bind the parties to stay in their respective markets or to do anything to avoid confusion, then such an agreement will carry little weight in determining the likelihood of confusion. *In re Mastic Inc.*, 829 F.2d 1114, 4 USPQ2d 1292 (Fed. Cir. 1987) (consent held not determinative). *See*: 2 J.T. McCarthy, *Trademarks and Unfair Competition* §23.25 (3d ed. 1995 rev.).

See LICENSE OF TRADEMARK.

• *Treatise Reference*: 2 J.T. McCarthy, *Trademarks and Unfair Competition* §18.25 (3d ed. 1995 rev.).

• *Case References*:

"The weight to be given more detailed [consent] agreements ... should be substantial. It can be safely taken that reputable businessmen-users of valuable trademarks have no interest in *causing* public confusion.... Thus when those most familiar with use in the marketplace and most interested in precluding confusion enter into agreements designed to avoid it, the scales of evidence are clearly tilted. It is at least difficult to maintain a subjective view that confusion will occur when those directly concerned say it won't.... As we read them, the very purpose and aim of the present agreements is the avoidance of public confusion." *In re E.I. du Pont de Nemours & Co.*, 476 F.2d 1357, 1363, 177 USPQ 563, 568 (C.C.P.A. 1973).

"The parties themselves have determined that confusion of the public by concurrent use of their marks is unlikely.... There is no reason to ignore their assessment of likelihood of confusion and not give substantial weight to their agreement as evidence that likelihood of confusion does not exist.... [I]t is well settled that in the absence of contrary evidence, a consent agreement itself may be evidence that there is no likelihood of confusion." *In re Four Seasons Hotels Ltd.*, 987 F2d 1565, 1569, 26 USPQ2d 1071, 1074 (Fed. Cir. 1993) (upheld the validity of a consent agreement as permitting the concurrent registration of FOUR SEASONS BILTMORE for a seaside resort hotel in Santa Barbara, California, and THE BILTMORE LOS ANGELES for a hotel in downtown Los Angeles, 120 miles south of the seaside resort).

consisting essentially of [patent] An introductory term used in patent claims, which commonly follows the claim preamble and introduces the ELEMENTS making up the claim. Use of the term "consisting essentially of" to introduce the elements of a CLAIM leaves the claim open only for the inclusion of other components, ingredients, or process steps that do not materially affect the basic and novel characteristics of the invention.

Thus, a claim using the introductory term "consisting essentially of" will be infringed only if any components or ingredients added in the accused device or product do not materially affect the basic and novel characteristics of the invention.

See COMPRISING, CONSISTING OF.

- *Treatise Reference*: 2 D. Chisum, *Patents* §8.06[1][b] (1994 rev.).

- *Case Reference*: "In *In re Janakirama-Rao*, [317 F.2d 951, 137 USPQ 893 (C.C.P.A. 1963)], this court held that the phrase 'consisting essentially of' limits the scope of a claim to the specified ingredients and those that do not *materially* affect the *basic* and *novel* charac-

teristic(s) of a composition. It cited *Ex Parte Davis*, 80 USPQ 448 (Pat. Off. Bd. App. 1948), which appears to have been the first published opinion construing the phrase 'consisting essentially of,' and quoted approvingly the following portion of the opinion: 'In the present case where the claims recite three ingredients and the reference discloses four, the important question is whether the term "consisting essentially of" excludes that fourth ingredient. We think that it does, since the "modifier" *materially changes* the *fundamental character* of the three ingredient composition.... [Emphasis added].' " *In re Hertz*, 537 F.2d 549, 551, 190 USPQ 461, 463 (C.C.P.A. 1976), cited with approval in *Atlas Powder Co. v. E.I. du Pont de Nemours & Co.*, 750 F.2d 1569, 1573, 224 USPQ 409, 411 (Fed. Cir. 1984).

consisting of [patent] A closed term used in patent claims, which commonly follows the claim preamble and introduces the ELEMENTS making up the claim. Use of the term "consisting of" to introduce the elements of a claim closes or restricts the claim to those elements or ingredients listed.

Closed Introductory Term. A claim using the introductory term "consisting of" will be infringed only if there are no additional components or ingredients added in the accused device or product. If the invention is claimed in the patent as "consisting of" elements A + B + C, the claim is not infringed by a device having elements A + B + C + X. "Consisting of" is a closed introductory term, while COMPRISING is the opposite—an open introductory term. A "consisting of" claim is narrower and is infringed only if the accused device has all of, but no more than, the elements recited in the patent claim.

"Consisting Essentially of." If the modifier "essentially" is added to make the phrase "consisting essentially of," then the claim is open only for the inclusion of other components, ingredients, or process steps that do not materially affect the basic and novel characteristics of the invention.

See CONSISTING ESSENTIALLY OF.

Introduction to One Element of a Claim. If the term "consisting of" is not used to introduce all the elements of a claim, but only to introduce one particular element within the body of a claim, then the term does not necessarily close that particular element to the exclusion of other features. In that event, it has been held that the addition in the accused device of other features does not necessarily avoid infringement. See *Mannesmann Demag Corp. v. Engineered Metal Prods. Co.*, 605 F. Supp. 1362, 226 USPQ 466 (D. Del. 1985), *aff'd*, 793 F.2d 1279, 230 USPQ 45 (Fed. Cir. 1986), quoted in case references below.

See COMPRISING, CONSISTING OF.

- *Treatise Reference*: 2 D. Chisum, *Patents* §8.06[1][b] (1994 rev.).

- *Case References*:

"The presence of the phrase 'consisting of' in claim 1 indicates that the list of elements is to be exclusive. By referring to '*a* longitudinally extending cord' (emphasis added), the patentee limits himself to one cord in the stringer. His claim will not cover stringers with more than one cord.... Since the patentee has limited his claim to only those stringers with 'a longitudinally extending cord,' the complainant cannot now claim that the respondents' three-cord stringer infringes the patent." *In re Certain Slide Fastener Stringers & Machs.*, 216 USPQ 907, 915 (U.S. Int'l Trade Comm'n 1981).

"When the phrase 'consisting of' appears in the *transitional phrase* of a claim, the claim is considered 'closed' to additional structures. A claim which is closed to additional structures cannot read on embodiments possessing any structure not expressly disclosed by the claim. P. Rosenberg, 2 *Patent Law Fundamentals* §14.05[2] (1984); D. Chisum, 2 *Patents* §8.06[1][b] (1984). In the present case, the 'consisting of' phrase does not appear in the transition phrase of the claim, but rather in the body of the claim as one of its limitations. [In view of the history of how the words 'consisting of' were added to the claim during prosecution,] I do not view the term, however, as excluding additions to the pipe coil ... which would not detract from its structural integrity as a *wall*." *Mannesmann Demag Corp. v. Engineered Metal Prods. Co.*, 605 F. Supp. 1362, 1380, 226 USPQ 466, 480 (D. Del. 1985), *aff'd on point*,

793 F.2d 1279, 1282, 230 USPQ 45, 47 (Fed. Cir. 1986) ("The [district] court correctly declined to read this usage of 'consisting of' as excluding all other elements from the claim as a whole.").

consonance [patent]
See DOUBLE PATENTING.

Constitution [patent–copyright–trademark]
The U.S. Constitution makes a specific grant of power to the U.S. Congress to pass statutes pertaining to patents and copyrights in Article I, section 8, clause 8. The wording of the clause is parallel, such that it authorizes Congress to promote "science" by giving to "authors" the exclusive rights to their "writings," and to promote the "useful arts" by giving to "inventors" the exclusive rights to their "discoveries." "Science" was used for its eighteenth century meaning of knowledge in general, and "useful arts" was used in the sense that "technology" is used today.

See ART.

Limited Times. The Constitution authorizes Congress to pass laws giving exclusive rights via patent and copyright "for limited times." Thus, such rights must have a limited and fixed duration.

See DURATION.

Trademarks. The Patent and Copyright Clause does not empower Congress to enact laws giving exclusive rights in trademarks. See *The Trademark Cases*, 100 U.S. 82 (1879). While there is no specific constitutional provision relating to laws protecting and registering trademarks, Congress has the power to do so as a part of its authority to regulate interstate and foreign commerce under the Commerce Clause of the Constitution.

See TRADEMARK, REGISTRATION OF TRADEMARKS.

- *United States Constitution*:

Patent and Copyright Clause: Article 1, section 8, clause 8: "The Congress shall have power ... To promote the progress of science and useful arts, by securing for limited times to authors and inventors the exclusive rights to their respective writings and discoveries."

Commerce Clause: Article 1, section 8, clause 3: "The Congress shall have power ... To regulate commerce with foreign nations, and among the several states, and with the Indian tribes."

- *Legislative Reference*: "The background, the balanced construction, and the usage current then and later, indicate that the constitutional [patent and copyright] provision is really two provisions merged into one. The purpose of the first provision is to promote the progress of science by securing for limited times to authors the exclusive right to their writings, the word 'science' in this connection having the meaning of knowledge in general, which is one of its meanings today. The other provision is that Congress has the power to promote the progress of useful arts by securing for limited times to inventors the exclusive right to their discoveries. The first patent law and all patent laws up to a much later period were entitled 'Acts to promote the progress of useful arts.' " H. Rep. No. 1923, 82d Cong., 2d Sess. 4 (1952); S. Rep. No. 1979, 82d Cong., 2d Sess. 3 (1952) (legislative history accompanying enactment of the 1952 Patent Code).

- *Case References*:

"The economic philosophy behind the clause empowering Congress to grant patents and copyrights is the conviction that encouragement of individual effort by personal gain is the best way to advance public welfare through the talents of authors and inventions in 'Science and useful Arts.' Sacrificial days devoted to such creative activities deserve rewards commensurate with the services rendered." *Mazer v. Stein*, 347 U.S. 201, 219, 100 USPQ 325, 333 (1954).

"[T]he federal patent power stems from a specific constitutional provision.... The clause is both a grant of power and a limitation.... The Congress in the exercise of the patent power may not overreach the restraints imposed by the stated constitutional purpose.... Congress may not authorize the issuance of patents whose effects are to remove existent knowledge from the public domain, or to restrict free access to materials already available. Innovation, advancement, and things which add to the sum of

useful knowledge are inherent requisites in a patent system which by constitutional command must 'promote the Progress of ... useful Arts.' This is the *standard* expressed in the Constitution and it may not be ignored." *Graham v. John Deere Co.*, 383 U.S. 1, 6, 148 USPQ 459, 462 (1966).

"The clause thus describes both the objective which Congress may seek and the means to achieve it. The objective is to promote the progress of science and the arts. As employed, the terms 'to promote' are synonymous with the words 'to stimulate,' 'to encourage,' or 'to induce.' To accomplish its purpose, Congress may grant to authors the exclusive right to the fruits of their respective works. An author who possesses an unlimited copyright may preclude others from copying his creation for commercial purposes without permission. In other words, to encourage people to devote themselves to intellectual and artistic creation, Congress may guarantee to authors and inventors a reward in the form of control over the sale or commercial use of copies of their works." *Goldstein v. California*, 412 U.S. 546, 555, 178 USPQ 129, 133 (1973).

"The [constitutional] Patent Clause itself reflects a balance between the need to encourage innovation and the avoidance of monopolies which stifle competition without any concomitant advance in the 'Progress of Science and the useful Arts.' ... Taken together, the novelty and nonobviousness requirements express a congressional determination that the purposes behind the Patent Clause are best served by free competition and exploitation of that which is either already available to the public, or that which may be readily discerned from publicly available material.... [T]he Patent and Copyright Clauses do not, by their own force or by negative implication, deprive the States of the power to adopt rules for the promotion of intellectual creation within their own jurisdictions." *Bonito Boats Inc. v. Thunder Craft Boats Inc.*, 489 U.S. 141, 146, 9 USPQ2d 1847, 1850, 1852, 1858 (1989).

"Original, as the term is used in copyright, means only that the work was independently created by the author (as opposed to copied from other works), and that it possesses at least some minimal degree of creativity.... Originality is a constitutional requirement.... [T]his Court [has] defined the crucial [Constitutional] terms 'authors' and 'writings.' In so doing, the Court made it unmistakably clear that these terms presuppose a degree of originality." *Feist Publications v. Rural Tel. Serv.,* 499 U.S. 340, 346, 18 USPQ2d 1275, 1278 (1991).

"In the Lanham [Trademark] Act, Congress set out what appears to be an unambiguous statement of the scope of federal trademark jurisdiction, namely, 'all commerce which may lawfully be regulated by Congress.' 15 U.S.C. §1127.... On its face, the Lanham Act provides a clear and unambiguous definition of federal trademark jurisdiction in terms of the general Constitutional law as interpreted by the Supreme Court." *In re Silenus Wines, Inc.,* 557 F.2d 806, 809–10, 194 USPQ 261, 264–65 (C.C.P.A. 1977).

constructive notice [trademark] A legal notice created by registration of a mark on the federal PRINCIPAL REGISTER to all the world of the registrant's claim of ownership of the mark.

Constructive Notice and Junior Users. The constructive notice created by federal registration deprives subsequent users of the common law defense of "good faith" adoption and use in a part of the United States in which the federal registrant's mark has not yet been used or become known. *Dawn Donut Co. v. Hart's Food Stores, Inc.,* 267 F.2d 358, 362, 121 USPQ 430, 432 (2d Cir. 1959). Thus, upon registration, the federal registrant knows that it has national rights, which cannot be reduced by subsequent use by a junior user in any part of the nation. However, although the registrant has nationwide rights, the injunctive remedy does not ripen until the registrant shows a likelihood of entry into the disputed territory. *Church of Scientology Int'l v. Elmira Mission of Church of Scientology,* 794 F.2d 38, 230 USPQ 325 (2d Cir. 1986) (entry by licensee sufficient).

Constructive Notice and Users Prior to Registration. Under Lanham Act §33(b)(5), 15 U.S.C. §1115(b)(5), an "intermediate junior user" cannot be deprived of its territorial trademark rights by the constructive notice of a registration issued after the junior user's first use.

Such a user is entitled to exclusive rights in its territory of use, even as against the federal registrant who is the national senior user. In effect, the §33(b)(5) defense "freezes" the junior user's market area as of the date of the senior user's federal registration. Any subsequent expansion of territory made while under the constructive notice of the registration is not in "good faith" and cannot be sustained as legal. *Thrifty Rent-A-Car Sys. Inc. v. Thrift Cars, Inc.,* 831 F.2d 1177, 4 USPQ2d 1709 (1st Cir. 1987). If the federal registrant with an INCONTESTABLE registration is the national junior user, its exclusive rights are limited under Lanham Act §15 by the territory of use established by the common law senior user.

Constructive Use. The 1989 revisions to the Lanham Act introduced the totally new, but related concept of a "constructive use" priority date—the date of filing the application for registration.

See CONSTRUCTIVE USE.

• *Treatise Reference*: 3 J.T. McCarthy, *Trademarks and Unfair Competition* §26.13 (3d ed. 1995 rev.).

• *Statutory Reference*: Lanham Act §22, 15 U.S.C. §1072: "Registration of a mark on the principal register provided by this Act, or under the Act of March 3, 1881, or the Act of February 20, 1905, shall be constructive notice of the registrant's claim of ownership thereof."

constructive reduction to practice [patent] See REDUCTION TO PRACTICE.

constructive use [trademark] A legally effective priority date, nationwide in scope, as of the date of filing an application for federal registration on the PRINCIPAL REGISTER.

Impact of the 1989 Constructive Use Provision. The Trademark Law Revision Act, effective in 1989, introduced a new concept to U.S. law: a federal statutory "constructive use" date for priority purposes. Contingent on the registration of the mark on the principal register, the *filing* of an application to register constitutes "constructive use" of the mark, conferring a "right of priority, nationwide in effect," except for three defined categories of persons, who prior to the application have either used or filed an application themselves. The Trademark Revision Commission stated that: " 'Constructive use' means that which establishes a priority date with the same legal effect as the earliest actual use of a trademark at common law." *Trademark Revision Commission Report*, 77 Trademark Rep. 375, 397 n.28 (1987).

Exceptions to Constructive Use. The three categories of persons who are not bound by the constructive use date are: (1) those who used the mark in the United States prior to the application; (2) those who filed their own U.S. application to register prior to the application; and (3) foreign applicants who filed a foreign application to register before the application date and qualify for that foreign filing date as their constructive date of priority under Lanham Act §44(d).

Constructive Use Establishes Early National Priority. One of the important goals of constructive use is to reduce the geographic fragmentation of trademark rights. Senate Judiciary Committee Report on S. 1883, S. Rep. No. 100-515, p. 29 (Sept. 15, 1988). This goal is achieved by fixing the priority date of a registrant at the date of filing of the application, rather than at the date of registration, as under previous law. One who makes first use of a conflicting mark anywhere in the nation after another has already filed an application after November 16, 1989, should have an inferior priority. This early nationwide priority given by §7(c) is a potent benefit of federal registration and creates a strong incentive to file an application as soon as possible.

Constructive Use and Constructive Notice. The newer concept of a "constructive use date" is in many ways more potent than the "CONSTRUCTIVE NOTICE" provision of §22, which will still destroy a junior user's ability to acquire an exclusive territory of use for the mark. But it is anticipated that in many situations, the "constructive use" provision dating back to the application date will often govern a territorial priority dispute. It is believed that the benefits of constructive use are applicable only to those registrations that resulted from applications filed after the effective date of the Trademark Law Revision Act: November 18, 1989. See 3

J.T. McCarthy, *Trademarks and Unfair Competition* §26.15[1] (3d ed. 1995 rev.).

See CONSTRUCTIVE NOTICE.

• *Treatise Reference*: 3 J.T. McCarthy, *Trademarks and Unfair Competition* §26.15 (3d ed. 1995 rev.).

• *Statutory Reference*: Lanham Act §7(c), 15 U.S.C. §1057(c):

Contingent on the registration of a mark on the principal register provided by this Act, the filing of the application to register such mark shall constitute constructive use of the mark, conferring a right of priority, nationwide in effect, on or in connection with the goods or services specified in the registration against any other person except for a person whose mark has not been abandoned and who, prior to such filing—

(1) has used the mark;

(2) has filed an application to register the mark which is pending or has resulted in registration of the mark; or

(3) has filed a foreign application to register the mark on the basis of which he or she has acquired a right to priority, and timely files an application under section 44(d) to register the mark which is pending or has resulted in registration of the mark.

Legislative History Reference: "Constructive use will fix a registrant's nationwide priority rights in a mark from the filing of its application for registration, whether that application is based on use or intent-to-use. This right of priority will have legal effect comparable to the earliest use of a mark at common law." Senate Judiciary Committee Report on S. 1883, S. Rep. No. 100-515, p. 29 (Sept. 15, 1988).

contestable registration [trademark]
See PRESUMPTION OF TRADEMARK VALIDITY.

continuation [patent] A second patent application for the same invention claimed in the first application, by the same inventor, containing the same disclosure as the first application and filed while the first is still pending. The continuation application is entitled to the filing date of the original.

For the second application to qualify as a continuation of the first: (1) both applications must be filed with at least one common inventor; (2) the same invention must be disclosed in both applications; (3) the applications must have been copending at some time; and (4) the second must cross-reference the first.

The first application is referred to as the PARENT APPLICATION; in a chain of three applications, the first is referred to as the GRANDPARENT APPLICATION.

- *Statutory Reference*: 35 U.S.C. §120 "An application for patent for an invention disclosed in the manner provided by the first paragraph of section 112 of this title in an application previously filed in the United States, ... which is filed by an inventor or inventors named in the previously filed application shall have the same effect, as to such invention, as though filed on the date of the prior application...."

- *Manual Reference*: "[A]n applicant may have recourse to filing a continuation in order to introduce into the case a new set of claims and to establish a right to further examination by the primary examiner." *Manual of Patent Examining Procedure* §201.07 (1994). See also *Manual of Patent Examining Procedure* §201.11 (1994).

- *Case References*:

"A continuing application enables an applicant to, inter alia, claim inventions disclosed but not previously claimed, to develop objective evidence of unobviousness, or to replace claims rejected for obviousness with narrower claims that can be approved." *In re Bauman*, 683 F.2d 405, 408, 214 USPQ 585, 588 (C.C.P.A. 1982).

"To consider an application a 'continuing application' means, of course, that it is entitled to the earlier 'parent'—or 'grandparent' etc.—application's filing date in determining what is '*prior* art' from the standpoint of validity." *Racing Strollers, Inc. v. TRI Indus., Inc.*, 878 F.2d 1418, 1421 n.*, 11 USPQ2d 1300, 1303 n.* (Fed. Cir. 1989).

" 'Continuation' and 'divisional' applications are alike in that they are both continuing applications based on the same disclosure as an earlier application. A 'continuation' application claims the same invention claimed in an earlier application, although there may be some variation in the scope of the subject matter claimed. See MPEP §201.07. A 'divisional' application, on the other hand, is one carved out of an earlier application which disclosed and claimed more than one independent invention, the result being that the divisional application claims only one or more, but not all, of the independent inventions of the earlier application. See MPEP §201.06. A 'CIP' application is a continuing application continuing a portion or all of the disclosure of an earlier application together with added matter not present in that earlier application. See MPEP §201.08." *Transco Prods. Inc. v. Performance Contracting, Inc.*, 38 F.3d 551, 555, 32 USPQ2d 1077, 1080 (Fed. Cir. 1994).

See CONTINUATION-IN-PART, PARENT APPLICATION, GRANDPARENT APPLICATION.

continuation-in-part [patent] A second patent application for the same invention claimed in the first application, by the same inventor, adding some new matter not contained in the disclosure in the first application and filed while the first is still pending. A continuation-in-part (CIP) differs from a CONTINUATION in that while it repeats at least some substantial portion of the disclosure of the earlier application, the continuation-in-part *adds* matter not disclosed in the earlier application.

Different Claims Entitled to Different Filing Dates. Those claims in the continuation-in-part application that are supported by the disclosure of the original (parent) application are entitled to the filing date of the parent. Claims that are dependent upon the new matter added in the continuation-in-part application are entitled to a filing date only of the continuation-in-part application, not the date of the parent application. *Litton Sys., Inc. v. Whirlpool Corp.*, 728 F.2d 1423, 1438, 221 USPQ 97, 106 (Fed. Cir. 1984) (see case reference below).

The first application is referred to as the PARENT APPLICATION and in a chain of three applications, the first is referred to as the GRANDPARENT APPLICATION.

Conditions. For the second application to qualify as a continuation-in-part of the first: (1) both applications must be filed with at least one common inventor; (2) the same invention must be disclosed in both applications; (3) the applications must have been copending at some time; and (4) the second must cross-reference the first.

Adding Postfiling Improvements. "[A] patentee can show he filed a CIP application to disclose improvements developed after the filing date of the parent application...." *Pennwalt Corp. v. Akzona Inc.*, 740 F.2d 1573, 1579 n.12, 222 USPQ 833, 836 n.12 (Fed. Cir. 1984).

• *Statutory Reference*: 35 U.S.C. §120. See statutory reference at CONTINUATION.

• *Manual Reference*: "Any claim in a continuation-in-part application which is directed *solely* to subject matter adequately disclosed under 35 U.S.C. §112 in the parent application is entitled to the benefit of the filing date of the parent application. However, if a claim in a continuation-in-part application recites a feature which was not disclosed or adequately supported by a proper disclosure under 35 U.S.C. §112 in the parent application, but which was first introduced or adequately supported in the continuation-in-part application, such a claim is entitled only to the filing date of the continuation-in-part application." *Manual of Patent Examining Procedure* §201.11 (1994).

• *Case References*:

"A C-I-P application is different from an original patent application, however, in that it often generates two effective filing dates applicable to different parts of the same patent. New matter in a C-I-P application has the filing date of *that* C-I-P application. The earlier filing date of the parent application pertains to material in the C-I-P application also disclosed in the prior application. 35 U.S.C. §120.... If matter added through amendment to a C-I-P application is deemed inherent in whatever the original parent application discloses, however, that matter is also entitled to the filing date of the original, parent application." *Litton Sys., Inc. v. Whirlpool Corp.*, 728 F.2d 1423, 1438, 221 USPQ 97, 106 (Fed. Cir. 1984).

"Law and policy liberally authorize the filing of C-I-P applications for a number of reasons, whether to enlarge the disclosure to include new technological information, thereby providing the public with knowledge of recent developments or improvements; or to enable more extensive prosecution or improved draftsmanship of specification or claims; or to provide a vehicle for prosecution of non-elected claims." *Paperless Accounting v. Bay Area Rapid Transit Sys.*, 804 F.2d 659, 663, 231 USPQ 649, 652 (Fed. Cir. 1986).

"A 'CIP' application is a continuing application continuing a portion or all of the disclosure of an earlier application together with added matter not present in that earlier application. See MPEP §201.08." *Transco Prods. Inc. v. Performance Contracting, Inc.*, 38 F.3d 551, 555, 32 USPQ2d 1077, 1080 (Fed. Cir. 1994).

contributory infringement [patent–trademark–copyright] Indirect infringement of intellectual property rights in which the defendant contributes to the direct infringement of another person.

1. Contributory Patent Infringement. Contributory infringement of a patent is the act of knowingly selling a nonstaple article specially made or adapted for use as part of a patented combination or for use in practicing a patented process. To constitute a "nonstaple," the article must be not suitable for substantial use in any other way than to infringe the patent.

Direct Infringement Is Necessary. There can be no contributory infringement unless there is proof of direct infringement. And there is no contributory infringement unless the seller of the nonstaple article knows that the combination or process for which the article is made is both patented and is infringing. *Preemption Devices Inc. v. Minnesota Mining & Mfg.*, 803 F.2d 1170, 1174, 231 USPQ 297, 300 (Fed. Cir. 1986). Direct evidence of direct infringement is not essential, and circumstantial evidence will suffice. *Moleculon Research Corp. v. CBS, Inc.*, 793 F.2d 1261, 1272, 229 USPQ 805, 813 (Fed. Cir. 1986).

Contributory Infringement of Method Patents. One important benefit of suing for contributory infringement inures to those who own a patent on a method that is widely practiced by many ultimate users who directly infringe the patented process. Since it is impractical to file hundreds of suits against users, the patent owner can sue for contributory infringement a manufacturer who sells to users an ingredient that is capable of use only in the patented process. "The drafters of the section explicitly recognized that without protection from contributory infringers, owners of method patents ... would have no effective protection." *Milton Hodosh v. Block Drug Co.*, 833 F.2d 1575, 1578, 4 USPQ2d 1935, 1937 (Fed. Cir. 1987).

Method Patent on Use of Unpatented Nonstaple. The patentee of a method patent on a use for a prior art unpatented chemical that has no known use other than in the patented method can legally license only those users who buy the unpatented chemical from the patentee. The patentee can remain the sole source of the nonstaple unpatented chemical by suing for contributory infringement competitors who sell the chemical. The refusal of the patentee to license others to sell the unpatented chemical is not a misuse of the patent. In upholding this practice, the U.S. Supreme Court noted: "The number of chemicals either known to scientists or disclosed by existing research is vast.... The number of these chemicals that have known commercial or social value, in contrast, is small. Development of new uses for existing chemicals is thus a major component of practical chemical research." *Dawson Chem. Co. v. Rohm and Haas Co.*, 448 U.S. 176, 188, 206 USPQ 385, 407 (1980).

See INDUCE INFRINGEMENT, STAPLE.

- *Statutory Reference*: 35 U.S.C. §271 (c): "Whoever sells a component of a patented machine, manufacture, combination or composition, or a material or apparatus for use in practicing a patented process, constituting a material part of the invention, knowing the same to be especially made or especially adapted for use in an infringement of such patent, and not a staple article or commodity of commerce suitable for substantial noninfringing use, shall be liable as a contributory infringer."

- *Case References*:

"The [doctrine of contributory patent infringement] exists to protect patent rights from subversion by those who, without directly infringing the patent themselves, engage in acts designed to facilitate infringement by others. This protection is of particular importance in situations ... where enforcement against direct infringers would be difficult, and where the technicalities of patent law make it relatively easy to profit from another's invention without risking a charge of direct infringement." *Dawson Chem. Co. v. Rohm and Haas Co.*, 448 U.S. 176, 188, 206 USPQ 385, 393 (1980).

"It is plain that §271(c)—part of the Patent Code enacted in 1952—made no change in the fundamental precept that there can be no contributory infringement in the absence of a direct infringement." *Aro Mfg. Co. v. Convertible Top Replacement Co.*, 365 U.S. 336, 341, 128 USPQ 354, 357 (1961).

"[A] majority of the Court is of the view that §271(c) does require a showing that the alleged contributory infringer knew that the combination for which his component was especially designed was both patented and infringing." *Aro Mfg. Co. v. Convertible Top Replacement Co.*, 377 U.S. 476, 488, 141 USPQ 681, 687 (1964).

"[A] finding of contributory infringement is normally the functional equivalent of holding that the disputed article is within the monopoly granted to the patentee.... Unless the commodity 'has no use except through practice of the patented method,' the patentee has no right to claim that its distribution constitutes contributory infringement." *Sony Corp. v. Universal City Studios, Inc.*, 464 U.S. 417, 441, 220 USPQ 665, 677 (1984).

2. Contributory Trademark Infringement. A manufacturer or distributor of goods who in some manner aids or encourages its distributing customers to pass off its goods as those of another, or to infringe another's trademark or trade dress, is liable as a contributory infringer. Some courts extend liability for contributory infringement further to include all those who knowingly play a significant role in accomplishing the infringement.

The 1982 Ives *Decision.* In the 1982 *Ives* case, the U.S. Supreme Court stated the general rule for contributory trademark infringement as covering a supplier who either: (1) intentionally induces a distributing customer to infringe, even if it merely suggests, even by implication, that a customer pass off its products as those of another; or (2) continues to supply products to a distributing customer whom it knows or has reason to know is engaging in trademark infringement. *Inwood Labs. Inc. v. Ives Labs. Inc.*, 456 U.S. 844, 854, 214 USPQ 1, 5 (1982). In the *Ives* case, a pharmaceutical company asserted a claim of contributory infringement of its registered word mark CYCLOSPASMOL, alleging that a competing maker of look-alike capsules, while not affixing the word mark to the drugs, contributed to the actions of some retail druggists who illegally substituted the generic look-alike for prescriptions written for CYCLOSPASMOL or mislabeled the look-alike as CYCLOSPASMOL. The plaintiff alleged that the defendant's acts of making a look-alike capsule and distributing catalogs comparing prices and showing the colors of the generic capsules facilitated or encouraged retail druggists to substitute or mislabel. The court of appeals found that this conduct supported a finding of contributory infringement (638 F.2d 538, 209 USPQ 449 (2d Cir. 1981)), but the Supreme Court reversed on the procedural point that the court of appeals did not state that the contrary findings of the district court were "clearly erroneous." It has been indicated that the formulation of *Ives* applies only to federal law and that the states are free to impose a more stringent rule with a greater risk of liability on manufacturers and distributors. *Ciba-Geigy Corp. v. Bolar Pharmaceutical Co.*, 747 F.2d 844, 224 USPQ 349 (3d Cir. 1984).

Participants in the Distributing Process. Many courts will hold liable everyone who knowingly participates in the preparation, distribution, and sale of infringing foods or services. *Stik Prods. Inc. v. United Merchants & Mfrs. Inc.*, 295 F. Supp. 479, 160 USPQ 777 (S.D.N.Y. 1968). In addition, since trademark infringement is a tort, the doctrine of joint tortfeasors is applicable. All those who act together to commit a tort are individually liable for the resulting injury. *Transgo, Inc. v. Ajac Transmission Parts Corp.*, 768 F.2d 1001, 227 USPQ 598 (9th Cir. 1985). Under the *Ives* test, a landlord of a flea market where counterfeit goods are sold may be civilly liable if it knew of the counterfeit sales or had reason to know of them. *Hard Rock Cafe Licensing Corp. v. Concession Servs. Inc.*, 955 F.2d 1143, 21 USPQ2d 1764 (7th Cir. 1992).

• *Treatise Reference*: 3 J.T. McCarthy, *Trademarks and Unfair Competition* §25.02 (3d ed. 1995 rev.).

• *Case References*:

"[L]iability for trademark infringement can extend beyond those who actually mislabel goods with the mark of another. Even if a manufacturer does not directly control others in the chain of distribution, it can be held responsible for their infringing activities under certain circumstances. Thus, if a manufacturer or distributor intentionally induces another to infringe a trademark, or if it continues to supply its product to one whom it knows or has reason to know is engaging in trademark infringement, the manufacturer or distributor is contributorily responsible for any harm done as a result of the deceit." *Inwood Labs. Inc. v. Ives Labs. Inc.*, 456 U.S. 844, 853–54, 214 USPQ 1, 5 (1982).

3. Contributory Copyright Infringement. Contributory infringement of a copyright is the act of supervising or directly financially benefiting from the direct infringement of another. There can be no contributory infringement unless there is proof of a direct infringement.

Statutory Support. Section 106 of the Copyright Act gives the owner of copyright the exclusive right "to do and to authorize" the listed exclusive rights of copyright. This phrase was intended by Congress in the 1976 revisions to impose liability for contributory infringement on one who only induces or permits another to engage in direct infringement. (See legislative history below.) Even the total lack of statutory language would not deprive the courts of using in copyright cases the rule of vicarious liability in general and the rule of contributory infringement in particular. *Sony Corp. v. Universal City Studios, Inc.*, 464 U.S. 417, 435, 220 USPQ 665, 675 (1984).

The Sony Betamax Case. In the 1984 *Sony* case, the U.S. Supreme Court said that it is not contributory infringement to sell a device used by some purchasers to engage in direct copyright infringement if the device is capable of substantial noninfringing uses. *Sony Corp. v. Universal City Studios, Inc.*, 464 U.S. 417, 220 USPQ 665 (1984) (see case references below). The Court borrowed from patent contributory infringement law the requirement that the article be a nonstaple, which is an article not suitable for substantial use in any other way than to infringe the patent. The majority of the Court in the *Sony* case held that the Sony "Betamax" video cassette recorder (VCR) is not like a nonstaple because a VCR is capable of substantial noninfringing uses by home television viewers making off-the-air taping. Such substantial noninfringing uses were said to be the time-shifting taping of copyrighted works whose owners do not object, like professional sports leagues, or the FAIR USE of works whose owners do object to off-the-air taping. Thus, the *Sony* decision effectively insulates from contributory copyright infringement exposure the makers and sellers of typewriters, word-processing computers, and photocopying machines, even if some buyers use those machines to infringe copyrights.

Joint Tortfeasors. In addition, copyright infringement is a tort, and all those who actively participate in infringement are liable as joint tortfeasors. *Costello Publishing Co. v. Rotelle*, 670 F.2d 1035, 1043, 212 USPQ 811, 816 (D.C. Cir. 1981).

Owner of Premises Where Infringing Performances Take Place Is Liable. A familiar example of contributory infringement is the contributory liability of owners of restaurants, night clubs, and dance halls for infringing performances on the premises by musical groups. Such liability is imposed even where the proprietor has neither knowledge of nor control over which songs are performed by independent contractor musicians. "The proprietor of a public establishment operated for a profit could otherwise reap the benefits of countless violations by orchestras, itinerant or otherwise, by merely claiming ignorance that any violations would take place." *Famous Music Corp. v. Bay State Harness Racing Ass'n*, 554 F.2d 1213, 1215, 194 USPQ 177, 178 (1st Cir. 1977). Congress has approved of these types of court rulings and has refused to exempt owners of establishments from liability for the copyright infringement of independent contractor performers. "To be held a related or vicarious infringer in the case of performing rights, a defendant must either actively operate or supervise the operation of the place where the performances occur or control the content of the infringing program, and expect commercial gain from the operation and either direct or indirect benefit from the infringing performance." H. Rep. No. 94-1476, 94th Cong., 2d Sess. 169–70 (1976).

• *Treatise References*: 2 *Nimmer on Copyright* §12.04 (1994 rev.); 2 P. Goldstein, *Copyright* §6.0 (1989); 1 N. Boorstyn, *Copyright* §10.06 (2d ed. 1994); M. Leaffer, *Understanding Copyright* §9.20 (1989).

• *Legislative History*: "The exclusive rights accorded to a copyright owner under section 106 are 'to do and to authorize' any of the activities specified in the five enumerated clauses. Use of the phrase 'to authorize' is intended to avoid any questions as to the liability of contributory infringers. For example, a person who lawfully acquires an authorized copy of a motion picture would be an infringer if he or she engages in the business of renting it to others for purposes of unauthorized public performance." H. Rep. No. 94-1476, 94th Cong., 2d Sess. 61 (1976).

• *Case References*:

"We recognize there are substantial differences between the patent and copyright laws. But in both areas the contributory infringement doctrine is grounded on the recognition that adequate protection of a monopoly may require the courts to look beyond actual duplication of a device or publication to the products or activities that make such duplication possible. The staple article of commerce doctrine must strike a balance between a copyright holder's legitimate demand for effective—not merely symbolic—protection of the statutory monopoly, and the rights of others freely to engage in substantially unrelated areas of commerce. Accordingly, the sale of copying equipment, like the sale of other articles of commerce, does not constitute contributory infringement if the product is widely used for legitimate, unobjectionable purposes. Indeed, it need merely be capable of substantial noninfringing uses [in order for its sale not to constitute contributory copyright infringement]." *Sony Corp. v. Universal City Studios, Inc.*, 464 U.S. 417, 442, 220 USPQ 665, 678 (1984).

CONTU [copyright–computer] An acronym for the National Commission on New Technological Uses of Copyrighted Works. Established in 1974 by Congress, CONTU was composed of experts in the field and was ordered to study copyright problems arising in connection with (1) computer uses of data and (2) photocopying machines. CONTU rendered its final report in 1979.

CONTU Recommendations Enacted. Congress enacted into law the following two computer-related recommendations of CONTU: (1) a definition of "computer program" in the Copyright Act, 17 U.S.C. §101; and (2) a new §117, which provides that it is not copyright infringement for the owner of a copy of a computer program to make another copy for the two limited purposes of "archival" (a back-up in the event the original copy is impaired or destroyed) or when necessary to use the program by loading the program into computer memory or onto a computer hard disk. The courts have accepted the recommendation of the CONTU majority that data or programs written in machine-readable language (OBJECT CODE) are copyrightable and protectible against copying. See, e.g., *Apple Computer, Inc. v. Franklin Computer Corp.*, 714 F.2d 1240, 1252, 219 USPQ 113, 123 (3d Cir. 1983) ("[W]e can consider the CONTU Report as accepted by Congress since Congress wrote into law the majority's recommendations almost verbatim."); *Lotus Dev. Corp. v. Paperback Software Int'l*, 749 F. Supp. 37, 54, 15 USPQ2d 1577, 1588 (D. Mass. 1990) (While the CONTU Report is not an "offical voice of Congress," its views are persuasive as to the meaning of what Congress intended.).

convention date [patent–trademark] A date of filing an application for patent or trademark registration in a foreign nation that is a party to the PARIS CONVENTION—one of the main intellectual property international treaties. Under the "right of priority" provisions of the Paris Convention, as implemented by domestic federal law, an applicant in the United States is entitled to have its U.S. application treated as though it were filed on the same day as its previous foreign filing date. Thus, qualified parties are given in the United States the priority benefits that flow from an earlier filing date abroad.

• *Treatise Reference*: "The right of priority means that, on the basis of a regular application for an industrial property right filed by a given applicant in one of the member countries, the same applicant (or its successor in title) may, within a specified period of time (six or 12 months), apply for protection in all the other member countries. These later applications will then be regarded as if they had been filed on the same day as the first (or earlier) application. In other words, these later applications enjoy a priority status.... The length of the priority period is different according to the various kinds of industrial property rights. For patents for invention and utility models the priority period is 12 months, for industrial designs and trademarks it is six months." WIPO, *Background Reading Material on Intellectual Property* 53–54 (1988).

1. Convention Priority Date for Patent. A person applying for a utility patent in the United States can be entitled to a convention priority filing date based on the filing of an application for the same invention in a qualified foreign country within the preceding 12 months. That is, the U.S. application is treated as if it were filed on the same day that the qualified foreign application was filed abroad. This provision of the PARIS CONVENTION is implemented in the U.S. Patent Code §119, 35 U.S.C. §119. The term is six months for a design patent. Patent Code §172, 35 U.S.C. §172.

Conditions. To be eligible for obtaining the benefit of the "convention date" of the foreign filing, several conditions must be met: (1) the U.S. filing must be within 12 months of the foreign filing; (2) the foreign filing must have been in an eligible nation that is a party to the Paris Convention; (3) the U.S. application must be for the same invention as the foreign application; (4) the foreign application must have been for a patent, not some other form of protection; and (5) the U.S. application and the foreign application must be filed by the same entity or an assignee of that entity.

Grace Period. However, Patent Code §119 specifically provides an important exception to obtaining the benefit of the foreign filing date: the foreign filing does not toll the one-year GRACE PERIOD, which requires that an application for patent must be filed in the United States within one year after description of the invention in a PRINTED PUBLICATION, PUBLIC USE of the invention, or placing the invention ON SALE.

• *Treatise Reference*: 3 D. Chisum, *Patents* §14.03 (1994 rev.).

• *Case Reference*: "Generally, an applicant may antedate prior art by relying on a previously filed foreign application to establish an effective date earlier than that of the reference.... Under section 119, the claims set forth in a United States application are entitled to the benefit of a foreign priority date if the corresponding foreign application supports the claims in the manner required by section 112." *In re Gosteli*, 872 F.2d 1008, 1010, 10 USPQ2d 1614, 1616 (Fed. Cir. 1989).

2. Convention Priority Date for Trademark Registration. Under Lanham Act §44(d), 15 U.S.C. §1126(d), an application in the United States for registration of a mark by a person whose country of origin is a party to the Paris Convention is entitled to a priority convention filing date as of the date of filing of a prior trademark application in a foreign country that is also a party to the Paris Convention. However, the following conditions must apply: (1) the U.S. application must be filed within six months from the date of the foreign application; and (2) if use in the United States is not claimed, the U.S. registration will not be granted until the

foreign registration is granted and proof of that is supplied to the U.S. Patent and Trademark Office.

• *Treatise References*: 3 J.T. McCarthy, *Trademarks and Unfair Competition* §29.05 (3d ed. 1995 rev.).

Convention of the International Union for the Protection of New Plant Varieties (UPOV) [patent–trademark] This international treaty organization guarantees to plant breeders in member nations national treatment and a right of priority in all other member nations. As of 1990, 19 nations were party to the treaty. The UPOV does not yet apply to protection of sexually reproduced plants protected under the Plant Variety Protection Act.

See PLANT PATENT.

Effect in the United States. In 1981, the UPOV came into effect in the United States. See *Manual of Patent Examining Procedure* §1612 (1994). Amendments to the U.S. Plant Variety Protection Act signed into law in 1990 and 1994 brought the Plant Variety Protection Act into harmonization with the UPOV. It was held that the UPOV was an executive agreement not ratified by the U.S. Senate and could not override conflicting federal patent statutes. *Ex Parte Hibberd*, 227 USPQ 443, 447 (Bd. Pat. App. & Int'f. 1985). See 1 D. Chisum, *Patents* §1.05 (1994 rev.).

Plant Names. The UPOV provides that a new plant variety shall be designated by a name destined to be its generic designation, and member nations will ensure that no rights in the name "shall hamper the free use of the denomination in connection with the variety, even after the expiration of the [plant patent] protection." See Schlosser, *The Registration of Plant Variety Denominations*, 29 IDEA 177 (1988); 1 J.T. McCarthy, *Trademarks and Unfair Competition* §12.11[4] (3d ed. 1995 rev.).

See text of the UPOV at M. Leaffer, *International Treaties on Intellectual Property* 53 (1990).

copies [copyright] As a noun, "copies" means the material objects that store or fix copyrightable information other than sounds. As a verb, "copies" means the act of "COPYING," an element required for copyright infringement.

Material Objects That Store Copyrightable Works. In the nomenclature of the Copyright Act, there are only two kinds of material objects in which a copyrightable work is capable of being "FIXED" or stored: "copies" and "PHONORECORDS." These two definitions are mutually exclusive. Phonorecords are any material objects that store sound, other than the soundtrack for an AUDIOVISUAL WORK such as a MOTION PICTURE. "Copies" are any material objects that store copyrightable works, including a motion picture with its accompanying soundtrack.

New Technology. In defining "copies," Congress left the door open for the accommodation of unforeseen developments in information storage technology by providing that a work can be "fixed by any method now known or later developed" and that it makes no difference if the work can only be perceived or communicated "with the aid of a machine or device." It has been held that the loading of software into a computer's RAM was the creation of a fixed "copy" of the software. *MAI Sys. Corp. v. Peak Computer Inc.*, 991 F.2d 511, 519, 26 USPQ2d 1458, 1464 (9th Cir. 1993). ("The representation is 'sufficiently permanent or stable to permit it to be perceived, reproduced, or otherwise communicated for a period of more than transitory duration.' ")

Singular Is Plural. The statutory definition of "copies" has one somewhat jolting grammatical twist in that the single original manifestation of a work, such as an original oil painting or stone sculpture, is defined as being "copies."

See COPYING, PHONORECORDS.

Statutory Reference: 17 U.S.C. §101: " 'Copies' are material objects, other than phonorecords, in which a work is fixed by any method now known or later developed, and from which the work can be perceived, reproduced, or otherwise communicated, either directly or with the aid of a machine or device. The term 'copies' includes the material object, other than a phonorecord, in which the work is first fixed."

copying [copyright–patent–trademark] The act of reproducing or imitating another's idea, concept, market fad, invention, or the like. Copying may or may not be illegal, depending on whether the original can be shown to be protectible INTELLECTUAL PROPERTY.

Copying Is Not Per Se Illegal. The first principle of unfair competition law is that everything that is not protected by an intellectual property right is free to copy. In fact, copying is an essential part of the whole fabric of an economic system of free competition. Every competitor is to some extent an imitator. Thus, the act of "copying," far from being intrinsically improper, is essential and should be lauded and encouraged, not condemned. There is absolutely nothing legally or morally reprehensible about exact copying of things in the public domain. See 1 J.T. McCarthy, *Trademarks and Unfair Competition* §§1.01[2], 1.15[3] (3d ed. 1995 rev.). For example, evidence that a junior user exactly copied unprotected descriptive, generic, or functional public domain words or shapes does not prove any legal or moral wrongs. *Murphy v. Provident Mut. Life Ins. Co.*, 923 F.2d 923, 17 USPQ2d 1299 (2d Cir. 1990) ("Absent some legally defined exclusive right, the law permits and encourages imitation and copying of marks that are in the public domain."). On the other hand, copying a feature that is the subject of intellectual property owned by another can be an illegal and tortious act, and even a crime in some circumstances. It is essential to keep this distinction in mind.

1. Copying in Copyright Law. "Copying" denotes two separate, albeit interrelated, concepts. To constitute an infringement of copyright, the accused work (1) must be a "copy" in the sense that it is substantially similar to the copyrighted work allegedly infringed; and (2) even if substantially similar, the accused work must have been "copied" from the copyrighted work, as opposed to the similarity being the result of coincidental, independent production or the result of being taken from the same prior source as was the copyrighted work. The requirement of copying under (2) distinguishes infringement of copyright from infringement of PATENTS and TRADEMARKS, neither of which require proof of copying.

Reasons for Similarity in Works. In an infringement suit, similarity between the works will usually be due to one of three possibilities: (1) the defendant had access to the plaintiff's work and copied from it, either consciously or unconsciously; (2) the defendant did not copy from the plaintiff's work and independent creation has resulted in a work that is coincidentally similar; or (3) both the plaintiff and the defendant based their works on a common prior source.

Circumstantial Evidence of Copying. Direct evidence of copying is rare indeed, for copying can be accomplished with little physical manifestation. Usually copying is proved by circumstantial evidence. Evidence that the accused work was the result of copying generally consists of proof that (1) the defendant had ACCESS to the copyrighted work and (2) the defendant's work is substantially similar to the copyrighted work. *Sid & Marty Krofft Television Prods., Inc. v. McDonald's Corp.*, 562 F.2d 1157, 1163, 196 USPQ 97, 101 (9th Cir. 1977); *Reyher v. Children's Television Workshop*, 533 F.2d 87, 90, 190 USPQ 387, 390 (2d Cir. 1976).

See ACCESS, SUBSTANTIAL SIMILARITY, UNCONSCIOUS INFRINGEMENT.

- *Treatise References*: 3 *Nimmer on Copyright* §13.01[B] (1994 rev.); 2 P. Goldstein, *Copyright* §7.2 (1989); M. Leaffer, *Understanding Copyright* §9.2 (1989); W. Patry, *Copyright Law and Practice* 556 (1994); 1 N. Boorstyn, *Copyright* §11.03 (2d ed. 1994).

- *Case References*:

"Proof of copying is crucial to any claim of copyright infringement because no matter how similar the two works may be (even to the point of identity), if the defendant did not copy the [copyrighted] work, there is no infringement.... However, because direct evidence of copying is rarely available, the plaintiff can rely upon circumstantial evidence to prove this essential element, and the most important component of this sort of circumstantial evidence is proof of access...." *Selle v. Gibb*, 741 F.2d 896, 901, 223 USPQ 195, 198 (7th Cir. 1984).

"As in most infringement cases of this kind, no direct evidence was developed that [defendant] or anybody else copied any version of [plaintiff's video game] product. There seldom is any direct evidence of copying in these matters. Therefore, copying may be established instead by circumstantial evidence of (1) the defendant's access to the copyrighted work prior to defendant's creation of its work, and (2) the substantial similarity of both the general ideas and expression between the copyrighted work and defendant's work.... In essence, the question of copying becomes a matter of reasonable inferences." *Data East USA Inc. v. Epyx Inc.*, 862 F.2d 204, 206, 9 USPQ2d 1322, 1324 (9th Cir. 1988).

2. Copying in Patent Law. A showing that competitors have found it necessary to copy the patent owner's patented device is relevant evidence of the NONOBVIOUSNESS and patentability of the invention. However, it must be proven that the copying was motivated by the superior merits of the patented aspects of the device, not by other reasons.

Copying is one of the types of objective evidence of real world recognition of the invention, known as SECONDARY CONSIDERATIONS, which argue in favor of the nonobviousness of the invention. "That Dennison, a large corporation with many engineers on its staff, did not copy any prior art device, but found it necessary to copy the cable tie of the claims in suit, is equally strong evidence of nonobviousness." *Panduit Corp. v. Dennison Mfg. Co.*, 774 F.2d 1082, 1099, 227 USPQ 337, 349 (Fed. Cir. 1985).

The fact that products embodying the invention were copied is closely related to evidence that the invention succeeded in solving a problem where there was a LONG FELT NEED and prior FAILURE OF OTHERS to solve the same problem or fill the same need.

The opposite of copying is INDEPENDENT DEVELOPMENT by others, which, in limited circumstances, can be evidence of the obviousness, and hence unpatentablity, of the invention.

See SECONDARY CONSIDERATIONS, COMMERCIAL SUCCESS, UNEXPECTED RESULTS, FAILURE OF OTHERS.

- *Treatise Reference*: R. Harmon, *Patents and the Federal Circuit* §4.6(c) (3d ed. 1994).

• *Case References*:

The Court of Appeals for the Federal Circuit has emphasized the need for proof of a nexus between copying and the merits of the claimed invention, noting that copying can be motivated by many other reasons. "It is our conclusion that more than the mere fact of copying by an accused infringer is needed to make that action significant to a determination of the obviousness issue.... Rather than supporting a conclusion of [non]obviousness, copying could have occurred out of a general lack of concern for patent property, in which case it weighs neither for nor against the nonobviousness of a specific patent.... Even widespread copying could weigh toward opposite conclusions, depending on the attitudes existing toward patent property and the accepted practices in the industry in question. It is simplistic to assert that copying per se should bolster the validity of a patent." *Cable Elec. Prods., Inc. v. Genmark, Inc.*, 770 F.2d 1015, 1028, 226 USPQ 881, 889 (Fed. Cir. 1985).

"The copying of an invention may constitute evidence that the invention is not an obvious one.... This would be particularly true where the copyist had itself attempted for a substantial length of time to design a similar device, and had failed." But the Court of Appeals for the Federal Circuit held that in this case alleged copying was not important because (1) the design project was given a low priority by the alleged infringer with no concerted effort to design a new product for some years; (2) the infringer did not entirely fail in its independent design efforts; and (3) the copying involved nonpatentable dimensions, not the basic concept of the patented invention. *Vandenberg v. Dairy Equip. Co.*, 740 F.2d 1560, 1567, 224 USPQ 195, 199 (Fed. Cir. 1984).

3. Copying in Trademark Law. Copying is not necessary to prove trademark infringement. The test is whether there is a likelihood of confusion, which can be created whether or not the accused infringer was personally aware of the senior user's mark and whether or not the accused infringer deliberately copied. However, proof of copying can be evidence that the infringement was willful, deliberate, or calculated, which is relevant to proving infringement by likelihood of confusion and to the recovery of remedies such as profits of the infringer and attorney fees, as well as establishing counterfeiting.

Evidence of Infringement. While willful or intentional infringement is not necessary to prove trademark infringement, proof of willful or calculated behavior may raise a presumption of a likelihood of confusion. If an intent to confuse can be inferred from evidence such as willful copying, then some courts will presume that the accused in fact succeeded in its purpose, and that confusion is indeed likely. see, e.g., *Spring Mills, Inc. v. Ultracashmire House, Ltd.*, 689 F.2d 1127, 1136, 217 USPQ 298, 306 (2d Cir. 1982). Other courts do not permit proof of deliberate copying to raise a presumption of likely confusion, but do consider such evidence as one of several factors to be weighed. *Schwinn Bicycle Co. v. Ross Bicycles, Inc.*, 870 F.2d 1176, 10 USPQ2d 1001 (7th Cir. 1989). See 2 J.T. McCarthy, *Trademarks and Unfair Competition* §23.34 (3d ed. 1995 rev.).

See WILLFUL INFRINGEMENT.

copying a claim [patent] A procedure in a patent INTERFERENCE proceeding by which an applicant copies either (1) the claim of an issued patent having the same subject matter so that both contesting inventors will have the same claim or (2) a claim suggested by the Patent and Trademark Office primary examiner. The applicant adopts or "copies" into its application by amendment the claim of the patent or the examiner's suggested claim that covers an inventive concept also covered by the application. This claim will then be defined as the contested COUNT. Who was the first to invent the subject matter defined by that count will be determined in the INTERFERENCE proceeding.

• *Rule Reference*: "The examiner may suggest that an applicant present a claim in an application for the purpose of an interference with another application or a patent. The applicant to whom the claim is suggested shall amend the application by presenting the suggested claim within a time specified by the examiner...." 37 C.F.R. §1.605(a).

● *Case References*:

"Having copied the claims from Bernier's '193 patent, DeGeorge must show by clear and convincing evidence that the disclosure on which he relies supports the copied claims that became the interference counts." *DeGeorge v. Bernier*, 768 F.2d 1318, 1321, 226 USPQ 758, 760 (Fed. Cir. 1985).

"The copier of claims for interference purposes must show support in the copier's specification for every material limitation of the proposed count." *Martin v. Mayer*, 823 F.2d 500, 503, 3 USPQ2d 1333, 1336 (Fed. Cir. 1987).

copyright [copyright] A federal right owned by every author of a work to exclude others from doing any of the following five activities in connection with the copyrighted work: (1) reproduction; (2) adaptation; (3) distribution to the public; (4) performance in public; or (5) display in public. 17 U.S.C. §106. For works created since January 1, 1978, copyright protection exists from the moment of creation and FIXATION of a work for all original works of authorship fixed in any tangible medium of expression. 17 U.S.C. §§102(a), 302(a). Under the IDEA-EXPRESSION dichotomy, copyright does not protect an abstract idea; copyright protects only a specific, concrete expression of an idea. 17 U.S.C. §102(b). To be valid, a copyrighted work must have ORIGINALITY and some modicum of CREATIVITY.

Right to Exclude, Not Right to Use. Copyright is not a right to use the copyrighted work; rather it is a right to exclude others from use of the work. Having a valid copyright on a DERIVATIVE WORK does not immunize that work from being an infringement of copyright in an underlying work on which the derivative work is based. Having a copyright on a photograph does not immunize the copyright owner from liability for other forms of illegal use of the photograph, such as not paying taxes for income from reproducing the photograph, publishing a photograph so as to invade the subject's privacy, or using the photograph in an advertisement, infringing the subject's right of publicity. See *Fox Film Corp. v. Doyal*, 286 U.S. 123, 128 (1932) (copyright ownership does not immunize owner from having to pay taxes on royalties from showing of copyrighted motion pictures); J.T. McCarthy, *The Rights of Publicity and Privacy* §11.14[C] (1995 rev.).

Copyright Legislation. The first U.S. copyright statute was passed in 1790. General revisions of the copyright law occurred in 1831 and 1870, and a major overhaul was accomplished with the 1909 Act. Starting in the 1950s, studies and congressional committee hearings lasted for decades and resulted in a major rewriting of the copyright law signed by the President in October 1976. This legislation did not generally become effective until January 1, 1978, a date of major significance in copyright analysis. A second major event occurred on March 1, 1989, when the United States made significant changes to domestic law in order to qualify to join the BERNE CONVENTION, the major copyright treaty organization. That legislation is known as the BERNE CONVENTION IMPLEMENTATION ACT (BCIA).

Copyright Formalities. Until the March 1, 1989, effective date of the Berne Convention Implementation Act (BCIA), copyright could be forfeited for failure to properly mark publicly distributed copies with a copyright NOTICE. For copies distributed since that date, while copyright cannot be lost by the distribution of copies containing no notice, the use of copyright notice is still highly recommended. The United States is unique in having a system of copyright REGISTRATION administered by a large government office maintaining copyright records. Registration with the Copyright Office has never created the rights of copyright nor has it marked the beginning of the DURATION of copyright. However, prompt registration maximizes the copyright owner's legal remedies against infringers and creates a PRESUMPTION OF COPYRIGHT VALIDITY.

Copyright Infringement. COPYING denotes two separate, but interrelated, concepts. To constitute an infringement of copyright, (1) the ACCUSED WORK must be a "copy" in the sense that it is substantially similar to the protected expression in the copyrighted work allegedly infringed; and (2) even if substantially similar, the accused work must have been "copied" from the copyrighted work, as opposed to the similarity being the result of coincidental, independent production. Evidence of copying usually consists of proof that the defendant had ACCESS to the copyrighted work and the defendant's work is substantially similar. Determining whether the accused work bears a SUBSTANTIAL SIMILARITITY to the copyrighted work is one of the most difficult areas of copyright law. The defense of FAIR USE is available for certain acts that would otherwise be an infringement but that have little impact on the market for the copyrighted work. The remedies of copyright infringement are an injunction and damages and/or PROFITS of the infringers. Copyright owners are also given the option to elect recovery of STATUTORY DAMAGES instead of actual damages and profits. Those who assist others to infringe can be liable for CONTRIBUTORY INFRINGEMENT of a copyright. Infringement need not be deliberate and knowing: it can be UNCONSCIOUS INFRINGEMENT.

Criminal Copyright Infringement. Anyone who infringes a copyright willfully and for purposes of commercial advantage is guilty of criminal copyright infringement. 17 U.S.C. §506(a).

Criminal infringement of copyright is a federal crime punishable by a maximum one-year imprisonment and/or a maximum fine of $250,000. 18 U.S.C. §2319. If the infringement consists of the reproduction or distribution during any 180-day period of at least 10 copies or phonorecords of one or more copyrighted works having a retail value of more than $2,500, then the maximum punishment is five years and/or a fine. A second or subsequent offense is punishable by up to 10 years in prison, a fine, or both. 18 U.S.C. §2319. See W. Patry, *Copyright Law and Practice* 1181 (1994).

Compulsory Licenses. As a result of legislative compromise between advocates of full copyright and advocates of free use, Congress created a COMPULSORY LICENSING system administered by the COPYRIGHT ROYALTY TRIBUNAL (CRT) for five types of uses of copyrighted works: (1) cable television; (2) the making of phonorecords of MUSICAL WORKS (the MECHANICAL LICENSE); (3) the use of musical works on jukeboxes (repealed as of 1993); (4)

the use of certain works on public broadcasting; and (5) the use of copyrighted works in certain satellite retransmissions.

See COMPULSORY LICENSING OF A COPYRIGHT.

Assignment and Licensing. Under the 1909 Copyright Act, the rule was one of "indivisibility": a copyright was an indivisible property right incapable of being split up into smaller units and assigned or exclusively licensed. That rule was done away with in the 1978 Copyright Act. See ASSIGNMENT OF COPYRIGHT. There is a clear line between the significance of an exclusive and a nonexclusive license of copyright. An exclusive licensee is regarded as the owner of the particular rights of copyright that are exclusively licensed. See LICENSE OF COPYRIGHT. Particular kinds of copyright licenses are BLANKET LICENSES of the PERFORMING RIGHTS SOCIETIES and BLOCK BOOKING of films. Copyright TRANSFERS are the subject of RECORDATION in the Copyright Office.

Federal and State Law Coexistence. The U.S. copyright statutes are passed by the U.S. Congress under a specific grant of power contained in the Patent and Copyright Clause of the CONSTITUTION. State law protection for certain works does not overlap with federal copyright, but can give protection to works not within the subject matter of the federal copyright statute and can even give protection to works within the subject matter of the federal copyright law so long as the state right is not equivalent to the exclusive rights of a federal copyright. In §301(a) of the Copyright Act, Congress set up a two-level test, stating that there is federal preemption only if: (1) the state right is "equivalent" to the exclusive rights of a federal copyright; *and* (2) the state right is "within the subject matter of copyright" as defined in §106 of the Act. The first element relates to the kinds of rights granted by state law, and the second element relates to the nature of the work in which rights are claimed. "Unfixed" works, such as an unrecorded spontaneous jazz music composition or an unrecorded, unscripted interview, are not covered by federal law and are clearly open to state law protection. 17 U.S.C. §301(b)(1). See FIXED.

International Relations. Since 1952 the United States has been a member of the UNIVERSAL COPYRIGHT CONVENTION, a multilateral treaty, which was tailored to the peculiarities of U.S. law. For various reasons, the United States did not join the main copyright treaty organization, the BERNE CONVENTION, until March 1, 1989. Prior to that time, U.S. authors and publishers had to use the so-called BACK DOOR TO BERNE to acquire the benefits of the Berne Convention.

See ORIGINALITY, CREATIVITY, COPYING, SUBSTANTIAL SIMILARITY, INFRINGEMENT OF COPYRIGHT, DERIVATIVE WORK, DURATION OF COPYRIGHT.

• *Treatise References*: *Nimmer on Copyright* (1994 rev.); P. Goldstein, *Copyright* (1989); W. Patry, *Copyright Law and Practice* (1994); N. Boorstyn, *Copyright* (2d ed. 1994); M. Leaffer, *Understanding Copyright* (1989).

• *Statutory References*:

17 U.S.C. §102:

(a) Copyright subsists, in accordance with this title, in original works of authorship fixed in any tangible medium of expression, now known or later developed, from which they can be perceived, reproduced, or otherwise communicated, either directly or with the aid of a machine or device. Works of authorship include the following categories:

(1) literary works;

(2) musical works, including any accompanying words;

(3) dramatic works, including any accompanying music;

(4) pantomimes and choreographic works;

(5) pictorial, graphic, and sculptural works;

(6) motion pictures and other audiovisual works; and

(7) sound recordings.

(b) In no case does copyright protection for an original work of authorship extend to any idea, procedure, process, system, method of operation, concept, principle, or discovery, regardless of the form in which it is described, explained, illustrated, or embodied in such work.

17 U.S.C. §106:

Subject to sections 107 through 118, the owner of copyright under this title has the exclusive right to do and to authorize any of the following:

(1) to reproduce the copyrighted work in copies or phonorecords;

(2) to prepare derivative works based upon the copyrighted work;

(3) to distribute copies or phonorecords of the copyrighted work to the public by sale or other transfer of ownership, by rental, lease, or lending;

(4) in the case of literary, musical, dramatic, and choreographic works, pantomimes, and motion pictures and other audiovisual works, to perform the copyrighted work publicly; and

(5) in the case of literary, musical, dramatic, and choreographic works, pantomimes, and pictorial, graphic, or sculptural works, including the individual images of a motion picture or other audiovisual work, to display the copyrighted work publicly.

• *Case References*:

"The economic philosophy behind the clause empowering Congress to grant patents and copyrights is the conviction that encouragement of individual effort by personal gain is the best way to advance public welfare through the talents of authors and inventions in 'Science and useful Arts.' Sacrificial days devoted to such creative activities deserve rewards commensurate with the services rendered." *Mazer v. Stein*, 347 U.S. 201, 219, 100 USPQ 325, 333 (1954).

"The [constitutional] clause thus describes both the objective which Congress may seek and the means to achieve it. The objective is to promote the progress of science and the arts. As employed, the terms 'to promote' are synonymous with the words 'to stimulate,' 'to encourage,' or 'to induce.' To accomplish its purpose, Congress may grant to authors the exclusive right to the fruits of their respective works. An author who possesses an unlimited copyright may preclude others from copying his creation for commercial purposes without permission. In other words, to encourage people to devote themselves to intellectual and artistic creation, Congress may guarantee to authors and inventors a reward in the form of control over the sale or commercial use of copies of their works." *Goldstein v. California*, 412 U.S. 546, 555, 178 USPQ 129, 133 (1973).

"Creative work is to be encouraged and rewarded, but private motivation must ultimately serve the cause of promoting broad public availability of literature, music, and the other arts. The immediate effect of our copyright law is to secure a fair return for an 'author's' creative labor. But the ultimate aim is, by this incentive, to stimulate artistic creativity for the general public good." *Twentieth Century Music Corp. v. Aiken*, 422 U.S. 151, 156, 186 USPQ 65, 67 (1975).

"[Defendant] argues that every copyright must further the ends of the Copyright Clause of the Constitution. [Plaintiff's] copyright, [defendant] says, does not further those ends and should not be enforced because [plaintiff] systematically destroys its broadcast videotapes and deprives the public of the benefit of its creative efforts. We agree that the Constitution allows Congress to create copyright laws only if they benefit society as a whole rather than authors alone. That is what Congress has done. But this does not mean that every copyright holder must offer benefits to society, for the copyright is an incentive rather than a command. And, a fortiori, a copyright holder need not provide the most complete public access possible." *Pacific & S. Co. v. Duncan*, 744 F.2d 1490, 1498, 224 USPQ 131, 136 (11th Cir. 1984).

Copyright Arbitration Royalty Panels

[copyright] A system of ad hoc arbitration panels that set the royalty rates for certain copyright compulsory licenses and in some cases is charged with apportioning the revenues to recipients.

Creation of the Panels. The Copyright Arbitration Royalty Panel (CARP) system was created by the Copyright Royalty Tribunal Reform Act of 1993 (Pub. L. No. 103-198, 107 Stat. 2304), which discontinued the COPYRIGHT ROYALTY TRIBUNAL (CRT). The CRT's duties were transferred to a system of ad hoc panels (CARPs) administered by the Librarian of Congress and the Copyright Office.

Composition of the Panels. Instead of a single administrative body like the former CRT, the new system features a division of authority. The Librarian of Congress and the Copyright Office are now responsible for doing the preliminary work necessary for the operation of both the distribution and the rate adjustment proceedings. This includes the selection and organization of the CARPs. Each CARP panel consists of three arbitrators, two of whom are chosen by the Librarian of Congress on recommendation of the Register of Copyrights. The third arbitrator, who is chosen by the other two arbitrators, acts as chair.

Responsibilities of the Panels. The primary task of the panels is to administer the COMPULSORY LICENSING system for certain uses of copyrighted materials. The panels are convened to make periodic adjustments in the compulsory license royalty rates for: (1) certain retransmissions of copyrighted programs by cable television; (2) the production of PHONORECORDS using copyrighted musical works; (3) the use of musical works on jukeboxes if voluntary licenses cannot be achieved; (4) the broadcast of certain copyrighted works on public noncommercial broadcasting stations if voluntary licenses are not achieved; and (5) certain satellite retransmissions of copyrighted material. The panels may also distribute device and media royalties collected from the sale of digital audio recording devices and media.

See COMPULSORY LICENSING OF A COPYRIGHT.

• *Treatise References*: 3 *Nimmer on Copyright* §14.11[A] (1994 rev.); 2 P. Goldstein, *Copyright* §12.4 (1989); W. Patry, *Copyright Law and Practice* 116 (1994).

Copyright Clearance Center [copyright]

The leading REPRODUCTION RIGHTS ORGANIZATION (RRO) in the United States, the Copyright Clearance Center (CCC) is a nongovernmental collective licensing organization that represents copyright owners. It licenses by prior agreement with rights holders the photocopying of their works by libraries, private corporations, and academic users. Royalties are paid by licensees to the CCC, which distributes them to the rights holders.

Services Available. CCC provides several services: (1) the Transactional Reporting Service (TRS), which gives users permission to photocopy any CCC-registered publication, and report and pay for copying after the fact; (2) the Annual Authorizations Service (AAS), which allows corporate users to purchase an annual license to photocopy for internal use material contained in any CCC-registered publication without reporting individual copying events; and (3) the Academic Permissions Service (APS), which was designed in the wake of *Basic Books v. Kinkos Graphics*, 758 F. Supp. 1552 (S.D.N.Y. 1991). The APS is a transactional license program for academic users at colleges and universities to obtain authorization to create course packets and anthologies using CCC-registered works. A digital uses license was in development for the corporate user and was planned to be available sometime in 1995.

Copyright Royalty Tribunal [copyright] A now-abolished independent administrative agency that set the royalty rates for certain copyright compulsory licenses and in some cases was charged with apportioning the revenues to recipients. Created by the 1978 Copyright Act revisions, the Copyright Royalty Tribunal (CRT) was abolished when the Copyright Royalty Tribunal Reform Act of 1993 became law. (Pub. L. No. 103-198, 107 Stat. 2304). The CRT's duties were transferred to a system of ad hoc COPYRIGHT ARBITRATION ROYALTY PANELS (CARPs) administered by the Librarian of Congress and the Copyright Office.

See COPYRIGHT ROYALTY ARBITRATION PANEL, COMPULSORY LICENSING OF A COPYRIGHT.

corporate receipt doctrine [copyright] A method of demonstrating that an alleged copyright infringer had ACCESS to a copyrighted work by showing that a third-party corporation, with whom both the copyright owner and the alleged infringer were dealing, had access to the copyrighted work.

Nexus Between Copyrighted Work and Accused Infringer. The majority of courts hold that in order to show that defendant had an opportunity to copy the plaintiff's work, a plaintiff must exhibit more than that defendant had a bare possibility of access. There must be a nexus between the alleged copier and the corporation that received the copyrighted work from the copyright owner. This nexus or relationship is shown by evidence that there is some "channel of communication" between the corporation to which the work was submitted by the copyright owner and the person who ultimately created the allegedly infringing work.

Channel of Communication. Once a channel of communication has been proven, most courts hold that the channel of communication between the corporate intermediary and the alleged copier must relate to the same subject matter. See *Meta-Film Assocs. v. MCA*, 586 F. Supp. 1346, 222 USPQ 211 (C.D. Cal. 1984) (no access because dealings involved unrelated subject matter); *Ferguson v. National Broadcasting Co.*, 584 F.2d 111, 200 USPQ 65 (5th Cir. 1976) (dealings on unrelated subject matter insufficient to establish chain of access). Nimmer suggests that proof of the fact of communication on any subject matter is sufficient for the trier of fact to find access. 3 *Nimmer on Copyright* §13.02[A] (1992 rev.).

• *Example 1*: Held to be not sufficient to sustain a finding of access was the submission of an unpublished screenplay to a director who was under contract to a film company and who had an office at the film company's lot, but whose only relationship to the alleged copiers was that they shared the same employer. *Meta-Film Assocs. v. MCA*, 586 F. Supp. 1346, 222 USPQ 211 (C.D. Cal. 1984).

• *Example 2*: The submission of an instrumental version of plaintiff's song to a director at defendant record company, who was supervised by a vice president, both of whom knew the alleged copiers, was sufficient to find a reasonable possibility of access. *Moore v. Columbia Pictures Indus.*, 972 F.2d 939, 23 USPQ2d 1864 (8th Cir. 1992).

correction, certificate of

See ACCESS, COPYING IN COPYRIGHT LAW

- *Treatise Reference*: W. Patry, *Copyright Law and Practice* 699 (1994) ("[A]ttempts to establish an inference of access through intermediaries such as literary agents, or through the so-called 'corporate receipt' theory, while theoretically possible, are seldom successful in practice."); 1 N. Boorstyn, *Copyright* §11.03[1][b] (2d ed. 1994).

- *Case Reference*: "[A]t a minimum, the dealings between the plaintiff and the intermediary and between the intermediary and the alleged copier must involve some overlap in the subject matter to permit inference of access." *Meta-Film Assocs. v. MCA*, 586 F. Supp. 1346, 1358, 222 USPQ 211, 220 (C.D. Cal. 1984).

- *Commentary Reference*: Brown, *The Corporate Receipt Conundrum: Establishing Access in Copyright Infringement Actions*, 77 Minn. L. Rev. 1409 (1993).

correction, certificate of   [patent–trademark–copyright]

1. Patent Certificate of Correction. A document issued by the Commissioner of Patents and Trademarks rectifying certain types of mistakes made in an issued patent. The following are types of mistakes:

(1) Mistakes incurred through the fault of the Patent and Trademark Office.

(2) Minor mistakes, such as clerical or typographical errors, incurred through the fault of the patent applicant. "A mistake is not of a minor character if the requested change would materially affect the scope of meaning of the patent." *Manual of Patent Examining Procedure* §1481 (1994 rev.).

(3) Erroneous inclusion or exclusion of a person as an inventor named on the patent if the error arose without deceptive intention.

The determination as to whether an error has been made, who is responsible, and if the error justifies issuance of a certificate of correction is made by the Certification of Correction Branch in the Patent and Trademark Office.

See AMENDMENT.

- *Statutory References*:

35 U.S.C. §254: *"Certificate of Correction of Patent and Trademark Office Mistake.* Whenever a mistake in a patent, incurred through the fault of the Patent and Trademark Office, is clearly disclosed by the records of the Office, the Commissioner may issue a certificate of correction stating the fact and nature of such mistake, under seal, without charge, to be recorded in the records of patents.... The Commissioner may issue a corrected patent without charge in lieu of and with like effect as a certificate of correction."

35 U.S.C. §255: *"Certificate of Correction of Applicant's Mistake.* Whenever a mistake of a clerical or typographical nature, or of minor character, which was not the fault of the Patent and Trademark Office, appears in a patent and a showing has been made that such mistake occurred in good faith, the Commissioner may, upon payment of the required fee, issue a certificate of correction, if the correction does not involve such changes in the patent as would constitute new matter or would require re-examination. Such patent, together with the certificate, shall have the same effect and operation in law on the trial of actions for causes thereafter arising as if the same had been originally issued in such corrected form."

35 U.S.C. §256: *"Correction of Named Inventor.* Whenever through error a person is named in an issued patent as the inventor, or through error an inventor is not named in an issued patent and such error arose without any deceptive intention on his part, the Commissioner may, on application of all the parties and assignees, with proof of the facts and such other requirements as may be imposed, issue a certificate correcting such error. The error of omitting inventors or naming persons who are not inventors shall not invalidate the patent in which such error occurred if it can be corrected as provided in this section...."

2. Trademark Registration Certificate of Correction. A document issued by the Commissioner of Patents and Trademarks rectifying certain types of mistakes made in a registration of a mark. The following are types of mistakes:

(1) Mistakes incurred through the fault of the Patent and Trademark Office (Lanham Act §7(g)).

(2) Mistakes incurred through the fault of the applicant for registration so long as the proposed change is not so major as to call for a new publication of the mark for opposition (Lanham Act §7(h)).

This rule prohibiting a change that would call for republication is probably coextensive with the amendment rule against changes that do not "alter materially the character of the mark." The object is to prevent presenting competitors with a registered mark that they have never had an opportunity to oppose. See *In re Holland Am. Wafer Co.*, 737 F.2d 1015, 222 USPQ 273 (Fed. Cir. 1984) (new version of trademark was an unpermitted "material alteration" of old version).

See AMENDMENT.

• *Statutory References*:

Lanham Act §7(g), 15 U.S.C. §1057(g): "Whenever a material mistake in a registration, incurred through the fault of the Patent and Trademark Office, is clearly disclosed by the records of the Office a certificate stating the fact and nature of such mistake shall be issued without charge and recorded and a printed copy thereof shall be attached to each printed copy of the registration...."

Lanham Act §7(h), 15 U.S.C. §1057(h): "Whenever a mistake has been made in a registration and a showing has been made that such mistake occurred in good faith through the fault of the applicant, the Commissioner is authorized to issue a certificate of correction or, in his discretion, a new certificate upon the payment of the required fee: *Provided*, That the correction does not involve such changes in the registration as to require republication of the mark."

3. Copyright Registration Correction. When information in a copyright registration was incorrect at the time the registration was made and when the error was not one that the Copyright Office should have recognized, the registration may be corrected by the filing of an application for a SUPPLEMENTARY REGISTRATION. This procedure is not appropriate to correct errors in the copyright NOTICE on copies of the work deposited with the registration.

The Register of Copyrights has the authority to "establish, by regulation, formal procedures for the filing of an application for supplementary registration, to correct an error in a copyright registration or to amplify the information given in a registration." 17 U.S.C. §408(d).

• *Rule Reference*: " ... (2) Supplementary registration may be made either to correct or to amplify the information in a basic registration.... (i) A 'correction' is appropriate if information in the basic registration was incorrect at the time that basic registration was made and the error is not one that the Copyright Office itself should have recognized; ... (iii) supplementary registration is not appropriate; ... (B) to correct errors in statements or notices on the copies or phonorecords of a work, or to reflect changes in the content of a work...." 37 C.F.R. §201.5(b).

corroboration [patent] The confirmation of the date of invention by additional evidence beyond the testimony of the inventor. The testimony of an inventor, without more, is not sufficient evidence of the date of invention by CONCEPTION and REDUCTION TO PRACTICE. The requirement of corroboration has been eased somewhat by the RULE OF REASON, under which all pertinent corroborating evidence is weighed and balanced to determine the credibility of the inventor's testimony of the date of invention. However, the rule of reason does not dispense with the necessity for some evidence of independent corroboration. While the inventor's oral testimony requires corroboration, corroborating evidence is not required to establish what a physical exhibit, such as a drawing, discloses or shows. "Only the inventor's testimony requires corroboration before it can be considered." *Price v. Symsek*, 988 F.2d 1187, 1195, 26 USPQ2d 1031, 1037 (Fed. Cir. 1993).

Nature of Corroborating Evidence. Corroborating evidence may be oral, for example, in the form of the testimony of one who witnessed and understood the reduction to practice of a new chemical composition. Or the evidence may be documentary, for example, in the form of the inventor's laboratory notebook, if the notebook was contemporaneously witnessed by another who understood what was described in the notebook. "Conception must be proved by corroborating evidence which shows that the inventor disclosed to others his 'completed thought expressed in such clear terms as to enable those skilled in the art' to make the invention." *Coleman v. Dines*, 754 F.2d 353, 359, 224 USPQ 857, 862 (Fed. Cir. 1985).

- *Treatise References*: 3 D. Chisum, *Patents* §§ 10.03–.06 (1994 rev.); 2 P. Rosenberg, *Patent Law Fundamentals* § 10.02[2] (1994 rev.).

- *Case References*:

"A corroboration analysis involves a reasoned examination and evaluation of all the pertinent evidence bearing on the credibility of the inventor.... In recent years, this court, by adopting a 'rule of reason,' has eased the requirement of corroboration with respect to the evidence necessary to establish the credibility of the inventor.... However, adoption of the 'rule of reason' has not altered the requirement that evidence of corroboration must not depend solely on the inventor himself.... Independent corroboration may consist of testimony of a witness, other than the inventor, to the actual reduction to practice or it may consist of evidence of surrounding facts and circumstances independent of information received from the inventor." *Reese v. Hurst v. Wiewiorowski*, 661 F.2d 1222, 1225, 211 USPQ 936, 940 (C.C.P.A. 1981).

"The objective sought in requiring independent corroboration of reduction to practice of a chemical composition invention is to insure that the inventor actually prepared the composition and knew it would work.... The standard is not inflexible and is not to be applied mechanically. Hence a 'rule of reason' approach is required.... Testimony of one who witnessed and understood the actual reduction to practice of a composition is strong evidence. Its absence need not be fatal, however, when other evidence is sufficient to corroborate such actual reduction to practice.... Though the requirement [of corroboration] does serve to impede fabrication and falsification, a finding of lack of corroborative evidence does not, of course, imply the

occurrence of such untoward conduct." *Minkus & Shaffer v. Wachtel*, 542 F.2d 1157, 1159–62, 191 USPQ 571, 573–75 (C.C.P.A. 1976).

"That some of the [laboratory] notebooks were not witnessed until a few months to one year after their writing does not make them incredible or necessarily of little corroborative value.... The notebooks clearly show facts underlying and contemporaneous with conception of the claimed invention and in conjunction with the testimony of [the inventors], and others, are altogether legally adequate documentary evidence under the law pertaining to conception, of the formation in the minds of the inventors of a definite and permanent idea of the complete and operative invention as it was thereafter applied in practice." *Hybritech Inc. v. Monoclonal Antibodies, Inc.*, 802 F.2d 1367, 1378, 231 USPQ 81, 89 (Fed. Cir. 1986).

"In this case ... we do not see how the laboratory notebook of Gortatowsky could be said to provide the necessary corroboration. In particular, it is noted that the notebook pages were not read and witnessed by anyone. In addition, Gortatowsky testified that he only attempted to keep his notebook entries in chronological order 'to a degree' and that it was his practice at times to leave blanks in the notebook which might be filled in at a later date. Thus, there isn't even adequate evidence here that the notebook itself was in existence and properly kept at the time alleged, let alone sufficient evidence in the notebook itself to in turn corroborate Gortatowsky's testimony." *Gortatowsky v. Anwar*, 442 F.2d 970, 972, 170 USPQ 41, 43 (C.C.P.A. 1971).

count [patent–general federal litigation]

1. Patent Interference Count. In an INTERFERENCE proceeding to determine who was the first inventor of the same invention, a count is the procedural vehicle for defining the invention common to the contesting inventors and over which the priority contest is fought. The count determines what evidence will be regarded as relevant on the issue of priority. All the claims in an interfering application or patent that define the same patentable invention will be designated to correspond to or be encompassed by a single count.

- *Rule Reference*: "A 'count' defines the interfering subject matter between (1) two or more applications or (2) one or more applications and one or more patents. When there is more than one count, each count shall define a separate patentable invention." 37 C.F.R. §1.601(f). "Each count shall define a separate patentable invention. Each application must contain, or be amended to contain, at least one claim which corresponds to each count." 37 C.F.R. §1.603.

- *Manual Reference*: "The following principles should be kept in mind: 1. Each count must be drawn to a separate patentable invention.… 2. A count should normally be sufficiently broad as to encompass the broadest corresponding patent claim of each of the parties.… 3. A count may not be so broad as to be unpatentable over the prior art.…" *Manual of Patent Examining Procedure* §2309.01 (1994).

- *Case References*:

"[T]he counts of the interference serve merely as a 'vehicle for contesting priority.' … The counts are not claims to an invention by either party. The purpose of the count is to determine what evidence is relevant to the issue of priority." *Case v. CPC Int'l, Inc.*, 730 F.2d 745, 749, 221 USPQ 196, 199 (Fed. Cir. 1984).

"The 'count' … is merely the vehicle for contesting priority which, in the opinion of the Commissioner, effectively circumscribes the interfering subject matter, thereby determining what evidence will be regarded as relevant on the issue of priority. The 'count,' as distinguished from a party's 'claim,' need not be patentable to either party in the sense of being fully supported by either party's disclosure." *Squirers v. Corbett*, 560 F.2d 424, 433, 194 USPQ 513, 519 (C.C.P.A. 1977).

- *Example 1*: "Application G contains patentable claims 1 (engine), 2 (6-cylinder engine), and 3 (engine with a platinum piston). Application H contains patentable claims 11 (engine) and 15 (engine with a platinum piston). Claims 1 and 2 of application G and claim 11 of appli-

cation H define the same patentable invention. Claim 3 of application G and claim 15 of application H define a [separate] patentable invention.… If an interference is declared, there will be two counts: Count 1 (engine) and Count 2 (engine with a platinum piston). Claims 1 and 2 of application G and claim 11 of application H would be designated to correspond to Count 1. Claim 3 of application G and claim 15 of application H would be designated to correspond to Count 2." *Manual of Patent Examining Procedure* §2309.01, Ex. 4 of count formulation (1994).

- *Example 2*: In 1987 a researcher at the University of Houston found that a yttrium, barium, copper, and oxygen compound would lose its electrical resistance at 90° K, a temperature much higher than previously known to be superconductive. But the researcher knew neither the chemical composition nor the crystalline structure of the material. The researcher went public and within a few weeks, other researchers figured out the exact nature of the superconducting material. Over a short span of time, the University of Houston and three other research teams filed patent applications on their inventions. The Patent and Trademark Office (PTO) declared an interference. The first step is for the PTO to formulate the count: to define the invention. For example, the count might define the invention as consisting of five parts: manufacture of the material; proof that it is a superconductor; analysis of the chemical composition of the compound; determination of its crystal structure; and preparation of a sample that is at least 90 percent pure. Whichever of the four contesting parties can show that it was first to invent all five elements would be granted priority and the patent. See Pool, *Superconductor Patents: Four Groups Duke It Out*, 245 Science 931 (Sept. 1, 1989).

See PHANTOM COUNT, LOST COUNT.

2. General Federal Litigation Count. In separating the allegations of fact and law made in a complaint or counterclaim, it is common to denominate as "counts" the separate legal theories of recovery alleged. For example, a complaint may label as "Count One" a claim for infringement of a federally registered trademark, "Count Two" as a claim for infringement of an unregistered mark under federal Lanham Act §43(a), and "Count Three" as a claim for infringement of an unregistered mark under the state common law of unfair competition.

counterfeiting [trademark] The act of producing or selling a product containing a sham mark that is an intentional and calculated reproduction of the genuine mark. A "counterfeit mark" is a false mark that is identical with, or substantially indistinguishable from, the genuine mark. Often, counterfeit goods are made to imitate a popular product in all details of construction and appearance so as to deceive customers into thinking they are purchasing the genuine merchandise. Counterfeiting is the most blatant and egregious form of PASSING OFF or trademark infringement.

PIRACY is usually used to refer to egregious infringement of copyright. However, trademark counterfeiters are also sometimes branded as "pirates" engaged in trademark piracy.

Criminal Remedies Against Counterfeiting. In 1984 Congress, for the first time, made trademark counterfeiting a federal crime. Pursuant to 18 U.S.C. §2320, the intentional trafficking in counterfeit goods or services is a federal crime subject to maximum penalties against a person of $2,000,000 and/or ten years in prison and a maximum fine of $5,000,000 against a corporation. All Lanham Act trademark affirmative defenses are available in a criminal prosecution. For criminal prosecution purposes, a "counterfeit mark" is a spurious mark used in connection with goods or services that is identical with or substantially indistinguishable from a mark registered for those goods or services on the federal principal register, whether or not the defendant knew such mark was registered, when the defendant's use is likely to cause confusion or mistake or to deceive. 18 U.S.C. §2320(d). It has been held that a "counterfeit" is not limited to goods that deceive only the immediate purchaser. The fact that the buyer of a counterfeit ROLEX watch knows that it is a fake does not mean that there is not confusion by those who observe the buyer wearing the watch or by recipients of it as a gift. *United States v. Gantos*, 817 F.2d 41, 2 USPQ2d 1536

(8th Cir. 1987); *United States v. Yamin*, 868 F.2d 130, 10 USPQ2d 1300 (5th Cir. 1989). Ignorance of the fact that selling counterfeit goods is a crime is no defense. *United States v. Baker*, 807 F.2d 427, 1 USPQ2d 1485 (5th Cir. 1986). The definition of "counterfeit mark" excludes a mark used on goods if, at the time of production, the maker was authorized to use the mark. This effectively excludes from the definition parallel imports, gray goods, and production overruns. 18 U.S.C. §2320(d)(1). See 3 J.T. McCarthy, *Trademarks and Unfair Competition* §30.33 (3d ed. 1995 rev.).

Civil Remedies Against Counterfeiting. In 1984 Congress, for the first time, empowered judges to grant ex parte seizure orders in counterfeit goods civil cases. The legislation also mandated certain monetary remedies.

The 1984 Act amended §§34, 35, and 36 of the Lanham Act, 15 U.S.C. §§1116, 1117, and 1118. The definition of "counterfeit mark" excludes a mark used on goods if the manufacturer was at the time of production authorized to use the mark. This effectively excludes parallel imports, gray goods, and production overruns from the definition. Lanham Act §34(d)(1)(B), 15 U.S.C. §1116(d)(1)(B). Prior to the 1984 Act, while some courts permitted ex parte restraining orders to seize counterfeit goods, there was uncertainty as to the appropriate circumstances and procedural steps required. Lanham Act §34(d), 15 U.S.C. §1116(d), grants the courts the power in counterfeit goods cases to issue ex parte orders for the seizure of counterfeit goods and records documenting the manufacture or sale of such goods. Various procedural steps must be observed by the plaintiff, and a prompt hearing on the seizure is required. As to remedies, the 1984 law added language requiring that unless the court finds extenuating circumstances, treble damages or PROFITS and a reasonable ATTORNEY FEE AWARD are to be given to an infringed trademark owner if the defendant counterfeiter intentionally dealt in the counterfeit goods and knew that the goods were counterfeit. Lanham Act §35(b), 15 U.S.C. §1117(b). In such cases, the court has discretion to award PREJUDGMENT INTEREST. The intent and knowledge elements are satisfied if a retailer is guilty of "willful blindness": if the seller "failed to inquire further because he was afraid of what the inquiry would yield." *Louis Vuitton S.A. v. Lee*, 875 F.2d 584, 10 USPQ2d 1935 (7th Cir. 1989). See 3 J.T. McCarthy, *Trademarks and Unfair Competition* §§30.16[2], 30.28[4] (3d ed. 1995 rev.).

Tariff Act Remedies Against Imported Goods Bearing a Counterfeit Mark. The Tariff Act was amended in 1978 to include more stringent import remedies against goods bearing a counterfeit mark. 19 U.S.C. §1526(e). The Tariff Act adopts by reference the Lanham Act §45 definition of "counterfeit" (see below). The standard of whether a mark on imported goods is a "counterfeit" is determined from the point of view of the "average purchaser," not the "expert" who minutely inspects and compares the marks. *Montres Rolex S.A. v. Snyder*, 718 F.2d 524, 528, 220 USPQ 10, 13 (2d Cir. 1983). Goods bearing a counterfeit mark are automatically seized and, in the absence of consent from the trademark owner, are forfeited. See 19 C.F.R. §133.23a. Unlike imports of goods merely bearing infringing marks, counterfeit goods may not be released by removing the offending mark or by diverting the goods to another nation. Unlike the case with ordinary infringing goods, the owner of the trademark that has been counterfeited is notified by the Customs Service of the seizure. After forfeiture, the Customs Service may dispose of the goods in several ways, including destruction or delivery to a federal agency such as a prison or to a charity. 19 C.F.R. §133.52(c). See 3 J.T. McCarthy, *Trademarks and Unfair Competition* §25.01[5][b] (3d ed. 1995 rev.); Annotation, 72 A.L.R. Fed. 858.

Criminal Copyright Infringement. Anyone who infringes a copyright willfully and for purposes of commercial advantage is guilty of criminal copyright infringement. 17 U.S.C. §506(a).

Criminal infringement of copyright is a federal crime punishable by a maximum one-year imprisonment and/or a maximum fine of $250,000. 18 U.S.C. §2319. If the infringement consists of the reproduction or distribution during any 180-day period of at least 10 copies or phonorecords of one or more copyrighted works having a retail value of more than $2,500, then the maximum punishment is five years and/or a fine. A second or subsequent offense is punishable by up to 10 years in prison, a fine, or both. 18 U.S.C. §2319. See W. Patry, *Copyright Law and Practice* 1181 (1994).

Phonorecord and Motion Picture Counterfeits. Federal law provides criminal penalties against a person who "knowingly traffics in a counterfeit label affixed ... to a phonorecord or a copy of a motion picture or other audiovisual work." 18 U.S.C. §2318. "Counterfeit label" is defined as "an identifying label or container that appears to be genuine but is not."

- *Statutory References*:

Lanham Act §45, 15 U.S.C. §1127: *Counterfeit*. "A 'counterfeit' is a spurious mark which is identical with, or substantially indistinguishable from, a registered mark."

Lanham Act §34(d)(1)(B), 15 U.S.C. §1116(d)(1)(B):

As used in this subsection the term "counterfeit mark" means—

(i) a counterfeit of a mark that is registered on the principal register in the United States Patent and Trademark Office for such goods or services sold, offered for sale, or distributed and that is in use, whether or not the person against whom relief is sought knew such mark was so registered; or

(ii) a spurious designation that is identical with, or substantially indistinguishable from, a designation as to which the remedies of this Act are made available by reason of [36 U.S.C. §380 dealing with the protection of Olympic marks and symbols];

but such term does not include any mark or designation used on or in connection with goods or services of which the manufacturer or producer was, at the time of the manufacture or production in question authorized to use the mark or designation for the type of goods or services so manufactured or produced, by the holder of the right to use such mark or designation.

- *Treatise Reference*: 3 J.T. McCarthy, *Trademarks and Unfair Competition* §25.01[5] (3d ed. 1995 rev.).

- *Commentary References*: *Symposium on Remedies Against Counterfeiting*, 14 AIPLA J. 231–336 (1986); Smith, *Obtaining Early and Effective Relief Against Trademark Counterfeiting*, 10 Hastings Comm/Ent 1049 (1988) ("The purpose of the seizure order is not only to obtain the records relating to the violation, but also to thwart the destruction, movement, and means of production.").

- *Case References*:

"[A]n award of little more than nominal damages would encourage a counterfeiter to merely switch from one infringing scheme to another as soon as the infringed owner became aware of the fabrication. Such a method of enforcement would fail to serve as a convincing deterrence to the profit maximizing entrepreneur who engages in trademark piracy." *Playboy Enters., Inc. v. Baccarat Clothing Co.*, 692 F.2d 1272, 1274, 216 USPQ 1083, 1084 (9th Cir. 1982).

"To stop counterfeiting, a trademark owner must be able to invoke section 1117(b), the treble-damage ... provision that Congress added to the trademark law in 1984. Treble damages are a particularly suitable remedy in cases where surreptitious violations are possible, for in such cases simple damages (or profits) will underdeter; the violator will know that he won't be caught every time, and merely confiscating his profits in the cases in which he is caught will leave him with a net profit from infringement." *Louis Vuitton S.A. v. Lee*, 875 F.2d 584, 588, 10 USPQ2d 1935, 1938 (7th Cir. 1989).

- *Definitional Reference*: "The pirating of trademarked products through commercial counterfeiting has reached epidemic proportions in recent years. The practice occurs where an unauthorized representation of a legally registered trademark is carried on goods which are similar to the product for which the trademark is registered. The object of the counterfeiter is to deceive the purchaser into believing that he or she is buying a legitimately branded product.

Commercial counterfeiting may thus involve patent and copyright infringements and passing off, as well as infringements of registered trademarks." WIPO, *Background Reading Material on Intellectual Property* 176 (1988).

Court of Appeals for the Federal Circuit

[patent–trademark] A federal court of appeal whose powers over intellectual property matters include exclusive appellate jurisdiction over civil suits that arise under the federal patent laws as well as appeals from decisions of administrative boards in the Patent and Trademark Office. The court is a coequal member of the national system of 13 federal appellate courts, but its appellate jurisdiction is defined by subject matter, not by the territorial location of the lower court. Federal Circuit decisions are reviewable on a writ of certiorari by the U.S. Supreme Court.

Abbreviation: CAFC

History and Jurisdiction. Effective October 1, 1982, the U.S. Court of Customs and Patent Appeals (CCPA) and the U.S. Court of Claims were merged into a new court called the U.S. Court of Appeals for the Federal Circuit (CAFC). Unlike the other 12 federal circuit courts of appeal, the jurisdiction of the CAFC is defined not by the place where the case was filed, but by the kind of subject matter of the case. The new court was given a wide range of appellate jurisdiction including both patent and trademark matters as well as reviews of certain decisions involving federal employees, federal contracts, import duties, and tax matters. 28 U.S.C. §1295.

Patent Matters. One of the reasons for the creation in 1982 of the Court of Appeals for the Federal Circuit was to achieve national uniformity in the application of the federal patent laws by putting to an end the disparate interpretations of the patent statutes being made in the various territorial federal circuit courts of appeal. *Panduit Corp. v. All States Plastic Mfg. Co.*, 744 F.2d 1564, 1574, 223 USPQ 465, 470 (Fed. Cir. 1984) ("It is, therefore, clear that one of the primary objectives of our enabling legislation is to bring about uniformity in the area of patent law."). For this reason, Congress gave the CAFC exclusive appellate jurisdiction over all claims involved in patent infringement suits that arise in federal district courts across the nation. 28 U.S.C. §1295(a)(1). Federal Circuit jurisdiction turns on whether the jurisdiction of the district court was based, in whole or in part, on the existence of a patent claim. *Christianson v. Colt Indus. Operating Corp.*, 486 U.S. 800, 807–08, 7 USPQ2d 1109, 1113 (1988). Thus, the CAFC may decide appellate matters involving nonpatent claims in a case where there is a claim arising under the patent laws. For such nonpatent claims, the CAFC will apply the law of the regional circuit involved. See, e.g., *Bandag, Inc. v. Al Bolser's Tire Stores, Inc.*, 750 F.2d 903, 223 USPQ 982 (Fed. Cir. 1984) (CAFC follows Ninth Circuit precedent on a trademark claim that is joined with a patent claim filed in a federal court in the state of Washington). The CAFC "follows the guidance of the regional circuits in all but the substantive law fields assigned exclusively to us by Congress." *Speedco Inc. v. Estes*, 853 F.2d 909, 914, 7 USPQ2d 1637, 1641 (Fed. Cir. 1988).

In addition, the Federal Circuit has appellate jurisdiction over patent matters involved in decisions of (1) the Patent and Trademark Office (PTO) BOARD OF PATENT APPEALS AND INTERFERENCES, relating to patent applications and INTERFERENCE proceedings; (2) the U.S. Claims Court, involving patent infringement suits against the U.S. government; and (3) the U.S. International Trade Commission, involving patent claims in cases concerning alleged unfair trade practices in import trade.

Trademark Matters. Most Federal Circuit reviews of trademark matters arise by three routes: (1) an appeal from an EX PARTE refusal of the PTO, affirmed by the Trademark Trial and Appeal Board (TTAB), to register a mark; (2) an appeal from an INTER PARTES decision of the TTAB, as in a CANCELLATION PROCEEDING or an OPPOSITION PROCEEDING; or (3) an appeal from a U.S. district court of a civil lawsuit involving a claim for patent infringement and a claim for trademark infringement.

Precedent. Soon after its creation, the Court of Appeals for the Federal Circuit en banc declared that it would be bound by the precedent of both of its predecessor courts as that precedent existed on September 30, 1982, just prior

to creation of the new court. *South Corp. v. United States*, 690 F.2d 1368, 215 USPQ 657 (Fed. Cir. 1982). Thus, patent and trademark decisions of the old CCPA are citable and binding as precedent unless they have been overruled by the new court en banc.

- *Treatise Reference*: R. Harmon, *Patents and the Federal Circuit* §§16–17 (3d ed. 1994); 2 J.T. McCarthy, *Trademarks and Unfair Competition* §21.04 (3d cd. 1995 rev.).

- *Case Reference*: "[J]urisdiction likewise extend[s] only to those cases in which a well-pleaded complaint establishes either that federal patent law creates the cause of action or that the plaintiff's right to relief necessarily depends on resolution of a substantial question of federal patent law, in that patent law is a necessary element of one of the well-pleaded claims." *Christianson v. Colt Indus. Operating Corp.*, 486 U.S. 800, 809, 7 USPQ2d 1109, 1113 (1988).

Court of Customs and Patent Appeals

[patent–trademark] An appellate court that had the power to hear appeals from patent and trademark administrative decisions of the Patent and Trademark Office. The separate existence of the Court of Customs and Patent Appeals (CCPA) came to an end in 1982 when it was merged with the U.S. Court of Claims to form the new U.S. COURT OF APPEALS FOR THE FEDERAL CIRCUIT (CAFC).

Soon after its creation, the Court of Appeals for the Federal Circuit en banc declared that it would be bound by the precedent of both of its predecessor courts as that precedent existed on September 30, 1982, just prior to creation of the new court. *South Corp. v. United States*, 690 F.2d 1368, 215 USPQ 657 (Fed. Cir. 1982). Thus, patent and trademark decisions of the old CCPA are citable and binding as precedent unless they have been overruled by the new court en banc.

Abbreviation: CCPA.

See COURT OF APPEALS FOR THE FEDERAL CIRCUIT.

creativity [copyright]

A modicum of artistic or literary ingenuity or intellectual input needed for a valid copyright.

Creativity and Originality Compared. The law's requirement for some minimal degree of creativity is a facet of the ORIGINALITY requirement. The Supreme Court has said that "originality is a constitutional requirement" that flows from the constitutional terms "authors" and "writings," which presuppose some amount of originality, which in turn requires "some minimal degree of creativity." *Feist Publications v. Rural Tel. Serv.,* 499 U.S. 340, 345, 18 USPQ2d 1275, 1278 (1991). While originality focuses upon the need for the author's independent effort, creativity imposes a minimal level of artistic or literary ingenuity. Nimmer has pointed out the independent significance of these two requirements. "[A] work may be entirely the product of the claimant's independent efforts, and hence original, but may nevertheless be denied protection as a work of art if it is completely lacking in any modicum of creativity." 1 *Nimmer on Copyright* §2.08[B][2] (1994 rev.). The Supreme Court, approving of Nimmer's analysis, held that: "Original, as the term is used in copyright, means only that the work was independently created by the author (as opposed to copied from other works), and that it possesses at least some minimal degree of creativity." *Feist Publications v. Rural Tel. Serv.,* 499 U.S. 340, 345, 18 USPQ2d 1275, 1278 (1991).

What Is Creativity? The courts have been vague in defining how much creativity is needed, keeping in mind Justice Holmes' famous caveat against lawyers and judges setting themselves up as adjudicators of artistic worth and public taste. *Bleistein v. Donaldson Lithographing Co.*, 188 U.S. 239 (1903). The Supreme Court has said that what is needed is a "creative spark" and that is easily found: "[T]he requisite level of creativity is extremely low; even a slight amount will suffice. The vast majority of works make the grade quite easily, as they possess some creative spark, 'no matter how crude, humble or obvious' it might be." *Feist Publications v. Rural Tel. Serv.,* 499 U.S. 340, 345, 18 USPQ2d 1275, 1278 (1991). Applying this test,

the D.C. Circuit held that while the individual graphic elements of each screen display of Atari's "Breakout" video game were not copyrightable, the selection and arrangement of elements were original and creative, not conventional, obvious, or inevitable. *Atari Games Corp. v. Oman,* 979 F.2d 242, 246–47, 24 USPQ2d 1933, 1937–38 (D.C. Cir. 1992).

Examples of Noncreative Works. The types of works denied copyright for want of creativity include fragmentary words or clichéd phrases (e.g., "hang in there" on a drink coaster) and words dictated by functional considerations (e.g., "stir well before using" or "open here"). Similarly, some courts have held that merely translating a preexisting work from one medium to another, without more does not demonstrate sufficient originality or creativity. For example, merely converting a motion picture from 35mm film to one-half-inch videocassette, while requiring some technical skill, does not embody even the minimal amount of creativity needed for a derivative copyright. The Supreme Court held that the arrangement of data in a telephone directory white pages lacked sufficient creativity for copyright protection. The alphabetical listing of names and phone numbers was entirely typical and obvious; it was "devoid of even the slightest trace of creativity." *Feist Publications v. Rural Tel. Serv.,* 499 U.S. 340, 362, 18 USPQ2d 1275, 1284 (1991).

Creativity and Compilations. Compilations containing only unprotectible data, such as unembellished facts, may possess the requisite creativity for valid copyright if the selection and arrangement of material entails a minimal degree of creativity. "[T]he selection and arrangement of the facts cannot be so mechanical or routine as to require no creativity whatsoever." *Feist Publications v. Rural Tel. Serv.,* 499 U.S. 340, 361, 18 USPQ2d 1275, 1284 (1991). Applying this test, the Eleventh Circuit en banc found insufficient originality and creativity and denied compilation copyright protection for a yellow-pages classified business directory that used an alphabetized list of business types and used divisions such as arranging churches by denomination or attorneys by area of specialty. *Bellsouth Advertising & Publishing Corp. v. Donnelley Information Publishing Inc.,* 999

F.2d 1436, 28 USPQ2d 1001 (11th Cir. 1993). See COMPILATION.

See ORIGINALITY, DERIVATIVE WORK.

- *Treatise References:* 1 *Nimmer on Copyright* §§2.01, 2.08[B][1] (1994 rev.); 1 N. Boorstyn, *Copyright* §2.02 (2d ed. 1994); 1 P. Goldstein, *Copyright* §2.2.1.2 (1989); M. Leaffer, *Understanding Copyright* §2.7[C] (1989); W. Patry, *Copyright Law and Practice* 151 (1994).

- *Case Reference:* "[T]he originality requirement is not particularly stringent. A compiler may settle upon a selection or arrangement that others have used; novelty is not required. Originality requires only that the author make the selection or arrangement independently (i.e., without copying the selection or arrangement from another work), and that it display some minimal level of creativity. Presumably, the vast majority of compilations will pass this test, but not all will. There remains a narrow category of works in which the creative spark is utterly lacking or so trivial as to be virtually nonexistent." *Feist Publications v. Rural Tel. Serv.,* 499 U.S. 340, 358–59, 18 USPQ2d 1275, 1283 (1991).

- *Example:* Art Rogers, a professional photographer, took a picture of two people holding eight puppies. Jeff Koons, a sculptor, later made an unauthorized copy of the photograph. When Rogers brought suit for copyright infringement, Koons argued that the photograph was typical, commonplace, and trite and contained no copyrightable expression due to lack of creativity. The court held that original elements of creative expression were copied, citing Rogers' efforts in posing the group for the photograph, choosing the lighting and taking and printing the picture. *Rogers v. Koons,* 960 F.2d 301, 22 USPQ2d 1492 (2d Cir. 1992).

critical date [patent] The date one year prior to the filing of a patent application. An event prior to that date can trigger the PUBLIC USE, ON SALE and PRINTED PUBLICATION bars to a patent. An inventor is given a one-year period after commercialization of the invention within which the inventor can decide whether or not to file an application for a patent on the invention.

An inventor cannot obtain a valid patent if he or she waits for more than the one-year statutory GRACE PERIOD to file a patent application after a product embodying the invention has been placed on sale, or there has been a public use of the invention, or the invention has been described in a printed publication.

See CRITICAL DATE, ON SALE, PUBLIC USE, PRINTED PUBLICATION, EXPERIMENTAL USE.

- *Statutory Reference*: 35 U.S.C. §102(b): "A person shall be entitled to a patent unless— …(b) the invention was patented or described in a printed publication in this or a foreign country or in public use or on sale in this country, more than one year prior to the date of the application for patent in the United States. ..."

- *Case Reference*: "The 'critical date,' the date one year before the filing of the patent application, is determined retrospectively. Therefore, those activities that will act as a bar must be of such a character that it is apparent at the time they are conducted that patent filing must be completed within a year." *Baker Oil Tools Inc. v. Geo. Vann Inc.,* 828 F.2d 1558, 1563, 4 USPQ2d 1210, 1213 (Fed. Cir. 1987).

- *Usage Example*: "CBS argues that the subject matter of the '201 patent was in 'public use' and 'on sale' by [inventor] Nichols, prior to the March 3, 1969, critical date (i.e., one year prior to filing of the patent application), thus rendering the patent invalid under section 102(b)." *Moleculon Research Corp. v. CBS, Inc.,* 793 F.2d 1261, 229 USPQ 805, 807 (Fed. Cir. 1986).

cross-read [patent] If a device infringing patent A must also infringe patent B and vice-versa, then the patents "cross-read" because the claims of one patent cannot be infringed without also infringing the other patent. In other words, there is DOUBLE PATENTING. *Carman Indus., Inc. v. Wahl,* 724 F.2d 932, 940, 220 USPQ 481, 487 (Fed. Cir. 1983).

If a device could be constructed that would infringe the claims of patent A but not the claims of patent B, then the claims do not "cross-read," and there is no violation of the rule against double patenting of the same invention type. *Shelcore, Inc. v. Durham Indus., Inc.*, 745 F.2d 621, 628, 223 USPQ 584, 590 (Fed. Cir. 1984).

See DOUBLE PATENTING.

crowded art [patents] A technology in which there have been many inventions within a short period of time.

Range of Equivalents. In applying the DOCTRINE OF EQUIVALENTS to determine whether a patent claim is infringed, a broad range of equivalents will infringe if the patent is a "pioneer" patent. But only a very narrow range of equivalents will infringe if the patent is a minor patent in a "crowded art." An "improvement patent in a crowded art" is entitled only to a "very narrow range of equivalents." *Hughes Aircraft Co. v. United States*, 717 F.2d 1351, 1362, 219 USPQ 473, 481 (Fed. Cir. 1983).

Number of Similar Contemporaneous Inventions. The word "crowded" refers to how many inventions in the technology are similar to the patented invention being considered. If the patented invention stands almost alone in the technology, it probably will be viewed as a "pioneer patent," and its claims will be read as covering a broad range of infringing equivalents. On the other hand, if the patented invention stands as a minor improvement in a crowd of similar minor improvements in the technology, its claims will be narrowly, if not literally, read in determining what is an infringement of those claims.

See also EQUIVALENTS, DOCTRINE OF; PIONEER PATENT.

• *Case References*:

A patent cannot "be considered a pioneer patent, because it issued in a crowded art." *Chemical Eng'g Corp. v. Essef Indus., Inc.*, 795 F.2d 1565, 1572 n.8, 230 USPQ 385, 391 n.8 (Fed. Cir. 1984).

"Because T&B's patent is not a pioneer patent, having issued in the crowded art of electrical connectors as an improvement over a prior standard 'D' connector, the claims should be given a range of equivalents narrow enough to distinguish over the prior art and thus, to avoid invalidity." *Thomas & Betts Corp. v. Litton Sys., Inc.*, 720 F.2d 1572, 1579, 220 USPQ 1, 6 (Fed. Cir. 1983).

crowded field of marks [trademark]
A market in which there are several similar marks used on similar goods or services.

Customers Can Distinguish Among Members of a Crowd. The greater the number of similar marks used on similar goods and services, the less distinctive and strong is any one of those marks. A mark hemmed in on all sides by similar marks on similar goods cannot be very distinctive. In such a "crowded" field of similar marks, each member of the crowd is relatively weak in its ability to prevent use by others in the crowd. Customers will not likely be confused between any two of the crowd and may have learned to carefully pick out one from the other. When many similar marks coexist for years, the public learns to differentiate one from the other.

• *Examples*: Many different companies use stripe design marks on sports shoes. This is a "crowded" field of marks, and any one design mark is entitled to only a very narrow scope of exclusive rights as a trademark. *In re Lucky Co.*, 209 USPQ 422 (T.T.A.B. 1980). Similarly, marks used to identify beauty pageants are a "crowded" field of similar marks consisting of a courtesy title and a geographic term, such as Miss U.S.A., Miss America, Mrs. America, and Miss World. In such a market, MRS. OF THE WORLD is not so close to the senior user's MISS WORLD as to be likely to cause confusion. *Miss World (UK) Ltd. v. Mrs. Am. Pageants Inc.*, 856 F.2d 1445, 8 USPQ2d 1237 (9th Cir. 1988).

Third-Party Uses and Registrations. Evidence of third-party use in wholly unrelated markets has little, if any, relevance. *Eclipse Assocs. Ltd. v. Data Gen. Corp.*, 894 F.2d 1114, 13 USPQ2d 1885 (9th Cir. 1990). The mere citation of third-party registration is not proof of third-party uses for the purpose of showing a crowded field and relative weakness of a mark. *In re Clorox Co.*, 578 F.2d 305, 198 USPQ 337 (C.C.P.A. 1978) (Markey, C.J., specially concurring).

See STRENGTH OF MARK.

• *Treatise Reference*: 1 J.T. McCarthy, *Trademarks and Unfair Competition* §11.26[1] (3d ed. 1995 rev.).

CRT [copyright]
See COPYRIGHT ROYALTY TRIBUNAL.

D

Dann Amendments [patent] Amendments to the Patent Rules effective from 1977 to 1982 that permitted "no fault" reissue and inter partes participation of protestors in reissue proceedings. The procedure was "no fault" because it permitted an applicant for reissue to obtain a ruling by the Patent and Trademark Office (PTO) on the validity of a patent in view of prior art not previously considered even without making the traditional declaration that the patent is "deemed wholly or partly inoperative or invalid." The procedure permitted inter partes participation by any member of the public, who could object to a pending reissue application and include citations to prior art or other information. The protestor could monitor proceedings by being supplied by the PTO with copies of all documents sent to the applicant.

The amendments were repealed as of July 1, 1982, in view of new legislation permitting REEXAMINATION. The amendments were named after the then Commissioner of Patents and Trademarks C. Marshall Dann.

- *Case Reference*: "The PTO permitted Celanese's participation in PPG's reissue applications only because of the now repealed 'Dann amendments.' Although proceedings before the PTO ordinarily are *ex parte*, in the late 1970s the regulations governing PTO reissue proceedings were amended by the so-called 'Dann amendments' to allow *inter partes* protestor participation…. The purpose of these amendments was to economize the time and expense for both the courts and the litigants…. In practice … the desired results were not achieved. After enactment of legislation providing for reexamination, the PTO repealed the 'Dann amendments' in 1982, thus eliminating extensive *inter partes* protestor participation in reissue proceedings." *PPG Indus. Inc. v. Celanese Polymer Specialties Co.*, 840 F.2d 1565, 1568, 6 USPQ2d 1010, 1013 (Fed. Cir. 1988).

DART [copyright] See DIGITAL AUDIO RECORDING TECHNOLOGY.

data base [copyright] A collection of information, such as a dictionary, encyclopedia, or a table of numerical data, regardless of the nature of the material object in which the data is recorded or stored. A data base may be copyrightable as a COMPILATION and is categorized as a LITERARY work. A computer data base fixes data in electronic storage devices, such as ROM, and is just as copyrightable as a data base fixed on the pages of a book.

In some cases, a computerized data base will differ from a COMPUTER PROGRAM in that a data base can be a passive, recorded bank of information while a computer program is active in that it is a listing of instructions used to bring about certain results in a computer.

See COMPUTER PROGRAM, COMPILATION.

- *Treatise References*: W. Patry, *Copyright Law and Practice* 201 (1994); M. Leaffer, *Understanding Copyright* §2.11[C] (1989); 2 P. Goldstein, *Copyright* §2.16.1.1 (1989).

CONTU Report Excerpt: "The automated data base represents a new technological form of a type of work long recognized as eligible for copyright. Dictionaries, encyclopedias and tables of numeric information are all forms of data bases which long antedate the computer, and for which copyright protection has been and will continue to be available under the copyright law. Under the new law, a data base is a compilation and thus a proper subject for copyright. This entitlement to copyright is not diminished by the fixation of the data base in a medium requiring the intervention of a computer to communicate its information content. Accordingly, a data base, whether printed in traditional hard copy or fixed in an electro-magnetic medium, is protected copyright under the terms of the new law." *Report of the National Commission on New Technological Uses of Copyrighted Works (CONTU)* 38 (1978).

deceptive mark [trademark]
    See DESCRIPTIVE MARK.

decompiling [computer–copyright]
    See DISASSEMBLING.

de facto secondary meaning [trademark]
Evidence tending to prove customer identification of a word or product feature with a single source, but which has no legal significance either because the word has already been determined to be a GENERIC NAME or because the feature has been determined to be "functional."
    See GENERIC NAME, FUNCTIONALITY.

defensive publication [patent]
    See STATUTORY INVENTION REGISTRATION.

definiteness of claims [patent]   A valid claim in a patent must be "definite" and not vague. See definition and references at INDEFINITENESS OF CLAIMS.

de minimis [general legal] A shortened form of the Latin legal maxim or saying "de minimis non curat lex," meaning the law does not concern itself with trifles. It is commonly used in legal briefs and judicial opinions to signify something so insignificant as to be disregarded. It is often used as a legal substitute for "minimal." E.g., "[S]ince only five items were sold in the United States, this is *de minimis* and cannot trigger liability for infringement" and "[T]he sale of only five items in the United States is a *de minimis* level of sales which does not trigger U.S. intellectual property law." The maxim is codified in the statutory law of some states. See, e.g., Cal. Civil Code §3533: "The law disregards trifles."

dependent claim [patent] A claim in a patent that refers back to a previous claim and defines an invention that is narrower in scope than the invention in the previous claim upon which this claim depends. A dependent claim must be written so as to be more restricted than the technology defined in the preceding claim on which the dependent claim rests. The usual reason that the patent attorney drafts a patent with several claims of varying scope is to provide some assurance that at least one claim will be upheld as valid and infringed should the patent ever be litigated in court.

Characteristics of a Dependent Claim. A dependent claim is immediately recognizable by its introduction that refers back to a previous claim. E.g., "[A] steam-driven paddle boat according to claim 1 in which the engine and the paddle wheel are connected by a variable speed drive shaft." Thus, a dependent claim always incorporates by reference everything in the previous claim on which it depends and adds some further limitation or restriction.

A Dependent Claim Narrows. A dependent claim narrows the claim on which it depends either by adding more elements to the claim or by making a further narrowing description of one or more of the elements of the previous claim. Claims in a patent are generally written in a series of claims of narrowing scope. For the purpose of determining infringement, a dependent claim necessarily incorporates all the limitations in the previous claim upon which the dependent claim depends. For example, if claim 1 is an independent claim and recites a boat, a paddle wheel, a steam engine, and a nuclear power source, then all four elements must be found before there can be literal infringement. If claim 2 is a dependent claim depending on claim 1 and adds the element of a variable speed drive shaft connecting the engine to the paddle wheel, then an infringement of claim 2 would have to have all five elements.

Chain of Narrowing Dependent Claims. Further dependent claims could be built on dependent claim 2. To continue the above example, claim 3 could be dependent on claim 2 and further add the narrowing element that the speed of the variable speed drive shaft be controlled by an electronic feedback circuit. Claim

3 would thus incorporate all the limitations of claims 1 and 2 and further narrow the definition. A further chain of progressively narrower dependent claims could be added.

Multiple Dependent Claim. A MULTIPLE DEPENDENT CLAIM refers to and depends upon more than one other claim in the alternative.

Each Claim Stands on Its Own. For purposes of infringement, each claim of a patent defines a separate invention. *Jones v. Hardy*, 727 F.2d 1524, 1528, 220 USPQ 1021, 1024 (Fed. Cir. 1984). That is, each claim of a patent defines a separate right to exclude. One claim of a patent may be infringed without another being infringed.

Claim Differentiation. Under the rule of CLAIM DIFFERENTIATION, limitations in a narrower dependent claim cannot be read into the meaning of a broader independent claim so as to narrow its scope to avoid ANTICIPATION or OBVIOUSNESS by the prior art.

Obviousness of Dependent Claims. Dependent claims are not invalid as obvious under Patent Code §103 if the independent claim upon which they depend is not obvious. *In re Fine*, 837 F.2d 1071, 5 USPQ2d 1596 (Fed. Cir. 1988).

Infringement of Dependent Claims. A dependent claim cannot be infringed unless the accused device is also covered by the parent independent claim. Thus, if the parent independent claim is found not to be infringed by the accused device, there is no point in going further to analyze the dependent claims. *Wahpeton Canvas Co. v. Frontier Inc.*, 870 F.2d 1546, 1553 n.9, 10 USPQ2d 1201, 1207 n.9 (Fed. Cir. 1989) ("One who does not infringe an independent claim cannot infringe a claim dependent on (and thus containing all the limitations of) that claim."). While the general rule is that a dependent claim cannot be found infringed unless the parent independent claim is infringed, there is an exception. The exception occurs when the independent claim is not infringed under the doctrine of equivalents because the asserted range of equivalents is so broad that it would encompass the prior art. In such a case, it does not necessarily follow that the range of equivalents of the narrower dependent claim would also encompass the prior

art. *Wilson Sporting Goods Co. v. David Geoffrey & Assoc.*, 904 F.2d 677, 14 USPQ2d 1942 (Fed. Cir. 1990).

See CLAIM; CLAIM DIFFERENTIATION, DOCTRINE OF.

- *Statutory References*:

35 U.S.C. §112, second paragraph: "The specification shall conclude with one or more claims particularly pointing out and distinctly claiming the subject matter which the applicant regards as his invention."

35 U.S.C. §112, third paragraph: "A claim may be written in independent or, if the nature of the case admits, in dependent or multiple dependent form."

35 U.S.C. §112, fourth paragraph: "Subject to the following paragraph [relating to multiple dependent claims], a claim in dependent form shall contain a reference to a claim previously set forth and then specify further limitation of the subject matter claimed. A claim in dependent form shall be construed to incorporate by reference all the limitations of the claim to which it refers."

35 U.S.C. §282: "Each claim of a patent (whether in independent, dependent or multiple dependent form) shall be presumed valid independently of the validity of other claims; dependent or multiple dependent claims shall be presumed valid even though dependent upon an invalid claim...."

- *Rule Reference*: 35 C.F.R. §1.75(c): "One or more claims may be presented in dependent form, referring back to and further limiting another claim or claims in the same application.... Claims in dependent form shall be construed to include all the limitations of the claim incorporated by reference into the dependent claim."

- *Manual Reference*: "The test as to whether a claim is a proper dependent claim is that it shall include every limitation of the claim from which its depends (35 U.S.C. §112, fourth paragraph) or in other words that it shall not conceivably be infringed by anything which would not also infringe the basic claim.... Thus, for example, if claim 1 recites the combination of elements A, B, C and D, a claim reciting the structure of claim 1 in which D was omitted or replaced by E would not be a proper dependent claim." *Manual of Patent Examining Procedure* §608.01(n) (1994).

- *Treatise References*:

"Use dependent claims extensively, most of the time when you wish to present a second claim that adds elements or features to a prior claim, whether the prior claim is dependent or independent. Either tell more about elements in the previous claim, or add elements to that claim, or both." J. Landis, *Mechanics of Patent Claim Drafting* §11, at 27 (3d ed. 1990).

"The most compelling reason for the presence of more than one claim in the patent application is the unpredictability of the protection afforded by only one claim in any subsequent litigation involving the patent containing it.... A multiplicity of claims provides greater assurance that at least one claim will validly afford the owner of the patent the protection he needs." J. White, *Chemical Patent Practice* 18 (11th ed. 1988).

deposit of biological materials   [patent]
See CELL DEPOSITORY.

deposit of copies [copyright] In the Copyright Act, Congress has required that the owner of copyright in a work published with notice of copyright in the United States must deposit two copies of the best edition with the Register of Copyrights. 17 U.S.C. §407.

Deposit: Purpose and Penalties. The main purpose of the deposit requirement is to provide copies for the Library of Congress. *Ladd v. Law & Technology Press*, 762 F.2d 809, 814, 226 USPQ 774, 777 (9th Cir. 1985) ("[T]he deposit requirement's purpose is to enforce contributions of desirable books to the Library of Congress."). Thus, the deposit requirement is a type of tax in order to provide free copies of books, records, periodicals, and films for the Library of Congress. Failure to comply with the deposit requirement will not impair copyright in the work. Rather, the sanction for failure to deposit is a series of fines. The Register of Copyrights can impose an initial fine of no more than $250 plus the retail cost of acquiring the copies for failure to deposit within three months of publi-

cation. An additional fine of $2,500 can be imposed for a willful or repeated refusal to comply with a demand for deposit. 17 U.S.C. §407(d).

Deposit Usually Accompanies Registration. Ordinarily, authors and publishers do not deposit copies unless they are making a REGISTRATION of a claim of copyright in the work. Registration requires a deposit of copies (two copies of a published work) as a condition of receiving a registration certificate. 17 U.S.C. §408(b). Thus, in the vast majority of cases, copies are deposited with the Library of Congress only as a part of an application for registration of a claim of copyright. The Register of Copyrights has put out regulations permitting or requiring the deposit of identifying material instead of, or in addition to, the deposit of copies or phonorecords. 37 C.F.R. §§202.20–.21. For example, for computer programs in machine-readable copies, the deposit may consist of the first and last 25 pages or equivalent units of the source code if reproduced on paper. 37 C.F.R. §202.20(c)(2)(vii)(A).

Deposit Is Constitutional. The deposit requirement has been upheld against a constitutional challenge that it is a taking of private property for public use without just compensation. "The Copyright Clause [of the Constitution] grants copyright protection for the purpose of promoting the public interest in the arts and sciences. Conditioning copyrights on a contribution to the Library of Congress furthers this overall purpose." *Ladd v. Law & Technology Press*, 762 F.2d 809, 814, 226 USPQ 774, 778 (9th Cir. 1985).

- *Treatise References*: 2 *Nimmer on Copyright* §7.17 *et seq.* (1994 rev.); 2 P. Goldstein, *Copyright* §§3.8–.10 (1989); M. Leaffer, *Understanding Copyright* §7.9 *et seq.* (1989).

- *Case Reference*:

"Although related to the deposit requirement in Section 407, which is designed to further the acquisitions policy of the Library of Congress, the deposit required by Section 408(b) serves the separate purpose of providing the Library's Copyright Office with sufficient material to identify the work in which the registrant claims a copyright. ... [A] key purpose of the Section

408(b) deposit requirement is to prevent confusion about which work the author is attempting to register. A second apparent claim of Section 408(b) is to furnish the Copyright Office with an opportunity to assess the copyrightability of the applicant's work. ... We conclude that there is no support in law or reason for a rule that penalizes immaterial, inadvertent errors on a copyright deposit." *Data Gen. Corp. v. Grumman Sys. Support Corp.*, 36 F.3d 1147, 1161–62, 32 USPQ2d 1385, 1393–95 (1st Cir. 1994).

derivation [patent] The act of taking the invention of another person and applying for a patent on that invention. Derivation relates to the question of whether the person who applied for a patent was in fact the person who invented the subject matter claimed in the patent. A person cannot patent an invention derived from another. Only the true inventor or inventors can be the applicants for a patent.

Help From Others. The rule against derivation does not prevent an inventor from using the services, ideas, and aid of others in the process of perfecting the invention. *Shatterproof Glass Corp. v. Libbey-Owens Ford Corp.*, 758 F.2d 613, 624, 225 USPQ 634, 641 (Fed. Cir. 1985).

Joint Inventors. Inventors may apply jointly for a patent even though they did not physically work together at the same time, did not make the same kind of contribution, or did not each make a contribution to the technology contained in every claim of the patent application. Sole inventor Alpha and joint inventors Alpha and Beta are regarded as different INVENTIVE ENTITIES, a legal characterization from which certain legal consequences flow, such as the determination of what is PRIOR ART.

See JOINT INVENTORS.

• *Statutory References*:

35 U.S.C. §102(f): "A person shall be entitled to a patent unless— ... he did not himself invent the subject matter sought to be patented...."

35 U.S.C. §116: "When an invention is made by two or more persons jointly, they shall apply for patent jointly .... Inventors may apply for a patent jointly even though (1) they did not physically work together or at the same time,

(2) each did not make the same type or amount of contribution, or (3) each did not make a contribution to the subject matter of every claim of the patent."

• *Treatise Reference*: "[Patent Code §102(f)] simply states a fundamental principle of American patent law—what you patent must be your own invention: you cannot patent another's invention, nor can you patent an invention imported from abroad." R. Harmon, *Patents and the Federal Circuit* §3.3 (3d ed. 1994).

• *Case References*:

"There is always an inventor; being an inventor might be regarded as a preliminary legal requirement, for if he has not invented something, if he comes with something he knows was invented by someone else, he has no right even to approach the door [of the Patent and Trademark Office]." *In re Bergy*, 596 F.2d 952, 960, 201 USPQ 352, 360 (C.C.P.A. 1979), *dismissed as moot*, 444 U.S. 924 (1980).

"A claim that a patentee derived an invention addresses originality - who invented the subject matter of the [patent claim]?... Under this attack on a patent or patent application, the proponent asserts that the patentee did not 'invent' the subject matter of the [claim] because the patentee derived the invention from another." *Price v. Symsek*, 988 F.2d 1187, 1190, 26 USPQ2d 1031, 1033 (Fed. Cir. 1993).

derivative work [copyright] A work which is based on a preexisting work and in which the preexisting work is changed, condensed, or embellished in some way.

A Derivative Work Is Built Upon an Underlying Work. Many works are built upon previous works, such as a play based on a novel, a motion picture based on a play, an English translation of an article in a Russian technical journal, a photograph of a sculpture, an orchestral version of a song scored only for voice, a new version of a computer program, and a new edition of a treatise. These are all "derivative works." The authors of such adaptations are entitled to their own derivative copyrights separate and apart from the copyright in the underlying work. The owner of copyright in the derivative work acquires no exclusive rights at all in the underlying work. The copyright in the underlying work and in the derivative work are separate from and independent of each other. 17 U.S.C. §103(b).

A Derivative Work Is Based On the Underlying Work. To be a derivative work, the new work must be more than merely "inspired by" a prior work. A derivative work must take more than merely unprotectible ideas or concepts from the underlying work. For example, the motion picture "Star Wars" is not a derivative work based on the 1930s "Buck Rogers" space adventure movie serials even if "Star Wars" borrowed general unprotectible themes or ideas of swashbuckling rocket jockeys battling evil aliens on strange planets. There is some difference of opinion as to the degree of similarity to the underlying work that must exist for an adaptation to be a "derivative" work. In Nimmer's view, to constitute a derivative work, the new work must be so "substantially similar" to the underlying work that in the absence of a license, it would be a copyright infringement of the underlying work (see SUBSTANTIAL SIMILARITY). See 1 *Nimmer on Copyright* §3.01 (1994 rev.). Under this view, the concepts of derivative work and copyright infringement are congruent. But in Patry's view, a work can be "derivative" without being substantially similar to the underlying work. See W. Patry, *Copyright Law and Practice* 159 n.153 (1994).

The Standard of Originality. The usual standard in determining the needed amount of originality in a derivative work is that it makes a variation on the underlying work that is more than "merely trivial." Some courts have imposed upon certain kinds of derivative works a higher than normal standard of ORIGINALITY, requiring that the derivative work constitute a "substantial variation" of the preexisting work. *Gracen v. Bradford Exch.*, 698 F.2d 300, 305, 217 USPQ 1294, 1298 (7th Cir. 1983)(must be "substantially different from the underlying work"). The stated reason for imposing this higher standard is to avoid "put[ting] a weapon for harassment in the hands of mischievous copiers intent on appropriating and monopolizing public domain work" by "extend[ing] copyrightability to minuscule variations." *L.*

Batlin & Son, Inc. v. Snyder, 536 F.2d 486, 492, 189 USPQ 753, 758 (2d Cir. 1976). While the types of derivative works to which this higher standard applies are not clearly defined, this rule appears limited to derivative works whose marketplace value is the result of the derivative work being based on a popular preexisting work. For example, such cases have involved a plastic version of a nineteenth century cast-iron penny bank; plastic dolls of popular Disney characters such as Mickey Mouse; and a painted collector's plate with a scene showing Judy Garland as Dorothy in the movie *The Wizard of Oz*. Compare *North Coast Indus. v. Jason Maxwell Inc.*, 972 F.2d 1031, 23 USPQ2d 1788 (9th Cir. 1992) (the test of originality of a derivative work is whether the difference between the work and a preexisting work is "non-trivial").

The Underlying Work Copyright Dominates the Derivative Work Copyright. If a derivative work is substantially similar to the underlying work, it would be a copyright infringement in the absence of a license. Thus, if the underlying work is in copyright, one who wishes to exploit the derivative work needs a copyright license from the owner of copyright in the underlying work or works. "The aspects of a derivative work added by the derivative author are that author's property, but the element drawn from the pre-existing work remains on grant from the owner of the pre-existing work." *Stewart v. Abend*, 495 U.S. 207, 223, 14 USPQ2d 1614, 1622 (1990). If there is no such license, then the use of the underlying work in the derivative work is illegal under copyright law.

No Derivative Copyright in Unlawful Portions. The Copyright Act states that copyright in the derivative work does not extend to any part of the derivative work in which such preexisting material is unlawfully used. 17 U.S.C. §103(a). This gives a potential infringer of the derivative copyright the opportunity to raise as a defense the argument that the plaintiff has not obtained a license from the owner of rights in the copyright in underlying material. This is a kind of JUS TERTII defense. Since typically the underlying work totally pervades each part of the derivative work, there will be no part of the derivative work in which the underlying work is not "unlawfully used," and hence no enforceable derivative copyright at all, at least not unless and until there is a license from the owner of copyright in the underlying work. See 1 P. Goldstein, *Copyright* §2.16 (1989).

Derivative Works Based Upon Some Pre-1978 Works. Prior to 1978, copyright was for an initial term of 28 years with a renewal term of another 28 years. See RENEWAL OF COPYRIGHT. An advance assignment of the renewal term or of a right to make a derivative work based on the copyrighted work was personal: it bound only the author/grantor, not the surviving spouse or heirs. If the author/grantor died before the vesting of the renewal term, then the assignment of the renewal term was void and the renewal term passed free of the author's grant to the statutory class of surviving spouse and children, executor of will, or next of kin if no will. 17 U.S.C. §304(a). The author had only an expectancy to assign—the expectancy that he or she would live to the vesting of the renewal term. In the "Rear Window" case, the Supreme Court held that if the author of a novel dies before the renewal period, then the assignee of the right to produce a derivative work, such as a movie studio that produces a motion picture of the novel, cannot continue to exploit the derivative motion picture without a new grant from the new owner of the renewal term. *Stewart v. Abend*, 495 U.S. 207, 14 USPQ2d 1614 (1990).

Derivative Work Vis-à-Vis a Compilation. A derivative work differs from both a COMPILATION and a collective work in that in the latter types of works, preexisting material is brought together without change, while in a derivative work, the preexisting material is changed in some way.

- *Treatise References*: 1 *Nimmer on Copyright* §3.01 (1994 rev.); 1 P. Goldstein, *Copyright* §2.16 (1989); M. Leaffer, *Understanding Copyright* §2.9 (1989); W. Patry, *Copyright Law and Practice* 158–67 (1994).

- *Statutory References*:

17 U.S.C. §101: "A 'derivative work' is a work based upon one or more preexisting works, such as a translation, musical arrangement, dramatization, fictionalization, motion picture version, sound recording, art reproduc-

tion, abridgment, condensation or any other form in which a work may be recast, transformed, or adapted. A work consisting of editorial revisions, annotations, elaborations, or other modifications, which, as a whole, represent an original work of authorship, is a 'derivative work.' "

17 U.S.C. §103:

(a) The subject matter of copyright as specified by section 102 includes compilations and derivative works, but protection for a work employing preexisting material in which copyright subsists does not extend to any part of the work in which such material has been used unlawfully.

(b) The copyright in a compilation or derivative work extends only to the material contributed by the author of such work, and does not imply any exclusive right in the preexisting material. The copyright in such work is independent of, and does not affect or enlarge the scope, duration, ownership, or subsistence of, any copyright protection in the preexisting material.

- *Legislative History*: "The most important point here is one that is commonly misunderstood today: copyright in a 'new version' covers only the material added by the later author, and has no effect one way or the other on the copyright or public domain status of the preexisting material. Between them the terms 'compilations' and 'derivative works'… comprehend every copyrightable work that employs preexisting material or data of any kind…. A 'derivative work' requires a process of recasting, transforming, or adapting 'one or more preexisting works'; the 'preexisting work' must come within the general subject matter of copyright set forth in section 102, regardless of whether it is or was ever copyrighted…. [Section 103(a)] prevents an infringer from benefiting, through copyright protection, from committing an unlawful act, but preserves copyright protection for those parts of the work that do not employ the preexisting work. Thus, an unauthorized translation of a novel could not be copyrighted at all, but the owner of copyright in an unauthorized anthology of poetry could sue someone who infringed the whole anthology, even though the infringer proves that publication of one of the poems was unauthorized." H.R. Rep. No. 94-1476, 94th Cong., 2d Sess. 57-58 (1976), 1976 U.S. Code Cong. & Admin. News 5659.

- *Example*: In 1900, L. Frank Baum published the book "The Wonderful Wizard of Oz." In 1902 Baum prepared a very successful derivative musical stage version based on the book with music by a collaborator. In succeeding years, Baum wrote a series of derivative books using the Oz theme and characters. In 1914, Baum founded his own motion picture organization, which produced several films including a derivative movie sequel using the characters and plot elements from the original "Wizard of Oz" book. After Baum's death in 1919, his publisher had Ruth Plumly Thompson write Oz sequel books for years, paying a royalty to Baum's widow. All these books appeared in derivative translations around the world. In 1939, MGM produced the classic motion picture *The Wizard of Oz*. In the 1970s, a play and motion picture entitled *The Wiz* featured an all-black cast and added new songs and material. These copyrighted works were derivative works that incorporated material from earlier derivative versions, and all could trace their origins to the underlying work, Baum's original 1900 book.

description requirement [patent] The requirement contained in Patent Code §112 that the invention claimed be the invention described in the DISCLOSURE of the patent. The disclosure portion of the patent must describe an invention having all the material features of the claims.

The Disclosure Must Support All the Claims. One of the primary purposes of the description requirement is to ensure that technology which is defined by a patent CLAIM added sometime after the original filing date of the patent application was sufficiently described in the original specification so that the filing date can truly be said to be the date of invention of the thing covered by the new claim. The description requirement usually becomes an issue when a claim is added by the patent applicant at some time after the original filing date and the claim is different in scope from the claims as originally filed. See 2 D. Chisum, *Patents* §7.04 (1994 rev.). The essence of the description requirement is "whether one skilled in the art, familiar with the practice of the art at the time of the filing date, could reasonably have found the 'later' claimed invention in the specification as filed." *Texas Instruments Inc. v. International Trade Comm'n*, 871 F.2d 1054, 1062, 10 USPQ2d 1257, 1263 (Fed. Cir. 1989).

The Requirements of the Patent Disclosure. Patent Code §112 sets forth three distinct requirements: (1) the description requirement—the invention that is claimed must be the invention that is described; (2) the ENABLEMENT requirement—the description must be in such full, clear, and concise terms as to enable any person skilled in the art to make and use it; and (3) the BEST MODE requirement—a description of the best embodiment of the invention known to the inventor at the time of the patent application.

Means Plus Function Elements and the Description Requirement. "While [patentees are] required to disclose some structure in the specification for all 'means' recitation in the claims, [patentees] are not required to disclose every means for implementing the stated function." *In re Hayes Microcomputer Prods. Inc.*, 982 F.2d 1527, 1535, 25 USPQ 2d 1241, 1246 (Fed. Cir. 1992). See also *DMI, Inc. v. Deere & Co.*, 755 F.2d 1570, 1574, 225 USPQ 236, 238 (Fed. Cir. 1985) ("Patentees are required to disclose in the specification some enabling means for accomplishing the function set forth in the 'means plus function' limitation. At the same time, there is and can be no requirement that the applicants describe or predict every possible means of accomplishing that function.").

See DISCLOSURE, SPECIFICATION.

- *Statutory Reference*: 35 U.S.C. §112, first paragraph: "The specification shall contain a written description of the invention, and of the manner and process of making and using it, in such full, clear, concise, and exact terms as to enable any person skilled in the art to which it pertains, or with which it is most nearly connected, to make and use the same, and shall set forth the best mode contemplated by the inventor of carrying out his invention."

• *Treatise References*: "The description requirement is different from enablement and requires that the invention be described in such a way that it is clear that the applicant invented what is claimed.... The purpose of the description requirement is to state what is needed to fulfill the enablement criteria.... Consideration of the written description requirement often arises in the context of 'new matter' problems ... [and] in the reissue context.... Thus, although it is not necessary that the claimed subject matter be described identically, the disclosure as originally filed must convey to those skilled in the art that the reissue applicant in fact had invented the subject matter later claimed." R. Harmon, *Patents and the Federal Circuit* §5.2(a) (3d ed. 1994). See 2 D. Chisum, *Patents* §7.04 (1994 rev.).

• *Case References*:

"This court has clearly recognized that there is a description of the invention requirement in 35 U.S.C. §112, first paragraph, separate and distinct from the enablement requirement.... A specification may contain a disclosure that is sufficient to enable one skilled in the art to make and use the invention and yet fail to comply with the description of the invention requirement." *In re Barker & Pehl*, 559 F.2d 588, 591, 194 USPQ 470, 472 (C.C.P.A. 1977) (claim invalid since invention claimed was not invention described in the disclosure).

"Satisfaction of the description requirement insures that subject matter presented in the form of a claim subsequent to the filing date of the application was sufficiently disclosed at the time of filing so that the prima facie date of invention can fairly be held to be the filing date of the application. This concept applies whether the case factually arises out of an assertion of entitlement to the filing date of a previously filed application under [the provision for a CONTINUATION application] ... or arises in the interference context wherein the issue is support for a count in the specification of one or more of the parties, ... or arises in an ex parte case involving a single application, but where the claim at issue was filed subsequent to the filing

of the application.... The specification as originally filed must convey clearly to those skilled in the art the information that the applicant has invented the specific subject matter later claimed." *In re Smith & Hubin*, 481 F.2d 910, 914, 178 USPQ 620, 623–24 (C.C.P.A. 1973).

"Although [the applicant] does not have to describe exactly the subject matter claimed, ... the description must clearly allow persons of ordinary skill in the art to recognize that [he or she] invented what is claimed. ... The test for sufficiency of support in a parent application is whether the disclosure of the application relied upon 'reasonably conveys to the artisan that the inventor had possession at that time of the later claimed subject matter.' " *In re Hayes Microcomputer Prods. Inc.*, 982 F.2d 1527, 1533, 25 USPQ 2d 1241, 1245 (Fed. Cir. 1992), quoting from *Vas-Cath Inc. v. Mahurkar*, 935 F.2d 1555, 1563, 19 USPQ 2d 1111, 1116 (Fed. Cir. 1991).

• *Example*: The Court of Appeals for the Federal Circuit held that in an INTERFERENCE, an applicant's specification disclosing a high frequency cable having an electrically conductive outer jacket surrounding inner layers of shielding, dielectric, absorptive, and conducting material did not adequately describe a claimed invention consisting of a "harness comprising a plurality of" such cables. "The issue is not whether one skilled in the art would have been able to make a harness using knowledge of the art, but rather did [applicant's] application sufficiently describe a harness of cables with conductive outer jackets. Section 112 ... does require specificity as to the claim limitations that characterize the interference count.... The description must be sufficiently clear that persons of skill in the art will recognize that the applicant made the invention having those limitations.... [The rival inventor in the interference proceeding] presented evidence ... that such bundling was not conventional as applied to cables with a conductive outer layer.... [W]e discern no disclosure in the [applicant's] specification of a plurality of cables, and no reference to a harness of cables wherein each cable had the conductive shield, all as required by count 6." *Martin v. Mayer*, 823 F.2d 500, 504–05, 3 USPQ2d 1333, 1337 (Fed. Cir. 1987).

descriptive mark [trademark] A word, picture, or other symbol that directly describes something about the goods or services in connection with which it is used as a mark. Such a term may be descriptive of a desirable characteristic of the goods; the intended purpose, function, or use of the goods; the size or color of the goods; the class of users of the goods; or the end effect upon the user. The issue of descriptiveness is usually tested from the viewpoint of the hypothetical customer who has that basic amount of knowledge about the product which is conveyed by advertising and promotion currently available in the marketplace. *G. Heileman Brewing Co. v. Anheuser-Busch, Inc.*, 873 F.2d 985, 10 USPQ2d 1801 (7th Cir. 1989).

Self-Laudatory Terms. Words that are self-laudatory of the goods or services are placed in the descriptive category, taking them at face value as describing the character or quality of the goods. Thus, words such as BEST, SUPERIOR, PREFERRED, and PLUS are usually classified as descriptive.

Secondary Meaning and Fair Use. A descriptive term is regarded as not being inherently distinctive and, to establish validity for registration or protection in court, needs proof of acquired distinctiveness, known as SECONDARY MEANING. Even if a secondary meaning is achieved, another merchant can make a FAIR USE of the term in a nontrademark sense.

See FAIR USE.

Suggestive Terms and the Test for Descriptive Terms. It is often very difficult to distinguish descriptive terms from "suggestive" terms, which suggest but do not directly describe. The distinction is often critical, for a "suggestive" term needs no proof of secondary meaning for registration or protection in court. Most courts will use some variation of the following three-point test: (1) The imagination test—how much imagination on the ordinary buyer's part is needed to cull a direct message from the term about the product or service. The more imagination needed, the more probable that the term is properly classified as "suggestive," rather than "descriptive." (2) The competitors' use test—are other sellers presently using this term to describe their products. (3) The competitors' need test—does the term so

directly convey some vitally important information about the product or service that others have a competitive need to use this term to convey that information. For example, while the term GREYHOUND for bus services implies that the bus is as fast as a greyhound dog, it takes some imagination to make that connection, and other bus lines have no competitive need to use that particular word to describe their own speedy service.

Doctrine of Foreign Equivalents. Under this guideline, words from foreign languages are usually translated into English and then tested for descriptiveness. While VOLKSWAGEN was held descriptive as meaning "Peoples' Car," it was protected upon proof of having acquired a secondary meaning as a trademark. See 1 J.T. McCarthy, *Trademarks and Unfair Competition* §11.14 (3d ed. 1995 rev.).

Style and Grade Designations. Words, letters, numbers, and symbols used to designate a particular style, grade, size, or type of a product are not protectible trademarks if they do not serve the purpose of identifying and distinguishing the source of goods as well as the style, grade, or size. Such designations are classified as "descriptive" and are only registered or protected upon proof of secondary meaning. For example, if a company's parts' numbers such as A7S are not shown to have acquired a secondary meaning as identifying only the products of one company, then a competitor is free to use its own variation such as L-A7S to designate its replacement parts. *J.M. Huber Corp. v. Lowery Wellheads, Inc.*, 778 F.2d 1467, 228 USPQ 206 (10th Cir. 1985). See 1 J.T. McCarthy, *Trademarks and Unfair Competition* §11.15 (3d ed. 1995 rev.).

Misdescriptive and Deceptive Terms. Marks that describe some characteristic or quality of the goods which they do not in fact possess are "misdescriptive." If a term is "deceptively misdescriptive" of goods or services, it is not registrable except upon proof that customers have become accustomed through advertising, promotion, and usage (1) not to expect that the goods or services have the described quality; and (2) to use the term as a mark to identify a source. Lanham Act §2(e), (f), 15 U.S.C. §1052(e), (f). For example, the term BAKED

TAM for a turkey meat product is deceptively misdescriptive, *American Meat Inst. v. Horace W. Longacre Inc.*, 211 USPQ 712 (T.T.A.B. 1981), as is CAMEO for jewelry that does not contain cameos. *In re Woodward & Lothrop, Inc.*, 4 USPQ2d 1412 (T.T.A.B. 1987). If the misdescriptiveness in a term is so significant that it will "materially affect" purchasing decisions, then the term may fall within the absolute "deceptive" bar of Lanham Act §2(a) and be unregistrable under any circumstances. *In re Budge Mfg. Co.*, 857 F.2d 773, 8 USPQ2d 1259 (Fed. Cir. 1988) (LOVEE LAMB for auto seat covers made of synthetic material held "deceptive" and unregistrable as falsely implying that product was made from natural lamb or sheep skin).

• *Treatise Reference*: 1 J.T. McCarthy, *Trademarks and Unfair Competition* §§11.05–.19 (3d ed. 1995 rev.).

• *Statutory Reference*: Lanham Act §2, 15 U.S.C. §1052:

No trademark by which the goods of the applicant may be distinguished from the goods or others shall be refused registration on the principal register on account of its nature unless it—

(a) consists of or comprises ... deceptive ... matter ...

(e) consists of a mark which, (1) when used on or in connection with the goods of the applicant is merely descriptive or deceptively misdescriptive of them ...

(f) except as expressly excluded in paragraphs (a), ... nothing here shall prevent the registration of a mark used by the applicant which has become distinctive of the applicant's goods in commerce. ...

• *Case References*:

"A 'merely descriptive' mark ... describes the qualities or characteristics of a good or service, and this type of mark may be registered only if the registrant shows that it has acquired secondary meaning; i.e., it 'has become distinctive of the applicant's goods in commerce.' §2(e), (f), 15 U.S.C. §1052(e), (f)." *Park 'N Fly Inc. v. Dollar Park & Fly*, 469 U.S. 189, 194, 224 USPQ 327, 329 (1985).

design around [patent] The act of consciously inventing and designing a new product or process that does not infringe the claims of a patent but does substantially the same or a better job than the patented invention. This is legitimate competitive behavior, which is encouraged as one of the benefits of the patent system.

Designing Around Is Legitimate Competitive Activity. In return for receiving the right to exclude inherent in the patent, the inventor gives up secrecy and fully discloses the invention to the public. This enables others to understand the invention and to be able to use it as a stepping stone to further develop the technology. This may take the form of "designing around" the patent claims in order to produce a product or process that may itself be a significant technical advance or may produce a product or process that is more efficient and less costly. This type of competitive behavior tends in the long run to result in more goods that consumers want at a price they are willing to pay.

Designing Around May Produce a Patentable Invention. The act of designing around a patent to produce a similar product or process will often result in a valuable technical innovation that may itself be patentable. It is by such a step-by-step process that the progress of technology is advanced. "[T]he incentive to innovation that flows from 'inventing around' an adversely held patent must be preserved." *Texas Instruments, Inc. v. International Trade Comm'n*, 805 F.2d 1558, 1572, 231 USPQ 833, 842 (Fed. Cir. 1986).

May Negate Willful Infringement. A good faith effort to design around patent claims that results nonetheless in a finding of patent infringement will still support a finding that the infringement was not WILLFUL and hence not trigger increased damages. That is, if a defendant in good faith thought that it had successfully designed around patent claims but was still found to have infringed, this is not a willful infringement, which would justify increased damages or an award of ATTORNEY FEES. *Rolls Royce Ltd. v. GTE Valeron Corp.*, 800 F.2d 1101, 1109, 231 USPQ 185, 191–92 (Fed. Cir. 1986).

Synonym: invent around.

• *Case Reference*: "Conduct such as Smith's, involving keeping track of a competitor's products and designing new and possibly better or cheaper functional equivalents is the stuff of which competition is made and is supposed to benefit the consumer. One of the benefits of a patent system is its so-called 'negative incentive' to 'design around' a competitor's products, even when they are patented, thus bringing a steady flow of innovations to the marketplace. It should not be discouraged...." *State Indus., Inc. v. A.O. Smith Corp.*, 751 F.2d 1226, 1235–36, 224 USPQ 418, 424 (Fed. Cir. 1985).

designer skilled in the art [patent]   The patent law test of OBVIOUSNESS defined in Patent Code §103 applies to design patents as well as to utility patents. The test of §103 is whether the subject matter would have been obvious at the time the invention was made to a person having ORDINARY SKILL in the art. For designs, such a person is a "designer skilled in the art" or a "designer of ordinary skill."

See SKILL IN THE ART.

• *Case References*:

"The proper test for determining obviousness of a claimed design under 35 U.S.C. §103 is whether the design would have been obvious to a designer of ordinary skill who designs articles of the type involved." *In re Carter*, 673 F.2d 1378, 1380, 213 USPQ 625, 626 (C.C.P.A. 1982).

"The Court finds that the typical toy designer, a person with college or art school background and several years experience designing toys, is able to design toys by himself, although there may be some toys beyond his ability to design alone.... [P]laintiff did not show that development of its patented invention required knowledge of plastics or of manufacturing processes not possessed by a toy designer of ordinary skill." *Shelcore, Inc. v. Durham Indus.,*

Inc., 221 USPQ 891, 896 (E.D. Pa.), *aff'd*, 745 F.2d 621, 223 USPQ 584 (Fed. Cir. 1984).

design patent [patent] A grant by the federal government of exclusive rights in a novel, nonobvious, and ornamental industrial design. A design patent confers the right to exclude others from making, using, and selling designs that closely resemble the patented design.

While governed by many of the same rules of validity as utility patents, design patents cover quite different aspects of products. While a utility patent covers functional aspects, a design patent covers ornamental aspects. Thus, both a design patent and a utility patent can cover different aspects of the same article, such as an automobile or a table lamp.

Validity. The tests for determining the validity of a design patent are identical to those used to determine the validity of a utility patent. *Litton Sys., Inc. v. Whirlpool Corp.*, 728 F.2d 1423, 1441, 221 USPQ 97, 108 (Fed. Cir. 1984). The test of OBVIOUSNESS is determined by the point of view of a DESIGNER SKILLED IN THE ART. A design patent can only validly cover ornamental aspects of design, not functional or utilitarian aspects. One purpose of design patents is to promote progress in the "decorative arts," not progress in the utilitarian design of technology. *Avia Group Int'l Inc. v. L.A. Gear Inc.*, 853 F.2d 1557, 1563, 7 USPQ2d 1548, 1553 (Fed. Cir. 1988). The presumption of validity of a design patent includes a presumption that the design is not functional. *Power Controls Corp. v. Hybrinetics, Inc.*, 806 F.2d 234, 240, 231 USPQ 774, 778 (Fed. Cir. 1986). A design patent is appropriate only for "industrial" design. It is not suitable for articles that are purely and only artistic such as a photograph, a painting, or a sculpture, as opposed to an ornamental design for utilitarian objects such as a microwave oven, an athletic shoe, or a watch face design.

See DESIGNER SKILLED IN THE ART.

Types of Designs or Pictures Appropriate for Design Patent. The language "new, original and ornamental design for an article of manufacture" has been found to include at least three kinds of designs: (1) a design for an ornament, impression, print, or picture to be applied to an article of manufacture (surface ornamentation);

(2) a design for the shape or configuration of an article of manufacture; and (3) a combination of the first two categories. *In re Schnell*, 46 F. 2d 203, 209, 8 USPQ 19, 25 (C.C.P.A. 1931). With respect to the first category of design patents, applicants have been required to show that a claimed design be more than a mere impression, print, or picture. Applicants must prove that the impression, print, or picture is specifically embodied in a particular article of manufacture. For example, the U.S. Patent and Trademark Office Board of Patent Appeals and Interferences has refused to provide design patent protection to computer icons based on the rule that "a picture standing alone is not protectable by a design patent." See, e.g., *Ex parte Strijland*, 26 USPQ2d 1259, 1261–62 (Bd. Pat. App. & Int'f. 1992) (rejected application for an icon alone, but indicated that if claim were for icon for computer screen and showed computer in dotted lines on drawing, claim might be statutory subject matter). Accord *Ex parte Donoghue*, 26 USPQ2d 1271 (Bd. Pat. App. & Int'f. 1992) (claimed design for computer icon is not patentable since it does not show the icon embodied in or applied to an article of manufacture—a computer); *Ex parte Donaldson*, 26 USPQ2d 1250 (Bd. Pat. App. & Int'f. 1992).

Infringement. Unlike a utility patent, a design patent has no word CLAIMS. A design patent is a picture patent. The drawing in the patent defines what is encompassed by it. It is the picture of the design in the patent drawing that must be compared with the appearance of the ACCUSED DEVICE. The test of INFRINGEMENT is the classic *Gorham* test of deception in the eye of the ordinary observer, supplemented by the POINT OF NOVELTY test. Since a design patent does not cover functional aspects of appearance, those aspects cannot form the basis for infringement. See INFRINGEMENT OF A DESIGN PATENT, POINT OF NOVELTY. Unlike utility patents, Patent Code §289 provides that the owner of a design patent can obtain the remedy of the infringer's profits.

See PROFITS.

Term. In 1982, the Patent Code was amended to provide a uniform 14-year duration for all design patents. 35 U.S.C. §173. This is in contrast to the DURATION for UTILITY PATENTS.

Convention Priority. With respect to design patents, the PARIS CONVENTION and the statute provide a six-month period within which to file in the United States after filing abroad in order to achieve a CONVENTION DATE of priority. 35 U.S.C. §172.

• *Statutory Reference*: 35 U.S.C. §171: "Whoever invents any new, original and ornamental design for an article of manufacture may obtain a patent therefor, subject to the conditions and requirements of this title. The provisions of this title relating to patents for inventions shall apply to patents for designs, except as otherwise provided."

• *Case References*:

"To qualify for protection, a design must present an aesthetically pleasing appearance that is not dictated by function alone, and must satisfy the other criteria of patentability." *Bonito Boats Inc. v. Thunder Craft Boats Inc.*, 489 U.S. 141, 148, 9 USPQ2d 1847, 1851 (1989).

"Many well-constructed articles of manufacture whose configurations are dictated solely by function are pleasing to look upon, for example a hexnut, a ball bearing, a golf club, or a fishing rod, the pleasure depending largely on one's interests. But it has long been settled that when a configuration is the result of functional considerations only, the resulting design is not patentable as an ornamental design for the simple reason that it is not 'ornamental'—was not created for the purpose of ornamenting." *In re Carletti*, 328 F.2d 1020, 1022, 140 USPQ 653, 654 (C.C.P.A. 1964).

"Design patents do not and cannot include claims to the structural or functional aspects of the article.... Thus it is the non-functional, design aspects that are pertinent to determinations of infringement.... [A] design patent is not a substitute for a utility patent. A device that copies the utilitarian or functional features of a patented design is not an infringement unless the ornamental aspects are also copied, such that the overall 'resemblance is such as to deceive.' " *Lee v. Dayton-Hudson Corp.*, 838 F.2d 1186, 1188–89, 5 USPQ2d 1625, 1626–27 (Fed. Cir. 1988).

"The test for infringement is not whether the accused product is substantially similar to the patentee's commercial embodiment of the claimed design.... Such a test risks relying on unclaimed and therefore irrelevant features as grounds for similarity or difference. It is legal error to base an infringement finding on features of the commercial embodiment not claimed in the patent.... When the trial court compared the accused design to [the patentee's] commercial embodiment without observing this obligation, it improperly expanded the patentee's right to exclude to unclaimed design features." *Sun Hill Indus. v. Easter Unlimited, Inc.*, 48 F.3d 1193, 1196–97, 33 USPQ2d 1925, 1927 (Fed. Cir. 1995).

design registration   [patent–international] A special type of intellectual property protection given in many nations for the novel and original ornamental or aesthetic aspects of a useful article. Generally not referred to as a "patent," such registration is exclusively for industrial design and not for the utilitarian or functional aspects of articles. The United States does not have a design registration system, although such systems have been proposed in Congress for several decades.

Duration. Typically, industrial design registration lasts from 5 to 15 years, although there is a wide range of variation among the nations. Some nations have a term of five years with two successive renewal periods for a maximum of 15 years.

Copyright and Design Registration. In most nations, industrial design registration differs from copyright in these important respects: (1) Under the industrial design law, protection is lost unless the design is registered before publication or public use, whereas copyright subsists without the formality of registration. (2) Industrial design registration is of limited duration on the order of 5 to 15 years, whereas copyright lasts for the life of the author plus 50 or more years. (3) An industrial design registration is usually infringed by a substantially similar design whether or not there has been copying; an independent creation can infringe. However, a copyright is only infringed by one who had access to the copyrighted work and copied

from it. Some nations, such as France and Germany, permit a creator to invoke the protection of either or both design registration and copyright; protection is cumulative. Other nations require the creator to choose to be protected by either design registration or copyright; if the creator has chosen one, the other cannot be used. For example, at the expiration of the design registration, copyright cannot be claimed.

International Relations. The PARIS CONVENTION treats industrial design registration as similar to patents and trademarks, giving it national treatment and priority rights. Article 5 *quinquies* of the PARIS CONVENTION requires that all member nations shall protect industrial designs. The HAGUE ARRANGEMENT is a multilateral treaty permitting an international registration system for industrial designs. The LOCARNO AGREEMENT is a multilateral treaty establishing a classification system for the registration of industrial designs.

U.S. Law. In the United States, apart from a design patent, there is no special intellectual property protection for industrial design. Bills have been introduced in Congress for many years without successfully resulting in legislation that would create a special form of industrial design protection.

See DESIGN PATENT, GESCHMACKSMUSTER.

• *Treatise References*: 2 S. Ladas, *Patents, Trademarks and Related Rights: National and International Protection* §§496–508 (1975); WIPO, *Background Reading Material on Intellectual Property* 187–206 (1988); 3 D. Chisum, *Patents* §14.03[4] (1994 rev.).

dictum [general legal] A Latin legal term that is a shortened form of *obiter dictum*, meaning a nonbinding, incidental remark or observation made by a judge in the course of a written opinion given in connection with a decision. Dictum included in a written opinion is not precedent for purposes of STARE DECISIS, is not the RATIO DECIDENDI of the decision, and need not be followed by courts in subsequent cases.

Use Note: The plural *dicta* is frequently misused as a singular noun. E.g., the following is incorrect: "This one sentence in the opinion in

Alpha v. Beta is merely dicta which does not bind this court."

• *Case References*:

Dictum is "a statement in a judicial opinion that could have been deleted without seriously impairing the analytical foundations of the holding—that, being peripheral, may not have received the full and careful consideration of the court that uttered it." Posner, J., in *Sarnoff v. American Home Prods. Corp.*, 798 F.2d 1075, 1084 (7th Cir. 1986).

"It would be nice if every statement made in an opinion could be automatically tested against every conceivable application to determine whether an exception or two should be noted; but that is a Utopian revery. Precedents are of value for what they *decide*, not for every sentence they contain." Rich, J., in *In re Ornum and Stang*, 686 F.2d 937, 946, 214 USPQ 761, 768 (C.C.P.A. 1982).

Digital Audio Recording Technology

[copyright] A technology brought to commercial form in 1986 which enables consumers to make perfect and flawless copies of recorded music. Audio tape copies made using this technology are almost impossible to distinguish from the original. With use of this technology, a copy made from a copy is just as clear as the original. Concerned with the prospect of widespread consumer copying of recorded music, several record companies, songwriters, music publishers, and performing rights societies negotiated a compromise with manufacturers of digital audio tape recording devices. This compromise became embodied in law in the Audio Home Recording Act ("AHRA") of 1992. (Act of October 28, 1993, Pub. L. No. 102-563, 106 Stat. 4237.) The Act sets out a system within which manufacturers are permitted to sell digital audio recording equipment and audiophiles are permitted to use them for home recording.

Audio Home Recording Act of 1992. This Act added Chapter 10 to the Copyright Act. 17 U.S.C. §§1001 *et seq.* The AHRA approved the compromise worked out between music producers and digital recording equipment producers by adopting the following three elements:

(1) The Act forbids the manufacture, importation, or distribution of digital recording equipment that is not equipped with a control device such as a "serial copy management system." 17 U.S.C. §1002(a). This is a control device that prevents recording equipment from copying a copy of a commercially sold digital audio recording of copyrighted music. Such a control device permits a home user to use a digital audio recorder to make a copy from an original commercially released compact disc, digital tape, or transmission, but prevents making a copy of the copy. The owner of such a machine equipped with this control device can make as many noncommercial copies as he pleases from the commercially sold "original," but the machine is disabled so that it cannot be used to make a copy from a copy. The law also forbids deactivation or circumvention of the control device. (2) The Act imposes a royalty on the distribution of digital audio recorders and blank digital tape. Recorder royalties are 2 percent of the transfer price of the equipment and are imposed on only the first person to make, distribute, or import. Blank digital tape royalties are 3 percent of the transfer price for each such tape made, sold, or imported and are imposed on only the first person to make, distribute, or import. Royalties are collected by the Copyright Office and distributed by a COPYRIGHT ARBITRATION ROYALTY PANEL convened by the Librarian of Congress. Royalties are distributed to owners of copyrights in musical works, performers, songwriters, and music publishers in a complicated formula defined in the statute. (3) The Act immunizes the ordinary person from copyright infringement liability for the private, noncommercial taping of copyrighted music, whether the equipment used is digital or analog. The immunity covers both tapes copied from a recording such as a compact disc as well as tapes copied from off-the-air transmissions. Immunity is also extended to protect the manufacturers and sellers of audio tape recorders and blank tape from any liability for contributory infringement where copying is made by buyers for private, noncommercial use.

• *Statutory Reference*: 17 U.S.C. §1001(3):

A "digital audio recording device" is any machine or device of a type commonly distributed to individuals for use by individuals, whether or not included with or as part of some other machine or device, the digital recording function of which is designed or marketed for the primary purpose of, and that is capable of, making a digital audio copied recording for private use, except for—

(A) professional model products, and

(B) dictation machines, answering machines, and other audio recording equipment that is designed and marketed primarily for the creation of sound recordings resulting from the fixation of nonmusical sounds.

- *Treatise References*: 1 N. Boorstyn, *Copyright* §6.12 (2d ed. 1994); 1 P. Goldstein, *Copyright* §5.2.2.3 (1994 Supp.); 1 *Nimmer on Copyright* §8A.01 (1994 rev.).

diligence [patent] Continuous inventive activity by the inventor who was first to conceive of the invention but second to reduce the invention to practice. In the United States, as between rival inventors, the patent is granted to the party who was FIRST TO INVENT. The process of invention starts with CONCEPTION and ends with a REDUCTION TO PRACTICE. Where the inventor who is first to conceive is not diligent, under Patent Code §102(g), he can lose the patent to a rival inventor who started second, but proceeded to complete the invention first by a reduction to practice.

Priority of Invention. Inventor Alpha who was first to conceive the invention will lose the patent to rival inventor Omega if Omega was second to conceive but first to reduce the invention to practice unless Alpha was continuously diligent from just prior to Omega's conception up to Alpha's reduction to practice. Alpha will receive the patent only if Alpha was diligent in reducing the invention to practice from a time just prior to Omega's conception. First-conceiver Alpha must show diligence because Alpha is attempting to win the patent over another who started later but who went on to finish first. Like the tortoise and the hare, tortoise Omega started later but actually reduced the invention to practice before Alpha did. Thus, the inventor who was the last to reduce to practice but first to conceive may still establish priority and win the patent by proving continuous and reason-able diligence toward reduction to practice during the critical period from just before the other person's conception until reduction to practice. See D. Chisum, *Patents* §10.07 (1994 rev.).

Diligence During the Critical Period. Whether or not the first inventor to conceive of the invention was diligent during the critical period will depend upon proof that the party first to conceive either engaged in constant effort such as tests and experimentation or has a valid explanation for inactivity. "[O]ne who was the first to conceive cannot recapture priority on the basis of his prior conception by spurting into renewed activity upon learning that another has entered the field." 2 P. Rosenberg, *Patent Law Fundamentals* §10.02[3] (1994 rev.). While the law gives strong weight to the purely mental act of conception, the law also requires that the first to conceive be diligent in continuing the inventive act to completion by a reduction to practice. 1 S. Ladas, *Patents, Trademarks and Related Rights: National and International Protection* §188 (1975).

Diligence in Filing a Patent Application. Diligence is also required if the first-to-conceive inventor relies upon a constructive reduction to practice by filing a patent application. There must have been diligence in preparing and filing the patent application.

See CONCEPTION, INTERFERENCE, REDUCTION TO PRACTICE.

- *Statutory Reference*: 35 U.S.C. §102(g): "In determining priority of invention there shall be considered not only the respective dates of conception and reduction to practice of the invention, but also the reasonable diligence of one who was first to conceive and last to reduce to practice, from a time prior to conception by the other."

- *Treatise References*: D. Chisum, *Patents* §10.07 (1994 rev.); 2 P. Rosenberg, *Patent Law Fundamentals* §10.02[3] (1994 rev.); 1 S. Ladas, *Patents, Trademarks and Related Rights: National and International Protection* §188 (1975).

- *Case References*:

"The reasonable diligence standard balances the interest in rewarding and encouraging invention with the public's interest in the earliest disclosure of innovation.... A review of case law on excuses for inactivity in reduction to practice reveals a common thread that courts may consider the reasonable everyday problems and limitations encountered by an inventor.... Delays in reduction to practice caused by an inventor's efforts to refine an invention to the most marketable and profitable form have not been accepted as sufficient excuses for inactivity." *Griffith v. Kanamaru*, 816 F.2d 624, 626–27, 2 USPQ2d 1361, 1362–64 (Fed. Cir. 1987).

"Because Oka is the senior party, Youssefyeh was required to establish reduction to practice *before* Oka's filing date, or conception before that date coupled with reasonable diligence from just before that date to Youssefyeh's filing date.... Oka, as the senior party, is presumptively entitled to an award of priority, and Youssefyeh, as the junior party in an interference between pending applications, must overcome that presumption with a preponderance of the evidence." *Oka v. Youssefyeh*, 849 F.2d 581, 584, 7 USPQ2d 1169, 1172 (Fed. Cir. 1988).

Diligence by a patent attorney in proceeding to a constructive reduction to practice by filing a patent application requires that the attorney worked reasonably hard on this particular application during the critical period. "Of course, it may not be possible for a patent attorney to begin working on an application at the moment the inventor makes the disclosure, because the attorney may already have a backlog of other cases demanding his attention.... Generally, the patent attorney must show that unrelated cases are taken up in chronological order, thus, the attorney has the burden of keeping good records of the dates when cases are docketed as well as the dates when specific work is done on the applications.... The question is under what circumstances may work on a related case be credited as diligence with respect to the instant application. We hold that work on the related case is to be credited toward reasonable diligence if the work on the related case 'contributes substantially to the ultimate preparation of the involved application.'" *Bey v. Kollonitsch*, 806 F.2d 1024, 1028–29, 231 USPQ 967, 970 (Fed. Cir. 1986).

• *Example*: Professor Griffith of Cornell University conceived in June 1981 of an invention for a drug useful in treating diabetes and reduced it to practice in January 1984. Inventor Kanamaru independently conceived second in time but reduced the invention to practice first by filing a patent application in November 1982. The burden was on Griffith to establish his diligence during the 14-month period from just before Kanamaru's filing date in November 1982 until Griffith's reduction to practice in January 1984. Professor Griffith was unable to prove diligence because of a three-month period of inactivity during the summer of 1983 and also because at other times he put aside this project to work on other experiments. The court rejected the excuse that delays were due to seeking funding for this project, caused by Cornell University's policy requiring researchers to seek outside funding. "The conclusion we reach from the record is that the [patentable] project was second and often third priority in laboratory research as well as the solicitation of funds. We agree that Griffith failed to establish a *prima facie* case of reasonable diligence or a legally sufficient excuse for inactivity to establish priority over Kanamaru." *Griffith v. Kanamaru*, 816 F.2d 624, 629, 2 USPQ2d 1361, 1364 (Fed. Cir. 1987).

dilution [trademarks] A type of infringement of a strong trademark in which the defendant's use, while not causing a likelihood of confusion, tarnishes the image or blurs the distinctiveness of the plaintiff's mark.

Dilution Doctrine Codified in State Law. As of 1994, the dilution doctrine had been codified in the statutes of approximately 26 states. The wording of the statutes is substantially the same, being based on the original version of the Model State Trademark Act. The wording of §12 of the Model State Trade Act is:

"Likelihood of injury to business reputation or of dilution of the distinctive quality of a mark registered under this Act, or a mark valid at common law, or a trade name valid at common law, shall be a ground for injunctive relief notwithstanding the absence of competition between the parties or the absence of confusion as to the source of goods or services."

As part of its 1992 revision of the state Model Bill, the United State Trademark Association incorporated into §13 of the state Model Bill the federal anti-dilution provisions which failed to be enacted into federal law in 1988. These provisions require that a mark be "famous" in the state and provide for a seven-part list of factors to consider in determining whether a mark has become "famous." The definition of dilution in the 1992 version of the Model State Trademark Bill is:

§1(K). "The term 'dilution' as used herein means the lessening of the capacity of a mark to identify and distinguish goods or services, regardless of the presence or absence of (a) competition between the parties, or (b) likelihood of confusion, mistake or deception."

Dilution Is Not a Part of Federal Law. Dilution is not codified in the federal Lanham Act and is applied by neither the courts nor the Patent and Trademark Office under federal substantive law. Nothing less than proof of a likelihood of confusion will suffice under the Lanham Act. *R.G. Barry Corp. v. Mushroom Makers, Inc.*, 612 F.2d 651, 204 USPQ 521 (2d Cir. 1979). While the TRADEMARK REVIEW COMMISSION recommended a form of federal anti-dilution law, the 1988 TRADEMARK LAW REVISION ACT did *not* contain any provision relating to dilution of marks. The original proposal for a federal anti-dilution statute is at 77 *Trademark Reporter* 454–62 (1987).

Types of Marks Protected Against Dilution. To possess the selling power and recognition protected by the anti-dilution statutes, the mark must be relatively strong and famous, at least within a certain group of people, product line, or territory. The Court of Appeals for the Second Circuit has stated that the plaintiff's mark must be "very famous" in the sense that it "has a distinctive quality for a significant percentage of the defendant's market." *Mead Data Central Inc. v. Toyota Motor Sales, Inc.*, 875 F.2d 1026, 1031, 10 USPQ2d 1961, 1966 (2d Cir. 1989).

Dilution by Tarnishment. A form of dilution that has often proven successful in the courts is the unpermitted use by a junior user of a famous mark in a setting that tarnishes the images associated with the famous mark. The classic exam-

ple is the sale of a poster reading "Enjoy Cocaine" in flowing script and red and white color identical to that used in labels and posters for the COCA-COLA soft drink. An injunction was issued based in part on dilution. *Coca-Cola Co. v. Gemini Rising, Inc.*, 346 F.Supp. 1183, 175 USPQ 56 (E.D.N.Y. 1972). In other examples, courts have found dilution by the use of trademarks in the context of X-rated movies, drug culture music, and a topless bar. 3 J.T. McCarthy, *Trademarks and Unfair Competition* §24.16 (3d ed. 1995 rev.). The dilution by tarnishment theory is not usually successful where the defendant's use is on a product whose status, reputation, and quality is of the same level as is the plaintiff's product.

Dilution by Blurring. The classic theoretical form of dilution is a blurring of the distinctiveness of a mark. That is, use of a famous mark by a junior user, even on a product far removed from that of the senior user, "dilutes" or reduces the substantially exclusive association that the mark has with the senior user, its goods or services, or the image associated with it. For example, the New York legislature, in enacting the New York dilution statute in 1954, said there was a need to prevent such hypothetical examples as "Dupont shoes, Buick aspirin tablets, Schlitz varnish, Kodak pianos, Bulova gowns, and so forth." N.Y. Legis. Ann. 49 (1954).

The Blurring Theory Is Not Often Successful. Because the classic "blurring" theory of dilution in theory creates a right of the owner of a well-known mark to stop almost any other use, the courts have been very reluctant to brand as illegal those uses which create dilution only by blurring. Only a handful of decisions have done so. See, e.g., *Ringling Bros.-Barnum & Bailey Combined Shows, Inc. v. Celozzi-Ettleson Chevrolet, Inc.*, 855 F.2d 480, 8 USPQ2d 1072 (7th Cir. 1988) (Ringling Brothers' circus slogan THE GREATEST SHOW ON EARTH found illegally diluted by defendant used car dealer's slogan THE GREATEST USED CAR SHOW ON EARTH).

The LEXIS v. LEXUS Case. In the famous LEXIS v. LEXUS case, the court found that there was no violation of the New York anti-dilution statute. Defendant's use of the mark LEXUS on a luxury automobile was held not to dilute illegally the mark LEXIS for a computerized legal research service. No tarnishment was found because the LEXUS was a top-of-the-line, high-quality luxury car. Blurring was held unlikely in the minds of the general public, for the LEXIS mark was not known to them. Blurring was said to be unlikely in the minds of attorneys, because their "recognized sophistication" enables them to avoid "any significant amount of blurring." *Mead Data Central Inc. v. Toyota Motor Sales, Inc.*, 875 F.2d 1026, 1031–32, 10 USPQ2d 1961, 1966 (2d Cir. 1989).

Dilution and Likelihood of Confusion. The classic form of trademark infringement is triggered by a likelihood of confusion. See INFRINGEMENT OF A TRADEMARK. That form of infringement is founded on the customer's right to be told the truth about the origin and sponsorship of goods and services. But the dilution theory rests not on the right of buyers to be free of confusion, but upon the right of the trademark owner to maximize the value of its trademark as a piece of property. In theory, dilution and a likelihood of confusion cannot coexist in the same person. In seeing the junior use, e.g., ROLLS ROYCE cosmetics, one either thinks that it is affiliated with or sponsored by the owner of the famous mark or that it is not and is separate. In the former case, there is a likelihood of confusion. In the latter case, the viewer is aware that the uses are not connected and that a term once uniquely associated with high-quality automobiles is now in use by another on cosmetics.

• *Treatise Reference*: 3 J.T. McCarthy, *Trademarks and Unfair Competition* §§24.13–.19 (3d ed. 1995 rev.).

disassembling [computers] REVERSE ENGINEERING of OBJECT CODE in a computer program to arrive at the SOURCE CODE.

Synonym: decompiling.

Disassembly to Obtain Unprotected Ideas and Concepts. It has been held to be a FAIR USE of a copyrighted computer program for a competitor to disassemble the program and make an intermediate copy solely in order to determine the uncopyrightable concepts embodied in the program. "We conclude that where disassembly is the only way to gain access to the ideas and functional elements embodied in a copyrighted computer program and where there is a legitimate reason for seeking such access, disassembly is a fair use of the copyrighted work, as a matter of law." *Sega Enters. Ltd. v. Accolade Inc.*, 977 F.2d 1510, 1527, 24 USPQ2d 1561, 1574 (9th Cir. 1992).

• *Case Reference*: "A program written in source code is translated into object code using a computer program called an 'assembler' or 'compiler', and then imprinted onto a silicon chip for commercial distribution. Devices called 'disassemblers' or 'decompilers' can reverse this process by 'reading' the electronic signals for '0' and '1' that are produced while the program is being run, storing the resulting object code in computer memory, and translating the object code into source code. Both assembly and disassembly devices are commercially available and both types of devices are widely used within the software industry." *Sega Enters. Ltd. v. Accolade Inc.*, 977 F.2d 1510 n.2, 24 USPQ2d 1561 n.2 (9th Cir. 1992).

Commentary Reference: "Reverse engineering of a computer program generally requires some use of the program, such as decompilation, disassembly, modular decomposition, or the like, which some have suggested might be considered a copyright infringement, since the program would be *copied* into a computer's memory.... However, the Fifth Circuit, in *Vault Corp. v. Quaid Software Ltd.*, 847 F.2d 255, 7 USPQ2d 1281 (5th Cir. 1988), held that Quaid's disassembly and decompilation to reverse engineer Vault's program were permitted under the provision of 17 U.S.C. §117 immunizing loading of a computer program into memory...." Jordan, *On the Scope of Protection for Computer Programs Under Copyright*, 17 AIPLA Q. J. 199, 201 n.12 (1989).

"To designate every decompilation a copyright infringement would be to transform copyright law into an extremely powerful version of trade secret protection law. This would be contrary to traditional principles of copyright law specifically and intellectual property law more generally, as well as the fundamental principles of competition underlying intellectual property law." Samuelson, Davis, Kapor & Reichman, *Existing Laws Fail to Protect Software Adequately*, Nat'l L.J., Feb. 20, 1995, at C33.

disclaimer [patent–trademark]   A formal statement by the owner of an intellectual property right that it does not make a claim to certain rights.

1. Patent Disclaimer A statement filed by an owner of a patent or of a patent to be granted, in which the owner gives up certain rights in the patent. There are two types of disclaimers of a patent: (1) A "statutory disclaimer" in which an entire claim or several claims in a patent are disclaimed and relinquished into the public domain. (2) A "TERMINAL DISCLAIMER" by which an applicant or patentee disclaims or dedicates to the public domain a certain period of time at the end of the term of a patent. This is usually done to overcome an "obviousness-type" of DOUBLE PATENTING objection.

See TERMINAL DISCLAIMER.

• *Statutory References*:
35 U.S.C. §253, first paragraph: "Whenever, without any deceptive invention, a claim of a patent is invalid, the remaining claims shall not thereby be rendered invalid. A patentee, whether of the whole or any sectional interest therein, may, on payment of the fee required by law, make disclaimer of any complete claim, stating therein the extent of his interest in the patent. Such disclaimer shall be in writing, and recorded in the Patent and Trademark Office; and it shall thereafter be considered as part of the original patent to the extent of the interest possessed by the disclaimant and by those claiming under him."

35 U.S.C. §253, second paragraph: "In like manner any patentee or applicant may disclaim or dedicate to the public the entire term, or any terminal part of the term, of the patent granted or to be granted."

35 U.S.C. §288: "Whenever, without deceptive intention, a claim of a patent is invalid, an action may be maintained for the infringement of a claim of the patent which may be valid. The patentee shall recover no costs unless a disclaimer of the invalid claim has been entered at the Patent and Trademark Office before the commencement of the suit."

• *Case Reference*: "We therefore agree with and adopt the Ninth Circuit's conclusions in *Jennings* that '[t]he failure of a patentee to disclaim an invalid patent claim does not prevent the patentee from enforcing any remaining claims in the same patent which are otherwise valid.'" *Allen Archery Inc. v. Browning Mfg. Co.*, 819 F.2d 1087, 1097, 2 USPQ2d 1490, 1497–98 (Fed. Cir. 1987) (the contrary rule of the 1939 Supreme Court decision in *Maytag* was changed by §§253 and 288 of the Patent Code of 1952).

2. Trademark Registration Disclaimer. This is a statement by a registrant of a COMPOSITE MARK that it is claiming only the whole composite mark as its registered mark and makes no claim to the particular portion or portions disclaimed.

Disclaimer of Unregistrable Parts of a Composite Mark. The Patent and Trademark Office trademark examining attorney sometimes will require that an applicant disclaim unregistrable matter that forms part of a registrable composite mark. A disclaimer makes it clear on the public record that the registration is presumptive evidence of the validity only of the composite mark as a whole, not of any individual unregistrable element of the composite. The standard form of disclaimer is: "No claim is made to the exclusive right to use _____ apart from the mark as shown." *Trademark Manual of Examining Procedure* §1213.09(a) (1993). The types of matter usually required to be disclaimed are those barred from registration under Lanham Act §2(e) as descriptive, geographically descriptive, or a surname in the absence of SECONDARY MEANING. If the registrable and unregistrable elements of a composite mark are integrated or merged together, the mark is regarded as a unitary mark, not a composite, and no disclaimer of parts is required. *Dena Corp. v. Belvedere Int'l Inc.*, 950 F.2d 1555, 21 USPQ2d 1047 (Fed. Cir. 1991); *Trademark Manual of Examining Procedure* §1213.06 (1993).

Admission of Descriptiveness. A disclaimer of a portion of a composite mark is an admission or concession that the disclaimed portion of the mark is an unregistrable descriptive component. *In re Pollio Dairy Corp.*, 8 USPQ2d 2012 n.4 (T.T.A.B. 1988).

A Disclaimer Is Irrelevant to a Determination of Likelihood of Confusion. For purposes of determining the likelihood of confusion created by an accused mark with a registered composite mark of which portions are disclaimed, the disclaimed portions must be considered and cannot be ignored. Likelihood of confusion is determined by the probable reaction of customers who see the mark as a whole and who neither know nor care about disclaimers on file in a government office. "The public is unaware of what words have been disclaimed during prosecution of the trademark application at the PTO." *In re National Data Corp.*, 753 F.2d 1056, 1059, 224 USPQ 749, 751 (Fed. Cir. 1985). The Lanham Act §6(b) explicitly states that no disclaimer has any effect on the registrant's common law rights in the disclaimed matter. The registrant can still allege infringement of its common law rights in the disclaimed material. *Official Airline Guides, Inc. v. Goss*, 856 F.2d 85, 8 USPQ2d 1157 (9th Cir. 1988).

See COMPOSITE MARK.

• *Treatise Reference*: 2 J.T. McCarthy, *Trademarks and Unfair Competition* §19.20–.22 (3d ed. 1995 rev.).

• *Statutory References*:

Lanham Act §6, 15 U.S.C. §1056:

(a) The Commissioner may require the applicant to disclaim an unregistrable component of a mark otherwise registrable. An applicant may voluntarily disclaim a component of a mark sought to be registered.

(b) No disclaimer, including those made under subsection (e) of section 7 of this Act, shall prejudice or affect the applicant's or registrant's rights then existing or thereafter arising in the disclaimed matter, or his right of registration on another application if the disclaimed matter be or shall have become distinctive of his goods or services.

Lanham Act §7(e), 15 U.S.C. §1057(e): " ... Upon application of the registrant and payment of the prescribed fee, the Commissioner for good cause may permit any registration to be amended or to be disclaimed in part: Provided, That the amendment or disclaimer does not alter materially the character of the mark...."

• *Manual Reference*: "The purpose of a disclaimer is to permit the registration of a mark which is registrable as a whole but which contains matter which would not be registrable standing alone, without creating a false impression of the extent of the registrant's right with respect to certain individual elements in the mark." *Trademark Manual of Examining Procedure* §1213 (1993).

• *Case References*:

[I]t is clear that [registrant's] common law right in the composite mark as used in commerce will remain unaffected without regard to deletion or disclaimer of the phrase in question or to the procurement of a federal registration.... The role of disclaimers within the law of trademarks was stated by this court in *In re Hercules Fasteners, Inc.*, 203 F.2d 753, 757, 97 USPQ 355, 357 (C.C.P.A. 1953), to be the following:

The purpose of a disclaimer is to show that the applicant is not making claim to the exclusive appropriation of such matter except in the precise relation and association in which it appeared in the drawing and description.

The effect of a disclaimer is to disavow any exclusive right to the use of a specified word, phrase, or design outside of its use within a composite mark.

In re Franklin Press, Inc., 597 F.2d 270, 273, 201 USPQ 662, 664–65 (C.C.P.A. 1979).

"[I]t is well settled that the disclaimed material still forms a part of the mark and cannot be ignored in determining likelihood of confusion.... Such disclaimers are not helpful in preventing likelihood of confusion in the mind of the consumer because he is unaware of their existence. Therefore, the disclaime[d] portions of the mark must be considered in determining the likelihood of confusion." *Giant Food, Inc. v. Nation's Foodservice, Inc.*, 710 F.2d 1565, 1570, 218 USPQ 390, 395 (Fed. Cir. 1983).

disclosure [patent] Those parts of a patent in which the inventor discloses and explains the invention in detail. In return for receiving the right to exclude in a patent, the inventor must give up secrecy and fully disclose the details of the invention to the public. This will enable others to understand the invention and be able to use it as a stepping stone to further develop the technology. Also, once the patent expires, the public is entitled to make and use the invention and is entitled to a full and complete disclosure of how to do so.

Specification and Claims Compared. The SPECIFICATION of a patent discloses and describes; the CLAIMS define. Whereas the disclosure portion of the specification describes the invention in technical detail, the claims define the scope of the invention. It is the role of the disclosure portion of the specification, not of the claims, to describe the invention. *Orthokinetics Inc. v. Safety Travel Chairs Inc.*, 806 F.2d 1565, 1575, 1 USPQ2d 1081, 1088 (Fed. Cir. 1986). "The disclosure of a patent is in the public domain save as the claims forbid. The claims alone delimit the right to exclude; only they may be infringed." *Environmental Instruments Inc. v. Sutron Corp.*, 877 F.2d 1561, 1564, 11 USPQ2d 1132, 1134 (Fed. Cir. 1989).

The Statutory Requirements of Disclosure. Patent Code §112 sets forth three distinct requirements for disclosure of the invention in the specification: (1) the DESCRIPTIVE requirement—the invention that is claimed must be the invention that is described; (2) the ENABLEMENT requirement—the description must be in such full, clear, and concise terms as to enable any person skilled in the art to make and use it; and (3) the BEST MODE requirement—description of the best embodiment of the invention known to the inventor at the time of the patent application.

A Patent Adds to the Prior Art as Well as Excludes. What the novice in the field often has some difficulty in fully appreciating is that a patent can serve two quite different purposes. Most obviously, the CLAIMS of the patent stake out a slice of technology from which the patent owner can exclude all others. But less easy to appreciate is that an equally important function of a patent is to disclose new technology to those working in the field. That invention which is described and disclosed in the patent will likely become part of the PRIOR ART for later inventors. Thus, while a patent ties up some claimed technology for the term of the patent, it also adds to the store of technical information immediately available to all.

See SPECIFICATION.

- *Statutory Reference:*

35 U.S.C. §112, first paragraph: "The specification shall contain a written description of the invention, and of the manner and process of making and using it, in such full, clear, concise, and exact terms as to enable any person skilled in the art to which it pertains, or with which it is most nearly connected, to make and use the same, and shall set forth the best mode contemplated by the inventor of carrying out his invention."

35 U.S.C. §112, second paragraph: "The specification shall conclude with one or more claims particularly pointing out and distinctly claiming the subject matter which the applicant regards as his invention."

- *Treatise Reference:* "Full disclosure of the invention and the manner of making and using it on issuance of the patent immediately increases the storehouse of public information available for further research and innovation and assures that the invention will be freely available to all once the statutory period of monopoly expires." 2 D. Chisum, *Patents* §7.01 (1989 rev.).

disclosure document [patent] A paper disclosing an invention and signed by the inventor, which is sent to the Patent and Trademark Office (PTO) for retention for two years as a record of the date of CONCEPTION of an invention. A fee of about $6.00 is charged by the PTO for filing a disclosure document. Contrary to the folklore circulating in some amateur inventor circles, a disclosure filed with the PTO disclosure-document program is not a cut-rate "patent" application. The only purpose of filing a disclosure document with the PTO is to serve as a more credible form of evidence of conception than the traditional practice of the inventor mailing a disclosure to himself by registered mail. The disclosure document will become important only if the inventor becomes engaged in a PRIORITY OF INVENTION battle with a rival inventor.

• *Manual Reference*: "The Disclosure Document is not a patent application, and the date of its receipt in the Patent and Trademark Office will not become the effective filing date of any patent application subsequently filed.... The two year retention period should not be considered to be a 'grace period' during which the inventor can wait to file his patent application without possible loss of benefits." *Manual of Patent Examining Procedure* §1706 (1994).

display [copyright] To show a copy of a copyrighted work, either directly or by means of a film, slide, television image, or any other device or process, including individual nonsequential images of a motion picture or other audiovisual work.

The exclusive right to "display the copyrighted work publicly" is granted to all types of copyrighted works except for SOUND RECORDINGS. 17 U.S.C. §106(5). The display right applies only to COPIES, and not PHONORECORDS.

What Is a "Display"? A work can be "displayed" by showing a copy directly. For example, one can "display" a painting or photograph by hanging it on a wall or "display" a sculpture by exhibiting it in a museum. A work is also "displayed" when an image is projected onto a screen or other surface or when an image is transmitted electronically. Showing an image of a copyrighted work on a computer screen is a "display." If the projection or transmission of the image can be seen in a public place, that constitutes a public display of the copyrighted work.

"Public" Display. The copyright owner does not have an exclusive right to all displays of the work: only "public" displays. The definition of "public" is the same as for PERFORMANCE. A display is public if it takes place either (1) at a place open to the public; or (2) at a place not open to the public if a substantial number of persons are gathered, except for a normal circle of a family and its social acquaintances. 17 U.S.C. §101.

"Copy" Versus "Display" in Computer Technology. The display of a copyrighted work on a computer screen is not necessarily a copy of that work. A copy is defined as a material object in which a work is FIXED. In order for a work to be fixed its embodiment in a copy must be "sufficiently permanent or stable to permit it to be perceived, reproduced, or otherwise communicated for a *period of more than transitory duration.*" 17 U.S.C. §101 (emphasis added). In the author's opinion, a transitory display of a copyrighted work by transmission of an image appearing on a computer screen is not fixed and therefore is not a copy. For example, when a case is called up from a computerized data base like Westlaw or Lexis, the image viewed on the computer screen would be a display of that case. If the case were downloaded to disk or printed, a copy would be created. The unauthorized transmission of an image of a copyrighted work from one computer to the screen of another computer could infringe the copyright owner's display right, but it would probably not also infringe the reproduction right unless the image was "fixed" by being saved into the computer's memory. See H.R. Rep. No. 94-1476, 94th Cong., 2d Sess. 62 (1976) ("Thus, the showing of images on a screen or tube would not be a violation of clause (1) [of §106] although it might come within the scope of clause (5).").

See COPIES, FIXED, TRANSMISSION.

Display and Performance Distinguished. The distinction between display and performance of a motion picture or other audiovisual work is in the number and sequence of the images shown. To display a motion picture or other audiovisual work means "to show individual images nonsequentially." 17 U.S.C. §101. The Copyright Act defines performance of a motion picture as "show[ing] its images in any sequence." 17 U.S.C. §101. If the images are shown individually and not in sequence there is no performance, but there is a display. See *Red Baron-Franklin Park, Inc. v. Taito Corp.*, 883 F.2d 275, 279 (4th Cir. 1989) (operation of video game constituted performance and not display because game images were shown in sequence). A public showing of a still image from a movie film would be a display and not a performance of the motion picture.

See PERFORMANCE.

Limitations on the Display Right—Owner of Copy. The buyer of a copy of a copyrighted work owns the copy but does not automatically own the copyright. The lawful owner of a lawfully made copy is entitled to display the copy publicly, without the authority of the copyright owner. 17 U.S.C. §109(c). This display privilege is similar to the FIRST SALE DOCTRINE as applied to the DISTRIBUTION RIGHT for phonorecords in §109(a). Those without ownership who merely possess a copyrighted work by rental, lease, or loan cannot display or authorize others to display it in public without permission from the copyright owner.

The permissible display of an owned copy of a work can be either direct or by projection. If by projection, it must be of no more than one image at a time to viewers present at the place where the copy is located. 17 U.S.C. §109(c). For example, the owner of a copy of a work may show it to the public directly in a gallery or a display case or indirectly by projection of a photographic slide, negative, or transparency to those "present at the place where the copy is located." But the display of a visual image of a copyrighted work would be an infringement if the image were transmitted by closed or open circuit television or by a computer system from one place to members of the public located elsewhere. Also, even where the viewers and the copy are located in the same place, projection of multiple images simultaneously is an infringement of the display right. Where each person in a lecture hall is supplied with a separate viewing apparatus, in order to lawfully project an image of a work on individual screens simultaneously, the copyright owner's permission would probably be required. H.R. Rep. No. 94-1476, 94th Cong., 2d Sess. 79–80 (1976).

Statutory Exceptions to the Display Right. Some of the §110 exceptions or defenses to conduct that would otherwise be an infringement of the exclusive right of public performance are equally applicable to the right of public display. Examples include the classroom exemption, the instructional broadcasting exemption, the religious services exemption, and the compulsory license for noncommercial broadcasting under §118.

See PERFORMANCE, TRANSMISSION.

• *Treatise References*: 2 *Nimmer on Copyright* §8.20 (1994 rev.); M. Leaffer, *Understanding Copyright* §§8.23–.24 (1989); 1 N. Boorstyn, *Copyright* §5.06 (2d ed. 1994); W. Patry, *Copyright Law and Practice* 1001 (1994).

• *Statutory References*:

17 U.S.C. §101: "To 'display' a work means to show a copy of it, either directly or by means of a film, slide, television image, or any other device or process or, in the case of a motion picture or other audiovisual work, to show individual images nonsequentially."

17 U.S.C. §101:

To perform or display a work "publicly" means

(1) to perform or display it at a place open to the public or at any place where a substantial number of persons outside of a normal circle of a family and its social acquaintances is gathered; or

(2) to transmit or otherwise communicate a performance or display of the work to a place specified by clause (1) to the public, by means of any device or process, whether the members of the public capable of receiving the performance or display receive it in the same place or in separate places and at the same time or at different times.

• *Legislative History*: "The committee's intention [in including a display right] is to preserve the traditional privilege of the owner of a copy to display it directly, but to place reasonable restrictions on the ability to display it indirectly in such a way that the copyright owner's market for reproduction and distribution of copies would be affected.... The concept of 'the place where the copy is located' is generally intended to refer to a situation in which viewers are present in the same physical surroundings as the copy, even though they cannot see the copy directly." H.R. Rep. No. 94-1476, 94th Cong., 2d Sess. 80 (1976).

dissection [trademark]

See COMPOSITE MARK.

distribution right [copyright] One of the five exclusive rights held by a copyright owner, under which the copyright owner has the exclusive right to distribute copies or phonorecords of the work to the public by sale, lease, or rental.

Scope of the Distribution Right. Unlike the other rights of copyright, the distribution right is infringed merely by a transfer of copies of the work, whether those copies were unlawfully or lawfully made. One reason for the distribution right is to give a copyright infringement claim against a wholesale or retail seller of infringing copies where the actual copying manufacturer is difficult to find. For example, a cartoonist has a copyright infringement claim against a retail store selling T-shirts imprinted with an infringing picture of a cartoon character protected by copyright. Without such a distribution right, the cartoonist would be without an effective claim, for the retail store would claim to be largely ignorant of where this particular item came from and the shirts may have been imprinted by a pirate manufacturer impossible to locate.

The Exception of the "First Sale Doctrine." The distribution right is subject to an important exception in the FIRST SALE DOCTRINE under which the distribution right is exhausted as to a particular lawfully made copy once there has been an authorized sale of that copy. However, there is an exception to this which imposes full copyright liability on the unlicensed commercial renting of phonorecords or computer programs. The first sale doctrine is triggered only by the authorized first sale of a lawfully made copy. Each sale in the chain of distribution of an unlawfully made, infringing, or pirated copy is itself an act of infringement of the distribution right.

See FIRST SALE DOCTRINE.

• *Treatise References*: 2 *Nimmer on Copyright* §8.11 (1994 rev.); 1 P. Goldstein, *Copyright* §5.5 (1989); M. Leaffer, *Understanding Copyright* §8.12 (1989); W. Patry, *Copyright Law and Practice* 834 (1994).

• *Statutory Reference*: 17 U.S.C. §106: "Subject to sections 107 through 118, the owner of copyright under this title has the exclusive right to do and to authorize any of the following: … (3) to distribute copies or phonorecords of the copyrighted work to the public by sale or other transfer of ownership, by rental, lease, or lending; …"

divestive publication [copyright]

See PUBLICATION.

divisional application [patent–trademark] An application to the Patent and Trademark Office to divide a single patent application, or a single application to register a mark, into more than one application.

1. Division of a Patent Application. A divisional application is an application for patent on a distinct invention, carved out of a pending application and disclosing and claiming only subject matter disclosed in the earlier or PARENT APPLICATION.

A divisional application is usually filed as a result of a requirement for RESTRICTION made by the PTO examiner.

The divisional application is entitled to the filing date of the original application, and neither the original nor the restricted divisional application can be cited against each other as prior art.

See *Manual of Patent Examining Procedure* §201.06 (1994).

See RESTRICTION.

• *Case References*:

"Giving a patent application the benefit of the earlier filing date of another earlier filed application has a statutory basis and does not rest on the mere claim or recitation of the applicant. Nor is the mere labeling of an application a 'division' enough." *Racing Strollers Inc. v. TRI Indus. Inc.*, 878 F.2d 1418, 1419, 11 USPQ2d 1300, 1301 (Fed. Cir. 1989) (en banc) (application for design patent can be a division of earlier filed utility patent application).

"'Continuation' and 'divisional' applications are alike in that they are both continuing applications based on the same disclosure as an earlier application. A 'continuation' application claims the same invention claimed in an earlier application, although there may be some variation in the scope of the subject matter claimed. See MPEP §201.07. A 'divisional' application, on the other hand, is one carved out of an earlier application which disclosed and claimed more than one independent invention, the result being that the divisional application claims only one or more, but not all, of the independent inventions of the earlier application. See MPEP §201.06." *Transco Prods. Inc. v. Performance Contracting, Inc.*, 38 F.3d 551, 555, 32 USPQ2d 1077, 1080 (Fed. Cir. 1994).

- *Statutory Reference*: 35 U.S.C. §121: "If two or more independent and distinct inventions are claimed in one application, the Commissioner may require the application to be restricted to one of the inventions. If the other invention is made the subject of a divisional application which complies with the requirements of section 120 of this title it shall be entitled to the benefit of the filing date of the original application. A patent issuing on an application with respect to which a requirement for restriction under this section has been made, or on an application filed as a result of such a requirement, shall not be used as a reference either in the Patent and Trademark Office or in the courts against a divisional application or against the original application or any patent issued on either of them, if the divisional application is filed before the issuance of the patent on the other application...."

2. Division of an Application to Register a Trademark. Under rules promulgated in 1989, it became possible to divide one application to register a mark for goods listed in one or more classifications into two or more separate applications. 37 C.F.R. §2.87. The purpose is to divide out some, but not all, of the goods or services into separate applications. Such a request to divide may be made: (1) at any time between the filing of the application and the time when the examiner approves the mark for publication; (2) during an OPPOSITION proceeding when division can be made upon motion granted by the TRADEMARK TRIAL AND APPEAL BOARD; or (3) pursuant to a request to divide an INTENT TO USE application filed along with a Statement of Use. By dividing the application, the applicant preserves the filing date and thus the CONSTRUCTIVE USE date as to all the goods and services covered by the original application. If the request is to divide out certain goods or services within a single PTO classification category, then an application fee for each new divided application must be paid.

An applicant may request division of an application for any reason. For example, in an INTENT TO USE application, the applicant may want to promptly go ahead to publication or registration for certain goods or services on which the mark has been used, while retaining the pending application for other goods or services on which the mark has not yet been used.

- *Rule Reference*: 37 C.F.R. §2.87.

- *Treatise Reference*: 2 J.T. McCarthy, *Trademarks and Unfair Competition* §19.15 (3d ed. 1995 rev.).

domination [patent] The situation that exists when a claim in patent A covers, includes, and encompasses technology claimed in patent B. The claim in patent A "dominates" patent B in the sense that the technology covered by patent B cannot be made, used, or sold without license from the owner of patent A. Patent A is called a "basic" patent, and patent B is called an "improvement" patent.

A Patent Is Not a Grant of a Right to Use. Contrary to popular belief, a patent is not a grant of a right to use the patented technology. Rather, it is a grant of a right to exclude others from using the technology defined in the patent claims. The patentee might not be able itself to use the technology of the patent because it is merely an improvement upon technology previously patented by another. In that event, a license from the previous patentee is needed. "A patent is not the grant of a right to make or use or sell. It does not, directly or indirectly, imply any such right. It grants only the right to exclude others." *Herman v. Youngstown Car Mfg. Co.*, 191 F. 579, 584 (6th Cir. 1911), quoted with approval in *Atlas Powder Co. v. E.I. du Pont de Nemours & Co.*, 750 F.2d 1569, 1580, 224 USPQ 409, 417 (Fed. Cir. 1984) (owner of improvement patent can be liable for infringing upon the claims of basic patent). See *Spindelfabrik Suessen-Schurr GmbH v. Schubert & Salzer AG*, 829 F.2d 1075, 1081, 4 USPQ2d 1044, 1048 (Fed. Cir. 1987) (patentee is not given the right to use patented technology: "His right is merely one to exclude others from making, using or selling...."); *In re Bergy*, 596 F.2d 952, 1081 n.3, 201 USPQ 352, 359 n.3 (C.C.P.A. 1979), *dismissed as moot*, 444 U.S. 924 (1980) ("The patent grant never has had anything to do with the patentee's right to make, use or vend...."); *Animal Legal Defense Fund v. Quigg*, 932 F.2d 920, 935, 18 USPQ2d 1677, 1689 (Fed. Cir. 1991) ("It should hardly need saying that the issuance of a patent gives no right to make, use or sell a patented invention."

"Domination" is not identical to the concept of the "same invention" for purposes of DOUBLE PATENTING.

- *Case References*: "By domination we refer, in accordance with established patent law terminology, to the phenomenon, which grows out of the fact that patents have claims, whereunder one patent has a broad or 'generic' claim which 'reads on' an invention defined by a narrower or more specific claim in another patent, the former 'dominating' the latter because the more narrowly claimed invention cannot be practiced without infringing the broader claim.... [O]ne patent dominates another if a claim of the first patent reads on a device built or process practiced according to the second patent disclosure." *In re Kaplan*, 789 F.2d 1574, 1577, 229 USPQ 678, 681 (Fed. Cir. 1986).

"[T]hat someone has a patent right to exclude others from making the invention claimed in his patent does not mean that his invention cannot infringe claims of another's patent broad enough to encompass, i.e., to 'dominate,' his invention." *Rolls-Royce Ltd. v. GTE Caleron Corp.*, 800 F.2d 1101, 1110 n.9, 231 USPQ 185, 191 n.9 (Fed. Cir. 1986).

double patenting [patent] The result when two patents are granted to one person containing claims that recite the same invention or obvious variations of the same invention. The law prohibits one person from obtaining more than one valid patent on the same invention or an obvious variation of the same invention. A finding of double patenting is a ground for refusing to issue the second patent or for holding invalid the second patent.

Burden of Proof. There is a heavy burden of proof on one seeking to prove double patenting. *Carman Indus., Inc. v. Wahl*, 724 F.2d 932, 940, 220 USPQ 481, 487 (Fed. Cir. 1983).

Two Types. There are two very distinct situations prohibited under the label "double patenting": (1) same invention-type double patenting; and (2) obviousness-type double patenting.

Terminal Disclaimer. A TERMINAL DISCLAIMER may overcome only the obviousness-type double patenting objection, not the same invention-type double patenting.

See TERMINAL DISCLAIMER.

- *Case Reference*: "[T]he law of double patenting is concerned *only* with what patents *claim*. 'Double patenting,' therefore, involves an inquiry into what, if anything, has been claimed twice." *General Foods Corp. v. Studiengesellschaft Kohle mbH*, 972 F.2d 1272, 1275, 23 USPQ2d 1839, 1840 (Fed. Cir. 1992).

- *Manual Reference*: "When two or more pending applications of (1) the same inventive entity, (2) the same assignee, or (3) having at least one common inventor, contain conflicting claims which are not patentably distinct, a 'provisional' double patenting rejection of either the same or obviousness-type should be made in each application. Such a rejection is 'provisional' since the conflicting claims are not, as yet, patented. *In re Wetterau*, 148 USPQ 499 (C.C.P.A. 1966)." *Manual of Patent Examining Procedure* §804 (1994).

- *Treatise Reference*: 3 D. Chisum, *Patents* §§9.01–.03 (1994 rev.).

1. Same Invention-Type Double Patenting. This rule prohibits an attempt to claim the same invention twice. This prohibition is based on Patent Code §101, which states that an inventor may obtain "a patent" on an invention. "The 'same invention' in this context means an invention drawn to identical subject matter." *In re Longi*, 759 F.2d 887, 892, 225 USPQ 645, 648 (Fed. Cir. 1985). "DOMINATION" is not identical to the concept of the "same invention." *In re Kaplan*, 789 F.2d 1574, 1577, 229 USPQ 678, 681 (Fed. Cir. 1986).

The Test of Same Invention-Type Double Patenting. "A good test, and probably the only objective test, for 'same invention,' is whether one of the claims would be literally infringed without literally infringing the other. If it could be, the claims do not define identically the same invention." *In re Vogel*, 422 F.2d 438, 441, 164 USPQ 619, 622 (C.C.P.A. 1970), quoted with approval and applied in *Studiengesellschaft Kohle mbH v. Northern Petrochemical Co.*, 784 F.2d 351, 355, 228 USPQ 837, 840 (Fed. Cir. 1986).

Cross-Reading. The foregoing test has sometimes been characterized as whether the two patents CROSS-READ. If they do cross-read, then there is double patenting. If a device infringing patent A must also infringe patent B and vice versa, then the patents cross-read because the claims of one patent cannot be infringed without also infringing the other patent. *Carman Indus., Inc. v. Wahl*, 724 F.2d 932, 940, 220 USPQ 481, 487 (Fed. Cir. 1983).

- *Example*: If one patent claims a composition and the other patent claims a process, then they claim different statutory classes and do not claim the "same invention." Therefore, there is no violation of the rule against same invention-type double patenting. *Studiengesellschaft Kohle mbH v. Northern Petrochemical Co.*, 784 F.2d 351, 355, 228 USPQ 837, 840 (Fed. Cir. 1986).

2. Obviousness-Type Double Patenting. This rule prohibits one from extending patent rights by obtaining claims in a second patent on an "obvious" modification of the same invention that is covered by the prior patent owned by the same person. This is a judicially created rule based on the public policy of preventing the extension of the duration of a patent by forbidding the issuance of claims in a second patent that are not distinct from the claims of the first patent.

The issue is "whether the claimed invention in the application for the second patent would have been obvious from the subject matter of the claims in the first patent, in light of the prior art." *In re Longi*, 759 F.2d 887, 892, 225 USPQ 645, 648 (Fed. Cir. 1985). While a rejection of double patenting of the obviousness-type is "analogous to" the nonobviousness rule of Patent Code §103, the prior patent underlying the double patenting rejection is "not considered prior art." *In re Longi, supra*, at 892 n.4.

Divisional Application. Patent Code §121 provides for RESTRICTION when independent and distinct inventions are claimed in one application. The applicant may respond to a requirement of restriction by filing a DIVISIONAL APPLICATION. The third sentence of §121 provides protection against a double patenting rejection where a divisional application is filed as a result of an examiner's division requirement. "[A] patent issuing on an application with respect to which a requirement for restriction under this section has been made, or on an application filed as a result of such a requirement, shall not be used as a reference against a divisional application or against the original application if the divisional application is filed before the issuance of the patent on the other application." 35 U.S.C. §121.

The double patenting protection under §121 does not apply if the divisional application was not filed in response to a restriction requirement actually imposed by the examiner or if the claims of the different applications or patents are not "consonant with the requirement made by the examiner...." *Manual of Patent Examining Procedure* §804.01(A) (1994). "Consonance requires that the line between the 'independent and distinct inventions' that prompted the restriction be maintained." *Gerber Garment Technology, Inc. v. Lectra Sys., Inc.*, 916 F.2d 683, 688, 16 USPQ2d 1436, 1440 (Fed. Cir. 1990). The claims must not have been changed in a material respect from the claims as they existed at the time the requirement was made. "Though the claims [in a divisional application] may be amended, they must not be so amended as to bring them back over the line imposed in the restriction requirement. Where that line is crossed the prohibition of the third sentence of Section 121 does not apply." *Id.* See RESTRICTION, DIVISIONAL APPLICATION.

The Test of Obviousness-Type Double Patenting. Step one of the analysis is to determine, by looking at the claims, what has been patented. Step two is to determine whether there exists a "patentable difference" between the claims of the first-patented invention and the claims of its variant. If the claims of the second invention define more than an obvious variation, the inventions are patentably distinct, and there is no double patenting. Comparison can be made only with what invention is *claimed* in the earlier patent and not by looking to the claim for anything that happens to be mentioned in it as though it were a prior art reference. *General Foods Corp. v. Studiengesellschaft Kohle mbH*, 972 F.2d 1272, 1275, 23 USPQ2d 1839, 1845 (Fed. Cir. 1992).

For example, patent A contains claims for a process for caffeine recovery. Patent B describes a process for decaffeination of coffee. One claim in patent A mentions the decaffeination process in patent B as providing a chemical solution from which caffeine can be recovered. Patent A does not invalidate the decaffeination process patent because the two patents do not claim the same invention, and neither process is a mere obvious variation of the other. *General Foods Corp. v. Studiengesellschaft Kohle mbH*, 972 F.2d 1272, 23 USPQ2d 1839 (Fed. Cir. 1992).

The "obviousness-type" of double patenting objection may be overcome by a TERMINAL DISCLAIMER.

• *Case References*:
"The public should ... be able to act on the assumption that upon the expiration of the patent it will be free to use not only the invention claimed in the patent but also modifications or variants which would have been obvious to those of ordinary skill in the art...." *In re Zickendraht*, 319 F.2d 225, 232, 138 USPQ 23, 27 (C.C.P.A. 1963).

The prohibition of obviousness-type double patenting may even apply to commonly owned applications made by different inventive entities. *In re Longi*, 759 F.2d 887, 895, 225 USPQ 645, 650 (Fed. Cir. 1985).

• *Treatise References*: "Obviousness-type double patenting is a judicially created doctrine grounded in public policy (as reflected in the patent statute). The purpose is to prevent the extension of the term of a patent, even when an express statutory basis for a rejection or defense is missing, by prohibiting the issuance of claims in a second patent that are not patentably distinct from those in a first patent.... This is so the public can, upon expiration of the first patent, be free to practice obvious variations of the invention claimed." R. Harmon, *Patents and the Federal Circuit* §15.5(a) (3d ed. 1994). See 3 D. Chisum, *Patents* §§9.01–.03 (1994 rev.).

doubt, rule of [copyright] A rule under which the U.S. Copyright Office will register a claim even though it has a reasonable doubt about the validity of the copyright. When a rule of doubt registration is made, the Copyright Office may send a letter to the applicant cautioning that, in its opinion, the claim may not be valid. See H.R. Rep. No. 388, 103d Cong., 1st Sess. 18 (1993); W. Patry, *Copyright Law and Practice* 1221 n.152 (1994).

Computer Program Deposits. In some instances, the U.S. Copyright Office will accept OBJECT CODE as a proper deposit as part of a registration of copyright for a COMPUTER PROGRAM. In making a deposit of the work in connection with registering a claim of copyright for a computer program, the Copyright Office believes that the best representation of the authorship in a computer program is a listing of the program in SOURCE CODE. Where the copyright claimant is unable or unwilling to deposit a identifying material in source code, depositing only object code instead, registration will proceed under the rule of doubt upon receipt of written assurance that the work as deposited in object code contains copyrightable authorship. Because object code is essentially unintelligible to copyright examiners, it is not possible to determine the presence of copyrightable material. *Compendium of Copyright Office Practices* §324.04 (1984). See 37 C.F.R. §202.20(c)(2)(vii) (specifying the nature of deposit of "[c]omputer programs and databases in machine-readable copies other than CD-ROM format").

• *Reference*: "The Copyright Office will register the claim even though there is a reasonable doubt about the ultimate action which might be taken under the same circumstances by an appropriate court with respect to whether (1) the material deposited for registration constitutes copyrightable subject matter or (2) the other legal and formal requirements of the statute have been met." *Compendium of Copyright Office Practices* §108.07 (1984).

dramatic rights [copyright]

See GRAND RIGHTS.

droit de suite [copyright–author's rights]

The laws of France, Italy, and Germany recognize a "droit de suite": the right of an artist to participate in proceeds from the subsequent sales of a work of art. The goal is to enable the artist to obtain some monetary gain from resale of a work of art as it increases in value over time. Each time the tangible work of art is resold, the artist is legally entitled to be paid a royalty based upon a portion of the proceeds from the resale.

Droit de Suite in the United States. The federal copyright act does not incorporate the droit de suite. The 1977 California Resale Royalties Act does adopt the droit de suite in that state. California Civil Code §986. Whenever an original work of fine art is resold and the seller resides in California or the sale takes place in California, the seller must pay to the artist 5 percent of the amount of the sale if the sale price is more than $1,000. In a 1992 study of the droit de suite, the Copyright Office took a generally negative view of implementing the right into federal law.

• *Treatise Reference*: 2 *Nimmer on Copyright* §8.22 (1994 rev.); W. Patry, *Copyright Law and Practice* 1014 (1994).

droit moral [copyright–author's rights]

See MORAL RIGHTS.

droits voisins [copyright]

See NEIGHBORING RIGHTS.

due diligence [general intellectual property]

An investigation undertaken in the course of an intellectual property transaction to verify and determine the ownership and scope of intellectual property legal rights being sold, licensed, or used as collateral. The purpose of a due diligence investigation is to provide the data needed to analyze and assess the business and legal risks associated with the intellectual property rights that are the subject of the transaction.

Due diligence procedures may include, among other things: (1) identification of all intellectual property involved in the transaction; (2) verification of ownership of the intellectual property; (3) determination of the enforceability or strength of the intellectual property assets; (4) review and verification of all documentation associated with the intellectual property, including registrations, licenses, security liens, FILE WRAPPERS, and claims of infringement; and (5) interviews of those persons with knowledge of the intellectual property, such as persons familiar with the subject of technical data claimed as trade secrets. If the intellectual property rights to be sold or licensed are international, then a due diligence investigation may include an inquiry into the patent and trademark records of several nations.

• *Example*: Alpha company wants to enter into an exclusive license agreement to make and sell toy figures based upon characters in Beta Studio's motion picture. The license will give Alpha permission to use the copyright and trademark rights associated with the characters in the movie. Because Alpha is licensing certain rights to the intellectual property, it will want to make sure that Beta owns the rights it is making available to Alpha. Alpha's attorneys may conduct a due diligence investigation to determine the scope and strength of Beta's intellectual property rights in the movie characters before Alpha enters into the license agreement.

• *Example:* Mega Corporation wants to acquire the Alta-Tech Corporation, a company that does research, development, production, and sales of specialized medical lasers. Mega's attorneys may conduct a due diligence investigation to determine the existence, scope, and strength of the patents, trade secrets, copyrights, and trademarks of the Alta-Tech Corporation before consummating the acquisition.

See ASSIGNMENT, LICENSE.

Dunkel Text [international–intellectual property] The Trade-Related Aspects of Intellectual Property Rights (*TRIPS*) agreement in *GATT* drafted by Director General Arthur Dunkel in December 1991. The "Dunkel Text," as amended, came into effect in 1994, as a result of the conclusion of the Uruguay Round of negotiations on December 15, 1993.

See GATT, TRIPS, URUGUAY ROUND AGREEMENTS ACT.

duration [patent–trademark–copyright– trade secret–right of publicity] The term or length of time that an intellectual property right lasts.

1. Duration of a Patent. The U.S. Constitution authorizes Congress to pass laws giving exclusive rights to inventors "for limited times." Thus, any patent must have a limited and fixed duration.

See CONSTITUTION.

Utility Patent. Prior to 1995, a U.S. patent on an invention had a duration of 17 years from the grant of the patent. As a result of the URUGUAY ROUND AGREEMENTS ACT, U.S. law was changed, effective June 8, 1995, to adopt a patent term of 20 years from the filing of the patent application. 35 U.S.C. §154(a). All U.S. patents that were in force on, or that issued on an application filed before, June 8, 1995, automatically have a term that is the greater of the 20-year term or 17 years from grant. However, MAINTENANCE FEES must be timely paid at three points during the duration of the patent grant in order to keep the patent alive.

Patent Extension. For patents on human drug products, medical devices, or food or color additives, the term of the patent may be extended under a special 1984 statute to compensate for the delay in awaiting federal regulatory agencies' approval of the product for commercial sale. 35 U.S.C. §156, 37 C.F.R. §§1.710–.785. As a result of the 1994 Uruguay Round Agreements Act changes, the new 20-year patent term is capable of being extended up to five years for delays in the issuance of a patent due to an INTERFERENCE, a secrecy order, or successful appeal to the BOARD OF PATENT APPEALS AND INTERFERENCES or the federal courts. 35 U.S.C. §154(b).

Design Patent. In 1982 the Patent Code was amended to provide a uniform 14-year term from grant for all design patents. 35 U.S.C. §173.

Plant Patent. A PLANT PATENT has the same duration as for a utility patent. 35 U.S.C. §161. The term of protection for certain sexually reproduced plants under the Plant Variety Protection Act was extended from 17 to 18 years in 1980 in order to facilitate U.S. entry into the CONVENTION OF THE INTERNATIONAL UNION FOR THE PROTECTION OF NEW PLANT VARIETIES (UPOV).

2. Duration of a Trademark. A trademark continues in duration as long as there is no ABANDONMENT of rights by nonuse or by acts that cause the term to lose its significance as an indicator of origin and to become a GENERIC NAME. The Trademark Law Revision Act of 1989 shortened the term of a federal trademark registration from 20 years to 10 years as part of an effort to reduce unused deadwood cluttering up the federal register. Registrations issued on or after November 16, 1989, have a duration of 10 years and may be renewed indefinitely so long as the mark is still in use. Lanham Act §§8, 9(a), 15 U.S.C. §§1058, 1059(a). Registrations based on applications pending in the Patent and Trademark Office on November 16, 1989, will last for review periods of 10 years. Lanham Act §51, 15 U.S.C. §1058 note.

3. Duration of a Copyright. The U.S. Constitution authorizes Congress to pass laws giving exclusive rights to authors "for limited times." Thus, any federal copyright must have a limited and fixed duration. See CONSTITUTION. Since the manner of measuring duration of federal copyrights was drastically changed effective January 1, 1978, that date is crucial in calculating the duration of copyrights.

Works Created After January 1, 1978: For works created after January 1, 1978, the basic duration is the life of the author plus 50 years. 17 U.S.C. §302. In the case of JOINT AUTHORS, the lifetime is measured by that of the longest-lived joint author. For ANONYMOUS WORKS, PSEUDONYMOUS WORKS, and WORKS MADE FOR

HIRE, the duration is 75 years from first publication or 100 years from creation, whichever expires first. 17 U.S.C. §302(c).

Proposal for Longer Term. In 1995, a proposal was made to increase the term of copyright to life plus 70 years, to make the U.S. term as long as the new life plus 70 term adopted by the nations of the European Union. The proposal would also add 20 years to the fixed-term durations. H.R. 989, introduced February 16, 1995. See 49 Pat. Trademark & Copyright J. (BNA) 497 (Feb. 13, 1995).

Works Created Before January 1, 1978:

Works Unpublished as of January 1, 1978. For works that had never been published as of January 1, 1978, the previous state "common law copyright" was "federalized" and given a duration the same as for works created after January 1, 1978. However, a minimum duration of until at least December 31, 2002, is provided, which is stretched until December 31, 2027, if the work is published before December 31, 2002. 17 U.S.C. §303.

Works in the First Term of Copyright on January 1, 1978. For works in the first 28-year term of copyright as of January 1, 1978, the 1978 Copyright Act revisions "stretched" the second RENEWAL term by 19 years to a total 47-year second term. Thus, the total term of such copyrights was increased to 75 years from the date of first publication with notice (28 + 28 + 19 = 75). 17 U.S.C. §304(a). However, such copyrights must be renewed, either automatically by operation of law or by registration by the copyright claimant. For example, the federal copyright on a textbook first published in 1970 would have to be renewed by 1998. Once renewed, the copyright will last until December 31, 2045.

Automatic Renewal. The 1992 revisions to the Copyright Act provided for automatic renewal of copyright for those works still needing renewal. That is, for works first published from 1964 to the end of 1977, copyright would not be lost for failure to renew. However, renewal is still strongly recommended, for Congress created certain bonus rights and remedies to reward those who register the renewal of their copyrights.

Works in the Renewal Term on January 1, 1978. For older works in the second 28-year renewal term as of January 1, 1978, under the 1978 Copyright Act revisions, the second term is automatically "stretched" by 19 years to a total 47-year term. Thus, the total term of such copyrights was increased to 75 years from the date of first publication with notice (28 + 28 + 19 = 75). 17 U.S.C. §304(b). For example, if a novel was first published in 1932 and the renewal copyright was timely filed by 1960, then the copyright lasts until December 31, 2007. Certain older works whose renewal terms would have expired between 1962 and 1976 were kept alive by special acts of Congress in anticipation of a "stretched" term, which was achieved in the copyright law revisions signed into law in 1976. Thus, a 1918 photograph whose copyright was renewed by 1946 would have expired under the old law in 1974. But a special act of Congress kept it alive until the revisions in the 1976 Act extended or stretched the duration of that copyright until December 31, 1993.

All terms of copyright run to the end of the calendar year in which they expire. 17 U.S.C. §305.

Restoration of Certain Copyrights of Foreign Origin. As a result of changes introduced in the 1994 URUGUAY ROUND AGREEMENTS ACT, U.S. protection for certain works of foreign origin that had fallen out of copyright or were never in copyright in the United States was "restored" if the work was still in copyright in its source country. The new version of 17 U.S.C. §104A restored U.S. copyright to almost all copyrighted works from nations that were members of the WTO or the BERNE UNION that were still protected in their source country but were not protected under U.S. copyright law. U.S. copyright for restored works lasts for the same duration as if the work had never been out of copyright in the United States. For example, a French novel published in the United States without copyright notice in 1945 would be treated as if it had been published with proper notice and properly renewed, such that copyright would last for 75 years. However, the new Act places certain requirements on the owner of such a restored copyright who wishes to enforce it against a "reliance party"— one who acted in reliance on the public domain status of the newly restored work. As a result of the NAFTA implementation act, U.S. copyright was restored in Mexican and Canadian motion pictures that had fallen out of copyright in the United States for failure to use proper copyright notice. Such NAFTA restoration required filing of a statement with the Copyright Office before January 1, 1995.

See RENEWAL OF COPYRIGHT.

• *Treatise References*: 2 *Nimmer on Copyright* §9.01 *et seq.* (1994 rev.); 1 P. Goldstein, *Copyright* §4.6 *et seq.* (1989); M. Leaffer, *Understanding Copyright* §6.2 (1989); W. Patry, *Copyright Law and Practice* ch. 6 (1994).

4. Duration of a Trade Secret. Protection of information as a trade secret lasts as long as the information remains secret. For example, the public disclosure of trade secret information in an issued patent, in a technical journal, or in easily ascertainable aspects of a publicly sold product ends trade secret legal protection.

• *Treatise References*: 1 Milgrim, *Trade Secrets* §2.05 (1994 rev.) ("Since secrecy is a requisite element of a trade secret, it follows that unprotected disclosure of the secret forfeits the trade secret status."); 1 M. Jager, *Trade Secrets Law* §6.03 (1994 rev.) ("It is horn book law that trade secrets are entitled to protection 'as long as they remain secret, i.e., until they are publicly disclosed.' ").

• *Case Reference*: "The property right in a trade secret ceases to exist after the secret has become public property through general disclosure. If a trade secret is patented there is no further right to secrecy. The patent is a legal disclosure with the right to a limited, temporary monopoly granted as the reward for the disclosure.... When the patent was granted on February 22, 1966, Scharmer's property right in a trade secret ceased prospectively. Thus, he had no right of action for misuse of a trade secret *subsequent* to that date." *Scharmer v. Carrollton Mfg. Co.*, 525 F.2d 95, 99, 187 USPQ 736, 739 (6th Cir. 1975).

5. Duration of the Right of Publicity. The right of publicity lasts at least for the duration of the life of the person. Several states by statute or common law have recognized a postmortem duration for the right of publicity. As of 1995, 13 states recognized a postmortem right of publicity: 10 by statute and 3 by common law. The statutes define durations after death ranging from 100 years (Indiana and Oklahoma), 50 years (California, Kentucky, Nevada), 40 years (Florida), 20 years (Virginia), 10 years minimum and as long thereafter as persona is used (Tennessee), and no stated duration (Nebraska). Courts in Georgia, Utah, and New Jersey have found a nonstatutory postmortem duration but have not defined its duration.

• *Treatise Reference*: J.T. McCarthy, *The Rights of Publicity and Privacy* §9.5 *et seq.* (1995 rev.).

E

early neutral evaluation [general legal]
See ALTERNATIVE DISPUTE RESOLUTION.

ejusdem generis [general legal] A Latin legal term meaning the same kind or class. It is a rule of statutory interpretation that where general words follow the enumeration of specific terms, the general words are read as applying only to other terms akin to those specifically enumerated.

For example, if a statute permits keeping on the grounds of a residence within the city limits "dogs, cats, birds, and other animals," "other animals" should be interpreted as referring to animals akin to those animals specifically named. The keeping of water buffalo in the backyard of a city residence should not be permitted under the general term "other animals."

• *Example*: The Copyright Act declares that a performance is public and hence infringing if someone "transmit[s] or otherwise communicate[s] a performance or display of the work ... to the public ... by means of any device or process...." The owner of a copyright in a motion picture argued that when a hotel rents a videodisc of a copyrighted motion picture to patrons to view in their hotel rooms on a videodisc player, the hotel "otherwise communicate[s]" movies "to the public." The court rejected this reading of the statute, using the rule of ejusdem generis to conclude that the general phrase "otherwise communicate" must be read as applying only to acts akin to the specific term "transmit." The Copyright Act defines "transmit" as communicating the images or sounds of a performance "beyond the place from which they are sent." Thus, "otherwise communicate" must be narrowly limited to sending out a signal by a device to be received by the public at a location beyond the place from which it is sent.

Therefore the court concluded that by renting videodiscs to its customers the hotel did not make an unpermitted transmission nor did it "otherwise communicate" the copyrighted motion picture to the public. *Columbia Pictures Indus., Inc. v. Professional Real Estate Invs. Inc.*, 866 F.2d 278, 282, 9 USPQ2d 1653, 1656 (9th Cir. 1989).

election of species [patent] A selection by a patent applicant, in response to a requirement by the Patent and Trademark Office patent examiner, of the species of the invention to which the claims will be restricted if no generic claim is held to be patentable.

"Election of species" is one form of RESTRICTION in a case where claims to particular species of the invention are independent and distinct inventions. Because two or more independent inventions may not be claimed in one patent application, and because the patent examiner may tentatively reject the broad, generic claim, the inventor must choose ("elect") which independent invention will be left in this application if the generic claim rejection stands.

Claims to separate species of the generic invention may be independent inventions if they claim mutually exclusive embodiments, such as when two or more different structures or steps can be used interchangeably to accomplish a result claimed in the generic claim. The generic claim defines the result broadly enough to encompass all the disclosed species, while the species claims cover the separate embodiments one at a time. See J. Landis, *Mechanics of Patent Claim Drafting* §58 (3d ed. 1990).

See RESTRICTION.

• *Rule Reference*: "Election of Species. In the first action on an application containing a

143

generic claim and claims restricted separately to each of more than one species embraced thereby, the examiner may require the applicant in his response to that action to elect that species of his or her invention to which his or her claim shall be restricted if no general claim is held allowable. However, if such application contains claims directed to more than a reasonable number of species, the examiner may require restriction of the claims to not more than a reasonable number before taking further action in that case." 37 C.F.R. §1.146.

• *Manual Reference*: "When there is no disclosure of relationship between species, ... they are independent inventions and election of one invention following a requirement for restriction is mandatory even though applicant disagrees with the examiner. There must be a patentable difference between the species as claimed.... Thus the reasons for insisting upon election of one species are the facts relied upon for the conclusion that there are claims restricted respectively to two or more patentably different species that are disclosed in the application...." *Manual of Patent Examining Procedure* §808.01(a) (1994).

element [patent] (1) A discrete part of a claim in a patent that defines a technological feature which is a limitation on the scope of the claim. (2) A discrete part of an ACCUSED DEVICE. (3) A discrete part of a physical embodiment of a patented invention.

Under the ALL ELEMENTS rule of the doctrine of EQUIVALENTS, each element of a claim or its substantial equivalent must be found in the accused device to constitute infringement. When applying the "all elements" rule, the word "element" is "used in the sense of a *limitation* of a claim." *Corning Glass Works v. Sumitomo Elec. USA Inc.*, 868 F.2d 1251, 1259, 9 USPQ2d 1962, 1968 (Fed. Cir. 1989).

For an ACCUSED DEVICE to constitute a LITERAL INFRINGEMENT, each and every element of the patent claim must be found in the accused device.

See CLAIMS, INFRINGEMENT.

• *Case References*:
"References to 'elements' can be misleading. 'Elements' often is used to refer to structural parts of the accused device or a device embodying the invention. 'Elements' is also used in the phrase '[a]n element of a claim' in 35 U.S.C. §112, ¶6. An element of an embodiment of the invention may be set forth in the claim (e.g., 'said connecting means' in clause (h) of the present claim.) It is the *limitation* of a claim that counts in determining both validity and infringement.... Because claims are composed of a number of limitations, the limitations have on occasion been referred to as 'claim elements' or 'elements of the claim,' but clarity is advanced when sufficient wording is employed to mean a component of an accused device or an embodiment of an invention and when it is intended to mean a feature set forth in or as a limitation in a claim." *Perkin-Elmer Corp. v. Westinghouse Elec. Corp.*, 822 F.2d 1529, 1533 n.9, 3 USPQ2d 1321, 1325 n.9 (Fed. Cir. 1987).

"Literal infringement requires that the accused device embody every element of the patent claim." *Mannesmann Demag Corp. v. Engineered Metal Prods. Co.*, 793 F.2d 1279, 1282, 230 USPQ 45, 46 (Fed. Cir. 1986).

"[I]t follows that each claim is an *entity* which must be considered *as a whole*. It cannot be said—though it often is, incorrectly, by the uninitiated—that a part of a claim is 'claimed' subject matter. For example, a claim to a process comprising the step A followed by step B followed by step C defines, as a matter of law, only the A-B-C process and one cannot properly speak of any single step as being 'claimed,' for it is not; all that is claimed is the process consisting of the *combination* of all three steps. Such a claim, therefore, creates no patent right or monopoly in step A, no right to prevent others from using step A apart from the combination of steps A-B-C. Step A is not 'patented.' " *General Foods Corp. v. Studiengesellschaft Kohle mbH*, 972 F.2d 1272, 1274, 23 USPQ2d 1839, 1840 (Fed. Cir. 1992).

• *Treatise Reference*: "Each element constitutes a limitation or narrowing of the scope of the claim." 4 D. Chisum, *Patents* §18.04[4] (1994 rev.).

embodiment [patent] An illustrative example of one use of an invention. Typically, one or more embodiments are included in a patent SPECIFICATION. An embodiment in a specification cannot be used to limit the scope of the claims if the claims are broader than the embodiment.

Embodiments included in a patent specification do not have to be finished examples of the inventions. The embodiments can be uses and functions of the invention contemplated by the applicant. While an applicant need not describe any working examples of the invention to comply with 35 U.S.C. §112, specific examples or embodiments can be the best way to teach one skilled in the art how to make and use the invention. See 2 Chisum, *Patents* §7.05[3] (1994 rev.).

- *Case References*:

"[C]laims are not to be interpreted by adding limitations appearing only in the specification.... [A]lthough the specifications may well indicate that certain embodiments are preferred, particular embodiments appearing in a specification will not be read into the claims when the claim language is broader than such embodiments." *Electro Medical Sys., S.A. v. Cooper Life Sciences, Inc.*, 34 F.3d 1048, 1054, 32 USPQ2d 1017, 1021 (Fed. Cir. 1994).

"There is no inconsistency between writing a paper (or giving a speech) on a particular embodiment of an invention and then claiming one's invention more broadly in a patent application. Patents often teach embodiments not carried out in the laboratory; scientific papers rarely do." *North Am. Vaccine, Inc. v. American Cyanamid Co.*, 7 F.3d 1571, 1578, 28 USPQ2d 1333, 1338 (Fed. Cir. 1993).

- *Example: Use of Several Embodiments in a Patent Specification.* A patent discloses an improvement in handbells of the type used by music groups. One of the improvements of the patent is the provision of a clapper mechanism which allows the loudness of the bell to be adjusted "on the fly"—while the bell is being played. Included in the specification of the patent are two embodiments: the first embodiment discloses a clapper with opposing "buttons" made of different materials of different hard-

ness which, when in contact with the bell, produce tones of different loudness. In the other embodiment, the clapper contains three opposing pairs of "striking surfaces" made of felt, slots cut into the clapper, and the hard rubber clapper itself. The different striking surfaces, when in contact with the handbell, produce either a louder or softer tone. *Malta v. Schulmerich Carillons, Inc.*, 952 F.2d 1320, 21 USPQ2d 1161 (Fed. Cir. 1991).

Preferred Embodiment. A type of embodiment which the inventor believes is the best example of how to make the invention. It can be used to satisfy the "best mode" requirement of 35 U.S.C. §112, first paragraph.

See BEST MODE.

Commercial Embodiment. A commercial use or application of the invention. For infringement purposes, the accused product is not compared to the commercial embodiment but to the patent claims.

- *Case Reference:* "The test for infringement is not whether the accused product is substantially similar to the patentee's commercial embodiment of the claimed design.... Such a test risks relying on unclaimed and therefore irrelevant features as grounds for similarity or difference. It is legal error to base an infringement finding on features of the commercial embodiment not claimed in the patent." *Sun Hill Indus. v. Easter Unlimited, Inc.*, 48 F.3d 1193, 1196–97, 33 USPQ2d 1925, 1927 (Fed. Cir. 1995).

enablement [patent] The requirement of §112 of the Patent Code that the disclosure of a valid patent must, when the application is filed, give a sufficiently clear explanation of the invention so as to enable a person having ordinary skill in the art (technology) to make and use the invention without undue experimentation.

Disclosure of Enablement Is the Patentee's Obligation. Enablement is a crucial condition of a valid patent, because what the inventor must give to the public in return for the grant of a limited period of exclusive rights (the patent) is a complete and candid description of the invention so as to enable others to understand it and to be able to use it as a stepping stone to further develop the technology. Also, once the patent expires, the public is entitled to use the invention and is entitled to a full and complete description of it in order to do so. "Full disclosure of the invention and the manner of making and using it on issuance of the patent immediately increases the storehouse of public information available for further research and innovation and assures that the invention will be freely available to all once the statutory period of monopoly expires." 2 D. Chisum, *Patents* §7.01 (1994 rev.).

The Disclosure Requirements of §112. Patent Code §112 sets forth three distinct requirements: (1) the DESCRIPTION REQUIREMENT—the invention is described so that those skilled in the art will know that the inventor was in possession of the invention at the time the application was filed; (2) the enablement requirement—the explanation must be in such full, clear, and concise terms as to enable any person skilled in the art to make and use it; and (3) the BEST MODE requirement—a description of the best embodiment of the invention known to the inventor at the time of the patent application. The first and second paragraphs of Patent Code §112 are parallel in that the first paragraph requires clarity in the SPECIFICATION by imposing the enablement requirement, while the second paragraph of §112 requires clarity in the claims by imposing the "definiteness" requirement.

See INDEFINITE CLAIMS.

Cell Depository. When an invention involves a microorganism or living cell that is not readily available to the public or cannot be reproduced without undue experimentation, to satisfy the enablement requirement it is necessary for the applicant for patent to deposit with a CELL DEPOSITORY a sample of the cells or microorganism.

Drawings. The drawings of the patent specification are to be considered along with the text in determining whether the enablement requirement is complied with. *In re Gay*, 309 F.2d 769, 774, 135 USPQ 311 (C.C.P.A. 1962).

See HOW TO MAKE, HOW TO USE, DESCRIPTION REQUIREMENT, BEST MODE.

- *Statutory Reference*: 35 U.S.C. §112, first paragraph: "The specification shall contain a written description of the invention, and of the manner and process of making and using it, in such full, clear, concise, and exact terms as to enable any person skilled in the art to which it pertains, or with which it is most nearly connected, to make and use the same, and shall set forth the best mode contemplated by the inventor of carrying out his invention."

- *Case References*:

"Enablement is a legal determination of whether a patent enables one skilled in the art to make and use the claimed invention .... [Compliance] is not precluded even if some experimentation is necessary, although the amount of experimentation must not be unduly extensive, ... and is determined as of the filing date of the patent application.... Further, a patent need not teach, and preferably omits, what is well known in the art.... We hold as a matter of law that the '110 patent disclosure is enabling." *Hybritech Inc. v. Monoclonal Antibodies, Inc.*, 802 F.2d 1367, 1384, 231 USPQ 81, 94 (Fed. Cir. 1986).

"Patents are not production documents, and nothing in the patent law requires that a patentee must disclose data on how to mass-produce the invented product, in patents obtained on either individual parts of the product or on the entire product.... Thus the law has never required that a patentee who elects to manufacture its claimed invention must disclose in its patent the dimensions, tolerances, drawings, and other parameters of mass production not necessary to enable one skilled in the art to practice (as distinguished from mass-produce) the invention. Nor is it an objective of the patent system to supply, free of charge, production data and production drawings to competing manufacturers.... [T]he law requires that patents disclose inventions, not mass-production data, and that patents enable the practice of inventions, not the organization and operation of factories." *Christianson v. Colt Indus. Operating Corp.*, 822 F.2d 1544, 1562, 3 USPQ2d 1241, 1254 (Fed. Cir. 1987), *vacated on jurisdictional grounds and remanded for retransfer to Seventh Circuit*, 486 U.S. 800, 7 USPQ2d 1109 (1988).

"A decision on the issue of enablement requires determination of whether a person skilled in the pertinent art, using the knowledge available to such a person and the disclosure in the patent document, could make and use the invention without undue experimentation. It is not fatal if some experimentation is needed, for the patent document is not intended to be a production specification." *Northern Telecom, Inc. v. Datapoint Corp.*, 908 F.2d 931, 941, 15 USPQ2d 1321, 1329 (Fed. Cir. 1990).

• *Example 1: Sufficient Enabling Disclosure.* Dahlem and Milles invented and received a patent on an improvement in hydraulic scrap shears, huge machines weighing several tons, which are used to cut large pieces of scrap metal into smaller pieces for recycling. In a patent infringement suit brought by the patent owner, the district court held the patent invalid on the ground that it was nonenabling because it did not disclose a hydraulic and electrical system for controlling the operation of hydraulic rams used to compact scrap metal in the shears. The Court of Appeals for the Federal Circuit found this to be error and reversed. "The unchallenged evidence of record established that hydraulic and electrical systems for metal scrap shears were well known to those skilled in the art, and that the selection and connection of the elements of such systems was simply a matter of plumbing.... It is clear that no undue experimentation was required in practicing the claimed invention." *Lindemann Maschinenfabrik GmbH v. American Hoist & Derrick Co.*, 730 F.2d 1452, 1463, 221 USPQ 481, 489 (Fed. Cir. 1984).

• *Example 2: Nonsufficient Enabling Disclosure.* Deutsch invented and received a patent on an improvement for a digital electronic organ. The Deutsch patent described and claimed a "sustain" feature whereby selected sounds fade gradually, rather than abruptly, after the organ key is released, mimicking the sound of a true pipe organ. The owner of the patent sued alleged infringer Kimball. In response to a specific question, the jury found that the Deutsch patent was invalid for lack of enablement in that it failed to describe in sufficient detail the "recognition logic block" part of the electronic circuit. The patent owner's witnesses testified that that part of the circuit could either be performed by a standard commercially available decoder unit or be easily designed by a person skilled in digital circuits. The defendant's witnesses testified that the patent did not provide enough information to build the circuit, one witness testifying that "even if I understand what [certain parts of the patent disclosure] probably do … I couldn't build it from this block diagram." The Court of Appeals for the Federal Circuit affirmed the jury decision of failure to meet the enablement requirement, saying that on this conflicting evidence, "a reasonable jury could have reached the conclusion here reached." *Allen Organ Co. v. Kimball Int'l Inc.*, 839 F.2d 1556, 5 USPQ2d 1769, 1777 (Fed. Cir. 1988).

enabling prior art [patent] For a piece of prior art to anticipate under Patent Code §102(b), a prior art reference must be enabling: it must describe sufficiently the invention so as to enable one skilled in the art to make and use the invention. However, a piece of prior art does not have to be enabling to render an invention obvious under Patent Code §103.

A Challenge to Prior Art. An inventor can argue that what would otherwise be a prior art patent disclosure is not valid because it discloses an inoperable invention. Under 37 C.F.R. §1.132, an applicant for a patent can submit evidence to the Patent and Trademark Office to substantiate the claim that a prior art reference is "inoperable." See 2 P. Rosenberg, *Patent Law Fundamentals* §15.07[2][c] (1994 rev.). However, for purposes of nonobviousness, an inoperative or unworkable device or patent is part of the prior art for all that it teaches.

See INOPERABLE PRIOR ART.

• *Treatise Reference*: R. Harmon, *Patents and the Federal Circuit* §3.2 (3d ed. 1994); 2 D. Chisum, *Patents* §5.03[3][a][ii] (1994 rev.).

• *Case References*:

"It is well settled that prior art under 35 U.S.C. §102(b) must sufficiently describe the claimed invention to have placed the public in possession of it.... Such possession is effected if one of ordinary skill in the art could have combined the publication's description of the invention with his own knowledge to make the claimed invention.... Accordingly, even if the claimed invention is disclosed in a printed publication, that disclosure will not suffice as prior art if it was not enabling.... It is not, however, necessary that an invention disclosed in a publication shall have actually been made in order to satisfy the enablement requirement." *In re Donohue*, 766 F.2d 531, 533, 226 USPQ 619, 621 (Fed. Cir. 1985).

"While a reference must enable someone to practice the invention in order to anticipate under §102(b), a non-enabling reference may qualify as prior art for the purpose of determining obviousness under §103." *Symbol Technologies, Inc. v. Opticon Inc.*, 935 F.2d 1569, 1578, 19 USPQ2d 1241, 1247 (Fed. Cir. 1991).

"A rejection for anticipation under section 102 requires that each and every limitation of the claimed invention be disclosed in a single prior art reference .... In addition, the reference must be enabling and describe the applicant's claimed invention sufficiently to have placed it in possession of a person of ordinary skill in the field of the invention." *In re Paulsen*, 30 F.3d 1475, 1478, 31 USPQ2d 1671, 1673 (Fed. Cir. 1994).

entire market value rule [patent] A rule permitting the recovery of damages for patent infringement based on the value of an entire apparatus containing several features, where the patented feature is the basis for customer demand for the entire apparatus. This can be used in awarding damages measured by LOST PROFITS as well as measured by a REASONABLE ROYALTY. Thus, damages for patent infringement can be based upon the sale of a whole product incorporating both unpatented and patented features if the patented feature constitutes the basis for customer demand for the whole product. But when recovery is sought on sales of unpatented components sold with patented components, the unpatented components must function together with the patented component in some manner so as to produce a desired end product or result. *Rite-Hite Corp. v. Kelley Co. Inc.*, 56 F.3d 1538, 1550, 35 USPQ2d 1065, 1073 (Fed. Cir. 1995) (en blanc) ("All the components together must be analogous to compo-

nents of a single asembly or be parts of a complete machine, or they must constitute a functional unit.")

• *Example.* The owner of a patent on a method of insulating the tank of a water heater by using polyurethane foam recovered its lost profits based on the lost sales of water heaters as a unit because of a competitor's infringement. The infringer's argument that foam insulation was not the basis for consumer demand for the water heaters was rejected because the infringer did not identify or present evidence of the value of any other elements allegedly contributing to demand. Thus, the patentee would have sold the water heaters as a unit but for the infringement. *State Indus. Inc. v. Mor-Flo Indus. Inc.*, 883 F.2d 1573, 12 USPQ2d 1026 (Fed. Cir. 1989).

• *Case Reference*: "The entire market value rule allows for the recovery of damages based on the value of an entire apparatus containing several features, when the feature patented constitutes the basis for customer demand.... It is the 'financial and marketing dependence on the patented item under standard marketing procedures which determines whether the non-patented features of a machine should be included in calculating compensation for infringement.' ... Where a hypothetical licensee would have anticipated an increase in sales of collateral unpatented items because of the patented device, the patentee would be compensated accordingly." *TWM Mfg. Co. v. Dura Corp.*, 789 F.2d 895, 901, 229 USPQ 525, 528 (Fed. Cir. 1986).

• *Treatise Reference*: "[T]he Federal Circuit has most definitely embraced the 'entire market' rule of damages.... The ultimate determining factor is whether the patentee or its licensee can normally anticipate the sale of the unpatented components together with the patented components. Where there is no evidence that the unpatented components have been or could be used independently of the patented structure, then the patentee would normally have anticipated the sale of the entire machine, and damages based upon the entire market value are appropriate." R. Harmon, *Patents and the Federal Circuit* §12.1(d) (3d ed. 1994).

entitlement proceeding [patent]   A proceeding in the Patent and Trademark Office to determine whether the inventor or the federal government is the owner of a patent on an invention allegedly made in the performance of work on the space program under a National Aeronautics and Space Administration (NASA) contract. The entitlement proceeding is before the Patent and Trademark Office BOARD OF PATENT APPEALS AND INTERFERENCES, which determines, in accordance with procedures used in an INTERFERENCE proceeding, whether NASA is entitled to receive the patent. National Aeronautics and Space Act of 1958, 42 U.S.C. §2457(d). For example, if the invention was actually REDUCED TO PRACTICE before the commencement of the NASA contract, then the private inventor is entitled to receive the patent. "[Title 42, section 2457 of U.S.C.] clearly treats an invention as property, the right to which is in the inventor or his assignee unless the invention was made (conception or first actual reduction to practice) in the performance of work under a NASA contract." *Williams v. NASA*, 463 F.2d 1391, 1400, 175 USPQ 5, 12 (C.C.P.A. 1972). A fundamental difference between an interference and an entitlement proceeding is that the former resolves the issue of which of two or more inventive entities will receive a patent, whereas the latter involves only one inventive entity and the only question is whether the government is entitled to ownership of the patent. *Sterzer v. NASA*, 230 USPQ 709 (Comm. Pat. & T.M. 1986).

EPO [patent–international] European Patent Office. See EUROPEAN PATENT.

equitable estoppel [patent] Equitable estoppel is an equitable defense to a claim for patent INFRINGEMENT. In 1992 the Federal Circuit in *Aukerman Co. v. Chaides Constr. Co.*, 960 F.2d 1020, 1042, 22 USPQ2d 1321, 1336 (Fed. Cir. 1992), expressly overruled the previous four-part test previously used and instead adopted a three-part test. The three elements necessary to bar a patentee's suit by reason of equitable estoppel are as follows: (1) the patentee, through *misleading conduct*, leads the alleged infringer to reasonably infer that the patentee

does not intend to enforce its patent against the alleged infringer; (2) the alleged infringer *relies* on that conduct; and (3) due to its reliance, the alleged infringer will be *materially prejudiced* if the patentee is allowed to proceed with its claim. Because the doctrine is an equitable one, the court also must take into consideration any other evidence and facts respecting the equities of the parties in exercising its discretion and deciding whether to allow the defense of equitable estoppel to bar the patentee's suit. *Aukerman Co. v. Chaides Constr. Co.*, 960 F.2d 1020, 1028, 1042–43, 22 USPQ2d 1321, 1325, 1336–37 (Fed. Cir. 1992).

First Factor—Misleading Conduct. "Conduct may include specific statements, action, inaction or silence where there was an obligation to speak." *Aukerman Co. v. Chaides Constr. Co.*, 960 F.2d 1020, 1028, 22 USPQ2d 1321, 1325 (Fed. Cir. 1992). If the defense is based on the patentee's inaction, then such inaction "must be combined with other facts respecting the relationship or contacts between the parties to give rise to the necessary inference that the claim against the defendant is abandoned." 960 F.2d at 1042, 22 USPQ2d at 1336.

Second Factor—Reasonable Reliance. "To show reliance, the infringer must have had a relationship or communication with the patentee which lulls the alleged infringer into a sense of security in going ahead with [further infringement]." *Aukerman Co. v. Chaides Constr. Co.*, 960 F.2d 1020, 1042, 22 USPQ2d 1321, 1337 (Fed. Cir. 1992).

Third Factor—Material Prejudice. As with the equitable defense of laches, in order to show material prejudice the infringer may produce evidence to establish either economic prejudice or evidentiary prejudice. *Aukerman Co. v. Chaides Constr. Co.*, 960 F.2d 1020, 1033, 1043, 22 USPQ2d 1321, 1328–29, 1337 (Fed. Cir. 1992). Economic prejudice may arise where defendant suffers monetary losses that would have been prevented by an earlier suit. Evidentiary prejudice may arise by reason of defendant's inability to present a full and fair defense on the merits due to loss of records, the death of a witness, or the unreliability of memories of long past events, thereby undermining the court's ability to judge the facts.

Equitable Estoppel Bars Patentee's Entire Claim. When an alleged infringer establishes the defense of equitable estoppel, the patentee's claim is entirely barred. This is in contrast to the equitable defense of laches where only prefiling damages are barred with proof of the elements of laches.

Laches Distinguished. LACHES focuses on the reasonableness of the patentee's delay in bringing suit; equitable estoppel focuses on what the defendant has been led to believe by patentee's conduct. Also, a laches defense will only bar presuit damages, whereas a defense of equitable estoppel can bar the entire infringement action. Furthermore, a showing of a six-year delay creates a presumption of laches, whereas no such presumption is applicable to the defense of equitable estoppel.

See LACHES.

• *Case References:*

"An equitable estoppel case ... has three important elements. [1] The actor, who usually must have knowledge of the true facts, communicates something in a misleading way, either by words, conduct or silence. [2] The other relies upon that communication. [3] And the other would be harmed materially if the actor is later permitted to assert any claim inconsistent with his earlier conduct." *Aukerman Co. v. Chaides Constr. Co.*, 960 F.2d 1020, 1041, 22 USPQ2d 1321, 1335–36 (Fed. Cir. 1992), quoting from Dobbs, *Remedies* §2.3 at 42 (1973).

"Although ... equitable estoppel may in some instances be based upon a misleading silence, mere silence must be accompanied by some *other* factor which indicates that the silence was sufficiently misleading as to amount to bad faith." *Hemstreet v. Computer Entry Sys. Corp.*, 972 F.2d 1290, 1295, 23 USPQ2d 1860, 1864 (Fed. Cir. 1992).

equivalents, doctrine of [patent] A rule of claim interpretation under which an accused product or process, although not a literal infringement, is still an infringement if it performs substantially the same function in substantially the same way to obtain substantially the same result as the claimed product or process. The doctrine of equivalents gives a degree of flexibility under which a court may expand the narrow and literal language of a patent claim. *Miles Labs. Inc. v. Shandon Inc.*, 997 F.2d 870, 876, 27 USPQ2d 1123, 1127 (Fed. Cir. 1993) ("The doctrine of equivalents thus prevents the risk of injustice that may result from a limited focus on words alone.")

Flexible Nature of the Doctrine of Equivalents. PIONEER patents are entitled to a broad range of equivalents, and minor patents in a CROWDED ART are entitled to only a very narrow range of equivalents. The rule of FILE WRAPPER ESTOPPEL is a limitation on the application of the doctrine of equivalents. Under the NOSE OF WAX rule, the doctrine of equivalents cannot be used to so twist and deform the words of a claim so as to make it cover something totally different from its plain meaning. A finding of equivalence is a finding of fact, reviewable on appeal under the clearly erroneous standard. *Great N. Corp. v. Davis Core & Pad Co.*, 782 F.2d 159, 166, 228 USPQ 356, 359 (Fed. Cir. 1986).

The "All Elements Rule." Under the ALL ELEMENTS RULE, each ELEMENT of a claim or its substantial equivalent must be found in the accused device to constitute infringement. That is, one does not merely compare the accused device as a whole with the claimed invention as a whole.

The Rule Cannot Stretch a Claim to Cover the Prior Art. An important limitation on the use of the doctrine of equivalents is that the claims cannot be accorded a construction that would cover the PRIOR ART. *Senmed Inc. v. Richard-Allen Medical Indus. Inc.*, 888 F.2d 815, 821, 12 USPQ2d 1508, 1513 (Fed. Cir. 1989). No owner of a patent should be able to use the doctrine of equivalents to get patent coverage that he should not have received in a literal claim granted by the PTO. Claims should be construed, if possible, as to sustain their validity. If claims were stretched to cover a proposed equivalent so that the result would be invalidity, the appropriate legal conclusion is one of non-infringement, not invalidity. *Carman Indus., Inc. v. Wahl*, 724 F.2d 932, 937 n.5, 220 USPQ 481, 485 n.5 (Fed. Cir. 1983). One test to avoid the foregoing problems is to construct a hypothetical literal patent claim sufficient in scope to encompass the accused product. That hypothetical claim is then tested against the prior art. If the conclusion is that the PTO would not have granted that claim over the prior art, then it would be improper to get comparable coverage under the doctrine of equivalents. *Wilson Sporting Goods Co. v. David Geoffrey & Assoc.*, 904 F.2d 677, 14 USPQ2d 1942 (Fed. Cir. 1990).

Time of Equivalence. It is not a requirement of equivalence that persons skilled in the art know of the equivalence when the patent application is filed or when the patent issues. That question is determined as of the time infringement takes place. *Atlas Powder Co. v. E.I. du Pont de Nemours & Co.*, 750 F.2d 1569, 1581, 224 USPQ 409, 417 (Fed. Cir. 1984).

The Graver Tank Case. The leading case defining the doctrine of equivalents is *Graver Tank & Mfg. Co. v. Linde Air Prods. Co.*, 339 U.S. 605, 608, 85 USPQ 328, 330 (1950). In *Graver Tank* the Supreme Court said that the accused device is equivalent to the claim and an infringement if the accused device performs substantially the same function in substantially the same way to obtain substantially the same result. This has been referred to as the "tripartite test of substantially the same function, way and result." *Atlas Powder Co. v. E.I. du Pont de Nemours & Co.*, 750 F.2d 1569, 1579, 224 USPQ 409, 416 (Fed. Cir. 1984). The Supreme Court in *Graver Tank* said that "to permit imitation of a patented invention which does not copy every detail would be to convert the protection of the patent grant into a hollow and useless thing." *Graver Tank & Mfg. Co. v. Linde Air Prods. Co.*, 339 U.S. 605, 607, 85 USPQ 328, 330 (1950).

The 1995 Hilton Davis Case. In this 1995 en banc decision of the Federal Circuit, the court faced the issue of whether a finding of infringement under the doctrine of equivalents requires a showing of some inequitable conduct by the infringer. A majority of the court answered in the negative, saying that the doctrine of equivalents is "not and equitable remedy available only on a showing of the equities" and that evidence of the "culpable conduct" is "not a prerequisite nor necessary for application of the doctrine." The court said that the doctrine of equivalents is a factual issue to be submitted to the jury and is not a "matter of equity to be

applied at the court's discretion." The court declared that the key to application of the doctrine is proof of "insubstantial differences" between the claim and the accused device and that "evidence beyond function, way and result," such as evidence of copying or designing around, can be relevant to that issue. *Hilton Davis Chem. Co. v. Warner Jenkinson Co.*, 62 F.3d 1512, 35 USPQ2d 1641 (Fed. Cir. 1995) (en banc).

Regarding application of the doctrine of equivalents in determining infringement of a claim drafted in "means for" format, see MEANS FOR.

See EQUIVALENTS, REVERSE DOCTRINE OF; ALL ELEMENTS RULE; FILE WRAPPER ESTOPPEL.

• *Case References*:

"[T]he test of equivalency extends beyond what is literally stated in a patentee's specification to be equivalent and encompasses *any* element which one of ordinary skill in the art would perceive as interchangeable with the claimed element." *Thomas & Betts Corp. v. Litton Sys., Inc.*, 720 F.2d 1572, 1579, 220 USPQ 1, 6 (Fed. Cir. 1983).

"Though the doctrine of equivalents is designed to do equity and to relieve an inventor from a semantic strait jacket when equity requires, it is not designed to permit wholesale redrafting of a claim to cover non-equivalent devices, i.e., to permit a claim expansion that would encompass more than an insubstantial change." *Perkin-Elmer Corp. v. Westinghouse Elec. Corp.*, 822 F.2d 1528, 1532, 3 USPQ2d 1321, 1324 (Fed. Cir. 1987).

"[A] finding of infringement under the doctrine of equivalents requires proof of insubstantial differences between the claimed and accused products or processes. Often the function-way-result test will suffice to show the extent of the differences. In such cases, the parties will understandably focus on the evidence of function, way and result, and the factfinder will apply the doctrine based on that evidence. Other factors, however, such as evidence of copying or designing around, may also inform the test for infringement under the doctrine of equivalents. No judge can anticipate whether such other factors will arise in a given case." *Hilton Davis Chem. Co. v. Warner Jenkinson Co.*, 62 F.3d 1512, 35 USPQ2d 1641 (Fed. Cir. 1995) (en banc).

"The doctrine of equivalents is limited in that the doctrine will not extend (1) to cover an accused device in the prior art, and (2) to allow the patentee to recapture through equivalence certain coverage given up during prosecution." *Pennwalt Corp. v. Durand-Wayland Inc.*, 833 F.2d 931, 934 n.1, 4 USPQ2d 1737, 1739 n.1 (Fed. Cir. 1987) (en banc).

• *Example 1: Mechanics; Equivalence Found.* A claim for a wheelbarrow recited as an element a cross brace between the handles with a channel in the cross brace to receive the handles. The accused wheelbarrow was almost identical, except that the cross brace was flat instead of having a channel. The flat cross brace in the accused wheelbarrow was held to be the equivalent of the channelled cross brace in the patent claim because the cross brace in the accused device performed the function of securing the handles in substantially the same way to produce the same result. *Radio Steel & Mfg. Co. v. MTD Prods., Inc.*, 731 F.2d 840, 221 USPQ 657 (Fed. Cir. 1984).

• *Example 2: Chemistry; Equivalence Found.* A claim for fluxes used in electric welding recited the use of an "alkaline earth metal silicate" for the flux. Other claims more broadly recited a "silicate," but those other claims were held invalid as overbroad. The patent owner actually used magnesium, an alkaline earth metal silicate. The accused device used manganese, a silicate, but not an earth metal silicate. The Supreme Court held that manganese was an infringing equivalent of the claim, noting that the literature taught that manganese could be substituted for magnesium in the patented welding flux. *Graver Tank & Mfg. Co. v. Linde Air Prods. Co.*, 339 U.S. 605, 85 USPQ 328 (1950).

• *Example 3: Computer Technology; No Equivalence Found.* A patent for an early version of a hand-held electronic calculator recited visual display means, shown in the specification as a thermal printer, which created dots on a tape to form numerals. Seventeen years later, the accused device used a liquid crystal display that was considerably smaller and used much less power than the thermal printer of the patented invention. It was held that the totality of technological changes in the accused device, including that of the display means, was too great a variation to support application of the doctrine of equivalents. *Texas Instruments, Inc. v. International Trade Comm'n*, 805 F.2d 1558, 231 USPQ 833 (Fed. Cir. 1986).

• *Example 4: Optical Communications; Equivalence Found.* One limitation in a patent on a type of optical fiber used in telecommunications recited a core to which a chemical had been added to increase the index of refraction of the core. In the accused device, a chemical was added to the cladding or outer shielding layer of glass in order to decrease the index of refraction of the cladding layer. However, the core-cladding differential in the index of refraction between the patent claim and the accused device was the same. The Court of Appeals for the Federal Circuit affirmed the finding of the district court that the substitution in the accused device of a negative chemical in the cladding was the equivalent of the claimed element of a positive chemical in the core of the fiber. It was found that the accused optical fiber performed substantially the same overall function in substantially the same way to obtain the same overall result of a refractive index differential between the core and cladding, which was necessary for the fiber to function as an optical waveguide. *Corning Glass Works v. Sumitomo Elec. USA Inc.*, 868 F.2d 1251, 1258–61, 9 USPQ2d 1962, 1967–70 (Fed. Cir. 1989).

equivalents, "means plus function" claims [patent] See MEANS-PLUS-FUNCTION CLAIM.

equivalents, reverse doctrine of [patent] An accused infringer's defense to what would otherwise appear to be a case of LITERAL INFRINGEMENT of a patent. Even though an ACCUSED DEVICE may be a literal infringement of a patent claim, the accused infringer may show under the "reverse doctrine of equivalents" that the accused device or process is so far changed that it performs the function of the claimed invention in a substantially different way.

Burden of Proof. Once the patentee has made a showing of literal infringement, the burden shifts to the accused infringer to establish the fact of noninfringement under the doctrine of reverse equivalents. Because an accused device that reads word-for-word on a patent claim will usually perform the same function in the same way to achieve the same result as the claimed invention, a defense based on the reverse doctrine of equivalents is not often successful.

The Graver Tank Case. The leading case defining both the doctrine of equivalents and the reverse doctrine of equivalents is *Graver Tank & Mfg. Co. v. Linde Air Prods. Co.*, 339 U.S. 605, 608–09, 85 USPQ 328, 330 (1950): "The wholesome realism of [the doctrine of equivalents] is not always applied in favor of a patentee but is sometimes used against him. Thus, where a device is so far changed in principle from a patented article that it performs the same or a similar function in a substantially different way, but nevertheless falls within the literal words of the claim, the doctrine of equivalents may be used [in reverse] to restrict the claim and defeat the patentee's action for infringement."

See EQUIVALENTS, DOCTRINE OF.

• *Case References*:

"One who takes a claimed structure and merely uses it in a way that differs from that in which a specification-described embodiment uses it, does not thereby escape infringement.... When a patentee establishes literal infringement, the accused infringer may undertake the burden of going forward to establish the fact of non-infringement under the reverse doctrine of equivalents.... [The] fact question is simple and direct: Is the accused product so far changed in principle that it performs the function of the claimed invention in a substantially different way? ... The test mandated in *Graver Tank* leaves room for the fact finder's application to varying circumstances. Words like 'so far,' 'principle' and 'substantially' are not subject to rigid pre-definition; nor will the 'principle' of a structural invention be always and immediately apparent." *SRI Int'l v. Matsushita Elec. Corp. of Am.*, 775 F.2d 1107, 1123–24, 227 USPQ 577, 587–88 (Fed. Cir. 1985).

"The reverse doctrine of equivalents is invoked when claims are written more broadly than the disclosure warrants. The purpose of restricting the scope of such claims is not only to avoid a holding of infringement when a court deems it appropriate but often is to preserve the validity of claims with respect to their original intended scope." *Texas Instruments v. International Trade Comm'n*, 846 F.2d 1369, 1372, 6 USPQ2d 1886, 1889 (Fed. Cir. 1988).

established royalty [patent]
See ROYALTY, REASONABLE.

estoppel by marking [patent]
See MARKING ESTOPPEL.

European Patent [patent–international]   A patent issued from the European Patent Office in Munich, Germany, which becomes effective as though it were a national patent in each nation that is a member of the European Patent Convention. It is not a true "European" or "Community" patent because it is the grant of a collection of national patents separately enforceable in each nation rather than the grant of one supranational patent. A European patent has basically the same effect and is subject to the same limitations as a patent granted by a nation in which the patent is to be enforced.

Description. The European Patent Convention came into force in 1977 and 16 nations are participants. Some smaller emerging Eastern European nations use the European Patent Office rather than set up their own patent office. A European patent lasts for 20 years from the date of filing, follows the priority rule of first to file, requires absolute novelty, and requires that the invention represent an "inventive step," which is analogous to the U.S. concept of NONOBVIOUSNESS. As of 1994, the European Patent Office had granted more than 250,000 patents and received over 650,000 applications.

Proposed Community Patent. A true EC-wide European Patent would become a reality upon full ratification of the Luxembourg Convention, providing for the creation of a single Community Patent. While EC member nations signed at Luxembourg in 1989 an agreement to set up a true Community Patent, the agreement has not been ratified by all member nations. There is even some doubt as to whether a true Community Patent in its proposed form will ever be ratified.

- *Treatise References*: 2 P. Rosenberg, *Patent Law Fundamentals* §19.03 (1994 rev.); 1 S. Ladas, *Patents, Trademarks and Related Rights: National and International Protection* §§394–420 (1975); M. Leaffer, *International Treaties on Intellectual Property* 141 (1990) (text of European Patent Convention).

- *Treaty Reference*: European Patent Convention, Article 64(1) & (3): "A European patent shall ... confer on its proprietor from the date of publication of the mention of its grant, in each Contracting State in respect of which it is granted, the same rights as would be conferred by a national patent granted in that State.... (3) Any infringement of a European patent shall be dealt with by national law."

European Trademark [international–trademark] A trademark registration granted by the European Community Trademark Office and enforceable throughout the nations that are members of the European Community. A Community Trademark will have a uniform effect throughout the European Community and have automatic legal force without the need for separate national legislation. Applications can be filed by a national of a nation belonging to the PARIS CONVENTION, so that U.S. trademark owners will be able to obtain a Community Trademark.

History of the European Community Trademark. Following many years of negotiations, in December 1993 the European Community's Council of Ministers approved the plan for a single trademark registration that provides for protection from infringement in all European Community nations. It is anticipated that applications for Community Trademarks cannot be filed until at least the beginning of 1996.

The Application. An application for a Community Trademark registration will be filed at the European Trademark Office located in Alicante, Spain. The application must be in one of the official languages of the European Community. In addition, the applicant must designate a second language from among the five official languages of the Trademark Office and accept use of that language in the event of an opposition, revocation, or invalidity proceeding. The official languages of the Trademark Office are English, French, German, Spanish, and Italian. If the application is not filed in one of those languages, the Office will translate it into the second language indicated by the applicant. For example, a Greek company could file an application in the Greek language and designate German as the "official language." The application would be translated into German, which would be the language used in the event of an opposition.

Examination of Applications. An examiner in the European Trademark Office will examine the application for an "absolute" ground of refusal going to the nature of the mark itself, such as genericness or descriptiveness without secondary meaning. A search will be conducted of earlier Community Trademark registrations and of earlier registrations from individual member nations and regional registration systems. But the Trademark Office will not refuse registration on the basis of a conflict with an earlier filed registration. Rather, the Office will inform the prior registrant of a Community Trademark registration of the pending application, giving it an opportunity to file an opposition. But the Office will not inform the prior registrant of a national or regional registration, who must find out about the pending application through publication in the Community trademark journal. An opposition based on prior registered or nonregistered rights must be filed within three months of publication of the mark.

Revocation. A Community Trademark registration may be challenged in a revocation proceeding brought by any person on the ground that the mark has not been put to genuine use within a continuous period of five consecutive years, that it has become generic or deceptive, or on other specified grounds. A registration may also be challenged on the ground that it was registered in violation of one of the initial grounds of refusal.

Term of Registration. The Community Trademark registration lasts for 10 years and is renewable for additional 10-year periods.

Enforcement. A Community Trademark is enforceable in any member nation in special Community trademark courts. Each member nation will designate national courts of first and second instance to serve as Community Trademark courts. These courts will apply the law of the European Community Trademark regulations. Proper venue is the nation of defendant's domicile or, if not domiciled in a member nation, of a member nation in which defendant has an establishment. If neither, then the same rules are applied to the plaintiff's place of domicile or establishment. If none of the forgoing rules apply, then the proper venue is Spain. For example, if plaintiff is Canadian and defendant Mexican and neither has an establishment in a European Community member nation, then the proper venue is Spain. All of the foregoing is subject to any agreement between the parties that a Community court in a different nation will hear the case or to the defendant entering an appearance before a Community court in another nation. In all cases, the Community court has jurisdiction to deal with acts of infringement committed anywhere within the European Community.

• *Treatise Reference*: R. Annand & H. Norman, *Blackstone's Guide to the Trademarks Act of 1994*, 235 *et seq.* (1994 U.K.).

eviction [patent] A patent licensee is "evicted" from its license when a final decision of invalidity of the licensed patent is rendered by a court of competent jurisdiction, even in a case in which the licensee is not a party.

Origin of the Term. The term "eviction" is obviously borrowed from landlord-tenant law. An early decision stated that "[m]any of the decisions treat a licensor as a landlord, and a licensee as his tenant who cannot dispute the title so long as he has the occupancy of the premises." *Whitle v. Lee*, 14 F. 789, 790 (D. Mass. 1882). Accord *Covell v. Bostwick*, 39 F. 421, 424 (S.D.N.Y. 1889). See Treece, *Licensee Estoppel in Patent and Trademark Cases*, 53 Iowa L. Rev. 525 (1967).

The Significance of Patent Eviction. Upon eviction, the licensee need pay no more royalties under the license, although it is liable for all preeviction royalties. *Drackett Chem. Co. v. Chamberlain Co.*, 63 F.2d 853, 855 (6th Cir. 1933); *Zenith Labs., Inc. v. Carter-Wallace, Inc.*, 530 F.2d 508, 513 n.10, 189 USPQ 387, 391 n.10 (3d Cir. 1976). Thus, even though this licensee never challenged the validity of the patent in or out of court, upon "eviction" it is freed from the payment of royalties thereafter. It cannot get a refund of preeviction royalties paid, and it must pay, even after eviction, royalties that accrued before eviction and were not paid. *Troxel Mfg. Co. v. Schwinn Bicycle Co.*, 489 F.2d 968, 973 (6th Cir. 1973); McCarthy, *"Unmuzzling" the Patent Licensee: Chaos in the Wake of Lear v. Adkins*, 45 Geo. Wash. L. Rev. 429, 461–62 (1977).

See LICENSE ESTOPPEL.

• *Treatise References*: 1 H. Einhorn, *Patent Licensing Transactions* §2.15 (1994 rev.).

examiner [patent] The Patent and Trademark Office employee who is assigned to examine and pass upon an application for a patent.

The "examiners-in-chief" are senior examiners who, together with the Commissioner, the Deputy Commissioner, and the Assistant Commissioners, may serve on the Board of Patent Appeals and Interferences. The Commissioner has the power to appoint certain senior examiners as temporary examiners-in-chief. 35 U.S.C. §7.

• *Use Example*: "Applications shall be taken up for examination by the examiner to whom they have been assigned in the order in which they have been filed...." 37 C.F.R. §1.101(a).

• *Statutory References*:

35 U.S.C. §7(a): "The examiners-in-chief shall be persons of competent legal knowledge and scientific ability, who shall be appointed to the competitive service."

35 U.S.C. §131: "The Commissioner shall cause an examination to be made of the application and the alleged new invention; and if on such examination it appears that the applicant

is entitled to a patent under the law, the Commissioner shall issue a patent therefor."

examining attorney [trademark] An attorney who is an employee of the Patent and Trademark Office and is assigned to examine and pass upon an application to register a trademark. Probably the most often used form of the title is "Trademark Examining Attorney."

• *Use Example*: "[N]ew applications normally are to be taken up for examination by the Examining Attorney to whom they have been assigned according to the dates on which the examining attorney receives the new applications." *Trademark Manual of Examining Procedure* §1102.02 (1993).

• *Statutory Reference*: Lanham Act §12(a), 15 U.S.C. §1062(a): "Upon the filing of an application for registration and payment of the fee herein provided, the Commissioner [of Patents and Trademarks] shall refer the application to the examiner in charge of the registration of marks, who shall cause an examination to be made...."

exceptional case [patent–trademark]
See ATTORNEY FEE AWARD.

exhausted combination [patent]
See OVERCLAIMING.

exhaustion doctrine [patent–trademark–copyright] A rule that some or all of the exclusive rights of intellectual property are exhausted as to a particular item upon the first authorized sale of that item by the owner of the intellectual property or its licensee.

1. Exhaustion of Patent Rights. Once a patented article is sold by the patent owner or its licensee without restriction, that article passes beyond the exclusive rights of the patent. The first authorized sale of a patented article "exhausts" the patent to the extent that an unconditional sale frees the purchaser from patent liability for use and resale of the article. *United States v. General Elec. Co.*, 272 U.S. 476, 489–90 (1926).

The Implied License Rationale. The exhaustion rule is often founded on the rationale that a purchaser of a patented article, in an unconditional sale, receives an implied license to use and resell the article without further obligation or payment to the patentee. The exhaustion rule as based upon an implied license is grounded on fairness and contractual expectation. If the patentee sells a patented machine to a purchaser without any express restriction, it is unfair for the patentee to require the purchaser to pay use royalties after the purchaser thought that it had fully paid the purchase price. For example, a buyer of a patented automobile would be astonished to find that the patentee-seller later sends a bill for a use royalty of $100 for every 1,000-mile turn of the odometer or that the seller forbids use of the auto outside the state in which it was purchased.

The Two-Part Test. The Court of Appeals for the Federal Circuit has laid down a two-part test necessary to find exhaustion and an implied license: (1) the thing sold by the patentee "must have no noninfringing use"; and (2) the circumstances of the sale must "plainly indicate that the grant of [an implied] license should be inferred." While an implied license can be negated by a clear agreement or statement at the time of sale of the patentee's imposition of use restrictions or use royalties, notification to the buyer after the purchase will not satisfy the second factor. *Met-Coil Sys. Corp. v. Korners Unlimited, Inc.*, 803 F.2d 684, 231 USPQ 474 (Fed. Cir. 1986) (postsale notice does not negate exhaustion and implied license); *Bandag, Inc. v. Al Bolser's Tire Stores, Inc.*, 750 F.2d 903, 924, 223 USPQ 982, 998 (Fed. Cir. 1984) (no implied license because sale did not meet factor one, since sold item had noninfringing uses).

Antitrust Law. Under the exhaustion doctrine, a patent owner has no greater power to restrict the terms on which a buyer of a patented product uses or resells it than does the seller of an unpatented product. The rule of antitrust law that applies to postsale restrictions on use and resale in general also applies with equal force to such restrictions on sold patented articles. *Munters Corp. v. Burgess Indus. Inc.*, 450 F.Supp. 1195, 194 USPQ 146 (S.D.N.Y. 1977).

Valid Restrictions. It is not accurate to say that the exhaustion doctrine prevents a patentee from placing any express restrictions on the use of a patented item that is sold. If the restriction is reasonably within the scope of the patent claims then it is valid. The Federal Circuit held that a district court erred in finding that a restriction on the use of a sold patented item was unenforceable under patent law. The patentee sold a patented device to hospitals with a restriction that it was to be used only once and then disposed of as biohazardous waste. Some hospitals violated the use restriction and sent the used devices to defendant, who reconditioned the devices and sold them for reuse. If the restriction is within the patent grant, then defendant may be liable for infringement. *Mallinckrodt Inc. v. Medipart Inc.*, 976 F.2d 700, 24 USPQ2d 1173 (Fed. Cir. 1992).

- *Treatise References*: 4 D. Chisum, *Patents* §16.03[2] (1994 rev.); W. Holmes, *Intellectual Property & Antitrust Law* §18.02 (1994 rev.).

- *Case References*:

"An incident to the purchase of any article, whether patented or unpatented, is the right to use and sell it, and upon familiar principles the authorized sale of an article which is capable of use only in practicing the patent is a relinquishment of the patent monopoly with respect to the article sold.... The patentee may surrender his monopoly in whole by the sale of his patent or in part by the sale of an article embodying the invention. His monopoly remains so long as he retains the ownership of the patented article. But sale of it exhausts the monopoly in that article and the patentee may not thereafter, by virtue of his patent, control the use or disposition of the article.... Hence the patentee cannot control the resale price of patented articles which he has sold...." *United States v. Univis Lens Co.*, 316 U.S. 241, 249–50, 53 USPQ 404, 407 (1942).

"The law is well settled that an authorized sale of a patented product places that product beyond the reach of the patent.... The patent owner's rights with respect to the product ends with its sale ... and a purchaser of such a product may use or resell the product free of the patent. This longstanding principle applies similarly to a sale of a patented product manufactured by a licensee acting within the scope of its license." *Intel Corp. v. ULSI Sys. Technology Inc.*, 995 F.2d 1566, 1568, 27 USPQ2d 1136, 1138 (Fed. Cir. 1993).

2. Exhaustion of Trademark Rights. Trademark rights are exhausted as to a given item upon the first authorized sale of that item. A distributor who resells branded goods without change is not a trademark "infringer" and needs no license. As to that product purchased and resold without change, the trademark is exhausted, or, alternatively, the buyer receives an implied license to use the mark in resales. The right to resell a branded item in an unchanged state carries with it the right to advertise that the dealer is selling that brand, so long as the advertising does not mislead customers into mistakenly believing that the dealer is an agent or an "authorized dealer" of the manufacturer. *Bandag, Inc. v. Al Bolser's Tire Stores, Inc.*, 750 F.2d 903, 223 USPQ 982 (Fed. Cir. 1984) (dealer's phone directory advertising falsely suggested that dealer was a franchisee of the manufacturer).

Altering a Branded Product. A purchaser may legally buy branded ingredients and rebottle them, repack them, or use them to make another product, and then offer the resulting product for sale under the original brand so long as labeling clearly discloses the facts. *Prestonettes, Inc. v. Coty*, 264 U.S. 359 (1924). Similarly, a buyer can recondition or repair a branded product and resell it under its original brand so long as the fact of repair or reconditioning is made quite clear in labeling. *Champion Spark Plug Co. v. Sanders*, 331 U.S. 125, 73 USPQ 133 (1947). However, it can be trademark infringement or false advertising to use an original equipment manufacturer's mark on a product in which the original product is buried or so changed as not to retain the characteristics of the original. See 3 J.T. McCarthy, *Trademarks and Unfair Competition* §§25.08–.10 (3d ed. 1995 rev.).

Reselling Unbranded Bulk Goods. The Fourth Circuit drew a line between reselling branded packaged goods and reselling unbranded bulk goods. It was held not to be trademark infringement for defendant to buy and resell SHELL-marked sealed packaged oil products even though defendant was not an "authorized dealer." But defendant was not permitted to resell under the SHELL mark bulk oil products, because the trademark owner can control the continuing quality of the unpackaged bulk oil only through its control over the handling, storage, and transportation practices of its authorized dealers. Without Shell's enforcement of its quality controls over handling of the bulk oil by a distributor, the oil sold by an unauthorized distributor was "not truly 'genuine.'" "The use of the Shell marks implies that the product has been delivered according to all quality control guidelines enforced by the manufacturer." *Shell Oil Co. v. Commercial Petroleum, Inc.*, 928 F.2d 104, 108, 18 USPQ2d 1156, 1158 (4th Cir. 1991).

- *Treatise Reference*: 3 J.T. McCarthy, *Trademarks and Unfair Competition* §25.11[1] (3d ed. 1995 rev.).

- *Case Reference*: "Under this doctrine [of exhaustion], as applied within the borders of a sovereignty, a markholder may no longer control branded goods after releasing them into the stream of commerce. After the first sale, the brandholder's control is deemed exhausted. Down-the-line retailers are free to display and advertise the branded goods. Secondhand dealers may advertise the branded merchandise for resale in competition with the sales of the markholder (so long as they do not misrepresent themselves as authorized agents)." *Osawa & Co. v. B & H Photo*, 589 F. Supp. 1165, 1173, 223 USPQ 124, 132 (S.D.N.Y. 1984).

Restatement Reference: "The trademark owner ordinarily cannot prevent or control the sale of goods bearing its mark once the owner has permitted those goods to enter commerce. It can be said that the rights of the trademark owner are exhausted once it authorizes the initial sale of the product under the trademark, or that the owner impliedly licenses others to further market the goods under the mark." *Restatement (Third) of Unfair Competition* §24, comment b (1995).

3. Exhaustion of Copyright Rights. A form of limited exhaustion of copyright upon sale is reflected in the FIRST SALE DOCTRINE. This is an exception to the exclusive right of a copyright owner to distribute copies or phonorecords of the copyrighted work. Under this exception, after the first sale of a lawfully made copy of the copyrighted work, anyone who is the owner of that copy can sell or dispose of that copy in any way without copyright infringement liability. This rule is codified in 17 U.S.C. §109(a). Thus, the distribution right is exhausted by the first authorized sale of a copy.

See FIRST SALE DOCTRINE.

Apart from the first sale doctrine, the general rule is that the transfer of ownership of a copyrighted object does not of itself transfer any rights of copyright. 17 U.S.C. §202.

ex parte [general legal] A legal proceeding in which only one party is involved with a court or other governmental agency. Ex parte, a Latin term, is commonly used as the opposite of IN-TER PARTES, which describes a proceeding in which there are two or more parties involved before a court or government agency.

For example, when a patent attorney is arguing with a Patent and Trademark Office examiner on behalf of an inventor applying for a patent, it is characterized as an ex parte proceeding; it is only the inventor seeking a patent from the government. But if the inventor is granted a patent and sues an alleged infringer in court, that lawsuit is characterized as an inter partes proceeding.

experimental use [patent] (1) An exception to the ON SALE and PUBLIC USE bars to a valid patent. (2) A defense to a charge of patent infringement.

1. Experimental Use as an Exception to the "On Sale" and "Public Use" Bars to Patent Validity. If the use made prior to the CRITICAL DATE is proven to be primarily for experiment in order to complete the invention, then there is no bar to a patent. Thus, if the use or sale is primarily for experimental purposes to bring the invention to a stage where it will work for its intended purpose, then that use or sale does not trigger the "on sale" or "public use" bars to patentability of the invention as to conduct that occurs prior to one year before the patent application filing date (the critical date).

"Exception" or Not. While the Court of Appeals for the Federal Circuit sometimes has said that experimental use is not accurately labeled an "exception" to the "on sale" or "public use" bars, it has, nevertheless on other occasions, referred to it as an "exception." The only significance of this semantic distinction appears to be the question of who has the burden of proving experimental use.

• *Case Reference*: "[I]t is incorrect to impose on the patent owner ... the burden of proving that a 'public use' was 'experimental.' These are not two separable issues. It is incorrect to ask 'Was it public use?' and then, 'Was it experimental?' Rather, the court is faced with a single issue: Was it public use under §102(b)? ... [This] means that if a prima facie case is made of public use, the patent owner must be able to point to or must come forward with convincing evidence to counter that showing...." *TP Labs., Inc. v. Professional Positioners, Inc.*, 724 F.2d 965, 971, 220 USPQ 577, 582 (Fed. Cir. 1984).

Burden of Proof. Although the statutory presumption of validity under 35 U.S.C. §282 puts the burden of proving invalidity on the party asserting it, once a prima facie case of "public use" or "on sale" activity is made by the challenger, the patent owner has the burden of coming forward with contrary evidence. *Sinskey v. Pharmacia Ophthalmics Inc.*, 982 F.2d 494, 498, 25 USPQ 2d 1290, 1293 (Fed. Cir. 1992).

Testing for Commercial Acceptance Is Not Experimentation. Market testing to gauge consumer demand does not qualify as an experimental use. The use must be to test the technical aspects of only those parts of a product that are claimed to be patentable. While commercial acceptance and feasibility is always important, it cannot be the primary purpose of the actions alleged to constitute experimentation. "The experimental use exception ... does not include market testing where the inventor is attempting to gauge consumer demand for his claimed invention. The purpose of such activities is commercial exploitation and not experimentation...." *In re Smith*, 714 F.2d 1127, 1134–35, 218 USPQ 976, 983 (Fed. Cir. 1983).

Experimentation Only by the Inventor. The experimental use rule works only to allow the inventor to refine his or her invention, not to permit others to do so. "If it is not the inventor or someone under his control or 'surveillance' who does these things, there appears to us no reason why he should be entitled to rely upon them to avoid the statute." *In re Hamilton*, 882 F.2d 1576, 1581, 11 USPQ2d 1890, 1894 (Fed. Cir. 1989).

Testing Can Be Public. Some inventions can only be tested properly by a use that is visible to and accessible by the general public. "The law ... recognizes that such testing and development may encompass, or even require disclosure to the public, without barring the inventor's access to the patent system." *Baker Oil Tools Inc. v. George Vann Inc.*, 828 F.2d 1558, 1563, 4 USPQ2d 1210, 1213 (Fed. Cir. 1987). The seminal case on this point is the nineteenth century Supreme Court case, *City of Elizabeth v. American Nicholson Pavement Co.*, 97 U.S. 126 (1878) (see case reference below).

Experimentation and Reduction to Practice. There is uncertainty as to whether there can be experimentation after a reduction to practice so as to excuse placing the invention ON SALE or in PUBLIC USE more than one year before the application for patent. The leading commentator stated that "the better and prevailing view is that experimental use can indeed continue even after the invention has been completed and reduced to practice as that term is normally used in patent law." 2 D. Chisum, *Patents* §6.02[7][b][i] (1994 rev.). However, a panel of the Court of Appeals for the Federal Circuit has stated that "experimental use, which means perfecting or completing an invention to the point of determining that it will work for its intended purpose, ends with an actual reduction to practice." *RCA Corp. v. Data Gen. Corp.*, 887 F.2d 1056, 1061, 12 USPQ2d 1449, 1453 (Fed. Cir. 1989). This uncertainty can probably be traced to a continuing imprecision as to the exact point in time when a "reduction to practice" occurs. See *In re Yarn Processing Patent Validity Litig.*, 498 F.2d 271, 282, 183 USPQ 65, 72 (5th Cir.

1974) (split of authority on experimentation issue due to differing definitions of "reduction to practice").

Experimental Sale. While it is possible for the inventor to avoid the "on sale" bar to patentability by proving that a sale was for experimental purposes, this is difficult. The primary purpose must be experimentation; commercial exploitation can be only incidental. *Baker Oil Tools Inc. v. George Vann Inc.*, 828 F.2d 1558, 1563, 4 USPQ2d 1210, 1213 (Fed. Cir. 1987) ("If the challenged use or sales activities were associated with primarily experimental procedures conducted in the course of completing the invention, ... a section 102(b) bar does not vest." Prior cases reviewed.).

See PUBLIC USE, ON SALE, REDUCTION TO PRACTICE, GRACE PERIOD.

• *Treatise Reference:* R. Harmon, *Patents and the Federal Circuit* §3.4(c) (3d ed. 1994).

• *Case References*:

"That the use of the pavement [covered by the patent] was public in one sense cannot be disputed. But can it be said that the invention was in public use? The use of an invention by the inventor himself, or by any other person under his direction, by way of experiment, and in order to bring the invention to perfection, has never been regarded as such a [public] use.... It is sometimes said that an inventor acquires an undue advantage over the public by delaying to take out a patent, inasmuch as he thereby preserves the monopoly to himself for a longer period than is allowed by the policy of the law; but this cannot be said with justice when the delay is occasioned by a bona fide effort to bring his invention to perfection, or to ascertain if it will answer the purpose intended." *City of Elizabeth v. American Nicholson Pavement Co.*, 97 U.S. 126, 134–37 (1878).

"This court has repeatedly recognized, when reviewing issues arising under the public use or on sale bar of section 102(b), that these issues must be determined by considering the totality of the circumstances. Factors we have considered include: the length of the test period; whether any payment was made for the invention; whether there is any secrecy obligation on the part of the user; whether progress records were kept; whether persons other than the inventor conducted the asserted experiments; how many tests were conducted; and how long the test period was in relation to test periods of similar devices." *In re Brigance*, 792 F.2d 1103, 1107–08, 229 USPQ 988, 991 (Fed. Cir. 1986).

• *Example 1: Experimental Use Found.* In the seminal and most famous experimental use case, Nicholson invented a new form of wooden block road paving material in the 1840s. In 1848 Nicholson had put down at his own expense a 75-foot length of his new paving on a heavily traveled toll road in Boston. The paving was put on a stretch of the road in front of the toll booth, where heavily loaded wagons stopped and started. That paving remained in use for six years, and thereafter Nicholson applied for a patent. The Supreme Court held that there was no disabling "public use" before the critical date (then two years prior to the patent application) because the use was "experimental." Thus the Nicholson patent was valid. The facts showed that the inventor inspected the road for wear almost every day and often examined the tollkeeper about the pavement and how travelers liked it. The court said that if the invention is of a machine, it can be tested indoors by the inventor without there being a "public use" that triggers the statutory period to file an application for a patent. "And though, during all that period, he may not find that any changes are necessary, yet he may be justly said to be using his machine only by way of experiment...." The Court remarked that this is not a "public use" even though the experimental machine produces things which are sold, (e.g., flour from a gristmill being tested) so long as the sale is incidental to the experimental purpose. But the nature of a road-paving material is that it cannot be tested for durability except on a public highway. The Court concluded: "Nicholson wished to experiment on his pavement.... Durability was one of the qualities to be attained.... Its character for durability could not be ascertained without its being subjected to use for a considerable time.... The public had the incidental use of the pavement, it is true; but was the invention in public use, within the meaning of the statute? We think not." *City of Elizabeth v. American*

Nicholson Pavement Co., 97 U.S. 126, 136 (1878).

- *Example 2: Experimental Use Found.* Two employees of Corn Products Co. invented and patented product claims on a food ingredient that was bland and colorless for use as a carrier for synthetic sweeteners in coffee whiteners. Prior to the CRITICAL DATE, Corn Products Co. shipped samples of the new compound to a few food manufacturers to test it for utility. Such testing was necessary because food ingredients like the new compound might interact adversely with other food ingredients in the manufacturers' products. The Court of Appeals for the Federal Circuit affirmed a finding that this was a true experimental use, not an invalidating "public use." "[T]he testing period was short, very small quantities of the samples were shipped, and they were free of charge. Because there was nothing in Corn Products' conduct that was 'inconsistent with experimentation,' ... the district court correctly determined that there had been no public use [prior to the critical date]." *Grain Processing Corp. v. American Maize-Prods. Co.*, 840 F.2d 902, 906, 5 USPQ2d 1788, 1792 (Fed. Cir. 1988).

- *Example 3: Experimental Sale and Use Found.* Prior to the critical date, the patentee had contracted to sell a new design of outdoor lighting assembly to the state, which conditionally approved payment for the device, subject to proof of its durability in an outdoor environment. The invention was mounted atop a 150-foot pole in a highway rest area closed to the public. After five months, state officials inspected the light pole, found the lighting assembly acceptable and authorized payment to the patentee. The Federal Circuit found that this was an experimental use and sale: "[A] sale that is primarily for experimental purposes, as opposed to commercial exploitation, does not raise an on sale bar. ... Because [patentee] did not attempt to use the invention when it first bid on the [state] contract, and did not offer to sell the [invention] to anyone else until after it was tested in the cold, rain, snow and wind—an environment in which it was designed to operate—we must agree with the district court that experimentation, and not profit, was the pri-

mary motive behind [patentee's] use." *Manville Sales Co. v. Paramount Sys., Inc.*, 917 F. 2d 544, 550, 16 USPQ 2d 1587, 1592 (Fed. Cir. 1990).

- *Example 4: No Experimental Use Found.* An employee of Hycor Corporation invented a machine for separating solids from waste water, sold by Hycor as the "Rotostrainer." Prior to the CRITICAL DATE, the Rotostrainer was submitted to the North Chicago sewage treatment plant and to two meat-packing plants to use without any obligation of secrecy imposed on employees at those plants. The Rotostrainer remained in use at the sewage treatment plant for almost two years, even though the inventor admitted that no more than four to five days of testing was required to determine effectiveness in a commercial setting. Hycor was unable to point to any significant documentary evidence of test reports. Photographs of the sewage treatment plant Rotostrainers were shown by Hycor to representatives of potential customers such as Oscar Mayer & Co. The Court of Appeals for the Federal Circuit affirmed the district court's holding that these were commercial activities constituting "public use" of the invention prior to the critical date and were not "experimental." These uses "of plaintiff's Rotostrainer by sewage treatment plants and food processors were intended to develop commercial demand for the Rotostrainer and to exploit its commercial value." The patent was held to be invalid. *Hycor Corp. v. Schlueter Co.*, 740 F.2d 1529, 1535, 222 USPQ 553, 557 (Fed. Cir. 1984).

- *Example 5: No Experimental Use Found.* A physician invented and patented intraocular lenses implanted in the human eye. The physician had implanted eight of the patented lenses in the eyes of patients and sold at least three lenses prior to the critical date. The doctor charged his usual surgical fee for implanting the lenses, the patients were charged a standard fee for the lenses, and the patients were not informed that they were being treated with "experimental" lenses. The Federal Circuit affirmed the holding that these activities prior to the critical date constituted "public use" and "sale" and were not "experimental": "Post-hoc affidavit testimony alone, years after the events described and purporting to show an inventor's subjective experimental intent, will never satisfy the burden of establishing experimental use in a case like this where there is not contemporaneous evidence of experimental purpose and the objective evidence is to the contrary." *Sinskey v. Pharmacia Ophthalmics Inc.*, 982 F.2d 494, 499, 25 USPQ2d 1290, 1294 (Fed. Cir. 1992).

• *Example 6: No Experimental Use Found.* Prior to the critical date, the patentee published price lists and sales letters offering for sale orthotics covered by its patent and sold about three hundred orthotics. An orthotic is a device worn inside a shoe to provide support for the foot. The patentee did not place any control or restrictions on the customers' use of the product and plaintiff never made customers aware of the experimentation. The Federal Circuit affirmed the holding that the patent was invalid under §102(b) and explained: "[T]he assertion of experimental sales, at a minimum, requires that customers must be made aware of the experimentation." *Paragon Podiatry Lab., Inc. v. KLM Lab., Inc.*, 984 F.2d 1182, 1186, 25 USPQ2d 1561, 1564 (Fed. Cir. 1993).

2. Experimental Use as a Defense to a Charge of Patent Infringement. There is a very limited experimental use exception as to activities that would otherwise infringe a patent. The only types of uses that fall within the exception are those made "for amusement, to satisfy idle curiosity or for strictly philosophical inquiry." *Roche Prods., Inc. v. Bolar Pharmaceutical Co.*, 733 F.2d 858, 863, 221 USPQ 937, 941 (Fed. Cir. 1984). See Bruzzone, *The Research Exception: A Proposal*, 21 AIPLA Q.J. 52 (1993).

Federally Mandated Testing of Patented Drug or Device. Federally mandated testing of a drug product just before the expiration of a patent on the product in order to be prepared to sell the product after patent expiration was held not to fall within the experimental use exception. *Roche Prods., Inc. v. Bolar Pharmaceutical Co., supra.* Amendments to the Patent Code in 1984 defined what does and does not constitute patent infringement in the context of obtaining federal approval for drugs. 35 U.S.C. §271(e). It was held that demonstration of a medical device at medical conferences in order to obtain physicians who will act as clinical investigators is reasonably related to the development of information for FDA approval and is not patent infringement under the 1984 amendments. *Telectronics Pacing Sys. Inc. v. Ventritex Inc.*, 982 F.2d 1520, 25 USPQ2d 1196 (Fed. Cir. 1992) ("By permitting the testing and regulatory approval process to begin well before a controlling patent had run its course, Congress must have intended to allow competitors to be in a position to market their products as soon as it was legally permissible." 25 USPQ2d at 1200.).

expression-idea dichotomy [copyright]
See IDEA-EXPRESSION DICHOTOMY.

F

failure of others [patent] A showing that the invention solved a technological problem that others had tried and failed to solve is relevant evidence of the nonobviousness and patentability of the invention. Failure of others is one of the types of objective evidence of real-world recognition of the invention, which are known as SECONDARY CONSIDERATIONS.

The failure of others to solve a specific technological problem, which was solved by this invention, tends to prove that this invention was not an "obvious" solution and hence is patentable under the OBVIOUSNESS bar of Patent Code §103. For example, the Court of Appeals for the Federal Circuit affirmed a finding of nonobviousness and the validity of a patent relating to a method and apparatus for inspecting turbine rotors in electrical generators by the use of ultrasonic waves to detect cracks and flaws within the rotors. "The evidence fully supports the district court's finding that others in the industry were unable to solve the problem. Westinghouse, a large corporation working on this matter, had tried but failed." *Alco Standard Corp. v. Tennessee Valley Auth.*, 808 F.2d 1490, 1500, 1 USPQ2d 1337, 1344 (Fed. Cir. 1986).

See OBVIOUSNESS, LONG-FELT NEED, SECONDARY CONSIDERATIONS, UNEXPECTED RESULTS.

- *Case References*:

"We can conceive of no better way to determine whether an invention would have been obvious to persons of ordinary skill in the art at the time, than to see what such persons actually did or failed to do when they were confronted with the problem in the course of their work. If the evidence shows that a number of skilled technicians actually attempted, over a substantial period, to solve the specific problem which the invention overcame and failed to do so,

notwithstanding the availability of all the necessary materials, it is difficult to see how a court could conclude that the invention was 'obvious' to such persons at the time." *Timely Prods. Corp. v. Arron*, 523 F.2d 288, 294, 187 USPQ 257, 261 (2d Cir. 1975).

The Court of Appeals for the Federal Circuit reversed a finding that claims were invalid as obvious in a patent on an air-deflecting device for reducing wind resistance encountered by a tractor-trailer vehicle. "The [district] court also did not take into account other objective evidence of long felt need and failure of others.... The district court did not consider the failure of the Maryland study to produce an effective solution to the wind resistance problem as an indication of long felt need. Instead, it viewed that failure as an indication that a later invention, based on a different principle, would have been obvious, because the inventor would know from such failure that he should try some other approach. Under this reasoning, it would be progressively more difficult, after a succession of failures, to secure a patent on an invention that provided a solution to a long felt need. This is contrary to the well established principle that the failure of others to provide a feasible solution to a long standing problem is probative of nonobviousness." *Uniroyal, Inc. v. Rudkin-Wiley Corp.*, 837 F.2d 1044, 1054, 5 USPQ2d 1434, 1440–41 (Fed. Cir. 1988).

fair use [copyright–trademark] A defense to a charge of either copyright or trademark infringement.

1. Copyright Fair Use.

The Statutory Guidelines of Fair Use. The defense of fair use to a charge of infringement of copyright has long been recognized as an equitable rule excusing certain types of other-

163

wise infringing conduct. Congress, in broadly defining the defense in §107 of the 1978 Copyright Act, intended to "restate the present judicial doctrine of fair use, not to change, narrow or enlarge it in any way." H.R. Rep. No. 94-1476, 94th Cong., 2d Sess. 66 (1976).

The Four Factors of §107. In §107, Congress laid down four factors to be considered and weighed by the courts in determining if a fair use defense exists in a given case: (1) the purpose and character of the accused use; (2) the nature of the copyrighted work; (3) the importance of the portion used in relation to the copyrighted work as a whole; and (4) the effect of the accused use on the potential market for or value of the copyrighted work. Congress viewed these four criteria as guidelines for "balancing the equities," not as "definitive or determinative" tests. Indeed, Congress observed that "since the doctrine [of fair use] is an equitable rule of reason, no generally applicable definition is possible." H.R. Rep. No. 94-1476, 94th Cong., 2d Sess. 65 (1976). The Supreme Court has observed that factor (4), relating to the effect on the potential market of the copyrighted work, "is undoubtedly the single most important element of fair use." *Harper & Row, Publishers, Inc. v. Nation Enters.*, 471 U.S. 539, 566, 225 USPQ 1073, 1083 (1985). Accord *Stewart v. Abend*, 495 U.S. 207, 238, 14 USPQ2d 1614, 1628 (1990).

Commercial and Noncommercial Uses. The U.S. Supreme Court held that the at-home use of a video cassette recorder (VCR) to record for time-shifting purposes copyrighted works broadcast on television was a noninfringing fair use. *Sony Corp. v. Universal City Studios, Inc.*, 464 U.S. 417, 220 USPQ 665 (1984). Many persons had believed that in that case, the Supreme Court laid down a general rule that if the use is for commercial gain, there is a presumption that there is no fair use. However, the Supreme Court later said that such a presumption applied only to verbatim copying: "But when, on the contrary, the second use is transformative, market substitution is at least less certain, and market harm may not be so readily inferred." *Campbell v. Acuff-Rose Music, Inc.*, 114 S. Ct. 1164, 1177, 29 USPQ2d 1961, 1970 (1994). There is no automatic presumption that

noncommercial uses are a fair use: "This listing [of four factors in §107] was not intended ... to single out any particular use as presumptively a 'fair' use. The drafters resisted pressure from special interest groups to create presumptive categories of fair use...." *Harper & Row, Publishers, Inc. v. Nation Enters.*, 471 U.S. 539, 561, 225 USPQ 1073, 1081 (1985).

Unpublished Works. In the "President Ford Memoirs Case," the U.S. Supreme Court held that the publication in *The Nation* magazine of verbatim excerpts from a stolen copy of the unpublished manuscript of Gerald Ford's memoirs was not a fair use where the author's right of first publication was preempted by the defendant's publication. "Under ordinary circumstances, the author's right to control the first public appearance of his undisseminated expression will outweigh a claim of fair use." *Harper & Row, Publishers, Inc. v. Nation Enters.*, 471 U.S. 539, 555, 225 USPQ 1073, 1079 (1985). In 1992, Congress added the following sentence to §107 at the end of the list of four factors: "The fact that a work is unpublished shall not itself bar a finding of fair use if such a finding is made upon consideration of all the above factors."

Scholarly and Transformative Uses. The reproduction of relatively small portions of copyrighted factual works for "scholarship" purposes is recognized as the classic example of what is easily recognized as fair use. That is, the copier makes a "transformative use" of the materials in order to better illustrate and illuminate a point. This use is "transformative" in that it does not merely supersede the original, but serves to advance knowledge and learning by transforming some or all of the first work into a second work containing new views and insights. As Professor Chafee remarked: "The world goes ahead because each of us builds on the works of our predecessors. 'A dwarf standing on the shoulders of a giant can see farther than the giant himself.' " Chafee, *Reflections on the Law of Copyright*, 45 Colum. L. Rev. 503, 511 (1945). Such uses do not usually damage the market for the copied work. In many instances, they may boost interest in and the value of the original work cited and reproduced. The Supreme Court has said that a "transformative work" is one that "adds something new, with a further purpose or different character, altering the first with new expression, meaning or message." The Court then observed: "Such works thus lie at the heart of the fair use doctrine's guarantee of breathing space within the confines of copyright ... and the more transformative the new work, the less will be the significance of other factors, like commercialism, that may weigh against a finding of fair use." *Campbell v. Acuff-Rose Music, Inc.*, 114 S. Ct. 1164, 1171, 29 USPQ2d 1961, 1965 (1994). The Supreme Court has noted that "[i]n general, fair use is more likely to be found in factual works than in fictional works." *Stewart v. Abend*, 495 U.S. 207, 238, 14 USPQ2d 1614, 1628 (1990).

Parody as Fair Use. Parody is viewed as a form of social and literary criticism, having socially significant value as free speech under the First Amendment. The Supreme Court has approved what is known as the "conjure up" test: the parodist is permitted a fair use of a copyrighted work if he takes only that amount of copyrighted material that is necessary to "recall" or "conjure up" the object of his parody. "When parody takes aim at a particular original work, the parody must be able to 'conjure up' at least enough of that original to make the object of its critical wit recognizable." *Campbell v. Acuff-Rose Music, Inc.*, 114 S. Ct. 1164, 1176, 29 USPQ2d 1961, 1969 (1994). The Supreme Court in the *Acuff-Rose* case held that a rap group's version of Ray Orbison's song "Pretty Woman" was a candidate for a parody fair use defense. The Court pointed out the difference between parody (in which the copyrighted work is the target) and satire (in which the copyrighted work is merely a vehicle to poke fun at another target): "Parody needs to mimic an original to make its point, and so has some claim to use the creation of its victim's (or collective victims') imagination, whereas satire can stand on its own two feet and so requires justification for the very act of borrowing." 114 S. Ct. at 1172, 29 USPQ2d at 1966.

Photocopying. The ubiquitous photocopying machine has brought inexpensive, quick, and mindless copying to everyone and creates problems of copyright and fair use, which are still largely unresolved. Some questions of whether photocopying is copyright infringement or a fair use can be resolved simply by asking: If you were not permitted to photocopy this, would you have bought multiple copies of the original? If the answer is yes, it is indicative of a negative impact on the potential market for the copyrighted work. But, like jaywalking and littering, photocopying infringement is so widespread and difficult to detect and police that it creates its own legal realities. To attempt to deal with multiple photocopies made by teachers for classroom use, some educators, authors, and publishers created some minimal guidelines in an "Agreement on Guidelines for Classroom Copying in Not-for-Profit Educational Institutions," reproduced in H.R. Rep. No. 94-1476, 94th Cong., 2d Sess. 72 (1976). See 3 *Nimmer on Copyright* §13.05[E][3] (1994 rev.). The photocopying made by a Texaco scientist who copied articles from professional journals was found to be an infringement, not a fair use. The court stressed the primarily archival purpose of providing the scientist with a personal set of papers for future reference, rather than filling an immediate research need for the articles. *American Geophysical Union v. Texaco Inc.*, 37 F.3d 881, 32 USPQ2d 1545 (2d Cir. 1994). Private groups such as the COPYRIGHT CLEARANCE CENTER serve as clearinghouses to grant licenses to corporate and library users who make substantial photocopying of certain newsletters and similar publications.

- *Treatise References*: 3 *Nimmer on Copyright* §13.05 (1994 rev.); 2 P. Goldstein, *Copyright* §10.1 (1989); M. Leaffer, *Understanding Copyright* §10.1 *et seq.* (1989); 1 W. Patry, *Copyright Law and Practice* ch. 9 (1994); 1 N. Boorstyn, *Copyright* §§12.02–.06 (2d ed. 1994); W. Patry, *The Fair Use Privilege in Copyright Law* (2d ed. 1995).

- *Statutory Reference*: 17 U.S.C. §107:

Notwithstanding the provisions of section 106, the fair use of a copyrighted work, including such use by reproduction in copies or phonorecords or by any other means specified by that section, for purposes such as criticism, comment, news reporting, teaching (including multiple copies for classroom use), scholarship, or research, is not an infringement of copyright. In determining whether the use made of a work in any particular case is a fair use the factors to be considered shall include—

(1) the purpose and character of the use, including whether such use is of a commercial nature or is for nonprofit educational purposes;

(2) the nature of the copyrighted work;

(3) the amount and substantiality of the portion used in relation to the copyrighted work as a whole; and

(4) the effect of the use upon the potential market for or value of the copyrighted work.

The fact that a work is unpublished shall not itself bar a finding of fair use if such a finding is made upon consideration of all the above factors.

• *Legislative History*: "The examples enumerated at page 24 of the Register's 1961 Report, while by no means exhaustive, give some idea of the sort of activities the courts might regard as fair use under the circumstances: 'quotation of excerpts in a review or criticism for purposes of illustration or comment; quotation of short passages in a scholarly or technical work, for illustration or clarification of the author's observations; use in a parody of some of the content of the work parodied; summary of an address or article, with brief quotations, in a news report; reproduction by a library of a portion of a work to replace part of a damaged copy; reproduction by a teacher or student of a small part of a work to illustrate a lesson; reproduction of a work in legislative or judicial proceedings or reports; incidental and fortuitous reproduction, in a newsreel or broadcast, of a work located at the scene of an event being reported.' " H.R. Rep. No. 94-1476, 94th Cong., 2d Sess. 65 (1976).

2. Trademark Fair Use. A defense to a charge of trademark infringement under which the junior user argues that it is not using a descriptive, geographically descriptive, or personal name designation in a trademark sense, but only to describe the defendant's goods or services, or their geographic origin, or to name the person running the business.

Descriptive Terms. A junior user is always entitled to use a term in good faith in its primary, descriptive sense. This is known as a noninfringing fair use. Such a defense is most often made as against a designation that is determined to be descriptive of the plaintiff's goods or services. Such a DESCRIPTIVE MARK requires proof of SECONDARY MEANING for registration and protection. Assuming such proof, the word or symbol has two meanings: (1) its old, "primary" meaning in the language, which existed prior to the plaintiff's usage; and (2) its new, "secondary" trademark meaning as an identifying symbol for the plaintiff's goods or services.

In the author's opinion, the better view is that one can make a noninfringing, descriptive "fair use" even if the senior user is not using the term in a descriptive sense with its goods or services. That is, the key is the junior user's descriptive use, not the senior user's descriptive use.

Example. Neither the plaintiff nor anyone else can have exclusive rights to the word or symbol in its primary meaning. Trademark rights relate only to the secondary meaning. For example, assume that a chain of discount consumer stores used the word PAYLESS as a mark and has achieved secondary meaning: the chain would have no right to prevent another's use of the word in its primary, descriptive sense. A competitive junior user would probably have a right to make a fair use in a nonservice mark sense, such as "At TARGET stores, we guarantee you will pay less!" or "Want to pay less? Come to TARGET stores."

Nontrademark Usage. The only type of use qualifying as a "fair use" is use in a nontrademark sense. Factors relevant to a determination if a word is being used as a trademark or not include type style, size, visual placement, and prominence. Fair use is both a defense at common law and is codified under Lanham Act §33(b)(4) as a defense against federally registered marks, including both incontestable and contestable registrations. Under the statute, four elements are needed to prove the defense: (1) the plaintiff's mark is "descriptive"; (2) the defendant's use of the term is not as a trademark or service mark; (3) the defendant uses the term "fairly and in good faith"; and (4) the defendant uses the term "only to describe" its goods or services.

Fair Use and Likely Confusion. In the author's opinion, the better view is that it is inconsistent to find both a likelihood of confusion *and* a fair use. *Lindey Pen Co. v. Bic Pen Corp.*, 725 F.2d 1240, 226 USPQ 17 (9th Cir. 1984). "Fair use" should be seen as merely one type of use that is not likely to cause confusion and is only a "defense" in that sense. 1 J.T. McCarthy, *Trademarks and Unfair Competition* §11.17[3] (3d ed. 1995 rev.).

Geographically Descriptive Terms. The term "fair use" is also extended to cover noninfringing, descriptive, nontrademark uses of geographically descriptive terms. That is, even if a senior user has achieved secondary meaning in a geographically descriptive term, anyone who is in fact located in that place has a limited right to tell consumers of the location. But the junior user must confine and adapt its usage of the geographical term so as not to cause a likelihood of confusion. This is also codified as a defense in Lanham Act §33(b)(4). See 1 J.T. McCarthy, *Trademarks and Unfair Competition* §14.07 (3d ed. 1995 rev.).

Personal Names. The term "fair use" is stretched even further to cover noninfringing trademark uses of one's own personal name. This is also codified as a defense in Lanham Act §33(b)(4). However, personal name cases have developed their own jurisprudence, not necessarily governed by the principles outlined above. While early law spoke of an "absolute right" of each person to use his or her own name in business, modern cases limit this to a qualified right: even the good faith same-name junior user will be required to take some precautions in the mode of use so as to eliminate or at least minimize the likelihood of confusion with the senior user. In many cases the courts have issued injunctions that permit the use of a surname but require the addition of the defendant's first name or initials; a change in the style, size, or color of lettering; the inclusion of some clarifying matter; the use of a disclaimer; or a combination of these conditions. In some cases where there is bad faith or confusion cannot be eliminated by halfway measures, an absolute and unconditional prohibition is required. See 1 J.T. McCarthy, *Trademarks and Unfair Competition* §13.03 (3d ed. 1995 rev.).

• *Treatise Reference*: 1 J.T. McCarthy, *Trademarks and Unfair Competition* §§11.17, 14.07, 13.03 (3d ed. 1995 rev.).

• *Statutory Reference*: Lanham Act §33(b), 15 U.S.C. §1115(b): "[Incontestably registered marks] shall be subject to the following defenses or defects: .... (4) That the use of the name, term or device charged to be an infringement is a use, otherwise than as a mark, of the party's individual name in his own business, or of the individual name of anyone in privity with such party, or of a term or device which is descriptive of and used fairly and in good faith only to describe the goods or services of such party, or their geographic origin; ...."

family of marks [trademark] Several marks that have some common element that distinguishes them as a recognizable "family." For example, Eastman Kodak Co. has a family of KODA- prefix marks including KODACOLOR and KODACHROME. In effect, the family "surname" or distinguishing element is recognized by customers as an identifying trademark in and of itself. Even though a junior use may not be that close to any one member of the family, it may use the distinguishing family "surname" or characteristic so as to be likely to cause confusion. That is, customers would be likely to think that this junior user's mark indicates a sponsorship or affiliation with the company that is identified by the family of marks. For example, the McDonald's quick food service system has a family of MC- prefix marks. Members of the family include: MCDONALD'S, EGG MCMUFFIN, CHICKEN MCNUGGETS, and MCPIZZA. A junior use of MCBAGEL for a bagel bakery and restaurant was held likely to cause confusion with the MC-family of marks. *McDonald's Corp. v. McBagel's, Inc.*, 649 F.Supp. 1268, 1 USPQ2d 1761 (S.D.N.Y. 1986). Similarly, a junior use of MCSLEEP for a chain of low-cost motels was held to infringe on the MC- family, *Quality Inns Int'l Inc. v. McDonald's Corp.*, 695 F. Supp. 198, 8 USPQ2d 1633 (D. Md. 1988), and a junior user's registration of MCPRETZEL for frozen pretzels was successfully opposed. *J & J Snack Foods Corp. v. McDonald's Corp.*, 932 F.2d 1460, 18 USPQ2d 1889 (Fed. Cir. 1991).

- *Treatise Reference*: 2 J.T. McCarthy, *Trademarks and Unfair Competition* §23.19 (3d ed. 1995 rev.).

famous mark [trademark] A concept under which a trademark or service mark is protected within a nation if it is well known in that nation even though the mark is not actually used or registered in that nation. Marks can become known in a nation in the absence of sales by various methods, for example, by advertising in internationally distributed media such as magazines or television, by travelers seeing the mark in other nations, or by discussion in local media by reporters and commentators.

Protection Without Registration. In many nations of the world, a mark is not protected from infringement or registration by another unless it is registered for those particular goods in that nation. Most nations do not recognize unregistered, or common law, rights in marks. The famous mark doctrine is an exception to that rule.

Variation in Domestic Enforcement. Although the basis of the modern treaties and domestic laws providing protection for famous or well-known marks is derived from the PARIS CONVENTION, the scope of protection afforded to famous marks is different in each country.

Spillover of Fame Between Nations. Under the famous mark doctrine, the law recognizes that knowledge and reputation of a mark that is well known in nation X, or in nations X, Y, and Z, can spillover, such that the mark becomes well known in nation A, even though the goods or services identified by the mark are not available in nation A. See Abnett, *AIPPI: Famous Trademarks Require a New Legal Weapon*, Trademark World 23 (Dec. 1990/Jan. 1991). For example, a Canadian court granted an injunction against the defendant's use of the name HILTON for a hotel in Vancouver, British Columbia, even though plaintiff, the United States HILTON hotel chain, at that time had no HILTON hotel in Canada and no Canadian registration. Plaintiff was well known in Canada by Canadians who traveled in the United States. *Hilton Hotels Corp. v. Belkin & Kalensky*, 17 WWR 86, 24 CPR 100 (1955). Another common use of the famous mark doctrine is to fight trademark pirates who rush to register a famous mark on goods on which it has not yet been registered in a nation by the legitimate foreign owner.

1. Famous Marks in the United States. U.S. trademark law has never had a separate doctrine or category of "famous marks." This is because U.S. law protects a mark against infringement or registration by another, even in the absence of registration, if it is so well known in the United States that confusion is likely to result. 3 McCarthy, *Trademarks and Unfair Competition* §29.01[4] (3d ed. 1995). For example, the famous MAXIM'S restaurant in Paris obtained an injunction against a person who opened an unauthorized MAXIM'S restaurant in New York. *Vaudauble v. Montmartre, Inc.*, 20 Misc 2d 757, 193 N.Y.S.2d 332, 123 USPQ 357 (New York 1959). The same concept has also been used to prevent the registration of a famous mark by an unauthorized person. For example, the promoter of the famous WIMBLEDON tennis championships in England successfully opposed the U.S. registration of "Wimbledon Cologne" with a picture of a tennis player. *All England Lawn Tennis Club, Ltd. v. Creations Aromatiques, Inc.*, 220 USPQ 1069 (T.T.A.B. 1983). Under U.S. law, famous or strong marks enjoy a wider latitude of protection in the determination of whether there will be a likelihood of confusion. *Kenner Parker Toys Inc. v. Rose Art Assocs., Inc.*, 963 F.2d 350, 22 USPQ2d 1453 (Fed. Cir. 1992).

2. Paris Convention, Article 6bis. The Paris Convention is the cornerstone of international protection of famous marks. But because the treaty does not define a famous mark, some countries have been hesitant to enforce protection. If protection is afforded, the scope of protection may be inconsistent from one country to another.

- *Treaty Reference*: Paris Convention for the Protection of Industrial Property, Article 6*bis*: "(1) The countries of the Union undertake, ex officio if their legislation so permits, or at the request of an interested party, to refuse or to cancel the registration, and to prohibit the use, of a trademark which constitutes a reproduction, an imitation, or a translation, liable to create confusion, of a mark considered by the competent authority of the country of registration or use to be well known in that country as being already the mark of a person entitled to the benefits of this Convention and used for identical or similar goods. These provisions shall also apply when the essential part of the mark constitutes a reproduction of any such well-known mark or an imitation liable to create confusion therewith....''

3. North American Free Trade Agreement (NAFTA), Article 1708(6). NAFTA Article 1708(6) expressly incorporates Article 6*bis* of the PARIS CONVENTION with the following modifications. First, NAFTA extends protection to service marks. Second, in determining whether or not a mark is famous, the standard used is how well the mark is known in a *relevant sector* of the public, not necessarily the general public. Thus, knowledge of the famous or well-known mark can be the result of actual use or promotion of the trademark only in a particular segment of trade.

• *Treaty Reference:* North American Free Trade Agreement, Article 1708(6): "Article 6*bis* of the Paris Convention shall apply, with such modifications as may be necessary, to services. In determining whether a trademark is well-known, account shall be taken of the knowledge of the trademark in the relevant sector of the public, including knowledge in the Party's territory obtained as a result of the promotion of the trademark. No Party may require that the reputation of the trademark extend beyond the sector of the public that normally deals with the relevant goods or services.''

4. General Agreement on Tariffs and Trade (GATT) Agreement on Trade-Related Aspects of Intellectual Property Rights, Including Trade in Counterfeit Goods (TRIPS), Article 16(2-3). Like NAFTA, the GATT TRIPS agreement extends protection to both goods and service marks even if the mark has not been registered in a member country. Also like NAFTA,

the mark need only be famous in a relevant segment of the public.

The special provisions of TRIPS Art. 16(3) apply to give protection beyond that of the Paris Convention. The famous mark rule applies even if the goods or services to which the allegedly infringing mark is being applied are *not* similar to the goods or services for which the famous mark has become well known. This is subject to three conditions: (1) the famous mark must be registered; (2) there must be such a connection between the respective goods or services that confusion is likely; and (3) it must be likely that the interests of the owner of the registered trademark will be damaged by such infringing use.

• *Treaty Reference:* GATT Agreement on Trade-Related Aspects of Intellectual Property Rights, (TRIPS), Article 16(2): "Article 6*bis* of the Paris Convention (1967) shall apply, mutatis mutandis, to services. In determining whether a trademark is well-known, Members shall take account of the knowledge of the trademark in the relevant sector of the public, including knowledge in the Member concerned which has been obtained as a result of the promotion of the trademark.''

Article 16(3): "Article 6*bis* of the Paris Convention (1967) shall apply, mutatis mutandis, to goods or services which are not similar to those in respect of which a trademark is registered, provided that use of that trademark in relation to those goods or services would indicate a connection between those goods or services and the owner of the registered trademark and provided that the interests of the owner of the registered trademark are likely to be damaged by such use.''

5. Examples of Domestic Implementation of the Famous Mark Doctrine.

United Kingdom: Trade Marks Act of 1994, Section 56. Prior to October 31, 1994, some cases indicated that protection of a famous mark depended on the presence of a trademark owner's good will in the United Kingdom. Following the enforcement date, an individual of a PARIS CONVENTION nation can restrain the use of another's trademark in the United Kingdom if the mark is identical or similar to the individual's mark, if the goods or services of the owners are similar or identical, and if the use of the infringing mark is likely to cause confusion, regardless of the presence of good will. However, if the proprietor of the famous mark acquiesces to the use of the mark by a third party and the party uses the mark for five years, the right to protect the famous mark is lost.

Brazil: In Industrial Property Code Art. 67, Brazil has adopted a special register of marks found to be "notorious" and entitled to protection as to all types of goods and services. Generally required for such registration is a market survey of Brazilians showing recognition of the mark in the range of 60–75 percent. Brazil also recognizes and applies the famous mark principles of Art. 6*bis* of the Paris Convention. L. Henrique do Amaral, *Famous Marks: The Brazilian Case*, 83 Trademark L. Rep. 394 (1993).

5. European Community Trademark Harmonization Directive, Article 5(2). Adopted in 1988, this directive gives registered famous trademarks a greater scope of protection, amounting to what U.S. law calls "anti-dilution" laws. See DILUTION. If, as a result of use in a country, a mark becomes famous or well known, protection of the mark extends beyond the use of an infringing mark on similar goods.

• *Treaty Reference*: European Community Trademark Harmonization Directive, Article 5(2): "Any Member State may also provide that the proprietor shall be entitled to prevent all third parties not having his consent from using in the course of trade any sign which is identical with, or similar to, the trade mark in relation to goods or services which are not similar to those for which the trade mark is registered, where the latter has a reputation in the Member State and where use of that sign without due cause takes unfair advantage of, or is detrimental to, the distinctive character or the repute of the trade mark."

fanciful mark [trademark] A coined term invented or selected for the sole purpose of serving as a trademark or service mark. Such marks comprise words either totally unknown before in the language or are completely out of common usage at the time, as with obsolete or scientific terms. Fanciful marks are inherently distinctive and need no proof of SECONDARY MEANING to be regarded as valid for registration or legal protection. Fanciful or coined marks are inherently the strongest of all marks, in that their uniqueness and inherent distinctiveness will likely make a substantial impact on the buyer's mind. In the author's opinion, the following marks would probably fall in this category: CLOROX bleach, KODAK cameras and film, EXXON gasoline, and YUBAN coffee.

• *Treatise Reference*: 1 J.T. McCarthy, *Trademarks and Unfair Competition* §11.03 (3d ed. 1995 rev.).

field of use restriction [general intellectual property–antitrust] A provision in an intellectual property license restricting the licensee to use of the licensed property only in a defined product or service market.

Examples of Field of Use Restrictions. Field of use restrictions are common in technology licensing and can take many different forms. For example, an electronic circuit protected by trade secret or patent might be licensed to manufacturers to sell electronic products embodying the invention only in a defined market such as the field for consumer electronics and not for military electronics. Or the licensee might be limited to selling to a defined group of distributors in a field. Alternatively, the licensee might be limited to the form or model of the product made under license, e.g., a laser only in a size suitable for medical use and not for communications use.

Used to Implement Differential Royalty Rates. Field of use licensing is used sometimes to implement a differential royalty schedule. The licensor can charge each licensed user in a field the price that maximizes the licensor's return from that use in that field. The field of use restriction prevents a licensee in a low-royalty rate field from invading the field of a high-royalty rate licensee. The patented technology may be more valuable to licensees in some fields of use than in others because the technology saves them more in manufacturing costs or because of greater demand for the technology in that field.

Antitrust Challenges. While some field of use restrictions have been challenged as being patent misuse or antitrust violations, such restrictions have generally been upheld as legal. *General Talking Pictures Corp. v. Western Elec. Co.*, 305 U.S. 124, 39 USPQ 329 (1938); *United States v. CIBA Geigy Corp.*, 508 F. Supp. 1118, 1126 (D.N.J. 1976) (approving of license restricting licensee to make and sell patented drug only in dosage form, not in bulk form, to prevent the licensee from selling in bulk to price-cutting generic drug companies who would resell in dosage form at low prices).

- *Treatise Reference*: ABA, *Antitrust Law Developments* 502 (2d ed. 1984); W. Holmes, *Intellectual Property and Antitrust Law* §18 (1994 rev.).

file wrapper [patent] The folder in which the Patent and Trademark Office keeps the papers of an application for a patent or for a trademark registration. See *Manual of Patent Examining Procedure* §717 (1994)

file wrapper estoppel [patent] A limitation on the doctrine of EQUIVALENTS that prevents the patent owner from arguing that an ELEMENT of the accused product or process is "equivalent" to an element of the patent claims when, in the prosecution of the patent application (its "file wrapper"), the inventor narrowed the claim to avoid cited PRIOR ART that covers the crucial element of the accused product or process. The synonym "prosecution history estoppel" is often used in place of the term "file wrapper estoppel."

Patentee Cannot Impose a Limitation to Receive the Claim and Then Ignore the Limitation in Interpreting the Claim. File wrapper estoppel "precludes a patentee from obtaining a claim construction that would resurrect subject matter surrendered during prosecution of his patent application.... [I]t limits a patentee's reliance on the doctrine of equivalents by preventing him from contending later in an infringement action that his claims should be interpreted as if limitations added by amendment were not present or that claims abandoned are still present." *Thomas & Betts Corp. v. Litton Sys., Inc.*, 720

F.2d 1572, 1579, 220 USPQ 1, 6 (Fed. Cir. 1983). File wrapper estoppel prevents a patentee from enforcing its claims against an otherwise equivalent feature in an accused device if that feature was excluded by claim limitations added by the patentee in order to avoid prior art and receive the patent. However, every narrowing amendment to the claims does not necessarily trigger an estoppel. In cases where a patentee's amendments were "not required in response to an examiner's rejection or critical to the allowance of claims, no estoppel has been found." *Mannesmann Demag Corp. v. Engineered Metal Prods. Co.*, 793 F.2d 1279, 1284–85, 230 USPQ 45, 48 (Fed. Cir. 1986).

Amendment of a Claim Is Not Required. Amendment of a claim in light of a prior art reference is not an indispensable condition to establish prosecution history estoppel. Even where there has been no citation in the prosecution history of a prior art reference disclosing an equivalent feature and an inventor never amended his or her claim to avoid a prior art reference, an inventor may still be estopped by his or her assertions made in support of patentability. "Unmistakable assertions made by the applicant to the Patent and Trademark Office (PTO) in support of patentability, whether or not required to secure allowance of the claim, also may operate to preclude the patentee from asserting equivalency between a limitation of the claim and a substituted structure or process step." *Texas Instruments, Inc. v. International Trade Comm'n*, 988 F.2d 1165, 1174, 26 USPQ2d 1018, 1025 (Fed. Cir. 1993).

Prosecution History Estoppel. Since the early 1980s, the Court of Appeals for the Federal Circuit has indicated a preference for the synonym prosecution history estoppel rather than file wrapper estoppel.

- *Treatise References*: 4 D. Chisum, *Patents* §18.05 (1994 rev.); R. Harmon, *Patents and the Federal Circuit* §6.3(b) (3d ed. 1994).

- *Case References*:

"[Plaintiff] cannot now contradict the representations it made in order to obtain the allowed claims.... When an accused device is the same as a disclosed embodiment, and claims covering the disclosed embodiment were rejected on appeal and cancelled, the yielded claim scope cannot be recovered in order to encompass the accused device through the doctrine of equivalents.... [Plaintiff] is thus estopped from asserting a scope of equivalency of the Turner patent claims that would encompass the [technology in the cancelled claim]." *Diversitech Corp. v. Century Steps Inc.*, 850 F.2d 675, 681, 7 USPQ2d 1315, 1320 (Fed. Cir. 1988).

Every narrowing amendment does not automatically bar all resort to the doctrine of equivalents: "Depending on the nature and purpose of an amendment, it may have a limited effect within a spectrum ranging from great to small to zero. The effect may or may not be fatal to application of a range of equivalents broad enough to encompass a particular accused product. It is not fatal to application of the doctrine [of equivalents] itself." *Hughes Aircraft Co. v. United States*, 717 F.2d 1351, 1363, 219 USPQ 473, 481 (Fed. Cir. 1983).

"By expressly stating that claim 12 was patentable because of the opposite-side gating limitation, particularly in light of their previous admission that same-side gating was known in the art, the inventors unmistakably excluded the same-side gating as an equivalent. Having represented that same-side gating does not work, and having distinguished cited prior art as not teaching the functional opposite-side gated process, TI cannot foreclose reliance upon its unambiguous surrender of subject matter." *Texas Instruments, Inc. v. International Trade Comm'n*, 988 F.2d 1165, 1175, 26 USPQ2d 1018, 1026 (Fed. Cir. 1993).

- *Example 1*: An inventor applies for a patent on a water-wheel device with paddles. The Patent and Trademark Office (PTO) cites as prior art a previous patent disclosing paddles within the circumference of the wheel. The inventor narrows the claim by amendment to cover only a water wheel with paddles extending laterally outwards of the water wheel. The patent issues. In an infringement suit, the patentee claims infringement by an accused water wheel with paddles within the circumference of the wheel, arguing that this is "equivalent" to the claim's outwardly extending paddles. The doctrine of "file wrapper estoppel" or "prosecu-

tion history estoppel" will prevent the patentee from using the doctrine of equivalents to argue "equivalency" to this element, which the patentee gave up by amendment.

- *Example 2*: In order to avoid prior art cited by the PTO, the patent applicant for a cooling-pipe system for a smelting furnace amended the claim from reading that the cooling pipes were "closely adjacent" to each other to read that the pipes were "in a contacting relation." In an infringement suit, the patentee argued that the accused device was equivalent because it had cooling pipes separated by only a 5/8 inch diameter bar, which the patentee argued was merely a "reshaping" of the pipes themselves. The court held that by giving up "closely adjacent" and narrowing by amendment to "contacting relation" (physically touching) in order to avoid cited prior art, the patentee was estopped from arguing equivalency. *Mannesmann Demag Corp. v. Engineered Metal Prods. Co.*, 793 F.2d 1279, 1285, 230 USPQ 45, 48 (Fed. Cir. 1986).

- *Example 3*: The inventor applied for a patent on a plastic slab used to transport hospital patients for the taking of x-ray photos. The claim as filed claimed a slab with a "plurality of openings" around the edges for hospital workers to move the slab. After the PTO rejected the claim as obvious in view of the prior art, the inventor narrowed the claim to only include a plastic slab with *both* round *and* rectangular openings. The inventor successfully argued to the PTO that none of the prior art references disclosed the presence of both rectangular and round openings. After the patent claim was granted as narrowed, the patent owner sued an alleged infringer whose patient carrier slab had no round openings—*only* rectangular openings. The Federal Circuit held that the patent owner was estopped from claiming that the rectangular openings of the accused device were the equivalent of the claimed plurality of round *and* rectangular openings. "The applicant thus surrendered the right to have a device that does not have both rectangular and round openings found to be equivalent to a claimed invention that does." *Dixie USA Inc. v. Infab Corp.*, 927

F.2d 584, 588, 17 USPQ2d 1968, 1970 (Fed. Cir. 1991).

• *Example 4*: In distinguishing its computer memory modules from the prior art during prosecution, the applicant-inventor distinguished the multiple row construction of memory chips on a printed circuit board taught by a prior invention. The applicant limited its claims to a module in which memory chips were physically located in a single row. Further, the applicant limited the scope of its claims to nine-chip modules in order to overcome prior art, which taught the use of eight chips. Prosecution history estoppel was applied to preclude the inventor from arguing that memory chips not located in a single row and memory modules having fewer than nine chips could infringe its claims. Since the accused memory modules did not have chips arranged in a single row and had fewer than nine chips they did not infringe under the doctrine of equivalents. *Wang Labs. Inc. v. Toshiba Corp.*, 993 F.2d 858, 868, 26 USPQ2d 1767, 1775–76 (Fed. Cir. 1993).

final rejection [patent–trademark] An action by an examiner in the Patent and Trademark Office officially ending the patent or trademark application process before the examiner.

1. Final Rejection of Patent Application. After a final rejection, the applicant for a patent is limited to the following actions: (1) an appeal of rejected claims to the BOARD OF PATENT APPEALS AND INTERFERENCES; (2) an amendment cancelling claims or complying with a requirement of form; (3) an amendment presenting rejected claims in better form for appeal; (4) a petition to the Commissioner of Patents and Trademarks from objections not involved in the rejection of a claim; or (5) upon a showing of good reasons why they are necessary and were not presented earlier, amendments of rejected claims. Any response to a final rejection or action, however, must include, as to each rejected claim in the application, either cancellation of the claim or an appeal from the rejection of the claim.

On October 1, 1982, the Patent and Trademark Office discontinued the practice of extending for one month the shortened statutory period for a response by the applicant to a final rejection upon the filing of a timely first response to a final rejection. Patent applicants are able to obtain additional time for a first or subsequent response to a final rejection only by petitioning under 37 C.F.R. §1.136(a) and paying the appropriate fee. See *Manual of Patent Examining Procedure* §706.07(f) (1994).

• *Rule References*:

37 C.F.R. §1.113(a): "On the second or any subsequent examination or consideration the rejection or other action may be made final, whereon applicant's … response is limited to appeal in the case of rejection of any claim (§1.191), or to amendment as specified in §1.116. Petition may be taken to the Commissioner in the case of objections or requirements not involved in the rejection of any claim (§1.181). Response to a final rejection or action must include cancellation of, or appeal from the rejection of, each rejected claim.…"

37 C.F.R. §1.116(a): "After final rejection or action (§1.113) amendments may be made cancelling claims or complying with any requirement of form which has been made. Amendments presenting rejected claims in better form for consideration on appeal may be admitted.… (b) If amendments touching the merits of the application … are presented after final rejection, or after appeal has been taken, or when such amendment might not otherwise be proper, they may be admitted upon a showing of good and sufficient reasons why they are necessary and were not earlier presented.…"

• *Manual Reference*: "[T]he applicant who dallies in the prosecution of his or her case, resorting to technical or other obvious subterfuges in order to keep the application pending before the primary examiner, can no longer find a refuge in the rules to ward off a final rejection.… Under present practice, second or any subsequent actions on the merits shall be final, except where the examiner introduces a new ground of rejection not necessitated by amendment of the application by applicant, whether or not the prior art is already of record.…" *Manual of Patent Examining Procedure* §706.07–.07(a) (1994).

2. Final Rejection of Application for Registration of Mark. The purpose of designating a rejection as "final" is to bring prosecution to a conclusion by controlling the type of response which is permissible, that is, only appeal or compliance. After a final rejection, the applicant for registration is limited to the following actions: (1) an appeal to the TRADEMARK TRIAL AND APPEAL BOARD; (2) compliance with a requirement of the examiner; (3) a petition to the Commissioner of Patents and Trademarks as to a matter not directly related to the merits of a rejection; or (4) without extending the time period of six months from the final rejection within which to appeal, a request for reconsideration of the grounds for the final rejection.

However, even after a notice of appeal has been filed, if the applicant submits new evidence together with an argument of how this new evidence changes the ground of final rejection, the applicant can request the Trademark Trial and Appeal Board to suspend the appeal and to remand the application for further EX PARTE examination by the examiner. 37 C.F.R. §2.142(d).

• *Treatise Reference*: 2 J.T. McCarthy, *Trademarks and Unfair Competition* §19.40[3] (3d ed. 1995 rev.).

• *Rule References*: 37 C.F.R. §2.64: (a) "On the first or any subsequent reexamination or reconsideration the refusal of the registration or the insistence upon a requirement may be stated to be final, whereupon applicant's response is limited to an appeal or to a compliance with any requirement, or a petition to the Commissioner if permitted by §2.63(b). (b) During the period between a final action and expiration of the time for filing an appeal, the applicant may request the examiner to reconsider the final action. The filing of a request for reconsideration will not extend the time for filing an appeal or petitioning the Commissioner, but normally the examiner will reply to a request for reconsideration before the end of the six-month period if the request is filed within three months after the date of the final action. Amendments accompanying requests for reconsideration after final action will be entered if they comply with the rules of practice in trademark cases and the Act of 1946."

• *Manual References*:
"The final action should include a statement that the refusal or the requirement is final. Where there is more than one ground set out as the basis for the final action, the letter may conclude with a paragraph containing wording such as 'This action is made FINAL,' or 'This is a FINAL action,' which will cover all grounds." *Trademark Manual of Examining Procedure* §1105.04(d) (1993).

"After a final action, the only response which an applicant may make as a matter of right is either appeal to the Trademark Trial and Appeal Board or petition to the Commissioner, whichever is appropriate in that particular case, or compliance with any requirement made by the Examining Attorney. Proper response to the final action must be taken within six months after the date of the final action." *Trademark Manual of Examining Procedure* §1105.04(g) (1993).

firmware [computer] Computer programs that are permanently encoded into a ROM (read only memory). "Hardware" in a computer system is the totality of physical elements in which information is stored, such as the central processing unit. "Software" in a computer system consists of the computer programs and related paper documentation.

ROMs and microprocessors have been classified as firmware. A COMPUTER PROGRAM stored in a ROM has been held to be copyrightable, as has the MICROCODE used to control a microprocessor.

See ROM.

• *Commentary Reference*: "Microcode is a set of encoded instructions—in other words, a program—that controls the fine details of the execution of one or more primitive functions of a computer. Microcode serves as a substitute for certain elements of the hardware circuitry that had previously controlled that function.... Although, strictly speaking, it is a program, it is considered a more integral part of the machine hardware than is software, hence its alternative name, 'firmware.' " Samuelson, *CONTU Re-*

visited: The Case Against Copyright Protection for Computer Programs in Machine Readable Form, 1984 Duke L. J. 663, 677 (1984).

- *Case Reference*: " 'Firmware' is a generic term used to describe any computer program permanently stored in ROM associated with microprocessor. A 'firmware listing' is a specific written computer program." *In re Hayes Microcomputer Prods. Inc.*, 982 F.2d 1527, 1536, 25 USPQ2d 1241, 1248 (Fed. Cir. 1992).

first sale doctrine [copyright] An exception to the exclusive right of a copyright owner to distribute copies or phonorecords of the copyrighted work. Under this exception, after the first sale of a lawfully made copy of the copyrighted work, anyone who is the owner of that copy can sell or dispose of that copy in any way without copyright infringement liability. This rule is codified in 17 U.S.C. §109(a).

Scope of the Doctrine. The first authorized sale exhausts the copyright owner's exclusive right to control distribution of copies. For example, the purchaser of a lawful copy of a book can resell it, commercially rent it out, give it away as a gift, or rip out the pages and destroy it. These are not acts of copyright infringement. However, if there is a transfer of possession but not ownership, as by rental, then there is no ownership and the first sale doctrine is not triggered. For example, if the owner of copyright in a computer program rents copies of the program to users, a user would infringe copyright if it resold that copy to another. This rule is codified in 17 U.S.C. §109(d).

Only Distribution Right Is Exhausted. It is important to note that the first authorized sale exhausts *only* the distribution right, not other rights of copyright. The purchaser of a lawfully made printed copy of the dialogue of a play does not have the right to reproduce it, adapt it to a movie version, or perform it in public. Similarly, the owner of a legal copy of a video tape of a copyrighted motion picture does not have the right to show that film in public—that would be an infringing public PERFORMANCE. These rights of reproduction, adaptation, and performance are not subject to the first sale doctrine. Apart from the first sale doctrine, the general

rule is that the transfer of ownership of a copyrighted object does not of itself transfer any rights of copyright. 17 U.S.C. §202.

Record Rental Exception. The 1984 record rental amendment creates one important exception to the first sale doctrine. This amendment imposes copyright infringement liability on the owner of a lawfully made PHONORECORD who, without license from the owners of both the MUSICAL WORK and SOUND RECORDING copyrights, commercially rents the phonorecord. 17 U.S.C. §109(b). This 1984 amendment contained a sunset provision effective in 1989, which was extended by Congress to 1997. The December 1993 NAFTA legislation eliminated the sunsetting provision, thereby making the record rental exception permanent.

Computer Program Rental Exception. The 1990 Computer Software Rental Amendments Act created another exception to the first sale doctrine. This amendment imposes copyright infringement liability on the owner of a lawfully made copy of a COMPUTER PROGRAM who, without license from the owner of the copyright, commercially rents the copy. 17 U.S.C. §109(b). This exception does not apply to the rental of products containing computer programs (such as automobiles), the rental of electronic audiovisual games, or the rental for nonprofit purposes by nonprofit libraries and educational institutions. This 1990 amendment originally contained a sunset provision effective in 1997, but the December 1994 URUGUAY ROUND AGREEMENTS ACT eliminated the sunsetting provision of the computer program rental exception, thus making the exception permanent.

Videotape Rentals. Under the first sale doctrine, one who purchases a copy of a videotape can thereafter rent it out commercially to others without infringing the copyright. Lobbying efforts have been made to expand the theory of the record rental exception to include the commercial rental of videotapes. Article 11 of the GATT TRIPS agreement provided that member countries need not provide rental rights in motion pictures unless rental leads to widespread copying that has a material effect on the copyright owner's exclusive right of reproduction. In introducing implementing legislation, the

U.S. government determined that videotape rental had not caused a widespread problem of copying in the United States and hence did not provide for rental rights for videotapes.

Infringing Copies. The first sale doctrine is triggered only by the authorized first sale of a lawfully made copy. Each sale in the chain of distribution of an unlawfully made, infringing, or pirated copy is itself an act of infringement of the distribution right.

Display Right. The theory of the first sale doctrine also extends to immunize from copyright infringement liability the owner of a lawfully made copy who without license displays that copy publicly. 17 U.S.C. §109(c).

See DISPLAY RIGHT, DISTRIBUTION RIGHT, EXHAUSTION DOCTRINE.

• *Treatise References*: 2 *Nimmer on Copyright* §8.12 (1994 rev.); 1 P. Goldstein, *Copyright* §5.6.1 (1989); M. Leaffer, *Understanding Copyright* §8.13 (1989); W. Patry, *Copyright Law and Practice* 842 (1994); 1 N. Boorstyn, *Copyright* §6.19 (2d ed. 1994).

• *Statutory References*:

17 U.S.C. §106: "Subject to sections 107 through 118, the owner of copyright under this title has the exclusive right to do and to authorize any of the following: ... (3) to distribute copies or phonorecords of the copyrighted work to the public by sale or other transfer of ownership, by rental, lease, or lending; ..."

17 U.S.C. §109(a): "Notwithstanding the provisions of section 106(3), the owner of a particular copy or phonorecord lawfully made under this title, or any person authorized by such owner, is entitled, without the authority of the copyright owner, to sell or otherwise dispose of the possession of that copy or phonorecord."

17 U.S.C. §109(d): "The privileges prescribed by subsections (a) and (c) do not, unless authorized by the copyright owner, extend to any person who has acquired possession of the copy or phonorecord from the copyright owner, by rental, lease, loan, or otherwise, without acquiring ownership of it."

first to file [patent–trademark]

1. Patent. First to file is a rule in which patent priority is determined by which inventor was the first to file a patent application, rather than who was first to actually invent. This is the rule followed by almost every nation in the world except the United States.

See INTERFERENCE.

Those who argue against such a rule posit that a first to file system discourages test construction and sufficient experimentation, resulting in a rush to file papers on untried, speculative, and incomplete inventions. See 2 P. Rosenberg, *Patent Law Fundamentals* §10.01[2] (1994 rev.).

See FIRST TO INVENT.

2. Trademark. First to file is a rule in which priority among conflicting applications to register trademarks is handled by publishing the application with the earliest filing date in the OFFICIAL GAZETTE for possible opposition by the applicant with the later filing date. 37 C.F.R. §2.83(a). Ownership of a trademark is determined by who was first to use, not who was first to file an application for registration. However, under the post-1989 INTENT-TO-USE system, an application for registration can be filed prior to actual use of a mark. The registration issues after use has been proven and includes with the rights of registration a CONSTRUCTIVE USE DATE as of the date of filing. 2 J.T. McCarthy, *Trademarks and Unfair Competition* §16.01 (3d ed. 1995 rev.).

first to invent [patent] A rule in which priority is determined by which inventor was the first to actually invent, rather than who was the first to file a patent application. First to invent is the rule followed in the United States. An INTERFERENCE proceeding is required to determine priority of invention.

See FIRST TO FILE, INTERFERENCE.

• *Case Reference*: "United States patent law embraces the principle that the patent right is granted to the first inventor rather than the first to file a patent application." *Paulik v. Rizkalla*, 760 F.2d 1270, 1272, 226 USPQ 224, 225 (Fed. Cir. 1985).

fixed [copyright] Recorded, transcribed, or stored for more than a fleeting duration. A work is copyrightable under federal law only if it is "fixed in any tangible medium of expression." 17 U.S.C. §102(a). Federal copyright law covers only "fixed" works because Congress has power under the Constitution to grant copyright only to "writings." See CONSTITUTION. "Unfixed" works are capable of protection under state law, which is not preempted by the federal Copyright Act. 17 U.S.C. §301(b)(1).

Unfixed Works Are Protectible Under State Law. "Unfixed" works unprotected by federal copyright are creations such as extemporaneous speeches, unscripted interviews, spontaneous comedy routines, unnotated dances, and ad lib musical compositions that are not recorded under the authority of the author. Unauthorized reproductions of such performances must be redressed under state law.

Bootleg Recording under the Uruguay Round Agreements Act. Until the December 8, 1994, enactment of the URUGUAY ROUND AGREEMENTS ACT, there was no specific federal law relating to the unauthorized recording of a live performance. Under that Act, 17 U.S.C. §1101 was added imposing liability on a person who makes an unauthorized recording of a live musical performance. Such a person is liable for all of the civil remedies available against a copyright infringer. Also, the addition of 18 U.S.C. §2319A makes bootlegging "knowingly and for purposes of commercial advantage or private gain" a federal crime. 17 U.S.C. §1101(d), added by the URUGUAY ROUND AGREEMENTS ACT, provides that the federal remedies are in addition to, not in lieu of, state law. Thus, parallel state protection against bootlegging continues after the 1994 federal law. Such protection would be available under state MISAPPROPRIATION law. Some states have statutes specifically aimed at bootlegging, e.g., California Penal Code §653s.

What Is a "Fixed" Work. The statutory definition states that a work is "fixed" when its embodiment is "sufficiently permanent or stable to permit it to be perceived, reproduced, or otherwise communicated for a period of more than transitory duration." 17 U.S.C. §101. It is a matter of degree exactly how long is a "period of more than transitory duration." The House Report (see legislative history below) indicates that a live and not simultaneously recorded television broadcast is not "fixed," because it is merely flickering dots on a cathode ray tube. Cases at the limit, such as chalk notes on a blackboard, a sand castle, or an ice sculpture, are harder to classify. While the House Report (see legislative history below) opined that data "captured momentarily" in the memory of a computer was not a fixation, that example was criticized in the *CONTU Report*, which stated that "[b]ecause works in computer storage may be repeatedly reproduced, they are fixed and, therefore, are copies." *National Comm'n on New Technological Uses of Copyrighted Works (CONTU) Final Report* 22 (1979). See COMPUTER PROGRAM. See 2 *Nimmer on Copyright* §8.08 (1994 rev.).

New Technology. Congress left the door open for the accommodation of unforeseen developments in information storage technology by providing in the definition of COPIES and PHONORECORDS that a work can be "fixed by any method now known or later developed" and that it makes no difference that the work can only be perceived or communicated "with the aid of a machine or device." 17 U.S.C. §101. Data stored in a computer ROM (read only memory) is "fixed" for the purpose of copyright law.

See ROM, RAM.

"Pseudo-Fixation." In the last sentence of the definition of "fixed," Congress stretched federal law to include many forms of live sports broadcasts and similar spontaneous live events. Thus, the Copyright Act extends the definition of "fixed" to include a "work" being broadcast and simultaneously recorded. The unauthorized reproduction or rebroadcast of a live sports broadcast, audio or video, which is being simultaneously recorded by the broadcaster, is *federal* copyright infringement even though the infringer is not in fact reproducing or rebroadcasting a "fixed" audio or video tape. This might be called "pseudo-fixation." The intent is clear: to bring such broadcasts within the protection of the federal law.

Constitutional Significance. Nimmer opines that fixation in tangible form is not just a statutory condition to copyright but is also a constitutional necessity. "That is, unless a work is reduced to tangible form it cannot be regarded as a 'writing' within the meaning of the constitutional clause authorizing federal copyright legislation." 1 *Nimmer on Copyright* §2.03[B] (1994 rev.).

See CONSTITUTION.

• *Statutory Reference*: 17 U.S.C. §101: "A work is 'fixed' in a tangible medium of expression when its embodiment in a copy or phonorecord, by or under the authority of the author, is sufficiently permanent or stable to permit it to be perceived, reproduced, or otherwise communicated for a period of more than transitory duration. A work consisting of sounds, images, or both, that are being transmitted, is 'fixed' for the purpose of this title if a fixation of the work is being made simultaneously with its transmission."

• *Legislative History*:

"[I]t makes no difference what the form, manner, or medium of fixation may be—whether it is in words, numbers, notes, sounds, pictures, or any other graphic or symbolic indicia, whether embodied in a physical object in written, printed, photographic, sculptural, punched, magnetic, or any other stable form, and whether it is capable of perception directly or by means of any machine or device 'now known or later developed.' … [T]he concept of fixation is important since it not only determines whether the provisions of the statute apply to a work, but it also represents the dividing line between common law and statutory protection…. [A]n unfixed work of authorship, such as an improvisation or an unrecorded choreographic work, performance, or broadcast, would continue to be subject to protection under State common law or statute, but would not be eligible for Federal statutory protection under section 102…. [T]he definition of 'fixation' would exclude from the concept purely evanescent or transient reproductions such as those projected briefly on a screen, shown electronically on a television or other cathode ray tube, or captured momentarily in the 'memory' of a computer." H.R. Rep. No. 94-1476, 94th Cong., 2d Sess. 52–53 (1976).

"[S]ection 301(b) explicitly preserves common law copyright protection for one important class of works: works that have not been 'fixed in any tangible medium of expression.' Examples would include choreography that has never been filmed or notated, an extemporaneous speech, 'original works of authorship' communicated solely through conversations or live broadcasts, and a dramatic sketch or musical composition improvised or developed from memory and without being recorded or written down…. [U]nfixed works are not included in the specified 'subject matter of copyright.' " H.R. Rep. No. 94-1476, 94th Cong., 2d Sess. 131 (1976).

• *Treatise References*: 1 *Nimmer on Copyright* §2.03[B] (1994 rev.); 1 P. Goldstein, *Copyright* §2.4 (1989); 1 N. Boorstyn, *Copyright* §2.04 (2d ed. 1994); W. Patry, *Copyright Law and Practice* 168 (1994).

flash of genius [patent] A now-superseded test of patentability of an invention under which patents would be granted only for those relatively few inventions that result from a "flash of genius." The test was viewed by some as meaning that an invention was not patentable if it resulted from long experimentation or trial and error rather than from a sudden "flash of genius." The test was held by the U.S. Supreme Court to have been abolished by Congress when it enacted the 1952 Patent Code.

History of the Test. In a 1941 decision, Justice Douglas, in writing the majority opinion for the Court holding invalid an invention for a form of automobile cigarette lighter, observed: "[T]he new device, however useful it may be, must reveal the flash of creative genius not merely the skill of the calling. If it fails, it has not established its right to a private grant on the public domain." *Cuno Eng'g Corp. v. Automatic Devices Corp.*, 314 U.S. 84, 91, 51 USPQ 272, 275 (1941). The Supreme Court in 1966 said that the "flash of creative genius" language did not really lay down "a more exacting standard" and "was but a rhetorical embellishment of language going back to 1883." Even if viewed as a test of invention, the Supreme Court said that it was abolished by Congress in the 1952 Patent Code: "It also seems apparent that Congress intended by the last sentence of §103 to abolish the test it believed this Court announced in the controversial phrase 'flash of creative genius,' used in *Cuno....*" *Graham v. John Deere Co.,* 383 U.S. 1, 15–16, 148 USPQ 459, 466 (1966). The Court quoted the Reviser's Note to §103: "The second sentence states that patentability ... is not to be negatived by the manner in which the invention was made; that is, it is immaterial whether it resulted from long toil and experimentation or from a flash of genius." *Graham,* 383 U.S. at 16 n.8.

• *Case Reference*: "Tests which call for an inquiry into the 'genius' revealed by a particular device are not longer viable. *Graham,* [*supra,*] 383 U.S. at 15. However, we do not believe that this unfortunate lapse into a bygone era tainted the [district] court's decision.... We do not believe that the mere reference to 'genius' requires reversal of the [district] court's opinion when it is clear that the dictates of *Graham* were followed." *Vandenberg v. Dairy Equip. Co.,* 740 F.2d 1560, 1565, 224 USPQ 195, 197 (Fed. Cir. 1984).

fragmented literal similarity [copyright]
See SUBSTANTIAL SIMILARITY.

franchising [trademark]
A business system in which the owner of a mark licenses others to operate business outlets using a trademark or service mark to identify products or services that are made and/or advertised by the licensor-franchisor. In one sense, a franchise system is built upon a framework of trademark or service mark licenses fleshed out with various rights and obligations of the franchisor and franchisee. A franchisee falls somewhere on a spectrum in between a fully independent entrepreneur and a hired clerk in a company-owned outlet.

Business Advantages of Franchises. From the franchisor's point of view, the franchise method is advantageous because it permits the franchisor to quickly set up and maintain a relatively large number of outlets using the capital investments of the franchisees. From the franchisee's point of view, the franchise method is attractive because the franchisee is given access to a proven and organized product or service that has been advertised and is known to customers. Rather than start from zero with its own mark and its own know-how, a small business person who opts to become a franchisee has the advantage of plugging into an existing system and becoming a partially independent entrepreneur.

Types of Franchises. While there are many different forms and kinds, franchises may be divided into three basic types.

(1) A manufacturing franchise is one in which the franchisor permits franchisees to make and sell products using either raw materials and/or specifications supplied by the franchisor. Examples are mattress and bedding manufacturing and the local bottling and canning of soft drinks.

(2) A distributing franchise is one in which the primary purpose is for the franchisee to serve as an outlet for products manufactured by or for the franchisor. Examples are franchised sales outlets for bicycles, automobiles, and gasoline.

(3) A licensing or "business format" franchise is one in which the franchisor is primarily licensing a business format or system, rather than selling goods identified with the franchisor. The best known example is the fast food franchise. In this type of franchise, the franchisee is primarily paying for the use of a franchisor's well-known and advertised mark together with training, operating specifications, and business know-how supplied by the franchisor.

Federal and State Franchise Investment Regulation. The advertising and selling of franchises is strictly regulated by both the Federal Trade Commission (FTC) and various state laws. For example, the FTC has minimum disclosure requirements, which detail the kind of information that must be disclosed to prospective franchisees. See 2 J.T. McCarthy, *Trademarks and Unfair Competition* §18.23 (3d ed. 1995 rev.). In some states, a violation of the state franchise disclosure law entitles the franchisee to rescind the agreement and recover royalties it has paid. *My Pie Int'l Inc. v. Debould, Inc.,* 687 F.2d 919, 220 USPQ 398 (7th Cir. 1982).

Tort Liability of Franchisor. Under various theories of tort and contract law, a franchisor generally will be held liable for the torts of franchisees. This includes legal responsibility for both personal injury and property damages resulting from defective products or negligently rendered services. See 2 J.T. McCarthy, *Trademarks and Unfair Competition* §18.24 (3d ed. 1995 rev.).

See TIE-INS, LICENSE OF TRADEMARK.

• *Treatise Reference*: 2 J.T. McCarthy, *Trademarks and Unfair Competition* §§18.22–.24 (3d ed. 1995 rev.).

• *Case Reference*: "[F]ranchising promises to provide the independent merchant with the means to become an efficient and effective competitor of large integrated firms.... [T]he manufacturer is assured qualified and effective outlets for his product, and ... the franchisee enjoys backing in the form of know how and financial assistance." *United States v. Arnold, Schwinn & Co.*, 388 U.S. 365, 386 (1967) (Stewart, J., concurring and dissenting.).

fraud on the Copyright Office [copyright] A knowingly false representation or concealment of fact made to the Copyright Office to induce the registration of a claim to copyright that would not have been issued but for the falsity.

Many cases have held that a nonfraudulent misstatement or a clerical error in the registration application will neither invalidate the copyright nor impair the PRESUMPTION created by the registration certificate. "Absent intent to defraud and prejudice, inaccuracies in copyright registration do not bar actions for infringement." *S.O.S. Inc. v. Payday Inc.*, 886 F.2d 1081, 1086, 12 USPQ2d 1241, 1245 (9th Cir. 1989); *Data Gen. Corp. v. Grumman Sgs. Support Corp.*, 36 F.3d 1147, 1161, 32 USPQ2d 1385, 1394 (1st Cir. 1994) (immaterial, inadvertent errors in applicatin for copyright registration do not jeopardize the validity of the registration) If the elements of fraud are proven, they could make out an "unclean hands" defense to the charge of copyright infringement.

If errors are discovered in a copyright registration certificate, a SUPPLEMENTARY REGISTRATION can be made to either correct or

amplify the information in the basic registration.

• *Treatise References*: 2 *Nimmer on Copyright* §7.20 (1989 rev.); 2 P. Goldstein, *Copyright* §9.6.2 (1989).

• *Case Reference*: "[T]he court clearly and justifiably believed that appellants' omissions in the copyright application were inadvertent and innocent. Only the "knowing failure to advise the Copyright Office of facts which might have occasioned a rejection of the application constitute reason for holding the registration invalid and thus incapable of supporting an infringement action ... or denying enforcement on the ground of unclean hands.... " *Eckes v. Card Prices Update*, 736 F.2d 859, 861–62, 222 USPQ 762, 764 (2d Cir. 1984).

fraud on the Patent and Trademark Office [patent–trademark]

1. Fraud in Obtaining a Patent.
See INEQUITABLE CONDUCT.

2. Fraud in Obtaining Registration of a Mark. Fraud in connection with obtaining a registration of a mark consists of a knowingly false representation to the Patent and Trademark Office regarding a material fact made with the intent to induce reliance, followed by reasonable reliance resulting in a registration or other similar benefit that would not have been granted but for the misrepresentation. *San Juan Prods., Inc. v. San Juan Pools, Inc.*, 849 F.2d 468, 473, 7 USPQ2d 1230, 1234 (8th Cir. 1988). Because a federal trademark registration does not "create" a trademark in the way that a federal patent grant does "create" the exclusive rights of a patent, the extremely stringent patent law requirements of disclosure have not been imported into trademark law. The trademark law standards for fraud are much closer to the traditional tort law criteria.

Fraud Does Not Extinguish Common Law Rights. Proof of fraud in obtaining a federal registration of a mark does not extinguish common law or Lanham Act §43(a) rights in a mark, unless the fraud rises to the level of an unclean hands defense to the whole trademark claim. *Gilbert/Robinson Inc. v. Carrie Beverage-Missouri Inc.,* 989 F.2d 985, 26 USPQ2d 1378 (8th Cir. 1993) (because common law rights continue, court permitted no damages for fraud in obtaining a registration under Lanham Act §38 because the infringer's exposure to infringement liability and injunction was not "in consequence of" the fraud on the PTO). See 3 J.T. McCarthy, *Trademarks and Unfair Competition* §31.21[1][b] (3d ed. 1995 rev.).

Trademark Fraud Is Difficult to Prove. A mere misstatement caused by an honest misunderstanding, inadvertence, or negligent omission does not constitute the kind of willful intent to deceive that is required. Also, the willful deception must concern a fact that is "material" in the sense that the registration would not have issued if the truth were known to the Patent and Trademark Office trademark examiner. Fraud must be proven by clear and convincing evidence. *Money Store v. Harriscorp Finance, Inc.,* 689 F.2d 666, 670, 216 USPQ 11, 15 (7th Cir. 1982).

Failure to Disclose Use by Others. The standard application oath signed by an applicant states that to the best of his or her "knowledge and belief" no other firm "has the right to use" a confusingly similar mark "in commerce." The oath is phrased in terms of a subjective belief as to the rights of others, such that it is difficult to prove objective falsity and fraud. Generally, an applicant has no duty to investigate and report to the PTO all other possible users of the same or a similar mark. *Money Store v. Harriscorp Finance, Inc.,* 689 F.2d 666, 670, 216 USPQ 11, 15 (7th Cir. 1982). Only if the rights of others are clearly established, for example, by a court decree or settlement contract, would there be a duty to disclose. *Rosso & Mastracco, Inc. v. Giant Food Inc.,* 720 F.2d 1263, 219 USPQ 1050 (Fed. Cir. 1983).

Lanham Act Provisions Relating to Fraud. It is a ground for a petition to cancel a registration of a mark at any time if "its registration was obtained fraudulently." Lanham Act §14(3), 15 U.S.C. §1064(3). Under §14 of the Lanham Act, fraud in obtaining a renewal of a registration amounts to fraud in obtaining a registration. *Torres v. Cantine Torresella S.r.l.,* 808 F.2d 46,

1 USPQ2d 1483 (Fed. Cir. 1986). A ground upon which to raise a defense or defect against an INCONTESTABLE REGISTRATION of a mark is "that the registration or the incontestable right to use the mark was obtained fraudulently." Lanham Act §33(b)(1), 15 U.S.C. §1115(b)(1). Under Lanham Act §38, 15 U.S.C. §1120, one who procures a registration by false or fraudulent representation is liable in damages to any person injured thereby. Any damages must be caused by use of the fraudulently procured registration, not solely from the false representation.

• *Treatise Reference*: 3 J.T. McCarthy, *Trademarks and Unfair Competition* §§31.21 (3d ed. 1995 rev.).

freeware [computers] See SHAREWARE.

functionality [patent–trademark–copyright] That aspect of design which makes a product work better for its intended purpose, as opposed to making the product look better aesthetically or to identifying the commercial source of the product.

The basic policy of U.S. intellectual property law is that there is only one valid source of exclusive rights in a publicly distributed feature which is functional and utilitarian: the law of utility patents. While generations of attorneys have strived mightily to use (or misuse) design patent, trademark, trade dress, and copyright law to achieve such exclusive rights, the courts have usually been quite diligent in preserving competition by denying such attempts to make an end-run around the strict requirements of utility patent law. If the plaintiff has no valid utility patent, then "reproduction of a functional attribute is legitimate competitive activity." *Inwood Labs., Inc. v. Ives Labs., Inc.,* 456 U.S. 844, 863, 214 USPQ 1, 9 (1982) (White, J., concurring).

1. Functionality and Design Patents. Design patents provide exclusive rights only for the ornamental aspects of industrial design, not for the utilitarian or functional aspects. It is only the nonfunctional, ornamental design elements that can form a basis for comparison with the accused design in determining infringement of a design patent. The presumption of validity of a design patent includes a presumption that the design is not functional. *Power Controls Corp. v. Hybrinetics, Inc.*, 806 F.2d 234, 240, 231 USPQ 774, 778 (Fed. Cir. 1986).

See DESIGN PATENT.

• *Case References*:

"When function dictates a design, [design patent] protection would not promote the decorative arts, a purpose of the design patent statute." *Avia Group Int'l Inc. v. L.A. Gear Inc.*, 853 F.2d 1557, 1563, 7 USPQ2d 1548, 1553 (Fed. Cir. 1988).

"Many well-constructed articles of manufacture whose configurations are dictated solely by function are pleasing to look upon, for example a hexnut, a ball bearing, a golf club, or a fishing rod, the pleasure depending largely on one's interests. But it has long been settled that when a configuration is the result of functional considerations only, the resulting design is not patentable as an ornamental design for the simple reason that it is not 'ornamental'—was not created for the purpose of ornamenting." *In re Carletti*, 328 F.2d 1020, 1022, 140 USPQ 653, 654 (C.C.P.A. 1964).

2. Functionality and Trademark–Trade Dress. A feature that is utilitarian cannot be protected or registered either as a trademark or trade dress. If the feature contributes utility to the product or assists in economy of manufacture or shipping, the feature is protectible only under the law of utility patents.

Utilitarian Functionality. The clear majority of courts hold that "functionality" means utility in the engineering sense: a feature that makes the product work better. "In general terms, a product feature is functional if it is essential to the use or purpose of the article or if it affects the cost or quality of the article." *Inwood Labs., Inc. v. Ives Labs., Inc.*, 456 U.S. 844, 851 n.10, 214 USPQ 1, 4 n.10 (1982).

Combination of Functional Features. The question is not whether the product as a whole is functional, but whether the particular feature or combination of features claimed as a mark or trade dress is functional. For example, while luggage made of lightweight nylon is functional, a particular combination of features may

not be functional. Such features, in one case, included parachute nylon in a variety of colors, trimmed in cotton carpet tape with matching cotton webbing straps, color-coordinated zippers with hollow rectangular metal zippers, and a repeating logo in an elongated ellipse. *Le Sportsac, Inc. v. K Mart Corp.*, 754 F.2d 71, 225 USPQ 654 (2d Cir. 1985). A combination of individually functional features can form a non-functional and protectible composite image. E.g., *Taco Cabana Int'l Inc. v. Two Pesos, Inc.*, 932 F.2d 1113, 19 USPQ2d 1253, 1257 (5th Cir. 1991), *aff'd*, 112 S. Ct. 2753, 23 USPQ2d 1081 (1992) (protection granted for trade dress in a distinctive combination of interior and exterior architectural design, layout, and decoration of chain of Mexican restaurants).

Burden of Proof. Under the majority view, functionality is a defense, and the burden of proof of proving it is on the party challenging the validity of the mark or trade dress. *Inwood Labs., Inc. v. Ives Labs., Inc.*, 456 U.S. 844, 863, 214 USPQ 1, 9 (1982) (White, J. concurring, "functionality is a defense to a suit under §43(a) of the Lanham Act"); *Vaughan Mfg. Co. v. Brikam Int'l, Inc.*, 814 F.2d 346, 1 USPQ2d 2067 (7th Cir. 1987).

Relevant Evidence. Evidence for and against the existence of functionality includes: (1) the existence of a utility patent that discloses the utilitarian advantages of the feature; (2) advertising or promotional literature of the proponent of trademark–trade dress rights that touts the utilitarian advantages of the feature; and (3) the existence of a reasonable number of alternative designs that perform the function equally well.

De Facto Secondary Meaning. Even if a functional feature has achieved consumer recognition (SECONDARY MEANING) as an indicator of origin, that feature cannot serve as a legally protected commercial symbol. The competitive right to copy unpatented functional features is a potent public policy that overrides the policy against customer confusion. Functionality trumps consumer recognition. Any consumer recognition of a functional feature does not count and is dismissed as mere "de facto secondary meaning." See 1 J.T. McCarthy, *Trademarks and Unfair Competition* §7.26[2] (3d ed. 1995 rev.).

Aesthetic Functionality. Some courts are of the view that aesthetic elements of a product are "functional" and hence unprotectible as trade dress. In the leading case espousing this view, the court refused to prevent a competitor from copying a floral design on hotel chinaware because the design was "functional" under this definition. " 'Functional' ... might be said to connote other than a trademark purpose. If the particular feature is an important ingredient in the commercial success of the product, the interest in free competition permits its imitation in the absence of a patent or copyright." *Pagliero v. Wallace China Co.*, 198 F.2d 339, 343, 95 USPQ 45, 48 (9th Cir. 1952). However, other courts have recognized that under this definition, the absurd result would be that "[t]he more appealing the design, the less protection it would receive." *Keene Corp. v. Paraflex Indus., Inc.*, 653 F.2d 822, 825, 211 USPQ 201, 203 (3d Cir. 1981). In the author's view, "aesthetic functionality" is an oxymoron, combining the opposing notions of aesthetics and utility. For these reasons, the majority of courts have rejected the theory of aesthetic functionality. See 1 J.T. McCarthy, *Trademarks and Unfair Competition* §7.26[4] (3d ed. 1995 rev.).

• *Treatise Reference*: 1 J.T. McCarthy, *Trademarks and Unfair Competition* §§7.26–.33 (3d ed. 1995 rev.).

3. *Functionality and Copyright.* Copyright provides exclusive rights only for the aesthetic, nonutilitarian aspects of the design of articles. In copyright law, an object that has some utilitarian function, other than to picture something or to convey information, is called a "USEFUL ARTICLE." The design or shape of a useful article is protected by copyright only to the extent that the aesthetic aspects can be identified separately and are capable of existing independently from the functional, utilitarian aspects of the design. This is known as the test of "separability and independence."

In so-called modern design, form largely follows function. Because of the difficulty of separating out the aesthetic from the functional aspects of modern design, this kind of unornamented design can only rarely qualify for copyright.

For a full discussion with references to statutes, legislative history, treatises, and cases, see USEFUL ARTICLE.

functional patent [patent]

See PATENT.

G

GATT [international trade–intellectual property] General Agreement on Tariffs and Trade, a multilateral treaty of over 100 nations. It is aimed primarily at reducing trade barriers and expanding and liberalizing world trade. GATT also provides a forum in which nations can resolve trade disputes and negotiate reduction of tariff and nontariff trade barriers. "GATT Rounds" are cycles of multilateral trade negotiations conducted since GATT was established in 1947. The latest was the "Uruguay Round," which began in 1986 and concluded in 1993. On December 8, 1994, President Clinton signed into law the URUGUAY ROUND AGREEMENTS ACT to implement GATT into U.S. law (Pub. L. No. 103-465, 108 Stat. 4809).

Intellectual Property Becomes a Topic for GATT. While intellectual property had not previously been a subject of discussion in GATT, in 1986, the United States proposed the enactment of rules and regulations that would recognize and adequately protect international intellectual property. The U.S. government had grown dissatisfied with the level of intellectual property protection provided by the WIPO conventions. The United States suggested that GATT adopt the following rules relating to intellectual property: an anti-counterfeiting code to discourage trade in counterfeit goods; a defined minimum level of protection for intellectual property; and a set of rules for multilateral dispute settlement procedures. Section 1101(b)(10) of the "Omnibus Trade and Competitiveness Act of 1988" declared it to be an objective of the United States in GATT negotiations to seek the enactment and effective enforcement by foreign countries of laws that recognize and adequately protect all forms of intellectual property. See Reichman, *Intellectual Property in International Trade: Opportu-*

nities and Risks of a GATT Connection, 22 Vanderbilt J. Transnat'l L. 747 (1989). Some developing nations insisted that WIPO, not GATT, was the correct forum for these matters. See WIPO.

The TRIPS Agreement. After seven years of negotiations, an intellectual property protection agreement was embodied in a section of the Uruguay Round Trade Accord on December 15, 1993. Entitled "Trade-Related Aspects of Intellectual Property Rights, Including Trade in Counterfeit Goods" or TRIPS, the agreement attempts to strengthen and harmonize intellectual property standards of protection throughout the world. One goal of TRIPS is to control, and eventually eliminate, the growing problem of international infringement and counterfeiting.

Creation of the World Trade Organization. The Uruguay Round of GATT negotiations also established the World Trade Organization or WTO. The purpose of the WTO is to facilitate the implementation of trade agreements and the protection of trade-related intellectual property rights. The WTO entered into force with respect to the United States on January 1, 1995.

• *Commentary Reference:* "GATT views trademark counterfeiting and intellectual property irregularities as distortions of legitimate trade. The solution, therefore, involved confronting TRIPS, or trade-related aspects of intellectual property, in order to maintain a level playing field." Lackert, *Practitioners Hopeful That GATT's Promise Won't Come Up Empty,* Nat'l L.J., May 16, 1994, at C41.

Gebrauchsmuster [international–patent] The German UTILITY MODEL. It has been held that the Gebrauchsmuster is a "patent" within the meaning of Patent Code §102(a), (b), and (d). See authorities cited at 1 D. Chisum, *Patents* §3.06[2] (1994 rev.).

genericide [trademark] The "death" of a trademark by means of its falling into majority usage as a generic name.

See GENERIC NAME.

• *Case Reference*: "The term genericide, although by now firmly ensconced in the literature, is a malapropism: It refers to the death of the trademark, not to the death of the generic name for the product. A more accurate term might be trademarkicide, or perhaps even generization, either of which seems to better capture the idea that the trademark dies by becoming a generic name." *Plasticolor Molded Prods. v. Ford Motor Co.*, 713 F. Supp. 1329 n.22, 11 USPQ2d 1023, 1036 n.22 (C.D. Cal. 1989), *vacated after settlement and consent decree*, 18 USPQ2d 1975 (C.D. Cal. 1991).

generic name [trademark] A word used by a majority of the relevant public to name a class or category of product or service. A generic name is incapable of exclusive appropriation or registration as a protectible trademark or service mark. For example, no one seller can have trademark rights in "personal computer" or "cellular phone." If one seller did have an exclusive right to call a thing by its recognized name, it would be tantamount to a monopoly on selling that type of product.

Tests and Evidence of Genericness. Whether a term is a generic name is ultimately determined by majority public usage of the term. The issue is whether the relevant public interprets and uses that term to name a whole class of goods or services or only to identify and distinguish one commercial source of those goods or services. While some may use "thermos" as a generic name, others may use it as a brand name or trademark. There is not necessarily just one generic name for a type of product; there may be several and each one is classified as "generic." For example, "mart," "store," and "market" are all generic names. There are two recognized types of consumer surveys that have been used to test for the generic usage of a term: the "Thermos Survey" and the "Teflon Survey."

See 1 J.T. McCarthy, *Trademarks and Unfair Competition* §12.02[8] (3d ed. 1995 rev.). Other evidence of generic or nongeneric usage includes usage by competitors, usage by plaintiff, dictionary definitions, and usage in the media.

De Facto Secondary Meaning. Once a name is determined to be generic, no amount of evidence of purported buyer association of the term with a single source will change the result. Such evidence is dismissed as mere evidence of "DE FACTO SECONDARY MEANING," which might arise during the period when a seller is the single source for a genus of goods. During the single-source period it is difficult but not impossible to determine whether the name is generic or a mark. The term used as a trademark of a patented product does not automatically become a generic name upon expiration of the patent.

Foreign Terms, Abbreviations, and Composite Terms. Under the doctrine of foreign equivalents, a foreign word is translated into English and then tested for generic meaning. Generic names from a foreign language will not be protected in the United States on the same principle that U.S. companies object to protection abroad for English language generic terms. For example, no one should obtain trademark protection for "personal computer" in Brazil and no one should be able to obtain trademark protection in the United States for foreign generic names. Easily recognizable abbreviations or misspellings are classified as generic names, e.g., "lite beer," "ROM" (read only memory). Composite terms with a generic component can be either strong trademarks (e.g., COCA-COLA) or merely a generic composite of generic terms (e.g., turbodiesel).

See COMPOSITE MARK.

The 1984 "Anti-Monopoly" Amendments. A 1984 revision to the definition of "ABANDONMENT" in the Lanham Act forbids the use of "purchaser motivation" as a test for abandonment. This was to preclude any future use of a generic-name test once used by the Court of Appeals for the Ninth Circuit, which inferred that a term is a generic name unless a majority of customers are motivated to buy the product because they know the corporate trade name of the producer and like the products of that company. *Anti-Monopoly, Inc. v. General Mills, Inc.*, 684 F.2d 1326, 216 USPQ 588 (9th Cir. 1982). The 1984 amendment also redefined "trademark" to make it clear that marks may distinguish unique products and products whose source is unknown by name to customers. Similar amendments were made to the §14 generic name ground for cancellation of a registration. Section 14 states that the generic status of a term is to be determined by the "primary significance of the registered mark to the relevant public...." Pub. L. No. 98-620, 98 Stat. 3335 (Nov. 8, 1984).

Federal Registration. In the 1989 amendments, the archaic term "COMMON DESCRIPTIVE NAME" in Lanham Act §§14 and 15 was replaced with the more modern term "generic name." This codified the interpretation the courts, including the Supreme Court, placed on "common descriptive name." A generic name cannot be federally registered as a mark. While the Lanham Act does not state that rule explicitly, it is the necessary implication of the Act under two views: (1) a generic name is the ultimate in descriptiveness, which is a bar to registration under Lanham Act §2(e)(1); (2) only a "trademark" is registrable and a generic name cannot be a "trademark" under the Lanham Act §45 definition. *In re Northland Aluminum Prods., Inc.*, 777 F.2d 1556, 227 USPQ 961 (Fed. Cir. 1985). A registration is properly refused if the word is a generic name of any of the goods for which registration is sought. *In re Analog Devices, Inc.*, 6 USPQ2d 1808 (T.T.A.B. 1988), *aff'd without published opinion*, 871 F.2d 1097, 10 USPQ2d 1879 (Fed. Cir. 1989). Under Lanham Act §14, the registration of a term that becomes a generic name can be cancelled at any time upon petition. A generic name is not registrable on the supplemental register because it is not capable of ever distinguishing the applicant's goods or services.

• *Examples*: Terms held to be unprotectible generic names in the United States include: "aspirin," "cellophane," "escalator," "thermos," "the pill," "light beer," "murphy bed," and "shuttle." See other examples at 1 J.T.

McCarthy, *Trademarks and Unfair Competition* §§12.03–.04 (3d ed. 1995 rev.).

• *Treatise Reference*: 1 J.T. McCarthy, *Trademarks and Unfair Competition* §§12.01–.18 (3d ed. 1995 rev.).

• *Statutory References*:

Lanham Act §14, 15 U.S.C. §1064: "A petition to cancel a registration of a mark, stating the grounds relied upon, may, upon payment of the prescribed fee, be filed as follows by any person who believes that he is or will be damaged by the registration of a mark on the principal register ... (3) at any time if the registered mark becomes the generic name for the goods or services, or a portion thereof, for which it is registered.... If the registered mark becomes the generic name for less than all of the goods or services for which it is registered, a petition to cancel the registration for only those goods or services may be filed. A registered mark shall not be deemed to be the generic name of goods or services solely because such mark is also used as a name of or to identify a unique product or service. The primary significance of the registered mark to the relevant public rather than purchaser motivation shall be the test for determining whether the registered mark has become the generic name of goods or services on or in connection with which it has been used."

Lanham Act §45, 15 U.S.C. §1127: *Abandonment*. A mark shall be deemed to be 'abandoned' when either of the following occurs: ... (2) When any course of conduct of the owner, including acts of omission as well as commission, causes the mark to become the generic name for the goods or services on or in connection with which it is used or otherwise to lose its significance as a mark. Purchaser motivation shall not be a test for determining abandonment under this paragraph.

• *Case References*:

"A generic term is one that refers to the genus of which the particular product is a species.... Generic terms are not registrable, and a registered mark may be canceled at any time on the grounds that it has become generic.... A 'merely descriptive' mark, in contrast, describes the qualities or characteristics of a good or service, and this type of mark may be registered only if the registrant shows that it has acquired secondary meaning, i.e., it 'has become distinctive of the applicant's goods in commerce.' §§2(e), (f), 15 U.S.C. §1052(e), (f)." *Park 'N Fly Inc. v. Dollar Park & Fly*, 469 U.S. 189, 194, 224 USPQ 327, 329 (1985).

"The genericness doctrine prevents trademarks from serving as the substitutes for patents, and protects the public right to copy any non-patented, functional characteristic of a competitor's product.... [I]f no commonly used alternative effectively communicates the same functional information, the term that denotes the product is generic. If we held otherwise, a grant of trademark status could effectively prevent a competitor from marketing a product with the same characteristic despite its right to do so under the patent laws." *A.J. Canfield Co. v. Honickman*, 808 F.2d 291, 305–06, 1 USPQ2d 1364, 1375–76 (3d Cir. 1986) (holding that "chocolate fudge" is a generic name for diet soft drinks that taste like chocolate fudge).

"When Judge Learned Hand said that whether a word is generic depends on what 'buyers understand by the word,' *Bayer Co. v. United Drug Co.*, 272 F. 505, 509 (S.D.N.Y. 1921), he was referring to a coined word for a commercial product that was alleged to have become generic through common usage. He was not suggesting that the meaning of a familiar, basic word in the English vocabulary can depend on associations the word brings to consumers as a result of advertising." *Miller Brewing Co. v. Schlitz Brewing Co.*, 605 F.2d 990, 995, 203 USPQ 642, 647 (7th Cir. 1979) (holding that "light beer" is a generic name of beer light in body and taste).

genetic engineering [patents] The development and application of scientific methods that permit direct manipulation of genetic material to change the hereditary traits of a cell or organism. Products and processes created by the use of genetic engineering are patentable.

Living Organism Patents Are Not New. Patents on products and processes involving living organisms are not recent events. The wine-making and beer-brewing industries have used living organisms for hundreds of years. In 1873 the U.S. Patent Office granted Louis Pasteur a patent on "yeast, free from organic germs of disease, as an article of manufacture." *Diamond v. Chakrabarty*, 447 U.S. 303, 314 n.9, 206 USPQ 193, 199 n.9 (1980).

The Chakrabarty Case. In the famous 1980 *Chakrabarty* case, the U.S. Supreme Court upheld the patentability of a living microorganism. The Court held that a patent claim covering a genetically engineered bacterium capable of degrading crude oil and helping to clean up oil spills was within a statutory patentable category as a "manufacture" or a "composition of matter." *Diamond v. Chakrabarty*, 447 U.S. 303, 206 USPQ 193 (1980) (see case reference below).

Patents on Higher Forms of Animals. In 1987 the Patent Office Board of Patent Appeals, by extrapolation from the *Chakrabarty* decision, held that a patent on a multicellular animal was within a patentable subject matter. The invention was of a process and the resulting animal for creating a sterile oyster, which would be edible year round. Since such oysters did not occur in nature, they were nonnatural living organisms in the same category as the bacteria in *Charkrabarty*. *Ex parte Allen*, 2 USPQ2d 1425 (Bd. Pat. App. 1987), *aff'd in unpublished opinion*, 846 F.2d 77 (Fed. Cir. 1988) (see case reference below).

Patent and Trademark Office Policy on Genetically Altered Animals and the Harvard Mouse. As a result of the *Allen* decision, on April 7, 1987, the Patent and Trademark Office (PTO) issued a statement that "[t]he Patent and Trademark Office now considers nonnaturally occurring nonhuman multicellular living organisms, including animals, to be patentable subject matter within the scope of 35 U.S.C. §101." The policy statement also said that a claim including a human being will not be considered patentable subject matter because it "is prohibited by the Constitution." 1077 TMOG 8 (Apr. 21, 1987). On April 12, 1988, the PTO granted the first "animal patent." U.S. Patent No. 4,736,866. This patent was on the so-called Harvard Mouse: a mouse genetically engineered to be susceptible to cancer for use in screening potentially carcinogenic products. In late 1988, du Pont Co. began marketing the patented mice to researchers who are studying the causes of and treatments for cancer. Wall St. J., Nov. 16, 1988, at B4. Members of the biotechnology industry have predicted the patenting of other transgenic genetically altered animals such as cows that produce more milk, hogs with less fat, and chickens that lay more eggs.

See TRANSGENIC.

Organized Opposition. A coalition of farmers' organizations and religious and animal welfare groups for some years has urged Congress to enact laws either limiting or eliminating patents on genetically engineered animals. For example, H.R. 4970, which passed the House in 1988 but died in the Senate, would have prohibited the patenting of human genetic material and provided exemptions for dairy and cattle producers.

• *Case References:*

"[W]e must determine whether [the inventor's] microorganism constitutes a 'manufacture' or 'composition of matter' within the meaning of the statute.... [The inventor's] microorganism plainly qualifies as patentable subject matter. His claim is not to a hitherto unknown natural phenomenon, but to a nonnaturally occurring manufacture or composition of matter—a product of human ingenuity 'having a distinctive name, character [and] use.' ... [T]he patentee has produced a new bacterium with markedly different characteristics from any found in nature and one having the potential for significant utility. His discovery is not nature's handiwork, but his own; accordingly it is patentable subject matter under §101." *Diamond v. Chakrabarty,* 447 U.S. 303, 309–10, 206 USPQ 193, 196–97 (1980).

"The issue, in our view, in determining whether the claimed subject matter is patentable under Section 101 is simply whether that subject matter is made by man. If the claimed subject matter occurs naturally, it is not patentable subject matter under Section 101.... The examiner has presented no evidence that the claimed polyploid oysters occur naturally without the intervention of man.... The record before us leads to no conclusion other than that the claimed polyploid oysters are non-naturally occurring manufactures or compositions of matter within the confines of patentable subject matter under 35 U.S.C. §101." *Ex parte Allen,* 2 USPQ2d 1425, 1426–27 (Bd. Pat. App. 1987), *aff'd in unpublished opinion,* 846 F.2d 77 (Fed. Cir. 1988).

geographic denomination [trademark–unfair competition] A general term referring to any use in advertising that conveys the message of geographic source. This term is intended to include APPELLATION OF ORIGIN, INDICATION OF SOURCE, and trademarks or service marks containing a geographic term. See McCarthy & Devitt, *Protection of Geographic Denominations: Domestic and International,* 69 Trademark Rep. 199 (1979).

geographic mark [trademarks] A mark that consists of terms which are descriptive of the geographic origin of goods or services. Such geographically descriptive terms are not inherently distinctive and require proof of SECONDARY MEANING for registration and protection in court as trademarks or service marks.

Nondescriptive Geographic Uses. Not every use of a geographic term in a mark is necessarily descriptive of territorial origin. The words "world" or "globe" or a picture of the world are not geographically descriptive because they convey nothing more than that the goods are of earthly origin. If the geographic term is not likely to denote to reasonable buyers that the goods come from the region or place named, then it is an arbitrary, not a descriptive or misdescriptive, mark. (See ARBITRARY MARK.) For example, NORTH POLE ice cream does not tell a reasonable person that the ice cream actually comes from the North Pole. Similarly, some prestige location names, such as FIFTH AVENUE watches or RODEO DRIVE perfume suggest high quality, not geographic origin. *In re Jacques Bernier Inc.,* 894 F.2d 389, 13 USPQ2d 1725 (Fed. Cir. 1990). If the place name is "obscure," in that few U.S. buyers would identify it with a geographic place, then it is not classified as a geographic mark. *Re Société Générale Des Eaux Minérales de Vittel S.A.,* 824 F.2d 957, 3 USPQ2d 1450 (Fed. Cir. 1987)

(American consumers would not know that Vittel, France, is renowned for its health spa and mineral water).

Fair Use. A merchant can make a fair use by making a noninfringing, descriptive, nontrademark use of geographically descriptive terms. That is, even if a senior user has achieved secondary meaning in a geographically descriptive term, anyone who is in fact located in that place has a limited right to tell consumers of the location. But the junior user must confine and adapt its usage of the geographical term so as not to cause a likelihood of confusion. This is also codified as a defense in Lanham Act §33(b)(4). See 1 J.T. McCarthy, *Trademarks and Unfair Competition* §14.07 (3d ed. 1995 rev.).

Deceptively Misdescriptive and Deceptive Terms. A term is "primarily geographically deceptively misdescriptive" under Lanham Act §2(e)(2) if the goods do not come from the place named, the term directly denotes a geographical place, and customers would believe that the goods originated from that geographic place. In holding that NANTUCKET for men's shirts was not geographically misdescriptive, the Court of Customs and Patent Appeals said: "If the goods do not come from the place named, and the public makes no goods-place association, the public is not deceived and the mark is accordingly not geographically deceptively misdescriptive." *In re Nantucket, Inc.*, 677 F.2d 95, 99, 213 USPQ 889, 893 (C.C.P.A. 1982). The goods-place association requirement does not need proof that the place is well known or noted for producing the goods. *In re Loew's Theatres, Inc.*, 769 F.2d 764, 226 USPQ 865 (Fed. Cir. 1985) (DURANGO for chewing tobacco not from the city of Durango in Mexico is geographically misdescriptive). If the geographic term is misdescriptive and the misrepresentation would materially affect the buyer's decision to purchase the goods, then the term may be classified as "deceptive" under Lanham Act §2(a) and unregistrable under any circumstances. *In re Quady Winery, Inc.*, 221 USPQ 1213 (T.T.A.B. 1984).

Changes Created by the 1994 NAFTA Amendments. Prior to the 1994 NAFTA Amendments to the Lanham Act, if the mark was "primarily geographically deceptively misdescriptive," it could be placed on the principal register if a showing of secondary meaning was made under §2(f) or placed on the supplemental register if such a showing could not be made. The ability to do this ended with the NAFTA Amendments, which were effective in 1994. Legislation enacted in December 1993 as part of U.S. implementation of the North American Free Trade Agreement (NAFTA) changed the Lanham Act such that a term that is "primarily geographically deceptively misdescriptive" cannot be registered under *any* circumstances on either the principal or supplemental registers. Lanham Act §2(f) was also amended to include a "grandfather" clause permitting the registration of "primarily geographically deceptively misdescriptive" terms that became distinctive before the December 8, 1993, enactment date of the NAFTA amendments. A similar "grandfather" clause in §23 permits registration on the supplemental register of such terms if they were in lawful use prior to December 8, 1993.

Changes Created by the 1994 Uruguay Round Agreements Act. The 1994 URUGUAY ROUND AGREEMENTS ACT amends §2(a) of the Lanham Act to prohibit the registration of a wine or spirits mark that is a geographical indication if it identifies a place other than the origin of the wine or spirits and the mark is first used after January 1, 1996.

See APPELLATION OF ORIGIN, INDICATION OF SOURCE.

• *Treatise Reference*: 1 J.T. McCarthy, *Trademarks and Unfair Competition* §§14.01 *et seq.* (3d ed. 1995 rev.).

• *Statutory Reference*: Lanham Act §2, 15 U.S.C. §1052:

No trademark by which the goods of the applicant may be distinguished from the goods of others shall be refused registration on the principal register on account of its nature unless it—

(a) Consists of or comprises ... deceptive ... matter;

...

(e) Consists of a mark which ... (2) when used on or in connection with the goods of the applicant is primarily geographically descriptive of them, except as indications of regional origin may be registerable under section 4, (3) when used on or in connection with the goods of the applicant is primarily geographically deceptively misdescriptive of them ..."

(f) Except as expressly excluded in paragraphs (a), ... and (e)(3) ... nothing herein shall prevent the registration of a mark used by the applicant which has become distinctive of the applicant's goods in commerce....

Geschmacksmuster [patent] A German DESIGN REGISTRATION. Registration is obtained by depositing with a local German office an application with a drawing, photograph, or sample of the article. Registration only protects against copying, not against independent duplication as would a U.S. DESIGN PATENT. Registration is effective on deposit, and a list of registered designs is published a short time after registration. This published list is contained within the Bundesanzeiger (Federal Gazette) and discloses the following: the general description of the deposited design, the class of articles deposited, the identifying number of deposited designs, the name and location of the registrant, the date and time of registration, the term of protection, and the city location of the deposited design. See 1 D. Chisum, *Patents* §3.06[2] (1994 rev.).

U.S. courts have held that a Geschmacksmuster is a patent within the meaning of Patent Code §102(d). *In re Carlson*, 983 F.2d 1032, 25 USPQ 2d 1207 (Fed. Cir. 1992). Also, the Federal Circuit, in a case of first impression, held that a Geschmacksmuster qualifies as a foreign patent for purposes of §102(a) and therefore constitutes prior art for use in the obviousness analysis under §103. *In re Carlson*, 983 F.2d 1032, 1036, 25 USPQ 2d 1207, 1211–12 (Fed. Cir. 1992).

• *Case Reference:* "We recognize that Geschmacksmustern on display for public view in remote cities in a far-away land may create a burden of discovery for one without the time, desire, or resources to journey there in person or by agent to observe that which was registered and protected under German law. Such a burden, however, is by law imposed upon the hypothetical person of ordinary skill in the art who is charged with knowledge of all the contents of the relevant prior art.... [A] hypothetical person is presumed to know all the pertinent prior art, whether or not the applicant is actually aware of its existence." *In re Carlson*, 983 F.2d 1032, 1037, 25 USPQ 2d 1207, 1211 (Fed. Cir. 1992).

get up [trademark] The various elements of packaging and presentation of a product. "Get up" sometimes appears as a synonym for "TRADE DRESS." "Get up" is much more commonly used in the United Kingdom than in the United States. In the United Kingdom, the "get up" of a product is protected under the separate body of law known there as "PASSING OFF."

• *Usage Example:* "The passing-off action was first developed to meet a classic case. As Lord Halsbury put it: 'nobody has any right to represent his goods as the goods of somebody else.' ... His means may consist of misappropriating the plaintiff's mark, business name or get-up. ..." W. Cornish, *Intellectual Property* 473 (1981).

gist of the invention [patent] The "heart" or "core" of the claimed invention. In determining whether a patent claim is invalid as obvious in view of the prior art, the claimed invention must be considered as a whole under Patent Code §103. Since the claimed invention is either obvious or nonobvious as a whole, redefining the invention to find its "gist" or "core" and then concluding that the gist is obvious is improper. Similarly, it is not proper in determining IN-FRINGEMENT of a patent claim to compare the gist of the patented invention with the gist of the ACCUSED DEVICE.

Consideration of the gist of the invention is sometimes appropriate in determining patent infringement under the DOCTRINE OF EQUIVALENTS. But specific claim limitations cannot be ignored as insignificant or immaterial in determining infringement. References to using the gist of the invention "must be read as shorthand" for the criteria of the doctrine of equivalents. *Perkin-Elmer Corp. v. Westinghouse Elec. Corp.*, 822 F.2d 1528, 1533 n.8, 3 USPQ2d 1321, 1325 n.8 (Fed. Cir. 1987).

See HEART OF THE INVENTION, OBVIOUSNESS.

• *Case References*:

" [T]his Court has made it clear ... that there is no legally recognizable or protected 'essential' element, 'gist' or 'heart' of the invention in a combination patent." *Aro Mfg. Inc. v. Convertible Top Replacement Co.*, 365 U.S. 336, 345, 128 USPQ 354 (1961).

"Although there is no legally recognized 'essence' or 'heart' of the invention in determining validity, ... it can be applicable in a determination of infringement under the doctrine of equivalents." *Atlas Powder Co. v. E.I. du Pont de Nemours & Co.*, 750 F.2d 1569, 1582, 224 USPQ 409, 418 (Fed. Cir. 1984).

"Though consideration of an invention's 'gist' is appropriate in some contexts, e.g., in determining infringement under the doctrine of equivalents, when determining obviousness there is no legally recognizable or protected 'essential' [sic] 'gist,' or 'heart' of the invention. *Loctite Corp. v. Ultraseal Ltd.*, 781 F.2d 861, 875, 228 USPQ 90, 99 (Fed. Cir. 1985).

good will [trademark] The value of a business or of a line of goods or services that reflects commercial reputation. A trademark or service mark is a symbol of the good will of the goods or services in connection with which the mark is used.

The Nature of Good Will. Good will reflects buyer momentum to continue doing business with a certain business or to continue buying the same brand. In this sense good will is a legal recognition of human buying habits. Good will is the value of a business beyond its tangible assets. A business with a well-established good will could see all of its tangible assets destroyed, yet still own the very valuable intangible asset of its reputation—its good will. Good will is sometimes characterized as the "going concern value" of a business. Good will together with its trademark symbol are legally classified as "property."

Trademark Infringement Is a Form of Theft of Good Will. Trademark infringement is a way of stealing or free riding on the good will symbolized by the mark that is being infringed. "The redress that is accorded in trademark cases is based upon the party's right to be protected in the good will of a trade or business." *Hanover Star Milling Co. v. Metcalf*, 240 U.S. 403, 412 (1918).

Good Will and Trademark Assignments and Licenses. Because a trademark or service mark is a symbol of good will, the "anti-assignment-in-gross rule" requires that when a trademark is sold or assigned, the party receiving the mark also receive the good will associated with or symbolized by that mark. See ASSIGNMENT OF TRADEMARK. Similarly, a trademark cannot be licensed without quality control to maintain the value of the good will represented by the licensed mark.

See LICENSING OF TRADEMARK.

Valuation of Good Will. Placing a value on good will and its trademark symbol is difficult because one is attempting to estimate the intangible value of reputation. Good will valuation is largely the domain of the economist and accountant, not the attorney. One valuation method recognized by the courts is to capitalize profits by multiplying the average annual net profits associated with good will by a multiple, which increases with the estimated strength of the good will. The Internal Revenue Service has its own approved methods of valuing good will for income tax purposes.

• *Treatise Reference*: 1 J.T. McCarthy, *Trademarks and Unfair Competition* §§2.07–.09 (3d ed. 1995 rev.).

• *Case References*:

" 'Goodwill' is the advantage obtained from use of a trademark. This includes public confidence in the quality of the product and in the warranties made on behalf of the product, and the 'name recognition' of the product by the public that differentiates that product from others. As Professor McCarthy explains: 'Good will is not a tangible, physical object that can be felt, seen and tasted. Its real existence is in the minds of the buying public. ... [It] is a business value which reflects the basic human propensity to continue doing business with a seller who has offered goods and services which the customer likes and has found adequate to fulfill his needs.... ' " *Premier Dental Prods. Supply Co. v. Darby Dental Supply Co.*, 794 F.2d 850 n.3, 230 USPQ 233, 235 n.3 (3d Cir. 1986).

"In truth, a trademark confers no monopoly whatever in a proper sense, but is merely a convenient means for facilitating the protection of ones's good will in trade by placing a distinguishing mark or symbol—a commercial signature—upon the merchandise or the package in which it is sold." *United Drug Co. v. Theodore Rectanus Co.*, 248 U.S. 90, 98 (1918).

grace period [patent] A one-year period given to an inventor after commercialization of the invention within which the inventor can decide whether or not to file an application for a patent.

Start of the Grace Period. The one-year grace period begins to run when a product embodying the invention is either: (1) placed ON SALE; (2) put into PUBLIC USE; or (3) described in a PRINTED PUBLICATION.

Significance of the Grace Period. An inventor cannot obtain a valid patent if he or she waits for more than the one-year grace period to file a patent application after a product embodying the invention has been placed "on sale," or there has been a "public use" of the invention, or the invention has been described in a "printed publication." It is against public policy to permit the invention to be commercially exploited for longer than the one-year grace period granted by Patent Code §102(b). "The 1-year grace period provided for by Congress in §102(b) represents a balance between ... competing interests." *General Elec. Co. v. United States*, 654 F.2d 55, 61, 211 USPQ 867, 873 (Ct. Cl. 1981).

Critical Date. The date one year prior to the filing date of the patent is known as the CRITICAL DATE. An event prior to that date can trigger the "public use" and "on sale" bars to a patent.

See CRITICAL DATE, ON SALE, PUBLIC USE, PRINTED PUBLICATION, EXPERIMENTAL USE.

• *Statutory Reference*: 35 U.S.C. §102(b): "A person shall be entitled to a patent unless— ... (b) the invention was patented or described in a printed publication in this or a foreign country or in public use or on sale in this country more than one year prior to the date of the application for patent in the United States...."

• *Case References*:

"Public policy favors prompt and widespread disclosure of inventions to the public, while giving the inventor a reasonable amount of time (1 year, by statute) to determine whether a patent is worthwhile, but precluding attempts by the inventor or his assignee from commercially exploiting the invention more than a year before the application for patent is filed." *Western Marine Elecs. v. Furuno Elec. Co.*, 764 F.2d 840, 845, 226 USPQ 334, 337 (Fed. Cir. 1985).

"After providing virtually all of their method to the public without applying for a patent within a year, [the inventors] foreclosed themselves from obtaining a patent on a method that would have been obvious from their publication to those of ordinary skill in the art, with or without the disclosures of other prior art." *In re O'Farrell*, 853 F.2d 894, 904, 7 USPQ2d 1673, 1681 (Fed. Cir. 1988) (patent application rejected on the ground of obviousness).

grandparent application [patent] The earliest patent application of an inventor in a chain of three applications disclosing at least in part the same invention. The same invention might or might not be claimed in the earlier application. The earliest application is referred to as the "grandparent" if the later parent application and subsequent application are CONTINUATION or CONTINUATION-IN-PART applications.

See PARENT APPLICATION.

• *Case Reference*: "To consider an application a 'continuing application' means, of course, that it is entitled to the earlier 'parent'— or 'grandparent' etc.—application's filing date in determining what is *'prior* art' from the standpoint of validity." *Racing Strollers Inc. v. TRI Indus. Inc.*, 878 F.2d 1418, 1421–22 n.*, 11 USPQ2d 1300, 1303 n.* (Fed. Cir. 1989).

• *Usage Example*: "[W]e must first decide whether the district court's holding that the Nemeth patent is entitled to only the April 1, 1974, filing date of the parent application, instead of the March 1, 1972, filing date of the grandparent application, is correct." *Pennwalt Corp. v. Akzona Inc.*, 740 F.2d 1573, 1578, 222 USPQ 833, 836 (Fed. Cir. 1984).

grand rights [copyright] Dramatic performing rights of music, as distinguished from "small," nondramatic performing rights.

Performing Rights Societies' Licenses. The grand-small distinction is important because the performing rights societies, such as ASCAP, license to live performers and to radio and television broadcasters only the small, nondramatic right to perform copyrighted MUSICAL WORKS, not the right to make a grand, dramatic performance of the musical works. "Grand rights" are not licensed from composers to a PERFORMING RIGHTS SOCIETY to be sublicensed. They are retained and licensed directly from the source: the owners of copyright in the music. For example, a television network that has an ASCAP blanket license cannot make a dramatic use of a song without a direct license from the owners of the copyright in that song.

Distinction Between Small and Grand Rights. There is disagreement as to how to draw the line between the grand (dramatic) and small (nondramatic) performance of musical works. Nimmer agrees with the definition in the ASCAP standard network television license that a performance of a musical work is dramatic if it aids in telling a story; otherwise it is not. 3 *Nimmer on Copyright* §10.10[E] (1994 rev.). The ASCAP standard television license defines a "dramatic performance" as "a performance of a musical composition on a television program in which there is a definite plot depicted by action and where the performance of the musical composition is woven into and carries forward the plot and its accompanying action." W. Patry, *Copyright Law and Practice* 240 (1994).

Dramatic Use: Sequence of Songs Tells a Story. In the *Jesus Christ Superstar* case, the Court of Appeals for the Second Circuit held that the performance of songs from the rock opera *Jesus Christ Superstar* was a dramatic performance, was outside the scope of the defendant's ASCAP license, and was enjoined. *Robert Stigwood Group, Ltd. v. Sperber*, 457 F.2d 50, 173 USPQ 258 (2d Cir. 1972). The

court found the defendant's presentation to be a "dramatic" performance because, although there was no dialogue outside of the songs and no scenery or costumes, the defendant performed 20 of the 23 songs in the plaintiff's opera, and all but one in the identical sequence as in the plaintiff's opera. The court found that "[t]he sequence of the songs seems to be the linchpin in this case" and enjoined the performance of any song in such a way as to follow another song in the same order as in the original opera.

• *Treatise References*: 3 *Nimmer on Copyright* §10.10[E] (1994 rev.); S. Shemel & M.W. Krasilovsky, *This Business of Music* 198–201 (1985); W. Patry, *Copyright Law and Practice* 240 (1994).

grant back [patent–antitrust] A provision in a patent license by which the patentee-licensor requires that the licensee assign or license back to the licensor patent rights on improvements developed by the licensee during the term of the license.

Antitrust and Misuse Analysis. Some forms of grant backs have been held to constitute misuse of a patent. The traditional view is the Supreme Court's holding in the 1947 *Trans-Wrap* case that no grant back is ever PER SE ILLEGAL but is always to be tested by the antitrust RULE OF REASON. *Transparent-Wrap Mach. Corp. v. Stokes & Smith Co.*, 329 U.S. 637, 72 USPQ 148 (1947). The procompetitive motivation for a grant back is the patentee's fear that it would be put at a competitive disadvantage by a licensee who develops and patents improvements and refuses to license the patentee to use them. This motivation can be satisfied by a nonexclusive license back. A grant back restriction that goes further than this raises the risk of being viewed as an attempt to discourage improvement inventions that might make the licensed invention obsolete. J.T. McCarthy, *Patent Grant-Backs: A New Look*, 2 APLA J. 67 (1974). In analyzing grant backs, the courts look to see if the restriction could have a restrictive or chilling effect on the development of improvements by licensees. *Santa-Fe Pomeroy, Inc. v. P & Z Co.*, 569 F.2d 1084, 1101, 197 USPQ 449, 464 (9th Cir. 1978).

- *Treatise Reference*: Holmes, *Intellectual Property and Antitrust Law* §23.01 (1994 rev.); ABA, *Antitrust Law Developments* 496 (2d ed. 1984).

graphical user interface [computer]

A computer user interface that incorporates significant graphic elements. Also known as a GUI or "gooey."

See USER INTERFACE

gray market goods [trademark–copyright]

Goods manufactured abroad with the permission of the trademark owner that are imported into the United States without the permission of the trademark owner. The classic case of gray goods, also known as PARALLEL IMPORTS, is where someone other than the designated exclusive U.S. importer buys genuine trademarked goods outside the United States and imports them for sale in the United States in competition with the exclusive U.S. importer.

- *Case References*:

"A gray-market good is a foreign-manufactured good, bearing a valid United States trademark, that is imported without the consent of the U.S. trademark holder." *K Mart Corp. v. Cartier Inc.*, 486 U.S. 281, 285, 6 USPQ2d 1897, 1899 (1988).

"The term 'gray-market goods' refers to foreign manufactured goods, for which a valid United States trademark has been registered, that are legally purchased abroad and imported into the United States without the consent of the American trademark holder. [Defendants] in the present case note that the term 'gray-market' unfairly implies a nefarious undertaking by the importer, and that the more accurate term for the goods at issue is 'parallel import.' We agree that the term parallel import accurately describes the goods and is, perhaps, a better term because it is devoid of prejudicial suggestion. For that reason, we use that term in this discussion. However, we also employ the term 'gray-market' goods because, for better or worse, it has become the commonly accepted and employed reference to the goods at issue." *Weil Ceramics & Glass, Inc. v. Dash*, 878 F.2d 659, 662 n.1, 11 USPQ2d 1001, 1003 n.1 (3d Cir. 1989).

" 'Gray market' or 'parallel imports,' are genuine products possessing a brand name protected by a trademark or copyright. They are typically manufactured abroad, and purchased and imported into the United States by third parties, thereby bypassing the authorized U.S. distribution channels." *Parfums Givenchy Inc. v. Drug Emporium*, 38 F.3d 477 n.6, 32 USPQ2d 1512 n.6 (9th Cir. 1994).

1. Trademark Law and Gray Market Goods. There are at least three separate statutory bases for possible exclusion of gray market goods from importation into the United States: (1) Tariff Act §526, 19 U.S.C. §1526; (2) the importation prohibition of Lanham Act §42, 15 U.S.C. §1124; and (3) the infringement of registered and unregistered marks prohibitions of Lanham Act §§32(a) and 43(b), 15 U.S.C. §§1114(a) and 1125(b).

Tariff Act. The Supreme Court has indicated that the "extraordinary protection" afforded by Tariff Act §526 is exclusively for domestic U.S. trademark owners with a registered mark and no corporate affiliation with the foreign manufacturer. *K Mart Corp. v. Cartier Inc.*, 486 U.S. 281, 6 USPQ2d 1897 (1988). Where the U.S. authorized importer and trademark owner is a subsidiary of the foreign manufacturer, the Tariff Act does not bar gray market imports. *Weil Ceramics & Glass, Inc. v. Dash*, 878 F.2d 659, 11 USPQ2d 1001 (3d Cir. 1989).

Lanham Act. The majority view is that if there are material physical differences between the gray market imports and the authorized imports, then the gray market imports are not "genuine" goods and can create a likelihood of confusion. *Lever Bros. Co. v. United States*, 877 F.2d 101, 11 USPQ2d 1117 (D.C. Cir. 1989), *on remand*, 981 F.2d 1330, 1338, 25 USPQ2d 1579, 1586 (D.C. Cir. 1993): "Trademarks applied to physically different foreign goods are not genuine from the viewpoint of the American consumer...." But if the authorized and the gray market imports are substantially physically the same, generally, the Lanham Act is no bar to importation unless the designated U.S. importer can show a likelihood of confusion by some other method. *Weil Ceramics & Glass, Inc. v. Dash*, 878 F.2d 659, 11 USPQ2d 1001 (3d Cir.

1989) ("Consumers who purchase [gray market] imported LLADRO porcelain get precisely what they believed that they were purchasing.").

State Disclosure Requirements. California, New York, and some other states require retailers of gray market goods to disclose certain information to consumers, such as product incompatibility with U.S. standards, the lack of English language instructions, and the lack of coverage by the manufacturer's warranty. Cal. Civil Code §§1797.8–.86 (1986); N.Y. Gen. Bus. Law §218-aa (1985).

• *Treatise Reference*: 3 J.T. McCarthy, *Trademarks and Unfair Competition* §29.19 (3d ed. 1995).

• *Case Reference*: "We conclude that the existence of any difference between the registrant's product and the allegedly infringing gray good that consumers would likely consider to be relevant when purchasing a product creates a presumption of consumer confusion sufficient to support a Lanham Act claim." *Societe Des Produits Nestle S.A. v. Casa Helvetia Inc.*, 982 F.2d 633, 641, 25 USPQ2d 1256, 1263 (1st Cir 1992).

2. Copyright Law and Gray Market Goods. The unauthorized importation into the United States of copies purchased outside the United States is an infringement of the U.S. copyright owner's exclusive right to distribute copies. 17 U.S.C. §602(a). The issue with respect to gray goods is whether the FIRST SALE DOCTRINE exempts importers who acquired ownership of the imported copies that were lawfully made abroad. The question is whether the phrase "lawfully made under this title" in 17 U.S.C. §109(a) exempts from infringement copies legally made and sold outside the United States.

The Ninth Circuit's view is that the language of §109(a) grants first sale protection only to copies legally made and sold in the United States. Sales abroad of foreign manufactured

U.S. copyrighted materials do not extinguish the U.S. copyright holder's exclusive distribution rights in the United States under §§106 and 602(a). *Parfums Givenchy Inc. v. Drug Emporium*, 38 F.3d 477, 32 USPQ2d 1512 (9th Cir. 1994) ("We ... [are] holding that sales *abroad* of foreign manufactured United States copyrighted materials do not terminate the United States copyright holder's exclusive distribution rights in the United States under §§106 and 602(a)." *Id.* at n.7).

However, it has been held that where goods are manufactured in the United States with copyrighted labels, shipped abroad, and subsequently re-imported, they are protected by the first sale defense and are not barred entry into the United States by the Copyright Act. "[H]aving sold its goods with copyrighted labels to foreign distributors, the manufacturer is barred by the first sale doctrine from establishing infringement through an unauthorized importation." *Sebastian Int'l v. Consumer Contacts Ltd.*, 847 F.2d 1093, 1094, 7 USPQ2d 1007, 1078 (3d Cir. 1988).

• *Treatise References*: 1 P. Goldstein, *Copyright* §5.6.1.2 (1989); 2 *Nimmer on Copyright* §8.12[B][6] (1994 rev.); W. Patry, *Copyright Law and Practice* 869 (1994).

• *Case Reference*: "[T]he importation right survives as to a particular copy unless and until there has been a "first sale' *in the United States*." *Parfums Givenchy Inc. v. Drug Emporium*, 38 F.3d 477, 481, 32 USPQ2d 1512, 1515 (9th Cir. 1994).

group of 77 [international] A group of developing nations that have banded together in a kind of lobbying group in international negotiations, especially with respect to PARIS CONVENTION revision negotiations, to jointly assert the position of developing nations as to international intellectual property issues.

H

Hague Arrangement [designs–patents]
The 1925 Arrangement of the Hague for the International Deposit of Designs is a multilateral treaty of about 15 nations, not including the United States, providing for an international registration system for INDUSTRIAL DESIGNS. While the international deposit establishes a definite date of creation of the design, the right to prevent infringement is governed by the national law of each country that is a party to the treaty.

See DESIGN REGISTRATION, LOCARNO AGREEMENT.

• *Treatise References*: "The Hague Agreement, achieved within the framework of the Paris Convention, permits persons entitled to make an international deposit to obtain protection for their industrial designs in a number of States with a minimum of formalities and cost by means of a single deposit made with the International Bureau of WIPO." WIPO, *Background Reading Material on Intellectual Property* 203 (1988). See 2 S. Ladas, *Patents, Trademarks and Related Rights: National and International Protection* §§522–44 (1975).

hard cases make bad law [general legal]
A common legal phrase usually used by an attorney seeking to distinguish precedent. The phrase signifies that the prior case need not be followed because in that case the judge bent the law too far ("bad law") in order to do justice in a case where applying mainstream legal rules would have resulted in injustice (a "hard case"). In other words, the argument is: "The judge in Gamma v. Zeta bent the law too far in order to arrive at a fair and just result in that case. But that is no reason to bend the law in the same way in this case where the facts are different and there is no need to deform the law to do justice."

Origins. The origin of this exact phrase is uncertain, but similar phrases appear in some early cases. E.g., "Hard cases, it has been frequently observed, are apt to introduce bad law." *Winterbottom v. Wright*, [1842] 152 Eng. Rep. 402; "Great cases, like hard cases, make bad law." Justice Holmes in *Northern Secs. Co. v. United States*, 193 U.S. 197, 400 (1904).

harmonization [international–intellectual property] The process of bringing the national intellectual property laws of the various nations into substantial uniformity and equivalence. The goal of the harmonization effort is to facilitate protection of intellectual property on an international basis by reducing the costs associated with compliance with widely varying requirements. The goal is not to achieve something like a "world patent," but to bring separate national laws into a more consistent pattern and to eliminate the more discordant rules.

Patent Harmonization Treaty. For several years, the World Intellectual Property Organization (see WIPO) sponsored international discussions and negotiations designed to lead to the adoption of a worldwide treaty to harmonize national patent laws. Drafts of the treaty discussed at the meetings would require member nations to adopt uniform laws on such topics as a first to file priority rule, publication within 18 months of filing, and a one-year worldwide grace period after disclosure. See 39 Pat. Trademark & Copyright J. (BNA) 213 (Jan. 18, 1990) (report of 1989 meeting). The U.S. Patent and Trademark Office (PTO) held hearings in the fall of 1993 to determine the attitude of U.S. inventors. The PTO concluded from the hearings that a consensus in the United States had not yet developed in support of a first to file rule. As a result of those hearings, the Secretary of Commerce announced in January 1994 that the United States would not seek to resume talks on the patent law harmonization treaty. As a result, WIPO suspended a scheduled second conference on the treaty. See 48 Pat. Trademark & Copyright J. (BNA) 274 (July 21, 1994).

European Harmonization. Harmonization is becoming a reality in the European Community, where directives such as the 1989 European Community Trademark Harmonization Directive and the 1991 Computer Software Directive require member nations to bring their national laws into congruence with the Community norms.

Harry Fox Agency [copyright] The largest MECHANICAL LICENSING AGENT in the United States. The Harry Fox Agency, established in 1927, represents more than 10,000 American music publishers and licenses a large percentage of uses of music in the United States on records, tapes, CDs, and computer chips. It is located at 205 East 42nd St., New York, NY 10017.

Main Function. The main function of the agency is the granting of mechanical licenses for the reproduction of musical works on phonorecords. While Copyright Act §115 creates a COMPULSORY LICENSE of these MECHANICAL RIGHTS, the custom of the trade is for the record producer not to rely on the compulsory license but to obtain a standard license from a mechanical licensing agent.

Other Functions. In addition, the Harry Fox Agency also acts as an agent and intermediary in negotiating voluntary licenses in the following cases: (1) granting SYNCHRONIZATION LICENSES, which are a license for the use of a musical work for use in motion pictures, broadcast and cable television programs, and CD videos; (2) negotiating licenses for the use of music in television and radio commercial advertising; (3) obtaining licenses of music for use in recordings for other than private use, such as commercial background music, in-flight music, syndicated radio services, karaoke, and multimedia; (4) obtaining licenses for the importation into the United States of recordings made abroad. The agency does not license the public performance of music (except in motion picture

theaters in the United States) or the reproduction of music in print or musical arrangements.

See MECHANICAL LICENSING AGENT.

• *Commentary Reference*: S. Shemel & M.W. Krasilovsky, *This Business of Music* 227–28 (1985); W. Patry, *Copyright Law and Practice* 805 (1994).

head start injunction [trade secret]
See REVERSE ENGINEERING INJUNCTION.

heart of the invention [patent] The "gist" or "core" of the claimed invention. In determining whether a patent claim is invalid as obvious in view of the prior art, the claimed invention must be considered as a whole under Patent Code §103. Since the claimed invention is either obvious or nonobvious as a whole, redefining the invention to find its "heart" and concluding that the "heart" is obvious is improper. Consideration of the heart or gist of the invention is sometimes appropriate in determining patent infringement under the DOCTRINE OF EQUIVALENTS.

See GIST OF THE INVENTION, OBVIOUSNESS.

• *Case References*:
"[T]his Court has made it clear ... that there is no legally recognizable or protected 'essential' element, 'gist' or 'heart' of the invention in a combination patent." *Aro Mfg. Inc. v. Convertible Top Replacement Co.*, 365 U.S. 336, 345, 128 USPQ 359 (1961), quoted and applied in *Vas-Cath Inc. v. Mahurkar*, 935 F.2d 1555, 1565, 19 USPQ 2d 1111, 1118 (Fed. Cir. 1991).

"Although there is no legally recognized 'essence' or 'heart' of the invention in determining validity, ... it can be applicable in a determination of infringement under the doctrine of equivalents." *Atlas Powder Co. v. E.I. du Pont de Nemours & Co.*, 750 F.2d 1569, 1582, 224 USPQ 409, 418 (Fed. Cir. 1984).

"Judge Boyle's reference to 'the heart of invention' was here a harmless fall-back to the fruitless search for an inherently amorphous concept that was rendered unnecessary by the statute, 35 U.S.C." *Stratoflex v. Aeroquip Corp.*, 713 F.2d 1530, 1540, 218 USPQ 871, 880 (Fed. Cir. 1983).

hindsight [patent] An improper conclusion that an invention is unpatentable because "obvious," by reading back into the PRIOR ART the teachings of the invention which came later.

The Obviousness Test. Under Patent Code §103, an invention is unpatentable if the differences between the invention and the prior art are such that "the subject matter as a whole would have been obvious at the time the invention was made" to a person skilled in the art. Thus, the proper time frame to apply the obviousness test is that moment just before the invention was made, not whether the invention appears obvious to a judge or jury after they learn all about the invention. *Stratoflex Inc. v. Aeroquip Corp.*, 713 F.2d 1530, 1538, 218 USPQ 871, 879 (Fed. Cir. 1983). But the judge or jury at trial is informed all about the prior art as well as the invention and is asked under §103 to decide if the invention was "obvious" at the time the invention was made.

Knowing the Invention Makes It Seem Obvious. The U.S. Supreme Court has cautioned against "slipping into the use of hindsight" and urged courts "to resist the temptation to read into the prior art the teachings of the invention in issue." *Graham v. John Deere Co.*, 383 U.S. 1, 36, 148 USPQ 459, 474 (1966). For example, impermissible "hindsight" is using knowledge of the solution to determine that the answer to the technical problem was "obvious," whereas to one without knowledge of the solution, the answer was not "obvious" at all.

Hindsight in Combining Prior Art. An example of the impermissible use of hindsight is to combine pieces of the prior art to argue that a combination invention is obvious. There must be something in the prior art that suggested the combination of these particular prior art devices and processes other than the hindsight gained from knowing that the inventor chose to combine these particular things in this particular way. *Uniroyal, Inc. v. Rudkin-Wiley Corp.*, 837 F.2d 1044, 1051, 5 USPQ2d 1434, 1438 (Fed. Cir. 1988).

See COMBINING PRIOR ART, OBVIOUSNESS.

• *Case References:*

"The present record reflects the insidious and powerful phenomenon known in patent law as the use of hindsight, for in this case a most careful and conscientious judge, after voicing the caveat against it, was nonetheless victimized by that phenomenon.… The test is whether the subject matter of the claimed inventions would have been obvious to one skilled in the art at the time the inventions were made, *not* what would be obvious to a judge after reading the patents in suit and hearing the testimony." *Panduit Corp. v. Dennison Mfg. Co.*, 774 F.2d 1082, 1090–92, 227 USPQ 337, 342–43 (Fed. Cir. 1985).

"To imbue one of ordinary skill in the art with knowledge of the invention in suit, when no prior art reference or references of record convey or suggest that knowledge, is to fall victim to the insidious effect of a hindsight syndrome wherein that which only the inventor taught is used against its teacher. It is difficult but necessary that the decisionmaker forget what he or she has been taught at trial about the claimed invention and cast the mind back to the time the invention was made (often as here many years), to occupy the mind of one skilled in the art who is presented only with the references, and who is normally guided by the then-accepted wisdom in the art." *W.L. Gore & Assocs., Inc. v. Garlock, Inc.*, 721 F.2d 1540, 1553, 220 USPQ 303, 313 (Fed. Cir. 1983).

"[The patentee's] device, once disclosed, seems obvious and simple. But that is the nature of most important creative ideas. Once we know of them, it seems as if we must always have done so. Science endeavors to move in the direction of simplicity. (Ptolemy had his Newton; and Newton, his Einstein. We increase knowledge importantly, so to speak, by shaving old ideas with Occam's razor.)" Frank, J. concurring in *Picard v. United Aircraft Corp.*, 128 F.2d 632, 638, 53 USPQ 563, 568 (2d Cir. 1942).

how to make [patent] One aspect of the ENABLEMENT requirement is that the specification of a patent must give a sufficiently clear description of the invention as to inform a person having ordinary skill in the art "how to make" the structure of the invention. The "how to make" requisite for a claim to a process could be called the "how to carry out" requirement.

- *Treatise Reference*: 2 D. Chisum, *Patents* §7.03[5] (1994 rev.).

See ENABLEMENT, HOW TO USE.

- *Statutory Reference*: 35 U.S.C. §112, first paragraph: "The specification shall contain a written description of the invention, and of the manner and process of making and using it, in such full, clear, concise, and exact terms as to enable any person skilled in the art to which it pertains, or with which it is most nearly connected, to make and use the same, and shall set forth the best mode contemplated by the inventor of carrying out his invention."

- *Case Reference*: "[W]e conclude that undue delay and experimentation would have been involved for the skilled worker to make the Christensen disclosure operative and, therefore, hold that Christensen has no right to make his claims corresponding to the counts because he lacks an enabling disclosure for 'how to make' the compound claimed." *Gosteli v. McCombie*, 230 USPQ 205, 209 (Bd. Pat. App. & Intf. 1986).

how to use [patent] One aspect of the ENABLEMENT requirement is that the specification of a patent must give a sufficiently clear description of the invention as to inform a person having ordinary skill in the art "how to use" the structure of the invention.

There is a relationship between the "how to use" requirement and the separate requirement that a patented invention have "UTILITY" in that if an invention is not shown to be useful or operative, then it would also fail to meet the "how to use" facet of the enablement requirement.

- *Treatise Reference*: 2 D. Chisum, *Patents* §7.03[6] (1994 rev.).

See ENABLEMENT, HOW TO MAKE.

- *Case Reference*: "[T]hese defenses are based on the specification's alleged failure to disclose adequately to one ordinarily skilled in the art 'how to use' the invention without undue experimentation—usually considered the 'how-to-use' defense under 35 U.S.C. §112." *Envirotech Corp. v. Al George Inc.*, 730 F.2d

753, 762, 221 USPQ 473, 480 (Fed. Cir. 1984).

hypothetical person skilled in the art

[patent] Under Patent Code §103, an invention is obvious and unpatentable if the invention would have been obvious in view of the prior art at the time the invention was made "to a person having ordinary skill in the art to which said subject matter pertains."

Ordinary Skill in the Art. The obviousness test is applied through the perception of a hypothetical person possessing ORDINARY SKILL in that technology, not the rare genius and not the judge or jury who during the trial has learned all about the details of the inventor's solution to the technological problem. Similarly, the test of whether an invention is obvious in view of prior art is not judged through the eyes of the actual inventor: that would result in granting patents to those inventors who are most ignorant of the prior art and denying patents to inventors who are fully aware of what went before.

Relevant Fields of Technology. It is proper to attribute to the hypothetical skilled person "knowledge of all prior art in the field of the inventor's endeavor and of prior art solutions for a common problem even if outside that field." *In Re Nilssen*, 851 F.2d 1401, 1403, 7 USPQ2d 1500, 1502 (Fed. Cir. 1988).

See ANALOGOUS ART.

For full definition and more references, see SKILL IN THE ART.

- *Case References*:

"It should be clear that that hypothetical person is not the inventor but an imaginary being possessing 'ordinary skill in the art' created by Congress to provide a *standard of patentability*, a descendant of the 'ordinary mechanic acquainted with the business' of *Hotchkiss v. Greenwood*. Realistically, courts have never judged patentability by what the real inventor/applicant/patentee could or would do. Real inventors, as a class, vary in their capacities from ignorant geniuses to Nobel laureates: the courts have always applied a standard based on an imaginary worker of their own devising whom they have equated with the inventor." *Kimberly-Clark Corp. v. Johnson & Johnson*

Co., 745 F.2d 1437, 1454, 223 USPQ 603, 614 (Fed. Cir. 1984).

"With the involved facts determined, the decisionmaker confronts a ghost, i.e., 'a person having ordinary skill in the art,' not unlike the 'reasonable man' and other ghosts in the law. To reach a proper conclusion under §103, the decisionmaker must step backward in time and into the shoes worn by that 'person' when the invention was unknown and just before it was made." *Panduit Corp. v. Dennison Mfg. Co.*, 810 F.2d 1561, 1566, 1 USPQ2d 1593, 1595–97 (Fed. Cir. 1987).

"We recognize that Geschmaksmustern [German design registrations] on display for public view in remote cities in a far-away land may create a burden of discovery for one without the time, desire, or resources to journey there in person or by agent to observe that which was registered and protected under German law. Such a burden, however, is by law imposed upon the hypothetical person of ordinary skill in the art who is charged with knowledge of all the contents of the relevant prior art. ... [A] hypothetical person is presumed to know all the pertinent prior art, whether or not the applicant is actually aware of its existence." *In re Carlson*, 983 F.2d 1032, 1036, 25 USPQ2d 1207, 1211 (Fed. Cir. 1992).

I

idea [patent] Patents do not protect ideas, theories, or concepts, only tangible inventions. See discussion and cases at CONCEPT.

idea-expression dichotomy [copyright] The fundamental rule of law that copyright does not protect an idea: copyright protects only specific expressions of an idea. This rule is codified in §102(b) of the Copyright Act.

Defining the "Idea." The difficulty in applying the idea-expression dichotomy is in deciding at what level of abstraction the "idea" of the plaintiff's work should be defined. If the idea is defined at a very high level of abstraction, there will necessarily be many different ways to express the idea. But if the idea is defined in very detailed and specific terms, there may be only a few ways to state the idea in different expressions. Courts often label as "ideas" those aspects of a work that the court wants to remain free for use by subsequent users and competitors. See: J. Ginsberg, *No "Sweat"? Copyright and Other Protection of Works of Information After Feist v. Rural Telephone*, 92 Colum. L. Rev. 338, 346 (1992) ("In copyright law, an 'idea' is not an epistemological concept, but a legal conclusion prompted by notions—often unarticulated and unproven—of appropriate competition.").

Computer Programs. For computer programs, there is a split of authority as to how to define the idea of a program. Under the minority view, the function of a program is the "idea" and the particular method chosen to accomplish that function is the protectible "expression." "Where there are various means of achieving the desired purpose, then the particular means chosen is not necessary to the purpose, hence, there is expression, not idea." *Whelan Assocs. Inc. v. Jaslow Dental Labs.*, 797 F.2d 1222,

1236, 230 USPQ2d 481, 490 (3d Cir. 1986). The alternative view is that a computer program is composed of many mini-programs, each with its own idea. The whole program is broken down into its constituent mini-programs; then the idea-expression dichotomy is applied to each, and nonprotectible elements are filtered out prior to applying the substantial similarity test. *Computer Assocs. In'tl v. Altai, Inc.*, 982 F.2d 693, 706, 23 USPQ2d 1241, 1252 (2d Cir. 1992). The *Altai* approach has become the majority view. See, e.g., *Autoskill Inc. v. National Educ. Support Sys., Inc.*, 994 F.2d 1476, 1491, 28 USPQ2d 1828, 1839 (10th Cir. 1993) ("This idea/expression dichotomy applies to computer programs.... Thus, in general, the portions of a computer program that are 'ideas' are nonprotectable, and the portions that represent 'expression' may be protected.") See 1 N. Boorstyn, *Copyright* §11.06 (2d ed. 1994); W. Patry, *Copyright Law and Practice* 326 (1994).

The Idea-Expression Dichotomy and Infringement. Under one view, the idea-expression dichotomy does not impose a limitation on copyrightability, but rather measures the degree of similarity between the plaintiff's work and the accused work that must exist to constitute "substantial similarity" for copyright infringement. *NEC Corp. v. Intel Corp.*, 10 USPQ2d 1177, 1179 (N.D. Cal. 1989). Some cases adopt the view that the degree of similarity required moves along a sliding scale: the fewer the number of expressions of a particular "idea," the narrower the scope of protection given any one of those expressions. *Concrete Mach. Co. v. Classic Lawn Ornaments Inc.*, 843 F.2d 600, 606, 6 USPQ2d 1357, 1362 (1st Cir. 1988). "[T]he fewer the methods of expressing an idea, the more the allegedly infringing work must resemble the copyrighted work in order to establish substantial similarity...." *Cooling Sys. & Flexibles, Inc. v. Stewart Radiator, Inc.*, 777 F.2d 485, 491, 228 USPQ 275, 280 (9th Cir. 1985). The limiting case is MERGER: when idea and expression merge, no copyright protection is given at all. Some courts have stated that when there is not total merger, but there are only a few or a limited number of ways to express an idea, the plaintiff must show near identity to prove infringement. This is sometimes known as the LITTLE VARIATION RULE.

• *Statutory Reference*: 17 U.S.C. §102(b): "In no case does copyright protection for an original work of authorship extend to any idea, process, procedure, system, method of operation, concept, principle, or discovery, regardless of the form in which it is described, explained, illustrated, or embodied in such work."

See MERGER, LITTLE VARIATION RULE.

• *Case References*:

"It is an axiom of copyright law that copyright protects only an author's expression of an idea, not the idea itself.... There is a strong public policy corollary to this axiom permitting all to use freely ideas contained in a copyrightable work, so long as the protected expression itself is not appropriated.... Thus, to the extent the similarities between plaintiff's and defendant's works are confined to ideas and general concepts, these similarities are noninfringing." *Data East USA Inc. v. Epyx Inc.*, 862 F.2d 204, 207–08, 9 USPQ2d 1322, 1325 (9th Cir. 1988).

"The expression/idea dichotomy is now expressly recognized in section 102(b) which precludes copyright for any 'idea.' This provision was not intended to enlarge or contract the scope of copyright protection but 'to restate ... that the basic dichotomy between expression and idea remains unchanged.' H.R. Rep. No. 1476 at 57, reprinted in 1976 U.S. Code Cong. & Ad. News at 5670.... Many of the courts which have sought to draw the line between idea and expression have found difficulty in articulating where it falls.... We ... focus on whether the idea is capable of various modes of expression. If other [computer] programs can be written or created which perform the same function as an Apple's [plaintiff's] operating system program, then that program is an expres-

sion of the idea and hence copyrightable." *Apple Computer Inc. v. Franklin Computer Corp.*, 714 F.2d 1240, 1253, 219 USPQ 113, 124 (3d Cir. 1983).

"When the idea and its expression are not completely inseparable, there may still be only a limited number of ways of expressing an idea. In such a case, the burden of proof is heavy on the plaintiff who may have to show 'near identity' between the works at issue.... Conversely, of course, 'as a work embodies more in the way of particularized expression, it moves further away from [merger of idea and expression] and receives broader copyright protection.' ... This broader protection is available in the typical case of an original work embodying only one of an infinite variety of ways of expressing an idea. At this end of the spectrum, '[d]uplication or near identity is not necessary to establish infringement.' " *Concrete Mach. Co. v. Classic Lawn Ornaments Inc.*, 843 F.2d 600, 606–07, 6 USPQ2d 1357, 1361–62 (1st Cir. 1988).

"[T]here are five other basic ideas embodied in the desktop metaphor: use of windows to display multiple images on the computer screen and to facilitate user interaction with the information contained in the windows; iconic representation of familiar objects from the office environment; manipulation of icons to convey instructions and to control operation of the computer; use of menus to store information or computer functions in a place that is convenient to reach, but saves screen space for other images; and opening and closing of objects as a means of retrieving, transferring and storing information.... No copyright protection inheres in these ideas." *Apple Computer Inc. v. Microsoft Corp.*, 35 F.3d 1435, 1443–44, 32 USPQ2d 1086, 1092 (9th Cir. 1994).

idem sonans [trademark] Sounding the same or alike. If conflicting trademarks sound alike, this phonetic similarity contributes to an ultimate finding of likely confusion between the marks and infringement. The term "idem sonans" is sometimes applied to this comparison of phonetic similarity between trademarks. In older general law, if two personal names were similarly pronounced, the rule of "idem sonans" provided that absolute accuracy in spelling a personal name was not required in a legal document or in civil or criminal proceedings; i.e., no advantage could be taken of a clerical error in spelling.

• *Treatise Reference*: 3 J.T. McCarthy, *Trademarks and Unfair Competition* §23.05 (3d ed. 1995 rev.).

• *Case Reference*: *Polylok Corp. v. Valley Forge Fabrics, Inc.*, 566 F. Supp. 263, 223 USPQ 567 (S.D.N.Y. 1983) (defendant's trademark POLYLOX sounds like plaintiff's trademark POLY-LOK. "This more than satisfies the 'idem sonans' rule.").

identity of invention [patent] One condition of ANTICIPATION and lack of NOVELTY. When one compares a single piece of prior art with the claimed invention, if there is an "identity of invention" between the two, then there is anticipation. Nonanticipation is a condition of the patentability of an invention, and "identity of invention" between a prior art reference and the claimed invention must be present for there to be anticipation.

See ANTICIPATION; INHERENCY; THAT WHICH INFRINGES IF LATER, ANTICIPATES IF EARLIER.

• *Case References*:

"A party asserting that a patent claim is anticipated under 35 U.S.C. §102 must demonstrate, among other things, identity of invention…. [O]ne who seeks such a finding must show that each element of the claim in issue is found, either expressly described or under principles of inherency, in a single prior art reference, or that the claimed invention was previously known or embodied in a single prior art device or practice." *Kalman v. Kimberly-Clark Corp.*, 713 F.2d 760, 771, 218 USPQ 781, 789 (Fed. Cir. 1983). Accord *Minnesota Mining & Mfg. v. Johnson & Johnson*, 976 F.2d 1559, 24 USPQ2d 1321 (Fed. Cir. 1992).

"Anticipation requires the presence in a single prior art disclosure of all elements of a claimed invention arranged as in the claim…. A prior art disclosure that 'almost' meets that standard does not 'anticipate.' Though it is never necessary to so hold, a disclosure that

anticipates under §102 also renders the claim invalid under §103, for 'anticipation is the epitome of obviousness'…. The reverse is not true, for the need to determine obviousness presumes anticipation is lacking." *Connell v. Sears, Roebuck & Co.*, 722 F.2d 1542, 1548, 220 USPQ 193, 198 (Fed. Cir. 1983).

• *Treatise Reference*: "Almost is not enough. A prior art disclosure that almost meets the standard of anticipation may render the claim invalid under §103, but it does not anticipate…. There are many ways to express the concept of identity. Anticipation is sometimes said to require that all limitations of a claim be found in a reference or 'fully met' by it…. Basically, anticipation requires identity of invention." R. Harmon, *Patents and the Federal Circuit* §3.2 (3d ed. 1994).

IFRRO [copyright] International Federation of Reproduction Rights Organizations. REPRODUCTION RIGHTS ORGANIZATIONS (RROs), such as the COPYRIGHT CLEARANCE CENTER, are nongovernmental collective licensing organizations composed of copyright owners. An RRO licenses photocopying of members' works by schools, universities, government, and/or private corporations without specific prior permission in return for royalty payments distributed to member copyright owners. The purpose of IFFRO is to facilitate on an international scale the collective administration of reprographic and related electronic, optical, or other reproduction rights in literary, scientific, and artistic works through the cooperation of national reproduction rights organizations.

implied license [patent–trademark copyright] See EXHAUSTION DOCTRINE.

improvement patent [patent]
See COMBINATION.

inconsistent positions, doctrine of [patent] A rule preventing a patent owner from taking a position concerning the scope of the patent claims that is inconsistent with the position taken in a prior patent infringement suit against a different defendant. However, the patent owner is not prevented from taking an inconsistent position if the opposing party in the second lawsuit fails to demonstrate either (1) personal reliance on the decision in the prior lawsuit; (2) prejudice to the defendant as a result of the first decision; or (3) the patent holder's apparent misuse of the court. *Hybritech Inc. v. Abbott Labs.*, 849 F.2d 1446, 1453–54, 7 USPQ2d 1191, 1198 (Fed. Cir. 1988).

incontestable registration [trademark]
See PRESUMPTION OF TRADEMARK VALIDITY.

incremental income approach [patent–trademark] A method of computing LOST PROFITS in determining damages for infringement of a patent or trademark. Under this approach, fixed costs are excluded when calculating profits.

While this approach has been accepted in measuring lost profits as damages in patent infringement cases, it has been rejected in some cases in computing an award of the infringer's profits in trademark infringement cases. *Warner Bros. Inc. v. Gay Toys Inc.*, 598 F. Supp. 424, 223 USPQ 503 (S.D.N.Y. 1984) (rejecting incremental income approach in a trademark case).

Case Reference: "The incremental income approach to the computation of lost profits is well established in the law relating to patent damages.... This approach recognizes that it does not cost as much to produce unit N + 1 if the first N (or fewer) units produced already have paid the fixed costs. Thus fixed costs—those costs which do not vary with increases in products, such as management salaries, property taxes, and insurance—are excluded when determining profits." *Paper Converting Mach. Co. v. Magna-Graphics Corp.*, 745 F.2d 11, 22, 223 USPQ 591, 599 (Fed. Cir. 1984).

indefiniteness of claim [patent] A patent claim will be found invalid if it is "indefinite" in failing to particularly point out and distinctly claim the invention. The test of definiteness is whether a person with SKILL IN THE ART can understand the language of the claim when it is read in light of the SPECIFICATION of the patent.

Importance of Definiteness of a Claim. Definiteness of a claim is important because the claims define the scope of the patent owner's right to exclude others. The trade is entitled to know with reasonable clarity where a patent claim leaves off and the public domain begins. A person skilled in the art should be able to read the claims in light of the whole patent and construct a device that does not infringe the claims.

Relationship Between Claim Definiteness and Operability. Whether an invention described by the claims is operable or not is irrelevant to the issue of whether a patent is sufficiently definite. "The invention's operability may say nothing about a skilled artisan's understanding of the bounds of the claim ... [although it] is possibly relevant, however, to the enablement requirement of §112, ¶ 1, or to utility under §101." *Miles Labs., Inc. v. Shandon Inc.*, 997 F.2d 870, 875, 27 USPQ2d 1123, 1126 (Fed. Cir. 1993).

Issue of Validity. Indefiniteness relates only to the validity of a claim, not to infringement of it. "A claim may be infringed, but the infringer would not be liable if the claim is invalid for indefiniteness under §112." *Kingsdown Medical Consultants Ltd. v. Hollister, Inc.*, 863 F.2d 867, 875 n.10, 9 USPQ2d 1384, 1391 n.10 (Fed. Cir. 1988).

Inexact Yet Definite Terms. Phrases such as "close to," "substantially equal," and "closely approximate" are ubiquitous in patent claims. Such terms will pass the indefiniteness test if they reasonably describe the claimed technology to those skilled in the art and serve to distinguish the claimed invention from the prior art. *Andrew Corp. v. Gabriel Elecs., Inc.*, 847 F.2d 819, 821, 6 USPQ2d 2010, 2012 (Fed. Cir. 1988) (claim containing these terms held to be sufficiently definite).

Claims and Specification. The first and second paragraphs of Patent Code §112 are parallel in that the first paragraph requires clarity in the specification by imposing the enablement requirement, while the second paragraph of §112 requires clarity in the claims by imposing the definiteness requirement.

Patentee Is His Own Lexicographer. In drafting the claims, the inventor may be his own "lexicographer" when there is a need to coin new expressions with which to precisely delineate a new technological development. *ZMI Corp. v. Cardiac Resuscitator Corp.*, 844 F.2d 1576, 6 USPQ2d 1557, 1560 (Fed. Cir. 1988). However, the patent specification must support the new definition of terms.

See CLAIMS, ENABLEMENT.

• *Statutory Reference*: 35 U.S.C. §112, second paragraph: "The specification shall conclude with one or more claims particularly pointing out and distinctly claiming the subject matter which the applicant regards as his invention."

• *Case References*: "The amount of detail required to be included in claims depends on the particular invention and the prior art, and is not to be viewed in the abstract but in conjunction with whether the specification is in compliance with the first paragraph of section 112: 'If the claims, read in the light of the specifications, reasonably apprise those skilled in the art both of the utilization and scope of the invention, and if the language is as precise as the subject matter permits, the courts can demand no more.' " *Shatterproof Glass Corp. v. Libbey-Owens Ford Co.*, 758 F.2d 613, 225 USPQ 634, 641 (Fed. Cir. 1985).

"The public is entitled to know the scope of the claims but must look to both the patent specification and the prosecution history, especially where there is doubt concerning the scope of the claims.... In defining the claimed 'word boost' feature [for a computer], the applicant directed the public to a circuit specifically disclosed in the specification, and also noted that equivalent circuits shown in prior publications would be found easily accessible to those skilled in the art. The claims were not indefinite." *Texas Instruments Inc. v. International Trade Comm'n*, 871 F.2d 1054, 1057, 10 USPQ2d 1257, 1263–64 (Fed. Cir. 1989).

Example of Sufficiently Definite Claim. Gafney invented and patented a form of collapsible pediatric wheelchair, which facilitates the placing of wheelchair-bound persons, particularly children, in and out of an automobile. The contested claim of the patent began: "In a wheel chair having a seat portion, a front leg portion,

and a rear wheel assembly, the improvement wherein said front leg portion is so dimensioned as to be insertable through the space between the door frame of an automobile and one of the seats thereof whereby...." An alleged infringer challenged the validity of the Gafney patent on the ground that use of the phrase "so dimensioned as to be insertable" was so vague and indefinite as to make the claim invalid. The Court of Appeals for the Federal Circuit rejected the challenge, noting that while the claim requires one to measure the space between a selected auto's door frame and seat and then "dimension" the legs of the wheelchair so that they will fit in that space in that particular make of automobile, one of ordinary skill in the art could easily determine the appropriate dimension. The court concluded:

"The claims were intended to cover the use of the invention with various types of automobiles. That a particular chair on which the claims read may fit within some automobiles and not others is of no moment. The phrase 'so dimensioned' is as accurate as the subject matter permits, automobiles being of various sizes.... The patent law does not require that all possible lengths corresponding to the spaces in hundreds of different automobiles be listed in the patent, let alone that they be listed in the claims." *Orthokinetics Inc. v. Safety Travel Chairs Inc.*, 806 F.2d 1565, 1576, 1 USPQ2d 1081, 1088 (Fed. Cir. 1986).

Example of Indefinite Claim. Greene and Godfrey invented a process for manufacturing acrylamide, an organic chemical widely used in various industries, from pollution control to food processing. The key claim in the patent began: "The process for hydrolyzing a nitrile ... comprising contacting said nitrile with water ... in the presence of copper ion, said copper ion being at least partially soluble in water...." It was held that the term "partially soluble" was too vague and imprecise to meet the definiteness requirement because the term had no established meaning to those skilled in the art. "Partially soluble" was neither defined in the patent specification nor was it a generally recognized term in the technology. *Standard Oil Co. v. American Cyanamid Co.*, 585 F. Supp. 1481, 1491, 224 USPQ 210, 217 (E.D. La.

1984), *aff'd on point*, 774 F.2d 448, 227 USPQ 293 (Fed. Cir. 1985).

independent claim [patent]
See DEPENDENT CLAIM.

independent development [patent]
Simultaneous, independent development of an allegedly patentable invention by others in an industry is evidence relevant to help a challenger prove that the invention is obvious and hence unpatentable.

"Secondary Considerations." Independent development is sometimes listed as one of the types of objective evidence of real world recognition of the invention, which are known as SECONDARY CONSIDERATIONS. However, unlike the other types of evidence within that category, independent development is not evidence of nonobviousness, but of the opposite—obviousness—and hence the nonpatentability of the invention. Almost simultaneous invention by others of the same solution to a technical problem supports a finding that the invention was obvious to those in the field.

Reasonably Contemporaneous Invention. While independent development by those other than the inventor is an indication of obviousness, that development must be reasonably contemporaneous with the work of the patentee. Development by competitors of similar technology some years after the filing of the patent application is outside of the "time the invention was made," which is the relevant time specified in 35 U.S.C. §103. *Stewart-Warner Corp. v. City of Pontiac*, 767 F.2d 1563, 226 USPQ 676 (Fed. Cir. 1985).

See SECONDARY CONSIDERATIONS, OBVIOUSNESS.

independent development injunction
[trade secret] See REVERSE ENGINEERING INJUNCTION.

independent inventor [patent] An inventor
who qualifies for a "SMALL ENTITY" discount on the payment of government fees connected with the filing, examination, and maintenance of patents.

An "independent inventor" is defined in 37 C.F.R. §1.9 as an individual who has not assigned or licensed the invention and is not under any contractual obligation to do so to a "nonsmall" entity. An employee of a large company will generally not qualify, because such a person generally has signed an employment agreement requiring the assignment to the employer of all inventions related to the business of the employer.

See SMALL ENTITY.

indication of source [trademark–unfair
competition] A term that refers to the geographic origin of production. This has been distinguished from an APPELLATION OF ORIGIN, which refers to both a product's geographic origin and its distinctive product characteristics caused by particular geographic conditions or methods of production. ROQUEFORT cheese is an example of an appellation of origin because it designates both geographic origin and product characteristics. "Paris" perfume is an indication of source because it refers only to geographic origin. The term GEOGRAPHIC DENOMINATION encompasses both categories.

Ladas suggests that the semantic difficulty between "appellation of origin" and "indication of source" is caused by the lack of direct English translation of the French terms "indications de provenance" (indications of source) and "appellations d'origine" (appellations of origin). "Source" in English does not have the same definite meaning of geographical origin that the word "provenance" has in French. 3 S. Ladas, *Patents, Trademarks and Related Rights: National and International Protection* §842 (1975). The second paragraph of Article 1 of the PARIS CONVENTION includes in the definition of INDUSTRIAL PROPERTY the categories of "indications of source or appellations of origin."

• *Commentary Reference*: "Indications of source and appellations of origin both serve to identify the source or origin of the products or services for which they are used. Appellations of origin, however, have an additional function. Whereas an indication of source shows only from where a product comes, an appellation of origin indicates, in addition, the characteristic qualities of a product which are determined by the geographical area from which it comes and to which the appellation refers." WIPO, *Background Reading Material on Intellectual Property* 14 (1988).

indivisibility of copyright [copyright] A now-obsolete theory that a copyright was an indivisible property right which was not capable of being split up into smaller units and sold or exclusively licensed. The rule of indivisibility was done away with in the 1978 Copyright Act revisions by 17 U.S.C. §201(d)(2). See discussion at LICENSE OF COPYRIGHT.

induce infringement [patent] One who actively aids another person in directly infringing a patent is himself liable for the separate statutory tort of inducement of infringement.

Direct Infringement Is Necessary. There cannot be inducement of infringement unless there is direct infringement. *Met-Coil Sys. Corp. v. Korners Unlimited, Inc.,* 803 F.2d 684, 687, 231 USPQ 474, 477 (Fed. Cir. 1986). That is, the person who is being induced must be a direct infringer of the patent claims. Proof of direct infringement can be either direct or circumstantial.

Knowledge of Direct Infringement. Patent Code §271(b) provides that "whoever actively induces infringement of a patent shall be liable as an infringer." Although the statute does not require that a person "knowingly" aid and abet the direct infringement of another, the case law and legislative history impose the requirements that the alleged infringer's actions induced infringing acts and that he knew or should have known his actions would induce actual infringement. *Manville Sales Co. v. Paramount Sys., Inc.,* 917 F. 2d 544, 553, 16 USPQ 2d 1587, 1594 (Fed. Cir. 1990) (no proof that defendant corporate officers had a specific intent to cause another to infringe).

Synonym: AID OR ABET INFRINGEMENT.

• *Case Reference*: "[I]t is well settled that corporate officers who actively aid and abet their corporation's infringement may be personally liable for inducing infringement under §271(b) regardless of whether the corporation

is the alter ego of the corporate officer." *Orthokinetics Inc. v. Safety Travel Chairs, Inc.,* 806 F.2d 1565, 1578, 1 USPQ2d 1081, 1090 (Fed. Cir. 1986).

• *Example.* Patent claims on the method of solving a Rubik's cube-type puzzle were directly infringed only by the puzzle user. Thus, the puzzle manufacturer could only be guilty of inducement to infringe, not direct infringement, of such a method claim. The manufacturer was found guilty of inducing its customers to directly infringe by circumstantial evidence of direct infringement consisting of "extensive puzzle sales, dissemination of an instruction sheet teaching the method of restoring the preselected pattern with each puzzle and the availability of a solution booklet on how to solve the puzzle." *Moleculon Research Corp. v. CBS, Inc.,* 793 F.2d 1261, 1272, 229 USPQ 805, 813 (Fed. Cir. 1986).

industrial design registration [patent–international] See DESIGN REGISTRATION.

industrial property [patent–trademark] A term once in vogue, but now generally outdated, in the United States, usually understood to designate the fields of patent, trade secret, trademark, and unfair competition laws, but not copyright laws or MORAL RIGHTS. One difficulty with the term is that the word "industrial" is ambiguous and does not unequivocally rule out literary and artistic property, as is intended by most users of the term. As generally defined, "industrial property" includes less ground than INTELLECTUAL PROPERTY and, hence, is intended to designate a narrower field.

• *References*:
"The nature of the rights included in the term 'industrial property,' and their classification in the whole scheme of legal rights, are great questions of juristic speculation, on which an agreement has not yet been reached." 1 S. Ladas, *Patents, Trademarks and Related Rights: National and International Protection* §1 (1975).

"The protection of industrial property has as its object patents, utility models, industrial designs, trademarks, service marks, trade names, indications of source or appellations of origin, and the repression of unfair competition." Paris Convention, Art. 1, Para. (2).

"[T]he expression 'industrial property' has acquired, at least in the European languages, a meaning which clearly covers not only inventions but also [trademarks and similar commercial designations]." WIPO, *Background Reading Material on Intellectual Property* 5 (1988).

inequitable conduct [patent] A variation on the equitable UNCLEAN HANDS defense in which the accused infringer asserts that the patent is not enforceable because the applicant, with the intent to deceive, obtained the patent by misrepresenting or withholding material information from the Patent and Trademark Office or by submitting false and material information to the PTO.

Fraud on the Patent Office. The type of misconduct now called "inequitable conduct" was once known as "fraud on the Patent Office," but the Court of Appeals for the Federal Circuit in the 1980s began using the new label "inequitable conduct." The court said that this was a conscious change made because the "fraud" label was easily confused with other forms of fraud. According to the court, the term "inequitable conduct" "encompasses affirmative acts of commission, e.g., submission of false information, as well as omission, e.g., failure to disclose material information." *J.P. Stevens & Co. v. Lex Tex, Ltd.*, 747 F.2d 1553, 1559, 223 USPQ 1089, 1092 (Fed. Cir. 1984). "Inequitable conduct" is a more neutral and bland phrase than "fraud on the Patent Office," a much more pejorative term. "[B]ut the change of name does not make the thing itself smell any sweeter." *Burlington Indus., Inc. v. Dayco Corp.*, 849 F.2d 1418, 1422, 7 USPQ2d 1158, 1161 (Fed. Cir. 1988).

Effect on Pending Applications. Since 1988, PTO policy has been not to investigate and reject applications for failure to comply with the disclosure obligations of Rule 56.1. The primary reason given for this change in policy was the belief that the PTO is not the best venue for determining the applicant's or her representative's intent to deceive. Patent and Trademark Office Implementation of 37 CFR 1.56, 1095 Official Gazette, Pat. Off. 16 (Oct. 11, 1988). See 5 Chisum, *Patents* §19.03[6] (1994 rev.); R. Harmon, *Patents and the Federal Circuit* §9.5(a) (3d ed. 1994).

Significance of Inequitable Conduct. When inequitable conduct is found after a patent has issued, all claims of the patent are rendered unenforceable, not merely those claims directly affected by the misconduct. In addition, under the doctrine of unclean hands, related patents in suit may also be rendered unenforceable. *Consolidated Aluminum Corp. v. Foseco Int'l Ltd.*, 910 F.2d 804, 810, 15 USPQ 2d 1481, 1487 (Fed. Cir. 1990).

Clear and Convincing Evidence. An accused infringer who asserts unenforceability of a patent based upon fraud or inequitable conduct must prove such conduct by CLEAR AND CONVINCING evidence.

State of Mind and Materiality of the Information. The challenger must make a threshold showing that the information misrepresented or withheld was material and that the applicant acted with the required kind of intent. The two key ingredients of inequitable conduct are "materiality" and "intent." These two are interrelated. A showing of a high degree of materiality can create an inference that the failure to disclose was willful, while a specific showing of wrongful intent can lower the standard of materiality. *Kimberly-Clark Corp. v. Johnson & Johnson*, 745 F.2d 1437, 1455, 223 USPQ 603, 614–15 (Fed. Cir. 1984). That is, the more material the omitted or misrepresented information, the less intent that must be shown to reach a conclusion of inequitable conduct. The stronger the proof of intent, the less material need be the information omitted or misrepresented. *Akzo N.V. v. E.I. du Pont de Nemours*, 810 F.2d 1148, 1153, 1 USPQ2d 1704, 1708 (Fed. Cir. 1987).

Materiality of the Information. There has been uncertainty as to the correct test for "materiality" of the information misrepresented to or withheld from the Patent and Trademark Office. However, a threshold test often used is that information is material if there is a substantial likelihood that a reasonable patent examiner would have considered it important in deciding whether to issue a patent. *Specialty Composites v. Cabot Corp.*, 845 F.2d 981, 992, 6 USPQ2d

1601, 1608 (Fed. Cir. 1988); *Molins PLC v. Textron, Inc.*, 48 F3d 1172, 33 USPQ 2d 1823, 1827 (Fed. Cir. 1995). Nondisclosed information can be "material" under this test even though, if disclosed, the information would not have rendered the invention unpatentable. That is, the test is not whether the patent would not have been granted "but for" the nondisclosure of the data. *Merck & Co. v. Danbury Pharmacal, Inc.*, 873 F.2d 1418, 10 USPQ2d 1682 (Fed. Cir. 1989). The 1992 version of Rule 1.56 defines materiality as information that establishes, by itself or in combination with other information, a prima facie case of unpatentability of a claim or information that refutes or is inconsistent with a position taken by the applicant before the PTO. 37 C.F.R. §1.56(b) (applicable to all applications pending or filed after March 16, 1992).

State of Mind and Intent. Intent need not be proven by direct evidence. It may be proven by showing acts the natural consequences of which were presumably foreseen by the actor. A finding that certain conduct amounts to "gross negligence" does not of itself justify an inference of an intent to deceive: the conduct in view of all the evidence, including exculpatory evidence of good faith, must "indicate sufficient culpability to require a finding of intent to deceive." *Kingsdown Medical Consultants Ltd. v. Hollister Inc.*, 863 F.2d 867, 876, 9 USPQ2d 1384, 1392 (Fed. Cir. 1988). Thus, grossly negligent conduct may or may not lead to an inference of intent to mislead. Mere evidence of simple negligence, oversight, or an erroneous judgment made in good faith is insufficient proof of the requisite intent. *Atlas Powder Co. v. E.I. du Pont de Nemours & Co.*, 750 F.2d 1569, 1578, 224 USPQ 409, 415 (Fed. Cir. 1984).

Unfounded Charges of Inequitable Conduct. The Court of Appeals for the Federal Circuit has indicated that it has little patience with unfounded charges of inequitable conduct in the procurement of a patent, saying that "the habit of charging inequitable conduct in almost every major patent case has become an absolute plague." *Burlington Indus., Inc. v. Dayco Corp.*, 849 F.2d 1418, 1422, 7 USPQ2d 1158, 1161 (Fed. Cir. 1988).

Synonym: FRAUD ON THE PATENT OFFICE. See INFORMATION DISCLOSURE STATEMENT.

• *Case References*: "The concept of inequitable conduct in patent procurement derives from the equitable doctrine of unclean hands: that a person who obtains a patent by intentionally misleading the PTO cannot enforce the patent. Inequitable conduct may be held although the common law elements of fraud are absent. To achieve a just application of this penalty in the variety of situations that may arise, this court established a balancing test ... whereby the materiality of the information that was not provided to the PTO is weighed against the intent of the actor." *Demaco Corp. v. F. Von Langsdorff Licensing Ltd.*, 851 F.2d 1387, 1394–95, 7 USPQ2d 1222, 1228 (Fed. Cir. 1988).

"The withholding of information must meet thresholds of both materiality and intent.... Once threshold findings of materiality and intent are established, the court must weigh them to determine whether the equities warrant a conclusion that inequitable conduct has occurred.... In light of all the circumstances, an equitable judgment must be made concerning whether the applicant's conduct is so culpable that the patent should not be enforced." *Molins PLC v. Textron, Inc.*, 48 F.3d 1172, 1178, 33 USPQ2d 1823, 1826–27 (Fed. Cir. 1995).

" 'Inequitable conduct' is not, or should not, be a magic incantation to be asserted against every patentee. Nor is that allegation established upon a mere showing that art or information having some degree of materiality was not disclosed. To be guilty of inequitable conduct, one must have intended to act inequitably. Thus, one who alleges a 'failure to disclose' form of inequitable conduct must offer clear and convincing proof of (1) prior art or information that is material; (2) knowledge chargeable to applicant of that prior art or information and of its materiality; and (3) failure of the applicant to disclose the art or information resulting from an intent to mislead the PTO. That proof may be rebutted by a showing that (a) the prior art or information was not material (e.g., because it is less pertinent than or merely cumulative with prior art or information cited to or by the PTO);

(b) if the prior art or information was material, a showing that applicant did not know of that art or information; (c) if applicant did know of that art or information, a showing that applicant did not know of its materiality; (d) a showing that applicant's failure to disclose art or information did not result from an intent to mislead the PTO." *FMC Corp. v. Manitowoc Co.*, 835 F.2d 1411, 1415, 5 USPQ2d 1112, 1115 (Fed. Cir. 1987).

"As a general rule, there is no duty to conduct a prior art search, and thus there is no duty to disclose art of which an applicant could have been aware.... However, one should not be able to cultivate ignorance, or disregard numerous warnings that material information or prior art may exist, merely to avoid actual knowledge of that information or prior art. When one does that, the 'should have known' factor becomes operative." *FMC Corp. v. Hennessy Indus. Inc.*, 836 F.2d 521, 526 n.6, 5 USPQ2d 1272, 1275 n.6 (Fed. Cir. 1987).

"The defense of inequitable conduct in a patent suit, being entirely equitable in nature, is not an issue for a jury to decide. ... [T]he decision respecting inequitable conduct is a discretionary decision to be made by the judge on his or her own factual findings. Thus, a disputed finding of intent to mislead or deceive is one for the judge to resolve, not the jury, albeit not on summary judgment if there is a genuine dispute. A patentee has no right to a jury trial respecting the factual element of culpable intent as part of the defense of inequitable conduct." *Paragon Podiatry Lab. v. KLM Labs., Inc.*, 984 F.2d 1182, 1190, 25 USPQ 1561, 1568 (Fed. Cir. 1993).

• *Rule Reference*: 37 CFR §1.56(a) (1992 rev.) "...Each individual associated with the filing and prosecution of a patent application has a duty of candor and good faith in dealing with the Office, which includes a duty to disclose to the Office all information known to that individual to be material to patentability. ... [N]o patent will be granted on an application in connection with which fraud on the Office was practiced or attempted or the duty of disclosure was violated through bad faith or intentional misconduct...."

• *Treatise Reference*: "The Federal Circuit has been very active in the area of fraud, or as it prefers to call it, 'inequitable conduct,' that is alleged to have occurred during the prosecution of patent applications before the PTO. A careful review of this activity leaves one with the distinct impression that the court will scrutinize charges of fraud very closely and will be disinclined to uphold an inequitable conduct defense in the absence of truly egregious conduct, such as falsification of data, or an admission of intent to deceive." R. Harmon, *Patents and the Federal Circuit* §9.5[a] (3d ed. 1994).

"Although a duty of candor applies to all contacts with the Patent and Trademark Office during the course of the prosecution of an application for a patent, areas of particular concern are (1) the statutory oath of inventorship, particularly as it relates to the question of prior public use by the inventor or his assignee; (2) the citation of known relevant prior art; (3) the use of affidavits concerning the date of invention; and (4) the use of affidavits presenting factual evidence on patentability." 5 Chisum, *Patents* §19.03[2] (1994 rev.).

• *Example 1: Inequitable Conduct Found.* Herst and Ngai, employees of the Peerless Electric Co., invented and patented a form of indirect-lighting fixture. In litigation, the district court found that the failure of Peerless during the pendency of the application to disclose to the Patent and Trademark Office prior art in the form of lighting fixtures previously advertised and sold by Peerless constituted inequitable conduct. While refusing to find that the applicants had intentionally misled the PTO, the district court did find that they were grossly negligent in not disclosing this relevant data to the PTO. The Court of Appeals for the Federal Circuit found that the district court correctly weighed materiality and gross negligence and affirmed the finding of inequitable conduct and unenforceability of the patent. The court remarked that "[i]n determining the equitable conduct issue, a district court need not make explicit findings on whether undisclosed art anticipates the claimed invention or whether it would have rendered the claimed invention obvious...." Thus, inequitable conduct can be found even where the claims were not held unpatentable over the undisclosed prior art. *Gardco Mfg. Corp. v. Herst Lighting Co.*, 820 F.2d 1209, 2 USPQ2d 2015 (Fed. Cir. 1987).

• *Example 2: Inequitable Conduct Found.* In the prosecution of a patent on a form of orthotic shoe inserts, the inventor's attorney presented three affidavits from professionals in the field who attested to the advantages of the invention over prior art devices. The Patent Office examiner was under the impression that these were "disinterested" affiants in view of the statement in each affidavit that: "I have not been in the past employed by nor do I intend in the future to become employed by the Paragon Podiatry Laboratories, a corporation which I understand is the assignee of the interest in the above captioned patent application." In fact, each of the affiants were stockholders in Paragon and one of them had been a paid consultant for Paragon. The Federal Circuit said that it agreed with the district court that an inference of intent to deceive the PTO was "strongly supported by the submission of these deceptive affidavits." Inequitable conduct was also found by applicant's failure to disclose precritical date commercial sales of the patented device. These two types of inequitable conduct were held sufficient to result in a summary judgment that the patent was unenforceable. *Paragon Podiatry Lab. v. KLM Labs., Inc.*, 984 F.2d 1182, 25 USPQ 1561 (Fed. Cir. 1993).

• *Example 3: No Inequitable Conduct Found.* Allen invented and patented a form of compound bow used in archery for hunting. An accused infringer argued that the patent was not enforceable because during the pendency of the application, the inventor failed to disclose the Wilkerson prior art patent to the patent examiner. During prosecution of the patent, Allen's patent attorney became aware of the Wilkerson patent and showed it to inventor Allen. Allen replied that the bow disclosed in Wilkerson was radically different from his invention. The district court found that the Wilkerson patent was in fact not material, that Allen and his patent attorney held a good faith belief that the Wilkerson patent was not material, and that there was no negligence or misconduct in failing to bring

the Wilkerson reference to the attention of the PTO. The Court of Appeals for the Federal Circuit affirmed the finding of no inequitable conduct, remarking that subjective good faith is always a relevant defense. *Allen Archery Inc. v. Browning Mfg. Co.*, 819 F.2d 1087, 2 USPQ2d 1490 (Fed. Cir. 1987).

information disclosure statement

[patent] A disclosure filed by an applicant for patent revealing PRIOR ART and other information that is material to the examination of the application. The statement is filed to comply with the duty of candor and good faith imposed on applicants for patent in 37 C.F.R. §1.56. This duty can be complied with by the filing of an information disclosure statement as provided for in 37 C.F.R. §§1.97–.98. An information disclosure statement includes a listing of patents, publications, or other relevant data, with a concise explanation of the relevance of each reference disclosed. The statement must be accompanied by a copy of each listed patent, publication, or other item. 37 C.F.R. §1.98(a).

See INEQUITABLE CONDUCT.

• *Rule References*:

"The [information disclosure] statement shall serve as a representation that the person preparing it has included therein what he or she believes to be the closest prior art or other information of which he or she is aware and shall not be construed as a representation that no better art exists or that a search has been made." *Manual of Patent Examining Procedure* §609 (1994).

"Applicants and other individuals substantively involved with the preparation and/or prosecution of a patent application have a duty to submit to the Office information which is material to patentability as defined in 37 CFR 1.56. ... An information disclosure statement filed in accordance with the provisions of 37 CFR 1.97 and 1.98 provides the procedure available to an applicant to submit information to the Office so that the information will be considered by the examiner assigned to the application." *Manual of Patent Examining Procedure* §609 (1994).

infringement [general intellectual property] An invasion of one of the exclusive rights of intellectual property.

The Nature of Exclusive Rights. Inherent in the institution of property in intellectual creations is the concept of exclusive rights: the owner of intellectual property owns certain rights exclusive to that person or firm. This means that the owner has the right to exclude. That is, the legal system will exclude others who without permission perform actions that invade those exclusive rights. For example, a U.S. patent gives to the patent owner the right in the United States to exclude others from making, using, selling, offering to sell, and importing products or processes covered by the claims of the patent. For example, one who without a license uses or sells an object that contains a part covered by the patent is committing patent infringement. On the other hand, a trademark gives to the owner the right to exclude others who are using a similar mark that is likely to confuse. Others who are without a license and make a use likely to confuse are committing trademark infringement.

Public Domain Is the Rule: Intellectual Property Is the Exception. Constant emphasis on protection of exclusive rights in legal analysis often obscures the basic principle of U.S. law that the principle of free copying of things in the public domain is the general rule. *Bonito Boats Inc. v. Thunder Craft Boats Inc.*, 489 U.S. 141, 151, 9 USPQ2d 1847, 1852 (1989). Legally protected areas of exclusive rights—such as patents, trademarks, and copyrights—are properly viewed as exceptions to the general rule of free copying and imitation.

See PUBLIC DOMAIN.

The Dimensions of Infringement Differ With Each Intellectual Property Right. When another person commits acts that invade the scope of the owner's intellectual property right, that is an "infringement." Each type of intellectual property has its own dimensions that define the kind of actions which constitute infringement. Actions that infringe a patent may or may not infringe a copyright or a trademark.

Analogy. Infringement is similar to a "trespass" on real estate. Legally defined rights in both fields of law are invaded by one who uses the property without permission. Real property can be rented out to a tenant. Intellectual property can be licensed to a licensee. Infringement of intellectual property is also a tort.

1. Infringement of a Utility Patent. A person or corporation who without permission makes, uses, sells, offers to sell, or imports a product or process covered by a claim of a patent is an infringer. 35 U.S.C. §271(a). It is only the CLAIMS of a patent that define what is an infringement of the patent. It is not proper to try to find the GIST of a patented invention or the HEART OF THE INVENTION and then compare that to the accused device, unless one is following the rules used in applying the DOCTRINE OF EQUIVALENTS. Each claim of a patent defines a separate exclusive right. One claim of a patent can be infringed without another claim being infringed.

Types of Infringement. The determination of direct patent infringement is a two-step process: (1) there must be a precise definition of what is patented; i.e., the language of the patent claim must be interpreted to delineate its precise scope and meaning; and (2) it must be determined if the claim as interpreted encompasses the accused product or process. There are two ways that the claim can encompass the accused product or process: (1) the claim reads on the ACCUSED DEVICE under the test of LITERAL INFRINGEMENT if each and every element of a claim is found in the accused product; or (2) the accused product or process is an infringement under the doctrine of equivalents if it performs substantially the same function in substantially the same way to obtain the same result as the claimed invention. These are forms of direct infringement. There can also be CONTRIBUTORY INFRINGEMENT, and it is also illegal to INDUCE INFRINGEMENT.

Copying Is Not Necessary. There is no requirement that an infringer of a patent copy the patentee's device (if any) or even be aware of the existence of the patent. A product or process that is the result of purely independent development is still infringing if it is covered by the claim of a patent.

Off-Shore Assembly. While generally only activities within the United States can infringe a U.S. patent, in some cases OFF-SHORE ASSEM-BLY can also infringe a U.S. patent. The traditional trilogy of exclusive rights of a patent (make, use, or sell) was expanded by the 1994 URUGUAY ROUND AGREEMENTS ACT to include importing into the United States and offering for sale in the United States as types of infringement.

See PATENT.

- *Case References*:

"This court has repeatedly stated that direct infringement requires a two-step analysis. The claimed invention must first be defined, a legal question of claim interpretation. Second, the trier of fact must determine whether the claims, as properly interpreted, cover the accused device or process. The second step involves a question of fact.... The burden is on ... the patent owner to prove infringement by a preponderance of the evidence.... Such proof must show that every limitation of the patent claims asserted to be infringed is found in the accused device, either literally or by an equivalent." *Smithkline Diagnostics Inc. v. Helena Labs. Corp.*, 859 F.2d 878, 889, 8 USPQ2d 1468, 1477 (Fed. Cir. 1988).

"Infringement, literal or by equivalence, is determined by comparing an accused product not with a preferred embodiment described in the specification, or with a commercialized embodiment of the patentee, but with the properly and previously construed claims in suit." *SRI Int'l v. Matsushita Elec. Corp. of Am.*, 775 F.2d 1107, 1121, 227 USPQ 577, 586 (Fed. Cir. 1985).

Title 35, §271(a) of the U.S. Code "incorporates the disjunctive language of the statutory patent grant which gives a patentee the 'right to exclude others from making, using or selling' a patented invention, 35 U.S.C. §154.... It is beyond argument that performance of only *one* of the three enumerated activities is patent infringement." *Roche Prods., Inc. v. Bolar Pharmaceutical Co.*, 733 F.2d 858, 861, 221 USPQ 937, 939 (Fed. Cir. 1984).

2. Infringement of a Design Patent. Unlike a utility patent, a design patent has no word CLAIMS. The picture of the design in the patent must be compared with the appearance of the ACCUSED DEVICE. The test of infringement is the classic *Gorham* test of deception in the eye of the ordinary observer, supplemented by the "point of novelty" test. Since a design patent does not cover FUNCTIONAL aspects of appearance, they cannot form the basis for infringement. Unlike utility patents, Patent Code §289 provides that the owner of a design patent can obtain the remedy of the infringer's profits.

See PROFITS.

The Gorham *Test.* The test laid down by the U.S. Supreme Court in the 1871 *Gorham* case remains the basic test for infringement of a design patent. The test requires that "if, in the eye of an ordinary observer, giving such attention as a purchaser usually gives, two designs are substantially the same, if the resemblance is such as to deceive such an observer, inducing him to purchase one supposing it to be the other, the first one patented is infringed by the other." *Gorham Co. v. White*, 81 U.S. 511, 528 (1871). While this test closely resembles the "likelihood of confusion" test of trademark infringement, it is not the same. There is no requirement that there be confusion as to the source of the goods since there is no requirement that the patent owner have used its design in the marketplace at all. *Unette Corp. v. Unit Pack Co.*, 785 F.2d 1026, 1029, 228 USPQ 933, 934 (Fed. Cir. 1986).

The "Point of Novelty" Test. This is a supplementary test of infringement of a design patent under which the accused device must take the novelty in the patented design that distinguishes it from the prior art. See POINT OF NOVELTY. Similarly, since a design patent does not encompass functional design aspects, an accused device that takes only functional aspects is not an infringement.

See FUNCTIONALITY.

- *Case Reference*: "Design patents do not and cannot include claims to the structural or functional aspects of the article.... Thus it is the non-functional, design aspects that are pertinent to determinations of infringement.... [A] design patent is not a substitute for a utility patent. A device that copies the utilitarian or functional features of a patented design is not an infringement unless the ornamental aspects are also copied, such that the overall 'resemblance is such as to deceive.' " *Lee v. Dayton-Hudson Corp.*, 838 F.2d 1186, 1188–89, 5 USPQ2d 1625, 1626–27 (Fed. Cir. 1988).

3. Infringement of a Trademark. Classic infringement of a mark consists of a junior user's use of a similar mark that creates a likelihood of confusion. Likelihood of confusion is the test of infringement of: (1) a federally registered mark under Lanham Act §32(a), 15 U.S.C. §1114(a); (2) unregistered marks and trade dress under Lanham Act §43(a), 15 U.S.C. §1125(a); (3) unregistered marks and trade dress under state common law; and (4) state registered marks. Likelihood of confusion with a previously registered or used mark is a ground for Patent and Trademark Office refusal to register a mark under Lanham Act §2(d), 15 U.S.C. §1052(d), as well as a ground for an OPPOSITION PROCEEDING or a CANCELLATION PROCEEDING.

Nature of Infringement. Trademark infringement is a type of UNFAIR COMPETITION. 1 J.T. McCarthy, *Trademarks and Unfair Competition* §2.02 (3d ed. 1995 rev.). Both trademark infringement and unfair competition are commercial torts. See TORT. All who act together to infringe a mark are liable as joint tortfeasors. See CONTRIBUTORY INFRINGEMENT.

Proof of Likelihood of Confusion. There are at least three types of proof of likelihood of confusion: (1) SURVEY evidence; (2) evidence of actual confusion; and (3) an argument based on an inference arising from a judicial comparison of the conflicting marks themselves and the context of their use in the marketplace. In a close case amounting to a tie, doubts are resolved in favor of the senior user. The majority of federal circuits view a finding on the likelihood of confusion issue as a finding of fact not reversible on appeal unless "clearly erroneous" under Federal Rule of Civil Procedure 52(a).

Factors to Consider in Judging Likelihood of Confusion. Each federal court of appeals has devised its own variation of a list of factors to be considered and weighed in judging infringement by a likelihood of confusion. For example, in the Second Circuit, the list is known as the *"Polaroid Factors."* The eight *"Polaroid Factors"* are: (1) strength of the mark; (2) degree of

similarity between the conflicting marks; (3) proximity of the goods or services; (4) likelihood that the senior user will bridge any gap between the goods or services of the parties; (5) actual confusion; (6) the junior user's good faith in choosing its marks; (7) the quality of the junior user's product; and (8) the sophistication of buyers. Originally conceived to apply only to cases of noncompeting goods, the *Polaroid* test now applies to all infringement cases. *Banff, Ltd. v. Federated Dep't Stores, Inc.*, 841 F.2d 486, 6 USPQ2d 1187 (2d Cir. 1988). The other circuits have devised very similar lists of factors. See 3 J.T. McCarthy, *Trademarks and Unfair Competition* §24.06[4] (3d ed. 1995 rev.).

Number of Persons Likely to Be Confused. A "likelihood" of confusion is synonymous with a "probability" of confusion. If a significant or appreciable number of prospective buyers are likely to be confused by the similar marks, then there is a likelihood of confusion and infringement of the mark. The courts have generally avoided deciding whether an "appreciable" number of buyers is to be measured by absolute numbers or a percentage. Survey evidence of as low as 11-percent confused persons has been held sufficient to corroborate a finding of a likelihood of confusion. Even a small percentage, if projected against a large universe of potential customers, would produce a large number of confused persons. *Quality Inns Int'l Inc. v. McDonald's Corp.*, 695 F. Supp. 198, 8 USPQ2d 1633 (D. Md. 1988).

Whose Confusion and About What. In most cases, the likely confusion of purchasers or prospective purchasers is the issue. But in some cases the persons confused would not be the purchaser, but others who view the goods after purchase. The person who buys a $20 counterfeit ROLEX watch at a flea market knows that it is a fake, but friends and the recipient of it as a gift do not know that. Such confusion of nonpurchasers is actionable. *United States v. Torkington*, 812 F.2d 1347, 2 USPQ2d 1292 (11th Cir. 1987). Confusion means more than that the junior user's mark merely "calls to mind" or is "reminiscent of" the senior user's mark. 2 J.T. McCarthy, *Trademarks and Unfair Competition* §23.01[4][e] (3d ed. 1995 rev.). Confusion need not be confusion that the junior user's goods or services come from the same source as that of the senior user's. Actionable confusion also includes confusion of connection, affiliation, or sponsorship between the parties. The trademark owner has protection against another's use of its mark on any product or service that would reasonably be thought to come from the same source or thought to be affiliated with, connected with, or sponsored by the trademark owner. 3 J.T. McCarthy, *Trademarks and Unfair Competition* §24.03 (3d ed. 1995 rev.). REVERSE CONFUSION is also actionable as a form of infringement.

Actual Confusion. The trigger of infringement is proof of the "likelihood of confusion," not the proof of "actual" confusion. The plaintiff is not required to prove any instances of actual confusion, especially since such evidence is often very difficult to come by. However, any evidence of instances of actual confusion is very strong proof of the fact of a likelihood of confusion. Proof that there was a long period of concurrent use of the conflicting marks with no known instances of actual confusion is some evidence that there will likely be no confusion in the future.

Evaluating Similarity Between the Marks. Conflicting marks are usually compared by the trilogy of sight, sound, and meaning. Where the goods and services are directly competitive, the degree of similarity required for infringement is less than in the case of dissimilar products. Under the "anti-dissection" rule, conflicting marks are to be compared in their entireties, not split up into component parts and only the parts compared. See COMPOSITE MARK. However, it is not a violation of the anti-dissection rule to separately view the component parts of a composite as a preliminary on the way to an ultimate determination of probable customer reaction to the conflicting composites as a whole. It is appropriate in determining the confusion issue to give greater weight to the "dominant" part of a composite mark, for it is that which may make the greatest impression on the ordinary customer. Similarly, it is appropriate to downplay the similarity of generic or highly descriptive portions of conflicting marks.

Dilution. Infringement of a mark by "dilution" is a totally different kind of legal theory than infringement by a likelihood of confusion. See DILUTION.

See CONTRIBUTORY INFRINGEMENT, STRENGTH OF MARK, SECONDARY MEANING, FAMILY OF MARKS, GENERIC NAME, FUNCTIONALITY, DILUTION.

- *Treatise Reference*: J.T. McCarthy, *Trademarks and Unfair Competition* §§23.01–.35, 24.01–.12 (3d ed. 1995 rev.).

- *Case References*:

"It is so easy for the honest business man, who wishes to sell his goods upon their merits, to select from the entire material universe, which is before him, symbols, marks and coverings which by no possibility can cause confusion between his goods and those of competitors, that the courts look with suspicion upon one who, in dressing his goods for the market, approaches so near to his successful rival that the public may fail to distinguish between them." *Florence Mfg. Co. v. J.C. Dowd & Co.*, 178 F. 73, 75 (2d Cir. 1910).

"In the consideration of evidence relating to trademark infringement, therefore, a court must expand the more frequent, one-on-one, contest-between-two sides, approach. A third party, the consuming public, is present, and its interests are paramount. Hence, infringement is found when the evidence indicates a likelihood of confusion, deception or mistake on the part of the consuming public.... A 'trademark' is not that which is infringed. What is infringed is the right of the public to be free of confusion and the synonymous right of a trademark owner to control his product's reputation." Chief Judge Markey in *James Burrough Ltd. v. Sign of Beefeater, Inc.*, 540 F.2d 266, 274, 192 USPQ 555, 561–62 (7th Cir. 1976).

4. Infringement of a Copyright. One who violates any one of the five exclusive rights of copyright is an infringer. 17 U.S.C. §501(a). These are the exclusive rights: (1) to reproduce the copyrighted work; (2) to prepare derivative works based on the copyrighted work; (3) to distribute copies or phonorecords of the copyrighted work to the public; (4) to perform the work publicly; and (5) to display the copyrighted work publicly. 17 U.S.C. §106.

Substantial Similarity of Expression. To prove a case of copyright infringement, the plaintiff must prove both ownership of a valid copyright and infringement of that copyright by invasion of one of the five exclusive rights. However, the work that the defendant is reproducing, adapting, distributing, performing, or displaying must be a copy of the copyrighted work. But exact, word-for-word, line-for-line identity does not mark the limit of copyright infringement. The courts have chosen the flexible phrase "SUBSTANTIAL SIMILARITY" to define that level of similarity which will, together with proof of validity and COPYING, constitute copyright infringement. The "substantial similarity" that must exist must be similarity of expression, not merely similarity of ideas or concepts, for copyright law does not protect an idea, concept, system, and the like. 17 U.S.C. §102(b). This is known as the "IDEA-EXPRESSION DICHOTOMY." Also, stock backgrounds and incidents are not protected from copying under the "SCÈNES À FAIRE" rule.

Copying Is Necessary. The accused work must have been "copied" from the copyrighted work, as opposed to the similarity being the result of coincidental, independent production or a taking from the same prior source as was the copyrighted work. The requirement of copying distinguishes infringement of copyright from infringement of PATENTS and TRADEMARKS, neither of which require proof of copying.

Causes of Similarity. In an infringement suit, similarity between the works will usually be due to one of three possible scenarios: (1) the defendant had access to the plaintiff's work and copied from it, either consciously or unconsciously; (2) the defendant did not copy from the plaintiff's work and independent creation has resulted in a work that is coincidentally similar; or (3) both the plaintiff and the defendant based their works on a common prior source. To prove copyright infringemment, the plaintiff must prove that the similarity is the result of the first scenario.

Circumstantial Evidence of Copying. Direct evidence of copying is rare indeed, for copying can be accomplished with little physical manifestation. Usually, copying is proven by circumstantial evidence. Evidence that the accused work was the result of copying usually consists of proof that (1) the defendant had ACCESS to the copyrighted work and (2) the defendant's work is substantially similar to the copyrighted work.

See COPYING IN COPYRIGHT LAW and ACCESS.

Unconscious Infringement. Copyright infringement need not be intentional and can be unconscious or subconscious. Because what one has seen or heard may be unconsciously stored in human memory, it is quite possible to copy without being conscious of the fact. See 3 *Nimmer on Copyright* §13.08 (1994 rev.).

See ACCESS, COPYING IN COPYRIGHT LAW, SUBSTANTIAL SIMILARITY, UNCONSCIOUS INFRINGEMENT, SCÈNES À FAIRE.

• *Treatise References*: M. Leaffer, *Understanding Copyright* §9.1 *et seq.* (1989); 3 *Nimmer on Copyright* §13.01 *et seq.* (1994 rev.); 2 P. Goldstein, *Copyright* §7.1 *et seq.* (1989).

5. Infringement of a Trade Secret. Unlike patent law, trade secret law does not afford protection against all who obtain or use the protected technical knowledge. Only improper methods of obtaining trade secret information constitute infringement or misappropriation of a trade secret. The classic improper and illegal methods of uncovering the trade secret information are: (1) industrial espionage, such as theft by breaking and entering or by electronic eavesdropping or wire tapping; (2) bribery, such as bribing an employee to breach a confidence and disclose information; (3) misrepresentation, such as obtaining data by misrepresenting oneself as an agent of a supplier of materials; and (4) breach of an explicit or implied contract or duty to maintain confidentiality, such as disclosure or use by an employee or a licensee under a promise not to disclose. In addition, there are other methods that may be improper under the circumstances, such as aerial photography of a competitor's chemical plant while it is in the process of construction. *E.I. du Pont de Nemours & Co., Inc. v. Christopher*, 431 F.2d 1012, 166 USPQ 421 (5th Cir. 1970).

See TRADE SECRET.

inherency [patent] A doctrine of patent law under which an unstated aspect of the prior art is treated as if it were expressly divulged because it is "inherent" in the prior art disclosure as a matter of scientific fact.

The Nature of Inherency. Those things that will always flow naturally from that which is disclosed in a prior art reference are regarded as being inherent and hence disclosed. "By disclosing in a patent application a device that inherently performs a function, operates according to a theory, or has an advantage, a patent applicant necessarily discloses that function, theory or advantage even though he says nothing concerning it." *Application of Smythe,* 480 F.2d 1376, 1384, 178 USPQ 279, 285 (C.C.P.A. 1973).

Anticipation. A challenger who argues that a patent claim is invalid as being anticipated under Patent Code §102 by a single piece of prior art must prove that each element of the claim is disclosed, either in so many words or by the rule of inherency, in that single piece of prior art. That is, there must be an IDENTITY OF INVENTION between the invention in question and what is disclosed in the prior art.

New Use for Old Product. One aspect of the rule of inherency is the maxim that one cannot obtain a product claim of a patent based on the discovery of a new use for an old product. That is, all uses of a product are deemed to be inherent in it. For example, the U.S. Supreme Court invalidated a patent for a frosted light bulb because the prior art disclosed the design of the bulb, even though the prior art did not disclose an advantage of the bulb that made it most useful—its strength. "If A without mentioning the element of strength patented a bulb which was extra strong, B could not obtain a patent on the bulb because of its strength, though he was the first to recognize that feature of it." *General Elec. Co. v. Jewel Incandescent Lamp Co.,* 326 U.S. 242, 247, 67 USPQ 155, 157 (1945). "The discovery of a new property or use of a previously known composition, even when that property and use are unobvious from the prior art, can not impart patentability to claims to the known composition." *In re Spada,* 911 F.2d 705, 708, 15 USPQ2d 1655, 1657 (Fed. Cir. 1990). "Congress has not seen fit to permit the

patenting of an old alloy, known to others through a printed publication, by one who has discovered its corrosion resistance or other useful properties...." *Titanium Metals Corp. v. Banner,* 778 F.2d 775, 782, 227 USPQ 773, 778 (Fed. Cir. 1985).

Process Claims for New Use for Old Product. One may obtain a PROCESS CLAIM for a novel process which consists of making a new use of an old product. *Dawson Chem. Co. v. Rohm and Haas Co.,* 448 U.S. 176, 206 USPQ 386 (1980) (patent on method of applying a chemical as a selective herbicide in the cultivation of rice); *Loctite Corp. v. Ultraseal Ltd.,* 781 F.2d 861, 875, 228 USPQ 90, 99 (Fed. Cir. 1985) ("Even if a composition is old, a process using a known composition in a new and unobvious way may be patentable."). But when a process claim for a new use of an old product is obtained, the patent extends only to that use, and not to the product itself. If the "old" product is currently protected by a patent, the new use patent does not include a right to use the old product, and one must get permission from the product patentee in order to practice the use covered by the process patent.

See ANTICIPATION, IDENTITY OF INVENTION.

• *Case References:*
"Under the principles of inherency, if a structure in the prior art necessarily functions in accordance with the limitations of a process or method claim of an application, the claim is anticipated. This is not to say that the discovery of a new use for an old structure based on unknown properties of the structure might not be patentable to the discoverer as a process.... [T]he law is, and long has been, that 'if a previously patented device, in its normal and usual operation will perform the function which an applicant claims in a subsequent application for a process patent, then such application for process patent will be considered to have been anticipated by the former patented device.' " *In re King,* 801 F.2d 1324, 1326, 231 USPQ 136, 138 (Fed. Cir. 1986).

"Inherency, however, may not be established by probabilities or possibilities. The mere fact that a certain thing *may* result from a given set of circumstances is not sufficient.... If, however, the disclosure is sufficient to show that the natural result flowing from the operation as taught would result in the performance of the questioned function, it seems to be well settled that the disclosure should be regarded as sufficient." *Hansgirg v. Kemmer*, 102 F.2d 212, 214, 40 USPQ 665, 667 (C.C.P.A. 1939), quoted with approval in *In re Oelrich*, 666 F.2d 578, 581, 212 USPQ 323, 326 (C.C.P.A. 1981).

"A product claim describes an article, new and useful.... [I]n the present case, the prior art discloses the method of making an article having the characteristics of the patented product, though all the advantageous properties of the product had not been fully appreciated.... Pipkin found latent qualities in an old discovery and adapted it to a useful end. But that did not advance the frontiers of science in this narrow field so as to satisfy the exacting standards of our patent system. Where there has been use of an article or where the method of its manufacture is known, more than a new advantage of the product must be discovered in order to claim invention.... It is not invention to perceive that the product which others had discovered had qualities they failed to detect." *General Elec. Co. v. Jewel Incandescent Lamp Co.*, 326 U.S. 242, 248–49, 67 USPQ 155, 157–58 (1945).

"The compound appellants are attempting to patent is not new—the use they discovered is, and they received a method patent for that. Their complaint that this is insufficient because their reward should be consistent with the full extent of their contribution is hollow. Their contribution was finding a use for the compound, not discovering the compound itself. Therefore they are being rewarded fully for their contribution; any more would be a gratuity." *In re Schoenwald*, 964 F.2d 1122, 1124, 22 USPQ2d 1671, 1673 (Fed. Cir. 1992).

- *Treatise Reference*: "Although inherency is usually encountered in the §102 [anticipation] setting, it can also arise in the context of [the obviousness test of] §103.... If the inherency does not result in anticipation, then one must ask whether the inherency would have been obvious." R. Harmon, *Patents and the Federal Circuit* §3.2 (3d ed. 1994).

- *Example of Inherency*. Subera invented and patented a system for the refrigeration and defrosting of open-front display cases used in supermarkets for the display of frozen foods. The invention incorporated three distinct and parallel bands of air, which form a curtain across the open front of the display case. The aspect of the Subera invention the patent owner argued was different from that disclosed in the prior art Aokage patent was that during the defrost cycle, only the second band of air was changed while the innermost air curtain was kept refrigerated. The prior art Aokage disclosure did not in so many words mention that a refrigerated band of air was maintained in front of the display case during the defrost cycle, as did the Subera patented invention. But the court found that in the Aokage prior art patent "the maintenance of the air curtain during the defrost cycle is an inherent feature of the claimed embodiment and naturally occurs when the air flow in the secondary band is reversed" during the defrost cycle. The Subera patent was found invalid as being "anticipated" by the prior art disclosed in the Aokage patent because "the Aokage patent taught each and every element of the Subera inventions under the principle of inherency." *Tyler Refrigeration v. Kysor Indus. Corp.*, 777 F.2d 687, 227 USPQ 845, 847 (Fed. Cir. 1985).

inoperable prior art [patent] A prior disclosure of an invention in which the invention fails to achieve its intended result.

A Challenge to the Status of Prior Art. An inventor can attempt to argue that what would otherwise be a PRIOR ART patent disclosure is not valid because it discloses an inoperable invention. Under 37 C.F.R. §1.132, an applicant for patent can submit evidence to the Patent and Trademark Office to substantiate the claim that a prior art reference is "inoperable." See 2 P. Rosenberg, *Patent Law Fundamentals* §15.07[2][c] (1994 rev.).

Partial Prior Art. It is not accurate to state that "a piece of prior art that doesn't work is not prior art." Rather, "[e]ven if a reference discloses an inoperative device, it is prior art for all that it teaches." *Beckman Instruments Inc. v.*

LKB Produkter AB, 892 F.2d 1547, 1551, 13 USPQ2d 1301, 1304 (Fed. Cir. 1989).

See ENABLING PRIOR ART.

INTA [trademarks] International Trademark Association. It was known as the United States Trademark Association prior to 1993. It is a nonprofit organization of over 2,800 corporate and law firm members from around the world devoted to promoting trademarks as essential to world commerce. The INTA publishes weekly bulletins and a quarterly newsletter, as well as the bimonthly *The Trademark Reporter*, a law review journal devoted to trademark topics. The INTA holds several meetings each year, including the annual meeting, which is attended by over 3,000 people from over 75 nations. INTA headquarters is located at 1133 Avenue of the Americas, New York, New York 10036.

See TRADEMARK REVIEW COMMISSION.

intellectual property [patent–trademark–unfair competition–copyright–trade secret–moral rights] Certain creations of the human mind that are given the legal aspects of a property right. "Intellectual property" is an all-encompassing term now widely used to designate as a group all of the following fields of law: patent, trademark, unfair competition, copyright, trade secret, moral rights, and the right of publicity.

Why "Intellectual"? The word "intellectual" is used to indicate that these kinds of "property" are distinct from real estate or personal property in that they are products of the human mind or intellect. These kinds of legal rights are intellectual property in the sense that the law grants property-type protection to nontangible creations of the human intellect. In one sense, intellectual property is legal recognition of a property right in certain kinds of information.

• *Usage References*:

" '[I]ntellectual property' shall include the rights relating to: [1] literary, artistic and scientific works; [2] performances of performing artists, phonograms, and broadcasts; [3] inventions in all fields of human endeavor; [4] scientific discoveries; [5] industrial designs; [6] trademarks, service marks and commercial names and designations; [7] protection against unfair competition; and all other rights resulting from intellectual activity in the industrial, scientific, literary or artistic fields." Convention Establishing the World Intellectual Property Organization, signed at Stockholm, July 14, 1967, Art.2 (viii).

"The objects mentioned under [1] belong to the copyright branch of intellectual property. The objects mentioned in [2] are usually called 'neighboring rights,' that is, rights bordering on copyright. The objects mentioned under [3], [5] and [6] constitute the industrial property branch of intellectual property. The object mentioned under [7] may also be considered as belonging to that branch.... The object mentioned under [4]— scientific discoveries—belongs to neither of the two branches of intellectual property. According to one opinion, scientific discoveries should not have been mentioned among the various forms of intellectual property since no national law or international treaty gives any property right in scientific discoveries. Scientific discoveries and inventions are not the same." WIPO, *Background Reading Material on Intellectual Property* 4 (1988).

See INDUSTRIAL PROPERTY.

intent to claim [patent] To obtain a REISSUE of a patent on the ground that the claims are too narrow and fail to adequately cover the true scope of the invention, it is necessary to establish that this was the result of "error." One way to establish such error is to show that the patent applicant had an "intent to claim" the subject matter of the reissue claim sought.

• *Case Reference*: "Language appearing first in [a 1942 U.S. Supreme Court opinion] has been picked up and has metamorphosed into a requirement that an applicant show his original 'intent to claim' the subject matter of the reissue claim sought. The phrase 'intent to claim' does not appear in the statute. It is but judicial shorthand, signifying a means of measuring whether the statutorily required *error* is present. Clearly, a showing that an applicant had an intent to claim matter that he did not claim can go a long way to support a finding that error occurred; and conversely, a showing that an applicant never had any such intent makes a finding of error extremely difficult if not impossible." *In re Weiler*, 790 F.2d 1576, 1581. 220 USPQ 673, 676 (Fed. Cir. 1986).

intent to use application [trademark] Since 1989 in the United States, an optional method of applying for federal registration of a mark based upon a declared good faith intention to use a mark on defined goods or services. For the first time in the United States, one could file an application not based upon prior use of the mark, but based on an intent to use (ITU).

Use-Based Applications Under Lanham Act §1(a). Prior to the Trademark Law Revision Act amendments effective November 16, 1989, a federal trademark application was void from the beginning if there was no use of the mark prior to filing of the application. The governing maxim was "no trade-no trademark." *Signature Guardian Sys., Inc. v. Lee*, 209 USPQ 81, 87 (T.T.A.B. 1980). This system was out of step with that used in the rest of the world and required a company with a new mark still in the planning or testing stages to make a token use of the mark on a small quantity of goods or services solely to provide a predicate for an application to register. And a company could never be sure that someone, somewhere in the nation, had not made a first use of a similar mark on similar goods or services just before that company's own first use. For these and other reasons, the TRADEMARK REVIEW COMMISSION recommended U.S. enactment of a system in which an application to register could be based on a declared intention to use a mark prior to actual use in the marketplace. These provisions were enacted into law and became effective November 16, 1989. However, applications based upon use under Lanham Act §1(a) can still be made and remain an optional route to federal registration.

Intent to Use Under §1(b). Since November 16, 1989, for the first time in U.S. law, one is permitted to commence the federal registration process by filing an application not based upon prior use of the mark, but upon a declared good faith intention to use the mark in the future. However, for domestic companies, the application will not mature into a registration unless and until the domestic applicant files a verified statement, together with specimens, that it has actually used the mark in interstate or foreign commerce. That statement will be either an AMENDMENT TO ALLEGE USE or a STATEMENT OF USE. But qualified foreign applicants with a foreign application or registration who file under Lanham Act §44 need not prove actual use in order to receive a U.S. registration. Such foreign applicants need only state a bona fide intention to use the mark in the U.S.

Filing a §1(d) Statement of Use. An ITU applicant has a maximum time of 36 months from receiving a "Notice of Allowance" within which to file a statement of use together with evidence of use. The "use" necessary is use in the "ordinary course of trade," not just token use, as was previously acceptable. The time gap between approval for publication and issuance of the notice of allowance during which the Statement of Use may not be filed is known as the BLACKOUT PERIOD. A six-month period within which to file the Statement of Use is available to everyone. Another six months is automatically available upon request to the Patent and Trademark Office (PTO) upon payment of a fee together with a verified statement of a continued bona fide intention to use. Thereafter, a maximum of four additional extensions in six-month increments may be obtained upon a sufficient showing of "good cause" to the PTO, together with a fee and a verified statement of a continued bona fide intention to use. 37 C.F.R. §§2.88, 2.89.

See STATEMENT OF USE.

Patent and Trademark Office Examination of ITU Application. PTO ex parte examination of a §1(b) ITU application proceeds in two stages:

(1) The first stage consists of examination for compliance with formalities and registrability in much the same way as was done previously. The mark will be examined to see if any of the Lanham Act §2 bars apply, such as descriptiveness under §2(e) or a conflict with a previously registered mark under §2(d). If found registrable, the examiner will pass the

mark to be published for opposition. If there is no successful opposition, the PTO will issue a Notice of Allowance. The date of the Notice of Allowance is critical, for it starts the clock running for an ITU applicant to submit the Statement of Use, described previously.

See OPPOSITION PROCEEDING.

(2) The second-stage examination will review the Statement of Use and specimen filed by the applicant to ensure that it tracks the mark and goods or services listed in the application. Normally, objections that could have been raised by the PTO during the first-stage examination cannot be raised in the second stage. The PTO will not refuse registration on a ground which could or should have been raised during the first stage unless failure to do so would be "clear error" in that it would result in issuance of a registration in violation of the Lanham Act. The Statement of Use cannot expand the scope of the goods or services. An ITU applicant can only delete or clarify the goods or services originally listed in the application; it cannot broaden the identification of goods or services.

Amendment of Application From ITU to Use Based. Under §1(c) of the Lanham Act, an ITU applicant who has made actual use of the mark may amend its application to a use-based application at any time after the filing of its application and before the application is approved for publication. Thereafter, an allegation of use may be made only by filing a §1(d) Statement of Use after the issuance of a Notice of Allowance. 37 C.F.R. §2.76.

See AMENDMENT TO ALLEGE USE.

Constructive Use. Early filing of an ITU application is essential to obtaining an early priority date. Contingent on the registration of the mark on the Principal Register, the *filing* of an application to register constitutes "constructive use" of the mark, conferring a "right of priority, nationwide in effect," except for three defined categories of persons, who prior to the application have either used or filed an application themselves.

See CONSTRUCTIVE USE.

- *Treatise Reference*: 2 J.T. McCarthy, *Trademarks and Unfair Competition* §§19.07–.08 (3d ed. 1995 rev.).

- *Statutory Reference*: Lanham Act §1(b), 15 USC §1051(b): "A person who has a bona fide intention, under circumstances showing the good faith of such person, to use a trademark in commerce may apply to register the trademark under this Act on the principal register hereby established...."

intercept survey [trademark]
See SURVEY.

interest, prejudgment [patent–trademark–copyright] See PREJUDGMENT INTEREST.

interference [patent–trademark]

1. Patent Interference. An administrative proceeding in the Patent and Trademark Office before the Board of Patent Appeals and Interferences to determine which of two or more inventors was the first to invent and therefore is entitled to the patent. Each inventor seeks to prove priority of invention, that is, that he or she was the first inventor of the technology common to all the contesting inventors. In interference practice, the technology or invention common to the inventors is called a "count." The underlying principle of an interference proceeding is that two patents must not be granted on the basis of only one count arrived at by each contesting inventor.

First to Invent System. An interference proceeding is necessary because the United States is virtually the only nation in the world that still follows the priority rule that the first to invent is entitled to the patent for an invention. Other nations follow the rule of "first to file": the first inventor to file an application for patent is entitled to the patent. However, in the United States, the first party in the interference proceeding who was the first to file a patent application is known as the SENIOR PARTY and is presumed to have been the first inventor. The burden is on the junior party to prove an earlier date of invention. The junior party can do this by establishing REDUCTION TO PRACTICE of the common invention before the filing date of the senior party or that the junior party conceived of the invention before that date and was reasonably diligent in proceeding to reduction to practice during the time period from just before that date to the junior user's filing date.

Priority of Invention. As a result of legislative changes enacted in 1994 in both the NAFTA implementation act and the GATT URUGUAY ROUND AGREEMENTS ACT, there was a substantial increase in the range of locations in which inventive activity would count toward patent priority in the United States. The 1994 NAFTA amendments increased the range of locations for inventive activity to include Canada and Mexico. The 1994 Uruguay Round Agreements Act further expanded the range of possible locations to include inventive activity that occurs within WORLD TRADE ORGANIZATION (WTO) member countries. These 1994 Uruguay Round Agreements Act amendments became effective as to patent applications filed on or after January 1, 1996, which was one year after the WTO Agreement became effective in the United States. In addition, an inventor cannot establish a date of invention earlier than January 1, 1996, with respect to activity in WTO nations.

See PRIORITY OF INVENTION.

Procedure. Patent law statutory amendments in 1984 combined the Board of Patent Interferences and the Board of Appeals of the PTO into a single Board of Patent Appeals and Interferences. Interference procedures were substantially revised in rules effective in 1985. See B. Collins, *Current Patent Interference Practice* (1989 rev.). An interference may be declared between conflicting pending applications or between an issued patent and a conflicting application. In most cases to provoke an interference, an applicant copies the claims of an issued patent or application into its own application. The applicant then requests an interference to determine priority of invention. After the Board of Patent Appeals and Interferences decides priority of invention, a party may seek to review the board's decision by either filing a direct appeal with the Court of Appeals for the Federal Circuit or by filing suit in federal district court.

See COUNT, PHANTOM COUNT, LOST COUNT, SENIOR PARTY, INTERFERENCE ESTOPPEL, REDUCTION TO PRACTICE.

• *Statutory Reference:* 35 U.S.C. §135. "Whenever an application is made for a patent which, in the opinion of the Commissioner, would interfere with any pending application, or with any unexpired patent, an interference may be declared.... The Board of Patent Appeals and Interferences shall determine questions of priority of the inventions and may determine questions of patentability."

• *Rule Reference.* "An 'interference' is a proceeding instituted in the Patent and Trademark Office before the board to determine any question of patentability and priority of invention between two or more parties claiming the same patentable invention." 37 C.F.R. §1.601(i). See *Manual of Patent Examining Procedure* §2300 *et seq.* (1994).

• *Case References:*

"[T]here were four claimants to priority of title. All four, acting independently, had made the same or nearly the same discovery at times not widely separate. The prize of an exclusive patent falls to the one who had the fortune to be first.... The others gain nothing for all their toil and talents." Justice Cardozo in *Radio Corp. of Am. v. Radio Eng'g Labs., Inc.*, 293 U.S. 1, 3 (1934).

"In order to establish priority in an interference, the party who files later is 'required to establish reduction to practice *before* [the] filing date [of the party who filed first], or conception before that date coupled with reasonable diligence from just before that date to [the] filing date [of the party who files later]." *Hahn v. Wong*, 892 F.2d 1028, 1032, 13 USPQ2d 1313, 1317 (Fed. Cir. 1989).

"When testing is necessary to show proof of actual reduction to practice, the embodiment relied upon as evidence of priority must actually work for its intended purpose.... [However], reduction to practice does not require 'that the invention, when tested, be in a commercially satisfactory stage of development.' ... Reduction to practice, however, does not require actual use, but only a reasonable showing that the invention will work to overcome the problem it addresses." *Scott v. Finney*, 34 F.3d 1058, 1061–63, 32 USPQ2d 1115, 1117–19 (Fed. Cir. 1994).

• *Treatise References:* "United States patent law embraces the principle that the patent right is granted to the first inventor rather than the first to file a patent application. As a consequence this country has, almost unique in the world, a procedure for resolving patent 'interferences.' … Interference proceedings are not only tortuous, they are virtually incomprehensible to the uninitiated. They are, in a word, arcane." R. Harmon, *Patents and the Federal Circuit* §15.2 (3d ed. 1994). See 3 D. Chisum, *Patents* §§10.01–.09 (1994 rev.).

2. Trademark Registration Interference. An administrative proceeding in the Patent and Trademark Office before the Trademark Trial and Appeal Board to determine, between pending applications for trademark registration, which applicant was the first to use the mark and therefore entitled to federal registration.

1972 Changes in Interference Practice. Revisions to the Trademark Rules in 1972 restricted trademark interference practice to the rare case in which a party could prove that he or she would suffer irrevocable harm if the only recourse was to file an opposition proceeding or a petition to cancel a registration. 37 C.F.R. §2.91. The net result since 1972 has been to virtually eliminate interference proceedings in trademark cases. The issue of priority formerly adjudicated in interference cases is now determined in other types of administrative proceedings: oppositions and petitions to cancel. If there are applications copending for marks that are confusingly similar, the allowable application with the earliest filing date is published in the Official Gazette for opposition. 37 C.F.R. §2.83(a). The other applicant then has an opportunity to file an opposition proceeding against registration of the published mark. Similarly, if an applicant finds that a registration is cited against his or her application, the possible recourse is to file a petition to cancel that registration.

• *Treatise Reference*: 3 J.T. McCarthy, *Trademarks and Unfair Competition* §20.24 (3d ed. 1995 rev.).

interference estoppel [patent] A rule pursuant to which if a party in a patent INTERFERENCE proceeding fails to seek to make the subject matter of a claim in the patent application a part of the interference COUNT, then that party may,

in some instances, be estopped or precluded from later obtaining a claim which is not patentably distinct from that count on which the opponent won on priority of invention in the interference proceeding.

The Court of Appeals for the Federal Circuit in dictum has lumped together under the label "interference estoppel" four types of estoppel: estoppel by dissolution; estoppel by judgment; equitable estoppel; and estoppel for failure to file a motion. *Woods v. Tsuchiya*, 754 F.2d 1571, 1579, 225 USPQ 11, 16 (Fed. Cir. 1985).

• *Case References*:

"The issue presented is whether [applicant], having never attempted to include in the interference subject matter which dominates the lost count, may now successfully claim that subject matter. The doctrine of interference estoppel is directed to finality of an interference, at least with respect to all issues which *might have been* presented in the interference…. Estoppel should be decided on the facts of each case with reference to principles of equity…. If claim 40 were patentably distinct from the lost count, it could not be denied to [applicant] on the sole ground of interference estoppel." *In re Kroekel*, 803 F.2d 705, 709–10, 231 USPQ 640, 643 (Fed. Cir. 1986).

"[T]he doctrine of interference estoppel holds that an interference settles not only the rights of the parties under the issues or counts of the interferences but also settles every question as to the rights to any claim which might have been presented or determined in the interference proceedings…. The basis or purpose of the doctrine of interference estoppel is to insure the resolution of priority in a single contest respecting all common subject matter disclosed by the parties." *Nelson v. Bowler*, 1 USPQ2d 2076, 2079 (Bd. Pat. App. & Int'f. 1986).

• *Rule References*:

"A judgment in an interference settles all issues which (1) were raised and decided in the interference, [and] (2) could have been properly raised and decided in the interference by a motion…. A losing party who could have properly moved, but failed to move … shall be estopped to take *ex parte* or *inter partes* action in the Patent and Trademark Office after the interference which is inconsistent with that party's failure to properly move...." 37 C.F.R. §1.658(c).

"The definition of interference estoppel is designed to encourage parties in interference cases to settle as many issues as possible in one proceeding. Section 1.658(c) creates an estoppel both as to senior and junior parties...." 1985 PTO Discussion Accompanying Adoption of New Interferences Rules, reproduced in D. Chisum, *Patents* App. 35, p. App 35-24 (1994 rev.).

• *Treatise Reference*: 2 D. Chisum, *Patents* §5.03[3][h] (1994 rev.).

See LOST COUNT.

inter partes [general legal] A legal proceeding in which more than one party is involved with a court or other governmental agency. While it is a Latin term familiar to all attorneys, the lay audience should know that inter partes is commonly used as the opposite of EX PARTE, which describes a proceeding in which there is only one party involved before a court or government agency.

For example, when a patent attorney is arguing with a Patent and Trademark Office examiner on behalf of an inventor applying for a patent, it is characterized as an ex parte proceeding; it is only the inventor seeking a patent from the government. But if the inventor is granted a patent and sues an alleged infringer in court, that lawsuit is characterized as an inter partes proceeding.

The phrase is sometimes given the English equivalent, inter party.

intervening rights [patent]   An infringer may have, under the second paragraph of Patent Code §252, a personal defense of intervening rights to continue what would otherwise be infringing activity if the activity or preparation for it was started before the grant of a reissue patent or before the grant of new claims after a REEXAMINATION of a patent.

• *Example*: If Zeta has been manufacturing an unpatented article and then Alpha obtains a reissue patent with broader claims which now cover that article, Zeta may have a personal defense to continue manufacture even if Zeta's manufacture started after the grant of the original patent to Alpha. Zeta, because of its pre-reissue activity, may have a personal intervening right to continue what would otherwise be an infringing activity after the reissue. The theory is that the public has the right to use what is not claimed in the original patent and no one who relies on this should be foreclosed from continuing to do so or made to pay damages based on pre-reissue activity.

Absolute and Equitable Intervening Rights. The first sentence of the second paragraph of Patent Code §252 has been characterized as defining an "absolute" intervening right, with the second sentence defining an "equitable" intervening right. "The absolute right extends only to anything made, purchased or used before the grant of the reissue patent. In other words, it cover products already made at the time of reissue.... The second sentence permits the continued manufacture, use, or sale of additional products covered by the reissue patent when the defendant made, purchased or used identical products, or made substantial preparations to make, use, or sell identical products, before the reissue date." *BIC Leisure Prods. Inc. v. Windsurfing Int'l Inc.*, 1 F.3d 1214, 1221, 27 USPQ2d 1671, 1676 (Fed. Cir. 1993).

Identical Claims. The first paragraph of Patent Code §252 makes it clear that the grant of a reissue patent does not affect any pending lawsuit or claim to the extent that the claims of the original and reissue patents are identical.

• *Statutory Reference:*

35 U.S.C. §252, first paragraph: "The surrender of the original patent shall take effect upon the issue of the reissued patent, and every reissued patent shall have the same effect and operation in law, on the trial of actions for causes thereafter arising, as if the same had been originally granted in such amended form, but in so far as the claims of the original and reissued patents are identical, such surrender shall not affect any action then pending nor abate any cause of action then existing, and the reissued patent, to the extent that its claims are identical with the original patent, shall constitute a con-

tinuation thereof and have effect continuously from the date of the original patent."

35 U.S.C. §252, second paragraph [The following sentence has been said to define an "absolute intervening right"]: "No reissued patent shall abridge or affect the right of any person or his successors in business who made, purchased or used prior to the grant of a reissue anything patented by the reissued patent, to continue the use of, or to sell to others to be used or sold, the specific thing so made, purchased or used, unless the making, using or selling of such thing infringes a valid claim of the reissued patent which was in the original patent." [The following sentence has been said to define an "equitable intervening right"]: "The court before which such matter is in question may provide for the continued manufacture, use or sale of the thing made, purchased or used as specified, or for the manufacture, use or sale of which substantial preparation was made before the grant of the reissue, and it may also provide for the continued practice of any process patented by the reissue, practiced, or for the practice of which substantial preparation was made, prior to the grant of the reissue, to the extent and under such terms as the court deems equitable for the protection of investments made or business commenced before the grant of the reissue."

• *Treatise References:* "Recapture through a reissue patent of what is dedicated to the public by omission in the original patent is permissible under specific conditions, but not at the expense of innocent parties. Therefore, one may be able to continue to infringe a reissue patent if the court decides that equity dictates such a result." R. Harmon, *Patents and the Federal Circuit* §15.3(b) (3d ed. 1994). See 3 D. Chisum, *Patents* §§15.01–.05 (1994 rev.).

• *Case References:*

"The statute sets forth a single straightforward test for determining whether the doctrine of intervening rights protects an alleged infringer. The only question to ask under this test is whether claims of the original patent which are repeated in the reissue patent are infringed. Section 252 assumes that a patentee having valid claims in a patent will retain those claims

in the reissued patent. If valid claims in the original patent appear unaltered in the reissue patent, the doctrine of intervening rights affords no protection to the alleged infringer.... When the doctrine of intervening rights is properly raised, the court must consider whether to use its broad equity powers to fashion an appropriate remedy." *Seattle Box Co. v. Industrial Crating & Packing Inc.*, 731 F.2d 818, 830, 221 USPQ 568, 576–77 (Fed. Cir. 1984).

The court permitted continuing infringing use of goods that were in inventory when the reissue patent was granted where the goods had been designed with advice of counsel to avoid infringement of the original patent and orders were received before the reissue. The defendant was permitted to dispose of inventory on hand at the time of reissue without liability for damages to the patentee. "The underlying rationale for intervening rights is that the public has the right to use what is not specifically claimed in the original patent." *Seattle Box Co. v. Industrial Crating & Packing Inc.*, 756 F.2d 1574, 1579, 225 USPQ 357, 361 (Fed. Cir. 1985).

• *Example:* Defendant was found to have infringed plaintiff's March 8, 1983, reissue patent claims on a form of sailboard. While defendant was liable to plaintiff for lost royalties, it had an absolute intervening rights defense to damages on 10,870 sailboards. This was based on the finding that defendant had 5,245 boards in inventory as of the reissue date and another 5,625 on order as of that date because a February 10, 1983 purchase order bound defendant to purchase those boards. "[T]he district court properly excluded the post-reissue sale of the 10,870 sailboards from the computation of damages." *BIC Leisure Prods. Inc. v. Windsurfing Int'l Inc.*, 1 F.3d 1214, 1220–22, 27 USPQ2d 1671, 1676–78 (Fed. Cir. 1993).

interview [patent–trademark] The appearance of an attorney representing an applicant for a patent or for a trademark registration, before the Patent and Trademark Office (PTO) examiner or a telephone conversation between those persons. An in-person or telephone conference interview often takes place between (1) the attorney representing an inventor or an applicant for a trademark registration and (2) the patent examiner or trademark attorney (examiner) employed by the PTO and representing the government. Such direct contacts are a traditional method of supplementing and expediting the usual on-paper interchanges between the government and the patent applicant or trademark registration applicant.

Under 37 C.F.R. §1.133, interviews with patent examiners must be conducted in the examiner's office within office hours. When reconsideration of an examiner's action is requested on the basis of what was said during the interview, the applicant must file a complete written statement of the reasons presented at the interview. An interview is not a substitute for a formal, written response by an applicant to an action by the PTO examiner.

• *Rule Reference*: "All business with the Patent and Trademark Office should be transacted in writing. The personal attendance of applicants or their attorneys or agents at the Patent and Trademark Office is unnecessary. The action of the Patent and Trademark Office will be based exclusively on the written record in the Office. No attention will be paid to any alleged oral promise, stipulation, or understanding in relation to which there is disagreement or doubt." 37 C.F.R. §1.2.

• *Manual References*: "An interview should be had only when the nature of the case is such that the interview could serve to develop and clarify specific issues and lead to a mutual understanding between the examiner and the applicant, and thereby advance the prosecution of the application.... It is the responsibility of both parties to the interview to see that it is not extended beyond a reasonable period, usually not longer than thirty minutes." *Manual of Patent Examining Procedure* §713 (1994). See parallel provisions in *Trademark Manual of Examining Procedure* §1107 (1993).

invent around [patent]

See DESIGN AROUND.

invention [patent] The human creation of a new technical idea and the physical means that can accomplish or embody the idea. In cases prior to the 1952 Patent Code, "invention" was often used as a synonym for a patentable invention. But today, an "invention" is not the same as a "patentable invention," which is an invention that passes the tests of the Patent Code. Under current law in the 1952 Patent Code, the question is not whether there is an invention, but rather whether the invention satisfies the key statutory legal tests such as novelty (ANTICIPATION) and NONOBVIOUSNESS.

See PATENT, OBVIOUSNESS, ANTICIPATION.

• *Case References*:

Old Definition: "What indicia of invention should the courts seek in a case where nothing tangible is new, and invention, if it exists at all, is only in bringing old elements together? ... It is agreed that the key to patentability of a mechanical device that brings old factors into cooperation is presence or lack of invention." *Great A. & P. Tea Co. v. Supermarket Equip. Corp.*, 340 U.S. 147, 150–51, 87 USPQ 303, 305 (1950).

Modern Definition: "The dispositive question is not whether the claimed device is an 'invention'; rather, it is whether the invention satisfies the standards of patentability." *Custom Accessories v. Jeffery-Allan Indus.*, 807 F.2d 955, 959, 1 USPQ2d 1196, 1198 (Fed. Cir. 1986).

"Apparently [the PTO examiner and solicitor] were thinking that 'invention' means 'patentable invention.' This has not been the language of the law since January 1, 1953." *Re Vogel & Vogel*, 422 F.2d 438, 440 n.1, 164 USPQ 619, 621 n.1 (C.C.P.A. 1970).

While it is proper to identify the difference between the invention and the prior art in determining nonobviousness, it is improper "to consider the *difference* as the invention. The 'difference' may have seemed slight ... but it may also have been the key to success and advancement in the art resulting from the invention." *Jones v. Hardy*, 727 F.2d 1524, 1528, 220 USPQ 1021, 1024 (Fed. Cir. 1984).

• *Commentary Reference*: "All an invention is, however, is something which has been found out, or devised or discovered. The question today is not what to call it but whether, under the statute, it is patentable. Hundreds of 'real' or 'true' inventions, all resulting from 'inventive acts' and the exercise of the 'inventive faculties,' are held unpatentable every day for lack of novelty.… [The obviousness test of Patent Code §103] is not a 'standard of invention' and it is not called a 'requirement of invention.' The presence or absence of 'invention' is not mentioned. The use of the term 'invention' was, in fact, carefully avoided with a view to making a fresh start, free of all the divergent court opinions and rhetorical announcements about 'invention.'" Rich, *The Vague Concept of "Invention" as Replaced by Sec. 103 of the 1952 Patent Act*, 46 J. Pat. Off. Soc'y 855, 862, 864–65 (1964).

inventive entity [patent] The person or persons who are regarded as the inventor or inventors of an invention. "Inventive entity" is a concept under which a sole inventor of one invention and joint inventors, including the sole inventor, of another invention, are regarded as separate "inventive entities." That is, if John Alpha is a sole inventor of Invention One and John Alpha and Sandra Beta are joint inventors of Invention Two, then these two inventions are deemed to have been made by separate "inventive entities." Distinct but overlapping groups of persons are treated as if they were separate inventors in determining what is a prior art reference of "others" or "another." See 1 D. Chisum, *Patents* §3.08[2] (1994 rev.).

Impact on What Is Prior Art. A basic rule is that an inventor's own prior work will not anticipate his later invention unless that work constitutes a bar under Patent Code §102(b). If Alpha invents and patents Invention One and Alpha and Beta jointly invent and patent Invention Two, then the disclosure of Patent One is prior art as to the invention claimed in Patent Two. *In re Land & Rogers*, 368 F.2d 866, 879, 151 USPQ 621, 633 (C.C.P.A. 1966). That is, the disclosure of the first inventive entity is that of "others" or "another" as to the claims of Invention Two made by a different inventive entity. *Ex Parte Des Ormeaux*, 25 USPQ2d 2040 (Bd. Pat. App. & Int'f. 1992) (Patent One of inventors A+B+C is the invention of "another" and is prior art, rendering obvious and unpatentable the invention claimed in application for Patent Two by inventors A+X.).

Joint Inventors. Under the law followed by some courts prior to the 1984 amendments to the Patent Code concerning joint inventors, a patent was invalid for failure to name the proper inventors unless the "inventorship entity" named was the true origin of *every* claim in a patent containing more than one claim. This was known as the ALL CLAIMS RULE. The 1984 amendment to Patent Code §115 "clearly repudiates the [all claims] rule." *Smithkline Diagnostics Inc. v. Helena Labs. Corp.*, 859 F.2d 878, 889, 8 USPQ2d 1468, 1477 (Fed. Cir. 1988).

Synonym: inventorship entity.

- *Treatise Reference*: 1 D. Chisum, *Patents* §2.03[1] (1994 rev.).

- *Statutory Reference*: 35 U.S.C. §116, first paragraph: "When an invention is made by two or more persons jointly, they shall apply for patent jointly.… Inventors may apply for a patent jointly even though (1) they did not physically work together or at the same time, (2) each did not make the same type or amount of contribution, or (3) each did not make a contribution to the subject matter of every claim of the patent."

inventive process [patent] The process of making an invention, which begins with CONCEPTION and usually ends with REDUCTION TO PRACTICE, actual or constructive. In some definitions, the inventive process continues until a patent is actually granted. The time when the inventive process begins and ends is important in determining who was the first to invent in an INTERFERENCE proceeding. It is also important in determining if there is an EXPERIMENTAL USE, which will excuse putting the invention ON SALE or in PUBLIC USE more than a year prior to filing an application for patent.

- *Treatise Reference*: 3 D. Chisum, *Patents* §§10.04–.05 (1994 rev.); 2 P. Rosenberg, *Patent Law Fundamentals* §10.01 (1994 rev.).

Synonym: inventive act.

- *Case Reference*: "The earliest phase in the development of any invention is its mental conceptualization by the inventor, the time when the first idea dawns. This is typically followed in short order by the second phase, in which the inventor attempts to embody his idea in a working model or prototype. Phase two ends when he has succeeded in rendering his idea a reality by constructing a working model that substantially embodies the claims later to be patented. Then begins the third phase, in which the inventor experiments with his model so as to satisfy himself that it needs no further refinement and to prove its fitness for the intended purpose. Once this is completed the inventor is free to initiate the last phase of concern to us, in which he secures a limited legal monopoly to himself under the patent laws. This last phase is initiated by his application for the patent and terminates when the patent is finally issued." *In re Yarn Processing Patent Validity Litig.*, 498 F.2d 271, 275, 183 USPQ 65, 67 (5th Cir 1974).

inventive step [patent–international] A European law condition of nonpatentability under which an invention cannot receive a valid patent if the invention does not involve an inventive step beyond the prior art. The requirement of an inventive step is analogous to the U.S. requirement of nonobviousness.

See OBVIOUSNESS.

• *Convention References:*

"Article 52. Patentable Inventions. (1) European patents shall be granted for any inventions which are susceptible to industrial application, which are new and which involve an inventive step...." European Patent Convention Article 52(1).

"Article 56. Inventive Step. An invention shall be considered as involving an inventive step if, having regard to the state of the art, it is not obvious to a person skilled in the art...." European Patent Convention Article 56.

inventor's certificate [patent–international] A form of reward to an inventor recognized primarily in socialist nations such as the former USSR as an alternative to a patent. Whereas a patent grants to the inventor the right to exclude, an inventor's certificate has two beneficiaries: the government and the inventor. The government has an exclusive right to use the invention and the inventor has a right to a reward based

on the savings achieved by putting the invention to use.

Nature of an Inventor's Certificate. Usually the applicant is free to choose between a patent and an inventor's certificate. But in some nations, inventors working in government enterprises who have received assistance from their employers in making the invention can only recover an inventor's certificate. Usually, the same requirements needed to obtain a patent are necessary to obtain an inventor's certificate.

U.S. Recognition of Inventor's Certificates. While there is no concept such as an inventor's certificate in domestic U.S. law, U.S. patent law does recognize a foreign inventor's certificate to be the equivalent of a foreign patent for some purposes. For example, the filing of an application for a foreign inventor's certificate can form the basis for a claim to a convention priority filing date (see CONVENTION DATE) in the United States. 35 U.S.C. §119; 37 C.F.R. §1.55(b).

Japanese Kokai. It has been held that the Japanese "Kokai," while allegedly analogous to an inventor's certificate, does not in fact fall within that category for purposes of U.S. law. *Ex parte Fujii*, 13 USPQ2d 1073 (Bd. Pat. App. & Int'f. 1989).

• *Treatise References*: WIPO, *Background Reading Material on Intellectual Property* 110–11 (1988); 3 P. Rosenberg, *Patent Law Fundamentals* §19.02[3] (1994 rev.); 3 D. Chisum, *Patents* §14.03[4] (1994 rev.).

• *Statutory References*:

35 U.S.C. §119, fourth paragraph "Applications for inventor's certificates filed in a foreign country in which applicants have a right to apply, at their discretion, either for a patent or for an inventor's certificate shall be treated in this country in the same manner and have the same effect for purpose of the right of priority under this section as applications for patents...."

35 U.S.C. §102: "A person shall be entitled to a patent unless— ... (d) the invention was first patented or caused to be patented, or was the subject of an inventor's certificate, by the applicant or his legal representatives or assigns in a foreign country prior to the date of the

application for patent in this country on an application for patent or inventor's certificate filed more than twelve months before the filing of the application in the United States."

investive publication [copyright]

See PUBLICATION.

ITU [trademark]

See INTENT TO USE APPLICATION.

J

Jepson claim [patent] A patent claim with a PREAMBLE that recites the old elements of a combination, followed by a transitional phrase indicating that the claimed invention is an improvement over the old combination, followed by the main body of the claim reciting the new elements of the invention.

Format of a Jepson Claim. The generalized format of a Jepson claim is: "A [type of machine] having [old elements A and B and C], wherein the improvement comprises [new elements, modification of old elements or doing something to the old elements]." Here, the transitional phrase "wherein the improvement comprises" is a signal that what follows is the allegedly novel part of the claim. Phrases that are equivalent to the term "wherein the improvement comprises" are acceptable so long as the claim is clear.

Admission of Prior Art. The PREAMBLE in a Jepson claim not only describes the setting of the new invention, but it also impliedly admits that what is recited in the preamble is old and in the PRIOR ART. *In re Fout*, 675 F.2d 297, 213 USPQ 532 (C.C.P.A. 1982) (by reciting a process in the Jepson preamble, applicants admitted that it was prior art). However, this implied admission can be overcome by a showing that what is in the Jepson preamble is in fact not in the prior art because it is the inventor's own work.

Scope of the Claim. The claimed invention consists of the elements mentioned in the preamble in combination with the elements recited in the improvement clause of the claim. "Although a preamble is impliedly admitted to be prior art when a Jepson claim is used, ... unless the preamble is the inventor's own work, ... the claimed invention consists of the preamble in combination with the improvement." *Pentec,*

Inc. v. Graphic Controls Corp., 776 F.2d 309, 315, 227 USPQ 766, 770 (Fed. Cir. 1985).

Origin of the Term "Jepson." The name is derived from a 1917 case in which this format of claim was approved. *Ex parte Jepson*, 1917 Comm. Dec. 62, 243 O.G. 525 (Ass't. Comm'r. Pat. 1917).

See PREAMBLE.

• *Rule Reference*: "Where the nature of the case admits, as in the case of an improvement, any independent claim should contain in the following order: (1) a preamble comprising a general description of all the elements or steps of the claimed combination which are conventional or known, (2) a phrase such as 'wherein the improvement comprises,' and (3) those elements, steps and/or relationships which constitute that portion of the claimed combination which the applicant considers as the new or improved portion." 37 C.F.R. §1.75(e).

• *Manual Reference*: "The [Jepson] form of claim ... is particularly adapted for the description of improvement type inventions. It is to be considered a combination claim. The preamble of this form of claim is considered to positively and clearly include all the elements or steps recited therein as art of the claimed combination." *Manual of Patent Examining Procedure* §608.01(m) (1994).

• *Treatise Reference*: "[Jepson] claims are frequently used where there is an improvement in one or more elements of an otherwise old and unchanged combination, or if one or more new elements are added to an old combination." J. Landis, *Mechanics of Patent Claim Drafting* §57 (3d ed. 1990).

230

• *Case References*:

"We agree that the preamble elements in a Jepson-type claim are *impliedly admitted* to be old in the art, ... but it is only an *implied admission*. The fact that none of the art cited by the examiner shows the combination recited in the claim preambles gives credence to [the inventors'] explanation for drafting the claims in Jepson format, which was not intended as an admission, but was to avoid a double patenting rejection in a co-pending case unavailable to the public. We think that a finding of obviousness should not be based on an implied admission erroneously creating imaginary prior art. That is not the intent of §103. We will not use [the inventors'] claim preamble as prior art against them in this situation." *In re Ehrreich*, 590 F.2d 902, 909–10, 200 USPQ 504, 510 (C.C.P.A. 1979).

"[T]here is an important distinction between the situation where the inventor improves upon his own invention and the situation where he improves upon the invention of another. In the former situation, where the inventor continues to improve upon his own work product, his foundation work product [recited in the preamble of a Jepson claim] should not, without a statutory basis, be treated as prior art solely because he admits knowledge of *his own work*." *Reading & Bates Constr. Co. v. Baker Energy Resources Corp.*, 748 F.2d 645, 650, 223 USPQ 1168, 1171–72 (Fed. Cir. 1984).

• *Example 1*: "In an electrical system of distribution of the class wherein a variable speed generator charges a storage battery and when the battery becomes sufficiently charged a voltage coil becomes effective to regulate the generator for constant potential, *the combination with* said voltage coil of a coil traversed by current flowing to the battery which is acted upon by decreasing battery current to reduce the potential maintained constant by the voltage coil." This is the original "Jepson claim" from *Ex parte Jepson*, 1917 Comm. Dec. 62, 243 O.G. 525 (Ass't. Comm'r. Pat. 1917).

• *Example 2*: "In an electromagnetic energy shield having a volume resistivity to be effective as an electromagnetic shield comprising a resin matrix loaded with particles coated with silver in an amount of about 40 to 80 volume percent, *the improvement being* that the silver coated particles are of a maximum size in the range of from 0.5 to 40 mils and wherein the resin is compressible." *In re Ehrreich*, 590 F.2d 902, 200 USPQ 504 (C.C.P.A. 1979) (Since the Jepson preamble recited applicant's own invention, which was the subject of another application, the material in the preamble was not prior art against the applicant.).

joint authors [copyright] The collaborating creators of a single copyrightable work who, at the time of creation, intend to merge their separate contributions to the work into a unitary whole.

Test of Joint Authorship. If there is joint authorship, then it follows that there is joint ownership of copyright in the work created. The key to a determination of whether there is joint authorship is the intention, at the time each person makes his or her contribution, that the separate contributions are to be absorbed or combined into an integrated unit.

• *Example*: The classic example is two songwriters, Rodgers writing the music and Hammerstein writing the words. When each writes his part, each intends it to be integrated with the contribution of the other into a unitary song with lyrics. However, if poet Alpha writes a poem with no intention that it ever be set to music, the contribution, years later, of composer Zeta in setting the poem to music is the creation of a DERIVATIVE WORK. Alpha and Zeta are not joint authors and are not joint owners of copyright because there is no single copyright.

Mere Assistants Are Not "Joint Authors." To qualify as a joint author, it is necessary that a person make some genuine copyrightable contribution to the work. Under the majority view, to be a joint author, one must supply more than mere secretarial assistance, overall directions, or unprotectible ideas: an AUTHOR is "the party who actually creates the work, that is, the person who translates an idea into a fixed, tangible expression entitled to copyright protection." *Community for Creative Non-Violence v. Reid*, 490 U.S. 730, 737, 10 USPQ2d 1985, 1989

(1989). In holding that a person who merely described to a computer programmer the sort of program to be written was not a joint author, an appellate court remarked: "The supplier of an idea is no more an 'author' of a [computer] program than is the supplier of the disk on which the program is stored." *S.O.S. Inc. v. Payday, Inc.*, 886 F.2d 1081, 1087, 12 USPQ2d 1241, 1245 (9th Cir. 1989). "Even though this issue is not completely settled in the case law, our circuit holds that joint authorship requires each author to make an independently copyrightable contribution." *Ashton-Tate Corp. v. Ross,* 916 F.2d 516, 521, 16 USPQ2d 1541, 1546 (9th Cir. 1990).

Joint Ownership Through Conveyance. Joint ownership of a copyright can be created in the absence of joint authorship. For example, a single author can assign copyright to several persons as co-owners or leave a copyright in a will to several heirs. Copyright may also constitute community property so as to create a special form of joint ownership between spouses in the marital relationship. *In re Marriage of Worth*, 195 Cal. App. 3d 768, 241 Cal. Rptr. 135 (1987); 1 *Nimmer on Copyright* §6.13 (1994 rev.).

Rights and Duties of Joint Owners of Copyright. As to the rights and duties of joint owners of copyright, Congress saw no need for a specific statute and approved of the case law rule that co-owners of a copyright are treated as tenants in common with each co-owner having "an independent right to license the use of a work, subject to a duty of accounting to the other co-owners for any profits." H.R. Rep. No. 94-1476, 94th Cong., 2d Sess. 121 (1976). While each co-owner of copyright can exploit or grant nonexclusive licenses to exploit the copyrighted work, a co-owner does not have the power to assign the entire copyright or grant an exclusive license without the written agreement of the co-owners. However, each co-owner can transfer his or her own interest in the joint work to a third party who will step into the shoes of the previous co-owner. 1 *Nimmer on Copyright* §6.11 (1994 rev.). On the death of one joint owner, his or her copyright interest passes to heirs, not to the surviving co-owner.

- *Treatise References*: 1 *Nimmer on Copyright* §6.01 *et seq.* (1994 rev.); 1 P. Goldstein, *Copyright* §4.2.1 (1989); M. Leaffer, *Understanding Copyright* §5.4 (1989); W. Patry, *Copyright Law and Practice* 363 (1994); 1 N. Boorstyn, *Copyright* §3.02 (2d ed. 1994).

- *Statutory Reference*: 17 U.S.C. §101: "A 'joint work' is a work prepared by two or more authors with the intention that their contributions be merged into inseparable or interdependent parts of a unitary whole.

- *Legislative History*: "[I]n the case of a 'joint work,' the coauthors of the work are likewise co-owners of the copyright. Under the definition of section 101, a work is 'joint' if the authors collaborated with each other, or if each of the authors prepared his or her contribution with the knowledge and intention that it would be merged with the contributions of other authors as 'inseparable or interdependent parts of a unitary whole.' The touchstone here is the intention, at the time the writing is done, that the parts be absorbed or combined into an integrated unit, although the parts themselves may be either 'inseparable' (as in the case of a novel or painting) or 'interdependent' (as in the case of a motion picture, opera, or the words and music of a song). The definition of 'joint work' is to be contrasted with the definition of 'collective work,' … in which the elements of merger and unity are lacking." H.R. Rep. No. 94-1476, 94th Cong., 2d Sess. 120 (1976).

joint inventors [patent] Two or more inventors of a single invention who jointly work or collaborate together in the INVENTIVE PROCESS.

Who Are Joint Inventors. Under the 1984 amendments to the Patent Code, inventors may jointly apply for a patent even though they did not physically work together at the same time, did not make the same kind of contribution, and did not each make a contribution to the technology contained in every claim of the patent application.

Some Collaboration or Connection Is Required. Persons cannot be joint inventors if they have had no contact and know nothing of each others' work. Even after the liberalizing 1984 amendments to §116, there must be some degree of collaboration or connection between the persons for them to constitute joint inventors. *Kimberly-Clark Corp. v. Procter & Gamble Distrib.*, 973 F.2d 911, 916–17, 23 USPQ2d 1921, 1926 (Fed. Cir. 1991).

The Old "All Claims" Rule. Under the law followed by some courts prior to the 1984 Patent Code amendments concerning joint inventors, a patent was invalid for failure to name the proper inventors unless each joint inventor named made an inventive contribution to *every* claim in a patent containing more than one claim. This was known as the ALL CLAIMS RULE. The 1984 amendment to Patent Code §116 "clearly repudiates the [all claims] rule." *Smithkline Diagnostics Inc. v. Helena Labs. Corp.*, 859 F.2d 878, 889, 8 USPQ2d 1468, 1477 (Fed. Cir. 1988).

- *Statutory References*:

35 U.S.C. §116, first paragraph: "When an invention is made by two or more persons jointly, they shall apply for patent jointly.... Inventors may apply for a patent jointly even though (1) they did not physically work together or at the same time, (2) each did not make the same type or amount of contribution, or (3) each did not make a contribution to the subject matter of every claim of the patent."

35 U.S.C. §116, second paragraph: "If a joint inventor refuses to join in an application for patent or cannot be found or reached after diligent effort, the application may be made by the other inventor on behalf of himself and the omitted inventor...."

35 U.S.C. §116, third paragraph: "Whenever through error a person named in an application for patent as the inventor, or through error an inventor is not named in an application, and such error arose without any deceptive intention on his part, the Commissioner may permit the application to be amended accordingly, under such terms as he prescribes."

35 U.S.C. §262: "In the absence of any agreement to the contrary, each of the joint owners of a patent may make, use or sell the patented invention without the consent of and without accounting to the other owners."

- *Rule Reference*: "Joint inventors must apply for a patent jointly and each must make the required oath and declaration: neither of them alone, nor less than the entire number, can apply for a patent for an invention invented by them jointly...." 37 C.F.R. §1.45(a).

- *Treatise References*: 1 D. Chisum, *Patents* §§2.02–.03 (1994 rev.); 2 P. Rosenberg, *Patent Law Fundamentals* §11.01 (1994 rev.).

- *Case References*:

"The exact parameters of what constitutes joint inventorship are quite difficult to define. It is one of the muddiest concepts in the muddy metaphysics of the patent law. On the one hand, it is reasonably clear that a person who has merely followed instructions of another in performing experiments is not a coinventor of the object to which those experiments are directed. To claim inventorship is to claim at least some role in the final conception of that which is sought to be patented.... [O]ne must be able to say that without his contribution to the final conception, it would have been less—less efficient, less simple, less economical, less something of benefit." *Mueller Brass Co. v. Reading Indus., Inc.*, 352 F.Supp. 1357, 1372, 176 USPQ 361, 372 (E.D. Pa. 1972).

"What is clear is that the statutory word 'jointly' is not mere surplusage. For persons to be joint inventors under Section 116, there must be some element of joint behavior, such as collaboration or working under common direction, one inventor seeing a relevant report and building upon it or hearing another's suggestion at a meeting. Here there was nothing of that nature. Individuals cannot be joint inventors if they are completely ignorant of what each other has done until years after their individual independent efforts. They cannot be totally independent of each other and be joint inventors." *Kimberly-Clark Corp. v. Procter & Gamble Distrib.*, 973 F.2d 911, 917, 23 USPQ2d 1921, 1926 (Fed. Cir. 1991).

jukebox [copyright]

See COMPULSORY LICENSING OF A COPYRIGHT.

junior party [patent] The second party in time to file a patent application in a patent INTERFERENCE proceeding to determine PRIOR-

ITY OF INVENTION. The junior party has the burden of proving by a preponderance of the evidence that he made the invention before the SENIOR PARTY'S filing date. However, if the junior party filed his application after a patent has already been granted to the senior party, proof of priority of invention beyond a reasonable doubt is required.

• *Case References*:

"Since the interferences involve pending applications, Morgan, as junior party, had the burden of proving his case for priority by a preponderance of the evidence." *Morgan v. Hirsh*, 728 F.2d 1449, 1451, 221 USPQ 193, 194 (Fed. Cir. 1984).

"Because Oka is the senior party, Youssefyeh was required to establish reduction to practice *before* Oka's filing date, or conception before that date coupled with reasonable diligence from just before that date to Youssefyeh's filing date…. Oka, as the senior party, is presumptively entitled to an award of priority, and Youssefyeh, as the junior party in an interference between pending applications, must overcome that presumption with a preponderance of the evidence." *Oka v. Youssefyeh*, 849 F.2d 581, 584, 7 USPQ2d 1169, 1172 (Fed. Cir. 1988).

• *Treatise Reference*: 3 D. Chisum, *Patents* §10.03[1][c] (1994 rev.).

jus tertii [copyright–trademark] The defense to a charge of infringement that the rights of a third party are superior to the asserted intellectual property rights of the plaintiff.

Outside intellectual property law, jus tertii is a disfavored defense. The majority rule in cases involving trespass to land and conversion of personal property is that it is no defense that the plaintiff does not have legal title to the property. "Possession is title against all the world but the true owner." 75 Am. Jur. 2d, *Trespass* 40. See discussion at 3 J.T. McCarthy, *Trademarks and Unfair Competition* §31.39 (3d ed. 1995 rev.).

1. Jus Tertii Defense in Copyright Cases: The Copyright Act, 17 U.S.C. §103(a), codifies a jus tertii defense as against alleged infringements of derivative copyrights. A defendant is permitted to challenge the validity of the plaintiff's copyright to the extent that the plaintiff has used preexisting copyrighted material illegally in the DERIVATIVE WORK which is allegedly infringed.

Copyright in a Derivative Work Making Unlawful Use of Underlying Material. A DERIVATIVE WORK has by definition SUBSTANTIAL SIMILARITY to the underlying work and would be a copyright infringement in the absence of a license. Thus, if the underlying work is in copyright, one who wishes to exploit the derivative work needs a copyright license from the owner of copyright in the underlying work or works. If there is no such license, then the use of the underlying work in the derivative work is illegal under copyright law. Copyright in the derivative work does not extend to any part of the derivative work in which such preexisting material is unlawfully used. 17 U.S.C. §103(a). This gives a potential infringer of the derivative copyright the opportunity to raise as a defense the argument that the plaintiff has not obtained a license from the owner of rights in the copyright in underlying material. This is a kind of jus tertii defense. Since typically the underlying work totally pervades each part of the derivative work, there will be no part of the derivative work in which the underlying work is not "unlawfully used" and hence no enforceable derivative copyright at all, at least not unless and until there is a license from the owner of copyright in the underlying work.

Compilations. While this defense also applies in theory to COMPILATIONS, in practice, because the compiler's copyrighted work is only that particular selection and arrangement of material, there is no "part of the work" in which the preexisting copyrighted material is unlawfully used and enforcement of the compilations copyright should not be precluded.

See DERIVATIVE WORK.

• *Treatise References*: 1 P. Goldstein, *Copyright* §2.16 (1989); 1 *Nimmer on Copyright* §3.06 (1994 rev.).

• *Statutory Reference*: 17 U.S.C. §103(a): "The subject matter of copyright as specified by section 102 includes compilations and derivative works, but protection for a work employing preexisting material in which copyright subsists does not extend to any part of the work in which such material has been used unlawfully."

• *Legislative History*: "[Section 103(a)] prevents an infringer from benefiting, through copyright protection, from committing an unlawful act, but preserves copyright protection for those parts of the work that do not employ the preexisting work. Thus, an unauthorized translation of a novel could not be copyrighted at all, but the owner of copyright in an unauthorized anthology of poetry could sue someone who infringed the whole anthology, even though the infringer proves that publication of one of the poems was unauthorized. Under this provision, copyright could be obtained as long as the use of the preexisting work was not 'unlawful,' even though the consent of the copyright owner had not been obtained. For instance, the unauthorized reproduction of a work might be 'lawful' under the doctrine of fair use or an applicable foreign law, and if so the work incorporating it could be copyrighted." H.R. Rep. No. 94-1476, 94th Cong., 2d Sess. 57–58 (1976).

2. Jus Tertii Defense in Trademark Cases:
Jus tertii may arise in the trademark setting if the defendant alleges that the plaintiff has no title to the allegedly infringed trademark because the plaintiff itself is an infringer of a third party who has rights allegedly superior to the plaintiff. In a 1913 decision, the U.S. Supreme Court indirectly indicated that jus tertii could provide grounds for an unclean hands defense to a charge of trademark infringement. *Ubeda v. Zialcita*, 226 U.S. 452 (1913). But modern cases uniformly reject the assertion of jus tertii in trademark cases. E.g., *Stock Pot Restaurant Inc. v. Stockpot, Inc.*, 737 F.2d 1576, 222 USPQ 655 (Fed. Cir. 1984); *Eagle Snacks Inc. v. Nabisco Brands, Inc.*, 625 F. Supp. 571, 228 USPQ 625 (D.N.J. 1985). However, the allegedly superior right of a third party is a relevant defense if the defendant is in privity with that third party and can claim rights flowing from that third party. *Lapinee Trade, Inc. v. Paleewong Trading Co.*, 687 F. Supp. 1262, 8 USPQ2d 1277 (N.D. Ill. 1988), *aff'd without opinion*, 876 F.2d 106 (7th Cir. 1989).

• *Treatise Reference*: "As a matter of policy, jus tertii should not be allowed as a defense in any trademark case. So long as plaintiff proves rights superior to defendant, that is enough. Defendant is no less an infringer because it is brought to account by a plaintiff whose rights may or may not be superior to the whole world. The plaintiff's speculative dispute with a third party does not concern the defendant." 4 J.T. McCarthy, *Trademarks and Unfair Competition* §31.39 (3d ed. 1995 rev.).

K

Kaminstein Legislative History Project
[copyright] A research tool tracing the development of the textual history of each section of the Copyright Act of 1976. The Kamenstein volumes detail the legislative history beginning with the initial recommendation by Copyright Register Abraham L. Kaminstein in 1961 up to passage of the Act in 1976. It is a useful research tool in that rather than simply setting out the various versions of the legislative text, it also includes text from hearings, reports, discussions, etc., in order to assist the researcher in understanding how the different versions of the statute changed in the legislative process.

knock-off [patent–trademark–copyright] An identical copy of a work or product protected by patent, trademark, trade dress, or copyright.

Synonyms: CHINESE COPY, COUNTERFEIT, PIRATE COPY.

* *Usage Examples*:

Patent Law: "Having determined that [plaintiff-patentee] Sensa-Gel's macerator was useful in non-infringing processes, the court found it a staple article, as was [defendant] OHI's machine that Senza-Gel called a 'knock-off' of the macerator...." *Senza-Gel Corp. v. Seiffhart*, 803 F.2d 661, 663, 231 USPQ 363, 364 (Fed. Cir. 1986). "Such [unauthorized] use [of the patented material] will also encourage other companies to infringe with similar 'knock-off' products and will disparage the reputation of the genuine Thighmaster product as it becomes intertwined in the consumer's mind with cheaper imitations." *Telebrands Direct Response Corp. v. Ovation Communications, Inc.*, 802 F. Supp. 1169, 1178 (D.N.J. 1992).

Trademark/Trade Dress Law: "Plaintiffs allege that the Swan [lamp] is a "knock-off" of the Dove lamp. They assert claims under the Lanham Act §43(a), 15 U.S.C. §1125(a).... " *PAF Srl v. Lisa Lighting*, 712 F. Supp. 394, 396, 12 USPQ2d 1161, 1162 (S.D.N.Y. 1989). "The parties use the term 'knock-off' to refer to copies nearly identical to the original. Here, [defendant] used a direct mold of [plaintiff's] ring." *CJC Holdings Inc. v. Wright & Lato Inc.*, 979 F.2d 60, 66 n.3, 25 USPQ2d 1213, 1216 n.3 (5th Cir. 1992).

Copyright Law: "[R]epresentatives of Whimsicality first discovered what they believed were infringing 'knock-off' Halloween costumes—i.e., lower priced, lower quality imitations ...." *Whimsicality, Inc. v. Rubie's Costumes Co.*, 721 F. Supp. 1566, 1569, 13 USPQ2d 1288, 1290 (E.D.N.Y.), *order aff'd in part, vacated in part*, 891, 13 USPQ 1296 F.2d 452, 13 USPQ 1296 (2d Cir. 1989).

know-how [trade secret] Information that enables one to accomplish a particular task or to operate a particular device or process. Know-how usually denotes a particular kind of technological information that enables the possessor of the information to accomplish a given task.

"Know-how" is not a legal term of art, although it occasionally appears as a synonym for TRADE SECRET. E.g., "Broadly speaking, know-how constitutes a body of knowledge outside the public domain, the possession of which has value." Goldscheider, *Technology Management* §17.01 (1989 rev.).

Sometimes, know-how might meet the qualifications for protection as a trade secret, and sometimes it might not. For example, much practical education consists of conveying know-how, such as teaching plumbers how to install a toilet or attorneys how to use a computerized legal research program, neither of which are legally protectible trade secrets. While such information is very valuable and useful, it is generally known in the trade. But teaching three employees in a company how to etch microchip circuits using a process known only within that company probably is protectible as a trade secret.

- *Case Reference*: "[T]he concept of 'know how' is … a very fuzzily defined area, used primarily as a short-hand device for stating the conclusion that a process is protectable. It covers a multitude of matters, however, which in the broad sense are not protectable, e.g., an employee's general knowledge and skill." *Van Prods. Co. v. General Welding & Fabricating Co.*, 419 Pa. 248, 263, 213 A.2d 769, 777, 147 USPQ 221, 227 (1965).

- *Treatise Reference*: 1 R. Milgrim, *Trade Secrets* §§2.09[2], 6.04[5] (1994 rev.).

L

label license [patent] A patent license that is granted to the purchaser of a product by a notice on the label of a patented product or a product used in a patented process. It is a business decision whether a portion of the purchase price should be apportioned as a separate royalty.

Label licenses can serve several purposes, including notice to potential CONTRIBUTORY infringers or to those who would INDUCE infringement. See 1 H. Einhorn, *Patent Licensing Transactions* §1.01[2] (1989 rev.).

Patent Misuse and Tying. The owner of a method patent who grants a license via a label license only to those who buy an unpatented component from the patentee may be guilty of misuse of the patent by tying in the sale of the unpatented product to the patent license. See *B.B. Chem. Co. v. Ellis*, 314 U.S. 495 (1942). However, if the unpatented product is not a "STAPLE," then such conduct is not patent misuse. *Dawson Chem. Co. v. Rohm & Haas Co.*, 448 U.S. 176, 206 USPQ 385 (1980).

See CONTRIBUTORY PATENT INFRINGEMENT, STAPLE, TIE-IN.

- *Example*: "This product and the process of using it as described in accompanying instructions are covered in U.S. Patent No. 8,197,671. The price of this product includes a prepaid non-exclusive royalty to use this product under this patent at the rate of 2 cents per ounce."

- *Case Reference*: "A patentee ... who does not affirmatively offer, or express a willingness to offer, a licensing program separate from the label license attached to a staple article of commerce, runs the risk that the court may, in conjunction with the particularized evidence in the case, conclude that a tying arrangement is im-plicit, and that a misuse of the patent has occurred.... We merely indicate that any patentee who sells the patented item only in conjunction with some other unpatented staple goods raises serious suspicions of tying behavior and misuse." *Rex Chainbelt Inc. v. Harco Prods., Inc.*, 512 F.2d 993, 1002, 185 USPQ 10, 16 (9th Cir. 1975).

laches [patent–trademark–copyright] An equitable defense to the assertion of infringement of intellectual property rights that arises when the intellectual property owner inexcusably delays in filing a lawsuit against an infringer, causing some prejudice to the alleged infringer. The interrelationship between delay and prejudice is expressed in the formula: the defense of laches = delay x prejudice. 4 J.T. McCarthy, *Trademarks and Unfair Competition* §31.02 (3d ed. 1995 rev.).

Compared to the Statute of Limitations. Unlike the absolute time frame of a STATUTE OF LIMITATIONS, laches is a fact-intensive defense involving a weighing and balancing of all points of equity and fairness in the case. It is generally much easier to establish a laches defense to the recovery of damages arising prior to the filing of the lawsuit than to bar prospective relief of an injunction and postfiling damages. *McLean v. Flemming*, 96 U.S. 245, 253 (1878).

Delay in Moving for a Preliminary Injunction. It is generally much easier to establish a laches defense to the granting of a motion for a preliminary injunction than to bar a permanent injunction after a full trial on the merits. Additionally, apart from laches, lack of diligence in promptly suing and moving for a preliminary injunction is weighty evidence that there is no irreparable injury in need of the prompt and extraordinary relief of a preliminary injunction.

Majorica, S.A. v. R.H. Macy & Co., 762 F.2d 7, 226 USPQ 624 (2d Cir. 1985).

See STATUTE OF LIMITATIONS.

1. ***Laches in Patent Cases.*** To invoke a laches defense in a patent infringement suit, an alleged infringer has the burden of proving two factors: (a) the patentee delayed filing suit for an unreasonable and inexcusable length of time and (b) the alleged infringer suffered significant prejudice attributable to the delay. *Aukerman Co. v. Chaides Constr. Co.*, 960 F.2d 1020, 1032, 22 USPQ2d 1321, 1328 (Fed. Cir. 1992) (en banc). However, laches is an equitable defense and establishment of these two factors does not mandate a laches defense. A court must also consider and weigh any excuse offered by patentee for its delay. Also, a patentee may defeat a laches defense if the infringer has engaged in particularly egregious or inequitable conduct which would change the equities significantly in patentee's favor. A court must weigh all pertinent facts including: the length of delay; the seriousness of the prejudice; the patentee's excuses; and the defendant's conduct or culpability. *Aukerman Co. v. Chaides Constr. Co.*, 960 F.2d 1020, 1033–34, 22 USPQ2d 1321, 1329 (Fed. Cir. 1992).

Delay in Bringing Suit. The length of delay which may be deemed unreasonable has no fixed boundaries but rather depends on the circumstances of each case. The period of delay is measured from the time the plaintiff knew or reasonably should have known of the defendant's alleged infringing activities to the date of suit.

Presumption of Laches Upon a Six-Year Delay. A presumption of laches arises in a patent infringement action when the patentee delays bringing suit for more than six years after the date that the patentee knew or should have known of the alleged infringer's activity. The six-year period is "borrowed" from the six-year patent statute of 35 U.S.C. §286. *Aukerman Co. v. Chaides Constr. Co.*, 960 F.2d 1020, 1034–35, 22 USPQ2d 1321, 1329–30 (Fed. Cir. 1992). This presumption has the effect of shifting the burden of going forward with the evidence to the patentee. However, the burden of

persuasion on the issue of laches remains with the defendant.

Eliminating the Presumption—The Double Bursting Bubble Theory. The laches presumption embodies what is known as the "bursting bubble theory of presumptions." Under this theory, a presumption is not merely rebuttable but completely vanishes upon the introduction of evidence sufficient to support a finding of the nonexistence of the fact to be presumed. In the six-year laches presumption there is a "double bursting bubble." That is, to eliminate the presumption of laches, the patentee may offer evidence showing either that the delay in filing suit was reasonable or that the defendant suffered no prejudice. Evidence negating either unreasonable delay or prejudice will eliminate the basis for the presumption. *Aukerman Co. v. Chaides Constr. Co.*, 960 F.2d 1020, 1037, 22 USPQ2d 1321, 1332 (Fed. Cir. 1992).

Prejudice Caused by Delay. Prejudice caused by the delay may be either economic or evidentiary in nature. "Evidentiary or 'defense' prejudice, may arise by reason of defendant's inability to present a full and fair defense on the merits due to loss of records, the death of a witness or the unreliability of memories of long past events, thereby undermining the court's ability to judge the facts." *Aukerman Co. v. Chaides Constr. Co.*, 960 F.2d 1020, 1033, 22 USPQ2d 1321, 1328 (Fed. Cir. 1992). Economic prejudice may arise where defendant suffers monetary losses which would have been prevented by an earlier suit.

Excuses for Delay. Excuses which have been recognized in some cases include: other litigation; negotiations with the accused; wartime conditions; minimal extent of infringement; and dispute over ownership of patent. *Aukerman Co. v. Chaides Constr. Co.*, 960 F.2d 1020, 1033, 22 USPQ2d 1321, 1329 (Fed. Cir. 1992).

Only Prefiling Damages Are Barred. Laches bars relief on a patentee's claim only with respect to damages accrued prior to filing of the infringement lawsuit. *Aukerman Co. v. Chaides Constr. Co.*, 960 F.2d 1020, 1041, 22 USPQ2d 1321, 1335 (Fed. Cir. 1992). To bar an injunction and postfiling damages, defendant will need to prove further the separate elements of equitable estoppel.

See EQUITABLE ESTOPPEL.

Equitable Estoppel Distinguished. A laches defense will only bar presuit damages; a defense of equitable estoppel can bar the entire infringement action. Laches focuses on the reasonableness of the patentee's delay in bringing suit; equitable estoppel focuses on what the defendant has been led to believe by patentee's conduct. A showing of a six year delay creates a presumption of laches; no such presumption is applicable to the defense of equitable estoppel.

See EQUITABLE ESTOPPEL.

• *Treatise References*: 4 D. Chisum, *Patents* §19.05[2] (1994 rev.); R. Harmon, *Patents and the Federal Circuit* §9.3 (3d ed. 1994).

• *Case References*:

"Once a presumption of laches arises, the patentee may offer proof directed to rebutting the laches factors. Such evidence may be directed to showing either that the patentee's delay was reasonable or that the defendant suffered no prejudice or both. By raising a genuine issue respecting either factual element of a laches defense, the presumption of laches is overcome." *Aukerman Co. v. Chaides Constr. Co.*, 960 F.2d 1020, 1038, 22 USPQ2d 1321, 1333 (Fed. Cir. 1992).

"[T]he presumption of laches which arises after defendant proves a six year delay is a 'double bursting bubble' which the plaintiff punctures with introduction of evidence sufficient to raise a genuine dispute as to either delay or prejudice. Here, [plaintiff] introduced evidence that the delay was attributable to its litigation with [other parties] as well as the re-examination proceeding with [those same parties] instigated some time after the notice letter had been sent to [the defendant]. This evidence was more than sufficient to raise a genuine dispute as to whether the delay was excusable. The bubble was burst; defendant was put to its proof on both factors." *Hemstreet v. Computer Entry Sys. Corp.*, 972 F.2d 1290, 1293, 23 USPQ2d 1860, 1863 (Fed. Cir. 1992).

2. Laches in Trademark Cases. Estoppel by laches has been a defense to either damages and/or an injunction in trademark cases for over 100 years in U.S. law. *McLean v. Flemming*, 96 U.S. 245, 253 (1878) ("Unreasonable delay in bringing a suit is always a serious objection to relief in equity."). Mere delay, without resulting prejudicial injury to the defendant, is not sufficient to prevent relief for infringement. Prejudice is proven by some action or expansion of the defendant taken in reliance on the trademark owner's failure to act.

Statutory Basis. The federal Lanham Trademark Act vests the courts with the power to grant injunctions and award profits and damages according to "the principles of equity." Lanham Act §§34, 35, 15 U.S.C. §§1116, 1117. This clearly includes the equitable defense of laches. Section 33(b)(8) permits laches to be raised as a defense or defect to infringement of an incontestably registered mark.

Defense to Damages Compared to Injunction. It is always easier for a defendant to make out an estoppel by laches defense precluding the recovery of presuit damages than precluding the prospective relief of an injunction. The courts are understandably reluctant to refuse to enjoin a proven likelihood of confusion of customers merely because the trademark owner has not moved with dispatch. In those cases where laches has been adjudged sufficient to preclude a final injunction, there have usually been some plus factors such as a dubious case of likelihood of confusion or a grossly long period of delay. Laches is generally not a defense when asserted by a deliberate and knowing trademark infringer. *Tisch Hotels, Inc. v. Americana Inn, Inc.*, 350 F.2d 609, 146 USPQ 566 (7th Cir. 1965) (Only in "the most exceptional circumstances" is delay a defense to an injunction "in a case of deliberate infringement.").

Traditional Exceptions. Classic reasons accepted for delay in suing are good faith settlement negotiations; other litigation pending concerning the same mark; reasonable lack of knowledge by the plaintiff until a reasonable time before filing suit; and a gradual encroachment by the defendant that did not prompt a lawsuit until the defendant's use first significantly impacted on the plaintiff's good will. 3

J.T. McCarthy, *Trademarks and Unfair Competition* §31.06 (3d ed. 1995 rev.).

Delay in Moving for a Preliminary Injunction. Even relatively short periods of delay, on the order of a few months, when coupled with some prejudice, can prevent the issuance of a preliminary injunction. Additionally, apart from laches, lack of diligence in promptly suing and moving for a preliminary injunction "undercuts any presumption that infringement alone has caused irreparable harm pendente lite." *GTE Corp. v. Wiliams*, 731 F.2d 676, 222 USPQ 803 (10th Cir. 1984). Delay, coupled with other equities, "tends to indicate at least a reduced need for such drastic, speedy action" as a preliminary injunction. *Citibank, N.A. v. Citytrust*, 756 F.2d 273, 225 USPQ 708 (2d Cir. 1985).

Use of State Statute of Limitations. The Court of Appeals for the Sixth Circuit has held that in federal Lanham Act cases, the analogous state statute of limitations will usually measure the time frame for laches. *Tandy Corp. v. Malone & Hyde, Inc.*, 769 F.2d 362, 226 USPQ 703, *reh'g denied*, 777 F.2d 1130, 228 USPQ 621 (6th Cir. 1985); not followed in *Clamp Mfg. Co. v. Enco Mfg. Co.*, 870 F.2d 512, 10 USPQ2d 1226 (9th Cir. 1989).

• *Treatise Reference*: 4 J.T. McCarthy, *Trademarks and Unfair Competition* §§31.01–.14 (3d ed. 1995 rev.).

3. Laches in Copyright Cases. While mere delay in suing for copyright infringement will not constitute a defense of laches, inexcusable delay coupled with resulting prejudicial reliance by the accused infringer may constitute a defense of laches. *Lottie Joplin Thomas Trust v. Crown Publishers, Inc.*, 592 F.2d 651, 199 USPQ 449 (2d Cir. 1978). Some copyright cases have held that laches will not prevent an injunction or an award of damages for postfiling acts unless the copyright owner's conduct constitutes an estoppel or an abandonment of copyright.

• *Treatise References*: 3 *Nimmer on Copyright* §§12.06, 13.07 (1994 rev.); 1 N. Boorstyn, *Copyright* §12.08 (2d ed. 1994); 2 P. Goldstein, *Copyright* §9.5.1 (1989).

Lanham Act [trademark] The premier federal law that (1) governs the registration and protection of TRADEMARKS, SERVICE MARKS, COLLECTIVE MARKS, and CERTIFICATION MARKS; (2) prohibits the infringement of most types of unregistered marks, TRADE NAMES, and TRADE DRESS; and (3) prohibits false advertising and trade libel.

The Lanham Act is the federal trademark act of 1946, codified at 15 U.S.C. §§1051–1127. Signed into law on July 5, 1946, it took effect on July 5, 1947, and has been amended many times since. The act is named after Fritz Garland Lanham (1880-1965), a lawyer from Fort Worth, Texas, and a Democratic representative in Congress for 28 years from 1919 to 1947.

Major amendments during the 1980s were: (1) The Trademark Counterfeiting Act of 1984; (2) The Trademark Clarification Act of 1984; and (3) The Trademark Law Revision Act of 1988.

See REGISTRATION OF A TRADEMARK, PRINCIPAL REGISTER, SUPPLEMENTAL REGISTER, PRESUMPTION OF VALIDITY, COUNTERFEIT.

• *Treatise Reference*: 1 J.T. McCarthy, *Trademarks and Unfair Competition* §§5.04–.05 (3d ed. 1995 rev.).

• *Statutory Reference*: Lanham Act §45, 15 U.S.C. §1127: "*Intent of Act.* The intent of this Act is to regulate commerce within the control of Congress by making actionable the deceptive and misleading use of marks in such commerce; to protect registered marks used in such commerce from interference by State, or territorial legislation; to protect persons engaged in such commerce against unfair competition; to prevent fraud and deception in such commerce by the use of reproductions, copies, counterfeits, or colorable imitations of registered marks; and to provide rights and remedies stipulated by treaties and conventions respecting trademarks, trade names, and unfair competition entered into between the United States and foreign nations."

late claiming [patent] A particular application of the rule against adding "NEW MATTER." That is, an inventor cannot by later amendment add new claims that relate to matter which was not disclosed in the original patent application.

The "Muncie Gear" Doctrine. The doctrine of "late claiming" is sometimes called the "Muncie Gear doctrine" after the seminal 1942 Supreme Court decision in *Muncie Gear Works Inc. v. Outboard Marine & Mfg. Co.*, 315 U.S. 759, 53 USPQ 1 (1942). The Supreme Court invalidated claims added by amendment beyond the statutory period after public use or sale if the claims were not supported by the disclosure of the original application for patent. See Ryan, *The Muncie Gear Doctrine and the Effect of §132 Upon It*, 62 J. Pat. Off. Soc'y 678 (1980).

A Facet of the Rule Against Adding "New Matter." There was some question among the circuit courts as to the correct interpretation of the *Muncie Gear* decision. Most courts took the following view as stated by the Court of Appeals for the Eighth Circuit: "The conclusion that *Muncie Gear* merely stands for a prohibition against new matter is further supported by the Court's concluding observation that 'the original application, wholly *failed to disclose* the invention now asserted....' " *Square Liner 360, Inc. v. Chisum*, 691 F.2d 362, 373, 216 USPQ 666, 674 (8th Cir. 1982). Similarly, the current view of the Court of Appeals for the Federal Circuit is that "late claiming" is merely an application of the rule against adding "new matter" to claims. New claims added by amendment must be supported by the original patent disclosure as filed in the sense that it complies with the DESCRIPTION and ENABLEMENT requirements. The Federal Circuit's position is now so definite that it has referred to the "inappropriate and long ago discredited 'late claiming' label," stating that the real issue is "whether the claims entered by amendment were supported by the disclosure in [the] original application." *Railroad Dynamics Inc. v. A. Stucki Co.*, 727 F.2d 1506, 1517, 220 USPQ 929, 940 (Fed. Cir. 1984).

• *Treatise References*: 3 D. Chisum, *Patents* §11.05 (1994 rev.); R. Harmon, *Patents and the Federal Circuit* §5.5 (3d ed. 1994).

• *Case Reference*: "The origin of what has been called a 'late claiming' doctrine is found in *Muncie Gear Works, Inc. v. Outboard Marine*

& Mfg. Co.... The interpretation of the Second Circuit ... is that *Muncie Gear* enunciated a new 'late claiming' doctrine whereby later-presented claims, whether or not directed to subject matter within the original disclosure, may be barred by intervening rights under §102(b).... We reject that interpretation in favor of one more widely endorsed, namely that the holding in *Muncie Gear*, that the claims were invalid 'if there was public use, or sale ... more than two years before the first *disclosure* thereof to the Patent Office' (emphasis added), is an application of the statutory prohibition against the introduction by amendment, after the filing date, of additional disclosure in an application and of claims directed thereto." *Westphal v. Fawzi*, 666 F.2d 575, 577, 212 USPQ 321, 322–23 (C.C.P.A. 1981), cited with approval in *Correge, Dominique & Ciprian v. Murphy*, 705 F.2d 1326, 1329 n.4, 217 USPQ 753, 755 n.4 (Fed. Cir. 1983).

Lear rule [patent]
See LICENSE ESTOPPEL.

letter of consent [trademark]
See CONSENT AGREEMENT.

letter of protest [patent–trademark]
See PROTEST.

license [patent–trademark–copyright] A permission to use an intellectual property right under defined conditions. While an ASSIGNMENT denotes the transfer of title, a license denotes only a permission to use within a defined time, context, market line, or territory. Whereas an assignment conveys title, in a nonexclusive license, title remains with the licensor. An analogy is the rental of real estate, where the tenant does not acquire ownership interests, no matter how long the tenancy. However, if the license is exclusive, the licensee's interest begins to resemble ownership of defined rights and there is much less of a resemblance to a rental of real estate.

Exclusive and Nonexclusive Licenses Compared. In intellectual property law, important distinctions exist between "exclusive licenses" and "nonexclusive licenses." An "exclusive" license does not necessarily mean that this is the one and only license granted by the licensor. More commonly, the license is "exclusive" as to a defined scope such as product line, context of use, territory, or time duration. In an exclusive license, the licensor expressly or impliedly promises the licensee that the licensor will not grant other licenses of the same rights within the same scope or field covered by the terms of the exclusive license. However, the owner of rights can grant as many nonexclusive licenses of the same rights as it chooses.

1. License of Patent. The demarcation between an assignment and an unlimited exclusive license is sometimes difficult to determine. Under the classic rule of *Waterman v. Mackenzie*, a patent license is any transfer of rights that does not amount to an ASSIGNMENT of the patent. An assignment is a transfer of either all rights of exclusivity in the patent, or of an undivided fractional portion (e.g., a 50 percent interest), or of all rights in a specified portion of the United States. 3 P. Rosenberg, *Patent Law Fundamentals* §16.01[1][a] (1994 rev.). Transfer of anything less than that is dubbed a "license." *Waterman v. Mackenzie*, 138 U.S. 252, 255 (1891) (see quotation below). "To determine whether a provision in an agreement constitutes an assignment or a license, one must ascertain the intention of the parties and examine the substance of what was granted." *Vaupel Textilmaschinen v. Meccanica Euro Italia*, 944 F.2d 870, 874, 20 USPQ2d 1045, 1048 (Fed. Cir. 1991).

The Right to Sue Infringers. The Patent Act of 1952 provides that a suit for infringement may be brought by "a patentee." 35 U.S.C. §281. A "patentee" includes the party to whom the patent was issued and the successors in title to the patent. 35 U.S.C. §100(d). The right to sue infringers is normally the privilege of the party that has title to the patent, such that a licensee usually cannot sue for infringement in its own name. *United States v. General Elec. Co.*, 272 U.S. 476, 489 (1926). However, an exclusive licensee can sue for infringement in the name of the patentee by joining the patentee as an involuntary party. *Independent Wireless Tel. Co. v. Radio Corp. of Am.*, 269 U.S. 459, 469 (1926) (see quotation below). "The policy underlying the requirement to join the owner when an exclusive licensee brings suit is to prevent the possibility of two suits on the same patent against a single infringer." *Vaupel Textilmaschinen v. Meccanica Euro Italia*, 944 F.2d 870, 874, 20 USPQ2d 1045, 1049 (Fed. Cir. 1991). See 6 D. Chisum, *Patents* §21.03[2][c] (1994 rev.) ("An exclusive licensee generally has standing to sue for infringement against anyone operating without authority in the stated area of exclusivity.").

Exclusive Patent License. Patent Code §261 specifically authorizes the grant of exclusive licenses of patents. An exclusive license is one in which the owner of the patent agrees not to grant licenses to others within the defined scope of the license. For example, there may be an exclusive license to use the patented technology of a form of laser in the industrial field, an exclusive license for the medical field, and an exclusive license for the military range-finding field. That type of defined FIELD OF USE license is known as a limited exclusive license, as distinguished from an unlimited exclusive license in which there are no other licenses of any kind under that patent. In patent law, the unmodified use of the term "exclusive license" usually refers to a promise by the patent owner not to grant any other licenses of any kind under that patent. Thus, there will usually be only a single "exclusive licensee" of a patent. In the absence of a provision to the contrary, grant of an exclusive license also precludes the licensor from practicing the patented invention. *Cutter Labs. Inc. v. Lyophile Cryochem Corp.*, 179 F.2d 80, 84 USPQ 54 (9th Cir. 1949); J. Dratler, *Licensing of Intellectual Property* §8.01 et seq. (1994); R. Nordhaus, *Patent License Agreements* §11 (1994 rev.). The licensor of an otherwise exclusive license may reserve the right to practice the invention. This is sometimes called a "sole exclusive license" because, while the licensor promises not to grant a license to anyone else, the licensor does not promise total exclusivity.

Nonexclusive Patent License. A nonexclusive license contains no limit on the licensor's power to grant further licenses. It is in effect a "mere waiver of the right to sue" for patent infringement. *DeForest Radio Tel. & Tel. Co. v.*

United States, 273 U.S. 236, 242 (1927). Thus, a license can be viewed as an arrangement in which the "licensee is purchasing the right to be free from infringement litigation." *Moraine Prods. v. ICI Am. Inc.*, 538 F.2d 134, 149, 191 USPQ 65, 77 (7th Cir. 1976). Unlike exclusive licenses, nonexclusive licenses have no statutory basis in Patent Code §261.

Other Aspects of Patent Licenses. A LABEL LICENSE is one which is on the label of a product and is granted to the purchaser of the product. The rule of LICENSEE ESTOPPEL was ended by the Supreme Court in 1969 in *Lear v. Adkins*, raising many difficult questions of litigation between patentee and licensee. While many other nations have extensive provisions for the government-ordered COMPULSORY LICENSING of patent, that is a rarity in the United States.

See LABEL LICENSE, LICENSEE ESTOPPEL, COMPULSORY LICENSE.

• *Statutory Reference*: 35 U.S.C. §261: "Applications for patent, patents, or any interest therein, shall be assignable in law by an instrument in writing. The applicant, patentee, or his assigns or legal representatives may in like manner grant and convey an exclusive right under his application for patent, or patent, to the whole or any specified part of the United States."

• *Case References*:

"In its simplest form, a license means only leave to do a thing which the licensor would otherwise have a right to prevent." *Western Elec. Co. v. Pacent Reproducer Corp.*, 42 F.2d 116, 118, 5 USPQ 105, 106 (2d Cir. 1930).

"The patentee or his assigns may, by instrument in writing, assign, grant and convey, either, 1st, the whole patent, comprising the exclusive right to make, use and vend the invention through the United States; or, 2d, an undivided part or share of that exclusive right; or, 3rd, the exclusive right under the patent within and throughout a specified part of the United States. A transfer of either of these three kinds of interests is an assignment, properly speaking, and vests in the assignee a title in so much of the patent itself, with a right to sue infringers; in the second case, jointly with the assignor; in

the first and third cases, in the name of the assignee alone. Any assignment or transfer, short of one of these, is a mere license, giving the licensee no title in the patent, and no right to sue at law in his own name for infringement. In equity, as at law, when the transfer amounts to a license only, the title remains in the owner of the patent; and suit must be brought in his name, and never in the name of the licensee alone, unless that is necessary to prevent an absolute failure of justice, as where the patentee is the infringer, and cannot sue himself. Any rights of the licensee must be enforced through or in the name of the owner of the patent, and perhaps, if necessary to protect the rights of all parties, joining the licensee with him as a plaintiff." *Waterman v. Mackenzie*, 138 U.S. 252, 255 (1891).

"It seems clear, then, on principle and authority, that the owner of a patent, who grants to another the exclusive right to make, use or vend the invention, which does not constitute a statutory assignment, holds the title to the patent in trust for such a licensee, to the extent that he must allow the use of his name as plaintiff in any action brought at the instance of the licensee in law or in equity to obtain damages for the injury to his exclusive right by an infringer, or to enjoin infringement of it. Such exclusive licenses frequently contain express covenants by the patent owner and licensor to sue infringers, that expressly cast upon the former the affirmative duty of initiating and bearing the expense of the litigation. But, without such express covenants, the implied obligation of the licensor to allow the use of his name is indispensable to the enjoyment by the licensee of the monopoly which by personal contract the licensor has given." *Independent Wireless Tel. Co. v. Radio Corp. of Am.*, 269 U.S. 459, 469 (1926).

"Based on the analysis in *Waterman* and *Independent Wireless Tel. Co.*, this court has recognized the following principles: The right to sue for infringement is ordinarily an incident of legal title to the patent. A licensee may obtain sufficient rights in the patent to be entitled to seek relief from infringement, but to do so, it ordinarily must join the patent owner. And a bare licensee, who has no right to exclude others from making, using, or selling the licensed products, has no legally recognized interest that entitles it to bring or join an infringement action." *Abbott Labs. v. Ortho Diagnostic Sys. Inc.*, 47 F.3d 1128, 1131, 33 USPQ2d 1771, 1774 (Fed. Cir. 1995).

"[A] patent license agreement is in essence nothing more than a promise by the licensor not to sue the licensee.... Even if couched in terms of '[l]icensee is given the right to make, use or sell X,' the agreement cannot convey that absolute right because not even the patentee of X is given that right. His right is merely one to exclude others from making, using or selling X...." *Spindlefabrik Suesenn-Schurr GmbH v. Schubert & Salzer*, 829 F.2d 1075, 1081, 4 USPQ2d 1044, 1048 (Fed. Cir. 1987).

"[A] license is fundamentally an agreement by the patent owner not to sue the licensee. In a normal negotiation, the potential licensee has three basic choices: forego all use of the invention; pay an agreed upon royalty; infringe the patent and risk litigation." *Fromson v. Western Litho Plate Co.*, 853 F.2d 1568, 7 USPQ2d 1606, 1613 (Fed. Cir. 1988).

- *Treatise References*: 6 D. Chisum, *Patents* §21.03[2][c] (1994 rev.); 3 P. Rosenberg, *Patent Law Fundamentals* §16.01[1][b] (1994 rev.); R. Nordhaus, *Patent License Agreements* §11 (1994 rev.); 1 H. Einhorn, *Patent Licensing Transactions* §1.01 (1994 rev.); H. Mayers & B. Brunsvold, *Drafting Patent License Agreements* (3d ed. 1991); J. Dratler, *Licensing of Intellectual Property* (1994).

2. License of Trademark. A trademark or service mark can be validly licensed only if the licensor exercises control over the nature and quality of the goods or services sold by the licensee under the licensed mark. In federal law, the licensee is known as a "related company." This does not denote any corporate ownership or affiliation, but only that the related company is a controlled licensee of the mark.

Naked Licensing. Licensing of a mark without adequate quality control is "naked licensing," which raises the risk that the public will be deceived into thinking that the goods or services provided by the uncontrolled licensee are of the same general nature and quality as those previously provided or as those provided by other licensees. This can result in the mark ceasing to serve as a symbol of quality and controlled source, causing the mark to become "abandoned" in the sense that the word or symbol no longer has significance as an identifying mark. For this reason, the law imposes on the trademark licensor the affirmative duty to police the mark as used by licensees. *Dawn Donut Co. v. Hart's Food Stores, Inc.*, 267 F.2d 358, 367, 121 USPQ 430, 437 (2d Cir. 1959). It has been held that uncontrolled licensing may estop the licensor from challenging the licensee's uncontrolled use of the mark. *Sheila's Shine Prods., Inc. v. Sheila Shine, Inc.*, 486 F.2d 114, 124, 179 USPQ 577, 583 (5th Cir. 1973).

Quality Control. There is considerable controversy as to how much and what kind of quality control over a licensee is necessary to comply with the law. Usually, the courts have not been satisfied with a contractual power to control and have required proof that the licensor in fact has exercised supervision and control over the nature and quality of the licensee's goods or services. While in ordinary situations total reliance on the licensee's discretion is not sufficient, if there has been a close and satisfactory relationship in the past, partial reliance on the licensee has been held sufficient. *Transgo, Inc. v. Ajac Transmission Parts Corp.*, 768 F.2d 1001, 227 USPQ 598 (9th Cir. 1985). The kind and extent of contractual standards and continuing supervision that is required will vary widely with the nature of the goods and services under license.

Valid Licensing. Lanham Act §5 provides that a licensee's use of the mark inures to the benefit of the licensor, the owner of the mark. That is, use of the mark by a licensee strengthens the mark owned by the licensor. The licensee builds up no ownership rights in the mark. The licensee is in the position of a renter of an apartment, who does not acquire title to the property, no matter how long the tenancy and no matter how many improvements are made. A trademark is an unusual kind of property in that it can be used by many licensees at the same time and the more use that is made of the mark, the stronger it becomes. There is no necessity for the name of the licensor to appear on licensed uses of a mark. *General Motors Corp. v.*

Gibson Chem. & Oil Corp., 786 F.2d 105, 110, 229 USPQ 352, 355 (2d Cir. 1986). Doubt as to whether initial rights in a mark could be acquired and sustained through use only by a controlled licensee was put to rest with a sentence added to the 1989 amendments to Lanham Act §5, which stated that such first use only by a licensee could establish valid rights in the licensor. While in some nations licensing is permitted only of registered marks and only by registered users, there are no such limitations in U.S. law.

See FRANCHISING, TIE-INS.

• *Treatise Reference*: 2 J.T. McCarthy, *Trademarks and Unfair Competition* §§18.13–.24 (3d ed. 1995 rev.).

• *Statutory References*:

Lanham Act §45, 15 U.S.C. §1127: *"Related Company*. The term 'related company' means any person whose use of a mark is controlled by the owner of the mark with respect to the nature and quality of the goods or services on or in connection with which the mark is used."

Lanham Act §45, 15 U.S.C. §1127: *"Abandonment*. A mark shall be deemed to be 'abandoned' … (2) [w]hen any course of conduct of the owner, including acts of omission as well as commission, causes the mark to become the generic name for the goods or services on or in connection with which it is used or otherwise to lose its significance as a mark.…"

Lanham Act §5, 15 U.S.C. §1055: "Where a registered mark or a mark sought to be registered is or may be used legitimately by related companies, such use shall inure to the benefit of the registrant or applicant for registration, and such use shall not affect the validity of such mark or of its registration, provided such mark is not used in such manner as to deceive the public. If first use of a mark by a person is controlled by the registrant or applicant for registration of the mark with respect to the nature and quality of the goods or services, such first use shall inure to the benefit of the registrant or applicant, as the case may be."

• *Case References*:

"Courts have long imposed upon trademark licensors a duty to oversee the quality of the licensee's products.… The rationale for this requirement is that marks are treated by purchasers as an indication that the trademark owner is associated with the product. Customers rely upon the owner's reputation when they select the trademarked goods. If a trademark owner allows licensees to depart from its quality standards, the public will be misled, and the trademark will cease to have utility as an informational device. A trademark owner who allows this to occur loses its right to use the mark.… Retention of a trademark requires only minimal quality control, for in this context we do not sit to assess the quality of products sold on the open market." *Kentucky Fried Chicken Corp. v. Diversified Packaging Corp.*, 549 F.2d 368, 386, 193 USPQ 649, 665 (5th Cir. 1977).

"The critical question in determining whether a licensing program is controlled sufficiently by the licensor to protect his mark is whether the licensees' operations are policed adequately to guarantee the quality of the products sold under the mark." *General Motors Corp. v. Gibson Chem. & Oil Corp.*, 786 F.2d 105, 110, 229 USPQ 352, 355 (2d Cir. 1986).

3. License of Copyright. In copyright law, there is a clear line of differentiation between the legal significance of exclusive and nonexclusive licenses. An exclusive licensee is regarded as the owner of the particular right of copyright that is exclusively licensed and has the right to sue for infringement of the licensed right.

Abolition of the Rule of Indivisibility of Copyright. The rule governing assignment of copyright under the 1909 Copyright Act was one of "indivisibility" of copyright: a copyright was an indivisible property right, which was not capable of being split up into smaller units and sold or exclusively licensed. The rule of indivisibility was done away with in the 1978 Copyright Act by §201(d)(2), which permits the assignment or exclusive license of any part or subpart of the bundle of rights comprising a copyright. H.R. Rep. No. 94-1476, 94th Cong., 2d Sess. 123 (1976). This and other provisions of the 1978 Act have largely done away with any practical distinction between an assignment and an exclusive license of the same rights of copyright. Both are categorized as a "transfer" of copyright ownership. An exclusive licensee of a right of copyright is regarded as the copyright owner of the particular right that is licensed.

Examples of Exclusive License of Copyright. For example, an author of a series of illustrated children's books could grant an exclusive license to Alpha Studios to produce a feature-length DERIVATIVE WORK motion picture using the copyrightable elements of the books, an exclusive license to Beta to create a daily newspaper cartoon based upon the illustrations in the books, an exclusive license to Gamma to use the characters from the books in puppet shows performed in the state of California for a one-year period, and an exclusive license to Zeta to make plush dolls smaller than 12-inches tall of characters from the books. Each of these licenses is a "transfer" of rights of copyright and each transferee has "all of the protection and remedies accorded to the copyright owner" by law. 17 U.S.C. §201(d)(2). For example, each transferee (exclusive licensee) has standing to sue third parties for copyright infringement for an invasion of its scope of exclusive rights within the original copyrighted work. There appears to be no limit on how narrowly the scope of exclusivity can be defined. This means that when several narrowly defined "exclusive" licenses are granted, at some point the distinction between "exclusive" and "nonexclusive" begins to blur. 3 *Nimmer on Copyright* §10.02[A] (1994 rev.).

One Copyright Per Work. There is never more than a single copyright in a work regardless of the owner's exclusive license of various rights to different persons. "Section 201(d)(2) provides for divisibility of rights, not divisibility of copyright." 3 *Nimmer on Copyright* §10.02[C][2] (1994 rev.). There is only one registration per copyrightable work. However, if a licensee creates a copyrightable DERIVATIVE WORK, that copyright can be separately owned and registered by the licensee.

Formality and Recording. To be valid, an exclusive license of copyright is a transfer that must be in writing and signed by the person conveying rights. 17 U.S.C. §204(a). This does not apply to nonexclusive licenses, which can be oral. RECORDATION of copyright licenses is advised to protect against prior or subsequent exclusive licensees of the same rights.

Scope of License for New Media. The development of new communications technology has created problems in determining the scope of the media which the license covers. When drafting a license agreement, the parties may be unaware of, or fail to take into account, the existence of novel technological developments which generate unforeseen applications for a previously licensed work. For example, does a grant of motion picture rights made before the advent of television include the right to exhibit a motion picture on television? The problem in determining the scope of a license is that courts must look to the intent of the parties as it is reflected in the written words of the contract (along with other permissible evidence). However, there may be no single intent as to future rights because the parties did not specifically contemplate the new medium at the time the license was granted.

Examples of "New Use" Cases. Generally, when a grant of rights includes the right to exhibit a work "by any means or methods now or hereafter known," it includes any and all media, even if the grantor did not anticipate at the time of contract a particular development in the manner of exhibiting motion pictures. Thus, a series of contracts granting motion picture distributors a license to exhibit plaintiff's films "by any present or future methods or means" and "by any means now known or unknown" was held to encompass the right to distribute the films by means of later-developed video technology, such as on video cassettes, even though the grantor did not have such rights in mind at the time of the grant. *Rooney v. Columbia Pictures Indus., Inc.*, 538 F. Supp. 211 (S.D.N.Y.), *aff'd without opinion*, 714 F.2d 117 (2d Cir. 1982). See *Platinum Record Co. v. Lucasfilm, Ltd.* 566 F. Supp. 226 (D.N.J. 1983). However, in a case involving a 1969 contract granting rights to "[t]he exhibition of [a] motion picture [containing a licensed work] ... by means of television," but containing a broad restriction reserving to the licensor "all rights and uses in and to said musical composition, except for those herein granted," the court held that the license did not encompass the right to revenues derived from sales of the motion picture in videocassette form. *Cohen v. Paramount Pictures Corp.*, 845 F.2d 851, 853–54, 7 USPQ2d 1570, 1571–72 (9th Cir. 1988). See *Rey v. Lafferty*, 990 F.2d 1379, 26 USPQ2d 1339 (1st Cir. 1993) (grant of rights to animated film episodes "for television viewing" did not encompass the right to distribute films in videocassette form, interpreting ambiguous copyright license against sophisticated licensee who was the drafting party).

- *Treatise References*: 3 *Nimmer on Copyright* §10.01 et seq. (1994 rev.); M. Leaffer, *Understanding Copyright* §5.8 (1989); 1 P. Goldstein, *Copyright* §4.4 (1989); W. Patry, *Copyright Law and Practice* 386 (1994).

- *Statutory References*: 17 U.S.C. §201:

(d) *Transfer of Ownership—*

(1) The ownership of copyright may be transferred in whole or in part by any means of conveyance or by operation of law, and may be bequeathed by will or pass as personal property by the applicable laws of intestate succession.

(2) Any of the exclusive rights comprised in copyright, including any subdivision of any of the rights specified by section 106, may be transferred as provided by clause (1) and owned separately. The owner of any particular exclusive right is entitled, to the extent of that right, to all of the protection and remedies accorded to the copyright owner by this title.

17 U.S.C. §101: "A 'transfer of copyright ownership' is an assignment, mortgage, exclusive license, or any other conveyance, alienation or hypothecation of a copyright, whether or not it is limited in time or place of effect, but not including a nonexclusive license."

17 U.S.C. §204(a): "A transfer of copyright ownership, other than by operation of law, is not valid unless an instrument of conveyance, or a note or memorandum of the transfer, is in writing and signed by the owner of the rights conveyed or such owner's duly authorized agent."

licensee estoppel [patent–trademark–copyright] A rule of contract interpretation under which a licensee of intellectual property is foreclosed from challenging the validity of the licensed property. The theory underlying the rule is that a licensee should not be permitted to enjoy the benefit of the licensed property while at the same time urging that the intellectual property which forms the basis of the agreement is void.

1. Licensee Estoppel in Patent Licenses. In the 1969 case of *Lear v. Adkins*, the Supreme Court held that the state law rule of licensee estoppel when applied to a patent license was preempted by federal patent policy. *Lear, Inc. v. Adkins*, 395 U.S. 653, 162 USPQ 1 (1969). Patent licensees were "unmuzzled" and permitted to challenge the validity of their licensor's patent.

Payment of License Royalties. The Supreme Court also held that a patent licensee cannot be forced to pay royalties pending its challenge in court. *Lear, Inc. v. Adkins*, 395 U.S. at 673. But issues concerning the timing of payment of royalties perplexed the lower courts. See McCarthy, *"Unmuzzling" the Patent Licensee: Chaos in the Wake of Lear v. Adkins*, 45 Geo. Wash. L. Rev. 429 (1977). One of the policies of the *Lear* decision is the encouragement of an early adjudication of patent invalidity. While the Supreme Court in *Lear* held that licensee Lear could avoid the payment of all royalties accruing after the Adkins' patent issued if Lear could prove invalidity, this was only because Lear challenged validity even before the Adkins' patent was finally granted. 395 U.S. at 437. The lower courts have held that it is the timing of the licensee's "challenge" to the validity of the patent which is crucial. Even if the patent is ultimately held invalid, there can be no refund of prechallenge royalties paid, because such a refund would discourage an early challenge to the patent. Also, the licensee has a choice either to challenge and continue paying royalties or to challenge and not pay and face an infringement charge. There is uncertainty whether postchallenge royalties paid by the successful paying and challenging licensee are refundable or not. See *Cordis Corp. v. Medtronic,*

Inc., 780 F.2d 991, 228 USPQ 189 (Fed. Cir. 1985) (issue not decided).

The Bystander Licensee. A bystander licensee who never challenged the validity of the patent is relieved from the obligation to pay royalties only upon EVICTION. Eviction is a final decision of invalidity rendered by a court in a litigation challenge initiated by another licensee. *Zenith Labs. v. Carter Wallace, Inc.*, 530 F.2d 508, 189 USPQ 387 (3d Cir. 1976).

Consent Decrees. While there had been a conflict in precedent, in 1991 the Federal Circuit held that it would follow its own rule that if the licensee and licensor settle a patent dispute and by a consent decree agree that the patent is valid, in a later dispute res judicata principles will bar that same licensee from raising the issue of patent invalidity, notwithstanding the rule of *Lear v. Adkins. Foster v. Hallco Mfg. Co.*, 947 F.2d 469, 20 USPQ2d 1241 (Fed. Cir. 1991) ("*Lear v. Adkins* does not abrogate general principles of res judicata with respect to the issue of the validity of a patent. If the consent decree here would foreclose subsequent challenges to validity of a patent under general rules of res judicata, the patent policy expressed in *Lear v. Adkins* does not change that effect....").

See ASSIGNOR ESTOPPEL, CHALLENGE.

• *Treatise References*: 4 D. Chisum, *Patents* §19.02[3] (1994 rev.); 3 P. Rosenberg, *Patent Law Fundamentals* §16.02[3] (1994 rev.).

• *Case References*:

"Surely the equities of the licensor do not weigh very heavily when they are balanced against the important public interest in permitting full and free competition in the use of ideas which are in reality a part of the public domain. Licensees may often be the only individuals with enough economic incentive to challenge the patentability of an inventor's discovery. If they are muzzled, the public may continually be required to pay tribute to would-be monopolists without need or justification." *Lear, Inc. v. Adkins*, 395 U.S. 653, 670, 162 USPQ 1, 8 (1969).

"In *Lear v. Adkins*, ... we held that a person licensed to use a patent may challenge the validity of the patent.... [We] relied on the desirability of encouraging licensees to challenge the

validity of patents, to further the strong federal policy that only inventions that meet the rigorous requirements of patentability shall be withdrawn from the public domain." *Aronson v. Quick Point Pencil Co.*, 440 U.S. 257, 264, 201 USPQ 1, 5 (1979).

"This public policy statement [of *Lear v. Adkins*] *does* permit a licensee to cease payments due under a contract while challenging the validity of a patent. It *does not* permit the licensees to avoid facing the consequences that such an action would bring. The holding of *Lear* only prevents the affirmative enforcement by the licensor of the royalty payment provisions of the license agreement while the patent's validity is being challenged by the licensee." *Cordis Corp. v. Medtronic, Inc.*, 780 F.2d 991, 228 USPQ 189 (Fed. Cir. 1985).

2. Licensee Estoppel in Trademark Licenses. The general rule is that the trademark licensee is estopped from challenging the validity of the licensed mark. 2 J.T. McCarthy, *Trademarks and Unfair Competition* §18.20 (3d ed. 1995 rev.). Most courts will permit an ex-licensee to challenge the validity of the mark as to facts that occur after the end of the license relationship. The patent rule of *Lear v. Adkins* has been distinguished as inapplicable to trademark licenses. *Beer Nuts, Inc. v. King Nut Co.*, 477 F.2d 326, 177 USPQ 609 (6th Cir. 1973).

3. Licensee Estoppel in Copyright Licenses. It is unclear whether the courts will carry the patent law policy of *Lear v. Adkins* into the copyright sphere to destroy the rule of licensee estoppel or will distinguish the *Lear* patent policy as distinct from copyright law policy. One court has implied that *Lear* is applicable so as to permit licensee challenges to copyright validity. *Golden West Melodies, Inc. v. Capitol Records, Inc.*, 274 Cal. App. 2d 713, 79 Cal. Rptr. 442, 163 USPQ 429 (1969). The Court of Appeals for the Seventh Circuit has distinguished *Lear* as inapplicable to copyright licenses and has upheld a no-contest clause in a copyright license. *Saturday Evening Post Co. v. Rumbleseat Press, Inc.*, 816 F.2d 1191, 2 USPQ2d 1499 (7th Cir. 1987), criticized in 3 *Nimmer on Copyright* §10.15[B] (1994 rev.).

likelihood of confusion [trademark]

See INFRINGEMENT OF A TRADEMARK.

Lisbon Arrangement [trademark–unfair competition] A multilateral treaty providing for an international system of registration and protection of APPELLATIONS OF ORIGIN, that is, of geographic denominations. Officially known as "The Lisbon Arrangement for the Protection of Appellations of Origin and Their International Registration," the treaty was formed at the 1958 Lisbon Conference of Revision of the PARIS CONVENTION.

The treaty provides for absolute protection against use of registered geographic names, regardless of whether another's use is likely to mislead. Uses of registered names are prohibited even if the true origin of the product is indicated and even if the word is modified by terms such as "kind" and "type." An appellation of origin cannot be deemed to be a GENERIC NAME by any member of the Lisbon Union so long as the term is protected in its country of origin. Approximately 16 nations (not including the United States) are members of the Lisbon Union under this treaty. Geographic names registered under the Lisbon Arrangement are published by WIPO in the periodical *Les Appellations d'origine. Reference*: 3 S. Ladas, *Patents, Trademarks and Related Rights: National and International Protection* §§861–64 (1975).

literal infringement [patent] A patent claim is literally infringed if each and every element of the claim is found in the accused product or process. The presence of additional elements in the accused product or process does not avoid literal infringement of the patent claim if the claim uses the traditional transitional phrase "comprising." See COMPRISING.

Literal Infringement of a Means Plus Function Claim. Literal infringement of a claim containing a "MEANS FOR" clause should be distinguished from infringement under the DOCTRINE OF EQUIVALENTS. Literal infringement of a "means for" or "means plus function" claim is determined by asking whether the corresponding means in the accused device is the same as or an equivalent of the corresponding structure described in the patent specification. *Texas In-*

struments, Inc. v. International Trade Comm'n, 805 F.2d 1558, 1562, 231 USPQ 833, 841 (Fed. Cir. 1986). That is, the ACCUSED DEVICE must perform an identical function, but the "means" can be an equivalent. *Spindelfabrik Suessen-Schurr GmbH v. Schubert & Salzer*, 829 F.2d 1075, 1085, 4 USPQ2d 1044, 1052 (Fed. Cir. 1987). Applying the mainstream doctrine of equivalents to a means plus function claim allows the accused device to perform a different but equivalent function and still be infringing.

See EQUIVALENTS, DOCTRINE OF; INFRINGEMENT.

• *Case References*:

"Literal infringement requires that the accused device embody every element of the patent claim.... The presence of additional elements is irrelevant if all the claimed elements are present in the accused structure." *Mannesmann Demag Corp. v. Engineered Metal Prods. Co.*, 793 F.2d 1279, 1282, 230 USPQ 45, 46 (Fed. Cir. 1986).

"[A]n accused device cannot escape infringement by merely adding features, if it otherwise has adopted the basic features of the patent.... Similarly an accused device that contains the same feature as the patented device cannot escape infringement because in it that feature performs an additional function it does not perform in the patented device." *Radio Steel & Mfg. Co. v. MTD Prods., Inc.*, 731 F.2d 840, 848, 221 USPQ 657, 663 (Fed. Cir. 1984).

• *Example 1:* Assume that a patent claim for an automobile recites the elements of: (1) a nuclear power source; (2) a means for producing steam from the nuclear power source; and (3) a steam engine driving the automobile. If the accused automobile contains all three elements, then there is literal infringement. The fact that the accused auto also contains a safety device for preventing the steam engine from overheating or that the steam is also used to heat the interior of the auto will not negate infringement.

• *Example 2:* The fact that the infringer has a patent on its improved combination does not avoid infringement. "[I]f Atlas patents A + B + C and du Pont then patents A + B + C + D, du

Pont is liable to Atlas for any manufacture, use or sale of A + B + C + D because the latter directly infringes claims to A + B + C." *Atlas Powder Co. v. E.I. du Pont de Nemours & Co.*, 750 F.2d 1569, 1580, 224 USPQ 409, 416 (Fed. Cir. 1984).

literary work [copyright] A category of copyrightable works expressed in words, numbers, or other indicia regardless of the kind of material object in which the data is recorded or stored. 17 U.S.C. §102(a)(1). "Literary" denotes no requirement of literary merit or content, for everything from a historical novel to a garden catalog, from a poem to a computer program falls within the category of "literary works."

• *Statutory Reference*: 17 U.S.C. §101: " 'Literary works' are works, other than audiovisual works, expressed in words, numbers, or other verbal or numerical symbols or indicia, regardless of the nature of the material objects, such as books, periodicals, manuscripts, phonorecords, film, tapes, disks, or cards, in which they are embodied."

• *Legislative History*: "The term 'literary works' does not connote any criterion of literary merit or qualitative value: it includes catalog directories, and similar factual, reference, or instructional works and compilations of data. It also includes computer data bases, and computer programs to the extent that they incorporate authorship in the programmer's expression of original ideas, as distinguished from the ideas themselves." H.R. Rep. No. 94-1476, 94th Cong., 2d Sess. 54 (1976).

little variation rule [copyright] When an idea is so specific that it necessarily can be utilized in only a very few forms of expression, then even a little variation in the defendant's work will avoid copyright infringement of the plaintiff's copyrighted expression of the idea.

Under the IDEA-EXPRESSION DICHOTOMY, copyright law protects only expressions of ideas, not ideas themselves. Under one (and in the author's opinion, better) view, the idea-expression dichotomy does not impose a limitation on copyrightability, but rather measures the degree of similarity between the plaintiff's work and the accused work that must exist to constitute "substantial similarity" for copyright infringement. Some courts take the view that the degree of similarity required moves along a sliding scale: the fewer the number of expressions of a particular "idea," the narrower the scope of protection given any one of those expressions. The limiting case is MERGER: when idea and expression merge, no copyright protection is given at all. Some courts have stated this principle by saying that when there is not total merger, but there are only a few or a limited number of ways to express an idea, the plaintiff must show near identity to prove infringement. This has been called the LITTLE VARIATION RULE, in that even a little variation over the plaintiff's expression will avoid infringement.

See IDEA-EXPRESSION DICHOTOMY, MERGER.

• *Example*: Freedman developed the idea of teaching persons to use the "point count system" of bidding in playing bridge by marking honor cards with a small arabic number so that the novice player could quickly learn the points assigned to certain cards. Freedman marketed a deck of cards that used his system. Freedman sued Grolier for copyright infringement for selling a deck of cards that used the same idea. Assuming there was no complete merger of idea and expression, there are only a very few ways to express or implement the Freedman concept or idea. The idea is not protectible by copyright and where the variations available to one who wishes to use the idea are very limited, even little variations in the mode of expression will avoid liability. That is, near identity of expression will be required to constitute infringement. Grolier's deck had numbers in a different color than Freedman's, double in size, and in a different style of print. These small variations avoided infringement. "When the expression of the idea can be carried out only in more or less stereotyped form—i.e., where the variations available to one who wishes to use an idea are quite limited—then it may be that even small variations or difference will be such as to preclude liability for copying." *Freedman v.*

Grolier Enters., 179 USPQ 476, 479 (S.D.N.Y. 1973).

• *Case Reference*:

"When the idea and its expression are not completely inseparable, there may still be only a limited number of ways of expressing an idea. In such a case, the burden of proof is heavy on the plaintiff who may have to show 'near identity' between the works at issue.... Conversely, of course, 'as a work embodies more in the way of particularized expression, it moves further away from [merger of idea and expression] and receives broader copyright protection.' ... This broader protection is available in the typical case of an original work embodying only one of an infinite variety of ways of expressing an idea. At this end of the spectrum, '[d]uplication or near identity is not necessary to establish infringement.' " *Concrete Mach. Co. v. Classic Lawn Ornaments Inc.*, 843 F.2d 600, 606–07, 6 USPQ2d 1357, 1361–62 (1st Cir. 1988).

Locarno Agreement [international–designs] The Locarno Agreement Establishing the International Classification of International Designs is a multilateral treaty, which established, in 1968, a classification system for the registration of industrial designs. There are 31 classes of goods with 211 subclasses. It is similar in purpose to the NICE AGREEMENT, which established an international classification system for the registration of trademarks. There are about 15 member nations party to the Locarno Agreement. The United States is not a member.

See DESIGN REGISTRATION.

• *Reference*: WIPO, *Background Reading Material on Intellectual Property* 205 (1988).

logo [trademark] A graphic representation or symbol of a company name or trademark which is usually designed for ready recognition. The term "logo" is derived from the word "logotype." "Logotype" is a typesetting term defined as a single piece of type bearing two or more letters, a syllable, or a word.

• *Usage Examples*:

"Appellee uses signs on its factories and trailer truck bodies resembling the 'd-DIXIE'

logotype which characterizes all of [its] marks. The same logotype is used on its office stationery." *American Can Co. v. Dixie Wax Paper Co.*, 407 F.2d 420, 424, 160 USPQ 721, 725 (C.C.P.A. 1969).

"A factor more probative of [the issue of likelihood of confusion] ... is the significance of the black and white diagonally-striped Venture logo prominently situated on the front of the original and relaunched Venture products." *Conopco, Inc. v. May Dep't Stores Co.*, 46 F.3d 1556, 1566, 32 USPQ2d 1225, 1232 (Fed. Cir. 1994).

"Deere ... is the world's largest supplier of agricultural equipment. For over one hundred years, Deer has used a deer design ('Deere Logo') as a trademark for identifying its products and services. Deere owns numerous trademark registrations for different versions of the Deere logo. Although these versions vary slightly, all depict a static, two-dimensional silhouette of a leaping male deer in profile. The Deere Logo is widely recognizable and a valuable business asset." *Deere & Co. v. MTD Prods. Inc.*, 4 F.3d 39, 41, 32 USPQ2d 1936, 1937 (2d Cir. 1994).

long felt need [patent] A showing that an invention satisfied a long felt need for a solution to a technical or marketplace problem is relevant evidence of the NONOBVIOUSNESS and patentability of the invention. Satisfaction of a long felt need is one of the types of objective evidence of real world recognition of the invention, which are known as SECONDARY CONSIDERATIONS.

The fact that an invention met a long felt need is closely related to evidence that the invention succeeded in solving a problem where there was prior FAILURE OF OTHERS to solve the same problem or fill the same need.

See FAILURE OF OTHERS, SECONDARY CONSIDERATIONS, UNEXPECTED RESULTS.

• *Case References*:

The Court of Appeals for the Federal Circuit reversed a finding that claims were invalid as obvious in a patent on an air-deflecting device for reducing wind resistance encountered by a tractor-trailer vehicle. "The [lower] court also did not take into account other objective evidence of long felt need and failure of others.... The district court did not consider the failure of the Maryland study to produce an effective solution to the wind resistance problem as an indication of long felt need. Instead, it viewed that failure as an indication that a later invention, based on a different principle, would have been obvious, because the inventor would know from such failure that he should try some other approach. Under this reasoning, it would be progressively more difficult, after a succession of failures, to secure a patent on an invention that provided a solution to a long felt need. This is contrary to the well established principle that the failure of others to provide a feasible solution to a long standing problem is probative of nonobviousness." *Uniroyal, Inc. v. Rudkin-Wiley Corp.*, 837 F.2d 1044, 1054, 5 USPQ2d 1434, 1440–41 (Fed. Cir. 1988).

"That there were other attempts, and various combinations and procedures tried in the past, does not render obvious the later successful one. The PTO's reliance on Dow's 'admission' of long felt need as prima facie evidence of obviousness is contrary to logic as well as law. Recognition of need, and difficulties encountered by those skilled in the field, are classical indicia of nonobviousness.... That these inventors eventually succeeded when they and others had failed does not mean that they or their colleagues must have expected each new idea to fail. Most technological advance is the fruit of methodical, persistent investigation.... " *In re Dow Chem.*, 837 F.2d 469, 472, 5 USPQ2d 1529, 1531 (Fed. Cir. 1988).

look and feel [computer–copyright] Those aspects of a COMPUTER PROGRAM that interface with the user, such as the design, arrangement, and manner in which the program presents information to the user. Elements of a computer program that contribute to its look and feel include command language; key strokes; text prompts; display windows; the layout of menus; and the sequence of screen displays. Look and feel differs from the STRUCTURE, SEQUENCE, AND ORGANIZATION of a computer program in that look and feel primarily relates to similarities of the visual and tactile impact of

programs rather than similarity in the structure of the computer program codes that generate the visual output.

Look and Feel and User Interface. The USER INTERFACE consists of what the user hears and sees on the screen, be it graphic or textual, and what the user does to make the program perform functions via keyboard or mouse. When a computer's visual displays incorporate significant graphic elements it is referred to as a graphical user interface (GUI or "gooey"). A GUI allows the user to see, point to, and manipulate graphical images, symbols, or words to instruct and interact with the computer program.

A Test of Infringement. Some courts have found copyright infringement when an accused infringer's program has the same look and feel as the copyrighted program. Other courts will refuse to grant exclusive rights of copyright to what appears to be merely a general functional concept or idea of the plaintiff's program. The user of a popular computer program progresses along a learning curve to master the particular user interface for that program. Producers of add-on or related software want to be able to use the same interface or look and feel in order to make their product appealing to users who have mastered a popular program. "The 'look and feel' of a program is perhaps the most important factor affecting the program's commercial success." Levy, *Single Computer Registration for Computer Programs: Outdated Perceptions Byte the Dust*, 54 Brooklyn L. Rev. 965, 976 (1988). The controversial issue remaining is to what extent copyright law can and ought to grant exclusive rights in the mere look and feel of a computer program. Some commentators reject the use of the term "look and feel" as too vague and sweeping to be able to provide a useful test of infringement.

Evolution of the Phrase. The term "look and feel" apparently evolved from the concept of "TOTAL CONCEPT AND FEEL" developed by the Court of Appeals for the Ninth Circuit. See, e.g., *Sid & Marty Krofft Television v. McDonald's Corp.*, 562 F.2d 1157, 1167 (9th Cir. 1977) ("It is clear to us that defendants' works are substantially similar to plaintiffs'. They have captured the 'total concept and feel' of the [plaintiff's television puppet] show."). One of the earliest references to the concept of "look and feel" was in Russo & Derwin, *Copyright in the "Look and Feel" of Computer Software*, 2 Computer Law. 1 (Feb. 1985).

The Apple v. Microsoft Case. In 1994, the Ninth Circuit decided a case that the whole computer industry had closely followed. Claiming that Microsoft's Windows infringed the copyrighted graphical user interface (desktop metaphor, windows, icons, and pull down menus) of Apple's Macintosh computer, in 1988 Apple sued Microsoft. In 1985, Apple had granted Microsoft a license to use the visual aspects of Windows 1.0. Apple claimed that later versions of Microsoft Windows became more "Mac-like" than the license allowed, and sued Microsoft. Microsoft was found not to have infringed. The Ninth Circuit agreed with the district court that most of the visual elements of the later versions of Windows fell within the scope of the Apple license and that the remaining unlicensed elements failed the test of virtual identity to Apple's copyrightable "unique selection and arrangement" of the elements of the graphical user interface. "When the range of protectable and unauthorized expression is narrow, the appropriate standard for illicit copying is virtual identity. For these reasons, the GUIs in Windows 2.03, 3.0 and NewWave cannot be compared for substantial similarity with the Macintosh interface as a whole. Instead, as the district court held, the works must be compared for virtual identity." *Apple Computer Inc. v. Microsoft Corp.*, 35 F.3d 1435, 32 USPQ2d 1086 (9th Cir. 1994).

The Lotus v. Borland Case. Defendant Borland, in its Quattro Pro spreadsheet program, gave users the option to use menu commands and command structures as used in the then industry-leader program Lotus 1-2-3. Lotus' claim that this constituted infringement of copyright in the menu command hierarchy of Lotus 1-2-3 was rejected by the First Circuit. The court held that the Lotus menu command hierarchy was an uncopyrightable "method of operation," barred from copyright by 17 U.S.C. §102(b). "The fact that there may be many different ways to operate a computer program, or even many different ways to operate a com-

puter program using a set of hierarchically arranged command terms, does not make the actual method of operation chosen copyrightable; it still functions as a method for operating the computer and as such is uncopyrightable." *Lotus Dev. Corp. v. Borland Int'l Inc.*, 49 F.3d. 807, 34 USPQ2d 1014 (1st Cir. 1995).

See STRUCTURE, SEQUENCE, AND ORGANIZATION; USER INTERFACE.

• *Case Reference*: "A computer program is made up of several different components, including the source and object code, the structure, sequence and/or organization of the program, the user interface, and the function, or purpose of the program.... The user interface, also called the 'look and feel' of the program, is generally the design of the video screen and the manner in which the information is presented to the user.... Whether the nonliteral components of a program, including the structure, sequence and organization and user interface, are protected depends on whether, in the particular facts of each case, the component in question qualifies as an expression of an idea, or an idea itself." *Johnson Controls Inc. v. Phoenix Control Sys. Inc.*, 886 F.2d 1173, 1175 n.3, 12 USPQ2d 1566, 1568–69 n.3 (9th Cir. 1989).

• *Commentary References*:

" 'Look and feel' is a term of somewhat vague definition, but it generally refers to a program's screen displays, both to the designs of the individual screen displays and to the sequencing of screen displays as an operator goes through various stages or operations in using the program." Jordan, *On the Scope of Protection for Computer Programs Under Copyright*, 17 AIPLA Q. J. 199, 210 (1989).

" 'Look and feel,' as that term has come to be used in the computer industry ... extends beyond the copyright notion of 'total concept and feel' and, to the extent it does, may reach items not protected by copyright, such as the placement of keys on a keyboard or a program's particular assignment of 'meaning' to a particular key. For that reason, the term is not helpful and we choose not to adopt it. On the other hand, the protection of a program's 'total concept and feel,' as manifest in its suite of user-perceptible manifestations, such as screen format, arrangement and content, interaction with the user, and printed reports, is a straightforward and salutary application of existing copyright law, not a development that should be viewed as controversial or disruptive." Clapes, Lynch, & Steinberg, *Silicon Epics and Binary Bards: Determining the Proper Scope of Copyright Protection for Computer Programs*, 34 UCLA L. Rev. 1493, 1572 n.282 (1987).

"[C]opyright law provides no general protection for the overall 'look and feel' of a computer program. Nevertheless, the courts are treating specific screen displays with non-functional features as valid pictorial or audiovisual works and/or compilations which will be afforded limited protection by copyright." Abramson, *"Look and Feel" of Computer Software*, 95 Case & Com. 3, 8 (Jan.–Feb. 1990).

" '[L]ook and feel' lawsuits are not really about the arrangement of user interface command terms but about the imitation of program behavior, a deeply important aspect of programs that has been obscured because it cannot be depicted using conventional copyright terms." Samuelson, Davis, Kapor & Reichman, *Existing Laws Fail to Protect Software Adequately*, Nat'l L.J., Feb. 20, 1995, at C33 (summarizing the arguments made in Samuelson, Davis, Kapor & Reichman, *A Manifesto Concerning the Legal Protection of Computer Programs*, 94 Colum. L. Rev. 2308 (1994)).

lost arts [patent] Technology once known long ago, the knowledge of which has been lost in succeeding generations. That such technological information once existed can only be inferred from knowledge or folklore that certain devices or processes were once known. A modern scientist or engineer who succeeded in apparently reproducing such a lost art would be regarded as a true "inventor" of something new and would be entitled to a patent, although such a person in a strict sense would not be the "first" inventor.

The rule of lost arts cannot be applied to technological information that is disclosed in an available but obscure technical publication or in an old patent. While the source of the information may be obscure and difficult to find, it is not "lost." It is a part of the PRIOR ART and hence

may render an apparently "new" invention old or obvious.

See PAPER PATENT.

- *Treatise Reference*: 1 D. Chisum, *Patents* §3.06[1] (1994 rev.).

- *Case References*:
"So, too, as to the lost arts. It is well known that centuries ago discoveries were made in certain arts the fruits of which have come down to us, but the means by which the work was accomplished are at this day unknown. The knowledge has been lost for ages. Yet it would hardly be doubted, if any one now discovered an art thus lost, and it was a useful improvement, that, upon a fair construction of the act of Congress, he would be entitled to a patent. Yet he would not literally be the first and original inventor. But he would be the first to confer on the public the benefit of the invention. He would discover what is unknown, and communicate knowledge which the public had not the means of obtaining without his invention." *Gayler v. Wilder*, 51 U.S. 477, 497 (1850).

"The doctrine of 'lost art' does not apply to earlier patents, as it does to prior uses. *Gayler v. Wilder....* A patent may have lain for years unheeded, as little a contribution to the sum of knowledge as though it had never existed, an idle gesture long since drifted into oblivion. Nevertheless, it will be as effective to invalidate a new patent, as though it had entered into the very life blood of the industry." Learned Hand in *Western States Mach. Co. v. S.S. Hepworth Co.*, 147 F.2d 345, 350, 64 USPQ 141, 146 (2d Cir. 1945).

lost count [patent] The technological subject matter involved when an inventor loses on the issue of priority in an INTERFERENCE PROCEEDING in the Patent and Trademark Office. Under the "doctrine of lost counts," the technology defined in the lost COUNT may in some circumstances constitute PRIOR ART against the losing party's attempt to obtain patent claims that vary in scope from the lost count. The losing party in the interference is barred from subsequently claiming the subject matter in the lost count.

Limitations on the Lost Count Rule. The subject matter of a lost count will not be considered to be prior art if it lacks a basis in §102, where, for example, the prevailing inventor in the interference won on the ground of a foreign priority filing date under §119. *In re McKellin*, 529 F.2d 1324, 188 USPQ 428 (C.C.P.A. 1976). The losing party to an interference can claim patentable subject matter other than that of the interference count, but only provided that the requirements of patentability are met. *In re Zletz*, 893 F.2d 319, 13 USPQ2d 1320 (Fed. Cir. 1989).

The Lost Count Rule as an Application of Res Judicata. The Federal Circuit has held that the subject of the lost count may preclude the losing party from obtaining a claim that is not patentably distinct from the lost count of the interference. "It is therefore proper, and consistent with the policies of finality and repose embodied in the doctrines of res judicata and collateral estoppel, to use that judgment [in the interference] as the basis for rejection of claims to the same patentable invention." *In re Deckler*, 977 F.2d 1449, 24 USPQ2d 1448 (Fed. Cir. 1992).

- *Case References*:

"It is well settled that a losing party in an interference is barred under §102(g) from subsequently claiming the subject matter lost, or subject matter which is obvious thereover within the meaning of §103.... [T]he 'prior art' here is the lost count. It is the subject matter of this count which is 'the invention of another' pursuant to §102(g). The rejection is on the lost count...." *Ex parte Kroekel*, 230 USPQ 191, 194 (Bd. Pat. App. & Int'f.), *aff'd on other grounds*, 803 F.2d 705, 231 USPQ 640 (Fed. Cir. 1986).

"If an applicant were granted a patent on claims to obvious variations of the invention of the counts which he lost in an interference because of his suppression and concealment, the public policy underlying the suppression and concealment doctrine would clearly be frustrated.... [W]e hold that the invention of the counts lost by appellant in the earlier interference is, because of his suppression and concealment, proper prior art under section 103 against the claims on appeal." *In re Suska*, 589 F.2d 527, 530, 200 USPQ 497, 499 (C.C.P.A. 1979).

- *Treatise References*: 2 D. Chisum, *Patents* §5.03[3][h] (1994 rev.); R. Harmon, *Patents and the Federal Circuit* §15.2(e) (3d ed. 1994) ("But the lost count of an interference is not prior art against a different invention, for 'prior art' in the sense of 35 U.S.C. §102(g) cannot be the basis of a §102(a) rejection, the invention not being publicly known or used.").

See COUNT, INTERFERENCE ESTOPPEL.

lost profits   [patent–trademark–copyright] The profits on sales lost by the intellectual property owner as a result of the infringer's actions. This is to be distinguished from an award or accounting of the *infringer's* profits. See PROFITS.

1. Lost Profits as a Measure of Damages for Patent Involvement. The owner of a patent who has proved infringement can claim that the measure of its actual damages is the amount of profits lost by the patentee because of the infringing sales.

Measurement of the Amount. To recover its lost profits, the patent owner must show that there is a reasonable probability that "but for" the infringement, the patent owner would have made the sales actually made by the infringer. "Evidence that shows a reasonable probability that the patent owner would have made the infringing sales made by the infringer will suffice." *Standard Havens Prods. Inc. v. Gencor Indus. Inc.*, 953 F.2d 1360, 1372, 21 USPQ2d 1321, 1331 (Fed. Cir. 1991). If the patentee can prove that he or she would have made the sales of the patented products but for the fact that the infringer made them, the infringer's profits are relevant in determining the amount of the patentee's lost profits. *Kori Corp. v. Wilco Marsh Buggies & Draglines, Inc.*, 761 F.2d 649, 653, 225 USPQ 985, 988 (Fed. Cir. 1985). However, it is not necessary for the patent owner to negate all possibilities that a purchaser might have bought a different product or might not have purchased the product at all. *Minnesota Mining & Mfg. v. Johnson & Johnson*, 976 F.2d 1559, 1577, 24 USPQ2d 1321, 1336–37 (Fed. Cir. 1992). When the litigating parties are the only suppliers of the product, it is "not inappropriate to infer that the patentee would have had the sales made by the infringers." *Marsh-McBirney Inc. v. Montedoro-Whitney Corp.*, 882 F.2d 498, 505, 11 USPQ2d 1794, 1798 (Fed. Cir. 1989).

The Infringer's Profits. In 1946 Congress eliminated statutory authority for the utility patent owner to recover the infringer's profits, inserting the present Patent Code §284 requiring an award of "damages adequate to compensate for the infringement." 35 U.S.C. §284. See *General Motors Corp. v. Devex Corp.*, 461 U.S. 648, 652, 217 USPQ 1185, 1188 (1983) ("In 1946 Congress excluded consideration of the infringer's gain by eliminating the recovery of his profits, ... the determination of which had often required protracted litigation."). However, recovery of the infringer's profits is an available remedy for the infringement of a design patent.

See PROFITS.

Special Rules. In computing lost profits, it is proper to use the INCREMENTAL INCOME APPROACH. Under the ENTIRE MARKET VALUE RULE, lost profits may be based on the sale of an entire apparatus containing both patented and unpatented features.

- *Case References*:

"If in all reasonable probability the patent owner would have made the sales which the infringer has made, what the patent owner in reasonable probability would have netted from the sales denied to him is the measure of his loss, and the infringer is liable for that." *Paper Converting Mach. Co. v. Magna-Graphics Corp.*, 745 F.2d 11, 23, 223 USPQ 591, 599–600 (Fed. Cir. 1984).

"To get lost profits as actual damages, the patent owner must demonstrate that there was a reasonable probability that, but for the infringement, it would have made the infringer's sales.... But '[t]he patent holder does not need to negate *all* possibilities that a purchaser might have bought a different product or might have foregone the purchase altogether.' ... A standard way of proving lost profits, first announced in *Panduit Corp. v. Stahlin Bros. Fibre Works*, 575 F.2d 1152, 1156, 197 USPQ 726, 730 (6th Cir. 1978), is for the patent owner to prove: '(1) demand for the patented product, (2) absence of acceptable noninfringing substitutes, (3) his

manufacturing and marketing capability to exploit the demand, and (4) the amount of the profit he would have made.' " *State Indus. Inc. v. Mor-Flo Indus. Inc.*, 883 F.2d 1573, 1577, 12 USPQ2d 1026, 1028 (Fed. Cir. 1989). Accord *Minnesota Mining & Mfg. v. Johnson & Johnson*, 976 F.2d 1559, 1577, 24 USPQ2d 1321, 1336–37 (Fed. Cir. 1992); *Rite-Hite Corp. v. Kelley Co. Inc.*, 56 F.3d 1538, 1545, 35 USPQ2d 1065, 1069 (Fed. Cir. 1995) (en banc) (*Panduit* test is a "useful, but non-exclusive, way for a patentee to prove entitlement to lost profits damages")

"The *Panduit* test, however, operates under an inherent assumption, not appropriate in this case, that the patent owner and the infringer sell products sufficiently similar to compete against each other in the same market segment. If the patentee's and the infringer's products are not substitutes in a competitive market, *Panduit's* first two factors do not meet the 'but for' test—a prerequisite for lost profits.... [D]uring the damages period, the sailboard market was not a unitary market in which every competitor sold substantially the same product. [The litigating parties] sold different types of sailboards at different prices to different customers.... On the facts of this case, [the patentee] did not show 'but for' causation under a correct application of *Panduit* or otherwise. The district court erred in awarding lost profits." *BIC Leisure Prods. Inc. v. Windsurfing Int'l Inc.*, 1 F.3d 1214, 1218, 27 USPQ2d 1671, 1674 (Fed. Cir. 1993).

"[T]o prove that there are no acceptable noninfringing substitutes, the patent owner must show either that (1) the purchasers in the marketplace generally were willing to buy the patented product for its advantages, or (2) the specific purchasers of the infringing product purchased on that basis." *Standard Havens Prods. Inc. v. Gencor Indus. Inc.*, 953 F.2d 1360, 1372, 21 USPQ2d 1321, 1331 (Fed. Cir. 1991).

2. Lost Profits as a Measure of Damages for Trademark Infringement. In an appropriate situation, the damages of the trademark owner may be measured by the profits lost as a result of the infringement. The plaintiff need only make a prima facie showing of reasonably forecast profits and the infringer has the burden of showing that some or all of the plaintiff's losses were caused by something other than the infringing acts. The infringer whose wrongful conduct makes it difficult for the plaintiff to demonstrate that lost sales were in their entirety due to sales of infringing items "cannot complain that the damages are somewhat speculative." *Brunswick Corp. v. Spinit Reel Co.*, 832 F.2d 513, 526, 4 USPQ2d 1497, 1506 (10th Cir. 1987).

- *Treatise Reference*: 3 J.T. McCarthy, *Trademarks and Unfair Competition* §30.27[2] (3d ed. 1995 rev.).

3. Lost Profits as a Measure of Damages for Copyright Infringement. Under 17 U.S.C. §504(b), the copyright owner can recover actual damages suffered "as a result of the infringement," including lost sales and profits. In the classic case of competing litigants, every sale made by the infringer is in theory a sale lost by the copyright owner. But if the litigants' products were significantly different or were sold at differing prices, it may not be accurate to assume that every sale of the infringer is one which would have been made by the copyright owner but for the infringement. *Stevens Linen Assoc., Inc. v. Mastercraft Corp.*, 656 F.2d 11, 14, 210 USPQ 865, 867 (2d Cir. 1981). Once the copyright owner has established the number of sales lost to the infringer, actual damages can be proven by the number of those sales times the copyright owner's profit per sale.

- *Treatise References*: 3 *Nimmer on Copyright* §14.02[A] (1994 rev.); 2 P. Goldstein, *Copyright* §12.1.1.1 a. (1989).

M

Madrid Arrangement [trademark] Some confusion is created by the fact that there are two international treaties known as the "Madrid Arrangement" or "Madrid Agreement." One relates to preventing false indications of geographic source, and the other creates an international trademark registration system.

1. The Madrid Source of Goods Treaty. Officially known as "The Madrid Arrangement Concerning the Prevention of False or Deceptive Indications of Source," this treaty was first created at the Madrid Revision Conference of the PARIS CONVENTION in 1890 and last revised at Stockholm in 1967. The treaty provides that goods bearing an indication by which one of the member nations, or a geographic place in it, is falsely indicated as the place of origin shall be seized upon importation. Approximately 30 nations are members of the Madrid Union created by this treaty. The United States is not a member.

• *Reference*: 3 S. Ladas, *Patents, Trademarks and Related Rights: National and International Protection* §847 (1975).

2. The Madrid Registration of Marks Treaty. Officially known as "The Madrid Arrangement Concerning the International Registration of Marks," this treaty was first created at the Madrid Revision Conference of the Paris Convention in 1890 and last revised at Stockholm in 1967. There are about 26 nations which adhere to the Madrid Registration Agreement. The United States is not a member.

Effect of International Registration. This treaty provides an international registration system known as the "Madrid Union," under which a mark already registered in the country of origin may be registered in the French language with the International Bureau (*WIPO*). This reg-

istration ensures the same protection in each of the member nations designated by the applicant as if the mark had been separately registered in that nation. An international registration is in effect a bundle of national applications, each subject to the domestic legislation of the designated nations. Each member nation designated by the applicant has 12 months to reject the application. If not rejected, the mark will be registered in the particular nation.

Central Attack. Under the rule of "central attack," for the first five years, if the home registration is cancelled, the international registration and all national registrations built on it are also cancelled. Only after five years does the international registration become fully independent.

• *Treatise Reference*: 2 S. Ladas, *Patents, Trademarks and Related Rights: National and International Protection* §§758–95 (1975) ("The International Bureau in registering a mark acts only as the alter ego of the national Patent Offices of the contracting countries, and an international registration is only a bundle of national registrations." Ladas, at p. 1471.).

Madrid Protocol [international–trademark] An independent international trademark registration agreement reached in 1989 which supplements the trademark registration treaty known as the MADRID ARRANGEMENT. While the Madrid Protocol closely parallels the Madrid Arrangement, it includes provisions that offer certain attractive options to those nations that had not previously joined the Madrid Union. It also creates a link between the Madrid Union and the trademark system of the European Community.

See EUROPEAN TRADEMARK.

Goal of the Treaty. The goal of the Protocol is to create a treaty organization that is attractive to the United States in that it will permit a U.S. company to file an intent to use (ITU) application in the United States and subsequently file in the U.S. Patent and Trademark Office (PTO) in English, using U.S. currency, an application for registration of the mark in any of the member countries. Thereafter, the appropriate trademark offices in each of those countries designated will examine the application under their domestic law. This streamlined process is designed to reduce to some extent the foreign trademark registration expenses of a U.S. company that wants to sell branded goods in the European market.

Features of the Treaty. A major feature introduced in the Protocol is that, unlike the Madrid Arrangement, which requires a home *registration*, the Protocol permits an international registration to be built upon a home country *application*. See Schechter, *Facilitating Trademark Registration Abroad: The Implications of U.S. Ratification of the Madrid Protocol*, 25 Geo. Wash. J. Int'l L. & Econ. 419, 432 (1991). This is attractive to U.S. companies because it permits a U.S. company to file a U.S. ITU application and use it immediately as the basis for seeking registrations in Madrid Protocol nations, giving the advantage of an early priority date abroad. Another advantage of the Protocol is the elimination of the "central attack" rule of the Madrid Arrangement, so that under the Protocol, registrations abroad are not contingent on the validity of the home registration after five years. Other innovations of the Protocol designed to attract U.S. adherence are the permitted use of the English language, a 10-year registration period, and the expansion from 12 months to 18 months of the time frame within which each nation must decide whether to refuse or register a mark under the Protocol.

History of the Protocol. When the Madrid Protocol closed for signature on December 31, 1989, it had been signed by 28 nations, including all 12 members of the European Community and all but 10 members of the Madrid Registration Treaty. In 1993, bills were introduced in the U.S. Congress to implement U.S. accession to the Madrid Protocol by adding a new Title XII to the Lanham Act. At a congressional hearing in May 1993, the PTO expressed support for accession to the Protocol and enactment of the proposed legislation. In May 1994, the Clinton administration announced that even though the administration had no problem with the substance of the Madrid Protocol, the United States would not implement it because certain provisions granting voting rights to intergovernmental organizations, such as the European Union, would create a precedent for double counting, which was at odds with the position taken by the United States in negotiations on other treaty organizations.

Madrid Union See MADRID ARRANGEMENT.

maintenance fees [patent] Fees required to be paid at defined intervals after the grant of a utility patent in order to keep the patent in force.

Patent Maintenance Fees in Other Nations. Most foreign patent systems for a long time have required the payment of maintenance fees as a condition of keeping a patent in force. Maintenance fees are also known as "annuities" or "renewal fees" or simply "taxes." 1 S. Ladas, *Patents, Trademarks and Related Rights: National and International Protection* §229 (1975). The schedule for payment of fees varies considerably among the nations. Some require annual fees from the date of filing an application to the end of the patent term. Other nations set the fees to be paid at defined intervals after the patent grant. Usually the fees are graduated, increasing in amount as the patent ages and proves its worth in the marketplace. Ordinarily the failure to make a timely payment of a maintenance fee results in the extreme sanction of forfeiture of the patent. Most nations provide a grace period to make late payments and impose a late payment surcharge. The PARIS CONVENTION Article 5 *bis* requires a period of grace of not less than six months for the payment of maintenance fees and permits a nation to make a late payment surcharge. See 1 S. Ladas, *Patents, Trademarks and Related Rights: National and International Protection* §332 (1975).

U.S. Patent Maintenance Fees. The United States did not have maintenance fees until 1980, when a schedule of three postgrant maintenance fees was adopted for patents based on applications filed on or after December 12, 1980. The intervals when fees are due after grant of the patent are 3 1/2 years, 7 1/2 years, and 11 1/2 years over the 17-year term of a utility patent. 35 U.S.C. §41(b). As of 1994, the three maintenance fees due for patents resulting from applications filed on or after December 12, 1980, were: $930, $1,870, and $2,820. 37 C.F.R. §1.20. A six-month grace period is provided, and if the required fee is not paid within the grace period, plus a late surcharge, the patent will expire.

Late Payment and Nonpayment. The Patent and Trademark Office may accept payment of a fee after the six-month grace period if upon a petition by the patentee, the delay is shown to the satisfaction of the Commissioner to have been either "unintentional" or "unavoidable." In 1992 Congress amended the Patent Code to permit patent owners whose patents expired due to nonpayment to have their patents reinstated upon a satisfactory showing that nonpayment was either unintentional or unavoidable. See *Contigram Communications Corp. v. Lehman,* 32 USPQ2d 1346, 1352 (E.D. Va. 1994) ("In passing the 1992 amendments, Congress intended to relax the standard for filing late patent maintenance fees and thereby increase the incidence of continued patent ownership."). If the delay was "unavoidable," payment may be made at any time; if the delay was only "unintentional," payment must be made within 24 months after the six-month grace period. 35 U.S.C. §41(c)(1). "Unavoidable" delay requires a showing that reasonable care was taken to ensure the timely payment of fees, and that the petition was filed promptly; it further requires an enumeration of the steps taken to ensure timely payment. 37 C.F.R. §1.378(b). In the event such a petition is granted, a special surcharge is due. 37 C.F.R. §1.20(i). The statute protects those who, in reliance on the expiration of a patent for nonpayment, make, use, or sell things covered by the patent and then find that the patent has not expired because the late payment was later held to have been unintentional or unavoidable, resulting in a resuscitated patent. 35 U.S.C. §41(c)(2).

The Small Entity Discount. Maintenance fees, like most patent fees, are reduced by 50 percent for a SMALL ENTITY. 35 U.S.C. §41(h). Maintenance fees are not required in order to maintain a DESIGN PATENT or a PLANT PATENT in force. 35 U.S.C. §41(b).

See SMALL ENTITY, PATENT.

Treatise Reference: 3 D. Chisum, *Patents* §11.02[1][d][iv] (1994 rev.).

Manual of Patent Examining Procedure [patent]
See *MPEP*.

manufacturing clause [copyright] A now-expired condition of U.S. statutory copyright law that required English language literary works to be manufactured, printed, and bound in the United States. Although appearing in varying forms of severity over the years since 1891, these statutory provisions all had one goal in common: to protect the U.S. printing industry against foreign competition. The manufacturing clause was widely criticized as holding the copyrights of U.S. authors hostage to benefit the domestic printing industry and printers' unions. The manufacturing clause expired on July 1, 1986.

The 1909 Act and "Ad Interim" Copyright. Under the 1909 Copyright Act, copyright in the United States was unable to be enforced for many books that failed to comply with the manufacturing clause. Nimmer is of the view that such copyrights were unenforceable but were not cast into the public domain. 2 *Nimmer on Copyright* §7.23[E] (1994 rev.). Under the 1909 Act, "ad interim," five-year provisional copyright protection was available for English language books and periodicals printed abroad. During the five-year period of ad interim protection, up to 1,500 copies could be imported from abroad. If, within the five-year period, an edition was printed in the United States, the work could claim a normal 28-year copyright term measured from the first publication abroad. 2 *Nimmer on Copyright* §7.23[F] (1994 rev.); 1 P. Goldstein, *Copyright* §3.18.2 (1989).

The 1978 Copyright Act. The severity of the manufacturing clause was considerably softened in the 1978 Copyright Act revisions to include several exceptions to the requirement of domestic printing. 17 U.S.C. §601 (now expired). Most importantly, violation of this softened version of the manufacturing clause did not invalidate copyright protection. But it was a complete defense to an infringement charge as to reproduction and distribution of copies of the work. However, the copyright owner could reinstate full rights by manufacturing an edition in the United States or Canada before an infringer commenced making copies.

The 1986 Demise of the Manufacturing Requirement. The 1978 Copyright Act version of the manufacturing clause contained a sunset provision dated July 1, 1982. In 1982 Congress passed an act to extend this for four years to July 1, 1986. President Reagan vetoed this extension of the manufacturing clause because it was an anti-free-trade measure, but Congress overrode the veto, and the provision was extended for four more years. By its own terms, the manufacturing clause expired on July 1, 1986. This helped to pave the way for U.S. membership in the BERNE CONVENTION, which became effective March 1, 1989.

• *Treatise References*: 2 *Nimmer on Copyright* §7.22 (1994 rev.); 1 N. Boorstyn, *Copyright* §§16.01–.07 (2d ed. 1994); 1 P. Goldstein, *Copyright* §§3.16–.18 (1989); M. Leaffer, *Understanding Copyright* §12.10 (1989).

march in [patent] Under certain circumstances, a federal agency that has funded research and allowed a small business or nonprofit organization to retain invention rights may require the contractor to grant patent licenses to any responsible applicant. This power of compulsory licensing is referred to as a "march-in right." If the contractor refuses to license, the federal agency may itself grant the license. March-in rights may be exercised if (1) the agency determines that commercialization of the invention is not being effectively pursued; (2) the license is necessary to satisfy health or safety needs; (3) the patent holder has not met the public use requirements specified by federal regulations; or (4) the patent holder has failed to agree that products incorporating the patented invention will be manufactured substantially within the United States. A march-in proceeding is initiated by the issuance of written notice by the agency to the contractor stating that the government has decided to exercise march-in rights. Before an agency may do so, the contractor must be provided a reasonable time to present facts and show cause why the proposed agency action should not be taken.

• *Statutory Reference*:

35 U.S.C. §203(1): "With respect to any subject invention in which a small business firm or nonprofit organization has acquired title under this chapter [35 U.S.C. §§200 et seq.], the Federal agency under whose funding agreement the subject invention was made shall have the right ... to require the contractor, an assignee or exclusive licensee of a subject invention to grant a nonexclusive, partially exclusive or exclusive license in any field of use to a responsible applicant ...."

mark [trademark] A TRADEMARK, SERVICE MARK, COLLECTIVE MARK, or CERTIFICATION MARK.

• *Statutory Reference*: Lanham Act §45, 15 U.S.C. §1127: "The term 'mark' includes any trademark, service mark, collective mark, or certification mark."

marking estoppel [patent] Some decisions hold that a company, usually a licensee, that marks product line A with the number of a patent owned by the plaintiff is estopped to deny that product line A is covered by the claims of the patent.

In the case most often cited in support of the rule of "marking estoppel," Crane licensed Aeroquip to manufacture products under Crane's patent. Aeroquip then modified its product, which the district court found did not infringe Crane's patent, but continued to mark Crane's patent number on the modified products. The district court found that Aeroquip was estopped to deny that it was liable for the payment of royalties on the modified products. The Court of Appeals for the Seventh Circuit found that the modified products did come within the claims of the patent and expressed "no opinion" on the marking estoppel issue. *Crane Co. v. Aeroquip Corp.*, 364 F. Supp. 547, 560, 179

USPQ 596, 581 (N.D. Ill. 1973), *aff'd in part and rev'd in part on other grounds*, 504 F.2d 1086, 1093, 183 USPQ 577, 581 (7th Cir. 1974). The Court of Appeals for the Federal Circuit has mentioned "marking estoppel" in passing but has found no reason to opine on its validity. *Smithkline Diagnostics Inc. v. Helena Labs. Corp.*, 859 F.2d 878, 890, 8 USPQ2d 1468, 1478 (Fed. Cir. 1988).

See MARKING OF PATENT.

marking of patent [patent]   Placing the word "patent" or its abbreviation "pat." together with the patent number on patented articles made by the patentee or the patentee's licensees.

Sets a Time Frame for Recovery of Damages. Damages for product patent infringement begin to accrue either when actual notice has been given to a specific infringer or when constructive notice has been given to the world by the patent holder. In order to comply with the constructive notice requirement, a patent owner who makes articles covered by the patent must mark them. If the patent holder has express or implied licensees, it must mark the articles. The only consequence of a failure to mark is the limitation on the recovery of damages from infringers. If the patent owner or its licensees fail to mark, the patent owner may recover damages only for acts of infringement that occur after the infringer received actual notice of infringement.

Delay in Marking. The Federal Circuit has held that: "[A] delay between issuance of the patent and compliance with the marking provisions of section 287(a) will not prevent recovery of damages after the date that marking has begun. ... [O]nce marking has begun, it must be substantially consistent and continuous in order for the party to avail itself of the constructive notice provision of the statute." *American Medical Sys. v. Medical Eng'g Corp.*, 6 F.3d 1523, 1537, 28 USPQ2d 1321, 1331 (Fed. Cir. 1993).

Limits of the Obligation to Mark. Of course, if the patent owner has neither made articles embodying the patent nor licensed others to do so, there is no marking requirement. The duty to mark relates only to a "patented article" and does not apply to unpatented products of a patented process or method. Similarly, the notice provisions do not apply where the patent claims cover a process or method. However, where the patent contains both apparatus and method claims, to the extent there is a tangible item to mark, there is an obligation to mark to recover damages under the method claims. *American Medical Sys. v. Medical Eng'g Corp.*, 6 F.3d 1523, 1538, 28 USPQ2d 1321, 1332 (Fed. Cir. 1993).

Parts of Combination. If a patentee makes only an element for use in a patented combination, it may either be marked "for use under U.S. X,XXX,XXX" or sold with a requirement that a licensee mark the patented combination product as "licensed under U.S. X,XXX,XXX." *Amstead Indus. Inc. v. Buckeye Steel Castings Co.* 24 F.3d 178, 185, 30 USPQ2d 1462, 1480 (Fed. Cir. 1994).

Mismarking. MISMARKING is the intentionally false designation on an article or in advertising that an item is patented or that a patent application is pending. Mismarking is specifically prohibited by statute.

See MISMARKING, MARKING ESTOPPEL, PATENT PENDING.

• *Treatise References*: 5 D. Chisum, *Patents* §20.03[7][c] (1994 rev.); R. Harmon, *Patents and the Federal Circuit* §9.4(b) (3d ed. 1994).

• *Statutory Reference*: 35 U.S.C. §287(a): "Patentees, and persons making or selling any patented article for or under them, may give notice to the public that the same is patented, either by fixing thereon the word 'patent' or the abbreviation 'pat.', together with the number of the patent, or when, from the character of the article, this can not be done, by fixing to it, or to the package wherein one or more of them is contained, a label containing a like notice. In the event of failure to so mark, no damages shall be recovered by the patentee in any action for infringement, except on proof that the infringer was notified of the infringement and continued to infringe thereafter, in which event damages may be recovered only for infringement occurring after such notice. Filing of an action for infringement shall constitute such notice."

Markush claim

• *Case Reference*: "The plain language of section 287(a) does not provide any time limit by which marking must begin, nor does the legislative history indicate any such limitation. Congress structured the statute so as to tie failure to mark with disability to collect damages, not failure to mark *at the time of issuance* with disability to collect damages. Furthermore, allowing recovery of damages from the point of full compliance with the marking statute furthers the policy of encouraging marking to provide notice to the public, even if initial marking after issuance of the patent is delayed. The sooner one complies with the marking requirements, the more likely one is to maximize the period of time for recoverable damages." *American Medical Sys. v. Medical Eng'g Corp.*, 6 F.3d 1523, 1537, 28 USPQ2d 1321, 1331 (Fed. Cir. 1993).

Markush claim [patent] A type of patent claim in which a group of related substances is defined by expressly naming the substances because there is no recognized generic name for that class of substances.

The Format of a Markush Claim. The general form of a Markush claim is "wherein R is a material selected from the group consisting of A, B, C, and D" or "wherein R is A, B, C, or D." For example, an element in the claim might include "a halogen selected from the group consisting of chlorine and bromine." The halogen group of chemicals consists of fluorine, chlorine, iodine, bromine, and astatine. Since there is no generic word for this particular set of two halogens selected from the five in the halogen group, Markush alternative language is needed to define that class. Or, in another example, assume an inventor found that in an electrical circuit the only metals that would work for a conductor were silver and copper. This element of the claim could be recited in Markush format as "a conductor selected from the group consisting of silver and copper."

Previous Patent Office Practice. Previously, Patent Office rules regarded claims with alternative language (e.g., A or B) as inherently ambiguous, failing to "distinctly" claim the matter as required by Patent Code §112, paragraph 2. This was the basis of the rejection that was overturned by the Commissioner in the 1924 *Markush* decision.

The Group Must Be of Related Compounds. In a Markush claim to a compound, the materials forming the Markush group must belong to a recognized physical or chemical class. *Manual of Patent Examining Procedure* §706.03(y) (1994 rev.). If they do not, the claim is subject to a rejection on the basis of "improper Markush grouping" or "lack of unity of invention." That is, there is more than one invention claimed. The concept of "lack of unity of invention" is the appropriate basis on which to reject a claim wherein "unrelated inventions are involved— inventions which are truly independent and distinct." *In re Harnish*, 631 F.2d 716, 722, 206 USPQ 300, 306 (C.C.P.A. 1980).

Group Members Must Be Related. In a Markush claim reciting a process or a combination, rather than a single compound, it is sufficient if (1) the members of the group are disclosed in the specification to have at least one property in common that is responsible for their function in the claimed invention and (2) it is clear that all the members of the group possess this property.

Usual Technologies. Markush claims are most often used in claiming chemical inventions in metallurgy, ceramics, pharmacy, pharmacology, and biology. But such a claim format is also acceptable, although rare, in claiming purely mechanical structures or processes.

History of the Term. Markush claims are named after patent applicant Eugene A. Markush, who appealed a rejection of a claim to the Assistant Commissioner of Patents. In a 1924 decision, the Commissioner approved of the form of the claim. *Ex parte Markush*, 1925 Comm. Dec. 126, 340 O.G. 839 (Asst. Comm'r. Pats. 1924). The name "Markush" became attached to the type of claim expression used in that case.

See CLAIMS, INDEFINITENESS OF CLAIMS.

• *Manual Reference*: "*Ex parte Markush*, 1925 CD 126, 340 OG 839, sanctions, in chemical cases, claiming a genus expressed as a group consisting of certain specified materials. This type of claim is employed when there is no commonly accepted generic expression which is commensurate in scope with the field which the applicant desires to cover.... It is improper to use the term 'comprising' instead of 'consisting of.' " *Manual of Patent Examining Procedure* §706.03(y) (1994).

- *Case References*:

"In the early years of the development of Markush practice, many of the cases involved the problem of clarity—avoiding the uncertainties of alternatives and the like. More recently, the cases have centered on problems of scope, which are related to enablement. Assuming enablement, however, there remains a body of Markush-type claims, particularly in the chemical field, concerned more with the concept of unity of invention. At least the term would be more descriptive and more intelligible internationally than is the more esoteric and provincial expression 'Markush practice.' ... [A]ll of [the inventor's] claimed compounds are dyes.... We hold, therefore, that the claimed compounds all belong to a sub-genus, as defined by [the inventor] which is not repugnant to scientific classification. Under these circumstances we consider the claimed compounds to be part of a single invention so that there is unity of invention.... The Markush groupings of claims 1 and 3-8 are therefore proper." *In re Harnish*, 631 F.2d 716, 722, 206 USPQ 300, 305 (C.C.P.A. 1980).

mask work [computer–copyright] A set of images or templates used in the manufacture of SEMICONDUCTOR CHIPS. A mask work is a kind of map or blueprint used to design and manufacture a semiconductor chip. The mask work defines the design of the chip in three dimensions, since a semiconductor chip consists of several layers of electronic circuits and elements that are laid down one atop another. The mask work images may be in pictorial or photographic form or broken down into digital numerical form for storage in a computer.

An Analogy. One useful analogy to a mask work is a series of separate maps showing the downtown area of a large city, each map showing a horizontal slice, starting with maps of underground and continuing vertically upwards to a map showing the top floor of the highest skyscraper. For example, the first in the series

of maps is a map of underground utilities and sewer connections, the second shows subway train tunnels and stations, the third shows street level, the fourth shows the second-floor level of building, etc. In similar fashion, mask works show the architecture of an electronic chip in three dimensions.

- *Statutory Definition.* The Semiconductor Chip Protection Act (see *SCPA*), 17 U.S.C. §901(a)(2), defines a "mask work" as "a series of related images, however fixed or encoded—(A) having or representing the predetermined, three-dimensional pattern of metallic, insulating or semiconducting material present or removed from the layers of a semiconductor chip product; and (B) in which series the relation of the images to one another is that each image has the pattern of the surface of one form of the semiconductor chip product."

See *SCPA*, CHIP.

means for claim [patent]
See MEANS-PLUS-FUNCTION CLAIM.

means-plus-function claim [patent] A patent claim, instead of reciting an element in precise detail, may recite "means for" performing a specified function. For example, a claim, instead of reciting that the handle of a pot is bolted or welded to the pot, may recite "means for securing the handle to the pot." This "means for" language will include all methods of performing the function as described in the patent disclosure and the equivalents of those methods. The purpose is to give an inventor a claim of sufficient scope to cover the true INVENTION without the need for the inventor to list a catalog of alternatives in the specification.

Literal Infringement Versus Equivalents. Literal infringement of a claim containing a "means for" clause should be distinguished from infringement under the doctrine of EQUIVALENTS. Literal infringement of a "means for" or "means-plus-function" claim is determined by asking whether the corresponding means in the accused device is the same as or an equivalent of the corresponding structure described in the patent specification as performing that function. *Texas Instruments, Inc. v. In-*

ternational Trade Comm'n, 805 F.2d 1558, 1562, 231 USPQ 833, 841 (Fed. Cir. 1986); *In re Hayes Microcomputer Prods. Inc.*, 982 F.2d 1527, 1541, 25 USPQ 2d 1241, 1251 (Fed. Cir. 1992). That is, the ACCUSED DEVICE must perform an identical function, but the "means" can be an equivalent. *Intel Corp. v. International Trade Comm'n*, 946 F.2d 821, 20 USPQ2d 1161 (Fed. Cir. 1991). Applying the mainstream doctrine of equivalents to a means-plus-function claim might allow the accused device to perform an equivalent function and still be infringing.

Means-Plus-Function Rules Must be Applied During Prosecution of a Patent. For some time, the Patent and Trademark Office (PTO) contended that it was entitled to read means-plus-function claims broadly, independent of any structure set out in the specification. But in 1994, the Federal Circuit en banc reversed this practice of the PTO. " [O]ne construing means-plus function language in a claim must look to the specification and interpret that language in light of the corresponding structure, material, or acts described therein, and equivalents thereof, to the extent that the specification provides such disclosure. ... [B]ecause no distinction is made in paragraph six [of 35 U.S.C. §112] between prosecution in the PTO and enforcement in the courts, or between validity and infringement, we hold that paragraph six applies regardless of the context in which the interpretation of means-plus-function language arises, i.e., whether as part of a patentability determination in the PTO or as part of a validity or infringement determination in a court." *In re Donaldson Co.*, 16 F.3d 1189, 1193, 29 USPQ 2d 1845, 1848–49 (Fed. Cir. 1994). See Finkle, *Means-Plus-Function Claims in Light of Donaldson and Other Recent Case Developments,* 10 Santa Clara Comp. & High Tech. L.J. 267(1994).

Need to Disclose Structure for the "Means" Element of the Claim. Because the scope of a "means for" element is determined by reference to the specification, it is imperative that the inventor disclose some structure or enabling means in the specification for all "means" recitations in the claims. *In re Hayes Microcomputer Prods. Inc.*, 982 F.2d 1527, 1535, 25

USPQ 2d 1241, 1246 (Fed. Cir. 1992). See *DMI, Inc. v. Deere & Co.*, 755 F.2d 1570, 1574, 225 USPQ 236, 238 (Fed. Cir. 1985) ("Patentees are required to disclose in the specification some enabling means for accomplishing the function set forth in the 'means plus function' limitation. At the same time, there is and can be no requirement that the applicants describe or predict every possible means of accomplishing that function.").

Single Means Claim. Only an element in a claimed combination of elements can be couched in means-plus-function format. A so-called SINGLE MEANS CLAIM that recites only a single element in "means for" format is not authorized by the statute and is improper.

Synonym: means for claim.

See SINGLE MEANS CLAIM.

• *Treatise References*: 4 D. Chisum, *Patents* §18.04[5] (1994 rev.); R. Harmon, *Patents and the Federal Circuit* §5.6 (3d ed. 1994).

• *Statutory Reference*: 35 U.S.C. §112, 6th paragraph: "An element in a claim for a combination may be expressed as a means or step for performing a specified function without the recital of structure, material, or acts in support thereof, and such claims shall be construed to cover the corresponding structure, material, or acts described in the specification and equivalents thereof."

• *Case References*:

"[W]here a claim sets forth a means for performing a specific function, without reciting any specific structure for performing that function, the structure disclosed in the specification must be considered, and the patent claim construed to cover both the disclosed structure and equivalents thereof." *Radio Steel & Mfg. Co. v. MTD Prods., Inc.*, 731 F.2d 840, 848, 221 USPQ 657, 663 (Fed. Cir. 1984).

"If all other limitations in such a claim are literally met, and the accused device is shown to contain an equivalent of the structure which was identified in the means-plus-function limitation of the claim and disclosed in the specification, infringement is said to be 'literal' as distinguished from infringement under the doctrine of equivalents." *Data Line Corp. v. Micro Technologies, Inc.*, 813 F.2d 1196, 1201, 1 USPQ2d 2052, 2055 (Fed. Cir. 1987).

"Anticipation is determined by comparison of the reference with the claims. The claims here define the invention in terms of several specific 'means-plus-function' elements. The limitations which must be met by anticipatory reference are those set forth in each statement of function…. Such a limitation cannot be met by an element in a reference that performs a different function, even though it may be part of a device embodying the same general overall concept." *RCA Corp. v. Applied Digital Data Sys., Inc.*, 730 F.2d 1440, 1445 n.5, 221 USPQ 385, 389 n.5 (Fed. Cir. 1984).

"It is not necessary to consider the prior art in applying section 112, paragraph 6. Even if the prior art discloses the same or an equivalent structure, the claim will not be limited in scope thereby. It is only necessary to determine what is an equivalent to the structure disclosed in the specification which is performing the function at issue. When the prior art is considered in the context of the doctrine of equivalents, however, the purpose is to ensure that the patent holder does not obtain a broader right to exclude under that doctrine than could have been obtained from the patent office…. Thus, under section 112, paragraph 6, the aids for determining a structural equivalent to the structure disclosed in the patent specification are the same as those used in interpreting any other type of claim language, namely, the specification, the prosecution history, other claims in the patent, and expert testimony." *Intel Corp. v. International Trade Comm'n*, 946 F.2d 821, 842, 20 USPQ2d 1161, 1179–80 (Fed. Cir. 1991).

"The doctrine of equivalents has a different purpose and application than section 112…. In sum, section 112 ¶6, and the doctrine of equivalents have separate origins and purposes. Section 112, ¶6 limits the broad language of means-plus-function limitations in combination claims to equivalents of the structure, materials or acts in the specification. The doctrine of equivalents equitably expands exclusive patent rights." *Valmont Indus. Inc. v. Reinke Mfg.*

Co., 983 F.2d 1039, 1042–44, 24 USPQ2d 1451, 1454–55 (Fed. Cir. 1993).

mechanical licensing agent [copyright] An agent of the owners of copyright in musical works who acts as an intermediary in granting licenses to record producers to produce recordings of the copyrighted music. These are known as MECHANICAL RIGHTS licenses. While Copyright Act §115 creates a COMPULSORY LICENSE of these mechanical rights, the custom of the trade is for the record producer not to rely on the statutory terms of the compulsory license but to obtain a standard license from a mechanical licensing agent.

Most nations do not have a mechanical rights compulsory licensing system as does the United States. In those nations, the analogous bodies are mechanical licensing societies, which are collective organizations of the owners of copyright in musical works. See S. Shemel & M.W. Krasilovsky, *This Business of Music* 229 (1985).

The largest mechanical licensing agent in the United States is the HARRY FOX AGENCY in New York City. Other smaller agencies are the American Mechanical Rights Association (AMRA) and the Copyright Service Bureau Ltd. See S. Shemel & M.W. Krasilovsky, *This Business of Music* 228 (1985).

See COMPULSORY LICENSING of musical works, HARRY FOX AGENCY.

mechanical rights [copyright] The right to use a copyrighted musical work to make and sell PHONORECORDS. A compulsory mechanical license is granted by Copyright Act §115, 17 U.S.C. §115. See COMPULSORY LICENSING of coypright.

Origin of the Term. The compulsory mechanical license was created by Congress in 1909 when for the first time it extended copyright protection to the act of "mechanically" recording a song on phonograph records and piano rolls. This is why the right to make a phonorecord of a song is still called a "mechanical right."

Compulsory Mechanical License. The compulsory license system created by Congress in 1909 is still in existence as modified by the

Copyright Act revisions effective in 1978. Congress originally created a compulsory licensing system for mechanical rights because it feared that a recording company might obtain a monopoly of songs, as apparently was the case in the early twentieth century with Aeolian Co., a leading manufacturer of piano rolls, which had exclusive contracts with most music publishers. See S. Shemel & M.W. Krasilovsky, *This Business of Music* 222–23 (1985); W. Patry, *Copyright Law and Practice* 797–800 (1994).

See COMPULSORY LICENSE.

• *Treatise References*: 2 *Nimmer on Copyright* §8.04 (1994 rev.); S. Shemel & M.W. Krasilovsky, *This Business of Music* ch. 20 (1985); M. Leaffer, *Understanding Copyright* §8.19[D] (1989).

mechanic skilled in the art [patent]
See SKILLFUL MECHANIC.

mediation [general legal]
See ALTERNATIVE DISPUTE RESOLUTION.

merchandising [general intellectual property] The licensing of publicly recognizable intellectual property for use on or in association with specific products or services to foster sales. For example, the licensing of the name and image of a popular motion picture character for use on children's toys and other products is a highly visible form of merchandising. E.g., *Warner Bros., Inc. v. Gay Toys, Inc.*, 658 F.2d 76, 211 USPQ 1017 (2d Cir. 1981), 724 F.2d 327 (2d Cir. 1983) (toy auto incorporating distinctive features of auto featured on a popular television series). Another form of merchandising would be the licensing of the trademark COCA-COLA for use on wearing apparel. Similarly, the licensing of a well-known athlete's identity to advertise athletic shoes is a merchandising license of the RIGHT OF PUBLICITY. Almost any form of intellectual property can constitute the "merchandising property" that forms the basis for a merchandising license.

See LICENSE, FRANCHISING.

Treatise References: G. Battersby & C. Grimes, *The Law of Merchandise and Character Licensing: Merchandising Law and Practice* (1994 rev.); J.T. McCarthy, *Trademarks and Unfair Competition* §§10.15–.22, 27.08[2] (3d ed. 1995 rev.); J.T. McCarthy, *The Rights of Publicity and Privacy* §§10.4–.15 (1995 rev.).

merchant's mark [trademark] A trademark or service mark used and owned by one who is a seller or distributor but not a maker or manufacturer of goods. It has long been recognized that one who sells goods made by another can have its own valuable trademark rights. *Menendez v. Holt*, 128 U.S. 514 (1888). If a distributor has goods manufactured for it according to its specifications or standards, the distributor clearly is the owner of the mark applied to the goods. However, the courts go further to hold that supplying such specifications to a manufacturer is not a condition precedent to ownership of a merchant's mark. It is sufficient that the merchant vouches for and stands behind the quality of the goods made by another. Only when ownership is disputed between manufacturer and merchant will "control" by the merchant be a critical enquiry. A single product may bear both the maker's mark and the merchant's mark, e.g., a men's suit with a label identifying MACY'S as the retail merchant and CHRISTIAN DIOR as the designer-maker.

Merchant's Service Mark. A merchant's service mark is a mark identifying the merchant as the source of such merchandising services as "retail department store services" or "retail grocery store services." *Trademark Manual of Examining Procedure* §1301.01(a) (1993).

See SERVICE MARK.

Origin of the Term. Prior to the 1989 Trademark Law Revision Act's rewriting of the Lanham Act definition of "trademark," the statute defined a trademark as including a word or symbol used by a "manufacturer or merchant" to identify and distinguish goods. Lanham Act §45, 15 U.S.C. §1127. This is the source of the word "merchant" as designating a seller's mark. While the duo of "manufacturer or merchant" disappeared from the definition of "trademark" in the 1989 revisions, this indicates no change of scope but was merely an attempt at modernizing the language of the statute.

- *Treatise Reference*: J.T. McCarthy, *Trademarks and Unfair Competition* §§16.15, 19.30[2] (3d ed. 1995 rev.).

merger [copyright–trademark] (1) *Merger in Copyright*: A congruence of an uncopyrightable idea with its copyrightable expression, so that to protect the expression would be to also protect the idea. (2) *Merger in Trademark*: A bar to the affirmative defense of prior use in a trademark infringement claim where the plaintiff is a former licensee and the defendant is a former licensor.

(1) Merger in Copyright. When an idea is capable of expression in only one manner, there is merger. Since ideas cannot be protected by copyright, when there is merger of idea and expression, there will be no protection of the expression. Merger will occur only when the idea is defined with such specificity that it is incapable of being expressed, used, or explained in more than one way. When there is merger, some courts will protect expression but only against "nearly identical copying." *Apple Computer Inc. v. Microsoft Corp.*, 35 F.3d 1435, 1444, 32 USPQ2d 1086, 1093 (9th Cir. 1994).

Copyright Does Not Protect an Idea. The fundamental rule of law is that copyright does not protect an idea, but only expressions of an idea. This IDEA-EXPRESSION DICHOTOMY is codified in §102(b) of the Copyright Act. It is immutable logic that if idea and expression merge into one, to protect expression would be to protect idea, which is forbidden in copyright law.

Differentiating "Idea" From "Expression." The difficulty in applying the merger rule is in defining exactly what is the idea. That is, at what level of abstraction should the idea of the plaintiff's work be defined? If the idea is defined at a very high level of abstraction, there will necessarily be many different ways to express the idea. But if the idea is defined in very detailed and specific terms, there may be only one way or a few ways to state the idea in different expressions. Whether or not there is merger will turn almost entirely upon the level of abstraction at which idea is defined. "Determining when the idea and its expression have merged is a task requiring considerable care; if the merger doctrine is applied too readily, arguably available forms of expression will be precluded; if applied too sparingly, protection will be accorded to ideas." *Kregos v. The Associated Press,* 937 F.2d 700, 705, 19 USPQ2d 1161, 1165 (2d Cir. 1991).

An Issue of Infringement. While it is not entirely clear, the better view is that the merger rule is not a bar to the validity of copyright but is simply a defense to a charge of infringement. That is, inseparability of idea and expression is evaluated in the context of a particular case, rather than trying to disqualify certain expression from copyright altogether. 3 *Nimmer on Copyright* §13.03[B][3] (1994 rev.); *NEC Corp. v. Intel Corp.*, 10 USPQ2d 1177, 1179 (N.D. Cal. 1989) (merger issue is question of "whether or not there is infringement rather than copyrightability"); *Kregos v. The Associated Press,* 937 F.2d 700, 705, 19 USPQ2d 1161, 1165 (2d Cir. 1991) (The Second Circuit uses the merger rule to determine whether infringement has occurred, rather than whether a copyright is valid: "Assessing merger in the context of alleged infringement will normally provide a more detailed and realistic basis for evaluating the claim that protection of expression would inevitably accord protection of the idea.").

Computer Program. The courts have developed a distinct set of rules for distinguishing idea from expression for computer programs. See COMPUTER PROGRAM, LOOK AND FEEL, USER INTERFACE, IDEA-EXPRESSION DICHOTOMY, LITTLE VARIATION RULE.

- *Statutory Reference*: 17 U.S.C. §102(b): "In no case does copyright protection for an original work of authorship extend to any idea, process, procedure, system, method of operation, concept, principle, or discovery, regardless of the form in which it is described, explained, illustrated, or embodied in such work."

- *Case References*:
"It is axiomatic that copyright protects only the expression of ideas and not the ideas themselves.... Thus, if an idea is indistinguishable from its expression, that is, if the idea is 'merged' into its expression, the expression

cannot be protected under the copyright laws. For example in *Herbert Rosenthal Jewelry Corp. v. Kalpakian*, 446 F.2d 738, 741–42 [170 USPQ 557, 558–59] (9th Cir. 1971), the court held that the idea of a jewel-encrusted bee pin could not be distinguished from the expression of that idea. As long as more than one manufacturer produced jewel-encrusted bee pins, the court found, it was inevitable that there would be a substantial similarity between the two forms of expression. In other words, the number of ways in which one can design a jewel-encrusted bee pin is strictly limited. Under such circumstances, to give one manufacturer a copyright on its bee pin would be to give that manufacturer a monopoly on the jewel-encrusted bee pin market because no other manufacturer could possibly conceive of a substantially different jewel-encrusted bee pin." *Broderbund Software, Inc. v. Unison World*, 648 F. Supp. 1127, 1133, 231 USPQ2d 700, 702 (N.D. Cal. 1986).

"Where an idea and the expression 'merge,' or are 'inseparable,' the expression is not given copyright protection.... In addition, where an expression is, as a practical matter, indispensable, or at least standard, in the treatment of a given idea, the expression is protected only against verbatim, or virtually identical copying." *Johnson Controls Inc. v. Phoenix Control Sys. Inc.*, 886 F.2d 1173, 1175, 12 USPQ2d 1566, 1568–69 (9th Cir. 1989).

"Defendants argue that the principle of merger between the idea and expression is applicable in this case because the idea or subject of the material at issue can be expressed only in a limited number of ways. The merger principle, when raised legitimately, is a variation of the idea/expression dichotomy.... When the idea and the expression of the idea coincide, then the expression will not be protected in order to prevent creation of a monopoly on the underlying 'art.' ... [A]n expression will be found to be merged into the idea when 'there are no or few other ways of expressing a particular idea.' ... It is on the basis of the merger principle that copyright has been denied to utilitarian ideas, such as forms.... We are, quite frankly, unpersuaded that the number of questions that can be devised to test students on their knowledge of square roots or dangling participles is so limited that [the plaintiff's examination] questions designed for this purpose represent a merger with the underlying ideas." *Educational Testing Servs. v. Katzman*, 793 F.2d 533, 539–40, 230 USPQ 156, 160 (3d Cir. 1986) (no merger found: preliminary injunction against copyright infringement affirmed).

"As long as selections of facts involve matters of taste and personal opinion,, there is no serious risk that withholding the merger doctrine will extend protection to an idea. That was surely the case with the selection of baseball cards.... It is also true of a selection of prominent families for inclusion in a social directory.... However, where a selection of data is the first step in an analysis that yields a precise result or even a better-than-average probability of some result, protecting the 'expression' of the selection would clearly risk protecting the idea of the analysis." *Kregos v. The Associated Press*, 937 F.2d 700, 705, 19 USPQ2d 1161, 1165 (2d Cir. 1991) (reversing lower court decision that selection of nine categories of baseball pitching statistics merged with the idea of an outcome predictive form), *on remand*, 3 F.3d 656, 27 USPQ2d 1881 (2d Cir. 1993) (no infringement found).

"Because Kregos' idea was of the soft type infused with taste or opinion, the court [in *Kregos v. The Associated Press, supra*] withheld application of the merger doctrine, permitting Kregos to exercise ownership. It accomplished this by assigning to the idea a different level of abstraction from the expression of it, so that the merger doctrine would not apply and the copyright owner would not lose protection.... *Kregos*, thus, makes a policy judgment as between two evils. Unbridled application of the merger doctrine would undo the protection the copyright law intends to apply to compilations. Complete failure to apply it, however, would result in granting protection to useful ideas. *Kregos* adopts a middle ground. In cases of wholesale takings of compilations,, a *selective* application of the merger doctrine, withholding its application as to soft ideas infused with taste and opinion, will carry out the statutory policy to protect innovative compilations without impairing the policy that requires public access to ideas of a more important and useful kind." *CCC Information Servs. Inc. v. Maclean Hunter Market Reports Inc.*, 44 F.3d 61, 71–72, 33 USPQ2d 1183, 1191–92 (2d Cir. 1994) (ordering entry of summary judgment of validity and infringement where data in copyright owner's guide books containing projected values for used cars were extensively copied into alleged infringer's data base; the used car valuations are "in the category of approximative statements of opinion.").

• *Treatise References*: 3 *Nimmer on Copyright* §13.03[B][3] (1994 rev.); 1 P. Goldstein, *Copyright* §2.3.2 (1989); W. Patry, *Copyright Law and Practice* 320 et seq. (1994).

• *Commentary Reference*: J. Ginsberg, *No "Sweat"? Copyright and Other Protection of Works of Information After Feist v. Rural Telephone*, 92 Colum. L. Rev. 338, 346 (1992) ("In copyright law, an 'idea' is not an epistemological concept, but a legal conclusion prompted by notions—often unarticulated and unproven—of appropriate competition.").

• *Example 1: No Merger Found.* The plaintiff asserts that the defendant has infringed its copyright on a lawn statue that shows a life-sized deer in a certain pose. The only significant difference between the parties' deer statues is that the defendant's deer head is turned in a different direction. The defendant asserts that there is no infringement because there is a MERGER of idea and expression. If one defines the idea as merely a life-sized animal lawn statue, then there are thousands of methods of expression by means of every animal from a lion to a deer in every pose imaginable. If one defines the idea as a deer statue, then there are several different media to use and dozens of sizes, ages, and poses of deer. If one defines the idea as a life-sized mature, female deer in a standing pose with one hoof raised in a posture of alertness prior to flight, etc., then there may be only one way or just a few ways to express such a detailed "idea." In reversing a denial of a preliminary injunction in a similar case, the court defined the "idea" as "a realistic-looking concrete deer," noting that even life-like animal statues, while allowing relatively few variations "are nonetheless somewhat stylized versions of these creatures in terms of posture and facial expression." No merger of idea and expression was found and minor differences (head pointing in different direction, two inches shorter and narrower) between the parties' statues were found not to avoid a finding of substantial similarity and infringement. *Concrete Mach. Co. v. Classic Lawn Ornaments Inc.*, 843 F.2d 600, 6 USPQ2d 1357 (1st Cir. 1988).

• *Example 2: Merger Found.* Kern River Gas Transmission Company drafted a set of maps depicting a proposed route for an interstate natural gas pipeline. The maps consisted of lines and mile markings drawn on topographical maps published by the United States Geological Survey. A competing pipeline company, Wy-Cal, copied Kern River's maps and submitted them to bid on the same job. Kern River sued Wy-Cal for copyright infringement. The court refused to issue a preliminary injunction to Kern River because the idea of the location of the pipeline merged with its expression embodied in the maps. Since the markings on Kern River's maps were the only effective way to convey the idea of the proposed location of a pipeline, they were unprotectible by copyright law. "The idea of the proposed location of a prospective pipeline is not copyrightable.... To extend protection to the lines [on the map] would be to grant Kern River a monopoly of the idea for locating a proposed pipeline in the chosen corridor, a foreclosure of competition that Congress could not have intended to sanction through copyright law, especially given the ALJ's finding ... that the Southern California enhanced oil recovery market could support only one pipeline." *Kern River Gas Transmission Co. v. The Coastal Corp.*, 899 F.2d 1458, 1464, 14 USPQ 2d 1898, 1902 (5th Cir. 1990). Compare *Mason v. Montgomery Data Inc.*, 967 F.2d 135, 23 USPQ2d 1676 (5th Cir. 1992) (real estate ownership maps of a county are copyrightable and not subject to the merger doctrine because the idea of bringing together available information on boundaries, landmarks, and ownership in an effective pictorial format could be expressed in a variety of ways).

method claim

(2) *Merger in Trademark.* A licensee of a trademark that was in use by the licensee prior to the license may not rely upon its prior independent use of the mark as a defense against an infringement claim brought against it by the licensor upon termination of the license. The licensee's prior trademark rights have been "merged" with that of the licensor at the time of licensing and have inured to the benefit of the licensor. See 1 J.T. McCarthy, *Trademarks and Unfair Competition* §25.07[2] (3d ed. 1995 rev.).

• *Case Reference:* "[T]he courts have repeatedly held that any separate existence and right to use a national organization's name or mark which a seceding local chapter might have had prior to affiliation with the national, was merged with that of the national when the local became a member of the national organization, thus rejecting contentions that prior independent existence and prior use of the mark in question entitled a seceding member to continue using the mark subsequent to disaffiliation." *Council of Better Business Bureaus v. Better Business Bureau,* 200 USPQ 282, 296 (S.D. Fla. 1978).

method claim [patent]
   See PROCESS CLAIM.

Mexico City Convention [copyright–international] A 1902 multilateral treaty between the United States and several Latin American nations relating to copyright protection. It has been largely superseded by the 1910 BUENOS AIRES CONVENTION ON LITERARY AND ARTISTIC COPYRIGHT.

microcode [computer–copyright] A computer program controlling a microprocessor. A microprocessor regulates certain basic switching functions within a computer. Microcode has been held to be copyrightable.

   See COMPUTER PROGRAM, IDEA-EXPRESSION DICHOTOMY, COPYRIGHT.

• *Definition Reference:* "The microcode defines the instruction set (repertoire) of a specific computer. It is often not accessible to programmers if the system is a large one and designed for nonuse by the owners and users, e.g., proprietary to the manufacturer." C. Sipple, *Computer Dictionary* 289 (4th ed. 1985).

• *Case Reference:* "A microcode consists of a series of instructions that tell a microprocessor which of its thousands of transistors to actuate in order to perform the tasks directed by the macroinstruction set. As such, it comes squarely within the definition of a 'computer program' which Congress added to the Copyright Act in 1980. ... NEC contends that Intel's microcode is a defining element of the computer itself. According to NEC, Intel's microcode does not come within the definition of a computer program because it cannot be used *in* a computer and also be a defining part of the computer. But, as stated at the outset, Intel's microcode is within the statutory definition of a 'computer program.' ... See also [*CONTU* Report] which asserted that '[p]rograms should no more be considered machine parts than videotapes should be considered parts of sound reproduction equipment.... [I]t is concluded that Intel's microcode was a proper subject for copyright protection.... ' " *NEC Corp. v. Intel Corp.,* 10 USPQ2d 1177, 1178–80 (N.D. Cal. 1989).

• *Commentary References:*
   "Microcode is a set of encoded instructions—in other words, a program—that controls the fine details of the execution of one or more primitive functions of a computer. Microcode serves as a substitute for certain elements of the hardware circuitry that had previously controlled that function.... Although, strictly speaking, it is a program, it is considered a more integral part of the machine hardware than is software, hence its alternative name, firmware." Samuelson, *CONTU Revisited: The Case Against Copyright Protection for Computer Programs in Machine Readable Form,* 1984 Duke L. J. 663, 677 (1984).

   "The physical/abstract duality of microcode, however, significantly narrows the scope of copyright protection. Specifically, as to those portions of the microcode that are not dictated by functional considerations, only identical or substantially identical copying will constitute infringement, and as to those portions of the microcode that *are* functionally dictated, there is no protection against copying." Laurie & Everett, *The Copyrightability of Microcode: Is It Software or Hardware Or Both?* 2 Computer Law. 1, 2 (1985).

microorganism depository [patent]
See CELL DEPOSITORY.

minitrial [general legal]
See ALTERNATIVE DISPUTE RESOLUTION.

misappropriation [unfair competition]
A judge-made common law form of unfair competition where the defendant has copied or appropriated some item or creation of the plaintiff which is not protected by either patent law, copyright law, trademark law, or any other traditional theory of exclusive rights.

Elements of Misappropriation. The following three elements are necessary to plead and prove a case of misappropriation: (1) the plaintiff has made a substantial investment of time, effort, and money in creating the thing misappropriated, such that the court can characterize that "thing" as a kind of property right; (2) the defendant has appropriated the "thing" at little or no cost, such that the court can characterize the defendant's actions as "reaping where it has not sown"; and (3) the defendant's acts have injured the plaintiff, such as by a direct diversion of profits from the plaintiff to the defendant or a loss of royalties that the plaintiff charges to others to use the thing misappropriated. See 1 J.T. McCarthy, *Trademarks and Unfair Competition* §10.25 (3d ed. 1995 rev.).

Examples of Things Misappropriated. The types of "things" that have been held to have been illegally misappropriated range from the unauthorized radio broadcast of professional baseball games (*Pittsburgh Athletic Co. v. KQV Broadcasting Co.*, 24 F. Supp. 490 (D.C. Pa. 1938)); tape and record piracy of pre-1972 recordings (*Goldstein v. California*, 412 U.S. 526, 178 USPQ 129 (1973)); the sale of stock market index futures based on the Dow Jones market average (*Board of Trade v. Dow Jones & Co.*, 108 Ill. App.3d 681, 439 N.E. 2d 526, 218 USPQ 636 (1982), *aff'd*, 98 Ill.2d 109, 456 N.E.2d 84 (1983)); and the taking of facts in race horse eligibility certificates (*U.S. Trotting Ass'n v. Chicago Downs Ass'n*, 665 F.2d 781 (7th Cir. 1981)).

The INS v. AP Case. The misappropriation doctrine was born in the 1918 Supreme Court decision of *International News Serv. v. Associated Press*, 248 U.S. 215 (1918). INS would take AP's hot news stories about World War I battles from publicly distributed New York newspapers that subscribed to the AP service. INS would then telegraph the story to the West Coast to Hearst newspapers, which would print the stories, sometimes ahead of the West Coast AP newspaper subscribers. Thus, INS appropriated hot news stories that had been gathered by AP at great expense and effort. There was no copyright infringement, for there was usually no copying of the exact words of an AP dispatch; rather there was an appropriation of the underlying factual information. The majority of the Supreme Court held that INS's actions constituted a new kind of unfair competition called "misappropriation" and approved of the lower court's injunction, which prohibited INS from taking AP public dispatches so long as the items remained hot news. In a famous dissent, Justice Brandeis argued that because the factual information of "hot news" is as uncopyrightable as bare ideas, it is not for judges to create new forms of exclusive rights: such protection must come from legislation drafted by Congress rather than by judge-made modifications of the common law of unfair competition. See Baird, *Common Law Intellectual Property and the Legacy of International News Service v. Associated Press*, 50 U. Chi. L. Rev. 411 (1983).

History of Misappropriation. From 1918 to 1964, the misappropriation doctrine was embraced by some courts but rejected by others. The Court of Appeals for the Second Circuit, generally in the person of Judge Learned Hand, consistently refused to recognize the misappropriation doctrine as law, confining *INS v. AP* to its facts. From 1964 to 1973, the Supreme Court *Sears-Compco* decisions cast a pall of federal preemption over the misappropriation doctrine, leading a minority of courts to reject the misappropriation doctrine as preempted by federal copyright law. From 1973 to 1978, the misappropriation doctrine was given a boost by the Supreme Court *Goldstein* decision, which upheld a state antimisappropriation statute prohibiting tape and record piracy. *Goldstein v. California*, 412 U.S. 526, 178 USPQ 129 (1973). From 1978 to the present, the preemption issue has been determined by applying the test of Copyright Act §301(a).

Federal Preemption. Traditionally, misappropriation has been a controversial legal theory because of the question of whether it is preempted by federal copyright law. Under the test of 17 U.S.C. §301(a), there is federal preemption of the state law misappropriation doctrine only if: (1) misappropriation is asserted in such a way that it is "equivalent" to the exclusive rights of copyright; *and* (2) misappropriation is asserted to protect something that comes "within the subject matter of copyright." For example, if the thing misappropriated is not FIXED (some live sporting events, improvised music, some parades), then state protection is not preempted. The misappropriation doctrine covers many different factual patterns: while some will be preempted by federal copyright law, some will not. When a misappropriation claim is nothing more than an alternative reformulation of a copyright claim, then the state claim is usually viewed as the "equivalent" of the federal copyright claim and is held to be preempted. For example, a claim of conversion and misappropriation of a design on a Christmas tree ornament was held preempted. *Mayer v. Josiah Wedgwood & Sons, Ltd.*, 601 F.2d 1523, 225 USPQ 776 (S.D.N.Y. 1985).

- *Treatise References*: 1 J.T. McCarthy, *Trademarks and Unfair Competition* §§10.23–.34 (3d ed. 1995 rev.); 1 *Nimmer on Copyright* §1.01[B][1] (1994 rev.); 2 P. Goldstein, *Copyright* §§15.14.2, 15.16.1.3(b) (1989); W. Patry, *Copyright Law and Practice* 1115–21 (1994).

- *Legislative History*: " 'Misappropriation' is not necessarily synonymous with copyright infringement, and thus a cause of action labeled as 'misappropriation' is not preempted if it is in fact based neither on a right within the general scope of copyright as specified by section 106 nor on a right equivalent thereto. For example, state law should have the flexibility to afford a remedy (under traditional principles of equity) against a consistent pattern of unauthorized appropriation by a competitor of the facts (i.e., not the literary expression) constituting 'hot' news, whether in the traditional mold of *International News Servs. v. Associated Press*, 248 U.S. 215 (1918), or in the newer form of data updates from scientific, business, or financial data bases." H.R. Rep. No. 94-1476, 94th Cong., 2d Sess. 132 (1976). *Caveat*: This observation must be read in light of the fact that it was written in connection with a bill that listed "misappropriation not equivalent to any of such exclusive rights" as one of the explicitly non-preempted state rights—a section stricken out of the final Copyright Act.

misdescriptive mark [trademark]

See DESCRIPTIVE MARK.

mismarking [patent] The act of falsely designating on an item or in advertising for it that the item is patented or that a patent application is on file and is pending. Mismarking, if done with the intent to deceive the public, is specifically prohibited by federal statute, 35 U.S.C. §292, which provides a maximum fine of $500 for each offense. Any person may file a private lawsuit for the penalty and recover one half of the penalty, the other half payable to the U.S. government. Since the fine is penal in nature, the statute is strictly construed. The requisite intent to deceive will not be inferred from facts which show that the mismarking was the result of a mistake, oversight, or inadvertence. *Arcadia Mach. & Tool Inc. v. Sturm, Ruger & Co.*, 786 F.2d 1124, 1125, 229 USPQ 124, 125 (Fed. Cir. 1986).

It has been held that mismarking is not a basis for the defense of unclean hands sufficient to prevent the patentee from prevailing in an infringement suit. *Republic Molding Corp. v. B.W. Photo Utils.*, 319 F.2d 347, 351, 138 USPQ 101, 104 (9th Cir. 1963) (improper use of "patent pending" before an application was filed is "no justification for invalidating the patent upon its subsequent issuance").

See MARKING OF PATENT, PATENT PENDING, MARKING ESTOPPEL.

- *Treatise References*: 4 D. Chisum, *Patents* §20.03[7][vii] (1992 rev.); R. Harmon, *Patents and the Federal Circuit* §9.4(c) (3d ed. 1994).

- *Statutory Reference*: 35 U.S.C. §292:

(a) ... Whoever marks upon, or affixes to, or uses in advertising in connection with any unpatented article, the word 'patent' or any word or number importing the same is patented, for the purpose of deceiving the public; or [w]hoever marks upon, or affixes to, or uses in advertising in connection with any article, the words 'patent applied for,' 'patent pending,' or any word importing that an application for patent has been made, when no application for patent has been made, or if made, is not pending, for the purpose of deceiving the public—

Shall be fined not more than $500 for every such offense.

(b) Any person may sue for the penalty, in which event one-half shall go to the person suing and the other half to the use of the United States.

misuse [patent–trademark–copyright] A defense to an infringement charge, the defense being based on the plaintiff's conduct in using the intellectual property in violation of the letter or the spirit of the antitrust laws. Misuse is a form of the traditional equitable defense of "unclean hands." Misuse is solely a defense, not a ground for an affirmative claim for relief.

1. Patent Misuse as a Defense. Misuse is a defense based upon the patentee's actions in obtaining or licensing the patent in violation of the policy of patent or antitrust law, regardless of a lack of injury or a lack of violation of the letter of antitrust law. Usually, this conduct consists of some attempt to extend the economic scope of the patent to include other articles or processes outside the scope of the patent.

Patent Misuse Is Broader Than Antitrust Law. The patent misuse defense is merely a type of "unclean hands." *Morton Salt Co. v. G.S. Suppiger*, 314 U.S. 488, 52 USPQ 30 (1942). Misuse is broader than the letter of antitrust law, for almost any conduct that offends the policy

of patent or antitrust could be held to be a misuse. Thus, conduct that constitutes a patent misuse defense does not necessarily have to constitute a violation of the antitrust provisions of the Clayton Act or the Sherman Act. *Zenith Radio Corp. v. Hazeltine Research, Inc.*, 395 U.S. 100, 140, 161 USPQ 577, 593 (1969) ("if there was such patent misuse, it does not necessarily follow that the misuse embodies the ingredients of a violation of either sec. 1 or sec. 2 of the Sherman Act"); *Senza-Gel Corp. v. Seiffhart*, 803 F.2d 661, 668, 231 USPQ 363, 368 (Fed. Cir. 1986).

Damage Is Not Essential. It is not necessary for a defendant in a patent infringement case to prove that it was damaged or injured in any way in order to assert the defense of misuse of the patent by the plaintiff. *Morton Salt Co. v. G.S. Suppiger*, 314 U.S. 488, 493, 52 USPQ 30, 33 (1942). Thus, the defendant can point to restrictions in a patent license between the patentee and third parties as a basis for a misuse defense.

Purge of Misuse. If patent misuse is proved, the patent is unenforceable unless and until the patentee has "purged" the misuse, if possible, by eliminating the offensive licensing conduct and dissipating the market effects of the misuse. *B.B. Chem. Co. v. Ellis*, 314 U.S. 495 52 USPQ 33 (1942); *Koratron Co. v. Lion Uniform, Inc.*, 409 F. Supp. 1019, 191 USPQ 576 (N.D. Cal. 1976).

Antitrust Violation. If the alleged patent infringer has suffered provable damages caused by the patentee's use of the patent in violation of the letter of antitrust law, it can assert a treble damage counterclaim as part of the patent litigation, e.g., *Walker Process Equip. Inc. v. Food Mach. Chem. Co.*, 382 U.S. 172, 147 USPQ 404 (1965).

Types of Conduct Constituting Patent Misuse. Misuse can be based upon almost any type of anticompetitive use of the patent that has been held to violate the antitrust laws. See ABA, *Antitrust Law Developments* 487 *et seq.* (2d ed. 1984); W. Holmes, *Intellectual Property and Antitrust Law* §1.07 (1994 rev.). However, patent misuse most often has been invoked in the context of patent TIE-INS conditioning a license of the patent on the purchase of something else, usually an unpatented product. For example, in the classic *Morton Salt* case, the owner of a patent on a machine used to deposit salt tablets in canned food licensed the use of its patented machines only to canners who also agreed to purchase all their unpatented salt from the patentee. Stretching the economic power of the patent to include unpatented salt led the Supreme Court to conclude that the patent had been sufficiently "misused" to deny relief against an infringer. *Morton Salt Co. v. G.S. Suppiger*, 314 U.S. 488, 52 USPQ 30 (1942). See, e.g., *Senza-Gel Corp. v. Seiffhart*, 803 F.2d 661, 231 USPQ 363 (Fed. Cir. 1986) (refusal to license use of patented process unless user leased patentee's machine is misuse of patent). However, the tie-in of a "nonstaple" is not a misuse of a patent. *Dawson Chem. Co. v. Rohm & Haas Co.*, 448 U.S. 176, 206 USPQ 385 (1980).

See CONTRIBUTORY INFRINGEMENT, STAPLE.

• *Treatise References*: 4 D. Chisum, *Patents* §19.04 (1994 rev.); ABA, *Antitrust Law Developments* 488 (2d ed. 1984); W. Holmes, *Intellectual Property and Antitrust Law* §1.07 (1994 rev.); J. Dratler, *Licensing of Intellectual Property* §5.04 (1994).

• *Commentary Reference*: J. Webb & L. Locke, *Intellectual Property Misuse: Recent Developments in the Misuse Doctrine*, 73 J. Pat. & Trademark Off. Soc'y 339 (1991).

• *Case References*:

"The doctrine of patent misuse is an affirmative defense to a suit for patent infringement, … and requires that the patentee has impermissibly broadened the 'physical or temporal scope' of the patent grant with anticompetitive effect…. To sustain a misuse defense involving a licensing arrangement held not to have been per se anticompetitive by the Supreme Court, a factual determination must reveal that the overall effect of the license tends to restrain competition unlawfully in an appropriately defined relevant market." *Windsurfing Int'l, Inc. v. AMF Inc.*, 782 F.2d 995, 1001–02, 228 USPQ 562, 566–67 (Fed. Cir. 1986).

"A successful patent misuse defense results in rendering the patent unenforceable until the misuse is purged. A successful complaint for antitrust violation results not only in unenforceability, but also, inter alia, in treble damages." *Senza-Gel Corp. v. Seiffhart*, 803 F.2d 661, 668 n.10, 231 USPQ 363, 368 n.10 (Fed. Cir. 1986).

"[T]he doctrine of patent misuse 'denies to the patentee after issuance the power to use [the patent] in such a way as to acquire a monopoly which is not plainly within the terms of the [patent] grant.' *Mercoid Corp. v. Mid-Continent Inv. Co.*, 320 U.S. 661, 665–66, 60 USPQ 21, 24 (1944). The doctrine is founded in the public interest in free competition…. As a consequence a party invoking the doctrine need demonstrate neither that the alleged misuse constitutes a violation of the federal antitrust laws nor that the alleged misuse has resulted in injury to the party itself…. However, courts will not find misuse of a patent if the patentee's practice 'creates no restraint of competition beyond the legitimate grant of the patent.' *Automatic Radio Mfg. v. Hazeltine Research, Inc.*, 339 U.S. 827, 833, 85 USPQ 378, 380 (1950). Generally, a determination that a patent has been misused will preclude a patentee from invoking the aid of the courts in enforcing his rights thereunder, at least for the period of the misuse … or until the effect of the misuse has been dissipated or purged." *Robintech, Inc. v. Chemidus Wavin, Ltd.*, 450 F. Supp. 817, 819–20, 197 USPQ 657, 658 (D.D.C. 1978), *aff'd*, 628 F.2d 142, 205 USPQ 873 (D.C. Cir. 1980).

"However, this is not a price-fixing or tying case, and the *per se* antitrust and misuse violations found in [prior cases] are not here present. The appropriate criterion is whether [the patentee's] restriction is reasonably within the patent grant, or whether the patentee has ventured beyond the patent grant and into behavior having an anticompetitive effect not justifiable under the rule of reason. Should the restriction be found to be reasonably within the patent grant, *i.e.*, that it relates to subject matter within the scope of the patent claims, that ends the enquiry." *Mallinckrodt Inc. v. Medipart Inc.*, 976 F.2d 700, 708, 24 USPQ2d 1173, 1179–80 (Fed. Cir. 1992) (district court erred in finding that a restriction on the use of a sold patented item was unenforceable under patent law).

2. Trademark Misuse as a Defense. Misuse of a trademark in violation of the antitrust laws can furnish a defense to a charge of trademark infringement only if the trademark has been "the basic and fundamental vehicle required and used to accomplish the violation." *Carl Zeiss Stiftung v. V.E.B. Carl Zeiss, Jena,* 298 F. Supp. 1309, 1315, 161 USPQ 414, 419 (S.D.N.Y. 1969), *modified on other grounds,* 433 F.2d 686, 167 USPQ 641 (2d Cir. 1970).

Rarely Successful. Because a patent usually has a much wider scope of exclusionary power than a trademark, it is much easier to find the necessary nexus between an antitrust violation and a patent than between an antitrust violation and a trademark. In no final reported case has a court actually refused to enforce a trademark because it was used in violation of antitrust law.

Statutory Basis. Lanham Act §33(b)(7) makes the defense of use of a trademark to violate the antitrust laws available to defeat the conclusive evidentiary force that would otherwise attach to a federal registration of a mark. 15 U.S.C. §1115(b)(7). Lanham Act §33(b)(7) does not define an unclean hands defense on the merits, but merely deprives an "incontestable" federal registration of its incontestable evidentiary status.

• *Treatise Reference*: 3 J.T. McCarthy, *Trademarks and Unfair Competition* §§31.24–.25 (3d ed. 1995 rev.).

3. Copyright Misuse as a Defense. The use of a copyright to violate the letter or spirit of the antitrust laws may constitute a misuse defense to an otherwise valid claim of copyright infringement. A majority of circuit courts have upheld the availability of the defense of copyright misuse, but have usually rejected the defense on its merits. See, e.g., *Service & Training Inc. v. Data Gen. Corp.*, 963 F.2d 680, 23 USPQ2d 1102 (4th Cir. 1992) (misuse defense based on alleged tie-in of repair services to copyright was considered and rejected on the merits). Few cases have sustained the defense. See, e.g., *Lasercomb Am. Inc. v. Reynolds*, 911 F.2d 970, 15 USPQ2d 1846 (4th Cir. 1990).

Another view is that misuse is not a defense because there is no copyright analogy to the patent misuse defense. See, e.g., *Orth-O-Vision Inc. v. Home Box Office,* 474 F. Supp. 672, 205 USPQ 644 (S.D.N.Y. 1978).

• *Treatise References*: 3 Nimmer on Copyright §13.09[A] (1994 rev.); 2 P. Goldstein, *Copyright* §9.6.1 (1989); ABA, *Antitrust Law Developments* 519 (2d ed. 1984).

• *Case References:*

"We are persuaded, however, that a misuse of copyright defense is inherent in the law of copyright just as misuse of patent defense is inherent in patent law. ... [S]ince copyright and patent law serve parallel public interests, a 'misuse' defense should apply to infringement actions brought to vindicate either right." *Lasercomb Am. Inc. v. Reynolds*, 911 F.2d 970, 973–76, 15 USPQ2d 1846, 1849–52 (4th Cir. 1990).

"Although it has yet to apply the copyright misuse defense, the United States Supreme Court has given at least tacit approval of the defense. *United States v. Loew's, Inc.,* 371 U.S. 38 (1962). In *Loew's,* the Court applied principles of patent misuse to a patentee's unlawful tying arrangements and held that recovery for infringement should be denied. The Court went on to apply, with reference to the copyrights, the same antitrust restrictions on tie-in sales. Numerous other cases suggest that the purpose and policy of patent misuse apply as well to copyright." *Atari Games Corp. v. Nintendo of Am. Inc.,* 975 F.2d 832, 846, 24 USPQ2d 1015, 1026 (Fed. Cir. 1992) (finding that plaintiff's own "unclean hands" prevented it from invoking the equitable defense of misuse).

• *Example.* Lasercomb, a company that developed and sold a computer program, included in its standard copyright licensing agreement clauses that forbid the licensee to develop or assist in developing any kind of similar software in this market. The court said that Lasercomb's use of its copyright in this manner was contrary to the public policy embodied in the copyright law. The court held that the misuse of copyright barred Lasercomb from suing for copyright infringement even though the defendants were not a party to the licensing agreement. "[W]hile it is true that the attempted use of a copyright to violate antitrust law probably would give rise to a misuse of copyright defense, the converse is not necessarily true—a misuse need not be a violation of antitrust law in order to comprise an equitable defense to an infringement action. The question is not whether the copyright is being used in a manner violative of antitrust law, ... but whether the copyright is being used in a manner violative of the public policy embodied in the grant of a copyright." *Lasercomb Am. Inc. v. Reynolds,* 911 F.2d 970, 978–79, 15 USPQ2d 1846, 1853 (4th Cir. 1990).

MITI [foreign commerce] Japanese Ministry of International Trade and Industry. MITI is "Japan's Commerce Department, Special Trade Representative's Office, and the Defense Advanced Research Projects Agency all rolled into one. And it still plays a day-to-day role in the management of Japanese enterprises, setting research agendas and acting as a safety net for risky technologies or dying industries." David E. Sanger, *Mighty MITI Loses Its Grip*, N.Y. Times, July 9, 1989, §3, at 1.

monopoly [general intellectual property]
(1) To the economist, the term "monopoly" is a socially neutral occurrence in which economic power is possessed by a seller who has some legal protection from competitors and faces a negatively sloped demand curve such that marginal revenue is significantly below selling price. (2) From the viewpoint of the antitrust laws, "monopoly" power is possessed by a seller who has a relatively high percentage of a precisely defined relevant economic market. If this kind of monopoly power has been achieved or maintained through exclusionary conduct, there can be a violation of the Sherman Act §2 prohibitions on "monopolization" or "attempt to monopolize." (3) To the populist social reformer, any form of privately held "monopoly" power is a social evil to be generally eliminated or at least strictly controlled by government. (4) To the traditional economic conservative, "monopoly" is primarily the unnecessary control by government over commercial affairs, to be

purged by the "privatization" of government-run enterprises.

The various forms of intellectual property are often mischaracterized as "monopolies" and their owners maligned as "monopolists." Often, such misnomers either are used as pejorative advocacy by the challenger of validity or reveal the writer's inherent bias against intellectual property rights.

1. A Patent Is Not a "Monopoly." A patent is personal property that has some of the aspects of the economist's "monopoly" but none of the anticompetitive attributes of the illegal antitrust law "monopoly." A patent is not a "monopoly" in the sense of the Sherman Act §2 prohibition on "monopolization" unless the patented technology has few if any economic substitutes and thus occupies a substantial portion of the relevant economic market. Without a rigorous analysis and definition of the relevant economic market, one cannot say that the claims of all, or even many, patents define a substantial portion of a true relevant market. *Walker Process Equip. Inc. v. Food Mach. Chem. Co.*, 382 U.S. 172, 177, 147 USPQ 404, 407 (1965).

Misuse of Term Persists. Notwithstanding the semantic confusion between the economist's neutral "monopoly" and the antisocial and pejorative connotations of the antitrust "monopoly," courts, attorneys, and writers still continue to refer to the "patent monopoly." For example, the Supreme Court revealed some of the ambiguity of the term "monopoly" when it remarked: "Although recognizing the patent system's desirable stimulus to invention, we have also viewed the patent as a monopoly which, although sanctioned by law, has the economic consequences attending other monopolies." *Blonder-Tongue Labs. v. University of Ill. Found.*, 402 U.S. 313, 343, 169 USPQ 513, 525 (1971).

See PATENT.

• *Statutory Reference*: 35 U.S.C. §261: "Subject to the provisions of this title, patents shall have the attributes of personal property."

• *Case References*:

"Though often so characterized a patent is not, accurately speaking, a monopoly, for it is not created by the executive authority at the expense and to the prejudice of all the community except the grantee of the patent.... The term 'monopoly' connotes the giving of an exclusive privilege for buying, selling, working, or using a thing which the public freely enjoyed prior to the grant. Thus a monopoly takes something from the people. An inventor deprives the public of nothing which it enjoyed before his discovery, but gives something of value to the community by adding to the sum of human knowledge." *United States v. Dubilier Condenser Corp.*, 289 U.S. 178, 187 (1933).

"To denounce patents merely because they create monopolies is to indulge in superficial thinking.... [T]here has seldom been a society in which there have not been some monopolies, i.e., special privileges. The legal and medical professions have their respective guild monopolies. The owner of real estate, strategically located, has a monopoly; so has the owner of a valuable mine.... The problem is not whether there should be monopolies, but, rather, what monopolies there should be, and whether and how much they should be regulated." Frank, J., concurring in *Picard v. United Aircraft Corp.*, 128 F.2d 632, 643 (2d Cir. 1942).

"Norton begins its ... argument with 'Patents are an exception to the general rule against monopolies....' A patent, under the statute, is property. 35 U.S.C. §261. Nowhere in any statute is a patent described as a monopoly. The patent right is but the right to exclude others, the very definition of 'property.' That the property right represented by a patent, like other property rights, may be *used* in a scheme violative of antitrust laws creates no 'conflict' between laws establishing any of those property rights and the antitrust laws. The antitrust laws, enacted long after the original patent laws, deal with appropriation of what should belong to others. A valid patent gives the public what it did not earlier have.... It is but an obfuscation to refer to a patent as an 'exception to the general rule against monopolies.' That description, moreover, is irrelevant when considering patent questions...." *Schenck, A.G. v. Norton Corp.*, 713 F.2d 782, 786 n.3, 218 USPQ 698, 701 n.3 (Fed. Cir. 1983).

A judgment of patent invalidity based on a jury verdict was reversed on various grounds, including an erroneous instruction to the jury charging it to subject the claimed invention "to careful scrutiny before endorsing [plaintiff's] right to the patent monopoly...." The court stated: "The language that the jury must give 'careful scrutiny' before 'endorsing' the 'patent monopoly' cannot be approved.... [I]t does incorrectly suggest that the jury must affirmatively find the patent valid, which is never appropriate. Further, this court has disapproved of a challenger's characterization of a patentee by the term 'monopolist,' which is commonly regarded as pejorative.... Instructions which supplement the statutory body of law governing patent validity by interjecting language to the effect that the public must be 'protected' against a 'monopoly,' a term found nowhere in the statute, are likely to be prejudicial and should be avoided." *Jamesbury Corp. v. Litton Indus. Prods., Inc.*, 756 F.2d 1556, 1558–59, 225 USPQ 253, 255 (Fed. Cir. 1985).

2. A Trademark Is Not a "Monopoly." Trademarks have sometimes been mischaracterized as "monopolies." Sometimes, the term "monopoly" has been used as an epithet to criticize the scope of legal protection of trademarks. E.g., Brown, *Advertising and the Public Interest*, 57 Yale L.J. 1165, 1206 (1948) (law of trademark infringement "really a doctrine of unfair intrusion on a monopoly"). Modern judicial decisions and writers almost unanimously reject application of the pejorative term "monopoly" to a trademark. For example, Chief Judge Markey of the Court of Appeals for the Federal Circuit rejected a defendant's argument that to protect the Levi Strauss pocket tab trademark would be to improperly protect a monopoly: "[Defendant's] pejorative use of 'monopoly' implies that Strauss's trademark right is harmful and anti-competitive. On the contrary, the pocket tab trademark gives the public a reliable indication of source and thus facilitates responsible marketplace competition." *Levi Strauss & Co. v. Blue Bell, Inc.*, 632 F.2d 817 n.5, 208 USPQ 713 n.5 (9th Cir. 1980).

A Trademarked Product Is Not Per Se an Antitrust "Monopoly." The U.S. Supreme Court has held that for the purpose of antitrust "monopolization" prohibited under Sherman Act §2, a trademark does not necessarily define its own relevant market. That is, a trademarked product is not automatically a "monopoly." "[T]his power that, let us say, automobile or soft-drink manufacturers have over their trademarked products is not the power that makes an illegal monopoly. Illegal power must be appraised in terms of the competitive market for the product." *United States v. E.I. du Pont de Nemours & Co.*, 351 U.S. 377, 393 (1956). Thus, it makes no sense to state: "The Ford Motor Co. has a monopoly of FORD brand autos." The relevant product market is automobiles, not one firm's brand of auto. However, in certain circumstances, a single brand could constitute a market. For example, a relevant market may consist of those who sell service and parts for Kodak-brand photocopying machines because the service and parts for Kodak equipment are not interchangeable with other manufacturer's service and parts. *Eastman Kodak Co. v. Image Technical Serv., Inc.*, 504 U.S. 451, 112 S. Ct. 2072, 2090 (1992).

• *Treatise Reference*: J.T. McCarthy, *Trademarks and Unfair Competition* §§2.05, 31.26[2][c] (3d ed. 1995 rev.).

• *Case References*:

"In truth, a trademark confers no monopoly whatever in a proper sense, but it is merely a convenient means for facilitating the protection of one's good will in trade by placing a distinguishing mark or symbol—a commercial signature—upon the merchandise or the pack in which it is sold." *United Drug Co. v. Theodore Rectanus Co.*, 248 U.S. 90, 99 (1918) (Pitney, J.).

"A trademark is indeed often spoken of as a monopoly; but in fact it is only part of the protection of the owner's business from diversion to others by means of deceit." Learned Hand, J. in *Artype, Inc. v. Zappulla*, 228 F.2d 695, 696, 108 USPQ 51, 53 (2d Cir. 1956).

moral rights [copyright–author's rights]
Some European continental legal systems and other nations expressly recognize certain rights of authors beyond those strictly recognized in copyright law. These are generally known as droit moral, or in German, urheberpersonlichkeitsrecht (UrhG). While varying in content among the nations, "moral rights" generally fall into three categories:

(1) the right of attribution and paternity: the right of an author to receive credit as the author of a work, to prevent others from falsely being named author, and to prevent use of the author's name in connection with works the author did not create.

(2) the right of integrity: the right of an author to prevent mutilation of a work; and

(3) the right of withdrawal: the right to withdraw a work from distribution if it no longer represents the views of the author.

Moral Rights in the United States. Because of the unfortunate translation of "droit moral" into English as "moral right," U.S. law has traditionally been reluctant to expressly incorporate this concept. However, certain moral rights have been indirectly incorporated into U.S. law. For example, the right of integrity was incorporated into the false advertising prohibitions of Lanham Trademark Act §43(a) in *Gilliam v. American Broadcasting Cos.*, 538 F.2d 14, 192 USPQ 1 (2d Cir. 1976). The right of paternity was also partially incorporated into Lanham Act §43(a) in *Smith v. Montoro*, 648 F.2d 602, 211 USPQ 775 (9th Cir. 1981) (actor has right to object to film credits that delete actor's name and falsely replace actor's name with another's name). The rights of integrity and paternity are partially codified in the laws of several states. For example, moral rights are partially codified as to works of "fine art" in the 1980 California Art Preservation Act, Cal. Civil Code §987. Ten other states have somewhat similar statutes.

The United States and the Berne Convention. On March 1, 1989, the United States joined the BERNE CONVENTION. Article 6 *bis* of the Berne Convention states that the author shall have the moral right to claim authorship of the work and to object to any distortion, mutilation, or other modification of the work which would be "prejudicial to his honor or reputation." In the 1989 Berne amendments (BCIA) to the U.S. Copyright Act, Congress stated that the Berne Convention was not to be self-executing and that the Berne Amendments neither "expand nor reduce" the moral rights of authors. 102 Stat. 2853, §2 (Oct. 31, 1988). Thus, the Berne Amendments to U.S. law, which were effective March 1, 1989, are completely neutral: they neither include nor exclude moral rights in U.S. law.

The Visual Artists Rights Act of 1990.

Limited Moral Rights for Visual Arts. For the first time in the United States, this Act creates a federal system of moral rights. Effective June 1, 1991, the Visual Artists Rights Act of 1990 amends Title 17 and creates certain rights of attribution and integrity for a very narrowly defined category of visual arts such as paintings, prints, sculpture, and those photographs that are produced for exhibition purposes. The Act does not include a wide range of media, such as posters, maps, globes, charts, technical drawings, diagrams, motion pictures and other audiovisual works, books, magazines, newspapers, periodicals, data bases, electronic publications, and advertising and packaging materials. 17 U.S.C. §101. Also not included are works made for hire and uncopyrightable works.

Limited Coverage and Rights. Once the exceptions to subject matter and to exclusive rights are sorted out, what remains is a limited prohibition on certain types of destruction or changes and instances of nonattribution or misattribution of artistic works shown in a traditional "artistic" setting such as an art gallery or museum. There is no prohibition on the use of reproductions of works of art which appear in media such as motion pictures, books, magazines, and advertisements. The statutory test of liability for unpermitted distortion, mutilation, or other modification of the work of art is that of the Berne Convention: whether it would be prejudicial to the "honor and reputation" of the artist.

Duration of Rights and Waiver. The Act creates: (1) lifetime rights for works of art created after June 1, 1991; and (2) rights expiring with the copyright in works created before June 1, 1991, but only if the artist still held the copyright at that time. An artist's rights under the Act may not be transferred, but may be specifically waived in writing on a per work and per use basis.

Preemption of State Law. State law that creates equivalent rights in works of visual arts covered by the federal law is preempted by the 1990 federal law. However, legislative history indicates that there might be no federal preemption of state law that creates equivalent rights in works not covered by the federal law, such as motion pictures.

See DROIT MORAL, DROIT DE SUITE, BERNE CONVENTION, BCIA.

• *Treatise References*: 2 *Nimmer on Copyright* §8.21 (1994 rev.); 2 P. Goldstein, *Copyright* §§15.23–.24 (1989); W. Patry, *Copyright Law and Practice* 1018 *et seq.* (1994); 1 N. Boorstyn, *Copyright* §5.07 (2d ed. 1994); 1 J.T. McCarthy, *Trademarks and Unfair Competition* §10.08[c] (3d ed. 1995 rev.).

motion picture [copyright] A general category of copyrightable works that consist of images which are related, are presented in a series, are intended to be shown by the use of a machine, and, when shown in succession, create an illusion of motion. Any sound accompanying the motion picture is also included in this category of work. Thus, the soundtrack is classified as part of the motion picture, not as a PHONORECORD. A license for the use of copyrighted music in connection with a motion picture is called a SYNCHRONIZATION LICENSE. A motion picture is a particular type of AUDIOVISUAL WORK.

Medium Is Irrelevant. The type of material object in which the motion picture is fixed is irrelevant: it can include film, videotape, computer disk, CD-ROM, or any other medium.

Slide Show. A series of slides shown in sequence is an audiovisual work but is not a motion picture because when shown it does not impart an impression of motion.

A Motion Picture Is "Performed." When a motion picture is shown, in the parlance of copyright it is a "PERFORMANCE" of the copyrighted film. That is, if one inserts a video cassette into a VCR to play it, one is "performing" the motion picture. If a still from a motion picture is shown, as in an advertisement for a movie or television show, it is a "DISPLAY," not a "performance."

See PERFORMANCE.

• *Statutory Reference*: 17 U.S.C. §101: " 'Motion pictures' are audio visual works consisting of a series of related images which, when shown in succession, impart an impression of motion, together with accompanying sounds, if any."

moveover [copyright–entertainment law]
In the distribution of motion pictures for exhibition in theaters, a privilege given to an exhibitor to move a film from one theater to another as a continuation of the run at the exhibitor's first theater. Moveovers also occur when an exhibitor is allowed to shift a film to a different screen at a multiplex or multiscreen theater complex.

Antitrust Issues. Moveovers are not inherently anticompetitive or illegal per se under the antitrust laws. But film-distributor discrimination against small, independent exhibitors in granting moveovers may be part of a combination that unreasonably restrains trade, which is illegal under Sherman Act §1. See *Harkins Amusement Enters., Inc. v. General Cinema Corp.*, 850 F.2d 477, 487 (9th Cir. 1988).

MPEP [patent] Manual of Patent Examining Procedure. The official internal working manual of procedure to be followed by patent EXAMINERS in reviewing applications for patent in the U.S. Patent and Trademark Office. The MPEP is often relied upon as a guide to patent attorneys and patent examiners on procedural matters during the PROSECUTION of patent applications.

Use of the MPEP in the Courts. The Court of Appeals for the Federal Circuit has remarked: "The MPEP has no binding force on us, but is entitled to notice so far as it is an official interpretation of statutes or regulations with which it is not in conflict." *Litton Sys., Inc. v. Whirlpool Corp.*, 728 F.2d 1423, 1439, 221 USPQ 97, 107 (Fed. Cir. 1984). *Accord Molins PLC v. Textron Inc.*, 48 F.3d 1172 n.10, 33 USPQ2d 1823 n.10 (Fed. Cir. 1995). A district court has remarked that the MPEP "is published by the United States Patent and Trademark Office and

serves as *the* authoritative reference for patent examiners and others working in the field." *Hewlett-Packard Co. v. Bausch & Lomb Inc.*, 692 F. Supp. 1118, 1122 n.3, 8 USPQ2d 1179, 1183 n.3 (N.D. Cal. 1988). However, the Federal Circuit has also noted that the MPEP is not infallible: "The MPEP is a loose leaf training and instruction manual for examiners which is continually revised in piecemeal fashion and it is not surprising to find inconsistencies in it." *Racing Strollers Inc. v. TRI Indus. Inc.*, 878 F.2d 1418, 1422, 11 USPQ2d 1300, 1303 (Fed. Cir. 1989).

multimedia [computer–copyright–general]
A technology that provides the interaction of video, music, and text through personal computers. Multimedia is typically thought of as three or more types of media united with some measure of interactivity and stored in digital form on a CD-ROM. With this technology, the computer user is able to call to the screen and manipulate information that has been digitized. This may include movies, novels, operas, paintings in a museum, the text of an encyclopedia, textbooks, etc.

Producers creating multimedia productions are confronted with the problem of working out agreements with the many creators and copyright owners whose works are incorporated in the productions. The copyright owners are at risk of receiving no reimbursement as the technology grows and more publishers use multimedia technology to package and deliver information.

multiple dependent claim [patent]
A DEPENDENT CLAIM in a patent that refers back in the alternative to more than one preceding claim. A multiple dependent claim adds narrowing limitations to the alternative claims upon which it depends.

• *Example*: A multiple dependent claim would be in the following form: "Claim 5. An electrical generator according to claims 3 or 4, further comprising …" or "Claim 16. An internal combustion engine as in claims 1, 7, 12 or 15, in which.…" The reference back must be in the alternative. The following form is not proper: "Claim 5. A modem according to claims 3 and 4, further comprising...."

Treated as a Plurality of Claims. A multiple dependent claim does not incorporate by reference all the limitations of all the alternative claims on which it depends. Rather, such a claim is like a plurality of single dependent claims, each of which incorporates by reference only those limitations of a single claim from which it depends.

See DEPENDENT CLAIM.

• *Statutory Reference*: 35 U.S.C. § 112, fifth paragraph: "A claim in multiple dependent form shall contain a reference, in the alternative only, to more than one claim previously set forth and then specify a further limitation of the subject matter claimed. A multiple dependent claim shall not serve as a basis for any other multiple dependent claim. A multiple dependent claim shall be construed to incorporate by reference all the limitations of the particular claim in relation to which it is being considered."

• *Manual Reference*: "35 U.S.C. § 112 indicates that the limitations or elements of each claim incorporated by reference into a multiple dependent claim must be considered separately. Thus a multiple dependent claim, as such, does not contain all the limitations of all the alternative claims to which it refers, but rather contains in any one embodiment only those limitations of the particular claim referred to for the embodiment under consideration. Hence a multiple dependent claim must be considered in the same manner as a plurality of single dependent claims." *Manual of Patent Examining Procedure* §608.01(n) (1994).

multiple performances doctrine
[copyright]

See PERFORMANCE.

Muncie Gear doctrine [patent]

See LATE CLAIMING.

musical work [copyright] A category of copyrightable work expressed in notation or sounds.

Medium and Originality. A musical work can be embodied and fixed in physical objects that are classified as either COPIES (sheet music) or PHONORECORDS (e.g., compact discs or tapes). The elements of originality in a musical work are melody, rhythm, and harmony. In the western musical tradition, these elements are strictly constrained by musical convention and popular taste.

Distinguished From a "Sound Recording" Copyright. A musical work copyright must be distinguished from a SOUND RECORDING copyright. For example, composer Cole Porter's song *Night and Day* is covered by a musical work copyright. But a post-1972 Frank Sinatra recording of *Night and Day* is covered by a sound recording copyright. The same is true of public domain musical works. While a Brahms piano concerto is in the public domain, a recording of it by Andre Watts can be protected by a sound recording copyright. Similarly, a sound recording can cover a recorded performance of a LITERARY WORK or a dramatic work.

Compulsory License for Recordings. Musical work copyrights are subject to the 17 U.S.C. § 115 COMPULSORY COPYRIGHT license for making phonorecords of musical works. The right to make a recording of a musical work is known as a MECHANICAL RIGHT.

Unconscious Infringement. The copyright in a musical work can be infringed by UNCONSCIOUS INFRINGEMENT where, for example, a composer has heard a melody years before and unconsciously incorporates it into what the composer consciously thinks is a new and original melody.

Musical Arrangement. A musical arrangement is a form of DERIVATIVE WORK and can be the subject of its own copyright protection.

See PHONORECORDS, SOUND RECORDING, COMPULSORY LICENSING OF A COPYRIGHT, MECHANICAL RIGHTS.

• *Treatise References*: 1 *Nimmer on Copyright* §2.05 (1994); 1 P. Goldstein, *Copyright* §2.8 (1989); 1 N. Boorstyn, *Copyright* §2.07 (2d ed. 1994).

• *Statutory Reference*: 17 U.S.C. §102(a): "Works of authorship include the following categories: … (2) musical works, including any accompanying words; …."

mutilation [trademark] The attempted registration as a mark of something less than the totality of the mark. The applicant "mutilates" his or her trademark, severs a part of it, and seeks registration of only that part. This is prohibited as an attempt to obtain protection for an element that is the applicant's exclusive property not alone, but only in combination with other words or symbols.

What Is the "Mark"? The key issue when an application is rejected for "mutilation" is whether the part of a COMPOSITE for which the applicant seeks registration creates a commercial impression separate and apart from the other matter in the composite or on the label. "It all boils down to a judgment as to whether that designation for which registration is sought comprises a separate and distinct 'trademark' in and of itself." 2 J.T. McCarthy, *Trademarks and Unfair Competition* §19.17 (3d ed. 1995 rev.), quoted with approval in *In re Chemical Dynamics, Inc.*, 839 F.2d 1569, 1571, 5 USPQ2d 1828, 1829 (Fed. Cir. 1988) (attempt to register only a portion of a picture mark rejected as a mutilation of the mark as a whole, since the parts of the picture are "interrelated elements of a single unified design").

N

NAFTA [international–intellectual property] North American Free Trade Agreement. An agreement between the United States, Canada, and Mexico which creates a North American free trade area and substantially reduces tariff and nontariff trade barriers between the markets of the three nations. NAFTA came into effect in the United States on January 1, 1994, as a result of the NAFTA Implementation Act, Pub. L. No. 103-182, 107 Stat. 2057, enacted December 8, 1993.

Objectives of NAFTA. In addition to national treatment and most-favored nation treatment, the objectives of NAFTA include: elimination of trade barriers between the United States, Canada, and Mexico; simplification of movement of goods and services between the nations; promotion of fair competition; substantial increase in investment opportunities; adequate and effective intellectual property rights protection and enforcement both internally and at the border; administration and dispute resolution procedures; and establishment of a framework to further expand and enhance the benefits to the Agreement. North American Free Trade Agreement, enacted Dec. 8, 1993, pt. 1, ch. 1., art. 102, 32 Int'l Legal Materials 289, 297 (1993).

NAFTA and Intellectual Property. NAFTA establishes a relatively high level of obligations with respect to intellectual property protection. The intellectual property provisions of NAFTA, contained in Part 6, Chapter 17, of the Agreement, are intended to harmonize patent, trademark, copyright, and trade secret standards of the United States, Canada, and Mexico. Generally, NAFTA requires that each country provide adequate and effective protection and enforcement of intellectual property rights. North American Free Trade Agreement, enacted Dec.

8, 1993, pt. 6, ch. 17, art. 1701, 32 Int'l Legal Materials 605, 670–71 (1993).

Basic Framework of Intellectual Property Protection. The first four articles of Chapter 17 set forth the basic framework for intellectual property protection under NAFTA:

(1) Article 1701 requires that each nation give effect to the intellectual property requirements of Chapter 17 of NAFTA and to the substantive provisions of four major international intellectual property treaties: the GENEVA PHONOGRAM CONVENTION; the BERNE CONVENTION; the PARIS CONVENTION; and the UPOV CONVENTION.

(2) Article 1702 makes clear that NAFTA establishes a floor for intellectual property protection and that the countries are free to implement more extensive protection of these rights in their domestic laws.

(3) Article 1703 embodies the principle of national treatment that each nation accord the nationals of the other two member nations no less favorable treatment than it accords its own nationals regarding protection and enforcement of intellectual property rights.

(4) Article 1704 permits nations to regulate licensing practices and abusive or anticompetitive conditions.

Intellectual Property Provisions. The Agreement sets out specific commitments regarding the protection of patents, trademarks, copyrights, trade secrets, plant breeders' rights, industrial designs, integrated circuits, and geographical indications. NAFTA was the first international intellectual property accord to require recognition of rights in trade secrets. U.S. enactment of the NAFTA implementing legislation has amended several provisions of U.S. intellectual property law concerning the protection of copyrighted works, patented products and processes, trademarks, and service marks. See Martin, *An Analysis of NAFTA's Intellectual Property Provisions*, 5 (No. 12) J. Proprietary Rts. 24 (Dec. 1993).

Changes Required in U.S. Intellectual Property Law.

1. Changes Required in Patent Law. The 1952 Patent Code, 35 U.S.C. §104, was amended to permit any patent applicant or patentee to establish a "date of invention" by reference to knowledge or use of the invention in Canada or Mexico. This change became effective as to patent applications filed on or after December 8, 1993, the enactment of the NAFTA legislation. In addition, an inventor cannot establish a date of invention earlier than December 8, 1993, with respect to activity in Canada or Mexico. This change was largely overwhelmed by the 1994 GATT TRIPS agreement implemented in the URUGUAY ROUND AGREEMENTS ACT, which expanded the range of possible locations to include inventive activity that occurs within World Trade Organization (WTO) member countries. Many of the 1994 URUGUAY ROUND AGREEMENTS ACT patent amendments became effective as to patent applications filed on or after January 1, 1996.

See PRIORITY OF INVENTION.

2. Changes Required in Copyright Law. Section 104A was added to the Copyright Act to protect certain Mexican and Canadian motion pictures that entered the public domain before March 1, 1989, because they lacked copyright notice. 17 U.S.C. §104A. Section 104A provides that copyright protection for such a motion picture may be reinstated for the remainder of the term of copyright protection which it would have been entitled had it been published with copyright notice. In order for the reinstatement of a motion picture's copyright to be effective, the copyright holder must have filed with the Copyright Office, before January 1, 1995, a statement of intent to have copyright protection restored. If this was done, the restored copyright protection would have become effective on January 1, 1995. 17 U.S.C. §104A. More substantial restoration provisions were contained in the 1994 GATT TRIPS legislative

package, known as the URUGUAY ROUND AGREEMENTS ACT.

NAFTA also eliminated the sunsetting provision of the Record Rental Amendment of 1984 in 17 U.S.C. §109, which requires a person wishing to rent lawfully obtained SOUND RECORDINGS to secure permission from the copyright holder.

3. Changes Required in Trademark Law. Sections 2 and 23 of the Lanham Act, 15 U.S.C. §§1052 and 1091 respectively, were amended to absolutely bar registration, on both the PRINCIPAL and SUPPLEMENTAL REGISTERS, of any mark that is "primarily geographically deceptively misdescriptive." However, because of "grandfather" clauses included in the §2(f) and §23(a) amendments, registration of such marks may be permitted if the mark became distinctive before the date NAFTA was enacted, December 8, 1993. Prior to NAFTA, §2 of the Lanham Act permitted a mark that was "primarily geographically deceptively misdescriptive" to be placed on the PRINCIPAL REGISTER if a showing of SECONDARY MEANING was made under §2(f) or placed on the SUPPLEMENTAL REGISTER, under §23(a), if such a showing could not be made. See GEOGRAPHIC MARK, PRINCIPAL REGISTER, SUPPLEMENTAL REGISTER.

NAFTA Enforcement Provisions. NAFTA imposes a basic obligation on the member nations to ensure that enforcement procedures permit effective action to be taken against any act of infringement of intellectual property rights covered by NAFTA, including expeditious remedies to prevent infringements and remedies to deter further infringements. North American Free Trade Agreement, enacted Dec. 8, 1993, pt. 6, ch. 17, art. 1714, 32 Int'l Legal Materials at 676 (1993). Each nation must provide that its judicial authorities have the authority to, among other things: make preliminary and final determinations based upon evidence presented; order a party in a proceeding to desist from an infringement; order an infringer of an intellectual property right to pay the right holder damages adequate to compensate for the injury suffered; and order an infringer to pay the right holder's expenses. North American Free Trade

Agreement, enacted Dec. 8, 1993, pt. 6, ch. 17, art. 1715, 32 Int'l Legal Materials at 677 (1993).

naked license [trademark]
See LICENSE OF TRADEMARK.

nanotechnology [patent] The building of a complex network of inter-working molecules for a variety of application by the precise placement of atoms or molecules. It is a method of engineering a system by the exact placement of atoms and molecules to make larger composites which perform a function such as a microscopic unit that identifies and destroys cancerous cells. By contrast, conventional microtechnology uses a top-down approach employing microscopic materials to make smaller and smaller features such as conventional microprocessors.

National Film Preservation Act [copyright] A special federal statute providing for the creation of a national register of significant motion picture films.

The Colorization Dispute and the 1988 Act. In the late 1980s some movie stars and directors complaining of the "colorizing" of older black-and-white motion pictures sought congressional action preventing such modification of films. The legislative response was the National Film Preservation Act of 1988 (Pub. L. No. 100-446, 2 U.S.C §178). Under the Act, the Librarian of Congress established a 13-member National Film Preservation Board to recommend up to 25 films per year that were deemed to be "culturally, historically, or aesthetically significant" for inclusion in the National Film Registry. The Act required that if registered films were materially altered, even if legal under the copyright laws, they had to disclose the alteration in wording required by the statute. The Act had a sunset provision that expired in three years.

The 1992 Act. The National Film Preservation Act of 1992 (Pub. L. No. 102-307, 2 U.S.C §201) reauthorized the National Film Registry and the National Film Preservation Board in the Library of Congress. The 1992 Act directed the Librarian of Congress to: (1) study and report to the Congress on the current state of film preservation and restoration activities, including the activities of the Library of Congress and other major film archives in the United States; (2) establish a comprehensive national film preservation program for motion pictures, in conjunction with other film archivists and copyright owners; and (3) establish a 18-member National Film Preservation Board to consult with the Librarian in the selection of up to 25 films per year for inclusion into the National Film Registry. Such films may then bear the seal of National Film Registry to indicate that they are included and are the Registry versions of the films. No film is eligible for inclusion on the registry until 10 years after its first theatrical release.

neighboring rights [copyright–international] A term used to express the concept of rights not equal to copyright but which relate to or are a "neighbor" of copyright. Neighboring rights consist of a bundle of exclusive rights of performers in their performances, recording companies in their SOUND RECORDINGS, and radio and television broadcasters in their broadcasts.

History of "Neighboring Rights." Before the technological revolution performers did not need the protection of copyright because their performances could not be fixed. Performances were only live and could not be exploited outside the place where they were given. But with the invention of sound recording, film, radio, and television, performers were vulnerable to the same threat of exploitation of unauthorized reproductions of their performances as copyright owners were in their COPIES.

The term "neighboring rights" was first used in 1948 during the Brussels Diplomatic Conference for the Revision of the Berne Convention. In some nations, performers, producers, and broadcasters are not considered "authors" and therefore their efforts are not protected by copyright laws. Various resolutions adopted at the Conference expressed the wish to protect the different interests of performing artists, phonogram producers, and broadcasting organizations without prejudicing the rights of authors. In 1961, members of the ROME CONVENTION agreed to bundle together the rights of these three different interests.

Significance of the Term in the United States. In U.S. copyright law, there was never any legal or philosophical barrier to direct copyright protection of rights of individuals and corporations in performances and new technologies, and so there was and is no need to use the term "neighboring rights." The only neighboring right that is not recognized in the United States is a performing right in a sound recording.

Neighboring Rights Versus Copyright. "Neighboring rights" confer a more limited level of protection than copyright. Copyright grants the copyright owner the exclusive right to reproduce, adapt, and publicly distribute, perform, and display a copyrighted work in whatever form and by whatever means. The owner of a neighboring right only has a right related to a particular form of the copyrighted work: the performer only for her performance, the producer only for his particular production of a sound recording, and the broadcaster only in the broadcast. Nora Mout-Bouwman, *Neighboring Rights: International and EC Aspects*, Global Intellectual Property Series 1993: Protecting Trademarks and Copyrights Successful Strategies at 245, 249 (PLI/Pat Literary Property Course Handbook Series No. G4-3906, 1993).

Droits Voisins. Neighboring rights are sometimes referred to under their French name "droits voisins."

WIPO Definition. The 1967 Convention Establishing the World Intellectual Property Organization in its definition of INTELLECTUAL PROPERTY includes "performances of performing artists, phonograms, and broadcasts." These are called "neighboring rights" because they are "rights bordering on copyright." WIPO, *Background Reading Material on Intellectual Property* 4 (1988).

International Relations. The major multinational treaty dealing with neighboring rights is the ROME CONVENTION, of which the United States is not a member. However, the United States is a member of two other neighboring rights treaties: the PHONOGRAM CONVENTION and the BRUSSELS SATELLITE CONVENTION.

- *Treatise Reference*: 2 P. Goldstein, *Copyright* §16.5 (1989); W. Patry, *Copyright Law and Practice* 139–41 (1994).

- *Commentary Reference*: "Rights neighboring to copyright, are, by definition, rights which are not genuine copyrights. They provide a strengthened protection against certain acts of unfair competition which can very loosely be associated with copyright infringements. Therefore they are situated 'in the vicinity' of copyright." H.C. Jehoram, *The Nature of Neighboring Rights of Performing Artists, Phonograms Producers and Broadcasting Organizations*, 15 Colum.-VLA J.L. & Arts 75, 76 (1990).

- *Reference*: Neighboring rights are "usually understood as meaning rights granted in an increasing number of countries to protect the interests of performers, producers of phonograms and broadcasting organizations in relation to their activities in connection with the public use of authors' works, all kinds of artists' presentations or the communication to the public of events, information, and any sounds or images. The most important categories are: the right of performers to prevent fixation and direct broadcasting or communication to the public of their performances without their consent; the right of producers of phonograms to authorize or prohibit reproduction of their phonograms and the import and distribution of unauthorized duplicates thereof; the right of broadcasting organizations to authorize or prohibit rebroadcasting, fixation and reproduction of their broadcasts. An increasing number of countries already protect some or all of these rights by appropriate rules, codified mainly within the framework of their copyright laws. Several countries also grant a sort of moral right to performers." WIPO, *Glossary of Terms of the Law of Copyright and Neighboring Rights* 167 (1980).

new matter [patent] New subject matter attempted to be added by amendment to a pending patent application or to be added in an application for a REISSUE patent. New matter cannot be added in either circumstance.

Impact of the New Matter Rule. While the new matter rule prohibits alterations and additions to the matter disclosed in the original application, it does not prohibit amendments that only clarify or fill out the original matter. New claims added by amendment must be supported by the original patent disclosure as filed in the sense that it complies with the DESCRIPTION and ENABLEMENT requirements. That is, an inventor cannot by later amendment add new claims that relate to matter that was not disclosed in the original patent application. This particular application of the rule against adding new matter by amendment was at one time known as LATE CLAIMING.

Violation of the Rule. If new matter does slip by in an amendment, the patent might be invalid under 35 U.S.C. §112. Typically, the issue arises in infringement suits in the context of a claim being supported only by new matter. "Then the claim is vulnerable to a validity attack on grounds of defective oath, or statutory bar, or both." R. Harmon, *Patents and the Federal Circuit* §5.5 (3d ed. 1994).

Continuation-in-Part Application. New matter is properly included by the filing of a CONTINUATION-IN-PART patent application, which is a second patent application for the same invention by the same inventor adding new matter.

See LATE CLAIMING, CONTINUATION-IN-PART.

• *Statutory References*:

35 U.S.C. §251: "No new matter shall be introduced into the application for reissue.... "

35 U.S.C. §132: "No amendment shall introduce new matter into the disclosure of the invention."

• *Rule Reference:* 37 C.F.R. §§1.118–19.

• *Manual Reference:* "In amended cases subject matter not disclosed in the original application is sometimes added and a claim directed thereto. Such a claim is rejected on the ground that it recites elements without support in the original disclosure under 35 U.S.C. §112, first paragraph.... New matter includes not only the addition of wholly unsupported subject matter, but also adding specific percentages or compounds after a broader original disclosure, or even the omission of a step from a method." *Manual of Patent Examining Procedure* §706.03(o) (1994 rev.). Regarding new matter

in a reissue application, see *Manual of Patent Examining Procedure* §1411.02 (1994 rev.).

• *Case References:*

A patent was held invalid in an infringement suit for failure to disclose BEST MODE. The patent owner applied for a REISSUE patent that would insert the missing description of best mode into the specification. The reissue application was rejected on the ground that it sought to add new matter. The Court of Customs and Patent Appeals affirmed the rejection. "[T]he reissue provisions of the Patent Act should be construed liberally in light of their remedial purpose, ... but this liberality has never been construed to permit insertion of new matter in contravention of the §251 proscription thereof.... [We] emphasize that the term 'new matter' presumably has the same meaning in §251 as it does in the last sentence of 35 U.S.C. §132, which prohibits introducing 'new matter' into the disclosure of the invention by amendment." *In re Hay*, 534 F.2d 917, 919, 189 USPQ 790, 791 (C.C.P.A. 1976).

"Whether particular technological information is 'new matter' depends on the facts of the case: the nature of the disclosure, the state of the art, and the nature of the added matter. A patent is presumed valid.... This presumption, which may be viewed as a presumption of administrative correctness, as applied to a new matter determination ... [means that] 'the fact that the Patent Office allows ... an amendment without objection thereto as new matter (within the meaning of Title 35 U.S.C. §132) is entitled to an especially weighty presumption of correctness.' " *Brooktree Corp. v. Advanced Micro Devices Inc.*, 977 F.2d 1555, 1574, 24 USPQ2d 1401, 1414 (Fed. Cir. 1992) (An amendment to claims for a computer chip adding the language "for video display" to the preamble was held to be merely an embellishment and not "new matter.").

• *Treatise Reference:* "When the scope of a claim has been changed by amendment in such a way as to justify an assertion that it is directed to a different invention than was the original claim, it is proper to enquire whether the newly claimed subject matter was described as the invention of the applicant in the patent application when filed. If the essence of the original disclosure supports the new claim limitation, the new limitation is not new matter." R. Harmon, *Patents and the Federal Circuit* §5.5 (3d ed. 1994). See 3 D. Chisum, *Patents* §11.04 (1994 rev.).

new use for old product [patent]
See INHERENCY.

Nice Agreement [trademark–international]
A treaty providing an international system for the classification of goods and services for the registration of trademarks and service marks. First entered into in 1957 in Nice, France, and last revised at Geneva in 1977, the international classification system is in use in more than 60 countries. About 30 nations adhere to the treaty.

The United States adhered to the Nice Agreement in 1972. All applications for federal registration of marks filed since September 1, 1973, are classified according to the International Classification Schedule, which is found in 37 C.F.R. §§6.1–.4.

• *Reference:* 3 S. Ladas, *Patents, Trademarks and Related Rights: National and International Protection* §§796–803 (1975). See text of treaty in M. Leaffer, *International Treaties on Intellectual Property* 499 (1990).

nonobviousness [patent]
See OBVIOUSNESS.

nonprofit organization [patent]
An organization that qualifies for the SMALL ENTITY discount on government fees connected with the filing, prosecution, and maintenance of patents.

A "nonprofit organization" is defined as a university, an IRS-defined tax-exempt nonprofit organization, or a nonprofit scientific or educational organization qualified under state law. 37 C.F.R. §1.9. Foreign nonprofit organizations also qualify if they would fall within the IRS tax-exempt definition or the state-qualified scientific or educational organization definition if they were located in the United States.

See SMALL ENTITY.

nonstaple [patent]
See STAPLE.

nose of wax [patent]
In a limitation on the DOCTRINE OF EQUIVALENTS, the Supreme Court in a nineteenth century decision emphasized that a claim in a patent cannot be so expansively read as to substantially change and expand the plain meaning of the words. The Supreme Court said: "Some persons seem to suppose that a claim in a patent is like a nose of wax which may be turned and twisted in any direction, by merely referring to the specification, so as to make it include something more than, or something different from, what its words express.... [I]t is unjust to the public, as well as an evasion of the law, to construe [the claim] in a manner different from the plain import of its terms." *White v. Dunbar*, 119 U.S. 47, 51 (1886).

Policy of the Analogy. The thought behind the "nose of wax" metaphor is that the words in a patent claim cannot be twisted one way to avoid invalidity by ANTICIPATION or OBVIOUSNESS and then twisted in the other direction to find LITERAL INFRINGEMENT. "Having construed the claims one way for determining validity, it is axiomatic that the claim must be construed in the same way for infringement." *Smithkline Diagnostics Inc. v. Helena Labs. Corp.*, 859 F.2d 878, 889 n.7, 8 USPQ2d 1468, 1477 n.7 (Fed. Cir. 1988).

Origin of Term. According to the *Oxford Dictionary*, a "nose of wax" is a thing easily turned or modified in any way desired. In the seventeenth century the phrase was in common use in referring to differing interpretations of Holy Scripture. E.g., "If the Scripture be contrary, then make it a nose of wax and wrest it this way and that till it agree."

• *Usage Example:* "[Defendants] contend that the district court violated the 'nose of wax' prohibition articulated in *White v. Dunbar* ... by giving the patent a narrow construction to find validity over the prior art and then giving it broad construction to find infringement." *Shields v. Halliburton Co.*, 667 F.2d 1232, 1234, 216 USPQ 1066, 1068 (5th Cir. 1982) (patent held valid and infringed).

See EQUIVALENTS, DOCTRINE OF.

notice [patent–copyright–trademark]   A formal sign or notification attached to physical objects that embody or reproduce an intellectual property right.

1. Notice of Patent.
See MARKING OF PATENT.

2. Notice of Trademark. An informal or formal notification used in connection with a word or other symbol indicating that trademark registration or trademark status is claimed in that word or other symbol.

Statutory Trademark Notice. The formal statutory notice of federal trademark registration is one of the following: the R in a circle symbol ®, "Reg. U.S. Pat. & Tm. Off.," or "Registered in U.S. Patent and Trademark Office." Lanham Act §29, 15 U.S.C. §1111. To recover profits or money damages in an infringement suit, the trademark registrant must give this "notice" of registration. But failure to give notice becomes immaterial if the alleged infringer has received "actual notice" in the form of a written or oral communication. In the absence of statutory notice, recovery of damages and profits prior to the date of receipt of actual notice may be precluded. Under the 1989 Trademark Law Revision Act, all forms of damages and attorney fee awards are available under Lanham Act §43(a), even for infringement of unregistered marks, perhaps making the trademark notice provisions irrelevant for such claims.

Proper and Improper Use of Trademark Notice. The use of the formal statutory notice is proper only with a mark that is already federally registered, either on the principal or the supplementary register. The statutory notice is not proper when used with a mark whose federal application for registration is still pending, or with a mark registered under a state statute. The Patent and Trademark Office, the Trademark Trial and Appeal Board, and the courts have been quite lenient in excusing inadvertent misuse of the statutory notice. Under the majority view, misuse of the statutory notice is not such "unclean hands" as to deny a trademark owner an injunction against the use of a confusingly similar, infringing mark. The use of the variation "Trademark Registered" to denote a mark registered under state law but not federally registered has been accepted as not being a misuse of the statutory notice.

Informal Trademark Notice. Many firms use informal trademark notices, such as "Brand," "TM," "Trademark," "SM," or "Service mark," adjacent to words or other symbols considered to be protectible marks. Such informal notices can serve several possible functions, such as: to inform competitors and the public that this word or symbol is considered to be an identifying mark, not a descriptive or generic term; to serve as a "no trespassing sign" to ward off competitors who may consider use of a similar mark; to use as evidence in registration or litigation of the user's intent that this word or symbol serve as an identifying mark.

- *Treatise Reference:* 2 J.T. McCarthy, *Trademarks and Unfair Competition* §§19.51–.55 (3d ed. 1995 rev.).

- *Statutory Reference:* Lanham Act §29, 15 U.S.C. §1111: "Notwithstanding the provisions of section 22 hereof, a registrant of a mark registered in the Patent and Trademark Office may give notice that his mark is registered by displaying with the mark as used the words 'Registered in U.S. Patent and Trademark Office' or 'Reg. U.S. Pat. & Tm. Off.' or the letter R enclosed in a circle, thus ®; and in any suit for infringement under this Act by such a registrant failing to give such notice of registration, no profits and no damages shall be recovered under the provisions of this Act unless the defendant had actual notice of the registration."

3. Notice of Copyright. A formal notification of copyright on publicly distributed copies of a copyrighted work. For public distribution of copies of a copyrighted work prior to the March 1, 1989, effective date of the Berne Convention Implementation Act of 1988 (BCIA), the affixing of a formal copyright notice to the copies was crucial to keep the copyright alive. For copies or phonorecords distributed after March 1, 1989, the affixation of notice is recommended to preclude the defense of innocence as a means of mitigating damages.

Three Eras of Law Regarding Copyright Notice. There are three separate copyright-notice "eras" or "epochs" divided by the effective legal requirements as to the use of copyright notice. Domestic Works that fell out of copyright and into the public domain in past years because of the public distribution of copies without the required notice are not revived by a subsequent change of law to a more lenient standard. The legal significance of a public distribution of copies that did not bear the required copyright notice is governed by the legal standards in effect on the date of the public distribution.

The "Old Era": 1909–1978. Distributions occurring prior to January 1, 1978, are governed by the 1909 Copyright Act, under which publication with notice marked the crucial borderline between state common law copyright protection for unpublished works and federal statutory copyright protection for works published with notice. An author could "secure copyright" under federal copyright law "by publication thereof with the notice of copyright required by this title." 1909 Copyright Act, §10. The highly technical notice provisions of the 1909 Act were sometimes draconian in effect, often resulting in the inadvertent and unfortunate forfeiture of copyright for failure to strictly adhere to the notice requirements. The form of notice required three elements: (1) the C in a circle symbol ©, the words "Copr." or "Copyright"; (2) the proprietor's name; and (3) the year date of first publication. The 1909 Act set down the specific location in which the notice must appear, such as on the title page or the immediately following page of the book. 1909 Copyright Act, §20. Sometimes, the courts would strain to avoid a forfeiture of copyright by labeling a certain distribution of copies without notice as a "limited publication," for which notice was not needed. See PUBLICATION.

The "Middle Era": 1978–1989. Distributions occurring between January 1, 1978, and March 1, 1989, are governed by the notice provisions of the 1978 Copyright Act, which considerably softened the rigid requirements of the 1909 Act but retained the need for notice as a condition subsequent of copyright protection. That is, the copyright itself could be forfeited if the notice requirements were not met and the savings or rescue provisions were not satisfied. The 1978 Act required the use of notice on "all

publicly distributed copies from which the work can be visually perceived, either directly or with the aid of a machine or device." 17 U.S.C. §401(a). This notice was required on all copies distributed anywhere in the world.

Middle Era Form of Notice. The form of notice on copies required three elements: (1) the C in a circle symbol © and the words "Copr." or "Copyright"; (2) the name of the copyright owner; and (3) the year date of first publication. 17 U.S.C. §401(b). The form of notice required for a SOUND RECORDING or a PHONORECORD required three elements: (1) the letter P in a circle; (2) the name of the owner of copyright of the sound recording; and (3) the year of first publication of the sound recording. 17 U.S.C. §402(b). Naming the wrong person in the notice did not invalidate the copyright but gave a special defense to one who obtained a "purported" license from the person named in the notice. 17 U.S.C. §406(a). While mistakenly using a notice year earlier than the actual year of first publication did not invalidate copyright, using a notice year more than one year later than the actual first publication year was an error rendering the whole notice void and the work was treated as if it bore no notice at all. 17 U.S.C. §406(b).

Middle-Era Rescue Provisions. Section 405(a) of the 1978 Copyright Act provided some savings or rescue provisions to avoid forfeiture of copyright if: (1) notice was omitted from no more than "a relatively small number of copies," with the case law generally, but not uniformly, adopting a percentage test of "relatively small"; and (2) registration of copyright was made within five years of publication without notice and a "reasonable effort is made to add notice to all copies or phonorecords that are distributed to the public in the United States after the omission has been discovered." 17 U.S.C. §405(a)(2).

The "New Era": 1989-Present. The Berne Convention Implementation Act of 1988 (BCIA), in order to allow U.S. membership in the BERNE UNION, abolished copyright notice as a condition of copyright effective March 1, 1989. However, for copies or phonorecords distributed after March 1, 1989, the affixation of notice is recommended to preclude the defense of lack of notice as a means of mitigating damages, as provided in new 17 U.S.C. §401(d). Other reasons for continuing to use notice of copyright during the "New Era" include: (1) the deterrence of infringement by using notice as a "no trespassing" sign, which provides a recognizable and clear warning that copyright is claimed and is likely to be enforced; and (2) the avoidance of the necessity of complying with little-known formalities found in the copyright laws of those nations that are members of the UNIVERSAL COPYRIGHT CONVENTION (UCC) but not the BERNE UNION.

Restoration of Certain Copyrights of Foreign Origin Published Without Notice. As a result of changes introduced in the 1994 URUGUAY ROUND AGREEMENTS ACT, U.S. protection for certain works of foreign origin that had fallen out of copyright for reasons such as publication without notice was "restored" if the works were still in copyright in its source country. See DURATION OF COPYRIGHT. As a result of the NAFTA implementation act, U.S. copyright was restored in Mexican and Canadian motion pictures that had fallen out of copyright in the United States for failure to use proper copyright notice. Such NAFTA restoration required filing of a statement with the Copyright Office before January 1, 1995.

See UNIT PUBLICATION DOCTRINE.

• *Treatise References: 2 Nimmer on Copyright* §7.02 *et seq.* (1994 rev.); 1 P. Goldstein, *Copyright* §3.5 (1989); 1 N. Boorstyn, *Copyright* §§9.01–.04 (2d ed. 1994); W. Patry, *Copyright Law and Practice* 421, 437, 453 (1994); M. Leaffer, *Understanding Copyright* §4.8 (1989).

•*Statutory Reference:* 17 U.S.C. §401(d): "Evidentiary Weight of Notice. If a notice of copyright in the form and position specified by this section appears on the published copy or copies to which a defendant in a copyright infringement suit had access, then no weight shall be given to such a defendant's interposition of a defense based on innocent infringement in mitigation of actual or statutory damages, except as provided in the last sentence of section 504(c)(2)."

novelty [patent] One of the conditions that an invention must meet in order to be patentable. Novelty is present if every element of the claimed invention is not disclosed in a single piece of PRIOR ART. Novelty is the opposite of ANTICIPATION. For example, an invention that is "anticipated" by the disclosure of a prior art patent or publication lacks "novelty."

See full description at ANTICIPATION.

• *Case Reference:* "Because of the above legal errors, the verdict of invalidity for lack of novelty (i.e., anticipation) cannot stand." *Jamesbury Corp. v. Litton Indus. Prods., Inc.,* 756 F.2d 1556, 1560, 225 USPQ 253, 256 (Fed. Cir. 1985).

nunc pro tunc [general legal] Latin legal term denoting a legal act done now with the intent to have it relate back to and become effective as of an earlier date. Literally meaning "now for then," the concept is useful to correct documents or situations by having later documents relate back so as to correct the intervening situation.

• *Example:* Where it was unclear whether a December assignment conveyed one patent or five patents, in the following September the parties signed a new assignment expressly conveying all five patents retroactive to the previous December. The court referred to this as a "nunc pro tunc provision" that sought to implement the parties' original understanding and intent, and said this suggested a recognition by the assignor that the original assignment covered all five patents and, with other facts, precluded a summary determination that only one patent was assigned as of December. *Merck & Co. v. U.S. Int'l Trade Comm'n,* 774 F.2d 483, 487, 227 USPQ 779, 781 (Fed. Cir. 1985).

O

object code [copyright–computer] The lowest level of computer language. Object code is "machine readable" by a computer and cannot be read by humans. Object code is often expressed in binary language, using "on-off" or "0-1" notation such as "01101001." COMPUTER PROGRAMS written in SOURCE CODE are readable by humans and are written in computer languages such as BASIC or FORTRAN. However, computers cannot understand source code, so to use the program, it must be translated into machine-readable object code. Computer programs written in both source code and object code are copyrightable and can qualify as trade secrets.

- *Case References*:

"As source code instructions must be translated into object code before the computer can act upon them, only instructions expressed in object code can be used 'directly' by the computer.... [A] computer program, whether in object code or source code, is a 'literary work' and is protected from unauthorized copying, whether from its object or source code version." *Apple Computer, Inc. v. Franklin Computer Corp.*, 714 F.2d 1240, 1249, 219 USPQ 113, 120–21 (3d Cir. 1983) (adopting the recommendation of the majority in the *CONTU* report).

"In every program, it is the object code, not the source code, that directs the computer to perform functions. The object code is therefore the final instruction to the computer." *Whelan Assocs. Inc. v. Jaslow Dental Lab.*, 797 F.2d 1222, 1231, 230 USPQ 481, 486 (3d Cir. 1986).

"Trandes put sufficient evidence before the jury to justify a conclusion that the [computer program] object code constituted economically valuable information and that Trandes took reasonable precautions to keep it secret. Because the object code meets the definitional requirements of [the trade secret statutes], it qualifies as a trade secret." *Trandes Corp. v. Guy F. Atkinson Co.*, 996 F.2d 655, 664, 27 USPQ2d 1014, 1022 (4th Cir. 1993).

objective evidence [patent] Evidence of the actual marketplace setting in which an invention was made. Such evidence is relevant to deciding whether the invention meets the most crucial test of patentability: nonobviousness. This term is defined herein under its synonym SECONDARY CONSIDERATIONS.

obviousness [patent] A condition of nonpatentability of an invention such that the invention cannot receive a valid patent if the invention could readily be deduced from publicly available information (PRIOR ART) by a person of ordinary skill in that technology.

Statutory Test of Obviousness. The obviousness criterion was introduced into U.S. law in §103 of the Patent Code of 1952. Prior to that time, the test of patentability required more ingenuity in making the technical innovation than would be the work of the "SKILLFUL MECHANIC." Under Patent Code §103, an invention is "obvious" and unpatentable if the differences between the invention and the prior art are such that "the subject matter as a whole would have been obvious at the time the invention was made" to a person skilled in that art. This standard is applied in the first instance by the Patent and Trademark Office in examining the application, and it is also the standard applied by the courts when deciding a challenge to the validity of an issued patent.

The Principle of the Inventive Step. In the United States, Congress is given the power to create patents only to promote the "progress" of

294

the "useful arts." See CONSTITUTION. The theory behind a requirement of nonobviousness is that more should be required to gain the reward of a patent than that the invention merely is different to any degree from the PRIOR ART. Not every slight realignment or trivial adjustment of what is known should receive the full panoply of patent rights and be an obstacle to free competition in the technological marketplace. Rather, there must be an inventive step that progresses or advances a certain distance beyond what is known. The length of that step is measured by the test of obviousness in that the invention reached by that step must not be obvious. A stride forward of that length is necessary for a patent and for the "progress" of the "useful arts" and technology. Something is obvious if it could have been readily seen or deduced from information available in the prior art.

Applying the Obviousness Test. The U.S. Supreme Court has read Patent Code §103 to require a four-part factual inquiry: (1) determine the scope and content of the prior art relied upon to challenge patentability; (2) identify the difference between that prior art and the claimed invention; (3) determine the level of ordinary SKILL IN THE ART at the time of the invention; and (4) consider the objective evidence of so-called SECONDARY CONSIDERATIONS. *Graham v. John Deere Co.,* 383 U.S. 1, 17, 148 USPQ 459, 467 (1966) (see quote below); *In re O'Farrell,* 853 F.2d 894, 902, 7 USPQ2d 1673, 1680 (Fed. Cir. 1988). These secondary considerations include such factors as COMMERCIAL SUCCESS, UNEXPECTED RESULTS, THE FAILURE OF OTHERS to achieve the results of the invention, a LONG FELT NEED which the invention fills, and COPYING of the invention by competitors. Having assembled all that factual data, the decision maker then must determine whether the claimed technology would have been either obvious or nonobvious to that hypothetical person of ordinary skill in the art. "It is difficult but necessary that the decisionmaker forget what he or she has been taught at trial about the claimed invention and cast the mind back to the time the invention was made (often as here many years), to occupy the mind of one skilled in the art who is presented

only with the [prior art] references, and who is normally guided by the then-accepted wisdom in the art." *W.L. Gore & Assocs., Inc. v. Garlock, Inc.,* 721 F.2d 1540, 1553, 220 USPQ 303, 313 (Fed. Cir. 1983).

Combining Prior Art. While it is not proper to combine prior art references in determining NOVELTY and ANTICIPATION under §102 of the Patent Code, combining prior art reference is proper and appropriate to determine obviousness under Patent Code §103. However, various bits of data or teachings of the prior art are not properly combined unless there is something in the prior art itself that suggests that those teachings could or should be combined. Both the suggestion for combining teachings to make the invention and its reasonable likelihood of success "must be founded in the prior art, not in the applicant's disclosure." *In re Dow Chem.,* 837 F.2d 469, 473, 5 USPQ2d 1529, 1531 (Fed. Cir. 1988). See COMBINING PRIOR ART.

Obvious to Try. Evidence indicating that what the inventor did was OBVIOUS TO TRY does not meet the test that the invention was obvious in the sense of Patent Code §103.

Hindsight Is Not Permitted. It is improper to use HINDSIGHT by reading back into the prior art the teachings of the invention that came later.

Issue of Law. Obviousness is a legal question the Federal Circuit independently reviews on appeal, even though it may be based on underlying factual findings of a trial court judge which are reviewed on appeal under the clearly erroneous standard. *In re Vaeck,* 947 F.2d 488, 493, 20 USPQ2d 1438, 1442 (Fed. Cir. 1991). While obviousness is a legal question, a jury may decide questions of anticipation and obviousness, either as special verdicts or en route to a verdict on the question of validity, which also may be decided by the jury. *Richardson v. Suzuki Motor Co.,* 868 F.2d 1226, 1234, 9 USPQ2d 1913, 1919 (Fed. Cir. 1989).

See SECONDARY CONSIDERATIONS, HINDSIGHT, SKILLED IN THE ART, ANALOGOUS ART, COMBINING PRIOR ART, SKILLFUL MECHANIC.

• *Statutory Reference*: 35 U.S.C. §103: "A patent may not be obtained though the invention is not identically disclosed or described as set forth in section 102 of this title, if the differences between the subject matter sought to be patented and the prior art are such that the subject matter as a whole would have been obvious at the time the invention was made to a person having ordinary skill in the art to which such subject matter pertains. Patentability shall not be negatived by the manner in which the invention was made...."

• *Case References*:

"The nonobviousness requirement extends the field of unpatentable material beyond that which is known to the public under §102, to include that which could readily be deduced from publicly available material by a person of ordinary skill in the pertinent field of endeavor.... Taken together, the novelty and nonobviousness requirements express a congressional determination that the purposes behind the [constitutional] Patent Clause are best served by free competition and exploitation of that which is either already available to the public, or that which may be readily discerned from publicly available material." *Bonito Boats Inc. v. Thunder Craft Boats Inc.*, 489 U.S. 141, 150, 9 USPQ2d 1847, 1852 (1989).

"While the ultimate question of patent validity is one of law, ... the §103 condition, which is but one of three conditions, each of which must be satisfied, lends itself to several basic factual inquiries. Under §103, the scope and content of the prior art are to be determined; differences between the prior art and the claims at issue are to be ascertained; and the level of ordinary skill in the pertinent art resolved. Against this background, the obviousness or nonobviousness of the subject matter is determined. Such secondary considerations as commercial success, long felt but unsolved needs, failure of others, etc., might be utilized to give light to the circumstance surrounding the origin of the subject matter sought to be patented. As indicia of obviousness or nonobviousness, these inquiries may have relevancy." *Graham v. John Deere Co.*, 383 US 1, 17, 148 USPQ 459, 467 (1966).

" 'Obviousness' as used in patent law, is not a term readily understood by a jury. Indeed, the term is overladen with layman's meanings different from its legal connotation, which can only add confusion to the decision-making process by the most conscientious jury. In this case such confusion is demonstrated by the jury's anomalous answers that there is no prior art, that the inventions were not obvious, but that the inventions were lacking in novelty." *Structural Rubber Prods. Co. v. Park Rubber Co.*, 749 F.2d 707, 723, 223 USPQ 1264, 1276 (Fed. Cir. 1984).

"With the involved facts determined, the decisionmaker confronts a ghost, i.e., 'a person having ordinary skill in the art,' not unlike the 'reasonable man' and other ghosts in the law. To reach a proper conclusion under §103, the decisionmaker must step backward in time and into the shoes worn by that 'person' when the invention was unknown and just before it was made. In light of *all* the evidence, the decisionmaker must then determine whether the patent challenger has convincingly established, 35 U.S.C. §282, that the claimed invention as a whole would have been obvious at *that* time to *that* person." *Panduit Corp. v. Dennison Mfg. Co.*, 810 F.2d 1561, 1566–68, 1 USPQ2d 1593, 1595–97 (Fed. Cir. 1987).

"[T]he following tenets of patent law ... must be adhered to when applying §103: (1) the claimed invention must be considered as a whole ... see, e.g., *Jones v. Hardy*, 727 F.2d 1524, 1529, 220 USPQ 1021, 1024 (Fed. Cir. 1984) (though the difference between claimed invention and prior art may seem slight, it may also have been the key to advancement of the art); (2) the references must be considered as a whole and suggest the desirability and thus the obviousness of making the combination ...; (3) the references must be viewed without the benefit of hindsight vision afforded by the claimed invention ...; (4) 'ought to be tried' is not the standard with which obviousness is determined ...; and (5) the presumption of validity remains constant and intact throughout litigation...." *Hodosh v. Block Drug Co.*, 786 F.2d 1136, 1143 n.5, 229 USPQ 182, 187 n.5 (Fed. Cir. 1986) (Rich, J.).

• *Treatise References*:

2 D. Chisum, *Patents* §§5.03–.05 (1994 rev.).

"Unlike a verdict on negligence to which the fact trier is expected to contribute the sense of the community, a decision on patent validity does not benefit from the fact trier's communal sense of patentability." R. Harmon, *Patents and the Federal Circuit* §4.2(b)(i) (3d ed. 1994).

"Something is obvious when it comes, so to say, automatically to one's mind. The English word 'obvious' has, as its root, the latin word *via* which means *way*. The solution which lies on your way, which you cannot fail to see because it lies on your way, is an obvious solution. Nonobviousness is, of course, not an objective criterion that can be measured on a scale or with a measuring rod. The judgment is made in the mind of a person." WIPO, *Background Reading Material on Intellectual Property* 84 (1988).

• *Example of Invention Held Obvious.* Robert Djorup invented and obtained two patents in the 1970s for a new form of electrical-sensing device to measure wind speed and direction. The device claimed in Djorup's '481 patent differed in two respects from the teachings of a well-known 1950 article by Lowell: (1) Lowell's article showed a V-shaped arrangement of wind sensors, whereas Djorup claimed side-by-side, closely spaced sensors; and (2) unlike Lowell, Djorup claimed an insulator to prevent air flow between the sensors. However, the Court of Appeals for the Federal Circuit held that the Djorup '481 patent was invalid as obvious because the disclosure of the prior Hayakawa patent suggested to one skilled in the art that Lowell's arrangement of sensors could be replaced with the two things that distinguished Djorup from Lowell. Thus, the two prior art references of Lowell and Hayakawa were combined to render Djorup's '481 patent claim obvious and invalid. *Environmental Instruments, Inc. v. Sutron Corp.*, 877 F.2d 1561, 11 USPQ2d 1132 (Fed. Cir. 1989).

• *Example of Invention Held Nonobvious.* Fine's invention concerned a system for detecting and measuring minute quantities of nitrogen compounds as small as one part in one billion. This would have use in detecting drugs and explosives concealed in luggage and closed containers. The Patent and Trademark Office (PTO) rejected Fine's patent application on the ground that it would be "obvious" under Patent Code §103 to substitute the nitric oxide detector disclosed in the prior art Warnick patent for the sulphur dioxide detector in the Eads' prior art sulfur detector to arrive at the Fine nitrogen detection invention. The Court of Appeals for the Federal Circuit reversed and ordered the PTO to grant to Fine the contested patent claims. The court held that it was not appropriate to combine the prior art references in this case because there was nothing in the prior art to suggest such a combination. "There is no suggestion in [the prior art] Eads [patent], which focuses on the unique difficulties inherent in the measurement of sulfur, to use that arrangement to detect nitrogen compounds. In fact Eads says that the presence of nitrogen is undesirable.... So instead of suggesting that the system be used to detect nitrogen compounds, Eads deliberately seeks to avoid them; it warns against rather than teaches Fine's invention.... In the face of this, one skilled in the art would not be expected to combine a nitrogen-related detector [as disclosed in Warnick] with the Eads system. Accordingly, there is no suggestion to combine [the] Eads and Warnick [prior art references]." *In re Fine*, 837 F.2d 1071, 1074, 5 USPQ2d 1596, 1599 (Fed. Cir. 1988).

obvious to try [patent] An impermissible test of the obviousness and patentability of an invention. Under this test, evidence of the PRIOR ART indicating that what the inventor did was OBVIOUS TO TRY constitutes obviousness of the invention, resulting in a conclusion that no patent should be (or should have been) granted for that invention.

The Court of Appeals for the Federal Circuit has held that "obvious to try" is *not* the proper test to apply in using the criterion of obviousness of Patent Code §103.

• *Case Reference*: "[T]his court and its predecessors have repeatedly emphasized that 'obvious to try' is not the standard under §103. However, the meaning of this maxim is sometimes lost.... The admonition that 'obvious to try' is not the standard under §103 has been directed mainly at two kinds of error. In some cases, what would have been 'obvious to try' would have been to vary all parameters or try each of numerous possible choices until one possibly arrived at a successful result, where the prior art gave either no indication of which parameters were critical or no direction as to which of many possible choices is likely to be successful.... In others, what was 'obvious to try' was to explore a new technology or general approach that seemed to be a promising field of experimentation, where the prior art gave only general guidance as to the particular form of the claimed invention or how to achieve it." *In re O'Farrell*, 853 F.2d 894, 903, 7 USPQ2d 1673, 1680–81 (Fed. Cir. 1988).

"An 'obvious-to-try' situation exists when a general disclosure may pique the scientist's curiosity, such that further investigation might be done as a result of the disclosure, but the disclosure itself does not contain a sufficient teaching of how to obtain the desired result." *In re Eli Lilly & Co.,* 902 F.2d 943, 945, 14 USPQ2d 1741, 1743 (Fed. Cir. 1990) (invention held obvious).

office action [patent–trademark] An official, written communication from an examiner in the Patent and Trademark Office (PTO), giving the position of the PTO on a pending patent application or a pending application to register a mark.

After an office action that is adverse in any respect, the applicant must respond within the time limit set. 37 C.F.R. §1.111(a) (patents); 37 C.F.R. §2.62 (trademarks).

See FINAL REJECTION.

• *Rule Reference*: 37 C.F.R. §1.2. "All business with the Patent and Trademark Office should be transacted in writing. The personal attendance of applicants or their attorneys or agents at the Patent and Trademark Office is unnecessary. The action of the Patent and Trademark Office will be based exclusively on the written record in the Office. No attention will be paid to any alleged oral promise, stipulation, or understanding in relation to which there is disagreement or doubt."

Official Gazette [patent–trademark] The U.S. Patent and Trademark Office publication, which contains official notices regarding pat-

ents and trademarks. The Official Gazette (OG) is published weekly in two sections or editions: the patent section (OG) and the trademark section (OGTM). When a mark has been published for opposition, it appears in the trademark section of the Official Gazette, which starts the time limit running for the filing of an OPPOSITION PROCEEDING to bar registration.

See PUBLICATION FOR OPPOSITION.

off-shore assembly [patent] The manufacture or assembly outside of the United States of a product, or by use of a process, patented in the United States. Under certain circumstances, such conduct outside of the United States can create liability for infringement of a U.S. patent.

1. Export of Parts of a Patented Combination for Assembly Off-Shore. The 1972 Supreme Court case of *Deepsouth Packing Co. v. Laitram Corp.*, 406 U.S. 518 (1972), concerned a defendant who manufactured in the United States all the parts of a patented machine and then shipped them in boxes to customers in foreign countries with instructions for quick assembly into a complete machine. The defendant was held to be neither a direct nor a contributory infringer of the plaintiff's U.S. patent on the assembled machine. The assembly of the complete machine was not a direct infringement because it occurred abroad, not within the United States. The defendant was not guilty of CONTRIBUTORY INFRINGEMENT because no act of direct infringement had occurred in the United States. Congress, in a 1984 amendment to the Patent Code, overruled the *Deepsouth* rule by converting a *Deepsouth* fact situation into an illegal infringement of a U.S. combination patent. 35 U.S.C. §271(f)(1).

The 1984 Amendment. The amended statute goes further than *Deepsouth* in that it reaches exportation of less than all of the component parts of the patented combination. That is, exportation of "a substantial portion of the components" is sufficient to constitute illegal inducement if the exporter induces off-shore assembly of the whole patented combination. See 4 D. Chisum, *Patents* §16.02[7] (1994 rev.).

2. Importation Into the United States of the Unpatented Product of an Off-Shore Use of a

Process Patented in the United States. The traditional rule was that it was not infringement to import a product made off-shore by use of a process covered by a U.S. patent. This was changed by a 1988 amendment to various parts of the Patent Code. The 1988 amendments provide for remedies against infringement in this situation but only if several complicated conditions are met. Briefly, unless the infringer is the person who practiced the patented process or had knowledge that a patented process was used, no remedies for infringement are available before the importer of the product had notice of infringement. It is the responsibility of the patent owner to give notice of infringement. In addition, the 1994 URUGUAY ROUND AGREEMENTS ACT amended Patent Code §271(g) to enable the holder of a U.S. process patent to prevent others from offering to sell in the United States products made by a patented process.

The 1988 Amendment. In suits alleging infringement of a process patent by importation, sale, or use of a product made from the patented process, the product is presumed to have been made by use of the patented process if (1) the court finds that there is a "substantial likelihood" that the product was made by the patented process; and (2) the plaintiff made a reasonable, but unsuccessful, effort to determine the process used. The burden of proving otherwise then rests with the alleged infringer. 35 U.S.C. §295.

- *Statutory Reference*:

35 U.S.C. §271(g): "Whoever without authority imports into the United States or offers to sell, sells or uses within the United States a product which is made by a process patented in the United States shall be liable as an infringer, if the importation, offer to sell, sale or use of the product occurs during the term of such process patent...."

35 U.S.C. §287(b)(2): "No remedies for infringement under section 271(g) of this title shall be available with respect to any product in the possession of, or in transit to, the person subject to liability under such section before that person had notice of infringement with respect to that product...."

OG [patent–trademark]
See OFFICIAL GAZETTE

old combination [patent]
See OVERCLAIMING.

on sale [patent] An inventor cannot obtain a valid patent if he or she waits for more than the one-year GRACE PERIOD to file a patent application after a product embodying the invention has been placed "on sale." It is against public policy for the inventor to commercially exploit the invention for longer than the one-year grace period of Patent Code §102(b). The date one year prior to the filing date of the patent is known as the CRITICAL DATE. An event prior to that date can trigger the "on sale" bar to a patent.

Policy. The policy behind the on sale bar is to give an inventor one year following the start of commercialization of the invention to decide whether to file an application for a patent. If no patent application is filed, the right to a patent is lost. "The 'on sale' bar forces the inventor to choose between seeking patent protection promptly following sales activity or taking his chances with his competitors without the benefit of patent protection...." *General Elec. Co. v. United States*, 654 F.2d 55, 61, 211 USPQ 867, 873 (Ct. Cl. 1981).

Sale of Product of a Process. The bar to a patent on a process is triggered when the inventor or his assignee places on sale a product made by the process. *D.I. Auld Co. v. Chroma Graphics Corp.*, 714 F.2d 1144, 219 USPQ 13 (Fed. Cir. 1983).

What Is Disclosed. To trigger the on sale bar, an advertisement or offer to sell need not itself disclose the invention in its patented details. "[M]erely offering to sell a product by way of an advertisement or invoice may be evidence of a definite offer for sale or a sale of a claimed invention even though *no* details are disclosed. That the offered product is in fact the claimed invention may be established by any relevant evidence, such as memoranda, drawings, correspondence, and testimony of witnesses." *RCA Corp. v. Data Gen. Corp.*, 887 F.2d 1056, 1060, 12 USPQ2d 1449, 1452 (Fed. Cir. 1989).

Anticipation and Obviousness. If the product placed on sale contains all the elements of the claimed invention, there is a direct ANTICIPA-TION bar under Patent Code §102(b) against a patent. In addition, the product placed on sale becomes part of the PRIOR ART for purposes of applying the OBVIOUSNESS bar against a patent. Thus, a valid patent is barred if the claimed invention is either completely embodied in or obvious in view of the product sold or offered for sale. *Baker Oil Tools Inc. v. Geo. Vann Inc.*, 828 F.2d 1558, 1563, 4 USPQ2d 1210, 1213 (Fed. Cir. 1987).

On Sale by Anyone. The bar of Patent Code §102(b) is not limited to offers to sell made by the inventor or someone under the inventor's control, but can result from the actions of an independent person. *J.A. LaPorte, Inc. v. Norfolk Dredging Co.*, 787 F.2d 1577, 1581, 228 USPQ 435, 437 (Fed. Cir. 1986).

Sale of Intellectual Property Rights. To trigger the "on sale" bar, the offer or sale must be of a tangible thing embodying the claimed invention or making it obvious. A sale of patent or other intellectual property rights in the invention is not a sale that triggers Patent Code §102(b). *Moleculon Research Corp. v. CBS, Inc.*, 793 F.2d 1261, 1267, 229 USPQ 805, 809 (Fed. Cir. 1986).

Experimental Sale. While it is possible for the inventor to avoid the "on sale" bar to patentability by proving that a sale was for experimental purposes, this is difficult (see EXPERIMENTAL USE). The primary purpose must be experimentation: commercial exploitation can be only incidental. *Baker Oil Tools Inc. v. Geo. Vann Inc.*, 828 F.2d 1558, 1563, 4 USPQ2d 1210, 1213 (Fed. Cir. 1987) ("If the challenged use or sales activities were associated with primarily experimental procedures conducted in the course of completing the invention, … a section 102(b) bar does not vest."). When sales are made in an ordinary commercial environment such that the goods are outside the inventor's control, an inventor's claim of an intent that the sales were to be "experimental" is insufficient to avoid the statutory bar in the absence of objective evidence. At a minimum, customers must be aware of the experimentation. *Paragon Podiatry Lab., Inc. v. KLM Labs., Inc.*, 984 F.2d 1182, 1187, 25 USPQ2d 1561, 1564–65 (Fed. Cir. 1993) (patent held invalid under §102(b)). The Federal

Circuit has set out some factors to be considered to determine whether the relationship with customers was experimental or creates an "on sale" bar, for example: (1) whether there was a need for testing by other than the patentee; (2) the amount of control exercised; (3) the stage of development of the invention; (4) whether payments were made and the basis thereof; (5) whether confidentiality was required; and (6) whether technological changes were made. *Continental Can Co. USA, Inc. v. Monsanto Co.*, 948 F.2d 1264, 1269, 20 USPQ2d 1746, 1750 (Fed Cir. 1991) (agreements between patentee's employer and customer for development of invention, where customer agreed to test the invention, did not place invention "on sale" under §102(b)).

An Offer to Sell a Product That Is Not Yet on Hand. The Court of Appeals for the Federal Circuit has adopted a modified version of what is known as the *"Timely* test" taken from *Timely Prods. Corp. v. Arron*, 523 F.2d 288, 302, 187 USPQ 257, 267–68 (2d Cir. 1975). This is a three-part test for determining whether patented subject matter is "on sale" in cases where the offer to sell concerns goods that have not yet been produced at the time of the offer to sell. Under this test, the patent is invalid if the patent application was filed more than one year after the solicitation of an order for a product not on hand which is to be produced later if: (1) the invention claimed is embodied in or is made obvious in view of the thing offered for sale; (2) the invention is "operable and commercially marketable" such that there has been a "REDUCTION TO PRACTICE"; and (3) the solicited sale is primarily for profit, not for experimental purposes. The Court of Appeals for the Federal Circuit in 1987 modified the second prong of the *Timely* test by stating that a reduction to practice is not an absolute requirement to find an "on sale" bar. *UMC Elecs. Co. v. United States*, 816 F.2d 647, 2 USPQ2d 1465 (Fed. Cir. 1987). However, the court added that "[w]e do not reject 'reduction to practice' as an important analytical tool in an on-sale analysis." The court noted that proof of a reduction to practice may "lighten the burden of the party asserting the [§102(b)] bar." 816 F.2d at 656, 2 USPQ2d at 1471.

Failure to Disclose Commercial Sales as Proof of Inequitable Conduct. The concealment of commercial sales information may be considered an intent to mislead the Patent and Trademark Office and render the claims unenforceable. "Absent explanation, the evidence of a knowing failure to disclose sales that bear all of the earmarks of commercialization reasonably supports an inference that the inventor's attorney intended to mislead the PTO." *Paragon Podiatry Lab., Inc. v. KLM Labs., Inc.*, 984 F.2d 1182, 1193, 25 USPQ2d 1561, 1569–70 (Fed. Cir. 1993). See INEQUITABLE CONDUCT.

See ANTICIPATION, OBVIOUSNESS, CRITICAL DATE, GRACE PERIOD.

• *Statutory Reference*: 35 U.S.C. §102: "A person shall be entitled to a patent unless— ... (b) the invention was ... in public use or on sale in this country, more than one year prior to the date of the application for patent in the United States...."

• *Case References*:

"[T]he 'on sale' bar has the following underlying policies: (1) a policy against removing inventions from the public domain which the public justifiably comes to believe are freely available due to commercialization; (2) a policy favoring prompt and widespread disclosure of inventions to the public; and (3) a policy of giving the inventor a reasonable amount of time following sales activity to determine whether a patent is worthwhile.... In the case of a patentee or patent applicant selling to an independently controlled distributor, all of the above policies warrant applying the 'on sale' bar. When a sale disclosing the invention is made by a person other than the patentee or patent applicant, as in this case, the policy against removing inventions from the public domain and the policy favoring early filing of patent applications justify application of the 'on sale' bar...." *In re Calvin*, 761 F.2d 671, 676, 226 USPQ 1, 4 (Fed. Cir. 1985).

"The date of the purchase agreement is, therefore, the effective date on which the invention became part of the public domain. That delivery of the device embodying the invention occurred later is immaterial." *J.A. LaPorte Inc. v. Norfolk Dredging Co.*, 787 F.2d 1577, 1583, 229 USPQ 435, 439 (Fed. Cir. 1986).

"[T]he overriding focus of Section 102(b) is preventing inventors from reaping the benefits of the patent system beyond the statutory term.... Accordingly, while what an offer or sale discloses to the public may tend to show whether the invention was on sale, the question is not whether the public knew of the invention, but whether the product sold or offered embodies the invention claimed.... Indeed, an offer or sale may invoke the statutory bar 'even though *no* details are disclosed.' " *Ferag AG v. Quipp Inc.*, 45 F.3d 1562, 1567, 33 USPQ2d 1512, 1516 (Fed. Cir. 1995).

• *Example 1*: Cole invented and patented an invention relating to a display system for generating alphanumeric characters on a television monitor. Cole assigned the patent to RCA. The Cole patent application was filed on October 16, 1963. On October 8, 1962, RCA had submitted a proposal to the Federal Aviation Administration (FAA) to sell monitors made according to the invention for use in air traffic control centers. The court held that this proposal to the FAA created a §102(b) bar, invalidating the patent. The court rejected the argument that the RCA proposal to the FAA was too vague and indefinite to constitute a definite offer to sell: "The requirement of a *definite* offer excludes merely indefinite or nebulous discussion about a possible sale.... RCA's bid was embodied in a lengthy written proposal providing background information, a detailed delivery schedule, a rate of completion of the proposed work and a separate section on financial data and costs.... Thus, there was a definite offer by RCA to sell which was proved to cover the subject invention, after that invention had been reduced to practice. That offer was made in this country more than one year prior to filing the application which matured into the Cole patent. Under these circumstances the claims are invalid under section 102(b)." *RCA Corp. v. Data Gen. Corp.*, 887 F.2d 1056, 1062, 12 USPQ2d 1449, 1454 (Fed. Cir. 1989).

• *Example 2*: Arron invented and patented an improvement for a battery-powered, electrically heated body garment. Arron filed the patent application on November 29, 1966. In the fall of 1965 Arron had shown to Alexander, a potential customer who sold by mail order, samples of electrically heated socks that Arron had also invented. Alexander ordered some of those heated socks from Arron and placed an advertisement for the heated socks in the November 1965 issue of "Outdoor Life," which reached its readers before the CRITICAL DATE of November 29, 1965. Even though the socks were not on hand and not available for delivery as of the critical date, the court held that the events of soliciting an order from Alexander and Alexander's "Outdoor Life" advertisement constituted a placing of the heated socks "on sale." This made the structure of the advertised socks a part of the "prior art" such that the claims of the Arron heated body garment patent were obvious under §103 in view of the heated socks on sale. Thus, the Arron patent was held invalid. *Timely Prods. Corp. v. Arron*, 523 F.2d 288, 294–95, 187 USPQ 257, 261 (2d Cir. 1975).

operating system program [computer–copyright] A COMPUTER PROGRAM that controls the internal operations of a computer. For example, DOS, or disk operating system, is an operating system that controls operations between the disk drive and the computer itself.

• *Case Reference*: "Computer programs can be categorized by function as with application programs or operating system programs. Application programs usually perform a specific task for the computer user, such as word processing, checkbook balancing, or playing a game. In contrast, operating system programs generally manage the internal functions of the computer or facilitate use of application programs.... [An uncopyrightable] 'process' is no more involved because the instructions in an operating system program may be used to activate the operating of the computer than it would be if instructions were written in ordinary English in a manual which described the necessary steps to activate an intricate complicated machine. There is, therefore, no reason to afford any less copyright protection to the instructions in an operating system program than to the instructions in an application program." *Apple Computer, Inc. v.*

Franklin Computer Corp., 714 F.2d 1240, 1251, 219 USPQ 113, 116, 122 (3d Cir. 1983).

opposition proceeding [trademark] An administrative INTER PARTES PROCEEDING before the TRADEMARK TRIAL AND APPEAL BOARD (TTAB) in which a person with a reasonable belief that he or she will be injured files a proceeding in opposition to the federal registration of a mark, which is the subject of a pending application. Oppositions are governed by Lanham Act §§13, 18, and 19.

Standing. Standing to oppose is conferred on anyone other than a mere intermeddler. Anyone with "a personal interest in the outcome beyond that of the general public" has standing. *Lipton Indus., Inc. v. Ralston Purina Co.*, 670 F.2d 1024, 1028, 213 USPQ 185, 188 (C.C.P.A. 1982).

Grounds. An opposition to registration may be based on any statutory ground that negates registration. *Lipton Indus., Inc. v. Ralston Purina Co.*, 670 F.2d 1024, 1029–30, 213 USPQ 185, 190 (C.C.P.A. 1982). Most often these grounds will be those bars to registration listed in Lanham Act §2. In determining likelihood of confusion in an opposition proceeding, it is the mark as shown in the application and as used on the goods or services listed in the application that must be considered, not the mark as actually used by the applicant. *Canadian Imperial Bank v. Wells Fargo Bank*, 811 F.2d 1490, 1 USPQ2d 1813 (Fed. Cir. 1987). The equitable defenses of LACHES, estoppel, and acquiescence are made available by Lanham Act §19, 15 U.S.C. §1069.

Evidence. The testimonial evidence in an opposition proceeding does not consist of live testimony before the Trademark Board, but of the written transcript of a testimonial deposition resembling a discovery deposition. The "trial" before the board consists of what in a court trial would be closing arguments by counsel supplementing their trial briefs.

• *Treatise Reference*: J.T. McCarthy, *Trademarks and Unfair Competition* §§20.1–.11 (3d ed. 1995 rev.).

ordinary observer test [copyright] A test of copyright infringement that asks if an "ordinary reasonable person" would perceive a substantial taking of protected expression. This is sometimes known as the "audience test," and some courts take the position that in applying the test, "analytic dissection and expert testimony are not appropriate." *Sid & Marty Krofft Television Prods., Inc. v. McDonald's Corp.*, 562 F.2d 1157, 1164, 196 USPQ 97, 103 (9th Cir. 1977).

Critics of the ordinary observer test point out that it looks at the totality of the conflicting works and is "concerned with surface illusion and the appearance of copying, not its reality." M. Leaffer, *Understanding Copyright* §9.6[B] (1989).

See full discussion and citations at SUBSTANTIAL SIMILARITY.

- *Treatise References*: 2 *Nimmer on Copyright* §13.03[E][2] (1994 rev.); 2 P. Goldstein, *Copyright* §7.3.2 (1989); M. Leaffer, *Understanding Copyright* §9.6[B] (1989).

ordinary skill in the art [patent] That level of technical knowledge, experience, and expertise possessed by the run-of-the-mill or ordinary engineer, scientist, or designer in the technology that is relevant to the invention.

See full definition and references at SKILL IN THE ART.

originality [copyright] To be copyrightable, a work must have originality in the sense that it owes its origin to this author and that it has at least a modicum of creativity.

Origin in Author, Not in Another. "Originality" simply means that to be copyrightable, the work must owe its origin to the person claiming to be the author: that the work is independently created, not mindlessly copied from another work. The Supreme Court has said that "originality is a constitutional requirement" that flows from the constitutional terms "authors" and "writings," which presuppose some amount of originality, which in turn requires "some minimal degree of creativity." *Feist Publications v. Rural Tel. Serv.*, 499 U.S. 340, 345, 18 USPQ2d 1275, 1278 (1991).

Originality and Creativity Compared. While originality focuses upon the need for the author's independent effort, creativity imposes a minimal level of artistic or literary ingenuity. Nimmer has pointed out the independent significance of these two requirements. "[A] work may be entirely the product of the claimant's independent efforts, and hence original, but may nevertheless be denied protection as a work of art if it is completely lacking in any modicum of creativity." 1 *Nimmer on Copyright* §2.08[B][2] (1994 rev.). The Supreme Court, approving of Nimmer's analysis, held that: "Original, as the term is used in copyright, means only that the work was independently created by the author (as opposed to copied from other works), and that it possesses at least some minimal degree of creativity." *Feist Publications v. Rural Tel. Serv.*, 499 U.S. 340, 345, 18 USPQ2d 1275, 1278 (1991).

Originality Is Different From Novelty. "Originality" does not imply that a work must be new, startling, novel, or unusual. It is clear that there is in copyright law no standard of novelty analogous to the standard of NONOBVIOUSNESS in patent law. Congress made it clear in the 1978 Copyright Act revisions that the copyright standard of "originality" does not include or imply any standard of "novelty." (See legislative history below.) "[T]he Constitution, as so interpreted, recognizes that the standards for patents and copyrights are basically different." *Alfred Bell & Co. v. Catalda Fine Arts*, 191 F.2d 99, 102–03, 90 USPQ 153, 156 (2d Cir. 1953) (J. Frank, J.). In theory, there is no reason why there could not be two valid copyrights on two substantially identical works if they were created independently of each other. This is very different from patent law. In a famous sentence, Judge Learned Hand put it this way: "[I]f by some magic a man who had never known it were to compose anew Keats' Ode on a Grecian Urn, he would be an 'author,' and if he copyrighted it, others might not copy that poem, though they might of course copy Keats." *Sheldon v. Metro-Goldwyn Pictures Corp.*, 81 F.2d 49, 54, 28 USPQ 330, 335 (2d Cir. 1936). These principles were reaffirmed by the Supreme Court in 1991 when it observed that: "Originality does not signify novelty; a work may be original even though it closely resembles other works so long as the similarity is fortuitous, not the result of copying." *Feist Publications v. Rural Tel. Serv.,* 499 U.S. 340, 345, 18 USPQ2d 1275, 1278 (1991).

Creativity. The Supreme Court in *Feist* said that a separate requirement called "creativity" arises as part of the constitutional requisite of "originality." The Court said that what is needed is a "creative spark" and that is easily found: "[T]he requisite level of creativity is extremely low; even a slight amount will suffice. The vast majority of works make the grade quite easily, as they possess some creative spark, 'no matter how crude, humble or obvious' it might be." *Feist Publications v. Rural Tel. Serv.,* 499 U.S. 340, 345, 18 USPQ2d 1275, 1278 (1991).

See CREATIVITY.

Higher Standard for Certain Derivative Works. Some courts have imposed upon certain kinds of derivative works a higher than normal standard of ORIGINALITY, requiring that the derivative work constitute a "substantial variation" of the preexisting work. *Gracen v. Bradford Exch.,* 698 F.2d 300, 305, 217 USPQ 1294, 1298 (7th Cir. 1983) ("substantially different from the underlying work"). The stated reason for imposing this higher standard is to avoid "put[ting] a weapon for harassment in the hands of mischievous copiers intent on appropriating and monopolizing public domain work" by "extend[ing] copyrightability to minuscule variations." *L. Batlin & Son, Inc. v. Snyder,* 536 F.2d 486, 492, 189 USPQ 753, 758 (2d Cir. 1976). While the types of derivative works to which this higher standard applies are not clearly defined, this rule appears limited to derivative works whose marketplace value is the result of the derivative work being based on a popular preexisting work. For example, such cases have involved transferring a preexisting work from one medium to another such as a plastic version of a nineteenth century cast-iron penny bank; plastic dolls of popular Disney characters such as Mickey Mouse; and a painted collector's plate with a scene showing Judy Garland as Dorothy in the movie *The Wizard of Oz.* Compare *North Coast Indus. v. Jason Maxwell Inc.,* 972 F.2d 1031, 23 USPQ2d 1788 (9th Cir. 1992) (The test of originality of a derivative work is whether the difference between the work and a preexisting work is "non-trivial.").

- *Treatise References*: 1 *Nimmer on Copyright* §§2.01, 2.08[B][1] (1994 rev.); 1 N. Boorstyn, *Copyright* §2.02 (2d ed. 1994); 1 P. Goldstein, *Copyright* §2.2.1.2 (1989); M. Leaffer, *Understanding Copyright* §2.7[C] (1989); W. Patry, *Copyright Law and Practice* 151 (1994).

- *Statutory Reference*: 17 U.S.C. §102: "(a) Copyright subsists, in accordance with this title, in original works of authorship fixed in any tangible medium of expression, now known or later developed, from which they can be perceived, reproduced, or otherwise communicated, either directly or with the aid of a machine of device."

- *Legislative History*: "The phrase 'original works of authorship,' which is purposely left undefined, is intended to incorporate without change the standard of originality established by the courts under the present copyright statute [of 1909]. This standard does not include requirements of novelty, ingenuity, or aesthetic merit, and there is no intention to enlarge the standard of copyright protection to require them." H. Rep. No. 94-1476, 94th Cong., 2d Sess. 51 (1976).

- *Case References*:

"Original, as the term is used in copyright, means only that the work was independently created by the author (as opposed to copied from other works), and that it possesses at least some minimal degree of creativity.... Originality is a constitutional requirement.... [T]his Court [has in past decisions] defined the crucial [Constitutional] terms 'authors' and 'writings.' In so doing, the Court made it unmistakably clear that these terms presuppose a degree of originality." *Feist Publications v. Rural Tel. Serv.,* 499 U.S. 340, 345–46, 18 USPQ2d 1275, 1278 (1991).

"It is clear then, that nothing in the Constitution commands that copyrighted matter be strikingly unique or novel. Accordingly, we were not ignoring the Constitution when we stated that a 'copy of something in the public domain' will support a copyright if it is a 'distinguishable variation'; or when we rejected the contention that 'like a patent, a copyrighted work must be not only original, but new.' ... All that is needed to satisfy both the Constitution and the statute is that the 'author' contributed something more than a 'merely trivial' variation, something recognizably 'his own.' Originality in this context 'means little more than a prohibition of actual copying.' No matter how poor artistically the 'author's addition, it is enough if it be his own.' " *Alfred Bell & Co. v. Catalda Fine Arts*, 191 F.2d 99, 102–03, 90 USPQ 153, 157 (2d Cir. 1953) (Frank, J.).

In holding that an illustrated poster advertising a circus was copyrightable, Justice Holmes issued his classic warning against lawyers and judges making artistic judgments in copyright cases: "The least pretentious picture has more originality in it than directories and the like, which may be copyrighted.... A picture is none the less a picture and none the less a subject of copyright that it is used for an advertisement. And if pictures may be used to advertise soap, or the theater, or monthly magazines, as they are, they may be used to advertise a circus.... It would be a dangerous undertaking for persons trained only to the law to constitute themselves final judges of the worth of pictorial illustrations, outside of the narrowest and most obvious limits." *Bleistein v. Donaldson Lithographing Co.*, 188 U.S. 239, 250–51 (1903).

"The copyright laws protect the work, not the amount of effort expended. A person who produces a short new work or makes a small improvement in a few hours gets a copyright for that contribution fully as effective as that on a novel written as a life's work.... The input of time is irrelevant. A photograph is the work of an instant and its significance may be accidental.... In 14 hours Mozart could write a piano concerto, J.S. Bach a cantata, or Dickens a week's installment of *Bleak House*. The Laffer Curve, an economic graph prominent in political debates, appeared on the back of a napkin after dinner, the work of a minute. All of these are copyrightable." *Rockford Map Publishers, Inc. v. Directory Serv. Co.*, 768 F.2d 145, 148, 226 USPQ 1025, 1027 (7th Cir. 1985).

Orphan Drug Act [patent] A law passed by Congress in 1983 giving seven years of market exclusivity for certain drugs developed to treat rare diseases. In 1993, Congress amended the Act so that all drugs, patented or not, which are expected to be useful in treating rare diseases or conditions can be given the seven-year exclusivity period. The goal is to give market exclusivity in order to induce drug companies to produce drugs that have only a small market.

Definition. To qualify as an orphan drug, the drug must reasonably be expected to be useful in treating rare diseases or conditions that affect less than 200,000 people in the United States. If the disease or condition affects more than 200,000 people in the United States, a drug can be designated an orphan drug if the cost of developing and making the drug available in the United States is not expected to be recovered from domestic sales of the drug.

Meeting Demand for Drug. If, after approval of the orphan drug certification, the holder cannot assure the availability of sufficient quantities of the drug to the public, the Secretary of Health and Human Services may, during the seven-year exclusivity period, approve another's application for the same orphan drug.

Orphan Drugs and Patents. An orphan drug designation, while not as broadly protective of market exclusivity as patent protection, may, as a practical matter, lengthen the exclusivity granted by a patent if the drug is given orphan drug status late in the life of a patent on the drug.

• *Statutory Reference*: 21 U.S.C. §360cc: "Except as provided in subsection (b) of this section, if the Secretary [of Health and Human Services]—(1) approves an application filed pursuant to section 355 of this title, or (2) issues a certification under section 357 of this title, or (3) issues a license under section 262 of Title 42 for a drug designated under section 360bb of this title for a rare disease or condition, the Secretary may not approve another application under section 355 of this title, issue another certification under section 357 of this title, or issue another license under section 262 of Title 42 for such drug for such disease or condition for a person who is not the holder of such approved application, of such certification, or of such license until the expiration of seven years from the date of the approval of the approved application, the issuance of the certification, or the issuance of the license."

• *Case Reference*: "In expanding the exclusivity provision to cover both patented and unpatented orphan drugs, the [House Committee on Energy and Commerce] noted that the provision would only benefit the sponsors of drugs with less than seven years of product patent protection available, and explained the difference between exclusivity under the Act and traditional patent protection. First, traditional patents generally offer much broader protection than orphan drug exclusivity, which is limited to treatment of a particular disease. ... Second, while the inviolability of a patent is limited only by the holder's ability to enforce his rights in court, orphan drug exclusivity exists only so long as the sponsor adequately supplies the market." *Genentech, Inc. v. Bowen,* 676 F. Supp. 301, 305 (D.D.C. 1987).

overbreadth [patent]
See UNDUE BREADTH.

overclaiming [patent] A now-obsolete reason for rejection or invalidation of a claim of a patent where an improved element in an old combination performs no new function in the old combination. It is also sometimes called the rule of "old combination" or "exhausted combination."

The Lincoln Engineering *Case.* The leading case that adopted this ground of invalidation of a patent was *Lincoln Engineering Co. v. Stewart Warner Corp.,* 303 U.S. 545, 37 USPQ 1 (1938). The Supreme Court held that where the invention was only an improvement in a single element of a combination of old elements, a patent claiming the entire combination was "void as claiming more than the applicant invented." It has been pointed out that characterizing this as "overclaiming" is both "a misnomer and illogical" because a claim to a combination of elements AX + B + C (AX being an improved version of A) is narrower in scope than a claim to the improved element AX alone. 2 D. Chisum, *Patents* §5.04[5][v] (1994 rev.). One does not claim "more" or "too much" by adding limitations to a claim. For this reason, "overclaiming," "old combination," or "exhausted combination" is not a separate ground for rejection of or invalidation of a patent claim to a combination of elements. See *Manual of Patent Examining Procedure* §706.03(j) (1994 rev.). *Lincoln Engineering* is not followed for that reason and also because "Lincoln Engineering was decided more than 20 years [sic] before the present patent code was enacted in 1952." *Radio Steel & Mfg. Co. v. MTD Prods., Inc.,* 731 F.2d 840, 845, 221 USPQ 657, 661 (Fed. Cir. 1984). Presentation of such a claim as a JEPSON CLAIM serves to make clear what is old and what is claimed to be new.

See UNDUE BREADTH.

• *Case References*:

"Many cases have said that the combination claim reciting only one new element with no new result is overclaiming or claiming more than the applicant invented. Such statements are indeed puzzling in view of the fact that the addition of elements to a claim *narrows* its scope and thereby creates a lesser monopoly. Others have said that the combination is not new, or is obvious, if no new coaction or result is obtained. This too is unsound, since it is not the result which is to be patented, but the recited machine, composition, etc." *In re Bernhart & Fetter,* 417 F.2d 1395, 1402, 163 USPQ 611, 618 (CCPA 1969).

"In *In re Bernhart & Fetter* [supra] ... the Court of Customs and Patent Appeals, whose decisions bind us, ... after discussing *Lincoln Engineering,* held that under the present statute the only proper basis for an old combination rejection is 'that portion of section 112 which requires that the claims specifically point out and distinctly claim the invention.' " *Radio Steel & Mfg. Co. v. MTD Prods., Inc.,* 731 F.2d 840, 845, 221 USPQ 657, 661 (Fed. Cir. 1985).

P

package licensing [patent] The license of several patents as a group. Where a patentee owns a "package" of several related patents and a licensee takes a license under all patents in the "package," there is a package license.

Antitrust and Patent Misuse Risks. Only if the licensee takes the package because of the patentee's "coercion" in a nonnegotiable "take all or none" position would package licensing raise the danger of being patent MISUSE or an antitrust violation by a TIE-IN of unwanted patents to the desired patents in the package. This might be accomplished by the patentee's unalterable demand that the same royalty revenue be paid by the licensee regardless of how many or few patents in the package the licensee desired to use. *American Sec. Co. v. Shatterproof Glass Corp.*, 268 F.2d 769, 122 USPQ 167 (3d Cir. 1959). Similarly, charging higher royalties for only some patents rather than for the whole package of patents can amount to coercion to take only the package. *Hazeltine Research, Inc. v. Zenith Radio Corp.*, 388 F.2d 25 (7th Cir. 1967), *aff'd and rev'd in part on other grounds*, 395 U.S. 100 (1969).

Interlocking Patents. Package licensing raises few if any antitrust or misuse risks if the technology cannot practicably be used without infringing all the patents in the package. *International Mfg. Co. v. Landon, Inc.*, 336 F.2d 723, 142 USPQ 421 (9th Cir. 1964).

Total Sales Royalty Base. Similar to package licensing is the situation where the patentee coerces the licensee into taking a license under one or more patents where running royalties are based upon sales of both patented and nonpatented items: a "total sales royalty base." Such conduct can constitute patent misuse. *Zenith Radio Corp. v. Hazeltine Research, Inc.*, 395 U.S. 100, 135, 161 USPQ 577, 591 (1969) ("We

hold that conditioning the grant of a patent license upon payment of royalties on products which do not use the teaching of the patent does amount to patent misuse.").

Block Booking. Patent package licensing is closely analogous to the BLOCK BOOKING of copyrighted motion picture films.

See TIE-IN of patent, MISUSE.

• *Treatise References*: W. Holmes, *Intellectual Property and Antitrust Law* §22 (1994 rev.); ABA, *Antitrust Law Developments* §504 (2d ed. 1984).

palming off [trademark]
See PASSING OFF.

Pan American Trademark Convention
[trademark] A multilateral treaty between the United States and several Latin American nations concerning trademark protection. There are three versions: 1910 (39 Stat. 1675); 1923 (44 Stat. 2494); and 1929 (46 Stat. 2907).

paper example [patent]
See PROPHETIC EXAMPLE.

paper patent [patent] (1) A patent whose invention has not been commercially made or used. (2) A patent whose invention has not yet been actually REDUCED TO PRACTICE.

Narrowing Construction. Some courts have held that where no embodiment of the patented invention has been produced for commercial use, a narrow rather than a broad construction of its claims in determining infringement is appropriate. *Lockwood v. Langendorf Bakeries, Inc.*, 324 F.2d 82, 88, 139 USPQ 220 (9th Cir. 1963); 2 D. Chisum, *Patents* §18.04[2] (1994 rev.). The theory behind this appears to be that

parallel imports

the claims of a "paper patent" are given a narrow range of EQUIVALENTS because the owner has failed to make commercial use of the invention himself, but seeks to exclude others from doing so. *Glendenning v. Mack*, 159 F. Supp. 665, 116 USPQ 249 (D. Minn. 1958).

Weight as Prior Art. Some decisions infer that paper patents have less weight as PRIOR ART. Refuting this view, Judge Learned Hand remarked: "The phrase, 'paper patent,' is a mere bit of rhetoric, usually employed as a makeweight by judges who wish to support the patent in suit, but are embarrassed by a [prior art] reference, of an escape from which they are not too confident. It is a meaningless platitude...." *Frank B. Killian & Co. v. Allied Latex Corp.*, 188 F.2d 942, 944, 89 USPQ 219, 221 (2d Cir. 1951). See 1 D. Chisum, *Patents* §3.06[1][c] (1994 rev.).

Unfinished Inventions. The second definition of "paper patent" was used in the following passage: "As the technology community will attempt to cope with this decision, it perforce will file more 'paper patents': patents on sketchy concepts, before they have been reduced to practice and before the inventor knows whether or how the invention will work, or whether it is worth developing." *UMC Elecs. Co. v. United States*, 816 F.2d 647, 664, 2 USPQ2d 1465, 1478 (Fed. Cir. 1987) (Smith, J. dissenting).

parallel imports [trademark–copyright]
See GRAY MARKET GOODS.

parent application [patent] An inventor's earlier patent application disclosing at least in part the same invention. The same invention might or might not be claimed in the earlier application. The earlier application is referred to as the "parent" if the later application is a CONTINUATION, a CONTINUATION-IN-PART, or a DIVISIONAL APPLICATION.

• *Manual Reference*: "The term 'parent' is applied to an earlier application of an inventor disclosing a given invention. Such invention may or may not be claimed in the first application. Benefit of the filing date of copending parent application may be claimed under 35

U.S.C. §120." *Manual of Patent Examining Procedure* §201.04 (1994 rev.). "Any claim in a continuation-in-part application which is directed *solely* to subject matter adequately disclosed under 35 U.S.C. §112 in the parent application is entitled to the benefit of the filing date of the parent application. However, if a claim in a continuation-in-part application recites a feature which was not disclosed or adequately supported by a proper disclosure under 35 U.S.C. §112 in the parent application, but which was first introduced or adequately supported in the continuation-in-part application, such a claim is entitled only to the filing date of the continuation-in-part application." *Manual of Patent Examining Procedure* §201.11 (1994 rev.).

• *Case References*:
"To consider an application a 'continuing application' means, of course, that it is entitled to the earlier 'parent'—or 'grandparent' etc.—application's filing date in determining what is '*prior* art' from the standpoint of validity. *Racing Strollers Inc. v. TRI Indus. Inc.*, 878 F.2d 1418, 1421 n.*, 11 USPQ2d 1300, 1303 n.* (Fed. Cir. 1989).

"The earlier filing date of the parent application pertains to material in the C-I-P application also disclosed in the prior application. 35 U.S.C. §120.... If matter added through amendment to a C-I-P application is deemed inherent in whatever the original parent application discloses, however, that matter also is entitled to the filing date of the original, parent application." *Litton Sys., Inc. v. Whirlpool Corp.*, 728 F.2d 1423, 1438, 221 USPQ 97, 106 (Fed. Cir. 1984).

"[A] patentee can show he filed a CIP application to disclose improvements developed after the filing date of the parent application rather than to obviate a PTO rejection." *Pennwalt Corp. v. Akzona Inc.*, 740 F.2d 1573, 1579 n.12, 222 USPQ 833, 836 n.12 (Fed. Cir. 1984).

" 'Continuation' and 'divisional' applications are alike in that they are both continuing applications based on the same disclosure as an earlier application. A 'continuation' application claims the same invention claimed in an earlier application, although there may be some vari-

308

ation in the scope of the subject matter claimed. See MPEP §201.07.... A 'CIP' application is a continuing application continuing a portion or all of the disclosure of an earlier application together with added matter not present in that earlier application. See MPEP §201.08. The term 'parent' is often used to refer to the immediately preceding application upon which a continuing application claims priority; the term 'original' is used to refer to the first application in a chain of continuing applications." *Transco Prods. Inc. v. Performance Contracting, Inc.*, 38 F.3d 551, 555–56, 32 USPQ2d 1077, 1080 (Fed. Cir. 1994).

See GRANDPARENT APPLICATION.

Paris Convention [patent–trademark] T h e principal international treaty governing patents, trademarks, and unfair competition. The Paris Convention for the Protection of Industrial Property, whose members form the "Paris Union," has more adherent nations (over 110 nations, including the United States) than any other treaty dealing with intellectual property rights. The World Intellectual Property Organization (WIPO) serves as the administering agency for the activities of the Paris Union.

Main Points of Treaty. The four main provisions reflected in the Paris Convention are:

(1) National treatment. Each member nation promises to give the same protection to foreigners who are citizens of Paris Convention member nations as it gives to its own citizens.

(2) Minimum level of protection. Each member nation promises to give at least a defined level of protection for certain rights, such as requiring effective protection against acts of unfair competition.

(3) Convention priority. On the basis of an application for patent, trademark, or design registration in a member nation, the applicant may within a specified time (6 months for trademarks, 12 months for patents) apply for protection in other member nations, with the later applications given priority as of the date of the first filing.

(4) Administrative framework. In creating a "Union," the Paris Convention creates a legal entity in international law with the responsibility to carry out certain tasks. The Paris Union

has three administrative bodies: the Assembly of all member nations; the Executive Committee elected by the Assembly; and the International Bureau of the World Intellectual Property Organization, headed by the Director General of WIPO.

Dates of Revisions. The Paris Convention was originally enacted in 1883. It subsequently was revised in Brussels (1900); Washington (1911); The Hague (1925); London (1934); Lisbon (1958); and Stockholm (1967). Four revision conferences were held in the 1980s: three in Geneva in 1980, 1982, and 1984, and one in Nairobi in 1981. These more recent conferences did not result in agreement on revisions.

GATT TRIPS Incorporates the Paris Convention. Article 2 of the 1993 GATT TRIPS agreement requires each WTO member country to abide by the substantive obligations of the Paris Convention and the BERNE CONVENTION. The ideas underlying TRIPS are that all GATT member nations should have minimum levels of protection for all forms of intellectual property and each nation should have effective and appropriate enforcement mechanisms, both internally and at the border, sufficient to make ownership of an intellectual property right meaningful in an economic sense. GATT TRIPS was implemented in the United States in the 1994 URUGUAY ROUND AGREEMENTS ACT.

• *References*: S. Ladas, *Patents, Trademarks and Related Rights: National and International Protection* (1975); Bodenhausen, *Guide to Paris Convention for the Protection of Industrial Property* (1968); WIPO, *Background Reading Material on Intellectual Property* 50 (1988). Information on the Paris Convention may be obtained from the World Intellectual Property Organization (WIPO), 34 Chemin des Colombettes, 1211 Geneva, Switzerland.

See CONVENTION DATE.

passing off [trademark] (1) The substitution of one brand of goods when another brand is ordered. (2) Trademark infringement where the infringer intentionally meant to mislead or deceive purchasers. (3) Trademark infringement where there is no proof of intent to deceive but likelihood of confusion is proven, that is, a synonym for run-of-the-mill trademark infringement. (4) In British-law countries, acts illegal under the common law, apart from registered "trademark" law, and consisting of the misrepresentation that the defendant's goods or services are those of a competitor, usually by way of using a similar mark.

Synonym: palming off.

Product Substitution. Passing off or palming off is often used to denote product substitution where the seller knowingly substitutes brand A in response to an order by the customer for brand X. This is illustrated in the many cases in which a restaurant's substitution of another brand of beverage in response to an order for COKE or COCA-COLA has been held to be illegal passing off or palming off. E.g., *Coca-Cola Co. v. Overland, Inc.*, 692 F.2d 1250, 216 USPQ 579 (9th Cir. 1982).

Ordinary Trademark Infringement. Passing off or palming off is often used as rhetorical hyperbole to refer to a case of ordinary trademark infringement, whether or not intent to deceive is involved.

British Law. In the nineteenth century, British common law developed an offshoot of the tort of fraud and deceit and called it "passing off" or "palming off." In the United States, this rule developed into the modern claim for trademark infringement, whether of a registered mark under federal law or of an unregistered mark under either federal or state law. In the United Kingdom, the jurisprudence took a different path, developing into two separate bodies of law, one called "trademark" law and restricted to infringement of registered marks, the other called "passing off" and restricted to common law liability for unregistered marks and trade dress. See W.R. Cornish, *Intellectual Property* 473 (1981).

Types of Passing Off. Passing off has been divided into four types: express, implied, regular, and reverse. Borchard, *Reverse Passing Off: Commercial Robbery or Permissible Competition?* 67 Trademark Rep. 1 (1977). Regular "express passing off" is defined as the classic form of trademark infringement, i.e., the infringer selling its own goods with a mark confusingly similar to that of the senior user. Regular "implied passing off" occurs when a company uses a picture or sample of its competitor's product, impliedly and falsely representing that its product is the competitor's product. Regular "implied passing off" has been held to be a form of false advertising in violation of Lanham Act §43(a). E.g., *Sublime Prods., Inc. v. Gerber Prods., Inc.*, 579 F. Supp. 248, 223 USPQ 383 (S.D.N.Y. 1984). For a description of the "reverse" versions of passing off, see REVERSE PASSING OFF.

Treatise Reference: J.T. McCarthy, *Trademarks and Unfair Competition* §25.01 (3d ed. 1995 rev.).

passive carrier [copyright] One who only provides cables or communications facilities for the use of others in the retransmission by cable, radio, or satellite of a copyrighted broadcast and who has no direct or indirect control over the content or selection of the main broadcast or over the recipients of the secondary transmission. These "passive carriers," such as long-distance carriers like AT&T, are exempt from copyright infringement liability under 17 U.S.C. §111(a)(3).

Most case law regarding the passive carrier exemption concerns the possible liability of intermediaries who relay signals from local television stations via satellite to the many local cable television systems across the nation. To come within the exemption, the party who provides the retransmission facilities cannot control: (1) the content of the primary broadcast; (2) the selection of the primary broadcast; and (3) the recipients of the secondary broadcast. Since a cable system usually selects both the primary broadcast and the recipients, a cable system does not generally fall within the exemption.

• *Treatise References*: 1 P. Goldstein, *Copyright* §5.8.2.c (1989); 3 *Nimmer on Copyright* §12.04[B][3] (1994 rev.); W. Patry, *Copyright Law and Practice* 947 (1994).

• *Statutory Reference*: 17 U.S.C. §111: "(a) The secondary transmission of a primary transmission embodying a performance or display of a work is not an infringement if— ... (3) the secondary transmission is made by any carrier who has no direct or indirect control over the content or selection of the primary transmission or over the particular recipients of the secondary transmission, and whose activities with respect to the secondary transmission consist solely of providing wires, cables, or other communications channels for the use of others: Provided, That the provisions of this clause extend only to the activities of said carrier with respect to secondary transmissions and do not exempt from liability the activities of others with respect to their own primary or secondary transmissions.... "

• *Case Reference*: "The [passive carrier] exemption thus allows carriers such as United Video to act as purely passive intermediaries between broadcasters and the cable systems that carry the broadcast signals into the home, without incurring any copyright liability. The cable system selects the signals it wants to retransmit, pays the copyright owners for the right to retransmit their programs, and pays the intermediate carrier a fee for getting the signals from the broadcast station to the cable system. The intermediate carrier pays the copyright owners nothing, provided it really is passive in relation to what it transmits, like a telephone company." *WGN Continental Broadcasting Co. v. United Video Inc.*, 693 F.2d 622, 624, 216 USPQ 97, 99 (7th Cir. 1982).

patent [patent] A grant by the federal government to an inventor of the right to exclude others from making, using, or selling the invention. After Jan. 1, 1996, the exclusive rights include offering to sell in the United States and importing into the United States. There are three very different kinds of patent in the United States: (1) a utility patent on the functional aspects of products and processes; (2) a DESIGN PATENT on the ornamental design of useful objects; and (3) a PLANT PATENT on a new variety of living plant. Thus, each type of patent confers the right to exclude others from a precisely defined scope of either technology, industrial design, or plant variety. Patents do not protect "ideas"—only structures and methods that apply technological concepts. *Jones v. Hardy*, 727 F.2d 1524, 1528, 220 USPQ 1021, 1026 (Fed. Cir. 1984).

The Source, Theory, and History of U.S. Patents: The U.S. patent statutes are passed by the U.S. Congress under a specific grant of power contained in the Patent and Copyright Clause of the federal CONSTITUTION. The patent system not only provides an economic incentive to inventors, but also provides an incentive to investors to invest risk capital in inventive activity—a very high-risk enterprise in which failure is more common than success. The first U.S. patent statute was enacted into law in 1790. Major revisions of the patent laws were made in the nineteenth century in 1836 and 1870. The last major revision was made in the 1952 Patent Code, which came into effect January 1, 1953. In 1975, the name of the Patent Office was changed to the Patent and Trademark Office. In 1991, U.S. Patent No. 5,000,000 was granted.

A Patent Analogized to a Contract. A patent may be analogized to a bargain between the inventor and the government. In return for a limited-term exclusive right over the technology defined in the patent CLAIMS, the inventor discloses in the patent specification information about the new technology of the invention. Without a patent system, commercial secrecy would be the inventor's only way to prevent imitators from taking a "free ride" on the hard work of the inventor. To fulfill his or her end of the patent bargain, the inventor must fully describe the invention in such detail as to enable those SKILLED IN THE ART to make and use the invention (see ENABLEMENT). The inventor must also disclose the BEST MODE known to the inventor of carrying out the invention.

The Nature of the "Bargain". In return for receiving the right to exclude, which is the gist of a patent, the inventor must give up secrecy and fully disclose the details of the invention to the public. This will enable others to understand the invention and be able to use it as a stepping stone to further develop the technology. Also, once the patent expires, the public is entitled to make and use the invention and is entitled to a full and complete disclosure of how to do so.

Parts of a Patent. Reflecting the bargain analogy, a patent has essentially two parts: the SPECIFICATION and the CLAIMS. In the specification, the inventor discloses the invention in detail through a description in words and drawings. In the claims, the inventor sets the bounds of the technology within which the patent owner has the legal right to exclude others from making, using, and selling.

Patent Infringement. It is the CLAIMS of a utility patent that define the scope of the patentee's right to exclude others from making, using, or selling products or processes that use the invention spelled out in the claims. The traditional trilogy of exclusive rights of a patent (make, use, or sell) was expanded by the 1994 URUGUAY ROUND AGREEMENTS ACT to include offering for sale and importation into the United States. The test of infringement of a utility patent is whether a claim READS ON the ACCUSED DEVICE. Infringement can be either by the rule of LITERAL INFRINGEMENT of the claims or by application of the doctrine of EQUIVALENTS. There are two types of claims: PRODUCT CLAIMS and PROCESS CLAIMS. The standard remedy for patent infringement is an injunction and damages, which are usually measured by either a reasonable royalty or LOST PROFITS.

See ROYALTY, REASONABLE.

Claim Construction Is for the Judge, Not the Jury. The Federal Circuit has held that construing the meaning of language in a patent claim is solely a question of law to be determined by a judge. It is not a question of fact for a jury. "[C]ompetitors should be able to rest assured, if infringement litigation occurs, that a judge, trained in the law, will similarly analyze the text of the patent and its associated public record and apply the established rules of construction, and in that way arrive at the true and consistent scope of the patent owner's rights to be given legal effect.... We therefore settle inconsistencies in our precedent and hold that in a case tried to a jury, the court has the power and obligation to construe as a matter of law the meaning of language used in the patent claim." *Markman v. Westview Instruments, Inc.*, 52 F.3d 967, 979, 34 USPQ2d 1321, 1329 (Fed. Cir. 1995).

A Patent Is Not a Grant of a Right to Use. Contrary to popular belief, a patent is not a grant of a right to use the patented technology. Rather, it is a grant of a right to exclude others from using the technology defined in the patent claims. The patentee itself might not be able to use the technology of the patent because it is merely an improvement upon technology previously patented by another. In that event, a license from the previous patentee is needed. "A patent is not the grant of a right to make or use or sell. It does not, directly or indirectly, imply any such right. It grants only the right to exclude others." *Herman v. Youngstown Car Mfg. Co.*, 191 F. 579, 584 (6th Cir. 1911), quoted with approval in *Atlas Powder Co. v. E.I. du Pont de Nemours & Co.*, 750 F.2d 1569, 1580, 224 USPQ 409, 417 (Fed. Cir. 1984) (owner of improvement patent can be liable for infringing upon the claims of basic patent). See *Spindelfabrik Suessen-Schurr GmbH v. Schubert & Salzer AG*, 829 F.2d 1075, 1081, 4 USPQ2d 1044, 1048 (Fed. Cir. 1987) (patentee is not given the right to use patented technology: "His right is merely one to exclude others from making, using or selling."); *In re Bergy*, 596 F.2d 952, 1081 n.3, 201 USPQ 352, 359 n.3 (C.C.P.A. 1979), *dismissed as moot*, 444 U.S. 924 (1980) ("The patent grant never has had anything to do with the patentee's right to make, use or vend."); *Animal Legal Defense Fund v. Quigg*, 932 F.2d 920, 935, 18 USPQ2d 1677, 1689 (Fed. Cir. 1991) ("It should hardly need saying that the issuance of a patent gives no right to make, use or sell a patented invention."); *Rolls-Royce Ltd. v. GTE Caleron Corp.*, 800 F.2d 1101, 1110 n.9, 231 USPQ 185, 191 n.9 (Fed. Cir. 1986) ("[T]hat someone has a patent right to exclude others from making the invention claimed in his patent does not mean that his invention cannot infringe claims of another's patent broad enough to encompass, i.e., to 'dominate,' his invention.").

Presumption of Validity. A patent is presumed to be valid. See PRESUMPTION OF PATENT VALIDITY. But the validity of a patent can always be challenged in litigation. However, if the challenge is not successful, it is not appropriate for a court to declare the patent "valid." Rather, the court simply declares that this challenger did not carry its burden of overcoming the presumption. "Thereupon, the patent simply remains valid until another challenger carries the [statutory] burden [of proof]." *Panduit Corp. v. Dennison Mfg. Co.*, 810 F.2d 1561, 1570, 1 USPQ2d 1593, 1598 (Fed. Cir. 1987).

Novelty and Nonobviousness. To be deserving of a valid patent, the invented technology defined in the patent claims must meet the two key tests of "newness": (1) the test of "novelty," meaning that it is not anticipated by being identical to technology disclosed in a single piece of PRIOR ART as defined in Patent Code §102 (see ANTICIPATION); and (2) the test of NONOBVIOUSNESS, meaning that the technology, although new, must be different enough that it is not OBVIOUS in view of the prior art. COMPUTER PROGRAMS and BIOTECHNOLOGY present special problems of protection. Under U.S. law, inventors are given a one-year GRACE PERIOD after commercializing the invention within which the inventor can decide whether or not to file a patent application.

Selling and Licensing Patents. Patents can be assigned outright or licensed, whether by exclusive or nonexclusive license (see ASSIGNMENT, LICENSE). Patent licenses must comply with the antitrust laws, usually by using the patent RULE OF REASON. Certain types of patent license transactions, such as PACKAGE LICENSING or FIELD OF USE RESTRICTIONS, are subject to abuse and might raise patent MISUSE concerns.

The Federal-State Relationship. It is clear that the states cannot grant protection that would conflict with the goals of the federal patent statutes. Thus, "the States may not offer patent-like protection to intellectual creations which would otherwise remain unprotected as a matter of federal law." *Bonito Boats Inc. v. Thunder Craft Boats Inc.,* 489 U.S. 141, 156, 9 USPQ2d 1847, 1854 (1989) (state law that prevents copying by making a mold directly from a product such as a boat hull held preempted by federal patent law). However, state law, such as TRADE SECRET protection, will be upheld if it can coexist and not conflict with the federal policies of encouraging patentable inventions and the prompt disclosure of innovations. *Kewanee Oil Co. v. Bicron Corp.,* 416 U.S. 470, 181 USPQ 673 (1974).

Duration of a Patent. Prior to 1995, a U.S. patent on an invention had a duration of 17 years from the grant of the patent. As a result of the URUGUAY ROUND AGREEMENTS ACT, U.S. law was changed effective June 8, 1995, to adopt a patent term of 20 years from the filing of the patent application. 35 U.S.C. §154(a). All U.S. patents that were in force on June 8, 1995, or

that issued on an application filed before June 8, 1995, automatically have a term that is the greater of the 20-year term or 17 years from grant. However, MAINTENANCE FEES must be timely paid at three points during the duration of the patent grant in order to keep the patent alive. Design patents have a 14-year term from grant. Under certain circumstances a patent term may be extended.

See DURATION.

International Relations. The United States, as a signatory of the PARIS CONVENTION, is a member of the premier international patent treaty organization, the Paris Union. A person applying for a patent in the United States can be entitled to a convention priority filing date based on the filing of an application for the same invention in a qualified foreign country within the preceding 12 months. That is, the U.S. application is treated as if it were filed on the same day that the qualified foreign application was filed abroad. This provision of the Paris Convention is implemented in the United States by Patent Code §119, 35 U.S.C. §119. See CONVENTION DATE. The United States is also a signatory of the PATENT COOPERATION TREATY (PCT), a multilateral treaty that eliminates some of the duplication connected with obtaining patent protection for the same invention in several nations. With the PCT, it is possible to file a single international application, which has the same effect as filing separate applications in each PCT nation the inventor designates in the international application. See PATENT COOPERATION TREATY. The United States is a party to the GATT trade-related Intellectual Property (TRIPS) agreement. Legislation implementing changes required by GATT TRIPS was called the URUGUAY ROUND AGREEMENTS ACT and enacted on December 8, 1994. It and the accompanying WTO (World Trade Organization) Agreement became effective in the United States on January 1, 1995. The United States is also a signatory to other patent-related treaties. See BUDAPEST TREATY, CONVENTION OF UNION FOR NEW PLANT VARIETIES.

See DURATION, INFRINGEMENT, NOVELTY, OBVIOUSNESS, PARIS CONVENTION, TRIPS.

Treatise References: D. Chisum, *Patents* (1994 rev.); R. Harmon, *Patents and the Fed-*

eral Circuit §15.2 (3d ed. 1994); P. Rosenberg, *Patent Law Fundamentals* (1994 rev.).

- *Case References*:

"First, patent law seeks to foster and reward invention; second, it promotes disclosure of inventions, to stimulate further innovation and to permit the public to practice the invention once the patent expires; third, the stringent requirements for patent protection seek to assure that ideas in the public domain remain there for the free use of the public." *Aronson v. Quick Point Pencil Co.*, 440 U.S. 257, 262, 201 USPQ 1, 4 (1979).

"The stated objective of the Constitution in granting the power to Congress to legislate in the area of intellectual property is to 'promote the Progress of Science and useful Arts.' The patent laws promote this progress by offering a right of exclusion for a limited period as an incentive for inventors to risk the often enormous costs in terms of time, research and development.... When a patent is granted and the information contained in it are circulated to the general public and those especially skilled in the trade, such additions to the general store of knowledge are of such importance that the Federal Government is willing to pay the high price of 17 years of exclusive use for its disclosure, which disclosure, it is assumed will stimulate ideas and the eventual development of further significant advances in the art." *Kewanee Oil Co. v. Bicron Corp.*, 416 U.S. 470, 480, 181 USPQ 673, 678 (1974).

"The federal patent system thus embodies a carefully crafted bargain for encouraging the creation and disclosure of new, useful and nonobvious advances in technology and design in return for the exclusive right to practice the invention for a period of years. ... [The inventor] may keep his invention secret and reap its fruits indefinitely. In consideration of its disclosure and the consequent benefit to the community, the patent is granted.... The attractiveness of such a bargain, and its effectiveness in inducing creative effort and disclosure of the results of that effort, depend almost entirely on a backdrop of free competition in the exploitation of unpatented designs and innovations.... To a limited extent, the federal patent laws must

determine not only what is protected, but also what is free for all to use." *Bonito Boats Inc. v. Thunder Craft Boats Inc.*, 489 U.S. 141, 150–51, 9 USPQ2d 1847, 1852 (1989).

"The patent document which grants the patentee a right to exclude others and hence bestows on the owner the power to license, consists of two primary parts: (1) a written description of the invention, which may ... include drawings, called the 'specification,' enabling those skilled in the art to practice the invention, and (2) claims which define or delimit the scope of the legal protection which the government grant gives the patent owner, the patent 'monopoly.' " *General Foods Corp. v. Studiengesellschaft Kohle mbH*, 972 F.2d 1272, 1274, 23 USPQ2d 1839, 1840 (Fed. Cir. 1992) (Rich, J.).

- *Commentary References*:

"The patent system ... added the fuel of interest to the fire of genius." Abraham Lincoln, *Lecture on "Discoveries, Inventions and Improvements,"* Feb. 22, 1860.

"The basic rationale of the patent system can be simply put. The economic case rests upon two propositions: first, that we should have more invention and innovation than our economic system would provide in the absence of special inducement; and second, that the granting of a statutory monopoly to inventors for a period of years is the best method of providing such special inducement." Turner, *The Patent System and Competitive Policy*, 44 N.Y.U. L. Rev. 450, 450–51 (1969).

patent annuity [patent]

See MAINTENANCE FEES.

Patent Cooperation Treaty [patent]

A multilateral treaty that became effective in 1978 and is administered by the World Intellectual Property Organization (WIPO).

The treaty is an option that facilitates the filing of parallel patent applications on the same invention in several nations. The common abbreviation is PCT.

Overview of the PCT. This treaty provides for the filing and processing of a patent application in one of the many "receiving offices" during the "international phase" of the patent application. After international phase processing, the application is sent to national or regional patent offices of PCT member nations for prosecution of the application under the law of each nation through to a national patent. A regional patent office is one such as the European Patent Office. The PCT application procedure has become more common as the number of member nations has increased. As of January 1, 1995, there were more than 70 nations that adhered to the treaty. The PCT neither creates an "international patent" nor changes the substantive requirements of patentability in the United States or in any other PCT nation.

International Phase. The PCT international phase can be viewed as a bridge between an applicant's home country application and the handling of the applicant's corresponding applications in nations that are members of the PCT. Under practice prior to the PCT, applicants would file several applications corresponding to their home country application separately and directly in each nation in which a patent was desired. Typically, this required a translation of the application and payment of filing fees in each country before the inventor had the results of an examination by the patent office in the inventor's home country. As a result, direct foreign filings often resulted in substantial costs even before the inventor had an evaluation of a patent office's view of the patentability of the invention and perhaps before the inventor had determined if the invention had economic value in the marketplace.

International Phase Procedures. During the international phase of the PCT application, the inventor can file a single application in a nearby "receiving office," usually without the need for a translation. For example, U.S. inventors can file their PCT applications in English at the U.S. Patent and Trademark Office, which is a designated PCT "receiving office." During this phase, the application is subjected to a patentability search of the prior art which can provide guidance to the inventor as to whether it will be worthwhile to further pursue patents in other nations. An optional final step in the international phase is an international examination of the claims in light of prior art identified in the search. This is an option for U.S.-based applicants as well as applicants whose home country is a party to the International Preliminary Examination portion of the PCT treaty.

Deferral of Time for Separate Processing in Each Nation. The international phase can extend up to two-and-one-half years from the date on which the original home country application was filed. During this period, translations and payment of national or regional patent office fees are deferred. This gives the applicant the opportunity to more fully evaluate the value of foreign applications.

Publication. Since one object of the PCT is early circulation of technical data in patent applications, PCT applications are published by WIPO 18 months after the date of the home country filing on which the PCT application is based.

National Stage. Any determination of the patentability (or lack of it) during the international phase is not binding on national or regional patent offices. These national or regional patent offices will evaluate independently the patentability of each application after the case passes from the PCT international phase to the national phase. However, rewording of the claims is permitted during the PCT international phase and may expedite national phase prosecution.

Adherents to the PCT. PCT can be used for most major nations, including the United States, Japan, Canada, and most western European nations. While more than 70 nations are members of the PCT, direct filings of patent applications must still be made in nations that are not members. Examples include India, Israel, and many African (e.g., South Africa) and South American nations, such as Brazil, Colombia, and Venezuela.

- *Treatise References*:

See 3 D. Chisum, *Patents* §14.02[4] (1994 rev.).

"The PCT assists the applicant in several ways. First of all, questions as to formalities are generally resolved in a single application filed with an Office which is convenient to him since usually this is his own national [Patent] Office. The international search report enables the applicant to have a clear picture whether it is likely that he will be able to obtain a patent and, therefore, whether it is worthwhile continuing with his application in the various countries which he has named in it. The international preliminary examination report gives the applicant an even better picture. Also, since amendments may be required during the preliminary examination, the scope of the protection which is sought better reflects the invention made by the applicant." WIPO, *Background Reading Material on Intellectual Property* 116 (1988).

Patent Depository Library [patent]

Sixty-two public, academic, and special-purpose libraries, located in 40 states, which maintain collections of U.S. patents received under the provisions of 35 U.S.C. §13. Most of these patent libraries maintain patents in numerical sequence and are more difficult to search by subject matter than is the main patent library at the U.S. Patent and Trademark Office in Crystal City, Virginia, near Washington, D.C.

Patent Harmonization Treaty [patent]

See HARMONIZATION.

patentee [patent]

The inventor to whom the patent was granted, and all persons to whom the patent is subsequently assigned. The Patent Act of 1952 provides that a suit for infringement may be brought by "a patentee." 35 U.S.C. §281. Similar to the use of the word "owner" in real estate law, each subsequent person who owns the patent succeeds to the title "patentee."

If the recipient and owner of the patent is the "patentee," it necessarily follows that it is the Patent and Trademark Office and the U.S. government that is the "patentor": the grantor of the exclusive rights in the patent. However, the word "patentor" is never commonly used.

See ASSIGNMENT, LICENSE.

• *Statutory Reference*: 35 U.S.C. §100: "(d) The word 'patentee' includes not only the patentee to whom the patent was issued but also the successor in title to the patentee."

patent marking [patent]

See MARKING OF PATENT, MISMARKING.

patent pending [patent]

A phrase often marked on products, indicating that a patent application is pending with claims that cover the marked product.

Purpose of the Warning. While there is no legal right to exclude until the patent is actually granted, the "patent pending" legend is used to warn potential imitators that a patent may soon issue. While the potential imitator of the product may legally copy under patent law until the date when the patent is granted, the unpredictability of when that might occur (or if at all) and how broad the patent claims might be is often sufficient to dampen the enthusiasm of the potential imitator and its investors.

Patents Do Not "Pend." Strictly speaking, the term "patent pending" is meaningless, for what is really meant is that an "application for patent is pending," because "[p]atents are never pending." *Arcadia Mach. & Tool Inc. v. Sturm, Ruger & Co.*, 786 F.2d 1124, 1125, 229 USPQ 124, 125 (Fed. Cir. 1986).

Mismarking. A false use of the "patent pending" legend is MISMARKING, which is specifically prohibited by 35 U.S.C. §292. It has been held that mismarking by using "patent pending" before an application was filed is "no justification for invalidating the patent upon its subsequent issuance." *Republic Molding Corp. v. B.W. Photo Utils.*, 319 F.2d 347, 351, 138 USPQ 101, 104 (9th Cir. 1963).

See MISMARKING.

• *Statutory Reference*: 35 U.S.C. §292(a), third paragraph: " Whoever marks upon, or affixes to, or uses in advertising in connection with any article, the words 'patent applied for,' 'patent pending,' or any word importing that an application for patent has been made, when no application for patent has been made, or if made, is not pending, for the purpose of deceiving the public—shall be fined not more than $500 for every such offense."

• *Case Reference:* Marking a product with a "patent pending" notice does not furnish a basis for finding a later infringement to be "willful." "To willfully infringe *a patent*, the patent must exist and one must have knowledge of it. A 'patent pending' notice gives one no knowledge whatsoever. It is nor even a guarantee that an application has been filed. Filing an application is no guarantee any patent will issue and a very substantial percentage of applications never result in patents. What the scope of claims in patents that do issue will be is something totally unforeseeable." *State Indus., Inc. v. A.O. Smith Corp.*, 751 F.2d 1226, 1236, 224 USPQ 418, 425 (Fed. Cir. 1985).

patent pool [patent] An interchange of patent rights by several companies. Either one or more of the patent owners, or some separate entity, has the right to license others under the pooled patents. Pools are competitively beneficial in that they may help resolve patent conflicts, make the assembled patents in the pool available to others, or resolve disputes over BLOCK-ING PATENTS. On the other hand, a patent pool is a horizontal agreement among competitors and carries the potential for abuse and as a cover for an anticompetitive cartel.

Antitrust Risks. In *Standard Oil Co. v. United States*, 283 U.S. 163 (1931), the Supreme Court applied the RULE OF REASON and found a pool of gasoline-refining patents to be reasonable and legal. A Canadian patent pool formed to prevent the export from the United States into Canada of radio and television sets was held illegal in *Zenith Radio Corp. v. Hazeltine Research, Inc.*, 395 U.S. 100, 114 (1969). Two of the best-known large patent pools are those of the automobile manufacturers and the aircraft manufacturers. See Caplan, *Patent Pools*, 2 APLA J. 81 (1974).

• *Treatise References*: ABA, *Antitrust Law Developments* 514 (2d ed. 1984); 1 H. Einhorn, *Patent Licensing Transactions* §7.09[1] (1994 rev.); W. Holmes, *Intellectual Property and Antitrust Law,* §14.01 et seq. (1994 rev.).

PCT [patent–international]
See PATENT COOPERATION TREATY.

performance [copyright] To recite, render, play, dance, or act a copyrighted work, including the broadcast by radio or television of a performance and the reception of such a broadcast.

The exclusive right to "perform the copyright work publicly" is granted to all types of copyrighted works except for pictorial and sculptural works and SOUND RECORDINGS. 17 U.S.C. §106(4).

What Is a "Performance"? According to copyright law, there are many ways to "perform" a work. While some of these ways are obvious, others cannot be intuitively arrived at and must be explained. Among the obvious ways to "perform" a work are: singing a song, reading a lecture aloud, acting a play from a script, and transmitting a radio or television broadcast by a station, cable system, or satellite retransmission. Among the less obvious ways to "perform" a work are: playing a compact disc in a playing machine, playing a video cassette in a VCR machine, and turning on a radio or television set. Many people find the last example perplexing, but there is no doubt that simply turning on a normal radio or television set does constitute a "performance" of those works broadcast over the air or by cable. Rep. No. 94-1476, 94th Cong., 2d Sess. 63 (1976). And if the radio or television set is turned on in a public place, that constitutes a public performance of copyrighted works which are broadcast.

"Public" Performance. The copyright owner does not have an exclusive right to make all performances of the work: only "public" performances. A performance is public if it takes place either (1) at a place open to the public; or (2) at a place not open to the public if a substantial number of persons is gathered, except for a normal circle of a family and its social acquaintances. Further, the transmission or broadcast of a performance over the air is public even if the person listening is alone in his or her own home. Assuming that the song "Happy Birthday" is still in copyright, singing it at a gathering of relatives and friends in a private home is not performing the song publicly. But if a musical group sings "Happy Birthday" to a patron in a public restaurant, that is a public performance. If a hotel rents video tapes to guests to view in their rooms, the viewing by a guest is not a public performance because hotel rooms, once engaged, are not "public." "While the hotel may indeed be 'open to the public,' a guest's room, once rented, is not."

Columbia Pictures Indus., Inc. v. Professional Real Estate Inv., Inc., 866 F.2d 278, 281, 9 USPQ2d 1653, 1655 (9th Cir. 1989).

The Doctrine of Multiple Performances. Under the doctrine of multiple performances, a single rendition of a work can be "performed" more than once as it is broadcast via radio or television and then either received and communicated by a normal receiving set or retransmitted by sophisticated cable and satellite systems. In 1931 the Supreme Court rejected the argument that when a radio station broadcasts the playing of copyrighted music from a phonograph record, there is only one performance and one potential liability for copyright infringement, and that is by the radio station. *Buck v. Jewell-LaSalle Realty Co.*, 283 U.S. 191, 9 USPQ 17 (1931). The Supreme Court recognized that there can be multiple performances at one time and that the LaSalle hotel, which had a master radio-receiving set that piped a radio broadcast into the private and public rooms of the hotel, was also making a "performance" of the work. However, in its later cable television decisions, the Supreme Court held that cable television systems were not "performing" by retransmitting television signals. *Fortnightly Corp. v. United Artists Television, Inc.*, 392 U.S. 390, 158 USPQ 1 (1968); *Teleprompter Corp. v. Columbia Broadcasting Sys. Inc.*, 415 U.S. 394, 181 USPQ 65 (1974). And in 1975 the Supreme Court held that reception of a radio broadcast in a small retail store was not a performance. *Twentieth Century Music Corp. v. Aiken*, 422 U.S. 151, 186 USPQ 65 (1975). While the doctrine of multiple performances "was for all practical purposes dead" prior to 1978, the 1978 Copyright Act revisions "revived" it in several provisions, such as those relating to "secondary transmissions." 2 *Nimmer on Copyright* §8.18[A] (1994 rev.). See TRANSMISSION.

"Performance," "Communication," and "Secondary Transmission." When one turns on an ordinary radio or television receiver in a public place, there is a "performance," which may or may not be exempt under 17 U.S.C. §110(5) (see exemption 5 below), but it is not a SECONDARY TRANSMISSION under 17 U.S.C. §111. This is because there is no "further trans-

mitting" of the broadcast. According to the Copyright Act, upon turning on the receiver, there is a "communication of a transmission" but not a "secondary transmission." As Nimmer has observed, "while every transmission involves a communication, not every communication involves a transmission." 2 *Nimmer on Copyright* §8.18[C][2] (1994 rev.).

Statutory Exceptions to the Performance Right. Copyright Act §110 defines 10 exceptions or defenses to conduct that would otherwise be an infringement of the exclusive right of public performance.

(1) *The Classroom Exemption.* Face-to-face teaching activities are exempt, such as performance of a play in a classroom.

(2) *The Instructional Broadcasting Exemption.* Certain instructional broadcasting is exempt, such as playing musical works in connection with transmissions made primarily for reception in classrooms.

(3) *The Religious Services Exemption.* Sacred music performed at a religious service is exempt, such as the performance of a musical setting of the mass or the singing of a hymn at a religious service.

(4) *The Nonprofit Exemption.* The public performance of nondramatic literary works and musical works is exempt if there is no profit motive (no purpose of direct or indirect commercial advantage), no payment to performers, and no admission charge, unless it is a charity benefit, in which case there can be an admission charge if the proceeds go to a genuine charitable cause and the copyright owner does not object. Note that this does *not* exempt nonprofit performances of stage plays and other dramatic works.

(5) *The Store Receiver Exemption.* Sometimes called the "*Aiken Chicken Shop*" exemption, 17 U.S.C. §110(5) is designed to codify the exemption created by the Supreme Court for a small retail establishment that plays an ordinary radio or television receiver for its patrons and employees. In that case, the owner of Aiken's Chicken Shop, a small restaurant in Pittsburgh with a floor area of 1,055 square feet, 620 square feet open to the public, used an ordinary FM radio receiver with four ceiling-mounted speakers to play music from WKJF-FM for the

enjoyment of its patrons. The Supreme Court held that this was not an infringing performance of copyrighted music broadcast over the station. *Twentieth Century Music Corp. v. Aiken*, 422 U.S. 151, 186 USPQ 65 (1975). Congress, in enacting the §110(5) exemption, stated that the factual situation in the *Aiken* case is intended to "represent the outer limit of the exemption and believes that the line should be drawn at that point." Rep. No. 94-1476, 94th Cong., 2d Sess. 87 (1976). Neither larger retail establishments nor places that use receiving apparatus of a kind not commonly used in private homes will usually fall within the *Aiken* exemption. E.g., *National Football League v. McBee & Bruno's, Inc.*, 792 F.2d 726, 731, 230 USPQ 30, 34 (8th Cir. 1986) (reception of television programs in a bar via a satellite dish not within exemption because satellite dishes were not "commonly found in private homes"). See AIKEN EXEMPTION.

(6) *The State Fair Exemption.* The performance of musical works at agricultural fairs or exhibitions is exempt.

(7) *The Record Store Exemption.* The performance of records to promote sales at a retail record store open to the public is exempt.

(8) and (9) *Handicapped Exemptions.* Certain nonprofit transmissions for handicapped persons are exempt.

(10) *The Fraternal Organization Exemption.* The performance of nondramatic literary and musical works at private charitable fundraising functions of veterans' and fraternal organizations is exempt.

See TRANSMISSION.

• *Treatise References*: 2 *Nimmer on Copyright* §§8.14–.15 (1994 rev.).; 1 P. Goldstein, *Copyright* §§5.7–.8 (1989); M. Leaffer, *Understanding Copyright* §8.15 et seq. (1989); 1 N. Boorstyn, *Copyright* §6.25 et seq. (2d ed. 1994); W. Patry, *Copyright Law and Practice* 875 et seq. (1994).

• *Statutory Reference*:

17 U.S.C. §101: "To 'perform' a work means to recite, render, play, dance, or act it, either directly or by means of any device or process, or, in the case of a motion picture or other audiovisual work, to show its images in any sequence or to make the sounds accompanying it audible."

17 U.S.C. §101:

To perform or display a work "publicly" means

(1) to perform or display it at a place open to the public or at any place where a substantial number of persons outside of a normal circle of a family and its social acquaintances is gathered; or

(2) to transmit or otherwise communicate a performance or display of the work to a place specified by clause (1) to the public, by means of any device or process, whether the members of the public capable of receiving the performance or display receive it in the same place or in separate places and at the same time or at different times.

• *Legislative History*: "One of the principal purposes of the definition [of public performance] was to make clear that ... performances in 'semipublic' places such as clubs, lodges, factories, summer camps, and schools are 'public performances' subject to copyright control. The term 'a family' in this context would include an individual living alone, so that a gathering confined to the individual's social acquaintances would normally be regarded as private. Routine meetings of businesses and governmental personnel would be excluded because they do not represent the gathering of a substantial number of persons.' " Rep. No. 94-1476, 94th Cong., 2d Sess. 64 (1976).

performing rights society [copyright]
Defined in the Copyright Act, 17 U.S.C. §116(e)(3), as "an association or corporation that licenses the public performance of nondramatic musical works on behalf of the copyright owners, such as the American Society of Composers, Authors and Publishers, Broadcast Music, Inc., and SESAC, Inc." The performing rights societies are authorized by their members, who are owners of copyright in musical works, to grant licenses of the nondramatic performing rights (small, as opposed to the GRAND RIGHTS) to users such as radio and television networks and stations. Usually, these are

BLANKET LICENSES of the right to use all musical works in the repertory of the society for a fixed or percentage fee.

See *ASCAP, BMI, SESAC,* BLANKET LICENSES, GRAND RIGHTS.

- *Case Reference*: *ACEMLA v. Copyright Royalty Tribunal,* 835 F.2d 446, 5 USPQ2d 1217 (2d Cir. 1987) (holding that an entity known as "Association de Compositores y Editores de Musica LatinoAmericana" was not a "performing rights society").

- *Treatise References*: 2 *Nimmer on Copyright* §8.19 (1994 rev.); 1 P. Goldstein, *Copyright* §5.9 (1989); M. Leaffer, *Understanding Copyright* §8.22 (1989); S. Shemel & M.W. Krasilovsky, *This Business of Music* ch. 18 (1985).

per se illegal [antitrust] A rule defining certain categories of contract, combination, or conspiracy in restraint of trade as being illegal under Sherman Act §2 without any detailed inquiry into the facts of a particular case. If a certain type of restraint does not fit within a per se category, then it is analyzed for illegality under Sherman Act §1 under the RULE OF REASON. Over a period of several decades the U.S. Supreme Court has defined several categories of business practices to be so much of a threat to competition and so without any redeeming procompetitive virtues as to deserve placement in the per se illegal category.

Traditional Per Se Categories. Conventional listings of the categories of per se illegal antitrust violations created by the Supreme Court are: (1) price-fixing agreements among competitors (horizontal price fixing); (2) division of markets among competitors; (3) group boycotts; (4) resale price maintenance agreements between a manufacturer and its distributors (vertical price fixing); and (5) tie-in sales (selling one thing only on condition that an unwanted thing must also be purchased).

Theory of Per Se Categories. The rationale for having judge-made per se illegal categories of restraints is that they create certainty in the law and ease the burden of prosecutors and private antitrust plaintiffs. The alternative rule of reason approach requires a full-blown weighing of all the competitive pros and cons, what Justice Marshall once characterized as a "ramble through the wilds of economic theory in order to maintain a flexible approach." *United States v. Topco Assocs.,* 405 U.S. 596, 609 n.10 (1972).

- *Case References:*

"There are, thus, two complementary categories of antitrust analysis. In the first category are agreements whose nature and necessary effect are so plainly anticompetitive that no elaborate study of the industry is needed to establish their illegality—they are 'illegal *per se*'; in the second category are agreements whose competitive effect can only be evaluated by analyzing the facts peculiar to the business, the history of the restraint, and the reasons why it was imposed. In either event, the purpose of the analysis is to form a judgment about the competitive significance of the restraint...." *National Soc'y of Professional Eng'rs v. United States,* 435 U.S. 679, 692 (1978).

"*Per se* rules of illegality are appropriate only when they relate to conduct that is manifestly anti-competitive. As the Court explained in *Northern Pac. Ry. Co. v. United States,* 356 U.S. 1, 5 (1958), 'there are certain agreements or practices which because of their pernicious effect on competition and lack of any redeeming virtue are conclusively presumed to be unreasonable and therefore illegal without elaborate inquiry as to the precise harm they have caused or the business excuse for their use.' " *Continental T.V. Inc. v. GTE Sylvania, Inc.,* 433 U.S. 36, 49 (1977).

"The costs of judging business practices under the rule of reason, however, have been reduced by the recognition of *per se* rules. Once experience with a particular kind of restraint enables the Court to predict with confidence that the rule of reason will condemn it, it has applied a conclusive presumption that the restraint is unreasonable.... For the sake of business certainty and litigation efficiency, we have tolerated the invalidation of some agreements that a fullblown inquiry might have proved to be reasonable." *Arizona v. Maricopa County Medical Soc'y,* 457 U.S. 332, 343–44 (1982).

"[W]e have some doubt—enough to counsel against application of the *per se* rule—about the extent to which this practice threatens the 'central nervous system of the economy,' … that is, competitive pricing as the free market's means of allocating resources. Not all arrangements among actual or potential competitors that have an impact on price are per se violations of the Sherman Act or even unreasonable restraints." *Broadcast Music, Inc. v. Columbia Broadcasting Sys., Inc.*, 441 U.S. 1, 23 (1979).

persona [right of publicity] Those elements of personality by which a given person can be identified when those elements appear in connection with advertising and goods or services. Those elements can include name, picture, vocal style, body movement, distinctive costume and makeup, and objects associated with a certain person. The term "persona" was adopted as a convenient shorthand for the various ways by which a human being can be identified when it was realized that the traditional phrase "name and likeness" was not adequate to describe the many aspects of a person that can identify him or her.

Occasionally "persona" is used to describe that bundle of commercial values embodied in the identity of a person. E.g., *Factors, Etc., Inc. v. Pro Arts. Inc.*, 579 F.2d 215, 216, 205 USPQ 751 (2d Cir. 1978) ("In 1956 Colonel Tom Parker, the manager of Elvis Presley, began the task of creating the 'Elvis persona.' ").

• *Treatise Reference*: J.T. McCarthy, *The Rights of Publicity and Privacy* §4.9 (1995 rev.) ("The term 'persona' is increasingly used as a label to signify the cluster of commercial values embodied in personal identity as well as to signify that human identity 'identifiable' from defendant's usage.").

• *Case References*: "The right of publicity … protects against the unauthorized appropriation of an individual's very persona which would result in unearned commercial gain to another." *Factors, Etc., Inc. v. Pro Arts, Inc.*, 652 F.2d 278, 289, 211 USPQ 1, 10 (2d Cir. 1981) (Mansfield, J., dissenting.).

The New York privacy and publicity statute "is intended to protect the essence of the person, his or her identity or persona from being unwillingly or unknowingly misappropriated for the profit of another." *Onassis v. Christian Dior-New York, Inc.*, 122 Misc. 2d 603, 472 N.Y.S.2d 254, 260 (Sup. Ct. 1984), *aff'd without opinion*, 110 A.D.2d 1095, 488 N.Y.S.2d 843 (App. Div. 1985).

personal name mark [trademark] A name of a real person used as a trademark or service mark. Personal names (both surnames and first names) are in that category of noninherently distinctive terms that need proof of SECONDARY MEANING for protection in court. A term that is "primarily merely a surname" cannot be registered on the federal principal register unless the applicant proves the acquisition of distinctiveness, that is, of secondary meaning. The Patent and Trademark Office most often proves surname significance by way of the number of listings of the name in telephone books or media stories. See, e.g., *In re Petrin Corp.*, 231 USPQ 902 (T.T.A.B. 1986). But a COMPOSITE MARK that includes a surname is not necessarily "primarily merely a surname." *In re Hutchinson Technology, Inc.*, 852 F.2d 552, 7 USPQ2d 1490 (Fed. Cir. 1988) (HUTCHINSON TECHNOLOGY held a composite mark that is not primarily merely a surname).

Federal Registration and the Right of Publicity. The Court of Appeals for the Federal Circuit has hinted in dictum that the prohibition of Lanham Act §2(a) might be triggered by an invasion of privacy or infringement of the RIGHT OF PUBLICITY. *University of Notre Dame du Lac v. J.C. Gourmet Foods, Inc.*, 703 F.2d 1372, 1376, 217 USPQ 505 (Fed. Cir. 1983). However, in the author's view, it is §2(c) of the Lanham Act that more closely approximates the policies underlying the state law concepts of privacy and the right of publicity. This provision forbids registration of a name or picture identifying a particular living person without the written consent of that person. See J.T. McCarthy, *The Rights of Publicity and Privacy* §6.17 (1995 rev.).

Fair Use of One's Own Name. The term "fair use" is stretched to cover noninfringing trademark uses of one's own personal name. This is codified as a defense in Lanham Act §33(b)(4).

While early law spoke of an "absolute right" of each person to use his or her own name in business, modern cases limit this to a qualified right: even the good faith same-name junior user will be required to take some precautions in the mode of use so as to eliminate or at least minimize the likelihood of confusion with the senior user. In many cases the courts have issued injunctions that, while permitting the use of a surname, require the addition of the defendant's first name or initials, a change in the style, size, or color of lettering, the inclusion of some clarifying matter, the use of a disclaimer, or a combination of these conditions. In some cases where there is bad faith or confusion cannot be eliminated by halfway measures, an absolute and unconditional prohibition is required. See J.T. McCarthy, *Trademarks and Unfair Competition* §13.03 (3d ed. 1995 rev.).

• *Treatise Reference*: J.T. McCarthy, *Trademarks and Unfair Competition* §§13.01–.12 (3d ed. 1995 rev.).

• *Statutory Reference*: Lanham Act §2, 15 U.S.C. §1052:

No trademark by which the goods of the applicant may be distinguished from the goods of others shall be refused registration on the principal register on account of its nature unless it—

(a) Consists of or comprises ... matter which may disparage or falsely suggest a connection with persons, living or dead....

...

(c) Consists of or comprises a name, portrait, or signature identifying a particular living individual except by his written consent, or the name, signature, or portrait of a deceased President of the United States during the life of his widow, if any, except by the written consent of the widow.

...

(e) Consists of a mark which ... (4) is primarily merely a surname.

(f) Except as expressly excluded in paragraphs (a), [and] ... (c), nothing herein shall prevent the registration of a mark used by the applicant which has become distinctive of the applicant's goods in commerce....

• *Case References*:

"[The courts] have routinely required second comers at a minimum to use full names, first as well as second in equal size.... The more recent trend is to forbid any use of the name as part of the proprietor's trademark, permitting use only in a subsidiary capacity, and ... with the first name attached. ... In either event, the junior user has almost uniformly been bound to display negative disclaimers." *Basile, S.p.A. v. Basile*, 899 F.2d 35, 38, 14 USPQ2d 1240, 1242 (D.C. Cir. 1990) (Reversing as too "mild" an injunction requiring a change of type style, enlargement of an associated logo, addition of a geographic modifier, and a statement of origin, "Courts have rarely approved so mild a cure as that adopted by the district court here.").

"Even where a junior user lacks an intent to capitalize on another's trademark, use of an infringing personal name may still be limited by an injunction carefully tailored to balance the interest in using one's name against the interest in avoiding confusion.... In other words, as long as the scope of the district court's injunction reflects a consideration of the judicial reluctance to enjoin use of a personal name, the court has acted properly." *E. & J. Gallo Winery v. Gallo Cattle Co.*, 967 F.2d 1280, 1288–89, 21 USPQ2d 1824, 1830 (9th Cir. 1992) (Defendant Joseph Gallo, brother of Ernest and Julio Gallo, of wine-making fame, was permitted in marketing cheese to "continue to explain to customers his participation in his business, but not as a trademark or trade name that causes confusion." The use permitted was nontrademark use on cheese labels such as "Joseph Gallo Farms" in small type below the trademark.).

petty patent [international–patent] Some nations, such as Germany and Japan, have a separate classification of patents known as "petty patents" or UTILITY MODELS. See UTILITY MODEL for full definition.

phantom count [patent] In an INTERFERENCE proceeding, a COUNT that defines the invention of the contesting parties but is not claimed as such by either rival inventor contesting priority. In an interference proceeding to determine who was the first inventor, the Patent and Trademark Office will devise a count to define the subject matter of the invention that is common to both contesting parties. This particular kind of count is called a "phantom" only because it defines subject matter that neither party asserts as a claim to an invention but does define a single inventive concept common to both inventors.

See COUNT, INTERFERENCE.

- *Rule Reference*: "When a count is broader in scope than all claims which correspond to the count, the count is a 'phantom count.' A phantom count is not patentable to any party." 37 C.F.R. §1.601(f).

- *Case References*: "The interference counts here are denominated 'phantom' counts because none are the same as claims in either Case's patent or CPC's application. The counts are broader than claims made by either party.... [A] phantom count [is one] which by definition neither party asserts as a claim.... [N]either claim 61 nor CPC's disclosure must support the phantom count." *Case v. CPC Int'l, Inc.*, 730 F.2d 745, 748–51, 221 USPQ 196, 198–201 (Fed. Cir. 1984).

"The phantom count merely represents the inventive concept which may in some cases portray two mutually exclusive, but patentably indistinct, sets of claims." *In re Kroekel*, 803 F.2d 705, 710, 231 USPQ 640, 643 (Fed. Cir. 1986).

"[B]oth parties carry out substantially the same process, differing only in what appears to be a patentably insignificant way. Under these circumstances, we believe that the phantom count procedure is proper in order to ensure that only one patent issues for one inventive concept." *Aeloby v. Arni*, 547 F.2d 566, 570, 192 USPQ 486, 491 (C.C.P.A. 1977).

- *Example*: "The PTO will continue to ... declare interferences where interfering patent and application claims are mutually exclusive provided the claims define the same patentable invention. Patent F contains claim 1 (benzine). Application Z contains patentable claim 11

(xylene). Benzene and xylene define the same patentable invention. If an interference is declared, there will be one count (benzene or xylene). Claim 1 of patent F and claim 11 of application Z would be designated to correspond to the count." *Manual of Patent Examining Procedure* Example 16, §2309.01 (1994 rev.).

phonogram [copyright] A copyrightable work that results from the fixation of sounds, regardless of the nature of the material object in which the sounds are fixed. Commonly known in the United States as a SOUND RECORDING, the term "phonogram" is defined in Article 1 of the PHONOGRAM CONVENTION as "any exclusively aural fixation of sounds of a performance or of other sounds." The type of material object in which a phonogram or sound recording is fixed is a phonorecord.

Phonogram Convention [copyright–international] The Convention for the Protection of Phonograms Against Unauthorized Duplication is a multilateral treaty under which member nations agree to prohibit the unauthorized duplication (PIRACY) of PHONOGRAMS, which are commonly known in the United States as SOUND RECORDINGS. Created in 1971 and adhered to by the United States in 1974, the Convention has about 40 member nations. Unlike the ROME CONVENTION, the Phonogram Convention does not create performing rights in sound recordings but only relates to duplication of the sounds themselves, as by electronic means. Domestic law formalities are satisfied under the Convention by placing on publicly distributed authorized duplicates the symbol of a P in a circle, the name of the producer, and the date of first publication. This is virtually identical to the notice prescribed in U.S. law in 17 U.S.C. §402.

See SOUND RECORDING, ROME CONVENTION, NOTICE OF COPYRIGHT.

- *Treatise References*: 2 P. Goldstein, *Copyright* §16.8 (1989) (see text of Convention and list of adherent nations at App. B-8 & B-9); W. Patry, *Copyright Law and Practice* 1263 (1994); see text of the Phonogram Convention and list of nations in *Nimmer on Copyright* Apps. 23 & 29 (1994 rev.).

phonorecords [copyright] The material objects that store or fix copyrightable sounds, other than the soundtrack accompanying a MOTION PICTURE.

Phonorecords and Copies Compared. In the nomenclature of the Copyright Act, there are only two kinds of material objects in which a copyrightable work is capable of being "fixed" or recorded: "copies" and "phonorecords." These two definitions are mutually exclusive and do not overlap. COPIES are any material objects that store copyrightable works, including an AUDIOVISUAL WORK such as a MOTION PICTURE with accompanying soundtrack. Phonorecords are any material objects that store sound, other than the soundtrack for an audiovisual work such as a motion picture.

Phonorecord and Sound Recording Compared. A SOUND RECORDING is a category of copyrightable work, not a category of material objects in which sounds are fixed or recorded. A sound recording is a copyrightable work consisting of the exact sounds rendered when one performs a work, such as singing, playing a musical instrument, or reading a book. In the wording of the Copyright Act, a "sound recording" can be fixed only in a "phonorecord," except for sounds accompanying an AUDIOVISUAL work such as a MOTION PICTURE. However, various categories of copyrightable works are capable of being fixed or recorded in either phonorecords or copies. For example, MUSICAL WORKS can be fixed in audio tapes, which are phonorecords, or in sheet music, which are copies. LITERARY WORKS, for example, could be fixed in compact discs, which are phonorecords, or in books, which are copies.

New Technologies. Congress, in defining phonorecords, left the door open for the accommodation of unforeseen developments in information storage technology by providing that a work can be "fixed by any method now known or later developed" and that it makes no difference that the sounds can only be perceived or communicated "with the aid of a machine or device." Thus, compact discs, not widely known when the copyright revision act was drafted in the 1970s, come comfortably within the definition of phonorecords. Even computer CHIPS that store sounds would come within the definition.

• *Statutory Reference*: 17 U.S.C. §101: " 'Phonorecords' are material objects in which sounds, other than those accompanying a motion picture or other audiovisual work, are fixed by any method now known or later developed, and from which the sounds can be perceived, reproduced, or otherwise communicated, either directly or with the aid of a machine or device. The term 'phonorecords' includes the material object in which the sounds are first fixed."

pioneer patent [patent] A patent on an invention that makes a significant advance in the technological art. The U.S. Supreme Court has defined a pioneer patent as one on an invention "of such novelty and importance as to mark a distinct step in the progress of the art, as distinguished from a mere improvement or perfection of what had gone before." *Westinghouse v. Boyden Power Brake Co.*, 170 U.S. 537, 562 (1898).

Broad Range of Equivalents. In applying the DOCTRINE OF EQUIVALENTS to determine whether a patent claim is infringed, a broad range of equivalents will infringe if the patent is a pioneer patent. Pioneer inventions are "normally entitled" to a "very broad range of equivalents." *Hughes Aircraft Co. v. United States*, 717 F.2d 1351, 1362, 219 USPQ 473, 481 (Fed. Cir. 1983). If the patented invention stands almost alone in field of technology, it will probably be viewed as a pioneer patent, and a court will grant a greater range of equivalency to claims that are not literally infringed. That is, its claims will be read as covering a relatively broad range of equivalents that will be regarded as an infringement. Pioneer status has to do with the position that the invention occupies in its technological art, not with whether or not it is a "combination of known elements." *MAC Corp. of Am. v. Williams Patent Crusher Co.*, 767 F.2d 882, 884 n.3, 226 USPQ 515, 517 n.3 (Fed. Cir. 1985).

Limits to the Expansion of Pioneer Patent Claims. The patent claims for a pioneer invention must be kept within reasonable bounds, for "even if the patent for a machine be a pioneer, the alleged infringer must have done something more than reach the same result." *Westinghouse v. Boyden Power Brake Co.*, 170 U.S. 537, 569 (1898). Even though patent claims for a pioneering invention in the art of hand-held electronic calculators were entitled to a broad range of equivalents, an accused calculator was still found not to infringe because of the totality of technological changes. *Texas Instruments, Inc. v. International Trade Comm'n*, 805 F.2d 1558, 231 USPQ 833 (Fed. Cir. 1986), *reh'g denied*, 846 F.2d 1369, 6 USPQ2d 1886 (Fed. Cir. 1988).

Crowded Art. Only a very narrow range of equivalents will infringe if the patented invention lies on the opposite end of the spectrum: a minor patent in a CROWDED ART. A crowded art is a field of technology crowded with many similar inventions. A patent cannot be considered a pioneer patent if it is in a crowded art. *Chemical Eng'g Corp. v. Essef Indus., Inc.*, 795 F.2d 1565, 1572 n.8, 230 USPQ 385, 391 n.8 (Fed. Cir. 1984).

See EQUIVALENTS, DOCTRINE OF; CROWDED ART.

- *Case References*:

"[W]hile a pioneer invention is entitled to a broad range of equivalents, an invention representing only a modest advance over the prior art is given a more restricted (narrower range) application of the doctrine." *Thomas & Betts Corp. v. Litton Sys., Inc.*, 720 F.2d 1572, 1579, 220 USPQ 1, 6 (Fed. Cir. 1983).

"The concept of 'pioneer' arises from an ancient jurisprudence, reflecting judicial appreciation that a broad breakthrough invention merits a broader scope of equivalents than does a narrow improvement in a crowded technology. But the 'pioneer' is not a separate class of invention, carrying a unique body of law. The wide range of technological advance between pioneering breakthrough and modest improvement accommodates gradations in scope of equivalency.... The place of a particular invention in this spectrum depends on all the circumstances ... and is decided as a factual matter." *Sun Studs Inc. v. ATA Equip. Leasing Inc.*, 872 F.2d 978, 987, 10 USPQ2d 1338, 1346 (Fed. Cir. 1989).

piracy [copyright–trademark] The act of exact, unauthorized, and illegal reproduction on a commercial scale of a copyrighted work or of a trademarked product. Often, the term "piracy" is used merely as rhetorical hyperbole for an obvious instance of copyright infringement.

Varying Meanings of "Piracy." While piracy is most often used to refer to egregious infringement of copyright, it is sometimes used to refer to the act of COUNTERFEITING—the intentional and systematic infringement of a trademark. For example: "The pirating of trademarked products through commercial counterfeiting reached epidemic proportions in recent years." WIPO, *Background Reading Material on Intellectual Property* 176 (1988). " 'Piracy' ... is a vague term that has no settled legal definition." Reichman, *Intellectual Property in International Trade: Opportunities and Risks of a GATT Connection*, 22 Vand. J. Transnat'l L. 747, 775 (1989).

Congressional Use. Congress has used the term "piratical" as hyperbole describing a clear case of copyright infringement. The House report defined "piratical articles" as "copies or phonorecords made without any authorization of the copyright owner." Rep. No. 94-1476, 94th Cong., 2d Sess. 169 (1976).

"Bootleg" Recording. A BOOTLEG RECORDING is an unauthorized recording of a live performance. A bootleg recording differs from a pirate recording in that a pirate recording is one that is electronically reproduced illegally from a genuine, authorized recording, not from a live performance.

- *Case Usage Examples*:

Copyright Law: "The prosecutor referred to [the defendant] as a 'racketeer' and 'tape pirate.' Given the fact that there was ample evidence to infer that he was a criminal copyright infringer and that he participated in racketeering activity, the references were not such impermissible exaggerations as to mischaracterize his role in the criminal ventures." *United States v. Drum*, 733 F.2d 1503, 1508 (11th Cir. 1984).

Copyright Law: "It is decidedly in the interests of creativity, not piracy, to permit authors to take well-known phrases and fragments from copyrighted works and add their own contributions of commentary or humor." *Warner Bros. Inc. v. American Broadcasting Cos.*, 720 F.2d 231, 242, 222 USPQ 101, 110 (2d Cir. 1983).

Trademark Law: "[A]n award of little more than nominal damages would encourage a counterfeiter to merely switch from one infringing scheme to another as soon as the infringed owner became aware of the fabrication. Such a method of enforcement would fail to serve as a convincing deterrence to the profit maximizing entrepreneur who engages in trademark piracy." *Playboy Enters., Inc. v. Baccarat Clothing Co.*, 692 F.2d 1272, 1274, 216 USPQ 1083, 1084 (9th Cir. 1982).

Trademark Law: "A ruling that the designs on these bracelets were not counterfeits of Rolex's trademark, despite the fact that only an expert could distinguish between the two, would remove a major disincentive that might otherwise prevent counterfeiters from pirating Rolex's mark." *Montres Rolex S.A. v. Snyder*, 718 F.2d 524, 528, 220 USPQ 10, 13 (2d Cir. 1983).

- *Definitional References*:

"*Piracy.* Commonly understood in the fields of copyright and neighboring rights as reproducing published works or phonograms by any appropriate means for public distribution and also rebroadcasting another's broadcast without proper authorization. Unlawful fixation of live performance is referred to in common parlance as 'bootlegging.' " *WIPO Glossary of Terms of the Law of Copyright and Neighboring Rights* 190 (1980).

"The unauthorized copying of copyrighted materials for commercial purposes and the unauthorized commercial dealing in copied materials is known as 'piracy.' " WIPO, *Background Reading Material on Intellectual Property* 222 (1988).

plagiarism [copyright] 1. The copying of ideas or expression of another author and using them as one's own work. 2. An informal, non-legal synonym for copyright infringement,

which requires the substantial copying of another's protected expression, not just the taking of ideas or concepts. See INFRINGEMENT OF COPYRIGHT, COPYING.

plant patent [patent] There are two distinct forms of special patent or patent-like protection available for new plant varieties: (1) under the 1930 Plant Patent Act (PPA), plant patents granted by the Patent and Trademark Office for asexually reproduced varieties; and (2) under the Plant Variety Protection Act of 1970 (PVPA), protection of new sexually reproduced and tuber-propagated varieties by the Department of Agriculture. In addition to special plant statutes, plants can also be protected by the mainstream Patent Code under 35 U.S.C. §101.

Patents for Nonplant Life Forms. The U.S. Supreme Court has held that the existence of the two separate statutory systems for protection of new plant varieties does not preclude the grant of mainstream utility patents for other life forms such as bacteria and multicellular higher life forms. *Diamond v. Chakrabarty*, 447 U.S. 303, 206 USPQ 193 (1980). See BIOTECHNOLOGY, TRANSGENIC.

International Relations. In 1981, the United States became a member of the CONVENTION OF THE INTERNATIONAL UNION FOR THE PROTECTION OF NEW PLANT VARIETIES (UPOV). In 1994, the Plant Variety Protection Act of 1970 was amended to bring the terms of the Act into conformance with the provisions of the Convention.

1. Plant Patents Under the Plant Patent Act of 1930 (PPA). A plant patent is a grant of exclusive rights from the federal government to a person who invents or discovers and asexually reproduces a distinct and new variety of plant other than a tuber-propagated plant or a plant found in an uncultivated state.

Purpose of Special Legislation. One purpose of the 1930 Plant Patent Act was to extend to agricultural products the incentives extended to industry in utility and design patents. *In re Bergy*, 596 F.2d 952, 982, 201 USPQ 352, 378–79 (C.C.P.A. 1979), *dismissed as moot*, 444 U.S. 924 (1980). Another purpose of having separate legislation was to put to rest two arguments that had prevented the patenting of plants under existing utility patent legislation: (1) the belief that even artificially bred plants were unpatentable products of nature; and (2) the notion that no plant could be adequately described in writing. *Diamond v. Chakrabarty*, 447 U.S. 303, 311–12, 206 USPQ 193, 198 (1980).

Validity of Plant Patents: The Patent Code states that unless otherwise specified, all the provisions governing utility patents will also govern plant plants. But to apply industrial concepts of NOVELTY and NONOBVIOUSNESS to plants requires some modification. See 1 D. Chisum, *Patents* §1.05[1] (1994 rev.). For example, in applying the nonobviousness criterion, it has been held that one should focus not on the newness of physical structure but upon the existence of new or unexpectedly superior qualities of the new plant variety, depending upon whether it is a food plant, a medicinal plant, or an ornamental plant. *Yoder Bros. Inc. v. California-Florida Plant Corp.*, 537 F.2d 1347, 1379, 193 USPQ 264, 292 (5th Cir. 1976). Because of the practical impossibility to obtain the same results by reproducing the "invention", the enablement requirement of the disclosure is relaxed for plant patent applications. The description of the plant and how it was "invented" need only be as reasonably complete as possible.

Qualifications of the Patent Holder. To be awarded a plant patent, the applicant must appreciate the novelty of the variety and the new variety must be asexually reproduced. See *Ex Parte Moore*, 115 USPQ 145, 147 (Pat. Off. Bd. App. 1957) (Merely becoming aware of the existence of a plant without any appreciation that it is a new variety is not sufficient. There must also be perpetuation of the variety by asexual reproduction. "It seems to us that although one may find a plant, he has not discovered a new variety if he has no appreciation that the plant is a distinct and new variety.").

Infringement of Plant Patents. A plant patent gives the exclusive rights to the asexual reproduction of the patented variety; the sale of the asexually reproduced plant; and the use of the asexually reproduced plant. Asexual reproduc-tion is reproduction other than by the use of seeds, e.g., cutting, grafting, budding. It is not infringement to sexually reproduce the plant, that is, by the use of seeds. "It is generally assumed that one infringes only if the accused plant is a direct or indirect asexual reproduction of the patentee's original parent plant." 1 D. Chisum, *Patents* §1.05[1][d] (1994 rev.).

- *Statutory References*:

Plant Patent Act of 1930. 35 U.S.C. §161: "Whoever invents or discovers and asexually reproduces any distinct and new variety of plant, including cultivated sports, mutants, hybrids and newly found seedlings, other than a tuber propagated plant or a plant found in an uncultivated state, may obtain a patent therefor, subject to the conditions and requirements of this title. The provisions of this title relating to patents for inventions shall apply to patents for plants, except as otherwise provided."

35 U.S.C. §162: "No plant patent shall be declared invalid for noncompliance with section 112 of this title if the description is as complete as is reasonably possible. The claim in the specification shall be in formal terms to the plant shown and described."

35 U.S.C. §163: "In the case of a plant patent the grant shall be of the right to exclude others from asexually reproducing the plant or selling or using the plant so reproduced."

- *Rule References*: 37 C.F.R. §1.163(a): "The specification must contain as full and complete a disclosure as possible of the plant and the characteristics thereof that distinguish the same over related known varieties, and its antecedents, and must particularly point out where and in what manner the variety of plant has been asexually reproduced. In the case of a newly found plant, the specification must particularly point out the location and character of the area where the plant was discovered."

37 C.F.R. §1.164: "The claim shall be in formal terms to the new and distinct variety of the specified plant as described and illustrated, and may also recite the principal distinguishing characteristics. More than one claim is not allowed."

- *Case Reference*: "In the case of plants, to develop or discover a new variety that retains the desirable qualities of the parent stock and adds significant improvements, and to preserve the new specimen by asexually reproducing it constitutes no small feat.... If the plant is a source of food, the ultimate question might be its nutritive content or its profligacy. A medicinal plant might be judged by its increased or changed therapeutic value. Similarly, an ornamental plant would be judged by its increased beauty and desirability in relation to other plants of its type, its usefulness in the industry, and how much of an improvement it represents over prior ornamental plants, taking all of its characteristics together." *Yoder Bros. Inc. v. California-Florida Plant Corp.*, 537 F.2d 1347, 1379, 193 USPQ 264, 292–93 (5th Cir. 1976).

2. The Plant Variety Protection Act of 1970 (PPA). Under this law the Department of Agriculture grants exclusive rights in certain sexually reproduced plants. While similar to plant patents, this form of protection is not called a "patent." 7 U.S.C. §2321 et seq. In 1994, to comport with provisions of the UPOV, the term of protection was extended from 18 to 20 years, except for trees and vines where the term of protection is 25 years. In 1994, protection was extended to first-generation hybrids, harvested plant parts, and tubers. See CONVENTION OF THE INTERNATIONAL UNION FOR THE PROTECTION OF NEW PLANT VARIETIES (UPOV).

Scope of Protection. A plant variety certificate gives the owner the right to exclude others "from selling the variety, or offering it for sale, or reproducing it, or importing it, or exporting it, or using it in producing (as distinguished from developing) a hybrid or different variety therefrom...." 7 U.S.C. §2483(a)(1) .

Farmer's or Crop Exemption. In recognizing the reality of farm life, a significant exemption from the patent-like protection offered by the PVPA has been carved out for farmers who, after planting, save enough seed of protected plants to plant the next year. If the farmer decides not to plant the saved seed, the farmer can sell the seed to another farmer for planting as long as the amount sold does not exceed the amount needed to seed the seller's field. Other requirements are that the growing of the plants not be a part of marketing and that both farmers not be engaged principally in selling seed for reproductive purposes. The Supreme Court held that this exemption applies only to seed that the farmer saved for replanting of the farmer's own acreage, not to saved seed that was grown for the purpose of sale for replanting. *Asgrow Seed Co. v. Winterboer*, 115 S. Ct. 788, 33 USPQ2d 1430 (1995).

- *Treatise Reference*: "The Act recognizes the ability of plant breeders to produce seeds expressing stable genetic characteristics.... The Act's primary purpose is to increase the selection of plant varieties available to the public." 1 D. Chisum, *Patents* §1.05[2] (1994 rev.).

- *Statutory Reference*:

Plant Variety Protection Act of 1970 (as amended 1994). 7 U.S.C. §2402(a): "The breeder of any sexually reproduced or tuber propagated plant variety (other than fungi or bacteria) who has so reproduced the variety, or the successor in interest of the breeder, shall be entitled to plant variety protection for the variety, subject to the conditions and requirements of this chapter ..."

- *Case Reference*: "[S]exually reproduced plants were not included under the 1930 [Plant Patent] Act because new varieties could not be reproduced true-to-type through seedlings.... By 1970, however, it was generally recognized that true-to-type reproduction was possible and that plant patent protection was therefore appropriate. The 1970 Act extended that protection." *Diamond v. Chakrabarty*, 447 U.S. 303, 313, 206 USPQ 193, 199 (1980).

"In 1970, Congress passed the Plant Variety Protection Act (PVPA), 84 Stat. 1542, 7 U.S.C. §2321 et seq., in order to provide developers of novel plant varieties with 'adequate encouragement for research, and for marketing when appropriate, to yield for the public the benefits of new varieties,' §2581. The PVPA extends patent-like protection to novel varieties of sexually reproduced plants (that is, plants grown from seed) which parallels the protection afforded asexually reproduced plant varieties (that is, varieties reproduced by propagation or grafting) under Chapter 15 of the Patent Act." *Asgrow Seed Co. v. Winterboer*, 115 S. Ct. 788,790, 33 USPQ2d 1430, 1431 (1995).

3. Protection by Utility Patent. Section 101 of the Patent Code can apply to inventions covering plants. However, the strict enablement and description requirements of utility patents must be followed. The "how-to-make" provision of section 112 can be satisfied by depositing seeds with a recognized public depository. In addition to the enablement requirement, the derivation of the new plant must meet the stricter nonobviousness requirement of the Patent Code.

While more difficult to obtain, a utility patent can offer a greater scope of exclusive rights than a plant patent. The patent holder does not have to prove derivation of the plant to prove infringement. Multiple parts of the plant, for example, seeds, fruit, flowers, cell tissue, transgenes, and transgenic products, can be claimed. See 1 Chisum, *Patents* §1.05[4] (1994 rev.).

• *Case References*:

"We disagree with these contentions that the scope of patentable subject matter under [Patent Code] section 101 has been narrowed or restricted by the passage of the PPA and the PVPA and that these plant-specific Acts represent the exclusive forms of protection for plant life covered by those acts." *Ex parte Hibberd*, 227 USPQ 443, 445 (Bd. Pat. App. & Int'f. 1985).

"There is no question that one having ... seeds available through the ATCC [American Type Culture Collection] depository would be enabled to grow a ... plant and produce additional seeds therefrom. The procedure to be used by appellant to deposit seeds of the plant does not differ from that used to deposit a culture of micro-organism as sanctioned by the Court of Customs and Patent Appeals in *In re Argoudelis*." *Ex parte C*, 27 USPQ2d 1492, 1495 (Bd. Pat. App. & Int'f. 1993).

point of novelty [patent] A supplementary test of infringement of a DESIGN PATENT under which the accused device must have that part of the patented design which distinguishes it from designs found in the PRIOR ART. It is not proper to define the overall design of a product as the

point of novelty. *Sun Hill Indus. v. Easter Unlimited, Inc.*, 48 F.3d 1193, 33 USPQ2d 1925 (Fed. Cir. 1995).

See INFRINGEMENT OF DESIGN PATENT, DESIGNER SKILLED IN THE ART.

• *Case References*: "[E]ven though the court compares two items through the eyes of the ordinary observer, it must, nevertheless, to find infringement, attribute their similarity to the novelty which distinguishes the patented device from the prior art. (This 'point of novelty' approach applies only to a determination of infringement.... This court has avoided the point of novelty approach in other contexts.)" *Litton Sys., Inc. v. Whirlpool Corp.*, 728 F.2d 1423, 1444, 221 USPQ 97, 110 (Fed. Cir. 1984).

"Beyond the substantial similarity requirement of *Gorham* and *L.A. Gear*, design patent infringement requires that the accused product 'appropriate the novelty in the patented device which distinguishes it from the prior art.' ... The patentee must prove both substantial similarity and appropriation of the 'point of novelty'.... [T]he trial court cannot evade the point of novelty test by relying on the claimed overall design as the point of novelty." *Sun Hill Indus. v. Easter Unlimited, Inc.*, 48 F.3d 1193, 1197, 33 USPQ2d 1925, 1927–28 (Fed. Cir. 1995) (accused design did not appropriate the four points of novelty of the patented design).

• *Example*: The three features of a Litton patented microwave oven design that distinguished it from prior microwave oven designs were a three-stripe border, the lack of a door handle, and a door latch release mounted on the bottom portion of the control panel. While there were several similarities between the appearance of the accused oven and the patented oven design, no infringement was found because the accused oven did not have those three features, which formed the "point of novelty." *Litton Sys., Inc. v. Whirlpool Corp.*, 728 F.2d 1423, 1444, 221 USPQ 97, 110 (Fed. Cir. 1984).

practice an invention [patent] To make use of an invention by making, using, or selling articles embodying the invention or by using a process.

Similarly, the phrase "practicing a patent" means (1) to make, use, or sell articles embodying the invention that is covered by the CLAIMS of the patent or (2) to use a process covered by the PROCESS CLAIMS of the patent.

The word "practice" is used here in the sense of a verb indicating pursuing or exercising a certain teaching, such as "practicing law" or "practicing medicine."

See PATENT.

preamble [patent] The formal introductory clause to a patent claim. A patent claim traditionally begins with an introduction or preamble, followed by the word COMPRISING, which introduces the formal elements of the claim. Generally, the preamble does not define a narrowing ELEMENT of the claim. The preamble usually only defines the setting or context in which the elements of the claim appear.

Effect of the Preamble. While generally the preamble does not limit the scope of a claim, the preamble may be read to shed light on the meaning of the claim and to define the invention. *De George v. Bernier*, 768 F.2d 1318, 1322 n.3, 226 USPQ 758, 761 n. 3 (Fed. Cir. 1985). In some cases the subject matter mentioned in the preamble does provide additional structural limitations of a claim. In order to avoid and distinguish the disclosures of the PRIOR ART, the patentee may wish to argue that the preamble is a limitation on the claimed invention. But in order to establish a case of infringement, the patentee may wish to argue that the preamble does not introduce an additional limitation that must be found in the ACCUSED DEVISE.

Jepson Claim. A JEPSON CLAIM is one in which the preamble of the claim rather extensively lays out the setting of the new invention and impliedly admits that what is recited in the Jepson preamble is old and in the prior art.

See COMPRISING, CONSISTING OF, CONSISTING ESSENTIALLY OF.

• *Treatise Reference:* R. Harmon, *Patents and the Federal Circuit* §5.6 (3d ed. 1994); 2 D. Chisum, *Patents* §8.06[1][b] (1994 rev.).

• *Case References*: "Other claims read: 'In a machine of the class described, the combination....' Such preliminary statement is com-

monly and properly used to specify the type of machine in which the claimed subsidiary combination of elements works an improvement over the prior art.... It would be difficult to describe an improvement in a washing machine without naming such a machine as the thing to which the patent is addressed, and equally difficult to refrain from referring to various parts of the machine, such as the tub or motor which actuates the washer. But it has never been thought that a claim limited to an improvement in some element of the machine is, by such reference, rendered bad as claiming a monopoly of tubs or motors used in washing machines." *Williams Co. v. United Shoe Mach. Corp.*, 316 U.S. 364, 369 (1942).

"No litmus test can be given with respect to when the introductory words of a claim, the preamble, constitute a statement of purpose for a device or are, in themselves, additional structural limitations of a claim.... The effect preamble language should be given can be resolved only on review of the entirety of the patent to gain an understanding of what the inventors actually invented and intended to encompass by the claim." *Corning Glass Works v. Sumitomo Elec. USA Inc.*, 868 F.2d 1251, 1257, 9 USPQ2d 1962, 1966 (Fed. Cir. 1989).

"The preamble of a claim does not limit the scope of the claim when it merely states a purpose or invented use of the invention.... However, terms appearing in a preamble may be deemed limitations of a claim when they 'give meaning to the claim and properly define the invention.'... In the instant case, review of the '456 patent as a whole reveals that the term 'computer' is one that 'breathes life and meaning into the claims and hence, is a necessary limitation to them.'" *In re Paulsen*, 30 F.3d 1475, 1479, 31 USPQ2d 1671, 1673–74 (Fed. Cir. 1994) (See Example 3 below.).

• *Example 1: Nonlimiting Preamble.* A claim reads in part: "A circuit for controlling the operation of a word processor printer *comprising* a buffer circuit, input circuit means...." In this claim, the presence of neither a "word processor" nor a "printer" would ordinarily constitute limiting ELEMENTS of the CLAIM, since they are mentioned only in the preamble. Only the things listed after the word "comprising" constitute limiting elements of the claim.

- *Example 2: Limiting Preamble.* The claim began: "An optical waveguide comprising ..." followed by (a) and (b), two defined structural elements making up a certain type of optical fiber. The patent specification defined an "optical waveguide" as having certain defined structural features. The court agreed that if the preamble did not limit the claim, then a prior art patent disclosure anticipated the claim by disclosing an optical fiber having the identical structure of the optical fiber defined in paragraphs (a) and (b) of the claim. But if the preamble limited the claim, then the claim was not invalid by anticipation, because the prior art patent disclosure did not disclose all the features of the claimed "optical waveguide" as it was structurally defined by the inventor in the patent specification. The court held that this preamble "does not merely state a purpose or intended use" but rather provides "positive limitations to the invention claimed." Since the prior art disclosure did not reveal all the structural limitations intrinsic to the claimed "optical waveguide," as defined by the inventor, the court concluded that the claim was not invalid because of anticipation. *Corning Glass Works v. Sumitomo Elec. USA Inc.*, 868 F.2d 1251, 1257, 9 USPQ2d 1962, 1966 (Fed. Cir. 1989).

- *Example 3: Limiting Preamble.* The term "computer" was used in the preamble of a claim to a portable computer contained within a compact, "clam shell" metal case. This term was held by the court to limit the scope of the claims which related to the mechanical elements of the case. Thus, to anticipate the claim, the prior art reference had to disclose some type of "computer." It did and the claim was invalid as being anticipated by the prior art reference. *In re Paulsen*, 30 F.3d 1475, 31 USPQ2d 1671 (Fed. Cir. 1994) (see quotation above).

preferred embodiment [patent]

See BEST MODE.

prejudgment interest [patent–trademark–copyright] Interest on a monetary judgment against an infringer awarded to a prevailing intellectual property owner measured from the date of infringement to the date of judgment.

1. Prejudgment Interest on Patent Infringement Awards. Patent Code §284 states that upon finding patent infringement, a court shall award damages "together with interest and costs as fixed by the court" but is silent on the subject of the interest running from a date earlier than the date of judgment. In the seminal 1983 *Devex* case, the U.S. Supreme Court held that under Patent Code §284 "prejudgment interest should ordinarily be awarded." *General Motors Corp. v. Devex Corp.*, 461 U.S. 648, 655, 217 USPQ 1185, 1188 (1983) (see quotation below). While the Court said that the statute leaves the court some discretion in awarding prejudgment interest, it "should be awarded under §284 absent some justification for withholding such an award." 461 U.S. at 657, 217 USPQ at 1189.

Interest on Lost Profits. While the Supreme Court decision in *Devex* dealt with an award of damages measured by a REASONABLE ROYALTY, the same principles of prejudgment interest apply to an award of damages measured by lost profits. *Gyromat Corp. v. Champion Spark Plug Co.*, 735 F.2d 549, 555, 222 USPQ 4, 9 (Fed. Cir. 1984).

Duration and Amount. The normal procedure is to award prejudgment interest from the date of infringement to the date of payment, since only such an award will give the patent owner complete compensation. The rate of prejudgment interest and whether it should be compounded or uncompounded are matters left largely to the discretion of the district court. *Bio-Rad Labs. Inc. v. Nicolet Instrument Corp.*, 807 F.2d 964, 968–69, 1 USPQ2d 1191, 1193–94 (Fed. Cir. 1986).

Postjudgment Interest. Postjudgment interest compounded at the 52-week Treasury Bill rate is mandated by 28 U.S.C. §1961.

- *Treatise References*: R. Harmon, *Patents and the Federal Circuit* §12.2(a) (3d ed. 1994); 5 D. Chisum, *Patents* §20.03[4][a] (1994 rev.).

- *Case References*:

"In the typical case an award of prejudgment interest is necessary to ensure that the patent owner is placed in as good a position as he would have been in had the infringer entered into a reasonable royalty agreement. An award of interest from the time that royalty payments would have been received merely serves to make the patent owner whole, since his damages consist not only of the value of the royalty payments but also of the foregone use of the money between the time of infringement and the date of the judgment." *General Motors Corp. v. Devex Corp.*, 461 U.S. 648, 655–56, 217 USPQ 1185, 1188 (1983).

"[S]ince the purpose of prejudgment interest is to compensate the patentee for its 'foregone use of the money [the royalty payments] between the time of the infringement and the date of the judgment,' *Devex*, 461 U.S. at 656, 217 USPQ at 1188, the merits of the infringer's challenges to the patent are immaterial in determining the amount of prejudgment interest." *Bio-Rad Labs. Inc. v. Nicolet Instrument Corp.*, 807 F.2d 964, 969, 1 USPQ2d 1191, 1195 (Fed. Cir. 1986).

2. Prejudgment Interest on Trademark Infringement Awards. Except as to COUNTERFEITING, the Lanham Act is silent on prejudgment interest. As to use of this remedy in ordinary trademark infringement cases, the statute neither allows nor prohibits it. The Court of Appeals for the Seventh Circuit has held that prejudgment interest should ordinarily be available in trademark infringement cases. "The time has come … to announce a rule that prejudgment interest should be presumptively available to victims of federal law violations. Without it, compensation of the plaintiff is incomplete and the defendant has an incentive to delay." *Gorenstein Enters. Inc. v. Quality Care-USA Inc.*, 874 F.2d 431, 436, 10 USPQ2d 1762, 1765 (7th Cir. 1989). Such an award was said to be "particularly appropriate" in trademark infringement cases where the violation is "intentional, and indeed, outrageous." *Id.* Other circuits are less enthusiastic about always awarding prejudgment interest in trademark cases.

In cases of trademark counterfeiting, Lanham Act §35(b), 15 U.S.C. §1117(b), gives the court discretion to award prejudgment interest from the date of service of the plaintiff's pleadings.

See COUNTERFEITING.

- *Treatise Reference*: J.T. McCarthy, *Trademarks and Unfair Competition* §30.28[3] (3d ed. 1995 rev.).

3. Prejudgment Interest on Copyright Infringement Awards. The Copyright Act is silent on prejudgment interest. The statute neither allows nor prohibits it. This has led to conflicting decisions by the courts of appeal. The Court of Appeals for the Ninth Circuit has held that prejudgment interest is an available remedy under the 1909 Copyright Act and presumably also under the present 1978 Act. The court ordered prejudgment interest based on an award of the defendant's profits that resulted from the infringing actions. *Frank Music Corp. v. MGM Inc.*, 886 F.2d 1545, 1550, 12 USPQ2d 1412, 1418 (9th Cir. 1989). On the other hand, the Court of Appeals for the Sixth Circuit has vacated an award of prejudgment interest on damages measured by lost profits of the copyright owner. The court said that the damages awarded were sufficient to promote creativity and to deter infringement. It is not clear whether the court was holding that prejudgment interest should never be awarded or should not be awarded based on the facts of this case. *Robert R. Jones Assocs. v. Nino Homes*, 858 F.2d 274, 282, 8 USPQ2d 1224, 1231 (6th Cir. 1988).

- *Treatise Reference*: 1 N. Boorstyn, *Copyright* §13.04 (2d ed. 1994); 1 P. Goldstein, *Copyright* §12.1.1 (1989); 2 *Nimmer on Copyright* §14.02[B] (1994 rev.).

preliminary injunction [patent–tradmark–copyright] An order by a court requiring the defendant to do or refrain from doing some action pending a full trial on the merits of the lawsuit. Sometimes in intellectual property litigation, the property owner, soon after filing the complaint, will make a motion for a preliminary injunction requiring the defendant to stop doing those things the plaintiff alleges are infringing the plaintiff's intellectual property right.

Procedure. In the federal courts, the procedure for obtaining a preliminary injunction is set by Federal Rule of Civil Procedure 65, which, among other things, requires notice to the adverse party, the posting of a bond, and an order that is specific and clear in its terms. Under Federal Rule of Civil Procedure 52(a), in granting or denying a motion for a preliminary injunction, the court must set forth its findings of fact and conclusions of law. While live witnesses are sometimes heard at a hearing on a preliminary injunction, most often the evidence consists only of documents and affidavits of witnesses.

Factors to Consider. Traditionally, a party seeking a preliminary injunction is required to show five basic factors: (1) that there is a probability of success at the ultimate trial on the merits of the claim; (2) that the plaintiff will undergo "irreparable injury" pending a full trial on the merits; (3) that a preliminary injunction will preserve the status quo which preceded the dispute; (4) that the hardships favor the plaintiff; and (5) that a preliminary injunction will favor the public interest and protect third parties.

Delay in Moving. The delay of the moving party in filing suit and in seeking a preliminary injunction can give rise to a defense on the traditional basis of LACHES, as well as undercut the alleged need for the immediate and extraordinary intervention of the court.

1. Patent Preliminary Injunction. To obtain a preliminary injunction against alleged patent infringement, the patent owner must prove two very basic elements: a strong probability of success on the merits at trial and irreparable injury. In 1985 the Court of Appeals for the Federal Circuit repudiated the older rule that a patentee had to show that the patent was valid "beyond question," substituting the rule that the patentee need only make a "clear showing" that the patent is valid and infringed in order to obtain a preliminary injunction. *Atlas Powder Co. v. Ireco Chems.*, 773 F.2d 1230, 227 USPQ 289 (Fed. Cir. 1985). Irreparable harm is presumed when a clear showing has been made of patent validity and infringement. *H.H. Robertson Co. v. United Steel Deck Inc.*, 820 F.2d 384, 2 USPQ2d 1926 (Fed. Cir. 1987).

Criteria for Patent Preliminary Injunction. To obtain a preliminary injunction pursuant to 35 U.S.C. §283, the patentee must establish its right through the weighing of four factors: (1) a reasonable likelihood of success on the merits; 2) irreparable harm; (3) the balance of the hardships tipping in the patentee's favor; and (4) the impact of the injunction on the public interest. *Hybritech Inc. v. Abbott*, 849 F.2d 1446, 1451, 7 USPQ2d 1191, 1195 (Fed. Cir. 1988). The four factors are to be balanced such that the weakness of plaintiff's case on one factor may be outweighed by the strength of the other factors. *Chrysler Motors Corp. v. Auto Body Panels of Ohio, Inc.*, 908 F.2d 951, 15 USPQ2d 1469 (Fed. Cir 1990). But the Federal Circuit has cautioned that a preliminary injunction in a patent case is a "drastic and extraordinary remedy that is not to be routinely granted." *Intel Corp. v. ULSI Sys. Technology Inc.*, 995 F.2d 1566, 1568, 27 USPQ2d 1136, 1138 (Fed. Cir. 1993).

Treatise References: 5 D. Chisum, *Patents* §20:04[1] (1994 rev.); R. Harmon, *Patents and the Federal Circuit* §13.2 (3d ed. 1994).

• *Statutory Reference*: 35 U.S.C. §283: "The several courts having jurisdiction of cases under this title may grant injunctions in accordance with the principles of equity to prevent the violation of any rights secured by patent, on such terms as the court deems reasonable."

• *Case Reference*: "It is well-settled that, because the principal value of a patent is its statutory right to exclude, the nature of the patent grant weighs against holding that monetary damages will always suffice to make the patentee whole. The patent statute provides injunctive relief to preserve the legal interests of the parties against future infringement which may have market effects never fully compensable in money. 'If monetary relief were the sole relief afforded by the patent statute then ... infringers could become compulsory licensees for as long as the litigation lasts.' We cannot hold that the district court abused its discretion by granting [the patentee's] motion for a preliminary injunction, for the period the litigation is pending, notwithstanding the potential availability of compensatory damages...." *Hy-*

britech Inc. v. Abbott Labs., 849 F.2d 1446, 1456–57, 7 USPQ2d 1191, 1200 (Fed. Cir. 1988).

2. Trademark Infringement Preliminary Injunction. To obtain a preliminary injunction against alleged trademark infringement, the courts generally weigh five factors: (1) whether the plaintiff can show a probability of success on the merits of the claim; (2) whether the plaintiff can show that it will suffer "irreparable injury" pending a full trial on the merits; (3) whether a preliminary injunction will preserve the status quo preceding the dispute; (4) whether the hardships tip in the plaintiff's favor; and (5) whether a preliminary injunction would favor the public interest. J.T. McCarthy, *Trademarks and Unfair Competition* §30.15[1] (3d ed. 1995 rev.). While each federal circuit has fashioned its own particular formulation, these five factors are balanced either explicitly or implicitly. The Court of Appeals for the Second Circuit has stated that a preliminary injunction should be granted if the moving party demonstrates (1) irreparable harm and (2) either (a) a probability of success on the merits or (b) sufficiently serious questions going to the merits to make them fair grounds for litigation and a balance of hardships tipping decidedly in the moving party's favor. *Church of Scientology Int'l v. Elmira Mission of Church of Scientology*, 794 F.2d 38, 230 USPQ 325 (2d Cir. 1986). The Court of Appeals for the Ninth Circuit has a similar rule.

Irreparable Injury Is Presumed. Most courts hold that a strong showing of probable confusion establishes irreparable harm. E.g., *Church of Scientology Int'l v. Elmira Mission of Church of Scientology*, 794 F.2d 38, 230 USPQ 325 (2d Cir. 1986) (denial of preliminary injunction reversed and injunction ordered); *Rodeo Collection Ltd. v. West Seventh*, 812 F.2d 1215, 2 USPQ2d 1204 (9th Cir. 1987) (irreparable harm "ordinarily presumed" from a showing of likely confusion, but denial of preliminary injunction affirmed where record does not support likely confusion). A plaintiff proves irreparable injury if it shows that it will lose control over the reputation of its trademark pending trial. *Power Test Petroleum Distribs., Inc. v. Calcu Gas, Inc.*, 754 F.2d 91, 225 USPQ 368 (2d Cir. 1985).

- *Treatise Reference*: J.T. McCarthy, *Trademarks and Unfair Competition* §§30.15–.23 (3d ed. 1995 rev.).

- *Statutory Reference*: Lanham Act §34(a), 15 U.S.C. §1116(a): "The several courts vested with jurisdiction of civil actions arising under this Act shall have power to grant injunctions, according to the principles of equity and upon such terms as the court may deem reasonable, to prevent the violation of any right of the registrant of a mark registered in the Patent and Trademark Office or to prevent a violation under section 43(a)...."

- *Case Reference*: "In a trademark action, a showing of confusion as to the source of a product ordinarily will establish that a risk of irreparable harm exists to the reputation of the trademark sought to be protected." *General Motors Corp. v. Gibson Chem. & Oil Corp.*, 786 F.2d 105, 109, 229 USPQ 352, 354 (2d Cir. 1986).

3. Copyright Infringement Preliminary Injunction. To obtain a preliminary injunction against alleged copyright infringement, the courts generally weigh four factors: (1) whether the copyright owner can show that it is likely to win on the merits; (2) whether the injury is irreparable; (3) whether the balance of hardships tip in the favor of the copyright owner; and (4) whether an injunction would promote the public interest. See, e.g., *West Publishing Co. v. Mead Data Central, Inc.*, 799 F.2d 1219, 230 USPQ 801 (8th Cir. 1986) (grant of preliminary injunction affirmed). The Courts of Appeals in the Second and Ninth Circuits employ a more complex test: the plaintiff must show either (1) a likelihood of success on the merits and the possibility of irreparable injury or (2) the existence of serious questions going to the merits and a balance of hardships that tips in the plaintiff's favor. See, e.g., *Apple Computer, Inc. v. Formula Int'l, Inc.*, 725 F.2d 521, 523, 221 USPQ 762, 763 (9th Cir. 1984) (grant of preliminary injunction affirmed).

To assist in the demonstration of the validity of the copyright, the plaintiff may point to the PRESUMPTION OF VALIDITY that flows from the registration certificate. If the copyright owner establishes a reasonable probability of success on the merits of the claim of validity and infringement, the courts will usually presume irreparable harm. *West Publishing Co. v. Mead Data Central, Inc.*, 799 F.2d 1219, 1229, 230 USPQ 801, 807 (8th Cir. 1986) ("In copyright infringement cases, the general rule is that a showing of a prima facie case raises a presumption of irreparable harm.").

- *Statutory Reference*: 17 U.S.C. §502(a): "Any court having jurisdiction of a civil action arising under this title may, subject to the provisions of [28 U.S.C. §1498] grant temporary and final injunctions on such terms as it may deem reasonable to prevent or restrain infringement of a copyright."
- *Treatise References*: 3 *Nimmer on Copyright* §14.06[A] (1994 rev.); 2 P. Goldstein, *Copyright* §11.1.2 (1989).
- *Case Reference*: "To be sure, irreparable harm is presumed when plaintiff establishes a *prima facie* case of copyright infringement.... However, it is equally settled that a party's delay in enforcement of copyrights rebuts that presumption." *Bourne Co. v. Tower Records Inc.*, 976 F.2d 99, 101, 24 USPQ2d 1309, 1311 (2d Cir. 1992) (reversing preliminary injunction because of copyright owner's long delay).

prequel [copyright] A story written after a previous story, putting the characters in a narrative set prior in time to that of the first story.

See SEQUEL.

presumption of validity   [patent–trademark–copyright] A presumption created by statute that an intellectual property right asserted by its owner is legitimate and sound in law.

1. Presumption of Patent Validity. Under Patent Code §282, a patent is presumed valid. This validity encompasses three key factors making up validity: novelty, utility, and nonobviousness. The decision maker must begin by assuming that the patent is valid and look to the challenger for proof that it is not valid.

Burden Is on the Challenger. The burden of establishing that a patent claim is invalid is always on the challenger. This burden of persuasion is permanent and is never destroyed.

The burden never shifts over to the patentee. The burden on the challenger is to prove invalidity by a CLEAR AND CONVINCING standard of proof.

Prior Art Cited by the Challenger. When the challenger cites no PRIOR ART other than that which has already been considered by the Patent and Trademark Office (PTO) examiner, then the challenger must surmount an additional evidentiary burden: the deference due to a government agency that is presumed to have properly done its job. When the challenger produces prior art that was not considered by the PTO examiner, the additional presumption that the PTO examiner correctly evaluated the prior art is not relevant because there is now new evidence not considered by the examiner. It is in this sense that the Court of Appeals for the Federal Circuit has said that the introduction of prior art not before the examiner "makes it easier for the party challenging the validity of the patent to carry his burden of proof." *Alco Standard Corp. v. TVA*, 808 F.2d 1490, 1497, 1 USPQ2d 1337, 1342 (Fed. Cir. 1986).

Each Claim Stands on Its Own. Each claim of a patent is presumed valid independently of the status of other claims. It is error for a court to find the whole patent invalid when fewer than all claims are in issue in litigation.

Courts Do Not Declare Patents Valid. Patents are born valid: courts do not declare patents valid. If the challenger succeeds in its challenge to validity, the court declares the patent invalid, and that finding collaterally estops the patentee from suing again on the same patent claims. If the challenger fails in its challenge, the court simply finds that the challenge fails, not that the patent is "valid." The statutory presumption of patent validity is not augmented by an earlier adjudication of "validity," that a different challenger failed to prove invalidity. *Allen Archery Inc. v. Browning Mfg. Co.*, 819 F.2d 1087, 1091, 2 USPQ2d 1490, 1493 (Fed. Cir. 1987). While the fact that the validity of a patent has previously been upheld in an earlier litigation is to be given weight in a subsequent suit on the issue of validity, the prior holding does not necessarily have a STARE DECISIS effect. *Gillette Co. v. S.C. Johnson & Son, Inc.*, 919 F.2d 720, 723, 16 USPQ2d 1923, 1926 (Fed. Cir. 1990).

Judgment of Invalidity Following a Finding of Noninfringement. Before the United States Supreme Court decision in *Cardinal Chem. Co. v. Morton Int'l Inc.*, 113 S. Ct. 1967, 26 USPQ2d 1721 (1993), the Court of Appeals for the Federal Circuit would vacate a declaratory judgment on the issue of patent validity whenever it determined that there was no infringement of the patent. The Federal Circuit held that validity issues raised in declaratory judgment counterclaims became "moot" once the appellate court found that the patent at issue was not infringed and that the dispute raised by the counterclaim did not extend beyond the patentee's infringement claim. See, e.g., *Vieau v. Japax, Inc.*, 823 F.2d 1510, 3 USPQ2d 1094 (Fed. Cir. 1987); *Fonar Corp. v. Johnson & Johnson*, 821 F.2d 627, 2 USPQ2d 1109 (Fed. Cir. 1987).

The Supreme Court held that a finding of noninfringement does not justify the Federal Circuit's practice of vacating declaratory judgments on patent validity because of mootness. The Court said that a party seeking a declaratory judgment of invalidity presents a claim independent of the patentee's charge of infringement. *Cardinal Chem. Co. v. Morton Int'l Inc.*, 113 S. Ct. 1967, 1775, 26 USPQ2d 1721, 1727 (1993). The Supreme Court emphasized "the importance to the public at large of resolving questions of patent validity" and of the risk of "relitigation and impos[ing] ongoing burdens on competitors who are convinced that a patent has been correctly found invalid." 113 S. Ct. at 1978, 26 USPQ2d at 1729.

• *Statutory Reference*: 35 U.S.C. §282: "A patent shall be presumed valid. Each claim of a patent ... shall be presumed valid independently of the validity of others claims.... The burden of establishing invalidity of a patent or any claim thereof shall rest on the party asserting such invalidity...."

• *Case References*:

"[Section] 282 creates a presumption that a patent is valid and imposes the burden of proving invalidity on the attacker. That burden is constant and never changes and is to convince the court of invalidity by clear evidence. Deference is due the Patent and Trademark Office decision to issue the patent with respect to evidence bearing on validity which it considered but no such deference is due with respect to evidence it did not consider. All evidence bearing on the validity issue, whether considered by the PTO or not, is to be taken into account by the tribunal in which validity is attacked." *American Hoist & Derrick Co. v. Sowa & Sons, Inc.*, 725 F.2d 1350, 1360, 220 USPQ 763, 771 (Fed. Cir. 1984).

"Under 35 U.S.C. §282, a patent is presumed valid, and the one attacking validity has the burden of proving invalidity by clear and convincing evidence.... Notwithstanding that the introduction of prior art not before the examiner may facilitate the challenger's meeting the burden of proof on invalidity, the presumption remains intact and on the challenger throughout the litigation, and the clear and convincing standard does not change." *Hybritech Inc. v. Monoclonal Antibodies, Inc.*, 802 F.2d 1367, 1375, 231 USPQ 81, 87 (Fed. Cir. 1986).

"Validity encompasses three 'separate tests of patentability': novelty, utility and nonobviousness.... Thus, included within the presumption of validity is a presumption of novelty, a presumption of nonobviousness and a presumption of utility, each of which must be presumed to have been met." *Structural Rubber Prods. Co. v. Park Rubber Co.*, 749 F.2d 707, 714, 223 USPQ 1264, 1269 (Fed. Cir. 1984).

"It is neither necessary nor appropriate for a court to declare a patent valid. A trial court is required by Congress, 35 U.S.C. §282 ... to say only whether the patent challenger carried its burden of establishing invalidity in the particular case before the court.... It is the judiciary's duty to follow statutes that require a trial court lacking a conviction of obviousness to hold that the challenger's burden was not carried. Thereupon, the patent simply remains valid until another challenger carries the §282 burden." *Panduit Corp. v. Dennison Mfg. Co.*, 810 F.2d 1561, 1569–70, 1 USPQ2d 1593, 1598 (Fed. Cir. 1987).

• *Treatise References*:

5 D. Chisum, *Patents* §19.02 (1994 rev.); R. Harmon, *Patents and the Federal Circuit* §1.5(a) (3d ed. 1994) ("A patent is born valid.

It remains valid until a challenger proves it was stillborn or had birth defects, or it is no longer viable as an enforceable right.").

"[S]ome circuit courts had held that the presumption was weakened or disappeared where prior art was introduced in the infringement case that had not been considered by the patent examiner. Since this is often the case in patent litigation, these holdings significantly weakened the effect of §282. Perhaps the single most significant consequence of the creation of the Federal Circuit for patent law is that the circuit follows CCPA precedents that held that the presumption of §282 is never weakened." E. Kitch & H. Perlman, *Legal Regulation of the Competitive Process* 880 (4th ed. 1991 rev.).

2. Presumption of Trademark Validity. A mark registered on the principal register established by the Lanham Act is presumed to be valid in two stages of registration: the "contestable" stage and the "incontestable" stage.

The Contestable Stage. From the time the mark is first registered, under Lanham Act §§7(b) and 33(a), the registration is prima facie evidence of the validity of the mark, its registration, the registrant's ownership of the mark, and the registrant's exclusive right to use the mark on the registered goods and services. However, Lanham Act §33(a) explicitly permits a challenger to raise any legal or equitable ground to attack the validity of the mark. The presumption of validity also includes a presumption that the mark is either inherently distinctive or has acquired distinctiveness through SECONDARY MEANING.

The Incontestable Stage. After five years of continuous use, the registrant can file a §15 affidavit, acquiring for the registered mark the benefits of "incontestability." The "incontestability" provisions of Lanham Act §33(b) permit the registration to mature into something more substantial than a mere rebuttable presumption of validity. That is, §33(b) states that the registration then becomes "conclusive evidence" of the validity of the mark, its registration, the registrant's ownership of the mark, and the registrant's exclusive right to use the mark on the goods and services specified in the §15 affidavit. However, the term "incontestability"

is a misnomer, for there may be several possible statutory exceptions that can be raised as a ground of challenge to the validity of the mark. Eight grounds of challenge are listed in §33(b) itself, and §33(b) incorporates by reference the exceptions of §15, which in turn incorporates other exceptions. However, two important challenges to the validity of a mark are cut off by the status of incontestability: (1) The mark is not inherently distinctive and lacks secondary meaning. The Supreme Court made this clear in *Park 'N Fly Inc. v. Dollar Park & Fly,* 469 U.S. 189, 224 USPQ 327 (1985). (2) The mark is inferior in priority to the challenger's previously used mark. Incontestable status does not relieve the registrant of proving infringement by way of a likelihood of confusion.

Format and Product-Line Scope of the Presumption. The presumptive validity of a registration extends only to the registered format of the mark and to the goods or services registered. *In re National Data Corp.,* 753 F.2d 1056, 224 USPQ 749 (Fed. Cir. 1985) (registration of COMPOSITE mark affords presumptive validity only to the mark as a whole, not to its component parts); *Levi Strauss & Co. v. Blue Bell, Inc.,* 778 F.2d 1352, 228 USPQ 346 (9th Cir. 1985) (registration for pants not presumptive evidence of secondary meaning for mark on shirts).

• *Treatise Reference*: J.T. McCarthy, *Trademarks and Unfair Competition* §§32.43–.45 (3d ed. 1995 rev.).

• *Statutory Reference*: Lanham Act §33, 15 U.S.C. §1115:

(a) Any registration … of a mark registered on the principal register provided by this Act and owned by a party to an action shall be admissible in evidence and shall be prima facie evidence of the validity of the registered mark and of the registration of the mark, of the registrant's ownership of the mark, and of the registrant's exclusive right to use the registered mark in commerce on or in connection with the goods or services specified in the registration subject to any conditions or limitation stated therein, but shall not preclude another person from proving any legal or equitable defense or defect, including those set forth in subsection (b), which might have been asserted if such mark had not been registered.

(b) To the extent that the right to use the registered mark has become incontestable under section 15, the registration shall be conclusive evidence of the validity of the registered mark and of the registration of the mark, of the registrant's ownership of the mark, and of the registrant's exclusive right to use the registered mark in commerce. Such conclusive evidence shall relate to the exclusive right to use the mark on or in connection with the goods or services specified in the affidavit filed under the provisions of section 15.... Such conclusive evidence of the right to use the registered mark shall be subject to proof of infringement as defined in section 32, and shall be subject to the following defenses or defects: [The list of eight "defenses or defects" follows].

• *Case Reference*: "The incontestability provisions, as the proponents of the Lanham Act emphasized, provide a means for the registrant to quiet title in the ownership of his mark.... The opportunity to obtain incontestable status by satisfying the requirements of §15 thus encourages producers to cultivate the good will associated with a particular mark.... We conclude that the holder of a registered mark may rely on incontestability to enjoin infringement and that such an action may not be defended on the grounds that the mark is merely descriptive." *Park 'N Fly Inc. v. Dollar Park & Fly*, 469 U.S. 189, 198, 205, 224 USPQ 327, 331, 334 (1985).

3. Presumption of Copyright Validity. Under Copyright Act §410(c), a copyright is presumed valid if it has been registered no later than five years after first publication of the work.

Extent of Presumption. The presumption of validity also extends to individual elements making up validity, such that the following elements are also presumed: originality, copyrightability of subject matter, compliance with statutory formalities, ownership, and a proper chain of title.

Renewals. Legislation in 1992 made optional the registration of renewal of certain older copyrights but, to encourage renewal registration, offered the benefits of the presumption of validity to the renewal term if registration was filed within one year before expiration of the initial 28-year term.

See RENEWAL.

• *Treatise References*: 3 *Nimmer on Copyright* §§12.11, 13.01[A] (1994 rev.); 2 P. Goldstein, *Copyright* §14.3 (1989); 1 N. Boorstyn, *Copyright* §9.05[5] (2d ed. 1994).

• *Statutory Reference*: 17 U.S.C. §410(c): "In any judicial proceedings the certificate of registration made before or within five years after first publication of the work shall constitute prima facie evidence of the validity of the copyright and of the facts stated in the certificate. The evidentiary weight to be accorded the certificate of a registration made thereafter shall be within the discretion of the court."

• *Legislative History*: "The principle that a certificate represents prima facie evidence of copyright validity has been established in a long line of court decisions, and it is a sound one. It is true that, unlike a patent claim, a claim to copyright is not examined for basic validity before a certificate is issued. On the other hand, endowing a copyright claimant who has obtained a certificate with a rebuttable presumption of the validity of the copyright does not deprive the defendant in an infringement suit of any rights; it merely orders the burdens of proof. The plaintiff should not ordinarily be forced in the first instance to prove all of the multitude of facts that underline the validity of the copyright unless the defendant, by effectively challenging them, shifts the burden of doing so to the plaintiff." Rep. No. 94-1476, 94th Cong., 2d Sess. 157 (1976).

• *Case References*:

"Before asking a court to consider the question of infringement, a party must demonstrate the existence and the validity of its copyright, for in the absence of copyright (or patent, trademark or state law) protection, even original creations are in the public domain and may be freely copied.... In many cases, the existence of a valid copyright can be established by the introduction into evidence of a Copyright Office certificate of registration.... It is clear, however, that a certificate of registration creates no irrebuttable presumption of copyright validity. Where other evidence in the record casts doubt on the question, validity will not be assumed." *Durham Indus., Inc. v. Tomy Corp.*, 630 F.2d 905, 908, 208 USPQ 10, 13 (2d Cir. 1980).

"Procedurally then, the plaintiff has the burden of proving the validity of his copyright; by obtaining a copyright certificate the plaintiff is entitled to a prima facie presumption of copyright validity (and the burden shifts to the defendant to prove lack of originality); upon proof by the defendant of the plaintiff's access to similar prior works, the burden of proving originality shifts back to the plaintiff." *Original Appalachian Artworks, Inc. v. Toy Loft, Inc.*, 489 F. Supp. 174, 179, 210 USPQ 634, 637 (N.D.Ga. 1980), *aff'd*, 684 F.2d 821, 215 USPQ 745 (11th Cir. 1982).

prima facie case [patent] A procedural tool for allocating the burden between the patent examiner and the applicant. The initial burden is on the examiner to present a "prima facie case" of unpatentability. If the examiner at the initial stage does not produce a prima facie case of unpatentability, then without more the applicant is entitled to the grant of the patent. However, if the burden is met, the burden of coming forward with evidence or argument shifts to the applicant. *In re Oetiker*, 977 F.2d 1443, 24 USPQ2d 1443 (Fed. Cir. 1992). On appeal, after evidence or argument is presented by the applicant in response, patentability is determined on the entire record, by a preponderance of evidence. The rule of a prima facie case has broad applicability to all technological classes of inventions.

- *Case Reference*: "The *prima facie* case is a procedural tool of patent examination, allocating the burdens of going forward as between examiner and applicant.... We think that the PTO is correct in treating the concept of the *prima facie* case as of broad applicability, for it places the initial burden on the examiner, the appropriate procedure whatever the technological class of invention. That a *prima facie* case

may be established, or rebutted, by different forms of evidence in various technologies does not restrict the concept to any particular field." *In re Oetiker*, 977 F.2d 1443, 1446, 24 USPQ2d 1443, 1444–45 (Fed. Cir. 1992).

principal register [trademark] The main federal register of marks established by the Lanham Act. Registrable on the principal register are TRADEMARKS, SERVICE MARKS, COLLECTIVE MARKS, and CERTIFICATION MARKS.

Criteria for Registration. The registration may be based upon either an INTENT TO USE application or a use-based application. But to obtain registration, the mark must have been in use in interstate commerce or in import or export trade, which means a bona fide use in the ordinary course of trade, not made merely to reserve rights in a mark. However, in a §44 application made by a qualified foreign firm with a foreign application or registration, the foreign applicant must state its bona fide intention to use the mark in the United States but, unlike domestic applicants, need not prove actual use in order to receive the registration. To be registrable, the mark must not fall within one of the statutory bars listed in Lanham Act §2. Under §2(d), the applicant's mark cannot be confusingly similar to a previously used or registered mark. Under §2(e), if the term is descriptive, geographically descriptive, or a personal name surname, it is registrable as a mark only upon proof under §2(f) of acquired distinctiveness, i.e., SECONDARY MEANING.

See DESCRIPTIVE MARK, GEOGRAPHIC MARK, PERSONAL NAME MARK.

Formalities of Registration. If the application is found acceptable by the Patent and Trademark Office (PTO) examiner, it is published for possible OPPOSITION by an interested person. If no opposition proceeding is filed, a registration is granted for a §1(a) use-based or §44 foreign entity application. If the application is a §1(b) INTENT TO USE application, a notice of allowance is sent to the applicant, who then has a fixed time with a maximum of 36 months to file a §1(d) statement of use with evidence that the mark has been placed in use. Registrations based on applications filed after or pending in the PTO on November 16, 1989, last for renewal periods of 10 years. Lanham Act §51, 15 U.S.C. §1058 note.

See DURATION.

Advantages Gained by Registration on the Principal Register. Among the advantages gained by registration are: (1) the registration is immediately prima facie evidence of the validity of the registered mark (see PRESUMPTION OF VALIDITY); (2) after five years of continuous use, the registration may become "incontestable," which will foreclose some but not all challenges to validity of the mark (see PRESUMPTION OF VALIDITY); (3) the registration is CONSTRUCTIVE NOTICE of the registrant's ownership, cutting off later claims of good faith use in territories remote from the registrant's use; (4) under the 1989 Trademark Law Revision Act amendments, at least for registrations issued on applications filed on or after November 16, 1989, the registrant has a CONSTRUCTIVE NOTICE priority date as of the date of filing of the application; and (5) under §2(d), PTO examiners will cite the registration as a bar to later applications to register a similar mark.

See REGISTRATION OF TRADEMARK, PRESUMPTION OF VALIDITY.

• *Treatise Reference*: J.T. McCarthy, *Trademarks and Unfair Competition* §§19.05–.19 (3d ed. 1995 rev.).

• *Statutory Reference*: Lanham Act §45, 15 U.S.C. §1127: "The term 'principal register' refers to the register provided for by sections 1 through 22 hereof, and the term 'supplemental register' refers to the register provided by sections 23 through 28 hereof."

printed publication [patent] A document, accessible to the public, that discloses technological data. A publication printed anywhere in the world that discloses technical information can be a bar to a patent and is prior art under Patent Code §102(a) if it was published before the present inventor's date of invention. Under Patent Code §102(b), it is also a statutory bar and PRIOR ART if it was published more than one year before the filing date of the present inventor's patent application. The "statutory bar" referred to is that of ANTICIPATION: lack of novelty. Such printed publications can also serve to make a later invention "obvious" and unpatentable under Patent Code §103.

Types of Printed Publications. A "printed publication" can include everything from manufacturers' catalogs to articles in scientific journals to academic theses on file in college libraries. The key is accessibility of the publication to that group of people concerned with this technology that is most likely to want to see the publication.

Printed Publication Can Trigger the Anticipation and Obviousness Bars. If the technical data disclosed in the printed publication contains all the elements of the claimed invention, there is a direct anticipation bar against a patent. In addition, the technical information disclosed becomes part of the prior art for purposes of applying the OBVIOUSNESS bar against a patent. Thus, a valid patent is barred if the claimed invention is either completely embodied in, or obvious in view of, the information disclosed in the printed publication. *Massachusetts Inst. of Technology v. AB Fortia*, 774 F.2d 1104, 1108, 227 USPQ 428, 431 (Fed. Cir. 1985).

The One-Year Grace Period. An inventor cannot obtain a valid patent if he or she waits for more than one year to file a patent application after the invention has been described in a "printed publication." It is against public policy to permit the inventor to disclose the invention more than one year before filing the patent application, which is the grace period created by Patent Code §102(b). The date one year prior to the filing date of the patent is known as the CRITICAL DATE. A printed publication disseminated prior to that date can trigger the bar to a patent.

See ANTICIPATION, OBVIOUSNESS, CRITICAL DATE.

• *Statutory Reference*: 35 U.S.C. §102:

A person shall be entitled to a patent unless—

(a) the invention was known or used by others in this country, or patented or described in a printed publication in this or a foreign country, before the invention thereof by the applicant for patent, or

(b) the invention was patented or described in a printed publication in this or a foreign country or in public use or on sale in this country, more than one year prior to the date of the application for patent in the United States....

• *Case References*:
"It is well settled that in determining whether a printed document constitutes a publication bar under 35 U.S.C. §102(b) the touchstone is public accessibility. This follows logically from the theory that the patent grant is in the nature of a contract between the inventor and the public. Hence, if knowledge of the invention is already accessible to the public there is a failure of consideration and no patent may be granted.... [W]e think it apparent that a printed document may qualify as a 'publication' under 35 U.S.C. §102(b), notwithstanding that accessibility thereto is restricted to a 'part of the public,' so long as accessibility is sufficient 'to raise a presumption that the public concerned with the art would know of [the invention].' " *In re Bayer*, 568 F.2d 1357, 1361, 196 USPQ 670, 673–74 (C.C.P.A. 1978).

"Accessibility goes to the issue of whether interested members of the relevant public could obtain the information if they wanted to. If accessibility is proved, there is no requirement to show that particular members of the public actually received the information." *Constant v. Advanced Micro-Devices Inc.*, 848 F.2d 1560, 1569, 7 USPQ2d 1057, 1062 (Fed. Cir. 1987) (claims of patent held invalid as anticipated by data in a product specification sheet distributed by Intel Corporation prior to the critical date).

• *Example 1*: Researchers at the Massachusetts Institute of Technology (MIT) invented and obtained a patent on an improvement in microcarriers: microscopic beads suitable for cell attachment and growth. Prior to the critical date, Dr. Levine, one of the members of the MIT research team, delivered an oral presentation describing part of the invention to an international scientific meeting of specialists in cell culture, which was held in Birmingham, Alabama. Before the conference, Dr. Levine gave a copy of his paper to the head of the conference. Afterward, copies were distributed on request, without any restrictions, to six persons. All of these events occurred before the critical date of

one year prior to the filing of the patent application by the MIT research team. The Court of Appeals for the Federal Circuit held that the "Birmingham paper" was a "printed publication" that became part of the PRIOR ART, in the light of which the patented invention was found to be obvious and invalid. *Massachusetts Inst. of Technology v. AB Fortia*, 774 F.2d 1104, 1108, 227 USPQ 428, 431 (Fed. Cir. 1985).

• *Example 2*: Professor Cronyn of Reed College invented a chemical compound that could be useful in treating cancer. The Patent and Trademark Office rejected his patent application under Patent Code §102(b) as being ANTICIPATED by data divulged in three student theses on file in the library at Reed College prior to the CRITICAL DATE, i.e., one year prior to the date that Cronyn filed his patent application. The Court of Appeals for the Federal Circuit held that these student theses were not "printed publications" within the meaning of the statute and reversed the rejection of Cronyn's application. In the 1978 *Bayer* case, the Court of Customs and Patent Appeals had held that a master's thesis did not become a "printed publication" upon its receipt by a university library. In the 1986 *Hall* case, the Federal Circuit had held that a doctoral thesis on file in the library of a German university was a "printed publication." The court explained these divergent results: "[T]he critical difference between the cases that explains the different results is that on the critical date in *Bayer* the thesis was 'uncatalogued and unshelved' and therefore was not accessible to the public, whereas in *Hall* the 'dissertation was accessible' because it had been indexed, cataloged and shelved." Here, the student theses were not accessible because "they had not been either catalogued or indexed in a meaningful way." *In re Cronyn*, 890 F.2d 1158, 1161, 13 USPQ2d 1070, 1072 (Fed. Cir. 1989).

prior art [patent] The existing body of technological information against which an invention is judged to determine if it is patentable as being a novel and nonobvious invention.

Prior Art Is Defined in Patent Code §102.
Prior art is that prior technological information as defined in several subsections of Patent Code

§102. That information is to be compared to the present invention to determine if the present invention is novel and nonobvious in view of that prior art. However, §102 is not the sole and exclusive source of what constitutes PRIOR ART. "Valid prior art may be created by the admissions of the parties." *In re Fout*, 675 F.2d 297, 300, 213 USPQ 532, 535 (C.C.P.A. 1982).

Dual Function of Patent Code §102. Patent Code §102 does double duty. Not only does it define ANTICIPATION as a bar to a patent for an invention, but several parts of it also define what constitutes "prior art" for purposes of applying the obviousness test of Patent Code §103. The antecedent of the words "the prior art" in §103 is in the phrase "disclosed or described as set forth in section 102."

Anticipation. If there is an IDENTITY of invention between a single prior art reference and the present claimed invention, then the present invention is unpatentable as being "anticipated" under §102. If the prior art references considered together would have made the present claimed invention obvious to a person skilled in the art, then the invention is not patentable under §103.

Person Having Skill in the Art. Under Patent Code §103, an invention is "obvious" and unpatentable if the differences between the invention and the "prior art" are such that "the subject matter as a whole would have been obvious at the time the invention was made" to a hypothetical person having ordinary "SKILL IN THE ART to which such subject matter pertains." See HYPOTHETICAL PERSON SKILLED IN THE ART. It is irrelevant whether or not the actual inventor was aware of the prior art references. *EWP Corp. v. Reliance Universal Inc.*, 755 F.2d 898, 907, 225 USPQ2d 20, 25 (Fed. Cir. 1985) (Rich, J.).

Prior Art and the Obviousness Test. Prior art is found in the kinds of disclosure accessible to the public, which are listed in §102. These include the disclosure of data in prior patents and printed publications such as technical journals and papers. Prior art will sometimes include technology that is in PUBLIC USE or ON SALE in the United States. Prior art can include certain prior publications and public uses not only of other persons, but also of the inventor himself.

Types of Prior Art. The kind of evidence most often relied upon as prior art to show obviousness is that listed in §102(a) as occurring before the date of the present invention: prior knowledge or use, prior patents, or printed publications. In addition, those things described in §102(b) can also qualify as prior art. Those are patents, publications, public uses, advertising, and sales that have effective dates more than one year prior to the present inventor's date of filing a patent application. *In re Kaslow*, 707 F.2d 1366, 1374, 217 USPQ 1089, 1095 (Fed. Cir. 1983) ("a public use or placing on sale under section 102(b) is 'prior art' which may support an obviousness rejection under section 103"). See 2 D. Chisum, *Patents* §5.03[2]-[3] (1994 rev.).

Analogous Prior Art. To qualify as "prior art," the data must be from the same technical field or from an ANALOGOUS ART. On the other hand, information from technology that is so far removed from the field of technology to which an invention pertains that the information is not considered to be "prior art" is known as a reference from a "nonanalogous art."

See ART, ANALOGOUS ART, ANTICIPATION, OBVIOUSNESS, SKILL IN THE ART.

• *Treatise Reference*: 2 D. Chisum, *Patents* §5.03 (1994 rev.); R. Harmon, *Patents and the Federal Circuit* §3.4 (3d ed. 1994).

• *Statutory References*:

35 U.S.C. §103: "A patent may not be obtained though the invention is not identically disclosed or described as set forth in section 102 of this title, if the differences between the subject matter sought to be patented and the prior art are such that the subject matter as a whole would have been obvious at the time the invention was made to a person having ordinary skill in the art to which such subject matter pertains...."

35 U.S.C. §102:

A person shall be entitled to a patent unless—

(a) the invention was known or used by others in this country, or patented or described in a printed publication in this or a foreign country, before the invention thereof by the applicant for patent, or

(b) the invention was patented or described in a printed publication in this or a foreign country or in public use or on sale in this country, more than one year prior to the date of the application for patent in the United States....

• *Case References*:

"Title 35 nowhere defines the term 'prior art.' Its exact meaning is a somewhat complex question of law which has been the subject of legal papers and whole chapters of books.... Basically, the concept of prior art is that which is publicly known, or at least known to someone who has taken steps which do make it known to the public ... or known to the inventor against whose application it is being applied." *In Re Bergy*, 596 F.2d 952, 965 n.7, 201 USPQ 352, 365 n.7 (C.C.P.A. 1979), *dismissed as moot*, 444 U.S. 924 (1980).

"[I]t has been unusual that opinions have explained the real reason for the denial of patent rights, which is the basic principle (to which there are minor exceptions) that no patent should be granted which withdraws from the public domain technology already available to the public.... It is available, in legal theory at least, when it is described in the world's accessible literature, including patents, or has been publicly known or in the public use or on sale 'in this country.' 35 U.S.C. §102(a) and (b). That is the real meaning of 'prior art' in legal theory—it is knowledge that is available, including what would be obvious from it, at a given time, to a person of ordinary skill in an art. Society, speaking through Congress and the courts, has said 'thou shalt not take it away.' " *Kimberly-Clark Corp. v. Johnson & Johnson Co.*, 745 F.2d 1437, 1453–54, 223 USPQ 603, 614 (Fed. Cir. 1984).

"[T]he remaining portions of §102 deal with 'prior art.' Three of them, (a), (e) and (g) deal with events prior to applicant's *invention* date and the other, (b), with events more than one year prior to the U.S. *application date*. These are the 'prior art' subsections." *In re Bass*, 474

F.2d 1276, 1290, 177 USPQ 178, 189 (C.C.P.A. 1973).

prior art statement [patent]
See INFORMATION DISCLOSURE STATEMENT.

priority of invention [patent] The first person to invent has priority of invention over others who invented the same patentable concept. The inventor with priority of invention is granted the patent. This is the rule followed in the United States. An INTERFERENCE proceeding is required to determine priority of invention.

First to Invent. Unlike most nations, the United States, as of 1995, does not use the "first to file" rule of determining who is the patentee of technology invented by more than one person at about the same time. Rather, the United States follows a "first to invent" rule. However, the first to file does gain an important procedural advantage, as described below.

First to File. In the United States, the party in the interference proceeding who is the first to file a patent application is known as the SENIOR PARTY and presumed to have been the first inventor. This is because the date of filing the patent application is presumed to be the date of invention. The burden is on the junior party to prove an earlier date of invention.

Place of Invention. As a result of legislative changes enacted in 1994 in both the NAFTA implementation act and the URUGUAY ROUND AGREEMENTS ACT, there was a substantial increase in the range of locations in which inventive activity would count toward patent priority in the United States. Under previous law, no evidence could be introduced in an interference proceeding by an inventor seeking to prove a date of invention if the evidence related to actions that took place outside the United States. The 1994 NAFTA amendments increased the range of locations for inventive activity to include Canada and Mexico. The 1994 Uruguay Round Agreements Act further expanded the range of possible locations to include inventive activity that occurs within WORLD TRADE ORGANIZATION (WTO) member countries. These 1994 Uruguay Round Agreements Act amendments became effective as to patent applications filed on or after January 1, 1996, one year after the WTO Agreement became effective in the United States. In addition, an inventor cannot establish a date of invention earlier than January 1, 1996, with respect to activity in WTO nations.

See INTERFERENCE, SENIOR PARTY, JUNIOR PARTY.

- *Statutory References*:

35 U.S.C. §102(g): "In determining priority of invention there shall be considered not only the respective dates of conception and reduction to practice of the invention, but also the reasonable diligence of one who was first to conceive and last to reduce to practice, from a time prior to conception by the other."

35 U.S.C. §104(a)(1): "In proceedings in the Patent and Trademark Office, in the courts, and before any other competent authority, an applicant for a patent, or a patentee, may not establish a date of invention by reference to knowledge or use thereof, in a foreign country other than a NAFTA country or a WTO member country, except as provided in sections 119 and 365 of this title."

- *Case Reference*: "In order to establish priority in an interference, the party who files later is 'required to establish reduction to practice *before* [the] filing date [of the party who filed first], or conception before that date coupled with reasonable diligence from just before that date to [the] filing date [of the party who files later].'" *Hahn v. Wong*, 892 F.2d 1028, 1032, 13 USPQ2d 1313, 1317 (Fed. Cir. 1989).

process claim [patent] A claim of a patent that covers a method by defining a series of steps to be followed in performing a process. A process claim is to be contrasted with a PRODUCT CLAIM or APPARATUS CLAIM, which covers the structure of a product.

Verb Introduction. A process claim can often be identified by the fact that each element of the claim will be introduced by a verb, as in the following example: "A method of retreading the road engaging surface of a tire comprising the steps of *forming* an assembly of a tire casing, tread and binding medium, *enclosing* said as-

sembly within an air-tight cover, *mounting* said tire casing on a rim...."

Control Over Products of Patented Process. A process claim usually gives exclusive rights only as to that use of that process. It cannot be interpreted so as to give rights on equipment used in performing the process, even if the claim could have been drafted to cover the equipment. An amendment to the Patent Code in 1988 for the first time gave an owner of a patent with a process claim a limited right to exclude others from acts such as using, selling, or importing unpatented products made by the patented process. However, that right to exclude is conditioned on several complicated procedural and notice requirements. See 4 D. Chisum, *Patents* §16.02[6] (1994 rev.). See 35 U.S.C. §271(g) & 295. See OFF-SHORE ASSEMBLY.

Product-by-Process Claim. A product whose structure is difficult to describe can sometimes be claimed by defining the process that produces the product. This is a PRODUCT-BY-PROCESS claim.

Synonym: METHOD CLAIM

- *Case Reference*: "It is commonplace that the claims defining some inventions can by competent draftsmanship be directed to either a method or an apparatus.... The inventor of such an invention has the option as to the form the claims in his patent will assume. There is nothing improper in this state of affairs, however, and the exercise of that option is to be respected in interpreting such claims as do ultimately issue from prosecution. Thus, the Carver [process] patent is not a patent on equipment for performing the method disclosed, even if its claims could have been so drafted." *Bandag, Inc. v. Al Bolser's Tire Stores, Inc.*, 750 F.2d 903, 922, 223 USPQ 982, 996 (Fed. Cir. 1984).

product-by-process claim [patent] A patent claim in which a product is claimed by defining the process by which the product is made.

Chemical Compounds. The product-by-process form of claim is most often used to define new chemical compounds. Many new chemicals, pharmaceuticals, and drugs can only practicably be defined by the process of making them.

Focus on Newness of Product. Even though a product-by-process claim recites the steps of a process, patentability is determined by the NOVELTY and NONOBVIOUSNESS of the product, not the process. A similar PRIOR ART product may preclude the patentability of a later product even if the two products are produced by patentably different processes. When the prior art discloses a product that appears to be either identical with or only slightly different from a product claimed in a product-by-process claim, the Patent and Trademark Office can reject the claim on the basis of ANTICIPATION under Patent Code §102 or OBVIOUSNESS under Patent Code §103. *Manual of Patent Examining Procedure* §706.03(e) (1994 rev.). As to prior art processes, the Patent and Trademark Office is not equipped to make products from processes cited to it and then make physical comparisons between the resulting products.

Scope of Claim. A product-by-process claim is not limited to a product prepared by the process set forth in the claims. Thus, it is possible that an identical product made by a different process could be an infringement. *Scripps Clinic & Research Found. v. Genentech, Inc.,* 927 F.2d 1565, 1583, 18 USPQ2d 1001, 1016 (Fed. Cir. 1991).

• *Treatise Reference*: 2 D. Chisum, *Patents* §8.05 (1994 rev.).

• *Case References*:

"Product-by-process claims are not specifically discussed in the patent statute. The practice and governing law have developed in response to the need to enable an applicant to claim an otherwise unpatentable product that resists definition by other than the process by which it is made. For this reason, even though product-by-process claims are limited by and defined by the process, determination of patentability is based on the product itself.... The patentability of a product does not depend on its method of production.... If the product in a product-by-process claim is the same as or obvious from a product of the prior art, the claim is unpatentable even though the prior product was made by a different process." *In re Thorpe,* 777 F.2d 695, 697, 227 USPQ 964, 966 (Fed. Cir. 1985).

"[T]he lack of physical description in a product-by-process claim makes determination of the patentability of the claim more difficult, since in spite of the fact that the claim may recite only process limitations, it is the patentability of the *product* claimed and *not* of the recited process steps which must be established." *In re Brown,* 459 F.2d 531, 533, 173 USPQ 685, 688 (C.C.P.A. 1972).

"Where a product-by-process claim is rejected over a prior art product that appears to be identical, although produced by a different process, the burden is upon the applicants to come forward with evidence establishing an unobvious difference between the claimed product and the prior art product." *In re Marosi,* 710 F.2d 799, 218 USPQ 289, 292-293 (Fed. Cir. 1983).

• *Example of Product-by-Process Claim.* The inventor wished to patent a new liquid composition used for imparting a smoked flavor to meat. The claim read: "A liquid smoke product comprising at least a portion of the material resulting from a process of: (a) contacting particulate wood solids with superheated steam having a temperature of at least 180°C to effect a thermal decomposition of said wood solids to form a smoking fluid; (b) withdrawing the smoking fluid from the wood solids; and (c) liquefying the smoking fluid to produce said liquid smoke product which may be stored and subsequently applied in the treatment of foodstuffs." The claim was found to be obvious in view of the prior art. The court stated that the Patent and Trademark Office bears a "lesser burden of proof in making out a case of prima facie obviousness" for product-by-process claims because of their "peculiar nature." *In re Fessmann,* 489 F.2d 742, 744, 180 USPQ 324, 326 (C.C.P.A. 1974).

product claim [patent] A claim of a patent that covers a structure, apparatus, or composition. A product claim is to be contrasted with a "process claim," which covers a method or process.

A product whose structure is difficult to describe can sometimes be claimed by defining the process that produces the product. This is a PRODUCT-BY-PROCESS claim.

profits [patent–trademark–copyright] In cases of infringement of a design patent, trademark, or a copyright, the plaintiff may be able to recover from the infringer those profits made by the infringer that are attributable to the infringing sales. In copyright and trademark cases, recovery of the profits made by the infringer from the infringing sales are a standard form of monetary recovery. The process of computing and awarding the infringer's profits is called an "accounting of profits."

The recovery of an infringer's profits is to be distinguished from the inclusion of the plaintiff's lost profits as an element of measuring the plaintiff's damages resulting from the infringement.

1. Patent Cases: Recovery of Infringer's Profits. The direct recovery of the patent infringer's profits is possible only with respect to infringement of a DESIGN PATENT, not a utility patent.

Infringer's Profits Are Not Recoverable for Infringement of a Utility Patent. In 1946 Congress eliminated statutory authority for the utility patent owner to recover the infringer's profits, inserting the present Patent Code §284, which requires an award of "damages adequate to compensate for the infringement." 35 U.S.C. §284. See *General Motors Corp. v. Devex Corp.*, 461 U.S. 648, 654, 217 USPQ 1185, 1188 (1983) ("In 1946 Congress excluded consideration of the infringer's gain by eliminating the recovery of his profits, ... the determination of which had often required protracted litigation."). Today, while such profits cannot be recovered per se, they can be taken into account as evidence in proving what is a REASONABLE ROYALTY or in measuring damages for infringement of a utility patent. 5 D. Chisum, *Patents* §20.02[4] (1994 rev.).

Design Patents. The special statutory section for DESIGN PATENTS provides that the infringer of a design patent "shall be liable to the owner to the extent of his total profit, but not less than

$250...." 35 U.S.C. §289. The Court of Appeals for the Federal Circuit has held that this statutory section does not apply to profits made on products not directly using the patented design. In that case, the patented design covered only a display rack used to sell eyeglasses. Profits made on the sale of eyeglasses were held not recoverable. *Trans-World Mfg. Corp. v. Al Nyman & Sons, Inc.*, 750 F.2d 1552, 1567-68, 224 USPQ 259, 268 (Fed. Cir. 1984).

• *Treatise Reference*: 5 D. Chisum, *Patents* §20.02[5] (1994 rev.).

2. Trademark Cases: Recovery of Infringer's Profits. The recovery of the trademark infringer's profits was and is a traditional remedy. Under federal law, the recovery of the infringer's profits is authorized by Lanham Act §35, 15 U.S.C. §1117.

Apportionment and Deductibility of Costs. The Lanham Act preserves two traditional doctrines of the recovery of profits from a trademark infringer: (1) it is the infringer's burden to prove any portion of total profits that were not due to use of the infringing mark; and (2) the plaintiff need prove the defendant's total sales only: the infringer has the burden of proof as to the allowability of any deductible costs to arrive at a profit figure. Allowable deductions include overhead, most operating expenses, and income taxes. Unprofitable years at an infringing outlet may be offset against the profitable years. *Burger King Corp. v. Mason*, 855 F.2d 779, 8 USPQ2d 1263 (11th Cir. 1988).

The Requirement of Wrongful Intent. Most courts will require some showing of deliberate or willful infringement before authorizing an accounting of profits. The traditional view is that an accounting of profits is not automatic upon a finding of infringement where an injunction will "satisfy the equities of the case." *Champion Spark Plug Co. v. Sanders*, 331 U.S. 125, 73 USPQ 133 (1947). Some form of bad faith or knowing infringement is needed before an accounting of profits is felt to be necessary. *Nalpac, Ltd. v. Corning Glass Works*, 784 F.2d 752, 228 USPQ 946 (6th Cir. 1986); Restatement (Third) of Unfair Competition, §37, comment e (1995).

Evidence of Actual Confusion. Some courts hold that proof of some instances of actual confusion is required as a basis for a recovery of damages or an accounting of profits. *Perfect Fit Indus., Inc. v. Acme Quilting Co.*, 618 F.2d 950, 205 USPQ 297 (2d Cir. 1980). Other courts will order an accounting in the absence of any evidence of actual confusion if the infringement was clearly intended, as in a COUNTERFEITING case. *Playboy Enters., Inc. v. Baccarat Clothing Co.*, 692 F.2d 1272, 216 USPQ 1083 (9th Cir. 1982).

Judicial Power to Increase Damages or Adjust Profits. Under Lanham Act §35, 15 U.S.C. §1117, the court is given the discretion to increase damages to treble damages and increase or decrease an award of profits by any amount if the court finds that the profit recovery is "either inadequate or excessive." Increasing damages and profits under Lanham Act §35(a) is common in COUNTERFEITING cases. Under Lanham Act §35(b), in counterfeiting cases, treble damages or profits are mandatory except in rare cases of "extenuating circumstances."

Competitive and Noncompetitive Cases. Where the litigants are competitors, the infringer's profits are a rough measure of the plaintiff's loss. Where the parties are not competitors, most courts will award the infringer's profits under a theory of unjust enrichment. *Maier Brewing Co. v. Fleischmann Distilling Corp.*, 390 F.2d 117, 157 USPQ 76 (9th Cir. 1968) (the object is to make deliberate trademark infringement unprofitable). Contra *Raxton Corp. v. Anania Assocs., Inc.*, 668 F.2d 622, 213 USPQ 903 (1st Cir. 1982) (an accounting of profits "not authorized" in noncompetitive cases).

- *Treatise Reference*: J.T. McCarthy, *Trademarks and Unfair Competition*, §§30.25-30.26 (3d ed. 1995 rev.)

3. Copyright Cases: Recovery of Infringer's Profits. The Copyright Act permits the recovery of both the copyright owner's damages and the infringer's profits, if the two are not cumulative and not merely two ways to measure the same injury. 17 U.S.C. §504(b).

Apportionment of Profits. The 1978 Copyright Act preserves two traditional doctrines of copyright remedies: (1) apportionment of profits; and (2) casting the burden of proof on the infringer. Under the doctrine of apportionment, only those profits "attributable to the infringement" are recoverable. But it is the infringer's burden to prove any proportion of its total sales that were not due to the use of the infringing work. In a famous case, the Supreme Court affirmed an apportioned award of 20 percent of the net profits made from exhibitions of a motion picture that infringed upon the plaintiff's copyrighted play. *Sheldon v. Metro-Goldwyn Corp.*, 309 U.S. 390, 44 USPQ 607 (1940). The remainder of the profits were due to the contribution to the movie of the motion picture studio and its producers, director, actors, camera operators, stage designers, costumers, make-up artists, etc. In another case, it was held that 50 percent of the profits on the sale of a magazine were due to the use of an infringing photograph of actress Raquel Welch on the cover of the magazine. *Sygma Photo News, Inc. v. High Soc'y Magazine, Inc.*, 778 F.2d 89, 228 USPQ 580 (2d Cir. 1985). However, it is the copyright owner's task to show those sales that were generated by an infringing advertisement, not just the total sales of a corporate infringer. *Taylor v. Meirick*, 712 F.2d 1112, 1122, 219 USPQ 420, 426 (7th Cir. 1983).

Deductible Costs. In arriving at a figure for "profit," the copyright owner need only introduce proof of the infringer's gross revenue, and then the infringer has the burden of proving appropriate elements of costs and expenses to be deducted. 17 U.S.C. §504(b). Generally, the infringer can deduct only those costs that are directly related to the infringing activity. Thus, overhead attributable to the production of the infringing items can be deducted, but only if it was of "direct assistance in the production, distribution or sale of the infringing product." *Kamar Int'l, Inc. v. Russ Berrie & Co.*, 752 F.2d 1326, 1332, 224 USPQ 674, 678 (9th Cir. 1984).

Prejudgment Interest and Indirect Profits. It has been held that an award of PREJUDGMENT INTEREST on the award of the infringer's profits is "consistent with the purposes underlying the profits remedy." *Frank Music Corp. v. MGM Inc.*, 886 F.2d 1545, 1552, 12 USPQ2d 1412,

1418 (9th Cir. 1989) (see case reference below). This case also upheld an award of indirect profits of 2 percent of a Nevada casino's hotel and gaming operations where the casino used without license the plaintiff's song in the casino's featured musical stage production.

See STATUTORY DAMAGES.

• *Statutory Reference*: 17 U.S.C. §504(b): "The copyright owner is entitled to recover the actual damages suffered by him or her as a result of the infringement, and any profits of the infringer that are attributable to the infringement and are not taken into account in computing the actual damages. In establishing the infringer's profits, the copyright owner is required to present proof only of the infringer's gross revenue, and the infringer is required to prove his or her deductible expenses and the elements of profit attributable to factors other than the copyrighted work."

• *Treatise References*: W. Patry, *Copyright Law and Practice* 1164–69; 3 *Nimmer on Copyright* §14.03 (1994 rev.); 2 P. Goldstein, *Copyright* §12.1 (1989); M. Leaffer, *Understanding Copyright* §9.12 (1989); 1 N. Boorstyn, *Copyright* §13.03 (2d ed 1994).

• *Case References*:

"It is true that if the infringer makes greater profits than the copyright owner lost, because the infringer is a more efficient producer than the owner or sells in a different market, the owner is allowed to capture the additional profit even though it does not represent a loss to him. It may seem wrong to penalize the infringer for his superior efficiency and give the owner a windfall. But it discourages infringement…. [S]ome of the 'windfall' may actually be profit that the owner would have obtained from licensing his copyright to the infringer had the infringer sought a license." *Taylor v. Meirick*, 712 F.2d 1112, 1121, 219 USPQ 420, 424 (7th Cir. 1983).

"Profits are awarded to the plaintiff not only to compensate for the plaintiff's injury, but also and primarily to prevent the defendant from being unjustly enriched by its infringing use of the plaintiff's property…. For the restitutionary purpose of this remedy to be served fully, the defendant generally should be required to turn over to the plaintiff not only the profits made from the use of his property, but also the interest on these profits, which can well exceed the profits themselves." *Frank Music Corp. v. MGM Inc.*, 886 F.2d 1545, 1552, 12 USPQ2d 1412, 1418 (9th Cir. 1989).

prophetic example [patent] A description in the patent SPECIFICATION of a manner and process of making a physical embodiment of the invention, which has not yet actually been made. Such examples may be made in certain inventions in order to satisfy the ENABLEMENT requirement for patent validity.

The burden is on the challenger of the patent to prove that the prophetic example, read in light of the specification as a whole, does not comply with the enablement requirement.

Synonym: paper examples.

See ENABLEMENT.

• *Case Reference*: "Because [the examples in the specification] are prophetic, argues du Pont, there can be no guarantee that the examples would actually work. Use of prophetic examples, however, does not automatically make a patent non-enabling. The burden is on one challenging validity to show by clear and convincing evidence that the prophetic examples together with other parts of the specification are not enabling. To the contrary the district court found that the 'prophetic' examples of the specification were based on actual experiments that were slightly modified in the patent to reflect what the inventor believed to be optimum, and hence, they would be helpful in enabling someone to make the invention." *Atlas Powder Co. v. E.I. du Pont de Nemours & Co.*, 750 F.2d 1569, 1577, 224 USPQ 409, 414 (Fed. Cir. 1984).

• *Manual Reference*: "Simulated or predicted test results and prophetic examples (paper examples) are permitted in patent applications. Working examples correspond to work actually performed and may describe tests which have actually been conducted and results that were achieved. Paper examples describe the manner and process of making an embodiment of the invention which has not actually been conducted. Paper examples should not be represented as work actually done. No results should be represented as actual results unless they have actually been achieved. Paper examples should not be described using the past tense." *Manual of Patent Examining Procedure* §608.01(p)(D) (1994 rev.).

proprietary [general intellectual property] Describing information that is property owned by someone. The term "proprietary rights" is often used to emphasize that protectible and exclusive intellectual property rights inure in certain scientific or engineering data and information (via PATENT or TRADE SECRET law) or in certain literary or artistic creations (via COPYRIGHT or related rights law) or in certain words, TRADE DRESS, or symbols (via TRADEMARK law).

"Proprietary" Legend on Documents. One sometimes sees the legend "proprietary" marked on certain business or technical documents: the person placing that legend on the document did so to indicate that the data contained in that document is protected by law as the exclusive property of that person and should not be used without permission.

See INTELLECTUAL PROPERTY.

prosecution [patent–trademark] The process of obtaining the grant of a patent or the registration of a trademark from the Patent and Trademark Office (PTO). Prosecution consists of filing an application with the PTO for the grant of a patent or the registration of a mark and carrying the application to a conclusion by dealing with the appropriate government EXAMINERS and other officials.

Patent Prosecution. Patent prosecution usually consists of preparation and filing of the disclosure, drawings, and claims of a patent application; filing of the responses and amendments to the objections of the PTO examiner; interviews with the PTO examiner; and timely payment of the appropriate fees.

Trademark Registration Prosecution. Trademark registration prosecution usually consists of preparation and filing of the application papers; filing of the responses and amendments to the objections of the PTO trademark examiner;

interviews with the PTO examiner; filing of the appropriate §§8 and 15 affidavits; and timely payment of the appropriate fees. The prosecution of intent-to-use applications also includes timely filing of a statement of use once the applicant has properly used the mark.

prosecution history estoppel [patent] See definition, case references, and examples at FILE WRAPPER ESTOPPEL. The Court of Appeals for the Federal Circuit since the early 1980s has indicated a preference for the synonym PROSECUTION HISTORY ESTOPPEL rather than the traditional term "file wrapper estoppel."

Synonym: FILE WRAPPER ESTOPPEL.

pro tanto [general legal] A Latin legal term meaning "to that extent" or "as far as it goes." "The patent laws which give a 17-year monopoly on 'making, using or selling the invention' are *in pari materia* with the antitrust laws and modify them *pro tanto*." *Simpson v. Union Oil of Cal.*, 377 U.S. 13, 24 (1964).

protest [patent–trademark] A written communication from a member of the public to the Patent and Trademark Office (PTO) presenting relevant evidence in support of an objection either to the grant of a patent or the registration of a trademark to an applicant. If the communication is accepted under PTO rules, the evidence or material in it will be considered by the examiner. Acceptance of the protest, however, does not turn an EX PARTE examination into an INTER PARTES proceeding involving the applicant and the sender of the protest. The communication is often in the form of a letter and called a "letter of protest," especially in trademark matters.

Synonym: LETTER OF PROTEST.

1. Protest to a Pending Patent Application. A protest by a member of the public against the grant of a pending patent application will be considered if it includes: (1) a listing of the patent, publications, or other information relied upon; (2) a concise explanation of the relevance of each listed item; (3) a copy of each listed patent, publication, or other information, or at least the pertinent portions; and (4) an English language translation of the pertinent parts of any non-English material submitted. 37 C.F.R. §1.291(b). The participation of the person who filed the letter of protest ends with the filing of the protest, and no further submission will be accepted or considered by the PTO unless the letter raises new issues that could not have been earlier presented and thus constitutes a new protest. 37 C.F.R. §1.291(c). Because pending patent applications are kept secret, persons other than the applicant rarely know of a pending application unless it is an application for a REISSUE patent.

• *Manual Reference*: "Any information which, in the protestor's opinion, would make the grant of a patent improper can be relied on in a protest under 37 C.F.R. §1.291(a). While prior art documents such as patents and publications are most often the subject of protests, 37 C.F.R. §1.291(a) is not limited to prior art documents. Protests may be based on any facts or information adverse to patentability.... The Office recognizes that when evidence other than prior art documents is relied upon problems may arise as to authentication and the probative value to assign to such evidence." *Manual of Patent Examining Procedure* §1901.02 (1994 rev.).

2. Protest to a Pending Application for Registration of a Mark. A letter of protest by a member of the public against a pending application for registration of a mark must contain evidence that could affect or prevent registration of the mark. The procedure permits parties other than the applicant to present evidence concerning the registration of a mark, thereby improving the quality of the examination process. If the letter or protest raises information relevant to the registrability of the application, it must contain proof and support of the information. Mere argumentation is not accepted. The protest is sent to the Director of the Trademark Examining Operation, who determines whether to forward the information in the protest to the examining attorney for consideration. *Trademark Manual of Examining Procedure* §1116 (1993).

Substance of Letter of Protest. The most frequent types of protest are: (1) when a person brings forth evidence that the term sought for registration is an unregistrable GENERIC NAME; (2) when a person brings forth a registration of a mark as to which the applied-for mark would cause a likelihood of confusion, barring registration under Lanham Act §2(d); and (3) when a person requests that prosecution of the application be suspended because of a pending application that is in potential conflict with the application. In a 1995 notice, the PTO instituted a policy under which a letter of protest received prior to publication will be forwarded to the examining attorney only if there is sufficient evidence in the letter to establish a PRIMA FACIE case that supports a refusal of registration such that publication for opposition, without consideration of the issue and evidence in the letter of protest, might result in a clear error by the PTO. 1172 OGTM 93 (Mar. 28, 1995).

Time for Filing. In a 1995 notice, the PTO changed its policy as to the timing of filing a letter of protest. Under the new practice, a letter of protest filed before publication must contain sufficient evidence to satisfy the "prima facie case" and "clear error" test mentioned above. The PTO, in the 1995 notice, did not change prior practice as to letters of protest received after publication for opposition. Generally, letters of protest filed more than 30 days after publication will not be accepted. *In re Pohn*, 3 USPQ2d 1700 (Comm. Pat. & T.M. 1987). A letter of protest received after publication will be accepted only if evidence in the protest shows that publication of the mark constituted "clear error." *Trademark Manual of Examining Procedure* §1116.02(b) (1993).

• *Treatise Reference*: J.T. McCarthy, *Trademarks and Unfair Competition* §19.40[6] (3d ed. 1995 rev.).

provisional application [patent] A method of establishing an early priority date of invention by the filing of a SPECIFICATION with the U.S. Patent and Trademark Office.

History. Provisional applications were introduced into the United States in Patent Code 35 U.S.C. §111(b) in the 1994 URUGUAY ROUND AGREEMENTS ACT. The beginning date for the filing of provisional applications was June 8,

1995. While GATT did not require the United States to adopt a provisional filing system, it was included as part of the GATT TRIPS legislative package known as the Uruguay Round Agreements Act.

Requirements. A provisional application requires neither a claim nor an oath signed by the inventor because a provisional application will not mature into a patent. But a valid provisional application must have the following elements:

(1) a specification complying with the requirements of the first paragraph of Patent Code §112. This includes the requirements of DESCRIPTION, ENABLEMENT and BEST MODE;

(2) a drawing, if necessary for understanding of the subject matter;

(3) the names of the inventor or inventors;

(4) the required filing fee; and

(5) a cover sheet to identify the application as provisional.

Characteristics. The theory of a provisional application is that it serves as a basis for a claim of priority over a competing inventor if the applicant later files a regular patent application within one year. Patent Code §119(e). The filing of a provisional application does not start the running of the 20-year duration of a patent—only the filing of a regular patent application starts the 20-year term. A provisional application is not examined by the Patent and Trademark Office and will not mature into a patent. A provisional application will automatically go abandoned one year from filing and may go abandoned earlier due to lack of fee payment or lack of response to a PTO requirement. A provisional application is a regular national filing that starts the PARIS CONVENTION priority date year running for purposes of claiming a CONVENTION DATE based on filing of the provisional application. Design patents are not covered by the provisional application procedures. A provisional application is kept in confidence by the PTO.

Benefits. A provisional application establishes an early date of invention for purposes of priority over competing inventors without all of the formalities of a regular patent application and at a lower cost. In 1995, the PTO filing fee for a provisional application was $150, with a 50 percent SMALL ENTITY discount. The filing of a provisional application provides an inventor with a one-year period before filing a regular patent application within which the inventor can further develop the invention, determine marketability, acquire funding, or seek licensing and manufacturing opportunities.

Domestic Inventors Given Parity With Foreign Convention Applicants. Another benefit of a provisional application is that it gives domestic applicants parity with foreign applicants who file in the United States and rely on a foreign CONVENTION DATE. A foreign applicant who files in its home country has 12 months to file in the United States, claiming priority, with the U.S. patent duration measured from the filing date in the United States, because under the PARIS CONVENTION, the duration of a patent cannot include the Paris Convention priority period. Patent Code §119(e), as amended, extends a similar period of time to domestic inventors who file a preliminary U.S. application followed in 12 months by a regular application. Thus, a domestic inventor filing a provisional application has up to 12 months in which to file a formal application but can claim priority based on the provisional application, with the period in between filings not included in the calculation of the patent term.

Conversion. A formally filed regular patent application may be converted to a provisional application by a petition filed within 12 months of filing but full filing fees paid in connection with the regular application will not be refunded.

provisional double patenting [patent]

A ground for rejection of a patent application by the Patent and Trademark Office when two pending applications of the same owner present a potential DOUBLE PATENTING situation.

See DOUBLE PATENTING.

• *Manual Reference*: "When two or more pending applications of (1) the same inventive entity, (2) the same assignee, or (3) having at least one common inventor, contain conflicting claims which are not patentably distinct, a 'provisional' double patenting rejection of either the same or obviousness-type should be made in each application. Such a rejection is 'provisional' since the conflicting claims are not, as yet, patented. *In re Wetterau*, 148 USPQ 499 (C.C.P.A. 1966)." *Manual of Patent Examining Procedure* §804 (1994 rev.).

pseudonymous work [copyright] A work in which the author is identified under a fictitious name. Copyright in a pseudonymous work created after January 1, 1978, lasts for a term of 75 years from first publication of the work or a term of 100 years from creation of the work, whichever expires first. But if, before the end of that term, the identity of the author is revealed in a registration of copyright or in the public records of the Copyright Office, the term of copyright is the life of the author plus 50 years.

See DURATION OF COPYRIGHT.

• *Statutory Reference*: 17 U.S.C. §101: "A 'pseudonymous work' is a work on the copies or phonorecords of which the author is identified under a fictitious name." Regarding DURATION, see 17 U.S.C. §302(c).

PTO [patent] The United States Patent and Trademark Office (PTO). In 1975, the name of the United States "Patent Office" was changed to the "Patent and Trademark Office" to reflect the growing role played by the office in registering trademarks. Pub. L. No. 93-596, 88 Stat. 1949. The PTO grants patents and registers marks and is a part of the Department of Commerce. It is located in Crystal City, Virginia, near Washington, D.C. The official address is: Commissioner of Patents and Trademarks, Washington, D.C. 20231.

publication [copyright] The distribution of copies or phonorecords of a work to the public without any restriction on use or disclosure.

Pre-1978 Publication. Prior to the 1978 Copyright Act, "publication" marked the crucial line between state common law copyright for unpublished works and federal statutory copyright for published works. This line of demarcation was eliminated in the 1978 amendments, and federal law took over for both published and unpublished works. However, acts of distribution that occurred prior to 1978 will still be judged by the pre-1978 dual system.

Pre-1978 Dual State-Federal Copyright System. Under the pre-1978 dual system of state common law protection for unpublished works and federal statutory protection for published works, federal protection was secured by publication with the required notice of copyright on each copy. 1909 Copyright Act, §10. Publication without notice, with only a narrow exception for certain mistakes, eliminated the possibility of federal copyright. Hence, the work lost common law copyright by publication, did not achieve federal copyright by publication with notice, and fell into the public domain. Events that occurred before 1978 will continue to be judged under that standard. 1 *Nimmer on Copyright* §4.05[B] (1994 rev.) ("[I]t is necessary to look to the law as it existed prior to January 1, 1978.").

Divestitive and Investitive Publication. During the pre-1978 period, to help authors avoid inadvertently having their works fall into the public domain on publication, the courts developed a two-tier system characterizing acts of dissemination: (1) "divestitive publication" or "general publication" consisted of acts of dissemination of the work that divested the author of the state common law copyright; and (2) "investitive publication" consisted of acts of dissemination of the work that, if made with the copyright notice affixed, invested the work with federal statutory copyright. To avoid forfeiture of copyright, acts of dissemination that might suffice as "investitive publication" were held not sufficient as "divestitive publication." When copies were distributed without the required notice on them, the courts would strain to find that a "divestitive publication" had not occurred and that there was only a "limited publication," i.e., acts that did not divest common law copyright. "The gap between investitive and divestitive publication under the 1909 Act gave copyright owners a margin for error." 1 P. Goldstein, *Copyright* §3.2.1 (1989). For example, a "limited publication" was found where advance copies of Martin Luther King, Jr.'s, famous "I Have A Dream" speech were distributed to the press without copyright notice on them. This was held not to divest the author of copyright because the copies were distributed to a "limited" group: the press. *King v. Mister Maestro, Inc.*, 224 F. Supp. 101, 140 USPQ 366 (S.D.N.Y. 1963). Similarly, it was held that the distribution of 158 Oscars without a copyright notice on them to recipients of Academy Awards from 1929 to 1941, was not such a general publication without notice that the Oscar fell out of copyright. The distribution was held to be to a selected group for a limited purpose. *Academy of Motion Picture Arts & Sciences v. Creative House Promotions Inc.*, 944 F.2d 1446, 19 USPQ2d 1491 (9th Cir. 1991).

The Significance of Post-1978 Publication. "Publication" continues to have significance under copyright law in several respects. For example, a copyright notice need not appear on unpublished copies; the year of first publication is to appear in the copyright notice; the term of copyright for ANONYMOUS and PSEUDONYMOUS works and WORKS MADE FOR HIRE is measured from the year of first publication; and under both the BERNE CONVENTION AND THE UNIVERSAL COPYRIGHT CONVENTION, works first published in a member nation by a citizen of a member nation must be given the same level of copyright protection as that nation gives to works of domestic origin.

The Meaning of "Publication" After January 1, 1978. The 1978 Copyright Act defined "publication" in such a way as to carry forward the pre-1978 case law holding that the distribution of copies is a "limited publication" and not a "divestitive publication" if the distribution was to a limited group for a limited purpose. *White v. Kimmell*, 193 F.2d 744, 92 USPQ 400 (9th Cir. 1952). The 1978 Act definition of publication requires distribution to "the public." While the definition on its face does not incorporate the "limited purpose" facet, Congress said that in this context, "public" means distribution to "persons under no explicit or implicit restrictions with respect to disclosure of its contents." Rep. No. 94-1476, 94th Cong., 2d Sess. 138 (1976). Thus, distribution or dissemination of copies to a limited group and for a limited purpose would probably not constitute "publication." 1 *Nimmer on Copyright* §4.13[B] (1994 rev.).

Public Performance and Display Is Not "Publication." It is a fundamental rule of copyright, as to both pre-1978 and post-1978 events, that performance of a work is not a "publication," no matter how extensive the publication. For example, it was held that the broadcast and televising to millions of Martin Luther King, Jr.'s, famous "I Have A Dream" speech was a performance of the speech, not a publication of it. *King v. Mister Maestro, Inc.*, 224 F. Supp. 101 (S.D.N.Y. 1963). This rule was codified in the 1978 Copyright Act in the last sentence of the definition of publication. While some pre-1978 cases held that the unrestricted public display of a work of art constituted "publication," the 1978 Act states that public display is never publication.

- *Treatise References*: 1 *Nimmer on Copyright* §4.01 et seq. (1994 rev.); 1 P. Goldstein, *Copyright* §§3.2–.3 (1989); M. Leaffer, *Understanding Copyright* §§4.3–.7 (1989); W. Patry, *Copyright Law and Practice* 414, 428 (1994); 1 N. Boorstyn, *Copyright* §4.01 et seq (2d ed. 1994).

Statutory Reference: 17 U.S.C. §101: " 'Publication' is the distribution of copies or phonorecords of a work to the public by sale or other transfer of ownership, or by rental, lease, or lending. The offering to distribute copies or phonorecords to a group of persons for purposes of further distribution, public performance, or public display, constitutes publication. A public performance or display or a work does not of itself constitute publication."

publication for opposition   [trademark] Once an application for registration on the federal PRINCIPAL REGISTER has been approved by the trademark examiner, the mark is published in the weekly Official Gazette of the Patent and Trademark Office, giving interested persons an opportunity to file an OPPOSITION proceeding to prevent registration. 37 C.F.R. §2.80. In the field of trademark law, the application is said to be "passed to publication" by the trademark examiner once an application to register on the principal register is approved.

Procedure. If the application is either a Lanham Act §1(a) use-based application or a Lanham Act §44 application by a foreign applicant, and no opposition is filed or an opposition is filed and dismissed, the application is prepared for issuance of the certificate of registration. 37 C.F.R. §2.81(a). If the application is an INTENT TO USE application (ITU) under §1(b), a Notice of Allowance is sent to the applicant. 37 C.F.R. §2.81(b). This starts the time running for the ITU applicant to file its Statement of Use of the mark in order to obtain registration.

Copending Applications. If multiple applications are pending at the same time on marks that are CONFUSINGLY SIMILAR, the mark with the earliest effective filing date is published for opposition. The application with the later filing date is suspended until the published or issued application is registered or the application abandoned. 37 C.F.R. §2.82.

Supplemental Register. Applications for registration on the SUPPLEMENTAL REGISTER are not published for opposition. Such marks are only published in the Official Gazette for information purposes upon registration. 37 C.F.R. §2.82.

See OPPOSITION, REGISTRATION OF MARK.

publication of pending patent application [patent] The publication by the government of material contained in a pending patent application after a legally-defined period of time has passed since the application was filed.

The Public Policy of Patent Publication. The publication of information in pending patent applications is an attempt to balance the right of the inventor to secrecy against the right of the public to benefit from knowledge of the invention and to anticipate the possible patent that may be granted. The longer the period of average pendency of patent applications, the longer that the technology disclosed in pending applications is withheld from the public. In addition, industry may be apprehensive about being caught by a future patent issued from a long-pending application. By adopting a system of publication, the goal is to prevent needless duplication of research and development, promote additional technological advances based on the information disclosed, and let industry know the scope of potential liability when a patent is granted. These policies have led several na-

tions, such as Germany and Japan, to provide for publication 18 months after the filing date.

Proposed Patent Publication in the United States. While the United States has never had a system of publication of pending patents, in 1994 the U.S. government made a commitment to Japan to introduce legislation and begin publishing patent applications by January 1, 1996. Starting in 1994 legislation was introduced into Congress to adopt an 18 month publication system. While such legislation did not pass the 103rd Congress, it will be re-introduced in the 104th Congress in 1995. In early 1995, the Patent and Trademark Office held hearings to determine ways to implement legislative changes which will require publication. Proposed was the creation of a publicly accessible electronic data base which mirrors the content of the published patent application files.

public display [copyright]
See DISPLAY

public domain [general intellectual property] The status of an invention, creative work, commercial symbol, or any other creation that is not protected by a form of intellectual property. Items that have been determined to be in the public domain are available for free copying and use by anyone.

Public Domain Is the Rule: Intellectual Property Is the Exception. Constant emphasis on protection of exclusive rights in legal analysis often obscures the basic principle of U.S. law that the principle of free copying of things in the public domain is the general rule. *Bonito Boats Inc. v. Thunder Craft Boats Inc.*, 489 U.S. 141, 151, 9 USPQ2d 1847, 1852 (1989). Legally protected areas of exclusive rights—such as patents, trademarks, and copyrights—are properly viewed as exceptions to the general rule of free copying and imitation. The Supreme Court has referred to "the important public interest in permitting full and free competition in the use of ideas which are in reality a part of the public domain." *Lear, Inc. v. Adkins*, 395 U.S. 653, 670, 162 USPQ 1, 8 (1969). "Sharing in the goodwill of an article unprotected by patent or trademark is the exercise of a right possessed by all—and in the free exercise of which the consuming public is deeply interested." Justice Brandeis in *Kellogg Co. v. National Biscuit Co.*, 305 U.S. 111, 122 (1938). The principle of free use of things in the public domain is an inherent right of the people and is not created by either the Constitution or any statute. It is probably a right reserved to the people by the Tenth Amendment to the U.S. Constitution.

Burden Is on the Party Asserting the Right to Exclude. Generally, the party seeking to establish a right to exclude another from using a creation or marketing tool has the burden to prove its entitlement to one of the forms of intellectual property. The burden of proving validity and infringement of an intellectual property right is on the party wishing to exclude. The using or copying party does not have the initial burden to prove that what it is using is in the public domain. In the United States, no one need obtain a special government license to copy or imitate. If someone feels that a particular copy or use is an infringement, that person must file a lawsuit and make an initial showing of the ownership and validity of an intellectual property right and an infringement of that right. *Durham Indus., Inc. v. Tomy Corp.*, 630 F.2d 905, 908, 208 USPQ 10, 13 (2d Cir. 1980) (see case reference below).

Copying Per Se Is Not Illegal. The popular folklore is that a "copycat" is a pirate and that all commercial copying is somehow illegal. That is not so. The copying of things that are in the public domain is not only tolerated but encouraged as a vital part of the competitive process. "Imitation is the life blood of competition." *American Safety Table Co. v. Schreiber*, 269 F.2d 255, 272, 122 USPQ 29, 43 (2d Cir. 1959). It is the ability to produce a product equivalent to that of one's competitor, but made at lower cost and sold for a lower price, that makes supply and demand work. The only kinds of imitation or copying that are illegal are those actions which under the law constitute infringement of one of the forms of intellectual property. "The world would be a duller place without the originators, but it would not work without the copyists." *B.H. Bunn Co. v. AAA Replacement Parts Co.*, 451 F.2d 1254, 1259, 171 USPQ 780, 783 (5th Cir. 1971).

Patents and the Public Domain. The grant of a patent does not "remove existing knowledge from the public domain," for there was no such knowledge until the inventor disclosed it in the patent. During the life of the patent, all workers in the field remain perfectly free to use and combine elements as they were used and combined prior to the invention. "They need only avoid [the inventor's] own novel combination and structure as claimed [in the patent]." *Panduit Corp. v. Dennison Mfg. Co.*, 810 F.2d 1561, 1573, 1 USPQ2d 1593, 1601 (Fed. Cir. 1987).

A Thing Is in the Public Domain Only If No Intellectual Property Right Protects It. One frequently sees statements such as: "Because the patent is invalid, the lamp is in the public domain." This is an erroneous overgeneralized conclusion because it considers only patent law and ignores the possibility that features of the lamp are protected by other types of intellectual property such as COPYRIGHT or TRADE DRESS. *Mine Safety Appliances Co. v. Electric Storage Battery Co.*, 405 F.2d 901, 902 n.2, 160 USPQ 413, 414 n.2 (C.C.P.A. 1969) (see case reference below). "[O]ne cannot come to the bottom-line conclusion that any item is 'in the public domain' until one has exhausted *all* of the possible areas of exclusive rights." J.T. McCarthy, *Trademarks and Unfair Competition*, §1.15[6] (3d ed. 1995 rev.) A more accurate usage is: "Because the patent is invalid, the lamp is in the public domain for purposes of patent law." Or, preferably, the following could be stated: "Because the patent is invalid, patent law cannot prevent manufacture of the lamp." On the copyright side, the phrase "because the term of the copyright has expired, the photograph has fallen out of copyright" is more accurate than "because the term of the copyright has expired, the photograph has fallen into the public domain." The fact that a firm does not have one form of intellectual property does not mean that it lacks ownership of another form of intellectual property in the same article or creation. For example, the fact that a picture has no copyright protection does not foreclose the possibility that it has been used in such a way as to achieve trademark significance. *Frederick Warne & Co. v. Book Sales, Inc.*, 481 F.Supp. 1191, 205 USPQ 444 (S.D.N.Y. 1979).

See COPYING, INTELLECTUAL PROPERTY.

• *Treatise Reference*: J.T. McCarthy, *Trademarks and Unfair Competition*, §§1.01, 1.15 (3d ed. 1995 rev.)

• *Case References*:

" … [I]mitation and refinement through imitation are both necessary to invention itself and the very lifeblood of a competitive economy.… [F]ree exploitation of ideas will be the rule, to which the protection of a federal patent is the exception. Moreover, the ultimate goal of the patent system is to bring new designs and technologies into the public domain through disclosure.… To a limited extent, the federal patent law must determine not only what is protected, but also what is free for all to use." Justice O'Connor in *Bonito Boats Inc. v. Thunder Craft Boats Inc.*, 489 U.S. 141, 146, 151, 9 USPQ2d 1847, 1850, 1852 (1989).

" … [T]he socio-economic policy supported by the general law is the encouragement of competition by all fair means, and that encompasses the right to copy, very broadly interpreted, except where copying is lawfully prevented by a copyright or a patent." Judge Rich in *App. of Deister Concentrator Co.*, 289 F.2d 496, 501, 129 USPQ 314, 319 (C.C.P.A. 1961).

"'Public domain' moreover, is a question-begging legal concept. Whether or not things are in or out of the public domain and free or not free to be copied may depend on all sorts of legal concepts including patent law, anti-monopoly law and statutes, the law of unfair competition, copyright law, and the law of trademarks and trademark registration. What we really do is to determine these *legal* rights; then we may express the ultimate conclusion by saying something is in the 'public domain'—or not in it." Judge Rich in *Mine Safety Appliances Co. v. Electric Storage Battery Co.*, 405 F.2d 901, 902 n.2, 160 USPQ 413, 414 n.2 (C.C.P.A. 1969).

"As Professor McCarthy has noted, close copying does not *necessarily* indicate that the defendant has attempted to capitalize on the secondary meaning of plaintiff's trademark or trade dress because '[t]here may have been many other motivations for defendant's actions.' 1 J.T. McCarthy, *Trademarks and Unfair Competition* (1973) §15:4, at 531. Further, '[i]t must … not be forgotten that there is absolutely nothing legally or morally reprehensible about exact copying of things in the public domain.' *Id.*" *Brooks Shoe Mfg. Co. v. Suave Shoe Corp.*, 716 F.2d 854, 860, 221 USPQ 536, 540 (11th Cir. 1983).

"Before asking a court to consider the question of infringement, a party must demonstrate the existence and the validity of its copyright, for in the absence of copyright (or patent, trademark or state law) protection, even original creations are in the public domain and may be freely copied.…" *Durham Indus., Inc. v. Tomy Corp.*, 630 F.2d 905, 908, 208 USPQ 10, 13 (2d Cir. 1980).

public performance [copyright]
See PERFORMANCE.

public use [patent] A commercial use of an invention by one who is not under any obligation of secrecy to the inventor. An inventor cannot obtain a valid patent if he or she waits for more than the one-year GRACE PERIOD to file a patent application after a product embodying the invention has been in "public use." It is against public policy to permit the inventor to commercially exploit the invention for longer than the Patent Code §102(b) one-year grace period. The date one year prior to the filing date of the patent is known as the CRITICAL DATE. An event prior to that date can trigger the PUBLIC USE bar to a patent.

"Public Use" Need Not Be "Public." The term "public use" is not taken literally. Rather, the courts have redefined the term to mean "commercial use." Public use is use by the inventor or by one who is not under any limitation, restriction, or obligation of secrecy to the inventor. *In re Smith*, 714 F.2d 1127, 1134, 218 USPQ 976, 983 (Fed. Cir. 1983). Commercial uses in which the patented part of the product is not seen by the public are still deemed to be a public use. For example, a public use would include the use of an internal part of a jet engine on a commercial airliner, a gear inside a watch used in public, and an undergarment worn by a person in public. "A commercial use is a public use even if it is kept secret." *Kinzenbaw v. Deere*

& Co., 741 F.2d 383, 390, 222 USPQ 929, 934 (Fed. Cir. 1984).

Public Use Can Trigger the Anticipation and Obviousness Bars. If the product placed in public use contains all the elements of the claimed invention, there is a direct ANTICIPATION bar under Patent Code §102(b) against a patent. In addition, the product placed in public use becomes part of the PRIOR ART for purposes of applying the OBVIOUSNESS bar against a patent. Thus, a valid patent is barred if the claimed invention is either completely embodied in, or obvious in view of, the product in public use. *Baker Oil Tools Inc. v. Geo. Vann Inc.*, 828 F.2d 1558, 1563, 4 USPQ2d 1210, 1213 (Fed. Cir. 1987).

Experimental Use Exception. The public use bar to a patent is subject to the EXPERIMENTAL USE exception. An experimental use exists if the primary purpose of the public use is shown to be an experiment to complete the invention and not just for testing for consumer acceptance or other commercial purposes.

See EXPERIMENTAL USE.

"Used by Others" Under §102(a). Patent Code §102(a) specifies that a patent is barred if the invention was "used by others" before the date of invention of this inventor. While, unlike §102(b), there is no explicit statutory requirement that that use be "public," there must be a kind of use that is accessible to the public. *Carella v. Starlight Archery Co.*, 804 F.2d 135, 139, 231 USPQ 644, 646 (Fed. Cir. 1986).

See ANTICIPATION, OBVIOUSNESS, GRACE PERIOD, CRITICAL DATE, PRINTED PUBLICATION, EXPERIMENTAL USE.

- *Treatise Reference*: 1 D. Chisum, *Patents* §3.05 (1994 rev.); R. Harmon, *Patents and the Federal Circuit* §3.4(c) (3d ed. 1994).

- *Statutory Reference*: 35 U.S.C. §102:

A person shall be entitled to a patent unless—

(a) the invention was known or used by others in this country, or patented or described in a printed publication in this or a foreign country, before the invention thereof by the applicant for patent, or

(b) the invention was patented or described in a printed publication in this or a foreign country or in public use or on sale in this country, more than one year prior to the date of the application for patent in the United States....

- *Case Reference*: "[C]ourts have discerned a number of factors which must be weighed in applying the statutory bar of §102(b). Operating against the inventor are the policies of (1) protecting the public in its use of the invention where such use began prior to the filing of the application, (2) encouraging prompt disclosure of new and useful information, (3) discouraging attempts to extend the length of the period of protection by not allowing the inventor to reap the benefits for more than one year prior to the filing of the application. In contrast to these considerations, the public interest is also deemed to be served by allowing an inventor time to perfect his invention, by public testing, if desired, and prepare a patent application." *TP Labs., Inc. v. Professional Positioners, Inc.*, 724 F.2d 965, 968, 220 USPQ 577, 580 (Fed. Cir. 1984).

- *Example 1*: Samuel Barnes invented a new form of steel corset stays. In 1855 he gave his friend a corset he had made containing corset steels that embodied the invention. She wore them, and in 1858 he gave her another set. Barnes married his friend, but not until 1866 did Barnes file an application for a patent on his form of steel corset stays. The Supreme Court held that there was a PUBLIC USE before the CRITICAL DATE (then two years prior to the patent application), which voided the Barnes patent. The Court emphasized that the fact that the invention could not be seen by the public eye did not disqualify this from being a "public use," referring to the analogy of an invention of a spring "hidden in the running gear of a watch," which would also be a "public use." There was no claim that Barnes' future wife was cautioned to preserve secrecy about the invention, nor was there a claim that her wearing the corset was within the EXPERIMENTAL USE exception. The Court concluded: "If an inventor, having made his device, gives or sells it to another, to be used by the donee or vendee, without limitation or restriction, or injunction of secrecy, and it is so used, such use is public, even though the use and knowledge of the use may be confined to one person." *Egbert v. Lippmann*, 104 U.S. 333, 336 (1881).

• *Example 2*: From 1957 to 1962 Nichols, while a graduate student in organic chemistry, worked on an invention consisting of a Rubik's Cube-type of cube puzzle with rotatable parts. He demonstrated a paper model of the puzzle to close friends and roommates. After he went to work as a research scientist, in 1968 Nichols constructed a working wood-block model of the puzzle, which he kept in his office. In January 1969 his employer expressed interest and Nichols explained its workings. In March 1970 Nichols filed a patent application on the puzzle. He assigned the resulting patent to his employer, which sued CBS, the owner of rights in the Rubik's Cube puzzle, for patent infringement. The court rejected CBS' challenge that the patent was invalid because of a "public use" prior to the CRITICAL DATE. Distinguishing *Egbert v. Lippmann* (see above), the court said that unlike Barnes, Nichols had not given an object embodying the invention to another person for free and unrestricted use. In the court's view, Nichols at all times retained control over the puzzle models he showed to others, such that he had "a legitimate expectation of privacy and of confidentiality." The court found "no evidence of commercially motivated activity by Nichols prior to the critical date." *Moleculon Research Corp. v. CBS, Inc.*, 793 F.2d 1261, 1265–67, 229 USPQ 805, 808 (Fed. Cir. 1986).

• *Example 3*: MacCarthy invented a new type of kaleidoscope containing liquid. Prior to the critical date, the developer of the inventor's device displayed a prototype of the invention to about 25 guests at a party hosted by the developer. The purpose of the display was to "generate discussion and garner feedback." Finding that this was a public use that invalidated the patent, the Federal Circuit distinguished its decision in *Moleculon Research* (see above example). The court said that in *Moleculon Research* the display to friends and colleagues of the inventor was subject to an implied restriction of confidentiality, with the inventor maintaining control over use of the device and of information concerning it. But in this case, there was no

evidence of any implied secrecy or confidentiality obligations on the observers at the party. *The Beachcombers, Int'l Inc. v. WildeWood Creative Prods. Inc.*, 31 F.3d 1154, 31 USPQ2d 1653 (Fed. Cir. 1994).

public use proceeding [patent] An administrative EX PARTE or INTER PARTES proceeding in the Patent and Trademark Office to determine whether an invention claimed in a pending application is barred from a patent because the invention was in PUBLIC USE or ON SALE more than one year before the filing of the patent application.

Inter Partes Proceeding. In an inter partes proceeding, the petitioner knows the content of the claims of the pending application. Inter partes proceedings are held at the discretion of the Commissioner when a protest has been filed regarding a REISSUE application. Since 1985, public use proceedings cannot be filed in INTERFERENCE actions by one of the parties in the interference. In the inter partes proceeding, after testimony is taken by both the petitioner and the patent applicant, an oral hearing is held in the PTO. See *Manual of Patent Examining Procedure* §720.04 (1994).

Ex Parte Proceeding. In an ex parte proceeding, the proceeding is initiated by one who has information that the subject matter of a pending patent application might be barred by 37 U.S.C. §102(b). The petitioner does not have the right to examine the pending application. After testimony from both the petitioner and applicant, there is ordinarily no oral hearing.

See PUBLIC USE, ON SALE.

• *Rule Reference*: 37 C.F.R. §1.292(a). "When a petition for the institution of public use proceedings ... is filed by one having information of the pendency of an application and is found, on reference to the examiner, to make a *prima facie* showing that the invention claimed in an application believed to be on file had been in public use or on sale more than one year before the filing of the application, a hearing may be had before the Commissioner to determine whether a public use proceeding should be instituted. If instituted, the Commissioner may designate an appropriate official to conduct the public use proceeding, including the setting of times for taking testimony which shall be taken as provided by §§1.671 through 1.685. The petitioner will be heard in the proceedings but after decision therein will not be heard further in the prosecution of the application for patent."

- *Treatise Reference*: 1 D. Chisum, *Patents* §3.05 (1994 rev.).

Q

quality control [trademark]
  See LICENSE OF TRADEMARK.

R

RAM [computer–copyright] Acronym for "random access memory." RAM is data stored in SEMICONDUCTOR CHIPS that may be read out without changing the stored information, that permits changing the stored information, and that retains data only so long as power is supplied. The memory is "random" because there is almost instantaneous access to any storage location point in the memory. In the usual personal computer, RAM is the temporary capacity of the computer to handle programs and files at any one moment. Usually, information stored in the RAM is erased when power to the computer is switched off.

The physical design of a RAM may be protected under the Semiconductor Chip Protection Act (SCPA).

Loading Software Into RAM Creates a "Copy." The act of loading a program into a computer's memory creates a copy of the program. 2 *Nimmer on Copyright* §8.08 (1994 rev.). Although loading software into the RAM only temporarily fixes the program, a copy is created under the Copyright Act 17 U.S.C. §101. "The representation is 'sufficiently permanent or stable to permit it to be perceived, reproduced, or otherwise communicated for a period of more than transitory duration.' " *MAI Sys. Corp. v. Peak Computer Inc.*, 991 F.2d 511, 519, 26 USPQ2d 1458, 1464 (9th Cir. 1993). For example, a computer system maintenance company that switches on its client's computer thereby causes copyrighted software to be loaded from either a hard disk, floppy disk, or ROM into the RAM memory of the computer's central processing unit (CPU). This act causes an unauthorized copy of the software to be made and constitutes copyright infringement in the absence of permission by the owner of the copyright in the software. *MAI Sys. Corp. v. Peak*

Computer Inc., 991 F.2d 511, 26 USPQ2d 1458 (9th Cir. 1993).

See COMPUTER PROGRAM, COPIES, FIXED

- *Case References*:

"[T]he units designated 'ROM' and 'RAM' are, respectively, a read only memory and a random access memory, terms well understood by those skilled in the art." *In re Iwahashi*, 888 F.2d 1370, 1372, 12 USPQ2d 1908, 1909 (Fed. Cir. 1989).

"[W]here … a copyrighted program is loaded into RAM and maintained there for minutes or longer, the RAM representation of the program is sufficiently 'fixed' to constitute a 'copy' under the [Copyright] Act." *Advanced Computer Servs. v. MAI Sys. Corp.*, 845 F. Supp. 356, 363, 30 USPQ2d 1443, 1449 (E.D. Va. 1994).

ratio decidendi [general legal] A Latin legal term literally meaning "the reason for deciding." It is the basic principle or rule of law upon which a court rests its written opinion in a decision.

- *Usage Example*: "The patent laws which give a 17-year monopoly on 'making, using or selling the invention' are *in pari materia* with the antitrust laws and modify them *pro tanto*. That was the *ratio decidendi* of the General Electric Case. We decline the invitation to extend it." *Simpson v. Union Oil of Cal.*, 377 U.S. 13, 24 (1964).

reads on [patent] If a claim of a patent "reads on" the ACCUSED DEVICE or process, then there is infringement of the patent claim. The claim "reads on" the accused device or process if each ELEMENT of the claim or its equivalent is present in the accused device or process. To ascertain if there is patent infringement "it must be determined whether the claim 'reads on' the accused product or process, that is, whether the claimed invention is being made, used or sold by the alleged infringer." *Standard Oil Co. v. American Cyanamid Co.*, 774 F.2d 448, 452, 227 USPQ 293, 295 (Fed. Cir. 1985).

Synonym: patent infringement.

See INFRINGEMENT OF PATENT; LITERAL INFRINGEMENT; EQUIVALENTS, DOCTRINE OF.

• *Case References*:

"If properly construed claims read on the infringing product, there is literal infringement." *Atlas Powder Co. v. E.I. du Pont de Nemours & Co.*, 750 F.2d 1569, 1579, 224 USPQ 409, 415 (Fed. Cir. 1984)."A determination of patent infringement under 35 USC 271(a) requires a two step analysis—first, the language the claim at issue must be interpreted to define its proper scope and, second, the evidence before the court must be examined to ascertain whether the claim has been infringed, whether the claim 'reads on' the accused product or process." *Minnesota Mining & Mfg. Co. v. Johnson & Johnson Orthopaedics Inc.*, 976 F.2d 1559, 1569, 24 USPQ2d 1321, 1330 (Fed. Cir. 1992).

reasonable royalty [patent–trademark–copyright]

See ROYALTY REASONABLE.

recapture [patent] The recapture rule forbids a patentee from regaining, through a REISSUE patent, claims that are of the same or broader scope than claims that were voluntarily cancelled or narrowed by the applicant during the prosecution of the original application. The rule is grounded in both equitable considerations as well as in the Patent Code. The statutory ground is that when a patent applicant responds to a Patent and Trademark Office rejection of a claim by cancelling or amending the claim, the action is ordinarily considered a deliberate, intentional act not qualifying as an "error" under the reissue statute. 35 U.S.C. §251.

• *Case References*:

"The [defendant] contends that [the patentee's] deliberate cancellation of the single feedline claims was not error. That act was taken to avoid a prior art rejection and, in the [defendant's] view, the recapture rule bars [the patentee] from securing similar claims through reissue.... The recapture rule bars the patentee from acquiring, through reissue, claims that are of the *same* or of *broader scope* than those claims that were cancelled from the original application. On the other hand, the patentee is free to acquire, through reissue, claims that are *narrower* in scope than the cancelled claims.... [T]he reissue claims [in this case] are sufficiently narrower than the cancelled claims to avoid the effect of the recapture rule.... The recapture rule is a creature of equity and it embodies the estoppel notions which the [defendant] now urges upon us." *Ball Corp. v. United States*, 729 F.2d 1429, 1434–36, 1439, 221 USPQ 289, 293–96 (Fed. Cir. 1984).

"The recapture rule does not apply here, however, because there is no evidence that [the patentee's] amendment of its originally filed claims was in any sense an admission that the scope of that claim was not in fact patentable." *Seattle Box Co. v. Industrial Crating & Packing Inc.*, 731 F.2d 818, 826, 221 USPQ 568, 574 (Fed. Cir. 1984).

"Error under the reissue statute does not include a deliberate decision to surrender specific subject matter in order to overcome prior art, a decision which in light of subsequent developments in the marketplace might be regretted. It is precisely because the patentee amended his claims to overcome prior art that a member of the public is entitled to occupy the space abandoned by the patent applicant. Thus, the reissue statute cannot be construed in such a way that competitors, properly relying on prosecution history, become patent infringers when they do so. In this case, [the patentee] narrowed its claims for the purpose of obtaining allowance in the original application and it is now precluded from recapturing what it earlier conceded." *Mentor Corp. v. Coloplast Inc.*, 998 F.2d 992, 996, 27 USPQ2d 1521, 1525 (Fed. Cir. 1993).

recordation of transfers [patent–trademark–copyright] The recording with the federal government of a transfer of ownership of a patent, trademark, or copyright.

1. Recordation of Transfer of Patent Ownership. Under Patent Code §261, the Patent and Trademark Office (PTO) will record assignments of a patent. Since the PTO does not inquire into the legal impact of a document, other documents relating to a patent, such as a license, will also be accepted for recordation. To be recordable, documents must identify the patent by number and date and preferably also by the name of the inventor and title of the invention. 37 C.F.R. §1.331.

See ASSIGNMENT OF PATENT, LICENSE OF PATENT.

- *Example.* Under Patent Code §261, if patentee Alpha assigns the patent to Beta and the assignment is not recorded within three months or prior to a later assignment, subsequent bona fide assignee Gamma will be the owner of the patent. The obligation is on Beta to protect itself by promptly recording the assignment so as to put others, such as Gamma, on notice of the transfer of title. However, as between Alpha and Beta, the failure to record the assignment does not affect their legal relationship.

- *Statutory Reference*: 35 U.S.C. §261, last paragraph: "An assignment, grant or conveyance shall be void as against any subsequent purchaser or mortgagee for a valuable consideration without notice, unless it is recorded in the Patent and Trademark Office within three months from its date or prior to the date of such subsequent purchase or mortgage."

- *Treatise Reference*: 3 P. Rosenberg, *Patent Law Fundamentals* §16.01[1][a] (1994 rev.).

- *Case Reference*: "It is well established that when a legal title holder of a patent transfers his or her title to a third party purchaser for value without notice of an outstanding equitable claim or title, the purchaser takes the entire ownership of the patent, free of any prior equitable encumbrance. [Citation omitted.] This is an application of the common law bona fide purchaser for value rule. Section 261 of Title 35

goes a step further. It adopts the principle of the real property recording acts, and provides that the bona fide purchaser for value cuts off the rights of a prior assignee who has failed to record the prior assignment in the Patent and Trademark Office by the dates specified in the statute. Although the statute does not expressly so say, it is clear that the statute is intended to cut off prior *legal* interests, which the common law rule did not." *FilmTec Corp. v. Allied-Signal Inc.*, 939 F.2d 1568, 1573–74, 19 USPQ2d 1508, 1512 (Fed. Cir. 1991).

2. Recordation of Transfer of Trademark Ownership. Lanham Act §10, 15 U.S.C. §1060, provides for permissive recordation with the Patent and Trademark Office (PTO) of an assignment of a trademark. An assignment is void as against a later bona fide purchaser unless it is recorded in the PTO within three months of the assignment or prior to any subsequent assignment to a bona fide purchaser. The PTO will accept for recordation some documents related to registered marks or applications to register even if they do not transfer title to the mark. Such documents include licenses, security interests in a mark, and agreements not to extend use of a mark. *Trademark Manual of Examining Procedure* §503 (1993 rev.).

Uniform Commercial Code. It has been held that the federal provision for recordation does not trigger an exception to the Uniform Commercial Code (UCC), because a security interest is not a presently operative assignment. Thus, the filing of a UCC financing statement in the debtor's state of incorporation perfects the creditor's security interest in a federally registered trademark. *In re Roman Cleanser Co.*, 43 B.R. 940, 225 USPQ 140 (Bankr. E.D. Mich. 1984), *aff'd*, 802 F.2d 207, 231 USPQ 301 (6th Cir. 1986).

- *Treatise Reference*: J.T. McCarthy, *Trademarks and Unfair Competition* §§18.01[7], 18.03 (3d ed. 1995 rev.).

3. Recordation of Transfer or License of Copyright. Under 17 U.S.C. §205, one can record with the Copyright Office of the Library of Congress all documents relating to copyright ownership, including assignments, exclusive licenses, and nonexclusive licenses.

Prerequisite to Filing a Lawsuit. For causes of action that arose prior to March 1, 1989, recordation of a transfer of a right of copyright to a plaintiff was a prerequisite to filing suit for copyright infringement. 17 U.S.C. §205(d). However, this requirement was eliminated by the BERNE CONVENTION IMPLEMENTATION ACT OF 1988.

Protection Against Conflicting Licenses. An important reason to record a transfer or a license is the protection of an assignee or licensee against a conflicting transfer of the same right of copyright to someone else by the same copyright owner. Without a method of government recording of a copyright TRANSFER, if Alpha sold the same right (e.g., exclusive license of motion picture rights) to Beta and later to bona fide purchaser without notice Gamma as well, Beta would usually prevail, for Alpha had nothing left to convey to Gamma. Under the copyright recording statute, Beta will prevail if Beta recorded the transfer within one month (or two months if made outside the United States) of signing the transfer. If Beta does not timely record, then as between Beta and Gamma, if Gamma records before Beta, Gamma owns the rights transferred. These rules presume that a claim to copyright in the work has been properly registered. A statutory scheme is provided to determine priority as between a conflicting transfer of copyright ownership and a nonexclusive license. See 17 U.S.C. §205(e).

Perfecting Security Interest. It has been held that the Copyright Act preempts state security filing for perfecting a security interest in a copyright. Thus, recording in the U.S. Copyright Office, not in a state under the Uniform Commercial Code, was held to be the proper method of perfecting a security interest in a copyright. *In re Peregrine Entertainment, Ltd.*, 116 B.R. 194, 16 USPQ2d 1017, 11 UCCRS2d 1025 (Bankr. C.D. Cal. 1990).

- *Treatise References*: 3 *Nimmer on Copyright* §10.07 (1994 rev.); M. Leaffer, *Understanding Copyright* §5.12 (1989); 1 P. Goldstein, *Copyright* §4.5.3 (1989); W. Patry, *Copyright Law and Practice* 394 (1994); 1 N. Boorstyn, *Copyright* §8.17 (2d ed. 1994).

- *Statutory Reference*: 17 U.S.C. §205(d): *"Priority Between Conflicting Transfers.* As between two conflicting transfers, the one executed first prevails if it is recorded, in the manner required to give constructive notice under subsection (c), within one month after its execution in the United States or within two months after its execution outside the United States, or at any time before recordation in such manner of the later transfer. Otherwise the later transfer prevails if recorded first in such manner, and if taken in good faith, for valuable consideration or on the basis of a binding promise to pay royalties, and without notice of the earlier transfer."

reduction to practice [patent] The physical part of the INVENTIVE PROCESS that completes and ends the process of invention for patent law purposes.

Creation of "Invention." Until there is a reduction to practice, there is really no "invention" because it is a reduction to practice that completes the inventive process and produces an "invention."

Two Kinds of Reduction to Practice. There are two distinctly different forms of reduction to practice: actual and constructive.

1. Actual Reduction to Practice. Actual reduction to practice is the physical construction of an apparatus that works for the intended purpose or the actual carrying out of the steps of a process invention. The apparatus or process must contain each and every element that is defined as constituting the invention. While the apparatus does not have to be commercially perfect, it must be more than just theoretically capable of producing the intended result: it must reasonably show that it will solve the problem it addresses. *Scott v. Finney*, 34 F.3d 1058, 1063, 32 USPQ2d 1115, 1119 (Fed. Cir. 1994).

Amount of Testing Required. While some devices are so simple and their purpose so obvious that mere construction is sufficient to constitute a reduction to practice, complex inventions may require laboratory tests that accurately duplicate actual working conditions in practical use. *Scott v. Finney*, 34 F.3d 1058,

1061–62, 32 USPQ2d 1115, 1118 (Fed. Cir. 1994).

Chemical Composition. To establish reduction to practice of a chemical composition, it is sufficient to prove "that the inventor actually prepared the composition and knew it would work." *Hahn v. Wong*, 892 F.2d 1028, 1032, 13 USPQ2d 1313, 1317 (Fed. Cir. 1989).

Experimentation and Reduction to Practice. There is uncertainty as to whether there can be EXPERIMENTATION after a reduction to practice so as to excuse placing the invention ON SALE or in PUBLIC USE more than one year before the application for patent. The leading commentator states: "[T]he better and prevailing view is that experimental use can indeed continue even after the invention has been completed and reduced to practice as that term is normally used in patent law." 2 D. Chisum, *Patents* §6.02[7][b][i] (1994 rev.). However, a panel of the Court of Appeals for the Federal Circuit stated that "experimental use, which means perfecting or completing an invention to the point of determining that it will work for its intended purpose, ends with an actual reduction to practice." *RCA Corp. v. Data Gen. Corp.*, 887 F.2d 1056, 1061, 12 USPQ2d 1449, 1453 (Fed. Cir. 1989). This uncertainty can probably be traced to a continuing imprecision as to the exact point when a "reduction to practice" occurs. See *In re Yarn Processing Patent Validity Litig.*, 498 F.2d 271, 282, 183 USPQ 65, 72 (5th Cir. 1974) (split of authority on experimentation issue due to differing definitions of "reduction to practice"). However, it is clear that an actual reduction to practice is not the same as commercialization of the invention: the physical apparatus or process need not be in a state of development that is fully acceptable for immediate commercial use.

Simultaneous Conception and Reduction to Practice. For some complex chemical compounds, conception will not occur until the invention has been reduced to practice. "We hold that when an inventor is unable to envision the detailed constitution of a gene so as to distinguish it from other materials, as well as a method for obtaining it, conception has not been achieved until reduction to practice has occurred, i.e., until after the gene has been isolated." *Amgen Inc. v. Chugai Pharmaceutical*

Co., 927 F.2d 1200, 1206, 18 USPQ2d 1016, 1021 (Fed. Cir. 1991).

• *Statutory Reference*: 35 U.S.C. §102(g): "In determining priority of invention there shall be considered not only the respective dates of conception and reduction to practice of the invention, but also the reasonable diligence of one who was first to conceive and last to reduce to practice, from a time prior to conception by the other."

• *Treatise References*:

"An invention is actually reduced to actual practice when the inventive concept has been embodied in some physical form and demonstrated to be a workable embodiment.... Irrespective of what kind and how much testing is required to make out actual reduction to practice, it is clear that it occurs not over an extended period of time but at a particular instant in time. Thus, reduction to practice is established when the *last* test needed to show operability is completed. The moment the requisite amount of testing that establishes workability is completed, the reduction to practice is perfected." *Kayton on Patents* 2-25–26 (1979).

"Actual reduction to practice occurs when the inventor constructs a product or performs a process that is within the scope of the patent claims and demonstrates the capacity of the inventive idea to achieve its intended purpose." 3 D. Chisum, *Patents* §10.06 (1994 rev.).

"An actual reduction to practice involves the physical construction or carrying out of the invention. An invention is actually reduced to practice when a prototype has been developed and sufficiently tested to demonstrate that it will work for its intended purpose. The actual reduction to practice of a process occurs when the constituent steps have been performed." 2 P. Rosenberg, *Patent Law Fundamentals* §10.01[2] (1994 rev.).

"Reduction to practice is the physical part of the inventive act. It is the application of the mental idea to the production of a practical result. It is the embodiment of the idea in some physical form. Reduction to practice is the production of something with knowledge that the thing will work practically for the intended purpose—a satisfactory demonstration by experiment to attain certainty." 1 S. Ladas, *Patents, Trademarks and Related Rights: National and International Protection* §188 (1975).

● *Case References*:

"In layman's terms, 'reduction to practice' connotes the initial construction of a working model of a new invention.... As a legal term of art, however, 'reduction to practice' includes not only this reduction to reality but also sufficient testing or experimentation to demonstrate that the device as it exists possesses sufficient utility to justify a patent, i.e., that the invention is suitable for its intended purpose.... Mere construction of the device ... does not reduce it to practice unless it is so simple that satisfactory operation is obvious." *In re Yarn Processing Patent Validity Litig.*, 498 F.2d 271, 280, 183 USPQ 65, 71 (5th Cir. 1974).

To prove an actual reduction to practice, the court required an inventor to prove that his physical embodiment of a computer-controlled robot production line not only had the capability of carrying out the invention, but that it had actually performed a crucial step of the invention. "[P]roof of actual reduction to practice requires demonstration that the embodiment relied upon as evidence of priority actually worked for its intended purpose.... [I]t was necessary for Newkirk to have demonstrated not only that his apparatus contained a means for altering the robot operation, but that he actually performed this step. Proof of actual reduction to practice requires more than theoretical capability; it requires showing that the apparatus of the count actually existed and worked for its intended purpose." *Newkirk v. Lulejian*, 825 F.2d 1581, 1582–83, 3 USPQ2d 1793, 1794 (Fed. Cir. 1987).

"In tests showing the invention's solution of a problem, the courts have not required commercial perfection nor absolute replication of the circumstances of the invention's ultimate use. Rather, they have instead adopted a common sense assessment. This common sense approach prescribes more scrupulous testing under circumstances approaching actual use conditions when the problem includes any uncertainties. On the other hand, when the problem to be solved does not present myriad variables, common sense similarly permits little or no testing to show the soundness of the principles of operation of the invention." *Scott v. Finney*, 34 F.3d 1058, 1063, 32 USPQ2d 1115, 1119 (Fed. Cir. 1994).

● *Example 1*: Murphy, an employee of McDonnell Douglas, conceived of a special sidewall vent for the DC-10 jet plane to solve a problem of explosive decompression that caused the main cabin floor to buckle and break when separation of the cargo door at high altitude caused sudden decompression in the cargo compartment below the main floor. The vent would permit rapid but controlled decompression of the main cabin. The COUNT of the INTERFERENCE proceeding (a count is the equivalent of a patent CLAIM) defined the invention as an airplane having a passenger cabin, a luggage compartment, an intervening door with openings, and ventilation devices. In July 1974, a full-sized prototype of the vent alone was tested in a small-scale test facility, which simulated the pressure of the main cabin floor. The following September, a full-sized prototype of the vent was tested in a full sized DC-10 fuselage. The July 1974 test was held not to be an actual reduction to practice of the invention because that test, unlike the September test, did not include all the elements defined in the count as constituting the invention. "The physical embodiment relied upon as an actual reduction to practice of the intention in interference must include every essential limitation of the count.... [I]t wasn't until the September 1974 tests in the body of a DC-10 that reduction to practice of the invention of the count took place." *Correge, Dominique & Ciprian v. Murphy*, 705 F.2d 1326, 1329, 217 USPQ 753, 755 (Fed. Cir. 1983).

● *Example 2*: Bell, an employee of Great Northern Corp., conceived of an improved molded polystyrene foam support for shipping very heavy rolls of cellophane. The key to the invention was the placement of a series of recesses molded into the supports to prevent cracking under the weight of stacked rolls of cellophane. Early tests resulted in cracked foam supports and were considered to be failures. Test shipments were made in February and

March 1977, using actual road tests. After that, further modifications in the number and size of the recesses were made because of slight cracking damage in the road tests. Testing continued until the summer of 1977. The court held that the invention was not completed and reduced to practice until sometime after the spring of 1977. "The [invention] was not reduced to practice until it was sufficiently tested to demonstrate that it would work for its intended purpose ... and that did not occur, in our view, until a location for the recesses, as defined in the claims, was determined that eliminated the cracking problem." *Great N. Corp. v. Davis Core & Pad Co.*, 782 F.2d 159, 165, 228 USPQ 356, 358 (Fed. Cir. 1986).

2. *Constructive Reduction to Practice.* A constructive reduction to practice is the filing of a patent application with the Patent and Trademark Office (PTO). A constructive reduction to practice does not involve any physical construction, but rather is accomplished by the formal filing, in the PTO, of a patent application that adequately discloses the invention. See *Vas-Cath Inc. v. Mahurkar*, 935 F.2d 1555. 19 USPQ2d 1111 (Fed. Cir. 1991).

• *Case Reference*: "[C]onstructive reduction to practice occurs when a patent application on the claimed invention is filed." *Hybritech Inc. v. Monoclonal Antibodies, Inc.*, 802 F.2d 1367, 1376, 231 USPQ 81, 87 (Fed. Cir. 1986).

reexamination [patent] A procedure created in 1980 by Congress pursuant to which any person, including the patent owner, can seek a review by the Patent and Trademark Office (PTO) of the validity of patent claims on the basis of additional PRIOR ART (consisting of patents or printed publications) not previously considered by the PTO. Third parties seeking reexamination of a patent include corporations and governmental entities. Licensees, potential licensees, patent litigants, and interference applicants can seek reexamination. *Manual of Patent Examining Procedure* §2212 (1994 rev.).

A request of reexamination can be made at any time during the life of the patent grant. A reexamination of an expired patent can be sought if the patent is involved or will likely be involved in litigation for damages due to past infringements. *Manual of Patent Examining Procedure* §2211 (1994 rev.).

Patent Reexamined in the Light of New Prior Art. When a substantial question exists about the correctness of the grant of a patent, on reexamination the PTO determines the correctness of that patent grant in light of the new evidence of prior art and either reaffirms the grant, substitutes a new grant by allowing amended or new claims, or withdraws the grant in whole or in part as to some or all claims. The presumption of patent validity, which is effective in court proceedings, is not applicable in the reexamination process.

Pros and Cons. On the one hand, the reexamination procedure gives the patent owner a method of strengthening the validity of her patent. On the other hand, it gives an accused infringer an opportunity to invalidate the patent outside of the courts.

INTERVENING RIGHTS of others are protected against being impinged upon by the grant of new or broader claims after reexamination. See *Kaufman Co. v. Lantech Inc.*, 807 F.2d 970, 1 USPQ2d 1202 (Fed. Cir. 1986).

Reexamination and Collateral Estoppel. A final federal court decision holding a patent not invalid is not binding on the PTO. While the examiner may accord deference to the court's finding of facts, the examiner may continue the reexamination procedure and eventually withdraw the patent grant. However, if a final decision of invalidity is made by a federal court, the PTO may discontinue the reexamination of patent claims. *Manual of Patent Examining Procedure* §2242 (1994 rev.).

Reexamination Compared to Reissue. Like a REISSUE proceeding, the reexamination of a patent is done to correct defects in issued patents. However, "[t]he purpose of the reissuance of patents is to enable correction of errors made by the inventor. ... The reexamination statute's purpose is to correct errors made by the government...." *Patlex Corp. v. Mossinghoff*, 758 F.2d 594, 604, 225 USPQ 243, 250 (Fed. Cir. 1985). And unlike a reissuance proceeding where all issues of patentability are open to scrutiny, in a reexamination proceeding, only prior art consisting of the cited patents and publications are considered by the PTO.

• *Treatise References*: "The innate function of the reexamination process is to increase the reliability of the PTO's action in issuing a patent by reexamination of patents thought 'doubtful.' When the patent is concurrently involved in litigation, an auxiliary function is to free the court from any need to consider prior art without the benefit of the PTO's initial consideration. In a very real sense, the intent underlying reexamination is to 'start over' in the PTO with respect to the limited examination areas involved—to reexamine the claims and to examine new or amended claims, as they would have been considered if they had been originally examined in light of all of the prior art of record in the reexamination proceeding." R. Harmon, *Patents and the Federal Circuit* §15.4 (3d ed. 1994). See 3 D. Chisum, *Patents* §11.07[4] (1994 rev.).

• *Statutory References*:

35 U.S.C. §301: *"Citation of Prior Art.* Any person at any time may cite to the Office in writing prior art consisting of patents or printed publications which that person believes to have bearing on the patentability of any claim of a particular patent...."

35 U.S.C. §302: *"Request for Reexamination.* Any person at any time may file a request for reexamination by the Office of any claim of a patent on the basis of any prior art cited under the provisions of section 301 of this title...."

Note. The procedures for reexamination by the Patent and Trademark Office are defined in 35 U.S.C. §§303–07.

• *Legislative History Reference*: "[Reexamination] will permit any party to petition the Patent Office to review the efficacy of a patent, following its issuance, on the basis of new information about pre-existing technology which may have escaped review at the time of the initial examination of the application." H. Rep. No. 66-1307, 96th Cong., 2d Sess. 3–4 (1980), *reprinted in* 1980 U.S. Code Cong. & Admin. News 6460, 6462.

• *Case References*:

"The reexamination statute enabled the PTO to recover administrative jurisdiction over an issued patent in order to remedy any defects in the examination which that agency had initially conducted and which led to the grant of the patent.... Congress had an important public purpose in mind when it enacted the reexamination statute. The statute was part of a larger effort to revive the United States industry's competitive vitality by restoring confidence in the validity of patents issued by the PTO.... The bill's proponents foresaw three principal benefits. First, the new procedure could settle validity disputes more quickly and less expensively than the often protracted litigation involved in such cases. Second, the procedure would allow courts to refer patent validity questions to the expertise of the Patent Office.... Third, reexamination would reinforce 'investor confidence in the certainty of patent rights' by affording the PTO a broader opportunity to review 'doubtful patents.' " *Patlex Corp. v. Mossinghoff*, 758 F.2d 594, 601–02, 225 USPQ 243, 248–49 (Fed. Cir. 1985).

"That one challenging validity in court bears the burden assigned by §282 [overcoming the presumption that a patent is valid], that the same party may request reexamination upon submission of art not previously cited, and that, if that art raises a substantial new question of patentability, the PTO may during reexamination consider the same and new and amended claims in light of that art free from any presumption, are concepts not in conflict. On the contrary, those concepts are but further indication that litigation and reexamination are distinct proceedings, with distinct parties, purposes, procedures and outcomes. In the former, a litigant who is attacking the validity of a patent bears the burden set forth in §282. In the latter, an examiner is not attacking the validity of a patent, but is conducting a subjective examination of claims in the light of prior art." *In re Etter*, 756 F.2d 852, 857–58, 225 USPQ 1, 4–5 (Fed. Cir. 1985) (en banc).

"[W]e see nothing untoward about the PTO upholding the validity of a reexamined patent which the district court later finds invalid. This is essentially what occurs when a court finds a patent invalid after the PTO has granted it. Once again, it is important that the district court and the PTO can consider different evidence. Accordingly, different results between the two forums may be entirely reasonable. And, if the district court determines a patent is not invalid, the PTO should continue its reexamination because, of course, the two forums have different standards of proof for determining invalidity. … On the other hand, if a court finds a patent invalid, and that decision is either upheld on appeal or not appealed, the PTO may discontinue its reexamination." *Ethicon Inc. v. Quigg*, 849 F.2d 1422, 1429, 7 USPQ2d 1152, 1157 (Fed. Cir. 1988).

registration [patent–trademark–copyright]

1. Invention Registration.
See STATUTORY INVENTION REGISTRATION.

2. Registration of a Trademark.
There are two very different federal registers established under the Lanham Act: the PRINCIPAL REGISTER and the SUPPLEMENTAL REGISTER. The principal register is the main register of marks and confers important benefits, such as the contestable and incontestable stages of the PRESUMPTION OF VALIDITY; CONSTRUCTIVE NOTICE of the registrant's ownership; and, since at least 1989, a CONSTRUCTIVE USE priority date as of the date of filing of the application. See PRINCIPAL REGISTER. On the other hand, the supplemental register confers none of those benefits and is only for terms such as DESCRIPTIVE words that have not yet achieved trademark status through SECONDARY MEANING but that are capable of doing so in the future.

See SUPPLEMENTAL REGISTER.

Types of Applications. Since the November 16, 1989, effective date of the 1988 TRADEMARK LAW REVISION ACT, there are three alternative ways to file an application to register on the principal register.

(1) *Use-Based Application*—A §1(a) use-based application, which is essentially the same as that used in the pre-1989 practice. This is an application based upon actual use of the mark in interstate or foreign commerce. However, unlike previous practice, the "use" that must precede application is not just "token" use but

real commercial use. Since 1989, trademark "use" is defined as "the bona fide use of a mark in the ordinary course of trade, and not made merely to reserve a right in a mark." Lanham Act §45, 15 U.S.C. §1127.

(2) *Foreign-Based Application*—A §44 application by a qualified foreign firm with an application or registration in a foreign nation. The applicant must state that it has a bona fide intention to use the mark in the United States on the goods or services listed but need not use or prove actual use in order to obtain the registration. Thus, even after 1989, qualified foreign applicants continued to enjoy an important benefit that domestic applicants did not: exemption from the requirement of proof of use before registration. In any application under §44, the applicant need not state a date of first use anywhere in the world and need not provide specimens of use. *Crocker Nat'l Bank v. Canadian Imperial Bank of Commerce*, 223 USPQ 909 (T.T.A.B. 1984); 37 C.F.R. §§2.21, 2.33. Under Lanham Act §44(d), 15 U.S.C. §1126(d), an application in the United States for registration of a mark by a person whose country of origin is a party to the PARIS CONVENTION is entitled to a priority convention filing date as of the date of filing of a prior trademark application in a foreign country that is also a party to the Paris Convention.

See CONVENTION DATE.

(3) *ITU Application*—A §1(b) INTENT TO USE APPLICATION filed by an applicant with a bona fide intention to use the mark on the goods or services listed. However, the registration will not be granted unless and until the applicant files a verified Statement of Use, together with specimens, proving that it has used the mark in interstate or foreign U.S. commerce. Since 1989 about half of all applications in the Patent and Trademark Office (PTO) have been filed as ITU applications.

Use of a Trademark in Interstate Commerce. To obtain a valid federal registration, it is necessary that the trademark be used in or affect interstate commerce. The traditional view of the PTO is that the statutory requirement of a sale or transportation "in commerce" demands a sale or transportation that physically crosses a state line or crosses a border of the United States.

However, the Court of Customs and Patent Appeals has indicated that use of a mark on even local sales of goods which have some significant effect on interstate or foreign commerce will suffice. *In re Silenus Wines, Inc.*, 557 F.2d 806, 192 USPQ 261 (C.C.P.A. 1977). SERVICE MARKS are governed by different standards of interstate commerce.

See SERVICE MARK.

Duration of Registration. The TRADEMARK LAW REVISION ACT effective in 1989 shortened the term of a federal trademark registration from 20 years to 10 years as part of an effort to reduce unused "deadwood" cluttering up the federal register. Registrations issued on or after November 16, 1989, have a duration of 10 years and may be renewed indefinitely so long as the mark is still in use. Lanham Act §§8, 9(a), 15 U.S.C. §§1058, 1059(a). Registrations based on applications pending in the PTO on November 16, 1989, will last for renewal periods of 10 years. Lanham Act §51, 15 U.S.C. §1058 note.

Section 8 Affidavit. A registration on either the PRINCIPAL REGISTER or the SUPPLEMENTAL REGISTER is automatically cancelled by the PTO on the sixth anniversary of its registration date unless the registrant files, within the fifth year, an affidavit (or equivalent declaration) listing the goods or services in connection with which the mark is in use in interstate or U.S. foreign commerce, attaching a specimen or facsimile showing current use of the mark. Lanham Act §8, 15 U.S.C. §1058. As of November 16, 1989, "token use" is not a basis on which to file a §8 affidavit. There must be a "use in commerce," meaning bona fide use in the ordinary course of trademark, not merely to reserve a right in a mark. The previous practice of making a special token shipment or sale as a basis for filing a §8 affidavit is no longer viable. The 1989 TRADE-MARK LAW REVISION ACT amendments also changed previous law by requiring the registrant to specify in the §8 affidavit the specific goods or services on or in connection with which the mark is in use in interstate or foreign U.S. commerce. Regulations require a specimen of use for each class of goods or services in the registration. 37 C.F.R. §§2.161–.162.

Disclaimer. An applicant can make a DIS-CLAIMER: a statement by a registrant of a COM-POSITE MARK that it is claiming only the whole composite mark as its registered mark and makes no claim to the particular portion or portions disclaimed.

See DISCLAIMER.

Infringement of Registered Mark. Infringement is determined by the likelihood-of-confusion test of Lanham Act §32(a), 15 U.S.C. §1114(a). The test is that of the modern "related goods" rule: the owner of a registered mark has protection against use of the mark on any product or service that would reasonably be thought by the public to come from the same source, or be thought to be affiliated with, connected with, or sponsored by the owner of the registered mark. Thus, the remedies of a registered trademark owner are not limited to the goods or services specified in the registration, but extend to any goods or services on which use of a similar mark is likely to cause confusion. *E. Remy Martin & Co., S.A. v. Shaw-Ross Int'l Imports Inc.*, 756 F.2d 1525, 1530, 225 USPQ 1131, 1134 (11th Cir. 1985). However, the presumptive validity of a registration extends only to the registered format and to the registered goods or services. *In re National Data Corp.*, 753 F.2d 1056, 224 USPQ 749 (Fed. Cir. 1985) (registration of COMPOSITE MARK affords presumptive validity only to the mark as a whole, not to its component parts); *Levi Strauss & Co. v. Blue Bell, Inc.*, 778 F.2d 1352, 228 USPQ 346 (9th Cir. 1985) (registration for pants is not presumptive evidence of secondary meaning for mark on shirts).

• *Treatise Reference*: J.T. McCarthy, *Trademarks and Unfair Competition* §§19.01–.56 (3d ed. 1995 rev.).

3. Registration of a Claim of Copyright. The United States is unique in the world in having a system of copyright registration as well as a large government office specifically charged with processing and maintaining records on copyright registrations. The federal office charged with this task is the Copyright Office, a department of the Library of Congress, and located in Washington, D.C. Contrary to popular belief, registration with the Copyright Office has never created the rights of copyright nor has it marked the beginning of DURATION of a copyright. Copyright for both published and unpublished works can be registered.

Registration Process. Registration is a simple process. The copyright claimant fills out the appropriate form (e.g., Form TX for nondramatic LITERARY WORKS) and sends it along with the fee ($20 in 1995) and the DEPOSIT of the appropriate number of copies of the work (e.g., two copies of a published work) to the Copyright Office in Washington, D.C., which makes an examination largely for form and issues a certificate of a claim to copyright. The certificate consists of the form filled out by the claimant. 17 U.S.C. §§409–10. The address is: United States Copyright Office, Library of Congress, Washington D.C. 20559.

Pre-1978 Works. As to works created before January 1, 1978, federal statutory copyright was obtained by publication with notice. 1909 Act, §10. Registration did not create the copyright: it merely recorded the claim to copyright. There was no time limit for registration to be made, except that to renew copyright for a second 28-year term, initial registration had to be made during the first 28-year term. See 2 *Nimmer on Copyright*, §9.05[B][2] (1994 rev.).

See RENEWAL.

Post-1978 Works. As to works created after January 1, 1978, the Copyright Act explicitly states that registration may be made "at any time during the subsistence of copyright" and that "registration is not a condition of copyright protection." 17 U.S.C. §408. The only time that registration would be crucial to save the copyright itself would be to cure the public distribution from 1978 to 1989 of copies without copyright NOTICE by registration within five years. 17 U.S.C. §405(a)(2). After the March 1, 1989, effective date of the BERNE CONVENTION REVISION ACT (BCIA), prompt registration of a claim of copyright is recommended for the following reasons: (1) registration is a condition precedent to filing suit in the United States for claims arising after March 1, 1989, for infringement of a work whose country of origin is the United States (17 U.S.C. §411(a)); (2) registration within five years of first publication creates a presumption of validity of the copyright and of the facts in the certificate (17 U.S.C. §410(c)); (3) prompt registration makes available the possibility of the recovery of STATUTORY DAMAGES and ATTORNEY FEES against an infringer (17 U.S.C. §412); and (4) registration is a condition of the constructive notice given by a RECORDATION of an assignment or license (17 U.S.C. §205(c)).

Errors in Registration. "It is well established that immaterial, inadvertent errors in an application for copyright registration do not jeopardize the validity of the registration.... In general, an error is immaterial if its discovery is not likely to have led the Copyright Office to refuse the application." *Data Gen. Corp. v. Grumman Sys. Support Corp.*, 36 F.3d 1147, 1161, 32 USPQ2d 1385, 1394–95 (1st Cir. 1994).

See DEPOSIT OF COPIES, PUBLICATION.

- *Treatise References*: 2 *Nimmer on Copyright* §7.16 et seq. (1994 rev.); 1 P. Goldstein, *Copyright* §§3.11–.15 (1989); M. Leaffer, *Understanding Copyright* §7.2 et seq. (1989); 1 N. Boorstyn, *Copyright* §9.05 (2d ed. 1994).

reissue [patent] The regranting by the Patent and Trademark Office of a patent in order to correct a patent that may be wholly or partly inoperative or invalid.

Reasons for Reissue. A reissue may be requested by a patent owner because the original claims are (1) too narrow and do not adequately protect the true scope of the invention; or (2) too broad and are invalid as claiming some aspects of prior art not invented by the patentee. A showing that an applicant had an INTENT TO CLAIM matter that was not originally claimed can go far to establish that error occurred, justifying a reissue for broader claims. "The most common bases for filing a reissue application are (1) the claims are too narrow or broad; (2) the disclosure contains inaccuracies; (3) applicant failed to or incorrectly claimed foreign priority; (4) applicant failed to make reference to or incorrectly made reference to prior copending applications." *Manual of Patent Examining Procedure* §1402 (1994 rev.).

Requirements for Reissue. To obtain a reissue of a patent, the patent owner must establish six things: (1) the patent is "deemed wholly or partly inoperative or invalid" because of a "defective specification or drawing" or because the patentee claimed "more or less than he had a right to claim in the patent"; (2) the defect came about "through error without any deceptive intention"; (3) the reissue does not introduce NEW MATTER; (4) an application for a reissue that enlarges the scope of the claims must be made "within two years from the grant of the original patent"; (5) the subject matter claimed in the application for reissue meets the legal requirements for a patent; and (6) the original patent has not yet expired. See 4 D. Chisum, *Patents* §15.03 (1994 rev.); 37 C.F.R. §§1.171–.179.

Application for Reissue. The application for the reissuance of a patent is essentially an application for the original patent including corrections. The matter to be omitted is enclosed in brackets and any additions underlined. A new oath and fee must accompany the reissue application as well as an offer to surrender the original patent. 37 C.F.R. §§1.171, 1.173.

Duration of Reissue. The duration of a reissue patent is coextensive with the unexpired portion of the superseded patent. There can be no stretching of the term of the patent by a reissue.

Recapture Rule. The RECAPTURE RULE forbids a patentee from regaining, through a reissue patent, claims that are of the same or broader scope than claims that were voluntarily cancelled or narrowed by the applicant during the prosecution of the original application.

Defense of Intervening Rights. An infringer may have a personal defense of INTERVENING RIGHTS to continue what would otherwise be infringing activity if the activity or preparation for it was started before the grant of a reissue patent.

Dann Amendments. Effective from 1977 to 1982, the DANN AMENDMENTS permitted "no fault" reissue and INTER PARTES participation of protestors in reissue proceedings.

• *Statutory Reference*: 35 U.S.C. §251: "Whenever any patent is, through error without any deceptive intention, deemed wholly or partly inoperative or invalid, by reason of a defective specification or drawing, or by reason of the patentee claiming more or less than he had a right to claim in the patent, the Commissioner shall, on the surrender of such patent and

the payment of the fee required by law, reissue the patent for the invention disclosed in the original patent, and in accordance with a new and amended application, for the unexpired part of the term of the original patent. No new matter shall be introduced into the application for reissue...."

• *Treatise References*: 4 D. Chisum, *Patents* §§15.01–.05 (1994 rev.); R. Harmon, *Patents and the Federal Circuit* §15.3 (3d ed. 1994).

"In enacting the reissue statute, Congress provided a statutory basis for correction of error. The statute is remedial in nature, based on fundamental principles of equity and fairness, and should be construed liberally. Nonetheless, not every event or circumstance that might be labeled error is correctable by reissue. The whole purpose of reissue, as far as claims are concerned, is to permit limitations to be added to claims that are too broad or to be taken from claims that are too narrow." R. Harmon, *Patents and the Federal Circuit* §15.3 (3d ed. 1994).

"A failure of the patent attorney to appreciate the full scope of invention is one of the most common sources of defects in patents. The fact that such error could have been discovered during the application stage with a more thorough patentability search or with improved communication between inventors and attorneys does not, by itself, preclude a patent owner from correcting defects through reissue." 2 P. Rosenberg, *Patent Law Fundamentals* §15.09[2][a][iv] (1994 rev.).

• *Case References*:

"[T]he central question ... [is] whether Weiler has established 'error' which can be remedied by reissue. The reissue statute was not enacted as a panacea for all patent prosecution problems, nor as a grant to the patentee of a second opportunity to prosecute *de novo* his original application.... Though the term 'error' is to be interpreted liberally, ... Congress did not intend to alter the test of 'inadvertence, accident or mistake' established in relation to the pre-1952 statutes.... Weiler's reliance on allegations of the inventor's ignorance of drafting and claiming technique and counsel's ignorance of the invention is unavailing. Those allegations could be frequently made, and, if accepted as establishing error, would require the grant of reissues on anything and everything mentioned in a disclosure.... Insight resulting from hindsight on the part of new counsel does not, in every case, establish error." *In re Weiler*, 790 F.2d 1576, 1582–53 n.4, 220 USPQ 673, 677 n.4 (Fed. Cir. 1986).

"[T]he statutorily required 'error' of section 251 has two parts: (1) error in the patent, and (2) error in conduct.... [T]he precedent of this court is that the [statutory] expression 'less than he had a right to claim' generally refers to the scope of a claim.... Thus, that provision covers the situation where the claims in the patent are narrower than the prior art would have required the patentee to claim and the patentee seeks broader claims. Conversely, the alternative that the patentee claimed 'more ... than he had a right to claim' comes into play where a claim is too broad in scope in view of the prior art or the specification and the patentee seeks narrower claims." *Hewlett-Packard Co. v. Bausch & Lomb Inc.*, 882 F.2d 1556, 1564–65, 11 USPQ2d 1750, 1755 (Fed. Cir. 1989).

"[T]he inquiry that must be undertaken to determine whether the new claims are 'for the invention' originally disclosed ... is to examine the entirety of the original disclosure and decide whether, through the 'objective' eyes of the hypothetical person having ordinary skill in the art, an inventor could fairly have claimed the newly submitted subject matter in the original application, given that the requisite error has been averred." *In re Amos*, 953 F.2d 613, 618, 21 USPQ2d 1271, 1275 (Fed. Cir. 1991).

"Reissue 'error' is generally liberally construed, and we have recognized that '[a]n attorney's failure to appreciate the full scope of the invention' is not an uncommon defect in claiming an invention.... However, the reissue procedure does not give the patentee 'a second opportunity to prosecute *de novo* his original application.' ... The deliberate cancellation of a claim of an original application in order to secure a patent cannot ordinarily be said to be an 'error' and will in most cases prevent the applicant from obtaining the cancelled claim by reissue.... If a patentee tries to recapture what he or she previously surrendered in order to obtain allowance of original patent claims, that

'deliberate withdrawal or amendment ... cannot be said to involve the inadvertence or mistake contemplated by 35 U.S.C. §251, and is not an error of the kind which will justify the granting of a reissue patent which includes the matter withdrawn.' " *Mentor Corp. v. Coloplast Inc.*, 998 F.2d 992, 995, 27 USPQ2d 1521, 1524 (Fed. Cir. 1993).

related company [trademark] A controlled licensee of a trademark or service mark. In federal law, any controlled licensee of a mark is known as a "related company." This does not denote any corporate affiliation but only that the related company is a licensee of the mark, with control being exercised by the licensor as to the nature and quality of the goods or services sold under the mark.

See LICENSE OF A TRADEMARK.

• *Statutory Reference*: Lanham Act §45, 15 U.S.C. §1127: *"Related Company*. The term 'related company' means any person whose use of a mark is controlled by the owner of the mark with respect to the nature and quality of the goods or services on or in connection with which the mark is used."

• *Treatise Reference*: J.T. McCarthy, *Trademarks and Unfair Competition* §18.16 (3d ed. 1995 rev.).

related goods or services [trademark] Goods or services that bear such a relationship to each other that persons are likely to believe that such goods or services, bearing a similar mark, come from the same source or are somehow connected with or sponsored by the same company.

A Legal, Not a Physical, Relationship. Sometimes judicial opinions and attorneys' law briefs use the term "related" to refer to some form of physical or use relationship between the conflicting goods or services of the litigants in a trademark infringement dispute. But this is incorrect. Goods are "related," not because of any inherent common quality or physical characteristic, but because when a similar mark appears on those goods, a reasonable person is likely to believe that those goods come from a common source or are put out by sources linked

373

by some form of sponsorship or affiliation. "The question is, are the uses related so that they are likely to be connected in the mind of a prospective purchaser?" *Fleischmann Distilling Corp. v. Maier Brewing Co.*, 314 F.2d 149, 159, 136 USPQ 508, 517 (9th Cir. 1963).

The "Related Goods" Test. The test of infringement of a registered mark is that of the modern "related goods" rule: the owner of a registered mark has protection against use of the mark on any product or service that would reasonably be thought by the public to come from the same source, or be thought to be affiliated with, connected with, or sponsored by the owner of the registered mark. Thus, the remedies of a registered trademark owner are not limited to the goods or services specified in the registration, but extend to any goods or services on which use of a similar mark is likely to cause confusion. *E. Remy Martin & Co., S.A. v. Shaw-Ross Int'l Imports Inc.*, 756 F.2d 1525, 1530, 225 USPQ 1131, 1134 (11th Cir. 1985). A related product is one "which would reasonably be thought by the buying public to come from the same source, or thought to be affiliated with, connected with, or sponsored by the trademark owner." *Sands, Taylor & Wood Co. v. Quaker Oats Co.*, 978 F.2d 947, 958, 24 USPQ2d 1001, 1010 (7th Cir. 1992), quoting from J.T. McCarthy, *Trademarks and Unfair Competition* §24.03[2] (3d ed. 1995 rev.).

See INFRINGEMENT OF A TRADEMARK.

• *Treatise Reference*: J.T. McCarthy, *Trademarks and Unfair Competition* §24.03 et seq. (3d ed. 1995 rev.).

• *Restatement Reference*: "Thus, the rule stated in this Section applies to all forms of confusion, including the false belief that the owner of the mark has formally certified the goods as meeting particular standards, as in the case of a certification mark, the false belief that the subsequent user of the mark is affiliated with the owner as a franchisee, agent or distributor, or the false belief that the subsequent user has the approval of the owner in manufacturing or marketing goods under the mark." *Restatement (Third) of Unfair Competition* §20, comment d (1995).

remake [copyright] An assignment or license of the right to make a remake is the grant of a right to produce one or more motion pictures based substantially upon the same story as contained in the original motion picture. While a SEQUEL puts the same characters in a different plot, a remake is a motion picture based substantially upon the same story, albeit with modernizing or updating elements.

See DERIVATIVE WORK.

renewal [trademark–copyright] The extension of a registration of a trademark or the extension of a copyright.

1. Renewal of Federal Trademark Registration. Prior to November 16, 1989, federal trademark registrations were issued for indefinitely renewable terms of 20 years. The Trademark Law Revision Act of 1989 shortened the term of a federal trademark registration from 20 years to 10 years as part of an effort to reduce unused "deadwood" cluttering up the federal register. Registrations issued or renewed on or after November 16, 1989, have a duration of 10 years and may be renewed indefinitely so long as the mark is still in use. Lanham Act §§8, 9(a), 15 U.S.C. §§1058, 1059(a); 37 C.F.R. §2.181(a)(2).

Material Alteration in Registered Mark. The registration of a mark that has been so changed as to be a "material alteration" of the mark as originally registered may not be amended or renewed. *In re Holland Am. Wafer Co.*, 737 F.2d 1015, 222 USPQ 273 (Fed. Cir. 1984). It may be fraud to submit to the Patent and Trademark Office an old form of label as a specimen of use in a renewal application after a material alteration has been made in the format of the mark. *Torres v. Cantine Torresella S.r.l.*, 808 F.2d 46, 1 USPQ2d 1483 (Fed. Cir. 1986).

• *Treatise Reference*: J.T. McCarthy, *Trademarks and Unfair Competition* §19.49 (3d ed. 1995 rev.).

2. Renewal of Copyright. For works first published before January 1, 1978, copyright duration was measured by an initial copyright term of 28 years, which could and still can be renewed for a second term. Originally, the 1909

Copyright Act provided for a second 28-year renewal term. 1909 Act, §24. The theory of the renewal term was the same as that for the modern TERMINATION OF GRANT: to protect authors from making a bad deal for the sale or license of their works. Authors were given a second chance after a period of years to get a better deal by renegotiating an assignment or license of the second term. The renewal term "creates a new estate ... clear of all rights, interests or licenses granted under the original copyright." *G. Ricordi & Co. v. Paramount Pictures, Inc.*, 189 F.2d 469, 471, 89 USPQ 289, 290 (2d Cir. 1951).

Assignments of Renewal Term. For a document to constitute an assignment of the renewal term in advance, it must clearly and explicitly refer to and include the second term. If assignment of the renewal term is explicit, then it is binding if the author lives to the vesting of the renewal term. *Fred Fisher Music Co. v. M. Witmark & Sons*, 318 U.S. 643, 57 USPQ 50 (1943); 2 *Nimmer on Copyright* §9.06[B][1] (1994 rev.); 1 P. Goldstein, *Copyright* §4.8.3.1 (1989). But an advance assignment of the renewal term is personal: it binds only the author/grantor, not the surviving spouse or heirs. If the author/grantor dies before the vesting of the renewal term, then the assignment of the renewal term is void and the renewal term passes free of the author's grant to the statutory class of surviving spouse and children, executor of will, or next of kin if no will. 17 U.S.C. §304(a); 2 *Nimmer on Copyright* §9.06[C] (1994 rev.). The author had only an expectancy to assign—the expectancy that he or she would live to the vesting of the renewal term. In the "Rear Window" case, the Supreme Court held that if an author, such as the author of a novel, dies before the renewal period, then the assignee of the right to produce a DERIVATIVE WORK, such as a movie studio that produces a motion picture of the novel, cannot continue to exploit the derivative motion picture without a new grant from the new owner of the renewal term. *Stewart v. Abend*, 495 U.S. 207, 14 USPQ2d 1614 (1990)

Time for Renewal. Renewal must be made during the 28th year after publication with notice, that is, between the 27th and 28th birthday of the copyright. All terms run to the end of the calendar year. 17 U.S.C. §305. For copyrights in their first term on January 1, 1978, the renewal term was "stretched" by Congress by 19 years to a total 47-year second, renewal term. Thus, the total duration of such renewed copyrights was increased to 75 years from the date of first publication with notice (28 + 28 + 19 = 75). 17 U.S.C. §304(a). However, such copyrights need to be renewed, either automatically by operation of law or by registration by the copyright claimant. For example, the federal copyright on a novel first published in 1975 will be renewed by December 31, 2003. Then, the copyright will last until the end of 2050.

Automatic Renewal. Revisions to the Copyright Act in 1992 provided for automatic renewal of copyright for those works still needing renewal. That is, for works first published from 1964 to the end of 1977, copyright would not be lost for failure to renew. However, renewal is still strongly recommended, for Congress created certain bonus rights and remedies to reward those who renew their copyrights. See: 37 C.F.R. §202.17; 2 *Nimmer on Copyright* §9.05[A][2] (1994 rev.); W. Patry, *Copyright Law and Practice* 501 (1994). For pre-1964 published works, failure to register the original term prior to renewal forecloses filing a renewal, thus causing a loss of copyright. See 2 *Nimmer on Copyright* §9.05[B][2] (1994 rev.).

Renewal Term "Stretched." For older works in federal copyright that were already in their renewal term as of January 1, 1978, the renewal term was automatically "stretched" 19 years for a total duration of 75 years from the date of first publication with notice. 17 U.S.C. §304(b).

See DURATION of copyright.

• *Treatise References*: 2 *Nimmer on Copyright* §9.02 et seq. (1994 rev.); 1 P. Goldstein, *Copyright* §4.8 (1989); M. Leaffer, *Understanding Copyright* §6.5 (1989); W. Patry, *Copyright Law and Practice* 470 (1994).

• *Case Reference*: "Thus, the renewal provisions were intended to give the author a second chance to obtain fair remuneration for his creative efforts and to provide the author's family a 'new estate' if the author died before the renewal period arrived.... [I]f the author dies before the commencement of the renewal period, the assignee holds nothing. If the assignee of all of the renewal rights holds nothing upon the death of the assignor before arrival of the renewal period, then a fortiori, the assignee of a portion of the renewal rights, e.g., the right to produce a derivative work, must also hold nothing.... [I]f the author dies before the renewal period, then the assignee may continue to use the original work only if the author's successor transfers the renewal right to the assignee." *Stewart v. Abend*, 495 U.S. 207, 220–21, 14 USPQ2d 1614, 1621 (1990)

reproduction rights organization [copyright] A nongovernmental collective-licensing organization composed of copyright owners. A reproduction rights organization licenses photocopying of members' works by schools, universities, government, and/or private corporations without specific prior permission in return for royalty payments distributed to member copyright owners. Such an organization in the United States is the COPYRIGHT CLEARANCE CENTER. Many national reproduction rights organizations are members of IFRRO.

reprography [copyright] The reproduction of written materials, drawings, pictures, etc., by a process using light rays or photographic methods, such as photocopying or microfilming. The word is a combination of repro[duction] and [photo]graphy.

See FAIR USE OF COPYRIGHT.

requirement for division [patent]

See RESTRICTION.

Restatement of the Law of Unfair Competition [trademark–trade secret–right of publicity] A summary of the law on the topics of false advertising, trademark, trade secret, and the right of publicity. Published in final form in 1995, this restatement of the law is already recognized as an authoritative reference for judges and attorneys.

Description of the Restatement. All restatements are created under the auspices of the American Law Institute, whose primary purpose is to create concise but comprehensive statements of the law in various fields. The Restatement of the Law of Unfair Competition is the result of an almost 10-year project. The influence of the *Restatement of the Law of Unfair Competition* is largely the result of the authority and experience of the 25 judges, expert practitioners, and professors who composed the Board of Advisors and of the diligence, skill, and clarity of the coreporters who actually prepared the material. The coreporters were Professors Robert C. Denicola and Harvey S. Perlman of the University of Nebraska College of Law. Like all restatements, the *Restatement of the Law of Unfair Competition* is composed of three parts: (1) the text of the restatement ("black letter" law); (2) the Comments on the text, including illustrative cases; and (3) the Reporters' Notes, containing case, statutory, and treatise citations supporting the text and notes.

Third Is the First. While the official citation form is to the "Third" Restatement of Unfair Competition, this denotes only that this is part of the third phase of all restatements, not that this is the third version of a *Restatement of the Law of Unfair Competition*. In fact, it is the first such restatement so named. It replaces similar coverage contained in the 1938 *Restatement of Torts*.

• *Restatement Reference*: *Restatement (Third) of Unfair Competition* §§1–49 (1995).

• *Commentary References:* H. Perlman, *The Restatement of the Law of Unfair Competition: A Work in Progress*, 80 Trademark Rep. 461 (1990); S. Edelman, *Restatement of the Law of Trademarks: A Review*, 81 Trademark Rep. 554 (1992).

research exemption [patent]

See EXPERIMENTAL USE, definition (2).

restoration [copyright]

See DURATION (of copyright).

restriction [patent] Narrowing down the scope of one patent application from more than one invention to only one invention. Under Patent Code §121, the Patent and Trademark Office may require that a patent application be

376

"restricted" to one of two or more independent and distinct inventions claimed in a single application. This is because two or more independent and distinct inventions may not be claimed in one patent application.

Divisional Application. The applicant may respond to a requirement of restriction by filing a DIVISIONAL APPLICATION. A divisional application is carved out of the PARENT APPLICATION and is entitled to the filing date of the original application. Neither the original nor the restricted divisional application can be cited against each other as PRIOR ART.

Double Patenting Challenge. If a restriction is required and complied with, then the patent owner is insulated from challenge for violating the rule against an "obviousness-type" of DOUBLE PATENTING.

Synonym: requirement for division.

See UNITY OF INVENTION, ELECTION OF SPECIES, DIVISIONAL APPLICATION.

• *Statutory Reference*: 35 U.S.C. §121: "If two or more independent and distinct inventions are claimed in one application, the Commissioner may require the application to be restricted to one of the inventions. If the other invention is made the subject of a divisional application which complies with the requirements of section 120 of this title it shall be entitled to the benefit of the filing date of the original application. A patent issuing on an application with respect to which a requirement for restriction under this section has been made, or on an application filed as a result of such a requirement, shall not be used as a reference either in the Patent and Trademark Office or in the courts against a divisional application or against the original application or any patent issued on either of them, if the divisional application is filed before the issuance of the patent on the other application...."

• *Rule Reference*: "If two or more independent and distinct inventions are claimed in a single application, the examiner in his action shall require the applicant in his response to that action to elect that invention to which his claim shall be restricted, this official action being called a requirement for restrictions (also

known as a requirement for division)...." 37 C.F.R. §1.142(a).

• *Manual References*:
"There are two criteria for a proper requirement for restriction between patentably distinct inventions: (1) The inventions must be independent ... or distinct as claimed ...; and (2) There must be a serious burden on the examiner if restriction is not required." *Manual of Patent Examining Procedure* §803 (1994 rev.).

"If it can be shown that the two or more inventions are in fact independent, applicant should be required to restrict the claims presented to but one of such independent inventions. For example: (1) Two different combinations, not disclosed as capable of use together, having different modes of operations, different functions or different effects are independent. An article of apparel such as a shoe, and a locomotive bearing would be an example. A process of painting a house and a process of boring a well would be a second example. (2) Where the two inventions are process and apparatus, and the apparatus cannot be used to practice the process or any part thereof, they are independent. A specific process of molding is independent from a molding apparatus which cannot be used to practice the specific process. (3) Where species under a genus are independent, for example, a genus of paper clips having species differing in the manner in which a section of the wire is formed in order to achieve a greater increase in its holding power." *Manual of Patent Examining Procedure* §806.04 (1994 rev.).

• *Case Reference*: "Congress in 1952 refused to truncate the term of patents issued following a restriction requirement, although the question was squarely before it." *Studiengesellschaft Kohle mbH v. Northern Petrochemical Co.*, 784 F.2d 351, 357, 228 USPQ 837, 841 (Fed. Cir. 1986).

reverse confusion [trademark] Customers dealing with the senior user of a mark under the confused and mistaken impression that they are dealing with one who is sponsored by or affiliated with the junior user of the mark. This confusion is created because the junior user has established itself as the source of goods or services identified by the mark through a relatively large advertising campaign.

Reverse Confusion Defined. The usual pattern of classic "forward confusion" occurs when customers are aware of the senior user's mark and mistakenly think that the junior user's goods or services are from the same source as, or are sponsored by, or connected with the senior user. In "reverse confusion," by contrast, most customers are aware only of the junior user's advertising and promotion of the mark and link the mark with the junior user. Such customers think that either the senior user is an infringer or that the senior user is sponsored by or affiliated with the junior user. Such a situation generally arises when the junior user's advertising and promotion of the mark is much larger than that of the senior user.

The Bigfoot Case and Its Progeny. The landmark decision establishing reverse confusion as a viable theory of legal recovery for trademark infringement is the 1976 BIGFOOT tire case, where the court upheld under Colorado state law a jury verdict of several million dollars against the Goodyear Tire Company based primarily upon the rule of reverse confusion. *Big O Tire Dealers, Inc. v. Goodyear Tire & Rubber Co.*, 408 F. Supp. 1219, 189 USPQ 17 (D. Col. 1976), *aff'd and award modified*, 561 F.2d 1365, 195 USPQ 417 (10th Cir. 1977), *cert. dismissed*, 434 U.S. 1052 (1978). Later decisions have followed the theory of the BIGFOOT decision and held that reverse confusion is actionable under federal law. See, e.g., *Banff, Ltd. v. Federated Dep't Stores, Inc.*, 841 F.2d 486, 6 USPQ2d 1187 (2d Cir. 1988) (reverse confusion actionable under Lanham Act §43(a) for infringement of unregistered marks); *Fuji Photo Film Co. v. Shinohara Shoji Kabushiki Kaisha*, 754 F.2d 591, 225 USPQ 540 (5th Cir. 1985) (reverse confusion actionable under Lanham Act §32(a) for infringement of registered mark). Reverse confusion can be relied upon by the PTO to refuse registration to a mark. *In re Shell Oil Co.*, 992 F2d 1204, 26 USPQ2d 1687 (Fed. Cir. 1993).

- *Treatise Reference*: 3 J.T. McCarthy, *Trademarks and Unfair Competition* §23.01[5] (3d ed. 1995 rev.).

- *Restatement Reference: Restatement (Third) of Unfair Competition* §20, comment f (1995) ("[T]he creation of reverse confusion falls within the traditional rules governing the infringement of trademarks.").

- *Case References*:

"A reverse confusion claim differs from the stereotypical confusion of source or sponsorship claim. Rather than seeking to profit from the goodwill captured in the senior user's trademark, the junior user saturates the market with a similar trademark and overwhelms the senior user. The public comes to assume the senior user's products are really the junior user's or that the former has become somehow connected to the latter. The result is that the senior user loses the value of the trademark—its product identity, corporate identity, control over its goodwill, and reputation and ability to move into new markets." *Ameritech Inc. v. American Information Technologies Corp.*, 811 F.2d 960, 964, 1 USPQ2d 1861, 1865 (7th Cir. 1987).

"[Plaintiff's] confusion theory is thus cognizable under the Lanham Act. Allowing such confusion claims comports with the dual purposes of the Act —namely, to protect the public from confusion as to the source of goods, and at the same time to protect the trademark holder from misappropriation of its mark.... Where, as here, the relevant issue is whether consumers mistakenly believe that the senior user's products actually originate with the junior user, it is appropriate to survey the senior user's customers." *Sterling Drug Inc. v. Bayer AG*, 14 F.3d 733, 741, 29 USPQ2d 1321, 1326 (2d Cir. 1994) (The American company owning the BAYER trademark in the United States successfully sued the German Bayer company, alleging reverse confusion in that the German company's recent actions in the United States were likely to confuse customers of the senior user American company's BAYER aspirin into mistakenly thinking that it was a product of the junior user German Bayer company.).

reverse doctrine of equivalents [patent]
See EQUIVALENTS, REVERSE DOCTRINE OF.

reverse engineering [trade secret]
A method of obtaining technical information by starting with a publicly available product and determining what it is made of, what makes it work, or how it was produced. The engineering effort goes in the reverse direction of usual engineering efforts, which start with technical data and use it to produce a product. Reverse engineering starts with the product and uses it to determine the technical data and know-how that was used to make the product.

Reverse Engineering to Reach a Trade Secret Is Not Infringement. Assuming that the product or other material that is the subject of the reverse engineering was properly obtained, the process of reverse engineering is not infringement of any trade secrets in the data embodied in a product and is legitimate and legal competitive behavior.

Reverse Engineering to Obtain Unprotected Ideas and Concepts Is Not Copyright Infringement. It has been held to be a FAIR USE of a copyrighted computer program for a competitor to disassemble the program and make an intermediate copy solely in order to determine the uncopyrightable concepts embodied in the program. "We conclude that where disassembly is the only way to gain access to the ideas and functional elements embodied in a copyrighted computer program and where there is a legitimate reason for seeking such access, disassembly is a fair use of the copyrighted work, as a matter of law." *Sega Enters. Ltd. v. Accolade Inc.*, 977 F.2d 1510, 1527, 24 USPQ2d 1561, 1574 (9th Cir. 1992).

See DISSASSEMBLING, TRADE SECRET, REVERSE PASSING OFF.

• *Restatement Reference*: "[O]thers remain free to analyze products publicly marketed by the trade secret owner and, absent protection under a patent or copyright, to exploit any information acquired through 'reverse engineering.' " *Restatement (Third) of Unfair Competition* §43, comment b (1995).

• *Case Reference*: "A trade secret, however, does not offer protection against discovery by fair and honest means, such as by independent invention, accidental disclosure, or by so-called reverse engineering, that is by starting with the known product and working backward to divine the process which aided in its development or manufacture." *Kewanee Oil Co. v. Bicron Corp.*, 416 U.S. 470, 476, 181 USPQ 673, 676 (1974).

reverse engineering injunction [trade-secret]
An injunction of limited duration against use of a trade secret. The injunction lasts for the estimated time it would take a hypothetical competitor to start with a legitimate public disclosure and work backward to discover the trade secret. This kind of limited-duration injunction deprives the infringer of any competitive advantage it obtained and attempts to put the trade secret owner in the position it would have been in but for the illegal taking of the secret.

Compromise of the Extremes. A classic factual scenario is a trade secret infringer who used improper means to obtain the secret, but the owner of the secret soon thereafter discloses the secret through legitimate means, such as the selling of a product or the issuance of a patent. The limited-duration reverse engineering injunction was developed as a compromise between the following two extremes:

(1) The *Shellmar* permanent injunction, which puts the infringer in a worse position than the rest of the world, who have been legally informed of the secret and can use it. The justification for a permanent injunction is that the infringer committed a tort by improperly acquiring the information while it was secret and should suffer the consequences. *Shellmar Prods. Co. v. Allen-Qualley Co.*, 87 F.2d 104 (7th Cir. 1936).

(2) The *Conmar* rule denying any injunction that would last beyond the trade secret owner's public disclosure. The justification is that since the information is no longer secret, there is no "property" to be protected, even though it was "property" when the defendant illegally acquired it. *Conmar Prods. Corp. v. Universal Slide Fastener Co.*, 172 F.2d 150, 80 USPQ 108 (2d Cir. 1949).

Injunction Limited to the Reverse Engineering Period. The reverse engineering injunction, a compromise of the two extremes, grants an injunction, but limits the duration to the time it would take a hypothetical legitimate competitor to reverse engineer the public disclosure and work backward to obtain the trade secret information. In *Winston Research*, one of the earliest cases using this approach, the injunction was limited to two years. *Winston Research Corp. v. Minnesota Mining & Mfg. Co.*, 350 F.2d 134, 146 USPQ 422 (9th Cir. 1965). See *Surgidev Corp. v. ETI Inc.*, 828 F.2d 452, 4 USPQ2d 1090 (8th Cir. 1987) (15 months a reasonable approximation of how long a diligent person would require to develop the protected information); *Lamb-Weston Inc. v. McCain Foods Ltd.*, 941 F.2d 970, 19 USPQ2d 1775 (9th Cir. 1991) (court upheld an eight-month preliminary injunction that was granted about 10 months after plaintiff's patents were granted; plaintiff's patents granted a month after the defendant's appropriation did not disclose specifications, materials, and manufacturing processes, which remained trade secrets).

If the Secret Cannot Be Reverse Engineered. If the secret, such as the step-by-step process of manufacture, cannot be reverse engineered from the public disclosure, then the reverse engineering period is infinite and a permanent injunction is called for. If the finding of no possible reverse engineering is not accurate and in fact some years later someone does reverse engineer, then the enjoined party can move to set aside the injunction on the ground that secrecy has ended.

Uniform Trade Secrets Act. The Commissioners' Comment to the Uniform Trade Secrets Act in effect in several states explains that §2(a) of the model act was intended to adopt the limited-duration approach of the reverse engineering injunction: "Section 2(a) of this Act adopts the position of the trend of authority limiting the duration of injunctive relief to the extent of the temporal advantage over good faith competitors gained by a misappropriator." See *Surgidev Corp. v. ETI Inc.*, 828 F.2d 452, 4 USPQ2d 1090 (8th Cir. 1987) (injunction measured by independent development required by Uniform Act). However, the actual language of §2(a) is less than explicit in adopting this principle.

Synonyms: head-start injunction, lead-time injunction, independent development injunction.

• *Treatise References*: 3 R. Milgrim, *Trade Secrets* §15.02[1][d] (1994 rev.); M. Jager, *Trade Secrets Law* §7.02[3][b] (1994 rev.).

• *Commentary Reference*: Barclay, *Trade Secrets: How Long Should an Injunction Last?* 26 UCLA L. Rev. 203 (1978).

• *Restatement Reference*: "[I]njunctive relief should ordinarily continue only until the defendant could have acquired the information by proper means. Injunctions extending beyond this period are justified only when necessary to deprive the defendant of a head start or other unjust advantage that is attributable to the appropriation. See Uniform Trade Secrets Act §2(a). More extensive injunctive relief undermines the public interest by restraining legitimate competition." *Restatement (Third) of Unfair Competition* §44, comment f (1995).

• *Case References*:

"A permanent injunction would subvert the public's interest in allowing technical employees to make full use of their knowledge and skill and in fostering research and development. On the other hand, denial of any injunction at all would leave the faithless employee unpunished where, as here, no damages were awarded; and he and his new employer would retain the benefit of a headstart over legitimate competitors who did not have access to the trade secrets until they were publicly disclosed. By enjoining use of the trade secrets for the approximate period it would require a legitimate [plaintiff's] competitor to develop a successful machine after public disclosure of the secret information, the district court denied the employees any advantage from their faithlessness, placed [plaintiff] in the position it would have occupied if the breach of confidence had not occurred prior to the public disclosure, and imposed the minimum restraint consistent with the realization of these objectives upon the utilization of the employees' skills." *Winston Research Corp. v.*

380

Minnesota Mining & Mfg. Co., 350 F.2d 134, 142, 146 USPQ 422, 427–28 (9th Cir. 1965).

"By enjoining the use of wrongfully acquired trade secrets for the approximate length of time it would require a legitimate competitor to develop a competitive product following a lawful disclosure of the information, the wrongdoer is deprived of any advantage from his wrongdoing, the developer of the trade secret is placed in the same position it would have occupied if the breach of confidence had not occurred, and the minimum restraint consistent with the other objections would be placed upon competitors and the utilization of the competitors' and the employees' skills." *Brunswick Corp. v. Outboard Marine Corp.*, 79 Ill. 2d 475, 404 N.E.2d 205, 207, 207 USPQ 1039, 1041 (1980).

reverse passing off [trademark] Selling a manufacturer's goods after removing the manufacturer's trademark from the goods and either substituting the distributor's mark or leaving the goods unbranded.

There are two distinct forms of "reverse palming off" or "passing off," both of which are quite different from REVERSE CONFUSION.

(1) "Express reverse passing off" occurs when the defendant removes or obliterates the original trademark on a product without permission and rebrands the goods with the defendant's own mark. This has been held by some courts to be a false designation in violation of Lanham Act §43(a). The Court of Appeals for the Ninth Circuit held that the claim that the defendant producer had removed the plaintiff-actor's name from film credits and had substituted the name of another person was a claim of express reverse passing off and stated a valid claim for false designation under Lanham Act §43(a). *Smith v. Montoro*, 648 F.2d 602, 211 USPQ 775 (9th Cir. 1981).

(2) "Implied reverse passing off" occurs when the defendant, without permission, removes the original trademark on a product and sells the plaintiff's goods in an unbranded state. Some have argued that such conduct deprives the trademark owner of the "advertising value" of having its marks on the goods when they reach the ultimate consumer. Borchard, *Reverse*

Passing Off: Commercial Robbery or Permissible Competition? 67 Trademark Rep. 1, 3, 17 (1977). But implied reverse passing off involves no real "false" representation, and the theory that it should be illegal rests primarily on a pure "property right" concept of a trademark. Several courts have held that implied reverse passing off is not illegal.

- *Treatise Reference*: 3 J.T. McCarthy, *Trademarks and Unfair Competition* §25.01[4] (3d ed. 1995 rev.).

revival [patent–trademark] Bringing back to active status an abandoned application for a patent or for a registration of a mark.

1. Revival of Abandoned Patent Application. In certain circumstances, a patent application that has become ABANDONED for failure to PROSECUTE may be revived and restored as an active application. The regulations prescribe certain conditions and time limits for revival of patent applications abandoned for failure to prosecute if the delay in responding was either unavoidable or was unintentional. 37 C.F.R. §1.137. The decision to revive is made by the Commissioner of Patents and Trademarks.

2. Revival of Abandoned Application to Register Mark. In certain circumstances, a trademark application that has become ABANDONED for failure to PROSECUTE may be revived and restored as an active application. The regulations permit the filing of a petition to revive on the ground that the delay to respond was unavoidable. A petition is made to the Commissioner of Patents and Trademarks. 37 C.F.R. §2.66.

right of publicity [general intellectual property] The inherent right of every human being to control the commercial use of his or her identity.

Tort and Property. Infringement of the right of publicity is a commercial TORT and a form of UNFAIR COMPETITION. *Factors Etc Inc. v. Creative Card Co.*, 444 F. Supp. 279, 283 (S.D.N.Y. 1977). The right of publicity is property and is properly categorized as a form of INTELLECTUAL PROPERTY. E.g., *Acme Circus Operating*

Co. v. Kuperstock, 711 F.2d 1538, 1541 (11th Cir. 1983) (right of publicity is "an intangible personal property right").

Evolution of the Right of Publicity. The concept of a property right in one's identity evolved from several sources, including the tort of invasion of privacy, as well as the law of COPYRIGHTS and TRADEMARKS. The concept and terminology "right of publicity" was first used by Judge Jerome Frank in *Haelan Labs., Inc. v. Topps Chewing Gum, Inc.*, 202 F.2d 866 (2d Cir. 1953). In a seminal law review article, Melville Nimmer filled in the outlines of the right. Nimmer, *The Right of Publicity*, 19 Law & Contemporary Prob. 203 (1954). As the right of publicity matured and grew, it became recognized as a right independent of privacy rights and distinct from, although related to, other types of intellectual property such as trademarks and copyrights. While an invasion of privacy rights triggers damages measured by "mental distress" and some injury to human dignity and the psyche, infringement of the right of publicity relates to commercial damage to the pocketbook, not the psyche.

Sources of Right of Publicity Law. Right of publicity law is state law. As of 1994, the right of publicity has been recognized in 25 states (by common law case decision in 11 states and by statute in 14 states). Statutes are found in California, Florida, Indiana, Kentucky, Massachusetts, Nebraska, Nevada, New York, Oklahoma, Rhode Island, Tennessee, Texas, Virginia, and Wisconsin. See J.T. McCarthy, *The Rights of Publicity and Privacy* §6.1[B] (1995 rev.).

Who and What Is Protected. The identity or PERSONA of everyone, both celebrities and noncelebrities, is protected against unauthorized use by the right of publicity. But the right of publicity does not protect the "persona" of a corporation, partnership, or an institute—only of a real person. *Eagle's Eye, Inc. v. Ambler Fashion Shop, Inc.*, 227 USPQ 1018, 1022 (E.D. Pa. 1985). Infringement of the right of publicity can be triggered by any unauthorized use in which the plaintiff is "identifiable." Identifiability can be by name, nickname, stage name, pen name, picture, photograph, or any object closely identified with a person. The use of celebrity look-alikes in advertising has been

held to meet the identifiable criterion and constitute an infringement. *Onassis v. Christian-Dior New York, Inc.*, 122 Misc. 2d 603, 472 N.Y.S.2d 254 (1984), *aff'd without opinion*, 110 A.D.2d 1095, 488 N.Y.S.2d 843 (1985) (use of Jacqueline Kennedy Onassis look-alike in advertisement for Christian Dior clothing); *White v. Samsung Elec. Am., Inc.*, 971 F.2d 1395, 23 USPQ2d 1583 (9th Cir. 1992), *reh'g en banc denied*, 989 F.2d 1512, 26 USPQ2d 1362 (9th Cir. 1993) (use of robotic caricature of television personality Vanna White in an ad for Samsung electronic products could be an infringement). Also, a person can be identifiable by a distinctive voice, as by a sound-alike in a television ad. *Midler v. Ford Motor Co.*, 849 F.2d 460, 7 USPQ2d 1398 (9th Cir. 1988) (use of Bette Midler sound-alike in ad for Ford automobiles could be an infringement); *Waits v. Frito-Lay, Inc.*, 978 F.2d 1093, 23 USPQ2d 1721 (9th Cir. 1992) (use of Tom Waits sound-alike in ad for Doritos chips held an infringement).

Infringement of the Right of Publicity. An unpermitted commercial use in which the plaintiff is identifiable triggers a prima facie case of infringement of the right of publicity. There are two different types of infringement:

(1) *Infringement of Identity Values in Persona.* The more familiar type of infringement, this is the unpermitted use of human identity to help sell a product. There is no need for any explicit or implicit message of endorsement, although an implied endorsement is not uncommon. No element of misrepresentation or falsity is needed to find an infringement of the right of publicity. *Rogers v. Grimaldi*, 875 F.2d 994, 1004, 10 USPQ2d 1825, 1832 (2d Cir. 1989) (right of publicity has no likelihood of confusion requirement).

(2) *Infringement of Performance Values in Persona.* This type of infringement is triggered by the unpermitted appropriation or imitation of an entertainer's performance or performance style. The most famous example is the 1977 case involving the unauthorized television news coverage of the act of Hugo Zacchini—the human cannonball. The Supreme Court upheld a finding that such a use of Zacchini's performance was an infringement of the Ohio

382

right of publicity law over a First Amendment news coverage defense. *Zacchini v. Scripps-Howard Broadcasting Co.*, 433 U.S. 564, 205 USPQ 741 (1977). Imitation can also trigger infringement of right of publicity performance values, as by an on-stage and filmed performance of Beatles imitators singing 29 Lennon-McCartney songs. *Apple Corps Ltd. v. Leber*, 229 USPQ 1015 (Cal. Super. Ct. 1986) ($7.5 million award). Entertainment impersonations of famous people are generally immune from liability under the First Amendment. See J.T. McCarthy, *The Rights of Publicity and Privacy* §8.15[B] (1995 rev.).

First Amendment Defense. The right of publicity cannot be used to prevent the use of someone's name or picture in the traditional media of communication, such as news reporting, unauthorized biography, or entertainment parody or satire. "The use of a person's identity in news reporting, commentary, entertainment, or works of fiction or nonfiction is not ordinarily an infringement of the right of publicity." *Restatement (Third) of Unfair Competition* §47, comment a (1995). There is no infringement of privacy or publicity rights to use one's photograph to truthfully illustrate the content of a newsworthy article in a magazine or newspaper. E.g., *Finger v. Omni Publications Int'l Ltd.*, 77 N.Y.2d 138, 564 N.Y.S.2d 1014 (1990) (no liability so long as there is a "real relationship" between picture and subject of article in magazine). But the use of a photograph of a person to draw attention to an advertisement is an infringement of the right of publicity. *Negri v. Schering Corp.*, 333 F. Supp. 101 (S.D.N.Y. 1971).

Commercial Speech. The difference between an infringing commercial use and an immune communicative use is often drawn on the ground that the latter constitutes "commercial speech" under the First Amendment. The Supreme Court may put a mix of advertising, news, social comment, and entertainment into the category of "commercial speech," which is subject to the lowest level of constitutional protection and immunity from liability. *Bolger v. Youngs Drug Prods. Corp.*, 463 U.S. 60, 67–68 (1983). Simply tacking a social message onto an advertisement does not turn commercial

speech into fully protected political or social speech. *Board of Trustees of the State Univ. of N.Y. v. Fox*, 492 U.S. 469 (1989). It will sometimes be difficult to categorize a given use as being a newsworthy communication immune from liability or a commercial exploitation that triggers liability. *Titan Sports Inc. v. Comics World Corp.*, 870 F.2d 85, 10 USPQ2d 1311 (2d Cir. 1989) (issue of fact whether fold-out poster in magazine is immunized from right of publicity infringement as being newsworthy communication).

Post-Mortem Right of Publicity. As of 1994, an after-death duration for the right of publicity has been recognized in 13 states: by statute in California, Florida, Indiana, Kentucky, Nebraska, Nevada, Oklahoma, Tennessee, Texas, and Virginia, and by common law case decision in Georgia, New Jersey, and Utah. Only one controlling decision still outstanding and not overruled by statute has rejected the concept of a post-mortem right. *Reeves v. United Artists*, 572 F. Supp 1231 (N.D. Ohio 1983), aff'd, 765 F.2d 79 (6th Cir. 1985). The most common post-mortem duration is 50 years, using the term of copyright as a model. However, Indiana and Oklahoma have a 100-year statute and Tennessee a statute that creates rights that last for at least 10 years and for as long thereafter as the right continues to be commercially exploited. There is no post-mortem duration of the right of publicity under the New York statute. See J.T. McCarthy, *The Rights of Publicity and Privacy* §9.5[A] (1995 rev.).

See DURATION.

Assignment and Licensing of the Right of Publicity. The right of publicity can be assigned and licensed. Unlike the licensing of a trademark, no quality control must be exercised by the licensor in a pure right of publicity license. J.T. McCarthy, *The Rights of Publicity and Privacy* §10.4[B] (1995 rev.). Right of publicity licenses are often limited in terms of duration, product line, and context of use. The erroneous belief that by becoming famous, one "waives" or "impliedly licenses" the use of one's identity for commercial purposes reveals a confusion of the right of publicity with the right of privacy. *Price v. Hal Roach Studios, Inc.*, 400 F. Supp. 836, 946 (S.D.N.Y. 1975) (by becoming public figures, entertainers Laurel and Hardy did not impliedly "waive" right to prevent unauthorized commercial exploitation). Some states have held that the right of publicity is marital property, the value of which must be accounted for in a divorce or dissolution of marriage. E.g., *Piscopo v. Piscopo*, 231 N.J. Super. 576, 557 A.2d 1040 (1988), *aff'd*, 232 N.J. Super. 559, 557 A.2d 1040 (App. Div. 1989).

See PERSONA.

• *Treatise Reference*: J.T. McCarthy, *The Rights of Publicity and Privacy* (1995 rev.).

• *Restatement Reference*: "The interest of a seller in attracting attention to a commercial solicitation is not sufficient to overcome the personal and economic interests protected by the right of publicity. Proof that prospective purchasers are likely to believe that the identified person endorses or sponsors the user's goods or services is not required for the imposition of liability.... The use of a person's identity in news reporting, commentary, entertainment, or works of fiction or nonfiction is not ordinarily an infringement of the right of publicity." *Restatement (Third) of Unfair Competition* §47, comment a (1995).

ROM [computer–copyright] An acronym for "read only memory," which is a SEMICONDUCTOR CHIP used to store data or computer programs. The information can be read out but is fixed and cannot be changed.

Chip Protection Act. The physical structure of a ROM chip may be protected under the Semiconductor Chip Protection Act (SCPA).

Copyright Protection. A computer program stored in a ROM is the subject of copyright protection, and copying copyrighted data directly from a ROM can be copyright infringement. See *Apple Computer, Inc. v. Franklin Computer Corp.*, 714 F.2d 1240, 1249, 219 USPQ 113, 121 (3d Cir. 1983) ("[W]e reaffirm that a computer program in object code embedded in a ROM chip is an appropriate subject of copyright"); *Stern Elecs., Inc. v. Kaufman*, 669 F.2d 852, 856, 213 USPQ 443, 445 (2d Cir. 1982) ("The audiovisual work [video game] is permanently embodied in a material object, the memory devices [PROMs], from which it can

be perceived with the aid of other components of the game.").

• *Case Reference*: "[T]he units designated 'ROM' and 'RAM' are, respectively, a read only memory and a random access memory, terms well understood by those skilled in the art." *In re Iwahashi*, 888 F.2d 1370, 1372, 12 USPQ2d 1908, 1909 (Fed. Cir. 1989).

Rome Convention [copyright–international] The "International Convention for the Protection of Performers, Producers of Phonograms and Broadcasting Organizations" is a multilateral treaty under which member states agree to protect performers from unauthorized broadcasting of a performance, to protect producers from unauthorized duplication of their PHONOGRAMS, and to protect broadcasting organizations from various types of unauthorized uses of their broadcasts. In some nations, these various rights are collectively known as NEIGHBORING RIGHTS (droits voisins). Created at Rome in 1961, the Convention has over 30 member nations. One reason that the United States is not a member is because the Convention provides for performance rights in SOUND RECORDING copyrights, a right not granted by U.S. copyright law. The United States is one of the few nations that protects a SOUND RECORDING under copyright law. Most nations do so under the neighboring rights system, as covered by the Rome Convention. See W. Patry, *Copyright Law and Practice* 1314 (1994). The Convention is jointly administered by WIPO and the International Labor Organization.

See SOUND RECORDING, PHONOGRAM CONVENTION, NEIGHBORING RIGHTS.

• *Treatise References*: WIPO, *Background Reading Material on Intellectual Property* 236 (1988). See text of the Convention in W. Patry, *Copyright Law and Practice* 2099 (1994); M. Leaffer, *International Treaties on Intellectual Property* 415 (1990).

royalty, reasonable [patent–trademark–copyright] A hypothetical royalty fee used as a measure of damages to compensate for the infringement of intellectual property.

1. Reasonable Royalty as a Measure of Damages for Patent Infringement. The Patent Code directs that a reasonable royalty is the minimum amount of recovery for compensatory damages for patent infringement. A reasonable royalty is the amount that a person desiring a license to make, use, or sell a patented item would be willing to pay as a royalty and still make a reasonable profit. *Trans-World Mfg. Corp. v. Al Nyman & Sons, Inc.,* 750 F.2d 1552, 1568, 224 USPQ 259, 269 (Fed. Cir. 1984). It is a purely hypothetical royalty resulting from negotiations between a willing licensor and a willing licensee, keeping in mind that this is not and was not in fact the situation of the litigants in the case.

Established Royalty. One logical measure of a hypothetical reasonable royalty is an actual, established royalty. *Nickerson Indus. Inc. v. Rol Mfg. Co.,* 847 F.2d 795, 798, 6 USPQ2d 1878, 1879 (Fed. Cir. 1988) ("Where an established royalty exists, it will usually be the best measure of what is a 'reasonable' royalty."). However, the license upon which the established royalty is based must be reasonably comparable to the hypothetical royalty that is to be established. Thus, "the defendant's infringing acts [must be] commensurate with those acts contemplated under the license for which the fee has been established." *Bandag, Inc. v. Gerrard Tire Co.,* 704 F.2d 1578, 1582, 217 USPQ 977, 980 (Fed. Cir. 1983) (established royalty was based on trademarks and other rights in addition to a patent license, whereas patent alone should be the basis for a reasonable royalty). "A single licensing agreement, without more, is insufficient proof of an established royalty ... [F]or a royalty to be established, it 'must be paid by such a number of persons as to indicate a general acquiescence in its reasonableness by those who have occasion to use the invention.' " *Trell v. Marlee Elecs. Corp.,* 912 F.2d 1443, 1446, 16 USPQ2d 1059, 1061 (Fed. Cir. 1990).

Entire Market Value Rule. Under the ENTIRE MARKET VALUE RULE, the royalty may be based on the sale of an entire apparatus containing both patented and unpatented features. "The entire market value rule allows a patentee to recover damages based on the value of an entire apparatus containing several features, when the feature patented constitutes the basis for customer demand." *Slimfold Mfg. Co. v. Kinkead Indus. Inc.,* 932 F.2d 1453, 1459 n.2, 18 USPQ2d 1842, 1847 n.3 (Fed. Cir. 1991) (Rich, J.). But when recovery is sought on sales of unpatented components sold with patented components, the unpatented components must function together with the patented component in some matter so as to produce a desired end product or result. *Rite-Hite Corp. v. Kelley Co. Inc.,* 56 F.3d 1538, 1550, 35 USPQ2d 1065, 1073 (Fed. Cir. 1995) (en banc) ("All the components together must be analogous to components of a single assembly or be parts of a complete machine, or they must constitute a functional unit.")

• *Statutory Reference*: 35 U.S.C. §284: "Upon finding for the claimant the court shall award the claimant damages adequate to compensate for the infringement but in no event less than a reasonable royalty for the use made of the invention by the infringer, together with interest and costs as fixed by the court...."

• *Treatise Reference*: 5 D. Chisum, *Patents* §20.03[3] (1994 rev.); R. Harmon, *Patents and the Federal Circuit* §12.1(c) (3d ed. 1994).

• *Case References*:

"An imaginary bid by an imaginary buyer, acting upon information available at the moment of the breach, is not the limit of recovery where the subject of the bargain is an undeveloped patent. Information at such time might be so scanty and imperfect that the offer would be nominal. The promisee of the patent has less than fair compensation if the criterion of value is the price that he would have received if he had disposed of it at once, irrespective of the value that would have uncovered if he had kept it as his own." *Sinclair Ref. Co. v. Jenkins Petroleum Co.,* 289 U.S. 689, 699, 17 USPQ 522, 526 (1933).

"Determining a fair and reasonable royalty is often ... a difficult judicial chore, seeming often to involve more the talents of a conjurer than those of a judge. Lacking adequate evidence of an established royalty, the court was left with the judge-created methodology described as 'hypothetical negotiations between willing licensor and willing licensee.' ... Forced to erect a hypothetical, it is easy to forget a basic reality—a license is fundamentally an agreement by the patent owner not to sue the licensee. In a normal negotiation, the potential licensee has three basic choices: forego all use of the invention; pay an agreed royalty; infringe the patent and risk litigation. The methodology presumes that the licensee has made the second choice, when in fact it made the third." *Fromson v. Western Litho Plate Co.*, 853 F.2d 1568, 1574–76, 7 USPQ2d 1606, 1612–14 (Fed. Cir. 1988).

" 'The key element in setting a reasonable royalty is the necessity for return to the date when the infringement began.' ... In this case, infringing products were being sold on the date of issuance of the '605 patent. Therefore, under *Fromson*, hypothetical royalty negotiations should have been considered to have occurred on the patent issuance date." *Wang Labs., Inc. v. Toshiba Corp.*, 993 F.2d 858, 870, 26 USPQ2d 1767, 1778 (Fed. Cir. 1993).

2. Reasonable Royalty as a Measure of Damages for Trademark Infringement. In a few cases, courts have awarded a reasonable royalty as a measure of damages to the trademark owner. *Boston Professional Hockey Ass'n v. Dallas Cap & Emblem Mfg. Inc.*, 597 F.2d 71, 202 USPQ 536 (5th Cir. 1979) (award of $20,000 measured by an amount that defendant offered to pay); *Sands, Taylor & Wood v. The Quaker Oats Co.*, 34 F.3d 1340, 32 USPQ2d 1065 (7th Cir. 1994), *reh'g denied, opinion slightly modified*, 44 F.3d 579, 33 USPQ2d 1543 (7th Cir. 1995) (affirming baseline award of $10.5 million as reasonable royalty on infringing sales).

Inadequate Compensation. In some cases, the problem with an award of a reasonable royalty is that the infringer is no worse off than if it had been licensed to use the mark, which it was not. The Court of Appeals for the Ninth Circuit has criticized and reversed a modest reasonable royalty award against a counterfeiter as doing little to take the economic incentive out of trademark infringement. *Playboy Enters. Inc. v. Baccarat Clothing Co.*, 692 F.2d 1272, 216 USPQ 1083 (9th Cir. 1982).

• *Treatise Reference*: 4 J.T. McCarthy, *Trademarks and Unfair Competition* §30.27[4] (3d ed. 1995 rev.).

• *Case Reference*: "[T]wo aspects of an award of a reasonable royalty make it difficult to ensure that the [Lanham] Act's policy of deterrence has been adequately addressed. First, because the award seeks to mirror the bargain at which the parties would have arrived had negotiations taken place, it becomes for the malefactor simply the cost of doing business. ... Second, as this case makes very clear, the valuation of a royalty payment is very difficult.... The court must review the probable happenings at a hypothetical bargaining table between parties that might well have never chosen to bargain with each other on a voluntary basis.... [A] court must take special care to ensure that the royalty payment has not undercompensated the victim. Enhancement of the damages ... is a permissible way of achieving that goal." *Sands, Taylor & Wood v. The Quaker Oats Co.*, 34 F.3d 1340, 1351, 32 USPQ2d 1065, 1073–74 (7th Cir. 1994), *reh'g denied, opinion slightly modified*, 44 F.3d 579, 33 USPQ2d 1543 (7th Cir. 1995).

3. Reasonable Royalty as a Measure of Damages for Copyright Infringement. Some courts have upheld an award of actual damages to a copyright owner based upon the loss of licensing royalties. E.g., *Cream Records Inc. v. Jos. Schlitz Brewing Co.*, 754 F.2d 826, 225 USPQ 896 (9th Cir. 1985) (where unauthorized use of a song in a commercial destroyed its licensing value for commercials, it is proper to award its licensing value as damages). The "value of use" measure of damages is somewhat akin to a reasonable royalty in that it awards as actual damages the fair market value of the infringer's use. *Deltak Inc. v. Advanced Sys., Inc.*, 767 F.2d 357, 362 n.3, 226 USPQ 919, 922 n.3 (7th Cir. 1985). In approving a jury instruction permitting an award of damages based on the reasonable value to the infringer of the copyrighted work, the Court of Appeals for the Ninth Circuit noted: "An author might license the use of his copyright either for a lump sum based on the reasonable value of the work or for a royalty derived from the licensee's profits, or for a combination of both." *Sid & Marty Krofft Television Prods. Inc. v. McDonald's Corp.*, 562 F.2d 1157, 1174, 196 USPQ 97, 111 (9th Cir. 1977).

For copies publicly distributed without copyright NOTICE from January 1, 1978, to March 1, 1989, in a suit against an innocent infringer misled by the absence of notice, 17 U.S.C. §405(b) authorizes a court to order, among other options, that "the infringer pay the copyright owner a reasonable license fee in an amount and on terms fixed by the court."

See COMPULSORY LICENSE.

Treatise References: 3 *Nimmer on Copyright* §14.02[A] (1994 rev.); 2 P. Goldstein, *Copyright* §12.1.1 b. (1989); 1 N. Boorstyn, *Copyright* §13.02 (2d ed. 1994).

• *Case Reference*: "[The copyright owner] is entitled to the lost fair market value of the architectural plans.... In calculating this figure, the court is to determine 'what a willing buyer would have been reasonably required to pay a willing seller' for plaintiff's work." *Eales v. Environmental Lifestyles Inc.*, 958 F.2d 876, 880, 22 USPQ2d 1059, 1062 (9th Cir. 1992).

RRO [copyright]

See REPRODUCTION RIGHTS ORGANIZATION.

rule of doubt [copyright]

See DOUBT, RULE OF.

rule of reason [patent–antitrust]

1. Patent Priority Rule of Reason. The rule of reason permits a flexible weighing of all evidence in CORROBORATION of an inventor's testimony as to the date when the invention was made. In proving the date an invention was made in a priority contest (INTERFERENCE PROCEEDING), the testimony of an inventor, without more, is not sufficient evidence of the date of invention by CONCEPTION and REDUCTION TO PRACTICE. Some additional evidence in corroboration of the inventor's testimony is needed. The requirement of corroboration is somewhat eased by the rule of reason, under which all pertinent corroborating evidence is weighed and balanced to determine the credi-

bility of the inventor's testimony of the date of invention. *Price v. Symsek*, 988 F.2d 1187, 1194, 26 USPQ2d 1031, 1037 (Fed. Cir. 1993) ("A 'rule of reason' analysis is applied to determine whether the inventor's prior conception testimony has been corroborated.").

For example, under the rule of reason, the dated signature, on a notebook page, of a witness sufficiently familiar with the particular field of technology to understand what is described on that page is evidence in corroboration of the inventor's testimony of the date of invention. *Grasseli v. Dewing*, 534 F.2d 306, 311, 189 USPQ 637, 641 (C.C.P.A. 1976).

See CORROBORATION, CONCEPTION, REDUCTION TO PRACTICE, INVENTIVE PROCESS.

• *Case References*:

"A corroboration analysis involves a reasoned examination and evaluation of all the pertinent evidence bearing on the credibility of the inventor.... In recent years, this court, by adopting a 'rule of reason,' has eased the requirement of corroboration with respect to the evidence necessary to establish the credibility of the inventor.... However, adoption of the 'rule of reason' has not altered the requirement that evidence of corroboration must not depend solely on the inventor himself.... Independent corroboration may consist of testimony of a witness, other than the inventor, to the actual reduction to practice or it may consist of evidence of surrounding facts and circumstances independent of information received from the inventor." *Reese v. Hurst, 661 F.2d 1222, 1225, 211 USPQ 936, 940 (C.C.P.A. 1981).*

"The objective sought in requiring independent corroboration of reduction to practice of a chemical composition invention is to insure that the inventor actually prepared the composition and knew it would work.... The standard is not inflexible and is not to be applied mechanically. Hence a 'rule of reason' approach is required.... Testimony of one who witnessed and understood the actual reduction to practice of a composition is strong evidence. Its absence need not be fatal, however, when other evidence is sufficient to corroborate such actual reduction to practice...." *Minkus & Shaffer v.*

Wachtel, 542 F.2d 1157, 1159, 191 USPQ 571, 573–75 (C.C.P.A. 1976).

• *Treatise Reference*: 3 D. Chisum, *Patents* §10.03 (1994 rev.); 2 P. Rosenberg, *Patent Law Fundamentals* §10.02[2] (1994 rev.).

2. Antitrust Rule of Reason. When a given contract, combination, or conspiracy in restraint of trade does not fall within a PER SE ILLEGAL category, it is illegal under Sherman Act §1 only if it is unreasonable under the rule of reason.

See PER SE ILLEGAL.

• *Case References*:

"Since the early years of this century a judicial gloss on this statutory language [of Sherman Act §1] has established the 'rule of reason' as the prevailing standard of analysis.... Under this rule, the factfinder weighs all of the circumstances of a case in deciding whether a restrictive practice should be prohibited as imposing an unreasonable restraint on competition." *Continental T.V. Inc. v. GTE Sylvania, Inc.*, 433 U.S. 36, 49 (1977).

"Contrary to its name, the Rule [of Reason] does not open the field of antitrust inquiry to any argument in favor of a challenged restraint that may fall within the realm of reason. Instead, it focuses on the challenged restraint's impact on competitive conditions.... [T]he Court has adhered to the position that the inquiry mandated by the Rule of Reason is whether the challenged agreement is one that promotes competition or one that suppresses competition." *National Soc'y of Professional Eng'rs v. United States*, 435 U.S. 679, 688, 691 (1978).

"Section 1 of the Sherman Act of 1890 literally prohibits *every* agreement 'in restraint of trade.' ... [W]e [have] recognized that Congress could not have intended a literal interpretation of the word 'every'; since ... [1911] we have analyzed most restraints under the so-called 'rule of reason.' As its name suggests, the rule of reason requires the factfinder to decide whether under all the circumstances of the case the restrictive practice imposes an unreasonable restraint on competition. The elaborate inquiry into the reasonableness of a challenged business practice entails significant costs. Litigation of the effect or purpose of a practice often is ex-

tensive and complex." *Arizona v. Maricopa County Medical Soc'y*, 457 U.S. 332, 342–43 (1982).

3. Patent-Antitrust Rule of Reason. This is a flexible test for determining if a patent owner's conduct in imposing conditions in licenses of the patent is in violation of the antitrust laws. The test is a vague one, merely stating that all license restrictions are legal under antitrust law if they are normally and reasonably adapted to the policy of the patent laws of permitting the inventor to realize income from market demand for the technology covered by the patent. Some commentators have referred to the U.S. Supreme Court's 1926 *General Electric* decision as creating a patent rule of reason.

• *Case Reference*: "Conveying less than title to the patent, or part of it, the patentee may grant a license to make, use and vend articles under the specifications of his patent for any royalty, or upon any condition the performance of which is reasonably within the reward which the patentee by the grant of the patent is entitled to secure." *United States v. General Elec. Co.*, 272 U.S. 476, 489 (1926).

• *Text References*:

"The classic yardstick for measuring the remuneration to which the patentee is entitled was announced in *United States v. General Electric*. The Court there formulated, as the test of determining whether or not the patentee's conduct is within the ambit of his grant, the standard that he may license 'for any royalty, or upon any condition the performance of which is reasonably within the reward which the patentee by the grant of the patent is entitled to secure.' This makes permissible all restrictions 'normally and reasonably adapted' to the patent policy of securing to the inventor rewards ancillary to his patent grant.... '[N]ormally and reasonably' within the reward encompasses the rights of exclusion only as defined by the claims of the patent. This limiting policy aims to prevent monopolistic extension beyond the discovery and resulting discouragement of invention." *Report of the Attorney General's Antitrust Committee* 231 (1955).

"The 'patent rule of reason' may be no more than a facet of another aspect of the more general rule of reason—the ancillary restraint doctrine. This way of phrasing the issue asks whether the restraint in question is reasonably necessary to carry out some main legitimate purpose. E.g., is the restraint reasonably 'ancillary' to a pro-innovation and pro-competitive goal of the license and does that restraint go no further than necessary to accomplish that goal?" S. Oppenheim, G. Weston, & J.T. McCarthy, *Federal Antitrust Laws* 880 (4th ed. 1984).

"In the vast majority of cases, restraints in intellectual property licensing arrangements are evaluated under the rule of reason. The Agencies' [Department of Justice and Federal Trade Commission] general approach in analyzing a licensing restraint under the rule of reason is to inquire whether the restraint is likely to have anticompetitive effects and, if so, whether the restraint is reasonably necessary to achieve pro-competitive benefits that outweigh those anticompetitive effects.... To determine whether a particular restraint in a licensing arrangement is given per se or rule of reason treatment, the Agencies will assess whether the restraint in question can be expected to contribute to an efficiency-enhancing integration of economic activity...." Department of Justice and Federal Trade Commission, *Antitrust Guidelines for Licensing of Intellectual Property* §3.4 (1995) (reprinted in 49 Pat. Trademark & Copyright J. (BNA) 714 (Apr. 13, 1995)).

S

satellite broadcasting [copyright]

See COMPULSORY LICENSING OF A COPYRIGHT, BRUSSELS SATELLITE CONVENTION.

scarecrow patent [patent] A potentially invalid or overbroad patent used by a patentee to threaten competitors with infringement suits in order to chill competition.

Declaratory Judgment Act. Before the passage of the Declaratory Judgment Act, 28 U.S.C. §2201, unless a patentee brought a suit for infringement, questions of validity of the patent or infringement by competitors could not be adjudicated. The Declaratory Judgment Act permits competitors to eliminate "scarecrow patents" without waiting to be sued. *Societe de Conditionnement en Aluminium v. Hunter Eng'g Co.*, 655 F.2d 938, 943, 210 USPQ 344, 348 (9th Cir. 1981). If an alleged infringer has a reasonable apprehension that the patentee will initiate a suit against him, a justiciable controversy exists and a suit for declaratory judgment for noninfringement and invalidity of the patent may be brought. See *Arrowhead Indus. Water, Inc. v. Ecolochem, Inc.*, 846 F.2d 731, 6 USPQ2d 1685 (Fed. Cir. 1988).

• *Case Reference:* The Declaratory Judgment Act was enacted to prevent a scenario where "a patent owner engages in a danse macabre, brandishing a Damoclean threat with a sheathed sword.... Guerrilla-like, the patent owner attempts extra-judicial patent enforcement with scare-the-customer-and-run tactics that infect the competitive environment of the business community with uncertainty and insecurity. ... The Act serves the policies underlying the patent laws by enabling a test of the validity and infringement of patents that are possibly being used only as what Learned Hand ... called 'scarecrows.' " *Arrowhead Indus. Water, Inc. v.*

Ecolochem, Inc., 846 F.2d 731, 734 & n.4, 6 USPQ2d 1685, 1688 & n.4 (Fed. Cir. 1988).

scènes à faire [copyright] Stock incidents, characters, or settings that are standard in writing about a certain topic or in expressing a certain concept. Such matter is not protected by copyright law (1) because it is not original; (2) by extension of the rule that "ideas" and "facts" are not copyrightable; or (3) by the view that the mere indispensable expression of an idea is either unprotectable or protectable only against virtually identical copying. The copyright law prohibits copyright for "any idea," as distinct from its expression. 17 U.S.C. §102(b). See Kurtz, *Copyright: The Scènes À Faire Doctrine*, 41 Fla. L. Rev. 79 (1989).

See IDEA-EXPRESSION DICHOTOMY, COPYRIGHT.

• *Case References:*

"Under that doctrine [of scènes à faire], a second author does not infringe even if he reproduces verbatim the first author's expression, if that expression constitutes 'stock scenes or scenes that flow necessarily from common unprotectable ideas.' " *Landsberg v. Scrabble Crossword Game Players, Inc.*, 736 F.2d 485, 489, 221 USPQ 1140, 1143 (9th Cir. 1984).

"Scènes à faire refers to 'incidents, characters or settings which are as a practical matter indispensable, or at least standard, in the treatment of a given topic'.... Such stock literary devices are not protectable by copyright." *Atari v. North Am. Philips Consumer Elecs.*, 672 F.2d 607, 616, 214 USPQ 33, 41 (7th Cir. 1982) ("standard game devices" in the PAC-MAN video game, such as the maze, scoring table, and tunnel exits, are unprotectible scènes à faire).

"Because it is virtually impossible to write about a particular historical era or fictional theme without employing certain 'stock' or standard literary devices, we have held that scènes à faire are not copyrightable as a matter of law." *Hoehling v. Universal City Studios, Inc.*, 618 F.2d 972, 979, 205 USPQ 681, 687 (2d Cir. 1980).

"Scènes à faire are afforded no protection because the subject matter represented can be expressed in no other way than through the particular scène à faire. Therefore, granting a copyright 'would give the first author a monopoly on the commonplace ideas behind the scènes à faire.' " *Whelan Assocs. Inc. v. Jaslow Dental Lab.*, 797 F.2d 1222, 1236, 230 USPQ 481, 491 (3d Cir. 1986).

After discussing the scènes à faire doctrine and the *Hoehling* case in Example 1 below, the court applied the doctrine to a computer program. "Professor Nimmer points out that 'in many instances it is virtually impossible to write a [computer] program to perform particular functions in a specific computing environment without employing standard techniques.' 3 Nimmer §13.03[F][3], at 13-65. This is a result of the fact that a programmer's freedom of design choice is often circumscribed by extrinsic considerations such as (1) the mechanical specifications of the computer on which a particular program is intended to run; (2) compatibility requirements of other programs with which a program is designated to operate in conjunction; (3) computer manufacturers' design standards; (4) demands of the industry being serviced; and (5) widely accepted programming practices within the computer industry. *Id.* at 13-66–71." *Computer Assocs. Int'l Inc. v. Altai Inc.*, 982 F.2d 693, 709, 23 USPQ2d 1241, 1255 (2d Cir. 1992).

- *Example 1*: Two novels about the 1937 crash of the German dirigible Hindenburg contained a scene in a German beer hall, in which the airship's crew engages in preflight revelry. These are "scènes à faire," unprotectible by copyright. *Hoehling v. Universal City Studios, Inc.*, 618 F.2d 972, 205 USPQ 681 (2d Cir. 1980).

- *Example 2*: "Elements such as drunks, prostitutes, vermin and derelict cars would appear in any realistic work about the work of policemen in the South Bronx. These similarities therefore are unprotectable as 'scènes à faire,' that is, scenes that necessarily result from the choice of a setting or situation." *Walker v. Time Life Films, Inc.*, 784 F.2d 44, 50, 228 USPQ 505, 509 (2d Cir. 1986).

- *Example 3*: "In this case, for example, use of overlapping windows inheres in the idea of windows. A programmer has only two options for displaying more than one window at a time: either a tiled system, or an overlapping system. As demonstrated by Microsoft's scènes à faire video, overlapping windows have been the clear preference in graphic interfaces. Accordingly, protectable substantial similarity cannot be based on the mere use of overlapping windows, although, of course, Apple's particular expression may be protected." *Apple Computer Inc. v. Microsoft Corp.*, 35 F.3d 1435, 1444, 32 USPQ2d 1086, 1093 (9th Cir. 1994).

SCMS [copyright] Abbreviation for Serial Copy Management System.

See DIGITAL AUDIO RECORDING TECHNOLOGY.

SCPA [computers] The Semiconductor Chip Protection Act of 1984, 17 U.S.C. §901, created a new kind of sui generis exclusive right to certain aspects of the structural design of SEMICONDUCTORY CHIPS. A MASK WORK is the protected subject matter. A mask work can be registered under the SCPA with the U.S. Copyright Office. A notice of protection consists of an M in a circle, or the words "mask work," or an M flanked by two asterisks, i.e., *M*. The SCPA does not prohibit independent development of a mask work: an identical but original second mask work is not an infringement of the first. See *Brooktree Corp. v. Advanced Micro Devices Inc.*, 977 F.2d 1555, 24 USPQ2d 1401 (Fed. Cir. 1992).

See MASK WORK, CHIP.

- *Treatise Reference*: R. Stern, *Semiconductor Chip Protection* (1986).

secondary considerations [patent]

Objective evidence of the actual marketplace setting in which an invention was made. This evidence is relevant to deciding what is perhaps the most crucial issue of whether an invention is patentable: whether the invention passes the hurdle of NONOBVIOUSNESS.

Synonym: objective evidence.

Categories of Secondary Considerations. This evidence, which consists of data showing how those actually in the marketplace viewed and reacted to the invention, usually consists of the following kinds of information: COMMERCIAL SUCCESS or the lack of commercial success of products covered by the patent claims in question; a LONG FELT NEED that was met by the invention of the patent claims in question; UNEXPECTED RESULTS achieved by the invention; the FAILURE OF OTHERS to make the invention; and COPYING of the invention by others. There must be a connection or nexus between such evidence and the claimed invention. Commercial success of a product may be due to several factors other than the nonobviousness of the invention underlying the product.

Independent Development by Others. The only type of secondary consideration that is probative of the obviousness and hence nonpatentability of the invention is that of INDEPENDENT DEVELOPMENT by others. Almost simultaneous invention by others of the same solution to a technical problem supports a finding that the invention was obvious to those in the field.

Why "Secondary"? The kinds of factual evidence are labeled "secondary considerations" not because they are second in importance but because they consist of circumstantial evidence that is relevant to the OBVIOUSNESS test through inference from objective evidence of the way real people have treated the invention. This is contrasted with personal inferences drawn from viewing the technological PRIOR ART and coming to a conclusion as to whether this invention was an obvious one. Prior to centralization of all patent appeals in the Court of Appeals for the Federal Circuit, some courts said that the secondary considerations were mere tie breakers, to be given weight only if there was doubt on the issue of obviousness of the invention. But the Federal Circuit has strongly indicated that these so-called secondary considerations are not secondary in importance. Rather, they are an important part of every obviousness inquiry and must always be weighed before a final conclusion is reached. "Objective evidence such as commercial success, failure of others, long-felt need and unexpected results must be considered *before* a conclusion on obviousness is reached and is not merely 'icing on the cake,' as the district court stated at trial." *Hybritech Inc. v. Monoclonal Antibodies, Inc.*, 802 F.2d 1367, 1380, 231 USPQ 81, 90 (Fed. Cir. 1986).

Objective Evidence. In the late 1980s, the Court of Appeals for the Federal Circuit indicated a preference for the term "objective evidence" as a more descriptive synonym for "secondary considerations." The court dubbed these kinds of facts as "objective" evidence because these "events proved to have actually happened in the real world (hence the description 'objective')." *Panduit Corp. v. Dennison Mfg. Co.*, 810 F.2d 1561, 1569, 1 USPQ2d 1593, 1598 (Fed. Cir. 1987). For example, evidence that those in the field tried and failed to achieve a solution to the technical problem this inventor solved is strong objective evidence that the invention was not "obvious" to persons skilled in the art. "We can conceive of no better way to determine whether an invention would have been obvious to persons of ordinary skill in the art at the time than to see what such persons actually did or failed to do when they were confronted with the problem in the course of their work." *Timely Prods. Corp. v. Arron*, 523 F.2d 288, 294, 187 USPQ 257, 261 (2d Cir. 1975).

Why Important? Evidence of secondary considerations is important because of the constant danger of using HINDSIGHT in viewing the difficulty or OBVIOUSNESS of making an invention. This is especially true when technically untrained judges and jurors attempt to decide whether a complex invention was obvious or not obvious at some time in the past to persons who were skilled and trained in that field of technology. Objective evidence of how those in that technical field and those in the marketplace treated the invention at the time is highly probative and relevant to answer the obviousness question.

Absence of Objective Evidence. The absence of objective evidence of secondary considerations certainly does not preclude a finding of nonobviousness. Such evidence is not a requirement of the patentability of an invention. The absence of such evidence is merely a neutral factor. *Custom Accessories, Inc. v. Jeffrey-Allan Indus., Inc.*, 807 F.2d 955, 960, 1 USPQ2d 1196, 1199 (Fed. Cir. 1986).

Origin of the Term. The term "secondary considerations" originated in the U.S. Supreme Court's seminal 1966 decision in *Graham v. John Deere.* There, the Supreme Court laid down the basic set of guidelines, a three-part factual inquiry to be made in determining the OBVIOUSNESS of an invention under Patent Code §103. After listing three factual inquiries, the Supreme Court added: "Such secondary considerations as commercial success, long felt but unsolved needs, failure of others, etc., might be utilized to give light to the circumstance surrounding the origin of the subject matter sought to be patented. As indicia of obviousness or nonobviousness, these inquiries may have relevancy." *Graham v. John Deere Co.*, 383 U.S. 1, 17, 148 USPQ 459, 467 (1966).

The Fourth Graham Inquiry. The Court of Appeals for the Federal Circuit has said that (1) attention must always be paid to "secondary considerations" or "objective evidence"; (2) such evidence is just as important as the three-part factual inquiry of the *Graham* case; and (3) this kind of evidence should be considered as the fourth factual inquiry under the Supreme Court's three-part *Graham* test. *Vandenberg v. Dairy Equip. Co.*, 740 F.2d 1560, 1567, 224 USPQ 195, 199 (Fed. Cir. 1984).

See OBVIOUSNESS, COMMERCIAL SUCCESS, COPYING, INDEPENDENT DEVELOPMENT, FAILURE OF OTHERS, LONG FELT NEED, UNEXPECTED RESULTS.

• *Case References:*

In speaking of "secondary considerations," the Supreme Court observed: "These legal inferences or subtests do focus attention on economic and motivational rather than technical issues and are, therefore, more susceptible of judicial treatment than are the highly technical facts often present in patent litigation.... Such inquiries may lend a helping hand to the judiciary which, as Mr. Justice Frankfurter observed, is most ill-fitted to discharge the technological duties cast upon it by patent legislation.... They may also serve to 'guard against slipping into use of hindsight,' ... and to resist the temptation to read into the prior art the teachings of the invention in issue." *Graham v. John Deere Co.*, 383 U.S. 1, 35–36, 148 USPQ 459, 474 (1966).

"It is jurisprudentially inappropriate to disregard any relevant evidence on any issue in any case, patent cases included. Thus evidence arising out of the so-called 'secondary considerations' must always when present be considered en route to a determination of obviousness.... Indeed, evidence of secondary considerations may often be the most probative and cogent evidence in the record. It may often establish that an invention appearing to have been obvious in light of the prior art was not. It is to be considered as part of all the evidence, not just when the decisionmaker remains in doubt after reviewing the art.... A nexus is required between the merits of the claimed invention and the evidence [of secondary considerations] offered, if that evidence is to be given substantial weight en route to conclusion on the obviousness issue." *Stratoflex Inc. v. Aeroquip Corp.*, 713 F.2d 1530, 1539, 218 USPQ 871, 879 (Fed. Cir. 1983).

"The rationale for giving weight to the so-called 'secondary considerations' is that they provide objective evidence of how the patented device is viewed in the marketplace, by those directly interested in the product. See ... *Safety Car Heating & Lighting Co. v. General Electric Co.*, 155 F.2d 937, 939, 69 USPQ 401, 403 (2d Cir. 1946) (L. Hand, J.): 'Courts, made up of laymen as they must be, are likely either to underrate, or to overrate, the difficulties in making new and profitable discoveries in fields with which they cannot be familiar; and, so far as it is available, they had best appraise the originality involved by the circumstances which preceded, attended and succeeded the appearance of the invention.' " *Demaco Corp. v. F. von Langsdorff Licensing Ltd.*, 851 F.2d 1387,

1391–92, 7 USPQ2d 1222, 1225 (Fed. Cir. 1988).

• *Treatise References*: "Lawsuits arise out of the affairs of people, real people facing real problems, and nowhere is this more true than in the obviousness setting. The Federal Circuit insists that what it terms the 'real world story' of the invention not be obscured by lawyer's games played with the patent and the prior art. That human, real world story forms a major part of the landscape of the case and often reflects the inadequacy of the prior art and compels a conclusion of nonobviousness." R. Harmon, *Patents and the Federal Circuit* §4.2(b)(i) (3d ed. 1994). See 2 D. Chisum, *Patents* §5.05 (1994 rev.).

secondary meaning [trademark]   A new meaning that attaches to a noninherently distinctive word or symbol, by which customers use that word or symbol as a trademark or service mark to identify and distinguish a single commercial source.

Secondary Meaning Is Acquired Distinctiveness. For noninherently distinctive trade symbols, such as a DESCRIPTIVE MARK, GEOGRAPHIC MARK, or PERSONAL NAME MARK, distinctiveness must be acquired in order to achieve the protectible status of a TRADEMARK or SERVICE MARK. *Taco Cabana Int'l Inc. v. Two Pesos, Inc.*, 112 S. Ct. 2753, 2757, 23 USPQ2d 1081, 1084 (1992). This acquired distinctiveness is known as "secondary meaning" because it is a meaning acquired second in time to the primary meaning of the word. Secondary meaning requires only that customers associate the word or symbol with a single, albeit anonymous, commercial source. There is no requirement that customers know the name of the company that produces the product. Under the anonymous source rule, now codified in the Lanham Act definition of a "trademark," "a term may function as an indicator of source and therefore as a valid trademark, even though consumers may not know the name of the manufacturer or producer of the product." *A.J. Canfield Co. v. Honickman*, 808 F.2d 291, 300, 1 USPQ2d 1364, 1371 (3d Cir. 1986). The issue of whether there is secondary meaning is a question of fact.

Evidence of Secondary Meaning. In general, the more descriptive and the less inherently distinctive the word, symbol, or trade dress, the greater must be the quantity and quality of evidence of secondary meaning to prove that level of distinctiveness necessary to achieve trademark, service mark, or trade dress status. Evidence of secondary meaning may consist of direct evidence, in the form of a customer survey, or circumstantial evidence, in the form of the input of the seller, e.g., sales volume, length of time used, and the quantity and quality of advertising and promotion exposing customers to the symbol. Under the majority view, evidence of copying permits, but does not compel, a finding of secondary meaning. *Bristol-Myers Squibb Co. v. McNeil-P.P.C., Inc.*, 973 F.2d 1033, 24 USPQ2d 1161 (2d Cir. 1992). A minority of courts go further to hold that proof of intentional, direct copying raises a presumption of secondary meaning. *M. Kramer Mfg. Co. v. Andrews*, 783 F.2d 421, 228 USPQ 705 (4th Cir. 1986).

Federal Registration. In applying to place on the federal principal register as a trademark or service mark a descriptive, geographically descriptive, or surname mark, Lanham Act §2(f), 15 U.S.C. §1052(f), permits the applicant to submit proof of acquired distinctiveness, which is the same thing as secondary meaning. Lanham Act §2(f) is not a provision on which registration is refused "but is a provision under which an applicant has a chance to prove that he is entitled to a federal trademark registration which would otherwise be refused." *Yamaha Int'l Corp. v. Hoshino Gakki Co.*, 840 F.2d 1572, 1580, 6 USPQ2d 1001, 1007 (Fed. Cir. 1988). There are three types of evidence of secondary meaning that may be relied on in applying for registration:

(1) Direct or circumstantial evidence tending to prove that the relevant buyer class uses the mark to identify the applicant.

(2) Proof of substantially exclusive and continuous use as a mark by the applicant for the five years preceding the date on which the claim of distinctiveness is made. This substitute form of evidence is authorized by Lanham Act §2(f), 15 U.S.C. §1052(f). Whether such evidence will be sufficient depends upon the descriptive-

ness of the term. *Trademark Manual of Examining Procedure* §1212.05 (1993 rev.).

(3) Evidence of ownership of one or more prior federal principal register registrations of the same mark for related goods or services. 37 C.F.R. §2.41(b), *Trademark Manual of Examining Procedure* §1212.04 (1993 rev.). This third type of evidence is generally appropriate only if the prior registration was based on a finding of secondary meaning in the mark. *In re Loew's Theatres, Inc.*, 223 USPQ 513 (T.T.A.B. 1984), *aff'd on other grounds*, 769 F.2d 764, 226 USPQ 865 (Fed. Cir. 1985).

Evidentiary Impact of Federal Registration. A registration of a mark on the principal register is prima facie evidence of the validity of the mark, which includes a presumption that the mark is either inherently distinctive or has acquired distinctiveness through secondary meaning. Lanham Act §§7(b), 33(a), 15 U.S.C. §§1057(b), 1115(a). If the registration of the mark has become incontestable, then the validity of the mark cannot be challenged on the ground that the mark is not inherently distinctive and lacks secondary meaning, for this is not one of the statutory challenges permitted to be made to such a registered mark. *Park 'N Fly Inc. v. Dollar Park & Fly*, 469 U.S. 189, 224 USPQ 327 (1985).

Fair Use. A junior user is always entitled to use a term in good faith in its primary, descriptive sense. This is known as a noninfringing fair use. Such a defense is most often made as against a designation that is determined to be descriptive of the plaintiff's goods or services. Such a DESCRIPTIVE MARK requires proof of secondary meaning for registration and protection. Assuming such proof, the word or symbol has two meanings: (1) its old, "primary" meaning in the language, which existed prior to the plaintiff's usage; and (2) its new, "secondary" trademark meaning as an identifying symbol for the plaintiff's goods or services. See FAIR USE.

De Facto Secondary Meaning. This is evidence tending to prove customer identification of a word or product feature with a single source but having no legal significance either because the word has already been determined to be a GENERIC NAME or because the feature has been

determined to be "functional." See discussion at GENERIC NAME, FUNCTIONALITY.

See FAIR USE; DE FACTO SECONDARY MEANING, DESCRIPTIVE MARK, GEOGRAPHIC MARK, PERSONAL NAME MARK.

• *Statutory Reference*: Lanham Act §2(f), 15 U.S.C. §1052(f): "Except as expressly excluded in paragraphs (a), (b), (c), (d) and (e)(3) of this section, nothing herein shall prevent the registration of a mark used by the applicant which has become distinctive of the applicant's goods in commerce. The Commissioner may accept as prima facie evidence that the mark has become distinctive, as used on or in connection with the applicant's goods in commerce, proof of substantially exclusive and continuous use thereof as a mark for the five years before the date on which the claim of distinctiveness is made...."

• *Case References*:

"Here we have a secondary meaning to the descriptive term 'Nu-Enamel.' ... The right arises ... from the fact that 'Nu-Enamel' has come to indicate that the goods in connection with which it is used are the goods manufactured by the respondent. When a name is endowed with this quality, it becomes a mark, entitled to protection." *Armstrong Paint & Varnish Works v. Nu-Enamel Corp.*, 305 U.S. 315, 336 (1938).

"The basic element of secondary meaning is a mental recognition in buyers' and potential buyers' minds that the products connected with the symbol or device emanate from or are associated with the same source." *Levi Strauss & Co. v. Blue Bell, Inc.*, 632 F.2d 817, 820, 208 USPQ 713, 716 (9th Cir. 1980).

"A company's promotional efforts may not succeed in endowing the trade dress of its product with secondary meaning; similarly, a company may achieve high sales, but fail to impress a trade dress on the public mind. But to say that proof of extensive advertising and substantial sales may not be probative of secondary meaning is to defy both logic and common sense." *Reader's Digest Ass'n v. Conservative Digest, Inc.*, 821 F.2d 800, 805, 3 USPQ2d 1276, 1279 (D.C. Cir. 1987).

- *Treatise Reference*: J.T. McCarthy, *Trademarks and Unfair Competition* ch. 15 (3d ed. 1995 rev.).

- *Restatement Reference*: " 'Secondary meaning' does not connote a subordinate or rare meaning. Instead it refers to a subsequent significance added to the previous meaning of the term." *Restatement (Third) of Unfair Competition* §13, comment e (1995).

- *Example*: Self-laudatory words, such as BEST for milk, are regarded as being descriptive and noninherently distinctive. The "primary meaning" is that this milk is purported to be the "best." To achieve exclusive trademark rights, the seller must use the word so that the word achieves a new, "secondary meaning" as denoting that all milk marked BEST comes from a single commercial source. Only when that is achieved does the seller have the right to prevent others from using the word BEST as a mark to identify their competitive or related products.

secondary transmission [copyright]
See TRANSMISSION.

semiconductor chip [computer–copyright] A multilayer semiconductor device that performs various electronic functions in a circuit. A semiconductor is a material having conductivity intermediate between a conductor, such as metal, and a nonconductor, such as glass. Silicon is currently the most popular semiconductor currently in use in making electronic chip products.

A "semiconductor chip product" is defined in §901(a)(1) of the Semiconductor Chip Protection Act (see SCPA) as a product "having two or more layers of metallic, insulating or semiconductor material deposited or otherwise placed on, or etched away or otherwise removed from, a piece of semiconductor material in accordance with a predetermined pattern; and intended to perform electronic circuitry functions."

See SCPA, ROM, CELL LIBRARY.

senior party [patent] The first party in time to file a patent application when that party is involved in a patent INTERFERENCE proceeding to determine PRIORITY OF INVENTION. Since the date of application is presumed to be the date of invention, the senior party is presumed to be the first inventor. The JUNIOR PARTY bears the burden of proving an earlier date of invention.

- *Case References*:
"Oka, as the senior party, is presumptively entitled to an award of priority, and Youssefyeh, as the junior party in an interference between pending applications, must overcome that presumption with a preponderance of the evidence." *Oka v. Youssefyeh*, 849 F.2d 581, 584, 7 USPQ2d 1169, 1172 (Fed. Cir. 1988).

"In order to establish priority in an interference, the party who files later is 'required to establish reduction to practice *before* [the] filing date [of the party who filed first], or conception before that date coupled with reasonable diligence from just before that date to [the] filing date [of the party who files later].' " *Hahn v. Wong*, 892 F.2d 1028, 1032, 13 USPQ2d 1313, 1317 (Fed. Cir. 1989).

See JUNIOR PARTY, INTERFERENCE.

sequel [copyright] A subsequent story using the same characters as in a previous story, but in a different plot. An assignment or license of the right to make a sequel of a story is a grant of the right to create subsequent stories employing the same characters in different plots or sequences. It has been held that the term "sequel" as used in the motion picture industry means a work that was written after another, regardless of whether the later story is set prior to, during, or subsequent to the time period of the first story.

While a sequel puts the same characters in a different plot, a REMAKE is a motion picture based substantially upon the same story, albeit with modernizing or updating elements. While a sequel will usually put the characters in a new story set later in time, a PREQUEL puts the characters in a new story set prior in time to the original story.

- *Case References*:
Sequels are "subsequent stories embodying the same character." *Goodis v. United Artists*

Television, Inc., 425 F.2d 397, 406, 165 USPQ 3, 9 (2d Cir. 1970).

"Although the denotative meaning of 'sequel' means a literary work continuing the course of a narrative begun in a preceding one, 'sequel' as used in the movie industry means only a work that follows another, regardless of whether the successive work is set prior to, during, or after the time period of the first work." *Trust Co. Bank v. MGM/UA Entertainment Co.*, 593 F. Supp. 580, 585, 223 USPQ 1046, 1050 (N.D. Ga. 1984), *aff'd*, 772 F.2d 740 (11th Cir. 1985).

Serial Copy Management System [copyright] See DIGITAL AUDIO RECORDING TECHNOLOGY.

service mark [trademark] A word, slogan, design, picture, or any other symbol used to identify and distinguish services. Marks used to identify services are protected at state common law, are registrable in almost all states, are federally registrable, and are protected as unregistered marks in the federal courts under Lanham Act §43(a).

Nature of Use Required for Federal Service Mark Registration. For service marks, there is no physical "thing" to which the mark can be affixed, so the Lanham Act does not specify any type of physical association that must exist between the service and the mark. Sufficient service mark usage includes use of the mark in advertising and promotional materials, use on the letterhead of a letter describing or promoting the service, and use on a business card used to solicit business. At one time the Court of Customs and Patent Appeals said that to prove that a certain term was being used to identify services, there must be a "direct association" in the advertising between the term and the service. The Court of Appeals for the Federal Circuit, however, later made it clear that the term "direct association" is merely a metaphorical guide and "does not create an additional or more stringent requirement for registration" of a service mark beyond that defined in the statute itself. *In re Advertising & Marketing Dev. Inc.*, 821 F.2d 614, 620, 2 USPQ2d 2010, 2014 (Fed. Cir. 1987).

Use of Service Mark in Interstate Commerce. To obtain a valid federal registration it is necessary that the service be rendered in interstate or foreign commerce. Many services rendered even within the confines of one state are necessarily rendered "in" interstate commerce in the sense that they "affect" interstate commerce. Thus, even a single, local gasoline service station or restaurant will be rendering services that affect interstate commerce. *Application of Gastown, Inc.*, 326 F.2d 780, 140 USPQ 216 (C.C.P.A. 1964). Similarly, the rendering of restaurant services from a single-location restaurant to out-of-state travelers is use in interstate commerce. *Larry Harmon Pictures Corp. v. Williams Restaurant Corp.*, 929 F.2d 662, 18 USPQ2d 1292 (Fed. Cir. 1991). However, some local services may be of such a nature that they do not have any substantial impact on interstate trade. *In re Conti*, 220 USPQ 745 (T.T.A.B. 1983) (local barber shop services do not impact interstate commerce). Minimal out-of-state advertising can change the result. *United States Shoe Co. v. J. Riggs West, Inc.*, 221 USPQ 1020 (T.T.A.B. 1984) (service mark of Kansas pool hall that advertised in New York held used in interstate commerce). See 2 J.T. McCarthy, *Trademarks and Unfair Competition* §19.36 (3d ed. 1995 rev.).

What Is a "Service"? While the Lanham Act does not define "service," the term is broadly interpreted and includes such things as hotel and restaurant services, retail sales services, airlines services, insurance, investment services, sponsorship of sporting events, entertainment services, and licensing services. However, a seller of goods or services cannot proliferate registrations by registering a plethora of service marks for ancillary services that every other competitor also offers, such as advertising, quoting prices, repairing defective goods, and demonstrating the use of products. *In re Orion Research, Inc.*, 523 F.2d 1398, 187 USPQ 485 (C.C.P.A. 1975) (guarantee to repair or replace products sold by applicant not a registrable "service"). "Ordinary and routine" promotional activities are not registrable "services." *In re Dr. Pepper Co.*, 836 F.2d 508, 5 USPQ2d 1207 (Fed. Cir. 1987). A mark developed by an advertising agency for a client's product can be used and registered as a mark of the agency to identify its advertising services as well as a trademark to identify the client's goods. *In re Advertising & Marketing Dev., Inc.*, 821 F.2d 614, 2 USPQ2d 2010 (Fed. Cir. 1987). It will sometimes be difficult to categorize a given use of a term in advertising as either a service mark identifying a corporate service or an unregistrable trade name identifying only the corporate entity.

See TRADEMARK, REGISTRATION OF TRADEMARK.

- *Treatise Reference*: 2 J.T. McCarthy, *Trademarks and Unfair Competition* §§19.29–.30 (3d ed. 1995 rev.).

- *Statutory Reference*:

Lanham Act §3, 15 U.S.C. §1053: "Subject to the provisions relating to the registration of trademarks, so far as they are applicable, service marks shall be registrable, in the same manner and with the same effect as are trademarks, and when registered they shall be entitled to the protection provided herein in the case of trademarks. Applications and procedure under this section shall conform as nearly as practicable to those prescribed for the registration of trademarks.

Lanham Act §45, 15 U.S.C. §1127:

The term "service mark" means any word, name, symbol, or device, or any combination thereof—

(1) used by a person, or

(2) which a person has a bona fide intention to use in commerce and applies to register on the principal register established by this Act,

to identify and distinguish the services of one person, including a unique service, from the services of others and to indicate the source of the services, even if that source is unknown. Titles, character names and other distinctive features of radio or television programs may be registered notwithstanding that they, or the programs, may advertise the goods of the sponsor.

SESAC [copyright] One of the PERFORMING RIGHTS SOCIETIES that licenses certain performing rights in copyrighted musical works. Established in 1930, SESAC is the second oldest performing rights society in the United States. The company changed its name in 1940 from the Society of European Stage Authors and Composers to SESAC because its repertory had grown well beyond the field of European classic music to encompass almost every type of music.

See also PERFORMING RIGHTS SOCIETIES, ASCAP, BMI, GRAND RIGHTS, BLANKET LICENSE, PERFORMANCE.

shareware [computers] A form of distribution of COMPUTER PROGRAMS in which the creator retains the copyright but permits free copying and distribution. After users have tried the shareware and have decided to use it on an ongoing basis, they are morally, but not legally, bound to send the creator a suggested donation. In return for the donation, the user often receives manuals, updates, telephone support, and other forms of support. Sometimes "shareware" is used to denote copyrighted software that is distributed for the purpose of testing and review.

Shareware and Patents. In 1989 Robert W. Kastenmeier, Chairman of the Subcommittee on Courts, Intellectual Property, and the Administration of Justice of the House Committee on the Judiciary, addressed the following question to the Patent and Trademark Office: "Assuming that a software program has a patentable feature and the inventor chooses to place the feature in the public domain as shareware or freeware, does the invention become part of the prior art serving to defeat a patent on a similar invention?" Jeffrey M. Samuels, Acting Commissioner of Patents and Trademarks, responded: "Any shareware or freeware which is placed in the public domain becomes part of the prior art and, where pertinent, could be used to reject an application seeking to patent a computer process." 39 Pat. Trademark & Copyright J. 59 (BNA) (1989).

Registry of Documents Relating to Shareware. Section 805(a) of Public Law No. 101-605, 104 Stat. 5089 (1990) (codified as note to

17 U.S.C. §205), authorized the creation of a registry of documents pertaining to computer shareware and public domain computer software in order to provide a means of notifying the public of the licensing terms of that program. Documents recorded in the Copyright Office under this statute will be included in the Computer Shareware Registry. 37 C.F.R. §201.26. Section 805(c) provides for the establishment of a voluntary system of depositing such software for the benefit of the Machine-Readable Collections Reading Room at the Library of Congress. It is important to note that participation with this registry is not a substitute for registering a claim to copyright a computer program under 17 U.S.C. §205.

Synonyms: freeware, user-supported software.

• *Rule Reference*: "The term computer shareware is accorded its customary meaning within the software industry. In general, shareware is copyrighted software which is distributed for the purposes of testing and review, subject to the condition that payment to the copyright owner is required after a person who has secured a copy decides to use the software." 37 C.F.R. §201.26(b)(1)

shoe [patent] The precomputerized Patent and Trademark Office (PTO) kept records of the PRIOR ART stored in wooden file drawers called "shoes," which were stored in cabinets called "shoe cases." There were millions of pieces of prior art located in thousands of these "shoes" stored in the search rooms of the PTO. Soon the PTO will complete its move to a fully computerized search operation and the storing of paper records in thousands of "shoes" will no longer be necessary.

Origin. The etymology of "shoe" is uncertain. One view is that in the early days of the Patent Office, records were stored in wooden boxes that were originally used to ship shoes.

shop right [patent] An implied-in-law non-exclusive license of a patent from an employee to the employer. A shop right is generally implied when an employee who is not specifically hired to invent uses the employer's facilities to invent, usually while on the job. The shop right rule grants to such an employer the royalty-free right to use the invention of the employee. It is based on the employer's presumed contribution to the invention through materials, time, and equipment. *California E. Labs. v. Gould*, 896 F.2d 400, 402–03, 13 USPQ2d 1984, 1985 (9th Cir. 1990).

• *Treatise Reference*: 5 D. Chisum, *Patents* §22.03[3] (1994 rev.).

• *Case References*:
"The so-called shop-right ... is that where a servant, during his hours of employment, working with his master's materials and appliances, conceives and perfects an invention for which he obtains a patent, he must accord his master a non-exclusive right to practice the invention." *United States v. Dubilier Condenser Corp.*, 289 U.S. 178, 188, 17 USPQ 154, 158 (1933).

"[I]f the employee was not hired to invent, the employer may establish a shop right. As commonly stated, a shop right will be found where the employer shows that the invention was developed by his employee during the employer's time or with the assistance of the employer's property or labor. A shop right permits the employer to use the subject of the patent for his own purposes, but not to sell or prohibit others from using it. The inventor retains a valid patent." *Wommack v. Durham Pecan Co.*, 715 F.2d 962, 965, 219 USPQ 1153, 1156–57 (5th Cir. 1983).

"Where the employee is not hired specifically to design or invent, but nevertheless conceives of a device during working hours with the use of the employer's materials and equipment, the employer is granted an irrevocable but non-exclusive right to use the invention under the 'shop right rule.' A shop right is an employer's royalty free, non-exclusive and non-transferable license to use an employee's patented invention." *Ingersoll-Rand Co. v. Ciavatta*, 110 N.J. 609, 542 A.2d 879, 886, 8 USPQ2d 1537, 1542 (1988).

shrink-wrap license [computers-copyright–trade secret] A paid-up "license" of intellectual property in computer software created by a notice placed on plastic wrapping that is "shrink wrapped" around a computer disk package. The notice on the wrapping states that by removing the wrapping, the purchaser agrees to the stated conditions of the license, which places restrictions on the use, sale, and cozpying of the computer program software.

The Court of Appeals for the Third Circuit held that the terms of a software manufacturer's shrink-wrap license were not binding on the purchaser, a value-added retailer, because these terms would materially alter the terms of the parties' prior agreement. The license did not bind this buyer because (1) the seller never obtained the buyer's express assent to the terms of the license, even though they differed substantially from those previously discussed by the parties; (2) the seller was aware, based on prior dealings, that the buyer objected to some of the terms; and (3) the terms of the license were not sufficiently important that the seller would forego its sales if it could not obtain consent. *Step-Saver Data Sys., Inc. v. Wyse Technology & the Software Link, Inc.,* 939 F.2d 91 (3d Cir. 1991).

Synonyms: tear-me-open license, box-top license, blister-pack license, consent-by-opening clause.

• *Case References*:

A provision of a Louisiana statute allowed enforcement of a shrink-wrap license provision that prohibits the buyer from adapting the program by DECOMPILATION or DISASSEMBLY. It was held that the state statutory provision conflicts with the federal rights of owners of a copy of computer programs and is thus preempted by federal law. The shrink-wrap license provision prohibiting decompilation or disassembly was found unenforceable, apparently because it was viewed as a contract of adhesion. *Vault Corp. v. Quaid Software Ltd.,* 847 F.2d 255, 7 USPQ2d 1281 (5th Cir. 1988).

"TSL never mentioned during the parties's negotiations leading to the purchase of the programs, nor did it, at any time, obtain Step-Saver's express assent to, the terms of the box-top license. Instead, TSL contented itself with attaching the terms to the packaging of the software, even though those terms differed substantially from those previously discussed by

the parties. Thus, the box-top license, in this case, is best seen as one more form in a battle of forms, and the question of whether Step-Saver has agreed to be bound by the terms of the box-top license is best resolved by applying the legal principles detailed in [U.C.C.] section 2-207." *Step-Saver Data Sys., Inc. v. Wyse Technology & the Software Link, Inc.,* 939 F.2d 91, 99–100 (3d Cir. 1991).

• *Commentary References*: Einhorn, *The Enforceability of "Tear-Me-Open" Software License Agreements,* 67 J. Pat. Off. Soc'y 509 (1985); Nelson, *Enforceability of Box-Top Licenses: A Proposal to End the Dilemma,* 2 Computer & High Tech. L.J. 171 (1986).

• *Statutory Reference*: 17 U.S.C. §§109, 117.

single means claim [patent] A claim that is drafted in "means for" or MEANS-PLUS-FUNCTION format and is invalid because the claim recites only a single element rather than a combination of elements. An example of a single means claim is: "An electronic multiplication processor comprising multiplication means for generating the multiplied output signals in response to input signals."

Reasons for Invalidity. A single means claim is invalid because the inventor claims exclusive rights in every conceivable means for achieving the stated result, while in return disclosing only those limited means known to the inventor. This is a violation of the ENABLEMENT requirement of Patent Code §112, first paragraph. While the final, sixth paragraph of §112 saves combination claims from this problem, no statutory section saves a single means claim.

SEE MEANS-PLUS-FUNCTION CLAIM, UNDUE BREADTH.

• *Statutory Reference*:

35 U.S.C. §112, first paragraph: "The specification shall contain a written description of the invention, and of the manner and process of making and using it, in such full, clear, concise, and exact terms as to enable any person skilled in the art to which it pertains, or with which it is most nearly connected, to make and use the same, and shall set forth the best mode contem-

plated by the inventor of carrying out his invention."

35 U.S.C. §112, sixth paragraph: "An element in a claim for a combination may be expressed as a means or step for performing a specified function without the recital of structure, material, or acts in support thereof, and such claims shall be construed to cover the corresponding structure, material, or acts described in the specification and equivalents thereof."

• *Case References*:

"Having made clear that, in our view, claim 35 denotes only a single means, we agree with the board that it is properly rejected under §112.... The proper statutory basis for the rejection of a single means claim is the requirement of the first paragraph of §112 that the enabling disclosure of the specification be commensurate in scope with the claim under construction. The long-recognized problem with a single means claim is that it covers every conceivable means for achieving the stated result, while the specification discloses at most only those means known to the inventor. See *O'Reilly v. Morse*, 56 U.S. 62, 112 (1853). Thus, the claim is properly rejected for what used to be known as 'undue breadth,' but has since been appreciated as being, more accurately, based on the first paragraph of §112.... The final paragraph of §112 saves *combination* claims drafted using means-plus-function format from this problem.... But no provision saves a claim drafted in means-plus-function format which is not drawn to a combination, i.e., a single means claim." *In re Hyatt*, 708 F.2d 712, 714–15, 218 USPQ 195, 197 (Fed. Cir. 1983).

• *Treatise References*: "A so-called single-means claim is improper because it covers every conceivable way of achieving the desired result, while the specification shows only a few at best. Invalidity results, not under some 'undue breadth' formulation, but for lack of enabling disclosure, because the single-means claim 'reads on subject matter as to which the specification is not enabling.' " R. Harmon, *Patents and the Federal Circuit* §5.2(d) (3d ed. 1994). See 2 D. Chisum, *Patents* §§8.03–.04 (1994 rev.).

SIR [patent]
See STATUTORY INVENTION REGISTRATION.

skillful mechanic [patent] A now-obsolete test of the patentability of an invention. The test was to ask whether more ingenuity was involved in making the technical innovation than would be the work of a skillful mechanic. If the answer was no, then the invention was not properly patentable. This test of newness and patentability was completely eliminated by §103 of the 1952 Patent Code, which substituted the test of OBVIOUSNESS.

Origin of the Term. The 1851 Supreme Court decision in *Hotchkiss v. Greenwood* approved of a jury instruction to the effect that the jury was to find the patent invalid if no more ingenuity or skill was required to come up with the invention than that of an "ordinary mechanic acquainted with the business." The statute in existence then was the Patent Act of 1836. The patented invention essentially involved nothing more than substituting ceramic or porcelain for wood or metal as a material for doorknobs. The jury found that the patent was not valid. The Supreme Court affirmed and said that unless "more ingenuity and skill ... were required ... than were possessed by an ordinary mechanic acquainted with the business, there was an absence of that degree of skill and ingenuity which constitute essential elements of every invention. In other words, the improvement is the work of the skillful mechanic, not that of the inventor." *Hotchkiss v. Greenwood*, 52 U.S. 248, 266 (1851). Thus, the Court developed two categories: patentable innovations that are the work of "inventors" and nonpatentable innovations that are merely the work of the "skillful mechanic." This led to the now-obsolete rule that a technical innovation had to be called an "invention" in order to be patentable.

See INVENTION.

Statutory Elimination of the Test. This "skilled mechanic" phrase became the standard test of the patentability of an invention. For example, in 1941 the Supreme Court could observe that: "Since *Hotchkiss v. Greenwood*, ... decided in 1851, it has been recognized that if an improvement is to obtain the privileged position of a patent more ingenuity must be involved than the work of a mechanic skilled in the art." *Cuno Eng'g Corp. v. Automatic Devices Corp.*, 314 U.S. 84, 90 (1941). But enactment of the 1952 Patent Code completely eliminated the "skilled mechanic" test of patentability. The OBVIOUSNESS test became the sole criteria of the newness of technical innovations.

See SKILL IN THE ART, OBVIOUSNESS, INVENTION.

• *Commentary Reference*: "The decision [in *Hotchkiss v. Greenwood*] made clear that patents are not to be granted on inventions which are no more than what the ordinary mechanic acquainted with the business would produce as a matter of course in the pursuit of his calling. Such mechanics are *expected* to produce *new* things, such as were involved in that case, which was the attaching of an old clay doorknob to an old metal shank in precisely the same manner that metal door knobs had been attached to such shanks before. Technically the assembly was *new*, but the court found novelty was not enough.... Due to the reasoning of the case, ... what came out of it after 1850 ... was an injection into the law of what has ever since been called the 'requirement for invention.' " Rich, *The Vague Concept of "Invention" as Replaced by Sec. 103 of the 1952 Patent Act*, 46 J. Pat. Off. Soc'y 855, 859–60 (1964).

skill in the art [patent] An ordinary level of proficiency in the particular technology in which an invention is made.

Hypothetical Person Having Ordinary Skill in the Art. Under Patent Code §103, an invention is "obvious" and unpatentable if the differences between the invention and the PRIOR ART are such that "the subject matter as a whole would have been obvious at the time the invention was made" to a person having ordinary "skill in the art" to which the invention relates. This person whose view of OBVIOUSNESS is critical to patentability is a hypothetical person having ordinary "skill in the art." The view of a judge, jury, or even the inventor is irrelevant. In order to construct a reasonable profile of this hypothetical person in a given case, it is necessary to determine the level of ordinary skill in this technology and determine with some par-

ticularity exactly what this hypothetical person is likely to know about the technology. Only then can an informed decision on obviousness be made.

The Graham Factors. The U.S. Supreme Court has read Patent Code §103 to require a four-part factual inquiry: (1) determine the scope and content of the prior art relied upon to challenge patentability; (2) identify the difference between that prior art and the claimed invention; (3) determine the level of ordinary "skill in the art" at the time of the invention; and (4) consider the objective evidence of so-called SECONDARY CONSIDERATIONS, which include such factors as COMMERCIAL SUCCESS, UNEXPECTED RESULTS, the FAILURE OF OTHERS to achieve the results of the invention, a LONG FELT NEED that the invention fills, and COPYING of the invention by competitors. *Graham v. John Deere Co.*, 383 U.S. 1, 17, 148 USPQ 459, 467 (1966). Having assembled all that factual data, the decisionmaker then must determine whether the claimed technology would have been obvious or nonobvious to that hypothetical person of ordinary "skill in the art."

Ordinary Skill in the Art. The statutory test is OBVIOUSNESS of the invention from the viewpoint of a person with merely "ordinary" skill in this technical field, not obviousness through the eyes of "the rare genius in the art, or to a judge or other layman after learning all about the invention." *Stratoflex Inc. v. Aeroquip Corp.*, 713 F.2d 1530, 1538, 218 USPQ 871, 879 (Fed. Cir. 1983). The test of obviousness is not made from the viewpoint of the inventor, for that would reward those "inventors" who were relatively ignorant of the state of the art and deny patents to those inventors who were fully informed. Neither is the test made from the perspective of the highly skilled inventor, to whom very few innovations are not "obvious."

Relevant Fields of Technology. It is proper to attribute to the hypothetical skilled person "knowledge of all prior art in the field of the inventor's endeavor and of prior art solutions for a common problem even if outside that field." *In re Nilssen*, 851 F.2d 1401, 1403, 7 USPQ2d 1500, 1502 (Fed. Cir. 1988).

See ANALOGOUS ART.

The Previous "Skillful Mechanic" Test. The old test of using the viewpoint of the SKILLFUL MECHANIC has been replaced since the advent of the 1952 Patent Code by the test of the person with skill in the art.

Enablement and Definiteness. The viewpoint of a person with skill in the art is also used in determining whether the specification of a patent complies with the ENABLEMENT requirement and whether a claim of a patent fails to be sufficiently specific and is INDEFINITE.

Design Patents. When the patentability of an industrial design, rather than of a utilitarian feature, is in question, the hypothetical person skilled in the art becomes a DESIGNER SKILLED IN THE ART.

See OBVIOUSNESS, DESIGNER SKILLED IN THE ART, HYPOTHETICAL PERSON SKILLED IN THE ART, HINDSIGHT, ANALOGOUS ART.

- *Statutory Reference*: 35 U.S.C. §103: "A patent may not be obtained though the invention is not identically disclosed or described as set forth in section 102 of this title, if the differences between the subject matter sought to be patented and the prior art are such that the subject matter as a whole would have been obvious at the time the invention was made to a person having ordinary skill in the art to which such subject matter pertains. Patentability shall not be negatived by the manner in which the invention was made...."

- *Case References*:

"Factors that may be considered in determining level of ordinary skill in the art include: (1) the educational level of the inventor; (2) type of problems encountered in the art; (3) prior art solutions to those problems; (4) rapidity with which innovations are made; (5) sophistication of the technology; and (6) educational level of active workers in the field.... Not all such factors may be present in every case, and one or more of these or other factors may predominate in a particular case. The important consideration lies in the need to adhere to the statute, i.e., to hold that an invention would or would not have been obvious, as a whole, when it was made, to a person of 'ordinary skill in the art'— not to the judge, or to a layman, or to those skilled in remote arts, or to geniuses in the art

at hand." *Environmental Designs, Ltd. v. Union Oil Co. of Cal.*, 713 F.2d 693, 696–97, 218 USPQ 865, 868–69 (Fed. Cir. 1983).

"With the involved facts determined, the decisionmaker confronts a ghost, i.e., 'a person having ordinary skill in the art,' not unlike the 'reasonable man' and other ghosts in the law. To reach a proper conclusion under §103, the decisionmaker must step backward in time and into the shoes worn by that 'person' when the invention was unknown and just before it was made." *Panduit Corp. v. Dennison Mfg. Co.*, 810 F.2d 1561, 1566, 1 USPQ2d 1593, 1595–97 (Fed. Cir. 1987).

"The *Graham* analysis includes a factual determination of the level of ordinary skill in the art. Without that information, a district court cannot properly assess obviousness because the critical question is whether a claimed invention would have been obvious at the time it was made to one with ordinary skill in the art.... The person of ordinary skill is a hypothetical person who is presumed to be aware of all the pertinent prior art. The actual inventor's skill is not determinative...." *Custom Accessories Inc. v. Jeffrey-Allan Indus., Inc.*, 807 F.2d 955, 962, 1 USPQ2d 1196, 1201 (Fed. Cir. 1986).

"The primary value in the requirement that the level of skill be found lies in its tendency to focus the mind of the decisionmaker away from what would presently be obvious to that decisionmaker and toward what would, when the invention was made, have been obvious, as the statute requires, 'to one of ordinary skill in the art.' " *Kloster Speedsteel AB v. Crucible Inc.*, 793 F.2d 1565, 1574, 230 USPQ 81, 86 (Fed. Cir. 1986).

- *Example 1*: The Court of Appeals for the Federal Circuit affirmed a finding of invalidity of a patent on a form of photosensitive night light, finding that a person of ordinary skill in the art would be aware of prior art in the related field of shades for overhead lighting fixtures. "In evaluating obviousness, the hypothetical person of ordinary skill in the pertinent art is presumed to have the 'ability to select and utilize knowledge from other arts reasonably pertinent to [the] particular problem' to which the claimed invention is directed.... Assuming arguendo that these four references [relating to overhead lighting fixtures] are not strictly within the field of [electric night lights], they are easily within a field analogous thereto, and their teachings are properly combinable with the earlier references...." *Cable Elec. Prods., Inc. v. Genmark, Inc.*, 770 F.2d 1015, 1025, 226 USPQ 881, 886 (Fed. Cir. 1985).

- *Example 2*: "The jury, among its special verdicts on the *Graham* factors, found that a person of ordinary skill in the pertinent art [of motorcycle suspension design] could be any of: (1) a motorcycle mechanic without formal technical education, (2) a person with experience in working on suspension systems for racing automobiles, but without formal technical training, (3) suspension system instructors, (4) professional motorcycle riders, and (5) someone possessing above-average mechanical skills." *Richardson v. Suzuki Motor Co.*, 868 F.2d 1226, 1237, 9 USPQ2d 1913, 1921 (Fed. Cir. 1989) (court affirming the jury verdict finding the patent claims nonobvious and not invalid).

- *Example 3*: "The Master determined that the level of ordinary skill in the casting art in 1979 would be a person having knowledge of chemistry equivalent to a bachelor's degree, having additional knowledge of resin systems and their curing mechanisms. Such a person would also have some experience in designing orthopedic casting materials and, more particularly, in developing backings for use in casting materials. Finally, a person of ordinary skill in the casting art would also have some knowledge of the clinical usage of casting materials." *Minnesota Mining & Mfg. Co. v. Johnson & Johnson Orthopedics, Inc.*, 976 F.2d 1559, 1573–74, 24 USPQ2d 1321, 1333 (Fed. Cir. 1992) (agreeing with master's conclusion and holding that patented invention would not have been obvious to one of ordinary skill in the art at the time of invention).

- *Treatise Reference*: "The hypothetical person skilled in the art is not the judge, nor a layman, nor one skilled in remote arts, nor a genius in the art at hand, nor the inventor—the invention is not to be evaluated through the eyes of the actual inventor. Indeed the court has said that the actual inventor's skill is irrelevant to the inquiry, and this for a very important reason. Inventors, as a class, ... are thought to possess a special something that sets them apart from workers of ordinary skill. Thus obviousness should not be determined by inquiring into what patentees—that is, inventors—would have known or likely would have done faced with the revelations of the prior art." R. Harmon, *Patents and the Federal Circuit* §4.3(a) (3d ed. 1994). See 2 D. Chisum, *Patents* §5.06 (1994 rev.).

small entity [patent] An independent inventor, nonprofit organization, or small business concern that qualifies for a 50 percent discount on the payment of many of the government fees paid to the Patent and Trademark Office for patent application filing and processing. These include filing fees, processing fees, issue fees, and maintenance fees. This fee discount for small entities was established in 1982.

Types of "Small Entities." The regulations define three categories of "small entity":

(1) An "independent inventor" is an individual who has not assigned or licensed the invention and is not under any contractual obligation to do so. (An employee of a large company will generally not qualify.)

(2) A "nonprofit organization" is an organization such as a university, an IRS-defined tax-exempt nonprofit organization, or a nonprofit scientific or educational organization qualified under state law. Foreign nonprofit organizations also qualify if they would fall within the IRS tax-exempt definition or the state-qualified scientific or educational organization definition if they were located in the United States.

(3) A "small business concern," according to the Small Business Administration definition, is a business that has less than 500 employees and that has not assigned or licensed and is not under any contractual obligation to assign or license the invention to other than a small entity. 37 C.F.R. §1.9.

Qualifying for the Fee Discount. To qualify for the reduced government patent fees, the applicant must file a verified statement with the patent application, stating under oath that the applicant qualifies as a small entity. Any attempt to fraudulently or improperly or through gross negligence establish status as a small entity is deemed to be a fraud practiced on the Patent and Trademark Office and could thereby endanger the validity of the patent itself. 37 C.F.R. §1.28(d).

SOU [trademark]
See STATEMENT OF USE.

sound recording [copyright] A category of copyrightable work consisting of the actual sounds that are recorded in a material object known as a PHONORECORD.

Exact Recorded Sounds. A sound recording is a type of work that comprises the exact sounds rendered when one performs a work, such as singing, playing a musical instrument, reciting a play, or reading a book. It also includes sounds of machines or nature, such as recorded sounds of birds singing, thunder booming, jet planes landing, or trains passing by. However, the sounds that accompany an AUDIOVISUAL WORK, such as a MOTION PICTURE, are not put in the category of a "sound recording," but are included as adjuncts of the audiovisual work.

First Federal Protection: February 15, 1972. The first federal copyright protection for sound recordings was effective February 15, 1972. Sound recordings first FIXED after that date became eligible for federal copyright protection. When the general copyright law revision was passed and became effective January 1, 1978, it incorporated most of the sound recording provisions previously enacted. But the law preserved state MISAPPROPRIATION law protection for sound recordings first fixed before February 15, 1972. 17 U.S.C. §301(c). On February 15, 2047, both federal and state protection will come to an end for such pre-1972 sound recordings. 17 U.S.C. §301(c).

"Sound Recording" Copyright and "Musical Work" Copyright Distinguished. A sound recording copyright must be distinguished from a MUSICAL WORK copyright. For example, composer Cole Porter's song *Night and Day* is covered by a musical work copyright. But a post-1972 Frank Sinatra recording of *Night and Day* is covered by a sound recording copyright. The same is true of public domain musical works. While a Mozart piano concerto is in the public

domain, a recording of a performance of it by Alicia de Larrocha can be protected by a sound recording copyright. Similarly, a sound recording can cover a recorded performance of a literary work or a dramatic work.

Special Limitations on Sound Recording Copyrights. As provided in 17 U.S.C. §114, copyright in a sound recording does not give the same scope of exclusive rights as for other types of copyrighted works, in three significant respects:

(1) *Duplication of Recorded Sounds.* The exclusive rights in a sound recording are limited to the exclusive rights to reproduce, adapt, and distribute the exact recorded sounds. That is, the exclusive right to reproduce is limited to the exclusive right to duplicate the sound recording in a form "that directly or indirectly recaptures the actual sounds fixed in the recording." Federal law protection is limited to what is popularly known as tape or record PIRACY: the actual electronic duplication of sounds. The Copyright Act explicitly states that a sound recording copyright does *not* give the right to prevent others from making an independent fixation of sounds that only "imitate or simulate" those in the copyrighted sound recording. Thus, a person who makes a recording that attempts to imitate the style of another performer's recording does not violate any rights in a federal sound recording copyright, although there may be a violation of the state law RIGHT OF PUBLICITY. *Midler v. Ford Motor Co.*, 849 F.2d 460, 7 USPQ2d 1398 (9th Cir. 1988).

(2) *Derivative Works.* The exclusive right to adapt the work, namely, to prepare derivative works based on the sound recording, is limited to the preparation of works in which the actual recorded sounds are "rearranged, remixed, or otherwise altered in sequence or quality," such as electronic rerecording in which the sounds are speeded up or slowed down, or sound bites are altered in pitch or combined with other sounds.

(3) *No Performance Rights in Sound Recordings.* There are no exclusive rights to perform the sounds in a sound recording copyright. For example, a radio station needs no license to play over the air the recorded sounds of a compact disc that is protected by a sound recording

copyright. Several other nations do grant performing rights in sound recordings and such rights are the subject of the treaty known as the ROME CONVENTION, to which the United States is not a member. See M. Leaffer, *Understanding Copyright* §8.27 (1989).

Authorship and Ownership of Sound Recording Copyright. The copyrightable elements in a sound recording copyright will usually, but not always, involve "authorship" both on the part of the performers whose performance is captured in the recording and on the part of the record producer responsible for setting up the recording session, capturing and processing the sounds, and compiling and editing them to make a final recording. Ownership of the copyright in a sound recording is left to bargaining among the performers and the producer. H.R. Rep. No. 92-487, 92d Cong., 1st Sess. 5 (1971). In the absence of any assignment contract or WORK-FOR-HIRE relationship, ownership of the sound recording copyright will either be in the recording artist or, if there is an original contribution by sound engineers, editors, and, producers, a JOINT AUTHORSHIP relationship. 1 *Nimmer on Copyright* §2.10[A][3] (1994 rev.).

Phonogram. In most nations, a "sound recording" is referred to as a PHONOGRAM and is the subject of a multilateral treaty known as the 1971 PHONOGRAM CONVENTION, in which the United States is a member nation.

See PHONORECORD, PHONOGRAM.

- *Treatise References*: 1 *Nimmer on Copyright* §§2.10, 8.05 (1994 rev.); 1 P. Goldstein, *Copyright* §§2.13, 5.2.1.2 (1989); M. Leaffer, *Understanding Copyright* §3.19 (1989); 1 N. Boorstyn, *Copyright* §§2.12, 6.09 (2d ed. 1994); W. Patry, *Copyright Law and Practice* 294 (1994).

- *Statutory References*:

17 U.S.C. §101: " 'Sound recordings' are works that result from the fixation of a series of musical, spoken, or other sounds, but not including the sounds accompanying a motion picture or other audiovisual work, regardless of the nature of the material objects, such as disks, tapes, or other phonorecords, in which they are embodied."

17 U.S.C. §114:

(a) The exclusive rights of the owner of copyright in a sound recording are limited to the rights specified by clauses (1) [reproduction], (2) [preparation of derivative works], and (3) [distribution] of section 106, and do not include any right of performance under section 106(4).

(b) The exclusive right of the owner of copyright in a sound recording under clause (1) of section 106 is limited to the right to duplicate the sound recording in the form of phonorecords, or of copies of motion pictures and other audio visual works, that directly or indirectly recapture the actual sounds fixed in a sound recording. The exclusive right of the owner of copyright in a sound recording under clause (2) of section 106 is limited to the right to prepare a derivative work in which the actual sounds fixed in the sound recording are rearranged, remixed, or otherwise altered in sequence or quality. The exclusive rights of the owner of copyright in a sound recording under clauses (1) and (2) of section 106 do not extend to the making or duplication of another sound recording that consists entirely of an independent fixation of other sounds, even though such sounds imitate or simulate those in the copyrighted sound recording....

- *Legislative History*: "The copyrightable elements in a sound recording will usually, though not always, involve 'authorship' both on the part of the performers whose performance is captured and on the part of the record producer responsible for setting up the recording session, capturing and electronically processing the sounds, and compiling and editing them to make the final sound recording. There may, however, be cases where the record producer's contribution is so minimal that the performance is the only copyrightable element in the work, and there may be cases (for example, recordings of birdcalls, sounds of racing cars, et cetera) where only the record producer's contribution is copyrightable." H.R. Rep. No. 94-1476, 94th Cong., 2d Sess. 56 (1976).

- *Example*: In 1995, the musical group The Red Rocks records a performance of Alice Abe's song *Hot Stuff*. Another musical group Cold Turkey then records *Hot Stuff*, attempting to imitate the unique style of the Red Rocks group. Cold Turkey has not infringed the sound recording copyright covering The Red Rocks' recording of *Hot Stuff* because, under 17 U.S.C. §114(b), it is not an infringement to make an "independent fixation of other sounds, even though such sounds imitate or simulate those in the copyrighted sound recording." However, there may be a violation of the state law right of publicity, if, for example, the recording is used as background for an advertisement. See J.T. McCarthy, *The Rights of Publicity and Privacy* §§8.14–.15 (1995 rev.). A disc jockey on radio station KZZZ who plays The Red Rocks' record of *Hot Stuff* over the air needs no license from The Red Rocks because there are no performance rights in a sound recording copyright. However, someone who buys a compact disc version of The Red Rocks' recording of *Hot Stuff*, electronically transfers it to multiple CD copies, and sells them has infringed upon the sound recording copyright in the recording. All of this is independent of the rights of Alice Abe in her "musical work" copyright in the song itself.

source code [copyright–computer] The highest level of computer language. Computer programs written in source code are readable by humans and are written in computer languages such as BASIC or FORTRAN. However, computers cannot understand source code, so to use the program, it must be translated into OBJECT CODE, which is machine readable. Computer programs written in both source code and object code are copyrightable and can qualify as trade secrets.

• *Case References*:

"As source code instructions must be translated into object code before the computer can act upon them, only instructions expressed in object code can be used 'directly' by the computer.... [A] computer program, whether in object code or source code, is a 'literary work' and is protected from unauthorized copying, whether from its object or source code version." *Apple Computer, Inc. v. Franklin Computer Corp.*, 714 F.2d 1240, 1248–49, 219 USPQ 113, 120–21 (3d Cir. 1983).

"The source code can and does qualify as a trade secret. The unique set of computer instructions that Trandes developed is information that (1) is not generally known, (2) is not readily ascertainable by proper means, and (3) if acquired by competitors would improve their ability to compete with Trandes." *Trandes Corp. v. Guy F. Atkinson Co.*, 996 F.2d 655, 663, 27 USPQ2d 1014, 1020 (4th Cir. 1993).

special 301 [international trade] Statutory provisions requiring annual review of trade agreement rights and foreign trade practices of U.S. trading partners that deny benefits to the United States or unjustifiably restrict or burden U.S. commerce. The Trade Act of 1974, as amended by the Special 301 provisions of the 1988 Omnibus Trade and Competitiveness Act, authorizes the United States Trade Representative (USTR) to identify and investigate potential violating countries, recommend the suspension of trade agreement concessions and the imposition of duties and import restrictions, and enter into agreements to eliminate the burdens or restrictions on U.S. trade. 19 U.S.C. §2411.

Why "Special 301"? Originally Title III of the Trade Act of 1974, chapter 1, section 301 provided for presidential responses to certain trade practices of foreign governments. Section 301 was amended by §1301(a) of the Omnibus Trade and Competitiveness Act of 1988 (OCTA). The §301 provisions are now embodied in 19 U.S.C. §§2411–20. Within the larger group of reforms enforcing U.S. trade rights is the smaller set of reforms referred to as "Special 301." This provision specifically addresses unfair foreign trade practices as they relate to intellectual property rights. 19 U.S.C. §2242 .

Special 301 and Intellectual Property Rights. In 1988, §1303 of the OCTA amended §182 of the 1974 Trade Act, 19 U.S.C. §2442, requiring the USTR to: (1) identify those foreign countries that deny "adequate and effective" protection to intellectual property or deny "fair and equitable market access" to businesses that rely on intellectual property protection; and (2) designate certain countries identified in subsection (1) as "priority foreign countries."

The Three Lists. In practice, the USTR annually identifies three categories of nations: (1) "priority foreign countries," whose practices are regarded as the most unacceptable; (2) a middle tier, "the priority watch list," for counties whose practices need careful monitoring; and (3) "the watch list," whose practices are of the lowest level of concern.

Rules for Identifying Priority Countries. Countries deemed to have the most unacceptable standards are designated as "priority foreign countries." The statute requires the USTR to identify as priority foreign countries only those countries that: (1) have the most onerous or egregious trade policies; (2) have the greatest adverse impact, either actual or potential, on U.S. products; and (3) are not entering into good faith negotiations or making progress in negotiations to provide adequate and effective protection of intellectual property rights. 19 U.S.C. §2242(b). The priority foreign nations identified are publicly listed and may become the subjects of a study by the USTR known as a "Special 301" investigation. 19 U.S.C. §2412 .

Special 301 Investigation. If, after an investigation, a country is found to have engaged in unreasonable trade practices, trade sanctions may be imposed by the United States. Under §304 of the Trade Act of 1974, 19 U.S.C. §2414, the USTR is required to determine whether an investigated foreign country is engaged in "unjustifiable, unreasonable, or discriminatory" trade practices. If so, the USTR must recommend trade sanctions to the President of the United States. If the President determines that it is in the best interests of the United States, he may take necessary action, which could include suspension of trade agreement concessions, the imposition of duties, and the withdrawal of privileges under GATT.

See GATT.

"Super 301" Enforcement of U.S. Trade Rights. Section 301 was added in 1988 to the Trade Act of 1974 by §1302 of the Omnibus Trade and Competitiveness Act of 1988, 19 U.S.C. §2420. Commonly referred to as "Super 301," it creates a process under which trade barriers and trade-distorting practices of all kinds of other nations are identified and investigated, with the possibility of ultimate presidential trade retaliation under §301 of the 1974 Trade Act. The process covers all sorts of trade barriers and distortions and is not specific to intellectual property. The Super 301 process, which was to last for only two years (1989 and 1990), expired in 1990. However, the President effectively renewed its main provisions in 1994 in an executive order. Executive Order 12,901, 59 Fed. Reg. 10,727 (Mar. 8, 1994).

History of Use of the Provisions. In 1989 the USTR did not name any "priority" nations to be investigated but identified eight countries as being placed on a "priority watch list" and 17 nations on a "watch list." 38 Pat. Trademark & Copyright J. (BNA) 119 (1989) ("PTCJ"). Due to "significant progress" made by those nations in the following year, the USTR in the spring of 1990 decided not to name any "priority" nations to be investigated. 40 PTCJ 9 (1990). On April 26, 1991, the USTR's first "priority foreign country" list included India, the People's Republic of China, and Thailand. 42 PTCJ 7 (1991). In 1992, the USTR named India, Taiwan, and Thailand as the "priority foreign countries." 43 PTCJ 569 (1992). Brazil, India, and Thailand were put on the list in 1993. 46 PTCJ 11 (1993). In 1994, the People's Republic of China was the sole country designated as a "priority foreign country" under §301. 48 PTCJ (1994). The United States and the People's Republic of China narrowly avoided a trade war by an agreement reached in February 1995. 49 PTCJ (1995). In 1995 the USTR did not name any nations to the "priority foreign countries" list but put 8 countries on the middle tier "priority watch list" and 24 nations on the lowest level "watch list." 50 PTCJ 12 (1995).

specification [patent] That part of a patent application which precedes the claim and in which the inventor specifies, describes, and discloses the invention in detail.

Specification and Claims Are Distinct. A strict reading of Patent Code §112 could lead to the conclusion that the claims of a patent are a part of the specification. ("The specification shall conclude with one or more claims....") But in practice, the specification and claims are always referred to by the courts and practitioners as separate and distinct parts of a patent.

E.g., "The claim must be read in light of the specification."

Different Functions of the Specification and the Claims. The specification describes; the claims define. Whereas the disclosure portion of the specification describes the invention in technical detail, the claims define the scope of the invention. It is the role of the disclosure portion of the specification, not of the claims, to describe the invention. *Orthokinetics Inc. v. Safety Travel Chairs Inc.*, 806 F.2d 1565, 1575, 1 USPQ2d 1081, 1088 (Fed. Cir. 1986). "The disclosure of a patent is in the public domain save as the claims forbid. The claims alone delimit the right to exclude; only they may be infringed." *Environmental Instruments Inc. v. Sutron Corp.*, 877 F.2d 1561, 1564, 11 USPQ2d 1132, 1134 (Fed. Cir. 1989). However, it is proper to use the disclosure of the specification to shed light on the meaning of the claims. This thought is usually encapsulated in the maxim: "The claims must be read in the light of the specification."

Statutory Requirements for an Adequate Specification. Patent Code §112 sets forth three distinct requirements for the specification: (1) the DESCRIPTION requirement—the invention that is claimed must be the invention that is described; (2) the ENABLEMENT requirement—the description must be in such full, clear, and concise terms as to enable any person skilled in the art to make and use it; and (3) the BEST MODE requirement—a description of the best embodiment of the invention known to the inventor at the time of the patent application.

See BEST MODE, DESCRIPTION REQUIREMENT, ENABLEMENT, DISCLOSURE, CLAIM, HOW TO MAKE.

- *Statutory References*:

35 U.S.C. §112, first paragraph: "The specification shall contain a written description of the invention, and of the manner and process of making and using it, in such full, clear, concise, and exact terms as to enable any person skilled in the art to which it pertains, or with which it is most nearly connected, to make and use the same, and shall set forth the best mode contemplated by the inventor of carrying out his invention."

35 U.S.C. §112, second paragraph: "The specification shall conclude with one or more claims particularly pointing out and distinctly claiming the subject matter which the applicant regards as his invention."

- *Case References*:

"It is entirely proper to use the specification to interpret what the patentee meant by a word or phrase in the claim.... But this is not to be confused with adding an extraneous limitation appearing in the specification, which is improper. By 'extraneous,' we mean a limitation read into a claim from the specification wholly apart from any need to interpret what the patentee meant by particular words or phrases in the claim." *E.I. du Pont & Co. v. Phillips Petroleum Co.*, 849 F.2d 1430, 1433, 7 USPQ2d 1129, 1131 (Fed. Cir. 1988).

"The patent document which grants the patentee a right to exclude others and hence bestows on the owner the power to license, consists of two primary parts: (1) a written description of the invention, which may ... include drawings, called the 'specification,' enabling those skilled in the art to practice the invention, and (2) claims which define or delimit the scope of the legal protection which the government grant gives the patent owner, the patent 'monopoly.' " *General Foods Corp. v. Studiengesellschaft Kohle mbH*, 972 F.2d 1272, 1274, 23 USPQ2d 1839, 1840 (Fed. Cir. 1992) (Rich, J.).

spectrum of distinctiveness [trademark]
See TRADEMARK.

split [copyright–entertainment law] In the distribution of motion pictures for theater exhibition, splits are agreements among exhibitors to divide a normally competitive market by allocating certain motion pictures to particular exhibitors and prohibiting bidding for licensing rights to those films.

Courts have found that split agreements can be viewed as competitor combinations, which are horizontal restraints on competition illegal per se under Sherman Act §1. See *Harkins Amusement Enters., Inc. v. General Cinema Corp.*, 850 F.2d 477 (9th Cir. 1988); *Movie 1+2 v. United Artists Communications, Inc.,* 909 F.2d 1245 (9th Cir. 1990).

SSO [computer–copyright] An abbreviation for STRUCTURE, SEQUENCE, AND ORGANIZATION.

staple [patent] A product that is suitable for substantial use in ways other than to infringe a patent. On the other hand, a "nonstaple" is a product that is not suitable for substantial use in any other way than to infringe the patent. The selling of a nonstaple may trigger liability for CONTRIBUTORY PATENT INFRINGEMENT.

Staples and Contributory Infringement. Contributory infringement of a patent is the act of knowingly selling a nonstaple article specially made or adapted for use as part of a patented combination or for use in practicing a patented process.

• *Example*: The sale of salt to persons who use it to directly infringe a method patent by use in a canning machine cannot be contributory infringement because salt is suitable for substantial noninfringing uses. Salt is a staple. But the sale of the chemical propanil to farmers, knowing that they will apply it to their crops in accordance with a method patent owned by Rohm & Haas was contributory infringement because propanil had no known commercial use other than in the patented process. Propanil was a nonstaple. See *Dawson Chem. Co. v. Rohm and Haas Co.,* 448 U.S. 176, 184, 206 USPQ 385, 391 (1980) (Propanil "is a 'nonstaple' article, that is, one that has no commercial use except in connection with [Rohm & Haas'] patented invention.").

See CONTRIBUTORY PATENT INFRINGEMENT.

• *Statutory Reference*: 35 U.S.C. §271(c): "Whoever offers to sell or sells within the United States or imports into the United States a component of a patented machine, manufacture, combination or composition, or a material or apparatus for use in practicing a patented process, constituting a material part of the invention, knowing the same to be especially made or especially adapted for use in an infringement of such patent, and not a staple article or commodity of commerce suitable for substantial noninfringing use, shall be liable as a contributory infringer" (as of Jan. 1, 1996).

• *Case References*:

"We follow the practice of the Court of Appeals and the parties by using the term 'nonstaple' throughout this opinion to refer to a component as defined in 35 U.S.C. §271(c), the unlicensed sale of which would constitute contributory infringement. A 'staple' component is one that does not fit this definition. We recognize that the terms 'staple' and 'nonstaple' have not always been defined precisely in this fashion.... [T]he staple-nonstaple distinction ... ensures that the patentee's right to prevent others from contributorily infringing his patent affects only the market for the invention itself." *Dawson Chem. Co. v. Rohm & Haas Co.,* 448 U.S. 176, 186 n.6, and 220, 206 USPQ 385, 392 n.6, and 406 (1980).

"Unless a commodity 'has no use except through practice of the patented method,' [*Dawson Chem. Co., supra*], the patentee has no right to claim that its distribution constitutes contributory infringement. 'To form the basis for contributory infringement the item must almost be uniquely suited as a component of the patented invention.' P. Rosenberg, *Patent Law Fundamentals* §17.02[2] (1982). '[A] sale of an article which though adapted to an infringing use is also adapted to other and lawful uses, is not enough to make the seller a contributory infringer. Such a rule would block the wheels of commerce.' Henry v. A.B. Dick Co., 224 U.S. 1, 48 (1912), overruled on other grounds, Motion Picture Patents Co. v. Universal Film Mfg. Co., 243 U.S. 502, 517 (1917)." *Sony Corp. v. Universal City Studios, Inc.,* 464 U.S. 417, 441, 220 USPQ 665, 678 (1984).

stare decisis [general legal] A Latin term literally meaning "to stand by things decided." It refers to the doctrine of precedent, under which judges must follow former judicial decisions when the same factual pattern comes up again. The basic policy of the rule of STARE DECISIS is one of fairness: litigants in similar situations will be judged by the same rules and results as litigants in previous cases.

See RATIO DECIDENDI, DICTUM.

Statement of Use [trademark] A verification, together with proof, that a mark that is the subject of an INTENT-TO-USE application for registration has in fact been used in trade.

Use Must Precede Registration. A U.S. trademark registration will not be granted unless and until the applicant files a verified statement, together with specimens, that it has used the mark in U.S. interstate or foreign commerce. The only exception is that qualified foreign companies are permitted to obtain a U.S. registration merely upon stating an intent to use without ever actually using or proving use in the United States. Proof of use is accomplished by filing either an Amendment to Allege Use (AAU) or a Statement of Use (SOU). The difference between these two methods of proving use of the mark is their timing. It is fundamental to U.S. trademark registration practice that use must precede registration. Without use, there is no "trademark" to be recorded on the federal register of marks. The "use" necessary is use in the "ordinary course of trade", not just token use.

Proof of Use. There are two methods for an ITU applicant to offer proof of use of the mark: (1) via an Amendment to Allege Use (AAU) during the pre-approval-for-publication period and (2) via a Statement of Use (SOU) during the post-notice-of-allowance period.

The time gap between approval for publication and issuance of the notice of allowance is known as the "BLACKOUT PERIOD" because during this period neither an SOU nor an AAU can be filed.

Requirements. Required in the Statement of Use is a verified statement that the applicant has used the mark, the dates of first use and first use in commerce, the type of commerce (interstate or import/export), and the mode or manner in which the mark is used. The SOU must include three specimens of the mark as used and the required fee. A Statement of Use is properly filed only when the mark has been used on or in connection with *all* of the goods or services specified in the application unless the applicant requests a division of the application to separate those goods and services on which the mark has been used from those on which it has not yet been used. See DIVISIONAL APPLICATION. Once

an SOU has been timely filed, it is examined, usually by the same examiner who conducted the earlier examination of this application. During this "second stage" examination, the Patent and Trademark Office (PTO) will not issue any requirements or refusals concerning matters that could have or should have been raised during the "first stage" examination unless failure to do so in the first stage examination constituted a "clear error." *Trademark Manual of Examining Procedure* §1105.05(f)(ii) (1993).

Extensions of Time to File SOU. A basic six-month period in which to file an SOU, beginning from the date of the notice of allowance, is automatically available to everyone. Another six months is automatically available upon request to the PTO and upon payment of a fee together with submission of a verified statement of a continued bona fide intention to use. 37 C.F.R. §2.89(a). Thereafter, up to four additional extensions in six-month increments may be obtained upon a sufficient showing of "good cause" to the PTO, together with a fee and a verified statement of a continued bona fide intention to use. Therefore, while the first six-month extension requires no showing beyond a verified statement of a continued bona fide intention to use, the four subsequent six-month extensions are "good cause" extensions. A showing of good cause need only provide general statements identifying the types of efforts the applicant has undertaken and need not state specific facts. The PTO will not require any evidence or explanation in a showing of good cause. *Trademark Manual of Examining Procedure* §1105.05(d)(ii) (1993). The total maximum time available from the original notice of allowance is 36 months.

• *Treatise Reference*: 2 J.T. McCarthy, *Trademarks and Unfair Competition* §19.07[5]–[6] (3d ed. 1995 rev.).

• *Statutory Reference*: Lanham Act §1(d), 15 U.S.C. §1051(d): "(1) Within six months after the date on which the notice of allowance with respect to a mark is issued under section 13(b)(2) to an applicant under subsection (b) of this section, the applicant shall file in the Patent and Trademark Office, together with such number of specimens or facsimiles of the mark as used in commerce as may be required by the Commissioner and payment of the prescribed fee, a verified statement that the mark is in use in commerce and specifying the date of the applicant's first use of the mark in commerce, those goods or services specified in the notice of allowance on or in connection with which the mark is used in commerce, and the mode or manner in which the mark is used on or in connection with such goods or services...."

• *Rule Reference*: The showing required in a "good cause" extension for filing an SOU must include: "A statement of applicant's ongoing efforts to make use of the mark in commerce on or in connection with each of the goods or services specified in the verified statement of continued bona fide intention to use. ... Those efforts may include, without limitation, product or service research or development, market research, manufacturing activities, promotional activities, steps to acquire distributors, steps to obtain required governmental approval, or other similar activities. In the alternative, a satisfactory explanation for the failure to make such efforts must be submitted." 37 C.F.R. §2.89(d)(2).

state of the art [patent] The condition of the relevant technology at a given time. When used without a temporal modifier, the phrase in popular usage is usually taken to mean the most current or up-to-date technology available, e.g., the advertising phrase "The ALPHA video camera incorporates state of the art electronics."

The phrase uses the word "art" in its older English usage sense of "technology."

See ART, PRIOR ART, SKILL IN THE ART.

• *Usage Examples*:

"At times the only evidence available may be that supplied by testimony of experts as to the state of the art, the character of the improvement, and the probable increase of efficiency or saving of expense...." *Sinclair Ref. Co. v. Jenkins Petroleum Co.*, 289 U.S. 689, 698, 17 USPQ 522, 525 (1933).

"In sum, in determining sufficiency of support it is the state of the art in 1953 and level of skill in the art at that time that is critical." *U.S. Steel Corp. v. Phillips Petroleum Co.*, 865 F.2d

1247, 1252, 9 USPQ2d 1461, 1465 (Fed. Cir. 1989).

"The district court stated: 'Until the time of the claimed invention, store-cut [window] shades were the state of the art.' " *Newell Cos. Inc. v. Kenney Mfg. Co.*, 864 F.2d 757, 783, 9 USPQ2d 1417, 1438 (Fed. Cir. 1988) (Newman, J., dissenting).

"In actions involving the validity or infringement of a patent the party asserting invalidity or noninfringement shall give notice ... to the adverse party ... of [information identifying] any patent [and] of any publication to be relied upon as anticipation of the patent ... or, ... as showing the state of the art...." 35 U.S.C. §282.

statute of limitations [patent–trademark–copyright] A statute declaring that no lawsuit can be validly maintained on a certain type of case unless the suit is filed within a specified period of years after the right to sue originated.

See LACHES.

1. Patent Statute. One cannot recover damages for any infringement committed more than six years before the filing of a complaint. 35 U.S.C. §286. This simply restricts the extent to which a patentee can recover prefiling damages: it does not bar an infringement suit altogether.

Not a "Statute of Limitations." The Court of Appeals for the Federal Circuit has held that §286 is not, strictly speaking, a "statute of limitations" that bars the bringing of a lawsuit. Rather, its only effect is to prevent the recovery of damages for any infringement committed more than six years prior to the filing of the complaint. "In the application of §286, one starts from the filing of a complaint or counterclaim and counts *backward* to determine the date before which infringing *acts* cannot give rise to a right to recover damages." *Standard Oil Co. v. Nippon Shokubai Kagaku Kogyo Co.*, 754 F.2d 345, 348, 224 USPQ 863 (Fed. Cir. 1985). The limitation of §286 restricts the period for which a patentee can recover presuit damages but places no other limitation on the filing of an infringement suit during the 17-year term of a patent. *Leinoff v. Louis Milona & Sons, Inc.*, 726

F.2d 734, 741, 220 USPQ 845, 850 (Fed. Cir. 1984).

Presumption of Laches Upon a Six-Year Delay. A presumption of laches arises in a patent infringement action when the patentee delays bringing suit for more than six years after the date that the patentee knew or should have known of the alleged infringer's activity. The six-year period is "borrowed" from the six-year patent statute of 35 U.S.C. §286. *Aukerman Co. v. Chaides Constr. Co.*, 960 F.2d 1020, 1034–35, 22 USPQ 2d 1321, 1329–30 (Fed. Cir. 1992). This presumption has the effect of shifting the burden of going forward with the evidence to the patentee. However, the burden of persuasion on the issue of laches remains with the defendant.

See LACHES.

• *Statutory Reference*: 35 U.S.C. §286: "Except as otherwise provided by law, no recovery shall be had for any infringement committed more than six years prior to the filing of the complaint or counterclaim for infringement in the action...."

2. Trademark Statute of Limitations. The federal Lanham Trademark Act has no statute of limitations but vests the courts with the power to grant injunctions and award profits and damages according to "the principles of equity." Lanham Act §§34–35, 15 U.S.C. §§1116–17. The courts have held that the appropriate statute of limitations for such federal claims is the state statute of limitations for analogous types of cases. The appropriate state statute is the one that best effectuates the federal policy in issue. See, e.g., *Fox Chem. Co. v. Amsoil, Inc.*, 445 F. Supp. 1355 (D. Minn. 1978) (Lanham Act §43(a) false advertising claim is governed by Minnesota six-year statute covering statutory liability); *PepsiCo., Inc. v. Dunlop Tire & Rubber Corp.*, 578 F. Supp. 196, 223 USPQ 21 (S.D.N.Y. 1984) (Lanham Act §43(a) false advertising claim is governed by New York six-year statute for fraud suits); *Johannsen v. Brown*, 797 F. Supp. 835, 25 USPQ2d 1227 (D. Or. 1992) (relevant statute for Lanham Act §43(a) count for false attribution of authorship is the Oregon two-year statute for claims of fraud.); *Official Airline Guides Inc. v. Goss*, 6 F.3d 1385, 28 USPQ2d 1641 (9th Cir. 1993) (relevant statute for Lanham Act §38 claim for fraud in registration is the Oregon two-year statute, which begins to run on the date of the alleged fraud).

• *Treatise Reference*: 4 J.T. McCarthy, *Trademarks and Unfair Competition* §31.11[1] (3d ed. 1995 rev.).

• *Restatement Reference*: "The role of statutes of limitations in trademark infringement actions remains uncertain. There is general agreement that it is the doctrine of laches rather than the statute of limitations that normally governs the availability of injunctive relief since infringement is typically a continuing wrong. A few cases indicate that the statute of limitations may bar claims for monetary relief with respect to damages incurred outside the statutory period." *Restatement (Third) of Unfair Competition* §31, comment a (1995).

3. Copyright Statute of Limitations. There is a three-year statute of limitations for the bringing of both civil and criminal copyright infringement cases. 17 U.S.C. §507. Many courts hold that when infringement has continued over a period of years, the copyright owner is limited to damages only for acts occurring within the three-year period preceding the filing of the lawsuit. *Roley v. New World Pictures, Ltd.*, 9 F.3d 479, 481, 30 USPQ2d 1654, 1656 (9th Cir. 1994). But a split of authority exists, for it has also been held that if one of the acts of infringement occurred within the three-year period, the copyright owner can reach back further than three years and recover damages for the entire course of the continuing conduct. *Taylor v. Meirick*, 712 F.2d 1112, 1118, 219 USPQ 420, 423 (7th Cir. 1983).

• *Case References*:

"[Plaintiff] argues that so long as any allegedly infringing conduct occurs within the three years preceding the filing of the action, the plaintiff may reach back and sue for damages or other relief for all allegedly infringing acts.... The district court rejected the application of this theory. We do so as well.... [T]he prevailing view [is] that the statute bars recovery on any claim for damages that accrued more than three

413

years before commencement of suit.... [W]e adopt this view." *Roley v. New World Pictures, Ltd.*, 9 F.3d 479, 481, 30 USPQ2d 1654, 1656 (9th Cir. 1994).

"When the final act of an unlawful course of conduct occurs within the statutory period, [the] purposes [of a statute of limitations] are adequately served, in balance with the plaintiff's interest in not having to bring successive suits, by requiring the plaintiff to sue within the statutory period but letting him reach back and get damages for the entire duration of the alleged violation." *Taylor v. Meirick*, 712 F.2d 1112, 1119, 219 USPQ 420, 423 (7th Cir. 1983).

• *Treatise References*: 3 *Nimmer on Copyright* §12.05 (1994 rev.); 2 P. Goldstein, *Copyright* §9.1 (1989); Patry, *Copyright Law and Practice* 1180 (1994).

statutory damages [copyright] A special monetary award that can be granted by a court for copyright infringement in an amount decided by the court within minimum and maximum limits set by the Copyright Act. Similar damages were available under the 1909 Copyright Act and were known as "in lieu" damages. The theory is that in many cases of proven copyright infringement, the copyright owner is damaged but in a manner and amount not readily susceptible of proof. Therefore, copyright owners may elect to rely on the discretion of the court to award a fair amount within the statutory limits.

Election of Remedies. At any time prior to final judgment in a case, the copyright owner may elect to recover, instead of actual damages and profits, an award of statutory damages for all infringements involved in the lawsuit. 17 U.S.C. §504(c)(1).

Statutory Limits. The Berne Convention Implementation Act (BCIA) doubled the maximum and minimum amounts of statutory damages for causes of action for infringement arising after March 1, 1989. For claims arising after that date, the court can award statutory damages of from $500 to $20,000 for most cases of copyright infringement. 17 U.S.C. §504(c)(1). If the copyright owner proves that the infringement was committed "willfully," the court has the

power to award statutory damages of up to $100,000. On the other hand, if the infringer proves that it was not aware and had no reason to believe that its acts constituted copyright infringement, the court can award statutory damages as low as $200.

Single and Multiple Statutory Limits. Copyright Act §504(c) gives the copyright owner the election to seek statutory damages "for all infringements involved in the action, with respect to any one work, for which any one infringer is liable individually, or for which any two or more infringers are liable jointly and severally." The maximum and minimum amounts apply to each copyrighted work that was infringed. For this purpose, all parts of a COMPILATION or a DERIVATIVE WORK constitute one "work." 17 U.S.C. §504(c)(1). Where the suit involves infringement of more than one separate and independent work, at least the minimum statutory damages for each work must be awarded. But only single statutory limits are applicable for each copyrighted work infringed, regardless of how many times a defendant has infringed or how many copies the infringer has produced. One does not multiply the minimum and maximum limits by the number of infringing copies. For infringement of a single copyrighted work by a single infringer, the statutory ceiling and floor dollar limits apply, no matter how many acts of infringement are involved in the lawsuit, and regardless of whether the acts were separate, isolated, or occurred in a related series. H.R. Rep. No. 94-1476, 94th Cong., 2d Sess. 162 (1976). The ceiling and floor dollar limitations are multiplied if separate works or separately liable infringers are involved in one lawsuit.

Innocence and Belief of Fair Use. For claims arising after March 1, 1989, the BCIA provides that an infringer cannot claim a defense of innocent infringement in mitigation of damages if proper notice of copyright appears on published copies or phonorecords of the work to which the infringer had access. 17 U.S.C. §§401(d), 402(d). The court has discretion to refuse to award any statutory damages if an infringer had a reasonable belief that the use made was a FAIR USE under Copyright Act §107, but only if the infringer was an employee of a nonprofit institution such as a school or library who infringed within the scope of employment or was a public broadcasting company. 17 U.S.C. §504(c)(2).

Registration. Under Copyright Act §412, a court has no discretion whatever to award statutory damages or ATTORNEY FEES unless the work was registered prior to the time that the defendant commenced the infringing act. The object of this provision is to encourage the early registration of claims to copyright. As to infringing acts that begin very soon after first publication of a work, the copyright owner is given a grace period of three months within which to register without losing these remedies. Even if registration does not occur within the three-month period after first publication, these remedies are available so long as registration precedes the commencement of infringement.

Judge or Jury. There is a split of authority as to whether the awarding of statutory damages is for the judge or for the jury.

• *Treatise Reference*: 3 *Nimmer on Copyright* §14.04 (1994 rev.); 2 P. Goldstein, *Copyright* §12.2 (1989); M. Leaffer, *Understanding Copyright* §9.13 (1989); 1 N. Boorstyn, *Copyright* §13.05 (2d ed. 1994); W. Patry, *Copyright Law and Practice* 1169 (1994).

• *Case References*:
"The [district] court has wide discretion in determining the amount of statutory damages to be awarded, constrained only by the specified maxima and minima. *L.A. Westermann Co. v. Dispatch Printing Co.*, 249 U.S. 100 (1919). The award will be overturned only for abuse of discretion.... The district court awarded for each of the six infringed songs the maximum damages permissible, in the absence of a specific finding of willfulness. The trial court is in a better position than we are to determine the appropriate damages. We affirm that decision." *Harris v. Emus Records Corp.*, 734 F.2d 1329, 1335, 222 USPQ 466, 470 (9th Cir. 1984).

"We have held that for the purpose of awarding enhanced statutory damages under §504(c)(2), an infringement is 'willful' if the defendant had 'knowledge that its actions constitute an infringement.' ... While an infringement may not be willful when a party, despite warnings to the contrary, 'reasonably and in good faith believes' that its conduct is innocent, ... this 'analysis is subject to the corollary that reckless disregard of the copyright holder's rights (rather than actual knowledge of infringement) suffices to warrant award of the enhanced damages.' " *N.A.S. Import Corp. v. Chenson Enters. Inc.*, 968 F.2d 250, 252, 23 USPQ2d 1387, 1388–89 (2d Cir. 1992) (reversing and remanding district court finding that the infringement was not willful; court of appeals said it was likely that defendant retailer knew that handbags with a copyrighted buckle design that it sold were counterfeit).

statutory disclaimer [patent]
See DISCLAIMER.

statutory invention registration [patent]
A patent-like document by which an inventor may officially and affirmatively put the invention into the public domain for defensive purposes.

A Defensive "Patent." A statutory invention registration (SIR) consists of a complete application for a patent together with a waiver of enforcement of patent rights in the form prescribed by the Patent and Trademark Office (PTO). Such a procedure is available to those inventors who do not desire patent rights in order to exclude others but want to be free from the claims of others to the same invention. This is accomplished through the SIR, which formally injects the invention into the public domain by disclosing the invention in a patent-like document available to all. While usually used by the federal government for inventions resulting from work at federal research agencies, the SIR is available to anyone.

Created in 1985. The SIR procedure became effective in 1985 as a result of statutory authorization in 35 U.S.C. §157. Federal regulations spell out the details of implementation in 37 C.F.R. §§1.293–97 (1985). The SIR replaced the previous "defensive publication program" that had been in use to serve the same purpose.

Characteristics of a SIR. A SIR is not a patent. It has the DISCLOSURE and defensive attributes of a patent but it has none of the rights to exclude embodied in a patent. A SIR is treated the same as a U.S. patent for all defensive purposes. A SIR is PRIOR ART, and the filing date of a SIR constitutes a CONSTRUCTIVE REDUCTION TO PRACTICE of the disclosed invention. SIRs are classified, cross-referenced, and placed in PTO search files; disseminated to foreign patent offices; and stored in PTO computer tapes. A published SIR is a fully viable publication for defensive purposes, usable as a prior art reference in the same manner as a patent.

Mismarking as "Patented." Because a SIR is not a "patented invention" for purposes of marking, the use of markings such as "patented" or "patent pending" on products or in advertising constitutes MISMARKING.

- *Statutory Reference*: 35 U.S.C. §157.

- *Rule Reference*: "An applicant for an original patent may request, at any time during the pendency of applicant's pending complete application, that the specification and drawings be published as a statutory invention registration...." 37 C.F.R. §1.293(a).

store receiver exemption [copyright]
See AIKEN EXEMPTION.

strength of mark [trademark] The power of a trademark or service mark to be recognized as an identifying symbol in the marketplace.

The Stronger the Mark, The Greater the Protection Given to It. The stronger a mark in the consciousness of potential customers, the greater the scope of protection the mark is given over the three possible differences that may exist between an alleged infringement and the allegedly infringed mark: (1) differences in appearance and format; (2) differences in the line of business of product and service; and (3) differences in territorial usage. To be confused, a buyer must be looking for something—in a case alleging traditional likely confusion, that something is the mark of the senior user. The stronger that mark, the more probable that there is an infringement. For example, while a junior user's use of CODAC on camera tripods could well cause confusion with the famous and strong mark KODAK, the mark IPEC on the same product may not infringe the obscure,

little-used, and little-known mark EPEK for batteries used for camera flash units.

Two-Prong Test of Strength. Under the "two-prong test," the strength of a mark is determined by weighing two factors:

(1) Conceptual Strength: The placement of the mark on the spectrum of distinctiveness. This can be called the "conceptual" strength of the mark in that it evaluates the inherent distinctiveness of the mark. On the spectrum of distinctiveness, a FANCIFUL or ARBITRARY term is relatively stronger than a DESCRIPTIVE term.

(2) Commercial Strength: The degree of marketplace recognition of the mark. This can be called the "commercial" strength of the mark. Unlike the first prong, which looks to potential, this prong focuses on the actual power of identification that the term has in the marketplace at the time registration is sought or at the time the mark is asserted in litigation to prevent a junior user's use.

Third-Party Uses. The greater the number of similar marks used on similar goods and services, the less distinctive and strong is any one of those marks. A mark hemmed in on all sides by similar marks on similar goods cannot be very distinctive. In such a "crowded" field of similar marks, each member of the crowd is relatively weak in its ability to prevent use by others in the crowd. Customers will not likely be confused between any two of the crowd and may have learned to carefully pick out one from the other. When many similar marks coexist for years, the public learns to differentiate one from the other.

Crowded Field of Marks. For example, many different companies use stripe design marks on sports shoes. This is a "crowded" field of marks and any one design mark is entitled to only a very narrow scope of exclusive rights as a trademark. *In re Lucky Co.*, 209 USPQ 422 (T.T.A.B. 1980). Similarly, marks used to identify beauty pageants are a "crowded" field of similar marks consisting of a courtesy title and a geographic term, such as Miss U.S.A., Miss America, Mrs. America, Miss World, etc. In such a market, MRS. OF THE WORLD is not so close to the senior user's MISS WORLD as to be likely to cause confusion. *Miss World (UK) Ltd. v. Mrs. Am. Pageants Inc.*, 856 F.2d 1445, 8 USPQ2d

1237 (9th Cir. 1988). See *General Mills Inc. v. Health Valley Foods*, 24 USPQ2d 1270, 1277 (T.T.A.B. 1992) (The field of "FIBER" composite marks for foods is crowded, such that there is no likely confusion between FIBER ONE and FIBER 7 FLAKES both for breakfast cereals high in fiber.).

Limits to Third-Party Evidence. Evidence of third-party use in wholly unrelated markets has little if any relevance. *Eclipse Assocs. Ltd. v. Data Gen. Corp.*, 894 F.2d 1114, 13 USPQ2d 1885 (9th Cir. 1990). The mere citation of third-party registration alone is not proof of third-party use for the purpose of showing a crowded field and relative weakness of a mark. *In re Clorox Co.*, 578 F.2d 305, 198 USPQ 337 (C.C.P.A. 1978) (Markey, C.J., specially concurring).

• *Treatise Reference*: 1 J.T. McCarthy, *Trademarks and Unfair Competition* §§11.24–.26 (3d ed. 1995 rev.).

• *Case Reference*: "The distinctiveness of a trademark determines its relative strength or weakness. In other words, the 'strength' of a mark denotes 'its tendency to identify the goods sold under the mark as emanating from a particular ... source.' ... To assess the strength of a mark, trademarks are generally categorized, in ascending degree of distinctiveness, as generic, descriptive, suggestive or arbitrary. Although this classification system is a helpful tool in conceptualizing this somewhat amorphous subject, it is not determinative, for the strength of a mark 'depends ultimately on its distinctiveness or its "origin-indicating" quality in the eyes of the purchasing public.' " *Plus Prods. v. Plus Discount Foods, Inc.*, 722 F.2d 999, 1005, 222 USPQ 373, 378 (2d Cir. 1983).

• *Restatement Reference*: "The distinctiveness or 'strength' of a mark measures its capacity to indicate the source of the goods or services with which it is used. The greater the distinctiveness of the mark, the greater the likelihood that prospective purchasers will associate the same or a similar designation found on other goods, services or businesses with the prior user. 'Strong' marks that have a high degree of distinctiveness are thus protected against the use of similar marks on a wider range of goods or services than are 'weak' designations that have less distinctiveness or market recognition." *Restatement (Third) of Unfair Competition* §21, comment i (1995).

structure, sequence, and organization

[computer–copyright] Those elements of a computer program beyond the literal OBJECT CODE and SOURCE CODE that some courts will protect from copying under the copyright laws. However, only if the overall structure, sequence, and organization of a particular program can be classified as EXPRESSION rather than an IDEA will it be copyrightable. Abbreviation: SSO.

Origin of the Term. In a controversial decision, the Court of Appeals for the Third Circuit held that the copyrightable "expression" in a computer program can include all aspects of the program that are not necessary to the basic purpose or function of the program. The court found that copyright protection in a computer program extends beyond just copying of the source code or object code to other, more general aspects of the program: "The question therefore arises whether mere similarity in the overall structure of programs can be the basis for a copyright infringement, or, put differently, whether a program's copyright protection covers the structure of the program or only the program's literal elements, i.e., its source and object codes.... By analogy to other literary works, it would thus appear that the copyrights of computer programs can be infringed even absent copying of the literal elements of the program.... We hold that ... copyright protection of computer programs may extend beyond the programs' literal code to their structure, sequence, and organization...." *Whelan Assocs. Inc. v. Jaslow Dental Lab.*, 797 F.2d 1222, 1234, 1248, 230 USPQ 481, 488–89, 500 (3d Cir. 1986). More recent decisions have rejected the "SSO" approach in favor of a "filtration" analysis under which nonprotectable aspects of the copyrighted program are filtered out before comparison with the accused program. See, e.g., *Computer Assocs. Int'l Inc. v. Altai Inc.*, 982 F.2d 693, 706, 23 USPQ2d 1241, 1252–53 (2d Cir. 1992).

See COMPUTER PROGRAM, LOOK AND FEEL, INFRINGEMENT OF COPYRIGHT, COPIES.

• *Case References*:

"A computer program is made up of several different components, including the source and object code, the structure, sequence and/or organization of the program, the user interface, and the function, or purpose of the program.... Whether the nonliteral components of a program, including the structure, sequence and organization and user interface, are protected depends on whether, on the particular facts of each case, the component in question qualifies as an expression of an idea, or an idea itself." *Johnson Controls Inc. v. Phoenix Control Sys. Inc.*, 886 F.2d 1173, 1175, 12 USPQ2d 1566, 1568–69 (9th Cir. 1989) (affirming preliminary injunction grounded on finding that the structure, sequence, and organization of plaintiff's program was protected expression and was copied). But compare *Brown Bag Software v. Semantec Corp.*, 960 F.2d 1465, 22 USPQ2d 1429 (9th Cir. 1992).

"*Whelan* has fared even more poorly in the academic community, where its standard for distinguishing idea from expression has been widely criticized for being conceptually overbroad.... Accordingly, we think that [the district court judge] wisely declined to follow *Whelan*.... We think that *Whelan's* approach to separating idea from expression in computer programs relies too heavily on metaphysical distinctions and does not place enough emphasis on practical considerations." *Computer Assocs. Int'l Inc. v. Altai Inc.*, 982 F.2d 693, 706, 23 USPQ2d 1241, 1252 (2d Cir. 1992) (using a "filtration" analysis).

• *Treatise References*: 3 *Nimmer on Copyright* §13.03[A][1][d] (1994 rev.); 2 P. Goldstein, *Copyright* §8.5.1.2 (1989); 1 N. Boorstyn, *Copyright* §11.06 (2d ed. 1994); W. Patry, *Copyright Law and Practice* 213 (1994).

• *Commentary References*:

"In *Whelan* the Third Circuit had to decide whether there can be 'substantial similarity' of computer programs under the copyright law without quantitatively significant line-for-line identity, when the only similarity shown is similarity in SSO.... As the Third Circuit acknowledged, life would be simpler (for judges, and for lawyers advising clients) if we needed to look only at the literal text of a program to determine whether there is substantial similarity. However, that has never been the law." Goldberg & Burleigh, *Copyright Protection for Computer Programs: Is the Sky Falling?* 17 AIPLA Q. J. 294, 300–04 (1989).

"In attempting to save the software industry from underprotection, the *Whelan* court inadvertently thrust it into overprotection, and contravened the explicit intent of Congress. The *Whelan* approach would treat as 'expression' every discretionary choice made during the design phase of program development, as though Congress had adopted the proposed amendments to section 102(b) that it and CONTU had, in fact, rejected." Samuelson, Davis, Kapor & Reichman, *A Manifesto Concerning the Legal Protection of Computer Programs*, 94 Colum. L. Rev. 2308, 1359 (1994).

style and grade designations [trademark]
See DESCRIPTIVE MARK.

submarine patent [patent] A patent that issues after its application has been secretly pending for many years while an industry matures under the assumption that no basic patent will issue. This type of patent is called a submarine patent because the patent application remains secretly submerged in the Patent and Trademark Office (PTO) for many years and then comes to the surface upon issuance, when its owner can "torpedo" an unsuspecting industry by threatening infringement suits and demanding royalties.

Before the 1995 change of the patent term to 20 years from the date of filing, a U.S. patent on an invention had a duration of 17 years from the grant of the patent. See DURATION. Because the 17-year clock did not begin running until the Patent Office determined that the inventor had met all the necessary requirements and formally "issued" the patent, the term could be extended by putting off the date of issuance. Delays might be caused by the filing of CONTINUATION or DIVISIONAL APPLICATIONS by the applicant or by requests made by the patent examiner. Occasionally, a patent remains pending for a remarkably long time. For example, one patent application was originally filed in 1954 and did not issue until 1994, a period of almost 40 years from filing to issuance. See 49 Pat. Trademark & Copyright J. 225, 226 (BNA) (Jan. 5, 1995).

The patent application process is kept secret. Therefore, industries do not know of applications during their pendency and may invest heavily in products thought to be in the public domain.

See PATENT PENDING, DURATION, PUBLICATION OF PENDING PATENT APPLICATION.

• *Commentary Reference*: Submarine patents are "those that hide unseen beneath the PTO 'patent pending' ocean and, after an industry sets sail unaware of the proprietary rights claims, surface with torpedoes ready to fire." D. Chisum, *The Harmonization of International Patent Law, Introduction*, 26 J. Marshall L. Rev. 437, 445 (1993).

subconscious infringement [copyright]

See UNCONSCIOUS INFRINGEMENT.

substantially [patent] A modifier often used in patent claims to introduce some degree of flexibility in determining LITERAL INFRINGEMENT of the claim. For example, using in a patent claim the phrase "X is substantially equal to A" rather than "X is equal to A" broadens the scope of the claim so as to encompass structures other than those in which X is absolutely identical to A in the ACCUSED DEVICE.

"Substantially" Broadens a Patent Claim. It is clear that introduction of the term "substantially" broadens the scope of a patent claim. For example, where Patent Code §305 prohibits enlarging the scope of a claim in a REEXAMINATION proceeding, it is not permissible to amend a claim by introducing the term "substantially." In one case, the amended claim changed the term "rounded bottom wall" to "substantially rounded bottom wall." Because "substantially rounded" encompasses more than simply "rounded" bottom walls, it covers structures not covered by the previous claim, impermissibly enlarging the claim as contrary to Patent Code

§305. *Ex parte Neuwirth*, 220 USPQ 71 (Bd. Pat. App. & Int'f. 1985).

• *Treatise Reference*: 2 P. Rosenberg, *Patent Law Fundamentals* §14.06[5][a] (1994 rev.); 2 D. Chisum, *Patents* §8.03 (1994 rev.).

• *Case Reference*: "The term 'substantially' in this element of the claim is one commonly used in patents to prevent the avoidance of literal infringement by minor changes which do not themselves cause a loss of the benefit of the invention.... Indeed, there is authority for the proposition that its presence should always be implied in every claim, even when not introduced. *Musher Foundation, Inc. v. Alba Trading Co., Inc.*, 150 F.2d 885, 889, 66 USPQ 183, 186–87 (2d Cir. 1945)." *National Research Dev. Corp. v. Great Lakes Carbon Corp.*, 188 USPQ 327, 333 (D. Del. 1975).

• *Example*: Nist invented and patented a system of double concave-shaped wood cradles and wooden spacer blocks for carrying long lengths of oil pipe during shipping to the Alaskan North Slope oil fields without bends or dents in transit. One portion of a key claim of the patent maintained as a limitation that the wooden spacer blocks were "of a height substantially equal to or greater than" the diameter of the oil pipes. The spacer blocks in the ACCUSED DEVICE were slightly shorter in height than the diameter of the oil pipes that they separated. The district court found that accused spacer blocks one sixteenth of an inch shorter than the diameter of a pipe was an infringement, but made no finding as to different blocks one quarter of an inch shorter. The Court of Appeals for the Federal Circuit affirmed the finding of infringement as to the one-sixteenth inch shorter blocks and remanded for consideration of the one-fourth inch shorter blocks. "Since 'substantially equal to' embraces 'slightly less than,' the district court's finding that [defendant's] 'slightly shorter' spacer blocks *were* 'substantially equal to' the pipe diameter is a finding of literal infringement which is not clearly erroneous.... The fact that a spacer block one-sixteenth of an inch less than a pipe diameter infringes a claim does not necessarily indicate that a spacer block one-quarter of an inch less than a pipe diameter also infringes that claim. There is a new literal infringement issue to decide: are spacer blocks one-quarter of an inch less than the diameter of the separated pipes 'substantially equal to' the diameter of those separated pipes? ... Since the claims issued for a [dimension] 'substantially equal to' the pipes' diameter, we recognize that some leeway is appropriate in determining literal infringement." *Seattle Box Co. v. Industrial Crating & Packing Inc.*, 731 F.2d 818, 828–29, 221 USPQ 568, 576 (Fed. Cir. 1984).

substantial similarity [copyright] The degree of resemblance between protected expression in the copyrighted work and the ACCUSED DEVICE that is sufficient to constitute copyright infringement. Exact word-for-word or line-for-line identity does not define the limits of copyright infringement. The courts have chosen the flexible phrase "substantial similarity" to define that level of similarity which will, together with proof of validity and COPYING, constitute copyright infringement.

Substantial Similarity of Expression. The "substantial similarity" that must exist must be similarity of "expression," not merely similarity of ideas or concepts, for copyright law does not protect an idea, concept, system, and the like. 17 U.S.C. §102(b). This is known as the IDEA-EXPRESSION DICHOTOMY. Similarly, stock backgrounds and incidents are not protected from copying under the SCÈNES À FAIRE doctrine.

Not a Statutory Test. The Copyright Act does not attempt to define the degree of similarity required. The statute merely defines an infringer as anyone who violates any of the exclusive rights of copyright. 17 U.S.C. §501(a). The "substantial similarity" test has been developed by the federal courts.

How Much Is Similar, Not How Little. A copier cannot escape a finding of infringement by pointing to those parts of his accused work that were not copied. As Judge Learned Hand remarked in a famous line: "[I]t is enough that substantial parts were lifted; no plagiarist can excuse the wrong by showing how much of his work he did not pirate." *Sheldon v. Metro-Gold-*

wyn Pictures Corp., 81 F.2d 49, 56, 28 USPQ 330, 337 (2d Cir. 1936).

More Than Merely Bring to Mind. "Substantial similarity" means more than that the accused work only serves to bring to mind the copyrighted work. "Stirring one's memory of a copyrighted character is not the same as appearing to be substantially similar to that character, and only the latter is infringement." *Warner Bros. Inc. v. American Broadcasting Cos.*, 720 F.2d 231, 242, 222 USPQ 101, 110 (2d Cir. 1983). To find infringement in works that are merely reminiscent of, or only evoke memories of, the copyrighted work would be tantamount to protection of basic ideas or concepts. Ideas or concepts are not copyrightable.

Nimmer's Two-Part Analysis of Substantial Similarity. Nimmer divided copyright infringement cases into two categories: (1) "fragmented literal similarity"; and (2) "comprehensive nonliteral similarity." 3 *Nimmer on Copyright* §13.03 (1994 rev.). Nimmer's terminology has been accepted and applied in the case law.

(1) The first category of "fragmented literal similarity" covers cases of partial verbatim, word-for-word, or line-for-line virtual identity. How much quantity of material can be taken before there is a "substantial" taking? No abstract rule can be stated other than that one cannot copy matter that constitutes an important part of the plaintiff's work, weighing both quality and quantity. In one instance, the copying of a few words would not be a "substantial" taking, while in another case it could be, especially if the plaintiff's work is concise and terse, such as a slogan or epigram. In cases of literal copying of a relatively small portion of a larger work, the result will often turn on the success of the defendant's invocation of the FAIR USE defense.

(2) The second category of "comprehensive nonliteral similarity" covers cases where there is no literal similarity of any part of the plaintiff's work, but there is a taking of the fundamental structure or pattern of the plaintiff's work. Various words have been used to describe the "thing" that has been copied, e.g., structure, essence, spine, and pattern. In the case of computer software, this has sometimes been called the STRUCTURE, SEQUENCE, AND ORGANIZATION

of the program. Some courts have developed copyright protection for what they call the TO-TAL CONCEPT AND FEEL of a work. In one view, the degree of similarity required moves along a sliding scale: the fewer the number of possible expressions for a particular "idea," the narrower the scope of protection given any one of those expressions. The limiting case is MERGER: when idea and expression completely merge, no copyright protection is given.

Applying the Substantial Similarity Test in the Courtroom. Most courts have used some form of a bifurcated test, asking first if there is copying and second if an audience of reasonable persons will perceive substantial similarities between the accused work and the protected expression of the copyrighted work. 2 P. Goldstein, *Copyright* §7.3 (1989). The Court of Appeals for the Ninth Circuit's version of this two-part test in the 1977 *Krofft* case is the best-known example. *Sid & Marty Krofft Television Prods., Inc. v. McDonald's Corp.,* 562 F.2d 1157, 1164, 196 USPQ 97, 103 (9th Cir. 1977). In *Krofft,* the first question is labeled the "extrinsic" test and asks if there is similarity of ideas. "Analytic dissection" and expert testimony are allowed. The second *Krofft* question is labeled the "intrinsic" test and asks if an "ordinary reasonable person" would perceive a substantial taking of protected expression. At this stage, "analytic dissection and expert testimony are not appropriate." The *Krofft* formulation is criticized by the leading commentators. 2 *Nimmer on Copyright* §13.03[E][3] (1994 rev.); 2 P. Goldstein, *Copyright* §7.3 n.6 (1989). The Ninth Circuit has substantially modified the *Krofft* test, bringing it more in line with the test followed in other circuits. See, e.g., *Shaw v. Lindheim,* 919 F.2d 1353, 15 USPQ2d 1516 (9th Cir. 1990); *Apple Computer Inc. v. Microsoft Corp.,* 35 F.3d 1435, 1443, 32 USPQ2d 1086, 1091–92 (9th Cir. 1994) ("As it has evolved, however, the extrinsic test now objectively considers whether there are substantial similarities in both ideas and expression, whereas the intrinsic test continues to measure expression subjectively.... [W]e use analytic dissection to determine the scope of copyright protection before works are considered 'as a whole.' ").

See IDEA-EXPRESSION DICHOTOMY; TOTAL CONCEPT AND FEEL; LOOK AND FEEL; STRUCTURE, SEQUENCE AND ORGANIZATION.

• *Case References:*

"It is an axiom of copyright law that copyright protects only an author's expression of an idea, not the idea itself.... There is a strong public policy corollary to this axiom permitting all to use freely ideas contained in a copyrightable work, so long as the protected expression itself is not appropriated.... Thus, to the extent the similarities between plaintiff's and defendant's works are confined to ideas and general concepts, these similarities are noninfringing." *Data East USA Inc. v. Epyx Inc.,* 862 F.2d 204, 207–08, 9 USPQ2d 1322, 1325 (9th Cir. 1988).

"It is of course essential to any protection of literary property, ... that the right cannot be limited literally to the text, else a plagiarist would escape by immaterial variations.... But, when the plagiarist does not take out a block in situ, but an abstract of the whole, decision is more troublesome. Upon any work, and especially upon a play, a great number of patterns of increasing generality will fit equally well, as more and more of the incident is left out.... [B]ut there is a point in this series of abstractions where they are no longer protected, since otherwise the playwright could prevent the use of his 'ideas,' to which, apart from their expression, his property is never extended.... Nobody has ever been able to fix that boundary, and nobody ever can.... As respects plays, the controversy chiefly centers upon the characters and sequence of incident, these being the substance.... The only matter common to the two [plays in this case] is a quarrel between a Jewish and an Irish father, the marriage of their children, the birth of grandchildren and a reconciliation.... [W]hile we are as aware as any one that the line, wherever it is drawn, will seem arbitrary, that is no excuse for not drawing it; it is a question such as courts must answer in nearly all cases. Whatever the difficulties a priori, we have no question on which side of the line this case falls. A comedy based upon conflicts between Irish and Jews, into which the marriage of their children enters, is no more susceptible of copyright than the outline of Romeo and

Juliet." Judge Learned Hand in *Nichols v. Universal Pictures Corp.*, 45 F.2d 119, 121–22, 7 USPQ 84, 86–88 (2d Cir. 1930) (This passage states what is known as Learned Hand's "abstractions test.").

• *Treatise References*:

"[I]f because of the camouflage of a different medium, the lay audience loses sight of the similarity, the fact remains that the plaintiff may have suffered a substantial appropriation of the fruits of his labor.... Thus, in this important area the immediate and spontaneous observations of a person untrained in the special requirements and techniques of the play, the novel, the short story, the motion picture, and most especially the computer may fail to note similarities, which, if analyzed and dissected, would be only too apparent." 3 *Nimmer on Copyright* §13.03[E][2] (1994 rev.).

"The court should be able to adapt its test of substantial similarity to the media involved, the variety of copyrightable subject matter, and the fact situation. For example, a single *ordinary observer test* may be all that is needed in less complicated fabric design or popular music cases. For more complicated literary works, experts may play a useful role in determining whether copying has taken place, and in separating protectable and non-protectable aspects of the work." M. Leaffer, *Understanding Copyright* §9.7 (1989).

"Cases often arise in which the defendant's work is similar to, and reduces the audience for, the plaintiff's work, but does not appropriate any protected subject matter from the work. This might occur if defendant's work attracts plaintiff's audience by borrowing a unique, though unprotected, plot device from plaintiff's play; a popular, but unprotected, setting from plaintiff's movie; an engaging, but unprotected, folk theme from plaintiff's musical composition; or an attractive, but common, configuration from plaintiff's fabric design." 2 P. Goldstein, *Copyright* §7.3 (1989).

See also 1 N. Boorstyn, *Copyright* §11.06 et seq. (2d ed. 1994); W. Patry, *Copyright Law and Practice* 556 et seq. (1994).

suggestive mark [trademark] a word, picture, or other symbol that suggests, but does not directly describe, something about the goods or services in connection with which it is used as a mark. A suggestive term is regarded as being inherently distinctive and needs no proof of SECONDARY MEANING for registration or protection in court. For example, GOLIATH for wood pencils suggests but does not directly describe large size, CITIBANK for banking only suggests a modern or urban bank, and GOLDEN DOOR for a health spa suggests but does not directly promise the wonderful effects that may flow from use of its facilities.

See full discussion at DESCRIPTIVE MARK.

summary judgment [general legal] A procedural device that permits a judgment to be granted as to all or part of a case if there is no real contest in the evidence which requires a trial. The judgment is "summary" in the sense that it is direct, prompt, and without delay.

Federal Rule of Civil Procedure 56. Under Rule 56(c) of the Federal Rules of Civil Procedure, summary judgment may be granted "if the pleadings, depositions, answers to interrogatories, and admissions on file, together with the affidavits, if any, show that there is no genuine issue as to any material fact...." The rule in state courts is very similar.

The Supreme Court's 1986 Trilogy of Cases. In a trilogy of cases decided in 1986, the U.S. Supreme Court endorsed the use of the summary judgment procedure, emphasizing that the "summary judgment procedure is properly regarded not as a disfavored procedural shortcut, but rather as an integral part of the Federal Rules as a whole, which are designed to secure the just, speedy and inexpensive determination of every action." *Celotex Corp. v. Catrett*, 477 U.S. 317, 327 (1986). The Supreme Court said that when the defendant moves for summary judgment, the defendant need not necessarily present affirmative evidence to prove the negative but may properly point out where and how there is a "hole" in the evidence produced by the plaintiff in discovery: "that there is an absence of evidence to support the nonmoving party's case." *Celotex*, 477 U.S. at 325. See *Anderson v. Liberty Lobby, Inc.*, 477 U.S. 242 (1986);

Matsushita Elec. Indus. Co. v. Zenith Radio Corp., 475 U.S. 574 (1986).

Patent Cases. "[T]he evidence must be viewed in a light most favorable to the non-movant and all reasonable inferences must be drawn in the nonmovant's favor." *Avia Group v. L.A. Gear Cal. Inc.*, 853 F.2d 1557, 1560, 7 USPQ2d 1548, 1550 (Fed. Cir. 1988). It is an "outmoded" view that summary judgment is not appropriate to determine the issues in a patent validity and infringement dispute. Summary judgment is as appropriate in a patent case as in any other. *Avia Group*, 853 F.2d at 1561, 7 USPQ2d at 1551 (affirming grant of plaintiff's motion for summary judgment of validity and infringement of design patent). See R. Harmon, *Patents and the Federal Circuit* §8.3 (3d ed. 1994).

Trademark Cases. In trademark cases, summary judgment for the defendant is appropriate "if the court is satisfied that the products or marks are so dissimilar that no question of fact [regarding a likelihood of confusion] is presented." *Universal City Studios, Inc. v. Nintendo Co.*, 746 F.2d 112, 116, 223 USPQ 1000, 1003 (2d Cir. 1984) (affirming grant of dismissal of trademark infringement claim). See *Lois Sportswear, U.S.A., Inc. v. Levi Strauss & Co.*, 799 F.2d 867, 230 USPQ 831 (2d Cir. 1986) (affirming summary judgment of infringement of trademark). See 1 J.T. McCarthy, *Trademarks and Unfair Competition* §§32.34–.37 (3d ed. 1995 rev.).

Copyright Cases. Summary judgment is most often used in copyright cases to dismiss without trial a claim of infringement where the only similarity between the two works is unprotected ideas or concepts. E.g., *Warner Bros. Inc. v. American Broadcasting Cos.*, 720 F.2d 231, 244–45, 222 USPQ 101, 108 (2d Cir. 1983). See 2 P. Goldstein, *Copyright* §7.4.2 (1989); 3 *Nimmer on Copyright* §12.10 (1994 rev.).

super 301 [international trade]

See SPECIAL 301.

super station [copyright] A local television station whose signals are rebroadcast, via satellite link, to a large number of homes across the nation via local cable systems.

WTBS in Atlanta, Georgia, is a well-known example of a super station. The possible copyright infringement liability of the intermediate satellite common carriers who provide the link between the broadcast station and local cable systems revolves around the issue of whether the satellite common carriers fall within the PASSIVE CARRIER exemption. See, e.g., *Hubbard Broadcasting, Inc. v. Southern Satellite Sys., Inc.*, 777 F.2d 393, 228 USPQ 102 (8th Cir. 1985).

• *Case Reference*: "WGN is an 'independent' television station in Chicago (that is, it is not affiliated with any of the television networks) and it is also a 'superstation,' meaning that its programs are carried, outside its local area, by cable television systems. To get those programs to the cable systems requires the services of an intermediate carrier such as United Video, a satellite common carrier that plucks broadcast signals off the air, including signals from WGN, and transmits them to cable systems." *WGN Continental Broadcasting Co. v. United Video Inc.*, 693 F.2d 622, 624, 216 USPQ 97, 99 (7th Cir. 1982).

• *Treatise Reference*: W. Patry, *Copyright Law and Practice* 948 (1994) (reporting that as of 1994 there were nine superstations, all telecasting major league baseball games).

supplemental register [trademark] A register of words, symbols, package trade dress, product or container shapes, or slogans that do not yet qualify for registrable trademark status but are capable of achieving trademark status upon the acquisition of SECONDARY MEANING. The supplemental register was originally created to enable domestic firms to register terms in the United States so that they could register abroad in those nations that required ownership of a home registration.

Effect of Supplemental Registration. Placement of a term on the supplemental register confers none of the substantive and procedural benefits of the PRINCIPAL REGISTER. A supplemental registration confers no substantive trademark benefits beyond those at common law. Terms accepted for the supplemental register are not subject to an opposition challenge but are vulnerable to a petition for CANCELLATION. One benefit of placement on the supplemental register is that the registered term is on file in the Patent and Trademark Office (PTO) and can be cited EX PARTE by the PTO against another's later application to register a confusingly similar mark, even on the principal register. *Application of Clorox Co.*, 578 F.2d 305, 198 USPQ 337 (C.C.P.A. 1978). Another benefit is the ability to use the official NOTICE of federal registration with the term.

Types of Terms on the Supplemental Register. The usual type of term registered on the supplemental register is one that is not registrable on the PRINCIPAL REGISTER under Lanham Act §2(e) because it is descriptive, geographically descriptive, or a personal name surname, and has not yet acquired SECONDARY MEANING. Often, when the applicant for the principal register meets with a FINAL REJECTION based on one of the Lanham Act §2(e) bars, the applicant will amend the application to switch it to an application for the supplemental register. 37 C.F.R. §2.75. However, it has been held that registration on the supplemental register is an implied admission that the registered term is not inherently distinctive (e.g., is descriptive) and falls within one of the §2(e) bars. In effect, the supplemental register is a roster of terms that have not yet achieved trademark status but might do so one day. But to be registrable, the term must possess the capability of someday acquiring full trademark status through secondary meaning. Thus, a GENERIC NAME cannot be on the supplemental register, for it has no such capability.

See DESCRIPTIVE MARK, GEOGRAPHICAL MARK, PERSONAL NAME MARK.

Impact of the 1989 Trademark Act Amendments. Under the 1989 Trademark Law Revision Act, a Lanham Act §1(b) INTENT TO USE application is not available for supplemental registration. The 1989 statute eliminated the previous requirement of a one-year period of use prior to supplemental registration. While Lanham Act §27 was amended to provide that supplemental registration does not constitute an admission that the mark has not acquired distinctiveness as of the date of registration, there is nothing in the amendment to preclude supplemental registration from being deemed an admission against interest that the term is not inherently distinctive.

See REGISTRATION OF TRADEMARK, SECONDARY MEANING.

- *Treatise Reference*: 1 J.T. McCarthy, *Trademarks and Unfair Competition* §19.09 (3d ed. 1995 rev.).

- *Statutory References*:

Lanham Act §23(a), 15 U.S.C. §1091(a): "All marks capable of distinguishing applicant's goods or services and not registrable on the principal register herein provided, except those declared to be unregistrable under subsections (1), (b), (c), (d) and (e)(3) of section 2 of this Act, which are in lawful use in commerce by the owner thereof, on or in connection with any goods or services may be registered on the supplemental register upon the payment of the prescribed fee and compliance with the provisions of subsections (1) and (e) of section 1 so far as they are applicable...."

Lanham Act §45, 15 U.S.C. §1127: "The term 'principal register' refers to the register provided for by sections 1 through 22 hereof, and the term 'supplemental register' refers to the register provided by sections 23 through 28 hereof."

supplementary registration [copyright]
A registration made subsequent to the basic application for registration of a claim to copyright in order to correct or amplify the information in a basic registration. 37 C.F.R. §201.5(b). A "correction" is appropriate if the information was incorrect at the time of the original registration. An "amplification" is appropriate either to reflect new facts or to clarify information previously given. A supplementary registration augments but does not supersede the original, basic registration. The basic registration is not expunged or cancelled.

Statutory Power. Pursuant to 17 U.S.C. §408(d), the Register of Copyrights is empowered to "establish, by regulation, formal procedures for the filing of an application for supplementary registration, to correct an error in a copyright registration or to amplify the information given in a registration."

Changes Not Appropriate for Supplementary Registration. Supplementary copyright registration is not appropriate to indicate changes in ownership or licensing of rights in the work or to correct errors in statements or copyright notices on copies of the work or to reflect changes in the content of the work. 37 C.F.R. §201.5(b)(2)(iii).

• *Statutory Reference*: 17 U.S.C. §408(d): "The information contained in a supplementary registration augments but does not supersede that contained in the earlier registration."

• *Rule Reference*: "After a basic registration has been completed, any author or other copyright claimant of the work, or the owner of any exclusive right in the work, or the duly authorized agent of any such author, other claimant, or owner, who wishes to correct or amplify the information given in the basic registration for the work may file an application for supplementary registration." 37 C.F.R. §201.5(b)(1).

suppression [patent] Acts by an inventor to withhold an invention from public knowledge by either (1) deliberately hiding the invention or (2) failing to apply for a patent within a reasonable time after invention. Such conduct can extinguish a first inventor's priority of invention so that a patent is granted to a later rival inventor. Suppression is generally regarded as synonymous with its statutory siblings: ABANDONMENT and CONCEALMENT. Patent Code §102(g) states that one who is the first to complete the invention by CONCEPTION and REDUCTION TO PRACTICE will lose the right of priority and the patent if that inventor thereafter abandons, suppresses, or conceals the invention.

The most common situation by which the first inventor loses out to a second inventor because of suppression is where after reduction to practice by the first inventor, no patent application is filed within a reasonable period and during that interval of inactivity the second inventor enters the scene.

• *Statutory Reference*: 35 U.S.C. §102: "A person shall be entitled to a patent unless— ... (g) before the applicant's invention thereof the invention was made in this country by another

who had not abandoned, suppressed, or concealed it...."

• *Treatise Reference*: 3 D. Chisum, *Patents* §10.08 (1994 rev.).

See case references and examples at CONCEALMENT and ABANDONMENT.

surname mark [trademark]
See PERSONAL NAME MARK.

surrender [patent–trademark]
1. Surrender of a Patent. Upon the grant of a REISSUE of a patent, the original patent is surrendered.

See REISSUE.

• *Statutory References:*
35 U.S.C. §251: "Whenever any patent is, through error without any deceptive intention, deemed wholly or partly inoperative or invalid, by reason of a defective specification or drawing, or by reason of the patentee claiming more or less than he had a right to claim in the patent, the Commissioner shall, on the surrender of such patent and the payment of the fee required by law, reissue the patent for the invention disclosed in the original patent, and in accordance with a new and amended application, for the unexpired part of the term of the original patent...."

35 U.S.C. §252: "The surrender of the original patent shall take effect upon the issue of the reissued patent...."

2. Surrender of a Trademark Registration. The owner of a trademark registration may surrender for cancellation all of a registration, or some of the classes of goods or services covered by the registration.

• *Statutory Reference*: Lanham Act §7(e), 15 U.S.C. §1057(e): "Upon application of the registrant the Commissioner may permit any registration to be surrendered for cancellation...."

• *Rule Reference*: "When there is more than one class in a registration, one or more entire class but less than the total number of classes may be surrendered as to the specified class or classes. Deletion of less than all of the goods or

survey

services in a single class constitutes amendment of registration as to that class." 37 C.F.R. §2.172.

See AMENDMENT OF TRADEMARK REGISTRATION.

survey [trademark] A poll or study of the state of mind of the relevant universe of persons, used as evidence on an issue of fact in a trademark lawsuit.

Issues Provable by Survey Evidence. Surveys as to the state of mind of prospective buyers have been accepted as evidence relevant to several issues in trademark and unfair competition litigation, including the existence of a likelihood of confusion; the existence of secondary meaning; whether a term is viewed as descriptive; whether a term is viewed as a generic name or a trademark; and what message is conveyed by advertising alleged to be false.

Relevant Universe. To be relevant, the survey must be of the relevant "universe" of persons whose attitudes and states of mind are in issue in a particular case. The group of persons surveyed should be neither too broad nor too narrow as compared to the relevant universe of persons. However, where the survey covers a slightly broader or narrower class of persons than would be the perfect target universe, this goes to the weight given the results, not to the admissibility of the survey.

Hearsay Objection. While at one time surveys were sometimes not admitted into evidence because of the hearsay objection, modern decisions, especially under the Federal Rules of Evidence, hold that hearsay is no objection to survey evidence. The results are reports of the states of mind of the persons interviewed which form the basis of the expert opinion of the survey director. *Piper Aircraft Corp. v. Wag-Aero, Inc.*, 741 F.2d 925, 223 USPQ 202 (7th Cir. 1984).

Survey Deficiencies. Survey questions, methodology, and execution are always subject to minute examination at trial, and some flaws may appear. However, technical deficiencies go to the weight to be accorded the survey results, rather than to their very admissibility as evidence. *Jellibeans, Inc. v. Skating Clubs of Ga., Inc.*, 716 F.2d 833, 222 USPQ 10 (11th Cir.

1983); *E. & J. Gallo Winery v. Gallo Cattle Co.*, 967 F.2d 1280, 1292, 21 USPQ2d 1824, 1833 (9th Cir. 1992) ("[I]t is routine to admit a relevant survey; any technical unreliability goes to weight, not admissibility."). Survey questions should be neither slanted nor misleading. Survey methodology, execution, and statistical compilation should comport with the professional standards of the trade.

Intercept Survey. A "probability" survey is one in which the results are statistically capable of being mathematically extrapolated to the universe of persons at large. A "mall intercept" or "random intercept" survey does not attempt to select persons according to pure probability analysis but selects or intercepts persons at certain public places. Such mall intercept survey results have been accepted as reliable evidence in the courts, especially by the use of Federal Rule of Evidence 703. 4 J.T. McCarthy, *Trademarks and Unfair Competition* §32.48[2][b] (3d ed. 1995 rev.).

• *Treatise Reference*: 4 J.T. McCarthy, *Trademarks and Unfair Competition* §§32.46–.55 (3d ed. 1995 rev.).

swearing back [patent] Making a sworn statement under oath showing that the applicant for patent completed the invention before the effective date of a prior art reference cited against the applicant by the Patent and Trademark Office examiner. That is, to overcome the prior art reference, the inventor is "swearing" under oath in an affidavit that he or she completed the invention in "back" of or prior in time to the effective date of that piece of PRIOR ART. If this affidavit is accepted, then that reference ceases to be prior" art as to this invention. Swearing back is a form of CARRY BACK.

Showing of Prior Invention. The showing in the affidavit must be sufficient to establish (1) REDUCTION TO PRACTICE of the invention prior to the effective date of the reference or (2) CONCEPTION of the invention prior to the effective date of the reference coupled with DUE DILIGENCE from prior to that effective date up to a later actual or constructive reduction to practice. See 37 C.F.R. §1.131(b).

Prior Art Patent. The swearing back procedure is effective as against a reference that is a U.S. patent only if that patent discloses and does not claim the same invention as the swearing inventor. If the U.S. patent does claim the same invention, then the only method of challenging it is through an INTERFERENCE proceeding. See *Manual of Patent Examining Procedure* §715.05 (1993 rev.).

Expanded Venues of Inventive Activity. As a result of legislative changes enacted in 1993 and 1994 in both the NAFTA implementation act and the GATT URUGUAY ROUND AGREEMENTS ACT, there was a substantial increase in the range of locations in which inventive activity would count toward patent priority in the United States. See INTERFERENCE. As a result, Rule 131 was amended as of May 31, 1995, to permit a party to rely on inventive activity not only in the United States, but also in any NAFTA or World Trade Organization country in order to prove a date of invention.

See CARRY BACK.

- *Rule Reference*: "37 C.F.R. §1.131(a)(1): When any claim of an application ... is rejected under 35 U.S.C. §102(a) or (e), or 35 U.S.C. §103 based on a U.S. patent to another which is prior art under 35 U.S.C. §102(a) or (e) and which substantially shows or describes but does not claim the same patentable invention, ... or on reference to a foreign patent or to a printed publication, the inventor of the subject matter of the rejected claim ... may submit an appropriate oath or declaration to overcome the patent or publication. The oath or declaration must include facts showing a completion of the invention in this country or in a NAFTA or WTO member country before the filing date of the application on which the U.S. patent issued, or before the date of the foreign patent, or before the date of the printed publication. When an appropriate oath or declaration is made, the patent or publication cited shall not bar the grant of a patent to the inventor ... unless the date of such patent or printed publication is more than one year prior to the date on which the inventor's ... application was filed in this country. (2) A date of completion of the invention may not be established under this section before Decem-

ber 8, 1993, in a NAFTA country, or before January 1, 1996, in a WTO Member country other than a NAFTA country." 37 C.F.R. §1.131(a) (as amended effective May 31, 1995).

- *Treatise References*: D. Chisum, *Patents* §§3.08[1], 10.03[1][c] (1994); 2 P. Rosenberg, *Patent Law Fundamentals* §§10.02[2], 15.07[1] (1994 rev.).

- *Manual Reference*: "The essential thing to be shown under 37 C.F.R. §1.131 is priority of invention and this may be done by any satisfactory evidence of fact. Facts, not conclusions, must be alleged, and they must be shown by evidence in the form of exhibits accompanying the affidavit or declaration.... A general allegation that the invention was completed prior to the date of the reference is not sufficient." *Manual of Patent Examining Procedure* §715.07 (1994 rev.).

- *Case References*:

"The purpose of filing a 131 affidavit is *not* to demonstrate prior invention per se, but merely to antedate the effective date of the reference.... Although the test for sufficiency of an affidavit under Rule 131(b) parallels that for determining priority of invention in an interference under 35 U.S.C. §102(g), it does not follow that Rule 131 practice is controlled by interference law.... Thus, 'the "conception" and "reduction to practice" which must be established under the rule need not be the same as what is required in the "interference" sense of those terms.'" *In re Eickmeyer*, 602 F.2d 974, 978–79, 202 USPQ 655, 660 (C.C.P.A. 1979).

"Confronted with rejections of claims based in part, if not primarily, on Rogers [article published in a technical society journal], [applicants] attempted to antedate, and thus remove, that reference as prior art, by filing declarations under 37 C.F.R. §1.131 (Rule 131).... [A]s [applicants] have shown no actual reduction to practice of the invention in this country and no constructive reduction prior to the date of Rogers, what Rule 131(b) says they have to show is conception in this country prior to Rogers' date coupled with 'due diligence from said date to ... the filing of the application.' ... [Applicants] would have us treat this case as though it were an interference between them and Rogers. … But Rogers is not an applicant and this is not an interference. … Interferences involve policy questions not present when antedating a reference." *In re Mulder & Wilms*, 716 F.2d 1542, 1543–45, 219 USPQ 189, 192–93 (Fed. Cir. 1982).

sweat of the brow [copyright] A now-superseded doctrine under which a copyright for a factual compilation was a reward for the hard work (sweat of the brow) that went into finding the facts. A subsequent compiler was not entitled to take even factual information from the previous work. The sweat of the brow, or industrious collection doctrine, was criticized for its extension of copyright protection beyond selection and arrangement of a compilation to include the facts themselves. This is contrary to a fundamental rule of copyright law: no one may through copyright obtain an exclusive right to facts or ideas. The doctrine was held by the U.S. Supreme Court to have been abolished by the 1976 revisions to the Copyright Act. *Feist Publications v. Rural Tel. Serv.*, 499 U.S. 340, 18 USPQ2d 1275 (1991).

History of the Doctrine. The classic formulation of the sweat of the brow doctrine was voiced in 1922: "The right to copyright a book upon which one has expended labor in its preparation does not depend upon whether the materials which he has collected consist or not of matters which are publici juris, or whether such materials show literary skills or originality, either in thought or in language, or anything more than industrious collection. The man who goes through the streets of a town and puts down the names of each of the inhabitants, with their occupations and their street number, acquires material of which he is the author. He produces by his labor a meritorious composition, in which he may obtain a copyright. …" *Jeweler's Circular Publishing Co. v. Keystone Publishing Co.*, 281 F. 83, 88 (2d Cir. 1922). As effective in 1978, 17 U.S.C. §102(b) is universally understood to prohibit any copyright in facts. And the addition of §103 in 1978 made clear that copyright in a compilation does not extend to the facts that are collected or arranged. In 1991, the Supreme Court reiterated that origi-

nality, not sweat of the brow, is the touchstone of copyright protection in directories and other fact based compilations. *Feist Publications v. Rural Tel. Serv.*, 499 U.S. 340, 359–60, 18 USPQ2d 1275, 1281 (1991).

See COMPILATION.

• *Case Reference*: "The 'sweat of the brow' doctrine had numerous flaws, the most glaring being that it extended copyright protection in a compilation beyond selection and arrangement—the compiler's original contributions—to the facts themselves…. 'Sweat of the brow' courts thereby eschewed the most fundamental axiom of copyright law—that no one may copyright facts or ideas." *Feist Publications v. Rural Tel. Serv.*, 499 U.S. 340, 359–60, 18 USPQ2d 1275, 1281 (1991).

synchronization license [copyright] A license for the use of a copyrighted musical work in connection with a MOTION PICTURE. "Motion picture" includes both film and video tape. Synchronization licenses are granted by MECHANICAL LICENSING AGENTS such as the HARRY FOX AGENCY.

syndex [copyright]
See SYNDICATED EXCLUSIVITY.

syndicated exclusivity [copyright] Federal Communications Commission (FCC) rules protect a local broadcaster from the importation into its market of distant signals that duplicate signals to which the broadcaster has purchased exclusive rights. Such rules allow the supplier of a syndicated program to agree with a broadcast television station that the station will be the exclusive presenter of the program in its local broadcast area. Thus, a broadcast station with exclusive rights to a syndicated program can forbid any cable television station to import the program into its local broadcast area from a distant station.

History of FCC Syndex Rules. Syndicated exclusivity (syndex) rules were promulgated by the Federal Communications Commission in 1965. After the 1978 revisions to the Copyright Act created a copyright compulsory license for cable broadcasts, the FCC concluded that syndex rules were no longer needed. In 1980 the rules were eliminated. But in 1988 the FCC promulgated new syndex rules after deciding that the 1980 decision was a mistake. The 1988 syndex rules were challenged in court as arbitrary and capricious but were upheld by the court of appeals. *United Video Inc. v. Federal Communications Comm'n*, 890 F.2d 1173, 12 USPQ2d 1964 (D.C. Cir. 1989). The court rejected the argument that FCC syndex rules were contrary to the cable television compulsory licensing system in §111 of the Copyright Act, noting that pursuant to 17 U.S.C. §111(c)(1), "the FCC can affect the copyright liability of cable television companies." The new syndex rules went into effect on January 1, 1990. See Note, *United Video, Inc. v. FCC: Just Another Episode in Syndex Regulation*, 12 Loy. L.A. Ent. L.J. 251 (1992).

See COMPULSORY LICENSING OF COPYRIGHT.

syndication rules [communications]
Restrictions placed upon the three major networks (ABC, CBS, and NBC) by the Federal Communications Commission in order to limit their power by limiting the networks' involvement in supplying television programs other than for their own or affiliated stations. These rules restricted the ability of the networks to sell syndication rights to network-produced programs and limited network purchase of syndication rights to programs purchased from outside producers. These rules are also known as "finsyn" for "financial and syndication" rules.

• *Development and History*. In 1970, the Federal Communications Commission (FCC) issued financial interest and syndication rules designed to limit the power of three major networks. The 1970 rules did not allow the networks to directly sell syndication rights to independent stations to any program produced by the network. The rules also barred the networks from purchasing syndication rights from outside program producers. If a network produced a program, it could sell syndication rights to an independent syndicator. The rules were designed to prevent the three networks from using their network distribution power to secure a dominant role in the production of television programs.

In 1991, the FCC issued revised finsyn rules, which were struck down in *Schurz Communications, Inc. v. FCC*, 982 F.2d 1043 (7th Cir. 1992). See also *Capital Cities/ABC, Inc. v. FCC*, 29 F.3d 309 (7th Cir. 1994). While the 1991 rules were meant to relax the restrictions, the court found that the Commission failed to show that the new rules were less rather than more restrictive. On remand, the FCC decided to repeal most of the restrictions. However, the remaining restrictions remained in effect until November 1995. *In re Evaluation of the Syndication and Financial Interest Rules: Second Report and Order*, 8 F.C.C.R. 3282 (1993); *Memorandum and Opinion on Reconsideration*, 8 F.C.C.R. 8270 (1993). Six months prior to the November 1995 deregulation, the FCC was scheduled to institute a proceeding to determine whether any restrictions needed to be continued.

Treatise Reference: W. Patry, *Copyright Law and Practice* 942–43 (1994).

synergism [patent] A now-rejected theory that to be patentably nonobvious under Patent Code §103, the elements making up a combination invention must combine to produce a result greater than the sum of its parts or one of the elements must function differently in the combination than it did separately.

Origin of Theory. The theory has roots in Justice Jackson's remarks in the 1950 *A&P* case: "[O]nly when the whole in some way exceeds the sum of its parts is the accumulation of old devices patentable.... Two and two have been added together, and still they make only four." *Great A & P Tea Co. v. Supermarket Equip. Co.*, 340 U.S. 147, 152, 87 USPQ 303, 305–06 (1950). Use of the word "synergism" to symbolize this theory of the test for a patentable invention stems from incidental use of the word in two Supreme Court cases in 1969 and 1976. In 1969 the Court stated: "A combination of elements may result in an effect greater than the sum of the several parts taken together. No such synergistic result is argued here." *Anderson's-Black Rock v. Pavement Co.*, 396 U.S. 57, 61, 163 USPQ 673, 674 (1969). In a 1976 case, a lower court upheld the validity of a patent, saying that the invention did "achieve a synergistic result," but the Supreme Court reversed, saying "[w]e cannot agree that the combination of these old elements ... can properly be characterized as synergistic." *Sakraida v. Ag Pro, Inc.*, 425 U.S. 273, 282, 189 USPQ 449, 453 (1976). The word "synergism" was much criticized as a slogan for a "get tough with patents" philosophy, which set an unreasonably high standard of patentability.

Rejection of Theory. The test of "synergism" has been almost uniformly rejected by the lower courts because in the real world, two and two never equals five and mechanical, hydraulic, or electrical elements can never perform different functions in combination than they do separately. "[S]ynergism is only a figure of speech, for in its literal sense synergism never has existed and never can exist in mechanical or hydraulic inventions when the term is defined as a whole result greater than the sum of its constituent parts." *Republic Indus., Inc. v. Schlage Lock Co.*, 592 F.2d 963, 970, 200 USPQ 769, 777 (7th Cir. 1979). Similarly, the Court of Appeals for the Federal Circuit and its predecessor courts "have considered and rejected the notion that a new result or function or synergism is a requirement of patentability." *American Hoist & Derrick Co. v. Sowa & Sons, Inc.*, 725 F.2d 1350, 1360 (Fed. Cir. 1984).

See OBVIOUSNESS, COMBINATION.

- *Case References*:

"A requirement for 'synergism' or a 'synergistic effect' is nowhere found in the [patent] statute.... When present, for example in a chemical case, synergism may point toward nonobviousness, but its absence has no place in evaluating the evidence on obviousness". *Stratoflex, Inc. v. Aeroquip Corp.*, 713 F.2d 1530, 1540, 218 USPQ 871, 880 (Fed. Cir. 1983).

"Virtually every invention is a combination of elements or process steps, and synergism, or its equivalent 'new and different result,' is not *required* for patentability." *Connell v. Sears, Roebuck & Co.*, 722 F.2d 1542, 1549, 220 USPQ 193, 199 (Fed. Cir. 1983).

T

teach [patent] To inform and instruct by way of the documents making up the PRIOR ART. The technological disclosures of the prior art, such as the SPECIFICATION of a previous patent or a PRINTED PUBLICATION, inform and instruct persons with SKILL IN THE ART. Thus, those prior art references "teach" the technology revealed in them and those references are said to be prior art "teachings."

See OBVIOUSNESS, PRIOR ART, SPECIFICATION.

- *Use Examples*:

"Thus, [the technical journal article by] Petersen must be read, not in isolation, but for what it fairly teaches in combination with the prior art as a whole. That teaching is that the interchange of the nitrogen and the unsaturated carbon atoms is isoteric and compounds so modified are expected to possess similar biological properties." *In re Merck & Co.*, 800 F.2d 1091, 1097, 231 USPQ 375, 380 (Fed. Cir. 1986).

"Obviousness cannot be established by combining the teachings of the prior art to produce the claimed invention, absent some teaching or suggestion supporting the combination. Under section 103, teachings of references can be combined *only* if there is some suggestion or incentive to do so." *ACS Hosp. Sys. Inc. v. Montefiore Hosp.*, 732 F.2d 1572, 1577, 221 USPQ 929, 933 (Fed. Cir. 1984).

teach toward–teach away [patent]

A PRIOR ART reference (such as the DISCLOSURE of a previous patent or a PRINTED PUBLICATION) that suggests or points in the direction of the present invention is said to "teach toward" the invention and is thus evidence that the present invention is obvious and not patentable. Conversely, a prior art reference that diverges from and points in a technical direction away from the present invention is evidence that the present invention is nonobvious and hence patentable (see OBVIOUSNESS).

Look at Prior Art References as Totality. The prior art must be looked at in its entirety, giving consideration to both technical data that teaches toward and teaches away from the present invention. Prior art "must be read as a whole and consideration must be given where the references diverge and teach away from the claimed invention." *Akzo N.V. v. International Trade Comm'n*, 808 F.2d 1471, 1481, 1 USPQ2d 1241, 1246 (Fed. Cir. 1986). It is error to find an invention obvious where the prior art references diverge from and teach away from the invention at hand. *W.L. Gore & Assocs. v. Garlock, Inc.*, 721 F.2d 1540, 1550, 220 USPQ 303, 311 (Fed. Cir. 1983).

Teaching Away. That a prior art reference discloses a technique used for a slightly different purpose from that utilized by the present inventor does not mean that that reference "teaches away" if those skilled in the art would readily see the application of the technique for the purpose it was put to in the present invention. *In re Heck*, 699 F.2d 1331, 1333, 216 USPQ 1038, 1040 (Fed. Cir. 1983)("[W]e do not consider [prior art reference] Maybech as 'teaching away.' Its specific use was different, but the broader disclosures of that patent were made known, were useful and were legally available to [the present inventor].").

See COMBINING PRIOR ART, TEACH, DISCLOSURE.

- *Case Reference*: "Obviousness cannot be established by combining the teachings of the prior art to produce the claimed invention, absent some teaching or suggestion supporting the combination. Under section 103, teachings of references can be combined *only* if there is some suggestion or incentive to do so." *ACS Hosp. Sys. Inc. v. Montefiore Hosp.*, 732 F.2d 1572, 1577, 221 USPQ 929, 933 (Fed. Cir. 1984).

technical trademark [trademark]   An archaic usage, referring to an inherently distinctive word affixed to a product. In early law, a common law "technical trademark" was an inherently distinctive word affixed to the goods. Only such things were protected as "trademarks." The category of "technical trademarks" was confined to words that were FANCIFUL, ARBITRARY, or SUGGESTIVE and did not consist of a personal name. Other words that had acquired distinctiveness through SECONDARY MEANING were protected as "trade names" by a separate body of law called "unfair competition." These definitions and distinctions have almost totally disappeared in modern case law and statutes. Under modern law, both inherently distinctive marks as well as noninherently distinctive marks with secondary meaning are protected and registered as "trademarks." The term "TRADE NAME" has taken on a new meaning as identifying a company.

• *Treatise Reference*: 1 J.T. McCarthy, *Trademarks and Unfair Competition* §§4.03–.04 (3d ed. 1995 rev.).

telephone interview [patent–trademark]
See INTERVIEW.

terminal disclaimer [patent] A voluntary giving up or surrendering of a certain period at the end of the term of a patent. The primary use of this is to overcome an objection based upon the rule against DOUBLE PATENTING. Patent Code §254 provides that any patentee may "disclaim or dedicate to the public the entire term, or any terminal part of the term, of the patent granted or to be granted."

Terminal Disclaimer Overcomes a Double-Patenting Objection. A terminal disclaimer is able to overcome only the "obviousness-type" double-patenting objection, not the "same invention type" of double patenting. The rule of obviousness-type double patenting prohibits prolongation of patent rights by obtaining claims in a second patent on an "obvious" modification of the same invention covered by the first patent. This is a judicially created rule based on the public policy of preventing the extension of the term of a patent by forbidding the issuance of claims in a second commonly owned patent that are not patentably distinct from the claims of the first patent. *In re Longi*, 759 F.2d 887, 892, 225 USPQ 645, 648 (Fed. Cir. 1985). In this situation, the inventor seeks a second patent on a modification or improvement upon what he or his assignee has already patented. The terminal disclaimer provides that the second patent will expire at the same time as the first, thus permitting public use of obvious modifications of the claims of the first patent.

Two Patents Expire at the Same Time. The terminal disclaimer causes the two patents to expire at the same time, obviates the arguable unlawful extension of the patent term, brings the improvements within the protection of the patent system, and thus gives an incentive for the public disclosure of improvement inventions. *In re Van Ornum & Stang*, 686 F.2d 937, 948, 214 USPQ 761, 770 (Fed. Cir. 1982). The net effect is as if all the claims of the two patents were in one patent that has one expiration date (see quote below).

Common Ownership Is Necessary. The regulations state that to overcome a double-patenting objection, a terminal disclaimer must include a provision that the second patent shall be enforceable only for and during the period that the patent is commonly owned with the first patent, which is the patent that formed the basis for the rejection. 37 C.F.R. §1.321(b). This provision ties together the termination and the ownership of the two patents and is valid because a common termination date assumes common ownership of the two patents throughout the life of the two patents. *In re Van Ornum & Stang*, supra. The effect of this clause in a terminal disclaimer is that a patent expires immediately when it ceases to be commonly owned with the other.

- *Treatise Reference*: 3 D. Chisum, *Patents* §9.04 (1994 rev.); R. Harmon, *Patents and the Federal Circuit* §15.5(c) (3d ed. 1994).

- *Case References*:

"When a terminal disclaimer causes two patents to expire together, a situation is created which is tantamount for all practical purposes to having all the claims in one patent." *In re Braithwright*, 379 F.2d 594, 601, 154 USPQ 29, 34 (C.C.P.A. 1967), quoted with approval in *In re Van Ornum & Stang*, 686 F.2d 937, 948, 214 USPQ 761, 770 (Fed. Cir. 1982).

"Only the claims are compared in a rejection for double patenting. Such a rejection by the patent office does not mean that the first-filed patent is a prior art reference under §102 against the later-filed application. Thus the 'obviation' of obvious-type double patenting by filing a terminal disclaimer has no effect on a rejection under §103 based on the first-filed patent. Such a rejection can not be overcome by a terminal disclaimer." *Quad Environmental Tech. v. Union Sanitary Dist.*, 946 F.2d 870, 874, 20 USPQ2d 1392, 1394 (Fed. Cir. 1991).

- *Manual Reference*: "[A] terminal disclaimer directed to a particular claim or claims will not be accepted; the disclaimer must be of a terminal portion of the term of the entire patent to be granted. The statute does not provide for conditional disclaimers and accordingly, a proposed disclaimer which is made contingent on the allowance of certain claims cannot be accepted." *Manual of Patent Examining Procedure* §1490 (1993 rev.).

termination of grant [copyright]   For certain grants of rights of copyright by assignment or license (either exclusive or nonexclusive), an author or his heirs are given the power after a period of years to terminate the grant and regrant the rights for a more favorable economic return.

Replacement of the Old Two-Term Copyright. The termination right first appeared in the copyright revisions effective in 1978 and replaced the two-term copyright that previously existed. The purpose of both the old two-term copyright and the present termination right is the paternalistic goal of protecting authors from making a bad deal for the sale or license of their works. Authors are given a second chance after a period of years to get a better deal. After termination the author can renegotiate the existing deal or resell or relicense the rights to others for a better price. Congress provided this sort of special protection because of the desire to have some provision "safeguarding authors against unremunerative transfers. A provision of this sort is needed because of the unequal bargaining position of authors, resulting in part from the impossibility of determining a work's value until it has been exploited." H.R. Rep. No. 94-1476, 94th Cong., 2d Sess. 124 (1976). Of course, the termination right will be exercised only if the market value of the work has increased since the first grant of rights was made.

The Two Types of Termination Rights. There are two distinct kinds of termination rights: one for grants made *before* January 1, 1978, and the other for grants made *after* January 1, 1978. For grants made *before* January 1, 1978, the Copyright Act, 17 U.S.C. §304(c), gives the author or the deceased author's surviving spouse, children, or grandchildren the right to terminate a grant for the period of the 19-year bonus term, which Congress added to the duration of federal copyrights that were in existence on January 1, 1978. The time to exercise the termination is a five-year window starting 56 years from the original date of copyright. For grants made *after* January 1, 1978, the Copyright Act, 17 U.S.C. §203, gives to the author or the deceased author's surviving spouse, children, or grandchildren the right to terminate an author's grant within a five-year window starting 35 years from the date of the grant. Grants made in 1978 will not be subject to termination until 2013.

Termination Procedures. The timing and formalities surrounding the termination of a grant are complicated and technical. Briefly, one exercising the termination of a grant serves notice on the grantee, specifying the date of termination within the five-year termination window. Notice may be served not less than 2 years and no more than 10 years before the termination date specified in the notice. 17 U.S.C.

§§203(a)(4), 304(c)(4). The notice must be in writing, signed, and recorded in the Copyright Office prior to the date of termination.

Right to Terminate Cannot Be Waived or Sold. The right to terminate a grant is absolute and inalienable. It cannot be waived or sold in advance. The copyright statute voids all contracts to waive or sell the termination right. 17 U.S.C. §203(a)(5).

Effect of Termination on Derivative Works. An authorized derivative work created under a copyright license before termination may continue to be utilized under the terms of the terminated grant. But after termination, no new derivative works can be created. 17 U.S.C. §§203(b)(1), 304(c)(6)(A). For example, a motion picture based on a short story may continue to be publicly performed even after the copyright owner of the story terminates the grant to the movie studio. But the movie studio may not thereafter make a television series based on the story.

Works Made for Hire. A WORK MADE FOR HIRE by an employee is not subject to termination of grant because there was no "grant" or transfer of title from employee to employer. Rather, the employer became the "author" and owner of copyright at the time of creation of the work by the employee. The Copyright Act specifically states that the termination right does not apply to works made for hire. 17 U.S.C. §§203(a), 304(c).

See WORK MADE FOR HIRE.

See ASSIGNMENT OF COPYRIGHT, LICENSE OF COPYRIGHT, DURATION OF COPYRIGHT.

- *Treatise References*: 3 *Nimmer on Copyright* §11.01 et seq. (1994 rev.); 1 P. Goldstein, *Copyright* §§4.9–.10 (1989); M. Leaffer, *Understanding Copyright* §§6.9–.15 (1989); 1 N. Boorstyn, *Copyright* §8.01 et seq. (2d ed. 1994); W. Patry, *Copyright Law and Practice* 493 (1994).

term of protection [patent–trademark–copyright–trade secret–right of publicity]
See DURATION.

territoriality of marks [trademarks]
A principle of international and domestic law that recognizes the separate existence of a trademark in each sovereign territory in which it has been registered. The contrary approach is the "universality" theory, which posits that a mark signifies the same source wherever the mark is used in the world.

Territoriality Principle Applied to Priority Disputes. Priority of trademark rights in the United States depends solely upon priority of use in the United States, not on priority of use anywhere in the world. Prior use in a foreign nation does not establish priority of use in the United States. Prior use of a trademark in a foreign country does not entitle its owner to claim exclusive trademark rights in the United States as against one who used a similar trademark in the United States prior to entry of the foreigner into the domestic American market. *Person's Co. v. Christman,* 900 F.2d 1565, 14 USPQ2d 1477 (Fed. Cir. 1990) (rule was extended to give U.S. trademark rights to one who copies in the United States a mark previously used abroad but which was not known in the United States).

Territoriality Principle Applied to "Gray Market" Imports. When seeking to prevent the importation of GRAY MARKET GOODS, a U.S. importer who has been assigned U.S. ownership of the mark of a foreign manufacturer will argue the "territoriality" principle to justify the separate identity of the mark in the United States. That is, if the mark identifies one source in the United States (the U.S. importer) and another source abroad (the foreign manufacturer), then gray market imports that originate with the foreign manufacturer but do not enter the United States through the U.S. trademark owner-importer are not "genuine" goods and must be illegal infringements. A single mark has a separate legal and factual significance in each nation where the local distributor and owner of local rights has developed an independent goodwill and reputation. *Osawa & Co. v. B & H Photo,* 589 F. Supp. 1163, 1171, 223 USPQ 124, 132 (S.D.N.Y. 1984).

In such a dispute over GRAY MARKET GOODS, the person who is importing the goods in competition with the authorized U.S. importer will argue the "universality" theory: the mark signifies the same manufacturing source everywhere in the world, and, therefore, these goods are "genuine" because they originate with the genuine manufacturing source and there can be no confusion or deception. Another way of phrasing this argument is to state it in terms of applying the "exhaustion" rule to international trade: once the foreign manufacturer releases marked goods into trade, anyone's trademark rights to control the sale of those goods anywhere in the world is "exhausted." Ladas criticizes application of the territoriality principle to justify prohibition of unauthorized gray market imports that are physically identical to the authorized imports. 2 S. Ladas, *Patents, Trademarks and Related Rights: National and International Protection* §732 (1975).

The 1923 Katzel Decision. The U.S. Supreme Court's decision in *A. Bourjois & Co. v. Katzel*, 260 U.S. 689 (1923), is widely viewed as rejecting the competing universality theory and accepting into U.S. law the territoriality principle. In the *Katzel* case, a French cosmetics firm sold its U.S. operations and assigned its JAVA trademark to the plaintiff, who continued to buy face powder in bulk manufactured by the French firm and who packed and sold it in the United States under the JAVA mark in boxes prominently displaying the name of the plaintiff as importer. The defendant, a third party, purchased authentic JAVA powder in France and imported it into the United States in competition with the plaintiff. The Court, by Justice Holmes, noted that the plaintiff packaged the product in a manner appropriate to the U.S. market and had achieved its own reputation in the United States as the source of JAVA products: "[Plaintiff] uses care in selecting colors suitable for the American market, in packing and in keeping up the standard, and has spent much money in advertising, etc., so that the business has grown very great and the labels have come to be understood by the public here as meaning goods coming from the plaintiff." 260 U.S. at 691. Thus, the sale of goods from the foreign source by anyone but the plaintiff would be likely to cause confusion as to source. The trademark infringement rationale of the Supreme Court's *Katzel* decision implied that U.S. purchasers are deceived and confused by these GRAY MARKET GOODS of the defendant because the JAVA mark had one meaning in the territory of the United States, another in the territory of France. "[JAVA] is the trademark of the plaintiff only in the United States and indicates in law, and, it is found, by public understanding, that the goods come from the plaintiff, although not made by it." 260 U.S. at 692.

The Territoriality Principle and the Paris Convention. The United States is a member of the Paris Union and a signatory of the PARIS CONVENTION, Article 6(3), which states: "A mark duly registered in a country of the [Paris] Union shall be regarded as independent of marks registered in other countries of the Union, including the country of origin." U.S. adherence to the Paris Convention has been viewed as committing U.S. law to the principle of territoriality embodied in Article 6(3). *Weil Ceramics & Glass, Inc. v. Dash*, 878 F.2d 659, 679, 11 USPQ2d 1001, 1017 (3d Cir. 1989) (Becker, J., concurring). The Paris Convention also provides that a mark and its goodwill can be validly assigned as to only one nation by the transfer of the right to sell the marked goods in one nation together with "that portion of the business or goodwill located in that country." Paris Convention, Art. 6 *quater*. Thus, the Paris Convention recognizes that a U.S. registered trademark for foreign-made goods can have a separate legal existence in the United States and that this separate mark and its goodwill are assignable. That is, manufacturer Alpha may own the mark in France, but exclusive importer Zeta may own the mark in the United States, if it is validly assigned by Alpha to Zeta.

Foreign Conduct and Law: Impact in the United States. Under the principle of territoriality, use, recognition, and registration of a trademark in a foreign nation do not establish rights in the United States. *Fuji Photo Film Co. v. Shinohara Shoji Kabushiki Kaisha*, 754 F.2d 591, 599, 225 USPQ 540, 546 (5th Cir. 1985) (see case reference below). However, if the reputation of a mark used only abroad extends to the United States, then that establishes certain trademark rights in the United States. *All England Lawn Tennis Club, Ltd. v. Creations Aromatiques, Inc.*, 220 USPQ 1069 (T.T.A.B. 1983) (WIMBLEDON tennis championships acquired fame in the United States sufficient to preclude registration of WIMBLEDON for cologne with a design of a tennis player). While the ownership of a mark may be affected by the decision of a court in the situs nation, foreign judgments rendered on foreign law have no general extraterritorial impact on trademark rights. *E. Remy Martin & Co., S.A. v. Shaw-Ross Int'l Imports, Inc.*, 756 F.2d 1525, 1531, 225 USPQ 1131, 1135 (11th Cir. 1985) ("[W]e are not bound to recognize or rely upon foreign law and disagreements abroad settled under it.").

See GRAY MARKET GOODS.

• *Treatise Reference*: 4 J.T. McCarthy, *Trademarks and Unfair Competition* §29.01 (3d ed. 1995 rev.).

• *Case References*:

"Since Holmes' decision [in *A. Bourjois & Co. v. Katzel*, 260 U.S. 689 (1923)], the universality principle has faded and has been generally supplanted by the principle of 'territoriality,' upon which the *Bourjois* rulings were based. This principle recognizes that a trademark has a separate legal existence under each country's laws, and that its proper lawful function is not necessarily to specify the origin or manufacture of a good (although it may incidentally do that), but rather to symbolize the domestic goodwill of the domestic mark-holder so that the consuming public may rely with an expectation of consistency on the domestic reputation earned for the mark by its owner, and the owner of the mark may be confident that his goodwill and reputation (the value of the mark) will not be injured through use of the mark by others in domestic commerce." *Osawa & Co. v. B & H Photo*, 589 F. Supp. 1165, 1171, 223 USPQ 124, 130 (S.D.N.Y. 1984).

"[Plaintiff] correctly assigns as error the trial court's admission of evidence of the parties' foreign trademark usage and occurrences. The concept of territoriality is basic to trademark law; trademark rights exist in each country solely according to that country's statutory scheme.... 'It is well settled that foreign use is ineffectual to create trademark rights in the United States.' ... It is equally well settled that 'when trademark rights within the United States are being litigated in an American court, the decisions of foreign courts concerning the re-

spective trademark rights of the parties are irrelevant and inadmissible.' " *Fuji Photo Film Co. v. Shinohara Shoji Kabushiki Kaisha*, 754 F.2d 591, 599, 225 USPQ 540, 546 (5th Cir. 1985).

that which infringes if later, anticipates if earlier [patent] A rule stating the equivalence between two separate tests of patent law: (1) the test of infringement of a patent; and (2) the test of what is ANTICIPATION in the prior art so as to invalidate a patent. This slogan or phrase encapsulates the equation between this test of validity and this test of infringement of a patent.

Source of the Rule. The rule can be traced as far back as *Peters v. Active Mfg. Co.*, 129 U.S. 530, 537 (1889) ("That which infringes, if later, would anticipate, if earlier.").

Modern Limitation on the Rule. The rule has been rephrased to make it clear that while there can be infringement by the DOCTRINE OF EQUIVALENTS, there cannot be anticipation merely by equivalency. The parallel to anticipation is the rule of LITERAL INFRINGEMENT. "While 'the classic test of anticipation' was indeed as stated, under the current statute 'anticipation' does not carry the same meaning as before and the 'classic test' must be modified to: That which would *literally* infringe if later in time anticipates if earlier than the date of invention." *Lewmar Marine, Inc. v. Barient, Inc.*, 827 F.2d 744, 747, 3 USPQ2d 1766, 1768 (Fed. Cir. 1987).

See ANTICIPATION, INFRINGEMENT OF PATENT, IDENTITY OF INVENTION.

tie-in [patent–trademark–copyright–antitrust] A form of MISUSE or antitrust violation in which the license or purchase of item A is conditioned upon the license or purchase of separate item B. This can be a violation of the Clayton Act or the Sherman Act or such a misuse of intellectual property as to deny relief in an infringement suit.

Antitrust Elements of a Tie-In. Traditional antitrust tie-in law states that conduct constitutes an illegal per se tie-in if: (1) there are two economically separable items; (2) a license or sale of the tied item is conditioned on the license or sale of the desired tying item; (3) the tying item has "sufficient economic power" to coerce a tie; and (4) a not-insubstantial amount of trade is tied up in the market for the tied item. *Northern Pac. Ry. Co. v. United States*, 356 U.S. 1, 6 (1958); *Eastman Kodak Co. v. Image Technical Servs., Inc.*, 504 U.S. 451 (1992). However, the Supreme Court, in 1984, retained the PER SE ILLEGAL rule for tie-ins by only a narrow 5-4 vote. *Jefferson Parish Hosp. Dist. No. 2 v. Hyde*, 466 U.S. 2 (1984). In practical effect, tie-ins are governed by a truncated version of the antitrust RULE OF REASON as described above.

See MISUSE.

1. Patent Tie-Ins. Conditioning the license of a patent on the purchase of unpatented supplies is the classic form of use of a patent to accomplish an illegal tie-in.

The Morton Salt Case. For example, in the classic *Morton Salt* case, the owner of a patent on a machine used in food canning to deposit salt tablets in canned food licensed the use of its machines only to canners who also agreed to purchase all of their needs for unpatented salt from the patentee. The stretching of the economic power of the patent to include the unpatented salt led the Supreme Court to conclude that the patent had been sufficiently "misused" to deny relief against an infringer. *Morton Salt Co. v. G.S. Suppiger*, 314 U.S. 488 (1942). See, e.g., *Senza-Gel Corp. v. Seiffhart*, 803 F.2d 661, 231 USPQ 363 (Fed. Cir. 1986) (refusal to license use of patented process unless user leased patentee's machine is misuse of the patent). If the defendant in *Morton Salt* had been in the tied market for salt, it might also have been able to assert an antitrust counterclaim for treble damages. Such conduct might also furnish a basis for a government antitrust case. See, e.g., *International Salt Co. v. United States*, 332 U.S. 392 (1947).

Method Patent Label Licenses. The owner of a method patent who grants a patent license via a LABEL LICENSE only to those who buy an unpatented component from the patentee may be guilty of an antitrust violation or misuse of the patent by tying in the sale of the unpatented product to the patent license. See *B.B. Chem. Co. v. Ellis*, 314 U.S. 495 (1942). However, if the unpatented product is not a STAPLE, then such conduct is not patent misuse. *Dawson Chem. Co. v. Rohm & Haas Co.*, 448 U.S. 176 (1980).

Product Separability. The Court of Appeals for the Federal Circuit has held that to determine product separability for misuse purposes, one need only "look to the nature of the claimed invention as the basis for determining whether a product is a necessary concomitant of the invention or an entirely separate product" and that, unlike the test for an antitrust violation, one need not look to consumer demand. *Senza-Gel Corp. v. Seiffhart*, 803 F.2d 661, 670 n.14, 231 USPQ 363, 370 n.14 (Fed. Cir. 1986).

Effect of 1988 Patent Code Amendments. The Supreme Court has held that when a patent is used as a tying item in a patent tie-in, sufficient economic power is presumed from the mere fact of the patent. However, as a result of 1988 amendments to the Patent Code, it is now necessary that there be proof that the patent holds market power in a relevant market in order to establish that a patent tie-in constitutes a defense of misuse. That is, it is not patent misuse that the patentee "conditioned the license of any rights to the patent or the sale of the patented product on the acquisition of a license to rights in another patent or purchase of a separate product, unless in the view of the circumstances, the patent owner has market power in the relevant market for the patent or patented product." 35 U.S.C. §271(d)(5).

See LABEL LICENSE, PROCESS CLAIM, STAPLE.

• *Treatise References*: ABA, *Antitrust Law Developments* 505 (2d ed. 1984); W. Holmes, *Intellectual Property and Antitrust Law* §20.01 (1994 rev.).

• *Case References*:

"[The patent owner] is making use of its patent monopoly to restrain competition in the marketing of unpatented articles, salt tablets, for use with the patented machines, and is aiding in the creation of a limited monopoly in the tablets not within that granted by the patent. A patent operates to create and grant to the patentee an exclusive right to make, use and vend the particular device described and claimed in the patent. But a patent affords no immunity for a monopoly not within the grant, ... and the use of it to suppress competition in the sale of an unpatented article may deprive the patentee of the aid of a court of equity to restrain an alleged infringement by one who is a competitor." *Morton Salt Co. v. G.S. Suppiger*, 314 U.S. 488, 491 (1942).

"[T]here are established limits which the patentee must not exceed in employing the leverage of his patent to control or limit the operations of the licensee. Among other restrictions upon him, he may not condition the right to use his patent on the licensee's agreement to purchase, use, or sell, or not to purchase, use, or sell, another article of commerce not within the scope of his patent monopoly." *Zenith Radio Corp. v. Hazeltine Research, Inc.*, 395 U.S. 100, 136, 161 USPQ 577, 591 (1969).

"A patentee ... who does not affirmatively offer, or express a willingness to offer, a licensing program separate from the label license attached to a staple article of commerce, runs the risk that the court may, in conjunction with the particularized evidence in the case, conclude that a tying arrangement is implicit, and that a misuse of the patent has occurred.... We merely indicate that any patentee who sells the patented item only in conjunction with some other unpatented staple goods raises serious suspicions of tying behavior and misuse." *Rex Chainbelt Inc. v. Harco Prods., Inc.*, 512 F.2d 993, 1002, 185 USPQ 10, 16 (9th Cir. 1975).

2. Trademark Tie-Ins. In the context of trademark franchising, a trademark licensor/franchisor may want to require that the licensee/franchisee purchase certain supplies only from the licensor or from designated sources connected with the licensor. Such restrictions may be tie-ins illegal under Sherman Act §1. The supplies are the tied item and the tying item is the license of the trademark, which the franchisee desires. While in the 1970s trademark tie-in prohibitions were quite strict, they have loosened up since then.

No Presumption of Sufficient Economic Power. Most courts will no longer presume the needed "sufficient economic power" in the tying market merely by the existence of the trademark and will require proof that the mark possesses the requisite power in a relevant economic market. *Mozart Co. v. Mercedes-Benz of N. Am. Inc.*, 833 F.2d 1342, 1346 (9th Cir. 1987). Usually, the franchisor's need to exercise quality control over items sold by franchisees under the licensed mark will not justify an otherwise illegal tie-in. A tie-in is avoided if the franchisor designates a reasonable number of approved sources for its franchisees. *Kentucky Fried Chicken Corp. v. Diversified Packaging Corp.*, 549 F.2d 368, 193 USPQ 649 (5th Cir. 1977).

Trademark Separate From Goods. Determination of whether the alleged tied goods are economically separate from the licensed mark is the issue that has provided a safety valve for franchisors. Under the majority view, the key is whether the mark serves to identify a distinctive business format or whether it serves to identify the source of the allegedly tied items. If the mark does the former, there can be a tie-in; if the mark does the latter, there can be no tie-in, for the mark cannot be viewed as a separate thing from the products whose source it identifies. For example, if a fried chicken fast-food franchisor requires that franchisees purchase all needed paper goods from the franchisor, the fast-food mark does not identify the source of such supplies, and there can be an illegal tie-in. *Siegel v. Chicken Delight Inc.*, 448 F.2d 43, 171 USPQ 269 (9th Cir. 1971). But if an ice cream manufacturer requires that franchisees sell only company-supplied ice cream in stores identified by the licensed mark, the mark identifies the source of the ice cream; there is no separability and no illegal tie-in. *Krehl v. Baskin-Robbins Ice Cream Co.*, 664 F.2d 1348 (9th Cir. 1982). Some courts go further and apparently would find no trademark-product separability in any situation. *Principe v. McDonald's Corp.*, 631 F.2d 303, 208 USPQ 377 (4th Cir. 1980).

Damage to the Franchisee. Some courts have found that even if there is an illegal franchise trademark tie-in, the franchisee is not damaged unless the price of the entire package of tying and tied items exceeds the competitive market price of the whole package. Usually, it will not. *Kypta v. McDonald's Corp.*, 671 F.2d 1282 (11th Cir. 1982); *Will v. Comprehensive Accounting Corp.*, 776 F.2d 665 (7th Cir. 1985).

The 1992 Kodak Case. While not involving a trademark tie-in, the Supreme Court's 1992 *Kodak* decision influenced the law of tie-ins by looking to the market for a single brand of product. The Court held that independent suppliers of service for Kodak photocopier machines should be allowed to go to trial to prove that Kodak intended to make independent service more difficult by selling replacement parts only to Kodak machine users who use Kodak-supplied service or repair their own machines. The claim was that Kodak had unlawfully tied the sale of service for Kodak machines to the sale of parts for Kodak machines. *Eastman Kodak Co. v. Image Technical Servs., Inc.,* 504 U.S. 451 (1992).

See TRADEMARK, FRANCHISING.

• *Treatise Reference*: 4 J.T. McCarthy, *Trademarks and Unfair Competition* §31.33 (3d ed. 1995 rev.).

3. Copyright Tie-Ins. Tie-ins involving copyrights have appeared in the context of BLOCK BOOKING, i.e., conditioning the license of desirable copyrighted motion picture films on also taking a license of undesirable films. Such conduct has been held to constitute an illegal tie-in. *United States v. Loew's Inc.,* 371 U.S. 38 (1962) (block booking of films for showing on television held illegal).

Computer Hardware-Software Tie-Ins. By analogy to the motion picture block booking tie-in cases, it has been held to be an illegal copyright tie-in for a computer manufacturer to tie in the purchase of computer hardware to the purchase of copyrighted software programs. That is, by contractual restriction, the programs could only be used on hardware made by the seller of the software. *Digidyne Corp. v. Data Gen. Corp.,* 734 F.2d 1336 (9th Cir. 1984). Such arrangements are sometimes called a BUNDLING of hardware and software.

See BLOCK BOOKING, BUNDLING.

• *Treatise Reference*: W. Holmes, *Intellectual Property and Antitrust Law* §36.05 (1994 rev.).

tie-out [patent–antitrust] A restriction in a patent license agreement by which the licensee agrees not to use or manufacture unpatented goods competitive with the patented item. While the term "tie-out" infers that such a license restriction is a form of TIE-IN, in fact it is not and bears little resemblance to a classic tie-in illegal under antitrust law.

Antitrust and Misuse Treatment. Tie-out restrictions have generally been viewed as per se MISUSE of a patent. *National Lockwasher Co. v. George K. Garrett Co.,* 137 F.2d 255, 58 USPQ 460 (3d Cir. 1943); *Berlenbach v. Anderson & Thompson Ski Co.,* 329 F.2d 782, 141 USPQ 84 (9th Cir. 1964). However, under traditional antitrust analysis, such a restriction would be viewed as an exclusive dealing arrangement, tested by the antitrust RULE OF REASON.

• *Treatise References*: W. Holmes, *Intellectual Property and Antitrust Law* §21 (1994 rev.); ABA, *Antitrust Law Developments* 512 (2d ed. 1984).

• *Case Reference*: "[T]here are established limits which the patentee must not exceed in employing the leverage of his patent to control or limit the operations of the licensee. Among other restrictions upon him, he may not condition the right to use his patent on the licensee's agreement to purchase, use, or sell, or not to purchase, use, or sell, another article of commerce not within the scope of his patent monopoly." *Zenith Radio Corp. v. Hazeltine Research, Inc.,* 395 U.S. 100, 136, 161 USPQ 577, 591 (1969).

TLRA [trademark]

See TRADEMARK LAW REVISION ACT.

TMEP [trademark] Trademark Manual of Examining Procedure. This is the official internal manual of procedure to be followed by trademark attorney EXAMINERS in reviewing applications for the registration of marks in the U.S. Patent and Trademark Office. The TMEP is often relied upon as a guide to attorneys and trademark examiners on procedural matters during the PROSECUTION of trademark registration applications. The second edition of the TMEP was published in June 1993 in looseleaf format and is periodically updated. A copy can be purchased from the Superintendent of Documents, U.S. Government Printing Office, Washington D.C. 20402.

TLT [trademark–international]

See TRADEMARK LAW TREATY.

tort [general legal-general intellectual property] The breach of a duty that is imposed on everyone by the law. For example, everyone has a duty not to commit assault or battery on another, and a breach of that duty by hitting someone with your fist is a tort. That is, assault and battery are "tortious" acts. The person who commits a tort is known as a "tortfeasor." When several persons cooperate to commit a tort, they are known as "joint tortfeasors."

The infringement of an intellectual property right is a commercial tort, and an infringer is a tortfeasor.

- *Case References*:

Patent Infringement: Orthokinetics Inc. v. Safety Travel Chairs, Inc., 806 F.2d 1565, 1579, 1 USPQ2d 1081, 1090 (Fed. Cir. 1986) (patent infringement is a tort); *Rite-Hite Corp. v. Kelley Co.*, 819 F.2d 1120, 1126, 2 USPQ2d 1915, 1919 (Fed. Cir. 1987) (referring to "the tort of infringement" and to an infringer as a "tortfeasor"); *North Am. Philips Corp. v. American Vending Sales Inc.*, 35 F.3d 1576, 1579, 32 USPQ2d 1203, 1205 (Fed. Cir. 1994) ("We hold that to sell an infringing article to a buyer in Illinois is to commit a tort there....").

Trademark Infringement: Lockridge v. United States, 218 Ct. Cl. 687, 200 USPQ 271, 272 (1978) ("[T]rademark infringement sounds in tort."); *The Keds Corp. v. Renee Int'l Trading Corp.*, 888 F.2d 215, 218, 12 USPQ2d 1808, 1810 (1st. Cir. 1989) (Trademark infringement is a tort.); *Dakota Indus. Inc. v. Dakota Sportswear Inc.*, 946 F.2d 1384, 1387, 20 USPQ2d 1450, 1452 (8th Cir. 1991) ("Infringement of a trademark is a tort.").

Unfair Competition: Golden Nugget Inc. v. American Stock Exch. Inc., 828 F.2d 586, 591, 4 USPQ2d 1466, 1469 (9th Cir. 1987) ("[T]he tort of unfair competition is extremely flexible...."); *G. Heilman Brewing Co. v. Anheuser-Busch Inc.*, 676 F. Supp. 1436, 1482, 6 USPQ2d 1481, 1512 (E.D. Wis. 1987), *aff'd*, 873 F.2d 985, 10 USPQ2d 1801 (7th. Cir. 1989) ("Common-law unfair competition is a tort which is governed by state law."); *Bonito Boats, Inc. v. Thunder Craft Boats, Inc.*, 489 U.S. 141, 158, 9 USPQ2d 1847, 1855 (1989) (referring to "the common-law tort of unfair competition").

Copyright Infringement: DeGette v. The Mine Co. Restaurant Inc., 751 F.2d 1143, 1145, 224 USPQ 763, 765 (10th Cir. 1985) (copyright infringement is a tort).

Infringement of a Trade Secret: Northern Petrochemical Co. v. Tomlinson, 484 F.2d 1057, 1060, 179 USPQ 386, 388 (7th Cir. 1973) ("A suit to redress theft of a secret is one grounded in tort....").

Infringement of the Right of Publicity: Martin Luther King, Jr. Found. v. American Heritage Prods., Inc., 250 Ga. 135, 296 S.E.2d 697, 703, 216 USPQ 711, 716 (1982) (infringement of the right of publicity is a tort); *Midler v. Ford Motor Co.*, 849 F.2d 460, 462 (9th. Cir. 1988) ("Appropriation of such common law rights is a tort in California."); *McFarland v. Miller*, 14 F.3d 912, 917, 29 USPQ2d 1586, 1590 (3d Cir. 1994) ("In New Jersey, [plaintiff's] claim to a right of publicity sounds in tort.").

total concept and feel [copyright] A test used by some courts as one way to define the level and degree of overall SUBSTANTIAL SIMILARITY needed to constitute INFRINGEMENT OF COPYRIGHT. Under this test, the copyrighted work is compared to the accused work as a whole, without removal of any unprotectible elements, to determine whether the overall feel or mood of the works is substantially similar.

Origin of Theory. The total concept and feel test originated in the context of copyright infringement of greeting cards. "[I]n total concept and feel the cards of United are the same as the copyrighted cards of Roth. ... [T]he characters depicted in the art work, the mood they portrayed, the combination of art work conveying a particular mood with a particular message, and the arrangement of the words on the greeting card are substantially the same as in Roth's cards." *Roth Greeting Cards v. United Card Co.*, 429 F.2d 1106, 1110, 166 USPQ 291, 294 (9th Cir. 1970). The total concept and feel doctrine evolved into the modern LOOK AND FEEL theory for substantial similarity. Both have fallen into disfavor.

See INFRINGEMENT OF COPYRIGHT, LOOK AND FEEL, SUBSTANTIAL SIMILARITY.

- *Case References*:

"It is clear to us that defendants' works are substantially similar to plaintiffs'. They have captured the 'total concept and feel' of the [plaintiff's television puppet] show." *Sid & Marty Krofft Television Prods. v. McDonald's Corp.*, 562 F.2d 1157, 1167, 196 USPQ 97, 105 (9th Cir. 1977).

"No copyright protection may be afforded to the idea of producing stuffed dinosaur toys or to elements of expression that necessarily follow from the idea of such dolls.... Under the intrinsic test, we may find substantial similarity of expression only if a reasonable observer would infer that [defendant's] dolls capture the 'total concept and feel' of [plaintiff's] designs." *Aliotti v. Dakin & Co.*, 831 F.2d 898, 902, 4 USPQ2d 1869, 1872 (9th Cir. 1987).

- *Treatise References*: 3 *Nimmer on Copyright* §13.03[A][1][c] (1994 rev.) (criticizing the test); 2 P. Goldstein, *Copyright* §7.3 (1989) (criticizing the test); W. Patry, *Copyright Law and Practice* 713 (1994) (criticizing the test); 1 N. Boorstyn, *Copyright* §11.08[2] (2d ed. 1994) (criticizing the test).

trade dress [trademark] The totality of elements in which a product or service is packaged or presented. These elements combine to create the whole visual image presented to customers and are capable of acquiring exclusive legal rights as a type of trademark or identifying symbol of origin.

Expansive Scope of "Trade Dress." At one time, "trade dress" referred only to the manner in which a product was "dressed up" to go to market with a label, package, display card, and similar packaging elements making up the total image. Cases involving imitation of the physical shape and appearance of the product itself were usually analyzed under the separate rubric of "product simulation." However, under the modern definition, "trade dress" has taken on a more expansive meaning and includes the shape and appearance of the product as well as that of the container and all elements making up the total visual image by which the product is presented to customers. *LeSportsac, Inc. v. K Mart Corp.*, 754 F.2d 71, 75, 225 USPQ 654, 656 (2d Cir. 1985) (protectible trade dress can include "the design of a product itself"); *Kohler Co. v. Moen, Inc.*, 12 F.3d 632, 641 n.11, 29 USPQ2d 1241, 1248 n.11 (7th Cir. 1993) (the modern "broad definition of trade dress as applied by the courts includes product configurations"). Trade dress is defined by looking to the total assembly of elements, not each individual element. Trade dress can consist of an assemblage of individually commonplace and nondistinctive features that are assembled in a distinctive way and used to identify source. E.g., *Roulo v. Russ Berrie & Co.*, 886 F.2d 931, 12 USPQ2d 1423 (7th Cir. 1989).

- *Examples of Trade Dress*. Since "trade dress" includes all factors making up the total image under which a product or service is presented to customers, it potentially covers almost all aspects of appearance. Things that have been held protectible under the category of "trade dress" include: the shape and appearance of a product; the shape and appearance of a container; the cover of a book or magazine; the layout and appearance of a place of business, such as a restaurant; the theme and "look" of a line of distinctive greeting cards; and the distinctive and recognizable shape of a automobile.

Trade Dress Law Is a Category of Trademark Law. Trade dress law is not a separate body of law with separate rules. It is merely one form of trademark law and is governed by the same rules of validity and infringement as trademark law. Federal Lanham Act §43(a) is often used as a vehicle by which to assert trade dress protection in the federal courts. In §43(a) cases, the traditional principles of trade dress and trademark law are applied. *Taco Cabana Int'l Inc. v. Two Pesos, Inc.*, 112 S. Ct. 2753, 23 USPQ2d 1081 (1992).

Rules of Trade Dress Law. The Supreme Court has held that if the elements making up the trade dress are so unusual or extraordinary as to be inherently distinctive, then proof of secondary meaning is unnecessary. *Taco Cabana Int'l Inc. v. Two Pesos, Inc.*, 112 S. Ct. 2753, 2760, 23 USPQ2d 1081, 1086 (1992) ("We see no basis for requiring secondary meaning for inherently distinctive trade dress protection under §43(a) but not for other distinctive words, symbols, or devices capable of identifying a producer's product."). The test of trade dress infringement is that of a likelihood of confusion. See INFRINGEMENT OF A TRADEMARK. Similarity of trade dress is to be determined by comparing the impression created by the overall similarity of all the elements making up the protectible trade dress and the accused trade dress. But each of the elements alleged to constitute the trade dress must be found in the accused product or advertisement. In some cases, the prominent use of a famous word mark on the accused look-alike product or package can prevent confusion. See, e.g., *Bristol-Myers Squibb Co. v. McNeil-PPC Inc.*, 973 F.2d 1033, 24 USPQ2d 1161 (2d Cir. 1992).

A Functional Composite Is Not Protectible. The rule that functional features are not protectible by trademark law applies with full force to trade dress cases. However, the question is not whether such a product per se is functional, but whether that particular feature or combination of features claimed as trade dress is functional. For example, while luggage made of lightweight nylon is functional, a particular combination of features is not functional. The features included parachute nylon in a variety of colors, trimmed in cotton carpet tape with matching cotton webbing straps, color-coordinated zippers with hollow rectangular metal zippers, and a repeating logo in an elongated ellipse. *Le Sportsac, Inc. v. K Mart Corp.*, 754 F.2d 71, 225 USPQ 654 (2d Cir. 1985). A combination of individually functional features can form a nonfunctional and protectible composite image. E.g., *Taco Cabana Int'l Inc. v. Two Pesos, Inc.*, 932 F.2d 1113, 19 USPQ2d 1253, 1257 (5th Cir. 1991), *aff'd*, 112 S. Ct. 2753, 23 USPQ2d 1081 (1992) (protection granted for trade dress in a distinctive combination of interior and exterior architectural design, layout, and decoration of chain of Mexican restaurants).

See TRADEMARK, INFRINGEMENT OF A TRADEMARK, FUNCTIONALITY, SECONDARY MEANING.

- *Treatise Reference*: 1 J.T. McCarthy, *Trademarks and Unfair Competition* §§7.23–.25, 8.01–.07 (3d ed. 1995 rev.).

- *Restatement Reference*: "The term 'trade dress' is often used to describe the overall appearance or image of goods or services as offered for sale in the marketplace. 'Trade dress' traditionally includes the appearance of labels, wrapper, and containers used in packaging a product as well as displays and other materials used in presenting the product to prospective purchasers. The design features of the product itself are also sometimes included within the meaning of 'trade dress,' although the substantive rules applicable to the protection of product designs differ in some respects from those applicable to packing and related subject matter." *Restatement (Third) of Unfair Competition* §16, comment a (1995).

- *Case References*:
"An infringement of the trade dress is proven if: (1) the plaintiff's trade dress is inherently distinctive or has acquired secondary meaning, (2) the plaintiff's trade dress is primarily nonfunctional, and (3) the defendant's trade dress is confusingly similar, engendering a likelihood of confusion in the marketplace." *Roulo v. Russ Berrie & Co.*, 886 F.2d 931, 935, 12 USPQ2d 1423, 1426 (7th Cir. 1989).

"Protection of trade dress, no less than of trademarks, serves the [Lanham] Act's purpose to 'secure to the owner of the mark the goodwill of his business and to protect the ability of consumers to distinguish among competing products.' " *Taco Cabana Int'l Inc. v. Two Pesos, Inc.*, 112 S. Ct. 2753, 2760, 23 USPQ2d 1081, 1086 (1992).

"Moreover, unless the trade dress is memorable—that is, striking or unusual in appearance, or prominently displayed on the product packaging, or otherwise somehow apt to be impressed upon the minds of consumers, so that it is likely to be actually and distinctly remembered—it cannot serve as a designator of origin." *Duraco Prods. Inc. v. Joy Plastic Enters.*

Ltd., 40 F.3d 1431, 1449, 32 USPQ2d 1724, 1738 (3d Cir. 1994).

trademark [trademark] (1) A word, slogan, design, picture, or any other symbol used to identify and distinguish goods. (2) Any identifying symbol, including a word, design, or shape of a product or container, which qualifies for legal status as a trademark, service mark, collective mark, certification mark, trade name, or trade dress.

Dual Meaning of "Trademark." The term "trademark" is often used in two different senses, one broad and one narrow. In its broader meaning, "trademark" or "trademark law" is a generic term used to indicate the whole field of protection of all forms of indications of origin, including marks used on goods, service marks, collective marks, certification marks, TRADE NAMES, and TRADE DRESS. Usually this is the meaning intended when one sees phrases like "the principles of trademark protection" or "slogans can be protected as trademarks." In its narrower meaning, "trademark" is used to designate only words and symbols used to identify and distinguish goods, as opposed to services (SERVICE MARKS), corporate entities (TRADE NAMES), or other subcategories of trade identity law. Thus, the designation "trademark" is like the designation "New York": sometimes it denotes a broad concept (New York State), sometimes it denotes a narrower part of that broad concept (New York City). Context supplies the meaning. Sometimes the word "MARK" is used as a synonym for the broader meaning of "trademark." A service mark identifies and distinguishes services rather than products and is protected and registered on the same legal principles as is a trademark.

State and Federal Sources of Legal Protection and Registration. Trademarks are protected by state common law, are registrable in almost all states, are federally registrable, and are protected as unregistered marks in the federal courts under Lanham Act §43(a). See REGISTRATION OF A TRADEMARK. When Lanham Act §43(a) is used as the vehicle for assertion of rights against infringement of an unregistered trademark, the federal substantive law rules applied are the traditional principles of trademark validity and infringement. *Taco Cabana Int'l Inc. v. Two Pesos, Inc.*, 112 S. Ct. 2753, 23 USPQ2d 1081 (1992); 3 J.T. McCarthy, *Trademarks and Unfair Competition* §27.03[1][b] (3d ed. 1995 rev.). Usually, there is no conflict caused by concurrent state and federal registration and regulation of trademarks. However, state law cannot narrow the rights of a federal registrant or permit the confusion of customers, which federal law seeks to prevent. But state law can expand the rights of the federal trademark registrant by granting greater rights to prevent confusion of customers. *Golden Door, Inc. v. Odisho*, 646 F.2d 347, 208 USPQ 638 (9th Cir. 1980). Similarly, state law can grant a remedy against infringement under conditions that are easier to meet than those required by federal law. *Tonka Corp. v. Tonk-A-Phone*, 805 F.2d 793, 231 USPQ 872 (8th Cir. 1986) (state law can permit award of ATTORNEY FEES even in the absence of a finding that the case is "exceptional," as required by federal law).

Federal Trademark Legislation. Federal trademark legislation began with a false step in the 1870 Act, which was held unconstitutional by the Supreme Court because the Act applied to all marks, regardless of whether or not they were used in interstate or foreign commerce. The Supreme Court held that the power of Congress to regulate trademarks does not flow from the Patent and Copyright Clause of the CONSTITUTION, but only from the Commerce Clause. *The Trademark Cases*, 100 U.S. 82 (1879). While limited trademark legislation was enacted in the wake of this decision, not until 1905 was the first modern federal trademark statute enacted. The present trademark legislation is the federal trademark act of 1946, known as the LANHAM ACT, codified at 15 U.S.C. §§1051–27. Signed into law on July 5, 1946, it took effect on July 5, 1947, and has been amended many times since. Special civil and criminal prohibitions against COUNTERFEITING were added by amendments in 1984. Part of the 1984 "*Anti-Monopoly*" amendments redefined "trademark" to make it clear that marks may distinguish unique products and products whose source is unknown by name to customers. This was designed to eliminate comments to the contrary by the Court of Appeals for the

Ninth Circuit in *Anti-Monopoly, Inc. v. General Mills, Inc.*, 684 F.2d 1326, 216 USPQ 588 (9th Cir. 1982). The TRADEMARK LAW REVISION ACT OF 1988, effective in 1989, made extensive changes to the Lanham Act, the most important of which was the adoption of an INTENT TO USE APPLICATION system. See REGISTRATION OF A TRADEMARK.

Functions of Trademarks. Trademarks perform four functions:

(1) Identification—to identify one seller's goods and distinguish them from goods sold by others. A trademark can identify a manufacturing source, a selling source (a MERCHANT'S MARK), or a source of sponsorship or authorization. For example, the mark of a university on clothing can signify that the university authorizes, endorses, and licenses the sale of such items by the maker.

(2) Source—to signify that all goods bearing the trademark come from, or are controlled by, a single, albeit anonymous, source. This could be a manufacturing source or a licensing source. The traditional rule that the buyer need not know or be able to identify the name of the source was codified in the Lanham Act definitions of trademark and service mark in 1984 amendments. *A.J. Canfield Co. v. Honickman*, 808 F.2d 291, 299, 1 USPQ2d 1364, 1371 (3d Cir. 1986). See 1 J.T. McCarthy, *Trademarks and Unfair Competition* §3.03[2] (3d ed. 1995 rev.).

(3) Quality—to indicate that all goods bearing the trademark are of an equal level of quality, whether that level is high, low, or a particular quality desired by customers, such as a reasonably priced, no-frills motel chain. The quality function is an outgrowth of the source theory of trademarks, which evolved to include not only the manufacturing source, but also the licensing source of standards of quality of goods bearing the mark.

(4) Advertising—to advertise, promote, and generally assist in selling the goods. Trademarks help advertise and sell the goods by providing a symbol upon which the buyer can fix his or her expectations and associations concerning the product and its qualities. Some trademarks can become so strong and well recognized in a culture that they symbolize not only the source of a product, but in addition they trigger a complex set of cultural meanings and associations connected to that product. For example: COCA-COLA, CHEVROLET CORVETTE, HARLEY-DAVIDSON, TEFLON, SONY WALKMAN, and McDONALD'S.

Spectrum of Distinctiveness. All trademarks are initially categorized for their validity as being either inherently distinctive or noninherently distinctive. The inherent distinctiveness of trademarks is determined by the placement of the mark on the spectrum of distinctiveness, which runs in ascending order of inherent distinctiveness as follows: (1) GENERIC NAME (not a trademark at all); (2) the category of DESCRIPTIVE MARKS, GEOGRAPHIC MARKS, and PERSONAL NAME MARKS; (3) SUGGESTIVE MARKS; and (4) the category of ARBITRARY MARKS and FANCIFUL MARKS. Terms in categories (3) and (4) are inherently distinctive terms that are protected as trademarks as soon as they are used in the marketplace to identify and distinguish. Terms in category (2) are noninherently distinctive terms and to reach the status of a protectible trademark, they must acquire distinctiveness through the acquisition of SECONDARY MEANING. *Taco Cabana Int'l Inc. v. Two Pesos, Inc.*, 112 S. Ct. 2753, 2757, 23 USPQ2d 1081, 1083 (1992). That is, they must become established among the relevant public as indicia of origin to identify and distinguish the source in addition to describing some attribute or geographic source or naming some person. See 1 J.T. McCarthy, *Trademarks and Unfair Competition* §§11.01–.23 (3d ed. 1995 rev.).

Strength of Mark. All terms that meet the minimum criteria for qualification as a trademark are not of equal strength, either inherently or through usage in the marketplace. The greater the power of a mark to be recognized as an identifying symbol, the greater its strength. The greater the strength of a mark, the more valuable it is economically, the more drawing power it has as a marketing tool, and the broader its scope of legal protection. See discussion at STRENGTH OF MARK.

Infringement of Trademark. In the vast majority of cases, the scope of the exclusive rights in a trademark is defined by the "likelihood of confusion test." A trademark is infringed by a junior user if the use causes likely confusion of source, affiliation, connection, or sponsorship. The test is a likelihood —a probability—of confusion, not actual confusion. Infringement can also be triggered by REVERSE CONFUSION. In a limited number of instances, the principle of trademark DILUTION may come into play, which creates liability for actions that do not cause a likelihood of confusion. Trademark infringement is a type of UNFAIR COMPETITION and is a commercial TORT. See discussion at INFRINGEMENT OF A TRADEMARK, CONTRIBUTORY INFRINGEMENT.

Assignments and Licenses. A trademark can be assigned along with the GOOD WILL symbolized by that trademark. An assignment devoid of such good will is invalid as an "assignment in gross." See ASSIGNMENT OF TRADEMARK. A trademark can be licensed so long as the licensor controls the nature and quality of the goods sold by the licensee under the trademark. A license with no such quality control is a "naked license," which potentially deceives the public and puts the trademark at risk.

See LICENSE OF TRADEMARK.

International Relations. The United States is a member of the Paris Union as a signatory of the PARIS CONVENTION. The trademark obligations of the United States under the Paris Convention are implemented in Lanham Act §44, 15 U.S.C. §1126.

Benefits Accorded to Foreign Applicants. Lanham Act §44 grants special benefits in filing an application for federal registration to a qualified foreign firm with an application or registration in a foreign nation. While the foreign applicant must state that it has a bona fide intention to use the mark in the United States on the goods or services listed, it need not use or prove actual use in order to obtain the registration. In any application under §44, the applicant need not state a date of first use anywhere in the world and need not provide specimens of use. 4 J.T. McCarthy, *Trademarks and Unfair Competition* §29.04 (3d ed. 1995 rev.). Under Lanham Act §44(d), 15 U.S.C. §1126(d), an application in the United States for registration of a mark by a person whose country of origin is a party to the PARIS CONVENTION is entitled to a priority convention filing date as of the date of filing of a prior trademark application in a foreign country that is also a party to the Paris Convention.

See CONVENTION DATE.

Territoriality. Under the principle of TERRITORIALITY, a trademark has a separate legal existence in each sovereign nation in which it has been registered or used. Registration or use in a foreign nation per se does not create trademark rights in the United States.

See REGISTRATION OF A TRADEMARK, STRENGTH OF A MARK, SECONDARY MEANING, INFRINGEMENT OF A TRADEMARK, COUNTERFEITING, PASSING OFF, SERVICE MARK, COLLECTIVE MARK, CERTIFICATION MARK, TRADE DRESS.

- *Treatise Reference*: J.T. McCarthy, *Trademarks and Unfair Competition* (3d ed. 1995 rev.).

- *Statutory Reference*: Lanham Act §45, 15 U.S.C. §1127: "The term 'trademark' means any word, name, symbol, or device, or any combination thereof—

"(1) used by a person, or

"(2) which a person has a bona fide intention to use in commerce and applies to register on the principal register established by this Act,

"to identify and distinguish his or her goods, including a unique product, from those manufactured or sold by others and to indicate the source of the goods, even if that source is unknown."

- *Restatement Reference*: "The test for infringement is whether the actor's use of a designation as a trademark, trade name, collective mark, or certification mark creates a likelihood of confusion.... The likelihood of confusion standard applies in infringement actions at common law as well as in actions arising under the Lanham Act and under state trademark registration and unfair competition statutes. Whether the use of a particular designation causes a likelihood of confusion must be evaluated in light of the overall market context in which the designation is used." *Restatement (Third) of Unfair Competition* §21, comment a (1995).

• *Case References*:

"His mark is his authentic seal; by it he vouches for the goods which bear it; it carries his name for good or ill. If another uses it, he borrows the owner's reputation, whose quality no longer lies within his control. This is an injury, even though the borrower does not tarnish it, or divert any sales by its use; for a reputation, like a face, is the symbol of its possessor and creator, and another can use it only as a mask.... The [senior user] need not permit another to attach to its good will the consequences of trade methods not its own." Judge Learned Hand in *Yale Elec. Corp. v. Robertson*, 26 F.2d 972, 974 (2d Cir. 1928).

"The protection of trademarks is the law's recognition of the psychological function of symbols. If it is true that we live by symbols, it is no less true that we purchase goods by them. A trademark is a merchandising short-cut which induces a purchaser to select what he wants, or what he has been led to believe he wants. The owner of a trademark exploits this human propensity by making every human effort to impregnate the atmosphere of the mark with the drawing power of a congenial symbol. Whatever the means employed, the aim is the same— to convey through the mark, in the minds of potential customers, the desirability of the commodity upon which it appears. Once this is attained, the trademark owner has something of value. If another poaches upon the commercial magnetism of the symbol he has created, the owner can obtain legal redress." Justice Frankfurter in *Misawaka Rubber & Woolen Mfg. Co. v. S.S. Kresge Co.*, 316 U.S. 203, 205 (1942).

"To say one has a 'trademark' implies ownership and ownership implies the right to exclude others. If the law will not protect one's claim of right to exclude others from using an alleged trademark, then he does not own a 'trademark,' for that which all are free to use cannot be a trademark." Judge Rich in *Application of Deister Concentrator Co.*, 289 F.2d 496, 501 n.5, 129 USPQ 314, 320 n.5 (C.C.P.A. 1961).

"[B]latant trademark infringement inhibits competition and subverts both goals of the Lan-

ham Act. By applying a trademark to goods produced by one other than the trademark's owner, the infringer deprives the owner of the goodwill which he spent energy, time and money to obtain.... At the same time, the infringer deprives consumers of their ability to distinguish among the goods of competing manufacturers." Justice O'Connor in *Inwood Labs. Inc. v. Ives Labs., Inc.*, 456 U.S. 844, 854 n.14, 214 USPQ 1, 6 n.14 (1982).

"Marks are often classified in categories of increasing distinctiveness; following the classic formulation set out by Judge Friendly, they are (1) generic; (2) descriptive; (3) suggestive; (4) arbitrary; or (5) fanciful. ... The latter three categories of marks, because their intrinsic nature serves to identify a particular source of a product, are deemed inherently distinctive and are entitled to protection...." *Taco Cabana Int'l Inc. v. Two Pesos, Inc.*, 112 S. Ct. 2753, 2757, 23 USPQ2d 1081, 1083 (1992).

"The courts and the Patent and Trademark Office have authorized for use as a mark a particular shape (of a Coca-Cola bottle), a particular sound (of NBC's three chimes), and even a particular scent (of plumeria blossoms on sewing thread).... If a shape, a sound, and a fragrance can act as symbols, why, one might ask, can a color not do the same?" *Qualitex Co. v. Jacobson Prods. Co.*, 115 S. Ct. 1300, 1302, 34 USPQ2d 1161, 1162 (1995) (upholding the registration of a single color for a product: a green/gold color used on dry cleaning press pads),

Trademark Law Revision Act [trademark]
A package of revisions to the federal Lanham Trademark Act establishing, among other things, an INTENT TO USE APPLICATION system in the United States. The Trademark Law Revision Act (TLRA) became effective on November 16, 1989.

History of the TLRA. In August 1987 the TRADEMARK REVIEW COMMISSION (TRC) issued its Report and Recommendations, published at 77 Trademark Rep. 375 (1987). Bills were introduced in both houses of Congress to enact the TRC's recommendations into law. Various committee hearings were held in the Senate and the House, leading to a different version in each house of Congress for a package of amendments to the Lanham Act. With the 100th Congress drawing to a close in the fall of 1988, a last-minute meeting in a Senate-House conference led to agreement on a compromise version. This version received congressional passage in both houses in October 1988. The Trademark Law Revision Act was signed into law by President Reagan on November 16, 1988, and became effective one year later.

- *Treatise Reference*: 1 J.T. McCarthy, *Trademarks and Unfair Competition* §5.05[4] (3d ed. 1995 rev.).

- *Legislative Citations*: Trademark Law Revision Act of 1988, Pub. L. No. 100-667, 102 Stat. 3935 (effective Nov. 16, 1989).

- *Legislative History Guide*: A very valuable collection of materials forming the legislative history of the 1988 Trademark Law Revision Act is contained in the U.S. Trademark Association (USTA) booklet "The Trademark Law Revision Act of 1988" available from the USTA. See also *Symposium on the 1988 Revision Act*, 79 Trademark Rep. 219–394 (1989).

Trademark Law Treaty [international–trademark] A multilateral treaty that harmonizes and unifies among its member nations many of the administrative requirements for trademark registration. The goal of the treaty is to reduce the costs of obtaining trademark registration in various nations around the world.

History of Treaty. Under the aegis of the WORLD INTELLECTUAL PROPERTY ORGANIZATION, negotiations resulting in the Trademark Law Treaty (TLT) were concluded in October 1994 in Geneva. At that final diplomatic conference, 35 of the 97 nations and international organizations represented signed the treaty. The United States also signed the TLT. As this goes to press, the treaty had not yet been ratified by the United States nor had implementing legislation yet been enacted by Congress. The treaty will become effective after ratification by five nations.

General Goals. The treaty not only harmonizes many registration formalities, but also eliminates some government requirements for trademark registration that had proven unduly burdensome to trademark owners. Because procedures for registration and recordation of changes in trademark registration differed widely among nations, harmonization results in reduced expenses and facilitates world trade.

Provisions. The treaty contains 25 articles and is supported by implementing regulations. Among its key provisions are the following. The TLT requires member nations to register service marks and equates service marks with trademarks for purposes of the treaty requirements. The TLT requires member nations use multiclass applications that permit a single application to cover goods and services falling in multiple classes. The TLT permits member nations to use an INTENT-TO-USE application system with proof of use required as a predicate to registration—system that the United States has had since 1989. The TLT prohibits the requirement of certain technical formalities, such as a certificate from a register of commerce or proof of registration in another country, except where CONVENTION DATE priority is desired. Under the TLT, it will no longer be necessary to notarize or otherwise legalize signatures on communications with the government registration office. (Art. (8)(4))

Changes in Ownership of Registrations. The TLT greatly simplifies the procedures for recording changes in name and ownership of trademark applications and registration. A standard international form is provided in the treaty regulations, and each nation must accept the request for change if made on an official form. However, a nation may require that the request be made in the local official language. A significant simplification is a provision permitting one form to serve to change ownership of multiple applications or registrations. Arts. 11(1)(h), 11(3). If a change in ownership results from a corporate merger, a nation may require a certified copy of an official document evidencing the merger. A nation may not require, as a condition of changing title to a registration, that an assignee prove that it received the business or relevant good will of the trademark. Art.

11(4)(iv). However, this provision does not preclude a nation, such as the United States, from enforcing a rule against assignments in gross.

Duration of Registration. The TLT harmonizes the term of registration and of succeeding renewals at 10 years.

Renewal of Registration. The TLT defines the conditions that may be required for renewal of registration. It specifically prohibits the requirement of a declaration or proof of actual use as a condition of renewal, as required by U.S. law. Art. 13(4)(iii). However, a nation can apply use requirements during the registration period outside of the renewal procedure.

See TRADEMARK REGISTRATION TREATY.

• *Textual Reference*: 49 Pat. Trademark & Copyright J. (BNA) 22, 30 (Nov. 10, 1994).

• *Commentary Reference*: G. Kunze, The Trademark Law Treaty, *Managing Intell. Prop.* 23 (Feb. 1995).

Trademark Manual of Examining Procedure [trademark]
See *TMEP*.

Trademark Registration Treaty [trademark–international] A multilateral treaty that would establish a multinational trademark filing arrangement for securing, administering, and maintaining national trademark registrations. Applications for registration of trademarks and service marks would be filed with WIPO in Switzerland. Such international filing would have the same effect in each of the nations party to the treaty which the applicant designates as would exist had the application been filed in each of those nations. In 1973 the Trademark Registration Treaty (TRT) was signed at Vienna by eight nations, including the United States, and by the end of 1973, 14 nations had signed. However, as of 1994, the TRT is only theoretically in force because only the former U.S.S.R. and four African nations had officially ratified the treaty. President Ford transmitted the TRT to the U.S. Senate in 1975 for ratification, and proposed implementing legislation was made public in 1978. But opposition to the treaty stalled further action. Because of the continued nonadherence of the United States, the treaty has never had any significant impact on international trademark matters.

• *Treatise Reference*: 4 J.T. McCarthy, *Trademarks and Unfair Competition* §29.10[3] (3d ed. 1995 rev.).

Trademark Review Commission [trademark] A special committee of trademark experts that studied U.S. trademark law and prepared a report recommending certain statutory changes in federal trademark law, including the adoption of an INTENT TO USE application system. Almost all the recommendations of the Trademark Review Commission (TRC) were enacted into law by Congress as part of the 1988 TRADEMARK LAW REVISION ACT, which became effective November 16, 1989.

History of the TRC. In 1985, the U.S. Trademark Association (USTA) chartered a special committee, the Trademark Review Commission (TRC) to study the U.S. trademark system and recommend improvements. The TRC was composed of approximately 30 members who met and corresponded for over two years. In August 1987 the TRC issued its Report and Recommendations, which is published at 77 Trademark Rep. 375 (1987). Bills were introduced in both houses of Congress to enact the TRC's recommendations into law. Various committee hearings were held in the Senate and the House, leading to a last-minute compromise in a Senate-House conference, which resulted in congressional passage in October 1988. The Trademark Law Revision Act (TLRA) was signed into law by President Reagan on November 16, 1988, and became effective one year later.

Trademark Trial and Appeal Board [trademark] An administrative tribunal in the Patent and Trademark Office, which: (1) decides appeals from a FINAL REJECTION of an application to register a mark; and (2) decides INTER PARTES proceedings involving challenges to the registration of marks.

Abbreviation: TTAB.

Inter Partes Cases. Since 1958, the INTER PARTES trademark proceedings of OPPOSITION, CANCELLATION, CONCURRENT USE PROCEEDING, and INTERFERENCE have been heard by the Trademark Trial and Appeal Board sitting as a fact-finding and decision-making body. Lanham Act §17, 15 U.S.C. §1067.

Ex Parte Appeals. Similarly, since 1958, EX PARTE appeals from denials of registration of marks have been heard by the Trademark Trial and Appeal Board sitting as an administrative appellate tribunal, reviewing the decisions made by the trademark attorneys examiners. Lanham Act §20, 15 U.S.C. §1070.

Procedure in TTAB Cases. Each case must be heard by at least three members of the Board. Lanham Act §17. Proceedings before the TTAB are governed by rules in 37 C.F.R. §§2.91–.145. Except as otherwise provided in those rules, procedure and practice in inter partes proceedings are governed by the Federal Rules of Civil Procedure. 37 C.F.R. §2.116(a). Pretrial discovery is permitted via depositions, interrogatories, requests for admission, and production of documents. Trial procedure differs considerably from that in federal courts, since "testimony" and "trial" in inter partes cases consist of testimony taken through a deposition-like procedure. Live testimony is not taken before the Board, but around the nation before court reporters. The Board thus "hears" testimony solely via a written transcript. Evidence not obtained and timely filed in compliance with the TTAB rules of procedure will not be considered, and the Board strictly enforces this rule. Motions in inter partes TTAB proceedings may be made either upon the express grounds set forth in the TTAB rules of procedure or upon grounds allowed in the Federal Rules of Civil Procedure. Resolution of cases on a motion for summary judgment became more common in the late 1980s. *Sweats Fashions, Inc. v. Pannill Knitting Co.*, 833 F.2d 1560, 4 USPQ2d 1793 (Fed. Cir. 1987).

Appeal From the Trademark Trial and Appeal Board. A party who is dissatisfied with the decision of the TTAB in an EX PARTE or INTER PARTES case has a choice of places to appeal. The party may appeal to: (1) the Court of APPEALS FOR THE FEDERAL CIRCUIT or (2) to a federal district court. Lanham Act §21, 15 U.S.C. §1071. If one party has already filed an appeal to the Federal Circuit, any adverse party may, within 20 days, elect to have the case reviewed by a federal district court. Thus, an appeal to the Federal Circuit can be made only with the consent of all parties. The purpose of the choice is to give the litigants the option of producing new evidence in a civil action in a federal district court, as opposed to an appeal to the Federal Circuit on the evidentiary record already produced before the TTAB. Also, additional claims can be added to a review before a district court. Federal district court review, while called a "de novo" review because new evidence may be introduced, is a unique proceeding because findings of fact made by the TTAB are given great weight and are not reversed unless new evidence is introduced that produces a "thorough conviction" that contrary findings are required. The Court of Appeals for the Federal Circuit will not reverse the factual findings of the TTAB unless they are found to be "clearly erroneous," but the ultimate determination of a likelihood of confusion is reviewed by the Federal Circuit on appeal as a legal conclusion.

See FINAL REJECTION, OPPOSITION PROCEEDING, CANCELLATION PROCEEDING.

- *Treatise Reference*: 3 J.T. McCarthy, *Trademarks & Unfair Competition* §§20.26–.34 (inter partes procedures); 21.01–.05 (ex parte appeals to the TTAB and appeals to the CAFC and federal district court) (3d ed. 1995 rev.).

- *Statutory References*:

Lanham Act §17, 15 U.S.C. §1067: "In every case of interference, opposition to registration, application to register as a lawful concurrent user, or application to cancel the registration of a mark, the Commissioner shall give notice to all parties and shall direct a Trademark Trial and Appeal Board to determine and decide the respective rights of registration ..."

Lanham Act §20, 15 U.S.C. §1070: "An appeal may be taken to the Trademark Trial and Appeal Board from any final decision of the examiner in charge of the registration of marks upon the payment of the prescribed fee."

trade name [trademark] A symbol used to identify and distinguish companies, partnerships, and businesses, as opposed to marks used to identify and distinguish goods or services.

Common Law and Federal Protection of Trade Names. Trade names, such as the names of corporate, professional, and business organizations, have long been protected at common law under the same principles of law as are trademarks. *American Steel Foundries v. Robertson*, 269 U.S. 372 (1926). Protected under similar principles are the names of charitable corporations, professional and fraternal groups, educational institutions, and religious groups and organizations. See 1 J.T. McCarthy, *Trademarks and Unfair Competition* §9.01 et seq. (3d ed. 1995 rev.). Federal Lanham Act §43(a) can be used as a vehicle by which to assert infringement of a trade name in federal court. *Railroad Salvage of Conn., Inc. v. Railroad Salvage, Inc.*, 561 F. Supp. 1014, 219 USPQ 167 (D.R.I. 1983); *Accuride Int'l, Inc. v. Accuride Corp.*, 871 F.2d 1531, 10 USPQ2d 1589 (9th Cir. 1989).

Governed by Rules Similar to That of Trademarks. The test of infringement of a trade name is that of trademark law: likelihood of confusion. A trademark or service mark use can infringe on valid trade name rights. Conversely, a trade name can infringe on valid trademark or service mark rights. The legal categorization does not determine the likelihood that the public will be confused or deceived by similar names and marks. Trademark and corporate trade name protection is "intertwined," governed by the same test of infringement and serves the same basic purposes. *Accuride Int'l, Inc. v. Accuride Corp.*, 871 F.2d 1531, 10 USPQ2d 1589 (9th Cir. 1989).

Federal Registration. One major distinction between trade names on the one hand and trademarks and service marks on the other hand is that if a word is used only as a trade name, then it is not federally registrable. For example, the name of a corporation cannot be federally registered unless it is also used in a trademark or service mark sense. The distinction is that a trade name usage of a corporate name is only to identify the business entity, while a trademark usage identifies and distinguishes the source of

particular goods. *Application of Antenna Specialists Co.*, 408 F.2d 1052, 161 USPQ 284 (C.C.P.A. 1969). For example, use of a corporate name with "Company" or "Inc." and an address and phone number tends to indicate use as a trade name only to identify the business entity and is not a registrable use. See 1 J.T. McCarthy, *Trademarks and Unfair Competition* §9.06 (3d ed. 1995 rev.).

Archaic Usage. In archaic usage, a trade name denoted noninherently distinctive terms that were not protected as TECHNICAL TRADEMARKS but were protected under the law of UNFAIR COMPETITION upon proof of SECONDARY MEANING.

• *Treatise Reference*: 1 J.T. McCarthy, *Trademarks and Unfair Competition* §§4.03[4], 4.04[4], 9.01–.06 (3d ed. 1995 rev.).

• *Statutory Reference*: Lanham Act §45, 15 U.S.C. §1127: *Trade Name, Commercial Name.* "The terms 'trade name' and 'commercial name' mean any name used by a person to identify his or her business or vocation."

trade secret [trade secret] Business information that is the subject of reasonable efforts to preserve confidentiality and has value because it is not generally known in the trade. Such confidential information will be protected against those who obtain access through improper methods or by a breach of confidence. Infringement of a trade secret is a TORT and a type of UNFAIR COMPETITION. Every alleged infringement of a trade secret involves two main issues: (1) whether there is valuable and secret business information; and (2) whether this defendant used improper means to obtain that information.

Sources of Trade Secret Law. Trade secret law is state law, not federal law. For many years, the criteria of the 1939 *Restatement of Torts* largely shaped and influenced the development of trade secret law in most states. The 1939 *Restatement* has been brought up to date by the 1995 *Restatement of Unfair Competition.* The 1979 Uniform Trade Secrets Act has become very popular and has been adopted (with various modifications) in about 40 states. See list at M. Jager, *Trade Secrets Law* §3.04 (1994 rev.).

It has been held that the misappropriation of a trade secret can form the nucleus of a valid allegation of a violation of the Racketeer Influenced and Corrupt Organizations Act (RICO). *Formax v. Hostert*, 841 F.2d 388, 5 USPQ2d 1939 (Fed. Cir. 1988).

Federal-State Relations. At one time, it was thought that federal patent law preempted state trade secret law as to some technical innovations. In a landmark 1974 decision, the Supreme Court removed any significant federal preemption obstacle to the application of state trade secret law even as to technical innovations that are clearly in a patentable category and are believed by the owner to be clearly patentable. "Congress, by its silence over these many years, has seen the wisdom of allowing the States to enforce trade secret protection. Until Congress takes affirmative action to the contrary, States should be free to grant protection to trade secrets." *Kewanee Oil Co. v. Bicron Corp.*, 416 U.S. 470, 493, 181 USPQ 673, 682 (1974).

Tort or Property. There is no doubt that "[c]onfidential business information has long been recognized as property." *Carpenter v. United States*, 484 U.S. 19, 26, 5 USPQ2d 1059, 1062 (1987). But Justice Holmes pointed out that a trade secret is a peculiar kind of property in that invasion of that property depends upon whether or not the particular defendant in the case abused a confidential disclosure. *E.I. du Pont de Nemours Powder Co. v. Masland*, 244 U.S. 100 (1917). Thus, a trade secret is a kind of relative property in that there is an infringement of the property only if there is a breach of a confidential relationship or the use of improper means to appropriate the confidential information. There are two different angles from which to look at a trade secret case:

(1) The "property view" where the defendant emphasizes the lack of secrecy precautions used by the plaintiff and the ease of REVERSE ENGINEERING to argue that there is really no "property" to be protected.

(2) The "tort view" where the plaintiff emphasizes the conduct of the defendant as being a tortious breach of confidence or use of improper means.

Some courts take the property view to hold that there is no trade secret if the information could have been ascertained by proper means, even if the defendant obtained it by improper means. See *Henry Hope X-Ray Prods., Inc. v. Marron Carrell, Inc.*, 674 F.2d 1336, 1341, 216 USPQ 762, 764 (9th Cir. 1982) (applying Pennsylvania law). But other courts use the tort view to hold that the issue is not how the defendant could have obtained the information, but whether the defendant in fact used improper, tortious means to obtain information that was not readily ascertainable. *Smith v. Dravo Corp.*, 203 F.2d 369, 375, 97 USPQ 98, 102 (7th Cir. 1953).

Requirement of Secrecy. The element of secrecy is a key requirement to the maintenance of a valid trade secret property right in commercial information. All secrecy is relative, for to have commercial value, secret information must be shared among workers who need to utilize that information to produce goods and services. Thus, "secrecy" implies that reasonable steps be taken to preserve the confidentiality of the information. Disclosure to persons who are under an obligation to maintain secrecy does not destroy the needed element of secrecy. *Metallurgical Indus., Inc. v. Fourtek, Inc.*, 790 F.2d 1195, 1199, 229 USPQ 945, 948 (5th Cir. 1986). But disclosure to persons who have no obligation of confidentiality "extinguishes the property right in the trade secret." *Sheets v. Yamaha Motors Corp.*, 849 F.2d 179, 184, 7 USPQ2d 1461, 1464 (5th Cir. 1988).

Reasonable Efforts to Maintain Secrecy. To maintain secrecy, the trade secret owner cannot remain passive, for in the absence of efforts to maintain secrecy, economically valuable technical data will leak. See *Motorola, Inc. v. Fairchild Camera & Instrument Corp.*, 366 F. Supp. 1173, 1186, 177 USPQ 614, 622 (D. Ariz. 1973) ("[P]laintiff's trade secret claims must fail because … no real effort was made by plaintiff prior to trial to keep them secret."). The kind of efforts that are reasonable under the circumstances will vary with the value of the data and the financial abilities of the company. "Only reasonable efforts, not all conceivable efforts, are required to protect the confidentiality of putative trade secrets." *Surgidev Corp. v. ETI Inc.*, 828 F.2d 452, 455, 4 USPQ2d 1090, 1092 (8th Cir. 1987). A small company should not be expected to maintain the kind of elaborate and expensive security system that a large company would maintain. At a minimum, reasonable efforts might include limiting access to the sensitive data on a "need to know" basis to key employees, having those employees sign confidentiality agreements, and alerting employees to the information that the employer considers to constitute trade secrets, such as by stamping "confidential" on key documents and keeping them in a secure location. The company must limit the access of outsiders to the information. See, e.g., *Sheets v. Yamaha Motors Corp.*, 849 F.2d 179, 183, 7 USPQ2d 1461, 1464 (5th Cir. 1988) (allowing persons under no obligation of secrecy to view allegedly secret invention supports finding of failure to take reasonable efforts to maintain secrecy).

Novelty. "Novelty, in the patent law sense, is not required for a trade secret." *Kewanee Oil Co. v. Bicron Corp.*, 416 U.S. 470, 476, 181 USPQ 673, 676 (1974). However, some degree of "novelty" is implicit in the requirement of "secrecy," for that which is not novel because it is known to all is not secret. "Novelty is only required of a trade secret to the extent necessary to show that the alleged trade secret is not a matter of public knowledge." *SI Handling Sys., Inc. v. Heisley*, 753 F.2d 1244, 1255, 225 USPQ 441, 447 (3d Cir. 1985). But the point is that the patent law standards of NOVELTY and NONOBVIOUSNESS have no application to trade secret law. Even "obvious" compilations of unpatentable engineering details or computer program listings can qualify as valuable and important trade secrets. See *Restatement (Third) of Unfair Competition* §39, comment f (1995) ("Although trade secret cases sometimes announce a 'novelty' requirement, the requirement is synonymous with the concepts of secrecy and value described in this section and the correlative exclusion of self-evident variants of the known art."); *Winston Research Corp. v. Minnesota Mining & Mfg. Co.*, 350 F.2d 134, 139, 146 USPQ 422, 425 (9th Cir. 1965) (even "mere choices of engineering design" are protectible as trade secrets).

Infringement of Trade Secret. There are proper and improper methods of uncovering or using the information that constitutes a legally protected trade secret. The classic improper and illegal methods of uncovering the trade secret information are: (1) industrial espionage, such as theft by breaking and entering or by electronic eavesdropping or wire tapping; (2) bribery, such as bribing an employee to breach a confidence and disclose information; (3) misrepresentation, such as obtaining data by misrepresenting oneself as an agent of a supplier of materials; and (4) breach of an explicit or implied contract or duty to maintain confidentiality, such as disclosure or use by an employee or a licensee under a promise not to disclose. In addition, there are other methods that may be improper under the circumstances, such as aerial photography of a competitor's chemical plant while it is in the process of construction. *E.I. du Pont de Nemours & Co. v. Christopher*, 431 F.2d 1012, 166 USPQ 421 (5th Cir. 1970).

Proper Methods of Obtaining Trade Secrets. Unlike patent law, trade secret law does not afford protection against all who obtain or use the protected technical knowledge. "While trade secret law does not forbid the discovery of the trade secret by fair and honest means, e.g., independent creation and reverse engineering, patent law operates 'against the world,' forbidding any use of the invention for whatever purpose for a significant length of time…. Where patent law acts as a barrier, trade secret law functions relatively as a sieve." *Kewanee Oil Co. v. Bicron Corp.*, 416 U.S. 470, 490, 181 USPQ 673, 681 (1974). The classic proper and legal methods of uncovering trade secret information are: (1) discovery by independent invention, such as a parallel and coincidental research effort that arrives at the same data; (2) discovery by REVERSE ENGINEERING, such as buying a product, disassembling it, and determining the information; (3) discovery by observation of a product that is in public use or is on public display; and (4) discovery by data available in publicly available literature, such as product specification sheets, promotional brochures, instruction sheets, or technical manuals.

Employee Mobility. Many trade secret infringement cases involve claims by an employer against a former employee. In such cases, public policy favoring employee mobility dictates that general skills and knowledge form the personal learning of every technical employee, who can use such information to increase personal skills for the benefit of any employer. But such general skills and knowledge must be distinguished from protected trade secrets, which comprise specific data that could have been acquired only from this employer as a result of work to solve a specific problem. *In re Innovative Constr. Sys., Inc.*, 793 F.2d 875, 879, 230 USPQ 94, 97 (7th Cir. 1986) (see quote below).

Remedies. Remedies for infringement of a trade secret include damages, profits, reasonable royalties, and an injunction. E.g., *Sperry Rand Corp. v. A-T-O Inc.*, 447 F.2d 1387, 171 USPQ 775 (4th Cir. 1971) (injunction and substantial actual and punitive damages awarded). As to the length of time that an injunction should last, many courts will issue a REVERSE ENGINEERING INJUNCTION which lasts for the estimated time it would take a hypothetical competitor to take a public disclosure and work backward to discover the trade secret.

See REVERSE ENGINEERING INJUNCTION.

Assignments and Licenses of Trade Secrets. Trade secret information can be sold by assignment or licensed to another. The Supreme Court held that there is no conflict with federal patent law when state law upholds a private license requiring the payment of use royalties which extends beyond the time when the trade secret became public through the licensee's sale of devices revealing the secret of construction. *Aronson v. Quick Point Pencil Co.*, 440 U.S. 257, 201 USPQ 1 (1979). There is no failure of consideration in such a license because, unlike a patent license, which is largely a waiver of a continuing right to sue, all the consideration from the owner of a trade secret flows to the licensee upon disclosure of the secret information. The method of paying for that disclosure can range from a single up-front payment to a use royalty which continues for any length of time.

Hybrid Patent-Trade Secret License. In the *Aronson* case, a patent application never matured into an issued patent. *Aronson v. Quick Point Pencil Co.*, 440 U.S. 257, 201 USPQ 1 (1979). But if a license conveys rights to use technology covered by both a patent application (which later matures into a patent) and trade secret, and the patent is held invalid, can the licensor continue to collect full use royalties based upon the continuing obligation to pay for the disclosure of the trade secret? If the patent and trade secret provisions in the license are "intertwined" as to time and amount, when the patent expires or is held invalid, so will end the ability of the licensor to collect the same royalty rate based on the trade secret. E.g., *Boggild v. Kenner Prods.*, 776 F.2d 1315, 228 USPQ 130 (6th Cir. 1985). However, if the patent and trade secret provisions are physically and contractually kept separate, with separate royalty rates, some think that then the trade secret royalties may be collectible regardless of the fate of the patent. The relevant policy is not to discourage the licensee from challenging the validity of the patent.

See LICENSEE ESTOPPEL.

Protection Against Trade Secret Disclosure in Other Types of Litigation. Courts have the power to issue a protective order limiting or precluding the disclosure in discovery or at trial of trade secret information in suits concerning other matters such as patent infringement, trademark infringement, and breach of contract. When a party seeking a protective order has shown that the information sought is a trade secret or confidential and that its disclosure might be harmful, the burden shifts to the party seeking discovery to establish that the information is relevant and necessary to its case. *American Standard Inc. v. Pfizer, Inc.*, 828 F.2d 734, 3 USPQ2d 1817 (Fed. Cir. 1987).

See KNOW-HOW, REVERSE ENGINEERING, REVERSE ENGINEERING INJUNCTION.

• *Treatise References*: R. Milgrim, *Trade Secrets* (1994 rev.); M. Jager, *Trade Secrets Law* (1994 rev.).

• *Statutory Reference*:

Uniform Trade Secrets Act, §1(4) (1985 rev.): " 'Trade secret' means information, including a formula, pattern, compilation, program, device, method, technique, or process, that:

"(i) derives independent economic value, actual or potential, from not being generally known to, and not being readily ascertainable by proper means by persons who can obtain economic value from its disclosure or use, and

"(ii) is the subject of efforts that are reasonable under the circumstances to maintain its secrecy."

• *Restatement References*:

"A trade secret is any information that can be used in the operation of a business or other enterprise and that is sufficiently valuable and secret to afford an actual or potential advantage over others." *Restatement (Third) of Unfair Competition* §39 (1995).

"A duty of confidence enforceable under the rules stated in §40 can be created by an express promise of confidentiality by the recipient of the disclosure. A duty of confidence may also be inferred from the relationship between the parties and the circumstances surrounding the disclosure. However, no duty of confidence will be inferred unless the recipient has notice of the confidential nature of the disclosure." *Restatement (Third) of Unfair Competition* §41, comment a (1995).

• *Case References*:

"A trade secret, however, does not offer protection against discovery by fair and honest means, such as by independent invention, accidental disclosure, or by so-called reverse engineering, that is by starting with the known product and working backward to divine the process which aided in its development or manufacture." *Kewanee Oil Co. v. Bicron Corp.*, 416 U.S. 470, 476, 181 USPQ 673, 676 (1974).

"In deciding whether to protect information, a balance must be struck between the competing interest of an employer in precluding others from exploiting specialized knowledge developed during the course of an employment relationship, and that of the former employee in the general use of his skills or training. Employers seek to protect information that they have spent time and effort gathering, and that gives them an advantage over competitors. Employees, however, quite understandably do not want such information protected if doing so would restrict their ability to find another position in the field in which they have developed exper-

tise." *In re Innovative Constr. Sys., Inc.*, 793 F.2d 875, 879, 230 USPQ 94, 97 (7th Cir. 1986).

transfer [copyright] An ASSIGNMENT, conveyance, or exclusive license of rights in a copyright, either by a voluntary private agreement or by operation of law, such as by order of a probate court pursuant to a devise in a will. A "transfer of copyright ownership" does not include a nonexclusive license. 17 U.S.C. §101.

Several Transfers of One Copyright. There can be a multiplicity of "transfers" of copyright ownership of several categories of the bundle of rights encompassed within a single copyright. For example, an author of a series of illustrated children's books could grant an exclusive license to Alpha Studios to produce a feature length DERIVATIVE WORK motion picture using the copyrightable elements of the books, an exclusive license to Beta to create a daily newspaper cartoon based upon the illustrations in the books, an exclusive license to Gamma to use the characters from the books in puppet shows performed in the state of California for a one-year period, and an exclusive license to Zeta to make plush dolls smaller than 12 inches tall of characters from the books. Each of these licenses is a "transfer" of rights of copyright, and each transferee has "all of the protection and remedies accorded to the copyright owner" by law. 17 U.S.C. §201(d)(2). For example, each transferee (exclusive licensee) has standing to sue third parties for copyright infringement for an invasion of its scope of exclusive rights within the original copyrighted work.

One Copyright Per Work. There is never more than a single copyright in a work regardless of the owner's exclusive license of various rights to different persons. 3 *Nimmer on Copyright* §10.02[C][2] (1994 rev.) ("Section 201(d)(2) provides for divisibility of rights, not divisibility of copyright."); 1 N. Boorstyn, *Copyright* §3.08 (2d ed. 1994) ("There is only one copyright in a work and it is not divisible; there are, however, different rights of copyright and they are divisible."). There is only one registration per copyrightable work. However, if a licensee creates a copyrightable DERIVATIVE WORK, that separate copyright can be separately owned and registered by the licensee.

Formalities of a Transfer. To be valid, a copyright transfer must be in writing and signed by the person conveying rights. 17 U.S.C. §204(a). This applies to assignments and exclusive licenses, but not to nonexclusive licenses, which can be oral.

See ASSIGNMENT OF COPYRIGHT, LICENSE OF COPYRIGHT.

• *Treatise References*: 3 *Nimmer on Copyright* §10.01 et seq. (1994 rev.); M. Leaffer, *Understanding Copyright* §5.8 (1989); 2 P. Goldstein, *Copyright* §4.4 (1989); W. Patry, *Copyright Law and Practice* 385 (1994); 1 N. Boorstyn, *Copyright* §3.08 (2d ed. 1994).

• *Statutory Reference*:

17 U.S.C. §101: "A 'transfer of copyright ownership' is an assignment, mortgage, exclusive license, or any other conveyance, alienation or hypothecation of a copyright, whether or not it is limited in time or place of effect, but not including a nonexclusive license."

17 U.S.C. §204(a): "A transfer of copyright ownership, other than by operation of law, is not valid unless an instrument of conveyance, or a note or memorandum of the transfer, is in writing and signed by the owner of the rights conveyed or such owner's duly authorized agent."

17 U.S.C. §201: "(d) Transfer of Ownership—

"(1) The ownership of copyright may be transferred in whole or in part by any means of conveyance or by operation of law, and may be bequeathed by will or pass as personal property by the applicable laws of intestate succession.

"(2) Any of the exclusive rights comprised in copyright, including any subdivision of any of the rights specified by section 106, may be transferred as provided by clause (1) and owned separately. The owner of any particular exclusive right is entitled, to the extent of that right, to all of the protection and remedies accorded to the copyright owner by this title."

transgenic [patent] Describing an animal or plant that has been transformed genetically. Transgenic animals carry a gene that has been introduced into the germline of the animal or an ancestor of the animal, at an early (usually one-cell) embryonic stage of development. For example, a "transgenic" cow would be a cow from a strain of cattle that has been altered by GENETIC ENGINEERING to produce more milk more efficiently and with a higher concentration of casein, an important ingredient in cheese. Other types of transgenic animals include mice that are susceptible to tumor formation and sheep that exhibit therapeutic proteins in their milk. A transgenic animal is patentable.

Examples of transgenic plants include plants that are resistant to herbicides, potatoes with lower starch concentrations, and tomatoes that ripen more slowly.

Patent Protection for Transgenic Animals. On April 12, 1988, the Patent and Trademark Office granted the first "transgenic animal patent." U.S. Patent No. 4,736,866. This patent was on the so-called Harvard Mouse: a mouse genetically engineered by researchers at Harvard University to be susceptible to cancer for use in screening potentially carcinogenic products. This transgenic mouse is sometimes called "oncomouse," oncology being that branch of medicine that deals with tumors. Claim 1 of the Harvard Mouse patent covers "[a] transgenic, non-human mammal all of whose germ cells and somatic cells contain a recombinant activated oncogene sequence introduced into said mammal, or an ancestor of said mammal, at an embryonic stage." Dependent claim 11 covers "[t]he mammal of claim 1, said mammal being a rodent." Dependent claim 12 covers "[t]he mammal of claim 11, said rodent being a mouse." In late 1988, E.I. du Pont de Nemours & Co. began marketing the patented mice to researchers who are studying the causes of and treatments for cancer. L. Hays, *du Pont Co. to Sell Gene-Spliced Mice to Scientists in Labs Studying Cancer,* Wall St. J., Nov. 16, 1988, at B5. Members of the biotechnology industry have predicted the patenting of other TRANSGENIC genetically altered animals such as cows that produce more milk, hogs with less fat, and chickens that lay more eggs. In 1992, three more patents which claimed transgenic mice were issued. See 45 Pat. Trademark & Copyright J. (BNA) 159 (Jan. 7, 1993). Since then, other patents on transgenic mice have been granted.

Organized Opposition. A coalition of farmers' organizations and religious and animal welfare groups have urged Congress to enact laws either limiting or eliminating patents on genetically engineered animals. H.R. 4970 passed the House in 1988 but died in the Senate. H.R. 4970 would have prohibited the patenting of human genetic material and provided exemptions for dairy and cattle producers. In 1993, S. 357 was introduced, which would have imposed a two-year moratorium on the granting of plant and animal patents so that a method for evaluating ethical, environmental, and economic considerations could be found. See 45 PTCJ 354 (Feb. 2, 1993). This bill also did not become law.

See GENETIC ENGINEERING.

transmission [copyright] The communication from one place to another of a performance of a copyrighted work by radio or television broadcasting, cable, or any other similar means.

Primary and Secondary Transmissions. Transmissions are broken down into a "primary transmission" and a simultaneous "secondary transmission." For example, a "primary transmission" is made by an originating television station broadcasting a copyrighted motion picture film. A "secondary transmission" is made by someone who simultaneously "further transmits" the signal. The secondary transmission could be made by a cable television operator or by a landlord or hotel owner who provides television reception service to tenants or guests. For certain cable operators, 17 U.S.C. §111(c) creates a COMPULSORY LICENSING system. For satellite rebroadcasters, a separate compulsory licensing scheme is provided. The landlord and hotel owner may be exempt under 17 U.S.C. §111(a)(1). Certain PASSIVE CARRIERS who only provide the physical facilities for retransmission are also exempt.

Secondary Transmission Is a "Performance." While it is not clear from the face of the 1978 Copyright Act, Nimmer is of the view that a secondary transmission of a performance is itself a performance that can trigger liability for infringing on the exclusive right to publicly perform a copyrighted work. 2 *Nimmer on Copyright* §8.18[B] (1994 rev.). The legislative history states that in the opinion of Congress, "a

cable television system is performing when it retransmits the broadcast to its subscribers...." H.R. Rep. No. 94-1476, 94th Cong., 2d Sess. 63 (1976). See W. Patry, *Copyright Law and Practice* 940 (1994) ("[C]able operators and others (such as hotels and apartment buildings) who retransmit copyrighted works are engaging in a performance. If that performance is to the public and unauthorized, infringement occurs, absent an exemption in Section 111 or a defense provided by another section of title 17.").

Exempt Secondary Transmissions. Some types of secondary transmissions are specifically exempt from infringement liability under the Copyright Act. For example, a landlord or hotel operator who merely relays broadcast signals to the private lodgings of guests or tenants and makes no direct charge for the service is exempt under 17 U.S.C. §111(a)(1). See 1 P. Goldstein, *Copyright* §5.8.2.1a. (1989).

Turning on a Receiving Set. Note that when one turns on an ordinary radio or television receiver in a public place, there is a "performance" that may or may not be exempt under 17 U.S.C. §110(5) (see PERFORMANCE), but it is not a "secondary transmission." This is because there is no "further transmitting" of the broadcast. In the parlance of the Copyright Act, this is a "communication of a transmission," but not a "secondary transmission." As Nimmer has observed, "[a]lthough every transmission involves a communication, not every communication involves a transmission." 2 *Nimmer on Copyright* §8.18[C][2] (1994 rev.).

See PERFORMANCE, PASSIVE CARRIER, COMPULSORY LICENSE OF COPYRIGHT, BRUSSELS SATELLITE CONVENTION, SUPERSTATION.

- *Treatise References*: 2 *Nimmer on Copyright* §8.18 (1994 rev.); 1 P. Goldstein, *Copyright* §5.8.2 (1989); W. Patry, *Copyright Law and Practice* 939 et seq. (1994); 1 N. Boorstyn, *Copyright* §6.27 et seq. (2d ed. 1994); M. Leaffer, *Understanding Copyright* §8.19 (1989).

- *Statutory References*:
17 U.S.C. §101. "To 'transmit' a performance or display is to communicate it by any device or process whereby images or sounds are received beyond the place from which they are sent."

17 U.S.C. §111(f) (first paragraph): "A 'primary transmission' is a transmission made to the public by the transmitting facility whose signals are being received and further transmitted by the secondary transmission service, regardless of where or when the performance or display was first transmitted."

17 U.S.C. §111(f) (second paragraph). "A 'secondary transmission' is the further transmitting of a primary transmission simultaneously with the primary transmission...."

transmit [copyright]
See TRANSMISSION.

traverse [patent] To deny or rebut an allegation of law or fact made by an adversary, especially that made by a patent EXAMINER for the Patent and Trademark Office. E.g., "Applicant traverses the Examiner's rejection on the ground that the drawing is inadequate." Traverse can also be used as a noun to denote a denial of an allegation. E.g., "Inventor Washington filed a traverse to the Examiner's rejection, Washington asserting that patentability was not barred by a lack of utility."

- *Rule Reference*: 37 C.F.R. §1.132: "When any claim of an application ... is rejected ... because the alleged invention is held to be inoperative or lacking in utility ... affidavits or declarations traversing these references or objections may be received."

- *Manual Reference*: "It is the responsibility of the primary examiner to personally review and decide whether affidavits or declarations submitted ... for the purpose of traversing grounds of rejection, are responsive to the rejection and present sufficient facts to overcome the rejection." *Manual of Patent Examining Procedure* §716 (1994 rev.).

TRIMS [international–intellectual -property] Trade-Related Investment Measures is an agreement under the authority of the General Agreement on Tariffs and Trade (GATT), which prohibits certain local content and trade balancing requirements. The TRIMS agreement reinforces GATT obligations by providing: (1)

that no party shall apply TRIMS that are inconsistent with GATT; and (2) an illustrative list of prohibited measures, identifying local content requirements and trade balancing requirements as falling within the prohibition.
See GATT.

TRIPS [international trade–intellectual property] Trade-Related Aspects of Intellectual Property is an agreement made under the authority of the General Agreement on Tariffs and Trade (GATT), which provides for the establishment of minimum international standards of intellectual property rights protection, the enforcement of those standards, and effective dispute settlement measures. U.S. legislation implementing changes required by GATT TRIPS was enacted on December 8, 1994, as the URUGUAY ROUND AGREEMENTS ACT. The accompanying WTO (World Trade Organization) Agreement entered into force with respect to the United States on January 1, 1995.

Objectives of TRIPS. Article 2 of the GATT TRIPS agreement requires each WTO member country to abide by the substantive obligations of the PARIS CONVENTION and the BERNE CONVENTION. The concept underlying TRIPS is that all GATT member nations should have minimum levels of protection for all forms of intellectual property and each nation should have effective and appropriate enforcement mechanisms, both internally and at the border, sufficient to make ownership of an intellectual property right meaningful in an economic sense. Further, there should be effective and expeditious procedures for multilateral settlement of disputes between governments. The agreement attempts to reduce tensions among countries that already protect intellectual property rights and to assist the less-developed nations of the world in implementing laws and regulations to enable them to promote technological innovation. One goal of the TRIPS agreement was to control and eventually eliminate international counterfeiting.

History of Intellectual Property in GATT. Traditionally, the World Intellectual Property Organization, WIPO, administered international intellectual property matters. But in the United States and in other developed countries, where intellectual property was an important commodity, WIPO was thought to be a less than optimal forum in which to raise the international level of intellectual property protection. See National Security & Int'l Affairs Div., Gen. Acct. Office, *Strengthening Worldwide Protection of Intellectual Property Rights* 22 (1987) ("The government sees greater opportunity for broad substantive progress by addressing this problem as an unfair trade practice within the new 'Uruguay' GATT round of multilateral trade negotiations."). In 1986, a GATT resolution was implemented with the aim of protecting intellectual property rights and dealing with international trade in counterfeit goods. After years of negotiations, Director General Arthur Dunkel drafted the proposed TRIPS agreement in December 1991. The "Dunkel Text," as amended, came into effect in April 1994, as a result of the conclusion of the Uruguay Round of negotiations on December 15, 1993.

General Provisions and Basic Principles. The general provisions and basic principles of TRIPS provide for, among other things, national treatment and most favored nation (MFN) status for GATT members. National treatment requires that a member nation give the citizens of other GATT member nations the same protection it gives to its own citizens. MFN status requires that any advantage, favor, privilege, or immunity granted by a member nation to the nationals of any other country be conferred immediately and unconditionally to the nationals of all other GATT members. *Final Act Embodying the Results of the Uruguay Round of Multilateral Trade Negotiations, Agreement on Trade-Related Aspects of Intellectual Property Rights, Including Trade in Counterfeit Goods*, December 15, 1993 (TRIPS) Pt. 1, Arts. 3–4, 33 Int'l Legal Materials 81, 85–86 (1994).

Standards Concerning Availability, Scope and Use. The TRIPS Agreement comprises detailed provisions defining protection for a broad spectrum of intellectual property rights. Part II of the agreement, which mandates minimum standards for the availability, scope, and use of each type of intellectual property, is divided into eight sections as follows:

1. Copyright and Related Rights.

2. Trademarks.

3. Geographical Indications.

4. Industrial Designs.

5. Patents.

6. Layout-Designs of Integrated Circuits.

7. Protection of Undisclosed Information.

8. Control of Anti-Competitive Practices in Contractual Licenses.

TRIPS Pt. II, Secs. 1–8, Arts. 9–40, 33 Int'l Legal Materials 87–99 (1994).

Enforcement of Intellectual Property Rights. The enforcement provisions of TRIPS require GATT nations to provide civil and administrative procedures and remedies available under their domestic laws to prevent infringement of intellectual property rights. Parties must provide, among other things, provisional remedies (e.g., preliminary injunction); border measures for prohibiting the importation of infringing goods; and criminal penalties for willful infringement of copyright and trademark. *TRIPS* Pt. III, Secs. 1–5, Arts. 41–61, 33 Int'l Legal Materials 99–105 (1994).

Dispute Prevention and Settlement. When a dispute concerning the interpretation or application of GATT arises between two or more member nations (e.g., when one country accuses another of violating its GATT obligations), GATT provides for consultations between disputing nations as a first step in securing a settlement. If consultations fail, the disputing nations may refer the dispute to the entire GATT membership. A panel is appointed to make recommendations to the disputing members through a panel report. A panel report is adopted unless all parties agree that it should not be adopted; it cannot be blocked by the offending party. The "teeth" of GATT's settlement provisions is the ability of all of the member nations to suspend the application of concessions or obligations under GATT to the nation violating its GATT obligations. See Monique L. Cordray, *GATT v. WIPO*, 76 J. Pat. & Trademark Off. Soc'y 121 (1994) (discussing GATT dispute prevention and settlement).

Phased-In Implementation. The TRIPS Agreement entered into force on January 1, 1995, with the establishment of the "World Trade Organization" (*WTO*). Under the "transitional arrangement" portion of TRIPS, GATT members which are considered "developed" countries must implement TRIPS within one year. "Developing" countries are entitled to delay application of the agreement for up to five years. The least developed countries may extend that five-year period to 10 years. *TRIPS* Pt. VI, Arts. 65–66, 33 Int'l Legal Materials 107–08 (1994). See WTO. U.S. legislation implementing changes required by GATT TRIPS was enacted on December 8, 1994, and the accompanying WTO (World Trade Organization) Agreement entered into force with respect to the United States on January 1, 1995.

Effect on U.S. Intellectual Property Law. Because GATT was adopted in the United States as an executive agreement and not as a treaty, it needed legislation to come into force under U.S. intellectual property laws. TRIPS "will not take effect with respect to the United States, and will have no domestic legal force, until the Congress has approved [it] and enacted any appropriate implementing legislation." *Memorandum for the United States Trade Representative*, 58 Fed. Reg. 67,263, 67,267 (1993) (executive summary of results of the GATT Uruguay Round of Multilateral Trade Negotiations).

Changes in U.S. Law. On December 8, 1994, President Clinton signed into law the Uruguay Round Agreements Act to implement GATT into U.S. law (Pub. L. No. 103-465, 108 Stat. 4809). Implementation of several of the changes in U.S. intellectual property law is measured from the date on which the WTO Agreement entered into force with respect to the United States. That date was January 1, 1995. For a description of those changes, see URUGUAY ROUND AGREEMENTS ACT.

• *Agreement Reference:* "*Objectives.* The protection and enforcement of intellectual property rights should contribute to the promotion of technological innovation and to the transfer and dissemination of technology, to the mutual advantage of producers and users of technological knowledge and in a manner conducive to social and economic welfare, and to a balance of rights and obligations." *Final Act Embodying the Results of the Uruguay Round of Multilateral Trade Negotiations, Agreement on Trade-Related Aspects of Intellectual Property Rights, Including Trade in Counterfeit Goods*, December 15, 1993, (TRIPS) Pt. 1, Art. 7, 33 Int'l Legal Materials 81, 86–87 (1994).

• *Commentary Reference:* "[T]he TRIPS Agreement is a far-reaching plan that attempts to strengthen and harmonize the standards of intellectual property protection offered throughout the world in an effort to control, and eventually eradicate, the ever-growing problems of international infringement and counterfeiting." L.B. Martin & S.L. Amster, *International Intellectual Property Protections in the New GATT Accord*, 6 J. Proprietary Rts., No. 2, at 9 (1994).

TRT [trademark–international]

See TRADEMARK REGISTRATION TREATY.

T-Search [trademark] The U.S. Patent and Trademark Office's computerized trademark search and retrieval system.

TTAB [trademark]

See TRADEMARK TRIAL AND APPEAL BOARD.

tying [patent–trademark–copyright–antitrust]

See TIE-IN.

U

UCC [copyright–international]
See UNIVERSAL COPYRIGHT CONVENTION.

unconscious infringement [copyright]
Copyright infringement that occurs when a person makes a work that has SUBSTANTIAL SIMILARITY to a preexisting copyrighted work to which that person had ACCESS but did not consciously intend to copy.

How Unconscious Copying Can Occur. Copying can occur "unconsciously" or, more accurately, "subconsciously" by the conscious creative mind being fooled into thinking that it is creating a new and original work when in fact it is merely repeating what has been stored, perhaps long before, in the subconscious memory. Since lack of intent to infringe is no defense to copyright infringement liability, unconscious copying is still illegal copyright infringement. However, the lack of conscious intent to infringe may lessen the severity and amount of remedies for infringement.

Legal Recognition of the Phenomenon. In his famous 1936 *Sheldon* decision, Judge Learned Hand observed that unconscious infringement is indeed full-fledged copyright infringement: "With so many sources before them [defendants] might quite honestly forget what they took; nobody knows the origin of his inventions; memory and fancy merge even in adults. Yet unconscious plagiarism is actionable quite as much as deliberate." *Sheldon v. Metro-Goldwyn Pictures Corp.*, 81 F.2d 49, 54, 28 USPQ 330, 336 (2d Cir. 1936). This rule was reaffirmed in the 1983 George Harrison case where former Beatle George Harrison was found to have unconsciously copied and infringed the 1963 Chiffons' popular hit song *He's So Fine* when in 1969 Harrison wrote *My Sweet Lord. Abko Music Inc. v. Harrisongs Music Ltd.*,

722 F.2d 968, 221 USPQ 490 (2d Cir. 1983) (see case reference below).

See INFRINGEMENT OF COPYRIGHT.

• *Case Reference*: "[Defendants] assert that allowing for subconscious infringement brings the law of copyright improperly close to patent law, which imposes a requirement of novelty.... We do not accept this argument. It is not new law in this circuit that when a defendant's work is copied from the plaintiff's, but the defendant in good faith has forgotten that the plaintiff's work was the source of his own, such 'innocent copying' can nevertheless constitute an infringement.... We do not find this stance in conflict with the rule permitting independent creation of copyrighted material. It is settled that '[i]ntention to infringe is not essential under the [Copyright] Act.' ... Moreover, as a practical matter, the problems of proof inherent in a rule that would permit innocent intent as a defense to copyright infringement could substantially undermine the protections Congress intended to afford to copyright holders." *Abko Music Inc. v. Harrisongs Music Ltd.*, 722 F.2d 968, 221 USPQ 490, 497–98 (2d Cir. 1983).

UNCTAD [international] United Nations Conference on Trade and Development. UNCTAD has promulgated the CODE ON TECHNOLOGY TRANSFER.

undue breadth [patent] A ground for rejection or invalidation of a claim in a patent for being too broad.

Three Types of Undue Breadth. As analyzed by Chisum, there are three senses in which a patent claim can be invalid as being of "undue breadth." 2 D. Chisum, *Patents* §7.03[7][a] (1994 rev.). These are:

(1) The patent claim may be too broad in that it covers old technology in the PRIOR ART as well as new technology. The legal sources of this challenge to a claim are the statutory tests of NOVELTY and NONOBVIOUSNESS. See *Manual of Patent Examining Procedure* §706.03(j) (1994 rev.).

(2) The patent claim may be too broad where it covers subject matter that the inventor does not in fact regard as part of the invention. The legal source of this challenge is the requirement that the patent have claims "particularly pointing out and distinctly claiming the subject matter which the applicant regards as his invention." 35 U.S.C. §112, second paragraph.

(3) The patent claim may be too broad where it covers technology that is not sufficiently explained in the specification as to meet the test of ENABLEMENT. The legal source of this challenge is the requirement of adequate enablement. 35 U.S.C. §112, first paragraph. This is the basis for rejection of a SINGLE MEANS CLAIM (see case references below).

See SINGLE MEANS CLAIM, OVERCLAIMING.

• *Case References*:

"[J]ust as a claim which is of such breadth that it reads on subject matter disclosed in the prior art is rejected under §102 rather than under the second paragraph of §112, a claim which is of such breadth that it reads on the subject matter as to which the specification is not 'enabling' should be rejected under the first paragraph of §112 rather than the second." *In re Borkowski*, 422 F.2d 904, 909, 164 USPQ 642, 646 (C.C.P.A. 1970).

A SINGLE MEANS CLAIM is a claim drafted in MEANS-PLUS-FUNCTION format that recites only a single element rather than a combination of elements. Such a claim is improper. "The long-recognized problem with a single means claim is that it covers every conceivable means for achieving the stated result, while the specification discloses at most only those means known to the inventor. See *O'Reilly v. Morse*, 56 U.S. 62, 112 (1853). Thus, the claim is properly rejected for what used to be known as 'undue breadth,' but has since been appreciated as being, more accurately, based on the first para-

graph of §112." *In re Hyatt*, 708 F.2d 712, 714, 218 USPQ 195, 197 (Fed. Cir. 1983).

"Stripped to its basics, defendants' argument is one of 'overbreadth,' but that word alone has long ago been discredited as a basis for determining the sufficiency of a specification. See ... *In re Hogan*, 559 F.2d 595, 605–06, 194 USPQ 527, 537 (C.C.P.A. 1977) ('Rejections under §112, first paragraph, on the ground that the scope of enablement is not commensurate with the scope of the claims, orbit about the more fundamental question: To what scope of protection is the applicant's particular contribution to the art entitled?')." *U.S. Steel Corp. v. Phillips Petroleum Co.*, 865 F.2d 1247, 1251, 9 USPQ2d 1461, 1464 (Fed. Cir. 1989).

• *Manual Reference*: "*Undue Breadth*. In applications directed to inventions in arts where results are predictable, broad claims may properly be supported by the disclosure of a single species.... However, in applications directed to inventions in arts where the results are unpredictable, the disclosure of a single species usually does not provide an adequate basis to support generic claims.... This is because in arts such as chemistry it is not obvious from the disclosure of one species, what other species will work." *Manual of Patent Examining Procedure* §706.03(z) (1989 rev.).

UNESCO [copyright–international] United Nations Educational, Scientific and Cultural Organization. UNESCO administers the UNIVERSAL COPYRIGHT CONVENTION. At the end of 1984 the United States withdrew from UNESCO.

unexpected results [patent] Surprising consequences that flow from an invention. A showing that the invention achieved unexpected results is relevant evidence of the nonobviousness and patentability of the invention. For example, evidence that experts in the field expressed surprise, amazement, or skepticism about the invention is evidence that the invention was not obvious to those skilled in the art. Unexpected results is one of the types of objective evidence of real world recognition of the invention,

which are known as SECONDARY CONSIDERA-
TIONS.

Supreme Court Adams *Battery Case.* The
U.S. Supreme Court rejected an invalidity challenge in a case where Adams invented a battery
with magnesium and cuprous chloride elec-
trodes. The battery was activated when water
was added. Adams sued the U.S. government
for infringement of his patent and won. The
prior art indicated that a battery such as the one
Adams constructed was theoretically inoperative and dangerous. "The court below found …
that the Adams' battery 'wholly unexpectedly'
has shown 'certain valuable operating advantages over other batteries.' … We conclude the
Adams battery was also nonobvious. As we
have seen, the operating characteristics of the
Adams battery have been shown to have been
unexpected and to have far surpassed then-existing wet batteries." *United States v. Adams*,
383 U.S. 38, 50–51, 148 USPQ 479, 483
(1966).

See SECONDARY CONSIDERATIONS, OBVI-
OUSNESS.

• *Case References*:

The patent at issue claimed a huge machine
for cutting large pieces of scrap metal into small
pieces for recycling. In reversing a finding of
invalidity, the Court of Appeals for the Federal
Circuit stated: "The district court ignored the
unexpected or surprising results achieved by the
claimed invention. Though no requirement for
such result is present in the statute, 35 U.S.C.
§103, … evidence of unexpected results may be
strong support for a conclusion of nonobviousness.… The record is clear that … no prior art
device of any type could economically process
rigidly massive scrap without pretreatment. Unchallenged testimony of experts was characterized by surprise and amazement that the
claimed invention was able to accomplish that
feat.… It is further clear from the uncontra-
dicted evidence that the claimed invention
achieved new and unexpected results nowhere
suggested in the prior art, and that the district
court overlooked the effect of that achievement
in reaching its determination of obviousness."
Lindemann Maschinenfabrik GmbH v. Ameri-
can Hoist & Derrick Co., 730 F.2d 1452, 1461–
62, 221 USPQ 481, 488 (Fed. Cir. 1984).

"When an article is said to achieve unexpected (i.e., superior) results, those results must
logically be shown as superior *compared* to the
results achieved with other articles.… Moreover, an applicant relying on comparative tests
to rebut a prima facie case of obviousness must
compare his claimed invention to the closest
prior art.… Here, appellants have not presented
any experimental data showing that prior heat
shrinkable articles split. Due to the absence of
tests comparing appellants' heat shrinkable articles with those of the closest prior art, we
conclude that appellants' assertions of unexpected results constitute mere argument and
conclusory statements in the specification
which cannot establish patentability." *In re De*
Blauwe, 736 F.2d 699, 705, 222 USPQ 191, 196
(Fed. Cir. 1984).

• *Treatise Reference*: "The fact that experts
at the time perceived the invention was an exceptional technological achievement is good
evidence of nonobviousness, as is unpredictability. An insight which is contrary to the
understanding and expectations of the art points
to patentability. Proceeding contrary to accepted wisdom of the art is strong evidence of
nonobviousness." R. Harmon, *Patents and the*
Federal Circuit §4.6(c) (3d ed. 1994). See 2 D.
Chisum, *Patents* §5.05 (1994 rev.).

unfair competition   [general intellectual property] Commercial conduct that the law
views as unjust, giving a civil claim against a
person who has been injured by the conduct.

"Unfair Competition" Covers Wide Range
of Kinds of Unjust Business Behavior. It is
illusive to try to give an abstract and overall
definition of "unfair competition." This category of law covers so many possible kinds of
conduct and there is so little agreement as to its
outer limits that a general definition is deceptive. However, some courts have made the attempt, using such vague synonyms as "the rule
of fair play," "means which shock judicial sen-
sibilities," "the morals of the marketplace," and
"the decent thing to do in trade." Perhaps the
best that can be done is to say that unfair com-

petition is composed of commercial "dirty tricks" that judges find offensive.

Examples of Acts of Unfair Competition. The best definition of unfair competition is by example. Trademark infringement has long been categorized as a species and subcategory of unfair competition. "[T]he common law of trademarks is but a part of the broader law of unfair competition." *Hanover Star Milling Co. v. Metcalf,* 240 U.S. 403, 413 (1916). Other legal categories recognized as being types of unfair competition are false advertising, product disparagement/trade libel, infringement of a trade secret, infringement of the right of publicity, and misappropriation. These are all "nominate torts" (torts with names) included under the overall umbrella of "unfair competition." See *Manufacturing Research Corp. v. Greenlee Tool Co.,* 693 F.2d 1037, 1044 (11th Cir. 1982) ("Unfair competition is a generic term that covers several species of specific torts."). Some even expand the term "unfair competition" so far as to include patent and copyright infringement.

Competition Is Not Necessary for Confusion. A competitive relationship between conflicting trademark owners does not indicate the boundary of trademark infringement. A likelihood of confusion of source, sponsorship, affiliation, or connection can readily occur if a similar mark is used even on noncompeting goods or services. "Confusion, or the likelihood of confusion, not competition, is the real test of trademark infringement." *Continental Motors Corp. v. Continental Aviation Corp.,* 375 F.2d 857, 861, 153 USPQ 313, 316 (5th Cir. 1967). It is a sterile literalism in a trademark infringement case to state that there cannot be "unfair competition" without competition between the litigants. 3 J.T. McCarthy, *Trademarks and Unfair Competition* §24.04[2] (3d ed. 1995 rev.).

State and Federal Codification of Prohibitions Against Unfair Competition. Some state statutes prohibit simply "unfair competition" or "unfair business practices." E.g., California Business & Professions Code §17203. *Barquis v. Merchants Collection Ass'n,* 7 Cal. 3d 94, 101 Cal. Rptr. 745, 496 P.2d 817 (1972) (collection agency that consistently files collection suits in improper counties of venue is engaged in "un-

fair competition"). Similarly, the Federal Trade Commission is authorized to proceed against "unfair methods of competition … and unfair acts or practices." FTC Act §5(a), 15 U.S.C. §45.

Lanham Act §43(a) Does Not Codify the Whole Law of "Unfair Competition." Lanham Act §43(a), 15 U.S.C. §1125(a), while often mistakenly denominated an "unfair competition" statute, is much narrower in scope than the whole genus of "unfair competition" law. Section §43(a) is confined to prohibitions on acts of trademark infringement, false advertising, and trade libel. Lanham Act §43(a) "does not prohibit a broad range of acts defined as unfair competition by the law of many states." *Toho Co. v. Sears, Roebuck & Co.,* 645 F.2d 788, 792, 210 USPQ 547, 551 (9th Cir. 1981). Thus, §43(a) is not a federal vehicle for the assertion of claims against such forms of unfair competition as MISAPPROPRIATION, theft of TRADE SECRETS, or infringement of the RIGHT OF PUBLICITY. In proposing the rewriting of Lanham Act §43(a), which was enacted as part of the 1989 TRADEMARK LAW REVISION ACT, the TRADEMARK REVIEW COMMISSION rejected attempting to codify the whole law of unfair competition in §43(a). *Report & Recommendations of the T.R.C.,* 77 Trademark Rep. 375, 435 (1987).

Antitrust Laws and Unfair Competition Laws Are Distinct. The federal antitrust laws are not prohibitions on acts of unfair competition. Sherman Act §1 prohibits combinations that engage in conduct that harms the overall competitive process, not just one competitor. "[I]t is the function of [Sherman Act] §1 to compensate the unfortunate only when their demise is accompanied by a generalized injury to the market." *Car Carriers, Inc. v. Ford Motor Co.,* 745 F.2d 1101, 1109 (7th Cir. 1984). 1 J.T. McCarthy, *Trademarks and Unfair Competition* §1.14 (3d ed. 1995 rev.). The Supreme Court has observed: "[T]he notion that proof of unfair or predatory conduct alone is sufficient to make out the offense of attempted monopolization is contrary to the purpose and policy of the Sherman Act.… The purpose of the [Sherman] Act is not to protect businesses from the working of the market; it is to protect the public from the failure of the market." *Spectrum Sports Inc. v. McQuillan*, 113 S. Ct. 884, 891 (1993).

Federal Pendent Jurisdiction. The U.S. federal courts retain a specific form of "pendent" or "supplemental" jurisdiction over certain nonfederal claims for unfair competition. 28 U.S.C. §2338(b). The statute grants jurisdiction over a claim of "unfair competition" when it is joined with a substantial and related claim under the federal copyright, patent, plant variety protection, or trademark laws. See 4 J.T. McCarthy, *Trademarks and Unfair Competition* §32.10 (3d ed. 1995 rev.). Thus, for example, a plaintiff could bring in federal court a complaint with count 1 for trademark infringement in violation of federal Lanham Act §43(a) and count 2 for trademark infringement in violation of state law. Similarly, a plaintiff could bring in federal court a complaint with count 1 for patent infringement and count 2 for trade secret infringement in violation of state law.

International Concept of Unfair Competition. In Article 10 *bis* of the PARIS CONVENTION, each signatory nation binds itself to assure "effective protection against unfair competition" and defines "unfair competition" as "any act of competition contrary to honest practices in industrial or commercial matters." The same article prohibits three specific types of unfair competition: all acts that create confusion with the company or goods or activities of a competitor; false allegations that discredit a competitor; and indications that are liable to mislead the public as to things such as the nature or qualities of the goods.

• *Treatise Reference*: 1 J.T. McCarthy, *Trademarks and Unfair Competition* §§1.01– .16 (3d ed. 1995 rev.).

• *Restatement Reference*: "It is impossible to state a definitive test for determining which methods of competition will be deemed unfair in addition to those included in the categories of conduct described in the preceding Comments. Courts continue to evaluate competitive practices against generalized standards of fairness and social utility. Judicial formulations have broadly appealed to principles of fairness and social utility. The case law, however, is far more circumscribed than such rhetoric might

indicate, and courts have generally been reluctant to interfere in the competitive process." *Restatement (Third) of Unfair Competition* §1, comment g (1995).

• *Case References*:

"The law of unfair competition has its roots in the common-law tort of deceit: its general concern is with protecting *consumers* from confusion as to source. While that concern may result in the creation of 'quasi-property rights' in communicative symbols, the focus is on the protection of consumers, not the protection of producers as an incentive to product innovation." Justice O'Connor in *Bonito Boats, Inc. v. Thunder Craft Boats, Inc.*, 489 U.S. 141, 157, 9 USPQ2d 1847, 1854–55 (1989).

" 'Unfair competition' and 'unfair or fraudulent business practice' are generic terms. Like the term 'nuisance' or 'negligence' they must be translated into specific situations of fact in order to be cognizable. The attribute of generality does not of itself, however, require a holding of nullity for vagueness…. [T]he concept of unfair competition runs deep in the stream of our jurisprudence and has been considered in numerous cases, articles and texts…. There is thus a definite background of experience and precedents to illuminate the meaning of the words…. No one need reasonably be misled thereby." *People ex rel. Mosk v. National Research Co.*, 201 Cal. App. 2d 765, 772, 20 Cal. Rptr. 516, 521, 133 USPQ 413, 416 (1962) (holding that a state statutory prohibition against "unfair competition" is not unconstitutionally void for vagueness).

"Unfair competition and patent law have long existed as distinct and independent bodies of law, each with different origins and each protecting different rights…. The law of unfair competition generally protects consumers and competitors from deceptive or unethical conduct in commerce…. Patent law, on the other hand, protects a patent owner from the unauthorized use by others of the patented invention, irrespective of whether deception or unfairness exists." *Mars Inc. v. Kabushiki-Kaisha Nipon Conlux*, 24 F.3d 1368, 1373, 30 USPQ2d 1621, 1624 (Fed. Cir. 1994) (holding that a claim of infringement of a foreign patent does not constitute a claim of unfair competition within the meaning of 28 U.S.C. §1338(b)).

unit of publication doctrine [copyright] A rule under which the affixation of copyright NOTICE to one element of a publication is regarded as sufficient notice for all elements of the publication. For example, it was held that a copyright notice on a computer instruction manual was sufficient to constitute notice for associated computer software tapes where the manual and the tapes, although physically separable, were always sold together, forming a "single commercial unit." *Koontz v. Jaffarian,* 787 F.2d 906, 229 USPQ 381 (4th Cir. 1986). The rule is reflected in 37 C.F.R. §202.19(b)(2).

See NOTICE.

- *Treatise Reference*: 2 *Nimmer on Copyright* §7.10[D] (1994 rev.); 1 P. Goldstein, *Copyright* §3.6.2.1 (1989); W. Patry, *Copyright Law and Practice* 445 (1994).

unity of invention [patent] (1) A requirement of the PATENT COOPERATION TREATY that an international patent application shall relate to only one invention or to a group of inventions so linked as to form a single general inventive concept. (2) A requirement of U.S. patent law that a claim, especially a MARKUSH CLAIM, not contain more than one independent and distinct invention.

Domestic Law Must Comply With the Treaty Definition. In *Caterpillar Tractor v. Commissioner of Patents and Trademarks,* 231 USPQ 590 (E.D. Va. 1986), the court held that a rule of the Patent and Trademark Office relating to the unity of invention requirement was invalid as inconsistent with a rule of the Patent Cooperation Treaty. Article 27 of the treaty provides that no national law can require compliance with requirements different from or additional to those in the treaty and its regulations. The Patent and Trademark Office regulations on unity of invention requirements were substantially rewritten in 1987. See 52 Fed. Reg. 20,038 (Apr. 28, 1987); 34 Pat. Trademark & Copyright J. (BNA) 137 (1987).

Foreign Rules. The laws of several nations have their own unity of invention requirements, as does Article 82 of the European Patent Convention. See Allam, *Chemical Patent Practice at the European Patent Office*, 13 AIPLA J. 19, 23 (1985) ("The unity requirements appear to be applied quite liberally by European Examiners.").

The Domestic Analogue. The U.S. domestic analogue to unity of invention is the requirement that two or more independent and distinct inventions may not be claimed in a single patent application. 37 C.F.R. §1.141 (1987 rev.).

See RESTRICTION.

Markush Claims. Unity of invention also has domestic significance as a ground of rejection of a MARKUSH CLAIM. In a Markush claim to a compound, the materials forming the Markush group must belong to a recognized physical or chemical class. If they do not, the claim is subject to a rejection on the basis of "improper Markush grouping" or "lack of unity of invention"; that is, there is more than one invention claimed. The concept of "lack of unity of invention" is the appropriate basis on which to reject a claim wherein "unrelated inventions are involved—inventions which are truly independent *and* distinct." *In re Harnish*, 631 F.2d 716, 722, 206 USPQ 300, 306 (C.C.P.A. 1980).

See PATENT COOPERATION TREATY, RESTRICTION, DIVISIONAL APPLICATION, MARKUSH CLAIM.

- *Rule Reference*: "(a) An international and a national stage application shall relate to one invention only or to a group of inventions so linked as to form a single general inventive concept ('requirement of unity of invention').... (b) An international or a national stage application containing claims to different categories of invention will be considered to have unity of invention if the claims are drawn only to one of the following combinations of categories: (1) a product and a process specially adapted for the manufacture of said product; or (2) a product and a process of use of said product; (3) a product, a process specially adapted for the manufacture of the said product, and a use of the said product; (4) a process and an apparatus or means specially designed for carrying out the said process; or (5) a product, a process specially adapted for the manufacture of said product, and an apparatus or means specially designed for carrying out the said process." 37 C.F.R. §1.475 (1993 rev.).

• *Case Reference*: "[T]here remains a body of Markush-type claims, particularly in the chemical field, concerned more with the concept of unity of invention. At least the term would be more descriptive and more intelligible internationally than is the more esoteric and provincial expression 'Markush practice.' ... [A]ll of [the inventor's] claimed compounds are dyes.... We hold, therefore, that the claimed compounds all belong to a sub-genus, as defined by [the inventor] which is not repugnant to scientific classification. Under these circumstances we consider the claimed compounds to be part of a single invention so that there is unity of invention.... The Markush groupings of claims 1 and 3-8 are therefore proper." *In re Harnish*, 631 F.2d 716, 722, 206 USPQ 300, 305 (C.C.P.A. 1980).

Universal Copyright Convention [copyright–international] Until the United States became a member of the Berne Union in 1989, the Universal Copyright Convention (UCC) was the major multilateral copyright treaty to which the United States was a party.

History of the UCC. The UCC was created in 1952 under the auspices of UNESCO to provide the international copyright community with a multilateral treaty to which the United States would become a party. Many provisions of the UCC were clearly fashioned so as to permit the then-existing copyright statutes of the United States to be in compliance. At that time, several provisions of the 1909 U.S. Copyright Act clearly prevented the United States from meeting the minimum standards for becoming a party to the BERNE CONVENTION. In one sense, the UCC was a halfway measure to enable the United States to move gradually towards full membership in the major international treaty organization: the Berne Union. That final step was taken by the United States effective March 1, 1989. Since the U.S. adherence to the Berne Convention, the importance and impact of the Universal Copyright Convention is much reduced. However, the UCC continues to have significance in that a few nations

may be members of the UCC but not members of Berne.

Main Points of Treaty.

(1) National Treatment: All member nations must give to foreign works eligible under the UCC the same degree of copyright protection given to works of domestic citizens.

(2) Copyright Notice: If the copyright owner uses the notice provided by the treaty, then the UCC excuses compliance with all copyright formalities that may be required by any nation, such as deposit, registration, fees, or special government certificates. The UCC copyright notice prescribed by the UCC for that purpose is "the symbol © accompanied by the name of the copyright proprietor and the year of first publication placed in such manner and location as to give reasonable notice of claim of copyright." UCC, Art. III.

(3) Minimum Standards: Certain minimum standards of copyright protection must be accorded in each member nation. However, these minimum standards are less rigorous than those of the BERNE CONVENTION.

(4) The Berne Safeguard Clause: To satisfy those who felt that the UCC was a step backwards from the progressive international standards of the Berne Convention, a "safeguard" clause was added in Article XVII, which has the effect of prohibiting a Berne member nation from renouncing Berne and relying on the more liberal standards of the UCC in copyright relations with a fellow Berne member nation.

See BERNE CONVENTION, BCIA.

• *Treatise References*: 3 *Nimmer on Copyright* §17.01[B][2] (1994 rev.); 2 P. Goldstein, *Copyright* §16.6 (1989); M. Leaffer, *Understanding Copyright* §12.3 (1989); Patry, *Copyright Law and Practice* 1257 (1994).

UPOV [patent–trademark] Union for Protection of New Plant Varieties.

See CONVENTION OF THE INTERNATIONAL UNION FOR THE PROTECTION OF NEW PLANT VARIETIES.

URAA [international trade–intellectual property] See URUGUAY ROUND AGREEMENTS ACT.

Uruguay Round Agreements Act [international trade–intellectual property] Legislation enacted in December 1994 in the United States to implement the GATT agreement. Title V of the Act enacted changes in U.S. intellectual property law to implement the Trade Related Intellectual Property (TRIPS) portions of the GATT Agreement.

Legislation Needed to Implement GATT. Because GATT is effected in the United States as an executive agreement and not as a treaty, it needs legislation to come into force under U.S. intellectual property laws. TRIPS "will not take effect with respect to the United States, and will have no domestic legal force, until the Congress has approved [it] and enacted any appropriate implementing legislation." *Memorandum for the United States Trade Representative*, 58 Fed. Reg. 67,263, 67,267 (1993) (executive summary of results of the GATT Uruguay Round of Multilateral Trade Negotiations).

Changes in U.S. Law. On December 8, 1994, President Clinton signed into law the Uruguay Round Agreements Act to implement GATT into U.S. law. (Pub. L. No. 103-465, 108 Stat. 4809). Most of the changes took effect as of Jan. 1, 1996. Some of the major impacts on U.S. domestic law are discussed below.

1. Changes Required in Patent Law. The term of U.S. patents was changed from 17 years from grant to 20 years from the date of filing of the application, effective June 8, 1995. All U.S. patents that were in force on, or that issued on an application filed before, June 8, 1995, automatically have a term that is the greater of the 20-year term or 17 years from grant. The new concept of a PROVISIONAL APPLICATION was introduced, permitting the filing of a specification and drawing without claims. Inventive activity in any World Trade Organization nation can be used as a basis for claiming PRIORITY OF INVENTION. Added to the exclusive rights of a patentee were the exclusive right to offer to sell and import the patented technology. The latter two changes take effect as of Jan. 1, 1996.

2. Changes Required in Trademark Law. The period of nonuse of a mark that triggers a presumption of abandonment was raised from two to three years. Registration of certain new geographic names for wines and spirits was barred unless the product comes from the place named.

3. Change Required in Copyright Law. For the first time, federal civil and criminal remedies were introduced against BOOTLEGGING— the unauthorized recording of live performances. U.S. copyright was restored for certain foreign works that were still in copyright in the country of origin but had fallen out of copyright in the United States because of, among other reasons, failure to comply with U.S. formalities or failure to renew. Persons who acted in reliance on the former public domain status of such works are given a limited form of protection.

Abbreviation: URAA.

See GATT, TRIPS, WTO.

useful article [copyright] An object that has some primarily functional, utilitarian use apart from picturing something or conveying information. The shape or design of a useful article is copyrightable only to the extent that it has aesthetic or nonfunctional aspects capable of being identified as separate, either physically or conceptually, from the useful, functional, and utilitarian aspects of the article. The job of separating the copyrightable aesthetic elements from the uncopyrightable functional elements of articles has proven to be a very difficult legal task. In many instances, the aesthetic design of a useful article is capable of protection under DESIGN PATENT and TRADE DRESS law as well as copyright.

What Is a "Useful Article"? A book or a photograph is not a "useful article" because the purpose is only to convey information or to portray the appearance of something. A book can be used to hold a door open and a photograph to cover a crack in the wall, but these are not the "intrinsic," normal, or primary functions of those objects. It has been held that toys are not "useful articles" because they are not the real thing but, like pictures, merely portray real objects. In holding that a toy airplane is not a "useful article," a court observed: "Other than the portrayal of a real airplane, a toy airplane, like a painting, has no intrinsic utilitarian function." *Gay Toys, Inc. v. Buddy L Corp.*, 703 F.2d

970, 973, 218 USPQ 13, 15 (6th Cir. 1983). Thus, toys are copyrightable per se without any need to separate the functional from the non-functional aspects. The traditional view has been that the design and cut of wearing apparel (apart from fabric designs) is uncopyrightable largely because clothing is a useful article. 1 *Nimmer on Copyright* §2.08[H][3] (1994 rev.).

Sole Versus Some Utilitarian Function. The 1978 Copyright Act expanded the category of useful articles from that in a previous regulation defining such an article to be something whose "sole intrinsic function is its utility." The 1978 Act merely requires that an article have "an intrinsic utilitarian function." 17 U.S.C. §101 (see statutory reference below). "The significant change from the prior law is that the courts need no longer determine whether an article's function is *solely* utilitarian. Now, if an article has *any* intrinsic utilitarian function, it can be denied copyright protection except to the extent that its artistic features can be identified separately and are capable of existing independently as a work of art." *Fabrica Inc. v. El Dorado Corp.*, 697 F.2d 890, 893, 217 USPQ 698, 700 (9th Cir. 1983).

Incorporating an Aesthetic Work Into a Useful Article. In *Mazer v. Stein*, the U.S. Supreme Court made it clear that an aesthetic, nonfunctional item, otherwise copyrightable, does not suddenly become uncopyrightable merely because it is used as part of a useful, functional article. The Court found that a small statue of a Balinese dancer, used as a base for a lamp, was copyrightable. *Mazer v. Stein*, 347 U.S. 201, 100 USPQ 325 (1954). Thus, a copyrightable picture does not lose its copyrightability merely because it appears on a functional dinner plate or the cover of a jewelry box.

Separating the Functional From the Aesthetic. The legislative history and the courts have said that copyrightable aesthetic, nonfunctional aspects of an article must be able to be identified as either physically or conceptually separable from the uncopyrightable functional, utilitarian aspects. The test of physical separability is easy to apply: one can readily envision removing the Victorian embellishments from an otherwise functional clock or grinding the floral relief off of the handle of an otherwise functional spoon. Application of the test of conceptual separability is more philosophical and difficult. See 1 P. Goldstein, *Copyright* §2.5.3.1 b. (1989).

- *Examples.* In most of the reported cases, the courts have found no separability and have denied copyright protection. Examples of unprotectible articles include parking lot outdoor lighting fixtures of sleek, modern design (*Esquire v. Ringer*, 591 F.2d 796, 199 USPQ 1 (D.C. Cir. 1978)); anatomically correct human torso forms used to display clothing in stores (*Carol Barnhardt, Inc. v. Economy Cover Corp.*, 773 F.2d 411, 228 USPQ 385 (2d Cir. 1985)); and a bicycle parking rack inspired by a nonfunctional wire abstract sculpture (*Bandir Int'l v. Cascade Pac. Lumber Co.*, 834 F.2d 1142, 5 USPQ2d 1089 (2d Cir. 1987)). One article held copyrightable was a belt buckle with an ornate swirling design molded into the shape of the buckle. *Kieselstein-Cord v. Accessories by Pearl, Inc.*, 632 F.2d 989, 208 USPQ 1 (2d Cir. 1980).

Modern Design. In so-called modern design, form usually follows function. Because of the difficulty of separating the aesthetic from the functional aspects of modern design, this kind of unornamented design only rarely can qualify for copyright.

Picture of a Useful Article: Copyright Act §113(b) codifies the law as it existed just prior to the January 1, 1978, date of the Copyright Act revision. Legislative history indicates that the state of the law then (and now) was that copyright in a picture of a useful article protects against reproduction of the picture in another picture but does not give an exclusive right to the manufacture of the article portrayed in the picture. H.R. Rep. No. 94-1476, 94th Cong., 2d Sess. 105 (1976); 1 *Nimmer on Copyright* 2.18[B] (1989 rev.). This makes good sense, for otherwise one could have an effective "mini-patent" if one could simply use the copyright on a photograph of utilitarian machine parts to prevent competitors from making those parts. One has to comply with the hurdles of obtaining and keeping a valid utility PATENT to accomplish that.

- *Treatise References*: 1 *Nimmer on Copyright* §2.08[B][3] (1994 rev.); 1 P. Goldstein, *Copyright* §2.5.3 (1989); M. Leaffer, *Understanding Copyright* §3.11 (1989); 1 N. Boorstyn, *Copyright* §2.10 (2d ed. 1994); W. Patry, *Copyright Law and Practice* 256 et seq. (1994).

- *Statutory References*:

17 U.S.C. §101: "A 'useful article' is an article having an intrinsic utilitarian function that is not merely to portray the appearance of the article or to convey information. An article that is normally a part of a useful article is considered a 'useful article.' "

17 U.S.C. §101: " 'Pictorial, graphic, and sculptural works' include two-dimensional and three-dimensional works of fine, graphic and applied art, photographs, prints and art reproductions, maps, globes, charts, technical drawings, diagrams and models. Such works shall include works of artistic craftsmanship insofar as their form but not their mechanical or utilitarian aspects are concerned; the design of a useful article, as defined in this section, shall be considered a pictorial, graphic, or sculptural work only if, and only to the extent that, such design incorporates pictorial, graphic, or sculptural features that can be identified separately from, and are capable of existing independently of, the utilitarian aspects of the article."

17 U.S.C. §113: "(a) Subject to the provisions of subsections (b) and (c) of this section, the exclusive right to produce a copyrighted pictorial, graphic, or sculptural work in copies under section 106 includes the right to reproduce the work in or on any kind of article, whether useful or otherwise.

"(b) This title does not afford, to the owner of copyright in a work that portrays a useful article as such, any greater or lesser rights with respect to the making, distribution, or display of the useful article so portrayed than those afforded to such works under the law, whether title 17 or the common law or statutes of a State, in effect on December 31, 1977, as held applicable and construed by a court in an action brought under this title.

"(c) In the case of a work lawfully reproduced in useful articles that have been offered for sale or other distribution to the public, copyright does not include any right to prevent the making, distribution, or display of pictures or photographs of such articles in connection with advertisements or commentaries related to the distribution or display of such articles, or in connection with news reports."

- *Legislative History*: "Unless the shape of an automobile, airplane, ladies' dress, food processor, television set, or any other industrial product contains some element that physically or conceptually can be identified as separable from the utilitarian aspects of that article the design would not be copyrighted under the bill. The test of separability and independence from 'the utilitarian aspects of the article' does not depend upon the nature of the design—that is, even if the appearance of an article is determined by aesthetic (as opposed to functional) considerations, only elements, if any, which can be identified separately from the useful article as such are copyrightable. And, even if the three-dimensional design contains some such elements (for example, a carving on the back of a chair or a floral relief design on silver flatware), copyright protection would extend only to that element, and would not cover the overall configuration of the utilitarian article as such." H.R. Rep. No. 94-1476, 94th Cong., 2d Sess. 55 (1976).

- *Case References*:

"While the [bicycle parking] rack may be worthy of admiration for its aesthetic qualities alone, it remains nonetheless the product of industrial design. Form and function are inextricably intertwined in the rack, its ultimate design being as much the result of utilitarian pressures as aesthetic choices. Indeed, the visually pleasing proportions and symmetricality of the rack represent design changes made in response to functional concerns. Judging from the awards the rack has received, it would seem in fact that [plaintiff] has achieved with the [bicycle] rack the highest goal of modern industrial design, that is, the harmonious fusion of function and aesthetics. Thus, there remains no artistic element of the [plaintiff's] rack that can be identified as separate and 'capable of existing independently of, the utilitarian aspects of the article.' Accordingly, we must affirm [the grant of summary judgment for defendant] on the copyright claim." *Bandir Int'l v. Cascade Pac. Lumber Co.*, 834 F.2d 1142, 1147–48, 5 USPQ2d 1089, 1094 (2d Cir. 1987).

"How, then is 'conceptual separateness' to be determined? In my view, the answer derives from the word 'conceptual.' For the design features to be 'conceptually separate' from the utilitarian aspects of the useful article that embodies the design, the article must stimulate in the mind of the beholder a concept that is separate from the concept evoked by its utilitarian function." *Carol Barnhardt, Inc. v. Economy Cover Corp.*, 773 F.2d 411, 422, 228 USPQ 385, 393 (2d Cir. 1985) (Newman, J., dissenting).

useful arts [patent] technology. See full definition and references at ART.

user interface [computer–copyright] Those elements of a computer program beyond the literal code that make up the medium of communication between a computer user and a program. The user interface consists of what the user hears and sees on the screen, be it graphic or textual, and what the user does to make the program perform functions via keyboard or mouse. When a computer's visual displays incorporate significant graphic elements it is referred to as a graphical user interface (GUI or "gooey"). A GUI allows the user to see, point to, and manipulate graphical images, symbols, or words to instruct and interact with the computer program. Some courts will protect the user interface from copying under the copyright laws.

User Interface Is Distinct From Literal Code. Copyright protection of the literal code of a computer program does not necessarily extend to the user interface because the two are conceptually dissimilar. The same interface can be created with different versions of literal code. Elements of interfaces have been characterized as "literary works" under 17 U.S.C. §102(a)(1), "pictorial, graphic and sculptural works" under 17 U.S.C. §102(a)(5), and "audiovisual works" under 17 U.S.C. §102(a)(6). Since 1988, a single computer program is entitled to only one copyright registra-

tion. The single registration covers the copyrightable authorship in both the literal code and the screen display or user interface generated by the program.

The Apple v. Microsoft *Case.* In 1994, the Ninth Circuit decided a case that the whole computer industry had closely followed. Claiming that Microsoft's Windows infringed the copyrighted graphical user interface (desktop metaphor, windows, icons, and pull-down menus) of Apple's Macintosh computer, Apple sued Microsoft in 1988. In 1985, Apple had granted Microsoft a license to use the visual aspects of Windows 1.0. Apple claimed that later versions of Microsoft Windows became more "Mac-like" than the license allowed and sued Microsoft. Microsoft was found not to have infringed. The Ninth Circuit agreed with the district court that most of the visual elements of the later versions of Windows fell within the scope of the Apple license and that the remaining unlicensed elements failed the test of virtual identity to Apple's copyrightable "unique selection and arrangement" of the elements of the graphical user interface. "When the range of protectable and unauthorized expression is narrow, the appropriate standard for illicit copying is virtual identity. For these reasons, the GUIs in Windows 2.03, 3.0 and New-Wave cannot be compared for substantial similarity with the Macintosh interface as a whole. Instead, as the district court held, the works must be compared for virtual identity." *Apple Computer Inc. v. Microsoft Corp.*, 35 F.3d 1435, 1439, 32 USPQ2d 1086, 1089 (9th Cir. 1994).

The Lotus v. Borland *Case.* Defendant Borland, in its Quattro Pro spreadsheet program, gave users the option to use menu commands and command structures as used in the then industry leading Lotus 1-2-3. Lotus' claim that this constituted infringement of copyright in the menu command hierarchy of Lotus 1-2-3 was rejected by the First Circuit. The court held that the Lotus menu command hierarchy was an uncopyrightable "method of operation," barred from copyright by 17 U.S.C. §102(b). "The fact that there may be many different ways to operate a computer program, or even many different ways to operate a computer program using a set of hierarchically arranged command terms, does not make the actual method of operation chosen copyrightable; it still functions as a method for operating the computer and as such is uncopyrightable." *Lotus Dev. Corp. v. Borland Int'l, Inc.*, 49 F.3d 807, 818, 34 USPQ2d 1014, 1023 (1st Cir. 1995).

See COMPUTER PROGRAM, GUI, LOOK AND FEEL, STRUCTURE, SEQUENCE AND ORGANIZATION,INFRINGEMENT OF COPYRIGHT, COPIES.

• *Treatise References*: W. Patry, *Copyright Law and Practice* 226 (1994).

• *Case References:*

"[U]nlike purely artistic works such as novels and plays, graphical user interfaces generated by computer programs are partly artistic and partly functional. They are a tool to facilitate communication between the user and the computer.... Design alternatives are further limited by the GUI's purpose of making interaction between the user and the computer more 'user friendly.' These, and similar environmental and ergonomic factors which limit the range of possible expression in GUIs, properly inform the scope of copyright protection." *Apple Computer Inc. v. Microsoft Corp.*, 35 F.3d 1435, 1444, 32 USPQ2d 1086, 1093 (9th Cir. 1994).

"Because of the functional quality of user interface, the abstraction portion of the three-step methodology may pose difficult questions. A user interface may often shade into the 'blank form' that epitomizes an uncopyrightable idea, ... or it can partake of high expression, like that found in some computerized games. In the middle of the abstractions spectrum sit user interfaces such as that of Lotus 1-2-3, whose menu structure, including its long prompts, contains numerous expressive features." *Engineering Dynamics Inc. v. Structural Software Inc.*, 26 F.3d 1335, 1344, 31 USPQ2d 1641, 1647 (5th Cir. 1994), *supplemental opinion*, 46 F.3d 408, 34 USPQ2d 1157 (5th Cir. 1995).

"Accepting the district court's finding that the Lotus developers made some expressive choices in choosing and arranging the Lotus command terms, we nonetheless hold that that expression is not copyrightable because it is part of Lotus 1-2-3's 'method of operation.' We do not think that 'methods of operation' are limited to abstractions; rather they are the means by which a user operates something. If specific words are essential to operating something, then they are part of a 'method of operation' and, as such, are unprotectable. This is so whether they must be highlighted, typed in, or even spoken, as computer programs no doubt will soon be controlled by spoken words." *Lotus Dev. Corp. v. Borland Int'l, Inc.*, 49 F.3d 807, 816, 34 USPQ2d 1014, 1022 (1st Cir. 1995).

• *Commentary Reference*: " '[L]ook and feel' lawsuits are not really about the arrangement of user interface command terms but about the imitation of program behavior, a deeply important aspect of programs that has been obscured because it cannot be depicted using conventional copyright terms." Samuelson, Davis, Kapor & Reichman, *Existing Laws Fail to Protect Software Adequately*, Nat'l L.J., Feb. 20, 1995, at C33 (summarizing the arguments made in Samuelson, Davis, Kapor & Reichman, *A Manifesto Concerning the Legal Protection of Computer Programs*, 94 Colum. L. Rev. 2308 (1994)).

USTA [trademarks] United States Trademark Association, the former name of the INTERNATIONAL TRADEMARK ASSOCIATION.

utility [patent] The usefulness of a patented invention. To be patentable, an invention must have "utility" in the sense that it can operate to perform some "useful" function for society. To be "useful," the invention must not only in fact be operable and capable of use, but it must also perform some societal function that is not clearly illegal.

Operability. Inherent in the utility requirement is the condition that a new product or process be operable; that is, it must be capable of being used to achieve the object proposed. However, the utility requirement does not mean that a patented device must accomplish all the objectives stated in the SPECIFICATION or achieve a particular characteristic set forth in the prosecution history in order to satisfy 17 U.S.C § 101. "[W]hen a properly claimed invention meets at least one stated objective, utility under §101 is clearly shown." *Stiftung v. Renishaw PLC*, 945 F.2d 1173, 1180, 20 USPQ2d 1094, 1100 (Fed. Cir. 1991). "To violate §101 the claimed device must be totally incapable of achieving a useful result...." *Brooktree Corp. v. Advanced Micro Devices Inc.*, 977 F.2d 1555, 1571, 24 USPQ2d 1401, 1412 (Fed. Cir. 1992). An invention is presumed to be operable as disclosed in the patent specification unless there is reason for one skilled in the art to question the truth of the statement of utility. *In re Langer*, 503 F.2d 1380, 1391, 183 USPQ 288, 297 (C.C.P.A. 1974).

Example of Rejection Due to Inoperability. An invention relating to the production of energy utilizing what is popularly know as "cold fusion" was rejected because of lack of enablement under §112 and as inoperative and lacking utility under §101. "In view of the compelling evidence that neither excess heat nor the traditional nuclear by-products have been detected by careful researchers conducting experiments under conditions that are highly analogous to appellants' electrolytic cell and, given the relative ease with which erroneous results can be achieved by failing to observe strict experiment design controls, ... we find that the examiner has established a reasonable basis for both challenging the operativeness of the claimed method as well as the utility of how to use the claimed method to achieve the fusion result claimed." *In re Dash*, 27 USPQ2d 1481, 1484 (Bd. Pat. App. & Int'f. 1993).

Effect on Laboratory Animals. Evidence of the efficacy of a new compound in treating disease in laboratory animals is regarded as evidence of the utility of that compound in treating humans. *In re Jolles*, 628 F.2d 1322, 1327, 206 USPQ 885, 890 (C.C.P.A. 1980) (see case reference below). Patent and Trademark Office guidelines for the examination of utility in biotechnology patent applications stated: "[D]ata generated using *in vitro* assays, or from testing in an animal model or a combination thereof almost invariably will be sufficient to establish therapeutic or pharmacological utility for a compound, composition or process. In *no* case has a Federal court required an applicant to support an asserted utility with data from human clinical trials." PTO, Utility Examina-

tion Guidelines, Legal Analysis III C (reprinted in 50 Pat. Trademark & Copyright J. (BNA) 297 (July 20, 1995).

Product of a Chemical Process. The U.S. Supreme Court held that to show the utility of a chemical process, the inventor must disclose in the specification that the product produced by the process has some known specific benefit, i.e., some practical utility. In that case, the inventor did not do so and the Supreme Court affirmed a finding of lack of utility for the process. *Brenner v. Manson*, 383 U.S. 519, 148 USPQ 689 (1966). The product of a new process is useful if it serves some identifiable purpose other than merely being the end product of a series of chemical reactions. The Patent and Trademark Office has adopted guidelines for the disclosure of utility in patent applications revealing drug or pharmaceutical activity (see Manual Reference below). In 1995 the P.T.O. announced Utility Examination Guidelines. See 50 Pat. Trademark & Copyright J. (BNA) 281 (July 20, 1995)

Utility Is Not Commercial Marketability. Utility does not impose a requirement of commercial marketability (see COMMERCIAL SUCCESS). "To require the product to be the victor in the competition of the marketplace is to impose upon patentees a burden far beyond that expressed in the statute." *Studiengesellschaft Kohle v. Eastman Kodak Co.*, 616 F.2d 1315, 1339, 206 USPQ 577, 598 (5th Cir. 1980). Similarly, a device does not lack utility merely because the particular embodiment disclosed in the patent specification performs crudely. "[T]he defense of non-utility cannot be sustained without proof of total incapacity." *E.I. du Pont de Nemours & Co. v. Berkley & Co.*, 620 F.2d 1247, 1260 n.17, 205 USPQ 1, 10 n.17 (8th Cir. 1980) (Markey, J.).

"Immoral" Inventions. While at one time patents on inventions relating to gambling devices were rejected as lacking "utility" because they were harmful to the public welfare, that view now seems obsolete. The Patent Office has rejected such an argument in permitting a patent on a new form of slot machine. *Ex Parte Murphy*, 200 USPQ 801 (Bd. Pat. App. & Int'f. 1977).

Infringer Is Estopped to Challenge Utility. An accused infringer who admits that its device falls within the scope of the patent claims also impliedly admits utility in the invention and is estopped from asserting invalidity for lack of utility. *E.I. du Pont de Nemours & Co. v. Berkley & Co.*, 620 F.2d 1247, 1258, 205 USPQ 1, 9 (8th Cir. 1980) (Markey, J.).

See ENABLEMENT.

• *Statutory Reference*: 35 U.S.C. §101: "Whoever invents or discovers any new and *useful* process, machine, manufacture, or composition of matter, or any new and *useful* improvement thereof, may obtain a patent therefor, subject to the conditions and requirements of this title. (Emphasis added.)

• *Case References*:

"The basic *quid pro quo* contemplated by the Constitution and Congress for granting a patent monopoly is the benefit derived by the public from an invention with substantial utility.... This is not to say that we mean to disparage the importance of contributions to the fund of scientific information short of the invention of something 'useful,' or that we are blind to the prospect of what now seems without 'use' may tomorrow command the grateful attention of the public. But a patent is not a hunting license. It is not a reward for the search, but compensation for its successful conclusion." *Brenner v. Manson*, 383 U.S. 519, 534–36, 148 USPQ 689, 695–96 (1966).

"An invention need not be the best or the only way to accomplish a certain result, and it need only be useful to some extent and in certain applications: '[T]he fact that an invention has only limited utility and is only operable in certain applications is not grounds for finding lack of utility.' " *Stiftung v. Renishaw PLC*, 945 F.2d 1173, 1180, 20 USPQ2d 1094, 1100 (Fed. Cir. 1991).

"[T]his court has accepted tests on experimental animals as sufficient to establish utility.... Utility was recognized by the court ... not because of any concern with the health or existence of the experimental animals, but rather because of the widespread pharmacological work in animals recognized as a screening procedure for testing new drugs. It is clear that such testing is relevant to show utility in humans." *In re Jolles*, 628 F.2d 1322, 1327, 206 USPQ 885, 890 (C.C.P.A. 1980).

• *Manual Reference*: "If the asserted utility of a compound is believable on its face to persons skilled in the art in view of the contemporary knowledge in the art, then the burden is upon the examiner to give adequate support for rejections for lack of utility.... On the other hand, incredible statements ... or statements deemed unlikely to be correct by one skilled in the art ... in view of the contemporary knowledge in the art will require adequate proof on the part of applicants for patents." *Manual of Patent Examining Procedure* §608.01(p), Pt. A, "Guidelines for Considering Disclosures of Utility in Drug Cases" (1994 rev.).

• *Treatise References*: "In some circumstances utility and enablement have a tendency to merge.... Certainly where a claim includes an incorrect or questionable theory or requires a means for accomplishing an unattainable result, it is invalid. The impossible cannot be enabled, and the invention would be inoperative as claimed, thus resulting in invalidity under both §101 and §112." R. Harmon, *Patents and the Federal Circuit* §2.3(b) (3d ed. 1994). See D. Chisum, *Patents* §4.01 (1994 rev.).

utility model [international–patent] Some nations, such as Germany and Japan, have a separate type of protection for inventions known as a UTILITY MODEL or PETTY PATENT ("GEBRAUCHSMUSTER" in German). The basic concept is to permit certain inventions such as mechanical devices, which do not rise to the level of the normal standards of patentable invention, to be given some degree of exclusivity and protection for a shorter period than for full-fledged patents.

Brief Description. Early utility model laws required that the subject matter be a movable article having three dimensions and a definite shape, such as tools or household implements. Processes are not eligible. More recent versions have expanded the possible subject matter. While some novelty is required, the degree of inventive advance can be more modest than that required for a full patent. Some nations, such as

Germany, do not examine for prior art, while other nations, such as Japan, did examine, at least prior to the 1993 Japanese revisions. The duration of protection for a utility model is usually much shorter than for a patent, averaging from 6 to 10 years. Utility models are covered by the provisions of the PARIS CONVENTION. The United States has never had any sort of protection similar to that of the utility model.

See GEBRAUCHSMUSTER.

• *Commentary References*: "The document that the inventor receives in the case of a utility model may be called, and in several countries is called, a patent. If it is called a patent, one must, in order to distinguish it from patents for invention, always specify that it is a 'patent for utility model.' " WIPO, *Background Reading Material on Intellectual Property* 110 (1988). See R. Liesegang, *German Utility Models After the 1990 Reform Act*, 20 AIPLA Q. J. 1 (1992).

See 2 S. Ladas, *Patents, Trademarks and Related Rights: National and International Protection* §548 et seq. (1975).

utility patent [patent]

See PATENT.

V

vague claims [patent] A valid claim in a patent must be definite and not vague. See full definition and references at INDEFINITENESS OF CLAIMS.

value-added retailer [computers] Companies that buy, combine, and resell computer hardware and software. These companies evaluate the needs of particular groups of potential computer users, compare those needs with the available technology, and develop and market a package of hardware and software to satisfy those needs. For example: a package consisting of word processing, data management, and communications software installed on appropriate hardware might be designed to satisfy the needs of physicians' and lawyers' offices.

vaporware [computers] A new computer hardware or software product that is not ready for market at the time it is announced to the public by the producer.

Good Vaporware and Bad Vaporware. The practice of announcing vaporware can be viewed as either good or bad depending on the circumstances. Vaporware can be good if used by manufacturers to give details about unfinished software to customers to facilitate their future software purchasing decisions or for help in improving the software. An example of the later is the release to potential customers of a "beta" version of a software program to test and refine it before it becomes available to the general public. The complicated development process for new computer software sometimes leads to premature announcement of coming attractions. Software development is very complex. Sometimes unavoidable delays are caused by the need to get "bugs" out of the product before

bringing it to the retail shelf after public announcement.

The practice of manufacturers announcing a product they have no intention of building or have no idea how to build has a negative connotation. This type of vaporware is not used to help customers or the development process. Vaporware that is used for the purpose of causing consumers to refrain from purchasing a competitor's product that has been developed and is either currently available or about to enter the market may be part of a course of conduct that is anticompetitive.

- *Commentary Reference*: "Vaporware [is] a term commonly used for computer products that are announced before they are ready for market." S. Yoder, *Computer Markers Defend "Vaporware,"* Wall St. J., Feb. 16, 1995, at B1.

venue [patent–trademark–copyright] The place in which a lawsuit must be filed. Federal rules of venue provide for a particular federal district or districts in which a particular type of civil lawsuit must be filed. Venue in the federal courts is an issue usually posed after it has been determined that the plaintiff has the right to bring suit in some federal court, that is, that there is federal jurisdiction. The issue of venue is separate from the question of personal jurisdiction, which is the power of a court in a certain state to exercise the right to require a person or corporation in another state to come and defend itself.

Remedy for Improper Venue. If a lawsuit is filed in violation of the federal venue rules, 18 U.S.C. §1406(a) provides that the action may be transferred to the federal court of proper venue.

Transfer for Convenience. Even if a case is filed in the place of proper venue, it may be transferred to another federal district for the convenience of parties and witnesses in the interest of justice. 28 U.S.C. §1404(a).

1. Venue in Patent Cases. There is a special venue statute for patent infringement suits, which in the past required that the suit be filed in the federal district in the state either in which the defendant corporation was incorporated (corporate "residence") or in which the defendant had committed acts of infringement and had a regular and established place of business. 28 U.S.C. §1400(b). The U.S. Supreme Court held that the special patent venue statute "is the sole and exclusive provision controlling venue in patent infringement actions, and that it is not to be supplemented by the provisions of [the general venue statute in] 28 U.S.C. §1391(c)." *Fourco Glass Co. v. Transmirra Corp.*, 353 U.S. 222, 229, 113 USPQ 234, 237 (1957). The only exception was for patent suits against aliens, which could be filed in any federal district. *Brunette Mach. Works, Ltd. v. Kockum Indus. Inc.*, 406 U.S. 706, 174 USPQ 1 (1972).

Effect of 1988 Changes in Federal Venue Statute. The Court of Appeals for the Federal Circuit (CAFC) has held that the 1988 revisions to the general federal venue statutes make them applicable to the special patent venue statute. According to 28 U.S.C. §1391(c), the word "resides" in §1400(b) is now expanded to mean any judicial district in which defendant is subject to personal jurisdiction. *VE Holding Corp. v. Johnson Gas Appliance Co.*, 917 F.2d 1574, 16 USPQ2d 1614 (Fed. Cir. 1990).

Personal Jurisdiction in Patent Infringement Actions. In 1994, the Federal Circuit in *Beverly Hills Fan Co. v. Royal Sovereign Corp.*, 21 F.3d 1558, 30 USPQ2d 1001 (Fed. Cir. 1994), established a new body of law defining the requirement of personal jurisdiction for patent infringement cases. The CAFC adopted a "stream of commerce" standard, which permits patent owners to sue in a state convenient to the patentee so long as the alleged infringer either directly or indirectly shipped goods into that state through established distribution channels. Federal district courts are now required to apply this new Federal Circuit law, instead of the law of the regional circuit, in cases that contain an allegation of patent infringement.

- *Statutory Reference*: 28 U.S.C. §1400(b): "Any civil action for patent infringement may be brought in the judicial district where the defendant resides, or where the defendant has committed acts of infringement and has a regular and established place of business."

- *Treatise References*: 5 D. Chisum, *Patents* §21.02[2] (1994 rev.); 3 P. Rosenberg, *Patent Law Fundamentals* §17.00[3] (1994 rev.); R. Harmon, *Patents and the Federal Circuit* §8.1(b) (3d ed. 1994).

- *Case References*:

"[I]n determining whether a corporate defendant has a regular and established place of business in a district, the appropriate inquiry is whether the corporate defendant does its business in that district through a permanent and continuous presence there and not ... whether it has a fixed physical presence in the sense of a formal office or store." *In re Cordis Corp.*, 769 F.2d 733, 737, 226 USPQ 784, 786 (Fed. Cir. 1985).

In determining that it could create and apply a nationally uniform body of Federal Circuit law regarding personal jurisdiction the court stated: "[W]e are not bound to apply Fourth Circuit law in this case because the [personal jurisdiction] issue here is intimately related to substantive patent law.... Although in one sense the due process issue in this case is procedural, it is a critical determinant of whether and in what forum a patentee can seek redress for infringement of its rights." *Beverly Hills Fan Co. v. Royal Sovereign Corp.*, 21 F.3d 1558, 1564, 30 USPQ2d 1001 (Fed. Cir. 1994).

2. Venue in Trademark Cases. Unlike the patent and copyright laws, federal trademark law has no special venue statute. Proper venue for trademark infringement suits is controlled by the general federal venue rules. Since 1990, for a federal question case, proper venue is the federal district or districts: (1) where any defendant "resides" if all defendants reside in the same state; (2) where a substantial part of the events or omissions giving rise to the claim occurred or a substantial part of property that is the subject of the action is situated; or (3) where any defendant may be found, if there is no district in which the suit can otherwise be filed. Since the 1988 amendments, a corporation is deemed to "reside" in any federal district in which it is subject to personal jurisdiction under the statutory and constitutional rules of personal jurisdiction. 28 U.S.C. §1391(c).

Where a Substantial Part of the Events or Omissions Giving Rise to the Claim Occurred. This language was inserted in 1990 to replace the previous test of the district "where the claim arose." The change was apparently intended to make it clear that there can be more than one district in which a claim arises. The traditional view is that a trademark claim arises not only where the infringing labels are affixed to the goods, but also wherever there is a sale using an infringing mark that causes likely confusion of customers. In the 1979 *Leroy* case, the Supreme Court indicated that where a claim arises in more than one district, elements of the convenience of witnesses and the defendant should be factored into the venue decision. *Leroy v. Great W. United Corp.*, 443 U.S. 173 (1979).

Where the Corporate Defendant "Resides." Since the 1988 amendment to 28 U.S.C. §1391(c), some venue disputes center around whether or not a corporate defendant "resides" in the forum district in the sense that there is personal jurisdiction over that corporation in that place. It is constitutional for a state to exercise personal jurisdiction over a corporation if it has "minimum contacts" with the state. The shipment of articles bearing an allegedly infringing mark into a state for resale usually constitutes sufficient minimum contacts. It has been held that by placing advertisements in nationally distributed magazines, the defendant sought to serve a national market and has minimum contacts even in a state where defendant never sold a single product bearing the infringing mark. *Oreck Corp. v. U.S. Floor Sys., Inc.*, 803 F.2d 166, 231 USPQ 634 (5th Cir. 1986).

- *Treatise Reference*: 4 McCarthy, *Trademarks and Unfair Competition* §32.22[3] (3d ed. 1995 rev.).

- *Statutory Reference*:

28 U.S.C. §1391(b) (as amended in 1990): "(b) A civil action wherein jurisdiction is not founded solely on diversity of citizenship may, except as otherwise provided by law, be brought only in (1) a judicial district where any defendant resides, if all defendants reside in the same State, (2) a judicial district in which a substantial part of the events or omissions giving rise to the claim occurred, or a substantial part of property that is the subject of the action is situated, or (3) a judicial district in which any defendant may be found, if there is no district in which the action may otherwise be brought."

28 U.S.C. §1391(c) (as amended in 1988): "For purposes of venue under this chapter, a defendant that is a corporation shall be deemed to reside in any judicial district in which it is subject to personal jurisdiction at the time the action is commenced. In a state which has more than one judicial district and in which a defendant that is a corporation is subject to personal jurisdiction at the time an action is commenced, such corporation shall be deemed to reside in any district in that State within which its contacts would be sufficient to subject it to personal jurisdiction if that district were a separate State, and, if there is no such district, the corporation shall be deemed to reside in the district within which it has the most significant contacts."

3. Venue in Copyright and Mask Work Cases. There is a special venue statute for copyright and MASK WORK cases that permits suit in the district in which the defendant "resides or may be found." 28 U.S.C. §1400(a). This effectively permits suit to be filed in any federal district in the state in which there is valid personal jurisdiction over the defendant. Prior to 1988, this resulted from decisions holding that a defendant is "found" in any district in which personal jurisdiction is valid. See, e.g., *Thomas Jackson Publishing, Inc. v. Buckner*, 625 F. Supp. 1044, 227 USPQ 1048 (D. Neb. 1985). After the 1988 amendments to 28 U.S.C. §1391(c), which equated the "resides" venue requirement to the personal jurisdiction standard, the same result for corporate defendants might be reached under the "resides" alternative. See previous discussion of trademark venue.

- *Treatise References*: 3 *Nimmer on Copyright* §12.01[D] (1994 rev.); 2 P. Goldstein, *Copyright* §13.3 (1989); 1 N. Boorstyn, *Copyright* §10.03 (2d ed. 1994).

- *Statutory References*:

28 U.S.C. §1400(a): "Civil actions, suits, or proceedings arising under any Act of Congress relating to copyrights or exclusive rights in mask works may be instituted in the district in which the defendant or his agent resides or may be found."

28 U.S.C. §1391(c) (as amended in 1988): "For purposes of venue under this chapter, a defendant that is a corporation shall be deemed to reside in any judicial district in which it is subject to personal jurisdiction at the time the action is commenced...."

virus [computers-copyright] A rogue program or set of computer instructions that, upon entering a computer system, replicates itself and infects other programs in the system. Viruses usually enter a computer system as part of contaminated software obtained from electronic bulletin boards, shareware programs, pirated software, or public-domain software, but they may enter from anywhere. Upon being activated, (frequently by a word, phrase, or date), a virus will replicate itself and initiate events. Benign viruses might simply display messages, while a malignant virus can erase files, change randomly selected bits of data, cause irreparable damage to the contents of hard disks, and adversely affect other programs. Examples include the "Yankee Doodle" virus that plays the tune *Yankee Doodle* at 5:00 p.m. or when Alt-Ctrl-Del is pressed, and the "Dark Avenger" virus that overwrites random sectors on the disk with its body.

See WORM.

Visual Artists Rights Act [copyright]
See MORAL RIGHTS

W

Walker Process counterclaim [patent–antitrust] An antitrust treble damage counterclaim asserted by an accused infringer against the patentee and alleging monopolization or attempt to monopolize in violation of Sherman Act §2. The exclusionary conduct part of the Sherman §2 charge is founded upon obtaining the patent by fraud on the Patent and Trademark Office (PTO), and the economic power part of the charge is founded upon use of the patent.

Origin of Term. The name is derived from *Walker Process Equip. Inc. v. Food Mach. Chem. Co.*, 382 U.S. 172, 147 USPQ 404 (1965), where the Supreme Court held that such a claim could be asserted.

Type of Fraud on the Patent and Trademark Office Required. The kind of fraud on the PTO required to establish the conduct part of a *Walker Process* claim is intentional fraud, not merely the kind of fraud that will suffice as INEQUITABLE CONDUCT resulting in unenforceability. In the latter case, the accused infringer merely "raises a shield," while in a *Walker Process* claim, the accused infringer "unsheathes a sword." *Korody-Colyer Corp. v. General Motors Corp.*, 828 F.2d 1572, 1578, 4 USPQ2d 1203, 1207 (Fed. Cir. 1987). Mere gross negligence or recklessness in failing to disclose information is not sufficient: there must be a knowing and willful misrepresentation of facts to the PTO. *Argus Chem. Corp. v. Fibre Glass-Evercoat Co.*, 812 F.2d 1381, 1 USPQ2d 1971 (Fed. Cir. 1987).

Similar to Common-Law Fraud. The kind of intentional fraud required for a *Walker Process* claim is very similar to common-law fraud: a misrepresentation of a material fact made to the PTO in order to obtain the patent, knowledge by the patentee of the misrepresentation, reliance by the PTO, and injury resulting from the reli-

ance. The Supreme Court in *Walker Process* recognized that mere "technical fraud" resulting from an "honest mistake" was insufficient and that it was "deal[ing] only with a special class of patents, i.e., those procured by intentional fraud." 382 U.S. at 176, 147 USPQ at 406.

Exclusionary Power in the Market. The power part of the Sherman §2 *Walker Process* claim cannot be satisfied by the mere existence of the patent. A patent does not automatically define its own relevant market. There must be proof that the patent occupies a significant percentage of a relevant product market. See MONOPOLY. The Supreme Court in *Walker Process* recognized that it is "necessary to appraise the exclusionary power of the illegal patent claim in terms of the relevant market for the product involved." 382 U.S. at 177, 147 USPQ at 407. "[T]he notion that proof of unfair or predatory conduct alone is sufficient to make out the offense of attempted monopolization is contrary to the purpose and policy of the Sherman Act...." *Spectrum Sports Inc. v. McQuillan*, 113 S. Ct. 884, 891 (1993).

- *Case Reference*: "The patent fraud proscribed by *Walker Process* is extremely circumscribed.... Wholly inadvertent errors or honest mistakes which are caused by neither fraudulent intent or design, nor by the patentee's gross negligence, do not constitute fraud under *Walker*.... '[K]nowing and willful fraud' as the term is used in *Walker*, can mean no less than clear, convincing proof of intentional fraud involving affirmative dishonesty, 'a deliberately planned and carefully executed scheme to defraud ... the Patent Office.' " *Cataphote Corp. v. DeSoto Chem. Coatings, Inc.*, 450 F.2d 769, 772, 171 USPQ 736, 738 (9th Cir. 1971).

"A patent does not of itself establish a presumption of market power in the antitrust sense.... The commercial advantage gained by new technology and its statutory protection does not convert the possessor thereof into a prohibited monopolist.... Absent a presumption of market power, Brennan alleged insufficient facts to satisfy the elements of an antitrust violation." *Abbott Labs. v. Brennan*, 952 F.2d 1346, 1354, 21 USPQ2d 1192, 1199 (Fed. Cir. 1991) (affirming dismissal of a *Walker Process* counterclaim under Federal Rule of Civil Procedure 12(b)(5) for failure to state a claim).

• *Treatise Reference*: W. Holmes, *Intellectual Property and Antitrust Law* §15.03 (1994 rev.); ABA, *Antitrust Law Developments* 490 (2d ed. 1984).

whereby clause [patent] A term used in patent claims that expresses the necessary result of limitations already recited in the claims. The existence of a "whereby" clause in a claim does not necessarily establish further limitations on the scope of the claim. For example, a method claim element that concludes with a clause that states "whereby the fluid will not directly engage the device and electrical connection means at a high velocity" was held to be a clause that "merely states the result of the limitations in the claim [and] adds nothing to the patentability or substance of the claim." This was because this whereby clause merely described the result of arranging the components in the manner recited in the claim. Thus it was proper to give the whereby clause no weight in determining infringement of the claim. *Texas Instruments v. U.S. International Trade Comm'n*, 988 F.2d 1165, 1172, 26 USPQ2d 1018, 1023–24 (Fed. Cir. 1993).

willful infringement [patent–trademark–copyright] Conduct that constitutes an illegal use of another's intellectual property where the infringer has no reasonable basis for believing that its actions are legal.

1. Willful Patent Infringement. Conduct that infringes a patent when the infringer knew of the patent and had no reasonable basis for believing that its actions were legal constitutes willful patent infringement. A finding of willful infringement is a basis for increasing damages up to treble the actual amount and/or to award attorney fees to the prevailing party. "Willfulness is shown when, upon consideration of the totality of the circumstances, clear and convincing evidence establishes that the infringer acted in disregard of the patent, that the infringer had no reasonable basis for believing it had a right to engage in the infringing acts." *Electro Medical Sys. S.A. v. Cooper Life Sciences Inc.*, 34 F.3d 1048, 1056, 32 USPQ2d 1017, 1023 (Fed. Cir. 1994).

Factors Considered. "In determining whether an infringer acted in bad faith as to merit an increase in damages against him, the court will consider the totality of the circumstances, ... including (1) whether the infringer deliberately copied the ideas or design of another; (2) whether the infringer, when he knew of the other's patent protection, investigated the scope of the patent and formed a good-faith belief that it was invalid or that it was not infringed; and (3) the infringer's behavior as a party to the litigation.... [A] finding of willful infringement is a finding of fact, not a conclusion of law." *Bott v. Four Star Corp.*, 807 F.2d 1567, 1572, 1 USPQ2d 1210, 1213 (Fed. Cir. 1986). These factors are not all inclusive. In addition, courts will look at (4) defendant's size and financial condition; (5) closeness of the case; (6) duration of defendant's misconduct; (7) remedial action taken by the defendant; (8) defendant's motivation for harm; and (9) any attempts by the defendant to conceal its misconduct. *The Read Corp. v. Portec Inc.*, 970 F.2d 816, 827, 23 USPQ 2d 1427, 1435–36 (Fed. Cir. 1992).

Designing Around. An unsuccessful attempt to DESIGN AROUND a patented product to avoid patent infringement does not necessarily result in willful infringement. *Westvaco Corp. v. International Paper Co.*, 991 F.2d 735, 744, 26 USPQ2d 1353, 1361 (Fed. Cir. 1993) ("Although this attempt to design around [the patentee's product] proved unsuccessful, as evidenced by the court's finding of infringement, [the infringer] should not be found to have willfully infringed based on its attempt.").

See DESIGN AROUND.

Obtaining Legal Advice. An infringer who is put on notice of the patentee's rights has an affirmative duty to exercise due care to determine whether or not there is an infringement. This duty can be satisfied by obtaining legal advice, although a failure to do so is not alone determinative of willfulness. *Delta-X Corp. v. Baker Hughes Prod. Tools Inc.*, 984 F.2d 410, 414, 25 USPQ 2d 1447, 1450 (Fed. Cir. 1993). On the other hand, seeking a legal opinion does not automatically immunize the infringer from a finding of willful infringement. There is no per se rule about obtaining legal advice. *Machinery Corp. of Am. v. Gullfiber AB*, 774 F.2d 467, 472, 227 USPQ 368, 372 (Fed. Cir. 1985). See *In re Hayes Microcomputer Prods. Inc.*, 982 F.2d 1527, 1544, 25 USPQ 2d 1241, 1254 (Fed. Cir. 1992) (Counsel's opinion letter was so broad and conclusory that it did not give the alleged infringer a reasonable basis for believing in good faith that the patent was invalid. Evidence showed that the opinion letter was more of a protective device than a genuine effort to determine before infringing whether the patent was invalid.). It has been held that when an infringer refuses to produce an exculpatory opinion of counsel when willful infringement is charged, an inference may be drawn either that no opinion was obtained or that, if obtained, it was unfavorable. *Electro Medical Sys. S.A. v. Cooper Life Sciences Inc.*, 34 F.3d 1048, 1056, 32 USPQ2d 1017, 1023 (Fed. Cir. 1994) (error for district court to award increased damages and attorney fees based solely on infringer's assertion of attorney-client privilege as basis for refusal to disclose advice of counsel; other evidence supported infringer's good faith belief that the patents were either invalid or not infringed).

Award of Attorney Fees. While a finding of willfulness does not automatically lead to an award of ATTORNEY FEES, in a given case, willfulness may be sufficient for declaring this to be an "exceptional case" appropriate for the award of attorney fees to the prevailing patent owner. *Avia Group Inc. v. L.A. Gear Calif., Inc.*, 853 F.2d 1557, 1566, 7 USPQ2d 1548, 1556 (Fed. Cir. 1988).

• *Statutory Reference*:
35 U.S.C. §284, second paragraph: "[T]he court may increase the damages up to three times the amount found or assessed."

35 U.S.C. §285: "The court in exceptional cases may award reasonable attorney fees to the prevailing party."

• *Treatise Reference*: 5 D. Chisum, *Patents* §20.03 (1994 rev.); R. Harmon, *Patents and the Federal Circuit* §14.2 (3d ed. 1994).

• *Case References*:
" 'Willfulness' in infringement, as in life, is not an all-or-nothing trait, but one of degree. It recognizes that infringement may range from unknowing, or accidental, to deliberate, or reckless, disregard of a patentee's legal rights. The role of a finding of 'willfulness' in the law of infringement is partly as a deterrent—an economic deterrent to the tort of infringement—and partly as a basis for making economically whole one who has been wronged.... The term 'willfulness' thus reflects a threshold of culpability in the act of infringement that, alone or with other considerations of the particular case, contributes to the court's assessment of the consequences of patent infringement. These consequences include the assessments provided by statute for multiplied damages and/or attorney fees." *Rite-Hite Corp. v. Kelley Co.*, 819 F.2d 1120, 1125–26, 2 USPQ2d 1915, 1919 (Fed. Cir. 1987).

"[A]wards of increased damages and attorney fees [should] not be allowed to thwart efforts to challenge the validity of patents believed in good faith to be invalid. A party who has obtained advice of competent counsel, or otherwise acquired a basis for a bona fide belief that a patent is invalid, can be said to serve the patent system in challenging that patent in a law suit conducted fairly, honestly, and in good faith. Such a party should not have increased damages or attorney fees imposed solely because a court subsequently holds that belief unfounded, particularly when the issues may be fairly described as 'close.' " *Kloster Speedsteel AB v. Crucible Inc.*, 793 F.2d 1565, 1581, 230 USPQ 81, 91–92 (Fed. Cir. 1986).

"Willfulness is a determination as to a state of mind. One who has actual notice of another's patent rights has an affirmative duty to respect those rights.... That affirmative duty normally entails obtaining advice of legal counsel although the absence of such advice does not mandate a finding of willfulness.... Those cases where willful infringement is found despite the presence of an opinion of counsel generally involve situations where opinion of counsel was either ignored or found to be incompetent." *The Read Corp. v. Portec Inc.*, 970 F.2d 816, 828–29, 23 USPQ 2d 1427, 1436–37 (Fed. Cir. 1992) (reversing jury finding of wilfulness where infringer obtained two independent written opinions of unrelated patent counsel).

"It is well settled that a potential infringer having actual notice of another's patent has an affirmative duty of due care that normally requires the potential infringer to obtain competent legal advice before infringing or continuing to infringe. ... However, legal advice is only one factor to be considered, and an opinion of counsel does not guarantee against a finding of willfulness. ... The emphasis here must be on 'competent' legal advice. ... [O]ral opinions are not favored. ... Such opinions carry less weight, for example, because they have to be proved perhaps years after the event, based only on testimony which may be affected by faded memories and the forces of contemporaneous litigation." *Minnesota Mining & Mfg. v. Johnson & Johnson,* 976 F.2d 1559, 1580, 24 USPQ2d 1321, 1339 (Fed. Cir. 1992) (willful infringement found and affirmed notwithstanding an oral opinion of invalidity from infringer's in-house counsel).

2. Willful Trademark Infringement. Proof that trademark infringement was willful, deliberate, or calculated is relevant to proving infringement by likelihood of confusion and to the recovery of remedies, such as profits of the infringer and attorney fees, as well as establishing counterfeiting.

Evidence of Infringement. While willful or intentional infringement is not necessary to prove trademark infringement, proof of willful or calculated behavior may raise a presumption of a likelihood of confusion. If an intent to confuse can be inferred from evidence such as willful copying, then some courts will presume that the accused in fact succeeded in its purpose and that confusion is indeed likely. E.g., *Paddington Corp. v. Attiki Importers & Distribs. Inc.*, 996 F.2d 577, 586, 27 USPQ2d 1189, 1195 (2d Cir. 1993) ("Where a second-comer acts in bad faith and intentionally copies a trademark or trade dress, a presumption arises that the copier has succeeded in causing confusion."). Other courts refuse to permit proof of deliberate copying to raise a presumption of likely confusion, but consider such evidence as one of several factors to be weighed. *Computer Care v. Service Sys. Enters., Inc.*, 982 F.2d 1063, 25 USPQ2d 1020, 1025 (7th Cir. 1992) ("Although deliberate copying does not create a *presumption* of consumer confusion, it is an 'important factor bearing on the likelihood of confusion.' "). See 3 J.T. McCarthy, *Trademarks and Unfair Competition* §23.32[2] (3d ed. 1995 rev.).

Counterfeiting. Willful infringement will sometimes constitute trademark COUNTERFEITING when there is a calculated attempt to pass off the infringing goods as genuine. Counterfeiting triggers special criminal and civil penalties.

Recovery of Infringer's Profits. The courts generally require some showing of deliberate or willful infringement before authorizing an accounting of profits. Some form of bad faith or knowing infringement is needed before an accounting of profits is felt to be necessary. *Nalpac, Ltd. v. Corning Glass Works*, 784 F.2d 752, 228 USPQ 946 (6th Cir. 1986).

See PROFITS.

Attorney Fees Award. The 1975 statutory authorization for the recovery of attorney fees in exceptional cases was intended to allow the recovery of fees "in infringement cases where the acts of infringement can be characterized as 'malicious,' 'fraudulent,' 'deliberate,' or 'willful.' " S. Rep. No. 93-1400, 93d Cong., 2d Sess. 2, *reprinted in* 1974 U.S. Code Cong. & Admin. News 7132, 7133. Most courts have found that an "exceptional" case justifying an award of fees to a prevailing plaintiff requires evidence of acts of intentional and deliberate infringement. See, e.g., *Centaur Communications, Ltd. v. A/S/M Communications, Inc.*, 830 F.2d 1217, 1229, 4 USPQ2d 1541, 1551 (2d Cir. 1987)

("Of course, deliberate and willful infringement can render a case 'exceptional' and thus support an award of attorneys' fees."); *CJC Holdings Inc. v. Wright & Lato, Inc.*, 979 F2d 60, 66, 25 USPQ2d 1212, 1216 (5th Cir. 1992) ("A district court normally should not find a case exceptional where the party presents what it in good faith believes may be a legitimate defense."). See ATTORNEY FEES AWARD.

• *Treatise Reference*: 3 J.T. McCarthy, *Trademarks and Unfair Competition* §§23.30–.35 (3d ed. 1995 rev.).

• *Restatement Reference*: "Although several cases have awarded an accounting of profits when the defendant deliberately but in good faith used a mark with knowledge of the plaintiff's prior use, application of the accounting remedy to uses undertaken in good faith can chill lawful behavior. A defendant who reasonably believes, for example, that its goods are sufficiently unrelated to those of plaintiff to avoid confusion, or that the plaintiff's mark is functional or generic, may be deterred from using the designation by the risk of substantial monetary liability unrelated to any injury to the plaintiff, thus effectively expanding the scope of the plaintiff's trademark rights. The better view limits an accounting of profits to acts intended to create confusion or to deceive potential purchasers." *Restatement (Third) of Unfair Competition* §37, comment e (1995).

• *Case References*:

"[A] late comer who deliberately copies the dress of his competitors already in the field must at least prove that his effort has been futile. Prima facie the court will treat his opinion so disclosed as expert and will not assume that it was erroneous.... He may indeed succeed in showing that it was; that however bad his purpose, it will fail in execution; if he does, he will win.... But such an intent raises a presumption that customers will be deceived." Judge Learned Hand in *My-T-Fine Corp. v. Samuels*, 69 F.2d 76, 77 (2d Cir. 1934).

"In assessing the likelihood of confusion to the public, an important factor is whether or not the second comer created the similar trade dress intentionally. If there was intentional copying the second comer will be presumed to have intended to create a confusing similarity of appearance and will be presumed to have succeeded." *Perfect Fit Indus., Inc. v. Acme Quilting Co.*, 618 F.2d 950, 954, 205 USPQ 297, 301 (2d Cir. 1980).

3. Willful Copyright Infringement. This is conduct that infringes a copyright where the infringer had no reasonable basis for believing that its conduct was legal. For example, where the defendant's work is essentially identical to the copyrighted work and no reasonable explanation is given, willful infringement will be found. *Camaro Headquarters, Inc. v. Banks*, 621 F. Supp. 39, 227 USPQ 170 (E.D. Pa. 1985).

Reckless Disregard. Willfulness includes both actual knowledge that one is infringing and reckless disregard of the copyright owner's rights. *RCA/Ariola Int'l, Inc. v. Thomas & Grayston Co.*, 845 F.2d 773, 779, 6 USPQ2d 1692, 1695 (8th Cir. 1988). Thus, the copyright owner can prove willfulness by showing that the infringer should have known its conduct was infringing or that it acted in reckless disregard of the plaintiff's copyright. *Wow & Flutter Music v. Len's Tom Jones Tavern, Inc.*, 606 F. Supp. 554, 556, 226 USPQ 795, 797 (E.D.N.Y. 1985). But one who has been put on notice that the copyright owner considers the conduct to be infringing, but who has a reasonable belief that it is not infringing, is not a willful infringer.

Effect on Statutory Damages. In recovering STATUTORY DAMAGES, if the copyright owner proves that the infringement was committed "willfully," the court has the power to award statutory damages up to $100,000 for each work infringed for each separately liable infringer. 17 U.S.C. §504(c)(1). To be criminally liable for copyright infringement, the defendant must be proven to have acted willfully. See 2 P. Goldstein, *Copyright* §11.4.1 b. (1989).

See STATUTORY DAMAGES.

• *Treatise References*: 2 P. Goldstein, *Copyright* §12.2.1.2 a. (1989); 3 *Nimmer on Copyright* §14.04[B][3] (1994 rev.); 1 N. Boorstyn, *Copyright* §13.05 (2d ed. 1994); W. Patry, *Copyright Law and Practice* 1169 (1994).

• *Case Reference*: "We have held that for the purpose of awarding enhanced statutory damages under §504(c)(2), an infringement is 'willful' if the defendant had 'knowledge that its actions constitute an infringement.' ... While an infringement may not be willful when a party, despite warnings to the contrary, 'reasonably and in good faith believes' that its conduct is innocent, ... this 'analysis is subject to the corollary that reckless disregard of the copyright holder's rights (rather than actual knowledge of infringement) suffices to warrant award of the enhanced damages.' " *N.A.S. Import Corp. v. Chenson Enters. Inc.*, 968 F.2d 250, 252, 23 USPQ2d 1387, 1388–89 (2d Cir. 1992) (reversing and remanding district court finding that the infringement was not willful; court said it was likely that defendant retailer knew that the handbags with a copyrighted buckle design that it sold were counterfeit).

WIPO [international] World Intellectual Property Organization. This is one of the 16 "specialized agencies" of the United Nations system of organizations. WIPO, located in Geneva, Switzerland, was created in 1967 and is responsible for the promotion of the protection of intellectual property throughout the world. It fulfills this responsibility through administration of many programs including promotion of cooperation among nations in intellectual property matters; administration of various "unions" and other treaty organizations founded on multilateral treaties; and the creation of model laws for adoption by developing nations. The four major unions that the WIPO administers are the PARIS CONVENTION, the BERNE CONVENTION, the MADRID ARRANGEMENT, and the ROME CONVENTION. Over 115 nations are members of WIPO.

WIPO Versus GATT. Western countries, especially the United States, desired a higher level of international intellectual property protection than that provided by the conventions administered by WIPO. As a result, in 1986, the U.S. government proposed to expand the "General Agreement on Tariffs and Trade" (GATT) to provide higher standards of international intellectual property protection. The "Trade-Related Aspects of Intellectual Property Rights" (TRIPS) agreement generally provides more detailed minimum standards of protection of intellectual property rights than do WIPO-administered treaties.

See GATT, TRIPS.

• *Information Reference*: Information may be obtained from the World Intellectual Property Organization (WIPO), 34 Chemin des Colombettes, 1211 Geneva, Switzerland.

• *Commentary Reference*: "The activities of WIPO are basically of three kinds: registration activities, the promotion of intergovernmental cooperation in the administration of intellectual property, and substantive or program activities. All these activities serve the overall objectives of WIPO to maintain and increase respect for intellectual property throughout the world, in order to favor industrial and cultural development by stimulating creative activity and facilitating the transfer of technology and the dissemination of literary and artistic works." WIPO, *Background Reading Material on Intellectual Property* 40 (1988).

World Trade Organization [international] See WTO.

working [patent–international]   The actual use of a patented invention either by making a product that embodies the invention or by using a process that includes the invention.

Foreign Working Requirements. Many nations require that within a specified time, the technology covered by a patent must be "worked" or actually used by the patentee or a licensee in that nation. If the patented technology is not "worked" within the time limit, any interested party may apply for and obtain from the government a nonexclusive COMPULSORY LICENSE to use the invention in that nation at a royalty rate set by the government. A petition for a compulsory license will often lead the parties into negotiations for a voluntary exclusive license. The importation of a patented article into the nation does not constitute working. The purpose of a working requirement is to force foreign patent owners to manufacture domestically rather than import goods made using the patented technology.

Working Under the Paris Convention and GATT TRIPS. The PARIS CONVENTION Article 5A places a minimum time limit on the working requirement in member nations. The time limit expires either four years from the date of filing the patent application or three years from the date of the grant of the patent for invention, whichever period expires last. This is a minimum time limit and a member nation is free to establish longer periods in which to work the invention. The Paris Convention requires that the patent owner must be given a longer time limit if legitimate reasons can be given for failure to work. For example, the patent owner might justify nonworking within the time limit by evidence of legal, economic, or technical barriers. The 1995 GATT TRIPS agreement in Article 31 places certain conditions on a nation's ability to order compulsory licensing for failure to work. For example, Article 31(f) requires that the compulsory license "shall be authorized predominantly for the supply of the domestic market of the Member [nation] authorizing such use."

No Patent Working Requirement in the United States. The United States has never had a statutory working requirement. The failure to use a patented invention has been held not to be "inequitable" conduct sufficient to be a bar to obtaining an injunction against an infringer. *Continental Paper Bag Co. v. Eastern Paper Bag Co.*, 210 U.S. 405 (1908). In the *Continental Paper Bag* case, the Supreme Court said that "it is the privilege of any owner of property to use or not use it," noting that the Court assumed that Congress was aware of the working requirements of foreign nations and had "selected another policy."

Nonuse Is Not Misuse of a Patent. The case law principle that nonuse is not misuse is now codified in the Patent Code. In 1988, Patent Code §271(d)(4) was added to provide that it is not a misuse of patent sufficient to deny relief against infringement if the patent owner has "refused to license or use any rights to the patent." Thus, the statute now prohibits claiming nonuse or a failure to work as a ground of defense in any patent infringement case.

See COMPULSORY LICENSE.

• *Treatise Reference*: 1 S. Ladas, *Patents, Trademarks and Related Rights: National and International Protection* §§247, 320 et seq. (1975); ABA, *Antitrust Law Developments* 497 (2d ed. 1984).

• *Case Reference*: "A patent owner is not in the position of a quasi-trustee for the public or under any obligation to see that the public acquires the free right to use the invention. He has no obligation either to use it or to grant its use to others. If he discloses the invention in his application so that it will come into the public domain at the end of the 17-year period of exclusive right he has fulfilled the only obligation imposed by the statute. 35 U.S.C. §33. This has been settled doctrine since at least 1896. Congress has repeatedly been asked, and has refused, to change the statutory policy by imposing a forfeiture or by a provision for compulsory licensing if the patent is not used within a specified time." *Hartford-Empire Co. v. United States*, 323 U.S. 386, 432 (1945).

work made for hire [copyright] (1) A work prepared by an employee within the scope of his or her employment or (2) a commissioned work that falls within a specified category of works and the parties agree in writing to treat it as a work made for hire.

Employer or Commissioning Party Is the "Author." In the case of a "work made for hire," the real person, partnership, or corporation for whom the work was prepared is considered to be both the "author" and the owner of copyright from the moment of creation of the work. 17 U.S.C. §201(b). This is the only situation in which someone other than the actual creator of the work is the "author." In an employment situation, the employer and employee can agree in a writing signed by both to modify their relationship and grant some or all rights to the employee. 17 U.S.C. §201(b).

Copyright Duration of a Work Made for Hire. The duration of copyright in a work made for hire is not the usual life of the author plus 50 years. Rather, regardless of whether the hiring party is a corporation or a real person, the duration of copyright in a work made for hire is 75 years from the first publication of the work or 100 years from creation of the work, whichever results in the shortest term. 17 U.S.C. §302(c).

No Right to Termination of a Transfer. Since vesting of copyright in the employer or commissioning party as the "author" in law is automatic, there is no voluntary transfer or assignment of the copyright, and the termination of transfer provisions of the Copyright Act are never triggered. 17 U.S.C. §§203(a), 304(c). The actual creator of the work can never exercise the termination provisions and reacquire the copyright because it never owned the copyright at any time.

Work Made for the Federal Government. If a work made for hire is created by an employee of the U.S. government and the U.S. government is the "author," then no copyright can be claimed in the work. 17 U.S.C. §105.

The Supreme Court 1989 CCNV *Decision.* In *Community for Creative Non-Violence v. Reid*, 490 U.S. 730, 10 USPQ2d 1985 (1989), the Supreme Court held that a specially ordered or commissioned work created by a freelance sculptor was not a work made for hire, and therefore the sculptor, not the commissioning party, was the owner of copyright in the sculpture. The Court rejected the theory that a right of control exercised by the commissioning party can in and of itself vest ownership of copyright in the commissioning party by turning the freelance, creating party into an employee. Rather, said the Court, the existence of an employment relationship is to be determined by the "general common law of agency." In determining whether a hired creative person is an employee under agency law, several criteria are considered, and no one factor is determinative.

Application of Criteria. In applying the *CCNV* test, the Second Circuit determined that each factor is not accorded equal weight. The factors should "be weighed according to their significance in the case." *Aymes v. Bonelli*, 980 F.2d 857, 861, 25 USPQ2d 1181, 1184 (2d Cir. 1992). Some factors will be significant in almost every situation: (1) the hiring party's right to control the manner and means of the creation; (2) the employee benefits provided by the hiring party; (3) whether the hiring party has the right

to assign more projects to the hired party; (4) the tax treatment of the hired party; and (5) the skill required to complete the project. Factors (2) and (4) are the most important and carry the most weight. In *Aymes*, the hiring party did not provide employee benefits or pay any payroll taxes for the hired party. These two factors were a "virtual admission" that the hired party was not an employee. *Id.* at 862.

- *Example.* One may apply the *CCNV* case's listing of the factors and criteria of agency law to the question of who owns copyright in a posed studio photograph in the absence of an express agreement: the hiring party or the photographer? In the author's opinion, a skilled freelance photographer, working in his own studio with his own photographic equipment, with the right to decide how many photos to take, the right to determine the poses and technical matters such as the light setting, type of camera, type of film, and camera aperture, will not be deemed to be an employee of the hiring party. This is especially so if the hiring party has no right to assign additional work, pays a flat fee on completion, and does not pay payroll or social security taxes or contribute to employee benefits. If the photo is of a person who hires the photographer, the fact that the subject has the right to control the general nature and style of the photos will not per se determine the work-for-hire status of copyright in the photos. Thus, if a person hires a photographer to take pictures of himself or herself and desires to own copyright in the resulting photos, that person should obtain a written assignment of copyright from the photographer. See J.T. McCarthy, *The Rights of Publicity and Privacy* §11.14[A][1] (1995 rev.).

Joint Work. Although a work may not be a work for hire, if the hiring party was involved in the development of the work and contributed some copyrightable material beyond mere ideas, the work might be considered a joint work. JOINT AUTHORS of a work are treated as co-owners.

- *Treatise References*: 1 *Nimmer on Copyright* §5.03 (1994 rev.); 1 P. Goldstein, *Copyright* §4.3 (1989); W. Patry, *Copyright Law and Practice* 373 (1994); 1 N. Boorstyn, *Copyright*

§3.03 (2d ed. 1994); M. Leaffer, *Understanding Copyright* §5.2 (1989),

• *Statutory References*:

17 U.S.C. §101: "A 'work made for hire' is—

"(1) a work prepared by an employee within the scope of his or her employment; or

"(2) a work specially ordered or commissioned for use as a contribution to a collective work, as a part of a motion picture or other audiovisual work, as a translation, as a supplementary work, as a compilation, as an instructional text, as a test, as answer material for a test, or as an atlas, if the parties expressly agree in a written instrument signed by them that the work shall be considered a work made for hire. For the purpose of the foregoing sentence, a 'supplementary work' is a work prepared for publication as a secondary adjunct to a work by another author for the purpose of introducing, concluding, illustrating, explaining, revising, commenting upon, or assisting in the use of the other work, such as forewords, afterwords, pictorial illustrations, maps, charts, tables, editorial notes, musical arrangements, answer material for tests, bibliographies, appendixes and indexes, and an 'instructional text' is a literary, pictorial or graphic work prepared for publication and with the purpose of use in systematic instructional activities."

17 U.S.C. §201(b): "In the case of a work made for hire, the employer or other person for whom the work was prepared is considered the author for purposes of this title, and unless the parties have expressly agreed otherwise in a written instrument signed by them, owns all of the rights comprised in the copyright."

17 U.S.C. §302(c): "In the case of ... a work made for hire, the copyright endures for a term of seventy-five years from the year of its first publication, or a term of one hundred years from the year of its creation, whichever expires first...."

• *Case References*: "Classifying a work as 'made for hire' determines not only the initial ownership of its copyright, but also the copyright's duration, §302(c), and the owner's renewal rights, §304(a), termination rights, §203(a) and right to import certain goods bearing the copyright, §601(b)(1).... The contours of the work for hire doctrine therefore carry profound significance for freelance creators—including artists, writers, photographers, designers, composers, and computer programmers—and for the publishing, advertising, music and other industries which commission their works." *Community for Creative Non-Violence v. Reid*, 490 U.S. 730, 737, 10 USPQ2d 1985, 1989 (1989).

"[T]he *Reid* test can be easily misapplied, since it consists merely of a list of possible considerations that may or may not be relevant in a given case. ... It does not necessarily follow that because no one factor is dispositive all factors are equally important, or indeed that all factors will have relevance in every case. The factors should not merely be tallied but should be weighed according to their significance in the case." *Aymes v. Bonelli*, 980 F.2d 857, 861, 25 USPQ2d 1181, 1184 (2d Cir. 1992).

work product [general legal]
See ATTORNEY WORK PRODUCT.

worm [computers-copyright] A self-replicating sequence intentionally inserted into a computer program which causes malfunction of the entire system when the user attempts to copy the program. A worm may travel from system to system via a network. While the terms "worm" and "virus" are sometimes used interchangeably, a worm differs from a virus in that a worm adds new information that copies itself over and over until overload occurs, while a virus alters or erases stored information.

See VIRUS.

WTO [international] The World Trade Organization, located in Geneva, Switzerland, was created at the end of the Uruguay Round of GATT negotiations in December 1993 to oversee the operation of GATT. The WTO entered into force with respect to the United States on January 1, 1995. See URUGUAY ROUND AGREEMENTS ACT. It is anticipated that the WTO will play much the same role in world financial and economic affairs as the United Nations does in political affairs.

Functions of the WTO. The WTO was established to facilitate the implementation, administration, and operation of the trade agreements reached in the Uruguay Round by bringing them under one institutional umbrella, requiring full participation of all countries in the new trading system and providing a permanent forum to address new issues facing the international trading system. *Memorandum for the United States Trade Representative*, 58 Fed. Reg. 67,263, 67,267 (1993) (executive summary of results of the GATT Uruguay Round of Multilateral Trade Negotiations). The agreements concluding the Uruguay Round of trade talks call for, among other things, implementation of agreements in the areas of trade in goods, trade in services, and protection of trade-related intellectual property rights and strengthened dispute settlement procedures. The WTO replaces GATT's old administrative structure, has greater powers to resolve disputes and police world trade, and occupies much the same status as the International Monetary Fund and World Bank. *Final Act Embodying the Results of the Uruguay Round of Multilateral Trade Negotiations, Agreement Establishing the World Trade Organization*, December 15, 1993, (WTO), Pt. II, Arts. I–III, 33 Int'l Legal Materials 13, 15–16 (1994).

The WTO Agreement. The WTO Agreement established the World Trade Organization as "the common institutional framework for the conduct of trade relations among its Members in matters related to the agreements and associated legal instruments included in the Annexes to this Agreement." *Final Act Embodying the Results of the Uruguay Round of Multilateral Trade Negotiations, Agreement Establishing the World Trade Organization*, December 15, 1993, (WTO), Pt. II, Art. II, 33 Int'l Legal Materials 13, 15 (1994). The WTO Agreement has four annexes:

Annex 1 includes substantive trade agreements on trade in goods (Annex 1A), the new General Agreement on Trade in Services (GATS, in Annex 1B), and the new Agreement on Trade-Related Aspects of Intellectual Property Rights (TRIPS, in Annex 1C).

Annex 2 consists of the Understanding on Rules and Procedures Governing the Settlement of Disputes.

Annex 3 provides for the Trade Policy Review Mechanism, a process of multilateral surveillance of national trade policies.

Annex 4 contains the "Plurilateral Trade Agreements," which were not negotiated in the context of the Uruguay Round.

The agreements in Annexes 1, 2, and 3 are integral parts of the WTO Agreement and are binding on all members of the WTO. The agreements in Annex 4 are binding only on those member nations that accept them. *Final Act Embodying the Results of the Uruguay Round of Multilateral Trade Negotiations, Introductory Note*, December 15, 1993, 33 Int'l Legal Materials 1, 2 (1994).

Structure of the WTO. The functions of the WTO are carried out by a Ministerial Conference, composed of representatives of all members, which meets at least once every two years. The Ministerial Conference has the authority to make decisions on all matters under the GATT agreements if so requested by a member nation. When the Ministerial Conference is not meeting, its functions are administered by the General Council, which is composed of representatives of all members. Under the General Council, there are separate councils for trade in goods, trade in services, and trade-related aspects of intellectual property rights. *Final Act Embodying the Results of the Uruguay Round of Multilateral Trade Negotiations, Agreement Establishing the World Trade Organization*, December 15, 1993, (WTO), Pt. II, Art. IV, 33 Int'l Legal Materials 13, 16 (1994). The WTO Secretariat, entrusted with the administrative duties of GATT, is an international agency, independent of any member government. The Director-General, appointed by the Ministerial Counsel, heads the Secretariat. *Final Act Embodying the Results of the Uruguay Round of Multilateral Trade Negotiations, Agreement Establishing the World Trade Organization*, December 15, 1993, (WTO), Pt. II, Art. VI, 33 Int'l Legal Materials 13, 17–18 (1994).

The Process of Decision Making. The WTO Agreement establishes institutional rules that will be applied to all the Uruguay Round agreements, and the WTO system will be available only to countries that are contracting parties to GATT. Each member nation has one vote. If attempts at reaching a consensus (virtually unanimous agreement with no objections) fail, a majority vote controls. In some special instances, a two-thirds or three-fourths majority is required. Nations may request waivers from new rules, but waivers can be granted only if three quarters of the WTO member nations agree. This tightened waiver provision prevents nations from becoming perpetual "free riders" by not meeting their GATT obligations. *Final Act Embodying the Results of the Uruguay Round of Multilateral Trade Negotiations, Agreement Establishing the World Trade Organization*, December 15, 1993, (WTO), Pt. II, Art. IX, 33 Int'l Legal Materials 13, 19 (1994).

Settlement of Disputes—Annex 2. New procedures (e.g., when one country accuses another of violating its WTO obligations) provide detailed rules and deadlines for settlement of disputes under the WTO Agreement. Disputes will be administered by a "Dispute Settlement Body" (DSB), which will make decisions by consensus. Disputes are considered by a panel of three experts and may be appealed to a seven-member appellate body. See *Final Act Embodying the Results of the Uruguay Round of Multilateral Trade Negotiations, Understanding on Rules and Procedures Governing the Settlement of Disputes*, December 15, 1993, 33 Int'l Legal Materials 112 (1994).

See GATT, TRIPS, URUGUAY ROUND AGREEMENTS ACT.

List of References Cited

Antitrust Law

ABA, *Antitrust Law Developments* (2d ed. 1984) (1 vol.)
C. Hills, *Antitrust Adviser* (3d ed. 1985) (1 vol.)
W. Holmes, *Intellectual Property and Antitrust Law* (1994 rev.) (1 vol.)
S. Oppenheim, G. Weston & J.T. McCarthy, *Federal Antitrust Laws*
  (4th ed. 1981) (1 vol.)

Copyright Law

N. Boorstyn, *Copyright* (2d ed. 1994) (2 vols.)
P. Goldstein, *Copyright* (1989) (3 vols. with supp.)
M. Leaffer, *Understanding Copyright* (1989) (1 vol.)
M. Nimmer & D. Nimmer, *Nimmer on Copyright* (1994 rev.) (4 vols.)
W. Patry, *Copyright Law and Practice* (1994) (3 vols.)
WIPO, *Glossary of Terms of the Law of Copyright and Neighboring
  Rights* (1980) (1 vol.)

International Law

G. Bodenhausen, *Guide to Paris Convention for the Protection of
  Industrial Property* (1968) (1 vol.)
W. Cornish, *World Intellectual Property Guidebooks:* U.K. (1981)
  (1 vol.: British law)
S. Ladas, *Patents, Trademarks and Related Rights: National and
  International Protection* (1975) (3 vols.)
WIPO, *Background Reading Material on Intellectual Property* (1988) (1 vol.)

Patent Law

D. Chisum, *Patents* (1994 rev.) (8 vols.)
R. Choat, W. Francis & R. Collins, *Patent Law* (3d ed. 1987) (1 vol.)
B. Collins, *Current Patent Interference Practice* (1989 rev.) (1 vol.)
J. Dratler, Jr., *Licensing of Intellectual Property* (1994) (1 vol.)
H. Einhorn, *Patent Licensing Transactions* (1994 rev.) (2 vols.)
R. Ellis, *Patent Assignments* (3d ed. 1955) (1 vol.)
R. Faber, *Landis on Mechanics of Patent Claim Drafting* (3d ed. 1990) (1 vol.)

R. Harmon, *Patents and the Federal Circuit* (3d ed. 1994) (1 vol.)

I. Kayton, *Kayton on Patents* (1979) (1 vol.)

H. Mayers & B. Brunsvold, *Drafting Patent License Agreements* (3d ed. 1991) (1 vol.)

R. Nordhaus, *Patent License Agreements* (1994 rev.) (1 vol.)

P. Rosenberg, *Patent Law Fundamentals* (1994 rev.) (3 vols.)

J. White, *Chemical Patent Practice* (11th ed. 1988) (1 vol.)

Right of Publicity Law

J.T. McCarthy, *The Rights of Publicity and Privacy* (1995 rev.) (1 vol.)

Trademark and Unfair Competition Law

J.T. McCarthy, *Trademarks and Unfair Competition* (3d ed. 1995 rev.)

Restatement (Third) of Unfair Competition (1995)

Trade Secrets Law

M. Jager, *Trade Secrets Law* (1994 rev.) (3 vols.)

R. Milgrim, *Milgrim on Trade Secrets* (1994 rev.) (4 vols.)

Other Subjects

C. Grimes & G. Battersby, *The Law of Merchandise and Character Licensing* (1994 rev.) (1 vol.)

R. Goldscheider, *Technology Management* (1989 rev.) (1 vol.)

E. Kitch & H. Perlman, *Legal Regulation of the Competitive Process, Cases, Materials & Notes on Unfair Business Practices, Trademarks, Copyright & Patents* (rev. 4th ed. 1991) (1 vol.)

M. Leaffer, *International Treaties on Intellectual Property* (1990) (1 vol.)

S. Shemel & M.W. Krasilovsky, *This Business of Music* (5th ed. 1985) (1 vol.)

R. Stern, *Semiconductor Chip Protection* (1986) (1 vol.)

Patent and Trademark Office Guides

Manual of Patent Examining Procedure (MPEP) (1994 rev.)

Trademark Manual of Examining Procedure (TMEP) (1993 rev.)

Note: For looseleaf treatises, the *Manual of Patent Examining Procedures* and the *Trademark Manual of Examining Procedure*, the date used in the citation is the date of the most recent revision consulted even if the pages of the exact section cited were not changed as of that date. For example, a treatise may be cited with a citation to its 1994 revised version while the page on which the exact section cited to was last updated or changed in 1989.

Appendix 1
Superintendents and Commissioners of Patents (and Trademarks)

1. Dr. William Thornton	1802–1828	"Chief" and adopted title "Superintendent"
2. Dr. Thomas P. Jones	1828–1829	
3. Dr. John D. Craig	1829–1835	"Superintendent" official title 1830
4. J.C. Pickett	1835	
5. Henry L. Ellsworth	1835–1845	1st "Commissioner" (title change 7/4/1836)
6. Edmund Burke	1845–1849	2nd Commissioner
7. Thomas Ewbank	1849–1852	3rd Commissioner
8. Silas Henry Hodges	1852–1853	4th Commissioner
9. Charles Mason	1853–1857	5th Commissioner
10. Joseph Holt	1857–1859	6th Commissioner
11. William Darius Bishop	1859–1860	7th Commissioner
12. Philip Francis Thomas	1860	8th Commissioner
13. David P. Holloway	1861–1865	9th Commissioner
14. Thomas C. Theaker	1865–1868	10th Commissioner
15. Elisha Foote	1868–1869	11th Commissioner
16. Samuel Sparks Fisher	1869–1870	12th Commissioner
17. Gen. Mortimer D. Leggett	1871–1874	13th Commissioner
18. John Marshall Thacher	1874–1875	14th Commissioner
19. Robert Holland Duell	1875–1876	15th Commissioner
20. Ellis Spear	1877–1878	16th Commissioner
21. Gen. Halbert Eleazer Paine	1878–1880	17th Commissioner
22. Edgar M. Marble	1880–1883	18th Commissioner
23. Benjamin Butterworth	1883–1885	19th Commissioner
24. Martin V.B. Montgomery	1885–1887	20th Commissioner
25. Benton J. Hall	1887–1889	21st Commissioner
26. Charles Elliott Mitchell	1889–1891	22nd Commissioner
27. William Edgar Simonds	1891–1893	23rd Commissioner
28. John S. Seymour	1893–1897	24th Commissioner

29. Benjamin Butterworth	1897–1898	—2nd term—
30. Charles Holland Duell	1898–1901	25th Commissioner
31. Frederick Innes Allen	1901–1907	26th Commissioner
32. Edward Bruce Moore	1907–1913	27th Commissioner
33. Thomas Ewing	1913–1917	28th Commissioner
34. James T. Newton	1917–1920	29th Commissioner
35. Robert Frederick Whitehead	1920–1921	30th Commissioner
36. Melvin H. Coulston	1921	31st Commissioner
37. Thomas E. Robertson	1921–1933	32nd Commissioner
38. Conway P. Coe	1933–1945	33rd Commissioner
39. Casper W. Ooms	1945–1947	34th Commissioner
40. Lawrence C. Kingsland	1947–1949	35th Commissioner
41. John A. Marzall	1949–1953	36th Commissioner
42. Robert C.Watson	1953–1961	37th Commissioner
43. David Lowell Ladd	1961–1963	38th Commissioner
44. Edward J. Brenner	1964–1969	39th Commissioner
45. William E. Schuyler, Jr.	1969–1971	40th Commissioner
46. Robert Gottschalk	1972–1973	41st Commissioner
47. C. Marshall Dann	1974–1977	42nd Commissioner
48. Donald W. Banner	1978–1979	43rd Commissioner
49. Sidney A. Diamond	1979–1981	44th Commissioner
50. Gerald J. Mossinghoff	1981–1985	45th Commissioner Assistant Secretary and Commissioner of Patents and Trademarks (10/25/82)
51. Donald J. Quigg	1985–1990	46th Commissioner
52. Harry F. Manbeck, Jr.	1990–1992	47th Commissioner
53. Bruce A. Lehman	1993–	48th Commissioner

Appendix 2
Assistant Commissioners of Trademarks

1. Daphne R. Leeds   1953–1959
2. Arthur Crocker   1959–1961
3. Horace B. Fay, Jr.   1961–1965
4. Edwin Reynolds   1965–1970
5. John Schneider   1970–1971
6. Rene D. Tegtmeyer   1971–1975
7. Bernard A. Meany   1975–1978
8. Sidney A. Diamond   1979–1961
9. Margaret M. Laurence   1980–1987
10. Jeffrey M. Samuels   1987–1993
11. Philip G. Hampton II   1994–

Appendix 3
Applications Filed and Patents Issued Since 1790

**Patents Granted From
1790 to 1836**

(Calendar Years)		(Calendar Years)	
Year	**Patents**	**Year**	**Patents**
1790	3	1814	210
1791	33	1815	173
1792	11	1816	206
1793	20	1817	174
1794	22	1818	222
1795	12	1819	156
1796	44	1820	155
1797	51	1821	168
1798	28	1822	200
1799	44	1823	173
1800	41	1824	228
1801	44	1825	304
1802	65	1826	323
1803	97	1827	331
1804	84	1828	368
1805	57	1829	447
1806	63	1830	544
1807	99	1831	573
1808	158	1832	474
1809	203	1833	586
1810	223	1834	630
1811	215	1835	752
1812	238	1836	599
1813	181		

Applications and Patents
1836 to 1994

Calendar Year	Total Applications	Patents			
		Inventions	Designs	Reissues	Total
1837	650[1]	424	—	11[2]	436
1838	900[1]	515	—	6	521
1839	800[1]	404	—	13	417
1840	765	458	—	10	468
1841	847	490	—	6	496
1842	761	488	1	13	501
1843	819	494	14	11	519
1844	1,045	478	14	7	497
1845	1,246	473	17	11	501
1846	1,272	566	59	13	638
1847	1,531	495	60	14	569
1848	1,628	583	46	23	652
1849	1,955	984	49	30	1,063
1850	2,193	883	83	26	992
1851	2,258	752	90	25	867
1852	2,639	885	109	20	1,014
1853	2,673	846	86	29	961
1854	3,324	1,755	57	28	1,840
1855	4,435	1,881	70	51	2,002
1856	4,960	2,302	107	83	2,492
1857	4,771	2,674	113	97	2,884
1858	5,364	3,455	102	126	3,683
1859	6,225	4,160	108	231	4,499
1860	7,653	4,357	183	232	4,772
1861	4,643	3,020	142	149	3,309
1862	5,038	3,214	195	116	3,525
1863	6,014	3,773	176	227	4,176
1864	6,932	4,630	139	248	5,017
1865	10,664	6,088	221	296	6,605
1866	15,269	8,863	294	290	9,457
1867	21,276	12,277	325	400	13,002
1868	20,420	12,526	446	420	13,392
1869	19,271	12,931	506	534	13,971
1870	19,171	12,137	737	439	13,313
1871	19,472	11,659	905	454	13,028
1872	18,246	12,180	884	529	13,593
1873	20,414	11,616	747	501	12,864
1874	21,602	12,230	886	483	13,599

[1]Estimate.
[2]The reissues for 1836 and 1837 are numbered with the other patents and thereafter are separately numbered.

Applications and Patents
1836 to 1994 (Continued)

Calendar Year	Total Applications	Patents			
		Inventions	Designs	Reissues	Total
1875	21,638	13,291	915	631	14,837
1876	21,425	14,169	802	621	15,592
1877	20,947	12,920	699	568	14,187
1878	20,260	12,345	590	509	13,444
1879	20,059	12,125	592	488	13,205
1880	23,012	12,926	515	506	13,947
1881	26,059	15,548	565	471	16,584
1882	31,522	18,135	861	271	19,267
1883	34,576	21,196	1,020	167	22,383
1884	35,600	19,147	1,150	116	20,413
1885	35,717	23,331	773	129	24,233
1886	35,968	21,797	595	116	22,508
1887	35,613	20,429	949	99	21,477
1889	40,575	23,360	723	75	24,158
1890	41,048	25,322	886	84	26,292
1891	40,552	22,328	836	80	23,244
1892	40,753	22,661	817	81	23,559
1893	38,473	22,768	902	99	23,769
1894	38,439	19,875	928	64	20,867
1895	40,680	20,883	1,115	59	22,057
1896	43,982	21,867	1,445	61	23,373
1897	47,905	22,098	1,631	65	23,794
1898	35,842	20,404	1,803	60	22,267
1899	41,443	23,296	2,139	92	25,527
1900	41,980	24,660	1,758	81	26,499
1901	46,449	25,558	1,734	81	27,373
1902	49,641	27,136	640	110	27,886
1903	50,213	31,046	536	119	31,701
1904	52,143	30,267	557	110	30,934
1905	54,971	29,784	486	129	30,399
1906	56,482	31,181	625	159	31,965
1907	58,762	35,880	589	151	36,620
1908	61,475	32,757	757	168	33,682
1909	65,839	36,574	687	160	37,421
1910	64,629	35,168	639	123	35,930
1911	69,121	32,917	1,010	157	34,084
1912	70,976	36,231	1,342	158	37,731
1913	70,367	33,941	1,683	164	35,788
1914	70,404	39,945	1,715	190	41,850
1915	70,069	43,207	1,545	182	44,934

Applications and Patents
1836 to 1994 (Continued)

Calendar Year	Total Applications	Patents			
		Inventions	Designs	Reissues	Total
1915	70,069	43,207	1,545	182	44,934
1916	71,033	43,970	1,759	198	45,927
1917	70,373	41,069	1,512	179	42,760
1918	59,800	38,569	1,207	165	39,941
1919	80,638	36,872	1,523	203	38,598
1920	86,893	37,164	2,485	233	39,882
1921	93,395	37,885	3,277	239	41,401
1922	89,028	38,414	1,627	256	40,297
1923	80,653	38,634	1,927	226	40,787
1924	80,888	42,594	2,671	235	45,500
1925	84,627	46,450	2,824	266	49,540
1926	86,116	44,750	2,602	275	47,627
1927	92,122	41,731	2,387	326	44,444
1928	92,725	42,376	3,188	335	45,899
1929	94,738	45,284	2,907	374	48,565
1930	94,203	45,243	2,712	367	48,322

		Inventions	Plants	Designs	Reissues	Total
1931	84,423	51,766	5	2,937	395	55,103
1932	71,864	53,473	46	2,944	393	56,856
1933	60,633	48,786	33	2,412	333	51,563
1934	61,572	44,429	32	2,921	371	47,753
1935	69,585	39,793	49	4,556	422	44,820
1937	72,984	37,695	55	5,137	384	43,271
1938	75,429	38,076	41	5,027	349	43,493
1939	71,689	43,090	45	5,593	352	49,080
1940	69,857	42,248	85	6,145	372	48,850
1941	59,901	41,122	62	6,486	309	47,979
1942	50,057	38,467	65	3,728	250	42,510
1943	48,724	31,074	47	2,229	173	33,523
1944	59,472	28,073	38	2,916	170	31,197
1945	76,119	25,702	17	3,524	121	29,364
1946	91,972	21,803	56	2,778	121	24,758
1947	83,313	20,139	52	2,102	130	22,423
1948	75,952	23,963	44	3,968	111	28,086
1949	74,810	35,131	93	4,450	118	39,792
1950	74,295	43,040	89	4,718	129	47,976

Applications and Patents
1836 to 1994 (Continued)

Calendar Year	Total Applications	Patents				
		Inventions	Plants	Designs	Reissues	Total
1951	64,949	44,326	58	4,163	134	48,681
1952	68,384	43,616	101	2,959	163	46,839
1953	79,486	40,468	78	2,714	151	43,411
1954	82,968	33,809	101	2,536	155	36,601
1955	83,266	30,432	103	2,713	187	33,435
1956	80,035	46,817	101	2,977	158	50,053
1957	79,242	42,744	129	2,362	150	45,385
1958	82,804	48,406	120	2,375	171	51,072
1959	83,833	52,470	101	2,769	177	55,517
1960	84,475	47,170	116	2,543	157	49,989
1961	88,340	48,368	108	2,487	189	51,152
1962	90,373	55,691	91	2,300	202	58,284
1963	90,982	45,679	129	2,965	198	48,971
1964	92,971	47,375	128	2,686	200	50,389
1965	100,150	62,857	120	3,424	246	66,647
1966	93,482	68,405	114	3,188	179	71,886
1967	90,544	65,652	85	3,165	196	69,098
1968	98,737	59,103	72	3,352	186	62,713
1969	104,357	67,559	103	3,335	233	71,230
1970	109,359	64,429	52	3,214	269	67,964
1971	111,095	78,317	71	3,156	246	81,790
1972	105,300	74,810	199	2,901	275	78,185
1973	109,622	74,143	132	4,033	314	78,622
1974	108,011	76,278	261	4,304	435	81,278
1975	107,456	72,002	150	4,282	378	76,812
1976	109,580	70,226	176	4,564	422	75,388
1977	108,377	65,269	173	3,929	407	69,778
1978	108,648	66,102	186	3,862	363	70,513
1979	108,209	48,854	131	3,119	308	52,412
1980	112,379	61,819	117	3,949	285	66,170
1981	113,966	65,771	183	4,745	364	71,063
1982	117,987	57,888	173	4,944	270	63,275
1983	112,040	56,860	197	4,562	361	61,980
1984	120,276	67,200	212	4,938	300	72,650
1985	126,788	71,661	242	5,066	276	77,245
1986	132,665	70,860	224	5,518	260	76,862
1987	139,455	82,952	229	5,959	245	89,385
1988	151,491	77,924	425	5,679	244	84,272
1989	165,748	95,539	587	6,092	317	102,535
1990	176,264	90,366	318	8,024	370	99,078
1991	177,830	96,514	353	9,568	263	106,698

Applications and Patents
1836 to 1994 (Continued)

Calendar Year	Total Applications	Patents				
		Inventions	Plants	Designs	Reissues	Total
1992	186,507	97,443	321	9,269	360	107,393
1993	188,739	98,344	442	10,630	332	109,748
1994	206,090	101,676	499	11,095	318	113,588

Appendix 4
Trademark Registrations and Renewals, 1870 to 1994

Calendar Year	Registrations	Calendar Year	Registrations
1870	121	1892	1,737
1871	486	1893	1,677
1872	491	1894	1,806
1873	492	1895	1,829
1874 . . . . :	559	1896	1,813
1875	1,138	1897	1,671
1876	959	1898	1,238
1877	1,216	1899	1,649
1878	1,455	1900	1,721
1879	872	1901	1,928
1880	349	1902	2,006
1881	834	1903	2,186
1882	947	1904	2,158
1883	902	1905	4,490
1884	1,021	1906	10,568
1885	1,067	1907	7,878
1886	1,029	1908	5,191
1887	1,133	1909	4,184
1888	1,059	1910	4,239
1889	1,229	1911	4,205
1890	1,415	1912	5,020
1891	1,762	1913	5,065

The tabulation of renewals has been made from an actual count of the renewals as published in the Official Gazette. The first renewals (4) were published in the O.G. of July 14, 1914. However, since the issue of July 14, 1914 published a renewal of a registration dated September 27, 1881 and renewed September 27, 1911, it is not known whether certain registrations may have been renewed and not published prior to those first appearing in 1914.

The Act of March 3, 1881, which granted registrations for a term of 30 years, did not provide for renewals; renewals for a term of 20 years were first provided for in the Act of February 20, 1905, which authorized renewals for registrations under the 1881 act. Therefore, the first registrations which became eligible were those whose 30-year term under the 1881 act expired in 1911. Original registrations under the 1905 Act did not become eligible for renewal until 1925.

Trademark Registrations and Renewals, 1870 to 1994 (Continued)

Calendar Year	Registrations	Renewals	Calendar Year	Registrations	Renewals
1914	6,817	48	1955	18,204	4,268
1915	6,262	57	1956	20,753	3,756
1916	6,791	55	1957	17,483	3,488
1917	5,339	52	1958	15,355	3,070
1918	4,061	38	1959	18,745	3,272
1919	4,208	64	1960	18,434	3,933
1920	10,282	73	1961	16,595	3,358
1921	11,654	117	1962	17,023	2,809
1922	12,793	254	1963	19,740	2,655
1923	14,845	251	1964	20,090	2,702
1924	15,749	227	1965	18,501	3,165
1925	13,815	2,278	1966	20,259	3,585
1926	14,955	4,273	1967	20,036	3,801
1927	14,579	3,063	1968	21,528	4,646
1928	14,133	2,049	1969	20,613	6,176
1929	14,514	1,750	1970	21,745	6,076
1930	13,246	1,661	1971	21,019	6,213
1931	11,400	1,643	1972	23,252	5,037
1932	9,603	1,587	1973	26,112	5,397
1933	9,130	1,671	1974	28,099	5,513
1934	11,362	2,445	1975	30,931	1,132
1935	10,886	1,874	1976	26,326	6,754
1936	10,722	1,888	1977	25,858	6,060
1937	11,242	1,524	1978	29,630	5,454
1938	11,204	1,051	1979	22,210	5,404
1939	10,521	1,398	1980	14,614	5,862
1940	9,974	2,547	1981	42,700	5,900
1941	8,530	2,765	1982	42,400	6,000
1942	6,795	2,894	1983	46,800	5,500
1943	5,594	3,835	1984	55,500	5,100
1944	6,025	4,052	1985	65,796	6,505
1945	7,490	4,210	1986	46,673	5,144
1946	8,106	5,725	1987	47,288	4,069
1947	8,976	6,139	1988	47,410	6,907
1948	11,472	5,056	1989	55,310	7,752
1949	15,968	3,788	1990	55,559	7,002
1950	16,817	3,564	1991	33,415	6,071
1951	17,376	3,350	1992	72,731	5,645
1952	16,172	3,419	1993	69,868	6,381
1953	15,610	3,103	1994	55,709	6,020
1954	15,946	3,491			

Appendix 5
Registers of Copyrights

Thorvald Solberg
    Register   1897–1930

William L. Brown
    Acting Register   1930–1934
    Register   1934–1936

Clement L. Bouve
    Register   1936–1943

Richard C. Dewolfe
    Acting Register   1944–1945

Sam Bass Warner
    Register   1945–1951

Arthur Fisher
    Acting Register   1951
    Register   1951–1960

Abraham L. Kaminstein
    Register   1960–1971

George D. Cary
    Register   1971–1973

Abe A. Goldman
    Acting Register   1973

Barbara Ringer
    Register   1973–1980

David L. Ladd
    Register   1980–1985

Donald C. Curran
    Acting Register   1985

Ralph Oman
    Register   1985–1994

Marybeth Peters
    Register   1994–

About the Author

J. Thomas McCarthy has been a Professor of Law at the University of San Francisco for almost 30 years. He is a member of the California and the U.S. Supreme Court Bars and is admitted to practice before the Patent and Trademark Office. He holds a B.S. degree in electrical engineering from the University of Detroit and a J.D. degree from the University of Michigan.

A prolific writer, Professor McCarthy is the author of the five-volume treatise *Trademarks and Unfair Competition*, published in its third edition in 1992 by Clark Boardman Callaghan. He is also the author of the one volume treatise, *The Rights of Publicity and Privacy*, published in 1987 by Clark Boardman Callaghan. He is the author of numerous articles in the field of Intellectual Property and related areas.

McCarthy was the recipient of the 1994 Jefferson Medal from the New Jersey Intellectual Property Law Association, of the 1965 Watson Award of the American Intellectual Property Law Association, and of the 1979 Rossman Award of the Patent and Trademark Society. He delivered the 1995 H.S. Manges Lecture at Columbia University and the 1989 Boal Memorial Lecture for the Brand Names Educational Foundation. He was the 1994 Biebel & French Distinguished Visiting Scholar in Law & Technology at the University of Dayton.

He was a member of the ALI advisory committee drafting the 1995 Restatement of the Law of Unfair Competition and is a member of the editorial board of the *Trademark Reporter*. A frequent speaker on Intellectual Property subjects, Professor McCarthy also serves as a consultant on trademark and right of publicity matters to corporations and law firms.

Other Intellectual Property Titles from BNA Books

International Treaties on Intellectual Property
Edited by Marshall A. Leaffer

Media Law
by Rex S. Heinke

Patent, Trademark, and Copyright Laws
Edited by Jeffrey M. Samuels

Patent, Trademark, and Copyright Regulations
Edited by James D. Crowne

Copyright Law and Practice (and GATT Supplement)
by William F. Patry

Copyright Laws & Treaties of the World
Compiled by UNESCO

The Fair Use Privilege in Copyright Law, 2nd Edition
by William F. Patry

Latman's The Copyright Law, 6th Edition
by William F. Patry

Biotechnology and the Federal Circuit
by Kenneth J. Burchfiel

Drafting Patent License Agreements, 3rd Edition
by Harry R. Mayers and Brian G. Brunsvold

International Patent Litigation: A Country-By-Country Analysis
Edited by Michael N. Meller

Patents and the Federal Circuit, 3rd Edition
by Robert L. Harmon

Intent-to-Use Trademark Practice
by Phillip H. Smith

Products Comparison Manual for Trademark Users
by Francis M. Pinckney

Unfair Competition and the Lanham Act
by Doris E. Long

All titles are available on a free 30-day examination basis. For ordering or other information please call **800-960-1220** or e-mail books@bna.com. BNA's home page on the Internet can be found at http://www.bna.com.